Encyclopedia of
Crime & Justice

Second Edition

EDITORIAL BOARD

Encyclopedia of Crime & Justice

Second Edition

Joshua Dressler, Editor in Chief

Volume 1
Abortion—Cruel & Unusual Punishment

MACMILLAN REFERENCE USA

GALE GROUP

THOMSON LEARNING

New York • Detroit • San Diego • San Francisco
Boston • New Haven, Conn. • Waterville, Maine
London • Munich

Macmillan Reference USA
An imprint of the Gale Group
300 Park Avenue South
New York, NY 10010

27500 Drake Road
Farmington Hills, MI 48331

Library of Congress Cataloging-in-Publication Data
Encyclopedia of crime and justice.—2nd ed. / Joshua Dressler, editor in chief.
    p. cm.
    Includes bibliographical references and index.
    ISBN 0-02-865319-X (set: alk. paper)—ISBN 0-02-865320-3 (v. 1: alk. paper)—ISBN 0-02-865321-1 (v. 2: alk. paper)—ISBN 0-02-865322-X (v. 3: alk. paper)—ISBN 0-02-865323-8 (v. 4: alk. paper)
    1. Criminology—Encyclopedias. 2. Criminal justice, Administration of—Encyclopedias. I. Title: Crime and justice. II. Dressler, Joshua.
HV6017 .E52 2002
364'.03—dc21
                                            2001042707

Portions of "Delinquent and Criminal Subcultures" have been adapted in part from "The Code of the Street" by Elijah Anderson by permission of W. W. Norton & Company Inc.

Printed in the United States of America
Printing number
 2 3 4 5 6 7 8 9 10

CONTENTS

EDITORIAL AND PRODUCTION STAFF

Linda S. Hubbard, *Editorial Director*

Anjanelle Klisz and Michael J. McGandy, *Project Editors*

Alja Collar, *Contributing Editor*

Deirdre Graves, Beth Richardson, and Barbara van Orden,
Editorial Assistants

Jonathan Aretakis, *Copy Editor*

Anthony Coulter, William Drennan, Carol Holmes, Evan Gabriel,
John Krol, and Greg Teague, *Proofreaders*

Laurie Andriot, *Indexer*

Datapage Technologies International, Inc., *Typesetter*

GGS Information Services, *Art Program*

Mary Beth Trimper, *Composition Manager*

Evi Seoud, *Assistant Production Manager*

Rhonda Williams, *Buyer*

Jennifer Wahi, *Art Director*

MACMILLAN REFERENCE USA

Elly Dickason, *Publisher*

Hélène G. Potter, *Editor in chief*

FOREWORD

Sanford H. Kadish, editor in chief of the original edition of the *Encyclopedia of Crime and Justice,* described the four-volume work that was published in 1983 as "an attempt, the first of its kind, to draw together in one set of volumes all that is known about criminal behavior and the response of societies to it" (Foreword, p. xxi). This was a lofty goal made even more daunting by the fact that the Editorial Board commissioned experts to write the essays in a manner that would "be accessible to as large an audience of interested readers as possible without sacrificing the sophistication of treatment required to achieve the special purposes of the Encyclopedia."

The *Encyclopedia of Crime and Justice* lived up to its promise. Whether one measures success by the number of citations to the Encyclopedia's essays in published journals, the many reports by librarians of the Encyclopedia's heavy usage, or the frequent calls to Macmillan for an updated edition, there is no question of the Encyclopedia's success in providing access to the world's knowledge of criminal behavior, its causes, and societies' responses to it.

Now, two decades later, in the infancy of a new century, this revised edition of the *Encyclopedia of Crime and Justice* is being made available to the public. Publication of the Encyclopedia is again premised on the belief that few (if any) issues are more important to a well-functioning society than those that relate to an understanding of criminal conduct, crime prevention, and punishment. But "criminal justice" is a daunting subject, necessarily interdisciplinary in nature. As a consequence, the revised edition of the *Encyclopedia of Crime and Justice,* like the original edition, serves a critical

need: to bring together in four volumes a vast array of knowledge that could not otherwise be obtained without canvassing countless libraries or sifting through often unreliable sources found on the Internet. In many cases, such a search would yield materials written in a manner accessible only to a narrow population of experts steeped in the specialized language of the field. In contrast, the Encyclopedia's authors have written essays highly accessible to laypersons, yet sophisticated in content.

The accessibility of the essays is a vital feature of the Encyclopedia. The Encyclopedia originally was prepared, and now is revised, with a deep appreciation of the fact that virtually everyone in society has reason to care about the subject matter of criminal justice and, therefore, has reason to use the works included in these four volumes. The issues that criminologists, criminal justice experts, and criminal lawyers study are matters with which "hard" scientists, philosophers, historians, theologians, poets, and, indeed, *all of us,* have wrestled for centuries to understand and resolve. "Experts" will find the Encyclopedia of considerable assistance, but its primary audience is "the rest of the world" who need to know, or who simply care, about crime and justice.

This edition of the Encyclopedia contains more than 250 essays of varying lengths, ranging from approximately eight hundred to twelve thousand words. (Most essays fall somewhere near the middle of this range.) The editorial board decided that essays should generally be broad, rather than narrow, in scope. This framework is consistent with the overriding goal of advancing knowledge of a subject by providing readers with in-depth, rather than thumbnail, coverage of topics. Each essay includes a bibliography, with selected references to additional scholarship in the field. The bibliographies typically include both classical works and important contemporary literature related to the topic, thus enabling the reader to delve more deeply into the subject with confidence. At the end of each essay, readers will find a list of related essays in the Encyclopedia that they may find useful in their research or education.

The authors of the essays were encouraged to provide fair and evenhanded approaches to their topics, setting out all reasonable sides of controversies. As recognized experts in their fields, the Encyclopedia's contributors were also urged to express their own opinions on current controversies in a balanced manner. The editors' primary concern was that knowledge be disseminated fairly.

Although users may find that the Encyclopedia has a predictably North American (even U.S.) bias to its coverage, the editors have worked diligently within the practical confines of producing an encyclopedia of manageable size to provide non-American perspectives. This is done in various ways: through selection of authors, whenever possible and relevant, with comparative law or foreign criminal justice knowledge; by asking all authors (in Sanford Kadish's well-chosen words) "to respect no national boundaries in presenting their subject, but rather to make an effort to deal with the best thought in the entire literature"; by citation in some bibliographies to comparative law references; and by including essays that deal explicitly with foreign law (for example, essays on criminal law in England, Continental Europe, Russia, and China) or cover criminal justice issues in a comparative manner (for example, the essay Criminal Procedure: Comparative Aspects).

Responsibilities for planning and editing the new edition fell to the editorial board, composed of seven members: Thomas J. Bernard, Professor of Criminal Justice and Sociology at The Pennsylvania State University; Deborah W. Denno, Professor of Law at Fordham University; Richard S. Frase, the Benjamin N. Berger Professor of Criminal Law at the University of Minnesota; John Hagan, the John D. MacArthur Professor of Sociology and Law at Northwestern University and Senior Research Fellow at the American Bar Foundation; Dan M. Kahan, Professor of Law at Yale Law School; Carol S.

Steiker, Professor of Law at Harvard Law School; and myself. Because we had the benefit of the original edition of *Encyclopedia of Crime and Justice,* the board's initial efforts focused on identifying topics to be added to the revised edition (there were many, such as essays on feminist criminology, international criminal courts, and sexual predators, to name a few) and determining whether any topics covered in the original Encyclopedia should be deleted, renamed, or integrated into another, perhaps reorganized, essay (for example, a number of such changes were made in the sex offenses field).

After the board determined the topics to be included in the revised Encyclopedia, each editor took responsibility for specific essays, based primarily on his or her expertise in the field. Each editor prepared descriptions of the articles to be written, designated word lengths for each essay, and proposed authors to commission for each topic. With regard to essay length, the board used the word allocations of the original Encyclopedia as a starting point and then decided whether, in light of changes in the field, either more or fewer words should be assigned for the revised edition. And, with new essays to add, the board had to work hard to ensure that the overall length of the Encyclopedia did not become unmanageable. In a few cases we were pleased to be able to update the text and bibliography of an essay from the original Encyclopedia; in the great majority of cases, however, entirely new essays were commissioned. The final task of the editors was to review, appraise, and (where needed) propose revisions in the submitted manuscripts, and to make final recommendations to the editor in chief on publication.

The administrative burdens of producing an encyclopedia of this magnitude are immense and fell upon the exceedingly able staff in New York, heroically managed by Hélène Potter. I do not know how many times I turned to Hélène for help, advice, and encouragement over the three-plus years that it took to bring this mammoth project to completion, but I know it was often. I deeply appreciate our contacts, even if nearly all of them were by way of the magic of electronic mail. And, special thanks go to Elly Dickason for her boundless energies in getting the project off the ground and for honoring me with the opportunity to serve as editor in chief of the *Encyclopedia of Crime and Justice.*

JOSHUA DRESSLER

LIST OF ARTICLES

LIST OF AUTHORS

Barry D. Adam
  University of Windsor
  HOMOSEXUALITY AND
    CRIME

Robert Agnew
  Emory University
  CRIME CAUSATION:
    SOCIOLOGICAL THEORIES

Larry Alexander
  University of San Diego
  MISTAKE

Emilie Allan
  The Pennsylvania State
    University
  GENDER AND CRIME

Albert W. Alschuler
  University of Chicago
    Law School
  GUILTY PLEA: PLEA
    BARGAINING
  JURY: LEGAL ASPECTS

Akhil Reed Amar
  Yale Law School
  CRIMINAL PROCEDURE:
    CONSTITUTIONAL ASPECTS
  SPEEDY TRIAL

Johannes Andenaes
  Juridiske Fakultet,
    Urbygningen, Norway
  DETERRENCE

Elijah Anderson
  University of Pennsylvania
  DELINQUENT AND CRIMINAL
    SUBCULTURES

Carol Archbold
  University of Nebraska
    at Omaha
  POLICE: ORGANIZATION AND
    MANAGEMENT

Richard Arum
  University of Arizona
  EDUCATION AND CRIME

Sandra Ball-Rokeach
  University of Southern
    California
  MASS MEDIA AND CRIME

William H. Barton
  Indiana University
  JUVENILE JUSTICE:
    COMMUNITY TREATMENT

Sara Sun Beale
  Duke University School
    of Law
  FEDERAL CRIMINAL
    JURISDICTION
  MAIL: FEDERAL MAIL FRAUD
    ACT
  SENTENCING: PROCEDURAL
    PROTECTION

Hugo Adam Bedau
  Concord, Massachusetts
  CAPITAL PUNISHMENT:
    MORALITY, POLITICS, AND
    POLICY

Thomas J. Bernard
  The Pennsylvania State
    University
  CRIMINOLOGY:
    INTELLECTUAL HISTORY

Denis Binder
  Chapman University School
    of Law
  ARSON: LEGAL ASPECTS
  RIOTS: LEGAL ASPECTS

Christopher Birkbeck
  Universidad de Los Andes,
    Merida, Venezuela
  DEVELOPING COUNTRIES,
    CRIME IN

Robert L. Bogomolny
  Searle/Monsanto, Inc.
  BANK ROBBERY

Steven G. Brandl
  University of Wisconsin
  FEDERAL BUREAU OF
    INVESTIGATION: HISTORY
  POLICE: CRIMINAL
    INVESTIGATIONS

Bartram S. Brown
  Chicago–Kent College
    of Law
  INTERNATIONAL CRIMINAL
    LAW

Jennifer Gerarda Brown
  Quinnipiac College School
    of Law
  DISPUTE RESOLUTION
    PROGRAMS

David Brownfield
  University of Toronto
    at Mississauga
  RELIGION AND CRIME

Pamela H. Bucy
  The University of Alabama
  School of Law
  CORPORATE CRIMINAL
    RESPONSIBILITY

Ann W. Burgess
  Boston College School
  of Nursing
  STALKING

James Alexander Burke
  Larkin, Axelrod, Trachte,
  and Tetenbaum L.L.P.,
  Newburgh, New York
  CONSPIRACY

Scott Burris
  Temple Law School
  HUMAN
    IMMUNODEFICIENCY
    VIRUS

Emily Buss
  University of Chicago
  Law School
  CONTRIBUTING TO THE
    DELINQUENCY OF MINORS

Jeffrey A. Butts
  The Urban Institute
  JUVENILE JUSTICE:
    JUVENILE COURT

José A. Canela-Cacho
  Earl Warren Legal Institute
  University of California,
  Berkeley
  INCAPACITATION

Mary Cheh
  George Washington
  University Law School
  FORFEITURE

Paul G. Chevigny
  New York University School
  of Law
  JUSTIFICATION: LAW
    ENFORCEMENT

Roland Chilton
  University of Massachusetts
  at Amherst
  CLASS AND CRIME

Scott Christianson
  Rensselaer Polytechnic
  Institute
  PRISONS: HISTORY

Russell Christopher
  Columbia University School
  of Law
  JUSTIFICATION: SELF-
    DEFENSE

Fred Cohen
  School of Criminal Justice
  State University of New
  York at Albany
  PROBATION AND PAROLE:
    PROCEDURAL PROTECTION

Lawrence E. Cohen
  University of California,
  Davis
  ECONOMIC CRIME: THEORY

Robert D. Crutchfield
  University of Washington
  URBAN CRIME

Francis T. Cullen
  University of Cincinnati
  REHABILITATION

G. David Curry
  University of Missouri,
  St. Louis
  JUVENILE AND YOUTH
    GANGS

Mirjan Damaška
  Yale Law School
  ADVERSARY SYSTEM

Malcolm Davies
  School of Law
  Thames Valley University
  COMPARATIVE CRIMINAL
    LAW AND ENFORCEMENT:
    ENGLAND AND WALES

Sharon L. Davies
  College of Law
  Ohio State University
  ARRAIGNMENT

Scott H. Decker
  University of Missouri,
  St. Louis
  JUVENILE AND YOUTH
    GANGS

Deborah W. Denno
  School of Law
  Fordham University
  CRIME CAUSATION:
    THE FIELD

Shari Seidman Diamond
  Northwestern University
  School of Law
  JURY: BEHAVIORAL ASPECTS

Donald A. Downs
  University of Wisconsin,
  Madison
  OBSCENITY AND
    PORNOGRAPHY:
    BEHAVIORAL ASPECTS

Donald Dripps
  University of Minnesota
  Law School
  CRIMINAL JUSTICE PROCESS
  EXCLUSIONARY RULE

Markus Dirk Dubber
  State University of
  New York at Buffalo
  School of Law
  CRIMINAL LAW REFORM:
    CURRENT ISSUES IN THE
    UNITED STATES
  CRUEL AND UNUSUAL
    PUNISHMENT

Amy V. D'Unger
  Emory University
  CRIMINAL CAREERS

Robin Shepard Engel
  The Pennsylvania State
  University
  POLICE: HISTORY
  POLICE: POLICE OFFICER
    BEHAVIOR
  URBAN POLICE

David P. Farrington
  Institute of Criminology
  Cambridge University
  CRIME CAUSATION:
    PSYCHOLOGICAL THEORIES

Malcolm M. Feeley
  University of California,
  Berkeley
  POLITICAL PROCESS AND
    CRIME

Floyd Feeney
  University of California,
  Davis
  ROBBERY

Barry C. Feld
  University of Minnesota
  Law School
  JUVENILE JUSTICE: HISTORY
    AND PHILOSOPHY
  JUVENILES IN THE ADULT
    SYSTEM

Theodore N. Ferdinand
Southern Illinois University,
Carbondale
STATISTICS: HISTORICAL
TRENDS IN WESTERN
SOCIETY

Herbert Fingarette
University of California,
Santa Barbara
EXCUSE: INTOXICATION

Claire Finkelstein
University of California,
Berkeley
CRIME: DEFINITION

George P. Fletcher
Columbia University School
of Law
EXCUSE: THEORY
JUSTIFICATION: THEORY

Edith E. Flynn
College of Criminal Justice
Northeastern University
CAREERS IN CRIMINAL
JUSTICE: CORRECTIONS
JAILS

David F. Forte
Cleveland–Marshall College
of Law
Cleveland State University
COMPARATIVE CRIMINAL
LAW AND ENFORCEMENT:
ISLAM

Lionel Frankel
College of Law
University of Utah
SHOPLIFTING

Richard S. Frase
University of Minnesota
Law School
AMNESTY AND PARDON
CORPORAL PUNISHMENT
CRIME COMMISSIONS
CRIMINALIZATION AND
DECRIMINALIZATION
CRIMINAL JUSTICE SYSTEM
VICTIMLESS CRIME

Robert M. Freeman
Shippensburg University
PRISONS: CORRECTIONAL
OFFICERS

Leon Friedman
Hofstra Law School
WAR CRIMES

Hualing Fu
The University of
Hong Kong
COMPARATIVE CRIMINAL
LAW AND ENFORCEMENT:
CHINA

Gilbert Geis
University of California,
Irvine
VICTIMS

Richard J. Gelles
School of Social Work
University of Pennsylvania
FAMILY ABUSE AND CRIME

Paul C. Giannelli
Case Western Reserve
University Law School
SCIENTIFIC EVIDENCE

Don C. Gibbons
Portland State University
TYPOLOGIES OF CRIMINAL
BEHAVIOR

A. R. Gillis
University of Toronto
PREVENTION:
ENVIRONMENTAL AND
TECHNOLOGICAL
STRATEGIES
WAR AND VIOLENT CRIME

Daniel Glaser
Needham, Massachusetts
UNEMPLOYMENT AND CRIME

P. R. Glazebrook
Jesus College
Cambridge University
CRIMINAL LAW REFORM:
ENGLAND

Peter Goldberger
Law Offices of Alan Ellis,
Ardmore, Pennsylvania
FORGERY

John S. Goldkamp
Temple University
BAIL

Abraham S. Goldstein
Yale Law School
PROSECUTION: HISTORY OF
THE PUBLIC PROSECUTOR

Kent Greenawalt
Columbia University
PUNISHMENT

Nancy G. Guerra
University of California,
Riverside
VIOLENCE

Sandra Guerra
University of Houston
Law Center
INFORMAL DISPOSITION

Pratheepan Gulasekaram
University of Chicago
CONTRIBUTING TO THE
DELINQUENCY OF MINORS

Joseph R. Gusfield
University of California,
San Diego
ALCOHOL AND CRIME: THE
PROHIBITION EXPERIMENT

Christopher Keith Hall
Amnesty International
INTERNATIONAL CRIMINAL
COURTS

Cheryl Hanna
University of Vermont
Law School
DOMESTIC VIOLENCE

Ann Fingarette Hasse
Oakland, California
EXCUSE: INTOXICATION

Kimberly Hassell
University of Nebraska
at Omaha
PREVENTION: POLICE ROLE

Gordon Hawkins
University of California,
Berkeley
CORPORAL PUNISHMENT
CRIME COMMISSIONS

Max Herman
Rutgers University
RIOTS: BEHAVIORAL
ASPECTS

Randy Hertz
New York University School
of Law
EXCUSE: INFANCY

Paul J. Hirschfield
Northwestern University
PREVENTION: COMMUNITY
PROGRAMS

Ross Homel
  Griffith University,
    Brisbane, Australia
    DRINKING AND DRIVING

Donald N. M. Horning
  St. Mary's College
    EMPLOYEE THEFT:
      BEHAVIORAL ASPECTS
    EMPLOYEE THEFT: LEGAL
      ASPECTS

Scott W. Howe
  Chapman University School
    of Law

Publicity in Criminal Cases

F. Patrick Hubbard
  School of Law
  University of South Carolina
    TRESPASS, CRIMINAL

James Willard Hurst
  University of Wisconsin
    TREASON

Douglas Husak
  Rutgers University
    DRUGS AND CRIME: LEGAL
      ASPECTS

Edward J. Imwinkelried
  School of Law
  University of California,
    Davis
    SCIENTIFIC EVIDENCE

James A. Inciardi
  University of Delaware
    ARSON: BEHAVIORAL AND
      ECONOMIC ASPECTS
    DRUGS AND CRIME:
      BEHAVIORAL ASPECTS

Stanley Ingber
  John Jay College of
    Criminal Justice
    LIBEL, CRIMINAL

Jerold H. Israel
  University of Florida College
    of Law
    GRAND JURY

Eric S. Janus
  William Mitchell College
    of Law
    SEXUAL PREDATORS

Sanford H. Kadish
  University of California,
    Berkeley
    CONSPIRACY

Dan M. Kahan
  Yale Law School
    ARSON: LEGAL ASPECTS
    ASSAULT AND BATTERY
    ATTEMPT
    BANK ROBBERY
    BRIBERY
    CONSPIRACY
    CRIMINAL LAW REFORM:
      HISTORICAL
      DEVELOPMENT IN THE
      UNITED STATES
    FORGERY
    HOMICIDE: LEGAL ASPECTS
    RIOTS: LEGAL ASPECTS
    ROBBERY
    SEDITION AND DOMESTIC
      TERRORISM
    SHAMING PUNISHMENTS
    SOLICITATION
    THEFT
    TREASON
    TRESPASS, CRIMINAL
    WHITE-COLLAR CRIME:
      HISTORY OF AN IDEA

Pamela S. Karlan
  Stanford Law School
    COUNSEL: RIGHT TO
      COUNSEL

Andrew Karmen
  John Jay College of
    Criminal Justice
    VIGILANTISM

Leo Katz
  University of Pennsylvania
    Law School
    EXCUSE: DURESS

William R. King
  Bowling Green State
    University
    CAREERS IN CRIMINAL
      JUSTICE: POLICE

David A. Klinger
  University of Missouri,
    St. Louis
    POLICE: POLICING
      COMPLAINANTLESS CRIMES
    POLICE: SPECIAL WEAPONS
      AND TACTICS (SWAT) TEAMS

Lyndee Knox
  Keck School of Medicine at
    the University of Southern
    California
    VIOLENCE

Daniel J. Kornstein
  New York, New York
    LITERATURE AND CRIME

Christopher P. Krebs
  Research Triangle Institute
    RACE AND CRIME

Barry A. Krisberg
  National Council on Crime
    and Delinquency
    CORRECTIONAL REFORM
      ASSOCIATIONS

Charis E. Kubrin
  University of Washington
    URBAN CRIME

Kenneth C. Land
  Duke University
    CRIMINAL CAREERS

Edward J. Latessa
  University of Cincinnati
    PROBATION AND PAROLE:
      SUPERVISION

William S. Laufer
  University of Pennsylvania
    STALKING

Frederick M. Lawrence
  Boston University School
    of Law
    HATE CRIMES

Barbara C. Leigh
  University of Washington
    ALCOHOL AND CRIME:
      BEHAVIORAL ASPECTS

Andrew D. Leipold
  College of Law
  University of Illinois
    PRELIMINARY HEARING

James Lindgren
  Northwestern University
    School of Law
    BLACKMAIL AND EXTORTION

Debra Livingston
  Columbia University School
    of Law
    PROSECUTION: UNITED
      STATES ATTORNEY
    VAGRANCY AND DISORDERLY
      CONDUCT

Bill Loges
  Baylor University
    MASS MEDIA AND CRIME

Edward J. Loughran
Council of Juvenile
Correctional
Administrators
JUVENILE JUSTICE:
INSTITUTIONS

David Luban
Georgetown Law Center
COUNSEL: ROLE OF COUNSEL

Gerard E. Lynch
Columbia University School
of Law
PROSECUTION:
PROSECUTORIAL
DISCRETION
RICO (RACKETEER
INFLUENCED AND
CORRUPT ORGANIZATIONS
ACT)

Daniel Macallair
Center on Juvenile and
Criminal Justice
SENTENCING: PRESENTENCE
REPORT

Doris Layton MacKenzie
University of Maryland
PROBATION AND PAROLE:
HISTORY, GOALS, AND
DECISION-MAKING

Tracey Maclin
Boston University School
of Law
WIRETAPPING AND
EAVESDROPPING

Ross Macmillan
University of Minnesota
STATISTICS: COSTS OF CRIME

Edward R. Maguire
University of Nebraska
at Omaha
POLICE: ORGANIZATION AND
MANAGEMENT
PREVENTION: POLICE ROLE

Paul Marcus
William and Mary School
of Law
ASSAULT AND BATTERY
ENTRAPMENT
SUICIDE: LEGAL ASPECTS

Bill McCarthy
University of California,
Davis
ECONOMIC CRIME: THEORY

Charles McClain
University of California,
Berkeley
CRIMINAL LAW REFORM:
HISTORICAL
DEVELOPMENT IN THE
UNITED STATES

Joan McCord
Temple University
FAMILY RELATIONSHIPS AND
CRIME

Candace McCoy
School of Criminal Justice
Rutgers University
SENTENCING: MANDATORY
AND MANDATORY
MINIMUM SENTENCES

Sarnoff A. Mednick
University of Southern
California
CRIME CAUSATION:
BIOLOGICAL THEORIES

Daniel J. Meltzer
Harvard Law School
APPEAL

Jennifer L. Meyer
Center for Drug and Alcohol
Studies
University of Delaware
ARSON: BEHAVIORAL AND
ECONOMIC ASPECTS

Alan C. Michaels
Ohio State University
College of Law
VICARIOUS LIABILITY

Tomas C. Mijares
Southwest Texas State
University
POLICE: POLICING
COMPLAINANTLESS CRIMES

Jennifer Modell
Baltimore, Maryland
CAREERS IN CRIMINAL
JUSTICE: LAW

John Monahan
University of Virginia School
of Law
PREDICTION OF CRIME AND
RECIDIVISM

Michael S. Moore
University of San Diego
Law School
ACTUS REUS
CAUSATION
RETRIBUTIVISM

Thomas H. Morawetz
University of Connecticut
School of Law
JUSTIFICATION: NECESSITY

Herbert Morris
School of Law
University of California,
Los Angeles
GUILT

Stephen J. Morse
School of Law
University of Pennsylvania
DIMINISHED CAPACITY
MENTALLY DISORDERED
OFFENDERS
PSYCHOPATHY

Clayton Mosher
Washington State
University, Vancouver
RURAL CRIME

Robert P. Mosteller
Duke University School
of Law
DISCOVERY
VICTIMS' RIGHTS

Joan Mullen
Abt Associates, Cambridge,
Massachusetts
PRETRIAL DIVERSION

Michael B. Mushlin
Pace University School
of Law
PRISONERS, LEGAL
RIGHTS OF

Stephanie M. Myers
University of Central Florida
POLICE: HANDLING OF
JUVENILES

Laura Nader
University of California,
Berkeley
COMPARATIVE CRIMINAL
LAW AND ENFORCEMENT:
PRELITERATE SOCIETIES

Mahesh K. Nalla
School of Criminal Justice
Michigan State University
POLICE: PRIVATE POLICE
AND INDUSTRIAL SECURITY

John T. Noonan, Jr.
U.S. Court of Appeals,
9th Circuit
BRIBERY

Victoria Nourse
  University of Wisconsin
  Law School
  FEMINISM: LEGAL ASPECTS

Barbara Owen
  California State University,
  Fresno
  PRISONS: PRISONS FOR
    WOMEN

John T. Parry
  University of Pittsburgh
  Law School
  COUNTERFEITING

Michael L. Perlin
  New York Law School
  EXCUSE: INSANITY

Richard Warren Perry
  University of California,
  Irvine
  PROSTITUTION

Joan Petersilia
  University of California,
  Irvine
  SENTENCING:
    ALTERNATIVES

Charles A. Phipps
  Columbia, South Carolina
  SEX OFFENSES: CHILDREN

Samuel H. Pillsbury
  Loyola Law School
  EXCUSE: INTOXICATION

Alex R. Piquero
  Dedham, Massachusetts
  CRIMINOLOGY AND
    CRIMINAL JUSTICE
    RESEARCH: METHODS
  CRIMINOLOGY AND
    CRIMINAL JUSTICE
    RESEARCH: ORGANIZATION

Nicole Leeper Piquero
  Dedham, Massachusetts
  CRIMINOLOGY AND
    CRIMINAL JUSTICE
    RESEARCH: METHODS
  CRIMINOLOGY AND
    CRIMINAL JUSTICE
    RESEARCH: ORGANIZATION

William T. Pizzi
  University of Colorado
  School of Law
  TRIAL, CRIMINAL

Ellen S. Podgor
  Georgia State University
  College of Law
  COMPUTER CRIME

Daniel D. Polsby
  George Mason University
  GUNS, REGULATION OF

Robert Prentky
  The Massachusetts
  Treatment Center
  RAPE: BEHAVIORAL ASPECTS

Nicole Rafter
  Northeastern University
  FEMINISM: CRIMINOLOGICAL
    ASPECTS

Kevin R. Reitz
  University of Colorado
  School of Law
  SENTENCING: ALLOCATION
    OF AUTHORITY
  SENTENCING: GUIDELINES

Daniel C. Richman
  Fordham University School
  of Law
  CROSS-EXAMINATION
  FEDERAL CRIMINAL LAW
    ENFORCEMENT
  OBSTRUCTION OF JUSTICE

Ira P. Robbins
  School of Law
  American University
  SOLICITATION

Paul H. Robinson
  Northwestern University
  School of Law
  MENS REA

Paul M. Roman
  University of Georgia
  ALCOHOL AND CRIME:
    TREATMENT AND
    REHABILITATION

Robin Room
  Stockholm University,
  Sweden
  ALCOHOL AND CRIME:
    BEHAVIORAL ASPECTS

Thomas Rotolo
  Washington State University
  RURAL CRIME

H. Ted Rubin
  State University of
  New York, Stonybrook

JUVENILE STATUS
  OFFENDERS

Vincent F. Sacco
  Queen's University, Ontario
  ORGANIZED CRIME

Shannon A. Santana
  University of Cincinnati
  REHABILITATION

Austin Sarat
  Amherst College
  POPULAR CULTURE

Joachim J. Savelsberg
  University of Minnesota
  MODERNIZATION AND CRIME

Stephen J. Schulhofer
  University of Chicago
  Law School
  ATTEMPT
  CORPUS DELICTI
  RAPE: LEGAL ASPECTS

Louis B. Schwartz
  School of Law
  University of Pennsylvania
  THEFT

Leslie Sebba
  Hebrew University
  of Jerusalem
  AMNESTY AND PARDON

Louis Michael Seidman
  Georgetown University
  Law Center
  CONFESSIONS

James F. Short, Jr.
  Washington State University
  CRIMINOLOGY: MODERN
    CONTROVERSIES
  DELINQUENT AND CRIMINAL
    SUBCULTURES

Katharine B. Silbaugh
  Boston University
  SEX OFFENSES: CONSENSUAL

Michael A. Simons
  St. John's University
  Law School
  PERJURY

John Simpson
  University of Toronto
  RELIGION AND CRIME

Richard G. Singer
  Rutgers Law School,
    Camden
    CONVICTION: CIVIL
      DISABILITIES
    STRICT LIABILITY

Jerome H. Skolnick
  New York University School
    of Law
    GAMBLING

Christopher Slobogin
  University of Florida College
    of Law
    EYEWITNESS
      IDENTIFICATION:
      CONSTITUTIONAL ASPECTS

Wesley J. Smith
  Oakland, California
    EUTHANASIA AND ASSISTED
      SUICIDE

Howard N. Snyder
  National Center for Juvenile
    Justice
    JUVENILE VIOLENT
      OFFENDERS

Cassia Spohn
  University of Nebraska
    at Omaha
    SENTENCING: DISPARITY

Darrell Steffensmeier
  The Pennsylvania State
    University
    AGE AND CRIME
    GENDER AND CRIME

Carol S. Steiker
  Harvard Law School
    CAPITAL PUNISHMENT:
      LEGAL ASPECTS
    CIVIL AND CRIMINAL DIVIDE

Jordan M. Steiker
  University of Texas School
    of Law
    HABEAS CORPUS

Geoffrey R. Stone
  University of Chicago
    Law School
    SEDITION AND DOMESTIC
      TERRORISM

William J. Stuntz
  Harvard Law School
    SEARCH AND SEIZURE

Scott E. Sundby
  Washington and Lee
    University School of Law
    BURDEN OF PROOF

Ralph B. Taylor
  Temple University
    ECOLOGY OF CRIME

Jasmine A. Tehrani
  University of Southern
    California
    CRIME CAUSATION:
      BIOLOGICAL THEORIES

Stephen C. Thaman
  St. Louis University School
    of Law
    COMPARATIVE CRIMINAL
      LAW AND ENFORCEMENT:
      RUSSIA

George C. Thomas, III
  Rutgers University
    DOUBLE JEOPARDY

Melissa Thompson
  University of Minnesota
    PREVENTION: JUVENILES AS
      POTENTIAL OFFENDERS

Charles R. Tittle
  Washington State University
    DEVIANCE

Jackson Toby
  Rutgers University
    SCHOOLS AND CRIME

Hans Toch
  School of Criminal Justice
  State University of
    New York at Albany
    PRISONS: PROBLEMS AND
      PROSPECTS

Austin T. Turk
  University of California,
    Riverside
    ASSASSINATION
    CRIME CAUSATION:
      POLITICAL THEORIES
    TERRORISM

Chris Uggen
  University of Minnesota
    PREVENTION: JUVENILES AS
      POTENTIAL OFFENDERS

Jeffery Ulmer
  Purdue University
    AGE AND CRIME

Mark Umbreit
  University of Minnesota
    RESTORATIVE JUSTICE

Barbara D. Underwood
  U.S. Department of Justice
    BURDEN OF PROOF

Mark Warr
  University of Texas at Austin
    FEAR OF CRIME
    PUBLIC OPINION AND CRIME

Robert R. Weidner
  Institute of Criminal Justice
  University of Minnesota Law
    School
    CRIMINAL JUSTICE SYSTEM

Thomas Weigend
  Universität zu Köln,
    Germany
    CRIMINAL LAW REFORM:
      CONTINENTAL EUROPE
    CRIMINAL PROCEDURE:
      COMPARATIVE ASPECTS
    PROSECUTION:
      COMPARATIVE ASPECTS

Joseph G. Weis
  University of Washington
    STATISTICS: REPORTING
      SYSTEMS AND METHODS

David Weissbrodt
  University of Minnesota
    Law School
    INTERNATIONAL CRIMINAL
      JUSTICE STANDARDS

Gary L. Wells
  Iowa State University
    EYEWITNESS
      IDENTIFICATION:
      PSYCHOLOGICAL ASPECTS

Stanton Wheeler
  Yale Law School
    WHITE-COLLAR CRIME:
      HISTORY OF AN IDEA

Charles H. Whitebread
  University of Southern
    California Law School
    BURGLARY
    KIDNAPPING

John Shepard Wiley, Jr.
  School of Law
  University of California,
    Los Angeles
    ECONOMIC CRIME:
      ANTITRUST OFFENSES
    ECONOMIC CRIME: TAX
      OFFENSES

James J. Willis
  University of Massachusetts,
    Boston
    POLICE: COMMUNITY
      POLICING

Bruce J. Winick
  University of Miami School
    of Law
    COMPETENCY TO STAND
      TRIAL

Edward M. Wise
  Wayne State University
    Law School
    ABORTION

Robert Witt
  University of Surrey,
    England
    CRIME CAUSATION:
      ECONOMIC THEORIES

Ann Dryden Witte
  Wellesley College
    CRIME CAUSATION:
      ECONOMIC THEORIES

Brian C. Wold
  Seattle, Washington
    STATISTICS: REPORTING
      SYSTEMS AND METHODS

Bradley R. E. Wright
  University of Connecticut
    INTELLIGENCE AND CRIME

Richard A. Wright
  Arkansas State University
    PRISONS: PRISONERS

Daniel B. Yeager
  University of Illinois College
    of Law
    ACCOMPLICES

Mark Yeisley
  Florida State University
    (deceased)
    RACE AND CRIME

Fred C. Zacharias
  University of San Diego
    School of Law
    GUILTY PLEA: ACCEPTING
      THE PLEA

Bruce Zagaris
  Washington, D.C.
    JURISDICTION

Margaret A. Zahn
  North Carolina State
    University
    HOMICIDE: BEHAVIORAL
      ASPECTS

Marvin Zalman
  Wayne State University
    VENUE

Franklin E. Zimring
  University of California,
    Berkeley
    CRIME COMMISSIONS

Eric M. Zolt
  Harvard Law School
    ECONOMIC CRIME: TAX
      OFFENSES

GUIDE TO LEGAL CITATIONS

The following brief guide to legal citations and the abbreviations used in them is designed primarily for readers unfamiliar with the literature of the law. It is confined to the abbreviations and citation forms used in this Encyclopedia. Readers wanting a comprehensive guide to legal citations and abbreviations should consult *A Uniform System of Citation* (the so-called Blue Book), now in its sixteenth edition, published by the Harvard Law Review Association and available at law school bookstores. Extensive lists of legal abbreviations and their meanings can also be found in the second edition of *Dictionary of Legal Abbreviations Used in American Law Books* by Doris M. Bieber (Buffalo, N.Y.: Hein, 1985). Readers wishing more comprehensive information about legal materials should consult the ninth edition of *The Hornbook on How to Find the Law* by Morris Cohen and Robert C. Berring (St. Paul: West, 1999) or the seventh edition of *Fundamentals of Legal Research* by J. Myron Jacobstein, Roy M. Mersky, and Donald J. Dunn (New York: Foundation Press, 1998).

The citation after the name of a case, statute, or treaty tells the reader where to find the full text of the court decision (in the case) or the full text of the material referred to. Below are typical American and British case and statute citations with brief explanations of their structure and the meaning of their various elements.

American state case: *People v. Hansen,* 9 Cal. 4th 300, 885 P.2d 1022 (1994)

American federal case: *United States v. Alkhabaz,* 104 F.3d 1492 (6th Cir. 1997)

1. The first element of a case citation consists of the names of the parties, with the plaintiff—or, in criminal cases, the prosecuting entity—listed first and the defendant last. In the example, therefore, this is the case of (the) People (of the State of California) versus Hansen. In criminal cases, such as the examples above, a governmental unit, rather than an individual, organization, or group is the plaintiff, designated "United States" in federal cases and "State," "People," or "Commonwealth" in state cases. In cases on appeal, such as these, it is usual to list the original plaintiff first in order to retain the same case name throughout the case's entire judicial history, but in some jurisdictions the case on appeal will begin with the name of the appellant (the party initiating the appeal), who is almost always the defendant in the original case.

2. The second element indicates where the case may be found in the appropriate volume of court reports, first in the official reporter (such reporters are published by the United States government and by most of the states) and second, in the unofficial (usually a regional) reporter. Within this element are listed, sequentially, the number of the volume, the abbreviated name of the court reporter, its series (if more than one series has been issued), and the page on which the text of the report (that is, the decision) begins. Further, within this element, the abbreviated name of the jurisdiction also indicates the level of court that decided the case. Thus, in the first example the abbrevi-

ation "Cal." indicates that the decision reported is that of the California Supreme Court (as contrasted to an abbreviation such as "Cal. App.," which would indicate a decision of one of the California courts of appeals). The case is reported in volume 9 of the official California Reports, fourth series, beginning on page 300, and also in volume 885 of the unofficial Pacific Reporter, second series, beginning on page 1022. In the second example, the abbreviation "F.3d" indicates that the decision reported is of one of the thirteen United States circuit courts of appeals (as contrasted to "U.S.," which would indicate the United States Supreme Court, or "F. Supp.," which would indicate a decision of one of the various federal district courts).

3. Within the parentheses is given the year in which the court decision was rendered. As the federal example shows, the parenthetical material may also indicate the specific court that handed down the decision, if the name of the reporter series itself does not convey that information; this is true of all citations to "F.3d." In the example, the parenthetical reference indicates which of the thirteen federal circuit courts of appeals rendered the decision—here, the sixth circuit. For those states that do not issue official state reporters, the abbreviated name of the state and the level of the court will be indicated within the parentheses before the date of decision, as in *State v. Reeves,* 916 S.W. 2d 909 (Tenn. 1996). Case decisions from states lacking an official reporter for one or more levels of their courts are published in the appropriate unofficial regional reporter. If the case has any further procedural history (for example, if the decision was later affirmed, modified, or reversed by a higher court), that information will be printed after the basic citation.

British case: *Regina v. McInnes,* (1971) 1 W.L.R. 1600 (C.A.)

The typical British case citation differs slightly in form from the American.

1. After the name of the parties (plaintiff or prosecuting entity first) appears the year in which the decision was published; this is not necessarily the same as the year in which it was rendered.

2. The number after the year is the volume number of that year's published reports. Each year's volumes begin with number 1; they are not numbered in sequence from the beginning of publication, as are American reports. This is followed by the name of the reporter (the official one first if more than one is listed) and the page on which the case report begins.

3. The final element, in parentheses, indicates which court rendered the decision. This element is omitted if the name of the official reporter, for example "A.C.," conveys that information.

American statutes: (1) Occupational Health and Safety Act (OSHA) of 1970, 29 U.S.C. § 651 (1988 & Supp. V. 1993); (2) Tax Reduction Act of 1975, Pub. L. 94-12, 89 Stat. 26 (codified as amended in scattered sections of 26 U.S.C.)

American statutes are cited in two different ways, depending on whether the text of the law in question is codified in one section (or a number of contiguous sections) of the United States Code (U.S.C.). Where this is so the statute is cited as in the first example.

1. The first element is the name of the act (either its actual name or the name by which it is popularly known), followed by the year of its enactment and an indication, if appropriate, of whether the act has been amended since its original passage.

2. The second element consists of the number of the Title (in the example, 29; each Title of the United States Code includes all the laws then in force relating to a particular subject matter, such as criminal law or copyright law) and the section number(s) where the statute has been placed in the code.

3. Finally, there appear in parentheses the edition of the United States Code (a new edition is published approximately every six years) and an indication of where to find any changes or amendments to the statute which have been enacted since the publication of that edition (a multivolume supplement to the code is published annually).

Where the provisions of the statute have been scattered among one or more Titles of the

United States Code, the law is cited as in the second example.

1. The first element consists of the name and date of the act.
2. The second element is the public law number. The first group of digits denotes which Congress enacted the legislation; the second group of numbers indicates the statute's number in the chronological sequence of all public laws passed by that Congress.
3. There follows the location of the statute's text in the United States Statutes at Large. Until 1946, a volume of this series was published for each Congress; since 1946 a volume has been published for each session of each Congress. The volume number precedes the abbreviation, and the page number on which the text of the statute begins follows it.
4. Finally, in parentheses, is listed the Title(s) (in the example, 26) of the code in or among which the text of the statute has been codified. If the act has been repealed or superseded, that fact will be indicated in parentheses.

British statute: Criminal Appeal Act, 1907, 7 Edw. 7, c. 23 (repealed)

British (or, before 1707, English) statutes are cited by the name of the act, the year of enactment, the year of the monarch's reign (in the example, the seventh year of Edward VII's reign; this practice was discontinued in 1963), and the position of the law in the numerical sequence of all the laws passed that year, the first law of each reign year being numbered chapter (c.) 1. If a particular section of the act is being cited, that will be indicated by "s." followed by the number of the section. If the act or some of its sections have been repealed, that fact will be indicated parenthetically, as in the example.

Internet Sources: United Nations Crime and Justice Information Network, *The Sixth United Nations Survey on Crime Trends and the Operations of Criminal Justice Systems (1995–1997)* (last modified, 13 March 2000) http://www.uncjin.org/Statistics/WCTS/WCTS86/wcts6.html

Citations to Internet sources are discouraged because of their transient nature. However, certain materials are unavailable in printed form or are very difficult to obtain, so Internet citations are used in such circumstances. The citation will include the author of the material, if any, and a full title of the material being cited. It is followed by the Uniform Resource Locator (URL), which is the electronic address for the material. It is customary to cite the most recent modification of the material (in the example above, on 13 March 2000). If no modification date is provided by the source, the citation should indicate the date the source-provider obtained access to the materials (which would be indicated as the date "visited").

JOSHUA DRESSLER

ABBREVIATION	FULL NAME	EXPLANATION
A.; A.2d	Atlantic Reporter (First Series; Second Series)	Unofficial reporter containing decisions of the highest courts and of some intermediate appellate courts of Connecticut, Delaware, Maine, Maryland, New Jersey, New Hampshire, Pennsylvania, Rhode Island, and Vermont. *Example:* 189 A.2d 646 (Me. 1933) = Volume 189, Atlantic Reporter, Second Series, page 646 (jurisdiction; year decision rendered).
A.B.M.R.	Army Board of Military Review	An appellate court that reviews decisions of army courts-martial.

ABBREVIATION	FULL NAME	EXPLANATION
A.C.	Appeal Cases (Great Britain)	Part of the official English Law Reports; reports appellate cases decided by the highest courts of England—the House of Lords and the Privy Council. This series of reports begins in 1891.
A.F.B.M.R.	Air Force Board of Military Review	An appellate court that reviews decisions of air force courts-martial.
aff'd,	affirmed	Indicates that the lower-court decision (which appears before *aff'd*) was affirmed by a decision of a higher court (which appears after *aff'd*). Compare *rev'd.*
All E.R.	All England Law Reports	Unofficial but widely cited series containing decisions of English courts, beginning with 1936.
App. Div.; App. Div. 2d (N.Y.)	New York Appellate Division Reports (First Series; Second Series)	Official reports of decisions of the intermediate appellate courts of New York State, the Appellate Division of the Supreme Court of the State of New York.
B.C. Ct. App.	British Columbia (Canada) Court of Appeals	An intermediate appellate court.
BGBI	Bundesgesetzblatt, Teil 1 (West Germany)	Weekly publication that prints the full official text of all West German federal laws, treaties, and decrees; published since 1949.
c.; ch.	chapter	
C.A.	Court of Appeal (England)	The appellate court in England, from which an appeal is possible only to the Appellate Committee of the House of Lords. It has two divisions: the Civil Division and the Criminal Division.
Cal.; Cal. 2d; Cal. 3d; Cal. 4th	California Reports (First Series; Second Series; Third Series; Fourth Series)	Official reports of decisions of the Supreme Court of California.
Cal. App.; Cal. App. 2d; Cal. App. 3d; Cal. App. 4th	California Appellate Reports (First Series; Second Series; Third Series; Fourth Series)	Official reports of decisions of the various California courts of appeals, which are intermediate appellate courts.
Cal. Rptr.; Cal. Rptr. 2d	California Reporter (First Series; Second Series)	Unofficial reporter that prints decisions of all the California courts.
Can. Crim. Code	Canadian Criminal Code	Codification of Canadian criminal law.

ABBREVIATION	FULL NAME	EXPLANATION
Can. S. Ct.	Supreme Court of Canada	Highest Canadian court.
C.C.A.	Court of Criminal Appeal (Great Britain)	Appellate court established by the Criminal Appeal Act of 1907; has been replaced by the Court of Appeal (Criminal Division).
C.C.C.	Canadian Criminal Cases Annotated	Reports of important decisions in criminal and quasi-criminal cases from dominion and provincial courts. Published since 1898; the second series begins with 1971.
C.F.R.	Code of Federal Regulations	A multivolume set, keyed to the Titles of the United States Code and revised annually. It gives the text of all administrative rules and regulations currently in force.
Cir. (as in 1st Cir.)	Circuit	A United States circuit court of appeals (an intermediate-level federal court). There are thirteen circuits; the number (or the letters D.C.) preceding the abbreviation indicates from which one the decision emanated.
Cmnd. (No.)	Command (Great Britain) (Number)	A designation affixed to certain reports issued by agencies of the British government and presented to Parliament at the command of the Crown.
C.M.R.	Court Martial Reports	Reports of the decisions of the various courts of military review and of the United States Court of Military Appeals. Published between 1951 and 1978.
Conn. Gen. Stat. (Ann.)	Connecticut General Statutes (Annotated)	A multivolume compilation, supplemented every year, containing all the laws and court rules currently in force in the jurisdiction (state).
C.P.	Court of Common Pleas (England)	One of the four superior courts at Westminster that existed until passage of the Judicature Acts in the second half of the nineteenth century. (The Judicature Acts fundamentally restructured the English court system.)
Cr. Cas. Res.	Court for Crown Cases Reserved (Great Britain)	A court of criminal appeal, established in 1848 to consider questions of law referred by a judge in certain of the lower courts before which a prisoner had been found guilty by verdict. If this court held that the point had been wrongly decided at the trial, the conviction was overturned. The court was abolished in 1907 by the Criminal Appeal Act, which created the Court of Criminal Appeal (C.C.A.).

ABBREVIATION	FULL NAME	EXPLANATION
Crim. App.	Criminal Appeal Reports (Great Britain)	Reports of cases brought under the Criminal Appeal Act of 1907; published since 1909.
C.R.N.S.	Criminal Reports, New Series (Canada)	Annotated reports (decisions) of criminal cases decided in the courts of the various Canadian provinces: 1st Series, 1946–1967; New Series, 1967–1978; 3d Series, 1978–.
Eng. Rep.	English Reports— Full Reprint	A compilation of all reported English cases between 1307 and 1865. Includes most of the material from the contemporary yearbooks.
Entscheidungen BGHSt	Entscheidungen des Bundesgerichtshofes in Strafsachen	Reports of decisions of the German Federal Republic's High Court of Criminal Appeals; published since 1951.
Entscheidungen RGSt	Entscheidungen des Reichsgerichts in Strafsachen	Reports of decisions of the highest court of criminal appeal under the German Empire, the Weimar Republic, and the Third Reich; published from 1880 through 1944.
Eur. Human Rights R.	European Human Rights Reports	Official reports of decisions of the European Court of Human Rights in Strasbourg, France.
Ex.	Court of Exchequer (England)	Originally established by William the Conqueror and later one of the four superior courts at Westminster, although inferior to the King's (Queen's) Bench and Common Pleas.
Exec. Order	Executive Order (United States)	Orders, with the force of law, promulgated by the President. These orders are collected in Title 3 of the Code of Federal Regulations.
F.; F.2d; F.3d	Federal Reporter (First Series; Second Series; Third Series)	Official reports of decisions of the federal courts other than the Supreme Court. "F." (begun in 1880) includes decisions of both the federal district courts and the circuit courts of appeals; "F.2d" (begun in 1913) and "F.3d" cover decisions of the courts of appeals and the Court of Claims.
F. Cas.	Federal Cases	Reports of decisions of the federal district courts and the federal circuit courts from the establishment of those courts through 31 December 1879.
Fed. Reg.	Federal Register	Official publication, issued daily, containing the text of new and proposed departmental and agency rules and regulations before they are entered in the Code of Federal Regulations. Also contains administrative notices, which are not transferred to the C.F.R.

ABBREVIATION	FULL NAME	EXPLANATION
Fed. R. Evid.	Federal Rules of Evidence	A set of rules governing the introduction and use of various kinds of evidence and the examination of witnesses in all federal trials, civil and criminal.
F.R.D.	Federal Rules Decisions	Reports of opinions, decisions, and rulings (by federal courts and other bodies) involving the Federal Rules of Criminal Procedure and the Federal Rules of Civil Procedure. Published since 1941; covers cases from 1940 on.
Fed. R. Crim. P.	Federal Rules of Criminal Procedure	Rules defining and prescribing proper procedure in all federal criminal cases. Most states have promulgated an analogous set of rules, often called the Code of Criminal Procedure (in New York it is called the Criminal Procedure Law, or CPL).
F. Supp.	Federal Supplement	Official reports of decisions rendered by the various federal district courts, the lowest federal courts.
G.A.O.R.	General Assembly Official Records (United Nations)	Official records of debates and resolutions of the United Nations General Assembly, beginning with its first session in 1946.
H.J. Res. (No.)	House Joint Resolution (Number)	A joint resolution proposed or passed by the House of Representatives of the United States Congress, by number.
H.L.	House of Lords (Great Britain)	As a legislative body, the House of Lords is the upper house of the United Kingdom Parliament; as a judicial body, it is the highest appellate court. It consists principally of the Lords of Appeal in Ordinary—former judges or barristers who are given life peerages and appointed to the House. They sit as Appellate Committees to hear cases and report their conclusions to the House.
H.R. (No.)	House of Representatives (Number)	A bill introduced in the House of Representatives of the United States Congress, by number.
I.L.M.	International Legal Materials	An American journal, published since 1962. Contains selected documents relating to international law, such as treaties and other international agreements, cases, regulations, legislation, and arbitration awards.
I.L.R.	International Law Reports	Unofficial reports of decisions of various international tribunals, and of national courts in cases in which the parties are of different nationalities.

ABBREVIATION	FULL NAME	EXPLANATION
I.R.C.	Internal Revenue Code	Compilation of the tax laws of the United States government. It is also Title 26 of the United States Code.
J.I.	Jury Instructions	Collection(s) of model or pattern instructions or charges given by judges to juries on various points of law.
K.B.	Court of King's Bench (England)	Historically, the highest common-law court in England. During the reign of a queen it is called the Queen's Bench (Q.B.). Under the Judicature Act of 1873 it was merged into the High Court of Justice.
L.N.T.S.	League of Nations Treaty Series	Official collection of bilateral and multilateral treaties and other international agreements signed between 1920 and 1946.
L.R.	Law Reports (England)	Official reports of English appellate cases. In an actual case citation a second abbreviation indicates which specific court or court division decided the case; an example is *Regina v. Prince,* L.R. 2 Cr. Cas. Res. 154 (1875).
Mich. Gen. Ct. R.	Michigan General Court Rules	Code of rules prescribing procedure for all cases, civil and criminal, brought in the courts of Michigan.
Misc.; Misc. 2d	Miscellaneous Reports (First Series; Second Series)	Official reports of the New York State trial courts.
M.J.	Military Justice Reporter	Reports of decisions of the United States Court of Military Appeals and of selected opinions of the courts of military review. Publication began in 1978; the cases reported date back to 1975.
N.E.; N.E.2d	Northeastern Reporter (First Series; Second Series)	An unofficial reporter containing decisions of the highest courts and of some intermediate appellate courts of Indiana, Illinois, Massachusetts, New York, and Ohio.
N.J.L.	New Jersey Law Reports	Compilation of cases decided by the New Jersey Supreme Court and the Court of Errors and Appeals. It was published from 1789 through 1948; subsequently it was merged into the New Jersey Reports (N.J.), which, however, include only decisions of the New Jersey Supreme Court.
N.W.; N.W.2d	Northwestern Reporter (First Series; Second Series)	Unofficial reporter containing decisions of the highest courts and of some intermediate appellate courts of Iowa, Michigan, Minnesota, Nebraska, North Dakota, South Dakota, and Wisconsin.

ABBREVIATION	FULL NAME	EXPLANATION
N.Y.S.; N.Y.S.2d	New York Supplement (First Series; Second Series)	Unofficial reports of the decisions of all New York State courts.
N.Z.L.R.	New Zealand Law Reports	Collection of decisions of the High (Supreme) Court of New Zealand, the highest appellate court, as well as decisions of other New Zealand appellate and special courts.
Op. Att'y Gen.	Opinions of the Attorney General of the United States	Contains formal advisory opinions of the attorneys general of the United States. Most states also publish advisory opinions of their attorneys general.
P.; P.2d	Pacific Reporter (First Series; Second Series)	An unofficial regional reporter containing decisions of the highest courts and of some intermediate appellate courts of Alaska, Arizona, California, Colorado, Hawaii, Idaho, Kansas, Montana, Nevada, New Mexico, Oklahoma, Oregon, Utah, Washington, and Wyoming.
Parry's T.S.	Parry's Consolidated Treaty Series	Unofficial collection of treaties and other international agreements signed between 1648 and 1919.
Pasch	Pascha (Easter)	The Easter term in the old English court calendar.
P.C.	Privy Council (England)	The principal council of the sovereign, composed of the cabinet ministers and other persons chosen by the monarch. Its Judicial Committee acts as a court of ultimate appeal in certain types of cases from Commonwealth countries.
Phil.	Philippine Reports	Compilation of decisions of the Supreme Court of the Philippines from c. 1900 to the present.
Pub. L.	Public Law	Public laws or acts passed by the United States Congress, as contrasted with private laws (laws passed for the benefit of an individual, a small group of individuals, or a particular locality).
Q.B.	Court of Queen's Bench (England)	See K.B.
Q.B.D.	Queen's Bench Division (England)	Same as Q.B.; see K.B.
rev'd,	reversed	Indicates that the lower-court decision (which appears before rev'd) was reversed by a decision of a higher court (which appears after rev'd). Compare aff'd.

ABBREVIATION	FULL NAME	EXPLANATION
§; §§	section; sections	
S. (No.)	Senate (Number)	A bill introduced in the United States Senate, by number.
S. Ct.	Supreme Court Reporter	Unofficial reporter containing decisions of the Supreme Court of the United States.
S.E.; S.E.2d	Southeastern Reporter (First Series; Second Series)	An unofficial regional reporter containing decisions of the highest courts and of some intermediate appellate courts of Georgia, North Carolina, South Carolina, Virginia, and West Virginia.
S.I.	Statutory Instruments (Great Britain)	A collection of rules, regulations, and orders issued by ministers, departments, and other authorized bodies. Published since 1948.
S.J. Res. (No.)	Senate Joint Resolution (Number)	A joint resolution proposed or passed by the United States Senate, by number.
So.; So.2d	Southern Reporter (First Series; Second Series)	An unofficial regional reporter containing decisions of the highest courts and of some intermediate appellate courts of Alabama, Florida, Louisiana, and Mississippi.
Star Chamber	Court of Star Chamber (England)	An early English court that evolved to remedy the inability of the common law courts to bring criminal offenders to justice. Its penalties were severe, its methods cruel, its procedures arbitrary, and its powers were sometimes illegally extended and exercised. Abolished in 1641, it has since become a synonym for the arbitrary and tyrannical exercise of authority.
Stat.	1. United States Statutes at Large	1. Official compilations of the text of newly enacted federal laws. Published for each Congress since the first (1789) and, since the Seventy-ninth Congress (1946), for each session of each Congress.
	2. Statutes	2. A compilation of all the currently effective laws of a given jurisdiction, usually a state.
Supp.	Supplement	
S.W.; S.W.2d	Southwestern Reporter (First Series; Second Series)	An unofficial regional reporter containing decisions of the highest courts and of some intermediate appellate courts of Arkansas, Kentucky, Missouri, Tennessee, and Texas.
T.I.A.S.	Treaties and Other International Acts Series	A collection of treaties and other international agreements and conventions to which the United States is a party. Published since 1945, by the Department of State.

ABBREVIATION	FULL NAME	EXPLANATION
Trade Cas. (CCH)	Trade Cases (Commerce Clearing House)	A privately published case reporter issued as part of a loose-leaf service. It contains cases and administrative decisions dealing with regulation of trade, including antitrust matters. Reference to the cases is typically by paragraph number.
T.S.	Treaty Series (United States Department of State)	Compilation of treaties and executive agreements to which the United States is a party that were signed between January 1908 and November 1944 (ends with No. 994).
U.N.T.S.	United Nations Treaty Series	Official collection of international treaties and other agreements signed since 1946. Continues the League of Nations Treaty Series.
U.S.	United States Reports	Official reports of all decisions of the Supreme Court of the United States.
U.S.C.	United States Code	Official compilation, by Title (subject matter), of all federal laws currently in force. Supplementary volumes are issued annually, and a new edition of the code appears approximately every six years. Two publishers produce annotated versions of the United States Code.
U.S.C.A.	United States Code Annotated	Same as the United States Code, but privately published and containing extensive annotations (summaries of judicial decisions), with references also to law review articles.
U.S.C.M.A.	United States Court of Military Appeals	Reports of cases decided by the named court and of appeals from the boards (since 1 August 1969, courts) of military review, which review the sentences of courts-martial in the various branches of the armed forces of the United States.
U.S. Code Cong. & Ad. News	United States Code Congressional and Administrative News	Unofficial compilation of public laws, legislative histories, executive orders, proclamations, reorganization plans, commentaries, and related materials, beginning with the Seventy-eighth Congress, second session (1944).
U.S.L.W.	United States Law Week	An unofficial weekly publication that prints the full text of the latest United States Supreme Court decisions (substantially before they appear in any of the reporters) and reports all the other actions taken by the Supreme Court. It also contains selected decisions of lower federal courts and of state courts.

ABBREVIATION	FULL NAME	EXPLANATION
U.S.T.	United States Treaties and Other International Agreements	Official collection of treaties and other international agreements to which the United States is a party; published since 1 January 1950.
W.L.R.	Weekly Law Reports (England)	An unofficial reporter, published since 1953, that contains decisions of all the high English courts.
Y.B.	Year Book (England)	Books of case reports in a series extending from the reign of Edward I (1272–1307) to the time of Henry VIII (1509–1547). The reports were written by the prothonotaries (chief scribes) of the courts, at Crown expense, and published annually. Most, but not all, of the Year Book cases are included in the English Reports—Full Reprint (Eng. Rep.).

A

ABORTION

In criminal law, *abortion* refers to induced abortion: the intentional destruction of a fetus in the womb, or an untimely delivery brought about with intent to destroy the fetus. An unintended miscarriage, or so-called *spontaneous abortion*, is not, for legal purposes, an abortion at all. *Termination of pregnancy* sometimes is used as a synonym for abortion. It is, however, a wider term, since pregnancy can be terminated by live birth: inducing labor, a common obstetrical practice, purposely terminates pregnancy, but would not be considered abortion. Abortion implies killing the fetus. This is what makes it controversial. Probably no contemporary public question has attracted more controversy than the question of whether abortion should be considered a crime or a matter of choice by a pregnant woman about how her body will be used.

Classical attitudes and canon law

Attitudes towards abortion have varied over time and across cultures. In the ancient world, it was widely practiced, for a number of reasons, as was infanticide. Roman law punished the wife who induced an abortion in order to thwart her husband or conceal an adultery; the harm lay not in killing the child but in depriving the husband of his right to decide whether or not to do so. Plato and Aristotle regarded both abortion and infanticide as forms of population control. Aristotle suggested that, "when local custom does not allow exposing infants for the purpose of keeping down numbers, the proper thing to do is to limit family size, and if a child is conceived in excess of the limit set, to induce an abortion before

it develops sensation and life: since whether abortion is right or not will depend on whether sensation and life have begun" (*Politics* 7.16, 1335b). This statement presupposes the common premodern belief that a fetus does not begin to live until some time after conception. The exact time was controversial. Aristotle himself put it at roughly forty days after conception for a male fetus, ninety days after for a female. A later Roman view took these two periods to be forty and eighty days respectively. Until then the fetus was thought to be an inanimate, inert part of the pregnant woman's body; its destruction could not be homicide. And even after "animation," prevailing opinion in Greco-Roman times permitted abortion, as it permitted infanticide after birth.

The Christian church, practically from the start, opposed both abortion and infanticide, on the ground of the sanctity of human life; in the case of abortion, association with sexual licentiousness provided a further reason for condemnation. But in determining when the soul enters the body, so as to make abortion homicide, early theologians were influenced by classical views regarding animation. A distinction was drawn between (1) abortion involving an inanimate or "unformed" fetus, which was regarded, like contraception, as an act that prevented a life from coming into being; and (2) abortion involving an animate, "formed," or "vivified" fetus, which amounted to the taking of a life that already had come into being. While not everyone accepted this distinction, it was incorporated into medieval law, both canon and civil law. There was considerable uncertainty, however, as to when animation or "ensoulment" took place. Gradually, between the fourteenth and sixteenth centuries, canon lawyers fixed the moment, as in Roman times, at forty days after conception for a male fetus, eighty days after for a female. This view was challenged in the seventeenth and eighteenth centuries, as Aristotelian biology began to fall into discredit. But only in the nineteenth century (just as secular laws on abortion were becoming more restrictive as well) did the Church definitively adopt the position that all abortion, at any stage of fetal development, should be treated as homicide.

Abortion in English law

Meanwhile, the uncertainty of canon lawyers allowed English law to give its own twist to the concept of animation. In the thirteenth century St. Thomas Aquinas had said that life is manifested principally in two kinds of actions: knowledge and movement. It could be taken to follow that *animus*, soul, or life, enters the body of the unborn infant when it first moves or stirs in the womb. This became the rule of English law. "Quickening" (literally, "coming to life") was held to occur not at a fixed time after conception, but at the moment when fetal movement is first detected—an event that varies with each pregnancy, but which usually happens near midterm, around the twentieth week.

It is not known exactly when this became the rule in England. The early twelfth-century text known as the *Leges Henrici Primi* took it for granted that animation occurs forty days after conception: abortion (which was treated only as an ecclesiastical offense) was said to be subject to three years' penance if it took place within those forty days, ten years' penance, as "quasi homicide," if it took place after animation (quickening). The identification of quickening with the first perception of fetal movement has been thought to date from the time of Henry de Bracton, a thirteenth-century judge and contemporary of Aquinas, who wrote the first systematic treatise on English law. But Bracton merely restated the canon law rule: "If one strikes a pregnant woman or gives her poison in order to procure an abortion, if the fetus is already formed or animated (quickened), especially if it is animated (quickened), he commits homicide." The usage by which a quickened fetus means one that has been felt moving in the womb could well be a much later development.

Although Bracton said that abortion of a quickened fetus was homicide, later writers insisted that it could not be homicide at common law. The proposition that abortion cannot be homicide is reiterated by practically every major writer on English criminal law, from William Staunford and William Lambard in the sixteenth century, through Edward Coke and Matthew Hale in the seventeenth century, to William Hawkins and William Blackstone in the eighteenth century. Homicide was agreed to require the prior birth of the victim. Murder might be charged, according to Hale, if the woman on whom an abortion was performed died as a result. Murder also might be charged, according to Coke, if a botched abortion injured a fetus that afterwards was born alive and then died from its prenatal injuries. But where a fetus, even a quickened fetus, was killed in the womb, resulting in stillbirth, whatever the crime, it would not be homicide at common law.

Killing the fetus might be a lesser crime. In England, abortion, both before and after quickening, was an ecclesiastical offense within the jurisdiction of the church courts. The extent to which it also could be prosecuted in the royal courts as a common law crime is a matter of controversy. Abortion after quickening, although not homicide, was said by Coke to be "a great misprison," by Blackstone to be "a very heinous misdemeanor." How far it actually was prosecuted is another question. As a practical matter, until the seventeenth century, the royal courts probably were content to leave the prosecution of abortion to church courts, which could compel, in ways the common law could not, testimony under oath about what had caused a miscarriage and whether a fetus had quickened.

The question of how far abortion constituted a common law crime became more important with the decline of ecclesiastical jurisdiction after the Reformation, especially after 1661 when the privilege against self-incrimination was extended to ecclesiastical tribunals. There are instances of prosecution for abortion in the royal courts during the seventeenth and eighteenth centuries. These are scattered, however, and the exact contours of the offense have been disputed, as they were disputed at the time. Again, difficulties of proof imposed limits on what could be prosecuted. Without reliable tests for pregnancy, testimony about fetal movement might be required to prove that a woman really had been pregnant, or that the abortion had killed a live fetus. Proof of quickening became, then, a practical if not a legal prerequisite; and the need for such proof would make it hard to prosecute a woman who had procured her own abortion. This, in fact, was seldom done.

In 1803 Lord Ellenborough's Act (43 Geo. 3, c. 58), an early effort to consolidate offenses against the person, put abortion on a statutory basis for the first time in England. Attempt to induce the abortion of a quickened fetus through the use of poison was made a capital felony, while the attempt by any means to induce an abortion before (or without proof of) quickening was made a felony punishable by transportation to a penal colony. In 1828, attempted abortion with instruments after quickening was made a capital felony as well. The Offenses Against the Person Act, 1837, eliminated capital punishment, abrogated the distinction based on quickening, and subjected all abortion, at any stage of pregnancy, to the same penalty—transportation for life or three years' imprisonment. The Offenses Against the Person Act, 1861, s.58, changed the maximum punishment to life imprisonment and expressly inculpated the woman who procured or attempted her own abortion. This section is still on the books, although the Abortion Act, 1967, made an exception for cases in which the abortion is performed by a registered medical practitioner on any of the fairly liberal grounds for abortion permitted by that act.

Abortion in American law: the nineteenth century

In the United States, the common law as stated by Blackstone generally was held to apply until superseded by statute in the nineteenth century. Abortion after quickening was treated as a common law misdemeanor; abortion before quickening was not considered a crime in the vast majority of states; and the liability of the woman who submitted to an abortion was questionable.

The first American abortion statute was enacted in Connecticut in 1821. It was influenced by the English statute of 1803 and made punishable by life imprisonment any attempt to induce the abortion of a quickened fetus through the use of poison. It was revised in 1830, two years after comparable revision of the English statute, to include attempts to induce abortion through the use of herbs or instruments. At the same time, the maximum penalty was reduced from life to ten years' imprisonment. Statutes based on Connecticut's 1821 law were enacted in Missouri in 1825 and in Illinois in 1827; these applied, by their terms, to all attempts to induce abortion

through use of poison, whether or not the fetus had quickened. In 1828 New York, as part of its Revised Statutes of 1829 (which took effect in 1830), enacted a more comprehensive set of provisions containing two further innovations. First, attempt to induce an abortion by any means, at any stage of pregnancy, was treated as a misdemeanor punishable by up to a year in jail, but abortion intended to destroy a fetus after quickening was specified to be second degree manslaughter. (In 1830, this was amended to make clear that it was manslaughter only if the fetus were actually killed.) Second, the New York statute made an exception for abortions necessary to preserve the mother's life or "advised by two physicians to be necessary for that purpose." A revision in 1845 included another innovation—a provision expressly making the woman who submitted to abortion guilty of a misdemeanor. (In 1881, this was amended to make the woman guilty of manslaughter, as the abortionist had been since 1830, if the abortion killed a quickened fetus.)

Every other state enacted abortion legislation during the nineteenth century (except Kentucky, which did so in 1910). Despite differences from state to state, a basic pattern emerged, which largely mirrored the innovations in New York. It prevailed throughout the United States until the 1960s; in about fifteen states, these old statutes, although unenforceable since 1973, remain on the books.

1. Abortion at any stage of gestation usually was made a criminal offense. Since most abortions take place in early pregnancy, this represented a drastic change in the law which previously had been understood to permit abortion before quickening. Some states continued to require proof of quickening; in some, as in New York, whether the abortion took place before or after quickening determined the level of punishment. But most rejected the quickening distinction and established the same penalty for all abortions.
2. States that used the quickening distinction to determine the level of punishment usually treated destruction of a quickened fetus as manslaughter, as New York did after 1830. A small number treated the destruction of a fetus at any stage of pregnancy as manslaughter. Most states, however, regarded abortion as a separate offense, not as a form of homicide.

3. In some states, the pregnant woman who procured her own abortion expressly was treated as a guilty party, as in New York after 1845. This was a largely symbolic condemnation: the woman was almost never prosecuted. Indeed, criminalizing her conduct could complicate prosecution of the abortionist because of evidentiary rules prohibiting compulsory self-incrimination and requiring the testimony of an accomplice to be corroborated.

4. Most statutes punished attempted as well as completed abortions in order to sidestep the problems involved in having to prove pregnancy as an element of the crime. Liability turned on whether the defendant acted with intent to destroy a fetus. Some of these statutes applied, however, only when the woman in fact was pregnant.

5. An exception was usually made, as in the New York statute of 1828, for abortions designed to save the mother's life. A few states permitted abortion to preserve the mother's health. Otherwise, the prohibition of abortion was absolute.

Nineteenth-century abortion statutes were adopted for several reasons. The immediate occasion for enactment often was consolidation of the criminal law in statutory form. An upsurge in anti-abortion legislation occurred after 1840, as abortion became more frequent, more visible, more widely advertised and publicly discussed. This legislation was actively promoted by the medical profession, which was beginning to organize itself, in part, around opposition to abortion. Medical opposition drew on new understandings of gestation as a continuous process, in which animation or quickening had no scientific significance. It also was linked to the struggle by physicians to monopolize the practice of medicine and exclude "irregular" (nonphysician) practitioners who were then the chief purveyors of abortion and abortifacients. It relied as well on social anxieties about declining birthrates among the established white population, and a sense that abortion had become a common recourse not only of single women "in trouble," but also of otherwise respectable middle-class married women who were unmindful of the fact that maternity was their only proper vocation. The United States was not alone in this: for similar reasons, most western countries adopted restrictive abortion laws during the nineteenth century, just as, beginning with England in 1967, most western countries, including the United States, relaxed restrictions on abortion within two decades of each other.

Twentieth-century abortion law reform

Despite legal prohibition, abortion remained available in the United States, under conditions that varied with time and place. During the 1930s, for instance, at least in large cities, abortion could be readily obtained through referral to private clinics. It was prosecuted, if at all, only when the woman who sought the abortion died. This changed in the 1940s and 1950s. Anti-abortion laws were enforced more strictly. Abortion became harder to obtain and more expensive. Hospitals created new rules to restrict therapeutic abortions. Women without money and good medical contacts where shut out of facilities for safe abortion. Injuries and fatalities from clandestine "back-alley" abortions increased.

Recognition that illegal abortion was widespread and often dangerous led in the 1950s and 1960s to calls for abortion law reform. Medical opinion reversed itself. Physicians began to complain about the hypocrisy and discrimination involved in applying statutory exceptions for abortions designed to preserve the mother's life, and chafed at restrictions imposed by law rather than as a matter of medical judgment. "Quality of life" was emphasized. In the early 1960s, highly publicized fetal deformities caused by thalidomide and rubella heightened sympathy for women seeking abortions. Concern about worldwide overpopulation produced more favorable attitudes toward all techniques for controlling reproduction. So did the "sexual revolution" of the 1960s, a flood of women in the workforce, and the beginnings of "second-wave" feminism.

The American Law Institute's Model Penal Code (1962) provided an important catalyst. The "tentative draft" of the code's section on abortion (§ 230.3) was first published in 1959. It proposed that abortion should be a felony, with the level of punishment to depend on whether the abortion took place up to or after the twenty-sixth week of pregnancy. It added, however, that "[a] licensed physician is justified in terminating a pregnancy if he believes there is a substantial risk (1) that continuation of the pregnancy would gravely impair the physical and mental health of the mother or (2) that the child would be born with grave physical or mental defect, or (3) that the pregnancy resulted from rape, incest, or other felonious intercourse."

During the decade or so between 1962 and 1973, nineteen states reformed their abortion laws. Some adopted all three of the Model Penal Code's expanded justifications for abortion; others followed it only in part. Four states (Hawaii, Alaska, New York, and Washington) went further and removed all limitations on the reasons for which abortions could be performed. The New York law enacted in 1970 was the most sweeping. It permitted all abortions within the first twenty-four weeks of pregnancy and did away with both residency and hospitalization requirements (thus encouraging the growth of free-standing abortion clinics).

Roe v. Wade and its aftermath

New York's was the only state abortion law that came close to surviving the Supreme Court's decision in *Roe v. Wade*, 410 U.S. 113 (1973). *Roe* held unconstitutional a Texas statute, dating from 1857, which prohibited all abortions except those procured on medical advice for the purpose of saving the mother's life. A companion case, *Doe v. Bolton*, 410 U.S. 179 (1973), struck down a Georgia law adopted in 1968 and based on the Model Penal Code's abortion provisions. The effect of these two decisions was to render invalid practically every abortion restriction on the books in the United States.

The decision in *Roe* was premised on a woman's constitutional right to control (in consultation with her physician) the use of her own body for reproductive purposes. This right was held to follow from the Court's previous decisions recognizing a fundamental right to "privacy" or personal autonomy. Because a "fundamental" right was involved, a state could not simply prohibit abortion on any terms it chose; it would have to adduce "compelling" reasons for overriding a woman's right to procreative choice. Since early abortion is safer than normal childbirth, concern for the mother's health would not provide a sufficiently compelling reason for restrictions on abortion during the first trimester, other than a requirement that it be performed by a licensed physician. Concern for the fetus could not be used to preempt a woman's right to elect abortion before "viability"—the point near the beginning of the third trimester at which a fetus is capable of surviving outside the womb, albeit only with artificial aid. After viability, concern for the fetus as "potential

life" was held to be sufficiently compelling to permit a state to regulate or even prohibit abortion, unless continued pregnancy threatened the mother's life or health. In other words, *Roe* invalidated almost all restrictions on abortion during the first six months of pregnancy except for those designed to protect maternal health in the second trimester, but permitted any and all restrictions during the third trimester except where abortion was necessary to preserve maternal health or life.

The *Roe* decision sparked enormous controversy. Opposition to *Roe* turned abortion into a central issue in national politics. Efforts to overrule *Roe* by constitutional amendment, or by packing the Supreme Court, so far have failed. The Court did depart from *Roe* and nearly overruled it in *Webster v. Reproductive Health Services*, 492 U.S. 490 (1989). Subsequently, however, the controlling opinion in *Planned Parenthood of Southeastern Pennsylvania v. Casey*, 505 U.S. 833 (1992), jointly delivered by Justices Sandra Day O'Connor, Anthony Kennedy, and David Souter, reaffirmed *Roe*'s "essential holding," although it significantly qualified *Roe* by allowing states to invoke both maternal health and concern for the life of the fetus as bases for restrictions that inhibit access to abortion at any stage of pregnancy, so long as those restrictions do not amount to an "undue burden" posing a "substantial obstacle" to the abortion of a nonviable fetus.

Since 1973 about two-thirds of the states have enacted new abortion laws designed to test the limits of *Roe*. These statutes curtail the availability of abortion in various ways: by denying the use of public funds or facilities for abortion; by requiring special precautions to prevent the abortion of a possibly viable fetus; by banning particular methods of abortion; and by imposing waiting periods and notification and consent requirements designed to discourage the choice of abortion.

1. Laws denying the use of public funds or facilities for abortion consistently have been upheld by the Supreme Court (e.g., *Maher v. Roe*, 432 U.S. 464 (1977); *Harris v. McRae*, 448 U.S. 297 (1980)), as was a Bush administration rule forbidding clinics that receive federal funds from counseling or even mentioning abortion (*Rust v. Sullivan*, 500 U.S. 173 (1991)). Indeed, it was in the abortion-funding cases that the distinction first emerged between "undue burdens" on pro-

creative choice and constitutionally permissible expressions of a legislative policy favoring maternity.

2. Laws prohibiting the abortion of a viable fetus are common and generally valid, provided they make exception for abortions necessary to preserve the mother's life or health. *Planned Parenthood Association of Kansas City v. Ashcroft*, 462 U.S. 476 (1983), narrowly upheld a Missouri statute mandating that a second doctor be present to look out for the fetus during post-viability abortions; *Thornburg v. American College of Obstetricians and Gynecologists*, 476 U.S. 747 (1986), struck down a similar Pennsylvania requirement that did not except situations where waiting for the second doctor would put the mother's life or health at risk. *Thornburg* also invalidated a requirement that post-viability abortions be performed in a way that would allow the unborn child to survive the procedure, if it could be done without significantly greater risk to the mother; this was read as impermissibly demanding that the mother bear an increased medical risk in order to save the fetus. *Webster v. Reproductive Health Services*, supra, upheld another Missouri statute prohibiting doctors from performing abortions on any woman believed to be twenty weeks pregnant or more without first undertaking tests to determine fetal viability.

3. Laws banning particular methods of abortion generally have been found to be invalid. *Planned Parenthood of Central Missouri v. Danforth*, 428 U.S. 52 (1976), struck down a prohibition of saline amniocentesis, at the time the usual and safest method for second trimester abortions. Most of the lower courts that passed on the spate of state laws prohibiting so-called partial-birth abortions found them to be invalid, as did the Supreme Court in *Stenberg v. Carhart*, 120 S. Ct. 2597 (2000). These laws criminalize abortions where "the person performing the abortion partially delivers vaginally a living unborn child before killing the unborn child and completing the delivery." This appears to refer to the procedure known as "intact dilation and extraction," in which, in order to minimize damage to the uterus and cervix, the fetus is partly moved into the birth canal before being destroyed. But no exception for maternal health is made in these laws; it is not required that the fetus be viable; and the statutory language is said to be vague enough to cover other permissible abortion procedures as well.

4. Laws imposing relatively minor impediments to abortion such as record-keeping requirements and a requirement of the patient's written consent generally have been upheld. Requirements that doctors make certain specified statements to a woman seeking abortion, so that her consent will be "informed," and mandatory twenty-four-hour waiting periods before the abortion can be performed, were struck down in *City of Akron v. Akron Center for Reproductive Health*, 462 U.S. 416 (1983), and in *Thornburg*, supra, on the ground that they were designed to intimidate women into forgoing abortion; such requirements were upheld, however, under the new standard adopted by the plurality opinion in *Planned Parenthood of Southeastern Pennsylvania v. Casey*, supra. A requirement of spousal consent was invalidated in *Danforth*, supra, on the ground that it effectively gave the husband a veto over his wife's exercise of a constitutional right; *Casey* similarly found that, for many women, even a requirement of spousal notification would pose a substantial obstacle to abortion and therefore was impermissible. A requirement of parental consent when an unmarried pregnant minor seeks an abortion was invalidated in *Danforth*; but such requirements generally have been upheld in subsequent cases, including *Casey*, when accompanied by alternative provision for a judge to approve the abortion in lieu of a parent. A law requiring that both of a minor's parents be notified of the abortion would be invalid without a similar provision for so-called judicial bypass (*Hodgson v. Minnesota*, 497 U.S. 417 (1990)); the validity of a requirement that only one parent be notified, without provision for judicial bypass, was left open in *Ohio v. Akron Center for Reproductive Health*, 497 U.S. 502 (1990), which upheld a law requiring notification to at least one parent, with a judicial bypass option.

Efforts to limit the availability of abortion have been relentless, an indication of the intensity of opposition to *Roe*. The anti-abortion "prolife" position is rooted partly in the belief that the fetus is already a human person whose destruction constitutes a form of homicide and should be punished as such. But it is not based exclusively on this belief. There are different strands of "pro-life" sentiment. Willingness to make exceptions for cases of medical necessity or of rape, and reluctance to classify abortion as first degree murder, suggest varying degrees of commitment to the premise that abortion is in no way different from any other form of homicide. In any event, opposition to abortion appears to be bound up as well with views about sexual morality and the nature of the relationship between men and women. *Roe v. Wade* is the outstanding symbol of the prevalence of an antithetical set of views that have, since the 1960s, subverted "traditional" family and religious values; taking up arms (in some cases quite literally) against abortion serves to reassert the importance of those values in an increasingly secular world. For the "pro-choice" side, *Roe* also has considerable symbolic significance, as well as the practical and liberating effect of giving women control over their fertility. For both sides, every millimeter of ground gained or lost in the struggle to preserve or curtail the right to abortion established in *Roe* is a signal victory or defeat in a continuing clash between deeply-held beliefs about the proper role and responsibility of women in the family and in society.

EDWARD M. WISE

See also CRIMINALIZATION AND DECRIMINALIZATION; HOMICIDE: LEGAL ASPECTS.

BIBLIOGRAPHY

BYRN, ROBERT M. "An American Tragedy: The Supreme Court on Abortion." *Fordham Law Review* 41 (1973): 807–862.

COLKER, RUTH. *Abortion & Dialogue: Pro-Choice, Pro-Life, & American Law*. Bloomington and Indianapolis: Indiana University Press, 1992.

DELLAPENNA, JOSEPH W. "The History of Abortion: Technology, Morality, and Law." *University of Pittsburgh Law Review* 40 (1979): 359–428.

DWORKIN, RONALD. *Life's Dominion: An Argument about Abortion, Euthanasia, and Individual Freedom*. New York: Knopf, 1993.

GARROW, DAVID J. *Liberty & Sexuality: The Right to Privacy and the Making of Roe v. Wade*. New York: Macmillan, 1994.

GLENDON, MARY ANN. *Abortion and Divorce in Western Law: American Failures, European Challenges*. Cambridge, Mass.: Harvard University Press, 1987.

KEOWN, JOHN. *Abortion, Doctors, and the Law: Some Aspects of the Legal Regulation of Abortion in England from 1803 to 1982*. Cambridge, U.K.: Cambridge University Press, 1988.

LUKER, KRISTIN. *Abortion and the Politics of Motherhood*. Berkeley: University of California Press, 1984.

MCDONAGH, EILEEN L. *Breaking the Abortion Deadlock: From Choice to Consent*. New York: Oxford University Press, 1996.

MEANS, CYRIL C., JR. "The Law of New York Concerning Abortion and the Status of the Foetus, 1664–1968: A Case of Cessation of Constitutionality." *New York Law Forum* 14 (1968): 411–515.

———. "The Phoenix of Abortional Freedom: Is a Penumbral or Ninth-Amendment Right about to Arise from the Nineteenth-Century Legislative Ashes of a Fourteenth-Century Common-Law Liberty?" *New York Law Forum* 17 (1971): 335–410.

MENSCH, ELIZABETH, and FREEMAN, ALAN. *The Politics of Virtue: Is Abortion Debatable?* Durham, N.C.: Duke University Press, 1993.

MOHR, JAMES C. *Abortion in America: The Origins and Evolution of National Policy, 1800–1900*. New York: Oxford University Press, 1978.

NOONAN, JOHN T., JR., ed. *The Morality of Abortion: Legal and Historical Perspectives*. Cambridge, Mass.: Harvard University Press, 1970.

REAGAN, LESLIE J. *When Abortion Was a Crime: Women, Medicine, and the Law in the United States, 1867–1973*. Berkeley and Los Angeles: University of California Press, 1997.

RODMAN, HYMAN; SARVIS, BETTY; and WALKER BONAR, JOY. *The Abortion Question*. New York: Columbia University Press, 1987.

TRIBE, LAURENCE H. *Abortion: The Clash of Absolutes*. 2d ed. New York: Norton, 1992.

WILLIAMS, GLANVILLE. *The Sanctity of Life and the Criminal Law*. New York: Knopf, 1957.

CASES

City of Akron v. Akron Center for Reproductive Health, 462 U.S. 416 (1983).

Doe v. Bolton, 410 U.S. 179 (1973).

Harris v. McRae, 448 U.S. 297 (1980).

Hodgson v. Minnesota, 497 U.S. 417 (1990).

Maher v. Roe, 432 U.S. 464 (1977).

Ohio v. Akron Center for Reproductive Health, 497 U.S. 502 (1990).

Planned Parenthood Association of Central Missouri v. Danforth, 428 U.S. 52 (1976).

Planned Parenthood Association of Kansas City v. Ashcroft, 462 U.S. 476 (1983).

Planned Parenthood of Southeastern Pennsylvania v. Casey, 505 U.S. 833 (1992).

Roe v. Wade, 410 U.S. 113 (1973).

Rust v. Sullivan, 500 U.S. 73 (1991).

Thornburg v. American College of Obstetricians and Gynecologists, 476 U.S. 747 (1986).

Webster v. Reproductive Health Services, 492 U.S. 490 (1989).

ACCOMPLICES

Accomplice liability rests on the premise that someone whom the law interchangeably calls an accomplice, accessory, aider and abettor, secondary party, or helper in the crime or crimes of his perpetrator, doer, or principal is derivatively liable for whatever crime or crimes the principal commits. Punishment for accomplice liability is shared equally among principals and their helpers. Proof of the helper's liability is heavily mediated by the actions of the principal. If the principal commits a crime, the equal blame goes to the helper as well, provided that the crime that occurs is one the helper knew about and whose success the helper intended when he provided his assistance.

Accomplice liability's legitimacy rests on its demand that the helper's contribution be significant enough to justify his punishment, but not so significant, dominant, or manipulative as to wipe out altogether the responsibility of the principal. Someone who helps or tries to help someone else commit a crime exerts somewhere from no, to some, to too much constraint on his principal's autonomy. *Too much* influence exerted by the accomplice does not produce a case of accomplice liability; rather, it produces a case of principal liability for the overreaching helper in his agent's (or would-be principal's) "innocent" wrongdoing. No influence, or perhaps more accurately, no *attempt* to influence or support the principal, does not produce a case of accomplice liability because the helper has not done *enough* to make him sufficiently caught-up or "causally" related to the principal's crime. Neither is there a case of accomplice liability if the helper and the principal do not put themselves to the same task, either because the helper does not really care whether the principal succeeds in or even attempts a crime, or because the principal commits a crime or crimes that depart from, or are in excess of, the parties' common scheme. Cases falling in between those cases where the helper does either too much or too little are what one could call "pure" or "core" cases of accomplice liability in which the helper: (1) exerts some (but not too much) influence on the principal; (2) intends that

the principal succeed in the jointly intended criminal act; and (3) the principal does in fact at least generally perform as the helper expects him to.

Principal liability: too much influence exerted by the helper

Cases of principal liability on the part of a would-be helper arise when the would-be helper acts in a way that allows us to say that it is *as though* the helper commits the crime himself. Certainly one can perform an action by getting others to do it. We say, for example, "Louis XIV built Versailles," even though the actual construction was not done by him. Indeed, we can think of cases where the principal is not a principal at all, but is simply, perhaps metaphorically, a tool, instrument, or means of someone else. Examples of such cases include cases where someone occupying what would otherwise be the position of the helper recruits a lunatic or a child to do the deed or tricks, forces, or even hypnotizes someone occupying what would otherwise be the position of the principal. These cases involve such coercion or manipulation of susceptible parties that the manipulated or coerced party's act is fishy enough for him to be called "not responsible" or for his act to be judged "not his own." Thus courts tend to reject the notion that providing a gun to a lunatic (the gun-provider being *unaware* of the lunatic's incapacity) to use to assault someone somehow makes the assault the gun-provider's and not the gun-wielding lunatic's. For one person's act to be wholly someone else's, the person to whom we attribute the act must act in a way that shows he *sees* his act as such; one cannot, after all, *use* someone else inadvertently. Were, for example, a ringleader to pay a safecracker to steal some jewels from a vault for a share of the profits, it is not as though the ringleader sees *himself* cracking the safe and stealing the jewels—he sees the safecracker doing it. The only evidence of his seeing himself doing it would be his placing such constraints on the safecracker's autonomy that it ceases to be the safecracker's intentional, purposeful, or deliberate act. Thus if the ringleader were to force the safecracker to crack the safe by putting a gun to his head or were he to trick the safecracker into believing that the safe and its contents really are the property of the ringleader, then the ringleader steals the jewels *through* the safecracker. In such a case, the ringleader would be the principal thief and not a helper at all, and the safecracker, who is *seemingly* the principal thief, would not be held responsible for his actions; instead, he would be viewed as an innocent means or instrument of the manipulative ringleader.

It is likewise an instance of principal as opposed to accomplice liability where *A* hands *B* a package into which *A* has secretly put a bomb for delivery to a victim *A* has in mind, or where *A* places *B* under duress by threatening *B* with a greater harm if *B* does not act on *A*'s behalf than if *B* does. There *A* acts through *B* by seeing *B* not as a killer, but as an innocent dupe—a giant fuse, if you will. *A* sees himself killing the victim by manipulating or forcing *B* into doing *A*'s dirty work for him. A harder case to classify is one in which a malicious felon places an innocent person or a police officer in circumstances where it is the innocent's right or the officer's duty to apply deadly force to repel the felon's threat of force, and the innocent or officer kills someone other than the malicious felon. In such cases the felon does not act *through* the innocent or officer because missing is the malicious felon's intention to *use* the killer. The felon's intention is likely that *no* such encounter materialize, except in so-called shield cases (where a third party is used by escaping suspects or those under siege as a shield against police gunfire), or in cases where one felon sends an innocent or confederate outside to a certain death in order to facilitate the malicious felon's escape. With such a bad intention and excessive risk at play, it is easy to see how in those cases we may conclude that the felon acts through the killer to deflect the justified use of deadly force away from the felon and toward another target.

When we are faced with questions of whether a would-be helper has manipulated the would-be principal to the point that the would-be principal's responsibility is wiped out altogether, the would-be helper/manipulator's conception of his own liability does not inhibit his conviction as principal. This is because the idea of "innocent agency" or "perpetration by means" is linked only to those cases where the principal *intends* to pursue an objective through the manipulative use of an agent. In other words, perpetrating harm *through* another is a narrower category of action than is *causing* another to do something harmful. Causing another to do something harmful, unlike perpetrating harm through another, is indifferent to whether the originating actor (whom we are considering treating as a manipulator) *intends* to reduce someone else to his

influence or control. In other words, causing can be mechanical whereas using cannot. Accordingly, the ringleader who recruits an insane safecracker—not knowing of the safecracker's affliction—may in some important sense *cause* the ensuing theft, but does not *commit* the theft through the insane thief. Missing there is the ringleader's intent to use, manipulate, or otherwise act through the safecracker. When, however, the harmful act *is* orchestrated by a user or manipulator who is counting on the agent's susceptibility, incapacity, or lack of responsibility, the idea of innocent agency or perpetration-by-means describes cases where the manipulated agent is a lunatic, a child, someone duped as to material facts, or anyone who cannot choose what is good and right due to coercion or any other constraint on the innocent agent that is known to the dominant party. In such cases it makes no difference whether the harm is committed by lying, stealing, frightening, shooting, stabbing, or nonconsensual intercourse (as in an infamous British case in which a husband misled an intoxicated man into thinking the husband's wife wanted intercourse with the intoxicated stranger) (*R. v. Cogan & Leak*, 1976 Q.B. (Eng. C.A.)). Each of these cases instantiates principal, not accomplice, liability on the part of the dominant party.

Core cases of accomplice liability

What must the helper do to be an accomplice to the principal's crime? In what way is it as though helpers who do *not* coerce or manipulate their principals commit their principal's crimes? The helper has merely helped. But helping, say, burglary, is not committing burglary. Nor is helping burglary *trying* to commit burglary, any more than *argue* is equivalent to "try to convince" or *warn* is equivalent to "try to alarm." Anglo-American law nevertheless treats a helper as a principal so long as the helper intentionally contributes to the principal's crime. In other words, if the helper pitches in the requisite contribution to the principal's crime, then the helper is punished identically to the principal since Anglo-American law long ago "abrogated" or statutorily eliminated the historically recognized distinction between the amount of punishment one deserves for, say, giving a burglar a crow bar and actually performing the breaking and entering oneself (*Standefer v. United States*, 447 U.S. 10 (1980) pp. 15–20; Smith). Whether a defendant is (1) a perpetrator (or "principal in the first degree") who actually performs the criminal act; (2) a perpetrator (or "principal in the second degree") who provides some assistance at the scene of the crime; or (3) a helper or an accomplice (or "accessory before the fact") whose aid is given in advance (as in the planning stages) or contemporaneous with but away from the scene makes no difference for purposes of punishment. Indeed, only a helper (or "accessory after the fact") whose assistance comes *after* the crime has taken place—typically in the form of concealment of the crime—receives a more lenient punishment than those criminals who make their contribution before or during the crime.

While this position of "equivalency" of punishment between those who commit crimes and those who help them is uncontroversial in Anglo-American law, there is some controversy over what sorts of help or contribution *count* as acts of accomplice liability. We know already that too much influence—too great a contribution—is not a case of accomplice liability at all, but rather a case of principal liability on the part of the would-be helper. So too is it possible that the would-be helper has not done *enough* for his contribution to count as an instance of accomplice liability. Although there are various formulations of how much the helper must add to the criminal venture, it is clear that encouragement of any sort, whether it be in the form of soliciting or asking the principal or another helper to commit or participate in a crime, cheering on the principal (or another helper), or merely promising the principal (or another helper) to help if necessary is enough to keep the helper on the hook for the principal's actions.

When accomplice liability is based on encouragement, the doctrine operates identically to the doctrine of conspiracy. The doctrine of conspiracy holds that parties who agree to commit a crime are jointly liable not only for the agreement, but also for the carrying out of the conspiratorial objectives (*Pinkerton v. United States*, 328 U.S. 640 (1946)). An agreement can be formal or explicit as well as implicit or arrived at through "nods and winks." Merely imitating another's behavior, however, falls short of an agreement, even if the imitation is mutual. Thus the Supreme Court has held that a conspiracy to fix prices cannot be proved in the absence of some communicated intention to pursue a specified pricing strategy. Simply pursuing such a strategy—even aware that it is strongly in other competitors' interests to do the same—is "consciously parallel" behavior, but does not make out a case

of conspiracy (*Interstate Circuit, Inc. v. United States*, 306 U.S. 208 (1939)). Many cases of accomplice liability, however, *are* also cases of conspiracy. Those that are not are cases that originate not with encouragement between parties, but when material aid such as a car, a crowbar, a gun, or poison are supplied, or when the helper serves as a getaway driver or lookout. In these instances—where there is no communication of the helper's intent to help—there is no conspiracy between the principal and the helper to commit a crime. Accordingly, the helper's shared responsibility for aiding the principal's crimes in these instances is based on the law of accomplice liability, as opposed to the laws both of accomplice liability *and* conspiracy.

When it is aid and not encouragement that the helper adds, it must be "actual" aid that "mattered" or "made a difference" to the principal's actions (Kadish, pp. 358–359). Only when the helper's actions could not have been successful in any case is there no accomplice liability. Thus the question "how much contribution?" comes down simply to whether the helper *meant* to contribute to the principal's crime, and any action that betrays such an intention will be deemed sufficient to constitute an act of accomplice liability. Thus it has been held that lending a man a smock to keep a battery victim's blood from staining the batterer's suit made enough difference to the batterer to justify our treating the smock-lender as a batterer (judgment of 10 May 1883, 8 RGSt 267; cited in Fletcher, pp. 677–678). So too might an angry judge's interception of a telegram have mattered in a murder, since if the victim had received the telegram, he could have anticipated the gunman behind him on reading the crucial wire: "Four men on horseback with guns following. Look out" (*State ex rel. Attorney General v. Tally*, 102 Ala. 25, 69, 15 So. 722, 734 (1894)). Even a door opened for a burglar *could* conceivably make a difference to burglary through the window.

The above are only exceptional examples; but even basic cases of accomplice liability, such as where a helper lends his principal a crowbar for a burglary or drives him to the sites of the crime, are not cases where the helper actually *causes* the crime, even if the principal has no crowbar of his own or cannot drive a car. It follows that an otherwise superfluous helper whose opening a bank door hastens a robbery by seconds is on the hook as accomplice to the robbery, as flimsy as his contribution may be. Thus the real issue here is not so much whether the helper has "caused" or even "made a difference" to the principal's crime, but rather, whether the helper has *put himself* to helping, or has *tried* to help.

What must the helper know about the principal's intentions? It is not enough that the helper encourage or aid the principal in the principal's crime or crimes. In order to be an accomplice in the principal's crime(s), the helper must in addition *know* what it is that is being helped, and must *intend* that the acts of encouragement or aid facilitate the principal's criminal venture. In other words, there must be some level of attunement between the parties before blame for the principal's actions can be shared equally by the helper. So, if the helper lends a crow bar to his neighbor unaware that the neighbor intends to use it for a burglary, then the helper is not an accomplice to the burglary, even though he has contributed material aid. Because the aid was provided in ignorance of what use it would be put to, the aid cannot, by itself, make out a case of accomplice liability against the helper. This is precisely the problem the law faces with providers of goods (e.g., retail hunting stores) and services (e.g., lessors of hotel rooms) who naively help along a criminal venture. A helper's contribution simply cannot count as accomplice liability unless the helper knows what the principal is up to.

Even when the helper does know what the principal is up to, there are two considerable problems to our finding the helper to be an accomplice in what the principal ultimately does: (1) the helper may be indifferent to how or even whether the helper's contribution operates on the principal; and (2) the principal may depart "upward" from the common scheme by committing excessive crimes not imagined by the helper, or depart "downward" from the common scheme by raising a complete or partial excuse from liability that may (or may not) be open to the helper.

The helper's level of commitment to the principal's criminal venture

Often the principal and helper have divergent levels of commitment to the contemplated crime. For example, the lessor of a hotel room that the lessor knows the lessee will use for gambling, drug distribution, or prostitution may well know to what unlawful use the premises will be put. But the lessor still may not, in the words of the celebrated Judge Learned Hand, have a sufficiently "purposive attitude towards" the venture so as to be "associated" with it in a way that demonstrates "that he wishes to bring [it] about" (*United States v. Peoni*, 100 F.2d 401 (2d Cir. 1938). Instead, the lessor may even prefer to lease the room to a law-abiding lessee (that way the lessor can avoid trouble) but is willing to rent to anyone who can pay the going rate. In such a case, the lessor's contribution to the crime counts as aid, but unless there is reason for us to believe that the lessor is somehow in on the scheme, the lessor's aid falls short of the "purposive attitude" toward the principal's crimes that the law of accomplice liability requires. No doubt a case of accomplice liability is made out if the lessor takes a commission from the lessee's venture or charges the lessee extra to insure against the risk the lessor incurs by leasing to a criminal who may for obvious reasons be bad for the lessor's business.

This means that a helper cannot be accidentally liable for or caught up in the principal's crimes, even when the crime that the principal has committed is one for which accident is not necessarily an excuse. For example, a (principal) driver can be convicted of drunk driving even if it is perfectly reasonable for him to believe he has had too little to drink to have become drunk. To be accomplice to the driver's drunk driving, however, the helper must do more than merely fail to take cost-justified precautions against doing or saying anything that may make the principal's drunk driving more likely. Instead, the helper must mean to facilitate drunk driving; he must, in Judge Hand's terms, demonstrate a purposive attitude toward bringing about the crime in question. So a bartender or social host may in fact be assisting drunk driving by keeping an inaccurate tally of how much their guest or customer has had to drink, they may know that such a result is likely, and nonetheless not have within the letter of the law helped drunk driving—not if such an outcome is not the bartender or social host's intention.

The principal's departures from the common scheme

When the principal departs "upward": the helper's liability for the principal's excess. Assuming that there is at least a crime toward which the helper has the requisite intention or "purposive attitude," then what happens if the principal commits other crimes in addition to or instead of the crime or crimes that the helper means to help? In evaluating the helper's responsibility for the principal's excessive criminality, the law is understandably unsympathetic to the claims of the too-finicky helper, who complains at trial that the principal deviated, however slightly, from the common scheme. Therefore if the helper asks the principal to take the victim's gold watch by snatching it from the victim's wrist, but the principal obtains it by threatening to expose the victim's criminal record to his golf club, a court would not let the helper off the hook for being an accomplice to the principal's blackmail. The criminal objective of stealing the watch remains the same—the principal's deviation only in means fails to demonstrate a lack of attunement between the parties. If, however, the helper lends a crowbar to the principal, believing that the principal intends to enter a house in order to steal a television, the helper will be off the hook for playing a role in, say, arson, if that is what the principal unexpectedly does instead upon entering the house. So long as there is attunement as to "essential matters" or so long as the crime in question is of the same "type" or within the "contemplation" of the range of crimes anticipated by the helper, the principal's departures will not save the helper from liability for what the principal ultimately does (*Northern Ireland v. Maxwell*, (1978) 3 All E.R. 1140; *Regina v. Bainbridge*, (1960) 1 Q.B. 129). Determining just what it was that was contemplated demands thorough knowledge of the enterprise, a matter that is made easier when there is a conspiracy: the more formal the better.

When the principal exceeds the helper's expectations, still a minority of courts have expanded the liability of the helper for the principal's excesses (*People v. Luparello*, 231 Cal. Rptr. 832 (Ct. App. 1987)). It is safe to say that decisions which hold helpers on the hook for their roles in, for example, intentional murder by a principal when the helper asked the principal to commit assault or at most kidnapping, reveal the most extended or outermost limits of a helper's liability. Yet the overwhelming majority of courts regularly do make this stretch when principals commit intentional *or* accidental killings—even unforeseeably or contrary to a carefully thought-out plan—during the course of certain "inherently dangerous felonies," such as burglary, robbery, arson, rape, kidnapping, and prison escape (Model Penal Code § 210.2(1)(b)). As a result, a getaway driver who means to aid in robbery is liable for the "murder" of a store clerk who dies of a heart attack when confronted by the armed principal robber. Outside of this area of homicide, known as "felony murder," helpers are typically held liable only for their principals' actions that are within, or at least adjacent to, their common scheme.

When the principal departs "downward": The helper's relation to the principal's excuses.   So far we have been focusing entirely on helpers' excuses that have to do with what the helper knows, intends, and does. But often the principal will have an excuse that will allow him to avoid altogether, or at a minimum reduce his responsibility for, what he has done. In such cases, courts have developed strategies for establishing the connection, if any, between the principal's full or partial excuses and the helper's liability.

Take for example a version of Shakespeare's *Othello*, in which Iago calmly and maliciously drives Othello into a blind rage and incites him to kill his wife Desdemona by making Othello believe (falsely) that Desdemona had been unfaithful to him. Let's assume that Othello's rage would make him eligible for the partial excuse of "provocation" or "extreme emotional disturbance," which precludes a murder conviction and instead makes his crime more accurately described as the less-grave offense of manslaughter. The excuse is only partial because Othello still deserves *some* punishment; it is not as though Iago acted (completely) *through* him. Othello was in a rage, but still knew what he was doing—knew that he was retaliating against his wife. While Othello is still partially responsible for what he has done, his rage reduces "down" to manslaughter an otherwise murderous act. Consequently Othello's punishment will be five or so years rather than the life imprisonment he would have been eligible for had he been thinking more clearly at the time of the killing.

But what is Iago's relation to Othello's partial excuse? There are four options open to us here, each of which is expressed in at least some Anglo-American court opinions: (1) allow Othello's rage to benefit Iago on the ground that a helper's liability cannot exceed whatever crime actually takes place. This view is appealing to the extent that it enforces the notion that a helper's liability is derivative of the principal's—the helper cannot help a crime that does not take place, whatever the reason may be that it fails. This view is unappealing, however, to the extent that it lets the helper borrow (perhaps unfairly) defenses such as intoxication, mistake, insanity, and duress, which may be utterly personal to the principal; (2) allow Othello's rage to benefit Iago only if Othello was "justified" in part in killing Desdemona as opposed to merely "excused." This has the appeal of letting the helper exploit a principal's actions that, at least in part, "interfere with the rights of no one." Unfortunately, to give the helper this benefit not only requires taking a position on which defenses are in fact justified as opposed to excused, but also threatens the unwelcome result of allowing a helper to claim he was justified in doing something when the very facts that make the act justified are unknown to him (as in battering someone whom unbeknownst to the batterer the principal had the right to repel in self-defense); (3) deny Iago the benefit of Othello's rage by "grafting" Othello's action onto Iago's intention in order to make out a case of murder on Iago's part and manslaughter on Othello's. While this way each party would have to raise his own defenses, the problems are considerable in that this would permit a defendant to be convicted as accomplice to a murder when no murder took place; and (4) conclude that Iago has attempted murder while Othello has committed manslaughter. This position (Model Penal Code § 5.01 (3)) recognizes that the helper's help has in an important sense failed or misfired (thus the reduced liability) and features the additional benefit of reflecting that accomplice liability is more about what the helper puts himself to than what he actually accomplishes. Whichever of these four strategies a jurisdiction adopts for dealing with problems of a helper's liability for the actions of a principal who may have a full or partial defense will determine whether the helper is punished even though the principal is not, whether the helper can borrow a principal's excuses (or his justifications), or a position somewhere in between.

What crimes can be helped?

Although the abrogation of the distinction between principals and helpers has equalized their punishments, the abrogation will never be able to eliminate altogether the distinction between helping and doing when it comes to identifying whether certain actors are liable at all for whatever it is that has happened. For example, suppose an antiprostitution law that criminalizes "selling sex." Obviously the prostitute is the seller, but what has the "John" or buyer of sex done? Sold sex? Helped the prostitute sell sex? Nothing criminal at all?

This problematical aspect of the law of accomplice liability comes up frequently in the context of two-party cases requiring the participation of two persons as opposed to the run-of-the-mill offense that requires a perpetrator and a victim. Dangerous games such as Russian roulette or drag racing are examples of such two-or-more-party offenses where the law of accomplices has an uncertain role to play. It is not all that unusual for courts to say that lucky survivors of dangerous games have somehow killed the unlucky players who have died from shooting themselves in the head or by driving their cars off the road into ditches or oncoming traffic.

For example, in *People v. Abbott & Moon*, 84 A.D.2d 11 (N.Y. App. Div. 1981), Moon was drag racing with Abbott, who killed Patricia Hammond and her two passengers, who had entered the intersection through which Moon was racing at 80–85 and Abbott at over 90 miles per hour at the time of the wreck. Although Moon was driving worse than unsafely, he was lucky enough to avoid ramming into anyone. While Abbott's liability for the three deaths was obvious, Moon's conviction of criminally negligent homicide and reckless driving also was upheld on appeal. The court explained that

[w]hile Moon did not personally control Abbott's vehicle which struck the three victims, it could reasonably be found that he "intentionally" aided Abbott in the unlawful use of the vehicle by participating in a high-speed race, weaving in and out of traffic, and thus shared Abbott's culpability. . . . Moon associated himself with the high-speed race on a busy highway and took part in it for nearly two minutes over a distance in excess of one mile. Actually his conduct made the race possible. He accepted Abbott's challenge and shared in the venture. Without Moon's aid Abbott could not have engaged in the high-speed race which culminated in the tragedy. (p. 15)

For this reading of complicity the New York appellate court cited criminal-law expert Wayne LaFave, who has noted that such a view "has much to recommend it" (LaFave and Scott, p. 673).

Although calling Moon an accomplice in the fatalities that arose out of his excessive risk-taking has an elemental appeal (he was, after all, a wrongdoer), it is analytically impossible. Consider again the passage quoted above in which the court observed: "Actually his *[Moon's] conduct made the race possible.*" Indeed it did, and this is precisely why each racer is analytically precluded from helping the race. Help can be withheld, or it wouldn't be helping at all. In other words, because the relation of helping (unlike doing or perpetrating) to the ultimate harm is synthetic or empirical, not analytic or true by definition, the actions of helping and doing are distinct and should be so treated. Thus if the crime analytically, elementally, or definitionally requires two or more parties, then the required parties cannot, merely by participating, possibly "help" an activity to which they are by definition essential. Certainly a buyer does not help a seller in an exchange transaction by paying for goods any more than an unmarried person helps a bigamist by marrying him or her, a betrothed couple help each other get married by marrying, or someone helps someone else kiss by simply kissing them.

Here we are not talking simply about cases of "joint principality," under which two parties divide the elements of an offense; for example, two parties rob when one commits the assault (the frightening of the person) and the other the larceny (the taking of the property). Since both the force or threat of force and the taking of the property are analytically, elementally, or definitionally necessary to any robbery, neither party is helping robbery; both are committing it. Oppositely, where the help of one party is necessary only as an empirical or synthetic matter—that is, where the helper does not fulfill a statutory definition of crime or one of its elements, but his actions happen to be necessary for the crime on these facts, then he is helping and not doing, no matter how he may characterize his own actions. For example, that a getaway driver may be necessary for a successful robbery must be observed to be known; getaway drivers are not analytically or definitionally necessary to robbery, which occurs whether or not the perpetrators have a car. Consequently, getaway drivers are helpers, not principals or joint principals, regardless of how they may characterize their actions.

Despite considerable confusion in court opinions—see *Commonwealth v. Atencio*, 189 N.E.2d 627, 630 (Sup. Jud. Ct. of Mass. 1963)—and academic commentary—see Fletcher, pp. 654–655—multiparty game cases, like exchange transactions, do not instantiate helping by one whose participation is analytically a necessary condition of the crime itself. This is not to say that drag racing and Russian roulette foreclose altogether the doctrine of accomplice liability. Spectators cheering on a drag race could be liable for helping the homicide. Well-known (and still controversial) decisions like *Wilcox v. Jeffrey*, 1 All E.R. 464 (King's Bench Division 1951), (where a magazine writer, for the purpose of writing about the performance, "helped" Cole-

man Hawkins play jazz illegally in the United Kingdom) have so held. Cheering spectators *are* helping drag racing (as Natalie Wood so enthusiastically did in Nicholas Ray's *Rebel Without a Cause*) and thus are liable as accomplices in the unlucky racer's demise. But a lucky drag racer who avoids disaster—who neither bumps, cuts off, nor swerves into another racer, driver, or pedestrian—"helps" nothing.

Although American law insists on treating helpers and doers identically, the cheering spectators should have an excuse, albeit a partial one: they were merely helping. Not only is the lucky survivor helping nothing, but neither is he jointly principal in the killing, given that the crime with which such defendants are customarily charged—manslaughter—has two elements: (1) excessive risk-taking and (2) causing death. Manslaughter is not, analytically, a two-or-more-party offense; nor is it divided into one (one steers, the other accelerates?) as obscene phone calling could be were one person to dial and the other to speak obscenely. Moon was charged with manslaughter, not with drag racing. To use the necessary participation as a means of describing the role as that of helping the unlucky player's actions papers over the grammatical, even moral, distinction between helping and doing.

DANIEL B. YEAGER

See also CONSPIRACY; RICO (RACKETEER INFLUENCED AND CORRUPT ORGANIZATIONS ACT); VICARIOUS LIABILITY.

BIBLIOGRAPHY

DRESSLER, JOSHUA. "Reassessing the Theoretical Underpinnings of Accomplice Liability: New Solutions to an Old Problem." *Hastings Law Journal* 37 (September 1985): 91.
FLETCHER, GEORGE. *Rethinking Criminal Law*. Little Brown, 1978.
Great Britain. "Assisting and Encouraging Crime." The Law Commission Consultation Paper No. 131. London: Her Majesty's Stationary Office, 1993.
KADISH, SANFORD. "Complicity, Cause, and Blame: A Study in the Interpretation of Doctrine." *California Law Review* 73 (March 1985): 323.
LaFAVE, W., and SCOTT, A., JR. *Criminal Law*, 2d ed. St. Paul, Minn.: West, 1986.
Model Penal Code § 2.06. Official Draft. Philadelphia: ALI, 1962.

ROBINSON, PAUL. "Imputed Criminal Liability." *Yale Law Journal* 93 (March 1984): 609.

SMITH, K. J. M. *A Modern Treatise on the Law of Criminal Complicity.* New York: Oxford University Press, 1991.

YEAGER, DANIEL. "Helping, Doing, and the Grammar of Complicity." *Criminal Justice Ethics* 15 (winter/spring 1996): 25.

YEAGER, DANIEL B. "Dangerous Games and the Criminal Law." *Criminal Justice Ethics* 16 (winter/spring 1997): 3.

CASES

Commonwealth v. Atencio, 189 N.E.2d 627 (Sup. Jud. Ct. of Mass. 1963).

Interstate Circuit, Inc. v. United States, 306 U.S. 208 (1939).

Northern Ireland v. Maxwell, (1978) 3 All E. R. 1140.

People v. Abbott & Moon, 84 A.D.2d 11 (N.Y. App. Div. 1981).

People v. Luparello, 231 Cal. Rptr. 832 (Ct. App. 1987).

Pinkerton v. United States, 328 U.S. 640 (1946).

Regina v. Bainbridge, (1960) 1 Q.B. 129.

Standefer v. United States, 447 U.S. 10, 15–20 (1980).

State ex rel. Attorney General v. Tally, 102 Ala. 25, 69, 15 So. 722, 734 (1894).

United States v. Peoni, 100 F.2d 401 (2d Cir. 1938).

Wilcox v. Jeffrey, All E.R. 464 (King's Bench Division 1951).

ACTUS REUS

Actus reus is a term of art in criminal law. Literally the Latin phrase means bad act. The technical, legal use of the phrase denotes one of the elements that must be proven by the prosecution before anyone can be liable to criminal punishment. The actus reus element is the act made criminal by some statute or other valid source of criminal law. Thus, a defendant is said to have committed the actus reus of some offense if he has done some act that is an instance of the type of action prohibited by the offense in question. Murder statutes, for example, typically prohibit the "killing of a human being"; the actus reus of murder is satisfied by any act that is an instance of the type of act so described—that is, any act that is a killing of a human being.

Actus reus versus mens rea

There are two contrasts with other elements of criminal liability that help to clarify the nature of actus reus. The first is the contrast with *mens rea*. Mens rea literally translated from the Latin means guilty mind. The technical legal use of the phrase denotes that prerequisite of criminal liability having to do with the state of mind of the accused when he committed the actus reus of some offense. Thus, one of the mens reas sufficient for murder is general intent: such requirement is often stated as a prohibition on *"intentionally* killing another human being." The word "intentionally" tells us what kind of mental state an accused must have to be guilty of this kind of murder (either an intent or a belief, as it turns out). The phrase "killing another human being" tells us two things: first, what must be done by way of action to be guilty of murder; and second, what object an accused's intention or belief must take in order to be guilty of murder (Moore, 1993). The first is the actus reus requirement, whereas the second is part of the mens rea requirement. The accused must both actually kill someone, and intend (or believe) that he is killing someone, in order to be guilty of this kind of murder.

The relationship between actus reus and mens rea is not always this close in all offenses. In what are often called specific intent offenses, for example, the object of the prohibited mens rea will not coincide with the act prohibited by law. Thus, the actus reus of common law burglary is the breaking and entering of the dwelling house of another at night, whereas the mens rea includes the requirement that the accused do such breaking and entering with the intent to commit a felony once inside. The commission of such a further felony is no part of the actus reus of burglary, but the intent to commit such a further felony is part of the mens rea of burglary.

In its actus reus/mens rea distinction the criminal law has mirrored a deep divide in morality. This is the divide between wrongdoing and culpability. Although it is disputed, morality is most often thought to contain certain prohibitions and requirements, such as "Do not kill" and "Help others in distress." Morality generally permits us either to do or to refrain from doing most acts, but morality forbids certain actions and requires others. To do an act morality forbids, or to refrain from doing an act morality requires, is to breach one's moral obligations. This is moral wrongdoing.

Morality likewise concerns itself with the culpability with which a wrongful act is done. Overall moral blameworthiness includes culpability as well as wrongdoing. One is free from moral blame for causing a harm to another if one neither intended to cause such a harm, believed one's act could result in such a harm, or unreasonably risked such a harm coming about because of one's actions.

The legal distinction between actus reus and mens rea is best seen as a reflection of this underlying moral distinction. The parallel is one of form, with criminal law and morality dividing criminal liability and moral responsibility (respectively) into these two elements. The difference, of course, lies in the content of legal versus moral norms; in many legal systems much that morality prohibits or requires the law does not, and vice versa.

Actus reus versus justificatory defenses

The second distinction illuminating the nature of actus reus is the distinction between the prima facie case for criminal liability and the defenses. The distinction is a procedural one having to do with allocation of certain burdens in an adversary system. The burdens here pertinent are two: one party or the other is given the burden of producing evidence from which a reasonable fact-finder could find in their favor, and one party or the other is given the risk of not persuading the fact-finder with her evidence. Thus, if the prosecution in a criminal case has both burdens on a certain issue, it will have a verdict directed against it if it fails to produce evidence on that issue and it will also lose if the fact-finder is undecided about which direction the evidence points on a certain issue.

The prima facie case in a criminal trial is that part of the elements of liability on which the prosecution has both of these burdens. Actus reus is best conceived as being as much of the prohibited action as is part of the prima facie case, but no more. Specifically what is excluded by this way of conceptualizing actus reus are the justificatory defenses (Moore, 1993).

Consider homicide again by way of example. Criminal codes do not in fact prohibit simply the "killing of a human being." Rather, they prohibit the killing of a human being except in self-defense, defense of others, prevention of certain crimes, in cases of necessity, and so on. Built into the seemingly simple prohibitions of the criminal law are those exceptional circumstances where the act in question is permitted or encouraged by the law. The actus reus of murder nonetheless remains the exceptionless, simple prohibition against killing a human being, for it is only this

much that the prosecution must sustain as part of its prima facie case. The defense has the burden of raising self-defense and the other justificatory defenses, so the absence of any justification of self-defense and the like is not part of the actus reus of murder.

A parallel limitation exists for mens rea. Certain defenses such as infancy, insanity, involuntary intoxication, duress, and provocation are not justificatory defenses; rather they only excuse prima facie illegal conduct. Some have urged an expansive definition of mens rea, so as to include absence of these excusing conditions as part of a "guilty mind." Preferable is the narrower conception of mens rea, paralleling the narrower conception of actus reus (Kadish). On this narrower conception, mens rea is present whenever the accused intends, believes, or unreasonably risks a prohibited action; such mens rea makes for a prima facie liability only, however, since such liability can be escaped by showing excusing circumstances in which the mental state arose.

It is controversial whether this second distinction in the criminal law reflects any underlying moral structure. On its face, the distinction is seemingly based only on the procedural convenience of dividing up the burdens of producing a trial between prosecution and defense in an adversarial system. On this view, the distinctions between actus reus and justification, and between mens rea and excuse, are morally arbitrary. That the actus reus of rape, for example, includes lack of victim consent, whereas the actus reus of criminal assault makes consent of the victim a defense (and thus not part of the actus reus), illustrates this apparent moral arbitrariness.

On the other hand, on some views of ethics morality consists of simple, exceptionless "absolutes" like "Thou shalt not kill." In this view of morality the justifications make actions permissible that are otherwise categorically prohibited. On this view one is morally permitted to kill in self-defense, for example, but it would be better if one did not take advantage of such permission (Moore, 1993). On this "stained permissions" view of the justifications like self-defense, the legal distinction between actus reus and the justificatory defenses reflects the underlying moral distinction between the categorical norms of obligation and the secondary norms of discretionary permissions. In such a view of morality the legal distinction between the actus reus of offenses and the justificatory defenses is not a morally arbitrary matter of procedural convenience.

Whatever may be the case about the moral basis for the two distinctions we have discussed, legally it is clear that actus reus is thus but one of four major elements in criminal liability. It joins mens rea, absence of justification, and absence of excuse as the four prerequisites for liability to punishment in the criminal law, and it joins mens rea in constituting the prima facie case for that liability.

The voluntary act principle

Having isolated actus reus within the overall requirements for criminal liability, it remains to examine its nature. The general nature of the requirement we have stated earlier: actus reus is the requirement that the accused have performed an action prohibited, at least prima facie, by the criminal law. We gain more insight into the nature of this requirement if we probe the nature of actions themselves. If the criminal law requires actions for liability, we would do well to understand what might be generally true of human actions.

This seemingly intuitive route for analysis runs into a long-existing, widely shared skepticism that denies the existence of any general truths about human actions as such. This skepticism admits that we can seek the nature of specific kinds of actions, such as killings, maimings, destroyings, and so on. Denied is that all such types of actions have any shared nature (Austin, 1956; Duff).

If such skepticism were true then the most we could say about the actus reus requirement of the criminal law is what we have said before: actus reus is the requirement that, before one is liable to punishment, one not do one of the many thousands of actions prohibited by the criminal law. Fortunately the metaphysics of human action is not as bleak as this skepticism would contend. There are two very general truths about human actions as such (and thus, about all those many human actions prohibited by Anglo-American criminal codes).

One of those truths is encapsulated within the criminal law's so-called *voluntary act principle*. The voluntary act principle states that there can be no actus reus (and thus, no criminal liability) unless the defendant performed a voluntary act. A voluntary act, in turn, is defined as a bodily movement caused by the "effort or determination of the actor, either conscious or habitual"

(Model Penal Code § 2.01(2)(d)). The voluntary act principle thus requires willed bodily movement by a defendant before criminal liability may attach.

To understand the voluntary act principle, it is helpful to subdivide it into four subprinciples. The first is the idea that voluntary acts are *events* and are not one of those more enduring things we call *states*. My firing of a gun yesterday is an event that occurred over a relatively brief interval of time and that involved change in the world. My being a person who likes to fire guns is a more enduring *state* not involving change but rather stasis.

The U.S. Supreme Court for a time attempted to articulate this distinction in its holdings prohibiting criminal punishment for *status* rather than *action*. In *Robinson v. California*, 370 U.S. 660 (1962), the Court held it unconstitutional for California to punish someone for the status of being an addict, recognizing that it was constitutionally permissible to punish someone for the actions of using drugs. Similarly in *Powell v. Texas*, 392 U.S. 514 (1968), the Court allowed the punishment of someone for being drunk in public because implicit in the actus reus of the crime was the action of going into public while one was drunk.

The second subprinciple is that voluntary actions are physical events involving the only physical mechanism within our immediate control, our own bodies. While there are mental events like deciding or intending to do something, voluntary acts are not these kinds of events. Rather, a voluntary act is (at least in part) the physical event of our bodies moving in response to our intentions to move them. The insight motivating this second aspect of the voluntary act principle is that the criminal law cares about harms in the world. The only means persons have at their disposal to bring such harms about is by use of their bodies. None of us has telekinetic powers so that only through bodily movement do our evil thoughts produce evil consequences.

The third subprinciple is that only *willed* bodily movements count as voluntary actions. Our bodies often "act" in the same way that inanimate objects "act," which is to say without our direction or control. If my body is thrown through a window, I cannot be said to have performed the voluntary act of breaking the window; in such cases, my body is no different than a stone that I happen to own breaking the window—in neither case have I broken the window. Similarly, if I am in the midst of an epileptic seizure, a hypogly episode, a reflex or shock reaction, hypnosis, somnambulistic or fugue state, or the like, I am not the author of the harms my body may cause. It is only bodily movements caused by my intention (or "willing") to so move that constitute voluntary actions (Moore, 1993).

Fourth and last, the results of my willed bodily movements are not proper parts of my voluntary actions nor do such results themselves constitute separate voluntary actions. John Austin stated this thesis explicitly: "a voluntary movement of my body. . .is an act. . .bodily movements are the only objects to which the term 'acts' can be applied with perfect precision and propriety" (p. 415). Oliver Wendell Holmes put this point even more succinctly: An action "is a willed muscular contraction, nothing more" (pp. 73–74). Consider the actions of killing someone by way of example. The English language suggests that we cannot kill another without causing the other's death. Are we to infer that the death of the victim, or the causing of it by one's bodily movements, are parts of the voluntary act of killing? Perhaps surprisingly, the answer is no. The only voluntary acts we do are the willed bodily movements by which we kill. What happens after that is no part of our voluntary act, nor is the death resulting a separate voluntary act we do. To paraphrase Holmes and Austin, all we ever do is move our bodies, and the rest is up to nature.

On this view, the causing of death by some bodily movement is a property of that act just as being "the most talked about killing of the decade" can be a property of an act of killing. One way to refer to the act in idiomatic English is by use of these causal properties: "The killing of Nicole," or "the most talked about killing of the decade." Yet the death of Nicole, the causing of it, the talk generated by it, are no part of the voluntary act of her killer. These descriptions are simply ways of referring to that willed bodily movement by use of familiar properties. We do the same thing when we talk of "the teacher of Alexander," referring to Aristotle. It is not an essential part of Aristotle that he taught Alexander, but use of this nonessential but familiar property is a good way to refer to him.

Lawyers and legal theorists often present the voluntary act principle as a distinctively legal principle. They often defend it as a special invention of the law, serving law's unique needs. In fact the four subtheses of the voluntary act principle simply restate some well-worn truths about human actions in metaphysics. Everything lawyers say about voluntary acts many philosophers would say about human actions generically. Human actions—all of them, not just the ones used in criminal codes—are events; they are those physical events known as bodily movements; they are only a subclass of such physical events, namely, only those bodily movements caused by an intention to so move; and the only actions there are are willed bodily movements, however much we refer to those actions via their causal properties (Davidson; Moore, 1993). The voluntary act principle should be seen for what it is, an analysis of the nature of human action as such. So seen, it is one-half of the story of what it is the actus reus principle of criminal law requires: to be an action at all—and thus, an action prohibited by the criminal code—there must be a willed bodily movement.

Common criticisms of the voluntary act principle

Critics of the classic analysis of actus reus are legion. Such critics attack all four aspects of the voluntary act principle, sometimes construing it as a creature of legal doctrine and other times taking it to be a general metaphysical truth about human actions. First, it is urged, there are criminal prohibitions of states and not only of events. In Samuel Butler's fictional Erewhon one could be punished for having tuberculosis, but even in Anglo-American criminal codes one can be punished for vagrancy, possession of various items (drugs, firearms, burglary tools, etc.), being in a vehicle where marijuana is smoked, and so on.

It is sometimes said that crimes of status are compatible with the voluntary act principle because acts may "consist of a state of affairs, rather than an event" (Gross, p. 60). This, however, is to obliterate the voluntary act requirement. Voluntary acts are essentially events and if crimes of status truly exist they contradict the voluntary act principle. Better is the response of the late Herbert Packer, who noted that crimes of status "are in fact very much on the way out" (Packer, p. 78). Not only are such laws rarely enacted today, but in America a number of constitutional infirmities are regularly found to afflict such laws so that even where they do remain on the books they are not valid (*Robinson v. California*).

An exception to this last observation must be made for possession crimes, which are both numerous and constitutionally valid. Such crimes seemingly prohibit the *state* of possessing something (weapons, drugs, etc.) and thus seem to be incompatible with the voluntary act principle.

Yet possession has become a term of art in Anglo-American criminal law. Although in ordinary English and in the law of property one might easily be said to possess something simply by being in the state of having it on one's person, criminal law requires more. "Possession" is defined in criminal law so that either an act of acquiring possession or an omission to rid oneself of possession are prerequisites to liability (Williams, 1961; Model Penal Code, § 2.01(4)). With "possession" so defined, possession crimes present no counter-examples to the voluntary act principle, or at least none greater than that presented by omissions generally (which we shall shortly discuss).

A second basis for denying that the voluntary act principle is part of the actus reus requirement stems from the supposed existence of criminal actions without any bodily movements on the part of the "actor." Sometimes this objection is cast as an observation about Anglo-American criminal law: certain crimes punish culpable mental acts alone without any execution into bodily movement. More often this objection is cast as a metaphysical observation about action: some actions can be done without any bodily movement.

The legal branch of the objection would be cogent if Anglo-American criminal law still punished thoughts alone, as in the ancient form of treason constituted by the mere "compassing the death of the king" (Williams, 1961; Fletcher, 1978). Yet modern statutes require execution of the most evil thought in bodily movement. This is true not only of treason, but also of attempt, solicitation, and conspiracy as well. Unlike the Romans, we have no crimes consisting only of mental events like dreaming of the death of the emperor (Scholz).

The metaphysical branch of the objection is more complicated. The objection is that one can literally do actions like killing without lifting a finger (Fletcher, 1995; Corrado; Annas; Brand). There are three sorts of examples here: (1) the actor ("A") pushes the victim ("V") into the water, and then stands still while V drowns; (2) A is attached to a device that will kill V if, but only if, A can stand on his head motionless for ten minutes, which A does, causing V's death; (3) A is driving when suddenly his old enemy, V, darts in front of his car, and A rather than swerving, remains motionless while his car runs over V, killing him.

In fact none of these sorts of cases present examples where A has killed V without a willed bodily movement by A. About (1), A's pushing V into the water is a voluntary act that caused V's death so that A did kill V, but not without moving his body. About (2), A again did kill V, but he again moved his body to do so. The trick is to see that A's activating the muscles needed to remain motionless are bodily movements too. For difficult routines where the "agent's body is about to be made to move by outside forces," to keep one's exterior body from moving by activating the appropriate muscles is to engage in willed bodily movement in the sense intended by the voluntary act principle (Vermazen, p. 95; see also Holmes; Moore, 1993, 1994). About (3), A does not kill V with his car. A will doubtlessly be liable for V's death, but not because A killed V; rather, A omitted to save V when A was duty-bound to do so because A's earlier acts of driving put V in danger (Moore, 1994). None of these examples disprove the voluntary act principle by producing instances of "motionless killings."

A third objection to the voluntary act principle stems from that principle's reliance on *willings* to mark the line between voluntary and involuntary bodily movements. The objection is that there are many voluntary actions where there is no datable mental state of willing. While this objection once had many adherents in both law (Hart) and philosophy (Ryle), more recent analyses have sustained the need for some state like willing, volition, endeavoring, intent to move, and so forth, to mark off voluntary action from mere involuntary movement (Moore, 1993, 1994; Bratman).

A fourth objection to the voluntary act principle disagrees with that principle's fourth thesis. Such an objection denies that the death I cause by shooting another is no proper part of my act. On this view my killing, my shooting, my pulling of the trigger, and my moving my trigger finger, are each distinct particular acts I did, not just four different descriptions of one act I did. On this view my act of killing is distinct from my act of moving my trigger finger, even though I did the former by doing the latter. The objection concludes that acts like killing others do not have at their core willed bodily movements or anything else. A killing is a killing, a burning is a burning, but they need share no feature universal to all actions, as is asserted to be the case by the voluntary act principle.

While there is a surprising amount to be said in favor of this objection (Goldman, 1970, 1994), common sense supports the voluntary act principle. When I move my trigger finger, when I move it slowly, when I move it smoothly, when I pull the trigger by moving it, and so on, I am doing one act, not as many acts as there are descriptions of it (Moore, 1993). Such a chain of descriptions of but a single act leaves open the possibility asserted to be true by the voluntary act principle: all actions are essentially willed bodily movements.

We have thus far deferred any discussion of omissions because they present the most serious objection to the view that the actus reus of all offenses includes a voluntary act. The objection also is a complicated one because those who voice it do not even agree what omissions are. The best conceptualization of omissions is that they are simply absent actions. An omission by actor A to save V from drowning is just the absence of any act by A of saving V. Such omission is not a ghostly act of saving or of anything else; rather, it is the absence of any such type of act. Such omissions are thus a kind of action no more than nonexistent elephants are a kind of elephant (Moore, 1993).

The voluntary act principle states that all actions are in essence willed bodily movements. An omission to save V at some time t thus might consist in A not moving his body at t. Yet motionless omitters are rare. Usually one who omits to save is busy doing something else at t—dancing a jig, buying a dishwasher, and so forth. What makes such persons omitters to save at time t is that none of their willed bodily movements at t has the causal property, saving-of-V's-life. One thus does not want to picture omitters as motionless statues because they need not be such (and they typically are not such).

Once we are clear as to what omissions are, we can see that Anglo-American law undeniably criminalizes some omissions. If we are the parent of a child who needs rescue, if we have undertaken such rescue even if we are not related to the child, if we have either innocently or culpably caused the condition of peril to the child, or if some statute specifically imposes a duty on us to rescue the child, we are under a positive legal duty to prevent the child's death. Despite numerous efforts to reconcile this liability with the voluntary act principle (Hughes; Gross; Epstein; Mack), the simple truth is that they are not reconcilable (Moore, 1993). Insofar as Anglo-American law criminalizes true omissions, it creates an exception to the principle that a willed bodily movement constitutes the essence of the actus reus of all criminal offenses. The voluntary act principle remains of great importance, how-

ever, because omission liability is rare in Anglo-American law and thus almost all the time it remains true that the actus reus requirement can be satisfied only by a willed bodily movement.

For the exceptional cases of omission liability we do need an account paralleling the voluntary act principle's account for act liability. If the essence of criminal omissions is not willed bodily movements, what might it be? Some have suggested that the essence of omissions is also to be found in willing. The analysis is that omissions are the willed absence of bodily movements (Fletcher, 1994). In this way one keeps as close a parallel to the voluntary act principle as possible. Yet willed absences of bodily movements is too narrow an analysis of omissions generically and it is even too narrow as an analysis of omissions made criminal by Anglo-American codes. If I negligently do not notice the child in distress, I negligently omit to save her. This is an omission, and if I am the child's parent, a criminal omission, yet I at no point willed the nonmovement of my limbs to refrain from saving her (Bentham).

The preferable line to take here is to see that the omissions we criminalize all have as their common element a capacity of the omitter not to have omitted. If I am to be held criminally liable for omitting to save my child, I must at a minimum have had the capacity to move my limbs in the relevant way—I was not asleep, in the middle of an epileptic seizure, under hypnosis, paralyzed, and so on, at the relevant times. Then I can be said to have voluntarily omitted to rescue the child.

This completes one-half of the analysis of actus reus in the criminal law. At a minimum, to satisfy the actus reus requirement of some offense one must satisfy the voluntary act principle (or in exceptional cases, the voluntary omission principle). We now need to see what else must be true in order to satisfy the actus reus requirement for criminal liability.

The properties common to complex types of actions

If criminal codes only prohibited actions like moving one's finger, then the actus reus requirement would be exhausted by the voluntary act principle. Yet for obvious reasons no criminal code consists exclusively (or even in part) of such prohibitions. We are morally and legally indifferent to such simple actions so no one has any reason to criminalize them. Rather, we criminalize more complex actions like killing another, destroying property, raping, maiming, and stealing. What else is true about all of these types of actions (beyond the fact that all are in essence willed bodily movements)?

What we seek here are useful generalizations about properties possessed by the thousands of actions prohibited by our criminal codes. It has been traditional to group all such properties into only two types: causal properties and noncausal properties of actions (Bentham; Austin; Williams; Model Penal Code § 1.13(9)). Killings of a human being, for example, are willed bodily movements having the causing of death of a human being as a property. The death is then said to be the *result element* of the actus reus of homicide. Death is so described because death of a human being must be the result of any willed bodily movement that is a killing of (i.e., a causing the death of) a human being. Killings of a police officer while in the performance of her official duties, by contrast, are willed bodily movements having not only the causal property of all killings but also having the noncausal properties that the person killed was a police officer and was on duty at the time. The facts that the victim was a police officer and that the victim was on duty at the time of the killing are then said to be the *circumstance elements* of the actus reus of cop-killing. These facts are described as "circumstances" because they are not caused by the defendant's willed bodily movement; they are simply facts ("circumstances") present at the time the defendant acted.

The criminal law's division of all properties of actions into these two kinds is uniquely legal. There is no corresponding division of the properties actions may possess in either philosophy or in ordinary thought. Philosophers of action often distinguish the properties actions may possess quite differently. Such philosophers often speak of causal properties, as do criminal lawyers, but noncausal properties are often divided up into conventional properties, mental properties, properties of the agent, properties of the victim, properties having to do with the manner, means, or instrumentality used, and so on (Rescher; Goldman; Bennet; Thalberg).

It is thus important to be clear why the criminal law is categorizing the properties actions may possess in order to assess the adequacy of its analysis. Perhaps surprisingly, the criminal law has little actus reus—oriented purpose in classifying the properties possessed by those actions criminal law prohibits. For we can determine whether a defendant satisfies the actus reus requirement for any crime without classifying the properties of action; we only need ascertain whether the act of the accused has the various properties each crime requires. Thus, the justification for classifying the properties of actions lies elsewhere, in the need of the criminal law to draw certain mens rea distinctions. These mens rea distinctions are between one who intends to cause a certain harm, one who knows to a practical certainty that his action will cause that harm, one who knows that his action will substantially and unjustifiably risk that harm, and one who unreasonably risks causing that harm even though he is unaware of that risk. These distinctions are used by the criminal law to grade the culpability with which a given wrongful act is done. The unaware but unreasonable risker is least culpable, and the intender is most culpable, with the knowing and reckless causers graded between these two extremes.

Such a grading scheme for culpable mens reas seemingly demands that the criminal law classify all properties of prohibited actions into causal or noncausal properties. The idea is that the grading scheme above described only makes moral sense with respect to the causal properties, but not the noncausal properties, of actions. Consider the crime of assault with intent to kill a police officer performing his official duties. Such a crime requires the most seriously culpable of the mental states, namely, an intent to kill; mere belief to a practical certainty that one's actions will result in death will not satisfy the mens rea requirement of this offense. Thus, a defendant who sets off a bomb against a prison wall in order to help some prisoners escape (while knowing that the guard next to the wall will be killed by the explosion) does not have the intent to kill; whereas another defendant who sets the bomb in order to kill the guard (in order that the guard cannot later identify the defendant) has the required intent to kill.

With regard to the causal property, causing-death-of-a-human-being, use of the intent/knowledge distinction seems to work well enough. The defendant who intends to kill is somewhat more culpable than the defendant who does not so intend but who only knows that his action will result in someone's death. But now imagine two more defendants, each of whom assault an on-duty police officer with the intent to kill him. The first of this pair of defendants knows that his intended victim is a police officer and knows that he is on duty; however, his reason for wanting to kill the officer has nothing to do with these facts, for this defendant hates the cop for personal reasons. By contrast the second defendant cares whether his intended victim is a police officer and whether that victim is on duty. We may suppose that this second defendant is engaged in a cop-killing contest between lifers in prison where there is no death penalty, and one "scores" in the contest only if one kills an on-duty policeman.

Defendant two is moved to kill the person he assaults by the fact that that person is an on-duty cop; defendant one is indifferent to these facts, although he knows that they exist. Both the common law and the Model Penal Code deny there to be any significant difference in culpability between these last two defendants. If one takes this view, then we do not want to distinguish between them when we grade culpability by mental states. We should thus lump those who literally intend to kill an on-duty cop with those who intend to kill a person who happens to be an on-duty cop (and who they know to be such), treating both as guilty of the most culpable grade of mental state.

We can define this most serious grade of culpability differently only if we can divide all criminal actions into two different aspects. This is where the causal versus noncausal property distinction is needed. If the property in question is causal, then the most serious grade of culpability requires intent as its mental state; if the property in question is noncausal, then the most serious grade of culpability allows belief to a practical certainty to suffice along with intent.

Other distinctions between the mental states that grade culpability are also thought to demand this distinction between causal and noncausal properties of action (Moore, 1993). Rather than pursue these, however, we should turn to three criticisms commonly made of this classification scheme.

Criticisms of the circumstance/consequence distinction

One is a moral criticism. The argument is that there is some difference in the culpability of the last pair of would-be cop-killers, and, indeed, as much difference as there is between the first pair of prison bombers. If this is so, then our reason for categorizing all properties of actions into two large clumps disappears.

It is hard not to have considerable sympathy for this moral criticism. Nonetheless, perhaps an enriched diet of examples can tip one back to-ward the orthodox criminal law categorization of actions. Consider this one. Two defendants each commit an assault with intent to have intercourse with a female who they know is not consenting. Defendant one is indifferent to the fact, seeking intercourse whether the victim consents or not; defendant two only likes nonconsensual sex, so that if the victim consented he would cease his assault. If both defendants are sufficiently close in culpability as to be lumped together in the most serious grade of culpability, then the criminal law may well be correct to draw its culpability distinctions differently for the noncausal property of consent than for the causal property of penetration.

It is also not quite true that the only reason for the criminal law to draw the causal/noncausal property distinction is in order to grade culpability systematically. If these kinds of properties differ in the universality with which they apply to criminal actions, that is a fact worth marking in systematizing criminal law. Although it is controversial—as we shall explore momentarily—all actions prohibited by Anglo-American criminal code have causal properties, while this is not true of noncausal properties. This is a fact worth marking, possible only if one distinguishes the two kinds of properties.

The second criticism of the causal/noncausal property classification is that it is incomplete. The argument is that certain actions are not divisible into their causal or their noncausal properties; rather such actions are said to have a nature that is neither. Such crimes are often termed "conduct" crimes, of which theft, rape, attempt, breaking and entering, and driving under the influence of alcohol are supposed to be examples.

This is a difficult criticism to get a handle on, since it seems so obviously false. Still, the criticism is a very popular one among criminal law theorists (Williams, 1983; Buxton; Fletcher, 1978), and it even infects the Model Penal Code when that Code (inconsistently) inserts "nature" of an action as an element in addition to "results" and "circumstances" (MPC § 2.02; see Moore, 1993). So the criticism must at least be taken seriously enough to be explained away as a mistake.

None of the supposed examples of "conduct crimes" turn out to require an analysis different than the orthodox analysis of action in criminal law. Take breaking and entering, for example. The actus reus of breaking and entering is breaking and entering a building not your own. That the building entered is owned by someone else is a noncausal property of the action required—a "circumstance element," in the language of the Model Penal Code (MPC § 1.13(9)). A breaking occurs when a willed bodily movement causes a window to be broken, and an entering occurs when a willed bodily movement takes place in the circumstance that an outward threshold of a building is crossed. There is no need for a nature to breaking and entering, since the actus reus of that offense is fully analyzable in the orthodox way.

The same analysis is adequate for the other supposed examples of "conduct crimes." The actus reus of rape is satisfied when a willed bodily movement causes penetration in the circumstance where there is a lack of victim consent. The actus reus of theft is satisfied when a willed bodily movement causes an item to move in the circumstances that the item in question is owned by another who has not consented to its taking. The actus reus of attempted murder is satisfied when a willed bodily movement causes a state of near success in killing to exist, and so on.

There are two apparent reasons explaining the persistence of this "conduct crimes" criticism despite its manifest falsity. One is due to the directness of the causal links between willed bodily movements and results in conduct crimes. Usually the causal chain between certain willed bodily movements and penetration in rape, for example, is very short. The shortness of the chain leads some to think that there is no causal link here at all. Yet a short causal chain is still a causal chain. In addition, once in a great while the chain is not so short, as when the defendant inserts the penis of another into the female (*Commonwealth v. Dusenberry*). Such cases make plain what was true all along: There is a causal property built into the actus reus of rape and other "conduct crimes," so that no sui generis "nature" of rape needs to be added into the analysis of that actus reus.

The second reason explaining the confusion about conduct crimes lies in certain linguistic facts. When we say, "The actus reus of theft is the moving of a chattel and such action of moving involves the causing of movement by that chattel," it may seem that the causal analysis is bogus. It sounds like saying, "The action of moving something involves moving that thing," which is trivial. Unnoticed is that the English language uses "moving" and "movement" in two quite different ways. "The moving of the chattel" refers to an action, whereas "the movement of the chattel" refers to a different event, the event of the chattel

moving. The latter event could be caused by an action of moving, or it might not. It is thus a significant assertion to say that "the willed bodily movement caused the movement of the chattel" and even to say, "The moving of the chattel caused the movement of the chattel." The causing of movement of a chattel is thus a causal property of moving a chattel, and no sui generis idea of "nature" need be added to analyze this action.

The third criticism of the orthodox division is that the causal/noncausal property distinction is wholly indeterminate. The potential indeterminancy appears when we consider how much to include as part of what is caused by an actor's willed bodily movements. Consider the actus reus of killing an on-duty policeman. The standard analysis is that the causing of a death of a human being is a causal property any act must possess to be an instance of this prohibited act-type, and that the victim of such killing is a police officer, and on duty, are noncausal properties any act must possess to be an instance of the prohibited act-type. Yet, why isn't causing the death of something the causal property, and the circumstance that the killed thing is a person or noncausal property? Alternatively, why isn't the causing of death of an on-duty policeman a causal property, with no noncausal property? Without some control on how we individuate properties—a notoriously tricky business (Armstrong)—it would seem that the orthodox classification scheme can be manipulated at will.

There is no dearth of suggestions as to how to deal with this problem. Some have suggested a temporal criterion: if the fact exists at the time of the willed bodily movement, then it is a noncausal property of that act. Others have urged a conventional criterion: what is "customarily regarded" as part of what is caused forms part of a causal property (Buxton, p. 31). Still others have urged a moral criterion: ask whether the intent/knowledge distinction marks any significant difference in culpability vis-à-vis the property in question, and if it does not, call the property noncausal (Moore, 1993). One might even urge a metaphysical criterion: include just so much of the state of affairs prohibited in the causal property as corresponds to true causal laws (see Armstrong). None of these suggested responses, however, has proved adequate to the objection.

Despite this unanswered criticism, the second general truth about actus reus retains wide acceptance: in addition to a willed bodily movement, the actus reus of all offenses includes the consequences of that movement and the circumstance in which that movement took place. These consequences and circumstances constitute the causal and the noncausal properties, respectively, that any willed bodily movement must possess if it is to satisfy the actus reus requirement of the criminal law.

MICHAEL S. MOORE

See also BURDEN OF PROOF; CRIME: DEFINITION; MENS REA; VICARIOUS LIABILITY.

BIBLIOGRAPHY

American Law Institute. *Model Penal Code.* Philadelphia: ALI, 1962.

ANNAS, JULIA. "How Basic Are Basic Actions?" *Proceedings of the Aristotelean Society* 78 (1978): 195–213.

ARMSTRONG, DAVID. *A Theory of Universals.* Cambridge, U.K.: Cambridge University Press, 1978.

AUSTIN, J. L. "A Plea for Excuses." *Proceedings of the Aristotelean Society* 57 (1956): 1–30.

AUSTIN, JOHN. *Lectures on Jurisprudence,* 5th ed. London: 1885.

BENNETT, JONATHAN. *Events and Their Names.* Indianapolis: Bobbs-Merrill, 1988.

BENTHAM, JEREMY. *Introduction to the Principles of Morals and Legislation (1789).* Buffalo, N.Y.: 1988.

BRAND, MYLES. "The Language of Not Doing." *American Philosophical Quarterly* 8 (1971): 45–53.

BRATMAN, MICHAEL. *Intentions, Plans, and Practical Reason.* Cambridge, Mass.: Harvard University Press, 1987.

BUXTON, R. "Circumstances, Consequences, and Attempted Rape." *Criminal Law Review* (1984): 25–34.

CORRADO, MICHAEL. "Is There an Act Requirement in the Criminal Law?" *University of Pennsylvania Law Review* 142 (1994): 1529–1561.

DAVIDSON, DONALD. *Essays on Actions and Events.* Oxford, U.K.: Oxford University Press, 1980.

DUFF, R. A. *Intention, Agency, and Criminal Liability.* Oxford, U.K.: Oxford University Press, 1990.

EPSTEIN, RICHARD. "A Theory of Strict Liability." *Journal of Legal Studies* 2 (1973): 151–204.

FLETCHER, GEORGE. *Rethinking Criminal Law.* Boston: Little, Brown, 1978.

———. "On the Moral Irrelevance of Bodily Movements." *University of Pennsylvania Law Review* 142 (1994): 1443–1453.

GOLDMAN, ALVIN. *A Theory of Human Action.* Englewood Cliffs, N.J.: Prentice-Hall, 1970.

———. "Action and Crime: A Fine-Grained Approach." *University of Pennsylvania Law Review* 142 (1994): 1563–1586.

GROSS, HYMAN. *A Theory of Criminal Justice.* New York: Oxford University Press, 1979.

HART, H. L. A. "Acts of Will and Responsibility." In *Punishment and Responsibility.* Edited by H. L. A. Hart, Oxford, U.K.: Oxford University Press, 1968. Pages 90–112.

HOLMES, OLIVER WENDELL. *The Common Law.* Boston: Little, Brown, 1881.

HUGHES, GRAHAM. "Criminal Omissions." *Yale Law Journal* 67 (1958): 590–637.

KADISH, SANFORD. "The Decline of Innocence." *Blame and Punishment.* Edited by Sanford Kadish. New York: Macmillan, 1987.

MACK, ERIC. "Bad Samaritanism and the Causation of Harm." *Philosophy and Public Affairs* 9 (1980): 230–259.

MOORE, MICHAEL S. *Act and Crime: The Philosophy of Action and Its Implications for Criminal Law.* Oxford, U.K.: Clarendon Press, 1993.

———. "More on Act and Crime." *University of Pennsylvania Law Review* 142 (1994): 1749–1840.

PACKER, HERBERT. *The Limits of the Criminal Sanction.* Stanford, Calif.: Stanford University Press, 1968.

RESCHER, NICHOLAS. "On the Characterization of Actions." *The Nature of Human Action.* Edited by M. Brand. Glenview, Ill.: Scott Foresman, 1970.

RYLE, GILBERT. *The Concept of Mind.* London: Hutcheson, 1949.

SCHOLZ, FRANZ. *Sleep and Dream.* Translated by H. J. Jewett. New York: 1893.

THALBERG, IRVING. *Perception, Emotion, and Action.* New Haven, Conn.: Yale University Press, 1977.

VERMAZEN, BRUCE. "Negative Acts." *Essays on Davidson's Actions and Events.* Edited by B. Vermazen and M. Hintikka. Oxford, U.K.: Oxford University Press, 1985.

WILLIAMS, GLANVILLE. *Criminal Law: The General Part.* 2d ed. London: Stevens and Sons, 1961.

———. "The Problem of Reckless Attempts." *Criminal Law Review* (1983): 365–375.

CASES

Commonwealth v. Dusenbery, 220 Va. 770, 263 S.E. 2d 392 (1980).

Powell v. Texas, 392 U.S. 514 (1968).

Robinson v. California, 370 U.S. 660 (1962).

ADVERSARY SYSTEM

The term *adversary system* sometimes characterizes an entire legal process, and sometimes it refers only to criminal procedure. In the latter instance it is often used interchangeably with "accusatorial procedure," and is juxtaposed to the "inquisitorial," or "non-adversary," process. There is no precise understanding, however, of the institutions and arrangements denoted by these expressions.

Nevertheless, several characteristics are commonly associated by American lawyers with the adversary criminal process. These include a relatively passive tribunal that ideally comprises both judge and jury; the presentation of evidence by the parties through their lawyers, who proceed by direct questioning and cross-examination of witnesses; the representation of state interests by one of the parties, the prosecutor; a presumption that the defendant is innocent until proved guilty; and the principle that he cannot be forced to testify against himself. The contours of the adversary system remain uncertain because the phrase has been used to describe three distinctive, albeit related, meanings.

The traditional meaning

In Anglo-American jurisdictions the phrase evokes both the aspirations and the actual features of Anglo-American criminal justice. It is incorporated to some extent into American constitutional law through provisions dealing with assistance of counsel and due process of law.

The attributes of "adversariness" change according to context. When techniques of ascertaining facts and deciding legal issues are discussed, a central feature is seen as a confrontational style: prosecution and defense prepare and present their cases to the court, and a decision is reached on the basis of the two alternative versions of fact and law. In this variant, partisan advocates are an essential aspect of the system, with their partisanship supported by canons of legal ethics (Fuller, p. 32). There is some equivocation, however, in the case of the public prosecutor, who is recognized to have a public responsibility that imposes limits upon the allowable degree of partisanship.

When the position of the criminal defendant is at issue, the focus shifts. The mainstay of the adversary system resides in the privilege against self-incrimination (*Malloy v. Hogan*, 378 U.S. 1, 7 (1964)), which implies high obstacles to conviction and an opposition to unbridled crime control. Any lowering of the evidentiary barriers erected to protect the defendant, such as the requirement of a unanimous jury verdict of guilt, is treated as a step away from the adversary ideal.

Adversary features are found not only in the contested trial but also in appellate proceedings, where arguments by the parties must ordinarily precede the decision of the appellate court. Even the pretrial phase of the criminal process is increasingly seen as displaying adversary characteristics. The privilege against self-incrimination, for example, now radiates into the earliest police inquiries, according protection to the suspect. The right to pretrial release and the hostility to preventive detention are also linked to the adversary system, particularly its emphasis on the presumption of innocence. On the other hand, the widespread practice of negotiations between the prosecution and the defense (plea bargaining) is usually treated as subverting adversariness. Where the defendant pleads guilty after such negotiations, the core of the adversary system, the contested trial, does not take place; moreover, the pressures used to encourage guilty pleas threaten the adversary principle that the defendant may not be forced to incriminate himself. At the same time, however, plea bargaining is quite "adversary" in the sense that it is dominated by the parties and their lawyers, rather than the court.

The adversary system has its distinctive source in liberal ideology. Consider, for example, the image so often used by lawyers of "balancing advantages" (or maintaining an "equality of arms") between the prosecution and the defense; such a goal makes sense only in light of liberal theories that treat the state interest as analogous to—and not superior to—private interests. The presumption of innocence, the requirement of proving guilt beyond a reasonable doubt, and related notions are also suffused with liberal values. Moreover, the passive attitude of the decision-maker has an affinity with the passive laissez-faire ideology.

It is this linkage to ideological currents that has produced two versions of the adversary system in its traditional meaning. In the "classical" variant, the ideal judge is propelled into action only to resolve disputes between the contending parties. The emergence of welfare-state liberalism has generated changes in this version of the idea; just as modern liberal governments intervene in the economy to correct failures of competitive markets, so, according to this view, an adversary judge should intervene in the trial to redress the competition of the parties. Whereas the classical variant celebrates the parties' dominance over the process, a later variant would curb this dominance (Fuller, p. 41). But there is disagreement over the extent to which the judge can intervene without negatively affecting the incentives of the prosecution and the defense for the zealous action required by the adversary system. Some see a solution to failures of party competition not in making the judge more active, but rather in replacing "ineffective" advocates by more capable ones.

It is plain that the adversary system in both its traditional senses is inextricably linked to legal ideology. It is praised in many quarters as a palladium of liberty and contrasted with an antipodal "inquisitorial" criminal process, that term serving to convey the worst features of continental European criminal justice prior to its reform in the wake of the French Revolution. Any departure from adversary features is said to imply a lapse into a system where searches are unbridled, the accused is detained without limits, his confession is coerced, counsel is denied him, and he is not accorded the benefit of doubt. This overdrawn polarization is reflected in such important judicial decisions as *Miranda v. Arizona*, 384 U.S. 436, 460 (1966).

The adversary system is extolled not only because of the protection it accords the accused, but also because its competitive style of presenting evidence and argument is thought to produce a more accurate result than an "inquisitorial" alternative, where the judge monopolizes proof-taking. According to this view, the judge who conducts an apparently nonpartisan inquiry cannot truly keep an open mind and lacks sufficient incentives to do a proper job. The possibility of a tension between the goals of obtaining accurate results and maintaining high barriers to conviction is often denied. It is occasionally conceded, however, that such barriers, while they lessen the possibility of convicting an innocent person, also increase the possibility that the guilty may escape conviction. Hence, by keeping these barriers high, as mandated by the adversary system, the accuracy of outcomes in the total number of cases irrespective of the kind of error can well be decreased. Where this is recognized, proponents of the adversary system accord decisive weight to liberal values: it is better to let a larger number of the guilty go free than to convict a smaller number of innocent persons.

The traditional Anglo-American concept of the adversary system has often been criticized by lawyers from other legal cultures. It has been vigorously questioned whether the clash of two zealous partisans represents the best instrument of discovering the truth. Moreover, the ample opportunities for the defendant to escape conviction have been said to exist mainly for those able to retain high-powered counsel. Finally, the practical importance of the adversary system in America has been doubted in view of the fact that most criminal cases never reach the stage of a contested trial but are settled through negotiations between prosecution and defense in the course of plea bargaining.

The adversary system as traditionally understood has its domestic enemies as well. Early in the twentieth century an eminent American legal scholar attacked it as inspired by a "sporting theory of justice" that treats substantively correct outcomes as relatively unimportant (Pound, p. 404). It is testimony to the continuing vitality of the traditional concept, however, that most critics castigate the alleged excesses of the system but fail to formulate alternatives to it. Only occasionally is inspiration for fundamental change sought in the non-adversarial modern criminal justice systems of Western Europe (Weinreb, pp. 117–146; Schlesinger, pp. 382–385).

The traditional concept of the adversary system evokes both actual features of Anglo-American criminal process and its aspirations. Inevitably, therefore, it combines both descriptive and prescriptive elements and cannot be expected to achieve rigorous internal consistency and coherence. It is not so much analytically precise as it is hortatory and rhetorical, aimed at mobilizing consent and at winning points in legal argumentation.

A model of conflict-solving procedure

A second way to view the adversary system is as a theoretical model. Conflict resolution is posited as the goal of the process, and the adversary model is then understood to comprise those procedures that implement this goal most effectively. In this second sense, then, the adversary system is a blueprint designed to promote the choice of certain procedures. Elements of the blueprint and features traditionally classed as adversary do not coincide.

Two methods have been used to construct the theoretical model of the adversary process. One method begins from the initial state of conflict between two sides and conceives of the ideal conflict-solving process as a simulation of, and substitute for, the private war between them. This leads to the central image of proceedings as a contest of two sides before the conflict-resolver. The task is then to develop procedural arrangements logically following from this central image. For example, if the adversary judge were permitted to inquire into facts not in dispute between the parties, the proceedings to determine these facts would "logically" cease to be a party contest. Consequently, the adversary model denies to the judge any independent powers to inquire into facts.

The other method starts from the desired end, which is said to be the acceptance of the court's decision by the disputants. The task here is to identify those procedures most likely to produce such acceptance, beginning with the premise that the goal of acceptance is promoted where the parties are permitted to exercise control over procedural action. In contrast to the first method, which relies on logical analysis, the second relies on observation and experiment. For example, whether participation of lawyers is an integral feature of the model hinges on whether such participation contributes to the control of the parties over the process.

As a model of a conflict-solving process, the adversary system is known in both continental European and Anglo-American legal cultures. Under the label "accusatorial proceedings" the model has a long history on the Continent.

The continental legal culture. Efforts to construct an ideal conflict-solving process are to be found in twelfth-century Roman Catholic ecclesiastical scholarship. By the fourteenth century, Italian students of procedure included in accusatorial proceedings many features now incorporated in the adversary system. But the most inclusive models of the conflict-solving process are products of rationalist "natural law" scholarship at the turn of the nineteenth century.

These models appear extremely "adversarial" even from the perspective of Anglo-American legal culture. Termed "the party-dominated process" (*Parteiverfahren*) by German legal theorists, they deserve brief description. Under them, the judge cannot initiate or continue proceedings without an actual dispute. Parties control the factual and, to a great extent, the legal boundaries of the case. Pleadings and stipulations are necessary devices to define and narrow issues, and the judge is not permitted to overrule such mutual arrangements. The court is also de-

nied the power to call witnesses on its own initiative. Even the court's powers of interrogation, otherwise very important on the Continent, are seriously curbed: only questions suggested by the litigants can be asked. Party "autonomy" is thought to be incompatible with the duty to testify, and thus a party can invoke a general "right to silence" if called to take the stand. Usually, minimal obligations are imposed on the litigants to disclose evidence or information. "Nobody is expected to supply weapons to his adversary" is the often-invoked maxim.

But this model, so rigorously designed as a contest of two sides before a passive judge, was recommended as a blueprint only for civil cases that were regarded as self-contained private controversies. Because no larger implications were perceived in such lawsuits, judicial passivity seemed appropriate, if not mandated by the requirement of judicial neutrality. Many continental European countries, therefore, enacted codes of civil procedure incorporating features of the recommended theoretical model. The rational implementation of policies toward crime was thought, however, to make the blueprint inapplicable in criminal cases. Though the logic of the party-dominated model might have permitted the prosecutor to represent the public interest in crime control, it was viewed as unacceptable to give the other party—the accused—mastery over defensive issues. If this were done, a substantively erroneous result might be imposed on the passive court. For example, an insane defendant could be convicted if, for some strategic reason of his own, he failed to raise the insanity defense.

European procedural theory thus developed a variety of modified blueprints for the criminal process, some of which were built on the "accusatorial principle" or on the "principle of contradiction" (Damaška, p.560). In their most radical form, they recommended a partial simulation of the party contest, with evidence collected mainly by a nonpartisan but active decision-maker. The facts alleged in the prosecutor's charge constitute the only limit on the court's inquiry.

The Anglo-American legal culture. In Anglo American countries, efforts to formulate organizing principles of procedure are mainly the product of the twentieth century. In civil procedure, for example, continental influences have led to the adoption of the twin principles of party prosecution (that the court will take no step in the case except on motion of a party) and of party presentation (that the scope and content of the controversy are to be defined by the parties). As a shorthand expression of the characteristics of the classical civil lawsuit, the two principles enjoy a certain currency in scholarly discourse.

In criminal procedure, theoretical study has been devoted principally to the discrepancy between the realities of law enforcement and the aspirations expressed in the traditional concept of the adversary system. But there was another factor that contributed to the emergence of theoretical models. A fascination with empirical science led to the desire to compare the efficiency of some features of the adversary system with the inquisitorial alternatives. Most of the empirical studies focused on alternative ways of developing factual and legal material for decision. For the narrow purposes of this research, an adversary "mini-model" was defined as an arrangement where proof and argument are presented to the decision-maker by two partisan advocates, whereas the inquisitorial mini-model was described as a unilateral official inquiry into facts and law. The two models were then used in laboratory experimentation to test their relative efficacy in counteracting the decision-maker's bias, producing reliable results, or attaining some other goal. For example, since in the adversary model the judge is required to listen passively to both sides of the case before making a decision, it was hypothesized that he or she would be less likely to become prematurely biased and draw a conclusion too early (Thibaut and Walker, 1975; Sheppard and Vidmar).

The models reviewed here are all based on the assumption that the goal of the process is the resolution of a conflict. They constitute useful guidelines for reform of procedural systems only insofar as these systems are directed toward the same goal. What then is the relation of theoretically posited goals to reality? Conflict resolution as a goal may be restricted to the contested trial in Anglo-American countries, and even there it may be a secondary or only a superficial aim. If the court refuses to accept the defendant's guilty plea, as it is empowered to do in the majority of common law jurisdictions, the case goes to trial despite the absence of a genuine controversy between the prosecution and the defense.

An archetype of Anglo-American process

In its third sense, the adversary system is a procedural type designed by comparative law scholars to capture characteristic features of the common law process, particularly when contrasted with continental systems. For some of these scholars the adversary type is the common denominator of all Anglo-American procedures, yet this conception is problematic. Consider, for example, the question whether the exclusion of illegally obtained evidence from the prosecution's case at trial represents a defining feature of the adversary type. Because the exclusionary rule has not been adopted by all Anglo-American jurisdictions, but has been adopted in several continental European countries, the answer is no (Hermann, p. 18). Under this approach the precise meaning of the adversary type remains hostage to changes in the law of a single common law country.

Other scholars conceive of the adversary type as an ideal of procedure that is not fully duplicated in any actual system. This second approach can best be exemplified by analogy with styles in art. To classify a work of art as pertaining to a particular style, it is thought sufficient that the work encompass some, though not all, elements of the stylistic ideal. Similarly, certain features can be viewed as typically adversarial, although they are found only in a small number of actual procedural systems. Of course, in order to be useful, the ideal type of the adversary process must provide a structure in which actual systems can be recognized, albeit in exaggerated or stylized form. This second approach is more widespread and will therefore be examined in some detail.

Most scholars describe the ideal type of the adversary process by focusing their attention on the trial stage of the criminal process and on the three-sided relation among the prosecution, the defense, and the court. This triadic relation is significantly different in continental and Anglo-American countries. In the former, the court tends to monopolize the courtroom activity; in the latter, the prosecution and the defense take the largest share of action. As a result, the ideal of the judge as a passive umpire, rather than an active seeker of the truth, is taken as the central ideal of the adversary system (Ploscowe, p. 433). But the focus on triadic relations leaves too much out of account. Both in Europe and in Anglo-American countries, important segments of the criminal process unfold in the absence of the judge and may involve other officials such as the police. Moreover, even if one considers only in-court proceedings, there are often four rather than three actors to consider—crime victims play an increasingly important role. Indeed, many European systems give the victim the rights to be heard as a party and be represented by counsel.

The contrast between Anglo-American and continental criminal procedure is best expressed in two basic notions. The first, underlying the inquisitorial type, regards the criminal process as an official inquiry. The second, underlying the adversary type, regards criminal procedure as a regulated contest between the prosecution and the defense. In discussing other meanings of the adversary system, the image of proceedings as a contest has already been encountered. But the comparative perspective highlights some aspects of this contest that are overlooked by a purely domestic vision.

First, under procedures of the adversary type the prosecution and the defense prepare two independent cases in advance of the trial (often with a view to possibly avoiding trial). Unlike the inquisitorial type, there is no nonpartisan agency preparing a single, or "integrative," case or case file. Problems of maintaining rough equality of the prosecution and the defense can thus arise long before the trial. Pretrial detention, for example, does not fit neatly into the adversary type, because it hampers the defendant in preparing his own independent case. Moreover, the resources and legal powers of investigation of the prosecutor are usually far greater than those of the defense. On the other hand, the exclusionary rule fits in smoothly. If in preparing its case the prosecution breached the law, it should not be permitted to reap advantages from such a "low blow."

Second, various forms of negotiation between the prosecution and the defense are a salient feature of the adversary type. Consider, for example, how easily the practice of plea bargaining fits the "style" of a process based on the notion of contest. It makes little sense to go on with such proceedings if the defendant refuses to oppose the demands of the prosecution. By contrast, in proceedings conceived of as an official inquiry, the defendant need not be asked how he pleads: the trial can go on irrespective of his attitude toward the prosecutorial charges. Inducements to facilitate the task of crime control agencies exist, of course, in both adversary and inquisitorial systems. But the two are characterized by the different loci of such inducements. In the adversary process, both sticks and carrots are used to persuade the defendant not to contest charges, so that the need for trial is obviated. In the inquisitorial process these inducements are used during the interrogation of the defendant: he is urged to reveal information facilitating the task of the officials conducting the inquiry.

So far we have dealt with the conventional position that attributes the same meaning to the words *adversary* and *accusatorial*. It has been suggested, however, that comparativists should draw a distinction between the two (Goldstein, p. 1016). Under this approach the adversary process is said to denote only a method of finding facts and deciding legal problems, and is characterized by two sides shaping issues before a relatively neutral judge. The accusatorial system, on the other hand, is a more encompassing concept, which includes the adversary method as its constituent element.

The meaning of this broader concept depends on the contrast with the inquisitorial system, and its non-adversary method of proof and trial. The contrast turns on the divergent attitudes of state officials. In the inquisitorial system, officials are self-propelling and affirmatively obligated to carry out state policies, but in the accusatorial system they step into action only when a controversy arises and they are requested by the participants to respond. Each attitude entails a variety of consequences and choices among procedural forms, the choice of the proper method of finding facts being only one of many. Ultimately, the contrast between the inquisitorial and the accusatorial modes of proceeding involves two polar views about the role of government in society; that is, whether government should be "reactive" or "proactive" (Goldstein, p. 1017).

The idea of linking the characteristics of the Anglo-American criminal process to political ideology is promising. Important features of the Anglo-American criminal process cannot be reduced to the abstract notion of contest, which is so central to the adversary type. Moreover, some features of Anglo-American justice are in conflict with procedures mandated by notions of a fair contest. For example, the right of the defendant to personally defend himself—a right unique to common law—follows from the tenets of the reactive liberal ideology, but it seriously strains notions of a fair contest (*Faretta v. California*, 422 U.S. 806 (1975)). If more common law characteristics are to be captured in procedural types, broader organizing principles are needed, and the ideology of reactive government provides one such principle. Consequently, it seems sensible to distinguish between the adversary type, which focuses on the contest design, and the accusatorial type, which centers on a political theory.

But even the broader concept of the accusatorial system fails to account for many striking characteristics of the Anglo-American criminal process when the latter is contrasted to continental systems. From the earliest known attempts to describe the peculiar nature of common law justice, the participation of the lay jury was regarded as its hallmark, and lay decision-making as one of its most characteristic elements. The law of evidence, for example, is the product of the interaction of the judge, the jury, and the lawyers (Langbein, p. 306). These features elude the adversary type organized around the notion of a contest; the latter can plainly take place with or without a jury. Nor does the accusatorial system, inspired by the reactive philosophy of government, require jury trials; lay adjudicators can be an arm of a totalitarian as well as of a laissez-faire government. Nevertheless, trial by jury reinforces the characteristic Anglo-American image of the criminal process as a contest of the accused and the state before outside arbiters. Where, as on the Continent, the apparatus of justice is dominated by hierarchically organized civil servants, this conception of the criminal process has little credibility—prosecutors and decision-makers are all too easily traceable to the center of state power. But the contest imagery has far greater plausibility in a procedural system where verdicts are reached by laypersons recruited to serve on the criminal court.

The difficulties involved in expressing the peculiar character of Anglo-American criminal procedure have given rise to increased skepticism as to whether any version of the adversary type can be useful. Those scholars of comparative law who subscribe to the common-denominator approach are clearly justified in their doubts: no single model can be set up to which all Anglo-American criminal procedures conform (Langbein and Weinreb, p. 1551). But even those scholars who are less demanding seem increasingly skeptical. Factors involved in describing the peculiar character of Anglo-American proceedings are too complex and heterogeneous to be captured in a single, internally consistent type of criminal justice. Moreover, as the world's criminal justice systems have become increasingly "hybridized," continental and other non–Anglo-American, "inquisitorial" systems have incorporated many adversary features traditionally seen as defining characteristics of common law systems.

MIRJAN DAMAŠKA

See also CRIMINAL JUSTICE SYSTEM; CRIMINAL PROCEDURE: COMPARATIVE ASPECTS; INTERNATIONAL CRIMINAL COURTS; INTERNATIONAL CRIMINAL JUSTICE STANDARDS; PROSECUTION: COMPARATIVE ASPECTS; TRIAL, CRIMINAL.

BIBLIOGRAPHY

DAMAŠKA, MIRJAN. "Evidentiary Barriers to Conviction and Two Models of Criminal Procedure: A Comparative Study." *University of Pennsylvania Law Review* 121 (1973): 507–589.
———. *Evidence Law Adrift.* New Haven: Yale University Press, 1997.
ESMEIN, ADHÉMAR. *A History of Continental Criminal Procedure, with Special Reference to France.* Translated by John Simpson. Boston: Little, Brown, 1913.
FRASE, RICHARD S. "Comparative Criminal Justice Policy, in Theory and in Practice." In *Comparative Criminal Justice Systems: From Diversity to Rapprochement.* Vol. 17 in *Nouvelles Études Pénales.* Toulouse, France: Eres, 1998. Pages 109–121.
FULLER, LON L. *The Adversary System: Talks on American Law.* Edited by Harold J. Berman. New York: Vintage Books, 1961.
GOODPASTER, GARY. "On the Theory of American Adversary Criminal Trial." *Journal of Criminal Law & Criminology* 78 (1987): 118–152.
GOLDSTEIN, ABRAHAM. "Reflections on Two Models: Inquisitorial Themes in American Criminal Procedure." *Stanford Law Review* 26 (1974): 1009–1025.
HERMANN, JOACHIM. "Various Models of Criminal Proceedings." *South African Journal of Criminal Law and Criminology* 2, no. 1 (1978): 3–19.
LANDSMAN, STEPHEN. *Readings on Adversarial Justice: The American Approach to Adjudication.* St. Paul, Minn.: West Publishing Co., 1988.
LANGBEIN, JOHN H. "The Criminal Trial before the Lawyers." *University of Chicago Law Review* 45 (1978): 263–316.
———, and WEINREB, LLOYD L. "Continental Criminal Procedure: Myth and Reality." *Yale Law Journal* 87 (1978): 1549–1568.
PLOSCOWE, MORRIS. "The Development of Present-day Criminal Procedures in Europe and America." *Harvard Law Review* 48 (1935): 433–473.
POUND, ROSCOE. "The Causes of Popular Dissatisfaction with the Administration of Justice." In *Report of the Twenty-ninth Annual Meeting of the American Bar Association.* Philadelphia: Dando, 1906. Pages 395–408.
SCHLESINGER, RUDOLF. "Comparative Criminal Procedure: A Plea for Utilizing Foreign Expe-

rience." *Buffalo Law Review* 26 (1976): 361–385.

SHEPPARD, BLAIR H., and VIDMAR, NEIL. "Adversary Pretrial Procedures and Testimonial Evidence: Effects of Lawyer's Role and Machiavellianism." *Journal of Personality and Social Psychology* 39 (1980): 320–332.

THIBAUT, JOHN W., and WALKER, LAURENS. *Procedural Justice: A Psychological Analysis*. Hillsdale, N. J.: Laurence Erlbaum Associates, 1975.

———. "A Theory of Procedure." *California Law Review* 66 (1978): 541–566.

VAN KESSEL, GORDON. "Adversary Excesses in American Criminal Trials." *Notre Dame Law Review* 67 (1992): 403–549.

WEINREB, LLOYD L. *Denial of Justice*. New York: Macmillan, 1977.

CASES

Faretta v. California, 422 U.S. 806 (1975).
Malloy v. Hogan, 378 U.S. 1, 7 (1964).
Miranda v. Arizona, 384 U.S. 436, 460 (1966).

AGE AND CRIME

The view that involvement in crime diminishes with age is one of the oldest and most widely accepted in criminology. Beginning with the pioneering research by Adolphe Quetelet in the early nineteenth century, criminological research consistently has confirmed that (the proportion of) the population involved in crime tends to peak in adolescence or early adulthood and then decline with age. This age-crime relationship is remarkably similar across historical periods, geographic locations, and crime types.

That the impact of age on criminal involvement is one of the strongest factors associated with crime has prompted the controversial claim that the age-crime relationship is universal and invariant (Hirschi and Gottfredson). However, considerable variation exists among offenses and across historical periods in specific features of the age-crime relationship (for example, peak age, median age, rate of decline from peak age). A claim of "invariance" in the age-crime relationship therefore overstates the case (Steffensmeier et al., 1989).

Age-crime patterns for the U.S.

The F.B.I.'s *Uniform Crime Report* (UCR) data, particularly the Crime Index (homicide, robbery, rape, aggravated assault, burglary, larceny-theft, auto theft) document the robustness of the age effect on crime and also reveal a long-term trend toward younger age-crime distributions in more modern times. Today, the peak age (the age group with the highest age-specific arrest rate) is younger than twenty-five for all crimes reported in the F.B.I.'s UCR program except gambling, and rates begin to decline in the teenage years for more than half of the UCR crimes. In fact, even the median age (50 percent of all arrests occurring among younger persons) is younger than thirty for most crimes. The *National Crime Victimization Survey* (NCVS), self-report studies of juvenile and adult criminality, and interview data from convicted felons corroborate the age-crime patterns found in the UCR data (Steffensmeier and Allan).

Explaining the youthful peak in offending. In a general sense, physical abilities, such as strength, speed, prowess, stamina, and aggression are useful for successful commission of many crimes, for protection, for enforcing contracts, and for recruiting and managing reliable associates (for a review, see Steffensmeier and Allan). Although some crimes are more physically demanding than others, persistent involvement in crime is likely to entail a lifestyle that is physically demanding and dangerous. Declining physical strength and energy may make crime too dangerous or unsuccessful, especially where there are younger or stronger criminal competitors who will not be intimidated, and this might help to explain the very low involvement in crime of small children and the elderly.

However, available evidence on biological aging reveals very little correspondence between physical aging and crime's decline in late adolescence. The research literature on biological aging (see especially Shock) suggests that peak functioning is typically reached between the ages of twenty-five and thirty for physical factors plausibly assumed to affect one's ability to commit crimes (strength, stamina, aerobic capacity, motor control, sensory perception, and speed of movement). Although decline sets in shortly after these peak years, it is very gradual until the early fifties, when the decline becomes more pronounced (Shock). Other commonly mentioned physical variables like testosterone levels peak in late adolescence but then remain at or near peak level until at least the mid-forties. In contrast, the age curves for crimes like robbery and burglary that presuppose the need for physical abilities peak in mid-adolescence and then decline very rapidly. In short, although biological and physiological factors may contribute toward an understanding of the rapid increase in delinquent behavior during adolescence, they cannot by themselves explain the abrupt decline in the age-crime curve following mid-to-late adolescence (which, in particular, is observed in contemporary, postindustrial nations).

A variety of social and cognitive factors can help explain the rapid rise in age-specific rates of offending around mid-adolescence. Teenagers generally lack strong bonds to conventional adult institutions, such as work and family (Warr). At the same time, teens are faced with strong potential rewards for offending: money, status, power, autonomy, identity claims, strong sensate experiences stemming from sex, natural adrenaline highs or highs from illegal substances, and respect from similar peers (Steffensmeier and Allan). Further, their dependent status as juveniles insulates teens from many of the social and legal costs of illegitimate activities, and their stage of cognitive development limits prudence concerning the consequences of their behavior. At the same time, they possess the physical prowess required to commit crimes. Finally, a certain amount of misbehavior is often seen as natural to youth and seen as simply a stage of growing up (Jolin and Gibbons; Hagan et al.).

For those in late adolescence or early adulthood (roughly ages seventeen to twenty-two, the age group showing the sharpest decline in arrest rates for many crimes), important changes occur in at least six spheres of life (Steffensmeier and Allan):

1. Greater access to legitimate sources of material goods and excitement: jobs, credit, alcohol, sex, and so on.
2. Age-graded norms: externally, increased expectation of maturity and responsibility; internally, anticipation of assuming adult roles, coupled with reduced subjective acceptance of deviant roles and the threat they pose to entering adult status.
3. Peer associations and lifestyle: reduced orientation to same-age-same-sex peers and increased orientation toward persons of the opposite sex or persons who are older or more mature.
4. Increased legal and social costs for deviant behavior.
5. Patterns of illegitimate opportunities: with the assumption of adult roles, opportunities increase for crimes (for example, gambling, fraud, and employee theft) that are less risky, more lucrative, or less likely to be reflected in official statistics.
6. Cognitive and analytical skill development leading to a gradual decline in egocentrism, hedonism, and sense of invincibility; becoming more concerned for others, more accepting of social values, more comfortable in social relations, and more concerned with the meaning of life and their place in things; and seeing their casual delinquencies of youth as childish or foolish.

As young people move into adulthood or anticipate entering it, most find their bonds to conventional society strengthening, with expanded access to work or further education and increased interest in "settling down." Leaving high school, finding employment, going to college, enlisting in the military, and getting married all tend to increase informal social controls and integration into conventional society (Steffensmeier et al., 1989). In addition, early adulthood typically involves a change in peer associations and lifestyle routines that diminish the opportunities for committing these offenses (Warr). Last, at the same time when informal sanctions for law violations are increasing, potential legal sanctions increase substantially.

Variations in the age curve

Although crime tends to decline with age, substantial variation can be found in the parameters of the age-crime curve (such as peak age, median age, and rate of decline from peak age). "Flatter" age curves (i.e., those with an older peak age and/or a slower decline in offending rates among older age groups) are associated with several circumstances:

1. Types of crime for which illegitimate opportunities increase rather than diminish with age.
2. Population groups for whom illegitimate opportunities and integration into adult society do not markedly increase with age (i.e., during young adulthood).
3. Cultures and historical periods in which youth have greater access to legitimate opportunities and integration into adult society.

Crime types. The offenses that show the youngest peaks and sharpest declines are crimes that fit the low-yield, criminal mischief, "hell-raising" category: vandalism, petty theft, robbery, arson, auto theft, burglary, and liquor law and drug violations. Personal crimes like aggravated assault and homicide tend to have somewhat "older" age distributions (median ages in the late twenties), as do some of the public order offenses, public drunkenness, driving under the influence, and certain of the property crimes that juveniles have less opportunity to commit, like embezzlement, fraud, and gambling (median ages in late twenties or thirties). However, even these older age-distributions (e.g., fraud) have shifted toward younger peak ages in recent years (see below).

Those offenses with flatter age curves are often those for which the structure of illegitimate opportunities increases rather than disappears with age. For example, some opportunities for fraud exist for young people (such as falsification of identification to purchase alcohol or gain entry to "adult" establishments), but since they are too young to obtain credit, they lack the opportunities for common frauds such as passing bad checks, defrauding an innkeeper, or credit card forgery. Similarly, young people have more opportunities for some kinds of violence (for example, street fights or gang violence) but less opportunity for other kinds of violence (for example, spousal violence).

Older people may also shift to less visible criminal roles such as bookie or fence. Or as a spin-off of legitimate roles, they may commit surreptitious crimes or crimes that, if discovered, are unlikely to be reported to the authorities, such as embezzlement, stock fraud, bribery, or price-fixing. Unfortunately, we know relatively little about the age distribution of persons who commit these and related lucrative crimes, but the fragmentary evidence that does exist suggests that they are likely to be middle age or older (Shapiro; Pennsylvania Crime Commission). Evidence also suggests that the age curves for lucrative crimes in the underworld like racketeering or loansharking not only peak much later but tend to decline more slowly with age (Steffensmeier and Allan; Steffensmeier).

Still less is known of the age distribution of "respectable" or upperworld offenders who commit lucrative business crimes like fraud, price-fixing, or bribery, since such data are not plentiful. However, data from *New York Times* articles on profitable business crimes (those involving gains of $25,000 or more) during the 1987–1990 period reveals a preponderance of middle-aged or older offenders, with a modal age between forty and fifty (Steffensmeier and Allan).

Minority differences. For black inner-city youths, the problems of youth described above are compounded by persistent racial discrimination and blocked conventional opportunity (Wilson, 1987; 1996). As inner-city blacks move into young adulthood, they continue to experience limited access to high quality adult jobs and are more likely to associate primarily with same-sex peers. As UCR data show, adult offending levels among blacks continue at higher levels than among whites, and the proportion of total black crime that is committed by black adults is greater than the proportion of total white crime that is committed by white adults (Steffensmeier and Allan). Arrest statistics for homicide/robbery from California further document the flatter age-crime curves among blacks than whites.

Cross-cultural and historical differences. In small preindustrial societies, the passage to adult status is relatively simple and continuous. Formal "rites of passage" at relatively early ages avoid much of the status ambiguity and role conflict that torment modern adolescents in the developed world. Youths begin to assume responsible and economically productive roles well before they reach full physical maturity. It is not surprising, therefore, to find that such societies and time periods have significantly flatter and less skewed age-crime patterns (for a review, see Steffensmeier et al., 1989).

Much the same is true for earlier periods in the history of the United States and other industrial nations, when farm youth were crucial for harvesting crops and working-class children were expected to leave school at an early age and do their part in helping to support their families. By contrast, "The typical job a teenager can get today provides neither the self-pride of economic independence not the socializing benefits of working alongside adult mentors. . .. Work relations seem to have been critical experiences for the socialization of many young men in the past. Such jobs integrated youths into adult society . . . instead of segregating them in a separate peer culture" (Coontz, p. 29).

Although youth has always been seen as a turbulent time, social processes associated with the coming of industrialization and the postindustrial age have aggravated the stresses of adolescence, resulting in increased levels of juvenile criminality in recent decades. The structure of modern societies, therefore, encourages crime and delinquency among the young because these societies "lack institutional procedures for moving people smoothly from protected childhood to autonomous adulthood" (Nettler, p. 241).

Unfortunately, reliable age statistics on criminal involvement are not available over extended historical periods. Nonetheless, we can compare age-crime distributions over the past sixty years or so in the United States and also compare these to early nineteenth-century age-crime distributions reported in Quetelet's pioneering study (see also Monkkonen). The age-crime plots for homicide clearly document the trend toward younger age distributions and younger peak ages.

The shift toward a greater concentration of offending among the young may be due partly to change in law enforcement procedures and data collection. Nevertheless, the likelihood that real changes have in fact occurred is supported by the consistency of the changes from 1830 to 1940 to 1980, and continuing into the mid-1990s. Support for the conclusion that real change has taken place over the past century also is found in the age breakdown of U.S. prisoner statistics covering the years 1890 to 1980 (Steffensmeier et al., 1989). As with the UCR statistics, the prison statistics show that age curves are more peaked today than a century ago and that changes in the age-crime curve are gradual and can be detected only when a sufficiently large time frame is used. Moreover, research shows that more-recent birth cohorts of juveniles are more violent than ones in the past (Tracey et al., 1990; Shannon, 1988).

Together, these findings are consistent with the view that contemporary teenagers in industrialized nations are subject to greater status anxiety than in previous periods of history and that the transition from adolescence to adulthood is more turbulent now than in the past (Greenberg, 1979, 1982; Glaser). In comparison to earlier eras, youths have had less access to responsible family roles, valued economic activity, and participation in community affairs (Greenberg 1982). This generational isolation has fostered adolescent subcultures oriented toward consumption and hedonistic pursuits (Hagen et al., 1998; Hagan). The weakened social bonds and reduced access to valued adult roles, along with accentuated subcultural influences, all combine to increase situationally induced pressures to obtain valued goods; display strength, daring, or loyalty to peers; or simply to "get kicks" (Hagan et al., 1998; Steffensmeier et al., 1989).

Sex differences in the age-crime relationship. Although age-crime parameters differ as described above, there appears to be considerable similarity in the age-crime relationship between males and females (Steffensmeier and Streifel). UCR arrest statistics from the 1930s to the 1990s show that the age curves of male and female offenders are very similar within any given period and across all offenses, with the exception of prostitution. To the extent that age differences between the sexes exist, the tendency is for somewhat lower peak ages of offending among females—apparently because of their earlier physical maturity and the likelihood that young adolescent females might date and associate with older delinquent male peers. But overall, although male levels of offending are always higher than female levels at every age and for virtually all offenses, the female-to-male ratio remains fairly constant across the life span (Steffensmeier and Streifel). Also, the trend toward younger and more peaked age-crime distributions holds for both sexes.

The single major difference in the age curves of males and females is for prostitution (and to some extent vagrancy, often a euphemism for prostitution in the case of female arrestees), with females having a much greater concentration of arrests among the young. Although this difference may be due in part to more stringent enforcement of prostitution statutes when young females are involved, the younger and more peaked female age curve is also a function of the extent to which opportunity structures for sexual misbehaviors differ between males and females. Clearly, sexual attractiveness and the marketability of sexual services are strongly linked to both age and gender: Older women become less able to market sexual services, whereas older men can continue to purchase sexual services from young females or from young males (Steffensmeier and Streifel).

Variations in criminal careers

The youthful peak and rapid drop-off in offending that constitutes the most common societal pattern for conventional crimes is actually but one of a number of patterns identified when criminal careers are tracked for individual offenders (Jolin and Gibbons).

"Aging out" of crime. Research suggests that exiting from a criminal career requires the acquisition of meaningful bonds to conventional adult individuals and institutions (Sampson and

Laub; Shover; Steffensmeier and Allan; Warr). One important tie to the conventional order is a job that seems to have the potential for advancement and that is seen as meaningful and economically rewarding. A good job shifts a criminal's attention from the present to the future and provides a solid basis for the construction of a noncriminal identity. It also alters an individual's daily routine in ways that make crime seem less likely. Other bonds that may lead people away from crime include involvement in religion, sports, hobbies, or other activities.

The development of conventional social bonds may be coupled with burnout or a belated deterrent effect as offenders grow tired of the hassles of repeated involvement with the criminal justice system, and the hardships of a life of crime. They may also have experienced a long prison sentence that jolts them into quitting or that entails a loss of street contacts which makes the successful continuation of a criminal career difficult. Or offenders may develop a fear of dying alone in prison, especially since repeated convictions yield longer sentences. Still other offenders may quit or "slow down" as they find their abilities and efficiency declining with increasing age, loss of "nerve," or sustained narcotics or alcohol use (Adler and Adler; Shover; Steffensmeier).

Older criminals. Older offenders fall into two categories: (1) those whose first criminal involvement occurs relatively late in life (particularly in shoplifting, homicide, and alcohol-related offenses); and (2) those who started crime at an early age and continue their involvement into their forties and fifties and beyond. What evidence is available on first-time older offenders suggests that situational stress and lack of alternative opportunities play a primary role. The unanticipated loss of one's job or other disruptions of social ties can push some individuals into their first law violation at any age (Jolin and Gibbons).

Older offenders who persist in crime are more likely to belong to the criminal underworld. These are individuals who are relatively successful in their criminal activities or who are extensively integrated into subcultural or family enterprises. They seem to receive relational and psychic rewards (e.g., pride in their expertise) as well as monetary rewards from lawbreaking and, as a result, see no need to withdraw from lawbreaking (Steffensmeier). Alternatively, such offenders may "shift and oscillate" back and forth between conventionality and lawbreaking, depending on shifting life circumstances and situational inducements to offend (Adler and Adler). These older offenders are also unlikely to see many meaningful opportunities for themselves in the conventional or law-abiding world. Consequently, "the straight life" may have little to offer successful criminals, who will be more likely to persist in their criminality for an extended period. But they, too, may slow down eventually as they grow tired of the cumulative aggravations and risks of criminal involvement, or as they encounter the diminishing capacities associated with the aging process.

Effects of age structure on crime rates

The dramatically higher age-specific offending rates for young people suggest that shifts in the age-composition of the population could produce sizable changes in societal crime rates. The so-called baby-boom generation born between the end of World War II and the early 1960s brought a large, steady increase in the proportion of the population aged twelve to twenty-five—the most crime-prone age group—during the 1960s and 1970s, a period when the nation's crime rate was also increasing steadily. Ferdinand found that about 50 percent of the increase in the index crime rate during the 1960s could be attributed to population shifts such as the baby-boom generation's movement into the crime-prone years. Similarly, Steffensmeier and Harer found that virtually all the reported decreases in the UCR and NCVS Index crime rates during the early 1980s could be attributed to the declining proportion of teenagers in the population—that is, to a "baby-bust" effect.

More recently, Steffensmeier and Harer reported that the large impact of age-composition on crime rates during the 1980s had diminished during the 1990s, and that the broad decline in both the UCR and NCVS crime rates since 1992 (the years of the Clinton presidency) cannot be solely attributed to changes in population age composition. One explanation of the recent downtrend has attributed the decline to dramatic increases in incarceration rates that presumably incapacitate or prevent crimes by locking up high-frequency offenders who commit a disproportionate amount of all crimes. However, the rise in incarceration rates extends backwards to at least the late 1970s, and therefore considerably predates the 1990s drop in crime. Therefore it appears unlikely that higher imprisonment rates explain much, if any, of the recent drop in crime—just as they do not account for the rise in crime in the late 1980s.

Alternative explanations for recent downward trends in crime rates include the strong economy and low unemployment of the 1990s, an abatement of the crack epidemic of the late 1980s, and the wide variety of community-level criminal justice initiatives undertaken in the 1990s, such as Operation Weed and Seed, Pulling America's Communities Together, SafeFutures, and community policing. Also, Steffensmeier and Harer speculate that offenders may be shifting from risky, low-return offenses like burglary (also robbery) to others that are more lucrative (drug dealing) or less risky (fraud).

Conclusion

Criminologists have long recognized that age is a very robust predictor of crime, both in the aggregate and for individuals. The most common finding across countries, groups, and historical periods shows that crime tends to be a young persons' activity. However, the age-crime relationship is not invariant, and in fact varies in its specific features according to crime types, the structural position of groups, and historical and cultural contexts. On the other hand, the age-crime relationship seems to be fairly similar for males and females. Finally, although they constitute a very small group, relatively little is known about older chronic offenders. Clearly, the structure, dynamics, and contexts of offending among older individuals is a rich topic for further research.

DARRELL STEFFENSMEIER
JEFFERY ULMER

See also CRIMINAL CAREERS; EXCUSE: INFANCY; FAMILY RELATIONSHIPS AND CRIME; JUVENILE AND YOUTH GANGS; JUVENILE VIOLENT OFFENDERS; POLICE: HANDLING OF JUVENILES; PREVENTION: JUVENILES AS POTENTIAL OFFENDERS.

BIBLIOGRAPHY

ADLER, PATRICIA, and ADLER, PETER. "Shifts and Oscillations in Deviant Careers: The Case of Upper-Level Drug Dealers and Smugglers." *Social Problems* 31 (1983): 195–207.

COONTZ, STEPHANIE. *The Way We Really Are: Coming to Terms with America's Changing Families.* New York: Basic Books, 1997.

Federal Bureau of Investigation. *Crime in the United States.* Washington, D.C.: U.S. Government Printing Office, 1935–1999.

FERDINAND, THEODORE. "Demographic Shifts and Criminality: An Inquiry." *British Journal of Criminology* 10 (1970): 169–175.

GLASER, DANIEL. *Crime in Our Changing Society.* New York: Holt, Rinehart, and Winston, 1978.

GREENBERG, DAVID. "Delinquency and the Age Structure of Society." *Contemporary Crisis* 1 (1979): 66–86.

———. "Age and Crime." In *Encyclopedia of Crime and Justice,* vol. 1. Edited by Sanford Kadish. New York: Macmillan, 1982. Pages 30–35.

HAGAN, JOHN. "Destiny and Drift: Subcultural Preferences, Status Attainments, and the Risks and Rewards of Youth." *American Sociological Review* 56 (1991): 567–581.

HAGAN, JOHN; HEFFLER, GERD; CLASSEN, GABRIELE; BOEHNKE, KLAUS; and MERKENS, HANS. "Subterranean Sources of Subcultural Delinquency Beyond the American Dream." *Criminology* 36 (1998): 309–342.

HIRSCHI, TRAVIS, and GOTTFREDSON, MICHAEL. "Age and the Explanation of Crime." *American Journal of Sociology* 89 (1983): 522–584.

JOLIN, ANNETTE, and GIBBONS, DON. "Age Patterns in Criminal Involvement." *International Journal of Offender Therapy and Comparative Criminology* 31 (1987): 237–260.

MONKKONEN, ERIC. "New York City Offender Ages: How Variable Over Time." *Homicide Studies* 3 (1999): 256–270.

NETTLER, GWYN. *Explaining Crime.* New York: McGraw-Hill, 1978.

Pennsylvania Crime Commission. *1990 Report—Organized Crime in America: A Decade of Change.* Commonwealth of Pennsylvania, Conshohoken, PA., 1991.

QUETELET, ADOLPHE. *Research on the Propensity for Crime at Different Ages.* (1833). Translated by Sawyer Sylvester. Cincinnati, Ohio: Anderson Publishing Co., 1984.

SAMPSON, ROBERT, and LAUB, JOHN. *Crime in the Making: Pathways and Turning Points through Life.* Cambridge, Mass.: Harvard University Press, 1993.

SHANNON, LYLE. *Criminal Career Continuity: Its Social Context.* New York: Human Sciences Press, 1988.

SHAPIRO, SUSAN. *Wayward Capitalists: Target of the Securities and Exchange Commission.* New Haven, Conn.: Yale University Press, 1984.

SHOCK, NATHAN. *Normal Human Aging: The Baltimore Longitudinal Study of Aging.* Washington, D.C.: U.S. Government Printing Office, 1984.

SHOVER, NEAL. "The Later Stages of Ordinary Property Offender Careers." *Social Problems* 30 (1983): 208–218.

STEFFENSMEIER, DARRELL. *The Fence: In the Shadow of Two Worlds.* Totowa, N.J.: Rowman & Littlefield, 1986.

STEFFENSMEIER, DARRELL, and ALLAN, EMILIE. "Criminal Behavior: Gender and Age." In *Criminology: A Contemporary Handbook.* Edited by Joseph Sheley. Belmont, Calif.: Wadsworth, 1995. Pages 83–114.

STEFFENSMEIER, DARRELL; ALLAN, EMILIE; HARER, MILES; and STREIFEL, CATHY. "Age and the Distribution of Crime." *American Journal of Sociology* 94 (1989): 803–831.

STEFFENSMEIER, DARRELL, and HARER, MILES. "Did Crime Rise or Fall During the Reagan Presidency? The Effects of an 'Aging' U.S. Population on the Nation's Crime Rate." *Journal of Research in Crime and Delinquency* 28 (1991): 330–359.

———. "Making Sense of a Recent U.S. Crime Trends, 1980–98: Age Composition Effects and Other Explanations." *Journal of Research in Crime & Delinquency* 36 (1999): 235–274.

STEFFENSMEIER, DARRELL, and STREIFEL, CATHY. "Age, Gender, and Crime across Three Historical Periods: 1935, 1960, and 1985." *Social Forces* 69 (1991): 869–894.

TRACEY, PAUL; WOLFGANG, MARVIN; and FIGLIO, ROBERT. *Delinquency Careers in Two Birth Cohorts.* New York: Plenum, 1990.

ULMER, JEFFERY, and SPENCER, J. WILLIAM. "The Contributions of an Interactionist Approach to Research and Theory on Criminal Careers." *Theoretical Criminology* 3 (1999): 95–124.

WARR, MARK. "Life-Course Transitions and Desistance from Crime." *Criminology* 36 (1998): 183–216.

WILSON, WILLIAM J. *The Truly Disadvantaged.* Chicago: University of Chicago Press, 1987.

———. *When Work Disappears.* Cambridge, Mass.: Harvard University Press, 1996.

ALCOHOL AND CRIME: BEHAVIORAL ASPECTS

In nineteenth-century American thought, the link between alcohol and crime was strong and certain. The showman P. T. Barnum was echoing countless other writers when he stated, in a temperance pamphlet published at mid-century, that "three-fourths of all the crime and pauperism existing in our land are traceable to the use of intoxicating liquors." These claims made by the temperance movement spurred research on the alcohol-crime relationship around the turn of the century, including John Koren's sophisticated multifactorial analysis in 1899 of the role of alcohol in causing crimes. Koren sounded a note of caution to those who would assume that alcohol caused crime: "When an offense is committed in a state of intoxication or by a habitual user of strong drink, the causal relations seem unmistakable, even inevitable, no matter how infinitely complicated the problem appears to the criminologist. . .. [But] we are still confronted with the question: Assuming that alcohol had never existed, how many and which of the criminal acts perpetrated during a period would not have been committed?" (Koren, pp. 49, 55).

In the polarized atmosphere of national Prohibition (1919–1933) and after repeal, empirical research on the linkage of alcohol and crime declined, with relatively little advance in research design or in theoretically relevant knowledge until Marvin Wolfgang's influential 1958 study *Patterns in Criminal Homicide*. In the years since Wolfgang described the frequency with which alcohol use accompanies homicides, the potential linkages between alcohol and crime have been explored by social and behavioral scientists from several disciplines.

Empirical evidence on alcohol and crime

Alcohol can be involved in crime in two ways: laws regulating its use or distribution can be violated, and its effects might generate behavior that violates other laws (Collins, 1991). (People may also commit crimes to obtain money for alcohol, but because alcohol is relatively inexpensive, this phenomenon does not occur as often as it does among drug users.) In the United States, alcohol-specific crimes include drunken driving, public drunkenness, underage drinking, and illicit production of alcohol. The present discussion is concerned with alcohol's role in non-alcohol-specific crimes. Most of the analyses on alcohol crime use one of three methods, with a focus either on criminal events, on people who commit crimes, or on populations with different alcohol policies and drinking patterns.

Studies of criminal events

Both drunkenness and the commission of a crime are events rather than conditions. Most of the empirical literature on alcohol and crime merely reports the percentage of criminal events in which alcohol was present either in the perpetrator or the victim. These figures come from studies of prisoners and jail inmates, surveys of victims, police reports, and official statistics. North American studies find that 55–60 percent of U.S. homicide offenders and 35–40 percent of Canadian homicide offenders were drinking alcohol prior to the crime. In Finland, Norway, and Sweden, countries with low homicide rates, alcohol is present in 65–80 percent of offenders in assaults. The corresponding share of drinking victims is also relatively high, about 45–50 percent (Pernanen, 1996).

In many violent offenses, both the offender and the victim have been drinking prior to the offense. The presence of alcohol in both parties appears to be associated with social interactions that increase the probability of violence. In 26 percent of the homicides studied by Wolfgang, the victim had precipitated the homicide by being the first to commence the interplay or resort to physical violence. Alcohol use was associated with victim precipitation: Alcohol was present, in either the victim or the offender, in 74 percent of the victim-precipitated events compared to 60 percent of other homicides. The victim was drinking in 69 percent of the victim-precipitated cases and in 47 percent of other cases (Wolfgang). Given that victims and perpetrators are often drinking together before the event, disentangling the role of alcohol in the two parties can be difficult (Pernanen, 1991).

For some interpersonal crimes, alcohol is more directly involved in victimization. For example, the vulnerability of drunken persons to robbery by "jackrollers" has long been recognized. People who are drinking are attractive targets: they are less able to protect themselves and to exercise sound judgment (Collins and Messerschmidt). Alcohol as a "victimogenic" factor is a relatively unexplored aspect of the alcohol and crime question, a limitation that probably reflects ideological concerns: establishing that victims are often drunk might diminish their perceived blamelessness (Miers).

Types of offenses

A common generalization about the role of alcohol in different types of crimes is that alcohol more often accompanies violent crime against people than property crime, but these findings are inconsistent (Collins and Messerschmidt; Graham, Schmidt, and Gillis). For example, a 1998 study of alcohol and crime produced by the U.S. Bureau of Justice Statistics showed that similar proportions of convicted offenders in state prisons had been drinking when they committed violent offenses (37.5 percent) or property offenses (31.8 percent) (Greenfeld). In samples of people who are arrested for crimes, however, there are larger differences in alcohol involvement in violent versus property crime (Wiley and Weisner).

Alcohol involvement in different kinds of crimes may involve different mechanisms. For example, although robbery involves premeditated violence, it is usually thought to be qualitatively different from the violence that typically occurs as a result of interpersonal conflict (Collins and Messerschmidt). And indeed, studies of offenders show that the percentage of alcohol involvement tends to be lower in robberies than in homicide and assault (Greenfeld). In property offenses, some offenders may drink to steady their nerves before committing the crime; thus, the motivation for the crime is independent of drinking (Collins, 1991). Drinking may even be a deterrent to professional property crime because it leads to unreliability, creating a barrier to admission to crime partnerships (Cordilia).

Biases in studies of events

The percentage of crimes in which the participants were drinking may be biased by several factors. First, these percentages are based on crimes that are detected and reported to the authorities, a select portion of all criminal events. Intoxicated offenders may be easier to apprehend, especially for incidents in public places where potential witnesses are more numerous; they are more likely to leave evidence connecting them to a crime and are more likely to be recidivists known by the police. If substance abusers are more likely to be recidivists, they may be overrepresented among prison inmates (Pernanen, 1989; 1996). These biases may lead to an inflated proportion of alcohol involvement in crime. Other factors might decrease the true proportion of alcohol involvement: for example, alcohol abusers may be diverted into treatment rather than sentenced, reducing the proportion of prison inmates who were drinking at the time of their crime (Pernanen, 1996).

Interpreting event-based studies

Information about the co-occurrence of alcohol and criminal events is widely reported, but does not establish a relationship between alcohol and crime. Knowing the proportion of offenders who were drinking at the time of the crime is not meaningful unless we know the proportion of drinkers among people who did not commit crimes; if these proportions are the same, then there is no association of drinking to crime. The National Research Council Panel on the Understanding and Control of Violent Behavior concluded that existing data was not "sufficient to show that alcohol use or intoxication increases the general risk of violence. To test that hypothesis with prevalence data, one would need a benchmark: the fractions of people not involved in violence or crime while drinking—with appropriate adjustments for demographic characteristics of participants, time of day, day of week, and place of occurrence" (Reiss and Roth, p. 184).

Collecting appropriate comparison information is difficult, and the appearance of alcohol in such a large proportion of some crimes had led some commentators to suggest that it is unlikely that such a large proportion of people in general would be drinking at a particular time. However, Evans notes that in the West of Scotland, the proportion of offenders who were intoxicated at the time of their offense corresponds with the proportion of men who would be expected to be intoxicated at similar times (Evans). Moreover, among convicted offenders, drinking at the time of the offense is no more than would be expected given typical drinking patterns (Kalish; Ladouceur and Temple). For example, data from the U.S. Bureau of Justice Statistics show that one-third of state prison inmates reported drinking heavily just before they committed the offense, but 20 percent of all inmates reported that they drank very heavily every day the entire year before entering prison (Greenfeld). Drinking before an offense may reflect a typical pattern rather than be specifically related to the commission of a crime.

Studies of people who commit crimes

A second tradition of research on alcohol and crime concerns the relationship between alcohol and criminal conditions—on the prevalence of alcoholism among criminals, on the criminal history of alcoholics, and on the intertwining of the "criminal career" and the "alcoholic career" (Collins, 1981). In general populations, heavier drinkers are more likely to have engaged in criminal behavior, and comparisons of prison populations to the general population show high rates of heavy drinking, drinking problems, and alcohol disorders among prisoners. For example, while 14 percent of men and 4 percent of women in the general population drink more than one ounce or more of alcohol per day, these proportions among inmates are 47 percent and 22 percent (Collins, 1993; Graham, Schmidt, and Gillis).

Relationships between drinking habits and criminality partly reflect the similarity in the demographic distribution of both alcohol use and criminal behavior in the population. Heavy drinking is more common among men than among women at all ages, and peaks among men in the general population in their early twenties. At the same time, men account for 80 to 90 percent of those arrested and convicted for serious crimes in the United States, with serious crimes peaking during the young adult years (Clark and Hilton; Collins, 1981). The near-coincidence in the distributions of heavy drinking and crime practically insures some positive correlation between heavy drinkers and criminals in the population. However, it is difficult to disentangle the causal connections between drinking problems and criminal behaviors. Developmental studies of adolescents show that aggressive behavior generally precedes alcohol use, and longitudinal studies of alcoholics suggest that criminality generally precedes the development of a drinking problem (Goodwin, Crane, and Guze; Pittman and Gordon; White). Both drinking and crime may have similar risk factors, and their relationship may be explained by coexisting predispositions to both drinking and crime (Collins, 1981; Lipsey et al.).

In the United States, relationships between criminal records and drinking problems are likely to be affected by ongoing changes in the alcoholism treatment and criminal justice systems. The courts' tendency to refer intoxicated offenders to alcoholism treatment—for both alcohol-specific and non-alcohol-specific crimes—is likely to produce samples of treated "alcoholics" who are younger and more criminally involved, while lowering the prevalence of "problem drinkers" in prison populations (Mosher; Schmidt and Weisner).

Studies of populations

In studies of populations, the unit of analysis is a population rather than an individual or an event. These analyses examine the covariation between alcohol consumption and violence at an aggregate level such as a country or a state. In studies incorporating *time series analysis*, per capita alcohol consumption is correlated with crime levels over a period of years. Such analyses show, for example, that increases in consumption are related to rises in homicide rates and assault rates in Sweden, assault rates in Norway, rates of violent crime and some property crime in the United Kingdom, and male homicide rates in Australia (Ensor and Godfrey; Lenke; Lester). In the United States, rates of rape, robbery, and assault (but not murder) tend to rise along with per capita consumption and fall with increases in state-level beer taxes (Cook and Moore 1993a; 1993b).

Time series analyses in different countries imply that the association of alcohol consumption and violent behavior tends to be higher in drinking cultures with a more "explosive" drinking pattern in which drinking to intoxication is common (Lenke). These quantitative findings echo the anthropological evidence collected by Craig MacAndrew and Robert Edgerton in their influential treatise *Drunken Comportment: A Social Explanation*. This evidence demonstrated wide variations in drunken behavior between different cultures and in the same culture at different historical periods, suggesting that the link between drinking and violence is at least as much a matter of cultural expectation and custom as of pharmacology (MacAndrew and Edgerton).

Natural experiments

In time series analyses, many co-occurring social trends could account for covariation in both drinking and crime. For example, per capita consumption and crime rates could both rise at the same time due to increases in the number of young men in the population in the postwar period. Although this problem can be partially solved with statistical techniques (Skog), trends may still be confounded with other trends. A more powerful analysis can be conducted by studying crime rates before and after sudden changes in alcohol availability or policies about alcohol distribution. Because population characteristics are unlikely to change drastically at exactly the same time as changes in alcohol availability, these "natural experiments" provide an opportunity to distinguish the effects of alcohol consumption from those of naturally-occurring trends (Lipsey et al.).

Restrictions or expansions of alcohol availability can arise from changes in alcohol policies, from changes in distribution caused by labor strikes, and as a result of social movements. Leif Lenke examined the consequences of several policy changes in Sweden, including rationing during the First World War, the repeal of a ration-book system in 1955, the legalization of sales of medium-strength beer in grocery stores in 1965 and of sales of strong beer in grocery stores in some provinces in 1967, and the discontinuation of Saturday opening hours at state-owned alcohol sales outlets in 1981. Although the results were not completely consistent, Lenke concluded that "When availability of alcohol has been reduced or increased, the rates of violent crimes have tended to follow the same direction" (p. 103). In Norway, assault rates declined following the closing of the state-owned alcohol sales outlets on Saturdays (Olsson and Wikstrom), and in the former Soviet Union, male homicide rates decreased by 40 percent following the alcohol reform of 1985 (homicide rates rose again when the reform broke down as a result of the illicit market and the dissolution of the Soviet Union) (Shkolnikov and Nemtsov).

A series of studies from the Nordic countries have examined the consequences of temporary reductions in alcohol availability due to labor strikes. In general, these studies show reductions in casualty ward injury admissions, assault and battery cases, and incidents of family violence during the strike period. For example, during a 1972 strike in Finland, there were noticeable reductions in levels of aggravated assault—a crime in which 80–90 percent of both perpetrators and victims in Finland are intoxicated (Mäkelä, 1980). During a second Finnish strike in 1985, there was a 20 percent drop in "rowdiness at licensed entertainment events" and a 20 percent reduction in crimes of violence (Österberg and Saila).

Major social or national movements that affect alcohol consumption can also affect alcohol-related violence. During the 1980 Gdańsk shipyard strike, out of which emerged the Polish Solidarity movement, the strikers imposed a prohibition on alcohol in the shipyard. The ban was quickly picked up and extended by the local government throughout the province, and temporary alcohol bans became a frequent symbolic gesture by both the Polish government and Solidarity as a signal of serious intent and yet a desire to avoid violence (Moskalewicz). Although drinking per se was not banned, a local survey showed that most residents did not drink at all during the prohibition, and that 84 percent of the respondents thought that the prohibition had reduced the number of violent incidents. According to the authorities, "a drop in the number of crimes was noted, although the militia activity in the town was reduced to a minimum" (p. 378). The local ambulance service reported an unusually quiet time (Bielewicz and Moskalewicz).

The drop in crime in Gdańsk may have resulted not only from the ban on alcohol sales but from an increased sense of common purpose, such as has been noted in grave times elsewhere to produce perturbations in social statistics. Gustav Aschaffenburg noted the effects of such a mixture of abstinence and common purpose in nineteenth-century Ireland: "Father Matthew succeeded, by the power of his personality and his enthusiastic speeches, in making total abstainers of 1,800,000 persons in the course of a few years. The result was that, whereas, in 1828, 12,000 serious crimes were committed in Ireland, in 1841 the number had sunk to 773, the sixteenth part!" Aschaffenburg added, however, that "[t]he slight permanence of this unexampled success proves, it is true, that the method employed was not the right one" (p. 129).

Interpreting population-level studies

Comparing rates of drinking and of crime across different countries or cultures provides only a weak demonstration of associations between the two. As Klaus Mäkelä notes, "cultural variations in drinking patterns are based on lasting historical traditions, and they may well be resistant to a certain degree to changes in the level of consumption. To take a somewhat extreme example, we have no reason to believe that the French would start drunken fights should they lower their consumption to the same level as the Scots or the Finns" (Mäkelä, p. 333). Studies of alcohol and crime are done mostly in societies that worry a lot about alcohol (Scandinavia, English-speaking countries) and that combine histories of explosive drunkenness with histories of strong temperance sentiments. Links between alcohol and crime may be weaker in other countries (for example, southern Europe) with different drinking customs.

Changes in policies that increase or decrease alcohol availability can result in changes in alcohol-related violence; however, examples of major changes in policy are rare (Graham, Schmidt, and Gillis). The effects of these changes have usually been studied in countries that have a government monopoly on alcohol distribution and a work force that is sufficiently unionized for a strike to have a significant impact on the availability of alcohol. Because strikes cause only short-term supply interruptions, longer-term effects are difficult to predict. When policies are changed permanently, it is difficult to disentangle the alcohol effects from the social motivations that gave rise to the policy in the first place (Pernanen, 1993).

Interpretation of population-level studies is also complicated by the fact that these studies cannot link individual criminal behavior to individual consumption and thus cannot directly address the question of whether individuals who consume alcohol are more likely to behave violently (Hennekens and Buring; Lipsey et al.). For example, as Pernanen and others have noted, when the supply of alcohol is cut down, the frequency of social interaction is also reduced, with a resulting decrease in the probability of interaction and, consequently, interpersonal crime. Changes in availability may lead to crime by making victims more vulnerable, attracting offenders and victims to high-risk environments, or affecting the frequency of male gatherings (Lipsey et al.). That is, it may not be drinking per se that reduces or increases levels of crime, but the effect may be through other factors that are influenced by the change in drinking.

Explaining the association of alcohol and crime

We turn at last to the vexed question of causation: does alcohol cause crime? Other than for the alcohol-specific offenses, for which the answer is a matter of definition, the answer must be "it depends what you mean." It is clear that drinking is only rarely followed by a criminal act; there is no general, consistent effect of alcohol on crime or violence analogous to its consistent effects on motor and cognitive functioning. Kai Pernanen proposes a "thought experiment" in which people are given increasing doses of alcohol. At sufficient doses, they all will start staggering or falling—but we do not know who, if anyone, will become aggressive (Pernanen, 1989). Connections between drinking and violence must be conditional: drinking in combination with other factors can result in a crime. If alcohol has any causal effects, they occur for some people and under some circumstances. Examining these circumstances and conditions constitutes an active area of research in experimental psychological studies on both animals and humans (Lang 1993).

On what level can we posit that alcohol increases the likelihood of crime? The question of causality usually implies that an individual who drinks is more likely to commit a crime than a sober person. To test this hypothesis requires research designs that show an association between drinking and crime at the level of the individual and the criminal event. Most of the existing research is inadequate to demonstrate such an association: studies of criminal events cannot demonstrate that individuals are more or less likely to commit crimes when drinking, and studies of drinking careers and criminal careers cannot disentangle the relationships between drinking, crime, and coexisting predispositions for both.

On a population level, however, we might propose that crime rates are affected by the level or patterning of alcohol consumption. This is a different kind of hypothesis, proposing only that changes in drinking can be followed by changes in crime on a population level, without requiring the variables to be connected within the individual committing the crime. This possibility highlights other pathways by which alcohol might lead to violence, for example, by making potential victims more vulnerable, by attracting offenders and victims to high-risk environments, or by increasing the number of male gatherings (Lipsey et al.). For example, criminologists have written about a "routine activity" approach to crime, in which criminal acts require convergence in space and time of likely offenders, suitable targets, and the absence of capable guardians against crime (Cohen). Drinking activities can contribute to this convergence by attracting people to certain locations, increasing the frequency of interactions with other people, and making people more vulnerable to attack (Parker and Cartmill; Parker and Rebhun).

Implications for alcohol policy

From a pragmatic policy perspective, it may not matter whether alcohol causes crime or at what level such an association exists. If evidence accumulates that a particular policy change is followed by decreases in crime and violence, the "true" cause of the decrease may be drinking or may be something else related to drinking, but specifying the precise causal mechanism is unnecessary for demonstrating effects on public health. For example, reductions in alcohol availability may be followed by reductions in crime by affecting the offender, the victim, or the interaction between them, but the effect on the crime rate is the same. The practical applications of such a view are wide-reaching and do not require a determination of causal influence in the conventional sense.

In the modern era, most studies of alcohol and crime in English-speaking countries have focused their attention on the relationship as it may exist within the individual psyche—occasionally extending the view to cover factors in the immediate situation of the criminal event. Much remains to be learned, indeed, about the role of alcohol in criminal events, and about the intertwining of drinking and criminal behaviors. But from the point of view of policy, such studies often focus on elements of the connection that are the hardest to change. The studies of change over time reawaken one to the existence of historical change and to the possibility of doing something to prevent crime by influencing the fact, context, and consequences of drinking. This is a worthy agenda for future research and experiment.

BARBARA C. LEIGH
ROBIN ROOM

See also ALCOHOL AND CRIME: TREATMENT AND REHABILITATION; DRINKING AND DRIVING; DRUGS AND CRIME: BEHAVIORAL ASPECTS; EXCUSE: INTOXICATION

BIBLIOGRAPHY

ASCHAFFENBURG, GUSTAV. *Crime and its Repression.* Translated by A. Albrecht. Boston: Little, Brown, 1913.

BARNUM, PHINEAS T. *The Liquor Business, Its Effects upon the Mind, Morals, and Pockets of Our People.* Whole World Temperance Tracts, no. 4. New York: Fowler and Wells, n.d.

BIELEWICZ, ANTONI, and MOSKALEWICZ, JACEK. "Temporary Prohibition: The Gdansk Experience." *Contemporary Drug Problems* 11, no. 3 (1982): 367–381.

CLARK, WALTER B., and HILTON, MICHAEL E. *Alcohol in America: Drinking Practices and Problems.* Albany, N.Y.: SUNY Press, 1991.

COHEN LAWRENCE E., and FELSON, MARCUS. "Social Change and Crime Rate Trends: A Routine Activities Approach." *American Sociological Review* 44 (1979): 588–607.

COLLINS, JAMES J. "Alcohol Careers and Criminal Careers." In *Drinking and Crime.* Edited by J. J. Collins. New York: Guilford Press, 1981. Pages 152–206.

———. "Drinking and Violations of the Criminal Law." In *Society, Culture, and Drinking Patterns Reexamined.* Edited by D. J. Pittman and H. R. White. New Brunswick, N.J.: Rutgers Center for Alcohol Studies, 1991. Pages 650–660.

———. "Drinking and Violence: An Individual Offender Focus." In *Alcohol and Interpersonal Violence: Fostering Multidisciplinary Perspectives.* NIAAA Research Monograph no. 24. Edited by S. E. Martin. Rockville, Md.: U.S. Department of Health and Human Services, 1993. Pages 221–235.

COLLINS, JAMES J., and MESSERSCHMIDT, PAMELA M. "Epidemiology of Alcohol-Related Violence." Special Issue, "Alcohol, Aggression, and Injury." *Alcohol Health & Research World* 17, no. 2 (1993): 93–100.

COOK, PHILIP J., and MOORE, MARK J. "Economic Perspectives on Reducing Alcohol-Related Violence." In *Alcohol and Interpersonal Violence: Fostering Multidisciplinary Perspectives.* NIAAA Research Monograph no. 24. Edited by S. E. Martin. Rockville, Md.: Department of Health and Human Services, 1993a. Pages 193–212.

———. "Violence Reduction through Restrictions on Alcohol Availability." Special Issue, "Alcohol, Aggression, and Injury." *Alcohol Health & Research World* 17, no. 2 (1993b): 151–156.

CORDILIA, ANN. "Alcohol and Property Crime: Exploring the Causal Nexus." *Journal of Studies on Alcohol* 46, no. 2 (1985): 161–171.

ENSOR, TIM, and GODFREY, CHRISTINE. "Modeling the Interactions between Alcohol, Crime and the Criminal Justice System." *Addiction* 88 (1993): 477–487.

EVANS, CHARLES M. "Alcohol and Violence: Problems Relating to Methodology, Statistics and Causation." In *Alcohol and Aggression.* London, U.K.: Croom Helm, 1968. Pages 138–160.

GOODWIN, DONALD W.; CRANE, J. BRUCE; and GUZE, SAMUEL B. "Felons Who Drink: An Eight-Year Follow-Up." *Quarterly Journal of Studies on Alcohol* 32 (1971): 136–147.

GRAHAM, KATHRYN; SCHMIDT, GAIL; and GILLIS, KELLY. "Circumstances When Drinking Leads to Aggression: An Overview of Research Findings." *Contemporary Drug Problems* 23, no. 3 (1996): 493–558.

GREENFELD, LAWRENCE A. "Alcohol and Crime: An Analysis of National Data on the Prevalence of Alcohol Involvement in Crime." Washington, D.C.: Bureau of Justice Statistics, 1998.

HENNEKENS, CHARLES H., and BURING, JULIE E. *Epidemiology in Medicine.* Boston: Little, Brown, 1987.

KALISH, CAROL B. "Prisoners and Alcohol." *Bureau of Justice Statistics Bulletin.* Washington, D.C.: Bureau of Justice Statistics, 1983.

KOREN, JOHN C. *Alcohol and Society.* New York: Holt, 1916.

LADOUCEUR, PATRICIA, and TEMPLE, MARK. "Substance Use among Rapists: A Comparison with Other Serious Felons." *Crime and Delinquency* 31, no. 2 (1985): 269–294.

LANG, ALAN R. "Alcohol-Related Violence: Psychological Perspectives." In *Alcohol and Interpersonal Violence: Fostering Multidisciplinary Perspectives.* NIAAA Research Monograph no. 24. Edited by S. E. Martin. Rockville, Md.: U.S. Department of Health and Human Services, 1993.

LENKE, LEIF. *Alcohol and Criminal Violence: Time Series Analyses in a Comparative Perspective.* Stockholm: Almqvist & Wiksell International, 1990.

LESTER, DAVID. "Alcohol Consumption and Rates of Personal Violence in Australia." *Drug and Alcohol Dependence* 31, no. 1 (1992): 15–17.

LIPSEY, MARK W.; WILSON, DAVID B.; COHEN, MARC A.; and DERZON, JAMES H. "Is There a Causal Relationship between Alcohol Use and Violence? A Synthesis of Evidence." In *Recent Developments in Alcoholism.* Edited by M. Galanter. Vol. 13, *Alcohol and Violence.* New York: Plenum, 1997. Pages 245–282.

MACANDREW, CRAIG, and EDGERTON, ROBERT B. *Drunken Comportment: A Social Explanation.* Chicago: Aldine, 1969.

MÄKELÄ, KLAUS. "Level of Consumption and Social Consequences of Drinking." In *Research Advances in Alcohol and Drug Problems,* vol. 4. Edited by Y. Irael et al. New York: Plenum, 1978. Pages 303–348.

———. "Differential Effects of Restricting Supply of Alcohol: Studies of Strike in Finnish Liquor Stores." *Journal of Drug Issues* (1980).

MIERS, DAVID. *Responses to Victimization: A Comparative Study of Compensation for Criminal Violence in Great Britain and Ontario.* Abingdon, England: Professional Books, 1978.

MOSHER, JAMES F. "Alcohol: Both Blame and Excuse for Criminal Behavior." In *Alcohol and Disinhibition: Nature and Meaning of the Link.* NIAAA Research Monograph no. 12. Edited by R. Room and G. Collins. Washington, D.C.: USGPO, 1983. Pages 437–460.

MOSKALEWICZ, JACEK. "Alcohol as a Public Issue: Recent Developments in Alcohol Control in Poland." *Contemporary Drug Problems* 10 (1982): 155–177.

OLSSON, ORVAR, and WIKSTROM, PERL-OLAF. "Effects of the Experimental Saturday Closing of Liquor Retail Stores in Sweden." *Contemporary Drug Problems* 11, no. 3 (1982): 325–353.

ÖSTERBERG, ESA, and SAILA, JIRKHAL-LIISA. *Natural Experiments with Decreased Availability of Alcoholic Beverages: Finnish Alcohol Strikes in 1972 and 1985.* Helsinki, Finland: Finnish Foundation for Alcohol Studies, 1991.

PARKER, ROBERT N., and CARTMILL, RAND S. "Alcohol and Homicide in the United States 1934–1995—or One Reason Why U.S. Rates of Violence May Be Going Down." *Journal of Criminal Law and Criminology* 88, no. 4 (1998): 1369–1398.

PARKER, ROBERT N., and REBHUN, LINDAL-ANNE. *Alcohol and Homicide: A Deadly Combination of Two American Traditions.* Albany, N.Y.: State University of New York Press, 1995.

PERNANEN, KAI. "Causal Inferences about the Role of Alcohol in Accidents, Poisonings and Violence." In *Drinking and Casualties: Accidents, Poisonings and Violence in an International Perspective.* Edited by N. Giesbrecht et al. New York: Routledge, 1989.

———. *Alcohol in Human Violence.* New York: The Guilford Press, 1991.

———. "Research Approaches in the Study of Alcohol-Related Violence." Special Issue, "Alcohol, Aggression, and Injury." *Alcohol Health & Research World* 17, no. 2 (1991): 101–107.

———. "The Social Cost of Alcohol-Related Crime: Conceptual, Theoretical and Causal Attributions." In *International Guidelines for Estimating the Costs of Substance Abuse.* Edited by E. Single et al. Ottawa: Canadian Center on Substance Abuse, 1996.

PITTMAN, DAVID J., and GORDON, C. WAYNE. "Criminal Careers of the Chronic Police Case Inebriate." *Quarterly Journal of Studies on Alcohol* 19 (1958): 255–268.

REISS, ALBERT J., and ROTH, JEFFREY A., EDS. *Understanding and Preventing Violence.* Washington D.C.: National Academy Press, 1993.

SCHMIDT, LAURA, and WEISNER, CONSTANCE. "Developments in Alcoholism Treatment." In *Recent Developments in Alcoholism.* Edited by M. Galanter. Vol. 11, *Ten Years of Progress.* New York: Plenum, 1993. Pages 369–396.

SHKOLNIKOV, VLADIMIR M., and NEMTSOV, ALEXANDER. "The Anti-Alcohol Campaign and Variations in Mortality." In *Premature Death in the New Independent States.* Edited by J. L. Bobadilla, C. Costello, and F. Mitchell. Washington D.C.: National Academy Press, 1997.

SKOG, OLE-JØRGEN. "Testing Causal Hypotheses about Correlated Trends: Pitfalls and Remedies." *Contemporary Drug Problems* 15 (1988): 565–606.

WHITE, HELENE R. "Longitudinal Perspective on Alcohol Use and Aggression during Adolescence." In *Recent Developments in Alcoholism.* Edited by M. Galanter. Vol. 13, *Alcohol and Violence.* New York: Plenum, 1997. Pages 81–103.

WILEY, JIM, and WEISNER, CONSTANCE. "Drinking in Violent and Nonviolent Events Preceding Arrest." *Journal of Criminal Justice* 23, no. 5 (1995): 461–476.

WOLFGANG, MARVIN E. *Patterns in Criminal Homicide.* Philadelphia: Pennsylvania University Press, 1958.

ALCOHOL AND CRIME: LEGAL ASPECTS

See ALCOHOL AND CRIME: THE PROHIBITION EXPERIMENT; ALCOHOL AND CRIME: TREATMENT AND REHABILITATION.

ALCOHOL AND CRIME: THE PROHIBITION EXPERIMENT

The Prohibition "experiment" is periodically cited as a test of the legal control of moral behavior. Implications are then drawn for other areas of morals legislation such as drug use, prostitution, abortion, and gambling. However, this analogy between a historical set of events and the scientific test of a hypothesis is both imperfect and misleading. What can be learned from the history of the legislation prohibiting the manufacture and sale of "intoxicating liquors" in the United States is neither as exact nor as unambiguous as the results of an experiment conducted under controlled conditions in a well-equipped laboratory. To speak of a "social experiment" in this context is to utilize a poetic metaphor that may deflect attention away from many important consequences and meanings embodied in the events. Prohibition was not undertaken or opposed in the spirit of experiment, nor was it administered as a controlled test of a hypothesis.

An adequate understanding of the implications of Prohibition for the effectiveness of criminalization and legal control cannot be confined to the 1920s. It must go back to the roots of Prohibition in the century-long temperance movement and the subsequent history of alcohol as a public issue in the United States. Context is essential to both action and understanding in human events. The analogy to an experiment is misapplied because it imagines social actions as understandable without a context or a history. It treats Prohibition as if it had a fixed meaning devoid of connotations provided by past or subsequent events.

The temperance movement

In December 1917 the United States Congress passed the Eighteenth Amendment outlawing the manufacture, sale, or transportation of "intoxicating liquors." In January 1919 the amendment was ratified by three-fourths of the states, and in January 1920 Prohibition became law. In February 1933 the Twenty-first Amendment, repealing Prohibition, was passed by Congress. It was quickly ratified before the end of that year, the first and, to date, the only amendment to the U.S. Constitution ever repealed. This brief encounter with legislation criminalizing commerce in hard liquor, beer, and wine was not an unexpected or bizarre interlude in American public life. It was only one phase in a long history of politics, legislation, common law, and exhortation about alcohol questions in the United States (Krout; Gusfield, 1963).

Popular belief and anti-Prohibitionist sentiment have often explained the passage of the Eighteenth Amendment as an aberration, put over on a quiescent public during wartime. Such an explanation ignores the fact that issues of drinking and its controls were very much in the foreground of American political, social, and legislative life from the 1820s through the 1920s. "Dry" and "wet" have been almost as essential in American politics as "left" and "right."

The antebellum movements. Although during the colonial period alcohol was widely perceived as a beneficial commodity and its excesses generally controlled, by the late eighteenth century widespread drunkenness had occasioned concern. In the decades preceding the Civil War, the temperance movement emerged in the form of organizations, such as the American Temperance Society and the Sons of Temperance, that were committed at first to minimizing and later to eradicating the use of beverage alcohol. A variety of state and local laws were passed, and by the

1850s thirteen states had been dry for varying lengths of time.

The temperance movement was a part of the general reformist impulse that marked American political and religious life in the first half of the nineteenth century. In its earliest phase, before 1826, the movement was dominated by a Federalist local aristocracy that saw in the manners and morals of a rowdy electorate a threat to its own fading power (Gusfield, 1963). By the 1820s temperance took on a tone of self-improvement as artisans, farmers, and industrial workers, often inspired by the religious revivalism of the period, sought their own perfection. During the next decade, improved transportation made whiskey less competitive with other uses of grain, and drinking became a costlier affair (Rorabaugh).

Temperance had become widely accepted in American life by the 1850s. If not necessarily followed by all or even most, it was the public ideal. In an expanding industrial and commercial society, employers and employees no longer thought of alcohol as a permissible accompaniment to the workday or a necessary aid to health and well-being. In an industrializing society, discipline, routinization, and steadiness of pursuit became virtues that contrasted with the erratic habits and spontaneous festivity of an earlier age (Tyrrell) Temperance, abolition, and penal reform were part of a drive toward a more humane and moral society and family (Clark). What in colonial America had been "the goodly creature of God" had become "demon rum" in the new democracy.

The clash of cultures. From one perspective, the rise of the temperance ideal of total abstinence was part of the transformation of the American population from a self-sufficient, rural society into an industrial and commercial one. However, that interpretation is too simple. Except for the Scandinavians, other industrializing societies have not developed so powerful or widespread a movement, nor one that has appeared and reappeared with such persistence for more than a century. Temperance in America owes much to the confrontation between the diverse cultures and religions that streams of immigration brought to the United States.

Most of the European peoples who immigrated to the United States were Roman Catholic. Their concentration in urban areas among the lower classes accentuated the clash with an American-born, Protestant, and rural population. The Irish and the Germans were the bêtes noires of temperance literature in the 1850s, joined by the Mediterranean and Slavic immigrants of the late nineteenth century. For these groups alcohol, in the form of beer, whiskey, or wine, was a part of daily life, and integral to the culture of the community. By the 1850s this was no longer the case among other Americans. Drinking and drunkenness had become isolated and marginal to the daily life of assimilated middle-class Americans—the acts of willful and weak sinners (Gusfield, 1963).

The vision of a dry America found a more pleasing reception among rural, nativist, and Protestant groups than among the new immigrants. Since its inception in 1869, the Prohibitionist party platforms displayed the rhetoric and aims of agrarian populism. Established in 1874, the Woman's Christian Temperance Union developed a number of programs to bring about the assimilation of immigrants into American culture, seeing in total abstinence a major form of acceptance of American values. Bringing the sinner and the immigrant into the mainstream of American life became a major objective of the temperance movement.

In this fashion the victories and defeats of the movement came to take on symbolic meanings of victory or defeat for the values of middle-class, American-born Protestants. Public approval of total abstinence emerged as a symbol, standing for the dominance of those whose way of life devalued and demeaned drinking and abhorred drunkenness. For some scholars the schism is seen in Catholic-Protestant and immigrant-native terms (Gusfield, 1963). For others it is couched in contrasts between religious theologies—basically between evangelical, fundamentalist, and denominational ("pietist") churches and ecclesiastical, hierarchical, and institutionalized ("liturgical") churches (Jensen). For both groups of scholars, however, the alcohol issue in the late nineteenth and the early twentieth century transcended the simple question of abstinence versus indulgence and acquired symbolic significance for a broader set of cultural, religious, and ethnic differences and conflicts.

The coming of Prohibition. By 1906, when the Anti-Saloon League began its agitation for state and national prohibition, the alcohol question had a long history as a significant factor in American politics. The league, by avoiding all other issues and acting as a pressure group in both major parties, was effective in organizing the power of Protestant churches and its members around a single issue—alcohol. Led by the league and its Methodist officials, the movement

for prohibition reached its zenith during the period of the great wave of immigration into American cities. In 1906 only three states had prohibition; by 1912 there were ten. In 1919, before the ratification of the Eighteenth Amendment, nineteen more states had passed restrictive legislation and more that 50 percent of the American population lived in dry areas.

The surge of Prohibitionist sentiment and power was abetted by the Progressive reform movement for clean and efficient government. The saloon had become a seat and a symbol of urban corruption, crime, and political manipulation of the electorate. It also played an important role in the lives of many immigrant and working-class groups, especially in the urban areas of the United States. The saloon was a major source of sociability, of financial aid, of news and food, and often an important avenue of economic mobility and of support for the urban political machine (Powers). Here, too, the religious and nativist conflicts gain further significance as part of the context for middle-class reform of the saloon as an established institution integrated into the cultures and leisure styles of the new urban immigrants, often from European societies where beer and liquor were more acceptable than in America.

Prohibition

When Prohibition was enacted, it was not as an experiment but as a major reform of American life and institutions. Although the temperance movement was concerned with the habitual drunkard, its main goal was total abstinence and the eradication of the liquor traffic. This totality gave the movement its moral character. The political conflict was not an argument over means for preventing alcoholism; it was a process of developing and defining the public values and life styles that would dominate in America—a conflict over the moral status of drinking and the cultural attitudes it implied.

The Prohibition amendment and its enforcing legislation, the Volstead Act (an Act to prohibit intoxicating beverages, and to regulate the manufacture, production, use, and sale of high-proof spirits for other than beverage purposes. . . , ch. 85, 41 Stat. 305 (1919) (repealed)), were thus attempts to define appropriate moral behavior relating to consumption of a commodity and to make the state an agent of cultural persuasion. The emphasis was sociological and institutional: to outlaw the manufacture and sale of liquor and thus make it unavailable. This strategy can be contrasted with alternate psychological approaches, such as that used in the slogan of the liquor industry in the 1980s: "The fault is in the man, not in the bottle." Here institutional change is ignored. For the partisan of Prohibition the problem was not "substance abuse" but "abusive substance."

Enforcement and crime. While Prohibition achieved much legislative support, there was in much of American political and social life a large and significant population that was hostile to its legislative passage and to its intended aspiration to change drinking habits in American life (Blocker, Kyvig). It must be noted that most state legislatures, where the Eighteenth Amendment was ratified, were dominated by rural constituencies since reapportioning had not occurred for decades. Enforcement was limited both in events and in punishments. If victory brought satisfaction to the Protestant, nativist, and rural segments of America, its symbolic character increased the resentment and alienation of populations who felt deeply insulted at a level of immediate, day-to-day existence. The expression "striking a blow for liberty" gave support and justification to those, especially in the large cities, who flouted the Prohibition law and kept the bootleggers in diamonds.

The Eighteenth Amendment and the Volstead Act declared a major American industry to be engaged in a criminal activity. Unlike the drug legislation of later decades, they did not criminalize the consumption or purchase of alcohol, but they did place the sale, manufacture, and transportation of a major commodity out of legal bounds. As has long been true of such proscribed goods and services as prostitution, illegal abortion, gambling, and illegal drugs, a lively black market emerged (Merz; Sinclair).

The special character of the commodity made Prohibition productive of organized crime in a manner distinct from that of other black markets. Since alcoholic beverages were still available in other countries, bootlegging was a major smuggling operation, as drugs were in the 1970s and 1980s (Cashman). Transportation was therefore a major aspect of the trade in alcohol. Bootlegging was an enterprise requiring venture capital and business organization, and money, protection against hijacking, and political protection were essential to such a complex undertaking. In such a market, political corruption is a necessary part of operating and competition is at least as volatile and unwelcome as in the manufacture and sale of automobiles. Much of the sensational gang warfare during Prohibition emerged from efforts to develop and to self-police agreements in restraint of trade. A number or bootleggers in effect died defending the tenets of free enterprise.

That Prohibition was a significant element in the development of organized crime is understandable, given the businesslike character of this victimless crime. Organized crime built on the existing gangs that had controlled prostitution and other black markets before 1920, and by the time of repeal, the underworld was more organized and efficient than it had been before.

The deterrent effects of Prohibition. Was the Prohibition experiment a success? The question possesses an inherent ambiguity that almost defies scientific analysis. Legislation often has meaning on different levels and for different periods of history. As legislation symbolizing the dominance of those classes and religious groups that supported Prohibition, the Eighteenth Amendment acquired significance simply by winning sufficient backing for its passage, regardless of its degree of enforcement. As legislation that sought to change the life styles of Americans, Prohibition could not be gauged until it had been on the books for at least a generation. In fact, some of its impact was not at all evident until after repeal, when restrictions on hours, conditions, and consumer ages displayed some of the lasting educative effects.

Whether or not Prohibition deterred drinkers presupposes the importance of the question's answer to justifications for or against the Eighteenth Amendment. The history of temperance indicates that the passage and continuation of Prohibition was as much a symbolic statement of the public disapproval of drinking as it was an intent to effectuate a change in behavior. The legal scholar should understand that the goal of deterrence does not exhaust the context of issues over which opponents and proponents fought. Prohibition was not championed only as a means of deterring drinking; it was also put forth as a means of reforming the moral attitudes of American life. Considering Prohibition as a moral reform, rather than an experiment in social control, it is doubtful if the arguments about its deterrent effects would have swayed many of its supporters or detractors.

Repeal did not return America to the same situation vis-à-vis alcohol that existed when the Eighteenth Amendment became law and the saloons became speakeasies. Certainly, the newspapers and magazines presented a lurid picture of an America awash in bathtub gin and in easy communication with the local bootlegger; an America that paid little attention to Prohibition except as a matter of ridicule and inconvenience. But such accounts are suspect of more than the pathetic fallacy of converting the experience of a circle of urban journalists into a universal principle. They reflected the world that many journalists saw about them—the world of the metropolitan upper middle class, precisely the group least Prohibitionist in sentiment and most able to spend the money to purchase liquors and wines. A more representative analysis of the 1920s suggests a more varied picture but also underscores the sheer difficulty of answering the question about the impact of the law.

Different accounts of the Prohibition period agree on certain conclusions, cautiously and with recognition of limits in the evidence:

1. Geographic areas where the law was least obeyed were those in which Prohibition had been least supported in elections—best characterized as metropolitan, Catholic, and Jewish. Conversely, areas where Prohibition was most strongly supported were those in which the law was most obeyed—rural, Protestant, and middle-class.
2. The major exception to this generalization was in urban working-class areas of all religious denominations, where the falloff in drinking appears to have been considerable.
3. Both the total consumption of alcohol and the number of deaths from cirrhosis of the liver were lower in the period after repeal than in the decade prior to Prohibition (Gusfield, 1968; Aaron and Musto).

The evidence supporting these conclusions is a variety of statistical data—total amount of grain produced and sold, arrests for drunkenness, hospital admissions for alcohol psychosis, mortality rates for cirrhosis of the liver, and tax revenues from post-repeal sales—all of which showed decreases. The use of many of these records for any quantitative estimate of alcohol consumption may be questionable, although the tax revenues offer more reliable data than most other sources. Arrest statistics for drunkenness provide especially poor data, since they depend very much on local policies and the categories used to describe a misdemeanor. Use of the data on deaths from cirrhosis of the liver depends on assumptions about the length of time between

the beginning of heavy drinking and the effects of the disease—a time period no longer thought to be very uniform. Alcohol consumption after 1933 was also affected by lower incomes during the Great Depression.

Despite such skepticism about their reliability, these data, together with supplementary material based on impressions of social workers in urban areas, all point in the same direction—toward a decline of alcohol use in pro-Prohibitionist areas and among the rural and urban working class. The available evidence suggests that, contrary to popular belief, Prohibition did decrease the total consumption of alcohol drinking in the United States. The burden of proof thus appears to rest on those who would assert otherwise (Blocker, Tyvig, Aaron and Musto, Gusfield).

The apparent consensus on the decline in drinking among the working class is consistent with information about other historical periods when costs of alcoholic beverages rose, and perhaps provides the major lesson of the Prohibition period for those interested in controlling total consumption of alcohol. The impact of restrictions on sale and manufacture resulted in a rise in price and a consequent decrease in demand in a segment of the market, especially notable among the less affluent. Not only did prices increase, but as in past periods in American history, transportation costs favored whiskey over beer. The percentage rise in the price of beer (the workingman's drink) was even greater than for hard liquors. Members of the affluent, whiskey-drinking upper middle class became the major customers for alcohol.

The further consequences of Prohibition and repeal. Although the Eighteenth Amendment came under sharper and more organized attack after the mid-1920s, with the victory of Herbert Hoover over Alfred E. Smith it seemed safe from the weapons of a wet siege. Yet four years later, by which time Hoover had become cool to it and Franklin Roosevelt had repudiated it, the Prohibition amendment was ready for the trash heap of history. Whatever else may have contributed to the waning of public passions for a sober America in the midst of the Great Depression, the blocked consumption of alcohol was both a minor issue and a drain on employment opportunities and potential tax revenues. Men of power and wealth who had embraced Prohibition, such as John D. Rockefeller and S. S. Kresge, now leaped off the wagon. Unions, which were always opposed or indifferent to it, now began to petition for redress of jobs.

In the drive for national Prohibition, the Anti-Saloon League had played a dominating role, the originator of the powerful one-issue pressure group (Kyvig, Kerr). Opposition to it had been weak. Both the liquor and beer industries had not played a major role as counters to the League. With Prohibition an active and organized opposition developed, with support from wealthy donors. Two of these organizations were especially important—the Association Against Prohibition Amendment (AAPA) and the Women's Organization for National Prohibition Reform (WONPR) (Kyvig).

With the Great Depression, the vision of a dry America creating prosperity through sober and distinguished living suffered a decline in belief. The immigrant generation had come of political age just as the Protestant establishment was tilting on its pedestal. The dramatic news of criminal violence and political corruption produced by Prohibition was too great a burden for a crumbling program to bear.

The repeal of the Eighteenth Amendment discredited attempts to control drinking through legal restrictions on the commercial traffic in alcoholic beverages. In addition, it diminished the political importance of the Prohibitionist constituency as shapers of public policy on alcohol after repeal. During the decade following repeal, the role of American Protestant churchmen as leaders of the anti-alcohol movement was taken over by academics, physicians, paraprofessionals, and recovered alcoholics. The stress shifted from the aim of achieving total abstinence and sobriety to the problem of chronic alcoholism—the behavior of a deviant minority of the population. As a corollary, strategies focused on treating the alcoholic rather than controlling the drinking of the general population.

Although American public discussion and action veered sharply away from legal controls, in several ways Prohibition left a legacy of acceptable legal constraints that went beyond those in existence before its passage. Per capita consumption of alcohol never returned to the high point of the early twentieth century, and the general drift away from whiskey and toward beer continued (Aaron and Musto). The comparatively high level of abstainers in the American population remained stable. In more that twelve thousand local-option elections during the two decades after repeal, there was very little change in local law (Gusfield, 1963). At the level of public opinion and personal choice, Prohibition appears to have done little to change attitudes toward drinking and abstinence.

However, the earlier lack of control over saloons was no longer acceptable. All states established Alcohol Beverage Control (ABC) boards. Although often proving to be less regulatory than anticipated, they have served to prevent issuance of licenses to those with underworld connections. The ABC legislation is one of a number of legislative measures enacted and accepted in American life that perpetuate and expand the concept of beverage alcohol as an "exceptional commodity" more dangerous than most commodities and consequently requiring special legal controls. Restrictions on hours, locations of sales, and special taxes have continued or increased. Laws against public drunkenness and against drinking and driving continue to be enforced, although public-drunkenness legislation is by no means universal in Western countries.

Perhaps most significant has been the increase in the number of minimum-age drinking laws. Availability of alcohol to minors became more restricted at the same time that availability to the general population was widened (Mosher). Indicative of the persisting view that alcohol is a dangerous and exceptional commodity is the failure of many states to alter laws prohibiting the sale of alcohol to persons under twenty-one. The repeal of laws lowering the age in some states has encountered little political resistance despite the decrease of the minimum age to eighteen for most legal purposes.

Although in the post-repeal period alcohol policy was dominated by an emphasis on treatment of alcoholics, by the 1970s attention was again beginning to turn toward questions of prevention through control measures such as taxation and restrictions on sale (Bruun et al.). The ambivalence of American society toward drinking remains characteristic, and still contrasts with wider acceptance of alcohol in most industrialized societies.

Although the consumption of alcohol, especially spirits, has diminished somewhat in recent decades, the system of control and permission has not altered in any significant respect since the early post-Repeal years.

JOSEPH R. GUSFIELD

See also CRIMINALIZATION AND DECRIMINALIZATION; EXCUSE: INTOXICATION; VICTIMLESS CRIME.

BIBLIOGRAPHY

AARON, PAUL, and MUSTO, DAVID. "Temperance and Prohibition in America: An Historical Overview." *Alcohol and Public Policy: Beyond the Shadow of Prohibition.* Edited by Mark Moore and Dean Gerstein. Washington, D.C.: National Academy Press, 1981, pp. 127–183.

BLOCKER, JACK S., JR. *American Temperance Movements: Cycles of Reform.* Boston: Twayne, 1989.

BRUUN, KETTIL et al. *Alcohol Control Policies in Public Health Perspective.* Finnish Foundation for Alcohol Studies, vol. 25. New Brunswick, N.J.: Rutgers Center of Alcohol Studies, 1975.

CASHMAN, SEAN D. *Prohibition: The Lie of the Land.* New York: Macmillan, 1981.

CLARK, NORMAN H. *Deliver Us from Evil: An Interpretation of American Prohibition.* New York: Norton, 1976.

ENGELMANN, LARRY. *Intemperance: The Lost War against Liquor.* New York: Free Press, 1979.

GUSFIELD, JOSEPH. "Prohibition: The Impact of Political Utopianism." *Change and Continuity in Twentieth Century America: The 1920s.* Edited by John Braeman, Robert H. Bremner, and David Brody. Columbus: Ohio State University Press, 1968, pp. 257–308.

———. *Symbolic Crusade: Status Politics and the American Temperance Movement.* Urbana: University of Illinois Press, 1969.

JENSEN, RICHARD. *The Winning of the Midwest: Social and Political Conflict, 1888–1896.* University of Chicago Press, 1971.

KERR, AUSTIN. *Organized for Prohibition: A New History of the Anti-Saloon League.* New Haven: Conn.: Yale University Press, 1985.

KROUT, JOHN A. *The Origins of Prohibition.* New York: Knopf, 1925.

KYVIG, DAVID. *Repealing National Prohibition.* Chicago: University of Chicago Press, 1979.

MERZ, CHARLES. *The Dry Decade.* (1931). Reprint, with a new introduction by the author. Seattle: University of Washington Press, 1969.

MOSHER, JAMES F. "The History of Youthful-drinking Laws: Implications for Current Policy." *Minimum Drinking-age Laws: An Evaluation.* Edited by Henry Wechsler. Lexington, Mass.: Health, Lexington Books, 1980, pp. 11–38.

POWERS, MADELON. *Faces along the Bar: Lore and Order and Workingman's Saloon, 1870–1920.* University of Chicago Press, 1998.

RORABAUGH, W. J. *The Alcoholic Republic: An American Tradition.* New York: Oxford University Press, 1979.

SINCLAIR, ANDREW. *Prohibition: The Era of Excess.* Preface by Richard Hofstadter. Boston: Little, Brown, 1962.

TYRRELL, IAN R. "Temperance and Economic Change in the Antebellum North." *Alcohol, Reform, and Society: The Liquor Issue in Social Context.* Edited by Jack S. Blocker, Jr. Westport, Conn.: Greenwood Press, 1979, pp. 45–68.

ALCOHOL AND CRIME: TREATMENT AND REHABILITATION

Providing treatment for persons who have committed crimes and who also have alcohol problems seems a straightforward subject for description and analysis. The approach should presumably center on the description of circumstances when criminals with alcohol problems do or do not receive treatment for these problems, factors affecting this differential use of treatment, and a review of evidence of the effectiveness of these interventions.

These issues will be dealt with in this entry, but they are not its primary focus. By contrast, the intersection of crime, alcohol problems, and treatment for alcohol problems offers unexpected opportunities for understanding the conceptual relationships between alcohol and crime. These understandings extend well beyond the somewhat tedious question of how drinking might "cause" crime. This intersection of three distinctive empirical phenomena also provides contextual understanding of the construction and implementation of social policy in Western nations.

The starting premise is that all alcohol problems are grounded in behavior that is "continuous" with crime, which provides a context for viewing why or why not treatment is readily provided to a wide range of persons with alcohol problems. According to Durkheimian theory (Erikson), crime is a constant in human societies. Important differences are found, however, in how and when crime is defined and acted upon in different structural and cultural circumstances. By contrast, neither alcohol problems nor their "treatment" are universal across different social structures. While it has been observed that alcohol is used in nearly all human societies, the notion of its "problematic" status is not a cultural universal (Macandrew and Edgerton).

Many dimensions of crime are dealt with exhaustively in this encyclopedia, but for present purposes it is significant to state simply that crime is more or less (but not perfectly) continuous with deviant behavior in everyday life. This is a basic Durkheimian perspective. If this continuum between deviance and crime is assumed, then crime is logically a subcategory of deviance. Where, however, is the "break" on the continuum wherein deviance becomes crime? It is useful in this entry to view the difference between deviance and crime as residing in three factors: the extent of norm violation, social visibility, and formalized social reaction.

Norm violation

Crimes are socially constructed in law. Law is implemented through the cataloging of certain behaviors as requiring formalized social reactions ranging from warnings, through arrests, trials, punishment, and ultimately to banishment or execution. The content of a criminal code may in large part describe the moral structure of the society wherein it is developed and implemented.

Crimes are, however, a subcategory within a broader set of phenomena called norm violations, or acts of deviance. All crimes are norm violations, but not all norm violations are crimes. Viewed historically, norm violations may move in and out of the category of crime, and an understanding of such shifts can be important in the analysis of social structure (Gusfield; Beauchamp). As described below, alcohol problems have been viewed as crimes in various ways at different points in American history, but in recent decades they have been almost wholly shifted to a noncriminal categorization.

Social visibility and formalized reactions

With the exception of those who perform socially invisible criminal acts known only to themselves but who "turn themselves in" due apparently to the weight of conscience, the vast remainder of criminals commit acts that are socially visible. The acts become visible through impacting others, through being viewed by others, and by being reported in some fashion. Acts in the broader category of deviant behavior of which crime is a part need not be socially visible. Their impact upon others may be unknown or ambiguous, others may not view the behavior, or social decisions may be made by affected or observing others that no advantage will be served by reporting the behavior. Without such reporting, the pathway to a formalized social reaction ends.

It is an axiom of sociology that there is a great deal of deviant behavior in society that does not have visible social consequences. Some of this deviance may prove, in retrospect, to be nascent crime, but in many other instances events of deviant behavior pass unnoticed and are absorbed into the ongoing flow of social life (Black). This distinction between deviance and crime is drawn out to establish the continuity between crime and deviance. This should set the stage for considering the conceptual status of alcohol problems, and in turn lead toward an understanding of the social meaning of "treatment."

Alcohol problems as double deviance

Central to this entry is the assertion that all alcohol problems spring from deviance, this being independent of medicalized and moral conceptions that may be attached to alcohol problems. As mentioned, alcohol problems have been subject to shifting definitions and categorizations across cultures and over history, experiences well documented in the history of American society. Colonial historians have observed that eighteenth-century drinking in the American colonies was far more extensive than drinking patterns known in subsequent periods, that drinking was woven into the fabric of nearly all phases of personal and social activity, and that "alcohol problems" were largely unknown, with the exceptions of grossly destructive behavior associated with drunkenness, and of persons who were unable to work and were community wards because of their excessive drinking (Rorabaugh).

As is well known, alcohol soon emerged as a social problem of major proportions, part of a massive set of social and ideological changes in the new republic occurring in the 1820s and 1830s. Interpreters have seen this period as one of the emergence of multiple social problems, not necessarily because of increased prevalence but because of transformed definitions. As part of these changes, alcohol consumption became problematic in America (Clark; Lender and Martin). Problem definitions began with labeling the consumption of liquor or "ardent spirits" as physically and mentally destructive, allowing, however, for the consumption of beer, cider, and wine.

After several decades, all alcohol consumption came to be seen as personally damaging and socially dangerous, and the temperance movement essentially defined all drinking as deviant. Eventually national Prohibition came to be seen as the solution to this alleged morass of problems, and it was enacted in 1920, leading to the distinctive definition of all alcohol-related activities within the conceptual arena of crime.

When Prohibition was repealed in 1933 (for a complex set of reasons still being debated), the definition of alcohol consumption within a criminal conception became obviously untenable. One set of responses moved toward the enactment of a great many rules as to when, how, and by whom alcoholic beverages could be consumed. A second set of responses set about to differentiate between problematic and nonproblematic drinking.

It was in this new area of research that the conception of the disease of alcoholism emerged (Jellinek summarizes these developments). Alcoholism was not defined by the consumption of a set amount of alcohol, but by behavioral patterns wherein persons completely "lost control" over their drinking. Such behavior often could be observed in terminally ill individuals who drank constantly, ate little, manifested severe psychiatric symptoms, and usually died or were permanently disabled due to organ damage. Other types of alcoholics could remain abstinent for considerable periods, but manifested this "loss of control" once drinking began again.

While there was consensus regarding the gravity of this behavioral syndrome, it was clear that any kind of effective intervention would have to address the problem at a considerably earlier stage in its development. Over several decades a well-organized campaign promoted the definition of alcohol problems into the medical arena and out of the criminal arena. Alcoholism as a crime was formally "decriminalized" in the 1960s, and by the 1970s the study of alcoholism as an illness was assigned to a federal research and treatment agency that ultimately became a unit of the National Institutes of Health.

Thus, from the beginning of the nineteenth century, when alcohol problems were barely recognized, there was a rapid shift toward viewing such problems as sin, then as crime, only to transform them into medical disorders by the last quarter of the twentieth century. These rapid and complex definitional changes have never been fully institutionalized in American culture, with the consequence that there are mixtures of definitions and ambivalences about how problems should be managed. These confusions have considerable implications for the likelihood that criminals will receive treatment for their alcohol problems.

One of the manifestations of these confusions is in the "double deviance" definition of alcohol problems. Alcohol problems are defined not by the amount of alcohol consumed or the pattern by which it is consumed, but by the problems in role performance that can be linked to the individual's drinking. Problem drinkers are essentially defined by how much trouble they have gotten into in association with their drinking. Double deviance arises in this way: one or more acts of deviance define an alcohol problem, which in turn defines the individual's drinking behavior as deviant. Persons who repeatedly engage in these patterns of behaviors are seen as unresponsive to negative feedback, and thus "alcohol dependent." Behavioral repetition by alcohol-dependent persons easily segues into "alcoholism."

While role performance impairment appears to be consistent with (in medical language) differential diagnosis at the individual level, it is clear that this definition is almost wholly dependent on social events. While self-diagnosis and self-referral of persons with serious alcohol problems is not unknown, it is very exceptional. Definitions of poor performance emanate from the judgments of significant others surrounding an individual, and thus are a "paradigm case" of socially defined deviance. The crucial understanding is that a problem drinker must also be a social deviant, placing all persons defined as problem drinkers on a continuum with criminals who have alcohol problems.

The prominence of deviance in treatment paradigms

In addition to facets of "crime" surrounding the definition of alcohol problems, there is also clear evidence of "punishment." Despite the widespread usage of medicalized language to describe the behaviors of persons with alcohol problems, they are punished in everyday life by social rejection, loss of friends, marital dissolution, job discipline, or job loss. Sometimes this occurs as part of the rehabilitation process, such as divorce following treatment or the loss of a job associated with treatment entry. Rarely do cries of social injustice arise when an alcohol-troubled person suffers these consequences. While these observations of punishment may seem pedestrian, their importance lies in the fact that alcohol problems are formally defined as medical issues. Crime and punishment are usually held to be independent of disease and medical care.

By linking admission of guilt and repentance to progress through the program, facets of punishment are embedded in the steps of Alcoholics Anonymous (AA), the most prominent mode of treatment for alcohol problems in the United States, and the modality that forms the basis for the vast majority of professionalized treatment programs for alcohol problems. It is important to keep in mind that passage through the twelve steps of AA should be sequential, and that there are no prescriptions regarding how far one must go in the sequence and still be an AA member in good standing. (A desire to stop drinking is, in fact, the sole requirement for membership.) In the eighth step AA members "made a list of all persons we had harmed and became willing to make amends to them all." Although seemingly simple, this step actually encompasses three distinct behaviors (making the list, overcoming resistances to approach others, and deciding to approach all such injured persons). These acts are concrete: writing, deciding, and encompassing a potentially vast array of others. Once this step is accomplished, the individual may move on to the ninth step, wherein he makes "direct amends to such people wherever possible, except when to do so would injure them or others." These expected reparations certainly place the AA member on a continuum with individuals with alcohol problems who have committed criminal acts.

Two further points elaborate this conception. First, there are a multitude of reasons for associating the emergence and social acceptance of the medical model of alcoholism with the invention and diffusion of AA (Beauchamp; Kurtz; Roman). The content of the eighth and ninth steps of the fellowship's program do, however, assert significant deviance with the alcoholic career. It is noteworthy that the eighth step does not suggest the optional possibility of "IF we have harmed others" wherein one might skip to subsequent steps. Herein lies substantial institutional evidence of the intertwining of the definition of alcohol problems and social deviance, well before the emergence of criteria in the American Psychiatric Association's Diagnostic and Statistical Manuals.

Second, the ninth step appears to be intertwined with the eighth step in that it seems illogical that one would become "willing" to make amends to "all" and then do nothing. This possibility must have been recognized by the founders of AA. It is evident that separate "packaging" of these potentially stress-filled and painful sets of actions very likely increases the probability that the reparative actions will be taken.

AA is the dominant modality in the treatment of alcohol problems, but the past few decades have seen the rapid emergence of professional research interest in addiction treatment, much of which has challenged the somewhat single-minded approach of AA and twelve-step programming in general. Prominent among the research-based strategies is the classification of alcohol and drug programs through the Addiction Severity Index (ASI), developed by a team of researchers at the University of Pennsylvania (McLellan et al., 1992a, 1992b). The ASI and a more recent inventory used with clients, the Treatment Services Review (TSR), are centered on the assumption that persons with addiction problems bring a multitude of problems to the treatment setting, including medical, psychological, familial, occupational, legal, and financial problems.

The authors of these inventories assert that most treatments fail because they focus only upon the addiction problems and such treatment typically ignores the accumulated consequences of deviant behavior associated with the development of alcohol problems. The ASI and TSR are focused on assessing clients across all of these problem areas and coordinating treatment services in each needed area in order that full rehabilitation may result. The more serious the alcohol problems, the higher the scores on the ASI and the greater the needs reflected in the TSR.

While the AA steps and the ASI/TSR approaches to addiction treatment have vastly different institutional origins and assumptions, they are remarkably similar in their emphasis upon the deviance that has accompanied the development of alcohol problems. Both approaches argue that successful treatment outcomes will not occur if only the problem of addiction is addressed. In very different ways, both point toward the necessity that problem persons address a range of difficulties in role performance that have been generated across most areas of their lives. In so doing, both approaches demonstrate the vast difference between the medicalized conception of alcohol problems and parallel conceptions associated with other disorders, their treatment, and expectations for recovery.

Why offer treatment to criminals with alcohol problems?

There are three contemporary justifications for the offering of treatment to persons with alcohol problems, all of which contrast to an earlier social welfare justification wherein treatment was offered because it was the morally correct choice. In the first of the contemporary justifications, the offering of treatment is essentially compelled by acceptance of the notion that alcohol problems are intermingled with alcohol dependency, and alcohol dependency is a medical or health problem. Sick persons deserve treatment and persons with alcohol dependency are sick persons.

The second justification is centered on social investment. This idea centers on the occupancy of significant social roles by persons with alcohol problems. Role occupancy in turn indicates that others are dependent upon the focal individual, allowing that in some circumstances this dependence may be symbolic and obligatory, such as the deference that is offered to the needs of elderly family members even though their "productivity" may be strictly symbolic at present but historically significant. Thus treatment is offered through allocating the resources owned by different interest groups, typically families or employers.

The third justification is focused on recidivism. Criminals with alcohol problems are seen as double deviants in a sense different from that used here, namely that there is a causal interdependence between their substance use and their criminality. While it is widely asserted that drinking facilitates crime, the element of differential association with bad company that accompanies drinking and illegal drug use is a secondary facilitating factor. Thus some data indicate that successful treatment of criminals' substance abuse problems will have a desirous effect on recidivism (Pearson and Lipton).

How are criminals linked to these justifications? Looking first at the illness-entitlement idea, it may be difficult to view criminals with alcohol problems as "sick." By definition, they have already received a cardinal label of criminality that implies "bad," not sick. "Bad" is the marker for imputing responsibility for deviant behavior, and the administration of the label "criminal" immediately excludes the possibility of an illness label. Thus, with the "sick" label absolving responsibility and the "bad" label imputing responsibility, "sick" and "bad" have a very difficult coexistence as labels for the same individual.

Thus the administration of criminal labels creates a logic-based resistance to the placement of a sick label on a criminal with alcohol problems. This is not to say, however, that the criminal justice system denies that alcohol problems exist among criminals. Instead, the alcohol problem is seen as something that may interfere with an individual's eventual return to society, as well as a possible contributor to recidivism, but it is clearly not the individual's cardinal problem, which is his or her criminality. There may be no reluctance in agreeing that a criminal's alcohol problem is secondary, or even lower in priority, but there cannot be the administration of a cardinal label wherein the criminal is seen as sick and thus deserving treatment.

Turning to the social investment justification, it is important to examine the role occupancy of the criminal. By being placed in prison, he or she occupies the prisoner role, and may be part of different social networks within the prison. Occupancy of social roles outside the prison is nonexistent or, at best, suspended. It is very rare for employers to hold open job positions for individuals while awaiting the completion of their incarceration. While fathers and mothers, as well as husbands and wives, may be deeply missed by their significant others during their incarceration, the demands of these vacant roles must be filled by others or not filled at all for the duration. Thus the social investment justification for providing treatment for alcohol problems is largely missing.

As mentioned, a principal goal of most prisons is the reduction of recidivism. Recidivism can also be understood in the terms of social roles. An individual who is a recidivist must return to a previous role in the community involving criminal behavior, or adopt a new criminal role configuration, for without such role occupancy, there can be no repeat offenses. Because roles in families and employment become "closed out" for individuals who are incarcerated (assuming they occupied such roles prior to incarceration), their opportunities following the completion of incarceration may be limited to prior roles involving engagement in criminal behavior. Indeed, this possibility may be enhanced if they were evaluated as particularly valuable in the performance of criminal acts by criminal peers, and these persons welcome them back into roles that may have been "held open" for them.

Given these facts, it is only logical to conclude that the major justification for the offering of treatment to criminals with alcohol problems is the traditional social welfare concept that it is the right thing to do. If this is correct, then it immediately explains why the offering of treatment for alcohol problems to criminals drifts down the list of priorities of what can be effectively carried out in the prison environment. The possibility of allocating resources for the treatment of alcohol problems essentially "competes" with other morally compelling programs, such as addressing criminals' mental health problems, dealing with their physical health, and providing them with skills so that they are attracted to noncriminal work opportunities when their incarceration is completed.

The published literature on the effectiveness of treatment invariably supports three general conclusions. First, that there are not enough available resources to afford the widespread availability of such treatment (Wright); second, that the extent of success in treatment is closely linked with the amount of time that criminals are retained in treatment programs (Farabee et al.); and third, that the long-term impact of this treatment on both recidivism and recovery from alcoholism is contingent on a vast range of factors that are extremely difficult to capture with available evaluation technology (Kinlock et al.; Hiller et al.).

Thus, it might be expected that investment in alcohol problem treatment for criminals would be found in an environment of munificent resources where a range of criminals' problems in living in the world were addressed. This would of course assume that the allocation of resources to alcohol problem treatment effectively competed with the demands and lobbying of other constituencies invested in morally compelling programs.

Conclusion

In conclusion, the relationships between alcohol problems, crime, and treatment may be said to offer conceptual excitement and empirical disappointment. The linkages between the three concepts tell us a great deal about the social and cultural attitudes toward alcohol problems that in turn explain the ways in which treatment is utilized and implemented. Deviant behavior, which is clearly on a continuum with criminal behavior, is an essential component of the definition of alcohol problems, and thus for access to treatment. Within the treatment and recovery process, the client's dealing with the facts of his or her deviance plays a central role.

By contrast, we find that treatment is made available to criminals with alcohol problems on a piecemeal basis at best. While there is evidence that some criminals with alcohol problems respond positively to treatment, there is a poor cultural "fit" between the widespread use of treatment and the administration of several major sectors of the criminal justice system.

Hence the empirical disappointment: While from some perspectives there is a very distinctive need for more treatment for criminals with alcohol problems, their deviance has carried them beyond the point where society regards treatment as a sound investment, or even as an appropriate investment. This is in sharp contrast to the salience of deviance in deciding and directing the administration of treatment to persons with alcohol problems whose behavior "falls short" of the criterion of criminality.

The amount of treatment available to the criminal population is minuscule relative to the apparent need. There is no clear way in which alcohol problem treatment could move up the list of priorities in the administration of criminal justice. Thus there is little reason to expect that the availability of alcohol problem treatment for the criminal population will increase at any time in the foreseeable future.

PAUL M. ROMAN

See also ALCOHOL AND CRIME: BEHAVIORAL ASPECTS; DRINKING AND DRIVING; DRUGS AND CRIME: BEHAVIORAL ASPECTS; EXCUSE: INTOXICATION.

BIBLIOGRAPHY

BEAUCHAMP, DAN. *Beyond Alcoholism*. Philadelphia: Temple University Press, 1980.
BLACK, DONALD. *The Social Structure of Right and Wrong*. Orlando, Fla.: Academic Press, 1993.
CLARK, NORMAN. *Deliver Us from Evil*. New York: W. W. Norton, 1976.
ERIKSON, KAI. *Wayward Puritans*. New York: John Wiley, 1966.
FARABEE, DAVID; PRENDERGAST, MICHAEL; CARTIER, JEROME; and WECHSLER, HARRY. "Barriers to Implementing Effective Correctional Drug Treatment Programs." *Prison Journal* 79 (1999): no. 2, 150–162.
GUSFIELD, JOSEPH. *Contested Meanings: The Social Construction of Alcohol Problems*. Madison: University of Wisconsin Press, 1996.
HILLER, MATTHEW; KNIGHT, KEVIN; and SIMPSON, DWAYNE. "Prison-based Substance Abuse

Treatment: Residential Aftercare and Recidivism." *Addiction* 94 (1999): no. 6, 833–842.

JELLINEK, ELVIN M. *The Disease Concept of Alcoholism.* New Haven, Conn.: The Hillhouse Press, 1960.

KINLOCK, TIMOTHY; HALON, THOMAS; and NURCO, DAVID. "Criminal Justice Responses to Adult Substance Abuse." In *Prevention and Societal Impact of Drug and Alcohol Abuse.* Edited by R. Ammerman, P. Ott, and R. Tarter. Mahwah, N.J.: Lawrence Erlbaum Associates, 1999, pages 201–220.

KURTZ, ERNEST. *Not-God: A History of Alcoholics Anonymous.* Center City, Minn.: The Hazleden Foundation, 1980.

LENDER, MARK, and MARTIN, JOHN. *Drinking in America: A History.* New York: The Free Press, 1982.

MACANDREW, CRAIG, and EDGERTON, ROBERT. *Drunken Comportment.* San Francisco: Aldine Publishing Co, 1967.

MCLELLAN, A. THOMAS; KUSHNER, H.; and WOODY, GEORGE. "The Fifth Edition of the Addiction Severity Index." *Journal of Substance Abuse Treatment* 9 (1992a): 199–213.

MCLELLAN, A. THOMAS; ALTERMAN, ARTHUR; WOODY, GEORGE; and METZGER, DAVID. "A Quantitative Measure of Substance Abuse Treatments: The Treatment Services Review." *Journal of Nervous and Mental Diseases* 180 (1992b): no. 2, 101–110.

PEARSON, FRANK, and LIPTON, DOUGLAS. "A Meta-analytic Review of the Effectiveness of Corrections-based Treatments for Drug Abuse." *Prison Journal* 79 (1999): no. 4, 384–410.

ROMAN, PAUL. "The Disease Concept of Alcoholism: Sociocultural and Organizational Bases of Support." *Drugs and Society* 2 (1988): 5–32.

RORABAUGH, WILLIAM. *The Alcoholic Republic.* New York: Oxford, 1979.

WRIGHT, KEVIN N. "Alcohol Use by Prisoners." *Alcohol, Health and Research World* 17 (1993): no. 2, 157–161.

AMNESTY AND PARDON

Examples of amnesty and pardon are as ancient as the records of organized society, and these institutions are recognized in almost every contemporary legal system. This universality may be seen as a reflection of the desire appertaining to all systems to "temper justice with mercy." More specifically, it signifies the need for any formal system to maintain a residual power to introduce occasional modifications in implementing its formal norms in order to meet the exigencies of unforeseen situations.

Terminology and etymology

The term *pardon* is first found in early French law and derives from the late Latin *perdonare* ("to grant freely"), suggesting a gift bestowed by the sovereign. It has thus come to be associated with a somewhat personal concession by a head of state to the perpetrator of an offense, in mitigation or remission of the full punishment that he has merited. *Amnesty*, on the other hand, derives from the Greek *amnestia* ("forgetting"), and has come to be used to describe measures of a more general nature, directed to offenses whose criminality is considered better forgotten. Yet, it is interesting to note that in ancient Greece, amnesties were in fact called *adeia* ("security" or "immunity"), and not *amnestia*. Moreover, the term *pardon* fell into disuse in French law, to be replaced by the term *grâce*.

Clemency is a broader term, often encompassing both amnesty and pardon (Weihofen). Gerald Ford's U.S. Presidential Clemency Board, on the other hand, specified that it was concerned with granting "clemency, not amnesty." Clemency, however, is not usually employed as a legal term.

Commutation and *remission* refer to a lowering of the severity of a penalty, for example, commuting a death sentence into life imprisonment, or remitting a portion of the prison term imposed. *Reprieve* refers to the postponement or temporary suspension of a penalty.

Historical overview

Early history. The roots of pardon and amnesty are found in ancient law. References to institutions somewhat resembling the modern pardon appear in ancient Babylonian and Hebrew law. The first amnesty is generally attributed to Thrasybulus in ancient Greece (403 B.C.E.); but fifteen centuries earlier the Babylonian kings, on accession to the throne, would declare a *misharum*, involving a general discharge from legal bonds of both a civil and a penal character. (An analogy may be found in the biblical "jubilee laws.") The Romans, on the other hand, developed a number of forms of clemency, and these influenced subsequent developments in European law.

In medieval Europe the power to grant pardon was held by various bodies, including the Roman Catholic Church and certain local rulers, but by the sixteenth century it usually was concentrated in the hands of the monarch. In post-

Reformation England, the royal prerogative of "mercy" was used for three main purposes: (1) as a precursor to the as-yet-unrecognized defenses of self-defense, insanity, and minority; (2) to develop new methods of dealing with offenders unrecognized by legislation, such as transportation or military conscription; and (3) for the removal of disqualifications attaching to criminal convictions.

Legislative amnesties were frequent in certain civil law countries, such as France, where they were used as an instrument of pacification after periods of civil strife (Foviaux). In England, however, this institution did not take root. The last "Acts of Grace" took place after the Jacobite risings of 1715 and 1745.

The eighteenth century: pardons and the classical school. During the eighteenth century the sovereign's power to grant pardons in individual cases came under attack, notably by Cesare Beccaria in his famous essay *On Crimes and Punishments.* Permitting the sovereign to interfere with the implementation of the laws was perceived as a threat to the concept of the separation of powers in derogation of the autonomy of both legislature and judiciary—although Montesquieu, with whom the concept of the separation of powers is associated, did not oppose the pardoning power. Such interventions were also seen as detrimental to the deterrent powers of the law, which were predicated on the inexorability of its implementation. Finally, the rampant use of pardons (particularly with respect to accomplices to crimes who informed against the principal perpetrators) was seen as a source not only of uncertainties but also of corruption and abuse.

These criticisms bore fruit after the outbreak of the French Revolution with the adoption of the Penal Code of 1791, which abolished all powers of pardon in relation to offenses triable by jury. However, the critics' victory was short-lived, for the pardoning power was revived when Napoleon Bonaparte became consul for life in 1802. Echoes of the eighteenth-century controversy, however, still reverberate today.

The nineteenth century: amnesty and the American Civil War. Article II, Section 2 of the U.S. Constitution bestows upon the president the power to "grant Reprieves and Pardons for offences against the United States, except in Cases of Impeachment." The first important questions arose in this regard when, in the wake of the Civil War, President Andrew Johnson purported to grant amnesty or a general pardon in favor of southern loyalists. The president was bitterly attacked, it being argued that the power he asserted was in the exclusive purview of Congress, and very different from that specified in the Constitution (L.C.K.). President Johnson seems, however, to have been vindicated in retrospect (at least as regards his constitutional position) by later measures of this type—notably, President Jimmy Carter's general pardon of the Vietnam draft evaders—which have gone unchallenged.

Clemency powers in the twentieth century

The constitutional nature of the clemency powers. Such conflicts in this area between the president and Congress have been symptomatic of the uncertainty attached to the constitutional nature of the clemency powers. Another example, the corollary of the Civil War issue, occurred in 1939 when California's legislature debated the grant of an *individual* pardon (to former labor leader Tom Mooney), and its legal powers to do so were challenged by some academic jurists (Radin).

Traditionally, these powers have been associated with the sovereign authority, and today they are most frequently entrusted to the head of state. This office is generally associated with the executive branch of government, particularly in presidential systems of government. For this reason, the exercise of pardon is often referred to as executive clemency. This, too, is the reason why impeachment has been excluded from the purview of the pardoning power in many jurisdictions: such a power might enable a chief executive to protect his ministers from parliamentary control. It is not altogether clear, however, whether it was in his executive capacity that the sovereign historically exercised these powers; he generally stood at the pinnacle of all three branches of government—legislative, executive, and judiciary—and the precise role of each branch in the decision-making process is controversial. Thus, the mechanism of decision-making, and the involvement of ministers and executive officials, judges, and sometimes even legislators in this process, have varied widely from one jurisdiction to another (Sebba, 1977; Stafford). Furthermore, although acts of clemency are in general immune from judicial review, the grounds for this immunity are sometimes stated to be the executive nature of the act—and sometimes its judicial nature.

Clemency powers extend to individual state governors in the United States, who occasionally exercise these powers to reflect contemporary changes in legal norms at the state level.

Contemporary functions of pardon and amnesty. The term *pardon* is often used generically to describe the power vested in the head of state to grant clemency in individual cases. In this sense it includes such subcategories as full pardon, conditional pardon, commutation, remission, and reprieve. Sometimes, however, it refers only to certain categories. Thus, the U.S. Constitution refers only to pardons and reprieves, the first term incorporating the remaining subcategories.

In recent times, pardons have served three main functions: to remedy a miscarriage of justice, to remove the stigma of a conviction (and the disabilities thereby entailed), and to mitigate a penalty. The first two objectives are usually achieved by means of a full pardon; the other forms are employed for the purpose of mitigating the sentence. These very different objectives have resulted in some confusion as to the legal effects of a pardon. Thus, a pardon is sometimes held to "blot out guilt"—a necessary outcome where the pardon was brought about by a miscarriage of justice, but an inappropriate result in other cases. A commutation substitutes one recognized form of penalty for another. A conditional pardon is more flexible, the only usual requirement being that the condition attaching to the pardon be reasonable. A remission simply implies cancellation of the penalty, wholly or partly. Finally, a reprieve denotes the deferment of a sentence's execution. This mode is typically adopted in capital cases; the penalty is then commuted to a prison term.

An amnesty typically (1) is enacted by legislation instead of being a purely executive act; (2) is applied generally to unnamed persons, that is, to persons who fulfill certain conditions or a description laid down by the law; and (3) is designed to remove ex post facto the criminality of the acts committed. Amnesties are deemed appropriate after a political, economic, or military upheaval. A newly installed regime may hold a different perception of conduct penalized by its predecessor, whereas a consolidated one may wish to indicate its self-confidence by forgiving its erstwhile opponents. These characteristics differentiate amnesty from pardon, which issues from the head of state rather than the legislature, impinges upon the penalty rather than the conviction, and is granted on an individual basis.

Pardons and amnesty compared. The above distinctions are difficult to apply in the United States and many other countries in the common law tradition, for three reasons. First, amnesties are rarely resorted to, and few conventions exist in this matter. Second, as noted above, the distribution of power between the legislature and executive in this area is unclear. Third, granting an individual pardon may, in removing the effects of the conviction, have effects as far-reaching as those of a European amnesty. Thus, the United States Supreme Court once went so far as to say that "the distinction between amnesty and pardon is one rather of philological interest than of legal importance" (*Knote v. United States*, 95 U.S. 149 (1877)). In at least one other case, however (*Burdick v. United States*, 236 U.S. 79, 95 (1915)), the Court has indicated the differences between these two concepts, and a state court once declared that "amnesty is the abolition or oblivion of the offence; pardon is its forgiveness'" (*State v. Blalock*, 61 N.C. (Phil. Law) 242, 247 (1867)).

This distinction may be illustrated by the measures taken with regard to the Vietnam War evaders and deserters by Presidents Gerald Ford and Jimmy Carter, respectively. Ford established a clemency board to consider for a presidential pardon individual petitioners who were willing to fulfill certain conditions. Carter, on the other hand, proclaimed that all persons convicted of certain offenses under the Selective Service Act were to be unconditionally pardoned, and all pending cases closed. Although the latter measure originated with the president rather than the legislature, and was described as a pardon, its generality, purpose, and breadth of scope suggested an amnesty.

In continental Europe, on the other hand, the older distinctions are becoming increasingly blurred. So-called amnesty laws have been introduced for varied purposes, often to remit penalties rather than to remove the criminality of the offense, and sometimes merely as a device for the reduction of prison populations. In France, for example, amnesties have been frequently enacted in recent years; these statutes often cover a broad range of offenses, and have a major impact on pending criminal caseloads and inmate populations. Further, a hybrid institution has been introduced, the *grâce amnistiante*, whereby the president is empowered to grant pardon (amnesty?) to selected individuals who fall within certain categories designated by the law. Finally, in Italy, the government has been delegated the power to pass legislation granting either amnesty or pardon (*indulto*).

Amnesty and Truth Commissions. Since the early 1980s, amnesty has developed as a popular method of expediting the transition to representative government. Broad grants of amnesty often followed the establishment of a "truth commission," organized by succeeding governments, nongovernmental organizations, churches, or the United Nations, and mandated to investigate human rights violations of a preceding regime. Used most frequently in Latin America, transitional governments have experimented with amnesty proceedings and "truth commissions" as an alternative to prosecution of human rights violations. However, some commentators have noted that broad grants of amnesty granted either before or after issuance of a truth commission's investigative findings may not comport with customary international law developed since World War II imposing a duty upon states to prosecute human rights violations. Although truth commission findings have often detailed broad cases of human rights violations, these truth commissions often lacked judicial functions to investigate alleged human rights violators. South Africa's Truth and Reconciliation Commission was the first government-initiated truth commission to be granted broad judicial investigatory powers, and also has power to offer conditional amnesty on narrow grounds. Suspected human rights violators who fail to apply for amnesty, which requires full disclosure of all such violations, are subject to investigation and prosecution.

The future of clemency

Although somewhat neglected by academic writers, clemency is clearly a perplexing area in the scheme of criminal justice. By their very nature amnesties tend to be controversial, since they denote a radical political reassessment of conduct previously designated as criminal. Constitutionally, however, they have presented less of a problem (outside the United States) because they are subject to the same processes and controls as other legislation. The pardoning power is considerably more problematic. The grant of relief from the processes of criminal justice to selected persons on an individual basis attracts criticism today no less than during the eighteenth century, especially where the decision-making process is often secretive and immune from judicial and political review. The suspicion of favoritism is thus frequently raised. Such criticism may be more vociferous when the pardon is a "blanket" one, unrelated to a specific indictment, as in the case of President Ford's pardon of his predecessor, Richard Nixon.

The functions of the pardon, too, are in modern times seen to be largely anomalous; most of its traditional functions are fulfilled by alternative institutions. Justice is individualized by other methods, such as the discretion of the sentencing judge, parole, and "good time" laws that reduce prison terms for good behavior. Allegations of miscarriages of justice may now lead to a new trial. Removal of the criminal stigma is now achieved in some jurisdictions by restrictions on the disclosure of criminal records or by their expungement. Many European legal systems achieve the same result by "rehabilitation" proceedings. The residual power of the chief executive to modify the inexorable harshness of the law may seem to have been rendered superfluous.

However, at least two considerations seem to operate in favor of retention of the pardoning function. First, the movement away from the rehabilitationist ideal has resulted in a lessening of the power of other existing institutions to individualize the penalty. Mandatory minimum and determinate sentencing laws have reduced and sometimes removed the court's discretion, and this is often coupled with the abolition of parole. Moreover, the death penalty, for which clemency powers have always been heavily used, is undergoing a resurgence. Paradoxically, the increasingly mandatory and severe character of the American penal system may necessitate the retention of the pardoning power for those exceptional cases which the formal norms of the written law prove unable to accommodate.

The second consideration in support of retention of the pardoning power is the evidence of history, which seems to indicate the inability of any legal system to survive without it.

LESLIE SEBBA
RICHARD S. FRASE

See also POLITICAL PROCESS AND CRIME; PUNISHMENT; REHABILITATION.

BIBLIOGRAPHY

BECCARIA, CESARE. *On Crimes and Punishments* (1764). Translated with an introduction by Henry Paolucci. Indianapolis: Bobbs-Merrill, 1963.

BELLO, JUDITH H., and WILHEM, DANIEL F. "South Africa—Promotion of National Unity and Reconciliation Act 1995—Amnesty—Truth Commissions—Constitutional Interpretation—Human Rights." *American Journal of International Law* 91 (1997): 360–364.

DUKER, WILLIAM F. "The President's Power to Pardon: A Constitutional History." *William and Mary Law Review* 18 (1977): 475–538.

FOVIAUX, JACQUES. *La Rémission des peines et des condamnations: Droit monarchique et droit moderne.* Preface by Robert Vouin. Paris: Presses Universitaires de France, 1970.

GAGNE, PATRICIA. *Battered Women's Justice.* New York: Twayne Publishers, 1998.

L.C.K. "The Power of the President to Grant a General Pardon or Amnesty for Offences against the United States." *American Law Register* 8 (n.s.) or 17 (o.s.) (1869): 513–532, 577–589.

MINOW, MARTHA. *Between Vengeance and Forgiveness.* Boston: Beacon Press, 1998.

MONTEIL, JACQUES. *La Grâce en droit français moderne.* Paris: Librairies Techniques, 1959.

MOORE, JOHN J., JR. "Problems with Forgiveness: Granting Amnesty under the Arias Peace Plan in Nicaragua and El Salvador." *Stanford Law Review* 43 (1991): 733–777.

MOORE, KATHLEEN DEAN. *Pardons, Justice, Mercy, and the Public Interest.* New York: Oxford University Press, 1989.

MORSE, WAYNE L., ed. *The Attorney General's Survey of Release Procedures,* vol. 3. *Pardon.* Washington, D.C.: U.S. Department of Justice, 1939.

Note. "Executive Clemency in Capital Cases." *New York University Law Review* 39 (1964): 136–192.

ORENTLICHER, DIANE F. "Settling Accounts: The Duty to Prosecute Human Rights Violations of a Prior Regime." *Yale Law Journal* 100 (1991): 2537–2615.

PASQUALUCCI, JO M. "The Whole Truth and Nothing but the Truth: Truth Commissions, Impunity, and the Inter-American Human Rights System." *Boston University International Law Journal* 12 (1994): 321–370.

RADIN, MAX. "Legislative Pardons: Another View." *California Law Review* 27 (1939): 387–397.

RWELAMIRA, M. R., and WERLE, G. *Confronting Past Injustices.* Durban, South Africa: Butterworths, 1996.

SCHABACKER, EMILY W. "Reconciliation or Justice and Ashes: Amnesty Commissions and the Duty to Punish Human Rights Offenses." *New York International Law Review* 12 (1999): 1–54.

SEBBA, LESLIE. "The Pardoning Power: A World Survey." *Journal of Criminal Law and Criminology* 68 (1977): 83–121.

———. "Amnesty: A Quasi-experiment." *British Journal of Criminology, Delinquency, and Deviant Social Behaviour* 19 (1979): 5–30.

STAFFORD, SAMUEL P. *Clemency: Legal Authority, Procedure, and Structure.* Denver: National Center for State Courts, 1977.

Truth and Reconciliation Commission of South Africa. Report, vols. 1–5. New York: Macmillan Reference, 1998.

U.S. Presidential Clemency Board. Report to the President. Washington, D.C.: The Board, 1975.

WEIHOFEN, HENRY, and RUBIN, SOL. "Pardon and Other Forms of Clemency." *The Law of Criminal Correction.* 2d ed. Edited by Sol Rubin. St. Paul: West, 1973. Pages 651–696.

CASES

Burdick v. United States, 236 U.S. 79, 95 (1915).
Knote v. United States, 95 U.S. 149 (1877).
State v. Blalock, 61 N.C. (Phil. Law) 242, 247 (1867).

APPEAL

Appellate review in criminal cases serves multiple purposes: correction of errors, supervision of trial court practice, articulation of legal standards, promotion of uniform decision-making, and provision of both procedural justice and its appearance. Although such review has come to be viewed as fundamental to criminal adjudication, the modern system of criminal appeals is a relatively recent phenomenon in Anglo-American law. England did not provide an adequate system of appellate review until enactment of the Criminal Appeal Act of 1907, 7 Edw. 7, c. 23 (repealed) (Meador, p. 16). In American states, appeals in criminal cases developed unevenly, but had become generally available by the end of the nineteenth century (Arkin, pp. 521–523). For its first one hundred years, the federal government did not give defendants a right to appeal from criminal convictions; criminal cases were reviewable only (1) when a federal circuit court—a three-judge court with trial jurisdiction—certified an issue of law on which the judges were divided, a rare occurrence (Arkin, p. 531); or (2) within the limited range of issues that could be raised by collateral attack on habeas corpus. A series of enactments spanning the period 1879–1970 created the present system of federal criminal review, which recognizes a right to appeal from the federal district court to the federal circuit court of appeals, with further, discretionary review available in the U.S. Supreme Court.

Appellate structures

Like the federal government, nearly forty states have two-tier appellate systems. Although the precise jurisdictional arrangements vary, the most typical pattern provides for one appeal as of right to an intermediate appellate court and for further review in the state's highest court primarily on a discretionary basis—though review as of right in the highest court (often directly from the trial level, thus bypassing the intermediate appellate court) is typically afforded from imposition of a death sentence. In two-tier systems, the state's highest court ordinarily concentrates on unifying and elaborating the law, and the intermediate appellate court, though also important in elaborating legal principles, focuses on error correction (Shapiro, p. 632). In the remaining states, appeals are heard directly by the state's highest court. The overwhelming majority of appellate courts hear civil and criminal appeals alike—a scheme thought preferable because a specialized criminal court "is unlikely to attract the continuing attention, interest, and concern of the entire bar" (American Bar Association, "Commentary on Standard," chap. 21, 1.2).

Appellate courts typically decide in multijudge panels, thus permitting several judges to review matters decided by a single trial judge. Traditionally, appeals have been decided after oral argument by published written opinion, but docket pressures have led many jurisdictions, in cases deemed routine, to abbreviate or eliminate oral argument and to affirm convictions by order or by unpublished opinions—practices that have generated considerable controversy (Stern § 2.2).

Appeals by the defense

Nature of the right. In *McKane v. Durston*, 153 U.S. 684, 687–88 (1894), the Supreme Court stated that a defendant has no federal constitutional right to an appeal. But in neither *McKane* nor in subsequent decisions that have reiterated that statement (e.g., *Ross v. Moffitt*, 417 U.S. 600, 606 (1974), and *Griffin v. Illinois*, 351 U.S. 12, 18 (1956)) did a state fail to provide any appellate review of criminal convictions. Doubts that the *McKane* dictum remains sound (e.g., Arkin;

Meltzer) are unlikely to be resolved, for every state now provides some method of appeal from criminal convictions in serious criminal cases. (In Virginia, West Virginia, and New Hampshire, formally no appeal as of right exists, but the procedures that each state's highest court follows in determining whether to grant discretionary review ensure substantive consideration of the appellant's contentions; Arkin, pp. 513–514.)

Except for common provisions requiring review when a death sentence is imposed, appeals in criminal cases are elective. Most jurisdictions require the trial court at sentencing to notify the defendant of the right to appeal (e.g., Rule 32(c)(5) of the Federal Rules of Criminal Procedure).

Equal protection and due process. Whether or not the U.S. Constitution confers a right to appeal, once state law confers such a right, a state may not, consistent with the Fourteenth Amendment, deny indigent defendants the right to meaningful appellate review. The Supreme Court first applied that principle in *Griffin*, holding that indigent defendants are entitled to a free trial transcript so that they would have "as adequate appellate review as defendants who have money enough to buy transcripts" (p. 19). The Court has read *Griffin* as "a flat prohibition against pricing indigent defendants out of as effective an appeal as would be available to others able to pay their own way"—*Mayer v. Chicago*, 404 U.S. 189, 196–197 (1971)—and thus has invalidated a rule conditioning the right to appeal on payment of a filing fee (*Burns v. Ohio*, 360 U.S. 252, 258 (1959)).

The *Griffin* principle was extended in *Douglas v. California*, 372 U.S. 353, 357–58 (1963), where the Supreme Court ruled that on a defendant's first appeal, granted as a matter of right, an indigent defendant is entitled to counsel to brief and argue the appeal. The right recognized in *Douglas* comprehends assistance of counsel that satisfies constitutional standards of effectiveness (*Evitts v. Lucey*, 469 U.S. 387 (1985)). But in *Ross v. Moffitt*, the Court declined to extend *Douglas* to require counsel for indigents who seek discretionary review before the state's highest court. Focusing less on equal treatment of rich and poor appellants and more on ensuring adequate access to appellate review, the Court reasoned that a "meaningful appeal" at the second tier was possible without counsel, for a lawyer would already have briefed and argued the first appeal, ensuring that the "defendant's claims of error are organized and presented in a lawyer-like fashion" (pp. 612, 615).

Because indigent criminal appellants, unlike most civil appellants, typically have everything to gain and nothing to lose by seeking review, *Douglas* gave rise to the troublesome question of the appropriate role for a court-appointed counsel who believes an appeal utterly without merit. In *Anders v. California*, 386 U.S. 738, 744 (1967), the Court held that a lawyer who, after a "conscientious examination" of the case, finds an appeal to be "wholly frivolous" should so advise the court and request permission to withdraw. The opinion in *Anders* added, however, that because the court, not counsel, must decide whether the appeal is frivolous, the lawyer's request must include "a brief referring to anything in the record that might arguably support the appeal" (p. 744), a copy of which must be furnished to the defendant, who then may raise additional points with the court. Some have criticized *Anders* for diverting limited resources from meritorious cases, though others have noted that appellate reversals sometimes occur even after appointed counsel has filed an "*Anders* brief" explaining the hopelessness of the case (Hermann, p. 709), and some states have further limited counsel's latitude by prohibiting withdrawal altogether (Warner, pp. 643–651). More recently, however, in *Smith v. Robbins*, 120 S. Ct. 726 (2000), the Supreme Court relaxed the strictures governing counsel, ruling that the *Anders* procedures are not the only way to satisfy the Constitution. In *Smith*, the Court approved a state procedure under which counsel's filing on appeal did not identify any arguable issues, but merely (1) summarized the case history; (2) attested that counsel had reviewed the record, consulted with his client, and supplied the client with a copy of the brief; and (3) requested that the court examine the record for arguable issues.

The final-order requirement. In general, appeal may be taken only from a final judgment, which typically means after conviction and imposition of sentence. The final judgment rule, though not unique to criminal cases, has been followed there with particular stringency because "the delays and disruptions attendant upon intermediate appeal," which the rule is designed to avoid, "are especially inimical to the effective and fair administration of the criminal law" (*DiBella v. United States*, 369 U.S. 121, 126 (1962)).

Most jurisdictions do, however, permit appeal from some set of orders not strictly final. In *Cohen v. Beneficial Industrial Loan Corp.*, 337 U.S. 541 (1949), a civil case, the Supreme Court concluded that a pretrial ruling should be deemed "final" for purposes of appeal in the federal system if (1) the lower court has fully decided the question; (2) the decision was not merely a step toward final disposition of the merits of the case but instead resolved a collateral issue; and (3) the decision involved an important right that would be lost, probably irreparably, if review had to await final judgment.

The Supreme Court has found the collateral order rubric of *Cohen* applicable in only three criminal cases. In *Stack v. Boyle*, 342 U.S. 1, 4 (1951), the Court ruled that a defendant may immediately appeal a pretrial order setting bail. (Whether under a variant of the collateral order doctrine or specific statutory authorization—as federal law now provides, see 18 U.S.C. § 3145—both defense and prosecution are typically authorized to appeal bail decisions.) Under the *Cohen* rationale, appeal has also been permitted from a trial court's denial of a motion to dismiss an indictment when the defendant claimed to be immune from prosecution under the double jeopardy clause (*Abney v. United States*, 431 U.S. 651, 662 (1977)) or the speech or debate clause (*Helstoski v. Meanor*, 442 U.S. 500, 508 (1979)); in both cases, the Supreme Court reasoned that the right at issue would be undermined by the mere occurrence of the trial. But the Court has not applied the *Cohen* doctrine expansively, refusing to permit an immediate appeal from a pretrial order that disqualified the defendant's counsel (*Flanagan v. United States*, 465 U.S. 259, 270 (1984)) or that denied a defense motion presenting the claim that the prosecution was vindictive (*United States v. Hollywood Motor Car Co.*, 458 U.S. 263, 270 (1982)) or that the defendant had been denied a speedy trial (*United States v. MacDonald*, 435 U.S. 850, 853 (1978)).

Many states follow *Cohen*'s collateral order doctrine or some similar approach that permits immediate appeal of some orders not strictly final. While a few states authorize interlocutory review more broadly—for example, where "appeal would be in the interest of justice" (Utah Code Crim. Proc. § 77–18a–1)—typically judicial authorization is required and is sparingly provided.

Bail pending appeal. Following conviction a defendant no longer enjoys the presumption of innocence, and thus the criteria governing release pending appeal are generally stricter than those applied pending trial. Some jurisdictions deny bail pending appeal for a category of more serious offenses; others make bail pending appeal, unlike bail pending trial, a matter of discretion rather than of right; still others make bail available only when the defendant demonstrates that the appeal raises a substantial question.

Appeals by the prosecution. Prosecution appeals typically require specific statutory authorization, and virtually every jurisdiction authorizes appeals from at least some orders. Some jurisdictions, including the United States, essentially permit government appeals from all decisions dismissing charges, whether before or after trial, except when further prosecution would be barred by the double jeopardy clause (e.g.,18 U.S.C. § 3731)—a bar that applies after a jury verdict of not guilty or after any other judgment deemed to constitute an acquittal.

Many jurisdictions also authorize interlocutory appeals by the prosecution from specified orders—most commonly, pretrial decisions to suppress evidence (e.g., 18 U.S.C. § 3731)—in part because if an erroneous decision to suppress leads to an acquittal, double jeopardy principles will preclude a government appeal. Because of the obvious concern about delay and disruption, interlocutory appeals are rarely permitted once trial has commenced.

Extraordinary writs

Either the defense or the prosecution may seek an extraordinary writ (e.g., mandamus or prohibition) from an appellate court to review decisions not otherwise appealable. Traditionally, such writs were available only in narrow circumstances—where, for example, the lower court failed to perform a ministerial duty or lacked jurisdiction. During the latter part of the twentieth century, many courts have relaxed the standards governing such writs (e.g., to comprehend a gross abuse of discretion or a serious legal error of general significance). Nonetheless, many jurisdictions express greater reluctance to issue such writs in criminal than in civil matters (e.g., *Will v. United States*, 389 U.S. 90 (1967)).

Mootness and related doctrines

No appeal will lie when post-trial events—for example, the death of the convict—render the case moot. Most jurisdictions have now departed from the traditional view that an appeal is moot whenever the sentence has been fully satisfied— that is, when the defendant has paid any fine and served the full period of any imprisonment or probation. A limited departure from the traditional position, in cases in which a fine has been paid, treats an appeal as alive if state law permits remittance of the fine upon overturning of the conviction.

A far broader and more common departure from the traditional view permits defendants to appeal, even where a sentence has been fully served, in order to avoid harmful collateral consequences of criminal convictions (e.g., possible enhanced punishment under recidivism statutes or testimonial impeachment should the convict testify in the future) (*Sibron v. New York*, 392 U.S. 40, 50–58 (1968)). When collateral consequences are presumed to exist, as they are in many jurisdictions, this doctrine approaches in practice, if not in theory, the view taken by a few jurisdictions that quite apart from collateral consequences, a conviction is never moot because the "stigma of guilt" remains even after the sentence has been satisfied (e.g.,*Jackson v. People*, 376 P.2d 991, 994 (Colo. 1962)). However, an appeal that challenges the legality not of the conviction but only of a sentence that has been fully served is likely to be deemed moot, unless collateral consequences from the harsher sentence can be demonstrated (*North Carolina v. Rice*, 404 U.S. 244, 248 (1971))

Concurrent sentence doctrine. Where a defendant had been sentenced to equal concurrent sentences on different counts, some appellate courts, after upholding the conviction on one count, will not consider challenges to the remaining counts. In *Benton v. Maryland*, 395 U.S. 784 (1969), the Supreme Court concluded that this so-called concurrent sentence doctrine could not, in light of *Sibron*, be justified on mootness grounds but stated that it "may have some continuing validity as a rule of judicial convenience" (p. 791). Following *Benton*, all but two of the federal circuits have embraced the concurrent sentence doctrine as a discretionary matter of judicial administration; only a few state courts have followed suit.

Scope of appellate review

In general. Appellate review, based as it is upon the written record assembled at the trial level, is often deferential, particularly with regard to discretionary trial management decisions, issues heavily intertwined with fact and testimonial credibility, and the trier of fact's determination of guilt. Review of the trial court's elaboration of legal standards is generally de novo, and many jurisdictions also review de novo the application of constitutional or other legal standards to the facts (e.g., *Ornelas v. United States*, 517 U.S. 690, 699 (1996)).

Conviction by guilty plea. Appeals from a conviction by guilty plea are typically limited to claims that the trial court lacked jurisdiction, that the procedure for entry of the plea was defective, that the sentence was illegal, and, in some states, that the charge failed to state an offense. Other objections are generally deemed to have been waived by entry of the plea. While convictions by plea far outnumber convictions after trial, appeals from conviction at trial far outnumber appeals from conviction by pleas (Davies, p. 558).

The federal government (see Fed. R. Crim. Proc. 11(a)(2)) and nearly half the states permit a defendant (typically only with government consent and court approval) to enter a conditional guilty plea, which reserves the right to appeal on a specified issue. If the appeal prevails, the defendant is then permitted to withdraw the earlier plea and to plead anew.

Review of sentence. In the United States, unlike many other countries, appellate review of a sentence imposed under traditional indeterminate systems rarely extended beyond ensuring that the sentence did not exceed the statutorily authorized punishment or was not influenced by factors that could not constitutionally be considered (e.g., *Dorszynski v. United States*, 418 U.S. 424, 431–32 (1974)). Appellate review of sentences has become far more common and somewhat more robust, however, in the last quarter of the twentieth century, for several reasons: (1) a number of states have extended review of sentencing decisions to embrace claims of clear abuse or clear mistake; (2) a significant minority of states have adopted determinate sentencing systems, which typically authorize appeals contending that the sentence violated applicable rules; and (3) review of death sentences is now routine to ensure compliance with the complex state and federal rules governing capital punishment.

Prosecution appeals of sentences have most commonly been authorized in determinate sentencing systems (e.g., 18 U.S.C. § 3742(b)), and in general do not violate the double jeopardy clause. However, the prosecution may not appeal the sentencer's refusal to impose a death sentence—a decision ordinarily treated as an "acquittal" of capital punishment (*Bullington v. Missouri*, 451 U.S. 430, 446 (1981)).

Issues not properly raised. Every jurisdiction prescribes rules of pretrial and trial practice governing when and in what fashion particular objections (e.g., to the adequacy of the charge, to the admission of evidence, or to jury instructions) must be made. To induce compliance with those rules and promote orderly judicial administration, appellate courts ordinarily will not consider objections that were not properly presented at the trial level and consequently not ruled upon by the trial court.

Limited exceptions to this rule are typically recognized. First, a procedural requirement that itself violates due process cannot bar appellate review (*Reece v. Georgia*, 350 U.S. 85 (1955)). In addition, most states permit a defendant to challenge the trial court's jurisdiction for the first time on appeal; states divide more evenly on whether they permit appeal of issues not raised below but based on newly announced legal decisions.

The most important and virtually universal exception authorizes appellate courts to consider "plain error," whether or not properly raised below. To qualify as plain error under the federal doctrine, an error must not only be clear and obvious, but must also be shown by the defendant to be prejudicial, in the sense of likely affecting the outcome of the case (*United States v. Olano*, 507 US. 725 (1993)). In determining whether to reach an issue raised for the first time on appeal, many states will consider, in addition to factors similar to those that govern under federal law, whether the legal issue is of general significance, whether it is constitutional in nature, and whether its consideration would promote judicial economy or the public interest.

In the end, plain error has proven hard to define and has a somewhat discretionary character. In practice, it is more likely to be found when defense counsel's representation was questionable or when the evidence of guilt is relatively weak.

Harmless error on appeal

In general. A determination on appeal that there was error at trial does not always require reversal. Rather, because minor errors are common and "[a] defendant is entitled to a fair trial but not a perfect one" (*Lutwak v. United States*, 344 U.S. 604, 619 (1953)), every jurisdiction follows some variant of the rule that harmless errors may be disregarded.

There is no agreement, however, as to just how the harmless-error standard should be formulated or how demanding it should be. On the first question, the most common approaches are (1) an "outcome-impact" approach, which focuses on whether the error influenced the jury in reaching its verdict; and (2) the "correct result" approach, which focuses on the force of the evidence against the defendant, error aside. The latter approach has often been criticized, on the grounds that it transforms the appellate court into a trier of fact and that even guilty defendants have a right to a fair trial, but it has not disappeared from the case law (Edwards, pp. 1192–1194). The decisions do not, however, always clearly apply a well-defined approach, often adverting to a range of factors in reaching a conclusion without specifying clearly the nature of the harmless error analysis. In any event, the verbal formulas may matter less than the attitude brought to the harmless error inquiry by the appellate judges. No doubt, the stronger the appellate court's belief that the defendant was guilty, the more likely it is that the error will be found harmless; indeed, concern has been expressed that appellate courts too readily find serious errors to be harmless when convinced of the defendant's guilt (Edwards, pp. 1191–1192).

States also vary in how strong a showing of harmlessness must be made. In the federal system, reversal is required if the appellate court determines that the error "had substantial and injurious effect or influence in determining the jury's verdict" (*Kotteakos v. United States*, 328 U.S. 750, 776 (1946)). In the states, standards range from demanding that the defendant prove it more probable than not that an error affected the outcome (*People v. Lukity*, 596 N.W.2d 607, 612 (Mich. 1999)) to requiring that the prosecution establish that an error was harmless "beyond a reasonable doubt" (*Commonwealth v. Story*, 383 A.2d 155, 162 (Pa. 1978)).

Errors involving constitutional rights. When the error is one of federal constitutional law, the question whether the error was harmless is governed by a federal standard. In *Chapman v. California*, 386 U.S. 18, 24 (1967), the Court, rejecting the view that federal constitutional error is never harmless, ruled that such error required reversal unless the prosecution could demonstrate that it "was harmless beyond a reasonable doubt." The basis for imposing this requirement on state courts is uncertain: it is unclear why a state should not be free to adopt a harmless error standard on appeal that is less favorable to the defendant than the *Chapman* standard, when the Supreme Court has insisted that the state could

eliminate appeals by the defendant altogether (Meltzer, p. 12).

While some have viewed the *Chapman* test as too strict, contending that an appellate court can rarely find the requisite degree of certainty that the error had no effect (Traynor, pp. 43–44), others have contended that by its nature the test may not be strict enough, for constitutional error (such as the admission of impermissible evidence) may have significantly shaped trial strategies in ways not apparent to the appellate court (Saltzburg, p. 990).

The Supreme Court has stressed that constitutional errors are presumptively subject to harmless error analysis (*Rose v. Clark*, 478 U.S. 570, 579 (1986))—even, for example, admission of a coerced confession (*Arizona v. Fulminante*, 499 U.S. 279, 285 (1991)), or the failure to instruct the jury of the need to find an essential element of the offense (*Neder v. United States*, 119 S. Ct. 1827, 1831 (1999)). The Court has, however, recognized a limited class of fundamental constitutional errors—including total deprivation of the right of counsel, denial of the right to self-representation, trial before a biased judge, racial discrimination in selection of the grand jury, denial of the right to a public trial, and improper instructions on proof beyond a reasonable doubt—that are "so intrinsically harmful" and that so infect the entire trial process that they defy harmless error analysis and require automatic reversal (*Neder v. United States*, p. 1833).

Effect of reversal on appeal

A retrial is ordinarily permitted after reversal of a conviction, except where retrial itself is the harm (as would usually be true when reversal was based on a claim of immunity, double jeopardy, or denial of a speedy trial) or where reversal was for insufficient evidence. Double jeopardy principles do not forbid imposition of a stiffer sentence after reconviction, but to protect a defendant's freedom to appeal, the Supreme Court ruled in *North Carolina v. Pearce*, 395 U.S. 711, 725 (1969), that due process requires that "vindictiveness against a defendant for having successfully attacked his first conviction must play no part in the sentence he receives after a new trial," and, indeed, that even an appearance of vindictiveness must be avoided. Consequently, in *Pearce* the Court held that a judge may impose a more severe sentence upon a defendant after a retrial only if the reasons for doing so are made part of the record and are based upon "objective information concerning identifiable conduct on the part of the defendant occurring after the time of the original sentencing proceeding" (p. 726).

The principle that *Pearce* announced has not been expansively applied. In *Colten v. Kentucky*, 407 U.S. 104 (1972), the Court held the principle inapplicable to sentences imposed after a defendant, convicted at trial, had exercised a statutory right to be tried de novo by a higher-level trial court. The Supreme Court stressed "that the court which conducted Colten's trial and imposed the final sentence was not the court with whose work Colten was sufficiently dissatisfied to seek a different result on appeal; and it is not the court that is asked to do over what it thought it had already done correctly" (pp. 116–117). Similarly, in *Chaffin v. Stynchcombe*, 412 U.S. 17, 35 (1973), the Court found little potential for vindictiveness, and hence no constitutional defect, when the jury at the retrial, not knowing what the sentence had been at the original trial, imposed a stiffer sentence. And in *Alabama v. Smith*, 490 U.S. 794, 801–02 (1989), the Court declined to apply the *Pearce* presumption of vindictiveness when a judge had imposed a longer sentence after trial than he had after an earlier guilty plea that was later vacated. The Court ruled that because the factors that counsel leniency after a guilty plea were no longer present and because a trial gives the judge a fuller understanding of the circumstances than does a plea colloquy, there was no basis to presume that a stiffer sentence was motivated by vindictiveness.

DANIEL J. MELTZER

See also BAIL; CAPITAL PUNISHMENT: LEGAL ASPECTS; COUNSEL: RIGHT TO COUNSEL; CRIMINAL PROCEDURE: CONSTITUTIONAL ASPECTS; DOUBLE JEOPARDY; GUILTY PLEA: ACCEPTING THE PLEA; HABEAS CORPUS; SENTENCING: GUIDELINES.

BIBLIOGRAPHY

American Bar Association. *Criminal Appeal.* In *Standards for Criminal Justice*, 2d ed. Vol. 4, chap. 21. Boston: Little, Brown, 1980.

ARKIN, MARC M. "Rethinking the Constitutional Right to Appeal." *UCLA Law Review* 39 (February 1992): 503–580.

DAVIES, THOMAS Y. "Affirmed: A Study of Criminal Appeals and Decision-Making Norms in a California Court of Appeal." *American Bar Foundation Research Journal* no. 3 (1982): 543–648.

EDWARDS, HARRY T. "To Err Is Human, but Not Always Harmless: When Should Legal Error Be Tolerated?" *New York University Law Review* 70, no. 6 (1995): 1167–1213.

FLANGO, CAROL R., and ROTTMAN, DAVID B. *Appellate Court Procedures.* Williamsburg, Va.: National Center for State Courts, 1997.

HERMANN, ROBERT. "Frivolous Criminal Appeals." *New York University Law Review* 47, no. 4 (1972): 701.

LAFAVE, WAYNE R., and ISRAEL, JEROLD H. *Criminal Procedure*, vol. 3, chap. 26, pp. 171–281. St. Paul, Minn.: West Publishing, 1984, 1991 supp.

MEADOR, DANIEL. *Criminal Appeals: English Practices and American Reforms.* Charlottesville: University Press of Virginia, 1973.

MELTZER, DANIEL J. "Harmless Error and Constitutional Remedies." *University of Chicago Law Review* 61, no. 1 (1994): 1–39.

ORFIELD, LESTER B. *Criminal Appeals in America.* Boston: Little, Brown, 1939.

ROSSMAN, DAVID. "'Were There No Appeal': The History of Review in American Criminal Courts." *Journal of Criminal Law & Criminology* 81, no. 3 (1990): 518–566.

SALTZBURG, STEPHEN A. "The Harm of Harmless Error." *Virginia Law Review* 59 (1973): 988.

SHAPIRO, MARTIN. "Appeal." *Law & Society Review* 14, spring (1980): 629–661.

STACY, TOM, and DAYTON, KIM. "Rethinking Harmless Constitutional Error." *Columbia Law Review* 88, no. 1 (1988): 79–143.

STERN, ROBERT L. *Appellate Practice in the United States*, 2d ed. Washington, D.C: Bureau of National Affairs, 1989.

STITH, KATE. "The Risk of Legal Error in Criminal Cases: Some Consequences of the Asymmetry in the Right to Appeal." *University of Chicago Law Review* 57, no. 1 (1990): 1–61.

TRAYNOR, ROGER. *The Riddle of Harmless Error.* Columbus: Ohio State University Press, 1970.

WARNER, MARTHA C. "Anders in the 50 States: Some Appellants' Equal Protection Is More Equal than Others." *Florida State University Law Review* 23, no. 3 (1996): 625–667.

CASES

Abney v. United States, 431 U.S. 651, 662 (1977).
Alabama v. Smith, 490 U.S. 794, 801–02 (1989).
Anders v. California, 386 U.S. 738, 744 (1967).
Arizona v. Fulminante, 499 U.S. 279, 285 (1991).
Benton v. Maryland, 395 U.S. 784 (1969).
Bullington v. Missouri, 451 U.S. 430, 446 (1981).
Burns v. Ohio, 360 U.S. 252, 258 (1959).
Chaffin v. Stynchcombe, 412 U.S. 17, 35 (1973).
Chapman v. California, 386 U.S. 18, 24 (1967).

Cohen v. Beneficial Industrial Loan Corp., 337 U.S. 121, 126 (1962).

Colten v. Kentucky, 407 U.S. 104 (1972).

Commonwealth v. Story, 383 A.2d 155, 162 (Pa. 1978).

DiBella v. United States, 369 U.S. 121, 126 (1962).

Dorszynski v. United States, 418 U.S. 424, 431–32 (1974).

Douglas v. California, 372 U.S. 353, 357–58 (1963).

Evitts v. Lucey, U.S. 387 (1985).

Flanagan v. United States, 465 U.S. 259, 270 (1984).

Griffin v. Illinois, 351 U.S. 12, 18 (1956).

Helstoski v. Meanor, 442 U.S. 500, 508 (1979).

Jackson v. People, 376 P.2d 991, 994 (Colo. 1962).

Kotteakos v. United States, 328 U.S. 750, 776 (1946).

Lutwak v. United States, 344 U.S. 604, 619 (1953).

Mayer v. Chicago, 404 U.S. 189, 196–97 (1971).

McKane v. Durston, 153 U.S. 684, 687–88 (1894).

Neder v. United States, 119 S. Ct. 1827, 1831 (1999).

North Carolina v. Pearce, 395 U.S. 711, 725 (1969).

North Carolina v. Rice, 404 U.S. 244. 248 (1971).

Ornelas v. United States, 517 U.S. 690, 699 (1996).

People v. Lukity, 596 N.W.2d 607, 612 (Mich. 1000).

Reece v. Georgia, 350 U.S. 85 (1955).

Rose v. Clark, 478 U.S. 570, 579 (1986).

Ross v. Moffit, 417 U.S. 600, 606 (1974).

Sibron v. New York, 392 U.S. 40, 50–58 (1968).

Smith v. Robbins, 120 S. Ct. 726 (2000).

Stack v. Boyle, 342 U.S. 1, 4 (1951).

United States v. Hollywood Motor Car Co., 458 U.S. 263, 270 (1982).

United States v. MacDonald, 435 U.S. 850, 853 (1978).

United States v. Olano, 507 U.S. 725 (1993).

Will v. United States, 389 U.S. 90 (1967).

ARRAIGNMENT

The term "arraignment" refers to the formal proceeding at which an accused is brought before the court to answer a criminal charge contained in an indictment or information. At arraignment, the presiding judicial officer informs the accused of the offense charged in the indictment or information and asks how the accused would like to plead. In most jurisdictions, this will result in a plea of guilty, not guilty, or *nolo contendere*.

Distinction from initial appearance and *Gerstein* probable cause proceeding

The term "arraignment" is habitually misused by courts and commentators when referring to another pretrial proceeding, the "initial appearance." The initial appearance is the proceeding at which an individual first appears before a judicial officer following arrest on a criminal charge. Unlike the arraignment proceeding—wherein a defendant is formally advised of charges contained in an indictment or information and asked to enter a plea—the purpose of the initial appearance is to have a judicial officer inform the defendant of the basis for the arrest, advise the defendant of her rights, and, if necessary, appoint counsel. Also unlike arraignment, defendants are not normally required to enter a plea at their initial appearances. In the federal system, the initial appearance is governed by Federal Rule 5(a), which requires arrested persons to be brought before the nearest available judicial officer "without unreasonable delay." Similar procedural rules exist in state criminal systems. Although frequently mislabeled as an "arraignment," even by Justices of the U.S. Supreme Court, it was this initial appearance, and not an arraignment, which was the subject of *Mallory v. United States*, 354 U.S. 449, 453–54 (1957) and *McNabb v. United States*, 318 U.S. 332 (1943).

If a defendant is arrested without a warrant, the bulk of an accused's initial appearance will often be devoted to the question of whether probable cause existed to justify the arrest. To justify a defendant's continued detention after a warrantless arrest, a judicial officer must approve the police officer's decision to arrest shortly after the arrest occurs (*Gerstein v. Pugh*, 420 U.S. 103 (1975)). Often this will take place at a defendant's initial appearance before the court, although technically the probable cause determination serves a purpose distinct from that of the initial appearance.

The probable cause proceeding is not an adversarial one. Defense counsel may appear with the accused at a *Gerstein* proceeding, but the Constitution does not require it. Neither must the prosecutor produce witnesses to provide evidence in support of the criminal allegations. Rather, the prosecutor's evidentiary obligations at this very early pretrial proceeding are satisfied once a law enforcement officer with knowledge of the investigation swears to the truth of the criminal allegations under oath and in the presence of the judicial officer. If the substance of those allegations amount to probable cause to believe that the arrestee has committed a criminal act, the prosecutor will have met her burden to justify the arrest. To satisfy the Fourth Amendment's requirement of a "prompt" resolution of this probable cause question, such an appearance and determination must take place as soon as reasonably feasible, but presumptively no later than forty-eight hours after arrest (*County of Riverside v. McLaughlin*, 500 U.S. 44 (1991)).

Distinction from other pretrial proceedings

Two other pretrial proceedings, bail hearings and preliminary examination hearings, are also sometimes confused with arraignments. Contributing to the confusion is the practice of some state and federal courts to combine the arraignment with other pretrial proceedings. For example, a jurisdiction might choose to combine arraignment with a bail proceeding, particularly if the accused has not appeared earlier on similar charges contained in a criminal complaint.

Purpose of arraignment

As stated above, although sometimes combined, arraignments serve a purpose distinguishable from that of initial appearances, *Gerstein* proceedings, bail proceedings, and preliminary examination hearings. At arraignment, the court formally informs a defendant of charges contained in an indictment or information, provides the defendant with a copy of the charging instrument, and takes the defendant's answer to those charges in the form of a plea. In open court, and outside the presence of a jury, the judicial officer reads or relays the substance of the indictment or information to the accused and requests that the accused enter a plea to the charge or charges. For this to occur, defendants must generally appear in person at the arraignment, and challenges to procedures permitting arraignments to occur via video teleconferencing have been heard by the courts. These challenges generally fail, however, if the defendant and counsel were able to see and hear the activities transpiring in the courtroom and the judge conducting the arraignment was able to see and hear the defendant throughout the proceeding.

As the foregoing description of the proceeding suggests, an arraignment is a largely formal procedure that, unlike other pretrial proceedings, takes little time to complete (if unaccompanied by an extended plea colloquy). The arraignment is nonetheless a critical juncture in the criminal process for many reasons. First, speedy trial obligations are often triggered on the date of arraignment. Second, should an accused flee after being arraigned, the prosecutor may choose to proceed in abstentia (i.e., proceed to trial in the defendant's absence). Third, from the point of arraignment, right to counsel is clear and failure to appoint counsel for an indigent defendant asked to enter a plea will bar valid conviction in the absence of a knowing and intelligent waiver (*Johnson v. Zerbst*, 304 U.S. 458 (1938) and *Gideon v. Wainwright*, 372 U.S. 335 (1963)). (The due process clause of the Fourteenth Amendment makes the Sixth Amendment's guaranty of counsel applicable to states.) Finally, after arraignment on an indictment or information, the charging instrument normally may not be materially altered absent re-arraignment on the new or amended charge.

Defects or delay in arraignment process

A failure to comply with arraignment requirements will not necessarily, nor even usually, result in a ruling vacating a conviction or dismissing an indictment. Rather, a defect in the arraignment process (even a failure to arraign the defendant on a charge) will affect a conviction only where actual prejudice resulting from the defect can be shown. Thus, in *Garland v. Washington*, 232 U.S. 642 (1914), the Supreme Court refused to vacate a conviction despite evidence that a defendant was never arraigned on a count in a superseding information. Disparaging the defendant's due process challenge as a mere "attempt to gain a new trial for want of compliance with what in this case could have been no more than a mere formality," the Court held that, absent proof that the defendant suffered actual injury from the failure to re-arraign on the superseding charge, the conviction would stand.

Similarly, although a delay in a defendant's arraignment may raise serious speedy trial concerns grounded in the Sixth Amendment or statutory law, a reversal or dismissal of the indictment is unlikely for the sole reason that arraignment was delayed. Courts called upon to consider dismissal of an indictment on such grounds typically consider four factors: (1) the length of the delay; (2) the reason for the delay; (3) whether the defendant asserted his rights to a more speedy disposition; and (4) the prejudice to the defendant resulting from the delay (*Barker v. Wingo*, 407 U.S. 514, 530 (1972)). Under these and similar standards, the mere passage of time between the return of an indictment and arraignment will not normally be determinative of constitutional speedy trial challenges. Rather, the delay must have actually prejudiced the accused to support such a claim.

Nature and consequences of various pleas entered at arraignment

As stated above, one of the principal reasons for arraignment is to enter the accused's plea to charges once an indictment or information has been filed. There are three pleas available to criminal defendants, guilty, not guilty, or nolo contendere, although many jurisdictions will accept a nolo contendere plea only with the express permission of the court.

Although courts may accept guilty pleas at arraignment (or even before if the defendant waives the right to an arraignment), the vast majority of criminal defendants who plead guilty do so after their arraignments have taken place. If a court accepts a defendant's guilty plea at arraignment, strict procedures designed to safeguard the accused's constitutional and statutory rights must be satisfied. Extended colloquy with the accused is called for to ensure that the plea is "intelligent and voluntary" (*Boykin v. Alabama*, 395 U.S 238 (1969)). This includes, among other things, a determination that the defendant understands the nature of the pending charge or charges, as well as the consequences of entering a guilty plea and the rights lost or waived by doing so. The court accepting a guilty plea must also determine that there is a factual basis for accepting the plea.

By far, most defendants plead not guilty at arraignment, at which time different things occur, depending on the jurisdiction. In many jurisdictions, particularly in the federal system, pleas at arraignment will be taken by a magistrate judge, who will then inform the defendant of the name of the trial judge assigned to preside over the case. In some jurisdictions, arguments for and against bail might also be heard. No matter the jurisdiction, the entry of a not guilty plea will in some sense signal trial readiness, although it is common for a considerable amount of time to pass between the entry of such a plea and trial to allow the parties to comply with discovery obligations and resolve pretrial motions.

Finally, in some jurisdictions a defendant may enter a plea of nolo contendere by which a defendant asserts that he does not contest the charges. Unlike pleas of guilty or not guilty, nolo contendere pleas are not available to a defendant as a matter of right, and some jurisdictions do not allow them. Others permit such pleas only with the consent of the court and sometimes the concurrence of the prosecutor. Where permitted, a nolo contendere plea will subject a defendant to the same sentence as a guilty plea. Unlike a guilty plea, however, evidence of a nolo contendere plea is inadmissible in a subsequent civil action to prove that the defendant committed the offense to which she entered a plea. It is, however, admissible in subsequent criminal proceedings to prove perjury or false statement.

SHARON L. DAVIES

See also BAIL; CRIMINAL JUSTICE PROCESS; CRIMINAL PROCEDURE: CONSTITUTIONAL ASPECTS; GUILTY PLEA: ACCEPTING THE PLEA; GUILTY PLEA: PLEA BARGAINING; PRELIMINARY HEARING; PRETRIAL DIVERSION; SPEEDY TRIAL; TRIAL, CRIMINAL.

BIBLIOGRAPHY

DRESSLER, JOSHUA. *Understanding Criminal Procedure*, 2d ed. § 1.03[C][6] at 10: Matthew Bender, 1997.

GILMORE, WARREN H. "Arraignment by Television: A New Way to Bring Defendants to the Courtroom." *Judicature* 63 (1980): 396.

KAMISAR, YALE; LAFAVE, WAYNE R.; ISRAEL, JEROLD H.; and KING, NANCY. *Modern Criminal Procedure*, 9th ed. St. Paul, Minn.: West Group, 1999. Pages 28–29; 1013–1014.

STEINBERG, COREY. Note, "'Justice Delayed Is Justice Denied'—The Abuse of Pre-Arraignment Delay." *New York Law School Journal of Human Rights* 9 (1992): 403.

THAXTON, RONNIE. Note, "Injustice Telecast: The Illegal Use of Closed-Circuit Television Arraignments and Bail Bond Hearings in Federal Courts." *Iowa Law Review* 79 (1993): 175.

WHITEBREAD, CHARLES H., and SLOBOGIN, CHRISTOPHER. *Criminal Procedure: An Analysis of Cases and Concepts*, 3d ed. New York, N.Y.: Foundation Press, 1993. Pages 487–545.

CASES

Barker v. Wingo, 407 U.S. 514, 530 (1972).
Boykin v. Alabama, 395 U.S. 238 (1969).
County of Riverside v. McLaughlin, 500 U.S. 44 (1991).

Garland v. Washington, 232 U.S. 642 (1914).
Gerstein v. Pugh, 420 U.S. 103 (1975).
Gideon v. Wainwright, 372 U.S. 335 (1963).
Johnson v. Zerbst, 304 U.S. 458 (1938).
Mallory v. United States, 354 U.S. 449 (1957).
McNabb v. United States, 318 U.S. 332 (1943).

ARREST AND STOP

See SEARCH AND SEIZURE.

ARSON: BEHAVIORAL AND ECONOMIC ASPECTS

The earliest scientific writings on arson were generated during the late eighteenth century by a group of German psychiatric theorists, who concluded that the crime was characteristic of physically and mentally retarded females from rural areas who were undergoing the stresses of puberty. These theorists classified arson under the rubric of "instinctive monomania" that, according to prevailing legal codes, defined arsonists as insane and not accountable for their actions. During the decades that followed, the terms "monomanie incendiaire" and "pyromania" appeared in the literature, which described arson as an impulsive act and a distinct mental disorder. From the 1820s through the 1930s, arson was studied in relation to psychiatry, psychology, and law. The prevailing issue concerned the medicolegal understanding of the term "irresistible impulse": was incendiarism generally impulsive behavior resulting from some form of mental aberration, and was a person legally responsible if motivated to commit a crime only by some irresistible impulse?

Later in the twentieth century, those studying arson began to examine other areas and motivations, and it was quickly learned that the phenomenon was not restricted to mentally ill or defective persons but could be found among otherwise "normal" individuals as well, whose actions emerged from a wide range of personal motives.

Offender types

Since the 1950s, studies of arsonists have generally focused on arrested, institutionalized, and paroled individuals. Six separate behavioral categories seem consistently to emerge. The works of the Columbia University psychiatrists Nolan Lewis and Helen Yarnell and numerous social and behavioral researchers have found that the offenders commit arson for purposes of revenge, vandalism, or crime concealment. Some seek to collect insurance; others set fires in search of excitement, or are impelled by an irresistible impulse (pyromaniacs).

Revenge.   Revenge arsonists, the most prevalent type, are persons who, as the result of arguments or feelings of jealousy or hatred, seek revenge by fire. The victims are typically family members and relatives, employers, or lovers. Even though victims are usually associates of the arsonist, hate groups tend to start fires in places of worship and religious dwellings in which the arsonist does not typically know the victim. In retaliation for real or imaginary wrongs, revenge arsonists set ablaze their victims' property or the premises in which they reside. These arsonists appear to be the most potentially dangerous of all the types. They set occupied dwellings afire with little thought as to the safety of those within, thinking only of the revenge they must have on their specific victims. Furthermore, they are often intoxicated at the time of the offense. No elaborate incendiary devices are employed, typically only matches and gasoline. Although their crimes are premeditated, they take few steps to conceal their identities and are thus easily detected by alert investigators.

Vandalism.   Vandalism arsonists include teenagers who willfully destroy property solely for purposes of fun and sport, although at times revenge motives may be partially present. As opposed to other arsonists, who work alone, vandalism arsonists usually have at least one accomplice. In terms of arrest, it is important to note that half of all persons arrested for arson are white males under the age of eighteen. They tend to set their fires at night in churches, school buildings, and vacant structures.

Crime concealment.   Crime-concealment arsonists set fire to premises where they have committed other offenses. The crime is usually burglary but sometimes murder, and the arson is an attempt to cover the traces of the criminal or obliterate the proof that another crime has taken place. Such fires are usually set at night in unoccupied dwellings or places of business.

Insurance claims.   Insurance-claim arsonists include insolvent property owners, small-business operators, and other individuals who, because of extreme financial pressure, incinerate their own property to collect the insurance on what has been destroyed. As a rule they do not set fire to occupied dwellings, and their offenses generally take place in the daytime.

Excitement. Excitement arsonists set buildings ablaze for the thrill connected with fires. Some like setting or watching fires, while others enjoy viewing the operations of the firefighters and fire equipment. (Occasionally a volunteer firefighter is found among them.) Their offenses take place at night, they rarely set ablaze anything but inhabited buildings, and they are usually intoxicated at the time of the offense.

Pyromaniacs. Pyromaniacs are pathological firesetters. They seem to have no practical reasons for setting the fires and receive no material profit from them. Their only motive seems to be some sort of sensual satisfaction, and the classic "irresistible impulse" is often a factor. The behavior of pyromaniacs was best described during the early 1950s by Lewis and Yarnell in their well-known study *Pathological Firesetting*:

The reasons for the fires are unknown; the act is so little their own that they feel no responsibility for the crime. . . . These offenders are able to give a classical description of the irresistible impulse. They describe the mounting tension; the restlessness; the urge for motion; the conversion symptoms such as headaches, palpitations, ringing in the ears, and the gradual merging of their identity into a state of unreality; then the fires are set. . . . Once they have started the fires, thrown the neighborhood into confusion, and are assured the fire engines are working, the tension subsides, and they can go home and drop into a peaceful sleep. The majority of pyromaniacs, incidentally, start fires in their own neighborhood. With some the impulse asserts itself episodically with extended periods of "normality" intervening; with others, it controls them night after night; in either instance they almost always have to set a fire when the impulse appears. Such offenders will continue, each fire being a facsimile of the first, until a more powerful force, usually embodied in the "arm of the law," steps in and commands them to stop. (p. 87)

These are the mysterious "firebugs" who terrorize neighborhoods by going on solitary firesetting sprees, often nocturnal, during which they touch off trash fires in one building after another without regard to property or life. Many suffer from low-level mental deficiencies, are persons who derive sexual satisfaction from watching fires, or are chronic alcoholics, and they encompass the full range of ages.

Many pyromaniacs bring arrest upon themselves by making certain that the identity of the firebug will be easily found, by being conspicuously present watching all of the fires, by repeatedly contacting police or fire officials as to the whereabouts of fires or with information about the "identity" of local arsonists, or by going directly to the police and asking to be protected from their own "criminal desires." Once they are arrested the irresistible impulse ceases, and for some it never returns. The sprees of pyromaniacs last from a few days to a few months or even years, but discovery and arrest tend to put an end to each particular episode.

Clearly, pathological firesetters are not a homogeneous group. Using Sigmund Freud's psychosexual stages, oral-stage and phallic-stage firesetters appear to meet the American Psychiatric Association's DSM-IV criteria for pyromania. Oral-stage firesetters experience feelings of happiness or well-being from watching a safe fire, but have a fear of fires that are out of control. They may also exhibit other non-firesetting, oral-stage behaviors, such as nail-biting, hoarding food, and vomiting when under stress to name but a few. The major indicator of phallic-stage firesetting is sexual arousal from watching fires.

These six types are those that are most familiar to criminal justice authorities, but there are other, less common, varieties. Lewis and Yarnell have identified a number of distinct arsonist types, including the "would-be hero" arsonists, who are motivated primarily by vanity. These individuals are described as "little" men with grandiose social ambitions whose natural capacities doom them to insignificance. They are basically exhibitionists who set significantly large fires, but instead of playing the role of hero by saving lives or helping to extinguish the flames, they turn in the alarms and identify themselves as those who discovered the fires. Lewis and Yarnell have also identified various categories of vagrant arsonists of all ages. These are basically wanderers who start brushfires or incinerate vacant buildings, railroad property, bridges, and farm property for the vicarious pleasure they derive from such destruction.

The arsonist-for-hire is an individual who is paid for the service of burning down property. This type of arsonist usually works alone. The arsonist-for-hire may be hired to destroy an office building, an automobile, or in rare cases, a person. Individuals who hire arsonists include mob figures, business owners, and average people seeking insurance money or revenge.

Arson for profit

Although the insurance-claim firesetter represents a longstanding type with economic motives for arson, since the early 1970s newer and more pervasive forms of arson for profit have become evident. A common pattern involves the purchase of property in decaying inner-city neighborhoods at a low price, followed by several changes of ownership in order to double or triple its paper value. Insurance is obtained, promises of rehabilitation are made, and fire then breaks out. An alternative pattern is manifested by owner-set fires in large inner-city apartment buildings, the rental profits from which have diminished over the years owing to decaying neighborhoods and economic recession. The annual taxes on such properties often exceed the rental income, reducing the market value to near zero. Incineration then becomes the only economically viable method of disposing of the building. Arson-for-profit is typically planned well ahead and the insured usually has a solid alibi far away from the crime scene. Another type of arsonist, often referred to as a "fire stripper," burns buildings and then scavenges them for plumbing, wiring, and fixtures exposed in the gutted structure.

Little is known about those involved in arson for profit, for few are arrested and convicted. Federal Bureau of Investigation data from the 1970s through the close of the 1990s reflect considerable consistency regarding those arrested for arson: the vast majority are white males under the age of twenty-five. But studies of imprisoned and paroled arsonists fail to detect many arson entrepreneurs, or "professional torches."

Fire insurance companies, however, have provided at least some insight into the dynamics of arson for profit and "arsonists for hire." So-called fire brokers, to give an example, specialize in locating failing businesses or decaying properties for persons who intend ultimately to "sell" them to an insurance company. Such brokers make arrangements for the legitimate sale of the targeted property, the inflated insurance, the fire, and the insurance settlement. Their fees range from 10 percent to 20 percent of the insurance value. These brokers generally work in conjunction with "arson co-ops," or rings that specialize in sophisticated methods of property incineration.

There is also evidence that organized crime is involved in the arson business, offering property owners package deals that begin with the fire and end with complete arrangements for settlement. Insurance investigators also believe that many fires result from extortion by underworld loan sharks, who arrange for incendiary fires and insurance settlements in order to force their principals to pay outstanding debts.

Arson and collective violence

The great Albany fire of 1793 has been documented as an illustration of how arson, combined with rioting, has been a mechanism for venting the grievances and frustrations of servitude and oppression. Similar phenomena were the inner-city riots of the 1960s, the prison uprisings during the 1970s and 1980s, and the rebellion in 1992 following the acquittal of the Los Angeles police officers charged with the videotaped beating of Rodney King. Studies of this behavior have shown that the fires associated with mob violence are not necessarily the work of arsonists but that they simply go hand in hand with the accompanying property destruction and looting. The persons participating in such incidents have rarely been arrested for arson and therefore have remained unstudied, but analyses of the spatial distribution of fires during riots suggest that these fires occur more often in neighborhoods where the median income is at or below the poverty line and where the participants have the least to lose in terms of personal property that could be destroyed by fire.

Statistical and economic issues

Since 1970 arson has been referred to as the fastest-growing major crime, and in 1979 the F.B.I. began including it as an "index crime" in its Uniform Crime Reports. Arson is the second leading cause of residential fire deaths. It is responsible for twenty-five percent of all fires in the United States. It is also an extremely violent crime that claims many lives each year. It is estimated that one in four fires is intentionally set and that no less than one thousand deaths and three thousand injuries each year result from arson. The number of arson fires annually is believed to exceed one-half million, with almost half involving buildings and other structures, 30 percent involving vehicles, and the balance directed at outdoor targets ranging from forests to city trash cans. The direct costs of arson in the United States approach $2 billion annually, but estimates suggest that the indirect costs—lost tax revenue and wages, unemployment insurance payments, relocation costs, and other economic ripple effects—are five to ten times higher.

The amount of information dealing with arson and arsonists is severely limited, owing to numerous difficulties in collecting comprehensive and reliable data. First, arson does not always appear to be a crime at the time of occurrence. Many fires are classified as suspicious, but subsequent investigations cannot always document whether a crime did indeed occur. Second, most police agencies are not adequately trained and equipped in the areas of fire science and investigation. Third, the legislative authority to investigate suspicious fires is typically in the hands of state and local fire marshals or municipal fire service companies, with the communication of arson data to law enforcement agencies only on a voluntary basis. Fourth, a significant proportion of firefighters in the United States serve as unpaid volunteers and this results in substandard investigation into the causes of fires. Fifth, rates and trends in arson are generally drawn from arrest statistics, and the unreliability of such data as measures of the incidence and prevalence of crime has been well documented. Sixth, and most important, arson is a low-risk crime, thus yielding few samples of offenders for scientific study. The offense is difficult to prove unless there is a confession or an unimpeachable witness—both unlikely, given the nature of the crime and the criminal. Furthermore, many prosecutors avoid filing formal charges unless the evidence is strong, because the conviction rates for arson are low; and most insurance companies are reluctant to question claims, because they fear civil suits for punitive damages if they turn down a legitimate claim.

JAMES A. INCIARDI
JENNIFER L. MEYER

See also ARSON: LEGAL ASPECTS; RIOTS: BEHAVIORAL ASPECTS.

BIBLIOGRAPHY

American Psychiatric Association. *Diagnostic and Statistical Manual of Mental Disorders*, 4th ed. Washington, D.C.: American Psychiatric Association, 1994.

Federal Bureau of Investigation. *Crime in the United States, 1998. Uniform Crime Reports.* Washington, D.C.: U.S. Department of Justice, 1999.

GERLACH, DON R. "Black Arson in Albany, New York, November 1973." *Journal of Black Studies* 7, no. 3 (March 1977): 301–311.

HAMLING, J. E. "A Psychodynamic Classification System for Pathological Firesetters with Strategies for Each Subgroup." World Wide Web document, 1995. http://www.ozemail.com.au/üjsjp/fireset.htm.

HURLEY, W., and MONOHAN, T. M. "Arson: The Criminal and the Crime." *British Journal of Criminology* 9, (1) (1969): 4–21.

INCIARDI, JAMES A. "The Adult Firesetter: A Typology." *Criminology* 8 (2) (1970): 145–155.

LEWIS, NOLAN D. C., and YARNELL, H. *Pathological Firesetting (Pyromania).* New York: Nervous and Mental Disease Monographs, 1951.

PETTIWAY, LEON E. "Urban Spatial Structure and Incidence of Arson: Differences between Ghetto and Nonghetto Environments." *Justice Quarterly* 5, (1) (1988): 113–129.

ARSON: LEGAL ASPECTS

Common law arson

By the mid-eighteenth century, common law arson was well established as the malicious and willful burning of the house of another by day or by night (Coke, p. 66). The common law viewed arson, like burglary, as a crime against the security of habitation rather than a crime against property. A *house* was defined for both crimes as the dwelling house of the occupant, in addition to the buildings located within the curtilage. *Curtilage* meant the yard or space of ground near the dwelling house, contained in the same enclosure and used in connection with it by the household, and the parcel of buildings or structures contained therein. Barns were generally included in the curtilage. It was quite foreseeable that a fire in any building within the curtilage could spread to the dwelling and endanger the occupants. Thus, a sufficient threat to quiet possession occurred even if the actual dwelling place escaped harm.

Since arson protected habitation, the burning of an unoccupied house did not constitute arson: there could be no arson if the fire occurred before the first resident moved in, after the dwelling was vacated, or in a period between residents. On the other hand, a dwelling retained its occupied status during the temporary absence of the occupant; it was unnecessary that he be present in the dwelling at the time of the burning.

The use of the building determined its status. A permanency of dwelling was necessary. Burning a place where transients stayed, such as a hotel, did not constitute arson under the common law. Neither did the burning of institutions, such as jails or hospitals, unless someone also lived in the building as a permanent resident.

Since arson was viewed as a crime against the security of habitation, the building burned had to be that of another. It was not arson to burn the house one occupied, whether or not the occupant owned it, even if the burning threatened the lives of others in the house. The burning of one's own dwelling to collect insurance did not constitute common law arson. It was generally assumed in early England that one had the legal right to destroy his own property in any manner he chose.

Arson was legally regarded as a heinous and aggravated offense both because it threatened human life and the security of habitation and because it evidenced a moral recklessness and depravity in the perpetrator. Arson was thus a capital offense until more lenient statutes were enacted in the nineteenth century.

Although it was not common law arson to burn one's own house, it was a common law misdemeanor ("houseburning") if the burning was intentional and the house was situated in a city or town, or, if beyond those limits, was still so near other dwellings as to create danger to them. Any malicious destruction of, or damage to, the property of another not amounting to common law arson constituted a common law misdemeanor known as malicious mischief.

The common law required an actual burning or ignition of some part of the building, at least to the extent of charring the wood. A mere smoking, scorching, or discoloration of the wood was insufficient. The general rule was that a slight charring, no matter how small, was sufficient.

Since the common law required that the fire damage the structure, setting fire to personal property within the building would not constitute arson unless the fire spread to the building itself. An attempted burning did not constitute arson. Similarly, it was no crime under the common law to prepare a building for a fire.

Corpus delicti. To have established the corpus delicti of arson at common law, the proof must have shown that there had been a burning of a structure or property protected by law, and that the fire had resulted from the criminal act of some person. It also had to be shown that the defendant was the criminal agency. The common law presumed that all fires resulted from accident, negligence, or natural causes. Therefore, direct or circumstantial evidence that the fire was of incendiary origin and that the defendant was the guilty party was required.

The requisite mens rea consisted of a willful and malicious intent to burn. The word *willful* meant the arsonist must have started the fire intentionally. The requisite intent could be viewed as the general, unlawful purpose to damage or destroy certain property. While the intent could be inferred from the act, more than negligence had to be shown. In some cases negligent burnings could be punished as a lesser offense, such as negligently burning prairie land or timberland.

Malice was an essential element of common law arson, and had to be established independently of any showing of willfulness. Malice was generally construed as a desire to injure the victim of the unlawful act, and was readily inferred from the nature of the act or the circumstances surrounding it, so that liability generally resulted if the burning were intentional. Motive was not an element of arson, although motive was often used to infer intent, such as overinsuring the property. The existence of a motive may have helped establish the corpus delicti of arson by showing both that the fire was intentional in origin and that the defendant was culpable. Conversely, the absence of a motive may have made proof of the essential elements less persuasive.

Direct evidence of arson is frequently unavailable since the crime is ordinarily committed under the cover of darkness, clandestinely, and in a manner intended to divert suspicion. Thus, circumstantial evidence, and reasonable inferences based thereon, were generally used to establish the crime and the culprit.

Statutory arson

Owing to the narrow confines of arson under the common law, statutes were enacted in every state beginning in the early 1800s (as, for example, in the *Acts Passed at the First Session of the Legislative Council of the Territory of Orleans. . ... p. 416), greatly expanding the crime to include the criminal burning of almost any type of property. The statutory scheme remained far from uniform through the early 1900s, but statutes generally protected property as well as habitation. The burning of one's dwelling constituted arson, whether or not the intent was to collect insurance. A few of the earliest statutes imposed a harsher penalty if the burning occurred at night. Modern statutes take note of the time of the arson only in determining the grade of degree of the crime. Statutory arson also included situations in which chattels (personal effects) were burned in a building without spreading to the structure. A few statutes followed the common law distinctions between dwelling house and other buildings. Some distinguished between occupancy and vacancy.

Statutes commonly divide arson into various degrees. First-degree arson is directed at the endangering of life rather than of property, whereas the lesser degrees relate to the value of the damaged property, the motive, or the type of property burned. The penalties differ according to the degree of arson.

A typical Alabama statute provided that arson of the first degree consisted of the willful burning of a dwelling or structure in which a person was present at the time, or of any inhabited dwelling. Arson of the second degree included the willful burning of a public building, manufacturing establishment, storage place, vessel, or uninhabited dwelling. Third-degree arson consisted of the willful burning of a house or vessel, bridge gate or causeway (Code of Ala., §§ 3289, 3290, 3293 (1923)). Many other statutes provide for aggravated arson, which covers that form of arson which does or could result in an injury to persons, and simple arson, which is all other arson.

Statutes generally require the act to be "willful" or "malicious," or some combination of these terms. Regardless of the word or phrase used, the interpretations have generally been in accordance with the common law.

Under the common law, damage caused by an explosive could not be considered arson since there was no burning. Many states have solved this problem by statutorily defining arson to include injury to property resulting from the use of an explosive, whether or not an actual burning occurs. Most modern statutes include "explosive" in the means of destruction or damage performed by arsonists (N.Y. Penal Law (McKinney) §§ 150.05—150.10, 150.20 (1999)).

Model arson statutes

The Model Arson Law, proposed in the early 1920s by the National Board of Fire Underwriters, enlarges criminal liability for preliminary behavior by punishing not only what would be attempted arson at common law, but also the preparation of a building for burning. In addition, a separate category is established for the intentional burning of any property insured against loss or damage by fire with the purpose of injuring or defrauding the insurer. This provision applies to the accused's own property. It should be noted that while arson requires only a general intent, arson to defraud requires a showing that the burning was specifically for the purpose of collecting insurance. Accessories to arson are liable as principals under the Model Arson Act.

The American Law Institute's Model Penal Code provisions on arson have not been widely followed (§ 220.1). Under these proposals arson is defined as the destruction of a "building or occupied structure" or the damaging of any property with intent to collect insurance. The Code's provisions differ from those of the abovementioned Model Arson Law in several ways. First, they include explosions as a category of arson. Second, they insert in the definition of intent a requirement that the act be done "with the purpose of destroying property." Third, they exclude the actor's own building or structure, unless it was insured. Finally, they unequivocally designate as arson the burning of any property, chattels as well as buildings, with the purpose of collecting insurance.

In addition to the crime so defined, the Code provides lesser felony penalties for reckless burnings or explosions that threaten bodily injury or damage to buildings or occupied structures of another. Other types of property damage by fire are treated as misdemeanors.

In 1978 several insurance associations prepared a model arson penal law, which is similar in several respects to the Model Penal Code. In the proposal a first-degree felony offense of "aggravated arson" encompasses cases of death or bodily injury resulting from arson. The second- and third-degree offenses resemble the Model Penal Code provisions, and include unoccupied structures. Specific penalties are provided for the damage of any property when the purpose is to defraud the insurer.

Consistent with the historical trend toward expansion, Congress enacted the Anti-Arson Act of 1982, Pub. L. No. 97-298, § 2(c), making it possible for the federal government to prosecute for the first time arsons involving nongovernmental property. The Act prohibits damage or destruction by fire (or explosives) of "any building, vehicle, or other real or personal property used in interstate or foreign commerce or in any activity affecting interstate or foreign commerce." 18 U.S.C. 844(i) (1994). Federal circuit courts are divided on how broadly to construe

the jurisdictional predicate of "affecting interstate . . . commerce," but some authority exists
for extending it to the destruction of private resi-
dences based solely on their owners' purchase of
natural gas that originated in another state or
their securing of mortgages from out-of-state
lenders. (*United States v. Jones,* 178 F.3d 479, 480
(7th Cir. 1999) (residential).)

DENIS BINDER
DAN M. KAHAN

See also ARSON: BEHAVIORAL AND ECONOMIC ASPECTS.

BIBLIOGRAPHY

*Acts Passed at the First Session of the Legislative Coun-
cil of the Territory of Orleans Begun and Held at
the Principal in the City of New-Orleans on Mon-
day the Third Day of December in the Year of Our
Lord One Thousand, Eight Hundred and Four and
of the Independence of the United States the Twenty-
ninth.* Published by Authority New-Orleans.
Printed by James N. Bradford, Printer to the
Territory, 1805.
American Law Institute. *Model Penal Code: Tenta-
tive Draft No. 11.* Philadelphia: ALI, 1960.
Arson Project. "Arson Fraud: Criminal Prosecu-
tion and Insurance Law." *Fordham Urban Law
Journal* 7 (1978–1979): 541–615.
BRAUN, WILLIAM C. "Legal Aspects of Arson."
*Journal of Criminal Law, Criminology, and Police
Science* 43 (1952): 53–62.
COHN, HERMAN H. "Convicting the Arsonist."
*Journal of Criminal Law, Criminology, and Police
Science* 38 (1947): 286–303.
COKE, EDWARD. *The Third Part of the Institutes of the
Laws of England: Concerning High Treason, and
Other Pleas of the Crown, and Criminal Causes.* 2d
ed. London: W. Lee & D. Pakeman, 1648.
CURTIS, ARTHUR F. *A Treatise on the Law of Arson,
Covering the Decisions of All American States and
Territories, and Including Those of England and
the British Colonies.* Buffalo, N.Y.: Dennis,
1936.
HOPPER, WILLIAM H. "Arson's Corpus Delicti."
*Journal of Criminal Law, Criminology, and Police
Science* 47 (1956): 118–130.
———. "Circumstantial Aspects of Arson." *Jour-
nal of Criminal Law, Criminology, and Police Sci-
ence* 46 (1955): 129–134.
Note. "Arson—Statutory Change of Common
Law Requisites." *Michigan Law Review* 25
(1927): 450–453.
Note. "Proof of the Corpus Delicti in Arson
Cases." *Journal of Criminal Law, Criminology,
and Police Science* 45 (1954): 185–191.
PANNETON, JOHN. "Federalizing Fires: The
Evolving Federal Response to Arson Related
Crimes." *American Criminal Law Review* 23
(1985): 151–206.
PERKINS, ROLLIN M. *Criminal Law* 2d ed. Mineola,
N.Y.: Foundation Press, 1969.
POULOS, JOHN. "The Metamorphosis of the Law
of Arson." *Missouri Law Review* 51 (1986): 295–
448.
SADLER, PAUL, JR. "The Crime of Arson." *Journal
of Criminal Law, Criminology, and Police Science*
41 (1950): 290–305.

ASSASSINATION

In the eleventh century the Shiite Ismaeli
convert Hasan ibn-al-Sabbah (c. 1050–1124),
"the Old Man of the Mountain," appeared in Islamic Persia and for nearly fifty years led the
struggle against both Sunni orthodoxy and
Turkish rule. Persecuted and hunted, he established the mountain fortress of Alamut, which
"became the greatest training center of fanatical
politico-religious assassins that the world has
known" (Franzius, p. 45). Hasan sent young men
(*fidais,* "devoted ones") singly or in small bands
to kill military, political, and religious leaders
aligned against him. Such was the suicidal fanati-
cism of Hasan's skilled killers that it was widely
believed they must be stimulated by hashish.
They were called "hashish-eaters," apparently
shortened in Arabic usage to *Assassins,* which may
also connote *Asasi* ("followers of the Asas," the
true teacher) and perhaps in addition, "followers
of Hasan" (Franzius, pp. 47–48).

Defining assassination

In time, assassin came generally to mean one
who killed an unsuspecting victim without warning, but the original sense of political purpose
was never quite lost, and has become increasingly
strong. To assassinate is to kill for a political reason—to secure or resist authority, to eliminate a
rival for power, to prevent or avenge a political
defeat, or to express a political grievance.

Political motivation distinguishes assassination from other deadly interpersonal violence.
Unfortunately for analytic rigor, motivation is
extremely difficult to establish. Indeed, after a
useful discussion of the problem, Havens, Leiden, and Schmitt remarked at the end of their research that "perhaps attempts to determine
motives are irrelevant, for once the act has been
committed the public manufactures its own mo-

tive in harmony with its own political predilections" (p. 150). Political motives, like others, are often hidden or unclear, and cannot merely be inferred from the political significance or prominence of a target (Kirkham, Levy, and Crotty). Heads of state may be the victims of nonpolitical violence; ordinary citizens such as tourists may die as political surrogates or pawns. Nonetheless, it has been generally assumed that only attacks on important officials and other influential persons are politically inspired, and that common folk are too insignificant to draw the assassin's fire. Both assumptions are questionable.

The meaning of the term *political* blurs as power concerns and struggles permeate society and as the interdependence and interpenetration of different loci and forms of authority increase. Any area of social life, from religion and education to industry and entertainment, can be politicized, serving as a base, vehicle, or object of power struggles. Whoever emerges as a leading figure may have, or be seen as having, political significance as actor or symbol, in the sense once associated almost exclusively with the leaders of governments and parties. Charismatic figures are especially likely to attract the attention of an established or aspiring power-wielder who sees the potential value and danger of anyone who sways others.

Contemporary justifications of assassination and terrorism began in nineteenth-century Russian anarchism and have led in their most extreme formulations to the conclusion that death is appropriate for all who live as "part of the problem"—that is, who try to carry on a normal life instead of joining in the war to destroy the existing world system, which is increasingly seen as culturally, economically, and militarily dominated by the United States. In such terms, every killing is an assassination, serving the political aim of demonstrating that all are guilty until injustice (as defined by the motivating ideology) is eliminated from the world.

One major consequence is that the meaning of *assassination* shifts not only to include common as well as prominent people, but also to include the killing of many as well as of one or a few. Assassination finally becomes synonymous with *terrorism*—which may be understood as random violence whose specific victims are selected mostly by chance instead of design, irrespective of the varying innocence and political power of individuals.

The logic of terrorist theory thus leads to a concept of assassination in which the element of specification is ultimately dissolved. Of course, even terrorists find it necessary to make distinctions and set priorities. Dangerous adversaries must be distinguished from innocent bystanders. Opportunities must be weighed with regard to potential risks and benefits. Resources have to be matched to opportunities. Targets have to be selected with due regard for their tactical importance. All this suggests that assassination is characterized by selection rather than by specification. The point is that victims are selected because of the anticipated impact of the timing, place, or manner of their death. Their attributes as individuals may or may not be relevant concerns and, in any case, will be secondary ones. Their individuality is irrelevant as such, although particular attributes (e.g., their perceived nationality or race) may be assessed as enhancing or reducing their significance as potential victims. Because significance is not only or necessarily a function of power or prominence, children and other noncombatants may be targeted precisely because their destruction is expected to weaken or deter support for the opposition. Symbols, positions, and relationships—not people—are the real targets of assassination.

Although agreeing that assassination is politically motivated killing, Ben-Yehuda emphasizes the need to distinguish between assassination and terrorism. His view is that assassination is defined by the targeting of specific individuals, while terrorism is (as suggested above) indiscriminate killing aimed at a general target—a collectivity or population. As he recognizes, and as illustrated by several of the cases he analyzes, it is difficult to maintain the distinction. Attempted or successful assassinations of particular actors may harm others in addition to or instead of the intended targets. Nontargeted others may be deliberately harmed because they are trying to protect or assist the target, or because they are potential witnesses. Companions or bystanders may be mistakenly or inadvertently harmed. And mistakes may occur, as when an agent dispatched by the Israeli Mossad misidentified and killed an innocent Arab in Lillehamer, Norway. Finally, the number of targets or victims of assassination may vary from one to many—which suggests that there may be a point at which the number becomes so great that the line between specific and general targeting is impossible to draw. In sum, the distinction between assassination and terrorism is at best tactical or analytical, not one dictated by empirical observations.

Thus, the most realistic definition of assassination is that it is politically motivated killing in which victims are selected because of the expected political impact of their dying. The victims of assassination are generally assumed to be few and to be individually targeted. When there are many victims, who appear to have been randomly selected by the circumstances of their being in "the wrong place at the wrong time," the event is more likely to be defined as terrorism than as assassination.

Assassination and the law

The legal status of assassination is ambiguous in both domestic and international law. Killing or endangering the sovereign, members of the royal family, or chief representatives of the sovereign has always been abhorrent in English common law, and was formally defined as treason in the fourteenth century ("Treason Act," 25 Edw. 3, stat. 5, c. 2 (1351) (England)). The concept of treason has since been extended beyond personal fealty to include violence against the constitutional system by anyone having a duty of allegiance. The law of treason has, however, rarely been invoked (Law Commission). Indeed, the English legal system has been characterized by its nonrecognition of political offenses as such. Political motivation has been accorded scant consideration as even a mitigating factor, in contrast to the tradition established in continental legal systems. There is no recognized political defense in English law. Thus, assassination as a form of treason is extremely circumscribed, and most assassinations are treated as common law crimes without political import.

The United States, Canada, and some other nations formerly British-ruled follow the English model on this question. In the United States, Congress reacted in 1963 to President John F. Kennedy's assassination by making it a federal offense punishable by death or life imprisonment to assassinate the president, president-elect, vice president, vice president-elect, or anyone legally acting as president (18 U.S.C. section 1751 (1976)). Subsequently, it was also made a federal offense to assassinate an incumbent or elected member of Congress. To war against the United States or to assist its enemies constitutes treason; and it is an offense to advocate the forcible or violent overthrow of the federal or any state government, or the assassination of any officer of such governments (18 U.S.C. sections 2381, 2385 (1976)). Otherwise, assassination is a common

crime to be dealt with by the state or other government in whose jurisdiction it occurs.

Even though a common crime, the killing of officials—especially police officers and federal agents—has been dealt with increasingly as a special offense meriting more stringent penalties; and any killings or attacks by antigovernment militants receive special attention under laws such as the Racketeering Influenced and Corrupt Organizations (RICO) statutes. Conviction in such cases typically results in significantly more severe sentencing (Smith). In effect, such homicides are perceived and treated as politically inspired—that is, as assassinations.

Until the nineteenth century the European monarchs generally agreed that regicide was intolerable, and considered the offender against government the most despicable of criminals. In 1833, Belgium initiated the doctrine that political offenders were not to be extradited. Most other nations followed suit, but the ensuing treaties typically required extradition of assassins and other violent offenders as common criminals unless their acts occurred in the course of a political disturbance or were "proportionate"—that is, not excessive in view of the aims and circumstances of the act (Kittrie). Beginning with the reaction against late nineteenth-century anarchist violence, the political defense of assassination and other political violence has been increasingly unlikely to prevent extradition. In particular, war crimes and crimes against humanity are widely considered to be extraditable offenses. However, there have been many exceptional cases; and the international community remains sharply divided on how to define and deal with terrorist killings and other politically motivated violence.

The legal situation is, then, that assassination may be defined domestically as treason, an "allied offense," or a common crime. Under international law, it may be defined as a nonextraditable political offense (albeit "complex" rather than "pure"), as an extraditable common crime, or as a crime against humanity or against the laws of war. In both domestic and international law, the legal status of any particular assassination depends on the political concerns and relative power of the various authorities and of any private parties involved in or interested in its occurrence.

Causes and patterns

How one approaches the problem of explaining assassination depends on one's assumptions about political violence. If violence for political reasons is considered to be unusual and unjustifiable, the causes of assassination are expected to lie in the psychopathology of individual killers. If political violence is thought to be aberrant but sometimes justifiable, or at least understandable, causes are sought in threatening or oppressive social conditions, which in principle can be changed so as to eliminate the violence. If violence is seen as an intrinsic dimension and a common instrument of politics, causes are to be found in the varying fortunes and tactics of social groups attempting to defend or increase their life chances. A developed scientific theory of assassination presumably would avoid moral assumptions about political violence and would encompass all three causal sources, treating them as sets of variables whose interrelationships result in an increasing or decreasing probability of assassination events. No such theory yet exists. Toward that goal, the following hypotheses are to be considered: (1) The more threatening or oppressive social conditions are for a particular group the more likely the group is to resort to assassination and other forms of violence; (2) individuals with certain psychopathologic characteristics are more likely to be selected for the actual work of killing; alternatively, those selected develop psychopathological characteristics because of the guilt, isolation, fear, suffering, or other experiences associated with their "dirty work."

Oppression, threat, and assassination. Research on the social causes of assassination indicates that oppression is probably less important than threat in affecting the probability of assassination. Gross has defined *oppression* as "acts of physical brutality, including killing and limitation of freedom, humiliation of persons, economic exploitation, deprivation of elementary economic opportunities, confiscation of property" (p. 86). He suggests that even foreign domination causes assassination only if it is perceived as oppression, if a political party exists with "an ideology and tactics of direct action," and if there are "activist personality types" ready to use violence (p. 89). Ethnic and nationalist conflicts appear to be far more important factors than socioeconomic conditions in encouraging assassination and other political violence. Political violence tends to be the work of higher-class visionaries and activists, in contrast to the lower-class predatory types who engaged in "common criminal violence" (p. 93).

The most systematic available evidence concerning the linkage between socioeconomic conditions and assassination is found in a cross-national comparative study for the United States National Commission on the Causes and Prevention of Violence (Kirkham et al.). Assassination is associated with political instability, which in turn reflects such factors as a low level of socioeconomic development, a high level of relative deprivation, and a high rate of socioeconomic change. Other contributing factors are a government neither very coercive nor very permissive, and high levels of externalized aggression and hostility toward foreigners, among minority and majority groups, and among individuals, as indicated by high homicide and low suicide rates. The United States is exceptional in combining an advanced level of socioeconomic development with the other features. It is noted that African Americans and other major sectors of the population do generally live under conditions internally approximating those found to be associated with relatively high levels of political violence. The findings suggest that socioeconomic conditions must interact with political and cultural factors to become significant in causing assassination and other political violence.

It appears that oppression becomes causally relevant only when it is interpreted as threat, whereas perceived threat in itself is sufficient to encourage political violence. One major implication of this general proposition is that economic conditions must become political factors to affect the level of political violence. A further implication is that political conditions must be interpreted as threatening in order to be causally significant. The process of interpretation is, then, the key to creating situations in which the probability of assassination and other political violence is significantly increased.

Threats may be real whether or not perceived. For a group to have fewer resources while another has more implies a present or potential threat to the life chances of the disadvantaged. The greater the differences, the greater the likelihood that the more advantaged group is living in part at the expense of the less advantaged (assuming they are bound together economically and politically in a real, if not necessarily formal, sense). Certainly, the less advantaged live more precariously and are more vulnerable to life's miseries. For them, it is not difficult to see or believe that inequality is threatening. At the same time, the more advantaged will readily see or believe that underclass discontent or gains are threatening. At any given moment, the available resources are finite; the pie cannot be shared without someone having less if another is to have more. Both sides are likely to feel threatened by change—particularly by high rates of socioeconomic change—because it is difficult to predict just who will win and who will lose in the course of events.

The perceived threat posed by existing or changing economic or political conditions does not of itself necessarily produce violence. What is required is that an enemy be identified and that potential assailants be mobilized. Historically, this last step has been accomplished by a campaign of vilification of visible members of a targeted group (government, party, class, religion, nationality, race, or ethnic category), as well as of the group as a whole (Gross; Kirkham et al.). Responsibility for the threatening economic or political conditions is placed squarely on the targeted individuals and groups, who are depicted as entirely reprehensible, irredeemably monstrous, and perhaps even subhuman.

Unchecked, vilification produces a climate of extremism because the targets of the campaign tend to respond in kind. In such a climate, some individuals experienced in using violence may be deliberately recruited as assassins (*hired killers*). Others (*political actors*) may progress in stages of activism from minimal political involvement to the conclusion that assassination is tactically essential. Still others (*expressive reactors*) may simply be caught up in the excitement of political conflict, finding in the rhetoric of vilification a means and focus for expressing their discontent, perhaps in assassination. Although individual cases exhibit some overlap and movement among them, these types—hired killers, political actors, and expressive reactors—must be analytically distinguished if the psychology of assassins is to be explored fruitfully.

The psychology of assassins.   Psychological profiles of assassins are derived from limited and unrepresentative samples biased in several ways. First, assassins who attack governmental and other institutional figures have been studied, rather than assassins acting on behalf of such figures. Second, assassins of chief executives and other prominent individuals have been studied, to the virtual exclusion of those who kill minor officials and ordinary people. Third, only assassins who have been caught have been studied, so that almost nothing is known about those who are deterred or who escape detection and capture. Fourth, analysis has focused on expressive reactors, with little or no attention having been given to hired killers and political actors. Fifth, the presumption of psychopathology has been strong in both the selection of subjects for study, usually by psychiatrists, and in the analysts' common tendency to see political (and other) violence as intrinsically abnormal and irrational. Finally, the possibility of organized, tactical assassination has tended to be dismissed in favor of an image of the assassin as typically a loner without coherent political motivation and unable to act in concert with others to further political aims.

Research on assassins and assailants of American presidents has found nearly all to be "mentally disturbed persons who did not kill to advance any rational political plan" (Kirkham et al., p. 62). Douglas and Olshaker argue that political intent or consequences are incidental, emphasizing instead the paranoid loser "assassin personality" (p. 219) as merely another type of murderer (delusional but not hallucinatory) essentially akin to senseless killers such as serial and spree murderers.

Ellis and Gullo found assassins other than "paid gunmen" and political agents to have long histories of psychological disturbance, to have experienced a life crisis shortly before the assassination, and to kill without aim or sense "as far as their political beliefs and aspirations are concerned" (pp. 190–250).

Harris has suggested that to understand assassins one must look beyond psychopathology to the more normal psychology of the "rebellious-rivalrous personality," a type who "finds authority and restrictions irksome and strives for a redistribution of hierarchical status by competing with the successful lime-lighted rival" (pp. 199–200). Similarly, after pointing out the narrow subjectivity of psychiatric evaluations of assassins, Clarke argues for a classification based on social contextual as well as situational and diagnostic evidence. He identifies four types of assassins, as well as a residual of "atypicals." His Type I, whose "extremism is rational, selfless, principled, and without perversity," appears to be equivalent to *political actors*. Types II (neurotics) and IV (psychotics) are analogous to *emotional reactors*, and Type III (psychopaths, sociopaths) is perhaps analogous to *hired killers* (pp. 13–17).

Though recognizing the quite limited explanatory power of psychopathology, Robins and Post nevertheless invoke the concept of a "paranoid style" in trying to explain why many people who are not clinically psychopathological may share a belief that their government or other forces are threatening their physical or cultural well-being. Applying such a label to social movements and organizations merely reinforces the assumption that there must be "something wrong" with people whose experiences and beliefs differ significantly from those of the observer, and whose perceptions of threat may not be entirely unwarranted.

From the limited evidence available, it may be concluded that the hypothesis of prior psychopathology is supported for expressive reactors and may have some relevance for explaining hired killers. However, these constitute only a minority of assassins, most of whom are clearly motivated by political concerns based on religious, nationalist, racial-ethnic, and other widely shared ideologies.

The impact of assassination

The impact of assassination varies according to the political milieu. Assassination undermines democratic institutions insofar as it deters able persons from seeking positions of leadership, reduces the public's sense of security, or leads to repression and vigilantism. In more totalitarian systems it encourages opportunism and autocracy, inhibits creative effort and cooperation, and therefore probably reduces the capacity for adapting to environmental and internal changes. Where economic and political instability are endemic, as in much of the developing world, assassination makes it even less likely that able leaders will emerge or have time enough to act effectively. In short, where political order is lacking, assassination helps to prevent its achievement; where it is established, assassination contributes to its erosion or ossification.

Assassination is most likely to be an effective tactic when the goal is a limited one (e.g., retaliation, discipline, elimination of a rival) and when it has organizational support (Ben-Yehuda). It is least likely to occur or affect political life when most people are content and when peaceful mechanisms for transferring power have been established. But insofar as political conflicts spill over or transcend national boundaries, "imported" assassinations may occur—particularly in more open societies such as the Western democracies. And finally, the globalization of conflicts facilitated by technological developments and driven by religio-political ideologies of cosmological struggle (Juergensmeyer) portends more assassination events irrespective of local conditions.

AUSTIN T. TURK

See also HOMICIDE: BEHAVIORAL ASPECTS; HOMICIDE: LEGAL ASPECTS; TERRORISM; VIOLENCE.

BIBLIOGRAPHY

BEN-YEHUDA, NACHMAN. *Political Assassinations by Jews.* Albany: State University of New York Press, 1993.

CLARKE, JAMES W. *American Assassins: The Darker Side of Politics.* Princeton, N.J.: Princeton University Press, 1990.

DOUGLAS, JOHN, and OLSHAKER, MARK. *The Anatomy of Motive.* New York: Scribners, 1999.

ELLIS, ALBERT, and GULLO, JOHN M. *Murder and Assassination.* New York: Lyle Stuart, 1971.

FRANZIUS, ENNO. *History of the Order of Assassins.* New York: Funk & Wagnalls, 1969.

GROSS, FELIKS. *Violence in Politics: Terror and Political Assassination in Eastern Europe and Russia.* Hague: Mouton, 1972.

HARRIS, IRVING D. "Assassins." In *Violence: Perspectives on Murder and Aggression.* Edited by Irwin L. Kutash, Samuel B. Kutash, Louis B. Schesinger, and others. Foreword by Alexander Wolf. San Francisco: Jossey-Bass, 1978. Pages 198–218.

HAVENS, MURRAY CLARK; LEIDEN, CARL; and SCHMITT, KARL M. *The Politics of Assassination.* Englewood Cliffs, N.J.: Prentice-Hall, 1970.

JUERGENSMEYER, MARK. *Terror in the Mind of God: The Global Rise of Religious Violence.* Berkeley: University of California Press, 2000.

KIRKHAM, JAMES F.; LEVY, SHELDON G.; and CROTTY, WILLIAM J. *Assassination and Political Violence: A Report to the National Commission on the Causes and Prevention of Violence.* Reprint, with an introduction by Harrison E. Salisbury. New York: Bantam Books, 1970.

KITTRIE, NICHOLAS N. "A New Look at Political Offenses and Terrorism." In *International Terrorism in the Contemporary World.* Edited by Marius H. Livingston, with Lee Bruce Kress and Marie G. Wanek. Westport, Conn.: Greenwood Press, 1978. Pages 354–375.

Law Commission. *Codification of the Criminal Law: Treason, Sedition, and Allied Offenses.* Working Paper No. 72. London: Her Majesty's Stationery Office, 1977.

ROBINS, ROBERT S., and POST, JERROLD M. *Political Paranoia: The Psychopolitics of Hatred.* New Haven, Conn.: Yale University Press, 1997.

SMITH, BRENT L. *Terrorism in America: Pipe Bombs and Pipe Dreams.* Albany, N.Y.: State University of New York Press, 1994.

ASSAULT AND BATTERY

Assault and battery are two distinct common law crimes that exist in all American jurisdictions, usually as statutory misdemeanors. Battery involves actual physical contact with the victim and is defined as conduct producing a bodily injury or an offensive contact. Assault, on the other hand, does not include physical contact with the victim and is classified as either an attempt at battery or an intentional frightening of another person. Although the term *assault and battery* is frequently used when a battery has been committed, one who commits a battery cannot be punished for committing an assault, since the lesser offense of assault blends into the actual battery.

Battery

Battery, which requires physical contact with the victim, is broken down into three separate elements: the defendant's conduct, his mental state, and the harm done to the victim. Although many statutes do not define battery with specificity, or even list these elements, it is a widely recognized principle of law that each of them must be met.

Conduct. A defendant's conduct in a case of battery encompasses the physical acts he performs in committing the crime. Battery may be committed either by directly touching a person or indirectly applying force to him. It is clear that intentionally striking someone should be classified as a battery, but it is less clear that a battery charge should result from an injury not directly caused by the defendant. The latter result is often reached by modern courts, however. Consequently, one may commit a battery by causing injury through poisoning. One may also be liable for directing another person to make a physical contact. Battery, therefore, may result when a person is forced to touch something that is repulsive to him or when one is injured in a dangerous situation intentionally created by the defendant. Additionally, if the other elements of battery are present, some cases have held persons criminally responsible when neglect of a duty to act causes injury to another—for example, when a lifeguard fails to warn swimmers of dangerous undercurrents.

Mental state. A defendant is held to be culpable in a battery charge if he acts with either an intent to injure or with criminal negligence. In some jurisdictions it is sufficient if he commits an unlawful act, regardless of his intent. Culpability is apparent when one acts with intent to injure, but one is usually not liable for committing a battery when he possesses no intent to injure. Hence, it is not a battery to grab someone in order to rescue him or to prevent him from doing something dangerous.

The use of criminal negligence to supply the requisite intent for battery is not always accepted, for negligence is not normally sufficient to prove the mental state needed for the criminal act. Some courts state that criminal negligence supplies the intent, thus equating this negligence with a simple intent to injure. Other states have statutes that make battery a minor misdemeanor when one acts in reckless disregard of the risk of causing injury to another.

If criminal negligence is held sufficient to warrant a charge of battery, the term *negligence* requires definition. For criminal liability, more than ordinary lack of due care should be required. Most jurisdictions defining batteries based on negligence require actions that create an unreasonable and high risk of harm to others. Although there is no single definition, it is generally accepted that the risk should be one a reasonable person would be clearly aware of, even if the defendant does not perceive it. It may seem wrong to criminally punish someone for harmful acts he does not intend. Nevertheless, one should be responsible for actions that would be recognized as harmful by most persons and that outrage and injure the general public.

In only a few jurisdictions is the unlawful-act standard applied to battery cases. The question of intent is again applicable, in connection with both the injury and the act itself. One who is consciously acting unlawfully should be responsible for the results of his actions, regardless of his intent. However, if he is unaware that he is acting unlawfully, it is more difficult to argue that criminal liability should automatically follow. Some states have dealt with this problem by ruling that liability results if the act is bad in itself (*malum in se*) but not if it is simply prohibited conduct (*malum prohibitum*); *malum prohibitum* acts, however, may be sufficient if the defendant is either criminally negligent or intends to cause injury.

Harm to the victim. The final element necessary for battery is the harmful result to the victim. This element is satisfied by virtually any type of bodily injury; indeed, many states have statutes that permit any offensive touching to qualify as a battery. Some cases have held that forcing a child to touch parts of the defendant's body created criminal responsibility, even when the defendant himself did not do any actual touching. In such situations, the defendant is viewed as having caused the act just as if he had touched the victim, since he initiated and controlled the situation, and the victim felt personally violated by the defendant.

Aggravated battery. The crime of aggravated battery, punishable as a felony and specifically defined by statute, exists in many states. Examples of such crimes are actions taken with intent to kill or to rape. Usually, the defendant must have intended to cause the specific result; otherwise, the crime is considered as a regular battery charge. Batteries based on criminal negligence are generally not considered sufficiently egregious to warrant a felony charge. Where a defendant did not intend to commit a felony, it seems unjust to convict him of the more serious charge.

Assault

An assault is classified as either an attempted battery or an intentional frightening of another person; physical contact is not an element of the crime in either of these situations. Many states do not define assault, and some states list it under attempt rather than under assault.

Attempted battery. In assaults resulting from attempted battery, there must be a specific intent on the part of the defendant to cause injury. The theory behind this requirement is that one cannot be guilty of attempting a battery if he lacks the intent to commit a battery. In some states there is an additional requirement of a present ability to commit the crime, on the assumption that a defendant cannot have attempted a battery if he was unable to act at the time.

Intentional frightening. Most states classify as assaults those acts that are designed to frighten another. Thus, one is liable for committing an assault when, intending to cause another person reasonable apprehension of immediate bodily harm, one acts to create such apprehension. In such assaults the defendant does not plan actually to harm the victim, but merely to frighten him. Some states do not classify an intentional frightening as a crime of assault, believing that such acts are not serious enough to warrant criminal punishment. There is a strong argument in favor of the viewpoint that intentional frightening should be left to tort law, where the defendant is held responsible more for causing harm to the plaintiff than for acting dangerously.

In the majority of states, the first requirement of intentional frightening as an assault is an actual purpose to frighten. It is not necessary that one have the ability to harm someone, because this assault focuses on intent rather than on present ability. Thus, when one points an unloaded gun at another with the intent to frighten, one is guilty of committing an assault even though it is impossible for him to fire.

A second requirement for a successful assault charge is that the victim actually be frightened by the defendant's actions. In addition, the defendant's conduct must be of the sort to arouse a reasonable apprehension of bodily harm in the average person. Thus, it is not sufficient to say something that frightens another, if a reasonable person would not be placed in fear of bodily harm by such conduct.

Proving fright on the part of the victim can be difficult. Some courts have created a distinction between immediate fear and reasonable apprehension stating that reasonable apprehension may be a response of which the victim is not immediately aware. One may be so startled by the defendant's acts that one's reaction is delayed, but this should not automatically mean that one is not frightened. When a person is threatened with a gun, it is irrelevant whether the gun is loaded. Just as an unloaded gun may be used to fulfill the intent requirement, it may also serve to cause apprehension. If a gun is used, the victim's apprehension is normally proven unless it is shown he knew the gun was unloaded.

Conditional assault. In addition to the above two types of assault, there is a third category, that of conditional assault. This is an assault that arises only under certain conditions, usually failure of the victim to act as the defendant directs. If a defendant threatens to shoot another unless that person leaves the property, he is guilty of committing an assault even though the victim departs. The defendant is not protected from an assault charge simply because the victim complied with the condition. The fact that the defendant would have harmed the victim if the condition had not been satisfied is enough to supply the requisite intent.

Aggravated assault. As with batteries, assaults may be charged in an aggravated form. Acts such as assault with intent to kill or to rape are punishable as felonies rather than misdemeanors. Many statutes provide that the use of a deadly weapon automatically creates an aggravated assault. What constitutes a deadly weapon, however, is not always certain. Most courts hold that a dangerous weapon per se is an instrumentality designed and constructed to produce death or great bodily harm. Thus, a riding crop is not a dangerous weapon per se even though it may be used to inflict excessive bodily harm. The riding crop may still be a dangerous weapon, however, if the trier of fact decides that it has been used in a way that makes it dangerous. Guns are almost always considered dangerous weapons per se.

Defenses to assault and battery

Although one is usually liable for committing either an assault or a battery when he commits the elements discussed above, there are defenses to both crimes. Perhaps the most popular defense is the claim of self-defense. The defendant will argue that he committed the assault or the battery only because it was necessary to protect himself from attack. In other situations the defendant may seek to prove that he acted properly to protect another from harm. Although that person may have been touched in a forcible or offensive way, the defendant's actions are justified because they were prompted by a desire to help or rescue the person who was in a dangerous situation.

The consent defense is claimed where the victim permits the defendant to commit certain acts. The issue of consent often arises in cases involving sexual assaults, where the victim alleges that an attack occurred, and the defendant claims consent was given. In other areas, consent may also act as a defense to a charge of assault and battery, such as a situation in which the defendant grabs someone while playacting. Many courts, however, hold that consent is no defense when the act violates public policy, especially when the battery is severe. Hence, a battery is normally committed when two people agree to fight each other.

The issue of consent has become very important in the areas of sports and domestic relationships. In sports, the issue is whether excessive violence in a game exposes players to criminal liability. Although the elements of battery are present, it is argued that the players consent to these actions before the game starts. Consent is presumed by the players' participation in the sport. The question remaining is to what specific acts the players have given their consent. When some participants become rougher than may be reasonably necessary, can it be assumed that an injured player consented to this violence? There is as yet no definite answer to this, but as more

sports-related prosecutions are brought, the answers will undoubtedly be forthcoming.

Interest in prosecuting domestic batteries has increased greatly as awareness of the problem developed. It is clear that in most domestic battery cases there is no actual consent given, so that consent should not operate as a defense to a criminal offense. The mere fact that the defendant was married to the victim should not operate as a defense. Still, government officials are properly reluctant to prosecute routinely in this area because of the presence in many cases of more appropriate forums for the resolution of disputes.

The common law crimes of assault and battery raise many interesting and difficult questions involving the elements of the offenses, the defenses to them, and the situations in which they should be charged. Perhaps most important is the need to clarify the societal interest in imposing criminal sanctions on such activities. Particularly when the defendant has not seriously injured the victim or did not intend adverse consequences, the civil tort remedy may be a preferable way of dealing with the problem.

PAUL MARCUS
DAN M. KAHAN

See also ATTEMPT.

BIBLIOGRAPHY

American Law Institute. *Model Penal Code: Tentative Draft No. 10.* Philadelphia: ALI, 1960.
American Law Institute. *Model Penal Code and Commentaries: Official Draft and Revised Commentaries.* 3 vols. Philadelphia: ALI, 1985.
HANSON CALVERT, LINDA S., and DERNIS, CRAIG. "Revisiting Excessive Violence in the Professional Sports Arena: Changes in the Past Twenty Years?" Seton Hall J. Sport L. 6 (1996): 127–166.
KEETON, W. PAGE. *Prosser and Keeton on the Law of Torts.* 5th ed. St. Paul: West, 1984.
LaFAVE, WAYNE R., and SCOTT, AUSTIN W., JR. *Handbook on Criminal Law.* St. Paul: West, 1972.
Note. "Consent in Criminal Law: Violence in Sports." *Michigan Law Review* 75 (1976): 148–179.
PERKINS, ROLLIN M. "An Analysis of Assault and Attempts to Assault." *Minnesota Law Review* 47 (1962): 71–91.

———. "Non-homicide Offenses against the Person." *Boston University Law Review* 25 (1946): 119–206.

ATTEMPT

To be punishable as a criminal attempt, conduct must consist of an intent to perform an act or to bring about a result that would constitute a crime, together with some substantial steps taken in furtherance of that intent. This article describes the historical development of criminal liability for attempts, the policies served (and disserved) by punishment in attempt cases, and the current scope of liability for attempts in American law.

History

There was no general crime of attempt in the early English common law. Historians have uncovered scattered decisions, dating back as far as the fourteenth century, in which courts did convict of felony the perpetrator of an unsuccessful attempt. But punishment of attempts was at the most sporadic, and was limited to cases in which rather serious harm had occurred in any event. During the sixteenth century, the Court of Star Chamber began to correct perceived shortcomings in the common law, by affording needed remedies that were unavailable in the common law courts. Cases involving attempts to coin money, threats, and attempted dueling were held punishable in the Star Chamber. The court apparently did not develop a general doctrine of criminal attempts, however (Hall, pp. 561, 567–568).

The Court of Star Chamber was abolished in 1641, and historians disagree about whether its jurisprudence had any influence on subsequent developments (cf. Sayre, p. 829; Meehan, pp. 153–154; Hall, p. 569). In any event, more than a century elapsed before anything like the modern theory of attempt was suggested in the common law courts. The first decision of consequence, *Rex v. Scofield,* Cald. 397 (1784), held that the defendant was properly charged with a misdemeanor for an unsuccessful attempt to burn down a house. Subsequently, in *Rex v. Higgins,* 102 Eng. Rep. 269, 275 (K.B. 1801), the court upheld an indictment charging an unsuccessful attempt to steal and stated in broad terms that "all such acts or attempts as tend to the prejudice of the community, are indictable."

The principle enunciated in *Higgins* was quickly accepted by courts and commentators, and it was soon considered settled that an attempt to commit either a felony or a misdemeanor was itself indictable as a crime. This remains the rule in the United States. In most jurisdictions, the rule is reflected in statutes specifying the punishment applicable to cases of attempt. The term *attempt* itself, however, is often left undefined, so that its meaning must be drawn from common law sources. In a few jurisdictions, the penal statutes may not provide explicitly for punishing criminal attempts, but such attempts nevertheless remain punishable as "common law crimes," unless the law of the jurisdiction requires that all criminal offenses be defined by statute.

Why did the law punishing attempts develop so slowly, and why did the general theory of attempts win acceptance only in relatively recent times? Part of the explanation lies in the availability, probably throughout history, of other means for dealing with threatening or dangerous behavior. In earlier times dangerous persons could be required to give a pledge as a guarantee of good behavior, under the systems of frankpledge and of surety for the peace. Moreover, some substantive crimes, such as vagrancy or unlawful assembly, could be used to punish attempt-like behavior, and such offenses as assault and burglary were undoubtedly developed as a means of reaching conduct that was merely preparatory to the infliction of actual harm. Even today, many statutes treat as completed substantive crimes conduct that involves only steps toward the commission of some specific offense, for example, possession of burglary tools with intent to commit burglary. A general crime of attempt was, and is, necessary only to the extent that there remain gaps in the network of substantive offenses relating to specific kinds of attempts.

Another factor in the belated acceptance of attempt principles may have been a tendency to view criminal law as concerned primarily with vengeance or retaliation. At the earlier stages of common law development, crime and tort were not yet neatly differentiated. Even though public prosecution and punishment now have become distinct from the private lawsuit to recover damages, the retaliatory principle—an eye for an eye—may still figure prominently in attitudes about punishment.

Policies

Why should the criminal justice system trouble itself to prosecute and punish persons whose conduct has not actually harmed other individuals or society generally? The question is important not only for appreciating the theoretical underpinnings of attempt crimes but also for understanding the various rules that govern the scope of attempted liability under prevailing legal doctrine.

For those modern theorists who view the criminal process as centered on a principle of retaliation for damage inflicted on society, punishment for attempt must remain a mystery or, perhaps, an unjustified aberration. Some writers, such as Lawrence Becker, have suggested that the attempt does actually injure society because the very real threat of harm upsets the social equilibrium and gives rise to a sense of tension or disorder (pp. 273–276). This insight applies particularly to situations involving highly dangerous and widely observed threats. The notion does not, however, afford a fully satisfying explanation for attempt liability. The importance of punishment in attempt cases usually seems much more closely tied to the gravity of the threatened harm than it is to an elusive "actual" harm associated with a disturbance of the social equilibrium.

Attempt liability therefore seems more plausibly explained, and justified, by reference to the forward-looking purposes of punishment—deterrence of future crime, restraint of the dangerous offender, and rehabilitation. The deterrence justification has been somewhat controversial and remains perhaps only a subsidiary justification for attempt liability. Some scholars suggest that punishing attempts cannot add significantly to the deterrent efficacy of the criminal law, because the person punished was in any event willing to risk the sanction authorized for the completed crime, which by hypothesis he intended to commit (Model Penal Code, 1960, commentary on § 5.05: Michael and Wechsler, pp. 1295–1298). The point cannot, of course, hold true for those crimes that, when successfully committed, are likely to go undetected (a "perfect" murder) or unpunished (treason is the classic example). Putting aside these relatively unusual examples, there remain many recurrent situations (such as "victimless" crimes investigated by police decoys), in which the penalties applicable to an attempt could significantly affect the calculus of risks involved in a given criminal plan (Schulhofer, pp. 1538–1539).

Restraint and rehabilitation appear to be the principal functions of punishment for attempt. A criminal attempt manifests a disposition toward dangerous behavior that often warrants confinement of the offender to protect the public and to permit rehabilitative efforts if possible. The man who shoots to kill but misses might in a sense be less dangerous than one who kills on the first shot (because the latter may appear a more skilled marksman), but both pose substantial threats to society. Indeed, the man whose attempt has failed may actually be more dangerous, since if not restrained he might try again to harm the intended victim.

Practical considerations of law enforcement reinforce these broad concerns of penal policy. Police on patrol should have power to investigate suspicious activity and, if possible, to prevent injury from being inflicted. If an officer observes someone about to commit a crime, he can warn the individual and, under some circumstances, detain him temporarily, but the officer would have no power to arrest the person unless there was probable cause to believe that a crime had already been committed. The law of attempts and related attempt-like crimes permits police officers to intervene effectively in potentially dangerous situations before serious, often irreparable, injury has occurred.

This "early intervention" function in attempt law draws attention to the dangers that accompany a vigorous extension of criminal liability for attempts. The law of crimes must not only provide for punishment when useful and otherwise justified, but must serve to safeguard *from* punishment those individuals whose behavior does not warrant criminal sanctions. This latter, safeguarding function has been associated with a tradition of limitations on the proper scope of criminal responsibility, including two notions particularly relevant here—reluctance to impose criminal liability in the absence of personal culpability, and an insistence that the behavior subject to criminal sanctions be clearly specified by standards that are reasonably ascertainable in advance. Both of these limiting notions can be infringed by expansive liability for attempts.

The culpability notion limits punishment to those whose conduct is morally blameworthy, in the sense that they have consciously chosen to do an act that society regards as wrong. Although the criminal law sometimes departs from the culpability requirement (strict liability offenses are an example), there is usually a sense that such departures are at best unfortunate and narrowly circumscribed exceptions. A penal law that authorized restraint and rehabilitation of any person identified as dangerous to society would in effect create a general power of preventive detention, in direct violation of the culpability requirement. Yet is this not precisely what occurs in the law of attempts? Attempt doctrine can escape the moral objections to general preventive detention, but only when the evil intentions are accompanied by definite acts (for without acts there has been no exercise of choice), and only when the acts proceed far enough to involve clearly culpable threats rather than blameless fantasy. The preceding concern prompts an unwillingness to punish all preparatory behavior as a criminal attempt, but courts and legislatures have been unable to delineate with precision the point at which preparations have gone far enough to warrant criminal liability. As a result, the behavior punishable as an attempt often cannot be distinguished readily from noncriminal preparation. Liability turns on a standard whose application cannot always be predicted reliably in advance.

Although attempt liability thus appears solidly grounded in the restraining and rehabilitating functions of the criminal law and, to a lesser extent, in the deterrent function, the concerns just mentioned have prompted some uneasiness about imposing criminal responsibility for attempts. As a result, legal doctrine continues to erect complex limitations on the scope of liability for unsuccessful efforts to commit crime.

Modern law

To indicate the scope of liability for attempts in modern American law, the following will be considered: (1) the required state of mind, or mens rea; (2) the required acts, or actus reus; (3) liability when the offender desists before completing the intended crime (the problem of "abandonment"); (4) liability when the accused could not possibly carry out the intended crime (the problem of "impossibility"); and (5) the severity of punishment for attempt (the problem of "grading").

The mens rea. A criminal attempt is traditionally defined as an intent to perform an act or to bring about a result that would constitute a crime, together with some substantial steps taken in furtherance of the intent. In accordance with this definition, it is apparent that the state of mind, or mens rea, required is the actual intent or purpose to achieve the proscribed result; mere recklessness or negligence will not suffice.

The usual requirements of intention or purpose can appear anomalous when the many situations are considered in which the *completed*

crime may be committed by recklessness, negligence, or even on a strict-liability basis. Suppose, for example, that a construction worker dynamites a hillside, with no intent to kill anyone, but with a reckless disregard for the lives of people residing nearby. If one of those people is killed by the explosion, the worker will be guilty of murder; recklessness is sufficient for liability. However, if the person injured by the explosion eventually recovers, the worker would not be guilty of murder and could not even be convicted of attempted murder because he was merely reckless and did not *intend* to kill.

How can this gap in attempts liability be explained? If in the event of death, the conduct should be punished as murder, then why does the identical behavior not remain a proper subject of penal sanctions when the victim luckily survives? One answer is definitional. An attempt, by the very meaning of the word, implies that the actor was *trying* to achieve the forbidden result, and this simply cannot be said of the construction worker. This view does not leave us with a very satisfying reason for not punishing the conduct, but rather focuses on the inelegance of referring to the conduct as an "attempt."

Some legislatures have relaxed to a limited degree the requirement of purpose or intention. one approach has been to create a specific offense of reckless endangerment, so that such conduct need not be prosecuted as an attempt (Pa. Cons. Stat. Ann. § 2705 (1983)).

The actus reus. The courts hold that certain preliminary activities, designated "mere preparation," are not punishable even when accompanied by the requisite intent. Attempt liability attaches only when the defendant goes beyond mere preparation and begins to carry out the planned crime.

How can one determine the location of this line dividing mere preparation from the punishable attempt? Suppose, for example, that a defendant announces his desire to blow up the office of a former employer, collects a supply of matches, old newspaper, and kerosene, buys dynamite and a long fuse, places the dynamite and other material in the building, and finally lights the fuse. At what point in this sequence of events has the defendant committed a punishable attempt? Cases confronting such questions have invoked a considerable variety of analytic devices and have come to widely divergent results. The most important approaches are those requiring either commission of the last necessary act, commission of an act proximate to the result, or commission of an act that unequivocally confirms the actor's intent. The Model Penal Code's approach combines elements of these three. After discussing these approaches, this section considers one other actus reus problem, the possibility of punishing "attempts to attempt."

The last-act test.   Under the last-act test, suggested in *Regina v. Eagleton,* 6 E. Cox, Crim. Cas. 559 (C.C.A.) (London, 1855), the disgruntled employee in the example above would be guilty of attempt only after lighting the fuse. At that point, although the attempt may still miscarry, the actor has done everything that appears necessary to carry it through to completion. The last-act test is designed not only to ensure that the defendant's intent is serious, but also to provide an incentive for him to desist by enabling him to avoid liability right up to the last possible moment. The last-act test seems much too strict, however, in terms of the "early intervention" function of attempt law. A defendant who follows a victim, draws a gun, and takes careful aim could not be charged with attempt, because he had yet to pull the trigger. For these reasons, no contemporary court would insist strictly upon commission of the last necessary act (Model Penal Code, 1960, commentary on § 5.01). Attempt liability attaches at an earlier point, and the needed incentive to desist is provided by a separate defense of "abandonment," discussed below.

The proximity test.   To avoid the practical difficulties of the last-act test, many courts apply a "proximity" test requiring only that a defendant's preparatory actions come rather close to completion of the intended crime. But how close is close enough? Two examples will indicate the difficulties of the proximity test. In *Commonwealth v. Peaslee,* 177 Mass. 267, 59 N.E. 55 (1901), the defendant arranged combustible material in a building and left. Later, intending to set off the blaze, he drove within a quarter mile of the building and then decided to turn back. Writing for the court, Justice Oliver Wendell Holmes suggested that this might be a punishable attempt. In *People v. Rizzo,* 246 N.Y. 334, 158 N.E. 888 (1927), the defendants spent considerable time driving around the streets of New York searching for a payroll clerk whom they intended to rob. The police arrested them before they could find the clerk, but the New York Court of Appeals held that this was not a punishable attempt. In such cases, courts may be thinking of proximity primarily in a physical or spatial sense; in *Peaslee* the defendant had driven most of the way to the building, whereas in *Rizzo* the payroll clerk

was never located at all and the defendants seemingly never came "close" to actually putting their plan into action. However, this sort of spatial proximity is not only hard to specify, but totally unrelated to the purposes of attempt law. Preliminary acts should become punishable when they establish that the intent is likely to be put into action, that the individual is sufficiently dangerous to require restraint, and that there is a dangerous probability of success requiring deterrence and early police intervention. From all of these perspectives the case for punishment is at least as strong in *Rizzo;* indeed, the defendant in *Peaslee* was, if anything, *less* deserving of punishment because he apparently chose voluntarily to abandon his plan. Some courts have attempted to adapt the proximity test more satisfactorily to the purposes of attempt law by focusing on whether the acts involve a dangerous proximity to success or demonstrate that the actor was unlikely to desist, but these approaches also prove difficult to apply with objectivity and consistency.

The equivocality approach.   Reluctance to punish "mere preparation" is based in part on concern that very preliminary acts may not confirm that the defendant seriously plans to put his intent into action. Accordingly, some authorities have suggested that to be punishable, a preliminary act must be "of such a nature as to be in itself sufficient evidence of the criminal intent with which it is done. A criminal attempt is an act which shows criminal intent on the face of it" (*Rex v. Barker,* [1924] N.Z.L.R. 865, 874 (C.A.)). American cases sometimes appear to speak approvingly of this requirement that the acts unequivocally confirm the criminal intent, and this approach does in theory appear consistent with the purposes of attempt law. Nevertheless, the equivocality approach, if applied literally, would often prove even stricter than the last-act approach. A defendant might approach a haystack, fill his pipe, light a match, light the pipe, and perhaps even toss the match on the haystack. The acts alone are not wholly unequivocal, but it is hard to imagine a court holding that regardless of any other evidence of intent, the acts themselves do not go far enough (Williams, p. 630).

The Model Penal Code approach. The Model Penal Code borrows from the concepts of proximity and equivocality but treats both in rather flexible fashion. Less suspicious of confessions and other direct evidence of intent, the Code relaxes the traditional insistence on very substantial preparation. Under the Code, an attempt must include "an act or omission constituting a substantial step in a course of conduct planned to culminate in . . . commission of the crime" (1962, § 5.01(1)(c)). The substantial-step requirement reflects proximity notions, but shifts the emphasis from the significance of the acts still required to the significance of what the defendant has already done. The Code also specifies that an act cannot be deemed a "substantial step" "unless it is strongly corroborative of the actor's criminal purpose" (§ 5.01(2)). The Code thus incorporates the concerns underlying the equivocality test, without being burdened by the impractical rigidity of that approach.

Attempts to attempt. Many substantive crimes are in effect attempts to commit some other offense. Assault, for example, is essentially an attempt to commit a battery; burglary (breaking and entering a structure with intent to commit a felony therein) is essentially an attempt to commit some other felony. Sometimes a defendant is charged with attempted assault or attempted burglary will argue that the alleged conduct should not be punishable because it amounts to no more than an attempt to attempt. Such arguments may suppose the conceptual impossibility of such an offense, or they may reflect the view that conduct not amounting to an attempt is necessarily "mere preparation." Neither position is plausible. Concerns about imposing attempt liability at an excessively early point need to be faced, but in principle there is no reason why preparations to commit burglary, for example, might not pass the realm of mere preparation, even though the burglary itself was not successfully perpetrated. Consider the case of a masked man caught in the act of picking the lock of an apartment door. In such a case, a charge of attempted burglary is clearly justified, and the courts so hold (Model Penal Code, 1960, commentary on § 5.01).

Abandonment. Once the defendant's conduct has moved from "mere preparation" into the realm of a punishable attempt, can he nevertheless avoid liability if he has a genuine change of heart and decides to abandon his plan? Many cases appear to give a negative answer to this question. Just as a defendant who has stolen property cannot avoid liability by making restitution, the courts often say that once the defendant's attempt goes far enough to be punishable, a crime has been committed and subsequent actions cannot change that fact, although they may have a bearing on the appropriate sentence (Perkins, pp. 319, 354).

Whatever the logic of this view, one of its consequences is to reinforce traditional objections to imposing liability at relatively early stages of preparatory conduct. In the absence of an abandonment defense, early liability eliminates a significant incentive to desist and appears unfair to the defendant who has had a genuine change of heart, as in *Peaslee*. Such concerns generate pressure to reject early liability even when there is no hint of possible abandonment by the defendants in the case actually at hand, as in *Rizzo*. In short, in the absence of an abandonment defense, the line between preparation and attempt may fall so early as to seem unfair to the defendant who voluntarily abandons his plan, yet fall too late to meet proper law enforcement objectives with respect to the defendant who apparently would have carried his plan through to completion.

One way to avoid this dilemma is to recognize that voluntary abandonment is a complete defense to a charge of criminal attempt. Although the common law decisions appear unsettled or in conflict with respect to the status of such a defense (Rotenberg, pp. 596–597), many statutory codifications have adopted it. For example, a New York statute (N.Y. Penal Law (McKinney) § 40.10(3)(1998)) provides a defense to an attempt charge when "under circumstances manifesting a voluntary and complete renunciation of his criminal purpose, the defendant avoided commission of the crime attempted" (cf. Model Penal Code, 1962, § 5.01(4)).

In jurisdictions that recognize an abandonment defense, it is necessary to determine when the abandonment is genuinely "voluntary." Given the rationale of the defense, it seems clear that abandonment should not be considered voluntary when prompted by realization that the police or the victim have detected the plan, or when the defendant is simply postponing the attempt until a more favorable opportunity presents itself. The Model Penal Code provides that "renunciation of criminal purpose is not voluntary if it is motivated in whole or in part, by circumstances, not present or apparent at the inception of the actor's course of conduct, which increase the probability of detection or apprehension or which make more difficult the accomplishment of the criminal purpose" (1962, § 5.01(4)).

Impossibility. Courts and commentators have struggled for generations over the question whether an accused should be punishable for attempt when, for reasons unknown to the defendant, the intended offense could not possibly be committed successfully under the circumstances. The problem arises in a great variety of settings. The accused, for example, may attempt to kill with a pistol that is unloaded of defective, or he may shoot at an inanimate decoy rather than at the intended victim. A would-be pickpocket may reach into an empty pocket, or a drug dealer may purchase talcum powder, believing it to be narcotics.

Some courts have sought to resolve such cases by distinguishing between "legal" and "factual" impossibility. Factual impossibility is said to arise when some extraneous circumstances unknown to the defendant prevents consummation of the crime, and in this situation the attempt is punishable. Legal impossibility, on the other hand, arises when the intended acts, even if completed, would not amount to a crime, and it is said that in this situation the attempt should not be punishable.

In application, these concepts of legal and factual impossibility have proved elusive and unmanageable. In one case involving a charge of attempt to smuggle letters out of prison without the knowledge of the warden, the plot was discovered by the warden, although the accused remained ignorant of this fact. The court treated the case as one of legal impossibility and reversed the conviction for attempt (*United States v. Berrigan*, 482 F.2d 171 (3d Cir. 1973)). It is apparent, however, that the situation could as readily be characterized as one of factual impossibility, and the same is true of attempts to pick an empty pocket, to shoot at a dead body believed to be alive, and so on. Some commentators have sought to clarify the categories by introducing further distinctions between "intrinsic" and "extrinsic" factual impossibility (Comment, pp. 160–162). One court has suggested a still more sophisticated taxonomy involving six ostensibly distinct categories (*Regina v. Donnelly*, (1970) N.Z.L.R. 980, 990 (C.A.)).

All of these efforts at classification ultimately founder, however, because generally speaking the reasons for punishing unsuccessful attempts apply as much to one category as to any of the others. When the defendant has fired at a decoy or used an unloaded weapon, the circumstances may, of course, raise a question about whether he actually intended to kill, but the question of intent must be faced and resolved with care in every type of "possible" or "impossible" attempt. In fact, the use of undercover agents or cleverly disguised decoys may provide particularly reliable *confirmation* of intent, even though such tactics would arguably raise a problem of "legal impossibility" under some of the traditional taxonomies. So long as it can be proved that the accused acted with intent to commit the offense and that his conduct would constitute the crime if the circumstances had been as he believed them to be, the defendant is just as culpable and in general just as dangerous as the defendant who successfully consummates the offense. Nearly all of the modern statutory codifications have taken this view, specifying that neither factual nor legal impossibility is a defense "if such crime could have been committed had the attendant circumstances been as such person believed them to be" (N.Y. Penal Law (McKinney) § 110.10 (1998)).

There remains one type of "legal impossibility" that fails to satisfy the proviso just quoted. Suppose that the accused has attempted to smuggle expensive lace past a customs officer but that (unknown to the accused) this item has recently been removed from the lists of goods subject to duty. Here, even if the accused had accomplished everything he set out to do, his acts will not violate any provision of law. It is true that the accused thought he would be committing a crime, but since the goal he seeks to achieve is not in fact prohibited, the purposes of attempt law do not call for punishment (Kadish and Paulsen, pp. 362–366). In this type of situation, sometimes called a case of "genuine" legal impossibility, the attempt would not be punishable even under revised statutory provisions that otherwise reject both factual and legal impossibility as defenses.

Grading.   Statutory provisions specifying the penalty applicable to a criminal attempt vary widely among American jurisdictions. A specific punishment may be provided for all attempts, or different penalty ranges may be specified according to the seriousness of the crime attempted. Under some statutes, for example, the maximum penalty is one-half that provided for the completed crime. Although a few states provide for the same maximum penalty for attempt and for the corresponding completed crime, this approach still appears to be the minority view; despite other variations in detail, in most jurisdictions an attempt will be punished much less severely than the completed crime (Model Penal Code, 1960, appendixes A and B to § 5.05).

What is the justification of this prevalent grading pattern? Relative leniency seems appropriate in the case of the defendants who have crossed beyond the domain of "mere preparation" but who nevertheless have yet to carry out every step that appears necessary to consummate the crime. When the attempt is incomplete in this sense, the intent and the dangerousness demonstrated are inevitably more ambiguous than when the actor has taken the decisive final step. Moreover, the lower penalty preserves some incentive for the actor to avert the threatened harm, even when he may be unable to meet the requirements for a complete defense of voluntary abandonment.

In contrast, the prevalent pattern of leniency for attempts appears difficult to justify when the defendant has carried out every step that appears necessary for successful completion of the offense, as, for example, when a defendant shoots at someone intending to kill, but the victim survives the wounds inflicted. In such a case the difference between a successful consummation of the crime and an unsuccessful attempt may result from fortuitous factors wholly beyond the control of the actor, and the sharp difference in applicable penalties appears anomalous.

It is sometimes suggested that the successful actor may be more dangerous or more culpable than the one whose attempt fails. Neither of these arguments can be considered valid over the general range of attempt situations (Schulhofer, pp. 1514–1517, 1588–1599). The Model Penal Code accepts that premise, and concludes that generally the maximum penalty for attempt should equal that for the completed crime. The Code provides, however, that in the case of the most serious felonies the penalty for attempt should be less severe than for the completed offense (1962, § 5.05(1)). The rationale for this limited exception to the general approach of equal treatment is that in this situation the use of severe sanctions can be minimized without impairing the deterrent efficacy of the law (Model Penal Code, 1960, commentary on § 5.05). The Model Penal Code rationale turns out to depend on a number of complex and problematic assumptions. Although the Code's goal of limiting the use of the most severe sanctions appears attractive, it proves difficult to show with any degree of generality that the Code's approach in fact has this effect; leniency for unsuccessful attempts may instead work to perpetuate unnecessarily severe and vindictively harsh sentences in the case of completed crimes (Schulhofer, pp. 1562–1585).

Intuitively, the most plausible explanation for more lenient treatment of attempts is that the community's resentment and demand for pun-

ishment are not aroused to the same degree when serious harm has been averted. This explanation, however, raises further questions. Can severe punishment (in the case of completed crime, for example) be justified simply by reference to the fact that society "demands" or at least desires this? To what extent should the structure of penalties serve to express intuitive societal judgments that cannot be rationalized in terms of such instrumental goals as deterrence, isolation, rehabilitation, and even retribution—that is, condemnation reflecting the moral culpability of the act? Conversely, to what extent should the criminal justice system see its mission as one not of expressing the intuitive social demand for punishment, but rather as one of restraining that demand and of protecting *from* punishment the offender who, rationally speaking, deserves a less severe penalty? Answers to these questions must be sought beyond the confines of attempt doctrine, for they reflect wider problems of democratic theory and normative political philosophy.

STEPHEN J. SCHULHOFER
DAN M. KAHAN

See also ASSAULT AND BATTERY; CONSPIRACY; SOLICITATION.

BIBLIOGRAPHY

American Law Institute. *Model Penal Code: Proposed Official Draft*. Philadelphia: ALI, 1962.
———. *Model Penal Code: Tenative Draft No. 10*. Philadelphia: ALI, 1960.
BEN-SHAHAR, OMRI, and HAREL, ALON. "The Economics of the Law of Criminal Attempts: A Victim-centered Perspective." *University of Pennsylvania Law Review* 145 (1996): 299–351.
BECKER, LAWRENCE C. "Criminal Attempt and the Theory of the Law of Crimes." *Philosophy and Public Affairs* 3 (1974): 262–294.
Comment. "Why Do Criminal Attempts Fail?: A New Defense." *Yale Law Journal* 70 (1960): 160–169.
DAVIS, MICHAEL. "Why Attempts Deserve Less Punishment than Complete Crimes." L. & Phil. 5 (1986): 1–32.
DUFF, R. ANTHONY. *Criminal Attempts*. New York: Oxford University Press, 1996.
HALL, JEROME. *General Principles of Criminal Law*. 2d ed. Indianapolis: Bobbs-Merrill, 1960.
KADISH, SANFORD H., and SCHULHOFER, STEPHEN. *Criminal Law and Its Processes: Cases and Materials*. 6th ed. Boston: Little, Brown, 1995.

MEEHAN, EUGENE R. "The Trying Problem of Criminal Attempt: Historical Perspectives." *University of British Columbia Law Review* 14 (1979): 137–161.

MICHAEL, JEROME, and WECHSLER, HERBERT. "A Rationale of the Law of Homicide." *Columbia Law Review* 37 (1937): 701–761, 1261–1325.

PERKINS, ROLLIN M. "Criminal Attempt and Related Problems." *UCLA Law Review* 2 (1955): 319–355.

ROTENBERG, DANIEL L. "Withdrawal as a Defense to Relational Crimes." *Wisconsin Law Review* (1962): 596–607.

SAYRE, FRANCIS B. "Criminal Attempts." *Harvard Law Review* 41 (1928): 821–859.

SCHULHOFER, STEPHEN J. "Harm and Punishment: A Critique of Emphasis on the Results of Conduct in the Criminal Law." *University of Pennsylvania Law Review* 122 (1974): 1497–1607.

SHAVELL, STEVEN. "Deterrence and the Punishment of Attempts." *J. Leg. Stud.* 19 (1990): 435–466.

WILLIAMS, GLANVILLE. *Criminal Law: The General Part.* 2d ed. London: Stevens, 1961.

B

BAIL

A common description of the American criminal process begins with the arrest of a person accused of crime who, after booking and possible interrogation by the police, is brought before a judge or judicial officer to have bail set. At this first judicial appearance, the judicial officer may read the charges to the accused, explain the need for and availability of counsel, schedule the defendant's next court date and then set an amount of bail that the defendant must post to gain release before trial. In popular understanding, bail is thought of as a dollar amount and *bail system* refers to the decision process and financial arrangements, often through bondsmen (compensated sureties), that determine release or confinement of defendants, before adjudication of their charges in the courts.

This traditional picture of bail, associating pretrial release with dollars to be paid by the defendant, represents a narrow conception of the bail function. With a history traced back to the Magna Carta, the statute of Westminster, and the emergence of English common law, bail originally had a broader meaning. Rather than denoting the practice of requiring an amount of currency or other form of financial assets from an accused for release, bail referred to the means employed to provide assurance that a person accused of a crime would face judicial proceedings. Depending on the historical epoch, this assurance could take different forms, from a person's oath to be present to stand trial when the judge made his appearance in the village or town, to placing an individual's property (such as cattle or other domestic animals) or the property of a close relation in the temporary custody of a local official to obtain greater certainty that an individual would be present for the judicial proceedings.

In the United States over the last century, with the growth of population centers and industrialization—and with the increasingly impersonal and anonymous nature of urban life—an individual's word or deposit of valued property was deemed insufficient to ensure that the defendant would appear for trial and submit to the judgment of the court. As the use of arrangements once workable in smaller, more rural societies became less practical, they were increasingly replaced by the use of *cash bail* to guarantee a defendant's release. The dollar became the currency for determining pretrial release or detention in America—in the form of cash bail or bond. The defendant's prospects for remaining free during adjudication were increasingly shaped by the economics of the larger, and more urban, society. Those who remained in jail before trial were persons who could not afford to post the dollar amount that had been set, while those who gained release somehow could. Dollars became the judge's assessment of the defendant's trustworthiness—of the likelihood that the defendant would attend court if released. The ability to post the required cash became the determinant of pretrial release.

The emphasis on financial terms in determining pretrial release or detention also created an irresistible opportunity for private entrepreneurs to enter the judicial process. For profit, *bondsmen* (more formally referred to as *compensated sureties*) could broker the release of detained defendants who could not afford their bail by being paid a premium (usually around 10 percent of the total bail). A defendant held in custody on $10,000 bail, for example, would pay a bondsman $1,000 to gain release before trial. In an adaptation of the earlier practice of having third parties vouch for the released defendant's appearance in court, the bondsman would guarantee the appearance of the defendant in court by putting up a surety bond. In exchange for the premium exacted from the defendant, the bondsman would in theory be responsible to the court for the defendant's entire bail in the event the defendant fled prosecution. This practice was based on the expectation that bondsmen would act as responsible third parties and make certain their clients would appear in court—for fear of having to forfeit the total amount of bail. At the same time, based on profit motive, bondsmen would have a strong incentive to write bonds for jailed defendants—and thus facilitate responsible release—because the premiums they accepted amounted to clear earnings, as long as the defendants appeared.

Advocates of *bail reform* questioned this primarily financial conception of the bail function, preferring to consider the bail decision as a *pretrial release decision*. In making the pretrial release decision instead of focusing on the dollars required for release, a judicial officer should determine whether the individual will await adjudication of criminal charges at liberty in the community, and if so under what conditions, or remain in jail under pretrial detention. Reform measures introduced in the 1960s sought to encourage greater use by judges of nonfinancial conditions of release in pretrial release determinations. These initiatives placed great emphasis on personal recognizance release (ROR or "release on own recognizance") and on conditions of supervision or participation in release programs that would help to ensure the defendant's appearance in court. Sparked by the pioneering efforts of the Vera Institute in New York City, bail reform advocates also promoted the establishment of pretrial services agencies to collect information about defendants for the pretrial release decision and to supervise them, if necessary, during the release period.

The purposes of the bail or pretrial release decision

Harsh criticism of bail practices occurred during most of the twentieth century, dating at least from the 1920s when Roscoe Pound, Felix Frankfurter, and others studied criminal justice in Cleveland, and Arthur Beeley studied the jail in Chicago. Caleb Foote's classic study of the

Philadelphia bail system and his sequel focusing on practices in the New York courts during the 1950s set the stage for the bail reform movement of the early 1960s. The body of criticism that grew over the last century excoriated the traditional cash bail system and the use of pretrial detention it fostered. The criticism questioned the legitimacy of the uses to which the bail decision was put, the existence of its highly discretionary exercise, the fairness of its application, and, even, its effectiveness.

Three purposes of the pretrial release decision are recognized in the United States at the beginning of the twenty-first century (American Bar Association). The two principal aims, to ensure a defendant's appearance in court and to protect the community from dangerous defendants, are related to a third, more general purpose, maintaining the integrity of the judicial process by preventing interference with victims or witnesses. The laws in many but not all American jurisdictions refer to both the appearance and community-protection aims of pretrial release decisions, if not necessarily the third purpose. However, explicit recognition of a community protection or "danger" agenda in law is a relatively recent development and has been the subject of debate discussed later in this entry.

Until the last decades of the twentieth century, judges or magistrates determined whether a defendant would be confined while awaiting trial with little statutory guidance. Moreover, this all-important liberty decision to release or confine the accused person through the device of cash bail was most often made by the lowest ranking local judicial official—sometimes a misdemeanor court judge, but often a quasi-judicial officer, magistrate, commissioner, or justice not trained in law. When guidance for that decision was provided, state and federal law concerned itself more with how (procedure) to decide bail than with why, and did not refer to a community protection goal. The language of the Eighth Amendment of the U.S. Constitution—"excessive bail shall not be required"—offered no guidance as to the purpose of bail.

In the 1960s, early proponents of bail reform argued that the only constitutionally acceptable purpose of bail was to ensure a defendant's appearance in court (Goldkamp, 1979). Reformers were critical of the then-existing bad system that they believed operated sub rosa to confine defendants perceived to be dangerous, an unconstitutional agenda in their view. The sub rosa detention system, framed in financial terms, resulted in the confinement of a great many poor defendants, based on anticipated future unlawful conduct, and on a subjective judicial prediction of dangerousness that broadly prejudged a defendant's guilt. At the same time, critics argued that when defendants were able to post the cash required, the cash-bail mechanism provided little incentive to defendants to return to court because their money was not refundable when paid to a bondman. To critics, cash bail and the bondsman's fee amounted to a way for defendants to purchase their release before trial, a sort of "ransom" for their freedom (Goldfarb), regardless of their intentions relating to court. The petty thief might not be able to raise a small amount of bail, while the drug dealer could produce large amounts of cash quite easily to gain release. Reform-minded critics advocated a system based less on financial considerations and more on nonfinancial methods for encouraging attendance, and rejected the argument that community safety was a legitimate concern for the release decision.

Opponents of the reform position agreed that an essential aim of pretrial release decisions was to ensure court attendance. However, they insisted that the bail decision had always also concerned itself legitimately with the public safety aim of protecting the community from dangerous defendants. Proponents of the public safety agenda asserted that too many "dangerous" defendants were being released to commit serious crimes in the community.

The preceding 1960s debate about the legitimate purpose(s) of bail was based on competing interpretations of the historical origins of bail in English common law. In looking for guidance from case law, both sides drew on Supreme Court decisions from the early 1950s: *Stack v. Boyle* (342 U.S. 1 (1951)) supported the reformers' appearance view and *Carlson v. Landon* (342 U.S. 524 (1952)) supported the danger-prevention function.

In *Stack*, the Supreme Court wrote that release before trial was "conditioned upon the accused's giving assurance that he will stand trial and submit to punishment if found guilty," and that bail "must be based on standards relevant to the purpose of assuring the presence of defendants." In *Carlson*, a (noncriminal) deportation proceeding involving the detention without bond of aliens, the Supreme Court appeared to condone a "danger" goal by approving the right of the state to designate classes of defendants for

whom bail could be denied by statute; it found in the present case that there was a "reasonable apprehension of hurt from the aliens charged with a philosophy of violence against the government" (541, 542). Danger-prevention advocates interpreted the concept of "apprehension of hurt" as supporting their view that judges are justified in weighing estimates of harm or danger to the community in making release decisions before trial in criminal cases. The debate about the legitimacy (and constitutionality) of a danger-prevention purpose of the bail decision reached a crescendo during and after the passage by Congress of the Bail Reform Act of 1966. In that landmark legislation, the only stated purpose of the pretrial release decision for accused persons was to ensure appearance in court (18 U.S.C.A. 3146(a)). A community protection aim ("danger to the community or any other person") appeared for the first time in an American law, but it applied only to the special case of a defendant seeking release after conviction, while awaiting sentencing or appeals (18 U.S.C.A. 3146(b)).

The American Bar Association's *Standards Relating to Pretrial Release*, published in 1968, mirrored the bail reform tenets and spirit of the federal legislation, but they also signaled a shift in the debate about the purpose of the pretrial release decision. Although draft standards for preventive detention based on danger were not approved by the ABA, they were discussed and included in an appendix as a model for discussion. Then, in 1970, Congress took the historic step of enacting legislation for the District of Columbia that permitted outright pretrial detention in noncapital cases of defendants posing a danger to "any other person or the community" (D.C. Code: 23–1321, 1322(a)). The D.C. Code was a modified version of the model outlined in the ABA's draft preventive detention standards. The "Preventive Detention Code" of the District of Columbia constituted the first enactment of a law in the United States authorizing preventive detention of criminal defendants based on estimations of their possible dangerousness (Goldkamp, 1985). The D.C. preventive detention law could not have been enacted without support from both bail reform advocates as well as supporters of the public safety agenda.

The early reform advocates attacked the discretionary and discriminatory practice of detaining defendants sub rosa through manipulation of financial bail. They demanded more objective and explicit procedures. Public safety advocates demanded that danger be an acknowledged and explicit concern of the bail process. The compromise was to accept community safety as a legitimate concern but only to allow it pursuant to narrowly defined procedures and criteria. Moreover, the D.C. law was notable because it expressly prohibited detention of defendants through the use of financial bail conditions. Thus, early reformers lost the argument against the public safety agenda, but gained more explicit procedures and a detention-decision mechanism that responded more to due process concerns, and a system that did not authorize confinement on the basis of cash.

Between 1970 and 1984, a growing number of states revised their laws to permit the consideration of dangerousness at the bail stage. No court ruled authoritatively on the constitutionality of the danger agenda until the D.C. Circuit of Appeals in *U.S. v. Edwards* (430 A.2d. 1321 (1981)) approved the provisions of the D.C. law (Goldkamp, 1985). Shortly thereafter, Congress enacted the Federal Bail Reform Act of 1984 (18 U.S.C.A.: 3141–3156). Adapting provisions and concepts from the D.C. law, Congress revised federal law to permit detention of defendants who pose a danger "to the community or any other person." In 1987 in *U.S. v. Salerno* (481 U.S. 739), the U.S. Supreme Court upheld the constitutionality of pretrial detention under the "danger" provision of the Federal Bail Reform Act of 1984. It declared "preventing danger to the community" to be "a legitimate regulatory goal." Although laws in all states do not explicitly recognize a community safety agenda for pretrial release or have preventive detention statutes, the effect of this legal history—the second transformation of bail—has been to make danger concerns at the bail stage legally acceptable.

The Eighth Amendment of the Constitution and defendant rights

The Eight Amendment of the United States Constitution, which provides only that "excessive bail shall not be required," offers no guidance as to the purposes of bail and the rights of defendants at bail. According to Caleb Foote (1965), bail under English law was construed as a device allowing a defendant to gain release before trial while providing assurance of attendance at court proceedings. Denial of bail, where it occurred, was reserved for those cases in which defendants were likely to flee because they were facing the death penalty. Foote argued that the Eighth Amendment of the Constitution represents an incomplete rendering of the principles of English law that gave birth to the institutions of bail and pretrial detention. Not only did English statutes enumerate the offenses under which a right to bail could be expected (it was restricted in capital cases), but the habeas corpus procedure was also a remedy for unlawful detention. In addition, the English Bill of Rights of 1689 proscribed the use of high bail as a means for securing detention. Foote reports that when these three ingredients (i.e., a specified right to bail, habeas corpus, and the excessive bail clause) were imported by the Americans, the habeas corpus remedy was incorporated under Article 1, section 9 of the Constitution, the excessive bail clause appeared in the Eighth Amendment, but a specific right to bail appeared nowhere. Thus, poorly translated from its English origins according to Foote, the Eighth Amendment contains some of the "most ambiguous language in the Bill of Rights" (1965, p. 969).

There are at least three interpretations of the "right to bail" deriving from the Eighth Amendment (Goldkamp, 1979, pp. 16–17). The first, finding no explicit reference to a right to bail in that amendment, conceives of no such right, and defers to statutory provisions to determine when bail must be set as a matter of right, and when it is discretionary. The second interpretation, in finding no explicit instruction from the Constitution or in statute, views bail as a matter of judicial discretion. The excessive bail clause, then, merely decrees that in cases in which a judge determines that bail will be set, it should not be excessive. A third interpretation finds a right to bail implicit in the Eighth Amendment and relies on a historical reading of English law for support.

This latter view, adopted by the early advocates of bail reform, is supported by the proposition that the constitutional prohibition of excessive bail can only stem from a presumption favoring the release of defendants before trial (Foote, 1965, pp. 979–981). This position assumes not only that there is a federally "guaranteed right to have bail set, but there also is a guaranteed Federal right to pretrial freedom, which may be abridged only under extreme, high-risk circumstances" (Fabricant, p. 312). Proponents of this interpretation point to language in *Stack* that (a) there is a presumption that defendants in all noncapital cases will be admitted to bail; and (b) that this presumption is based on the "traditional right to freedom before conviction" deriving from the presumption of innocence, as long as release is "conditioned upon the accused's giving assurance that he will stand trial and submit to punishment if found guilty" (342 U.S. 1, 4–5 (1951)).

The reasoning of *Stack* served as the basis for the broad principles of bail reform. Indeed, this conditional right to release is reflected in the language of the Federal Bail Reform Acts of 1966 and 1984 in two ways: (a) in the presumption favoring release of defendants on personal recognizance; and (b) in the presumption favoring release under the least restrictive conditions necessary to ensure appearance. However, the community safety aim was included in the 1984 act. It and the District of Columbia's preventive detention law specify exceptions to the release presumptions, namely, when the defendant's release cannot be "conditioned on . . . giving assurance" of compliant pretrial behavior. Indeed, the presumption in favor of release is reversed for specified categories of defendants facing serious charges and posing serious risks of flight or threat to the community or other persons. Defendants in the designated categories are presumed detained, pending a pretrial detention hearing to determine whether any "condition or combination of conditions" will ensure appearance and public safety. At that hearing, such defendants are placed in the position of having to counter the government's contention that they pose such a risk of harm or flight that they should remain in confinement.

Liberty decisions based on prediction: due process issues

Beyond the issue relating to the constitutional purposes of the bail process and the rights of defendants at bail, other serious problems are associated with the cash-based bail system. These problems derive from the discretionary and predictive nature of the bail decision, its cash-oriented form, and its problematic effects upon defendants and the community. In a period of a few minutes in a high-volume and overcrowded courtroom, and often with little information for guidance, a judge or other judicial officer in his or her discretion must weigh the risk a defendant poses of fleeing the court's jurisdiction (thus thwarting prosecution) or of posing a danger to the community, victims, witnesses, or jurors.

Predicting human behavior is a difficult undertaking in whatever setting, and regardless of whether subjective or statistical methods are employed. In deciding pretrial release at the first ju-

dicial stage, the problem faced by the judge, challenging under the best of circumstances, seemingly requires talents of judicial prognostication. The judge must "predict" the likelihood that a defendant will flee or commit a crime by reasoned guess or experienced hunch. The task is made more difficult because the judge is not asked to make a broader assessment, for example, of whether the defendant will ever reoffend, but is instead required to predict more narrowly what will occur during the narrow pre-adjudication period. The judge, who cannot really know what will happen in the short-term future, is nevertheless compelled to make a reasonable pretrial release decision balancing the interests of the defendant with those of the community and the justice system in effective prosecution and safety.

One of the due process arguments raised by critics of pretrial detention procedures is that the "danger" being predicted—posing a threat to "the safety of the community or to any other person"—is impermissibly vague in its definition. The more vague the description of danger, the more difficult for a defendant to show that he or she would avoid "it." Since 1970 a growing number of states have incorporated danger provisions in statutes and constitutions (Goldkamp, 1985). The shift from statutory silence to specific mention of the danger purpose in state laws represents a movement in the direction of greater explicit recognition of that goal and represents an improvement over practices that addressed danger sub rosa. However, the danger language that has been employed in bail laws may not resolve the vagueness concerns critics have voiced.

In a number of states, for example, rather general danger concerns are indicated, such as "the public would be placed in significant peril" (Colorado), danger to the "safety of the community" (Delaware), "danger to the public" (Vermont), or the defendant's release would be "inimical to public safety" (Minnesota). Unusual danger references include a Georgia law that considers the potential "threat" a defendant may pose to "any property within the community," while laws in at least six states allude to the possible danger defendants may pose to themselves. More specific danger references relate to "serious crime" (a number of states), to "physical harm to persons" (Florida), to "threaten[ing] another with bodily harm" (Minnesota), and "to protect members of the community from serious bodily harm" (Wisconsin). The imprecision of the danger targeted by pretrial detention not only poses a substantive problem for due process, it makes judicial prediction all the more problematic.

Reform-oriented critics of the bail process have argued that pretrial detention laws are unconstitutional and they deprive defendants of their liberty without the due process guaranteed under the Fifth and Fourteenth Amendments of the U.S. Constitution. Critics have argued that the future conduct being predicted (danger, threat to the community, etc.) is too vague, that the ability to predict at the bail stage is too error-prone, and that the criteria relied upon to make the bail predictions are often inappropriate to justify depriving an accused of liberty, given the presumption of innocence. Even under optimal prediction conditions, the ratio of incorrect to correct detention decisions ranges from about four to one to about three to one (Angel et al.).

According to critics, detention of a defendant before trial raises a presumption of dangerousness or flight risk (and, worse, of guilt) that the defendant has no means of refuting and leaves the defendant with the dilemma of having to prove the negative, that he or she would not be dangerous if released. Once confined, it is logically impossible for a defendant to demonstrate that a predicted act would not have occurred. Studies have also shown that detained defendants not only suffer the disadvantages of confinement, but are more likely to be convicted and sentenced to confinement upon conviction than their released counterparts. And reform advocates have argued that the best predictive intentions of the bail judiciary notwithstanding, pretrial detention is tantamount to punishment before trial, just as in *Alice in Wonderland* where punishment preceded the trial.

These due process arguments have been rejected by the courts. *U.S. v. Edwards* tested the constitutionality of the D.C. preventive detention law. And, in *U.S. v. Salerna* the U.S. Supreme Court considered a challenge to the constitutionality of pretrial detention under the federal procedures specified in the Bail Reform Act of 1984 in *U.S. v. Salerno*. (The Supreme Court addressed similar issues in the juvenile context in a case testing the constitutionality of New York juvenile detention law in *Schall v. Martin* (467 U.S. 253 (1984)).)

The courts evaluated the procedures authorized by the statutes. The procedures specified under the federal and D.C. laws include notice, a right to be present at the detention hearing, a right to be represented by counsel, a right to tes-

tify or present witnesses, and a right to confront and cross-examine prosecution witnesses. The challenged laws also list detention criteria to be taken into consideration by the judicial officer in determining whether "no condition or combination of conditions of release" will ensure the attendance of the defendant in court or protect the safety of the community or any other person. *Schall*, *Edwards*, and *Salerno* were consistent in finding that, despite the imperfections of detention decision-making and the difficulties of predicting future behavior, pretrial detention is an appropriate regulatory function and the procedures in the respective detention laws meet minimum requirements of due process.

Disparity in bail and detention: equal protection issues

Criticism of cash-based bail practices have extended beyond questions about the fairness (and substance) of the procedures employed to arrive at a pretrial detention decision to concern regarding the disparate consequences of those practices. Bail reform advocates have argued that the discretionary cash-based system produces unfair results from an equal protection perspective, because similar defendants charged with the same offenses and with the similar backgrounds are often treated differently.

Unfettered judicial discretion in bail proceedings results in outcomes described by critics as random and arbitrary. The likelihood of detention has varied among judges in the same court and across courts, and even by a single judge over time. Studies of bail decisions have found at least as much disparity—unequal treatment of similar individuals—as was found in studies of sentencing and parole that sparked major reforms of those justice decisions (Goldkamp, 1979).

Reform advocates have targeted cash bail as the source of unequal treatment of defendants at bail. They have claimed that the cash-based charge-governed system institutionalizes economic discrimination against the poor. According to this reform perspective, the treatment of defendants has been unequal because some can afford their freedom and some cannot. Critics of such bail practices do not believe a person's ability to afford cash bail, a reflection of economic background, is related to determining the likelihood that he or she will fail to attend court. Unfortunately, because of the economic basis of cash-based pretrial release, at least in most urban settings, racial bias is also a result. African Americans and other minorities, who disproportionately are numbered among the poorest of the poor, also disproportionately fill the jails as pretrial detainees.

This economic effect has been accentuated by the role of the bondsman, who selects those persons he would assist on the basis of profit motive. Persons without assets and ties are not viewed as good business risks and are not accepted by bondsmen, who have an economic interest in doing business with only the most reliable of defendants (those with sufficient assets). In addition, persons charged with minor crimes who cannot afford even low amounts of bail are also not accepted by bondsmen because the fees to be earned are too small.

Implicit in the equal protection criticism of American bail practices is the assertion that the two classes of accused produced through cash bail—those released and those detained before trial—are formed by inappropriate, illegitimate, or invidious distinctions (Goldkamp, 1979). Rather than finding that the dividing line between release and confinement is formed on the basis of race and wealth, a rational and fair system would shape release on the basis of factors relating to appearance and public safety. In short, a constitutional analysis of bail practices would require that the factors determining pretrial release be demonstrably and logically, if not empirically, related to the risk of flight and crime.

Bail reform strategies

During the last decades of the twentieth century, a number of studies examined the factors most predictive of pretrial misconduct. These studies did not find support for the conventional judicial wisdom that the more serious the defendant's criminal charges, the greater the risk of flight or crime posed. Risk of pretrial misconduct was found to vary by charge type, but not by charge seriousness in the way generally assumed. In fact, almost the opposite of the conventional wisdom was found to apply: lower-level drug, property, and nuisance crimes were associated with higher rates of failure to appear in court and of pretrial crime; more seriously charged defendants produced relatively lower rates of failure. These actuarial studies of failure-to-appear and pretrial crime did not find that race or economic background were predictors of defendant performance on release (flight or crime), despite their association with the use of pretrial detention under the cash-bail system.

Bail reform in its first generation attacked the problem of unequal treatment at bail in two principal ways: (a) by encouraging the use of more objective criteria in the release decision process (and discouraging the traditional, unthinking reliance on the charge standard); and (b) by reducing reliance on financial bail as the principal currency of release. One of the initial goals of the pioneering Vera Institute in the early 1960s was to encourage judges not to rely on the charge standard, and to consider instead other factors reflecting on a defendant's ties to the community, family relationships, and connections to work or study. The Vera Institute also pioneered by creating a special bail reform agency (later to be known as "pretrial services agency") to support the collection and presentation to the judge of information more objectively related to the risk of a defendant's failure to appear.

The bail reform aim of making the pretrial release decision more rationally related to the purposes of bail (by improving the criteria considered by the judge) also promoted a second important goal of bail reform: to encourage greater use of ROR and other nonfinancial forms of release. The Vera "community ties" strategy sought to encourage a presumption that defendants should, on the whole, be released on personal recognizance. To address the cases of defendants who achieved immediate own-recognizance release, bail reformers sought to further reduce reliance on cash bail through implementation of conditional release options, including release conditions requiring programs of supervision or treatment of the defendants, thus adding to the judge's confidence that defendants would appear in court.

A third bail reform strategy, for defendants gaining neither ROR nor conditional release, encouraged use of deposit of 10 percent bail, when financial conditions were to be set. Under the "deposit bail" procedure, defendants would deposit with the court a small percentage of the total amount of bail (10 percent of the total), equivalent to what might otherwise have been the bondsman's fee. When the defendant attended all court proceedings, the deposit would be refunded. Developed in Illinois in 1965, the reasoning behind this reform initiative was that the prospect of recovering bail deposited would provide defendants with a strong incentive to appear in court, in contrast to paying a nonrefundable fee to the bondsman for release. The use of nonfinancial forms of pretrial release and deposit bail grew noticeably through the 1960s and beyond, accompanied by a dramatic growth in pretrial services agencies modeled after the early Vera reform prototype.

Building on an analysis of the effects of bail reform, Goldkamp and his colleagues have experimented with another strategy for addressing the core problems associated with traditional bail practices in Boston, Phoenix, and Miami during the 1980s and 1990s (Goldkamp et al.). Their "pretrial release guidelines" experimental approach was premised on the belief that the problems with bail are linked with the unfettered exercise of judicial discretion. They argued that bail reform has been less successful than desired because it has failed to engage judges centrally in the reform process. Therefore, the guidelines strategy was designed as a self-help judicial approach, in which researchers worked with judges in a collaborative process of study and review of actual practices, followed by formulation of a set of judicial policies to serve as a presumptive decision guide for the judges or commissioners who had bail responsibilities.

The rationale for the pretrial release guidelines approach is that if members of the judiciary play a role in identifying the problem, make use of strong data to test various assumptions about the use of detention and release, and take a leadership role in shaping improved bail policies, judicial pretrial release guidelines will have a greater impact on release and detention practices than has been achieved by the bail reform movements to date. Positive results were reported in studies of judicial pretrial release guidelines (Goldkamp et al.), particularly in Philadelphia where the guidelines served as a blueprint for major system reform as well as a tool for dealing with jail overcrowding.

Bail, release and detention in the twenty-first century

Bail practices in the United States have changed considerably in law and practice since Pound and Frankfurter excoriated the bondsmen as "anomalous" and as "that extra legal parasite" in their study of justice in Cleveland in 1922, and since Arthur Beeley found in his study of the Chicago jail that many "dependable" defendants who could have been released safely and be expected to return to court were held in detention merely because they were poor and unable to post the cash bail. The bail reform movement developed pretrial services agencies to assist in pretrial release decisions and encouraged greater nonfinancial release. The first generation of bail reform shaped the landmark legislation in the Federal Bail Reform Act of 1966 and transformed the way important liberty decisions were conducted. The second generation of reform built on these accomplishments and explicitly recognized the community protection agenda of the pretrial release and detention process, establishing procedures for determining pretrial detention and its review.

With much accomplished, there is also much that remains unresolved or only partly addressed. Traditional cash-based detention practices remain the norm in most non-federal jurisdictions at the outset of the twenty-first century. Few states have adopted the federal or District of Columbia models of pretrial release decision-making. And, when features of these laws have been adopted by states, they have been accepted in a piecemeal fashion, breaking key elements away from the overall reform concept, and failing to incorporate the due process framework for detention decisions in routine cases. No state that has added preventive detention procedures to determine dangerousness has adopted the District of Columbia provisions prohibiting detention through cash bail. The result is that by allowing the discretionary cash-bail system (and the use of bondsmen and their bond schedules) to continue to exist, the detention provisions remain obscure and seldom employed. The use of nonfinancial bail has increased since the 1960s; "low risk" defendants with strong community ties are no longer commonly held in jail. However, the nation's historically overcrowded jails are still filled with the poorest of the poor, principally urban minorities, who are held on financial bail they cannot raise. Efforts to work with the judiciary to review and improve judicial pretrial release decisions are still rare.

JOHN S. GOLDKAMP

See also APPEAL; ARRAIGNMENT; CAPITAL PUNISHMENT: LEGAL ASPECTS; CIVIL AND CRIMINAL DIVIDE; JAILS; PREDICTION OF CRIME AND RECIDIVISM; PRELIMINARY HEARING; TRIAL, CRIMINAL.

BIBLIOGRAPHY

ANGEL, ARTHUR; GREEN, E.; KAUFMAN, H.; and VAN LOON, E. "Preventive Detention: An Empirical Analysis." *Harvard Civil Rights–Civil Liberties Law Review* 6 (1971): 301.

American Bar Association. *Pretrial Release Standards* rev. ed. Chicago: American Bar Association, 1985.

BEELEY, ARTHUR. *The Bail System in Chicago.* Chicago: University of Chicago Press, 1927.

FABRICANT, NEIL. "Bail as a Preferred Freedom and the Failures of New York's Revision." *Buffalo Law Review* 18, no. 1 (1968–1969): 303.

FOOTE, CALEB. "Compelling Appearance in Court: Administration of Bail in Philadelphia." *University of Pennsylvania Law Review,* 102 (1954): 1031.

———. "The Coming Constitutional Crisis in Bail: I." *University of Pennsylvania Law Review* 113 (1965): 959.

FRANKFUTER, FELIX, and POUND, ROSCOE. *Criminal Justice in Cleveland.* Cleveland: Cleveland Foundation, 1922; Montclair, N.J.: Patterson-Smith, 1968.

GOLDFARB, RONALD. *Ransom: A Critique of the American Bail System.* New York: John Wiley and Sons, 1965.

GOLDKAMP, JOHN S. *Two Classes of Accused: A Study of Bail and Detention in American Justice.* Cambridge, Mass.: Ballinger Publishing Co., 1979.

———. "Danger and Detention: A Second Generation of Bail Reform." *Journal of Criminal Law and Criminology* 76, no. 1 (1985): 1–74.

GOLDKAMP, JOHN S.; GOTTFREDSON, MICHAEL R.; JONES, PETER R.; and WEILAND, DORIS. *Personal Liberty and Community Safety: Pretrial Release in the Criminal Courts.* New York: Plenum, 1995.

CASES

Carlson v. Landon, 342 U.S. 524 (1952).
Schall v. Martin, 467 U.S. 253 (1984).
Stack v. Boyle, 342 U.S. 1 (1951).
U.S. v. Edwards, 430 A.2d. 1321 (1981).
U.S. v. Salerno, 481 U.S. 739 (1987).

BANK ROBBERY

Under the federal Bank Robbery Act of 1934, as amended, 18 U.S.C §§2113, 3231 (1999), banks, credit unions, and savings and loan associations that are (1) organized under federal law; (2) part of the federal system; or (3) federally insured are protected. This section of the United States Code defines *bank* as any banking or trust institution that is organized and operating under United States law and that is either a member of the Federal Reserve System or has its deposits insured by the Federal Deposit Insurance Corporation (FDIC). Concurrently, this statute also applies to those savings and loan associations that have their accounts insured by the FDIC (§2113(f), (g)).

The act makes it a federal offense for anyone to take or attempt to take by force and violence or intimidation anything of value belonging to one of the protected institutions, or anything that is in one of the protected institution's care, custody, control, management, or possession (§ 2113(a)). The statute divides the offense of bank robbery into various stages, making criminal the acts that constitute the steps of the crime.

First, the entering of a protected bank or savings and loan association with the *intent* to commit a felony therein is a crime. Second, Section 2113(b) addresses the stage of taking and carrying away the property of the protected institution. The escape phase of the robbery is regarded as part of the robbery itself, not as a separate event that takes place afterward. Hence, any party assisting or participating in that phase of the robbery becomes a principal to the crime itself (*United States v. von Roeder*, 435 F.2d 1004 (10th Cir. 1970), *vacated and remanded sub nom. Schreiner v. United States*, 404 U.S. 67 (1971)). Third, Section 2113(c) deals with what one does with the stolen property. Any other party who becomes involved in this stage of the act is subject to the same punishment he would have incurred if he had robbed the bank. Fourth, Section 2113(d) makes the acts described in sections 2113(a) and 2113(b) subject to a heavier penalty if anyone's life is put in jeopardy with the use of a dangerous weapon or device or if the person committing or attempting to commit the offense assaults any person. Finally, Section 2113(e) allows a jury to authorize the death penalty if any offense described within the act is accompanied by a killing or a kidnapping.

The question is commonly posed whether an unlawful entry and a robbery that follows are two separate offenses, consecutively punishable. The United States Supreme Court in *Prince v. United States*, 352 U.S. 322 (1957) answered in the negative. The Court concluded that the unlawful-entry provision was included in the act to cover an instance in which a person entered a bank intending to rob it but became frustrated before doing so. Conversely, the Court stated, where one entered a bank intending to rob it and did rob it, the two crimes merged. The provision of the act that addresses the receiving of stolen property is intended not to increase the robber's punishment, but rather to punish the ones who eventually and knowingly receive the stolen money (*Heflin v. United States*, 358 U.S. 415 (1959)).

Section 2113(e), which deals with kidnapping and murder, especially where these acts are committed after the robbery and in an attempt to avoid apprehension, may provide separate and distinct crimes from the robbery provision (*United States v. Parker*, 283 F.2d 862 (7th Cir. 1960); *Duboice v. United States*, 195 F.2d 371 (8th Cir. 1952); *Clark v. United States*, 184 F.2d 952 (10th Cir. 1950)). However, it has been suggested that the entire statute creates a single offense, with various degrees of sentences allowed for the increasing severity of the crime (*United States v. Drake*, 250 F.2d 216 (7th Cir. 1957); *Simunov v. United States*, 162 F.2d 314 (6th Cir. 1947); *Wells v. Swope*, 121 F. Supp. 718 (N.D. Cal. 1954)). From the Supreme Court's decision in *Prince*, this latter view appears to be supported, even though the Court did not expressly overrule the other cases.

Depending on the facts of the alleged violation of the Bank Robbery Act, various sentences may be imposed on the offender on the different counts of the indictment without constituting double jeopardy (*United States v. Koury*, 319 F.2d 75 (6th Cir. 1963)). However, if the defendant is charged with separate counts of jeopardizing the lives of different persons, this is generally regarded as but one offense, and only one sentence may be imposed (*McDonald v. Johnston*, 149 F.2d 768 (9th Cir. 1945); *McDonald v. Hudspeth*, 129 F.2d 196 (10th Cir. 1942)). Analogous to this reasoning, as shown in *United States v. McKenzie*, 414 F.2d 808 (3rd Cir. 1969) and *Holbrook v. Hunter*, 149 F.2d 230 (10th Cir. 1945), where one is charged with committing a robbery and also with assault, only one sentence may be imposed.

ROBERT L. BOGOMOLNY
DAN M. KAHAN

See also FEDERAL CRIMINAL JURISDICTION; FEDERAL CRIMINAL LAW ENFORCEMENT; ROBBERY.

BIBLIOGRAPHY

Comment. "A General Sentence Is To Be Imposed for a Conviction Consisting of Several Counts Charging Violation of the Federal Bank Robbery Act but the Term Shall Not Exceed the Maximum Permissible Sentence on the Count That Carries the Greatest Maximum Sentence." *Houston Law Review* 9 (1972): 579–586.

CONKLIN, JOHN E. *Robbery and the Criminal Justice System*. Philadelphia: Lippincott, 1972.
DRECHSLER, C. T. "Annotation: Validity and Construction of Federal Bank Robbery Act." *American Law Report Annotated*, 2d series, vol. 59. Rochester, N.Y.: Lawyers Cooperative, 1958. Pages 946–1011.
LEE, PATRICIA E. "Bank Robbery Act: Fraud or Larceny." *George Washington Law Review* 50 (1982): 656–670.
O'KEEFE, JOSEPH JAMES. *The Men Who Robbed Brink's: The Inside Story of One of the Most Famous Holdups in the History of Crime, as Told by Specs O'Keefe to Bob Considine, in Cooperation with the FBI*. New York: Random House, 1961.
WHARTON, FRANCIS. *Wharton's Criminal Law*, vol. 4. 14th ed. Edited by Charles E. Torcia. Rochester, N.Y.: Lawyers Co-operative, 1978.

BLACKMAIL AND EXTORTION

Extortion refers to obtaining property or compelling action by the use of threats or by the misuse of public office. The terms *blackmail* and *extortion* are often used interchangeably; yet in ordinary speech, they connote somewhat different behavior. Blackmail generally refers to hush money, and extortion refers to certain forms of public official misconduct and to those making threats of physical harm to person or property. Few "blackmail" statutes remain on the books, with most statutes prohibiting such behavior as extortion, theft, or criminal coercion.

Extortion is of two types: (1) extortion by threats or fear; and (2) extortion under color of office. Extortion by threats or fear (coercive extortion) can refer to any illegal use of a threat or fear to obtain property or advantages from another, short of violence, which would constitute robbery. Extortion offenses include not only threats obtaining property, but also those compelling any action against one's will (also called criminal coercion).

Statutes usually set out the kinds of threats that make up coercive extortion—for example, the threat to commit a crime, injure person or property, or expose a crime or contemptible information. The distinction traditionally drawn between robbery by intimidation and some forms of extortion is that a person commits robbery when he threatens to do immediate bodily harm, whereas he commits extortion when he plans to do bodily harm in the future. Historically, extortion under color of office is the seeking or receipt of a corrupt payment by a public official (or a pretended public official) because of his office or his ability to influence official action.

Extortion by a public official

Extortion is an older term than blackmail. In England, among the earliest extant statutes setting out the crime of extortion was the First Statute of Westminster (1275), 3 Edw. ch. 26 (repealed), which prohibited extortion by a sheriff or other royal official. According to William Hawkins, extortion at common law was "the taking of money by any officer, by colour of his office, either where none at all is due, or not so much is due, or where it is not yet due" (vol. 1, p. 316).

One sees much the same kind of public corruption case in the late 1200s as in modern cases. Then, as now, extortion has usually embraced takings by various methods: coercion, false pretenses, or bribery. Some American courts attempted to separate bribery and extortion, occasionally even claiming that the two crimes were mutually exclusive (Symposium, pp. 1717–1732). Nonetheless, a solid majority of cases (especially cases before 1850 and cases after 1970) hold that bribery and extortion overlap sometimes even affirming bribery and extortion convictions for the same transaction.

Coercive extortion by a public official is the seeking or receiving of a corrupt benefit paid under an implicit or explicit threat to give the payer worse than fair treatment or to make the payer worse off than he is now or worse than he expects to be. The payee is guilty of extortion; the payer is the victim of extortion. Thus, coercive extortion has at least three baselines (fair treatment, expected treatment, and the status quo).

For example, it is extortion if a public official threatens to deny a public contract to a bidding contractor who clearly deserves to receive it unless the bidder pays off the official. The official would receive the payoff under a threat to give the contractor worse than fair treatment. In many jurisdictions the contractor would not have done anything illegal since he was forced to buy back only what he deserved in the first place, but in others he would be guilty of bribery. In most payoff situations, however, we will not clearly know who actually deserved to get a public contract. Usually, the official makes the bidder aware that he will not get the contract unless he pays off the official, and if the bidder pays, he will defi-

nitely get the contract. If the bidder does not pay, he gets less than fair treatment (coercive extortion). If he pays, he gets more than fair treatment (bribery). Thus the same envelope filled with cash can be both a payment extorted under a threat of unfairly negative treatment and a bribe obtained under a promise of unfairly positive treatment.

Blackmail and extortion by a private person

The first references to "blackmail" date from the sixteenth century, when Scotland made it a crime to obtain property by certain written threats of physical harm to person or property (1567 Scot. Parl. Acts, ch. 27). In 1722 the Waltham Black Act authorized the death penalty throughout the country for making certain written threats that demanded property as the price for refraining from physically endangering person or property (9 Geo. I, ch. 22, § 1 (1722) (repealed)). It was not until 1843 that Parliament finally extended blackmail to cover threats to expose evidence of embarrassing but noncriminal behavior (6 & 7 Vict., ch. 96, @ 3 (1843) (repealed)).

There were many other English statutes that did not mention blackmail but punished blackmail behavior; for example, the Elizabethan Informers' Statute (18 Eliz. I, ch. 5 (1576)) made it criminal for individuals to take money to suppress prosecutions. Further, at English common law, extortion by private citizens was punished, at least where the fear was the exposure of a crime that would lead to confinement (Lindgren, p. 674).

In the United States in 1796, New Jersey passed perhaps the first American statute prohibiting threats to expose any crime, not just a capital or infamous crime. In 1827, Illinois passed a statute prohibiting threats to expose "infirmities or failings" (Act of 1827, § 108 1827 Ill. Laws 145), sixteen years before similar threats were made illegal in England. In the influential Field Code (Proposed Penal Code of the State of New York (1865)), extortion was divided into three crimes: extortion (coercion seeking property), extortion under color of official right, and criminal coercion (seeking to compel action).

Modern American statutes vary considerably in the ways they define blackmail or extortion by a private person. Some statutes require that the threat accomplish its purpose. Under such a statute an unsuccessful threat may usually be prosecuted as a criminal attempt. But most modern statutes do not require that the extortionate threat succeed; the making of the threat is enough. The statutes also vary with regard to what must be demanded for the behavior to be illegal. Some statutes, for example, prohibit the obtaining of "property," or "any valuable thing." Many extortion or coercion statutes prohibit compelling action or inducing someone "to do or refrain from doing any act against his will" (Lindgren, pp. 676–677).

American blackmail and extortion statutes, unlike those in England, usually enumerate the types of prohibited threats. The most common are: (1) the threat of personal injury; (2) the threat to injure property (whether or not such an injury is physical); (3) the threat to accuse of a crime; and (4) the threat to expose any matter that would damage personal or business reputation or would expose the victim to hatred, contempt, or ridicule. Many other threats are prohibited under some state statutes: (1) the threat to commit any offense or any felony; (2) the threat to physically confine; (3) the threat to impair credit; (4) the threat to expose a secret; (5) the threat to strike or boycott, if a labor representative is seeking a personal payoff for not striking or boycotting; (6) the threat to give or withhold testimony; (7) the threat of a public official to take or withhold action against anyone or anything; and (8) the threat to inflict any other harm that would not benefit the threatener.

Because some of these prohibited threats often have legitimate uses, some jurisdictions give the threatener an affirmative defense that he genuinely believed that the property sought was due him or that he was only trying to right a wrong or obtain restitution. Other jurisdictions allow this "claim of right" defense only when the amount sought was previously ascertained, as with a preexisting debt. But some jurisdictions have not yet recognized the claim-of-right defense in any form.

Modern federal statutes

Federal statutes make many particular kinds of extortion or blackmail illegal. For example, extortion by officials of the federal government is a crime (18 U.S.C. § 872). It is blackmail to demand or receive a valuable thing by offering not to inform against anyone who has violated federal law (18 U.S.C. § 873). It is also prohibited to mail or transmit in interstate commerce certain threats with the intent to extort, including threats to accuse of a crime or to injure person, property, or reputation (18 U.S.C. §§ 875–877). The Travel Act (18 U.S.C. § 1952) also punishes certain kinds of blackmail and extortion.

The federal extortion statute that has generated the most litigation is the 1946 "Hobbs Act" (18 U.S.C. § 1951), which prohibits racketeering in interstate commerce. The act prohibits robbery and extortion when these would affect interstate commerce. The U.S. Supreme Court interpreted official extortion under the Hobbs Act in two cases from the early 1990s. In *McCormick v. United States*, 500 U.S. 257 (1991), the Court held that there was a requirement of an explicit quid pro quo in official extortion cases involving campaign contributions. Then, in *Evans v. United States*, 504 U.S. 255 (1992), the Court held that (1) there is no requirement of inducement for official extortion; (2) official extortion does not require coercion; (3) bribery is not a defense to extortion; (4) official extortion is not limited to false pretenses; and (5) the government "need only show that a public official has obtained a payment to which he was not entitled, knowing that the payment was made in return for official acts." Thus, bribery and extortion under color of official right substantially overlap.

The most controversial interpretations of the Hobbs Act have been in the area of labor extortion. In *United States v. Teamsters Local 807*, 315 U.S. 521 (1942), the Court restricted the operation of the Hobbs Act's predecessor so that is did not cover labor violence used to seek work or wages. In *Enmons v. United States*, 410 U.S. 396 (1973), the Court held that no extortion had occurred, although a union had allegedly blown up a power station to enforce its demands for higher wages. Apparently, only two basic types of union extortion are illegal under the Hobbs Act: where the work sought is totally unwanted or unneeded, and where a union official is seeking a personal payoff or kickback. In essence, the Court has refused to apply the Hobbs Act to unions that seek almost any legitimate objective, no matter what means are used to obtain that objective.

The paradox of blackmail

One of the most intractable intellectual problems in the criminal law is what Glanville Williams called the paradox of blackmail (p. 163). The problem is that combining two rights makes a wrong. For example, if I threaten to expose a businessman's income-tax evasion unless he gives me a lucrative contract, I have committed blackmail. I have a legal right to expose and to threaten to expose the tax evasion, and I have a legal right to seek a lucrative contract, but if I combine these rights I have committed blackmail. If both ends and means are otherwise legal, why is it blackmail to combine these legal ends and means? Since the 1920s, many theories have been offered to explain this paradox, and a few scholars, led by Walter Block, argue that blackmail ought to be legal since it violates no basic legal right of the "victim" (e.g., Block, p. 225). Even among scholars trying to resolve the paradox, there is no consensus on its resolution (Symposium, pp. 1565–2168).

One approach that is at least descriptively powerful is to look at the relationships between the parties. Consider first informational blackmail. Here the blackmailer threatens to tell others damaging information about the blackmail victim unless the victim heeds the blackmailer's request, usually a request for money. The blackmailer obtains what he wants by using extra leverage. But that leverage belongs more to a third person than to the blackmailer. The blackmail victim pays the blackmailer to avoid involving third parties; he pays to avoid being harmed by persons other than the blackmailer. When the reputation of a person is damaged, he is punished by all those who change their opinion of him. They may "punish" him by treating him differently or he may be punished merely by the knowledge that others no longer respect him.

Thus when a blackmailer threatens to turn in a criminal unless paid money, the blackmailer is bargaining with the state's chip. The blackmail victim pays to avoid the harm that the state would inflict. Of course, this does not effect a legally binding settlement, but the leverage is effective precisely to the extent that the victim believes that he has reached an effective settlement. Likewise, when a blackmailer threatens to expose damaging but noncriminal behavior unless paid money, he is also turning third-party leverage to his own benefit. What makes his conduct blackmail is that he interposes himself parasitically in an actual or potential dispute in which he lacks a sufficiently direct interest. In effect, the blackmailer attempts to gain an advantage in return for suppressing someone else's actual or potential interest. The blackmailer is negotiating for his own gain with someone else's leverage or bargaining chips.

This misuse of another's leverage is perhaps seen most clearly in noninformational blackmail—for instance, where a labor union leader threatens to cause a strike unless he is given a personal payoff. There the labor leader is turning group power and a group dispute to personal benefit. Whoever seeks a personal payoff by credibly wielding the power of a third party to harm the victim is a blackmailer.

James Lindgren

See also Bribery; Organized Crime; Robbery; Theft.

BIBLIOGRAPHY

Block, Walter. "The Case for Decriminalizing Blackmail." *Western State University Law Review* 24 (spring 1997): 225–246.
Hawkins, William. *A Treatise of Pleas of the Crown*, 6th ed. Edited by Thomas Leach, 1788.
Hepworth, Mike. *Blackmail: Publicity and Secrecy in Everyday Life*. London: Routledge & Kegan Paul, 1975.
Lindgren, James. "Unraveling the Paradox of Blackmail." *Columbia Law Review* 84 (1984): 670–717.
Perkins, Rollin M. *Criminal Law*, 2d ed. Mineola, N.Y.: Foundation Press, 1969.
Symposium. "Blackmail." *University of Pennsylvania Law Review* 141 (1993): 1565–2168.
Williams, Glanville. "Blackmail." *Criminal Law Review* (1954): 79–92, 162–172, 240–246.

CASES

Enmons v. United States, 410 U.S. 396 (1973).
Evans v. United States, 504 U.S. 257 (1991).
McCormick v. United States, 500 U.S. 257 (1991).
United States v. Teamsters Local 807, 315 U.S. 521 (1942).

BRIBERY

The act or practice of benefiting a person in order to betray a trust or to perform a duty meant to be performed freely, bribery occurs in relation to a public official and, derivatively, in private transactions. This article will deal with both species in terms of (1) the tradition; (2) modern law; and (3) problems.

The tradition

Roots. Like many American legal concepts, the notion of bribery has its roots in the ancient Near East. As in most archaic societies, peaceful relations with strangers were here established in two ways, by gift and by contract. The gods or God were similarly made approachable by offerings or covenants. Against the norm of reciprocal relations ran two concepts. First, the ruler was the protector of the powerless, of "the widow and the orphan," as texts from Lagash (2400 B.C.), Babylon (1700 B.C.), and Israel (600 B.C.) expressed it. Second, man was judged by the gods impartially, as shown by the sales in the judgment scene of the Egyptian Book of the Dead (2500 B.C.). A ruler who aids the powerless is not responsive to gifts, nor is one who judges in the place of the gods. These religious insights crystallized in an image of a judge who does not take gifts for his judgment, an ideal apparent in Egyptian texts by 1500 B.C. The ideal received an expression of great influence on Western culture in Deuteronomy (seventh century B.C.), where it was stated that God in judging "does not take reward" (Deut. 10:17) and man in judging should not "take reward" (Deut. 16:19). The total biblical message on reciprocity was mixed but provides the main religious outlook from which the bribery prohibition of the West developed.

Biblical hostility to bribery was reinforced by a political tradition that appeared in the Greek city-states and had a strong impact on the ideals of the Roman Republic. The classic expression was provided by Cicero in his prosecution of Verres (whose name in Latin means "hog"), among the worst of whose offenses was "taking money for judgment," a crime described as "the foulest" (*Against Verres*, pp. 2, 3, 78). The essential sanction was supernatural, and climactically Cicero called on various gods to punish Hog.

The antibribery ethic, reflecting the biblical and classical sources, was conveyed by Christian moralists like Augustine and reinforced by the special aversion developed against a subspecies of bribery, the sin of simony, or sale of spiritual offices or goods. Denounced as a heresy, simony was the periodic object of reformers from Gregory I (A.D. 600) to Gregory VII (A.D. 1073). The notion of a spiritual domain that should not be sold complemented that of nonvendible justice. Papal pronouncements such as Innocent III's *Qualiter et quando* of 1205 (Gregory IX, "Decretales") insisted that judges must put aside "favor and fear" and "have God alone before their eyes."

Secular law followed suit. The antibribery ethic was firmly set out in Henry de Bracton's great mid-thirteenth-century treatise on English law (pp. 302–303), where the taking of bribery was condemned by biblical and Roman law and

the judge who takes was said to be "corrupted by filth." Two notions, central to the idea of a judge in English law, were embodied in the antibribery ethic: trust should not be betrayed, acts of judgment cannot be sold. All subsequent development flows from these two ideas.

Literature and linguistics. The strongest teacher of the prohibition of bribery was literary. At the center of the European tradition stood Dantes *Divine Comedy*, in which bribery and simony constituted sins of fraud, more reprehensible than sins of violence because they involved misuse of man's intellect; those who sold secular justice were punished even more severely than the ecclesiastics, by immersion in a boiling, sticky pitch. Lucca, where "No becomes Yes for money," is eternally stigmatized as a symbol of civic corruption (*Inferno*, canto 21). Shakespeare fixed the English literary-moral tradition, especially with passages on bribes and corruption in *Julius Caesar* (act 4, scene 3) and with an entire play, *Measure for Measure*, which contrasts Christian spiritual reciprocities with foul redemption by a bribe. From Shakespeare to Henry Adams (*Democracy*) and Robert Penn Warren (*All the King's Men*), the moral offensiveness of criminal bribery has been a significant theme in English and American literature.

The classical languages had a single word—*shohadh* in Hebrew, *doron* in Greek, and *munus* in Latin—meaning gift, reward, bribe. The ambiguity reflected moral and legal ambivalences. By the sixteenth century, English used *bribe* unambiguously in its present moral and legal sense. By the same period *to bribe, bribery,* and *briber* were in use, as well as the colloquial expression *to grease*, meaning *to bribe*. *Bribee, graft,* and *grafter* are nineteenth-century terms, the latter two American. *Slush fund*, a source from which bribes are paid, and *payoff* are twentieth-century Americanisms. The association of bribes with dirt, dirty hands, and grease goes back to classical times. Euphemisms for bribe are *gift, gratuity, reward, contribution,* and *kickback. Conflict of interest* is sometimes used for a good-faith dilemma, sometimes as a euphemism for a situation produced by bribery.

Paradigms. In the Anglo-American tradition there have been several cases in which the defendant was so prominent that his prosecution was exemplary. (1) The paradigmatic trial of a bribe-taking judge was that of Francis Bacon, chancellor of England, convicted by the House of Lords in 1621. (2) The classic trial of a corrupt administrator was that of Governor-General

Warren Hastings of Bengal, impeached by the House of Commons in 1787. Although ultimately acquitted, Hastings was irretrievably damaged in reputation, and his prosecution by Edmund Burke, modeled on Cicero's of Hog, set the standards for the nineteenth-century British civil service. (3) The trial of Oakes Ames, a Massachusetts congressman and a central figure in the Union Pacific–Credit Mobilier scandal, served as a double paradigm for bribers and legislators. Ames was censured by the House of Representatives in 1873 for bribing members of Congress. Legislative investigation created each paradigm. In each, multiple acts of bribery were established. The essential sanction in each was public shame.

Modern law

Nonstatutory sanctions.   Bribery, along with treason, is one of two crimes for which the United States Constitution (art. ii, sec. 4) specifically prescribes impeachment for the President, Vice-President, and "all civil officers of the United States." Two federal judges have been impeached and convicted of corruption; more than a dozen others have resigned in the face of threatened impeachment. Indication of investigation has produced other resignations, most notably of a Justice of the Supreme Court.

Since 1873, Congress has censured members for bribe-taking or bribe-giving, and in 1980 it actually expelled a member after his criminal conviction. A more common sanction has been electoral, although belief that a candidate is a bribe-taker is more apt to act as a comparative disadvantage than an absolute disqualification. Lawyers convicted of bribery are subject to disbarment. In descending order of frequency, electoral disadvantage, forced or prudential resignation, disbarment, censure, impeachment, and expulsion have been sanctions for bribery in high American office. In enforcing them, the role of the press has been crucial.

Statutes.   Modern statutes, state and federal, have four common characteristics. (1) They apply equally to receivers and givers. (2) They are comprehensive, including as officials all employees of government and those acting in a government capacity, such as jurors and legislators. More recent statutes include party officials and even party employees. (3) They treat bribery as a crime that can be committed by the briber even though the bribee is not influenced. (4) They treat bribery as a felony.

American statutes differ in that some treat a bribe as any "benefit," thereby including nonpe-cuniary favors, whereas others restrict the term to pecuniary benefits. Some, such as the New York Penal Code, permit extortion to be a defense for the bribe-giver (N.Y. Penal Law (McKinney) § 200.05 (1999)), but this defense is disapproved by the Model Penal Code (§ 240.1). Older statutes use *corruptly* to qualify the condemned giving and receiving, whereas more recent ones eliminate *corruptly* and speak more specifically. An essential component of modem statutes is an antigratuity provision making it criminal to confer any benefit on an official "for or because of any official act" (18 U.S.C. § 201(c)(1)(A)(1994)). Excepted, of course, are benefits provided by law. The provision eliminates a need to show that the benefit was "to influence" performance. The giver is guilty if he gave for the act; the recipient is guilty if he took on account of the act. Some statutes also criminalize compensation for a past official act, obviating difficulty in proving bribery (Model Penal Code § 240.3). Some statutes also criminally forbid private employment in a matter on which, as an official, one had acted, assimilating such conflicting interest to a bribe. An example of such a statute is the Bribery, Graft, and Conflicts of Interest Act of 1962, as amended, 18 U.S.C. §§ 201–208 (1999)).

Prosecutions.   Neither the state nor the federal statutes have been systematically and uniformly enforced against all offenders. Usually either political investigation or particularly outrageous corruption has triggered prosecution. Routine federal cases show topicality: bribees were prohibition agents in the 1920s, draft-board members in the 1940s, revenue agents in the 1950s. Celebrated convictions include those of Secretary of the Interior Albert Fall for accepting bribes in connection with the Teapot Dome oil leases (*Fall v. United States*, 49 F.2d 506 (D.C. Cir. 1931)) and of Circuit Court Judge Martin Manton (*United States v. Manton*, 107 F.2d 834 (2d Cir. 1938)).

The 1970s were marked by a more sustained federal effort, in particular by the temporary Watergate Special Prosecution Force, by the permanent Office of Public Integrity in the Justice Department, and by the project known as Abscam, where the use of decoys and the filming of transactions led to the conviction of half a dozen members of Congress and a senator.

Auxiliary legislation.   Evidentiary difficulty in proving bribery, conceptual difficulty in distinguishing bribes from campaign contributions, and experience with the effect of money on elections have led to the adoption of state and federal laws generically known as anticorrupt practice acts. Typically, these limit the amount of campaign contributions, require that they be made only to identified committees, specify that they be reported, and prohibit certain classes of contributors from contributing anything. Offenses under such statutes have, in general, been misdemeanors rather than felonies. The laws have been limited and sometimes invalidated by federal or state constitutional requirements.

For the most part the effectiveness of these statutes has rested chiefly on their being observed by law-abiding corporate managers, lawyers, auditors, and campaign officials. Before the 1970s there was almost no criminal enforcement of the federal law against corporations, contractors, or candidates. The Securities and Exchange Commission (SEC), by requiring the confession of illegal contributions by corporations with stock registered under the Securities Exchange Act, and the Watergate Special Prosecution Force, showed that the laws were often violated. John McCloy's report on Gulf Oil was particularly revealing, disclosing that a slush fund had been maintained for fifteen years, from which leading American politicians, including Senate Majority Leader Lyndon Johnson, were supplied with envelopes containing cash. The difference between such access payments and bribes was difficult to detect.

While federal agencies began to give vigor in the 1970s to the Corrupt Practices Act, federal involvement in prosecuting state and local bribery underwent an enormous expansion. Mail fraud law was used to catch the bribery of Governor Otto Kerner of Illinois. Failure to report the income led to the prosecution of Vice-President Spiro Agnew for bribes taken as governor of Maryland. In addition, on the books were (1) the Travel Act of 1961, as amended, 18 U.S.C. § 1952 (1999), making it a federal felony to use interstate facilities to commit what was bribery under state law; and (2) the much older Hobbs Act, 18 U.S.C. § 1951 (1999), covering any act affecting interstate commerce and defining extortion as obtaining property from another person with that person's consent "under color of official right." This definition was interpreted to include payoffs expressly or tacitly sought by a governor, a state legislator, a city alderman, or a policeman (for example, *United States v. Braasch*, 505 F.2d 139 (7th Cir. 1974)).

These laws were eventually overshadowed by the Racketeer Influenced and Corrupt Organi-

zations (RICO) Act of 1970, 18 U.S.C. 1962 (1999) § 1961, punishing as "racketeering" any "pattern" (two or more acts) of bribery. Under this act, bribe-taking bail bondsmen, sheriffs, and traffic court employees—typical small-time grafters—as well as state revenue officials, state senators, and a state governor, were federally indicted as racketeers. Acquittal under state law was no defense to the federal crime, and state statutes of limitations did not apply. Armed by RICO with powerful weapons, the Justice Department became a formidable adversary of local corruption. By the 1970s, state officials were being federally prosecuted at the rate of several hundred per year.

Foreign corrupt practices.   In the 1970s the SEC took the position that payments of bribes overseas constituted material information, to be disclosed on reports to the SEC. More than four hundred American companies confessed to making such payments. A small percentage of registered corporations, they included such giants as Lockheed Corporation, which spent $6 million a year in overseas bribes. In response to public furor, Congress enacted the Foreign Corrupt Practices Act of 1977, 15 U.S.C. §§ 78dd-1–dd-2 (1999). This legislation was notable in four respects: (1) The statute made it a crime to bribe an official of *another* country, an extension of jurisdiction never attempted before in regard to bribery. (2) It applied only to bribers, whereas other bribery laws apply to bribees as well. (3) Under criminal penalty, it required one class of bribers, those registered under the securities laws, to make a public report of its crime. (4) As to all bribers, it was *more* stringent than federal law on bribery in the United States in that (a) it applied to bribing political parties; (b) it applied to all domestic businesses and all American citizens; and (c) it specified a heavier financial punishment, up to $1 million. The act's effect has depended on cooperation by lawyers, auditors, corporate managers, and outside directors.

Commerce and contests.   Criminal statutes against the bribery of private persons began with New York in 1881. They were enacted in England and several states in the early twentieth century, numbered seventeen by 1934, and doubled by 1980. The earlier statutes tended to specify employments—gardeners in Maryland, chauffeurs in Illinois! The more recent tendency, reflected in the Model Penal Code, has been to include all employees, agents, and fiduciaries. Seeking to reach payola in the recording business, the Code, followed by several states, also includes anyone who professionally is a disinterested expert. The statutes in substance make it a crime to confer a benefit on a fiduciary with intent to influence the recipient's conduct in his principal's affairs. Consent of the principal is a defense, and penalties vary. The statutes have sometimes been invoked civilly to invalidate a contract, but they have rarely led to criminal convictions. Persons injured have more incentive to hold the bribee liable for the bribe or to make the briber turn over his gain.

Between 1947 and 1980, thirty-four states made it a crime to influence sporting contests by bribes to officials or participants. The state statutes are rarely used, but occasionally they have been harshly applied—for example, ten years' sentence of imprisonment was imposed for fixing a basketball game in Iowa. Concern with the effect on sports of professional gamblers connected with organized crime led in 1964 to a federal law which has been extended to apply to jockeys rigging their own race (18 U.S.C. § 224 (1999)). Responding to rigged television contests, the Model Penal Code (§ 224.9) and eight states have included not only sports but every "publicly exhibited contest." The Code and three states specified a criminal penalty for any participant who knows that the contest has been fixed.

Dynamism.   Modern bribery law has tended to expand enormously those subject to the criminal law, to increase the acts covered, to multiply indirect attacks on bribery, to develop more effective techniques of detecting the crime, to expand federal jurisdiction at home and abroad, to increase the number of prosecutions, and to increase the severity of sanctions. The movement of the law has been the reverse of Henry Maine's famous dictum, "from status to contract." The law here has gone from reciprocity to nonreciprocity, determined by status. Its continued expansion could be confidently predicted, were it not for three problems now to be addressed.

Problems

Quantification.   Bribery is not normally reported by briber or bribee, nor boasted of. No statistics exist as to the number or amount of bribes or the percentage of transactions affected by them. Consequently, although many historians speak of a government, a country, or an era as "corrupt," there is no quantifiable evidence on which they rest their judgments. By extrapolation from the disparate data available, guesses conceivably might be made that would compare one regime with another as more or less corrupt. But such comparative guesses have not been developed. Historians often take an era in which there is greater legislation against bribery or greater prosecution of it and conclude that this period was more corrupt than an era without legislative or prosecutorial activity. Nothing could be more fallacious. Greater activity indicates greater opposition to bribery and has no necessary connection with an increase in bribery. To take a contemporary American comparison, were the 1970s more corrupt than the 1950s? No one has done the work that can provide a rational answer to this question.

Since bribery is an unquantified phenomenon, it is impossible to say whether the multiplication of laws and prosecutions is reducing it, keeping even with it, or falling behind. In the absence of a quantitative basis for evaluating the efficacy of criminal law in this area, the success of the law is measured in terms of its symbolic impact. The law is more specially vindicated when a powerful person is subjected to it. Hence bribery prosecutions often have a political aspect.

Prosecutorial discretion.   Prosecutorial discretion determines to a very large degree the application of the law. Discretion exists at the federal level as to state crimes. Virtually any local bribery has an aspect touching interstate commerce and thus could be federally prosecuted. Prosecution depends on decisions by regional district attorneys and by Washington. Discretion also exists at the charging level. For example, a campaign contribution by a corporation, criminal under federal law, can be prosecuted for having been made or accepted (a misdemeanor); for not being reported (a misdemeanor usually treated lightly); for being made by a federal contractor (a felony; most corporations are federal contractors to some extent); for being a gratuity (a more serious felony); or for being a bribe (a very serious felony).

Prosecutors again have discretion to interpret custom to modify the statutes. A Christmas present to a mailman, for example, is a federal felony if the anti-gratuity law is read literally. Prosecutorial discretion saves the law from being absurd. In a more debatable exercise of discretion, no prosecutor charged Governor Nelson Rockefeller of New York with a crime for giving large loans, as much as $500,000, to public employees in literal violation of an antigratuity statute. In a more central area of concern, many legislative deals or compromises fall literally within the terms of a bribery statute. The older type of statute, providing that giving must be done "corruptly," has left the prosecutor to interpret this vague term with the help of custom to exclude the legislative arena.

Historically, prosecutors have depended on chance to bring cases to their attention. To take the example of a particularly elaborate investigation, the congressmen prosecuted in Abscam became targets when criminal middlemen boasted that they could deliver them. No overall plan to test the members of Congress existed. Since the mid-1970s it has been the conscious policy of the Justice Department to give priority to cases involving high federal or state officials—members of Congress, judges, and governors. This exercise of discretion, rationally defensible, could be followed by a second exercise of discretion, to monitor closely the activities of, say, all members of Congress. Experienced observers suggest that almost any area of government, if probed, will yield evidence of corruption. To what extent shall the prosecutor with limited resources wait for an informant? To what extent shall he probe? The bite of the law depends on his decision. The political power resident in his exercise of discretion is substantial. Coupled with the political aspect of many bribery cases, prosecutorial discretion means that bribery, to an extent unusual in the criminal law, is a crime whose prosecution depends on political, but not necessarily partisan, choices.

Rigorism, cynicism, and relativism. Reciprocities run through human relations, including the political. They can as easily be removed from society as moisture from the atmosphere. Confronted with their ubiquity, one can take three positions. (1) *The rigorist*—every bargain, even looked-for reciprocation in the area of political judgments, is wrong. Each judgment is to be made on its merits. The standards applied to judges should apply equally to presidents, legislators, and voters. (2) *The cynical*—most political reciprocities go uncondemned and unpunished. Legislators logroll, presidents use patronage, voters are rewarded by bills that favor their interest. The isolation of a few specific trades as corrupt is hypocritical pretense. In the main, reciprocities rule. A Marxist view of Western society approaches the cynical, even though actual communist societies afford a basis for even greater cynicism. (3) *The relativist*—custom determines which reciprocities are bad and which are acceptable. No trade is intrinsically evil. The antibribery ethic is sufficiently enforced by a few

spectacular cases showing the kinds of trades our society rejects.

Each of these positions has an effect on the criminal law. The internal dynamism of the antibribery ethic pushes toward rigorism. The result is perceptible in the Model Penal Code and modern statutes struggling with definitions that will not make a criminal prosecutor the judge of legislative compromises and election promises. The cynical view is the inevitable reaction to rigorism when it becomes apparent that all reciprocity cannot be eliminated. This view undermines enforcement and even observance of the law. The relativist position is that of the liberal, comfortable with society as it is, who believes that ideal disinterestedness in political judgments can be encouraged if not guaranteed and that its violation can be vindicated in flagrant instances. The relativist, however, has little reason to condemn corruption abroad and, viewing what constitutes corruption as arranged by social convention, has a small moral investment in the criminal law. The removal of moral fire from the law weakens its efficacy.

Conclusion

There exists, however, a fourth position, the social-personalist one. It holds bribery to be a moral issue, that is, it affects both the good of society and the good of persons—the good of society by its impact on the ideals of the society, the good of persons by involving them in acts unworthy of their nature. A breach of trust and a sale of what should not be sold, bribery violates a divine paradigm set out in Jewish tradition and Christian tradition. Because of its deep moral content, the antibribery ethic requires embodiment in the law.

The social-personalist position denies the cynic's charges of hypocrisy, insisting that selective, symbolic, and dramatic enforcement is educative. It challenges the relativist's belief that all is conventional, pointing to fundamental needs for trust, gratuitous action, and disinterested judgment that are protected, although imperfectly and variously. It has affinities with the rigorist position, rejoicing in the expansion of the ethic, especially its belated inclusion of legislators; yet it differs from the rigorist position by rejecting its reliance on criminal sanctions, in particular imprisonment. Rooted in history, the fourth position favors attacking bribery in multiple ways.

In particular, three measures should be considered. (1) *Increasing the legal profession's efforts against bribery.* Lawyers have been very frequently involved in modern bribery as advisers, bagmen, couriers, directors, lobbyists, or recipients. Meanwhile law schools, like legal scholars of every era, ignore the profession's involvement. A key class of participants could be educated, disciplined, and motivated to take a more active stand against bribery. (2) *Extending the requirements of the Foreign Corrupt Practices Act to all corporations as to domestic bribes and political contributions.* There is no reason to be more concerned with corruption overseas than at home. The record-keeping provisions and heavy financial penalty of the act are appropriate deterrents to use against all corporations. (3) *Relying more on disgrace, censure, and electoral reprisals than on imprisonment.* At a time when there are general doubts about incarceration, it is odd to rely on it as a remedy here. Historically, bribery has been punished by shame attached to acts unworthy of human persons.

JOHN T. NOONAN, JR.
DAN M. KAHAN

See also FEDERAL CRIMINAL LAW ENFORCEMENT; OBSTRUCTION OF JUSTICE; WHITE-COLLAR CRIME: HISTORY OF AN IDEA.

BIBLIOGRAPHY

American Law Institute. *Model Penal Code and Commentaries: Official Draft and Revised Comments.* 3 vols. Philadelphia: ALI, 1980.

BOND, EDWARD A., ed. *Speeches of the Managers and Counsel in the Trial of Warren Hastings.* 4 vols. London: Longman, 1859–1861.

BORKIN, JOSEPH. *The Corrupt Judge: An Inquiry into Bribery and Other High Crimes and Misdemeanors in the Federal Courts.* New York: Clarkson Potter, 1962.

BRACTON, HENRY DE. *On the Laws and Customs of England.* vol. 2. Translated with revisions and notes by Samuel E. Thorne. Cambridge, Mass.: Harvard University Press, Belknap Press, 1968.

CICERO, MARCUS TULLIUS. *Against Verres.* Translated by L. H. G. Greenwood. Cambridge, Mass.: Harvard University Press, 1928–1935.

GREGORY IX (POPE). "Decretales" (1234). *Corpus Juris Canonici,* vol. 2. 2d Leipzig ed. Edited by Emil Albert Friedberg and Aemilius Ludwig Richter. Graz, Austria: Akademische Druck und Verlagsanstalt, 1955, cols. 1–927.

LINDGREN, JAMES. "The Theory, History, and Practice of the Bribery-Extortion Distinction." *University of Pennsylvania Law Review* 141 (1993): 1695–1740.

LOWENSTEIN, DANIEL HAYS. "Political Bribery and the Intermediate Theory of Politics." *University of California Los Angeles Law Review* 32 (1985): 784–851.

MCCLOY, JOHN J.; PEARSON, NATHAN W.; and MATTHEWS, BEVERLY. *The Great Oil Spill: The Inside Report—Gulf Oil's Bribery and Political Chicanery.* New York: Chelsea House, 1976.

NOONAN, JOHN T., JR. *Bribes.* New York: Macmillan, 1984.

Note. "Campaign Contributions and Federal Bribery Law." *Harvard Law Review* 92 (1978): 451–469.

Note. "Control of Nongovernmental Corruption by Criminal Legislation." *University of Pennsylvania Law Review* 108 (1960): 848–867.

RUFF, CHARLES F. C. "Federal Prosecution of Local Corruption: A Case Study in the Making of Law Enforcement Policy." *Georgetown Law Journal* 65 (1977): 1171–1228.

BURDEN OF PROOF

The principal purpose of most trials is to resolve a dispute about facts. Both parties present evidence to a fact finder, either judge or jury, who evaluates the evidence and resolves the controversy. A number of rules of law guide the fact finder in evaluating the evidence; most important of these are the rules that tell the fact finder who should have the benefit of the doubt.

These rules are typically expressed as statements about which party must carry the burden of proof, and how heavy the burden is. For example, in most civil cases, the plaintiff has the burden of proof, and the burden is to prove the case "by a preponderance of evidence." In criminal cases, it has long been the general rule that the prosecution has the burden of proof, and the burden is to prove guilt "beyond a reasonable doubt."

The reasonable doubt rule

In 1970 the U.S. Supreme Court declared that the Constitution required the reasonable doubt rule in criminal cases. In the case of *In re Winship,* 397 U.S. 358 (1970), the Court held that the "Due Process Clause protects the accused against conviction except upon proof beyond a reasonable doubt of every fact necessary to constitute the crime with which he is charged" (p. 364).

Winship restated the general understanding of the rule governing proof in a criminal case, and therefore it was not especially controversial. At the same time, however, by articulating a constitutional basis for the rule, *Winship* laid the foundation for litigation over the proper scope of this newly articulated constitutional rule.

One question is whether the rule applies in contexts that are not criminal prosecutions, but are similar in some respects to criminal cases. *Winship* itself extended the rule from ordinary criminal cases to certain types of juvenile delinquency proceedings. In general, the Court has declined to hold that the rule is required in noncriminal proceedings, although it has held that sometimes the Constitution requires the government to prove its case by the intermediate standard of "clear and convincing evidence." For example, the state must prevail by clear and convincing evidence in proceedings for compulsory psychiatric hospitalization (*Addington v. Texas*, 441 U.S. 418 (1979)) and in proceedings to terminate parental rights (*Santosky v. Kramer*, 455 U.S. 745 (1982)).

A second controversial question is whether the rule applies to every issue in a criminal case, or whether particular issues may be excluded from the rule. Although most states have long adhered to the general rule that the prosecution must prove guilt beyond a reasonable doubt, each state also has developed its own idiosyncratic list of exceptions, requiring defendants to prove such issues as self-defense, duress, insanity, entrapment, renunciation, and mistake.

State criminal codes frequently use the term *defense* or *affirmative defense* to describe an issue where the burden of proof is assigned to the defendant. Other codes simply state that the burden of proof for all issues is on the state except where the statute expressly states otherwise.

Both the reasonable doubt rule and some of its exceptions have relatively ancient roots. The reasonable doubt rule has been recognized in Anglo-American law at least since 1798, and probably for several centuries before that (May; Morano; Green). Exceptions to the rule were also apparently recognized in the eighteenth and nineteenth centuries (Fletcher). But not until the rule acquired constitutional standing in 1970 did courts begin to seek criteria to govern its application, and the search has not been an easy one.

In a pair of very similar cases decided soon after *Winship*, the Court reached virtually opposite conclusions. Both cases involved statutes that shifted to the defendant the burden of proving that the crime was not murder but only the less serious crime of manslaughter. In *Mullaney v. Wilbur*, 421 U.S. 684 (1975), the Court had invalidated a state statute requiring the defendant to prove provocation, but two years later, in *Patterson v. New York*, 432 U.S. 197 (1977), the Court, without overruling *Mullaney*, upheld a statute requiring the defendant to prove "extreme emotional disturbance." The Court found a critical distinction in the way the two statutes were written: the *Mullaney* statute defined murder as including the absence of provocation, while the *Patterson* statute defined murder without reference to extreme emotional disturbance, which it defined separately as a defense. The Court seemingly gave states considerable leeway to make drafting choices that would determine which facts constitute elements of a crime, and must therefore be proved beyond a reasonable doubt.

In the following decade, the Court said little more about when the reasonable doubt rule applied. In the few cases it did decide, the Court favored the approach it took in *Patterson*, giving considerable leeway to the states in this regard. In *Martin v. Ohio*, 480 U.S. 228 (1987), for instance, the Court held that even though the defendant would have been entirely innocent of murder if her claim of self-defense were true, the state could require her to prove she had acted in self-defense because the state had not defined murder as including the absence of self-defense.

The rule's scope became controversial again, however, as legislatures increasingly began to draft statutes that specified particular *sentencing factors*, and courts began to consider whether such factors should be governed by the reasonable doubt rule. A sentencing factor is a fact that determines not what crime a defendant committed, but what sentence the defendant can receive. For example, drug laws frequently dictate that the sentence for possessing or selling drugs shall be increased by a certain number of years as the quantity possessed increases. A sentencing factor also may take the form of a "mandatory minimum," which means that if the factor is present, the defendant must serve at least a specified number of years, greater than the minimum sentence otherwise prescribed for the crime. A sentencing factor, therefore, may be of critical importance in determining how many years a defendant will serve in prison.

While the idea that certain facts, like possessing large quantities of drugs, should lead to harsher sentences is not particularly controversial, the procedure for determining those facts has become quite controversial. Statutes commonly provide that sentencing factors are determined at a sentencing hearing by a judge using a "preponderance of the evidence" standard. In *McMillan v. Pennsylvania*, 477 U.S. 79 (1986), the Court upheld a statute authorizing a judge to impose a mandatory minimum five-year sentence if the judge found by a preponderance of the evidence that the defendant had possessed a firearm during the commission of a criminal offense. By the late 1990s, however, members of the Supreme Court began voicing concern that sentencing factors were in effect circumventing the protections of the reasonable doubt rule. In 2000, the issue reached a constitutional boiling point in *Apprendi v. New Jersey*, 120 S. Ct. 2348 (2000).

In *Apprendi*, the defendant had fired shots into the home of an African-American family that had recently moved into an all-white neighborhood. A state statute provided that using a firearm to shoot into a home would ordinarily carry a sentencing range of five to ten years, but that if the crime was motivated by racial bias, the sentencing range rose to ten to twenty years. Despite Apprendi's denial at the sentencing hearing that he had acted out of racial bias, a judge found by a preponderance of the evidence that Apprendi had been so motivated and sentenced him to twelve years—two more years than the maximum sentence of ten years he could have received if the judge had not found the sentencing factor to be present.

The Supreme Court held that because Apprendi received a sentence that was greater than the maximum sentence he otherwise could have received without the sentencing enhancement, due process required that the sentencing factor of racial bias be proven to a jury beyond a reasonable doubt. But the *Apprendi* case does not necessarily apply the reasonable doubt rule to every sentencing factor that increases a defendant's punishment; the Court declined to disturb an earlier decision holding that when a defendant's prior convictions are used to increase his maximum sentence, the prior crimes need not be proved to a jury beyond a reasonable doubt (*Almendarez-Torres v. United States*, 523 U.S. 224 (1998)), and it also implied that when aggravating factors are required before the death penalty can be imposed, the aggravating factors need not be proved to a jury beyond a reasonable doubt. The scope of the rule in this area remains unclear, including whether the reasonable doubt rule applies to sentencing factors that increase the defendant's punishment within the statutory range, but do not increase the maximum punish-ment authorized by statute. Because sentencing factors are so widely used to calculate sentences, the answer to this question is crucial to the future of sentencing in the United States.

The courts are likely to struggle in the coming years with this question and other situations involving the reasonable doubt rule. In resolving such questions, it is useful to consider the rule's purposes.

Reasons for the rule

In justifying its holding, the *Winship* Court invoked the two distinct functions that generally are attributed to the reasonable doubt rule. First, the rule is meant to reduce the likelihood of erroneously convicting an innocent defendant. It puts a thumb on the defendant's side of the scales of justice to implement "a fundamental value determination of our society that it is far worse to convict an innocent man than to let a guilty man go free" (*Winship*, p. 372, Justice Harlan concurring).

Second, the rule symbolizes for society the great significance of a criminal conviction by singling out criminal convictions as peculiarly serious among the adjudications made by courts. The rule reaffirms the special opprobrium that attaches to criminal convictions, and the special importance of protecting individuals against the state's power to convict.

There are, of course, empirical questions about whether the rule in practice has its intended effect. The available studies are inconclusive, but they suggest that the instruction on the burden of proof can affect the outcome of a case (L.S.E. Jury Project; Simon, 1969, 1970; Simon and Mahan).

Issues that should be governed by the rule

Commentators have suggested different approaches for deciding which issues should be governed by the reasonable doubt rule. At one extreme, the rule might apply to every issue, without exception, governing the proof of every fact that the criminal law makes relevant to a criminal conviction. At the other extreme, the rule might apply only to those issues for which the legislature has made no explicit exception. The Supreme Court has plainly rejected both extreme positions in *Mullaney* and *Patterson*. Under these cases some exceptions are permitted, but there are constitutional limits on the legislature's power to make exceptions. Although the Court has not specified the criteria for permissible exceptions, commentators have suggested several.

First, and least controversial, is the view that the Constitution permits an exception for issues in a criminal case that do not directly relate to guilt or innocence. In the course of a criminal prosecution, it may be necessary to decide whether the case is properly before the court, whether particular items may be admitted into evidence, or whether the defendant is mentally competent to stand trial. These decisions may well determine whether it is possible as a practical matter to convict the defendant, but they do not determine whether the defendant is in fact guilty. For that reason, the Constitution does not impose the reasonable doubt rule on such determinations, although the rule may nonetheless be required as a matter of state law.

A second, more controversial proposal is an exception for issues that present special problems of proof. It is suggested that the defendant should bear the burden of proof on an issue if the defendant has better access than the prosecution to the evidence. The rationale is that a defendant with control over the relevant evidence has a great incentive to withhold the evidence, mislead the jury, and prevail because of the prosecution's inability to meet its burden of proof. This strategy could be prevented by a rule shifting the burden of proof to the defendant. On this theory, the burden of proof might be assigned to the defendant on the issue of insanity or of intent. The problem with shifting the burden to the defendant for this reason is that it accomplishes too much. It not only elicits evidence from the defendant, but it also continues to tilt the scales against the defendant even after the evidence has been produced. A better solution to the problem of access to evidence would shift to the defendant the burden of coming forward with enough evidence to raise the issue, and then leave with the government the ultimate burden of proof after all the evidence is in.

A third proposed criterion for identifying exceptions to the reasonable doubt rule has become the center of a major debate. This controversy raises basic questions about the relationship between substantive law and procedure, as well as about the relationship between state legislatures and the federal Constitution on matters of criminal law. Some commentators have argued that the reasonable doubt rule should not apply to any fact that the legislature could constitutionally have omitted from its substantive criminal law.

They argue that if the legislature has the constitutional power to make a fact irrelevant to guilt, then it must also have the power to choose its own rules for proving that fact. Put differently, if the legislature has created a gratuitous defense, then that issue is exempt from the requirement that the government prove its case beyond a reasonable doubt.

Other commentators argue that legislative power to eliminate a defense does not entail the power to shift to the defendant the burden of proof. They maintain that both the practical and the symbolic functions of the reasonable doubt rule apply with full force where a gratuitous defense is concerned.

The controversy is set forth in a pair of articles by Barbara Underwood and by John Jeffries and Paul Stephan. Jeffries and Stephan argue that it is both illogical and unwise to impose strict procedural requirements on the proof of a gratuitous defense. It is illogical, they say, because only if the Constitution requires the state to prove a particular fact as a prerequisite to conviction does the Constitution also require the state to prove that fact beyond a reasonable doubt. It is unwise, they argue, because legislatures have often been willing to enact new defenses to crime only in conjunction with rules that shift the burden of proof to the defendant. To prohibit such compromises, they contend, would stifle criminal law reform.

Underwood argues, by contrast, that the power to eliminate an issue from the criminal law does not entail the power to alter the rules of proof for that issue. In her view, the Constitution allocates to the states very broad power to define the substantive criminal law, but it imposes rigorous procedural requirements on the process of proving whatever facts the state has made criminal. Thus, the Constitution does not permit a state to adopt a controversial defense, and then limit it by shifting the burden of proof to the defendant. Instead, the state must resolve controversies over criminal law policy by making adjustments and compromises in the content of the substantive criminal law.

For example, a state legislature might be divided over a proposal to exempt from the narcotics law those who possess narcotics solely for personal use. A procedural compromise would be to adopt the defense in full, and to limit it by shifting the burden of proof to the defendant. A substantive compromise would be to adopt the defense in part, exempting only those who possess narcotics for personal use in specified small quantities, or in the privacy of the home. If the Constitution prohibits the procedural compromise, then the legislature must adopt or reject the defense or find a substantive compromise.

It is, of course, difficult to determine whether in fact criminal law reform would be stifled if the burden-shifting device were prohibited. Legislatures might instead adopt reforms without burden-shifting, or they might find satisfactory substantive compromises. Moreover, the argument that burden-shifting is necessary for legislative reform does not require an exception from the reasonable doubt rule for all gratuitous defenses. It requires an exception only for those new gratuitous defenses that result from legislative compromise.

Linking the reasonable doubt rule to only those facts that the Court says are constitutionally required to constitute a crime is equally questionable. Commentators have long urged the Court to develop a body of constitutional criminal law, but the Court has been highly reluctant to do so. In *Montana v. Egelhoff*, 518 U.S. 37 (1996), for instance, the Court struggled with the issue of whether the state could help meet its burden of proving that the defendant had intentionally killed the victim by barring him from showing that he was intoxicated. A bare majority of the Court held that the state could bar the intoxication defense, but it was badly split in its reasoning, and the case's difficulties suggest that the Court rarely will plunge into the quagmire of reviewing state substantive criminal law. Given the paucity of constitutional criminal law, if the rule applies only to constitutionally necessary facts, then it may have almost no application at all (Sundby, 1989a).

Moreover, the gratuitous character of a defense is not by itself sufficient to exempt that defense from other constitutional requirements of fair procedure. Even a defendant raising a gratuitous defense has the right to have that issue determined at a trial by jury, with counsel and confrontation of adverse witnesses. If an issue is exempt from the requirement of proof beyond a reasonable doubt, the reason must not be solely that the defense is gratuitous, but that for some reason it is less important to protect the defendant against error.

Presumptions as burden-shifting devices

Closely related to rules that regulate the burden of proof are rules of law that establish presumptions. These rules come in many variations, but they all instruct the fact finder to infer one fact from evidence that directly proves some other fact.

The Supreme Court has recognized that some forms of presumptions shift the burden of proof to the defendant in an unconstitutional manner. In *Sandstrom v. Montana*, 442 U.S. 510 (1979), the Court found constitutional error in an instruction that "the law presumes that a person intends the ordinary consequences of his voluntary acts" (p. 513). That instruction, in a prosecution for "deliberate homicide," shifted to the defendant the burden of proving he did not intend to cause death.

By contrast, in *County Court v. Allen*, 442 U.S. 140 (1979), the Court upheld an instruction that "upon proof of the presence of the machine gun and the hand weapons, you may infer and draw a conclusion that such prohibited weapon was possessed by each of the defendants who occupied the automobile at the time when such instruments were found" (p. 161, n. 20). That instruction, in a prosecution for criminal possession of a weapon, was held to be merely permissive and not burden-shifting, because it left the jury free to credit or reject the inference.

From these and earlier cases, several principles emerge. If the reasonable doubt rule applies to an issue, then the rule cannot constitutionally be circumvented by a presumption. Both the issue of intent in *Sandstrom* and the issue of possession in *County Court* were clearly subject to the reasonable doubt rule. For such issues, there can be no mandatory presumptions, even if they are rebuttable, because such presumptions are burden-shifting. The state may, however, use presumptions that merely authorize a permissible inference or invite the fact finder to consider it.

Neither *Sandstrom* nor *County Court* dealt with issues outside the scope of the reasonable doubt rule. For such issues there can be no constitutional objection to the burden-shifting character of a presumption, although the Constitution requires that any presumption, whether burden-shifting or not, have some rational basis.

BARBARA D. UNDERWOOD
SCOTT E. SUNDBY

See also CRIMINAL PROCEDURE: CONSTITUTIONAL ASPECTS; SENTENCING: PROCEDURAL PROTECTION; TRIAL, CRIMINAL.

BIBLIOGRAPHY

ALEXANDER, LARRY. "The Supreme Court, Dr. Jekyll, and the Due Process of Proof." *Supreme Court Review* 191 (1996): 191–217.

ALLEN, RONALD J. "Structuring Jury Decision-making in Criminal Cases: A Unified Constitutional Approach to Evidentiary Devices." *Harvard Law Review* 94 (1980): 321–368.

DANE, FRANCIS C. "In Search of Reasonable Doubt: A Systematic Examination of Selected Quantification Approaches." *Law and Human Behavior* 9 (1985): 141.

DRIPPS, DONALD A. "The Constitutional Status of the Reasonable Doubt Rule." *California Law Review* 75 (1987): 1665.

FLETCHER, GEORGE P. "Two Kinds of Legal Rules: A Comparative Study of Burden-of-Persuasion Practices in Criminal Cases." *Yale Law Journal* 77 (1968): 880–935.

GREEN, THOMAS A. "The Jury and the English Law of Homicide, 1200–1600." *Michigan Law Review* 74 (1976): 413–499.

JEFFRIES, JOHN C., JR., and STEPHAN, PAUL B. "Defenses, Presumptions, and Burden of Proof in the Criminal Law." *Yale Law Journal* 88 (1979): 1325–1407.

L.S.E. Jury Project. "Juries and the Rules of Evidence." *Criminal Law Review* (1973): 208–223.

MAY, JOHN W. "Some Rules of Evidence of Reasonable Doubt in Civil and Criminal Cases." *American Law Review* 10 (1876): 6.

MORANO, ANTHONY A. "A Reexamination of the Development of the Reasonable Doubt Rule." *Boston University Law Review* 55 (1975): 507–528.

NESSON, CHARLES R. "Reasonable Doubt and Permissive Inferences: The Value of Complexity." *Harvard Law Review* 92 (1979): 1187–1225.

SALTZBURG, STEPHEN A. "Standards of Proof and Preliminary Questions of Fact." *Stanford Law Review* 27 (1975): 271–305.

SCHWARTZ, LOUIS B. "'Innocence'—A Dialogue with Professor Sundby." *Hastings Law Journal* 41 (1989): 153.

SHAPIRO, BARBARA A. *"Beyond a Reasonable Doubt" and "Probable Cause": Historical Perspectives on the Anglo-American Law of Evidence.* Berkeley: University of California Press, 1991.

SIMON, RITA JAMES. "Judges' Translations of Burdens of Proof into Statements of Probability." *Trial Lawyer's Guide* (1969): 103–114.

———. "'Beyond a Reasonable Doubt': An Experimental Attempt at Quantification." *Journal of Applied Behavioral Science* 6 (1970): 203–209.

SIMON, RITA JAMES, and MAHAN, LINDA. "Quantifying Burdens of Proof—A View from the Bench, the Jury, and the Classroom." *Law and Society Review* 5 (1971): 319–330.

SUNDBY, SCOTT E. "The Reasonable Doubt Rule and the Meaning of Innocence." *Hastings Law Journal* 40 (1989a): 457.

———. "The Virtues of a Procedural View of Innocence—A Response to Professor Schwartz." *Hastings Law Journal* 41 (1989b): 161.

UNDERWOOD, BARBARA D. "The Thumb on the Scales of Justice: Burdens of Persuasion in Criminal Cases." *Yale Law Journal* 86 (1977): 1299–1348.

UVILLER, H. RICHARD. "Acquitting the Guilty: Two Case Studies on Jury Misgivings and the Misunderstood Standard of Proof." *Criminal Law Forum* 2 (1990): 1.

CASES

Addington v. Texas, 441 U.S. 418 (1979).
Almendarez-Torres v. United States, 523 U.S. 224 (1998).
Apprendi v. New Jersey, 120 S. Ct. 2348 (2000).
County Court v. Allen, 442 U.S. 140 (1979).
In re Winship, 397 U.S. 358 (1970).
Martin v. Ohio, 480 U.S. 228 (1987).
McMillan v. Pennsylvania, 477 U.S. 79 (1986).
Montana v. Egelhoff, 518 U.S. 37 (1996).
Mullaney v. Wilbur, 421 U.S. 684 (1975).
Patterson v. New York, 432 U.S. 197 (1977).
Sandstrom v. Montana, 442 U.S. 510 (1979).
Santosky v. Kramer, 455 U.S. 745 (1982).

BURGLARY

Burglary is a criminal offense that may be generally described as the unauthorized entry of a dwelling (or another delineated building) with the intent to commit a crime therein. Every jurisdiction has its own precise statutory definition of the crime of burglary, with corresponding case law to carve out the limits and meanings of that particular definition. One will immediately notice that the crime of burglary is not dependent upon the success of the unauthorized entrant intending to commit a crime. The mere intent to commit a crime (when added to the other elements) is sufficient to constitute violation of a burglary statute. This is not to be confused with larceny, which involves the actual taking of property. The entry may occur by the use of force, such as breaking a door or window, or may occur by simply walking through an open doorway, as long as the person entering has no right to be present.

Origins of the offense

Modern burglary statutes are the result of a long evolution from the early burglary laws found in England. The crime of burglary was one of the earliest of laws that was reduced to writing in Anglo-Saxon jurisprudence. Burglary probably dates back in relation to the ancient Anglo-Saxon crime of "hamsoaken" ("hamesecken"), or housebreaking. William Blackstone describes burglary as "nocturnal housebreaking," and descendant from ancient law (p. 958). The early laws reflect the age-old maxim that "a man's home is his castle." Indeed, the legal systems of many different countries have historically contained laws to punish those who would invade or tamper with another's home. This was seen as a particularly violent and punishable act, both because of the element of personal danger likely to be involved in breaking into another's home, and also because it was a crime against the home itself, which has a sanctified place in many human cultures. There were strict definitions as to what constituted a house and what time of day was sufficient to be called nighttime in order to satisfy a burglary charge.

Burglary was defined in the common law as breaking and entering into a dwelling house belonging to another, at night, with the intent to commit a felony therein. If the dwelling was open so that no "breaking" was necessary to enter, there could be no burglary. Entering a dwelling was satisfied if the perpetrator merely reached his arm through a window—the focus being on the intrusion to the home itself rather than the body position of the perpetrator. The definition of a dwelling house was often extended to include appurtenances nearby. English common law had precise definitions as to what was night and what was daytime, but no American jurisdiction has followed this approach.

Modern statutory scheme

The old common law requirement of a "breaking" is rarely found in modern statutes. Instead there is often found such language as "unauthorized entry" or "unlawful entry." There may also be varying degrees of burglary (first degree, second degree, and so on) depending on the level of seriousness. States have expanded the scope of burglary so that the crime intended by the entrant may not necessarily need to be classified as a felony for the elements of burglary to be met.

As noted above, only the intent to commit a crime, not the success in completing it, is required to make out the elements of burglary. One might note that the proximity to success that is accomplished by the burglar is not taken into account by the statutory schemes. Therefore, it can be said that the intent to commit a crime found in the burglary definition is a somewhat more relaxed standard than the standard used to define an attempt to commit a crime (itself punishable in other criminal situations), the latter generally being defined by the actor's steps taken to effectuate the act and his proximity to the completion thereof. A burglar is guilty of burglary the moment he unlawfully enters a building intending to commit a crime. Whether he makes it one step into the building or actually completes the crime does not alter his guilt for the burglary statutes.

Under many statutes a burglar may be subject to two punishments if he or she completes the intended act. A perpetrator may be punished for both burglary and the crime committed therein. Under ordinary attempt law, the attempt is only punished when the crime remained incomplete.

Because modern statutory schemes have expanded the old common law element of a home to include a structure or building, critics have noted that the law of burglary has so far evolved from its modern origins that the original rationales for this cause of action no longer apply. Nevertheless, burglary is a widely recognized crime in modern American culture, and is clearly an offense that will remain cognizable by legal authorities.

Current trends in America

In 1996 the average maximum sentence for those receiving incarceration for burglary was forty-one months. Twenty-nine percent of all convicted burglars, however, received no jail or prison sentence whatsoever, receiving instead probation.

Burglary rates have been dropping significantly in the last twenty years. According to the Federal Bureau of Investigation, the amount of burglaries being committed per capita in the United States has declined by over one third since the late 1970s (measuring the number of "household" burglaries). Nevertheless, the Department of Justice reports that in 1998 alone there were 4.1 million "household" burglaries in the United States.

Another survey reports that in 1996 more burglaries occurred during daylight hours than at night, and overwhelmingly in urban settings. Additionally, burglaries represented only 1 percent of all felony convictions nationwide (*Statistical Abstract of the United States*).

CHARLES H. WHITEBREAD

See also ATTEMPT; THEFT; TRESPASS, CRIMINAL.

BIBLIOGRAPHY

American Jurisprudence. *Burglary.* West Publishing Group, 1964. Current through April 1999 Cumulative Supplement.

BLACKSTONE, WILLIAM. *Commentaries on the Laws of England (1769).* 4th ed. Edited by George Chase. New York: Banks Law Publishing Company, 1974.

United States Department of Justice. *Bureau of Justice Statistics Bulletin.* July 1999.

United States Department of Commerce. *Statistical Abstract of the United States, 1998.* 118th ed. Washington, D.C.: Bernan Press, 1998.

C

CAPITAL PUNISHMENT: LEGAL ASPECTS

Until the twentieth century, the law of capital punishment in the United States was almost entirely in the hands of individual states. State legislatures could decide whether to have capital statutes at all, what crimes to render eligible for capital punishment, what procedures to follow in capital trials, and what methods of execution to use. The federal legislature—Congress—also exercised similar policy discretion over the use of capital punishment for federal crimes. However, criminal law has always been primarily the province of state as opposed to federal power, and the vast majority of American executions have been conducted by states rather than by the federal government.

State legislative innovations

From the founding of the Republic through the nineteenth century and into the twentieth century, states made a number of changes in their capital statutes. In both the nineteenth and twentieth centuries, there were periodic waves of legislative abolition, starting with Michigan in 1846 and concluding with New Mexico in 1969, but of the twenty-two states that voted to abolish capital punishment for ordinary murder during this period, eleven eventually reinstated the death penalty. As of early 2001 only twelve states and the District of Columbia do not have capital punishment statutes (Massachusetts, the twelfth state, had its capital murder statute struck down under that state's constitution by the Massachusetts Supreme Judicial Court in 1984).

The states also made changes over the years in the crimes eligible for capital punishment.

Perhaps the most significant change was commenced by Pennsylvania in 1794 when it became the first state to divide murder into "degrees," rendering only "first-degree" murder—murder accompanied by "premeditation and deliberation"—eligible for the death penalty. This innovation was widely followed, and it restricted the scope of the death penalty to a smaller pool of convicted murderers. In addition to murder, a number of other crimes were commonly covered by capital statutes well into the twentieth century, including rape, kidnapping, and armed robbery, as well as extraordinary crimes such as treason, espionage, and sabotage.

As for capital trial procedures, the states wrought surprisingly little change on their own over the years before the federal constitution was held to compel such change late in the twentieth century. Before the constitutional era, capital trials did not tend to differ markedly from ordinary felony trials, although capital sentencing was generally placed in the hands of juries rather than judges, who conducted most other, ordinary criminal sentencing. Finally, states made a number of changes over the years in the methods of executions they employed. While public hanging was by far the most prevalent mode of execution at the time of the founding, death by electrocution, by lethal gas chamber, and by lethal injection later almost completely displaced hanging, with lethal injection being by far the most common mode employed today. No American jurisdiction currently conducts any executions in public, despite occasional interest from members of the public and the media.

Early constitutional intervention

Before the twentieth century, there was no intimation from the U.S. Supreme Court that the federal constitution placed any special restrictions, substantive or procedural, on the use of capital punishment by the states or the federal government. Rather, it was assumed that the scope of capital statutes, the conduct of capital trials, and the manner of execution were all policy choices entrusted completely to the states or to the political branches of the federal government.

The first significant constitutional ruling regarding the use of capital punishment arose in an unusual and unusually fraught context—the trial of the Scottsboro Boys, nine young black men accused of raping two white women on a freight train near Scottsboro, Alabama, in the early 1930s. The men were arrested, indicted, and tried in short order, and convicted and sentenced to death on the basis of extremely flimsy evidence after extremely abbreviated legal proceedings. The case led to a number of appeals in both state and federal courts, but the most famous and legally significant ruling to result from the case was the Supreme Court's holding that, at least in capital cases, trial judges had an obligation to ensure that indigent defendants who could not adequately represent themselves be appointed counsel to represent them (*Powell v. Alabama*, 287 U.S. 45 (1932)). This requirement of appointed counsel was not broadly extended to noncapital defendants until the 1960s. While the Scottsboro case is justly famous both for its illumination of the treatment of black defendants in southern criminal courts and for its anticipation of the later use of the due process clause of the Fourteenth Amendment to "incorporate" the Bill of Rights to apply to the states as well as the federal government, it also is a landmark in the legal regulation of capital punishment. The Supreme Court's ruling signaled, for the first time, that the federal constitution might specially limit the use of the death penalty, long thought to be an unfettered prerogative of state criminal justice systems.

Perhaps because Scottsboro was so distinctive a case, the Supreme Court did not quickly move to elaborate upon the U.S. Constitution's significance in capital cases. Indeed, except for holding in 1947 that a botched electrocution that failed to result in death did not constitutionally bar a second try (*State of Louisiana ex rel. Francis v. Resweber*, 330 U.S. 853 (1947)), the Court did not make any further significant constitutional rulings regarding capital punishment until the late 1960s. The Warren Court, headed by Chief Justice Earl Warren, revolutionized criminal procedure generally during the 1960s by holding that almost all of the specific criminal procedural protections contained in the Bill of Rights were applicable not only to federal cases but to state criminal trials as well. The Warren Court also broadly construed these constitutional protections, requiring, for example, that arrested suspects be given warnings before being questioned and that attorneys be present during many line-ups (*Miranda v. Arizona*, 384 U.S. 436 (1966); *United States v. Wade*, 388 U.S. 218 (1967)). In addition to seeing such revolutionary expansion of the constitutional rights of the accused, the 1960s were also a time of declining popular support for the use of capital punishment. A Gallup poll conducted in 1966 showed for the first (and it has turned out to be the only) time in the twentieth century that more of those polled opposed capital punishment for murder than supported it. At the same time, the NAACP Legal Defense Fund was successfully pursuing a "moratorium" strategy in criminal courts around the country, attempting to prevent any executions from going forward by raising every legal claim conceivably available. It is not surprising, therefore, that the Supreme Court chose this time to reenter the death penalty debate.

In 1968, the last year of the Warren Court, the Court gave a small but significant victory to the abolitionist forces when it ruled that states could not automatically exclude from capital trial juries all of those with conscientious scruples against capital punishment, as many jurisdictions did as a matter of course. (*Witherspoon v. Illinois*, 391 U.S. 510 (1968)). Rather, such potential jurors can now be removed for cause only if their attitudes about capital punishment would prevent or substantially impair the performance of their duties as jurors. Abolitionist litigators were emboldened by this ruling, which many hoped or believed would lead to the constitutional abolition of capital punishment entirely.

These hopes were crushed, however, only a few years later when, in 1971, the Supreme Court heard and rejected the first sweeping challenge to the American practice of capital punishment. The Court held that the due process clause of the Fourteenth Amendment was not violated by the existence of completely standardless capital sentencing procedures—in which the sentencing jury was told it had absolute discretion to impose a sentence of life or death for whatever reasons it deemed appropriate—nor did the constitution require that capital trials and sentencing procedures be bifurcated into two separate hearings (*McGautha v. California*, 402 U.S. 183 (1971)). This decisive defeat seemed to mark the end of constitutional challenges to the administration of capital punishment.

Constitutional abolition in *Furman v. Georgia*

In a startling turnaround, however, the very next year the Supreme Court heard the very same challenge to American capital sentencing practices, but this time under the Eighth Amendment's proscription of cruel and unusual punishments. Once again, abolitionist lawyers argued that standardless capital sentencing procedures violated the federal constitution—and this time, they prevailed. The Supreme Court's ruling in (*Furman v. Georgia*, 408 U.S. 238 (1972)), had the effect of abolishing the death penalty as it was then administered in the United States, invalidating the statutes of thirty-nine states, the District of Columbia, and the federal government.

But the reasoning behind the Court's landmark ruling was far from clear. The Court was closely divided—5 to 4—and each of the five Justices in the majority authored his own opinion and refused to join the opinion of any other Justice. Only two Justices—William J. Brennan and Thurgood Marshall—were convinced that the death penalty in all cases constituted cruel and unusual punishment. The other Justices in the majority were more concerned with the procedures used to impose the death penalty and with the patterns of its application. The fact that so many defendants charged with serious felonies were eligible for the death penalty while so few were actually sentenced to death led Justice Potter Stewart to compare receiving the death penalty with being struck by lightning. Justice William O. Douglas feared that the application of the death penalty was not merely arbitrary, but actually discriminatory against racial minorities, the poor, and the politically unpopular. The absence of any guidance to sentencing juries to prevent such questionable patterns of imposition, concluded Justice Byron White, demonstrated the lack of legislative will behind the death penalty. The dissenting Justices, who also produced a range of separate opinions, objected that the majority was using the Eighth Amendment to usurp a legislative function and speculated that state legislatures might be able to remedy their flawed capital sentencing schemes.

Just as many believed that the Supreme Court's rejection of due process challenges to capital punishment spelled the end of constitutional abolition, many believed that the Court's decision in *Furman* spelled the end of capital punishment in America. This latter belief proved as ill-founded as the former. *Furman* created an angry backlash in many states, and thirty-five states almost immediately redrafted their capital sentencing schemes in order to attempt to salvage the death penalty in the wake of the Court's constitutional ruling. Four years after its seemingly final pronouncement in *Furman*, the Court granted review to consider five of the new statutes, from the states of Florida, Georgia, Texas, Louisiana, and North Carolina.

Post-*Furman* constitutional regulation

The Court's five decisions in 1976 both revived the practice of capital punishment in America and established an ongoing role for courts to supervise death penalty practices under the Constitution. The Court struck down two of the challenged statutes—those from Louisiana and North Carolina because they required mandatory imposition of the death penalty upon conviction of certain crimes (*Roberts v. Louisiana*, 428 U.S. 325 (1976)); (*Woodson v. North Carolina*, 428 U.S. 280 (1976)). While such statutes were an understandable reaction to *Furman*'s concern about unbridled jury discretion, the Court nonetheless concluded that there was an overwhelming societal consensus against mandatory capital sentencing and thus that such sentencing ran afoul of the "evolving standards of decency" that the Eighth Amendment enshrined in the Constitution. The Court upheld the three remaining statutes on the ground that they appropriately guided the discretion of capital sentencing juries (*Gregg v. Georgia*, 428 U.S. 153 (1976); *Proffitt v. Florida*, 428 U.S. 242 (1976); *Jurek v. Texas*, 428 U.S. 262 (1976)). The Florida and Georgia statutes, though somewhat different from one another, both provided for jury consideration of "aggravating" and "mitigating" factors during a separate capital sentencing hearing, as the drafters of the Model Penal Code had suggested well before *Furman*, and this model has become the dominant one in post-*Furman* capital sentencing. Texas required that its sentencing juries answer a set of "special issues" or questions that would then form the basis for the trial judge's imposition of either death or a lesser sentence. In its three opinions upholding the new statutes from Florida, Georgia, and Texas, the Court did not attempt to list in any definitive fashion the prerequisites for a valid capital punishment scheme; rather, the Court upheld each statutory scheme on the basis of its own peculiar mix of procedural protections. The 1976 opinions permitted executions to resume in the United States in 1977, but the provisional tone and approach of these opinions established an ongoing role for the Supreme Court in regulating the use of capital punishment in the post-*Furman* era.

In subsequent opinions, the Supreme Court elaborated on the constitutional role of both "aggravating" and "mitigating" evidence. Aggravating factors, according to the Court, play a constitutionally significant role in both narrowing the class of the death eligible and channeling the sentencer's discretion during the penalty phase. However, the Court made clear that the narrowing function need not necessarily be performed by aggravating factors when it held that state legislatures could narrow—i.e., make smaller—the class of those eligible for the death penalty simply by drafting capital murder statutes that excluded some murderers from the definition of capital murder (*Lowenfield v. Phelps,* 484 U.S. 231 (1988)). But the Court has never required states to narrow the class of death eligible to some particular size. As a result, most states capital sentencing schemes have seen a proliferation of statutory aggravating factors that render most, though not all, murderers eligible for the death penalty. Indeed, it seems likely, and at least one empirical study in Georgia (Baldus et al.) has expressly concluded, that the vast majority of persons convicted of murder who would have been eligible for the death penalty prior to *Furman* remain death eligible under the "reformed" capital statutes.

The second function of aggravating factors— the channeling of sentencer discretion during the penalty phase—also has been rendered less than indispensable by the Court. On the one hand, the Court has insisted that statutory aggravating factors cannot be excessively broad or vague, and thus it has occasionally struck down extraordinarily capacious aggravators, such as one widely adopted from the Model Penal Code that asks whether the murder was "especially heinous, atrocious or cruel." On the other hand, the Court has permitted state courts to salvage such aggravators by giving them "narrowing" constructions, and it has held some dubiously

broad constructions to be sufficiently narrowed, such as the Idaho Supreme Court's "cold-blooded, pitiless slayer" construction of one of its aggravators (*Arave v. Creech,* 507 U.S. 463 (1993)). Moreover, while the Court has held that if states include aggravating factors in their sentencing schemes, such factors may not be overly broad and vague, it has never held that states must include aggravators or their equivalent as part of constitutionally valid penalty phase proceedings.

As for mitigating factors, the Court has concluded that such evidence plays an entirely different role in capital sentencing. While aggravators narrow or channel discretion, mitigators create the opportunity for the exercise of discretion through individualized sentencing. A few years after rejecting mandatory capital sentencing, the Court went further and held that the Eighth Amendment also requires that sentencers be permitted to consider all relevant mitigating evidence that might call for a sentence less than death (*Lockett v. Ohio,* 438 U.S. 586 (1978); *Eddings v. Oklahoma,* 455 U.S. 104 (1982)). Hence, states are not free to limit the range of mitigating factors to a statutory list, the way they frequently do with aggravators. And capital sentencing proceedings now have the potential—at least when the defendant has access to sufficient resources and competent counsel—to become in-depth explorations of the defendant's background and personal moral culpability for the crime at issue. As many members of the Court have noted, however, the constitutional roles of aggravating and mitigating evidence are in some tension with each other. The sentencer's discretion to impose death must be confined, but the sentencer's discretion not to impose death must be unlimited. In the words of Justice Antonin Scalia, to acknowledge that there is an inherent tension between these two commands "is rather like saying that there was perhaps an inherent tension between the Allies and the Axis Powers in World War II" (*Walton v. Arizona,* 497 U.S. 639, 664 (1990) (Scalia, J., concurring)).

Perhaps because it has insisted that sentencing juries be required to consider any and all mitigating evidence offered by the defense, the Supreme Court has been reluctant to hold that the existence of particular mitigating evidence categorically excludes some defendants from the class of the death eligible. In particular, the Court has rejected claims that the Constitution categorically forbids the execution of either juveniles or persons with mental retardation, although it has required that state legislatures make clear their intention, if it exists, to render eligible for capital punishment those offenders who are younger than sixteen at the time of their crimes (*Thompson v. Oklahoma*, 487 U.S. 815 (1988)). In addition, although the Court initially approved a categorical exemption for defendants who were convicted of felony murder but did not themselves kill or intend to kill, the Court later narrowed this ruling. The narrowed exemption permits defendants to be executed for murders committed by others during the course of joint felonies if the defendant played a substantial role in the felony and evinced a reckless disregard for human life (*Tison v. Arizona*, 481 U.S. 137 (1987)). The only other categorical exemption from capital punishment mandated by the Court came only one year after it revived the death penalty in 1976, in a pair of cases forbidding the imposition of the death penalty for the crime of rape, for which death had been imposed frequently, and for kidnapping, for which death had been imposed occasionally (*Coker v. Georgia*, 433 U.S. 584 (1977); *Eberheart v. Georgia*, 433 U.S. 917 (1977)). Since these decisions in 1977, all executions have been of convicted murderers. Whether crimes not specifically dealt with by the Court—such as the rape of children, hijacking, or treason—might still be constitutionally valid predicates for the imposition of capital punishment remains to be determined.

The Court's rejection of the death penalty for rape was ostensibly based on the disproportion between the crime of rape and the punishment of death and not on the widely known fact that the death penalty for rape was disproportionately imposed on black men who raped white women in southern states. Such claims of racial discrimination in the application of capital punishment were widely made in state and lower federal courts in the 1950s and 1960s; indeed, Justice Douglas's opinion in *Furman* itself in 1972 explicitly made reference to racial discrimination as a reason to reject the American system of capital punishment. The Court managed to avoid a head-on confrontation with the issue of race until 1987, when it heard and decided the claim of a black defendant sentenced to death in Georgia for the murder of a white victim (*McCleskey v. Kemp*, 481 U.S. 279 (1987)). McCleskey's lawyers presented a detailed empirical study of capital sentencing in Georgia in which researchers found, among other things, a strong statistical correlation, after multiple regression analysis, between the white race of the victim and the im-

position of the death penalty. The researchers also found that among murder defendants whose victims were white, black defendants were much more likely to receive the death penalty than white defendants. The Court split 5–4 on the question, but ultimately ruled against McCleskey. The Court held that defendants claiming racial discrimination in the imposition of capital punishment may not rely on statistical evidence of racial bias; rather, such defendants must offer particularized proof of intentional racial discrimination in the prosecution or decision of their individual cases. Direct proof of such discrimination, of course, is difficult if not impossible to obtain even when such discrimination occurs. Moreover, the nature of the strong statistical correlation found—between death and the race of the victim rather than the race of the defendant—suggests that the bias involved might often be what is sometimes called "unconscious" racial discrimination, in which (largely white) sentencers tend to empathize selectively with victims whose race is the same as their own and sentence accordingly; evidence of this sort of discrimination can come only from the hearts and mouths of decision-makers if statistical methods of proof are ruled out. After the Court's ruling, concerns about racial discrimination in capital sentencing moved from the judicial to the legislative arena. Congress considered but refused to adopt a proposed "Racial Justice Act," which would have precluded the carrying out of executions in jurisdictions in which certain showings of racial disproportion could be made until such disproportion was corrected. A number of states considered similar measures, with one state (Kentucky) actually adopting a weaker version of the failed federal statute (Kentucky, *Revised Statutes* (1998) at 532. 300–309).

The statistical evidence offered in *McCleskey*—and reproduced in other jurisdictions, including the northern city of Philadelphia—suggests that the Court's constitutional regulation of capital punishment in the post-*Furman* era has failed to address many of the concerns raised in 1972 about the arbitrary or discriminatory administration of capital punishment. Central to this failure, in the eyes of many expert observers of the judicial process, has been the lack of competent counsel in capital cases. Despite the Court's assertion that capital cases on occasion call for more stringent procedural protections than noncapital criminal cases, the Court has been unwilling to tighten in capital cases the fairly lax constitutional standard for "effective assistance of counsel" guaranteed to all criminal defendants by the Sixth Amendment. At the same time, the Court cut back substantially in the post-*Furman* era on the availability of federal habeas corpus review of state criminal convictions, a cutback that was partly codified and partly even intensified by Congress's redrafting of the habeas statute in the Anti-Terrorism and Effective Death Penalty Act, which was passed in 1996. The widespread lack of competent counsel in capital cases, coupled with the tightening of federal review, has led to growing concerns about the fairness and reliability of capital sentencing in the United States.

Growing concerns about fairness and reliability

For much of the last quarter of the twentieth century, the Supreme Court played a seemingly intensive, even intrusive, role in the regulation of capital punishment. It issued several significant opinions every year on constitutional challenges to the administration of capital punishment, and many perceived the resulting doctrines to be complex and confusing. Ultimately, however, the Court's constitutional requirements for valid capital statutes are fairly undemanding, and the Court has rejected a variety of more sweeping challenges that would have truly changed the nature and availability of capital punishment in America—such as challenges to the execution of juveniles and the mentally retarded, challenges to racial disproportion in capital sentencing, and challenges regarding the quality of counsel and the availability of federal review in capital cases. However, at least for awhile, the appearance of intensive regulation seemed to trump the reality of its absence, and complaints about undue judicial intervention in capital sentencing were widely heard and helpful in easing the passage of the "habeas reform" statute in 1996.

In the last few years of the twentieth century, however, concerns about the fairness and reliability of the administration of capital punishment seemed to grow significantly. In the year 2000, the governor of a state—Republican Governor George Ryan of Illinois—declared a moratorium on executions, citing evidence that innocent people had been erroneously convicted and sentenced to death. More than two dozen municipalities—including Atlanta, Baltimore, Philadelphia, and San Francisco—imposed similar measures, and President Bill Clinton, in the last months of his presidency, stayed what would

have been the first federal execution in thirty-seven years to await the completion of a study by the Department of Justice on racial and geographical disparities in administration of the federal death penalty. In the same year, the legislature of New Hampshire—the only retentionist state with no one on "death row"—became the first state legislature in the post-*Furman* era to vote to abolish the death penalty; its vote, however, was vetoed successfully by Democratic Governor Jeanne Shaheen.

These developments suggest that the weakness of federal constitutional regulation of capital punishment is becoming more apparent both to political actors and to the public at large. It is possible that the new century may bring about a turn in the fate of the institution of capital punishment in the United States.

CAROL S. STEIKER

See also CAPITAL PUNISHMENT: MORALITY, POLITICS, AND POLICY; CRUEL AND UNUSUAL PUNISHMENT; HABEAS CORPUS; HOMICIDE: LEGAL ASPECTS; JUVENILES IN THE ADULT SYSTEM; JUVENILE VIOLENT OFFENDERS; MENTALLY DISORDERED OFFENDERS; RACE AND CRIME; SENTENCING: ALLOCATION OF AUTHORITY; SENTENCING: ALTERNATIVES; SENTENCING: DISPARITY; SENTENCING: GUIDELINES; SENTENCING: MANDATORY AND MANDATORY MINIMUM SENTENCES; SENTENCING: PRESENTENCE REPORT; SENTENCING: PROCEDURAL PROTECTION; VICTIMS' RIGHTS.

BIBLIOGRAPHY

ACKER, JAMES R.; BOHM, ROBERT M.; and LANIER, CHARLES S., eds. *America's Experiment with Capital Punishment: Reflections on the Past, Present, and Future of the Ultimate Penal Sanction.* Durham, N.C.: Carolina Academic Press, 1998.

BALDUS, DAVID C.; WOODWORTH, GEORGE G.; and PULASKI, CHARLES A., JR. *Equal Justice and the Death Penalty: A Legal and Empirical Analysis.* Boston, Mass.: Northeastern University Press, 1990.

BILIONIS, LOUIS D. "Legitimating Death." *Michigan Law Review* 91 (June 1993): 1643–1702.

BRIGHT, STEPHEN B. "Counsel for the Poor: The Death Sentence Not for the Worst Crime but for the Worst Lawyer." *Yale Law Journal* 103 (May 1994): 1835–1883.

GIVELBER, DANIEL. "The New Law of Murder." *Indiana Law Review* 69 (1994): 375–422.

GROSS, SAMUEL R., and MAURO, ROBERT. *Death and Discrimination: Racial Disparities in Capital Sentencing.* Boston, Mass.: Northeastern University Press, 1989.

KENNEDY, RANDALL L. "*McCleskey v. Kemp*: Race, Capital Punishment, and the Supreme Court." *Harvard Law Review* 101 (May 1988): 1388–1443.

MELTSNER, MICHAEL. *Cruel and Unusual: The Supreme Court and Capital Punishment.* New York: Random House, 1973.

PATERNOSTER, RAYMOND. *Capital Punishment in America.* New York: Lexington Books, 1991.

SIMON, JONATHAN, and SPAULDING, CHRISTINA. "Tokens of Our Esteem: Aggravating Factors in the Era of Deregulated Death Penalties." In *The Killing State: Capital Punishment in Law, Politics, and Culture.* Edited by Austin Sarat. New York: Oxford University Press, 1999.

STEIKER, CAROL S., and STEIKER, JORDAN M. "Sober Second Thoughts: Reflections on Two Decades of Constitutional Regulation of Capital Punishment." *Harvard Law Review* 109 (December 1995): 355–438.

WEISBERG, ROBERT. "Deregulating Death." *Supreme Court Review 1983* (1983): 305–395.

WHITE, WELSH S. *The Death Penalty in the Nineties: An Examination of the Modern System of Capital Punishment.* Ann Arbor, Mich.: University of Michigan Press, 1991.

ZIMRING, FRANK. "Inheriting the Wind: The Supreme Court and Capital Punishment in the 1990s." *Florida State University Law Review* 20 (Summer 1992): 7–19.

CASES

Arave v. Creech, 507 U.S. 463 (1993).
Coker v. Georgia, 433 U.S. 584 (1977).
Eddings v. Oklahoma, 455 U.S. 104 (1982).
Eberheart v. Georgia, 433 U.S. 917 (1977).
Furman v. Georgia, 408 U.S. 238 (1972).
Gregg v. Georgia, 428 U.S. 153 (1976).
Jurek v. Texas, 428 U.S. 262 (1976).
Lockett v. Ohio, 438 U.S. 586 (1978).
Lowenfield v. Phelps, 484 U.S. 231 (1988).
McCleskey v. Kemp, 484 U.S. 279 (1987).
McGautha v. California, 402 U.S. 183 (1971).
Miranda v. Arizona, 384 U.S. 436 (1966).
Powell v. Alabama, 287 U.S. 45 (1932).
Proffitt v. Florida, 428 U.S. 242 (1976).
Roberts v. Louisiana, 428 U.S. 325 (1976).
State of Louisiana ex rel. Francis v. Resweber, 330 U.S. 853 (1947).
Thompson v. Oklahoma, 487 U.S. 815 (1988).
Tison v. Arizona, 481 U.S. 137 (1987).
Walton v. Arizona, 497 U.S. 639 (1990).
Witherspoon v. Illinois, 391 U.S. 510 (1968).
Woodson v. North Carolina, 428 U.S. 280 (1976).

CAPITAL PUNISHMENT: MORALITY, POLITICS, AND POLICY

Throughout the world, from earliest recorded times, the death penalty has played a prominent role in social control. Abolition of the death penalty became a matter for political discussion in Europe and America beginning in 1764, when the young Italian jurist Cesare Beccaria (1738–1794) published his little book, *On Crimes and Punishments*. Beccaria's criticism of torture and the death penalty typified the Enlightenment zeal for rational reform of prevailing social practices. Beccaria's alternative to the death penalty was life in prison at hard labor. In short order Catherine of Russia decreed an end to the death penalty, and so did Emporer Leopold in the province of Tuscany in the Austro-Hungarian Empire. Maximilien Robespierre, a powerful leader in the French Revolution, attacked the death penalty as murder. In England, by the end of the eighteenth century, Parliament was being petitioned to reduce the number of capital felonies, which numbered in the hundreds; complete abolition was never a serious prospect.

The death penalty in America, 1793–1982

During the seventeenth century, the criminal justice systems in the American colonies took their main features from the mother country. A mandatory hanging carried out in public after conviction in a jury trial was the widely used punishment for murder and other traditional felonies (arson, rape, robbery, burglary). In the new nation, the first significant step toward reform of the death penalty was taken in Pennsylvania in 1793, when the legislature created "degrees" of murder and confined the death penalty to offenders convicted of murder in the "first-degree"—willful, deliberate, and premeditated murder and felony murder (any homicide committed in the course of arson, rape, robbery, and burglary). By the middle of the nineteenth century many states had adopted this reform as a more precise conception of what ought to count as criminal homicide deserving the death penalty.

During the nineteenth century, state legislatures from Maine to Pennsylvania regularly received petitions from religious groups, notably the Society of Friends (Quakers), in favor of complete abolition. During this period two important further reforms were initiated. One ended public executions, thus confining the hangman and his necessary but sordid duties to the relative privacy of the prison yard. (Debauchery among the onlookers at public executions was widely regarded in this country and in England as a disgrace that needlessly fueled demands for abolition.) The other reform abandoned the mandatory death sentence upon a conviction of a capital felony in favor of giving the trial jury the power to choose between a death sentence and "mercy," in the form of a long prison term. A third trend—statutory abolition of all death penalties—advanced, stumbled, and by the Civil War vanished. Nevertheless, between 1847 (when Michigan abolished the death penalty for murder, though not for treason) and 1887 (when Maine abolished the death penalty), several states experimented with complete abolition.

With the advent of the Progressive Era, nine states across the nation, from Tennessee to Washington, repealed all their capital statutes; all but two (Minnesota and North Dakota) restored it within a few years, as public reaction to the experiment in most states brought it to an end. Execution by lethal gas chamber was first used in Nevada in 1923 and within a few years was adopted in many other states as a method superior in its humanity both to hanging and to electrocution.

During the Depression and World War II, agitation for abolition in the state legislatures came to a virtual halt. In 1958 the first prominent interest in evaluating and abolishing the death penalty occurred in Delaware, when the legislature (under the influence of local political leadership and the pathbreaking *Report* of the Royal Commission on Capital Punishment in England in 1953) repealed all that state's death penalty statutes. Influenced by the example of Delaware, several other states in the 1960s debated whether to abolish the death penalty; abolition efforts were successful in Vermont, West Virginia, and Iowa. No doubt the highpoint of the mid-century abolition movement occurred in 1964 in Oregon, when in a popular referendum the public voted to repeal the state constitutional provision for the death penalty.

Beginning in 1967, a new strategy to abolish the death penalty nationwide began to unfold, directed by the NAACP Legal Defense and Educational Fund (LDF) in New York. Mindful of the way in which African American defendants were especially vulnerable to the death penalty, and

the way the administration of the death penalty was both highly discriminatory and in general arbitrarily imposed, the LDF decided to attack it nationwide, not in the legislatures but in the federal courts, and on federal constitutional grounds. LDF attorneys argued that the evidence showed the death penalty in the United States violated "equal protection of the laws" and "due process of law," and that it was a "cruel and unusual punishment"—not in this or that case, not just in the South as part of the legacy of slavery and Jim Crow, but uniformly and generally across the nation. This strategy, inspired by the Civil Rights movement of the early 1960s, led to a moratorium on executions (though not on death sentences) as the Supreme Court debated the constitutional status of the death penalty.

In 1972, the Court held that the death penalty was unconstitutional as administered, because of its arbitrary and discriminatory application (*Furman v. Georgia*). Many state legislatures promptly revised and reenacted their death penalty statutes, hoping they would pass constitutional muster. Four years later the Court held that several varieties of these new capital statutes had indeed cured the problems of the prior statutes and that, in any case, the death penalty as such was not unconstitutional; more precisely, the death penalty did not violate the constitutional prohibition against "cruel and unusual punishment" (*Gregg v. Georgia*). In 1977, after the moratorium had lasted nearly a decade, executions resumed, first in Utah and then across the nation. During this period a new method of execution found increasing favor across the land: death by lethal injection. First adopted, in Oklahoma, in 1977, lethal injection was first used in Texas in 1982.

Current status

As of 1998, Amnesty International reported that some sixty nations worldwide (including all western European countries) counted as "abolitionist for all crimes." Another fifteen countries were listed as "abolitionist for ordinary crimes only," that is, these countries retained the death penalty only for "exceptional crimes" such as those provided by military law. Another twenty-eight countries were listed as "abolitionist de facto," because although their statutes still authorized the death penalty in certain cases, no executions had been carried out for at least a decade. Finally, ninety-four countries—mostly in Africa, the Middle East, and Asia—were listed as retaining and using the death penalty for murder and other felonies. Interpreters of the international scene have insisted that there is a slow but steady rejection of the death penalty worldwide, a trend that isolates the United States and conspicuously prevents it from exercising international leadership in protecting human rights, as these rights are increasingly defined under international human rights law.

By 1998, in the United States, thirteen states (and the District of Columbia) had abolished the death penalty: Alaska, Hawaii, Iowa, Maine, Massachusetts, Michigan, Minnesota, New Mexico, North Dakota, Rhode Island, Vermont, West Virginia, and Wisconsin. Since 1977 each of thirty states has carried out at least one execution.

Among the death penalty states (and the federal government), thirty-two use lethal injection to carry out the death penalty, eleven use the electric chair, seven use the gas chamber, four use hanging, and three use firing squad. Fourteen of these jurisdictions give the prisoner a choice between death by lethal injection and one of the other four methods.

Early in 1999 the LDF reported a total of 3,565 persons under death sentence in thirty-seven states (twenty-nine of these prisoners were awaiting execution under federal law, including eight under military law). By race, whites constituted 56 percent of the total, African Americans 35 percent; other nonwhites (American Indians, Asians, Hispanics) totaled 9 percent. The vast majority (99 percent) were male. The U.S. Bureau of Justice Statistics reported that as of the end of 1998, 65 percent of the nation's death row population were recidivist felons with a prior criminal record, including 9 percent who had a conviction of some form of criminal homicide. During the 1990s, the nation's death row population grew on the average at a rate of about 250 prisoners per year. The average length of time spent under death sentence prior to execution was about ten years. Of the 6,424 persons sentenced to death between 1973 and 1998, more than a third (38 percent) were not executed; some died awaiting execution, others committed suicide, and still others were commuted or resentenced by court order.

Executions in the 1990s went from a low of fourteen in 1991 to a high of seventy-four in 1997, for an annual average of about forty. The nation's high-point in executions during the twentieth century was reached in 1935, however, when 199 offenders were executed. During the 1930s the percentage of convicted murderers executed was far higher than in the 1990s.

Capital crimes

Historically, a wide variety of crimes have been punishable by death. As recently as 1965 in the United States one or more jurisdictions authorized the death penalty not only for murder, but also for kidnapping, treason, rape, carnal knowledge, armed robbery, perjury in a capital case, assault by a life-term prisoner, burglary, arson, train wrecking, sabotage, and desecration of a grave, to mention only a dozen. Executions for these crimes, except for rape, were rare. Supreme Court decisions in the 1970s, however, rejected mandatory death penalties (even for murder by a prisoner serving a life term for murder), and the death penalty for such nonhomicidal crimes as rape and kidnapping. In subsequent years, Congress has enacted statutes punishing several nonhomicidal crimes with death (notably, the crime of trafficking in large quantities of drugs). Whether the Supreme Court will sustain or reject the death penalty for such crimes remains to be seen.

In other countries murder is by no means the only capital crime. In Egypt and Algeria, terrorists are subject to the death penalty. Rebellion and obdurate apostasy are subject to the death penalty in Saudi Arabia and Yemen. Threats of a coup d'etat in Sierra Leone led to summary executions in 1992. Certain drug offenses in Malaysia and Indonesia carry a death penalty. In 1992, China added more than two dozen new capital crimes to its penal code. Although virtually all of western European nations have abolished the death penalty for all crimes, it retains popular and governmental support in much of Asia, Africa, and the Middle East.

Public opinion

American public opinion appears to support the death penalty for murder and has done so throughout the twentieth century, except for a brief period in the mid-1960s. In the 1990s, nearly 80 percent of the public approved of capital punishment; about 5 percent were undecided and the rest opposed it. However, more careful investigations of public attitudes have shown that given the option of life imprisonment without the possibility of parole (LWOP), the public support for the death penalty drops by a significant amount, in some cases by half (from 80 percent to 40 percent). This research supports the view that while the public generally accepts the death penalty for murderers, it prefers their long-term imprisonment. And capital trial juries, all of them vetted to exclude anyone strongly opposed to the death penalty, coupled with plea bargaining practices, produce death sentences in only about 10 percent of the murder cases where it might be issued. Understandably, opponents of the death penalty view public support of executions as "a mile wide but only an inch deep."

No doubt public support for the death penalty is a powerful political factor in explaining the decline of executive clemency in capital cases and the willingness of most legislatures, state and federal, to expand the list of capital crimes. (Executive clemency in capital cases dropped from an annual average of twenty-two in the 1960s to two in the 1990s.) In Europe, however, despite popular majorities in many countries that have supported the death penalty for decades, parliaments have not only abolished it, they have gone further and made abolition a condition of entry into the Council of Europe.

Administration

In 1997 the House of Delegates of the American Bar Association called for a nationwide moratorium on executions, pending fundamental improvements in its administration. Salient problems affecting the fairness of the death penalty included failure to provide adequate trial counsel for the defendant, inadequate resources for counsel to investigate the crime and locate witnesses, and inadequate resources to verify alibi testimony and retain expert witnesses. Several other investigative bodies in the 1990s, notably the International Commission of Jurists (1996) and the UN Commission on Human Rights (1999), went further and called for the United States to abolish the death penalty entirely, on the ground that the record to date showed that these administrative problems were beyond remedy.

During the 1990s the Capital Jury Project, funded by the National Science Foundation, studied the behavior of jurors and juries in capital cases. Over a thousand juror interviews were conducted in more than a dozen death penalty states. Research found that trial jurors do not adequately understand the judge's instructions designed to guide them in deciding whether to sentence the defendant to death, and that even where they do understand these instructions, they often ignore them.

By far the most prominent worry has been prompted by perceived racial disparities in death sentences and executions. For decades, the men and women on American death rows have been disproportionately nonwhite when measured against their proportion of the total population. (The numbers have not been so disproportionate when measured against the racial distribution of all persons in prison.) In the early 1970s, research on the death penalty for rape showed a powerful race-of-victim effect: virtually no one was sentenced to death for the rape of a nonwhite woman, and a black man accused of raping a white woman was ten times as likely to be convicted, sentenced to death, and executed as a white man charged with the same crime.

In the early 1980s a massive research project was launched in order to determine whether much the same pattern could be found in the death penalty for murder. The results of this research, conducted by David Baldus and his associates for the appellant's argument in *McCleskey v. Kemp* (1987) and later published in their book as *Equal Justice and the Death Penalty* (1990), showed that "defendants charged with killing white victims were 4.3 times as likely to receive a death sentence as defendants charged with killing blacks" (p. 401). Nevertheless, the Supreme Court, by a vote of 5 to 4, refused to order revision or nullification of any death penalty statutes or procedures, arguing that this research failed to "prove that the decisionmakers in [McCleskey's] case acted with discriminatory purpose." Efforts in subsequent years to persuade Congress to enact a Racial Justice Act (designed to permit a challenge to any death sentence believed to be based on racial grounds and to require the government to rebut the challenge, if possible, with appropriate evidence to the contrary) were unsuccessful. Meanwhile, a 1990 report on racial disparities in death sentencing conducted by the U.S. General Accounting Office confirmed the "race of victim influence . . . at all stages of the criminal justice system process" (p. 5).

Miscarriages of justice

Of all the worries associated with the death penalty, probably none is more potent than the horrifying thought that an innocent person might be executed. Western civilization itself could be said to rest on two cases of execution of the innocent: the death of Socrates in Athens in 399 B.C. and the death of Jesus of Nazareth in Jerusalem in A.D. 33. Death for witches is the most extreme case, for if witchcraft is impossible (even though belief in its efficacy remains widespread to this day in various parts of the world), then everyone burned at the stake or hanged for this crime was innocent.

There is no doubt, however, that scores of innocent defendants have been arrested, tried, convicted, and sentenced to death—only to be saved (often literally at the last minute) because new evidence was discovered that persuaded an appellate court to overturn the sentence or convinced a governor to extend clemency. Virtually every American death penalty jurisdiction has at least one sobering story of this sort to tell. And there are scattered cases from the nineteenth century in which the state government, in the twentieth century, admitted to carrying out a wrongful execution. The Haymarket anarchists in Chicago a century ago was one such case; Governor John Peter Altgelt spared the lives of the three surviving defendants in 1893. The most recent, widely publicized, and flagrant example of this problem appeared in Illinois late in 1998: Between 1977 and 1988 in Illinois, almost as many death row inmates were released on grounds of their innocence (ten) as were executed (eleven).

Arguments for and against

Arguments in defense and criticism of the death penalty can take any of several forms: secular versus religious, and empirical versus a priori.

Religious arguments. Jews, Christians, and Muslims have often defended the death penalty on the strength of texts in the Bible and the Koran. In 1995, however, the Vatican released a papal encyclical—*Evangelium Vitae* (The Gospel of Life)—arguing that the death penalty was permissible only under very special conditions, and that in modern civil society it was not permissible because none of those conditions prevailed. The encyclical argued that the basic doctrinal paradigm for how God wants murderers to be punished is to be found in the story of Cain and Abel (Genesis 4:8–16). Abel was murdered for no good reason by his brother, Cain, and upon discovery God inflicted on him a threefold punishment: he was cursed, he was stigmatized so all would know he was a murderer, and he was banished. He was not killed; indeed, God threatened

dire punishment on anyone who would "raise his hand" against Cain. Early in the history of the Biblical peoples as this story is, it is unquestionably vivid and telling. Whether its impact is negated by later passages in the Bible, in which the death penalty for many crimes is endorsed, is a matter of controversy among scholars.

Christians often appeal to "the sanctity of life," or at least the sanctity of human life; but this appeal cuts both ways in the controversy over the death penalty. Its opponents think executions fly in the face of the sanctity of human life; but its friends will cite this religious idea as their most important reason for favoring this punishment. If we are created in "the image of God" (Genesis 9:6), and if this is the source and nature of the sanctity of our lives, then the crime of murder is the gravest and most radical violation of that sanctity imaginable. It requires an adequate response to the offender's crime, and the only adequate response is to put the offender to death.

There is much more in the Bible relevant to the death penalty besides the story of Cain and Abel and the *imago dei*, and Jews, Christians, and Muslims have been adroit and energetic in interpreting their scriptures to support their preferred view about the death penalty. In secular societies, however, or in nations whose religious history is nonbiblical (apart from western imperialism), other arguments are required to establish public policy and the principles governing the criminal justice system.

Secular arguments. Defenders of the death penalty typically divide between those who rely on consequentialist (crime preventive) considerations, and those who rely on deontic (retributive) considerations. Arguments of the former kind depend on empirical evidence but the latter do not; they rely on moral intuitions and a priori reasoning. In a day when the death penalty was used for a wide variety of crimes and long-term imprisonment had yet to be practiced, it was plausible to stress the death penalty as a necessary means to the end of public safety. The death penalty could be used as a means to that end in either or both of two ways: as a *deterrent*, striking fear in would-be felons, or as incapacitation, effectively preventing recidivism in any form.

The chief source of support for the claim of superior deterrence was essentially this argument: Persons fear death more than imprisonment; the greater the fear the better the deterrent. That argument involves two empirical claims, raising the question of what (if any) evidence can be enlisted in their support. Little or no empirical evidence had been brought to bear on them until half a century ago. In the early 1950s in the United States, social scientists compared homicide rates in adjacent states (some with, others without the death penalty), homicide rates in all abolition states versus the rates in death penalty states, and homicide rates in a given state before and after abolition. In none of these comparisons was any evidence found of a superior deterrent effect thanks to the death penalty.

The debate was heightened in the mid-1970s, when statistical methods borrowed from econometrics purported to show that each execution during the middle years of this century was correlated with eight or so fewer homicides. Close scrutiny established that the purported special deterrent effect (the claim that each execution *caused* eight or so fewer homicides) was an artifact of the methodology and not a reliable, reproducible result. By the mid-1980s, social scientists had lost interest in further research of this sort. The most recent review of a half century of deterrence research concluded: "Neither economists nor sociologists, nor persons from any other discipline (law, psychology, engineering, etc.) have produced credible evidence of a significant deterrent effect for capital punishment. And not a single investigation to date has produced any indication that capital punishment deters capital murders—the crime of direct theoretical and policy concern" (Bailey and Peterson, p. 154).

Research on incapacitation, by contrast, has been infrequent and less rigorous. A study of the behavior in prison and (where relevant) after release of more then five hundred offenders on death row who were resentenced in the 1970s as ordered by the Court in *Furman* showed that a half dozen of these murderers killed again. Many committed other felonies, but hundreds (if the evidence is reliable) were guilty of no further crimes. Since there is no reliable way of predicting which convicted murderers will recidivate, recidivist murder can be prevented only by executing every person convicted of murder. This will strike all but a few as excessively draconian as well as immoral (because it involves "punishing" some prior to their having recidivated, and it involves "punishing" others who will not become guilty of any recidivist crimes at all). Bureau of Justice statistics show that among death row prisoners in the 1990s, perhaps one in eleven had a previous conviction of some form of criminal homicide. Obviously, imprisonment failed to incapacitate these recidivist offenders. But there is no known method by means of which the courts or prison authorities could have identified the nine percent who would become recidivist murderers. Since a mandatory death penalty is unconstitutional, it is not clear what can practically and legally be done to reduce further (and ideally eliminate) this recidivism by convicted murderers.

However, as the Supreme Court's rulings in the 1970s limited the death penalty to the punishment of murder and prohibited mandatory death penalties as well, the role of empirical arguments on behalf of the superior preventive effects of the death penalty has steadily shrunk, in favor of the a priori argument that relies entirely on desert and retribution. Here the essential argument goes as follows: Justice requires *lex talionis*, that is, that the punishment fit the crime; the punishment that best fits the crime of murder is the death penalty. Or, in a slightly different version: Murderers deserve to die, and justice requires that we inflict deserved punishments.

The classic objection to any argument of this form, in which the proper punishment for a crime is held to lie in making the punishment as close to the crime as possible, is that it cannot be generalized—or can be generalized only with absurd results. There is no punishment of this sort to "fit" a kidnapper who has no children, a bankrupt embezzler, or a traitor, a homeless arsonist, and a host of other serious offenders. As for the crimes of rape and torture, we could rape and torture the convicted offender, but the very idea is (or ought to be) morally repugnant. A retributivist can, of course, abandon *lex talionis* in favor of a principle of proportionality: the graver the crime the more severe the deserved punishment. This principle has great intuitive appeal; abolitionists who advocate life without the possibility of parole accept this principle. However, it does not require the death penalty. On the assumption that murder is the worst crime, all this principle requires is that murderers receive the severest punishment permissible. In sum, whereas retributivists have a plausible answer to the question, Who deserves to be punished? (Answer: all and only the guilty), they do not have a plausible answer to the next question, What is the deserved punishment? Their most plausible answer—murderers deserve the most severe punishment permissible—does not by itself provide any defense of the death penalty.

Opponents of the death penalty often point to the incompatibility of this practice with respect for the right to life, the value of even the worst lives, and human dignity. None of these normative considerations, however, quite succeeds in providing a rational ground to oppose *all* executions. Since at least the time of John Locke (1632–1704), defense of the death penalty can be made consistent with our "natural" and "inalienable" right to life on the understanding that the murderer forfeits his right to life. Even apart from forfeiture, it can be argued that the right to life is not absolute; few think it is morally wrong to take the life of an unjust aggressor if there is no other way to prevent an innocent person from being murdered. As for the value of human life, either this is a disguised way of asserting that the death penalty is morally wrong (and thus cannot be a reason for that judgment except by begging the question) or it is an empirical claim about convicted murderers (and thus open to doubt because of the belief that in the case of some murderers, whatever value is to be found by them or by society in their lives is cancelled or outweighed by the value to others of executing them). As for human dignity and the death penalty, proponents of the death penalty will argue that it no more confers immunity from a lawful execution than does the right to life. Perhaps the most that can be said about these three normative considerations is that they put the burden of argument on the defenders of the death penalty.

A better argument against the death penalty starts from a well-known liberal principle of state interference: society, and government as its instrument, ought not to intervene coercively in individual lives except to pursue a goal of paramount social importance and then only by the least invasive, restrictive, destructive means. With this as the major premise (roughly equivalent to the principle familiar in constitutional law of "substantive due process"), the abolitionist can then concede as a minor premise that reducing violent crime is a goal of paramount social importance. The crucial step in the argument is the next one, the twofold empirical claim that longterm imprisonment is (a) a sufficient means to that end; and (b) a less restrictive, coercive means to that end. The evidence for (a) is partly negative (the failure of social science to discover any persuasive evidence of the superiority of the death penalty as a deterrent, and the practical and legal impossibility of killing all convicted murderers to maximize incapacitation), and partly positive (the record of successful social control both in prison and in the general public without recourse to the death penalty in a dozen

different American abolition jurisdictions spanning a century and a half). The evidence for (b) is partly direct (convicted murderers themselves show by the relative rarity both of suicide, or even attempted suicide, on death row and of death prisoners who "volunteer" for death by refusing appeals that they believe that death for them is far more invasive and destructive than even LWOP) and partly indirect (opponents of the death penalty believe that death is more severe than LWOP, and so do its supporters).

International law of human rights

Probably the most influential factor in shaping the future of the death penalty is international human rights law. In 1966 the International Covenant on Civil and Political Rights was adopted by the General Assembly of the UN, and it came into force in 1976. The Covenant provided that "no one shall be subjected to torture or to cruel, inhumane or degrading punishment or torture." It was clear that this language was on a collision course with the death penalty. The United States ratified the Covenant but took explicit exception to two other provisions: the prohibition against executing juveniles (persons under eighteen at the time of the crime) and pregnant women. In 1989 the General Assembly adopted the Second Optional Protocol to the Covenant, asserting that "No one within the jurisdiction of a State party to the present Optional Protocol shall be executed." This protocol came into force in 1991. Concurrently, the Organization of American States adopted in 1990 a Protocol to the American Convention on Human Rights to Abolish the Death Penalty. Interpreting and enforcing these protocols continues to challenge signatory nations, and the United States is by no means the only country seeking for ways to disregard their mandate. Nevertheless, these developments in conjunction with the condition placed on nations wishing to join the Council of Europe that they abolish the death penalty suggest the direction in which the future will unfold (Council of Europe 1998; Schabas).

HUGO ADAM BEDAN

See also CAPITAL PUNISHMENT: LEGAL ASPECTS; CRUEL AND UNUSUAL PUNISHMENT; HABEAS CORPUS; JUVENILE JUSTICE: HISTORY AND PHILOSOPHY; JUVENILE VIOLENT OFFENDERS; MENTALLY DISORDERED OFFENDERS; PUNISHMENT; RACE AND CRIME: SENTENCING: DISPARITY; VICTIMS' RIGHTS.

BIBLIOGRAPHY

American Bar Association, House of Delegates. "Recommendation [of a moratorium on executions pending reforms in the administration of the death penalty]." *Law and Contemporary Problems* 61, no. 4 (1998): 219–231.

BAILEY, WILLIAM C., and PETERSON, RUTH D. "Murder, Capital Punishment, and Deterrence: A Review of the Literature." In *The Death Penalty in America: Current Controversies*. Edited by H. A. Bedan. New York: Oxford University Press, 1997. Pages 135–161.

BALDUS, DAVID; PULASKI, JR., CHARLES; and WOODWORTH, GEORGE G. *Equal Justice and the Death Penalty: A Legal and Empirical Analysis*. Boston, Mass., Northeastern University Press, 1990.

BECCARIA, CESARE. *On Crimes and Punishments and Other Writings*. Edited by Richard Bellamy. Cambridge, U.K.: Cambridge University Press, 1995.

BEDAU, HUGO ADAM. "The Decline of Executive Clemency in Capital Cases." *New York University Review of Law & Social Change* 18, no. 2 (1990–1991): 255–272.

———. *The Death Penalty in America: Current Controversies*. New York: Oxford University Press, 1997.

———. "Abolishing the Death Penalty Even for the Worst Murderers." In *The Killing State: Capital Punishment in Law, Politics, and Culture*. Edited by Austin Sarat. New York: Oxford University Press, 1999. Pages 40–59.

BLOCK, BRIAN P., and HOSTETTLER, JOHN. *Hanging in the Balance: A History of the Abolition of Capital Punishment in Britain*. Winchester, U.K.: Waterside Press, 1997.

BOWERS, WILLIAM J. "The Capital Jury Project: Rationale, Design, and Early Findings." *Indiana Law Journal* 70 (1995): 1043–1102.

DAVIS, MICHAEL. *Justice in the Shadow of Death: Rethinking Capital and Lesser Punishments*. Lanham, Md.: Rowman & Littlefield, 1996.

EVANS, RICHARD J. *Rituals of Retribution: Capital Punishment in Germany 1600–1987*. Oxford, U.K.: Oxford University Press, 1996.

Great Britain. Royal Commission on Capital Punishment 1949–1953. *Report*. London: H.M.S.O., 1953.

HODGKINSON, PETER, and RUTHERFORD, ANDREW. *Capital Punishment: Global Issues and Prospects*. Winchester, U.K.: Waterside Press, 1996.

HOOD, ROGER. *The Death Penalty: A World-wide Perspective*. 2d ed. Oxford, U.K.: Clarendon Press, 1996.

International Commission of Jurists. *Administration of the Death Penalty in the United States*. Geneva: International Commission of Jurists, 1996.

JOYCE, JAMES AVERY. *Capital Punishment: A World View*. New York: Thomas Nelson, 1961.

MACKEY, PHILIP ENGLISH, ed. *Voices against Death: American Opposition to Capital Punishment, 1787–1975*. New York: Burt Franklin, 1976.

MASUR, LOUIS P. *Rites of Execution: Capital Punishment and the Transformation of American Culture, 1776–1865*. New York: Oxford University Press, 1989.

MEGIVERN, JAMES J. *The Death Penalty: An Historical and Theological Survey*. Mahwah, N.J.: Paulist Press, 1997.

MELTSNER, MICHAEL. *Cruel and Unusual: The Supreme Court and Capital Punishment*. New York: Random House, 1973.

NAACP Legal Defense and Educational Fund, Inc. *Death Row, U.S.A.*, Spring 1999. New York, N.Y.: NAACP Legal Defense and Educational Fund, Inc., 1999.

POJMAN, LOUIS P., and REIMAN, JEFFREY. *The Death Penalty: For and Against*. Lanham, Md.: Rowman & Littlefield, 1998.

POPE JOHN PAUL II. *The Gospel of Life* (Evangelium Vitae). New York: Random House, 1995.

RADELET, MICHAEL L.; BEDAU, HUGO ADAM; and PUTNAM, CONSTANCE E. *In Spite of Innocence: Erroneous Convictions in Capital Cases*. Rev. ed. Boston, Mass.: Northeastern University Press, 1994.

RADELET, MICHAEL L., and ZSEMBIK, BARBARA A. "Executive Clemency in Post-*Furman* Capital Cases." *University of Richmond Law Review* 27 (1993): 289–314.

SARAT, AUSTIN, ed. *The Killing State: Capital Punishment in Law, Politics, and Culture*. New York: Oxford University Press, 1999.

SCHABAS, WILLIAM A. *The Abolition of the Death Penalty in International Law*. 2d ed. Cambridge, U.K.: Cambridge University Press, 1977.

SCOTT, GEORGE RYLEY. *The History of Capital Punishment*. London: Torchstream Books, 1950.

U.S. Bureau of Justice Statistics. *Capital Punishment 1998*. Washington, D.C.: U.S. Department of Justice, Office of Justice Programs, 1999.

U.S. General Accounting Office. *Death Penalty Sentencing: Research Indicates Pattern of Racial Disparities*. Washington, D.C.: General Accounting Office, 1990.

U.S. Staff Report, Subcommittee on Civil and Constitutional Rights, House Judiciary Committee, 103d Congress, 1st Session. *Innocence and the Death Penalty: Assessing the Danger of Mistaken Executions*. Washington, D.C.: Subcommittee on Civil and Constitutional Rights, 1993.

CAREERS IN CRIMINAL JUSTICE: CORRECTIONS

The criminal justice system is composed of the agencies of police, courts, and corrections. The corrections system, representing the community's response to suspected and convicted juvenile and adult offenders, is a significant component of criminal justice. Corrections agencies, operating at local, municipal, state, and federal levels, include jails, prisons with varying degrees of security, and a wide array of quasi-institutional as well as community-based programs. Among the most frequently applied community-based programs are probation, parole, and halfway houses, easing the transition of offenders from prison or jail to the community. Recent rapid expansions of intermediate sanctions have provided corrections with a widening range of community-based options. They include home detention, electronic monitoring, intensive supervision probation and parole programs, restitution, community service, substance abuse monitoring, fines, day reporting programs, shock incarceration, and regimented discipline programs more commonly known as boot camps. Juvenile corrections programs operate on the parens patriae principle, under which local, state, and federal jurisdictions assume responsibility for juveniles in order to protect "the child's best interest." As such, it is the role of juvenile corrections to "treat" and "help" the children in their charge, whether they are "dependent and neglected," in "need of supervision," or deemed "delinquent." By contrast, the penal sanctions imposed on convicted adult offenders serve a multiplicity of purposes ranging from deterrence and incapacitation to punishment and rehabilitation.

Even though people are the most effective resource for helping offenders and for effecting crime control and crime reduction, they remain underutilized and, for the most part, inappropriately applied in corrections. Major manpower problems range from a continuing shortage of specialized professional personnel, to poor working conditions, to unsound utilization of available human and scarce fiscal resources. Of all the components of criminal justice, the corrections system suffers the poorest image and is characterized by mission conflict. System fragmentation is yet another serious problem. Given the multiplicity of overlapping but seldom intercommunicating agencies at the local, state, and federal levels, planning, resource allocation, restructuring, and standardization have been next to impossible. As a result of these problems, correctional manpower has developed haphazardly. There has never been a national manpower strategy, nor has there been a systematic study of correctional employment. It is the purpose of this article to discuss the historical development of correctional careers, to describe the current job market and job requirements, and to review employment conditions for workers in correctional institutions, probation, and parole. Additional topics of discussion are career development and opportunities, salaries, and unionization in the professions.

Corrections, probation, and parole

One of the earliest references describing work in prisons comes from the notable prison reformer John Howard. In his classic work, *The State of the Prison in England and Wales* (1777), Howard writes that there is nothing more important to effective prison management than a warden who is honest, sober, and free of other vices, such as gambling. Responding to the serious abuses heaped upon prisoners in his day, Howard recommended that wardens and guards be salaried and not depend on fees customarily levied on inmates. Howard's prison staffing recommendations were remarkably parsimonious: a warden, a matron (for female prisoners), some guards, a manufacturer (to furnish inmates with work), and a few taskmasters to provide the necessary vocational training. Although prison staffing patterns have changed much since Howard's writing, his outline of the essential prison manpower and personal characteristics of staff are valid to this day.

Since its inception, correctional practice has developed haphazardly in Europe and subsequently in America. Near the end of the eighteenth century, Americans began to embrace Cesare Beccaria's enlightened concept of imprisonment as punishment, first enunciated in his seminal *Essays on Crimes and Punishment* (1764). During the Penitentiary Movement era (1790–1825), American prisons became models for European reformers seeking to humanize criminal punishment. Capital and corporal punishment was gradually replaced by confinement in penitentiaries. Prisoners would be redeemed through labor, religious reflection, isolation, and silence. Yet in spite of these efforts every informed observer since Beaumont and Tocqueville has remarked on the pervasive contradictions in goals and philosophy within the American correctional system. Not surprisingly, these contradictions have historically affected recruitment of personnel and work performance. To this day corrections personnel—and the public as their employer—are doubtful as to whether corrections should punish and isolate offenders or rehabilitate and reintegrate them back into society.

The correctional officer work force in America, from the earliest prisons and jails until the mid-twentieth century, lacked training and preparedness for the job. Officers came into corrections largely by chance, seldom by choice. Employment prerequisites and salaries were low. Most obtained their jobs through political patronage, the vestiges of which remain today. What training occurred was done on the job. It was not until 1930 that the first formal training program was initiated in New York City under the auspices of the Federal Bureau of Prisons (Schade). The three-month training program covered such topics as the history of crime and punishment, inmate classification and management, and discipline and segregation of inmate categories. Thereafter, it became largely the task of professional organizations, unions, and state civil-service provisions to set the performance standards for corrections. Of particular note is the work of the National Prison Association (NPA). First formed in 1830, it was renamed the American Correctional Association (ACA) in 1954. As the largest organization of corrections professionals and volunteers, the ACA has been instrumental in lifting the image of the profession. It has carried the responsibility for developing standards for the profession, which today serve as the benchmarks for the accreditation of prisons and jails. In a similar vein, selection standards, the quality of recruits, and training programs have improved significantly. The combined efforts of the professional organizations, unions, and state civil service commissions have resulted in improved working conditions, better pay, and most of all, the professionalization of institutional corrections.

Probation as an alternative to imprisonment also has its roots in ancient England. As early as the 1300s the English courts had the option of placing certain low risk offenders into the custody of upstanding citizens who would vouch for their conduct. By comparison, probation in America has a shorter history. John Augustus (1784–1859) is generally recognized as the father of American probation. Augustus was a successful shoemaker in Boston. While visiting criminal courts he was distressed to see petty criminals being consigned to jail because they were unable to pay even modest fines. After bailing selected offenders, Augustus would help find a job for them and provide assistance to their families if needed. At time of sentencing, Augustus would vouch for the individual in court. He would also point to the progress being made toward the person's reformation. Judges, in turn, usually responded by imposing modest fines and court costs, rather than sentence the individual to time in jail (Glueck). The idea of probation as an alternative to incarceration quickly took root in state court systems. By 1925, Congress authorized probation at the federal level and probation had become not only accepted but also the most widely used form of community-based supervision.

Parole is the supervised early release of prisoners from correctional confinement. Alexander Maconochie is credited with first conceiving the practice in the 1840s. Captain Maconochie of the Royal Navy was the superintendent of an English penal colony on Norfolk Island located between New Caledonia and New Zealand (1840–1844). Responding to the brutalities of prison management of his day, Maconochie thought that prisoners should be provided with incentives for rehabilitation and opportunities for earning their way out of confinement. He devised a system of credits or "marks" to be awarded for good conduct, hard labor, and industriousness. As inmates earned marks, they could apply them toward less restrictive prison settings and eventually toward an early release. A "ticket of leave" was the final step in the release process and meant that a prisoner was discharged without constraint and free to pursue his life.

Careers in jails and correctional institutions

Nature of the work. Correctional officers are responsible for supervising persons who have been arrested and detained in jails pending trial. They also supervise individuals who have been convicted of crimes and sentenced to serve time in jails, reformatories, and prisons. Comprising over 60 percent of most institutional staff, they are responsible for maintaining order and institutional discipline. Officers enforce institutional rules and regulations. They monitor and control inmates throughout their incarceration twenty-four hours a day, seven days a week. Officers must periodically search inmates and the prison environment for contraband, such as weapons or drugs. Officers are in charge of internal and perimeter security. They must periodically inspect locks, window screens, grilles, doors, and gates to prevent escapes or other malfeasance. Officers also inspect inmate mail, control visitors, and escort inmates within the facility or transport them to outside locations, such as court hearings, facilities transfers, or hospitals for medical care. Officers bear responsibility for maintaining safe, sanitary, and secure conditions in prisons and jails. Unlike police officers, they do not have any law enforcement responsibilities outside their institutions. By the same token, correctional officers are expected to function as change agents in the correctional process. They are informal counselors in charge of the health, safety, and general welfare of their inmates by providing guidance and tracking an inmate's life and behavior in the institution.

Correctional officers report orally and in writing on inmate activities and conduct. This includes reports on security breaches, disciplinary infractions, and violence. Similar to role call in policing, officers attend short briefings before the beginning of their shifts to learn about events, problems, and inmates with special needs. Logs are kept for each shift, reflecting inmate counts, unusual occurrences, and incidents, if any. At times, officers must deal with inmates who may be self-destructive, violent, or uncooperative. They must write citations for behavior infractions and attend disciplinary hearings during which incidents are reviewed and adjudicated. Unlike police, corrections officers work unarmed in prisons and jails. Exceptions to this rule are special prisons designed for holding highly dangerous offenders and prisons in lockdown conditions due to collective violence incidents, and similar emergencies. In lieu of weapons, officers are equipped with communications devices with which they can summon help if needed. Depending on the shift or available manpower, correctional officers may work on a tier or cell block alone, or with another officer. In direct supervision facilities, an officer may be in the midst of fifty to one hundred inmates or more. Officers must rely on their intelligence, training, and interpersonal communications skills to maintain order and control over their inmates. Their only other means for motivating inmates are a series of progressive sanctions involving a small number of privileges, such as visits to the canteen, time spent in day rooms, visitation, and so on.

There are approximately 450,000 workers in the nation's correctional agencies (Camp and Camp). Of these, the vast majority is uniformed (or line) staff, located throughout roughly fifteen hundred correctional facilities spanning many security levels. The latter range from maximum, medium, minimum, community-level, intake, multi-level, to high/close. Line staffing patterns follow a paramilitary and highly hierarchical structure: correctional officer, sergeant, lieutenant, captain, and major. There are fifty state-level correctional agencies, controlled by directors or commissioners. These positions are usually gubernatorial appointments. Only a few are a part of a state's civil service structure. Penal facilities are operated by wardens. They generally serve at the pleasure of the director or commissioner of corrections. By contrast, most, but not all, jails are under the control of popularly elected sheriffs. Police and sheriffs' departments in county and municipal jails, as well as large precinct station houses, also employ large numbers of correctional (or detention) officers. There are approximately thirty-three hundred jails in the country. They hold and process more than twenty-two million arrestees a year. On any given day, jails detain and hold about half a million inmates. Given the nature of jail operations, they have a high turnover of their inmate populations. Jail clientele vary much, ranging from petty criminals to highly dangerous felons.

Pay. Salaries for line staff have greatly improved in recent years, with annual starting pay ranging from a low of $15,324 in Louisiana to a high of $34,070 in New Jersey (Camp and Camp). The national average starting salary for a correctional officer was pegged at $22,500 in 2001. A combination of annual pay increases and pay incentives for post-secondary education, hazardous duty, or overtime can easily raise pay above $50,000 for line staff, with lieutenants and captains earning as much as $70,000 to $75,000. Salaries for agency directors reflect their many responsibilities and range from a low of $32,000 to $130,000.

Qualifications and education. Historically, correctional officers were white males from rural areas with low-level education. However, due to the previously discussed quickening process of professionalization, this dismal picture is changing rapidly. Employment criteria for entry-level positions require that candidates be at least eighteen to twenty-one years of age and have a high school education (or equivalent). Applicants must be in good health, of good moral character, meet fairly strict physical fitness requirements, and undergo a psychological assessment. Additional criteria include U.S. citizenship and the absence of a criminal record. These entry-level requirements resemble those for policing. Although relatively modest when compared to other professions, there is a distinct trend in the profession favoring educational attainments beyond high school. This salutary development is attributable to a number of factors. First, with increases in professionalization, the field has become more attractive to better-educated individuals looking for a career in corrections. This development is reinforced by the fact that most corrections agencies, including the Federal Bureau of Prisons (FBP), have made time spent as a correctional officer the cornerstone of a correctional career. Second, equal employment opportunity has opened the field to a more diverse workforce, including people of color and women, many of whom have post-secondary education experience. And third, post-secondary education, such as the acquisition of an associate's, bachelor's, or master's degree, are becoming increasingly important in promotion considerations and leadership selections. In sum, the ideal officer candidate will be highly motivated, with a good education. Above all, the individual will be have good judgment, maturity, a strong sense of fairness, and the ability to think and act quickly and decisively.

Selection. The vast majority of today's correctional agencies follow well-established and mostly nondiscriminatory selection processes. Nonetheless, a majority of jurisdictions do give preference points to veterans. The underlying rationale is to reward veterans for their military service and to assist them in the readjustment to civilian life. Another reason for favoring veterans is the assumption that a military background will be of advantage in corrections due to the paramilitary nature of the work. While the military model is now considered out of place by many national organizations, such as the FBP and the American Correctional Association, veteran's preference remains in place. Once selected, candidates must pass a written examination and a physical fitness test. They must undergo drug testing, a medical examination, a psychological assessment, and extensive background checks. Following successful completion of this process, candidates are given oral interviews by a selection board representing management, security, human services, and corrections officers. Successful candidates will then be offered employment, contingent upon successfully completing academy training (ranging from six to twelve weeks), and a probationary period (ranging from six to twenty-four months).

Pre-service and in-service training. Federal, state, and a majority of local corrections agencies provide pre-service training in training academies. The training follows the guidelines established by the American Correctional Association and the American Jail Association. Academies are paramilitary in nature and teach a variety of topics. Subjects include: the legal parameters under which the agencies operate; rules and regulations; security procedures, team work, and self-defense; firearms proficiency; search and seizure; inmate characteristics and needs; inmate management, counseling, and supervision; suicide prevention and emergency medical aid; disciplinary procedures and report writing; inmate rights and responsibilities.

Regular in-service training is now a staple in all corrections agencies. The Federal Bureau of Prisons (FBP) is in a leadership position by requiring at least 200 hours of additional training to occur during the first year of employment. On top of this requirement is another 120 hours of specialized training at the FBP's residential training center at Glynco, Georgia, within the first sixty days of employment. State and local corrections agencies have annual in-service programs ranging from forty to one hundred hours. Given the potential for violence in corrections institutions, each agency trains and assigns correctional officers to tactical response teams (better known as Special Weapons and Tactics Teams, or SWAT). It is the responsibility of these teams to respond to prison and jail disturbances, riots, hostage situations, forced cell moves, escapes, and similarly dangerous situations. SWAT teams emphasize physical and mental fitness, training, and teamwork.

Job outlook. The U.S. Department of Labor notes highly favorable job opportunities for correctional officers in the first decade of the twenty-first century. This is due to a number of factors. First, the number of juvenile and adult offenders under some form of correctional supervision is rising. Prisons and jails are expanding, and more juvenile delinquents are waived into adult court than ever before. Second, the adoption of mandatory sentencing laws, such as three strikes, has increased the time offenders spend in prisons and jails. Third, reduced usage of parole, coupled with a tightening of parole violation procedures, is spurring demand for more manpower. Fourth, there is an ongoing need to replace correctional officers due to retirement, transfer to other occupations, such as policing, and internal promotion. The totality of these effects will generate thousands of job openings in the foreseeable future.

Career development. With experience, further education, and in-service and skills training, qualified correctional officers have excellent opportunities for advancement to higher ranks. They may be promoted to supervisory positions, such as shift commanders, unit or program supervisors, training or tactical commanders, or some combination. Additional opportunities exist for qualified and enterprising officers to be promoted to administrative posts, assistant superintendent, superintendent or warden.

Most federal, state, and local corrections agencies provide career development incentives for their employees. For example, many increase an officer's pay upon completion of postsecondary education degrees. There is also support for professional development, such as pursuing additional training and skill development programs, and for attending professional association meetings. Many agencies also look favorably on extracurricular activities, such as volunteer work with schools, youth development programs, such as sports or the Boy Scouts and Girl Scouts, or similar activities that serve to enhance the agency's image in the community.

Careers in probation and parole

The nature of the work. Probation and parole officers share common goals. They supervise, support, and provide needed services to offenders so that they can return to free society as law-abiding and productive citizens. Whether an offender is on probation or on parole is determined by his or her legal status. An offender, under a probationary sentence, will be under the supervision of a probation officer. If the court imposes a "split-sentence," the offender serves a short time in a correctional institution, usually in a house of correction. Thereafter, he or she is supervised by a probation officer for the remainder of the sentence. Offenders serving time in prisons or jails are often placed on parole upon their release. Both probationers and parolees are given a conditional release under the supervision of a probation or parole officer for specific length of time.

Probation and parole straddle the worlds of police, courts, corrections, and social work. Probation agents are officers of the court and fulfill a multiplicity of interrelated functions. At the police level, they provide information for the possible diversion of an offender from criminal justice to alternatives, such as community assistance programs. Parole officers usually work for the executive (federal, state, and local) branches of government. They notify local police and victims when certain individuals (for example, sex offenders) are released from prison. Release notifications are determined by law and vary considerably by jurisdiction. Both probation and parole officers assist police in the location and apprehension of probation absconders or parole violators.

At the court level, probation officers conduct presentence investigations. They prepare reports on the offenders for prosecutorial and judicial decisions, such as bail or other pretrial release. They supervise offenders placed by the courts on pretrial release. Probation officers routinely make sentence recommendations, including the use of special conditions to be placed on individual offenders. Once offenders are placed on probation, the officers supervise and monitor their activities. They prepare reports for the courts, which reflect an offender's relative progress. As warranted, the reports may recommend probation revocation in case of serious rule violations or the commission of new crimes. They may modify the conditions of probation as needed, or they may recommend an early discharge for good behavior. Parole officers, in turn, make recommendations on sentence length through parole decisions. They provide liaison between the police, the courts, and the executive branches of government. They also coordinate the supervision process for offenders with split sentences. While the decision to parole is usually made by parole boards, it is the parole officer who prepares the cases for hearings, formulates the recommendations for action, and supervises the offender in the community. This activity includes enforcing the conditions of an offender's release, including substance abuse monitoring. Officers assist offenders in finding and retaining work and housing. They also provide the necessary linkages to community services, such as medical or mental health treatment, vocational training, and drug treatment.

Through their sentencing recommendations, probation officers exert a major impact on institutional corrections, since they help determine who will go to prison or jail, and for how long. They serve as a liaison between the courts and the various corrections agencies. Probation officers also administer the community release phase of an offender's split sentence. Parole officers, in turn, coordinate the release of inmates from institutions. This involves the preparation of offenders' dossiers for the release hearing, as well as the procurement of housing, work, and community assistance as needed. The supervision of parolees has long been recognized as a vital component of an offender's reintegration into the community. Unfortunately, recent criminal justice reforms have abolished parole in many jurisdictions. Although some corrections systems have replaced parole with another form of community supervision, any reduction in post-release supervision is detrimental to community safety and crime reduction.

Probation and parole work emphasizes casework, reflecting the influence of social work on the professions. This focus first emerged in the middle of the twentieth century, when officers were expected to form therapeutic relationships with their "clients." In the process, the development of social work skills was emphasized, and work consisted of probing interviews, counseling, providing insight, and modifying offender behavior. With the demise of the "medical model" during the late 1970s and early 1980s, the focus changed from diagnosis and treatment to a much broader perspective of probation and parole work. Today's probation and parole officers fulfill a multiplicity of functions. They are agents of law enforcement, responsible for the supervision of the offenders assigned to their care, and, indirectly, for the safety of their communities. They are also social workers in the broadest sense of the word. As such, they work with individuals, groups, and communities. They recognize that factors such as poverty, lack of education, unemployment, underemployment, marginality, inadequate housing, and ill health are connected to crime and can affect an offender's rehabilitation.

Since it is the responsibility of probation and parole officers to enforce court orders, they must, as the occasion arises, arrest those they supervise, conduct physical searches, seize evidence, and decide whether to revoke probation or parole or whether to file charges for new court proceedings. One of the latest trends in community corrections is the development and growth of collaborative projects between police, probation, parole, and other social service agencies. For example, Operation Night Light in Boston is a highly acclaimed juvenile crime reduction program in which probation officers and police not only share information, but also engage in joint patrols and curfew checks. The program has succeeded in reducing gang violence, homicides, and violence committed with firearms. It is currently being duplicated in other cities and states.

Pay. In 1999, the average starting salary for probation officers was $27,197. With time in grade, the average salary rises to $36,622, with the highest salaries ranging from a low of $36,275 in South Dakota to a high of $93,411 in the federal system (Camp and Camp). That same year, the average starting salary for parole officers was $28,491. With time in grade, the average salary rises to $37,319, with the highest salaries ranging from a low of $30,036 in West Virginia to a high of $64,212 in California.

Qualifications and education. A bachelor's degree in social work (BSW) is generally the minimum requirement for employment as a social worker. In corrections, majors in criminal justice, education, psychology, sociology, police science, and related fields are also acceptable for entry-level work. Federal positions require one year of graduate-level courses in addition to the degree. By contrast, some agencies accept experience plus passing a university equivalency test as substitute for formal education requirements. However, there is a trend toward increasing educational requirements in the professions. Similar to the corrections track, candidates must be citizens of the United States, have no felony convictions, and must pass a battery of job-related general physical abilities tests, psychological and physical examinations, as well as drug tests. In some jurisdictions, probation and parole officers must also be willing to complete training necessary for certification as peace officers.

Probation and parole officers must have excellent communication and human interaction skills. Agents must also have good oral and writing skills, analytical aptitude, and be willing and able to work under stressful conditions.

In-service training. A majority of agencies require the completion of an intensive basic training course within the first year of employment. California, for example, requires a 200-hour basic training course and certification by the California State Board of Corrections. Similar training is provided to parole agents, who also must complete several weeks of academy training. In many jurisdictions, probation and parole officers are also expected to complete one year of supervised casework.

Job outlook. According to the U.S. Department of Labor, the employment of probation, parole, or community supervision officers is expected to rise faster than the average for all occupations during the first decade of the twenty-first century. At year-end 1998, the number of adult men and women in the United States being supervised in the community exceeded four million, reflecting a growth rate of about 3.1 percent per annum (Bureau of Justice Statistics). The number of federal, state, and local probation officers will continue to rise due to a number of factors. First, prison overcrowding in many jurisdictions has led many judges to sentence larger numbers of offenders to probation, including higher risk cases. Second, widespread adoption and expansion of intermediate sanctions, such as electronic monitoring, day reporting, education and work furloughs, and community service, is increasing demand for supervisory agents and workers in each of these areas.

Looking at parole, each year approximately 600,000 federal and state inmates are released to the community. Many more parolees are released from local houses of correction. Because prisons and jails, at all levels of government, have retained few treatment programs in this era of resource cutbacks and lost faith in rehabilitation, the prisoner reentry population has greater needs than ever before. Therefore, the need for parole and related supervisory agents is expected to rise, as will their caseload. Meeting the myriad of needs of this population, such as finding and keeping a job, increasing their skills and education, improving their family ties, and dealing with their persistent and destructive substance abuse problems, will be critical if a new crime wave is to be prevented.

Career development. Most probation and parole officers begin their career as trainees and receive on-the-job-training for six to twelve months. With experience, further education, and in-service and new skills training, qualified officers can advance to higher grades. Depending on qualifications and ambition, officers can also advance to supervisory positions and, with time, to administrative posts. Most agencies encourage their employees to advance their education and to attend professional-training events to keep at the cutting edge of their work. Of note here are the activities of the American Probation and Parole Association (APPA), an international association composed of individuals from the United States and Canada actively involved with adult and juvenile probation, parole, and community-based corrections. The APPA provides national training workshops, symposia, and training institutes on a regular basis.

Issues in correctional careers

Employment of women and minorities. Historically, prison and jail staffs have been principally white males. However, the demographics of correctional employees have changed dramatically during the past two decades. In 1999, women comprised 32.5 percent of all agency staff in adult correctional agencies, while 29.6 percent of all agency staff were nonwhite (Camp and Camp). Today, minorities and women are a vital part of the correctional workforce. What is more important, they function in every capacity of the work environment, as correctional officers, supervisors, and senior managers, as well as superintendents and wardens. Although women, African Americans, and Hispanics remain underrepresented when compared to their presence in the general population, correctional agencies are committed to spending time, effort, and resources to make their institutions culturally diverse. These efforts are based on the conviction that effective institutional management depends on a heterogeneous staff that can relate to and communicate with an equally heterogeneous inmate population.

Labor relations and unions. Public unions in corrections are a relatively recent phenomenon. While correctional officer unions did not emerge until the late 1950s and 1960s, they are now established in almost every state. Operating under the provisions of the National Labor Relations Act (NLRA), first passed by Congress in 1935, correctional employees have the right to organize and to be represented by a union of their choice. Employers, in turn, are required to enter into agreements with the union regarding their workers' terms and conditions of employment. Both employers and unions must follow established collective bargaining procedures. While private-sector union members have the right to strike as a last resort during labor negotiations, public-sector workers such as correctional or police officers are prohibited, for the most part, from any strike activities. One of the fastest-growing unions is the American Federation of State, County, and Municipal Employees (AFSC-ME), which represents a large number of corrections employees. There are many other unions at the national, state, and local levels, each of which is committed to improve working conditions for their members. Most unions are concerned with issues of safety, pay, fringe benefits, performance evaluations, disciplinary procedures, job protection, training, recruitment, and career advancement. Unions have also been a driving force behind the previously discussed accreditation of many correctional institutions by the Commission on Accreditation for Corrections.

Compared with previous practice, unions have made labor-management relations more complex. Employers can no longer hire and fire workers in an arbitrary manner. With the help of the unions, workers are now entitled to legal representation in all work-related matters. On the negative side, unions have on occasion taken strong adversarial positions toward management. And when management and labor are bogged down in protracted and stormy disputes, the ensuing mutual distrust serves to corrode the mission of corrections. Since unions are likely to remain a permanent part of the correctional landscape, management's best approach will be tolerance, coupled with the development of sufficient collective-bargaining skills to preserve its administrative prerogatives.

Working conditions.   Work in correctional institutions can be stressful and at times hazardous. Jails and prisons, with their fences, barbed wire, gray walls, incessant din, artificial lighting and stale air, are gloomy places at best and highly inhospitable, dangerous abodes at worst. While newer institutions provide more pleasant work environments, the majority of facilities are older, overcrowded, and lack air conditioning. In 1998, there were almost fifteen thousand assaults committed by inmates on staff. Over two thousand of these staff members required medical attention (Camp and Camp), which averages out to 304 such assaults per week. Given the large number of inmates held under lock and key in the country, the rate is not inordinately high. Nonetheless, it speaks to the difficulty of the job.

Supervising and managing difficult, distressed, and sometimes dangerous inmates, whether they are located in institutions or in the community, make corrections work a difficult and demanding profession. It is interesting to note that most stress experienced by correctional workers emanates from, or is influenced by, the correctional organization. For example, a major source of stress is role conflict and role ambiguities. This is because officers must strike a delicate balance between maintaining control and providing assistance to inmates, probationers, and parolees. Characteristics intrinsic to the job are other sources of stress. For example, security levels of prisons and work assignment to specific shifts are highly correlated with stress. Perceived dangerousness and officer-client-inmate contact go to the heart of corrections work. There is evidence that probation and parole officer stress and burnout are consistently tied to such stressors as hostile and antagonistic client contracts, critical decisions involving dangerous offenders, work overload, and insufficient resources (Champion). Finally, organizational characteristics as they relate to administrative and supervisory matters are still another, major source of stress. Included here are flawed supervisory activities and leadership, faulty communications between departments, institutions, program staff and the officers, lack of decision latitude, feelings of alienation and powerlessness, and a lack of participation and input in the organizational decision-making process. Given the many challenges presented by working in this field, it will be the task of today's correctional managers to improve their organizational climates so that stress is either reduced or eliminated. In addition, managers must marshal to the fullest their workers' commitment to their work and to the mission of their organizations.

EDITH E. FLYNN

See also CAREERS IN CRIMINAL JUSTICE: LAW; CAREERS IN CRIMINAL JUSTICE: POLICE; PRETRIAL DIVERSION; PREVENTION: POLICE ROLES; PRISONS: CORRECTIONAL OFFICERS; PRISONS: HISTORY; PRISONS: PRISONERS; PRISONS: PRISONS FOR WOMEN; PRISONS: PROBLEMS AND PROSPECTS; PROBATION AND PAROLE: HISTORY, GOALS, AND DECISION-MAKING; PROBATION AND PAROLE: PROCEDURAL PROTECTION; PROBATION AND PAROLE: SUPERVISION; SENTENCING: PRESENTENCE REPORT.

BIBLIOGRAPHY

BEAUMONT, GUSTAVE DE, and TOCQUEVILLE, ALEXIS DE. *On the Penitentiary System in the United States and Its Application in France* (1833). Translated by Francis Leiber. Introduction by Thorsten Sellin. Carbondale: University of Southern Illinois Press, 1964.

BECCARIA, CESARE. *On Crimes and Punishment,* 2d ed. Translated by Edward D. Ingraham. Philadelphia: Philip H. Nicklin, 1819.

Bureau of Justice Statistics. *Probation and Parole in the United States, 1998.* Washington, D.C.: U.S. Department of Justice, Office of Justice Programs, 1999.

CAMP, CAMILLE, and CAMP, GEORGE. *The Corrections Yearbook, Adult Corrections.* Middletown, Conn.: Criminal Justice Institute, Inc. 1999.

CHAMPION, D. J. *Probation and Parole in the United States.* Columbus, Ohio: Merrill Publishing Co., 1990.

GLUECK, SHELDON. Introduction. *John Augustus— First Probation Officer* by John Augustus. The original *Report of his Labors* (1852). Montclair, N.J.: Patterson Smith, 1972.

HOWARD, JOHN. "The State of the Prisons in England and Wales" (1777). In *Penology.* Edited by George Killinger and Paul Cromwell. St. Paul, Minn.: West, 1973. Pages 5–11.

SCHADE, T. "Prison Officer Training in the United States: The Legacy of Jessie O. Stutsman." *Federal Probation* 50, no. 4 (1986): 40–46.

U.S. Department of Labor. "Correctional Officers." *Occupational Outlook Handbook 2000-01 Edition.* Washington, D.C.: U.S. Government Printing Office, 2000.

CAREERS IN CRIMINAL JUSTICE: LAW

A career in criminal law can be very rewarding and a valuable learning experience. The field is attractive to those who have a strong sense of justice and who are interested in public service. Furthermore, it is a good choice for individuals interested in trial work and litigation. Criminal lawyers generally work either as prosecutors or as defense attorneys. Defense attorneys work either for a public defender organization, as solo practitioners, or in a law firm. Prosecutors work for the government either at the local, city, or county prosecutor's office, the criminal division of the state attorney general's office, or the U.S. attorney's office. In both prosecution and defense work, there are opportunities to work with state or federal criminal laws, or to do appellate appeals rather than trial work. Both the local prosecutor's offices and public defender organizations hire graduates right out of law school, or after a short time in practice.

Legal education

In the past, most individuals starting out as criminal defense attorneys or prosecutors had minimal background in criminal law. In fact, even today, most law schools only require one basic criminal law class although there are opportunities to take additional courses in advanced criminal law and criminal procedure. However, the contemporary law student's exposure to the practical side of criminal law has been enhanced by the development of legal clinics and skills courses. The history of legal education presents an interesting pattern from practical training in its inception, to a more doctrinal and analytical approach, and currently back to an emphasis on practical training in conjunction with traditional theoretical methods.

During the colonial era, Americans who wished to become lawyers obtained a legal education at one of the British Inns of Court. However, those who could not afford a trip to England were trained in an apprenticeship system whereby aspiring lawyers worked under the tutelage of a practicing lawyer. During the American Revolution and thereafter, the apprentice system became more widespread. During these apprenticeships, students would learn the practical skills of a lawyer by doing legal work for the mentor who would also advise and suggest readings in substantive law. However, given the differences in various mentors' styles and skill in teaching as well as the competing demands of the mentor's practice, satisfaction with the apprentice system dwindled. Proprietary law schools then began to emerge. These were private schools that were headed by some of the more skilled and popular mentors. Instruction was conducted on a group basis and students received formal lectures on the law, thereby systematizing legal education for the first time.

Eventually, university-affiliated law schools began to emerge. Harvard Law School was established in 1817, and in 1870 the school fostered a revolution in legal teaching when Christopher Columbus Langdell became its dean. Langdell developed the case method of legal instruction, which was based on the assumption that law was a science and that the most appropriate way to teach this science was through the study of appellate cases. The method for teaching these cases has been called the "Socratic Method"; students were called upon to state the facts of the case, and what the court decided, and to analyze the court's reasoning and abstract the legal principles. The professor would then test the student's understanding by posing a series of hypotheticals and asking the student to apply the reasoning of the case to the new fact patterns. While this method remains a popular teaching method in law schools today, it has been criticized for failing to adequately prepare students for the practice of law. It has been further criticized for being unnecessarily confrontational and unsuitable to the increasingly diverse law school population. Many contemporary law professors have modified the Socratic method or used it in conjunction with other teaching methods.

As early as the 1930s, legal realists argued that law should be taught in terms of how it operated in the real world. However, clinical programs did not gain popularity in law schools until the 1960s, when there was increased funding for provision of services to low-income citizens as well as a growing sense that law schools were failing to adequately prepare students for the practice of law. Today, almost every law school in the country has one or more clinical offerings. There are two types of clinics operating in law schools: in-house clinics and externship placement clinics. In-house clinics are generally small legal offices in law schools that represent low-income clients in a variety of cases. Students take on actual cases under the supervision of a faculty member. In externship clinics, students receive course credit for participating in certain lawyering activities away from the law school in a field placement. In those cases, students are supervised and trained by a supervisor who is generally a practicing attorney at the organization in which the student is placed. There are criminal defense clinics and prosecution clinics in both formats. Alongside the development of legal clinics has been an increase in skills-based courses that teach students such things as interviewing, counseling, negotiation, and pretrial and trial practice through simulation, role playing, mock court hearings, and skills exercises. More and more students interested in careers in criminal law take in-house clinics, externships, or skills courses during their three years in law school, and are thus perhaps more prepared for work as criminal lawyers than their predecessors.

The prosecuting attorney

Most law graduates interested in prosecution seek work at the state court level in the local prosecutor's office. Office titles for local prosecutors include city attorney, district attorney, county attorney, prosecuting attorney, commonwealth attorney, and state's attorney. City attorneys generally prosecute minor criminal violations classified as misdemeanors under local ordinances or state criminal statutes. Prosecutors at the county or multi-county (district) level prosecute felony offenses (and, in some jurisdictions, serious misdemeanors). While some local prosecutors' offices hire law graduates to work in their appellate divisions, the bulk of law graduates entering the field work as trial-level assistant prosecutors. Larger prosecutors' offices also have specialized units dealing with particular types of crime such as narcotics, juvenile prosecution, domestic violence, and sex crimes. Most entry-level attorneys do not work in the specialized units but may be promoted there after several years on the job.

In larger jurisdictions, the local prosecutor's office hires a number of law graduates each year and typically will begin interviewing candidates in the fall of their third year of law school. Candidates are asked to take part in a series of interviews focusing on their knowledge of criminal procedure, their ability to handle complex ethical issues, and their dedication to public service. District attorneys offices generally look for candidates with internship or clinical experience in a district attorney's office or legal experience in other governmental offices. They also look for students who enjoy public speaking and can think on their feet, wrestle with difficult problems, and make sound decisions. Skills in trial advocacy or moot court experience are also looked upon favorably. Some of the larger prosecutors' offices provide a week to several weeks of training before sending new assistants to work. However, much of the training in both small and large prosecutors' offices occurs on the job. For law graduates who want to get a significant amount of early responsibility and substantial trial practice, the prosecutor's office is a very good place to work.

The salaries for entry-level assistant prosecutors vary widely and depend largely upon the size of the county and office. Salaries in 1998 ranged from a high of $51,000 to as low as $23,000 (*National Law Journal*, 1 June 1998, p. B13). In larger offices, new assistant prosecutors are required to make a three-year commitment. Since advancement in the prosecutors' office is limited, many assistant prosecutors move on after three years. Many go on to private practice as criminal defense attorneys, others enter politics or work at a firm in a different practice area.

Some assistant prosecutors work at the state attorney general's office. In most states, the attorney general has jurisdiction to prosecute violations of state criminal laws, and deals with issues of statewide significance such as organized and white collar crime, drug trafficking, fraud and embezzlement, and criminal enforcement of environmental protection laws. Assistant State's Attorneys generally appear regularly in state court, but also spend a great deal of time conducting investigations and drafting motion papers.

Prosecutors can also work at the federal level in Washington, D.C., or in the local United States Attorney's office. United States Attorney's offices are divisions of the U.S. Department of Justice, and are responsible for the prosecution of most federal crimes. (Some federal prosecutions are handled by Department of Justice attorneys based in Washington.) Crimes that are uniquely federal include evasion of federal income taxes, counterfeiting, and immigration violations; however, many other federal crimes (especially drug offenses) are also violations of state law that could be prosecuted by state authorities. For the most part, Assistant U.S. Attorneys are hired three to six years out of law school.

Prosecutors occupy a unique position in the criminal justice system in that they exercise a considerable amount of discretion. From the initial arrest to the final disposition, prosecutors determine which defendants are prosecuted, the type of plea bargains that are struck, and the severity of sentences imposed. Before a case comes to trial, prosecutors may decide to accept a plea bargain, divert suspects to a social services agency for an alternative to incarceration program, or dismiss the case entirely for lack of evidence. Attorney General and Supreme Court Justice Robert H. Jackson believed that the prosecutor has "more control over life, liberty and reputation than any other person in America" (Jackson, p. 31). This broad discretion occasionally can lead to abuse, such as when a prosecuting attorney decides not to prosecute a friend or to overzealously prosecute an enemy. But such behavior is not the norm.

The tasks of an assistant prosecutor are varied. They interview victims, witnesses, police officers, and experts, conduct fact investigations, counsel victims, and negotiate pleas. Furthermore, they do such administrative work as issuing subpoenas, monitoring lineups, ordering lab reports, conducting hearings and trials, and drafting motions. Caseloads of large prosecutors'

offices are quite high, and assistant prosecutors must learn to juggle competing demands. Beginning prosecutors will deal with less serious crimes such as trespass, petty theft, and misdemeanor assaults before they advance to burglary, car theft, robbery, rape, and homicide.

Prosecutors are unique not only because of the breadth of their discretion, but also because their client is the state rather than the individual victim. In this role, the prosecutor must act on behalf of the public good. The Model Code of Professional Responsibility states that "[t]he responsibility of the public prosecutor differs from that of the usual advocate; his duty is to seek justice, not merely to convict" (Model Code of Professional Responsibility, EC 713). While called upon to act as a zealous advocate, the prosecutor must also ensure that a defendant's trial is fair and that the proceedings appear fair to the public. This dual role of protecting the process and securing convictions can be difficult, and prosecutors often struggle to determine which role takes priority in a given situation. The stresses of this conflict as well as the enormous caseloads held by many prosecutors leads to significant burnout. However, many prosecutors find great satisfaction in their jobs and see themselves both as crusaders against crime and champions on behalf of crime victims.

Criminal defense

Individuals who enter the field of criminal defense have a strong interest in helping people, and believe in safeguarding the Constitution. Such individuals generally have a dedication to serving the underrepresented and to protecting individuals against the power of the state. The majority of criminal defense lawyers work as public defenders, contract attorneys, or assigned counsel, and serve those too poor to retain private counsel. This is primarily because the majority of those accused of crime are poor people. According to a 1997 National Legal Aid and Defender Association report, public defenders and court appointed counsel typically represented over 75 percent of the criminally accused in the United States (Hartmann, p. 2).

While taken for granted today, the right to counsel for indigent defendants is a relatively new concept and arose over a long period of time. The Sixth Amendment of the Bill of Rights of the U.S. Constitution grants any individual accused of a crime the right to effective assistance of counsel. However, for many years this constitutional guarantee applied only to criminal defendants who had the financial resources to hire a private attorney. It was not until 1963, in the case of *Gideon v. Wainwright*, 372 U.S. 335 (1963), that the right to appointed counsel was extended to all indigent defendants facing a felony in state court, and it was not until 1972 that this right was extended to misdemeanor cases involving a sentence of imprisonment (*Argersinger v. Hamlin*, 407 U.S. 25, 1972).

In response to these decisions, federal and state governments have devised a variety of means to provide legal services to indigent criminal defendants. There are three basic models for the delivery of legal services to the indigent criminally accused. Public defender programs are public or private nonprofit organizations with a staff of full-time attorneys who provide defense services to indigent defendants. Some of the larger defender organizations have specialized practices in areas such as juvenile defense, capital defense, and appellate work. The second model is the assigned counsel system, in which individual criminal cases are assigned to private attorneys on a systematic or ad hoc basis. In this system, the judge assigns the case either to an attorney in the courtroom, one who is on a special list, or the first attorney who comes to mind. The state or county compensates these attorneys on a case-by-case basis. The third model is that of a contract system in which states contract with an individual attorney, group of attorneys, or some other entity to provide representation in a certain number of cases or all cases within a jurisdiction. Many states use a combination of these models.

Representation on the federal level is similar to that on the state level. There are assigned counsel, contract attorneys, and federal public defender organizations. Attorneys hired to work as federal defenders are experienced criminal or trial attorneys from state or local public defender organizations or large private firms. This is because federal criminal cases tend to be complex, requiring more sophisticated trial skills. Federal defenders work on issues involving organized crime, large-scale drug cases, white-collar crime, or fraud cases.

Attorneys in all three types of defender systems have suffered the consequences of underfunding by both state and federal governments. A 1992 report revealed that the defense function received less than one-third of the federal, state, and local funds expended by the prosecution (Bureau of Justice Statistics, p. 2). A 1997 report by the National Legal Aid and Defender Associa-

tion concluded that "[t]here is a crisis in defender services. Historically underfunded, the strain on the indigent defense component of the criminal justice system has been exacerbated by the federal government's declared 'war on drugs' fought with a zero tolerance policy that promotes the criminalization of more behavior and Draconian penalties (such as 'three strikes' and mandatory sentencing laws) . . . . This failure to fairly fund the indigent defense component of the criminal justice 'eco-system' has resulted in 'overburdened public defenders, the incarceration of the innocent, court docket delays, prison overcrowding, and the release of violent offenders into the community' " (Hartman, p. 1).

Despite the financial concerns of public defender organizations, they have long been recognized as a training ground for criminal defense attorneys. Many of the larger offices provide excellent training programs and ongoing supervision. Moreover, because most courts require contract or assigned attorneys to have some experience, most defense attorneys begin their careers at public defender offices. Public defender organizations hire graduates out of law school and seek those who have had internships in similar organizations, trial skills, and a demonstrated commitment to public interest law. Salaries for entry-level public defenders range from $29,000 to $44,000 (*National Law Journal*, 1 June 1998, p. B14). New public defenders have a great deal of early responsibility, and handle their own cases from the beginning. Typically, new public defenders handle misdemeanors for several years and then advance to felonies.

Defense attorneys spend most of their day in court. They represent their clients at arraignment, bail hearings, pretrial motions, plea bargaining, trials, and sentencing hearings. Defense attorneys also evaluate the strengths and weaknesses of the prosecutor's case and advise their clients about the legal consequences of certain actions. They are called upon to listen closely to the client and explain the law and the development of the case and strategies in terms the client can understand. Defense attorneys also engage in plea bargaining and can negotiate for probation, a drug treatment program, or other alternatives to incarceration. Trial work is also an important part of the defender's job, and they use cross-examination and other techniques to reveal weaknesses in the state's case. Criminal defense attorneys also conduct investigations of crime scenes, interview witnesses, and perform legal research. They draft motions to suppress evidence or confessions, and conduct suppression hearings.

In *United States v. Wade*, 388 U.S. 218, 256 (1967), Supreme Court Justice White, comparing defense attorneys with prosecutors, stated that "defense counsel has no comparable obligation to ascertain or present the truth. Our system assigned him a different mission. He must be and is interested in preventing the conviction of the innocent, but, absent a voluntary plea of guilty, we also insist that he defend his client whether he is innocent or guilty." This duty to prevent conviction and fight against violations of the defendants' rights must not, however, exceed the attorney's ethical obligation. Defense attorneys cannot mislead the court by providing false information, nor can they knowingly allow the use of false testimony. This weighty responsibility is clearly stressful and, combined with heavy caseloads and limited resources and the knowledge that the client's freedom is at stake, leads to tremendous burnout in the field. A 1978 study of criminal defense attorneys found that those who enjoyed their role of defender in criminal cases stayed with the public defender's office because of the financial security. Those who left did so after two to three years, and far more went to the prosecutor's office than to private practice in the criminal field (Wice, p. 85). Some public defenders, however, move on to the appellate or federal level. Many of those who stay on as public defenders at the trial level are sustained by the fact that they are playing an essential role in the adversarial system of this country and, in so doing, are protecting the rights of all citizens.

JENNIFER MODELL

See also CAREERS IN CRIMINAL JUSTICE: CORRECTIONS; CAREERS IN CRIMINAL JUSTICE: POLICE; COUNSEL: RIGHT TO COUNSEL; COUNSEL: ROLE OF COUNSEL; CRIMINAL JUSTICE SYSTEM; PROSECUTION: COMPARATIVE ASPECTS; PROSECUTION: HISTORY OF THE PUBLIC PROSECUTOR; PROSECUTION: PROSECUTORIAL DISCRETION; PROSECUTION: UNITED STATES ATTORNEY.

BIBLIOGRAPHY

Bureau of Justice Statistics. *Justice Expenditure and Employment, 1990*. Washington, D.C.: U.S. Department of Justice, 1992.
COLTON, AMY M. "Note: Eyes to the Future, Yet Remembering the Past: Reconciling Tradition with the Future of Legal Education." *University of Michigan Journal of Law Reform* 27 (1994): 963.

DEFRANCES, CAROL J., and STEADMAN, GREG W. "Prosecutors in State Courts, 1996." *Bureau of Justice Statistics Bulletin*. Washington, D.C.: Bureau of Justice Statistics, National Institute of Justice, 1998.
ENGLISH, MICHAEL Q. "Note: A Prosecutor's Use of Inconsistent Factual Theories of a Crime in Successive Trials: Zealous Advocacy or a Due Process Violation." *Fordham Law Review* 68 (1999): 525.
HARTMAN, MARSHALL J. *Blue Ribbon Committee on Indigent Defense Services*. Washington, D.C.: National Legal Aid and Defender Association, 1997.
JACKSON, ROBERT H. "The Federal Prosecutor." Address delivered at the Second Annual Conference of United States Attorneys, 1 April 1940. Repr. in *Journal of the American Institute of Law & Criminology* 31 (1940): 3.
MOUNTS, SUZANNE. "Public Defender Programs, Professional Responsibility, and Competent Representation." *Wisconsin Law Review* (1982): 473.
NEUBAUER, DAVID W. *America's Courts and the Criminal Justice System*. Belmont, Calif.: Wadsworth, 1996.
WICE, PAUL B. *Criminal Lawyers: An Endangered Species*. Beverly Hills, Calif.: Sage, 1978.

CAREERS IN CRIMINAL JUSTICE: POLICE

Job and career opportunities in policing are many and varied. The early years of American policing were typified by political appointment of officers and frequent turnover in departmental personnel (Fogelson). This is no longer the case. Policing currently offers an attractive and stable profession to many people. The realm of employment in policing is quite vast, therefore the following section will present a brief overview of potential job opportunities with law enforcement agencies in the United States in two parts. The first section will describe the various types of agencies, how many people they currently employ, salaries, and employment requirements. This overview should give the reader a fair understanding of the field of policing. The second part will detail three issues about American policing: the gender and ethnic make-up of officers, the use of specialist versus generalist officers, and the use of civilian employees.

Current career opportunities in policing

Because the United States has no national police force, policing is done by a myriad of police agencies. This sometimes confusing quilt of organizations is more easily understood if divided into six organizational types: private, local, sheriff's, federal, special, and state. The employment opportunities for each of these six organizational types are described below.

Private policing.   Private policing has a long history, dating back before the creation of full-time police departments staffed by trained and paid officers. Although the exact number of private police departments and officers is unknown, private policing is believed to be the largest employer of officers in the United States. For example, some estimate the number of private agencies at between 57,000 and 92,000 (Ricks, Tillett, and Van Meter). Regardless, "it is safe to say that the private police outnumber the public police, both in terms of agencies and personnel" (Langworthy and Travis, p. 133). These agencies do a wide range of functions. Some agencies provide uniformed patrol of property, or security (such as for armored cars). Sometimes private policing involves undercover investigations of employees or surveillance of people. Private policing can also involve protecting information or money, such as by investigating embezzlement or insurance fraud. Finally, some private police agencies specialize in providing personnel security to people or corporations (such as executive body guards).

The requirements for becoming a private police officer vary. In some cases, all that is required is a GED or high-school diploma, passing a background check, and a period of training provided by the company. Some private security companies require a college degree, and some require state certification as a peace officer (which requires that employees attend and complete a state-certified police academy).

Overall, the field of private policing probably presents the largest pool of potential jobs for those interested in policing. Prospective employees should research the companies employing people in their area, to see what the job entails and what the entrance requirements are. Unfortunately, some private policing jobs do not pay well, employee turnover is great, and the hours long and tedious. On the other hand, some private policing jobs pay very well, offer great benefits, and challenge their employees. Those considering employment in private policing should begin by investigating the available jobs.

Local policing.   Local police provide law enforcement, along with a wide range of other services, to cities, towns, townships, villages, and tribal populations. In terms of employment opportunities, local policing presents the second largest pool of potential jobs for those seeking a career in law enforcement. There are roughly 14,628 local police agencies employing about 383,873 full-time officers (Maguire, Snipes, Uchida, and Townsend).

Generally, local police officers are expected to provide law enforcement, service (such as assisting at fires and disasters), and order maintenance (such as providing crowd control at parades) to their community. In fact, studies indicate that officers do much more service and order maintenance than law enforcement during an average day (Parks, Mastrofski, Dejong, and Gray). Officers assigned to patrol should expect to spend a large part of their workday patrolling, talking and listening to people, and doing paperwork. Rarely does an officer's workday yield an arrest, and even less frequently a high-speed car chase or shootout.

The entrance requirements for becoming a police officer vary from state to state and from one department to the next. Therefore, prospective police officers should investigate the specific entrance requirements of any departments they would like to work for. Most local police departments require that applicants be between the ages of twenty-one and thirty-five, have a high-school diploma (or GED), and have no felony convictions. Agencies vary in the combinations of these attributes. For example, some departments will not consider applicants with a felony arrest, while others disqualify only applicants with felony convictions. Some departments will disqualify applicants based on their juvenile criminal record, while other departments will not. Besides criminal records, other common entrance requirements are that applicants possess a particular level of uncorrected vision and hearing, and have no serious physical disabilities. Most departments have discarded their height requirements. Although few departments require a college degree, it is important to note that a considerable number of people enter policing with two or more years of college (Walker).

New police recruits will generally attend a police academy for their basic training. Nationally, local police departments require an average of 480 academy hours, followed by an average of 295 hours of "on the job" training with a field training officer (U.S. Department of Justice).

Once working, new police officers will usually be assigned to patrol. The entry-level salary for new officers varies considerably across the United States. In 1997, the median entry-level annual salary for new officers in local police agencies was $29,794. Of course, pay increases come with promotions, and for these same local departments, the median salary for sergeants during 1997 was $44,683. Following academy and field training, police officers can expect an average of twenty-four hours per year of "in service" training (U.S. Department of Justice).

Sheriff's agencies. The third most frequent employers of law enforcement officers in the United States are the 3,156 sheriff's agencies, which employ roughly 137,985 sworn deputies (Maguire et al.). Generally, sheriffs are elected officials who are responsible for an entire county. In turn, sheriffs hire deputies who provide a wider range of services than do local police. For example, most sheriffs are responsible for running jails, providing court security, serving summonses and other court orders, and providing law enforcement to unincorporated areas of a county. Rarely do local police agencies perform such a wide range of functions (Falcone and Wells). Prospective employees should research the sheriff's agencies they would like to work for; in some states they do not have arrest powers, do not do general patrol, and only run the jails and serve summonses. Generally, however, new deputies can expect to be assigned to one of the three major responsibilities of sheriff's agencies: court operations, jail operation, or patrol. Therefore, unlike new officers in local police agencies, new deputies are not necessarily assigned to patrol or general law enforcement duties.

Generally, the entrance requirements for becoming a sheriff's deputy are the same as for local policing (see above). In 1997, deputies were required to attend an academy for an average of 397 hours, followed by a mean of 190 hours of field training. Deputies can also expect an average of twenty-two hours per year of additional in-service training. As with local policing, salaries for deputies vary greatly. The median first year deputy's salary in 1997 was $23,296 and the minimum sergeant's salary in 1997 was $34,428.

Federal law enforcement. About thirty different federal agencies employ about 69,000 armed and sworn agents who patrol, provide security, or investigate violations of certain federal laws (Maguire et al.). The most famous of these agencies is probably the Federal Bureau of Investigation (FBI). However, a number of other federal entities employ their own uniformed police officers (such as the U.S. Capitol Police), or investigators (such as the Internal Revenue Service). According to the Bureau of Justice Statistics, in 1998 four federal agencies accounted for three-fifths of federal officers: The Immigration and Naturalization Service (16,552 officers), the Federal Bureau of Prisons (12,587 officers), the FBI (11,285 officers), and the Customs Service (10,539 officers) (Reaves). (Although all of these officers are authorized to make arrests and to carry firearms, many of them—and most of the Bureau of Prisons employees—are correctional officers.)

Despite the relatively large number of federal officers, becoming a federal officer is one of the hardest law enforcement jobs to attain. First, the requirements for federal officers are generally more stringent than for other law enforcement positions. As with all law enforcement jobs, the requirements vary agency by agency. However, the FBI's requirements for employment are illustrative. In order to be considered as an FBI agent, applicants must be U.S. residents between the ages of twenty-three and thirty-seven, be in excellent physical condition, and meet particular vision and hearing requirements. Furthermore, prospective agents must have a four-year college degree and possess skills or a degree in one of four areas—a law degree, a degree in accounting, proficiency in certain foreign languages, or three years of relevant, full-time work experience. However, merely meeting these requirements does not guarantee someone a job as an FBI agent. Prospective agents must also undergo extensive background checks, physicals, interviews, and careful selection by the FBI. Very few applicants eventually become FBI agents. Following hire, agents must attend the FBI's training academy in Quantico, Virginia, for sixteen weeks. Following training, agents are assigned to one of the FBI's fifty-six regional field offices.

The requirements for federal law enforcement jobs vary from one agency to the next, and change over time. Therefore, prospective employees should contact the agencies they are considering (or visit each agency's web page) and request a copy of their current employment requirements.

Special police. The fifth most frequent employers of police officers in the United States are special police agencies. Special police agencies provide law enforcement, service, and order maintenance to either limited geographic areas (such as state parks, college campuses, transit systems, and public housing), or enforce a limited number of laws over a wider area (such as liquor enforcement for an entire state). It is estimated that there are 3,280 special police agencies employing 58,689 officers (Maguire et al.).

The duties of special police officers vary depending upon the agency. If the agency serves a geographic area, such as a campus or transit system, officers will be expected to provide service, order maintenance, and law enforcement (just as local police agencies do) to people in that geographic area. On the other hand, if the special police agency concentrates on the enforcement of particular laws (e.g., natural resources policing, fire investigation, or liquor enforcement) officers might not have patrol duties. Instead, such special police officers may be expected to conduct investigations or undercover work.

As with all police agencies in the United States, the requirements for being hired vary from one agency to the next. Overall, however, the requirements of being hired as a special police officer are similar to those of local police agencies (see above). In 1997, special police officers were required to complete an average of 600 academy hours, followed by 358 hours of field training. On average, special police officers in the United States received 30 hours of annual in-service training. The median salary for a special police officer in 1997 was $28,921, and the minimum sergeant's salary in 1997 was $49,371.

State police.   Finally, the sixth group of employers of law enforcement officers in the United States are the forty-nine state police or highway patrols (hereafter both will be called "state police"). With the exception of Hawaii, each state has its own state police. The full duties of these agencies differ from state to state, but generally state police are expected to patrol the interstates and state routes, enforce traffic laws, and investigate crimes committed on state property. In some states the state police patrol the unincorporated areas of the state. Likewise, in some states the state police run the state crime lab and a state police academy. Therefore, smaller local police agencies may request assistance from their state police for some criminal investigations, and sometimes the state police train local police officers at the state police academy. As with the rest of law enforcement in the United States, the exact duties and responsibilities of the state police differ from one state to the next.

State police officers can expect primarily to conduct patrol and enforce motor vehicle laws on that state's highways. In some cases, officers provide service, order maintenance, and law enforcement to rural communities that do not have their own police departments. As with most police agencies, state police are generally expected to conduct criminal investigations of crimes that occur within their jurisdiction, or that involve violations of specific state laws.

State police officers' academy training lasts for an average of 800 hours, followed by an average of 392 hours of field training, and 28 hours of in-service training annually. State police officers earn an average annual salary of $27,651, and the maximum salary for sergeants is $48,176.

Issues in employment

The following section discusses three issues concerning employment in police agencies; the gender and ethnicity of sworn officers, the use of generalist or specialist officers, and the use of civilian employees.

Employment of women and minorities.   The early American police were primarily white males. Although the first Irish and Italian police officers were hired in the latter 1800s (not without controversy), and some departments later hired female officers, neither women nor ethnic minorities were represented significantly among the ranks of law enforcement officers until the 1970s. In 1997, women composed between 5 and 11 percent of sworn officers in local, sheriff's, special, and state police agencies. Ethnic minorities account for between 12 and 25 percent of sworn officers in these same agency types (U.S. Department of Justice). Of course, there is great variation from one agency to the next in terms of how many women and ethnic minorities each employs. As a rule of thumb, larger agencies have higher percentages of both. Depending on the agency, between 8 and 25 percent of sworn federal officers are female, and between 8 and 42 percent are ethnic minorities (Reaves, 2000).

Generalist versus specialist officers.   Police agencies, like most organizations, must choose between two ways of allocating employees to performing the work of that organization. Organizations can use generalists, who perform a wide-range of functions, or can use specialists, who are highly trained to perform a single or limited number of tasks. This is analogous to the differences between a general family physician and a brain surgeon. The general family physician is a generalist capable of handling a wide range of illnesses and ailments, but who may not have ex-

Table 1

Agencies, sworn personnel, and average first-year salary for U.S. law enforcement agencies in 1997

Agency type	Number of agencies	Number of sworn officers	Average salary first-year officer
Private police	57,000-92,000	Unknown	Unknown
Local police	14,628	383,873	$29,794
Sheriffs	3,156	137,985	$26,830
Federal	30	69,000	$35,658[1]
Special police	3,280	58,689	$28,921
State police	49	53,336	$27,651

[1]This estimate is based on the current entry grade (GS 10) for new F.B.I. agents. This figure may not apply to all sworn federal law enforcement positions.

pertise in any one medical area. The brain surgeon, on the other hand, is a highly trained specialist in one area, but might not have the broad knowledge or experience of a general family physician.

Analogously, police organizations perform a wide range of tasks, such as enforcing vice and narcotics laws, working with juveniles, performing crime prevention, and analyzing crime data. Police agencies must decide whether their patrol officers will perform most of these tasks, or if specially trained officers will concentrate on only one or two of these tasks. Some departments, especially smaller ones, rely upon generalists; their regular patrol officers perform most of the agency's tasks. For example, officers will patrol their beats, respond to crime scenes where they will collect and preserve physical evidence, counsel juveniles who may be getting into trouble, and attend neighborhood meetings. Other departments choose to assign their officers as specialists. Thus, some of their officers also patrol a beat. However, if there is a crime scene, it is another officer's responsibility to collect and preserve the evidence. Another officer may work with juveniles in the community. And a fourth officer may work as a community liaison who attends community meetings.

This difference between specialist and generalist officers has important implications for those considering a career in law enforcement. Generalists get to do a wide range of tasks, but some occur very infrequently. Specialists get to work at one or two specific tasks, but often do little else. For example every patrol officer would be expected to write speeding tickets in an agency without a special traffic enforcement unit. On the other hand, an agency with a special unit will assign some officers to focus on enforcing of traffic laws. These officers will spend the majority of

their day writing traffic tickets, but doing little else.

Not only does specialization dictate what officers will do during their average work day, it also structures the chances for changing one's job and for promotion. Some special units have a lot of prestige, freedom, or rewards attached to them. For example, officers in SWAT teams, K-9 units, or working as homicide detectives are often revered by other officers and the public, may have greater flexibility in the hours they can work, and may be better paid; these are prestigious assignments. Of course, some special assignments are not, such as working at the police impound yard, checking evidence into the property locker, or working as a dispatcher. This is not to say that such jobs are not important, nor that everyone dislikes them. However, there are pros and cons to working as a specialist or as a generalist.

Employment of civilians. Law enforcement agencies often hire people to work as non-sworn employees (called civilian employees or civilians). Nationally, about 25 percent of the employees of local, state, and special police agencies are civilians. Of course, because civilian employees are not trained as peace officers, they do not carry guns and do not have arrest powers. However, civilians perform a wide range of important duties for police agencies, and those seeking employment in policing should not overlook these opportunities.

As with the other aspects of policing in America, the jobs and responsibilities performed by civilian employees vary from one agency to the next. The most common duties performed by civilians are answering emergency switchboards and dispatching patrol officers, performing clerical or secretarial duties, maintaining police vehicles, or doing custodial chores around police buildings. Some agencies also hire civilians to perform very specialized tasks. Most of the better positions require a college degree or extensive experience. Such specialized civilian positions include running computer hardware or writing software programs for agency computers. Some agencies hire civilians to serve as advocates for victims of crime. Some agencies also hire civilians as crime scene technicians, processing physical evidence, or as lab technicians, working in police crime labs. A few police agencies also employ civilians in community liaison or public relations capacities.

Sometimes police agencies employ civilians as uniformed security officers. Because these security officers do not have arrest powers, or are unarmed, they are not technically considered law enforcement officers. However, security personnel perform a wide range of duties that would normally be performed by sworn patrol officers, such as securing buildings, assisting people, responding to first aid calls and emergencies, patrolling a beat, and investigating crimes. Furthermore, some city police departments have hired civilians who were trained to respond to nonemergency 911 calls. These civilians meet with crime victims and complainants, take a report if necessary, and advise people what they should do about their problem. By using these trained civilians to handle nonemergency calls, sworn officers are freed to concentrate on more serious matters.

WILLIAM R. KING

See also CAREERS IN CRIMINAL JUSTICE: CORRECTIONS; CAREERS IN CRIMINAL JUSTICE: LAW; CRIMINAL JUSTICE SYSTEM; FEDERAL BUREAU OF INVESTIGATION: HISTORY; POLICE: COMMUNITY POLICING; POLICE: CRIMINAL INVESTIGATIONS; POLICE: HANDLING OF JUVENILES; POLICE: HISTORY; POLICE: ORGANIZATION AND MANAGEMENT; POLICE: POLICE OFFICER BEHAVIOR; POLICE: POLICING COMPLAINANTLESS CRIMES; POLICE: PRIVATE POLICE AND INDUSTRIAL SECURITY; POLICE: SPECIAL WEAPONS AND TACTICS (SWAT) TEAMS; URBAN POLICE.

BIBLIOGRAPHY

FALCONE, DAVID N., and WELLS, L. EDWARD. "The County Sheriff as a Distinctive Policing Modality." *American Journal of Police* 14, no. 3/4 (1995): 123–149.

FOGELSON, ROBERT M. *Big City Police.* Cambridge, Mass.: Harvard University Press, 1977.

LANGWORTHY, ROBERT H., and TRAVIS, LAWRENCE F., III. *Policing in America: A Balance of Forces,* 2d ed. Columbus, Ohio: Prentice Hall, 1999.

MAGUIRE, EDWARD R.; SNIPES, JEFFREY B.; UCHIDA, CRAIG D.;, and TOWNSEND, MARGARET. "Counting Cops: Estimating the Number of Police Departments and Police Officers in the United States." *Policing: An International Journal of Police Strategies and Management* 21, no. 1 (1998): 97–120.

PARKS, ROGER B.; MASTROFSKI, STEPHEN D.; DEJONG, CHRISTINA; and GRAY, M. KEVIN. "How Officers Spend Their Time with the Community." *Justice Quarterly* 16, no. 3 (1999): 483–518.

REAVES, BRIAN A. *Federal Law Enforcement Officers, 1998.* Washington, D.C.: U.S. Department of Justice, Bureau of Justice Statistics, 2000.

RICKS, TRUETT, A.; TILLETT, BILL G.; and VAN METER, CLIFFORD W. *Principles of Security,* 3d ed. Cincinnati, Ohio: Anderson Publishing Co., 1994.

U.S. Department of Justice, Bureau of Justice Statistics. Law Enforcement Management and Administrative Statistics (LEMAS): 1997 Sample Survey of Law Enforcement Agencies. Computer file. ICPSR version. U.S. Dept. of Commerce, Bureau of the Census [producer], 1998. Ann Arbor, Mich.: Inter-university Consortium for Political and Social Research [distributor], 1999.

WALKER, SAMUEL. *The Police in America: An Introduction,* 3d ed. Boston, Mass.: McGraw-Hill College, 1999.

CAUSATION

Role of causation in the criminal law

The place of causation in criminal law doctrines.   The part of the substantive criminal law commonly called the "special part" consists of several thousand prohibitions and requirements. Criminal codes typically prohibit citizens from doing certain types of action and sometimes (but much less frequently) require citizens to do certain types of actions. Causation enters into both the prohibitions and the requirements of a typical criminal code, for such statutes either prohibit citizens from *causing* certain results or require them to *cause* certain results. In either case causation is central to criminal liability.

It is sometimes urged that *omission liability* (that is, liability for *not* doing an act required by law) is noncausal, and there is a sense in which this is true. A defendant who omits to do an act the law requires him to do is not liable for having caused the harm that the act omitted would have prevented; rather, he is liable for not preventing the harm (Moore, 1993, pp. 267–278). Yet notice that to assess whether a defendant is liable for an omission to prevent some harm, a causal judgment is still necessary: we have to know that no act of the defendant prevented (i.e., caused the absence of) any such harm. For if some act of the defendant did cause the absence of a certain harm, then the defendant cannot be said to have omitted to have prevented the harm. One can, for example, only be liable for omitting to save another from drowning if none of one's acts have the causal property, saving-the-other-from-drowning (Moore, 1993, pp. 29–31).

It is also sometimes said that many prohibitions of the criminal law do not involve causation. Criminal law typically prohibits theft, rape, burglary, conspiracy, and attempt, and (so the argument goes) these are types of actions that have no causal elements in them. Although this view has been elevated to a dogma accepted by both American and English criminal law theorists (Fletcher, 1978, pp. 388–390; Fletcher, 1998, pp. 60–62; Buxton, p. 18; Williams, p. 368), it is manifestly false. A theft occurs, for example, only when an actor's voluntary act causes movement ("asportation") of the goods stolen. Similarly a burglary occurs only when there is a breaking and an entering of a building, and these occur only when a defendant's voluntary act *causes* a lock on a window to be broken and *causes* the alleged burglar to be in the building in question (Moore, 1993, pp. 213–225). The temptation to accept the dogma (of noncausal criminal actions) stems from the fact that many of the results the criminal law prohibits are usually brought about rather directly. Penetration in rape, for example, usually is not the result of a lengthy chain of events beginning with the rapist's voluntary act. But this is not always the case, as where the defendant inserts the penis of another into the victim (*Dusenberry v. Commonwealth*, 220 Va. 770, 263 S.E2d 392(1980)); and in any case, that the causal conclusion is often easy to reach should not obscure the fact that a causal judgment is involved in all actions prohibited or required by the criminal law.

The place of causation in criminal law policy. It is a much debated question whether the criminal law should be so result-oriented. Why is the defendant who intends to kill another and does all he can to succeed in his plan less punishable when he fails to cause the harm intended than when he succeeds? Utilitarians about punishment typically justify this causation-oriented grading scheme by alluding either to popular sentiment or to the need to give criminals incentives not to try again. Retributivists about punishment typically invoke a notion of "moral luck" according to which a defendant's moral blameworthiness increases with success in his criminal plans (Moore, 1997, pp. 191–247). In any case, for one set of reasons or another, causation is an element of criminal liability for all completed crimes, in addition to mens rea and voluntariness of action.

Causation in criminal law and causation in tort law. Many of the leading cases on causation, most of the causal doctrines finding some acceptance in the law, and most of the theorizing about causation, originate in the law of tort and not in the criminal law. The reasons for this are not hard to discern. Unlike the thousands of specific actions prohibited or required by the criminal law, tort law largely consists of but one injunction: do not unreasonably act so as to cause harm to another. Such an injunction places greater weight on causation. It leaves open a full range of causal questions, much more than do injunctions of criminal law such as, "do not intentionally hit another."

Criminal law thus has been a borrower from torts on the issue of causation. Such borrowing has not been uniform or without reservations. Aside from the greater demands of directness of causation implicit in specific criminal prohibitions (noted above), the criminal sanction of punishment is sometimes said to demand greater stringency of causation than is demanded by the less severe tort sanction of compensation. Still, the usual form such reservations take is for criminal law to modify causation doctrines in tort by a matter of degree only (Moore, 1997, p. 363 n.1). Foreseeability, for example, is a test of causation in both fields, but what must be foreseeable, and the degree with which it must be foreseeable, is sometimes thought to be greater in criminal law than in torts. Such variation by degree only has allowed causation in criminal law and in torts to be discussed via the same tests, which we shall now do.

Conventional analysis of causation in the law

The two-step analysis. The conventional wisdom about the causation requirement in both criminal law and torts is that it in reality consists of two very different requirements. The first requirement is that of "cause-in-fact." This is said to be the true causal requirement because this doctrine adopts the scientific notion of causation. Whether cigarette smoking causes cancer, whether the presence of hydrogen or helium caused an explosion, are factual questions to be resolved by the best science the courts can muster. By contrast, the second requirement, that of "proximate" or "legal" cause, is said to be an evaluative issue, to be resolved by arguments of policy and not arguments of scientific fact. Suppose a defendant knifes his victim, who then dies because her religious convictions are such that she refuses medical treatment. Has such a defendant (legally) caused her death? The answer to such questions, it is said, depends on the policies behind liability, not on any factual issues.

The counterfactual analysis of cause-in-fact. By far the dominant test for cause-in-fact is the common law and Model Penal Code "sine qua non," or "but-for" test (MPC §2.03(1)). Such a test asks a counterfactual question: "but for the defendant's action, would the victim have been harmed in the way the criminal law prohibits?" This test is also sometimes called the necessary condition test, because it requires that the defendant's action be necessary to the victim's harm. The appeal of this test stems from this fact. The test seems to isolate something we seem to care a lot about, both in explaining events and in assessing responsibility for them, namely, did the defendant's act make a difference? Insofar as we increase moral blameworthiness and legal punishment for actors who do *cause* bad results (not just try to), we seemingly should care whether a particular bad result would have happened anyway, even without the defendant.

The policy analysis of legal cause. There is no equivalently dominant test of legal or proximate cause. There are nonetheless four distinguishable sorts of tests having some authority within the legal literature. The first of these are what we may call "ad hoc policy tests" (Edgarton). The idea is that courts balance a range of policies in each case that they adjudicate where a defendant has been found to have caused-in-fact a legally prohibited harm. They may balance certain "social interests" like the need for deterrence with certain "individual interests" like the unfairness of surprising a defendant with liability. Courts then decide wherever such balance leads. Whatever decision is reached on such case-by-case policy balancing is then cast in terms of "proximate" or "legal" cause. Such labels are simply the conclusions of policy balances; the labels have nothing to do with causation in any ordinary or scientific sense.

The second sort of test here is one that adopts general rules of legal causation. Such rules are adopted for various policy reasons also having nothing to do with causation, but this "rules-based" test differs from the last by its eschewal of case-by-case balancing; rather, *per se* rules of legal causation are adopted for policy reasons. Thus, the common law rule for homicide was that death must occur within a year and a day of the defendant's harmful action, else the defendant could not be said to have legally caused the death. Analogously, the "last wrongdoer rule" held that when a single victim is mortally wounded by two or more assailants, acting not in concert and acting seriatim over time, only the last wrongdoer could be said to be the legal cause of the death (Smith, p. 111). Such sorts of tests also found a temporary home in tort law with its "first house rule," according to which a railroad whose negligently emitted sparks burned an entire town was only liable for the house or houses directly ignited by its sparks, not for other houses ignited by the burning of those first burnt houses (*Ryan v. New York Central R.R.*, 35 N.Y. 210, 91 Am. Dec.49 (1866)). There is no pretense in such rules of making truly causal discriminations; rather, such rules were adopted for explicit reasons of legal policy.

The third sort of test here is the well-known foreseeability test (Moore, 1997, pp. 363–399). Unlike the "rules-based" test, here there is no multiplicity of rules for specific situations (like homicide, intervening wrongdoers, railroad fires, etc.). Rather, there is one rule universally applicable to all criminal cases: was the harm that the defendant's act in fact caused foreseeable to him at the time he acted? This purportedly universal test for legal causation is usually justified by one of two policies: either the unfairness of punishing someone for harms that they could not foresee, or the inability to gain any deterrence by punishing such actors (since the criminal law's threat value is nonexistent for unforeseeable violations).

Some jurisdictions restrict the foreseeability test to one kind of situation. When some human action or natural event intervenes between the defendant's action and the harm, the restricted test asks whether that intervening action or event was foreseeable to the defendant when he acted (Moore, 1997, p. 363 n.1). This restricted foreseeability test is like the restricted rules we saw before and is unlike the universal test of legal causation the foreseeability test usually purports to be.

The fourth and last sort of test here is the "harm-within-the-risk" test (Green). Like the foreseeability test, this test purports to be a test of legal cause universally applicable to all criminal cases. This test too is justified on policy grounds and does not pretend to have anything to do with factual or scientific causation. Doctrinally, however, the test differs from a simple foreseeability test.

Consider first the arena from which the test takes its name, crimes of risk creation. If the defendant is charged with negligent homicide, for example, this test requires that the death of the victim be within the risk that made the actor's action negligent. Similarly, if the charge is manslaughter (for which consciousness of the risk is required in some jurisdictions), this test requires that the death of the victim be within the risk the awareness of which made the defendant's action reckless.

Extension of this test to nonrisk-creation crimes requires some modification. For crimes of strict liability, where no mens rea is required, the test requires that the harm that happened be one of the types of harms the risk of which motivated the legislature to criminalize the behavior. For crimes requiring knowledge or general intention for their mens rea, the test asks whether the harm that happened was an instance of the type of harm foreseen by the defendant as he acted. For crimes requiring purpose or specific intent for their mens rea, the test asks whether the harm that happened was an instance of the type of harm the defendant intended to achieve by his action.

What motivates all of these variations of the harm-within-the-risk test is the following insight: when assessing culpable mens rea, there is always a "fit problem" (Moore, 1997, pp. 469–476). Suppose a defendant intends to hit his victim in the face with a stick; suppose further he intends the hit to put out the victim's left eye. As it happens, the victim turns suddenly as he is being hit, and loses his right ear. Whether the harm that happened is an instance of the type of harm intended is what the present author calls the "fit problem." Fact finders have to fit the mental state the defendant had to the actual result he achieved and ask whether it is close enough for him to be punished for a crime of intent like mayhem. (If it is not close enough, then he may yet be convicted of some lesser crime of battery or reckless endangerment.)

The essential claim behind the harm within the risk test is that "legal cause" is the inapt label we have put on a problem of culpability, the fit problem. Proponents of this test urge that legal cause, properly understood, is really a mens rea doctrine, not a doctrine of causation at all.

Problems with the conventional analysis

Problems with the counterfactual test. Very generally there are four sorts of problems with the counterfactual test for causation in fact. One set of these problems has to do with proof and evidence. As an element of the prima facie case, causation-in-fact must be proven by the prosecution beyond a reasonable doubt. Yet counterfactuals by their nature are difficult to prove with that degree of certainty, for they require the fact finder to speculate what would have happened if the defendant had not done what he did. Suppose a defendant culpably destroys a life preserver on a seagoing tug. When a crewman falls overboard and drowns, was a necessary condition of his death the act of the defendant in destroying the life preserver? If the life preserver had been there, would anyone have thought to use it? Thrown it in time? Thrown it far enough? Have gotten near enough to the victim that he would have reached it? We often lack the kind of precise information that could verify whether the culpable act of the defendant made any difference in this way.

A second set of problems stems from an indeterminacy of meaning in the test, not from difficulties of factual verification. There is a great vagueness in counterfactual judgments. The vagueness lies in specifying the possible world in which we are to test the counterfactual (Moore, 1997, pp. 345–347). When we say, "but for the defendant's act of destroying the life preserver," what world are we imagining? We know we are to eliminate the defendant's act, but what are we to replace it with? A life preserver that was destroyed by the heavy seas (that themselves explain why the defendant couldn't destroy the life preserver)? A defendant who did not destroy the life preserver because he had already pushed the victim overboard when no one else was around to throw the life preserver to the victim? And so on. To make the counterfactual test determinate enough to yield one answer rather than another, we have to assume that we share an ability to specify a possible world that is "most similar" to our actual world, and that it is in *this* possible world that we ask our counterfactual question (Lewis, 1970).

The third and fourth sets of problems stem from the inability of the counterfactual test to match what for most of us are firm causal intuitions. The third set of problems arise because the counterfactual test seems too lenient in what it counts as a cause. The criticism is that the test is thus overinclusive. The fourth set of problems arise because the counterfactual test seems too stringent in what it counts as a cause. The criticism here is that the test is underinclusive.

The overinclusiveness of the test can be seen in at least four distinct areas. To begin with, the test fails to distinguish acts from omissions, in that both can be equally necessary to the happening of some event (Moore, 1993, pp. 267–278; Moore, 1999). Thus, on the counterfactual test both my stabbing the victim through the heart and your failure to prevent me (though you were half a world away at the time) are equally the cause of the victim's death. This is, to put it bluntly, preposterous.

It is important to see that there is a counterfactual question to ask about omissions before we blame someone for them. We do need to know, counterfactually, if the defendant had not omitted to do some action, whether that action would have prevented the harm in question. Yet the counterfactual test of causation would turn this question about an ability to prevent some harm, into a question of causing that which was not prevented. It is a significant objection to the counterfactual theory that it blurs this crucial distinction.

A second way in which the counterfactual test is overinclusive is with regard to coincidences. Suppose a defendant culpably delays his train at t_1; much, much later and much further down the track at t_2, the train is hit by a flood, resulting in damage and loss of life (*Denny v. N.Y. Central R.R.*, 13 Gray (Mass.) 481 (1859)). Since but for the delay at t_1, there would have been no damage or loss of life at t_2, the counterfactual test yields the unwelcome result that the defendant's delaying caused the harm.

While such cases of overt coincidences are rare, they are the tip of the iceberg here. Innumerable remote conditions are necessary to the production of any event. Oxygen in the air over England, timber in Scotland, Henry the VIII's obesity, and Drake's perspicacity were all probably necessary for the defeat of the Spanish Armada (Moore, 1993, pp. 268–269), but we should be loath to say that each of these was equally the cause of that defeat.

A third area of overinclusiveness stems from the rockbed intuition that causation is asymmetrical with respect to time (Moore, 1999). My dynamite exploding at t_1 may cause your mother minks to kill their young at t_2, yet your mother minks killing their young at t_2 did not cause my dynamite to explode at t_1. The counterfactual test has a difficult time in accommodating this simple but stubborn intuition.

To see this, recall the logic of necessary and sufficient conditions. If event c is not only necessary for event e but also sufficient, then (of necessity) e is also necessary for c. In such a case c and e are symmetrically necessary conditions for each other and, on the counterfactual analysis, each is therefore the cause of the other. Intuitively we know that this is absurd, yet to avoid this result we must deny that some cause c is ever sufficient (as well as necessary) for some effect e. And the problem is that almost all proponents of the necessary condition test readily admit that every cause c is, if not sufficient by itself, then sufficient when conjoined with certain other conditions c'; c'', etc. (Mill, 1965, book 3, chap. 5, sec. 3). Sufficiency seems to well capture the commonsense view that causes make their effects inevitable. Yet, with such inevitability of effects from their causes come a necessity of those effects for those causes. Therefore, every effect is also a cause of its cause?

The fourth sort of overinclusiveness of the counterfactual analysis can be seen in cases of epiphenomena. One event is epiphenomenal to another event when both events are effects of a common cause (Moore, 1999). I jog in the morning with my dog. This has two effects: at t_2, my feet get tired; at t_3, my dog gets tired. Intuitively we know that my feet getting tired did not cause my dog to get tired. Yet the counterfactual analysis suggests just the opposite. My jogging in the morning was not only necessary for my feet getting tired, it (sometimes at least) was also sufficient. This means (see above) that my feet getting tired was necessary to my jogging in the morning. Yet we know (on the counterfactual analysis) that my jogging in the morning was necessary to my dog getting tired. Therefore, by the transitivity of "necessary," my feet getting tired was necessary to my dog getting tired. Therefore, the tiring of my feet *did* cause the tiring of my dog, contrary to our firm intuitions about epiphenomena.

The fourth set of problems for the counterfactual test has to do with the test's underinclusiveness. Such underinclusiveness can be seen in the well-known overdetermination cases (Moore, 1999; Wright, 1985, pp. 1775–1798), where each of two events c_1 and c_2 is independently sufficient for some third event e; logically, this entails that neither c_1 nor c_2 is necessary for e, and thus, on the counterfactual analysis of causation, neither can be the cause of e. Just about everybody rejects this conclusion, and so such cases pose a real problem for the counterfactual analysis.

There are two distinct kinds of overdetermination cases. The first are the concurrent-cause cases: two fires, two shotgun blasts, two noisy motorcycles, each are sufficient to burn, kill, or scare some victim. The defendant is responsible for only one fire, shot, or motorcycle. Yet his fire, shot, or noise joins the other one, and both simultaneously cause some single, individual harm. On the counterfactual analysis the defendant's fire, shot, or noise was not the cause of any harm because it was not necessary to the production of the harm—after all, the other fire, shot, or noise was by itself *sufficient*. Yet the same can be said about the second fire, shot, or noise. So, on the but-for test, neither was the cause! And this is absurd.

The preemptive kind of overdetermination cases are different. Here the two putative causes are not simultaneous but are temporally ordered. The defendant's fire arrives first and burns down the victim's building; the second fire arrives shortly thereafter, and would have been sufficient to have burned down the building, only there was no building to burn down. Here our intuitions are just as clear as in the concurrent overdetermination cases but they are different: the defendant's fire did cause the harm, and the second fire did not. Yet the counterfactual analysis again yields the counterintuitive implication that neither fire caused the harm because neither fire was necessary (each being sufficient) for the harm.

Situated rather nicely between these two sorts of overdetermination cases is what this author has called the asymmetrical overdetermination cases (Moore, 1999). Suppose the defendant nonmortally stabs the victim at the same time as another defendant mortally stabs the same victim; the victim dies of loss of blood, most of the blood gushing out of the mortal wound. Has the nonmortally wounding defendant caused the death of the victim? Not according to the counterfactual analysis: given the sufficiency of the mortal wound, the nonmortal wound was not necessary for, and thus not a cause of, death. This conclusion is contrary to common intuition as well as legal authority (*People v. Lewis*, 124 Cal. 551, 57 P. 470 (1899)).

Defenders of the counterfactual analysis are not bereft of replies to these objections. As to problems of proof they assert that counterfactuals are no harder to verify than other judgments applying causal laws to unobservable domains (such as those parts of the past for which there is no direct evidence, or those aspects of the universe too far removed for us to observe, or those future events beyond our likely existence). As to the problem of indeterminacy, they assert that we test counterfactuals in that possible world that is relatively close to our actual world; usually this means removing the defendant's action only, and then suspending enough causal laws so that events that normally cause such action just did not on this occasion (Wright, 1988). As to the problems of omissions and asymmetry through time, they assert that we should simply stipulate that a cause is not only a necessary condition for its effect, but it is also an event (not the absence of an event) that precedes (not succeeds) the event which is its effect. Such stipulations are embarrassingly ad hoc, but they do eliminate otherwise troublesome counterexamples. With regard to coincidences and epiphenomenal pairs of events, they assert that there are no causal laws connecting classes of such events with one another; one *type* of event is not necessary for another *type* of event, however necessary one particular event may be for its putative (coincidental or epiphenomerical) "effect." With regard to the embarrassment of riches in terms of how many conditions are necessary for any given event or state, they typically bite the bullet and admit that causation is a very nondiscriminating relation; however our usage of "cause" is more discriminating by building in pragmatic restrictions on when certain information is appropriately imparted to a given audience. As to the problem posed by the concurrent overdetermination cases, they usually urge that if one individuates the effect finely enough in such cases, one will see that each concurrent cause is necessary to *that* specific effect (American Law Institute, 1985). A two-bullet death is different than a one-bullet death, so that each simultaneous, mortally wounding bullet is necessary to the particular death (i.e., a two-bullet death) suffered by the victim shot by two defendants. Similarly, in the preemptive overdetermination cases, they assert that the first fire to arrive was necessary to the burning of the house, but the second was not, because had the first fire not happened the second fire still would have been prevented from burning the house (Lewis, 1970).

There are deep and well-known problems with all of these responses by the counterfactual theorists (Moore, 1999). Rather than pursue these, we should briefly consider modifications of the counterfactual test designed to end run some of these problems. With regard to the problem posed by the overdetermination cases, the best known alternative is to propose the NESS test: an event c causes an event e if and only if c is a necessary element in a set of conditions sufficient for e (Mackie; Wright, 1985). It is the stress on *sufficiency* that is supposed to end run the overdetermination problems. In the concurrent cause cases, where the two fires join to burn the victim's house, each fire is said to be a necessary element of its own sufficient set, so each fire is a cause. In the pre-emptive case, where the fires do not join and one arrives first, the first fire is a necessary element of a sufficient set, and so is the cause; but the second fire is not because absent from its set is the existence of a house to be burned.

There are problem with this NESS alternative too (Moore, 1999). For example, it is not stated how one individuates sets of conditions. Why aren't the two fires part of the same set, in which event neither is necessary? Also, in the preemptive case, isn't the addition of the condition, "existence of the victim's house at the time the second fire would be sufficient to destroy it," already sliding in the causal conclusion that the first fire already caused the house not to exist? Again these problems are not conclusive, and debate about them will no doubt continue for the foreseeable future. Such problems cause grave doubt to exist about any version of the counterfactual test among many legal theoreticians. Such academic doubts seem to have shaken the doctrinal dominance of the test very little, however.

Problems with the policy tests for legal cause.   The main problem with both the ad hoc and the rule-based policy tests is that they seek to maximize the wrong policies. The general "functionalist" approach of such tests to legal concepts is correct: we should always ask after the purpose of the rule or institution in which the concept figures in order to ascertain its legal meaning. Yet the dominant purpose of the law's concept of causation is to grade punishment proportionately to moral blameworthiness. One who intentionally or recklessly causes a harm that another only tries to cause or risks causing, is more blameworthy (Moore, 1997, pp. 191–247). We must thus not seek the meaning of causation in extrinsic policies; rather, the legal concept of causation will serve its grading function only if the concept names some factual state of affairs that determines moral blameworthiness. By ignoring this dominant function of causation in criminal law, the explicit policy tests constructed an artificial concept of legal cause unusable in any just punishment scheme.

This problem does not infect the foreseeability and harm-within-the-risk tests. For those tests do seek to describe a factual state of affairs that plausibly determines moral blameworthiness. They are thus serving the dominant policy that must be served by the concept of causation in the criminal law. Their novelty lies in their reallocation of the locus of blame. On these theories, "legal cause" is not a refinement of an admitted desert-determiner, true causation; it is rather a refinement of another admitted desert-determiner, namely, mens rea (or "culpability").

Precisely because it is a culpability test, however, the foreseeability test becomes subject to another policy-based objection, that of redundancy. Why should we ask *two* culpability questions in determining blameworthiness? After we have satisfied ourselves that a defendant is culpable—either because she intended or foresaw some harm, or because she was unreasonable in not foreseeing some harm, given the degree of that harm's seriousness, the magnitude of its risk, and the lack of justification for taking such a risk—the foreseeability test bids us to ask, "was the harm foreseeable?" This is redundant, because any harm intended or foreseen is foreseeable, and any harm foreseeable enough to render an actor unreasonable for not foreseeing it, is also foreseeable.

The only way the foreseeability test avoids redundancy is by moving toward the harm-within-the-risk test. That is, one might say that the defendant was culpable in intending, foreseeing, or risking some harm type H, but that what his act in fact caused was an instance of harm type J; the foreseeability test of legal cause becomes nonredundant the moment one restricts it to asking whether J was foreseeable, a different question than the one asked and answered as a matter of mens rea about H. Yet this is to do the work of the harm-within-the-risk test, namely, the work of solving the "fit problem" of mens rea. Moreover, it is to do such work badly. Foreseeability is not the right question to ask in order to fit the harm in fact caused by a defendant to the type of harm he either intended to achieve or foresaw that he would cause. If the foreseeability test is to be restricted to this nonredundant work it is better abandoned for the harm-within-the-risk test.

The main problem for the harm-within-the-risk test itself does not lie in any of the directions we have just explored. The test is in the service of the right policy in its seeking of a true desert-determiner, and the test does not ask a redundant question. To grade culpability by the mental states of intention, foresight, and risk we have to solve the fit problem above described. The real question for the harm-within-the-risk test is whether this grading by culpable mental states is all that is or should be going on under the rubric of "legal cause."

Consider in this regard two well-known sorts of legal cause cases. It is a time honored maxim of criminal law (as well as tort law) that "you take your victim as you find him." Standard translation: no matter how abnormal may be the victim's susceptibilities to injury, and no matter how unforeseeable such injuries may therefore be, a defendant is held to legally cause such injuries. Hit the proverbial thin-skulled man or cut the proverbial hemophiliac, and you have legally caused their deaths. This is hard to square with the harm-within-the-risk test. A defendant who intends to hit or to cut does not necessarily (or even usually) intend to kill. A defendant who foresees that his acts will cause the victim to be struck or cut, does not necessarily (or even usually) foresee that the victim will die. A defendant who negligently risks that his acts will cause a victim to be struck or cut is not necessarily (or even usually) negligent because he also risked death.

The second sort of case involves what are often called "intervening" or "superseding" causes. Suppose the defendant sets explosives next to a prison wall intending to blow up the wall and to get certain inmates out. He foresees to a practical certainty that the explosion will kill the guard on the other side of the wall. He lights the fuse to the bomb and leaves. As it happens, the fuse goes out. However: a stranger passes by the wall, sees the bomb, and relights the fuse for the pleasure of seeing an explosion; or, a thief comes by, sees the bomb and tries to steal it, dropping it in the process and thereby exploding it; or, lightning hits the fuse, reigniting it, and setting off the bomb; and so on. In all variations, the guard on the other side of the wall is killed by the blast. Standard doctrines of inter-

vening causation hold that the defendant did not legally cause the death of the guard (Hart and Honore, 1985, pp. 133–185, 325–362). Yet this is hard to square with the harm-within-the-risk test. After all, did not the defendant foresee just the type of harm an instance of which did occur? Because the harm-within-the-risk question asks a simple type-to-token question—was the particular harm that happened an instance of the type of harm whose foresight by the defendant made him culpable—the test is blind to freakishness of causal route.

The American Law Institute's Model Penal Code modifies its adoption of the harm-within-the-risk test in section 2.03 by denying liability for a harm within the risk that is "too remote or accidental in its occurrence to have a [just] bearing on the actor's liability or on the gravity of his offense." Such a caveat is an explicit recognition of the inability of the harm-within-the-risk test to accommodate the issues commonly adjudicated as intervening cause issues.

Such a recognition is not nearly broad enough to cover the inadequacy of the harm-within-the-risk approach. The basic problem with the test is that it ignores *all* of the issues traditionally adjudicated under the concept of legal cause. Not only is the test blind to freakishiness of causal route in the intervening cause situations, and to the distinction between antecedent versus after-arising abnormalities so crucial to resolution of the thin-skulled-man kind of issue, but the test also ignores all those issues of remoteness meant to be captured by Sir Francis Bacon's coinage, "proximate causation." Even where there is no sudden "break" in the chain of causation as in the intervening cause cases, there is a strong sense that causation peters out over space and time (Moore, 1999). Caesar's crossing the Rubicon may well be a necessary condition for my writing this article, but so many other events have also contributed that Caesar's causal responsibility has long since petered out. The logical relationship at the heart of the harm-within-the-risk test—"was the particular harm that happened an instance of the type of harm whose risk, foresight, or intention made the defendant culpable?"—is incapable of capturing this sensitivity to remoteness. As such, the harm-within-the-risk test is blind to the basic issue adjudicated under "legal cause." The harm-within-the-risk test asks a good question, but it asks it in the wrong place.

Less conventional approaches to causation in the criminal law

The problems with the conventional analysis of causation have tempted many to abandon the conventional analysis, root and branch. This generates a search for a unitary notion of causation that is much more discriminating (in what it allows as a cause) than the hopelessly promiscuous counterfactual cause-in-fact test of the conventional analysis. Indeed, the search is for a unitary concept of causation that is so discriminating that it can do the work that on the conventional analysis is done by both cause-in-fact and legal cause doctrines. It is far from obvious that causation is in fact a sufficiently discriminating relation that it can do this much work in assigning responsibility. Nonetheless, there are four such proposals in the academic literature, each having some doctrinal support in the criminal law.

Space time proximateness and the substantial factor test.   The oldest of the proposals conceives of causation as a metaphysical primitive. Causation is not reducible to any other sort of thing or things, and thus there is little by way of an *analysis* that one can say about it. However, the one thing we can say is that the causal relation is a scalar relation, which is to say, a matter of degree. One thing can be *more* of a cause of a certain event than another thing. Moreover, the causal relation diminishes over the number of events through which it is transmitted. The causal relation is thus not a fully transitive relation, in that if event c causes e, and e causes f, and f causes g, it may still be the case that c does *not* cause g.

On this view of causation, all the law need do is draw the line for liability somewhere on the scale of causal contribution. On matters that vary on a smooth continuum, it is notoriously arbitrary to pick a precise break-point; where is the line between middle age and old age, red and pink, bald and not-bald, or caused and not caused? This approach thus picks an *appropriately* vague line below which one's causal contribution to a given harm will be ignored for purposes of assessing responsibility. Let the defendant be responsible and liable for some harm only when the degree of his causal contribution to that harm has reached some non-*de minimus*, or "substantial," magnitude. This is the "substantial factor" test, first explicitly articulated by Jeremiah Smith (1911) and then adopted (but only as a test of cause in fact, not of causation generally) by the American Law Institute in its *Restatement of Torts*. To the common objection that the test tells us lit-

tle, its defenders reply that that is a virtue, not a vice, for there is little to be said about causation. It, like obscenity, is something we can "know when we see it," without need of general definitions and tests.

Force, energy, and the mechanistic conception of cause.   Other theorists have thought that we can say more about the nature of the causal relation than that it is scalar and diminishes over intervening events. On this view the nature of causation is to be found in the mechanistic concepts of physics: matter in motion, energy, force (Beale; Epstein; Moore, 1999). This test is similar to the substantial factor view in its conceiving the causal relation to be scalar and of limited transitivity.

This view handles easily the overdetermination cases that are such a problem for the conventional analysis. When two fires join, two bullets strike simultaneously, two motorcycles scare the same horse, each is a cause of the harm because each is doing its physical work. When one nonmortal wound is inflicted together with a larger, mortal wound, the victim dying of loss of blood, each is a cause of death because each did some of the physical work (loss of blood) leading to death.

Such a mechanistic conception of causation is mostly a suggestion in the academic literature because of the elusive and seemingly mysterious use of "energy" and "force" by legal theorists. One suspects some such view is often applied by jurors, but unless theorists can spell out the general nature of the relation being intuitively applied by jurors (as is attempted in Fair), this test tends to collapse to the metaphysically sparer substantial factor test.

Aspect causation and the revised counterfactual test.   There is an ambiguity about causation that we have hitherto ignored but which does find intuitive expression in the decided cases. The ambiguity lies in the sorts of things that can be causes and effects, what are called the "relata" of the causal relation. The usual assumption is that causal relata are whole events; in the phrase "the firing of his gun caused the death of the victim," the descriptions "the firing of his gun" and "the death of the victim" each name events. Sometimes, however, we might say, "it was the fact that the gun fired was of such large caliber that caused the victim to die." That it was a large-caliber-gun firing is an aspect of the event. The whole event was the firing of the gun; one of that event's properties was that it was a large-caliber-gun firing.

Lawyers adopt this shift in causal relata when they distinguish the defendant's action as a cause, from some wrongful aspect of the defendant's action which is not causally relevant. Thus, when an unlicensed driver injuries a pedestrian, they say: "while the driving did cause the injuries, the fact that it was unlicensed driving did not."

A restrictive notion of causation can be found by restricting things eligible to be causal relata to aspects of a defendant's action that make him culpable (either by foresight, intent, or risk). Typically, this restriction is married to some counterfactual conception of causation (Wright, 1985). The resulting conception of causation promises fully as discriminating a notion as was achieved by the harm-within-the-risk approach of the conventional analysis (for notice that this conception really is just harm-within-the-risk conceptualized as a true causal doctrine rather than a construction of legal policy). Such a conception of causation must thus face the challenges faced by the harm-within-the-risk conception, namely, the inadequacy of either analysis to deal with intervening causation, remoteness, freakishness of causal route, and so on. In addition, this proposed conception faces metaphysical hurdles not faced by the harm-within-the-risk analysis, for it must make sense of the idea of *aspects* of events being causes, rather than events themselves.

Hart and Honore's direct cause test. Beginning in a series of articles in the 1950s and culminating in their massive book, *Causation in the Law* (1959), Herbert Hart and Tony Honore sought to describe a unitary conception of causation they saw as implicit both in the law and in everyday usages of the concept. One can see their concept most easily in three steps. First, begin with some version of the counterfactual analysis: a cause is a necessary condition for its effect (or perhaps a NESS condition). Second, a cause is not *any* necessary condition; rather, out of the plethora of conditions necessary for the happening of any event, only two sorts are eligible to be causes. Free, informed, voluntary human actions, and those abnormal conjunctions of natural events we colloquially refer to as "coincidences," are the two kind of necessary conditions we find salient and honor as "causes" (versus mere "background conditions"). Third, such voluntary human action and abnormal natural events cause a given effect only if some other voluntary human action or abnormal natural event does not intervene between the first such event and its putative effect. Such salient events, in other words, are breakers of causal chains as much as they are initiators of causal chains, so that if they do intervene they relegate all earlier such events to the status of mere background conditions.

Hart and Honore built on considerable case law support for their two candidates for intervening causes (Carpenter, pp. 471–530). Indeed, it is arguable that the basic distinction between principal and accomplice liability depends in part on this conceptualization of causation (Kadish). One concern for this view of causation, nonetheless, is the worry that it is incomplete with respect to the remoteness range of issues usually dealt with under the rubric of "legal cause" in the law. Causation fades out gradually as much as it breaks off suddenly in the law, and the Hart and Honore analysis ignores this.

MICHAEL S. MOORE

See also ATTEMPT; CIVIL AND CRIMINAL DIVIDE; HOMICIDE: LEGAL ASPECTS; PUNISHMENT.

BIBLIOGRAPHY

American Law Institute. *Model Penal Code: Proposed Official Draft*. Philadelphia: American Law Institute, 1962.

———. *Model Penal Code and Commentaries*. Philadelphia: American Law Institute, 1985.

BEALE, JOSEPH. "The Proximate Consequences of an Act." *Harvard Law Review* 33 (1920): 633–658.

BUXTON, R. "Circumstances, Consequences, and Attempted Rape." *Criminal Law Review* (1984): 25–34.

CARPENTER, CHARLES. "Workable Rules for Determining Proximate Cause." *California Law Review* 20 (1932): 229–259, 396–419, 471–539.

EDGARTON, HENRY. "Legal Cause." *University of Pennsylvania Law Review* 72 (1924): 211–244, 343–376.

EPSTEIN, RICHARD. "A Theory of Strict Liability." *Journal of Legal Studies* 2 (1973): 151–204.

FAIR, DAVIS. "Causation and the Flows of Energy." *Erkenntnis* (1979): 219–250.

FLETCHER, GEORGE. *Rethinking Criminal Law.* Boston: Little Brown, 1978.

———. *Basic Concepts of Criminal Law.* Oxford, U.K.: Oxford University Press, 1998.

GREEN, LEON. *Rationale of Proximate Cause.* Kansas City, Mo.: Vernon Law Book Co., 1927.

HART, H. L. A., and HONORE, TONY. *Causation in the Law.* Oxford, U.K.: Oxford University Press, 1959.

KADISH, SANFORD. "Causation and Complicity: A Study in the Interpretation of Doctrine." *California Law Review* 73 (1985): 323–410.

LEWIS, DAVID. "Causation." *Journal of Philosophy* 70 (1973): 556–567.

MACKIE, JOHN. *The Cement of the Universe.* Oxford, U.K.: Oxford University Press, 1974.

MILL, J. S. *A System of Logic,* 8th ed. London: Longman, 1961.

MOORE, MICHAEL. *Act and Crime: The Implications of the Philosophy of Action for the Criminal Law.* Oxford, U.K.: Clarendon Press, 1993.

———. *Placing Blame: A General Theory of the Criminal Law.* Oxford, U.K.: Oxford University Press, 1997.

———. "Causation and Responsibility." *Social Philosophy and Policy* 16 (1999): 1–51.

SMITH, JEREMIAH. "Legal Cause in Actions of Tort." *Harvard Law Review* 25 (1911): 103–128, 223–252, 253–269, 303–321.

WILLIAMS, GLANVILLE. "The Problem of Reckless Attempts." *Criminal Law Review* (1983): 365–375.

WRIGHT, RICHARD. "Causation in Tort Law." *California Law Review* 73 (1985): 1737–1828.

———. "Causation, Responsibility, Risk, Probability, Naked Statistics, and Proof: Pruning the Bramble Bush by Clarifying the Concepts." *Iowa Law Review* 73 (1988): 1001–1077.

CHARGING

See PROSECUTION: PROSECUTORIAL DISCRETION.

CIVIL AND CRIMINAL DIVIDE

The structure of the American legal system presupposes a clear distinction between civil and criminal wrongs in that the system provides distinctive legal processes and distinctive legal responses to the two kinds of wrongs. The clearest, strongest version of the civil/criminal distinction goes something like this: A civil action is brought by a private, injured party to seek compensation for an unintentional harm unlawfully caused by another party, whereas a criminal action is brought by the state to punish a defendant for a deliberate offense against the community. Civil actions are pursued in civil courts and are governed by rules of civil procedure and by a few special constitutional provisions relating to civil cases, whereas criminal actions are pursued in criminal courts and are governed by rules of criminal procedure and by a larger number of special constitutional provisions relating to criminal cases. Civil actions give rise to distinctive civil remedies like money damages or injunctions, whereas criminal actions give rise to distinctive criminal punishments like imprisonment or the death penalty.

As is the case with most generalities, in law and everywhere else, there is some truth to the clear, strong version of the civil/criminal divide, but the reality is much less clear and much more complex. Moreover, throughout the twentieth century, the movement was consistently away from clarity and toward complexity, even confusion, of the civil/criminal distinction. This destabilization of the distinction has taken place on both a conceptual and an institutional level; that is, the theoretical rationales for the distinction have been called into question, and the institutional structures that promoted the distinction have been altered. This entry will explore the many ways in which the clear, strong version of the civil/criminal distinction needs to be qualified and offer some explanations for the acceleration of these qualifications in the recent past.

Before "destabilization" of the civil/criminal distinction

To speak of the "destabilization" of anything is to imply that there was a time of stability. In the case of the civil/criminal distinction, this would be a somewhat misleading implication. The distinction between criminal and civil wrongs, and the nature of the processes used to address them, have never been static, but rather have continuously changed over time, often dramatically. For example, in Roman law, often cited by contemporary legal scholars as evidence of the ancient pedigree of the civil/criminal divide, robbery and theft were classified as (private) torts rather than as the (public) crimes we now consider them. And in early English common law, the civil/criminal distinction was neither a distinction between two intrinsically different wrongs, nor a bifurcation of procedural regimes, but rather was reflected in a choice among writs, of which there were at least four, that could be pursued by a victim of a wrong or by officers of the Crown. It was not until the mid-eighteenth century that any systematic defense of a civil/criminal distinction in English law was offered—by William Blackstone in his enormously influential *Commentaries on the Laws of England,* initially published as a series of lectures between 1765 and 1769, and now known simply as Blackstone's *Commentaries.*

Blackstone divided English law generally into "private wrongs" and "public wrongs" and in turn divided legal sanctions into compensation (for private wrongs) and punishment (for public wrongs). Blackstone was the first to bifurcate the law into two such clearly distinct systems.

Despite this checkered history, the civil/criminal distinction was established enough by the time of the founding of the American republic to be written into the federal constitution—not once, but many times. The framers of the U.S. Constitution clearly did not find the distinction particularly ambiguous, because they made reference to it in numerous places throughout the Bill of Rights without feeling any need to explain what constituted, for example, "criminal cases" for purposes of the Sixth Amendment, "self-incrimination" for purposes of the Fifth Amendment, or "punishments" for the purposes of the Eighth Amendment. Early American judicial cases, too, assumed a sharp and knowable divide between the realms of civil and criminal law. For example, many American common law courts rejected early claims for "punitive" damages in civil tort cases, relying upon a clear distinction between the intrinsically punitive function of the criminal law and the intrinsically compensatory purpose of civil law. Asked one such court, "How could the idea of punishment be deliberately and designedly installed as a doctrine of civil remedies? Is not punishment out of place, irregular, anomalous, exceptional, unjust, unscientific, not to say absurd and ridiculous, when classed among civil remedies?" (*Fay v. Parker*, 53 N.S. 342, 382 (1873)). While punitive damages eventually were accepted as part of the American tort system, courts throughout the nineteenth and early twentieth century continued to speak with assurance about the clear distinction between "criminal prosecutions" and "the enforcement of remedial sanctions," as the U.S. Supreme Court did as late as 1938. (*Helvering v. Mitchell*, 303 U.S. 391, 402 (1938)).

Current blurring or "destabilization" of the civil/criminal distinction

Despite such confident pronouncements of the clarity of the civil/criminal distinction, and despite the ease with which lawyers can delineate (or at least recognize) the clear, strong version of the distinction, even casual observers of the current U.S. legal regime would note at least the following five obvious qualifications.

First, the notion of civil actions as "private" and criminal actions as "public" is most clearly challenged by the many instances in which the government is cast in the role of plaintiff in civil suits. Starting with the New Deal policies of the 1930s, accelerating in the second half of the twentieth century, and continuing to the present, the federal government has been cast in the role of enforcer of a growing body of regulatory law, and this enforcement often takes the form of "civil enforcement actions" by government agencies against individuals or entities. For example, federal agencies such as the Environmental Protection Agency (EPA) and the Security and Exchange Commission (SEC) often bring civil suits, either alone or in conjunction with criminal charges, in order to address violations of extensive federal regulatory regimes in their areas. Such lawsuits challenge the paradigm of the civil suit initiated by a private party to redress individual injury. In addition, the government is also styled as a civil plaintiff when it seeks a delinquency determination against a wayward youth or when it seeks a civil commitment order against someone thought to be mentally ill and dangerous. Such cases demonstrate conclusively that civil lawsuits are not only an avenue of private redress, but also an important mode of governmental regulation.

The flip side of this qualification is the growing role of private parties in criminal actions. The victim's rights movement has called for a greater voice for individual victims in prosecutorial decision-making in criminal cases. The movement seeks rights for victims to be notified about the progress of criminal cases, to be present at all judicial proceedings, to have a say in plea bargaining, and to be heard at sentencing. This call for growing participation by victims in the criminal process necessarily qualifies the concept of a criminal action as a wholly public one brought by the state on behalf of the collective; rather, it seeks to render the criminal process also as a mode of private redress or retribution on behalf of individual victims.

Second, and relatedly, the strong version of the civil/criminal distinction is likewise challenged by civil remedies that look "punitive" and by criminal punishments that look "remedial." As some early nineteenth-century courts recognized, "punitive" damages—civil awards beyond the amount necessary to make a plaintiff whole—are meant to deter future offenses rather than to compensate plaintiffs for injuries. The acceptance of punitive damages in the American tort system thus sits uneasily with the distinction between compensatory and retributive justice upon which the strong version of the civil/criminal distinction relies. Similarly, the growing use of civil fines and forfeitures by regulatory enforcement agencies as well as the growing use of civil forfeiture by ordinary criminal enforcement agencies, especially in drug cases, have begun to create what some scholars have called a "middle ground" between civil and criminal sanctions. In this middle ground, governmental agencies use putatively "civil" sanctions in ways that parallel, often intentionally, criminal punishments, with the goal of deterrence paramount, and the goal of compensation secondary or nonexistent. Similarly, the use of noncriminal incarceration for juveniles and the dangerous mentally ill likewise imports nonremedial goals into the civil justice system—this time incapacitation or rehabilitation—in settings that are strongly reminiscent of prisons. On the flip side, it is not unusual for criminal courts to order, as a part of a criminal defendant's punishment, that the defendant make restitution to the victim. The victims's rights movement urges greater resort to such awards, just as they urge an enhanced procedural role for victims in criminal cases. This use of the criminal justice system to promote compensation, like the use of civil sanctions to deter or incarcerate, must qualify the purported bright line between civil remediation and criminal punishment.

Third, the strong version of the civil/criminal distinction sees civil wrongs as unintentional, primarily negligent, while criminal wrongs are intentional, the product of a *mens rea* or "guilty mind." Once again, while this generalization contains some truth, there is more overlap in culpable mental states in civil and criminal cases than the strong version suggests. The general tort standard is one of negligence—that is, failing to act as a reasonable person would act under the circumstances, whether or not the harm caused was inflicted intentionally or unintentionally. Moreover, American tort law permits a fair amount of "strict liability"—that is, liability without regard to any fault at all, such as manufacturer's responsibility for faulty products even when they acted reasonably in producing and distributing them. But in addition to these standards of negligence and strict liability, American tort law also contains a substantial category of "intentional" torts, which require a more culpable mental state and thus move closer to the criminal category of mens rea. As for criminal cases, in general

it is true that ordinary tort negligence is commonly deemed insufficient for criminal liability. Most criminal statutes that use negligence as a culpable mental state rely on the common law concept of *criminal negligence*, which denotes a greater deviation from reasonableness than mere tort negligence. Criminal negligence is often described as "gross" or "wanton" negligence; the Model Penal Code describes it as a "gross deviation" from the standard of care that a reasonable person would observe (MPC § 2.02 (2) (d)). However, while disfavored, ordinary tort negligence is occasionally incorporated into criminal statutes. Moreover, even strict liability is no stranger to American criminal law. The doctrine of felony murder, which treats even unintentional killings during the course of a felony as murders, is the oldest and most famous form of strict criminal liability. But the twentieth century also saw the proliferation of so-called public welfare offenses, in which strict liability criminal sanctions are imposed for various kinds of unintentional regulatory offenses like the mislabeling of drugs or the adulteration of food offered for sale. Thus, there is no clear or absolute demarcation between the mental states sufficient for civil as opposed to criminal liability.

Fourth, the strong version of the civil/criminal distinction posits two distinct procedural systems, one for civil cases and one for criminal. Once again, there is a general truth here that needs to be qualified. It is true that there are separate rules of procedure for civil and criminal cases and that the federal constitution and most state constitutions contain a fairly long list of special procedural rights reserved for criminal cases, such as the protection against double jeopardy, the prohibition of ex post facto laws, the burden of proof beyond a reasonable doubt, the provision of free legal counsel, the exclusion of unconstitutionally seized evidence, the privilege against self-incrimination, and the proscription of cruel and unusual punishments and excessive fines. But some putatively civil suits have been held to require some or all of the special procedural regime reserved for criminal cases. Two paradigmatic examples: The Supreme Court held that a putatively civil statute imposing the sanction of forfeiture of citizenship in fact constituted punishment that required the application of the entire special criminal procedural regime in the federal constitution (*Kennedy v. Mendoza-Martinez*, 372 U.S. 144 (1963)). In addition, the Court held that juvenile delinquency proceedings must receive almost all of the special constitutional criminal procedural protections with the exception of trial by jury (*In re Gault*, 387 U.S. 1 (1967)). Beginning in the late 1980s, there has been an explosion of litigation about whether civil fines and forfeitures or new forms of incapacitative incarceration are subject to any or all of the special criminal procedural protections. (See, e.g., *Kansas v. Hendricks*, 521 U.S. 346 (1997), holding that the double jeopardy prohibition does not apply to the indefinite civil commitment of "sexually violent predators" after the conclusion of their prison terms; *United States v. Ursery*, 518 U.S. 267 (1996), holding that the double jeopardy prohibition does not apply to civil forfeitures imposed in addition to criminal punishment; *Austin v. United States*, 509 U.S. 602 (1993), holding that the Eighth Amendment's prohibition of excessive fines applies to civil forfeitures that are "punitive"; *United States v. Halper*, 490 U.S. 435 (1988), holding that the double jeopardy prohibition does apply to noncompensatory civil fines imposed in addition to criminal punishment.) This litigation explosion has led a number of scholars to urge a procedural "middle ground" to accompany the "middle ground" of sanctioning that lies between "pure" civil and criminal sanctions.

Fifth and finally, the strong version of the civil/criminal distinction suggests that the two sorts of wrongs give rise to distinctive legal responses, with money damages being the paradigmatic civil remedy and imprisonment being the paradigmatic criminal punishment. At an earlier time in American history, before the widespread use of incarceration, criminal penalties were distinctive in that they were usually capital or corporal. However, the nineteenth century saw the waning of the gallows, the whipping post, and the stockade, and the concomitant growth of prisons and monetary fines as the predominant forms of criminal punishment. These forms of punishment are not as distinct from civil remedies because incarceration is widely used as a civil restraint (for juvenile delinquents, pretrial detainees, pre-deportation detainees, and the civilly committed), and monetary payouts are ubiquitous in the civil system as either damages or fines. Thus, there is more overlap between criminal and civil sanctions than the strong version of the distinction would recognize.

In sum, the clear, strong version of the civil/criminal distinction is only generally or approximately true; it must be qualified by important overlaps—overlaps that are largely, though not exclusively, the product of the twentieth century.

Explanations for the current blurring or "destabilization" of the civil/criminal distinction

Of course, one would be hard pressed to find many bright-line distinctions, in law or elsewhere, that can be maintained with absolute clarity. The complexity of the world in general, and the legal world in particular, demands a certain degree of flexibility, particularly in sharp, binary divisions. However, the fuzziness at the edges of the civil/criminal distinction has definitely been increasing, and at an accelerating rate, throughout the last century and particularly throughout the last few decades. The causes of this accelerating increase are themselves complex and interdependent. They can usefully be divided into conceptual and institutional challenges to the civil/criminal distinction, each of which, in turn, has promoted and reinforced the other.

The two most significant conceptual or intellectual challenges to the civil/criminal distinction have their roots in the nineteenth century, but have become much more influential in the last two to three decades. The first big conceptual challenge has been the growing dominance of consequentialism or utilitarianism in legal thought—what has come to be known in recent times as "law and economics." Economic analysis of law has fundamentally recast the nature of civil and criminal sanctions in a way that portrays them as related parts of a unitary scheme of state control of private behavior. The clear, strong version of the civil/criminal distinction would make a sharp distinction between (private) compensatory justice and (public) retributive justice. However, the advent of utilitarianism and its application to jurisprudence in the eighteenth and nineteenth centuries—beginning with the famous work of Jeremy Bentham and Cesare Beccaria—led to a reconception of the civil sanction as forward-looking in addition to backward-looking, able to shape future choices through deterrence in addition to restoring some preexisting status quo. At the same time, economic analysis of criminal law also emphasized its deterrent function, in addition to its nonconsequential justification in placing blame and giving offenders their "just deserts." Indeed, the strong economic view of criminal law would reject the moral dimension of the criminal law altogether and conceptualize it as entirely derivative of civil law, offering a sanction when civil remedies are unavailing, primarily in the case of insolvent defendants. Economic analysis of law thus portrays civil and criminal law not as separate or independent, but rather as complementary means of promoting a unitary system of "optimal sanctioning." This convergence on deterrence as the unifying rationale of civil and criminal law presents a compelling intellectual challenge to the traditional civil/criminal distinction.

The second big intellectual challenge to the civil/criminal distinction has come not from economics, but rather from the cognitive and behavioral sciences. Just as economic analysis of law has blurred the distinction between civil penalties and criminal punishments with its focus on deterrence in both the civil and criminal contexts, so too the developing science of human behavior has made less salient the distinction between treatment and punishment with its increasing emphasis on incapacitation (rather than rehabilitation) in both the civil and criminal contexts. In the nineteenth century—the century of the invention of the prison, the asylum for the mentally ill, and the home or school for the juvenile delinquent—there was widespread belief in rehabilitation as a plausible goal of all types of incarceration, though in quite different ways. Prisons were thought to have the potential to rehabilitate offenders through silence, work, discipline, and penitence (hence the name "penitentiary"). Prisoners were to wear degrading uniforms (the prisoner's "stripes"), walk in lockstep, and work, eat, and pray in silence. On the other hand, asylums for the mentally ill were thought to rehabilitate through a model of medical "treatment" and "cure," and homes or reform schools for juvenile delinquents were thought to rehabilitate by providing a family surrogate (hence the name "home"). The twentieth century saw a waning of this confident faith in the malleability of human character and behavior, especially by governmental intervention with such "total institutions" as the mental hospital, the juvenile home or reform school, and the prison. This waning of faith led to the widespread deinstitutionalization of the mentally ill in the 1960s and 1970s and to a de-emphasis on rehabilitation for those among the mentally ill who remained incarcerated. At the same time, the goal of rehabilitation was also de-emphasized for juvenile delinquents and for incarcerated prisoners of the criminal justice system. Instead, all of these institutions—the putatively "civil" institutions of mental hospital and juvenile home or reform school, and the "criminal" institution of prison—all emphasized a common goal: protecting society by incapacitating the "dangerous." In the twentieth century, it thus became less compelling to distinguish the "mad" in need of treatment from the "bad" in need of punishment; rather, it was more important to identify the "dangerous" in need of segregation. This convergence on dangerousness as the key determinant of incarceration parallels the convergence on deterrence as the key rationale for sanctions; both convergences threaten the idea of separate and distinct civil and criminal realms.

These two conceptual or intellectual shifts have been paralleled by two major shifts in the structure and uses of legal institutions. First, the twentieth century saw unprecedented growth in what has come to be known as "the administrative state"—the regulation of vast spheres of life by administrative agencies, which often have broad sanctioning authority that is both civil and criminal. This organizational structure challenges the civil/criminal distinction in two ways: it casts the government in the role of civil plaintiff as a regulatory strategy, and it merges civil and criminal authority in a single administrative unit. This structure thus reinforces the deterrence theory that is one of the primary conceptual challenges to the civil/criminal distinction and is, in turn, reinforced by that theory. Second, existing forms of "civil" incarceration have come to resemble much more the dominant form of "criminal" incarceration—the prison. In the 1970s, the juvenile justice system saw a shift away from indeterminate, rehabilitative commitment of delinquents, toward determinate, graduated commitments graded according to the seriousness of the juvenile's offense. In addition, during the last few decades, legislatures have made it progressively easier to commit juveniles to long periods of incarceration and to try juveniles as adults in criminal court. On the mental health side, legislatures have progressively narrowed the scope of the insanity defense, and some jurisdictions have even formally authorized verdicts of "guilty, but mentally ill" in order to ensure the long-term incarceration of those among the mentally ill who demonstrate their dangerousness through the commission of serious crimes. In addition, numerous jurisdictions have created new forms of "civil" incarceration to incapacitate dangerous offenders who might otherwise escape long-term criminal custody. The most common example of this development is the recent resurgence of interest in the civil commitment of sex offenders, especially of those who are about to be released from criminal confine, as reflected in "sexually violent predator" statutes like the one upheld by the U.S. Supreme Court in *Kansas v. Hendricks*. These doctrinal and institutional trends subordinate the distinction between "mad" and "bad" to the need for protection from the "dangerous." These trends thus reinforce—and are reinforced by—the conceptual change in perceptions about the possibility of rehabilitation.

The future of civil/criminal distinction

The conceptual and institutional challenges to the civil/criminal distinction show few signs of abating, and thus the question is raised of whether the distinction can or should survive. Economists openly urge a more global approach to sanctioning that would substantially reduce if not entirely eliminate the distinctiveness of civil and criminal sanctions and systems. Some other scholars openly advocate for the recognition of some "middle ground" of sanctioning in which there are mixed rationales for sanctions and a mixed procedural regime that is more protective than the civil one, but less restrictive than the criminal one. Yet other scholars urge that the civil/criminal distinction be more strongly maintained and policed, both to limit strategic avoidance by the government of the strict limitations on criminal sanctioning and in order to protect the distinctive moral voice of the criminal law. It is too early to say which, if any, of these approaches will prevail in legislatures and courts; but the choice will be an important one in the twenty-first century.

CAROL S. STEIKER

See also BAIL; BURDEN OF PROOF; MENS REA; PUNISHMENT; SCIENTIFIC EVIDENCE; SEXUAL PREDATORS.

BIBLIOGRAPHY

BLACKSTONE, WILLIAM. *Commentaries on the Laws of England (1765–1769)*. 4 vols. Chicago: University of Chicago Press, 1979.

CHAPMAN, JOHN W., ed. *Compensatory Justice: Nomos XXXIII*. New York and London: New York University Press, 1991.

CHAPMAN, JOHN W., and PENNOCK, J. ROLAND, eds. *Criminal Justice: Nomos XXVII*. New York and London: New York University Press, 1985.

CHEH, MARY M. "Constitutional Limits on Using Civil Remedies to Achieve Criminal Law Objectives: Understanding and Transcending the Criminal-Civil Law Distinction." *Hastings Law Journal* 42 (July 1991): 1325–1413.

COFFEE, JOHN C. "Paradigms Lost: The Blurring of the Criminal and Civil Law Models—And What Can Be Done about It." *Yale Law Journal* 101 (June 1992): 1875–1893.

KADISH, SANFORD H. "Some Observations on the Use of Criminal Sanctions in Enforcing Economic Regulations." *University of Chicago Law Review* 30 (1963): 423–449.

KING, NANCY J. "Portioning Punishment: Constitutional Limits on Successive and Excessive Penalties." *University of Pennsylvania Law Review* 144 (November 1995): 101–196.

MANN, KENNETH. "Punitive Civil Sanctions: The Middleground between Criminal and Civil Law." *Yale Law Journal* 101 (June 1992): 1795–1873.

ROBINSON, PAUL H. "Foreword: The Criminal-Civil Distinction and Dangerous Blameless Offenders." *Journal of Criminal Law and Criminology* 83 (Winter 1993): 693–717.

Symposium. "The Civil-Criminal Distinction." *Journal of Contemporary Legal Issues* 7 (spring 1996): i–269.

Symposium. "The Intersection of Tort and Criminal Law." *Boston University Law Review* 76 (February/April 1996): 1–373.

STEIKER, CAROL S. "Foreword: Punishment and Procedure: Punishment Theory and the Criminal-Civil Procedural Divide." *Georgetown Law Journal* 85 (April 1997): 775–819.

ZIMRING, FRANKLIN E. "The Multiple Middlegrounds between Civil and Criminal Law." *Yale Law Journal* 101 (1992): 1901–1908.

CASES

Austin v. United States, 509 U.S. 602 (1993).

Fay v. Parker, 53 N.S. 342 (1873).

Helvering v. Mitchell, 303 U.S. 391 (1938).

In re Gault, 387 U.S. 1 (1967).

Kansas v. Hendricks, 521 U.S. 346 (1997).

Kennedy v. Mendoza-Martinez, 372 U.S. 144 (1963).

United States v. Helper, 490 U.S. 435 (1988).

United States v. Ursery, 518 U.S. 267 (1996).

CLASS AND CRIME

The longstanding controversy over the importance of social class in the production of criminal conduct is often an argument over the meaning of class and the measurement of crime. Criminal conduct is far from a unitary phenomenon. In general, for a crime to be committed, there must be some intentional conduct that is prohibited by a criminal law. Occasionally, the law may require specific conduct such as filing a tax return. Under these circumstances, a law-making body can create a link between class and crime simply by making rules designed to control the conduct of the rich or the poor. If the legislature creates a law making it a crime to be found in public without money or a permanent address, they will have created a link between poverty and crime. If they make it a crime to engage in "insider trading" on the stock market, they will have created a crime that is almost certain to involve those with access to management decisions that might change stock prices. This kind of law would create a link between wealth and crime.

Definition of crime

Although official definitions of crime are legislative, in practice crime is defined by administrative policies and enforcement practices. While most crime is some form of theft or assault and most of it results in physical harm or property loss for individuals, there are crimes where no loss of property is involved and no injury is inflicted on others. Enforcement policies and practices will determine who is arrested for such crimes. The areas in which these offenses are perpetrated, as well as the prior income and employment status of prison and jail inmates suggest that drug laws and laws against gambling and prostitution have generally worked against the poor more than they have against the rich.

Those who study crime and delinquency also define crime. The definition of crime was greatly expanded when criminologists began asking people to report their own illegal or improper behavior. In some of the early self-report studies, conduct that is only illegal when minors do it was defined as criminal (Nye and Short). In some self-report studies conduct was defined as delinquent even when it was so common than almost everyone could be classified as delinquent. At the other extreme, criminologists have classified some conduct as criminal that does not violate existing law. These writers believe that all forms of economic exploitation, racial discrimination, or creation of unsafe or unhealthy work environments are harmful and should be made criminal. Because they define such conduct as criminal, they argue that crime is evenly distributed across class levels or that it is linked to upper class status (Pepinsky and Jesilow).

Measuring crime

Some measures of crime are based on police, court, correctional, or official survey reports. These efforts produce information on victims and offenders. Reports of offenses known to the police and victimization survey results provide victim-based information. However, such victim information is sometimes used to infer offender characteristics. On occasion, victim-based measures are simply treated as if the offender-victim distinction is unimportant. That is, the focus on victims in such studies is never mentioned. Occasionally, offender information, such as that provided by the Supplementary Homicide Reports (SHR) program or by police reports of arrests, is used to modify victim information. A few studies have used arrest data in combination with offenses known to the police to create race-specific offense rates (Sampson; Ousey). More often, offender information is used to look at offender characteristics or the relationship between victims and offenders (Chilton and Jarvis). It is sometimes used to compute rates for studies that examine the relationship of offense rates to other economic and social characteristics of urban areas.

A different set of crime measures are created when interviews or questionnaires are used to ask people about crimes they have committed. Those asked about their criminal conduct can be juveniles or adults, male or female. They may live in the same community or be part of a national sample. The measures of crime used in such studies vary widely. Respondents may be asked to select, from a list, offenses they have committed at some point in their lives or at some time during the last year. They may or may not be asked about the frequency with which they have engaged in such conduct. The acts presented range from very minor offenses, or offenses that are only illegal for children, to very serious offenses. Measures of crime are sometimes created by counting the number of different types of crime reported and sometimes by using the frequency of crimes reported or by counting specific offenses such as assault or burglary.

Definition of class

In addition to issues of the definition and measurement of crime, disagreements about the meaning and measurement of social class make it difficult to conclude whether or not class is linked to crime. Looking at social class categories as essentially a matter of differences in wealth and income, we can say in a general way that those who own a great deal of property and have high incomes are rich or upper class; those who own little or nothing and have low incomes are poor or lower class. Beyond this general notion the issue is quickly complicated. No commonly accepted set of classes exists. And a wide variety of gradational scales designed to measure social class have been developed. Self-report studies generally use reports of parent's occupation to create social class scores. At least one self-report study of adults asked for work information and used it to assign each respondent to a specific social class depending on his or her business ownership and employee or employer status (Dunaway et al.).

Studies of geographic distribution are more likely to infer the social class of an area based on measures that reflect the income and assets of those living in the area. Measures often used are the median income of the residents of each area, the proportion of home ownership, the median value of homes, median rent, the proportion of the population in poverty, median education, and the prevalence of dilapidated housing. Variations on these indications of area wealth and deprivation are sometimes used. Results vary according to the measures used and their construction and, more often, according to the size of the areas used—census tracts, cities, Metropolitan Statistical Areas (MSA), or states. An additional complication in discussions of the social class of geographic areas arises because it is possible to see people as rich or poor in either an absolute or relative sense. This has produced studies of inequality and crime in addition to, and sometimes instead of, poverty and crime. In such an approach the emphasis is on the gap between those with high incomes and those with low incomes.

Early work

For the first half of the twentieth century, the question of the link between class and crime was examined in three basic ways. First, investigators looked at the impact of economic conditions on crime rates, asking if crime increases with an economic downturn. A basic assumption in this approach was that poor economic conditions are harder on the poor than the middle class and that this produces increased crime. A second approach examined the social class of prisoners or others formally identified as offenders to ask about the social class backgrounds of people convicted of crime. Generally, convicts were and are poor. In a third approach, crime rates for specific geographic areas were compared with a set of social and economic characteristics of the areas. These studies asked if areas with indications of high poverty rates and low social class were also areas with high crime rates. In general the answers to this question were yes. All three of these approaches probably influenced the development of theories either attempting to explain the reasons for the class-crime relationship or assuming such a relationship (Merton; Cohen; Cloward and Ohlin).

Some of the earliest empirical efforts to study class and crime used measures of the general economic conditions of regions of a country in combination with official crime rates for the regions to ask if poor economic conditions were associated with high crime rates (Bonger). Although those carrying out these studies often found that poor regions had high crime rates, they also found poor regions in which the crime rates were low. This led Bonger to conclude that the gap in income and wealth between the rich and poor might be more important than the overall poverty or affluence of an area.

When similar studies were done for areas within cities in the early decades of the twentieth century, most suggested a clear link between crime or delinquency rates and the social and economic characteristics of urban areas. By the 1940s there was general agreement that both property crimes and crimes of violence were higher in areas with low average incomes, high transiency, low educational achievement, and high unemployment (Shaw and McKay).

In addition, examinations of the characteristics of prisoners during the first half of the twentieth century indicated that a disproportionate percentage were poor, uneducated, and unemployed before incarceration (Glueck and Glueck). In general, most of these early examinations suggested there was a class-crime link. Moreover, since the relationship could be interpreted as showing that poverty and unemployment produced much ordinary crime, the findings at the early studies were consistent with conclusions reached by a number of philosophers and social thinkers.

Shifts in focus

In the 1940s and 1950s there was a shift in focus in criminology. The first aspect of the shift came when Edwin Sutherland introduced the notion of "white collar crime" to call attention to offenses committed by high status people in conjunction with their occupations. As he saw it, this occurred in two ways. Some high status individuals, acting alone, engaged in large-scale theft by embezzlement or fraud. In addition, groups of high status individuals, acting in concert, engaged in what he called "corporate crime." This frequently involved corporate efforts to reduce competition through some form of price-fixing. It sometimes involved the intentional manufacture and sale of toxic or dangerous products. Thus, "white collar crime" shifted the focus from the poor to the wealthy and is sometimes used to argue against the notion that poverty increases most forms of crime.

A second shift in focus came at about the same time when some criminologists fixed their attention on young people and on middle-class delinquency. Two research procedures were important in this shift. One was the development of self-reported crime studies (Nye and Short). The other was the use of techniques that required researchers to spend time with and observe the actions of middle-class young people. Both of these developments led investigators to conclude that there was a great deal of unreported criminal and delinquent conduct committed by middle-class children. Interest in the observation of middle-class children waned but interest in confessional studies was strong in the 1960s and 1970s and remained strong through the end of the century.

Almost all of the self-report studies used samples of young people in school who were assured of anonymity. Some national samples of minors were selected along with a few studies of adults. In some studies, the children were interviewed more than once and some were followed into adulthood. Most of these studies found weak or nonexistent links between social class and juvenile delinquency or crime. However, some studies using national samples to measure the frequency of self-reported delinquency found that lower-class youth reported nearly four times as many offenses as middle-class youth and one and one-half times as many as working-class youth (Elliott and Ageton).

In trying to reconcile the conflicting results of a number of individual-level confessional studies with those comparing area characteristics with area crime rates, some questioned the accuracy, representativeness, and scope of the surveys. Others played down or ignored the problems presented by the survey approach and concluded that the impact of social class on crime was a myth (Tittle, Villemez, and Smith).

In 1979, John Braithwaite published a careful review of a large number of area and confessional studies and a balanced discussion of the advantages and limitations of each. After reviewing studies carried out through the mid-1970s, he concluded that lower-class children and adults commit the types of crime handled by the police at higher rates than middle-class children and adults. On the "myth" of the class-crime relationship, he warns us "be wary of reviews that pretend to be exhaustive but are in fact selective" (p. 63).

Braithwaite also discussed a related shift in focus that called attention to discrimination in the system of justice. In general, researchers focused on police or court bias and argued that most of the differences in economic background that appear when offenders were compared with people in the general population do not reflect a difference in criminal conduct but reflect biases in the operation of the system of justice. After a lengthy review, Braithwaite felt in 1979 that the tide of evidence was "turning against the assertion that there is an all-pervasive bias against the lower class offender in the criminal justice system" (p. 143).

These shifts in focus and the development of national crime victimization surveys in the 1970s prompted some criminologists to play down or dismiss official measures of crime as biased and misleading. While this approach made it easier to reject the class-crime link shown in most studies of official crime data, it created a need to rely more heavily on surveys, anecdotes, estimates, and ideology in discussions of the topic. In addition it led some to conclude that victimization surveys are more accurate sources of data on crime than police records. Such a focus ignores the great absence of information on suspects and offenders in the victimization data and the many other limitations of the approach. National Crime Victimization Survey (NCVS) results are reported only for the country as a whole. And only a small set of offenses are used. Even then, the sizes of the samples used make the responses on rape, for example, very shaky. No information is collected on homicide.

However, the NCVS does identify each victim's reported income. These data usually suggest that low-income respondents are more likely to report being victims of burglary and assault than high-income respondents. Unfortunately, the NCVS collects very little information on the offenders involved. Still, the social class of the victims and the characteristics of urban residential patterns suggest that the offenders are also people with low incomes.

Later work

Using slightly different kinds of analysis, studies of the geographic distribution of crime in the 1950s and 1960s generally reinforced the findings of Shaw and McKay that official delinquency rates for small urban areas were linked to indicators of poverty and disadvantage (Chilton). Research done in the last two decades of the century continued in both styles. A renewed interest in studies looking at the geographic distribution of crime produced additional evidence in support of a class-crime link. Patterson's 1991 review of twenty-two studies of poverty and crime published from 1976 to 1986 found that some of the studies used data for different sets of cities, for MSAs, and for areas within cites. Although most of the studies showed positive effects of poverty on crime, some did not. In his analysis of fifty-seven areas within Tampa, Florida, Patterson found that levels of absolute poverty were associated with higher rates of violent crime.

During the same period, some researchers using reports of individuals suggested that while social origin might play a minor role in explaining juvenile criminality, the effect of the subject's own social position is important for adult criminality (Thornberry and Farnworth). Others suggested that the correlations between self-reported delinquency and social class are weak and should be weak in part because of the offenses used and in part because traits associated with high and low social class scores are related to different kinds of crime. Responding to the general absence of studies on the impact of social class on adult crime, Dunaway and his colleagues used three different measures of social class to analyze the responses of an adult sample for a single city.

Dunaway and colleagues' "underclass" measure focused on unemployment, receiving public assistance or food stamps, or living in public housing. Another measure used income and education as gradational measures of class. Their third measure of social class focused on a respondent's business ownership and position as an employer or employee. As a measure of crime they used the total number of offenses reported when respondents were asked to check one or more offenses from a list of fifty that they might have committed over the preceding year. This approach gives equal weight to an admission of marijuana possession, illegal gambling, driving while drunk, income tax fraud, threatening to hit a family member, stealing, burglary, robbery, and assault with intent to kill.

Recognizing the problematic nature of this range of offenses, they created a separate violence measure that included some relatively minor offenses but also included serious assaults, rape, and robbery. Using the violence subset as a measure of crime, they reported an inverse relationship between crime and some of their social class measures. When the full set of offenses is used to measure crime, only income is inversely related to crime. While arguing that there was little impact of class on crime if categorical measures of class are used, they note that family income negatively affects crime by both men and women, that the results vary by race in that the class-crime relationship was stronger for white respondents than for black respondents, and that violence is related to social class when income is used to measure class.

In a New Zealand study, Wright and others report that their Socioeconomic Status Score (SES) had both a negative and a positive indirect affect on delinquency. Using data for 1,037 children born in 1972 and 1973 and reassessed eight times since birth, they found no association between parental SES and delinquency at age twenty-one before they looked at several mediating factors. They interpret this as the result of high self-reported delinquency scores for middle-class young people that are high for reasons different from the reasons for high self-reported delinquency scores of lower class young people. They argue that there can be causality without correlation.

While this may explain the results observed in many individual-level studies, another possible explanation of the conflicting results between self-report studies and area studies is the distinctly different locations of the people and situations studied. Studies of geographic location are usually carried out for urban areas, Metropolitan Statistical Areas, urban counties, cities, or census tracts. Confessional studies have frequently been carried out in small towns and areas with very small minority populations. These studies have often been unable to tap both the high and the low ends of the social class distribution. Nowhere is this clearer than in the way the two approaches deal with race. One classic self-report study dropped all black respondents from the analysis (Hirschi). Other self-report studies attempt to hold constant the impact of race. Such procedures are rare in studies of geographic areas. The area studies include minority populations in the crime counts and in the population counts. Whether the areas are census tracts, cities, or Metropolitan Statistical Areas, the populations studied are almost always urban and multiracial.

U.S. public health statistics on homicide as a cause of death indicate that this is a leading cause of death for black males (Anderson, Kochanek, and Murphy). About 40 percent of all homicide victims are black males though black males make up about 6 or 7 percent of the U.S. population (U.S. Bureau of the Census). Although the 40 percent figure has fluctuated some since 1960, the victimization rate for black males has been remarkably consistent for forty years—ranging from 33 to 49 percent. Forty percent was also the figure provided by the Uniform Crime Reports' Supplementary Homicide reports for 1995 (Snyder and Finnegan).

The Federal Bureau of Investigation's Supplementary Homicide Reports (SHR) also suggest that black offenders are responsible for most homicides with black victims. They suggest that 48 to 50 percent of offenders in homicide cases are black males and that most homicides are intraracial (Federal Bureau of Investigation). More importantly, black males have been overrepresented in both the victimization figures and the offender figures for over thirty-five years. During the period 1960 to 1990, the average percentage of homicide victims reported as black males was about 39 percent. In addition, the SHR offender information suggests that, on average, about 44 percent of the people reported as homicide offenders were described as black males. There is little doubt that black males are, and have for some years been, greatly overrepresented as both victims of homicide and as homicide offenders.

The traditional response to any discussion of this situation is the suggestion that these high homicide-offending rates for black males are more a function of social class than biological or cultural differences. However, it is almost as traditional to suggest that we lack sufficient information on social class to claim empirical support for the social class explanation. One way to clarify this murky situation would be through the construction of race- and gender-specific homicide rates for census tracts. Peterson and Krivo analyzed homicide victimization rates for 125 U.S. cities and found that black homicides were linked to racial segregation. Parker and McCall's city-level analysis of interracial and intraracial homicide provides another indication of the probable utility of race-specific data. Using race-specific independent variables for about one hundred U.S. cities, they conclude that economic deprivation affects the intraracial homicide rates for whites and blacks.

In a study that used arrest counts to create race-specific offense rates, Ousey reported a large gap between black and white homicide rates. The black rates were five times as high as the white rates. Although he found that measures of poverty and deprivation had an impact on both black and white homicide rates, he found that the effects of these variables were stronger for whites than for blacks. He suggests that extensive and long-term disadvantage may have produced cultural and normative adaptations that have produced this gap in the rates.

Because social status is the term used in the self-report studies wherein young people are asked about their parents' occupations and their own delinquency, it may be misleading in a discussion of race, class, and crime. Even a term such as "economic conditions" is too vague to describe the ways in which vast differences in income and assets and a pervasive system of racial separatism probably contribute to high homicide rates in some areas of U.S. central cities. For an understanding of this issue, asking why the homicide rates are so high in specific areas of U.S. cities is probably more useful than asking individuals how much crime they have committed and comparing their reports with the social class implied by reports of a parent's occupation.

The patterns of homicide rates by race suggest that the rates are probably linked to exclusion and segregation—economic, racial, and ethnic—but especially to the separation and isolation of large segments of the urban population based on income and assets. This separation is frequently based on race or ethnicity but it is increasingly linked to a combination of racial separatism and poverty. In most studies using census tracts or other relatively small areas, a concentration of the poor in areas with high homicide rates was related to low median incomes, low educational attainment, higher proportions of low-paying occupations, unemployment, and underemployment in the areas. These indicators in turn are probably closely related to housing conditions, living arrangements, and family composition. In these same areas, additional research will probably show reduced public service facilities (parks, pools, libraries, recreation centers) and reduced expenditures for schools and possibly even for police services. In short, expanded and race-specific studies of the geographic distribution of homicide rates will probably show that areas with high homicide rates are areas with concentrations of poor individuals and poor families, regardless of race or ethnicity.

To the extent that these rates reflect the impact of exclusion, isolation, and impoverishment, a continuing focus on short-term trends will leave the extensive and persistent long-term differences unexamined and unexplained—especially the relatively stable and unusually high rates of homicide victimization and homicide offending reported for black males. To understand this long-term trend we will probably have to look to widespread practices and procedures that persist over time and continue to exclude and isolate a large number of black males from full participation in the economic, political, and social life of American society. It is in this sense that race is closely linked to class as a cause of violent crime in the United States. The class effects are compounded by racial separatism and racial discrimination.

Moreover, as John Hagan has suggested, the relationship between class and crime may be class- and crime-specific. It is also probably race- and gender-specific. He is probably also right in his assertion that not only does class have an impact on crime but some kinds of crime, or at least some responses to crime, have an impact on the social class of some offenders (Sampson and Laub). This is why he is right in his assessment that "the simple omission of class from the study of crime would impoverish criminology."

All of this suggests that the class-crime relationship will continue to generate research, comment, and debate well into the twenty-first century. As more of the research on this issue is focused on specific offenses and specific types of offenses, there may be greater coherence in the results than is now available. The development of standard measures of social class and greater attention to the kinds of questions being asked when using officially aggregated information as distinct from the kinds of questions asked in cohort or confessional studies may reduce some of the confusion surrounding the issue. However, the issue will remain controversial for reasons unrelated to scholarship or social research because of the implications for social policy suggested by any set of clear conclusions in one direction or the other.

ROLAND CHILTON

See also CRIME CAUSATION: BIOLOGICAL THEORIES; CRIME CAUSATION: ECONOMIC THEORIES; CRIME CAUSATION: POLITICAL THEORIES; CRIME CAUSATION: PSYCHOLOGICAL THEORIES; CRIME CAUSATION: SOCIOLOGICAL THEORIES; EDUCATION AND CRIME; GENDER AND CRIME; RACE AND CRIME; UNEMPLOYMENT AND CRIME; WHITE-COLLAR CRIME: HISTORY OF AN IDEA.

BIBLIOGRAPHY

ANDERSON, ROBERT N., KOCHANEK, KENNETH D.; and MURPHY, SHERRY L. *Report of Final Mortality Statistics, 1995*. Vol. 45, no. 11, supplement 2. Monthly Vital Statistics Report. Washington, D.C.: U.S. Department of Health and Human Services, Centers for Disease Control and Prevention, National Center for Health Statistics, 1997.

BONGER, WILLIAM A. *Criminality and Economic Conditions*. Boston: Little, Brown, and Company, 1916.

BRAITHWAITE, JOHN. *Inequality, Crime, and Public Policy*. Boston: Routledge and Kegan Paul, 1979.

CHILTON, ROBERT. "Delinquency Area Research in Baltimore, Detroit, and Indianapolis." *American Sociological Review* 29, no. 1 (1964): 71–83.

CHILTON, ROBERT, and JARVIS, JOHN. "Using the National Incident-Based Reporting System (NIBRS) to Test Estimates of Arrestee and Offender Characteristics." *Journal of Quantitative Criminology* 15, no. 2 (1999): 207–224.

CLOWARD, RICHARD A., and OHLIN, LLOYD E. *Delinquency and Opportunity: A Theory of Delinquent Gangs*. New York: The Free Press, 1960.

COHEN, ALBERT K. *Delinquent Boys*. New York: The Free Press, 1955.

DUNAWAY, R. GREGORY; CULLEN, FRANCIS T.; BURTON, JR., VELMER S.; and EVANS, T. DAVID. "The Myth of Social Class and Crime Revisited: An Examination of Class and Adult Criminality." *Criminology* 38, no. 2 (2000): 589–632.

ELLIOTT, DELBERT S., and AGETON, SUZANNE S. "Reconciling the Differences in Estimates of Delinquency." *American Sociological Review* 45, no. 1 (1980): 95–110.

Federal Bureau of Investigation. *Crime in the United States*. Washington, D.C.: U.S. Government Printing Office, 1960–1996.

GLUECK, SHELDON, and GLUECK, ELEANOR T. *500 Criminal Careers*. 1939. Reprint, New York: Kraus Reprint Corp., 1965.

HAGAN, JOHN. "The Poverty of a Classless Criminology—The American Society of Criminology 1991 Presidential Address." *Criminology* 30, no. 1 (1992): 1–19.

HIRSCHI, TRAVIS. *Causes of Delinquency*. Berkeley: University of California Press, 1969.

KOVANDZIC, TOMISLAV V.; VIERAITIS, LYNNE M.; and YEISLEY, MARK R. "The Structural Covariates of Urban Homicide: Reassessing the Impact of Income Inequality and Poverty in the Post-Reagan Era." *Criminology* 36, no. 3 (1998): 569–600.

MERTON, ROBERT K. "Social Structure and Anomie." *American Sociological Review* 3 (October 1938): 672–682.

NYE, F. IVAN, and SHORT, JAMES F. "Scaling Delinquent Behavior." *American Sociological Review* 22, no. 3 (1957): 326–331.

OUSEY, GRAHAM C. "Homicide, Structural Factors, and the Racial Invariance Assumption." *Criminology* 37, no. 2 (1999): 405–426.

PARKER, KAREN F., and PATRICIA L. M. "Adding Another Piece to the Inequality and Crime Homicide Puzzle: The Impact of Structural Inequality on Racially Disaggregated Homicide Rates." *Homicide Studies* 1, no. 1 (1994): 35–60.

PATTERSON, E. BRITT. "Poverty, Income Inequality, and Community Crime Rates." *Criminology* 29, no. 4 (1991): 755–776.

PEPINSKY, HAROLD E., and JESILOW, PAUL. *Myths That Cause Crime*. Washington, D.C.: Seven Locks Press, 1992.

PETERSON, RUTH D., and KRIVO, LAUREN J. "Racial Segregation and Black Urban Homicide." *Social Forces* 71, no. 4 (1993): 1001–1026.

SAMPSON, ROBERT J. "Urban Black Violence: The Effect of Male Joblessness and Family Disruption." *American Journal of Sociology* 93, no. 2 (1987): 348–382.

SAMPSON, ROBERT J., and LAUB, J. "Stability and Change in Crime and Delinquency over the Life Course: The Salience of Adult Social Bonds." *American Sociological Review* 55 (1990): 609–627.

SHAW, CLIFFORD R., and MCKAY, H. D. *Juvenile Delinquency in Urban Areas*. Chicago: University of Chicago Press, 1942.

SNYDER, HOWARD, and FINNEGAN, TERRENCE A. *Easy Access to the FBI's Supplementary Homicide Reports: 1980–1994*. Data Presentation and Analysis Package. Washington, D.C.: Office of Juvenile Justice and Delinquency Prevention, 1996.

SUTHERLAND, EDWIN H. "White Collar Criminality." *American Sociological Review* 5, no. 1 (1940): 1–12.

THORNBERRY, TERENCE P., and FARNWORTH, MARGARET. "Social Correlates of Criminal Involvement: Further Evidence on the Relationship Between Social Status and Criminal Behavior." *American Sociological Review* 47, no. 4 (1982): 505–518.

TITTLE, CHARLES R.; VILLEMEZ, WAYNE A.; and SMITH, DOUGLAS A. "The Myth of Social Class and Criminality: An Empirical Assessment of the Empirical Evidence." *The American Sociological Review* 43, no. 5 (1978): 643–656.

U.S. Bureau of the Census. *Statistical Abstract of the United States 1994*. Washington, D.C.: U.S. Government Printing Office, 1995.

WRIGHT, BRADLEY R. E. et al. "Reconsidering the Relationship between SES and Delinquency: Causation but Not Correlation." *Criminology* 37, no. 1 (1999): 175–194.

COMPARATIVE CRIMINAL LAW AND ENFORCEMENT: CHINA

A striking contradiction of the reform era of the People's Republic of China (PRC) since the late 1970s has been the coexistence of dramatic changes in the social and economic field and the sustained stagnation of political and legal institutions. The Chinese Communist Party (CCP) has insisted upon adherence to both the existing political system and to continuous economic reform. This contradictory doctrine has resulted in divergence between political conservatism and economic liberalization. Legal dualism has emerged as a result of the divergence. Public law, including laws regulating China's criminal process, lags far behind private law. Civil and commercial law, spearheaded by foreign investment legislation, is, in general, more certain, predictable and liberal, and has made real progress over the past twenty years. Criminal law, on the other hand, remains characterized by, inter alia, political interference in the legal process, arbitrary police power, wanton use of the death penalty, and so on.

Continuing economic reforms have placed increasingly heavy pressure on the political and legal system. Political institutions have undergone significant changes during the reform years, but today these political and legal institutions are strained and barely able to adapt to the vibrant economy and society. The criminal justice system is confronting the tension between the demand for social and political liberalization and the demand for political stability. Social and economic progress in China has given rise to an increasing demand for professionalism and procedural justice in the criminal justice system and a growth in the general public's cognizance of its rights. In contrast, the deterioration in social order and the perceived threat to political stability requires the criminal justice system to play an instrumental role in controlling crime and disorder. Reform of the criminal law and criminal justice system should be seen within this larger political context.

Concept of crime

Classification of crime. China enacted its Criminal Law (CL) in 1979 and substantially amended it in 1997. The law defines crime as any act that endangers society and is subject to punishment. An act that endangers society is not deemed a crime, however, where "the circumstances are obviously minor and the harm done is not serious" (CL, Art. 13). An act that endangers society but with minor circumstances or consequences is referred to as an unlawful act. PRC criminal law draws a clear distinction between a criminal and an unlawful act. A criminal act is defined by the Criminal Law, investigated and prosecuted according to the procedures set out in the PRC Criminal Procedure Law (CPL) and subject to criminal penalties. An unlawful act is defined by administrative laws and regulations, punished by administrative organs according to administrative procedures, and subject to administrative penalties.

The PRC's legislature, the National People's Congress (NPC), or its Standing Committee determines the threshold separating a criminal act from an unlawful act by specifying the extent of seriousness of the consequences and circumstances to which an act warrants a criminal penalty. The legislature may define the seriousness of the consequences by setting a fixed amount enumerated in Chinese currency, renminbi, or use other criteria to determine the consequences of the offense, which will trigger application of the Criminal Law. For example, accepting a bribe will only be considered an offense if the amount of the bribe exceeds 5,000 yuan (CL, Art. 383). The Criminal Law applies if the amount reaches the specified minimum. Otherwise, such acts are considered "unlawful" and thus subject only to administrative penalties. The triggering amount, while a key determinant for criminal liability, is not conclusive. A crime may still be declared, even if the minimum amount has not been reached, where aggravating circumstances exist.

Increasingly, the legislature has defined the parameters of criminal acts more clearly by specifying a trigger amount. Yet, the Criminal Law largely continues to set only general standards, applying ambiguous terms such as *light, serious,* or *very serious* in relation to various circumstances and *large, huge,* and *especially huge* in relation to their consequences. The Criminal Law leaves detailed criteria to be determined by the Chinese courts and other institutions in the application and enforcement of the Criminal Law. The Supreme People's Court (SPC) and the Supreme People's Procuracy (SPP), severally, jointly, or in conjunction with other executive institutions, are principally responsible for filling the lacunae left by the legislature. The ministries under the State Council, the Ministry of Public Security (MPS) in particular, have played an active role in constructing China's criminal law regime, though this role seems to have declined in recent years.

Politicization of crime. The ideological foundation of this duality is the doctrinal classification of social conflict as among the *people* or between the *people* and their *enemy*. The former is antagonistic, the latter is nonantagonistic. This doctrine was formed in 1957 by the CCP and still applies to a large degree. China continues to be a state under the people's democratic dictatorship, which has been interpreted as democracy for the people and dictatorship against the enemy. The criminal justice system occupies a unique position in the Communist theory of the state, and is instrumental in this dictatorship/democracy dichotomy. Criminal Law in general is identified with dictatorship against the enemy, and the criminal justice system stands in the front line of this struggle.

Enemy is a key but fluid concept. In the early years of the Communist rule, the *enemy* included spies, saboteurs, career criminals, landlords, and capitalists who were hostile to the new government. Once they were eliminated, their positions were replaced by counter-revolutionaries, bad elements, and rightists. During the economic reform of the 1980s, new enemies, including serious criminal offenders, political dissidents, separatists, and religious cults have become targets of the CCP dictatorship. Whoever challenges the CCP leadership and undermines the socialist system can be treated as an enemy of the state.

As the two contradictions are fundamentally different, the methods for solving them also differ. The CCP's ideology provides a bifurcated system. Criminal law is reserved to suppress the enemy. A crime is not simply a violation of criminal law but a challenge to the established political order. A guilty verdict means more than a mere conviction; it transforms the convicted person into an enemy of the state. Consequently the police, the procuracy and the court are not merely places to enforce the law, they are also places of dictatorship. Criminalization principally means repression.

But the repressive approach does not apply to the *people*. Conflicts among the people were to be dealt with by the methods of democracy, that is, didactic, informal, and rehabilitative methods, which would be accomplished through criticism, persuasion, and mediation, backed by administrative penalties.

Crime and punishment. There are five types of principal punishment in China's criminal law:

1. Public surveillance
2. Criminal detention
3. Fixed term imprisonment
4. Life imprisonment
5. Death penalty of immediate execution and death penalty with a two-year stay.

The figures for criminal convictions have gradually increased since the early 1980s. In 1987, Chinese courts tried approximately 300,000 criminal cases, and convicted more than 300,000 persons. In 2000, courts tried more than half a million criminal cases and convicted more than 600,000 persons. It has been a general practice for Chinese courts to sentence approximately 40 percent of the offenders to five or more years' imprisonment, life imprisonment, or death.

The death sentence has been most controversial. The number of capital offenses in China has grown since 1979. There were twenty-eight capital offenses in the 1979 Criminal Law. By 1983, there were forty-two capital offenses, and the figure grew to nearly seventy by 1993. There were three new death penalty offenses added to the statute book each year on average from 1981 to 1993. The 1997 amendment to the criminal law limited the use of the death penalty for a number of offenses, such as theft and robbery, to more serious circumstances, but the number of capital offenses remained the same.

Since death penalty statistics are classified as a top state secret by the Supreme People's Court, the number of offenders executed each year is unknown. Informed estimates vary from four thousand to forty thousand per year. The vast majority of the death penalties were imposed for five types of offenses: murder, robbery, rape, serious assault, and serious theft. In the latter half of the 1990s, capital drug offenses have been on the rise due to the seriousness of the problem in China and the tough stance the government is taking.

Minor offenses and administrative penalties. The police punish minor offenses that are not regarded as having breached the criminal law. Those punishments are referred to as administrative because the police make the decisions. There is no public hearing and no defense is available. There are a variety of legislative and administrative regulations that authorize different types of administrative penalties. The police have great discretion in imposing such sanctions. A court can only subsequently review administrative penalties.

There are two main types of administrative penalties. One is the public order punishment, authorized by the Regulations on Penalties for Public Security 1957 (the Regulations). The Regulations are administrative in nature, punishing petty theft and other activities disrupting public order. Punishment is administered by the police and may include a warning, a fine, or administrative detention of not more than fifteen days. Over three million public-order offenses are handled by the police each year.

The other type of administrative punishment is Reeducation Through Labor (RTL), an administrative penalty with no clear legislative authority. The police control the intake process and also administer the RTL institutions. The government created the RTL in 1957 "to reform into self-supporting new persons those persons with the capacity to labor who loaf, who violate law and discipline, or who do not engage in proper employment" (The State Council Decision on the Problem of Re-education through Labor). It has been gradually expanded to include minor offenses, where the circumstances or consequences are not serious. As a result, a great variety of offenders, ranging from thieves to prostitutes, drug addicts, and political dissidents, have received RTL penalties. Approximately 150,000 offenders are incarcerated under the RTL regime each year.

The term of incarceration was indefinite until 1979 when the government set a limit of three years' incarceration, with a possible extension of one year. The target population of RTL is restricted to residents of large and medium-sized cities.

The institutions of criminal justice

One needs to look into the relations between criminal justice institutions and the CCP and the interrelations between those institutions to understand the structure of criminal justice in China.

The Chinese Communist Party. China is still a one-party state. The CCP is the leading political party; its policies dominate the criminal justice system. Institutionally, the CCP exercises its immense power in three principal ways. First, it appoints and removes persons, most of them being CCP members, to and from senior positions in criminal justice institutions at each level. Key positions, including the presidents of the people's court and of the people's procuracy and chiefs of police are tightly controlled by the CCP. The appointment and removal, as a rule, is approved by the respective people's congress.

Second, the CCP has a vast array of powerful institutions with specific political responsibilities to which the government is accountable. Two CCP institutions have had great effect on the criminal justice system, the Political and Legal Commission (PLC) and the Commission of Disciplinary Inspection (CDI). The PLC at the central and local levels is the ultimate authority to which the court, procuracy, and police and other law-related institutions are responsible. The PLC makes criminal justice policies, determines work priority, coordinates different legal institutions and settles their internal conflict. PLCs at the local level in particular frequently intervene in the daily operation of the criminal justice institutions.

The third control is the exclusion of the criminal justice institutions from investigating crimes perpetrated by CCP officials. It is long-standing policy that the CCP is above the law in many aspects. Where a CCP official commits a crime in the course of executing his or her duty, corruption in particular, the CCP, through its CDIs at the national and local levels, has the power to investigate the offense, and to determine whether the criminal law should be applied. Therefore the police cannot initiate a criminal investigation into the CCP or its ranking members, the prosecution cannot authorize the arrest of a ranking CCP member without the prior approval of a competent CCP authority,

and the courts have been compliant to the demands of the CCP. In relation to this type of offense, the CCP is effectively beyond the reach of the criminal law, and the criminal justice system merely performs a legal formality, giving legal effect to the CCP's decision.

Local/central relations. The CCP leadership is fragmented, however. China does not have a centralized legal leadership, and the power of central criminal justice authorities—the MPS, the SPC, and the SPP—are limited. There is always a tension between the local CCP committee and the central criminal justice authorities over the control of local criminal justice institutions.

Local criminal justice institutions are accountable to both the central criminal justice authorities and the local CCP committee. This particular system of accountability is referred to as a combination of line and area, the latter taking priority. The central criminal justice authorities exercise the professional leadership (the line) and determine the structure, function, and redistribution of power inside the institutions. However the professional leadership is restricted by the control of the local CCP Committee (the area), which controls the budget, personnel, and other financial sources of the local criminal justice institutions.

The vertical system and dual leadership create a fragmented structure of authority in the criminal justice system. But given the political and financial dependence of local criminal justice institutions on the local CCP committee, the control exerted by the local CCP committee is more substantial and indeed overwhelming, negating the centralized command at a national level.

Institutional mutual independence. While the criminal justice institutions are dependent on the CCP and compliant to its demand, they are independent from each other. Governing the relations among the criminal justice institutions is the Criminal Procedural Law (CPL), enacted in 1979, and substantially amended in 1996. Under the CPL, one institution does not have legal supremacy over the other in the criminal process. They have the equal authority to interpret and enforce laws in relation to their own rights and duties, largely without external supervision.

Criminal process in China is divided into three legal steps: investigation, prosecution, and trial. There are three corresponding institutions in charge of each step: the investigative organs (mainly the police), the procuracy, and the courts. The police, the procuracy, and the courts exercise their respective powers independently in accordance with the law and are meant—in theory, at least—to operate free of any interference by any administrative organ, public organization, or individual (CPL, Art. 5). The relationship between the three organs is that they "shall divide responsibilities, coordinate their efforts and check each other to ensure the correct and effective enforcement of law." (CPL, Art. 7).

The judiciary is not supreme in the criminal process, it is one of the government departments. Where a conflict occurs between the different institutions, those involved have to reach a consensus through negotiation, otherwise the dispute has to be settled by the PLC. There is a clear tendency for the criminal justice institutions to avoid confronting each other.

Powers and process of the criminal justice institutions

The police and police powers. The police is the most powerful institution in China's criminal process for three reasons. First, the police hold a special place in Chinese politics. Until the late 1970s, the Minister of Public Security maintained close, even personal, ties with top CCP and state officials, and played the role of a leader in China's legal institutions. While the role of the MPS in national politics was substantially diminished during the reform era largely due to the rising power of the SPP and the SPC, police at the regional levels continue to dominate the criminal justice system.

The chief of police, as part of the local political elite, generally holds three key positions: member in the Standing Committee of the local Party Committee; chairman of the local PLC; and deputy mayor/governor in the regional government. He is the law of the place. China has been searching for a proper balance between the powers of the police, procuracy, and the court to ensure checks and balances. A development since the mid-1990s is the requirement that the chairman of the PLC at the local and national levels hold no position in legal institutions. Notwithstanding this change, the CCP will continue to lead the local legal system through the police, given its political influence.

Second, the criminal process is structured in such a way that the police play a dominant role. There are few procedural requirements within the investigative process, and there are few measures to protect a suspect's rights. The law en-courages the police to ascertain the true facts of an offense with little regard to procedural rectitude. Once the police have found the truth, as they perceived it, all the subsequent processes become a mere verification of that determination. The files prepared by the police become central to the entire prosecuting process, and the only issue at stake is whether the files can withstand the scrutiny of prosecutors, judges, and lawyers.

Finally, the police can bypass the criminal procedures and avoid accountability by utilizing administrative penalties. Punishment for public order offenses and RTL can be imposed by the police summarily and with little external supervision. The police powers in this regard are extremely broad, and also severe, leading to one to three years' incarceration. Administrative penalties offer the police sufficient scope to dispose of most minor offenses.

The procuracy. The procuracy is a unique institution in Chinese law. It is equal to the court in its constitutional status. The procuracy performs multiple functions as an investigative, prosecutorial, supervisory, and judicial body.

It investigates crimes, mostly corruption, committed by state functionaries in executing their duty. The procuracy has been criticized for its lack of action against government corruption and blamed for its rampage. But given the relationship between the CCP and China's legal system, and the role of the CDIs in investigating crimes by CCP members, the procuracy's authority to investigate crimes committed by the CCP officials is limited.

Second, the procuracy institutes public prosecution against all crimes in court. After the investigators conclude their investigations, they transfer the case to the procuracy for public prosecution. Where the procuracy considers the facts to be clear, the evidence reliable and complete, and the offense serious enough to warrant criminal sanction, it shall initiate a public prosecution in a court with competent jurisdiction, unless the case is "obviously minor" or where other statutory conditions exist. Where a case is not prosecuted, the police, the victim, and the suspect can apply to the procuracy to review the decision. Alternatively, the victim may institute a prosecution in court directly (CPL, Arts. 144–146).

Third, the procuracy supervises the application and enforcement of law by other legal institutions. In relation to the police, the procuracy has the power to demand that the police initiate a criminal investigation over a complaint; to review and approve arrests to be made by the police; and, after the police completes its investigation, to request the police to conduct supplementary investigations if the evidence is insufficient, and to decide not to prosecute if the police are unable to supply additional evidence. In relation to the court, the procuracy supervises the legality of judicial work including reviewing the legality of criminal and civil trials. In the case of criminal trials, the supervisory role necessarily creates a conflict in a criminal trial between procurators as prosecutors before the court and procurators as supervisors above the court.

Finally, the procuracy performs a limited judicial function. Before the 1996 CPL reform, the procuracy had the power to find a suspect guilty of an offense without initiating a public prosecution. Under the law, the procuracy was able to grant an exemption from prosecution where the procuracy deemed it unnecessary to impose a criminal punishment, while simultaneously finding the person guilty of a criminal offense. The exemption system was finally abolished in 1996. The only existing judicial function of the procuracy is that the SPP has the authority to interpret laws in its procuratorial work. As it happens, most of the judicial interpretations of criminal law are given by the SPC and the SPP, either severally or jointly.

The court. Chinese courts are composed of several chambers according to the subject areas of the law. Criminal law chamber may be further divided according to the nature and seriousness of the offenses. Heading each chamber is a chief judge, who is responsible for allocating cases to judges in the chamber and supervising their work.

Once the prosecution initiates proceedings against a suspect, and transfers the case to a particular chamber, the chamber forms a collegial panel, composed solely of judges or of judges and lay judges (referred to as people's assessors) at the discretion of the court. The chief judge of the chambers is responsible to the president of the court and the adjudicative committee of the court. The adjudicative committee is the power center of a court. It is chaired by the president of the court, and composed of vice-presidents of the court, chief judge of the chambers and heads of political and services departments of the courts.

Criminal trials in China have been referred to as inquisitorial, and since the 1996 CPL reform, the criminal trial has been in a gradual transformation from an inquisitorial model to an adversarial model. Before the CPL reform, the prosecution was required to submit all the evidence to the court once it finished its investigation, and the trial judges were required to investigate the case thoroughly, including interviewing the accused and examining evidence, before the case was tried. Where the court found prosecution evidence to be insufficient, it was bound to remand the files to the procuracy for supplementary investigations. A case would not be tried unless the trial judge was certain about the facts and the law. Naturally, the trial was merely an occasion to announce a decision made before the trial started, and a "not guilty" verdict was a near impossibility.

The 1996 CPL reform abolished the use of pretrial judicial investigation. Under the new procedures, the prosecution provides a Bill of Prosecution and a list of evidence to be produced in court; the court will decide to try the case if there is prima facie evidence of criminal wrongdoing. Without pretrial judicial investigation, the prosecution now bears the burden of proof. The defense is able to play a more meaningful role. It can cross-examine the prosecution evidence and produce its own evidence to challenge the allegation. The defense can make strong arguments on behalf of the accused without necessarily challenging the authority of the court. Judges are now expected to be more neutral and passive arbitrators, evaluating evidence and arguments presented before the court. "Not-guilty" verdicts have become a real possibility in Chinese courts.

The implementation of reform has been difficult and confusing, however. For the most part, the former inquisitorial trial style remains unchanged. Most witnesses still do not testify in court, and the trial continues to be based on affidavits. Trial judges remain active during the trials and interrogate defendants as frequently as in the past. Judges found themselves unable to decide without first reading the files prepared by the prosecution; the trial itself is too brief to provide solid factual and legal bases for a proper decision. The court now reads the files after the trial. The consequence of the reform is that the decision-making process is postponed from before the trial to after the trial. The court hearing is still a formality.

Another issue concerns the actual decision-maker in a trial. Chinese law emphasizes the independence of the court as an institution, not that of the judge as an individual. A judge is part of the judicial hierarchy and is bound to follow orders from the chief judge, the president, and the adjudicative committee. There are doubts as to who in a court is entitled to decide a trial. In ordinary cases, it is the collegial panel that "shall render a judgment" after the hearings and deliberations. However, in "difficult, complex or major cases" in which the collegial panel finds it difficult to make a decision, the collegial panel should refer the case to the president of the court. The president will then decide whether to submit the case to the judicial committee for discussion and an eventual decision (CPL, Art. 149). The collegial panel is bound to execute the decision of the judicial committee. Given the vagueness of the phrase "difficult, complex or major case" and given the hierarchical nature within a people's court, the fact remains that those who hear a case might not decide its outcome.

The trend of liberalization and its limits

There are a number of amendments to China's substantive criminal law that are of significant symbolic value. They include the abolition of counterrevolutionary crimes, replacing them with crimes endangering state security; and the abolition of the principle of analogy, which allowed a court to punish an act or omission according to the most closely analogous article in the criminal law where the act or omission was not expressly prohibited by the law. Both counterrevolutionary crimes and the principle of analogy were notorious concepts in Chinese criminal law and their abolition is regarded as a major step forward in developing the rule of law in China.

Another important change of great important symbolic value is the acceptance in the Criminal Law of the principles of no crime except in accordance with law and equality before the law (CL, Arts. 3 and 4). But it is the changes in the criminal procedure that have more practical implications.

Controlling police powers

Two major developments in ensuring police accountability are the restriction of police power to detain and arrest and the development of judicial review on police administrative decisions.

Abolishing Shelter for Examination. Chinese criminal law is characterized by the use of extralegal measures in the criminal process, effectively sidelining procedural requirements and accountability. Where legal procedure is deemed to be adversely affecting crime control, extralegal processes will be created. When the CPL was enacted in 1979, it created certain procedural requirements for detention and arrest. But the procedures were regarded as having rendered law enforcement impossible and even contributing to the increase in crime. As a result, the police used an extralegal measure, called Shelter for Examination, effectively bypassing the procedural limits on detention and arrest.

Under Shelter for Examination, the police were able to shelter a suspect for examination for a period of not more than three months for those suspected of committing an act falling within a specific category of crime in accordance with the MPS internal rules. It was estimated that the police held in custody the vast majority (more than 80%) of the accused without regard to the criminal procedure requirements. Moreover, the Shelter for Examination was itself abused by the police, who had not only used it to detain persons indefinitely, but also extended it to detain all types of criminal suspects.

Since 1996, the police have stopped using Shelter for Examination in lieu of detention and arrest. The abolition is, however, partial. Certain elements of the Shelter for Examination have been legalized and merged into the formal criminal process. In that sense, it can be argued that the police will be able to do legally what they were doing illegally. The law, to a certain extent, has legalized what it intended to abolish.

The rule of law and judicial scrutiny of police power. Law and legality have become increasingly relevant for the police since the late 1970s. The recurring emphasis on "socialist legality" is expected to alleviate the crisis faced by the party and justify its continuing rule during the post-Mao period. The elementary requirement of socialist legality is that police power has to be derived from law and is exercised through properly defined legal procedures. Since 1979, police powers have been increasingly given a legislative basis and incorporated into the legal process. While there is a very large gap between the formal law and police practice, legalization has provided a mechanism to highlight police abuse of powers and made the exercise of police power more public and visible.

One of the most important legal developments is to subject certain acts of the government to limited judicial review. As a result, the wide range of police administrative powers is now subject to review by the courts. Judicial review of police decisions has passed down a tortuous road in

China since its authorization by the NPC Standing Committee in 1986. The initial police reaction was hostile. The police were concerned that judicial review would promote judicial authority, destabilizing the balance of power between the police and the court. More importantly, if a court found a police decision unlawful and invalid, it would damage the image and status of the police. By the time the NPC enacted the Administrative Litigation Law in 1989, the power of a court to review police administrative decisions was widely recognized and reluctantly accepted by the police.

Judicial review has made important contributions in controlling police behavior by imposing administrative penalties and ensuring the legality of police work. The courts have overruled or changed a significant percentage of police decisions in judicial review cases. The external supervision by the court also forces the police to strengthen its internal review and quality control. One major limitation of judicial review is that it is restricted to reviewing the legality of a concrete administrative act (i.e., the application of laws and regulations); the courts cannot review the lawfulness of an abstract administrative act (i.e., the laws and regulations themselves).

Fair trial

In response to the increasing attack on the lack of transparency in judicial decision-making and judicial corruption, the SPC has initiated a number of reforms, such as increasing the entry standard for judges, improving their judicial skills through training, and implementing public trial as required by law. However, the reforms are limited to the court itself, and do not affect their relations with external institutions. Importantly, they do not touch upon some of the fundamental aspects in relation to a fair trial.

Presumption of innocence. Chinese law is silent on the presumption of innocence and the burden of proof. Indeed, the concept itself was criticized as bourgeois. Since China's socialist legal system practiced the principle of "deciding a case according to facts," presumptions and any procedural rules were not allowed a place in the criminal law. In the rigorous pursuit of "truth," rules protecting the rights of the accused were often swept aside. The 1996 CPL amendment gives the court the exclusive authority to determine the guilt or innocence of an accused. Article 12 of the CPL provides that no one is guilty of a crime without a people's court rendering a judgment according to law. While the increasing authority of the court in the criminal process and trial reform in China may be the first step toward developing the presumption of innocence in China, the existing law provides no remedies on this principle.

The right to silence. Under Chinese law, a suspect has no right to remain silent. A suspect has the duty to answer questions truthfully when asked by investigators, but may refuse to answer questions that are irrelevant to the case (CPL, Art. 93). There is no penalty if the suspect refuses to answer and, moreover, there is no legal duty to assist the police under Chinese law. It is an offense only when a person knowingly gives false testimony in criminal proceedings, which is punishable by a maximum sentence of three years' imprisonment (CL, Art. 305). It is routine practice for police to administer physical punishment on suspects to obtain confessions.

The police and procuracy at local levels have been experimenting with pilot projects equivalent to the right to silence, often without the authorization of central authorities. In 2000, the procuracy in a small city in a northeastern province started, on a trial basis, utilizing a mechanism referred to as zero confession. It is intended to eliminate reliance upon confessions in criminal investigations and requires the investigators to search for other evidence. While the rules have received wide support from judges, lawyers, and academia in public debate, the central authority, that is, the SPP, has not given its blessings to the local invention.

Exclusion of evidence. Under the CPL, unlawfully obtained evidence is not excluded in court. Article 43 of the CPL prohibits extortion of confessions through threat, enticement, deceit, or other unlawful means, but there is no effective and sufficient remedy for breach of this rule, unless the circumstances are serious enough to amount to a criminal offense. Given the equal legal status of the police and the procuracy, there is little a court can do when facing allegations of torture by the police or by the procuracy. In practice, the standard court procedure is to do nothing except to declare the allegation of torture as unfounded.

The SPC, however, has attempted to exclude certain types of unlawfully obtained evidence, and issued rules in 1994 prohibiting the use of any statement obtained through unlawful means. When the CPL was amended in 1996, this exclusionary rule was not consolidated into the CPL.

Nevertheless, the SPC restated its rules on the admissibility of unlawfully obtained statements in the 1998 SPC Interpretation, according to which statements of witnesses, victims, and the accused obtained through torture, threat, enticement, fraud, or other unlawful means should not be used as evidence in adjudicating a case (SPC Interpretation of the CPL, Art. 61).

Right to counsel. Defense counsel had little role in the criminal process before the 1996 CPL reform. First, political interference in criminal defense was frequent. As state legal workers, lawyers were bound to accept orders from the government in carrying out their defense. For example, lawyers were frequently admonished not to direct their mind to trivial matters and technicalities, and they were not allowed to raise not-guilty defenses without the prior approval of the government.

Second, judges' involvement in the pretrial investigation seriously diminished the role of defense counsel. After reading through the prosecution files and verifying the evidence, trial judges would necessarily have formed a prejudiced view on the case. They had difficulties accepting alternative views from the parties. A challenge to the charge was not so much a challenge to the prosecution's case as a direct attack on the court's credibility.

Third, the law did not allow any involvement of a defense counsel at the investigation and prosecution stages of a criminal case. In other words, a defense lawyer had no right to enter a police station and the prosecutor's office to obtain information or meet with and correspond with the accused. Practically, no legal representation was allowed until a week before the trial.

Legal reform since the mid 1990s has expanded the right to counsel. In the Lawyers Law 1996, the NPC Standing Committee changed the status of lawyers from state functionaries to members of a more autonomous All China Lawyers Association. The legislative change reflects the independent nature of the legal profession and reinforces the tendency of lawyers to become more independent. The importance of this change is that, despite the criticism against Chinese lawyers for their lack of ethics and competence, they have become independent from the state, economically, and to certain extent, politically.

There has been less political interference in lawyers' defense work in criminal trials during the 1990s, and the legal profession, essentially a private business, cannot be tightly controlled by the government. One indication of such a development is the frequent use of a not-guilty plea in a criminal trial, even in the politically sensitive cases of political dissidents. Chinese lawyers are representing interests that may not be synonymous with those of the CCP.

The introduction of some adversarial elements into criminal proceedings means, if anything, that the prosecutors have the burden of proof and of leading evidence under a relatively neutral panel of judges. Defense counsel has the opportunity to put up a rigorous defense and play a more meaningful role. More importantly, defense counsel is no longer limited to defending an accused at the trial stage. Defense counsel duties now extend to providing legal advice and assistance at the early stage of criminal investigation (CPL, Art. 96).

The right to counsel at the investigative stage is closely regulated by the police, however. First, a lawyer needs to give notice to the police of such a meeting, and the police have forty-eight hours to make the necessary arrangements. In serious and complicated cases, the meeting may not be arranged until five days after an application is made (MPS Procedural Rules, Art. 44). Second, where a case concerns state secrets, a meeting between a lawyer and client requires police approval (CPL, Art. 96). Finally, the police have the discretion to be present during the meeting according to "the necessity and circumstances" of the case. An officer present has the power to limit the content of the conversation and even to stop the meeting if it appears to him that legal procedures and police rules have been violated during the meeting (MPS Procedural Rules, Art. 48). Because of these rigid limitations, the police are able to make the right to counsel at the investigative stage virtually impossible.

The routine and arbitrary criminal process

There is a tension between the demand for order and stability and the demand for reform and liberalization. This tension has created a dual criminal justice system in China. On the one hand, there is the routine and institutionalized criminal process, in which legal bureaucrats process criminal cases within their perspective institutions according to legal procedures, institutional position, and personal interests. This routine system, despite the drawbacks and abuses, is characterized by increasing professionalism and relative institutional autonomy.

On the other hand, there is the arbitrary criminal system, which is periodically superimposed by the CCP on the routine criminal process. When that occurs, the criminal justice institutions lose their institutional autonomy, and the institutional mandate gives way to the political imperative. There is a sudden political takeover of the criminal justice system. This arbitrary system is characterized by periodic campaigns against crime, commonly referred to as hard strikes (*yanda*).

Common crimes and the public's fear of them have been perceived as threats to the party's political order and a challenge to the party's legitimacy. To restore public confidence, the party resorted to *yanda*. In July 1983, the former paramount leader Deng Xiaoping ordered the police to launch several mass campaigns against violent crimes and to solve the crime problem within three years. Under political pressure, the police rendered swift and brutal justice to ensure political stability. It was expected that the legitimacy deficit could be compensated for by effective crime control. *Yanda* did not stop in 1986; it continued and has become a permanent feature of China's criminal justice system.

Over the last decade, *yanda* has become more aggressive. The term *campaign* has been replaced by *war* or *battle*. The soldiers and armed police have become more visible in the operation. The period of the operation is prolonged to a campaign with different battlefields and well-planned phases. It took three years to accomplish the national war on theft. The war expands; there are different battles on different crimes organized by different levels of government, often carried out simultaneously. Rights of the accused and legal procedural requirements are routinely bypassed and ignored by the police during *yanda*. Police, prosecution, and judges are required to work in a streamlined fashion in order to expedite the process. Criminal defense is virtually suspended and capital punishment is encouraged. Justice is rendered as speedily and as severely as possible. Those who committed violent crimes are regarded as the enemy of the state and treated as such.

While the *yanda* approach to crime can temporarily suppress the impetus of crime and reassure the public, the police have paid a high price for this problematic method of crime control. The military style of policing results in high casualties among the officers, prolonged work hours for the front-line officers, and degeneration of public relations, and, more importantly,

has subverted routine law enforcement. The success in controlling crime is highly exaggerated. Each *yanda* creates a wave of arrests and convictions. But when it is over, another crime wave is soon recorded, causing another *yanda*. The periodic crackdown on crime created a vicious circle of crime and policing in post-Mao China.

Each *yanda* leads to a detection of a great number of crimes and the arrest of a great number of suspects. It demonstrates the seriousness of crime, the urgent need for a solution and the indispensable position of the police. The criminal justice institutions have strategically used crime statistics to bargain for more powers and resources, and at the same time to prove their effectiveness in combating crime. Streets are safer immediately after a terror of *yanda*, and the public feel more satisfied with social order. *Yanda* thus becomes the self-fulfilling prophecy that the police are indispensable to the legitimacy of the CCP and the security of the state.

By the late 1980s, it became abundantly clear to the police that *yanda* was not the solution to the problem of crime and public disorder. Without *yanda*, society becomes ungovernable, but *yanda* relies on destructive internal warfare to maintain order. China is addicted to this type of crime control, and it appears to be very difficult to break the habit.

Conclusion

Reform in the criminal process in China should be seen in the light of a conflict between the political need for stability on the one hand, and the domestic and international pressures to liberalize the criminal justice system on the other. China remains a one-party state under the dominance of the CCP despite economic liberalization, and the primary concern of the CCP has been the maintenance of social and political order. "Stability overwhelms everything," as the CCP has insisted. Whenever the CCP perceives that crime is posing a threat to stability and challenging its legitimacy, it will mobilize the criminal justice system to strike hard at crime, disregarding most of the legal requirements. Gradual and piecemeal reform and liberalization have been interrupted by periodical campaigns against crime. Criminal law and criminal justice are fundamentally political.

At the same time, a progressive force is taking root in China, pushing for liberalization of criminal law and the criminal justice system and the implementation of rights already existing in

Chinese law. The growth in the economy is creating a middle class and a vibrant society that demands its rights. International pressures, especially China's pending participation in the World Trade Organization (WTO) and the possible ratification of the International Covenant of Civil and Political Rights, will add momentum to the liberation of China's criminal justice system.

HUALING FU

See also ADVERSARY SYSTEM; COMPARATIVE CRIMINAL LAW AND ENFORCEMENT: RUSSIA; CRIMINAL PROCEDURE: COMPARATIVE ASPECTS; PROSECUTION: COMPARATIVE ASPECTS.

BIBLIOGRAPHY

BRADY, JAMES P. *Justice and Politics in People's China: Legal Order or Continuing Revolution?* London: Academic Press, 1982.

CHEN, ALBERT H. Y. *An Introduction to the Legal System of the People's Republic of China.* Singapore: Butterworths Asia, 1992.

FU, H. L. "Criminal Defence in China: The Possible Impact of the 1996 Criminal Procedure Law Reform." *The China Quarterly* 153 (1998): 31–48.

KRAUS, RICHARD C. *Class Conflict in Chinese Socialism.* New York: Columbia University Press, 1981.

Lawyers Committee for Human Rights. *Opening to Reform? An Analysis of China's Revised Criminal Procedure Law.* New York: Lawyers Committee for Human Rights, 1996.

———. *Lawyers in China: Obstacles to Independence and the Defense of Rights.* New York: Lawyers Committee for Human Rights, 1998.

LENG, SHAO-CHUAN, and CHIU, HUNGDAH. *Criminal Justice in Post-Mao China: Analysis and Documents.* Albany: State University of New York Press, 1985.

LI, VICTOR. *Law without Lawyers: A Comparative View of Law in China and the United States.* Boulder, Colo.: Westview Press, 1978.

LIEBERTHAL, KENNETH. *Governing China: From Revolution through Reform.* New York: W. W. Norton & Company, 1995.

LIEBERTHAL, KENNETH, and OKSENBERG, MICHAEL. *Policy Making in China: Leaders, Structures, and Processes.* Princeton, N.J.: Princeton University Press, 1988.

LUBMAN, STANLEY, ed. *China's Legal Reform.* Oxford, U.K.: Oxford University Press, 1996.

———. *Bird in a Cage: Legal Reform in China after Mao.* Stanford, Calif.: Stanford University Press, 1999.

COMPARATIVE CRIMINAL LAW AND ENFORCEMENT: ENGLAND AND WALES

In the United Kingdom there are three separate criminal justice systems, one each for Scotland, Northern Ireland, and England and Wales. This entry will focus on the system in England and Wales, a jurisdiction with a population of fifty-two million people.

In many jurisdictions the criminal laws or penal code can be traced to a key constitutional date when a new system of government was introduced bringing changes to the role of government in general and to criminal procedures in particular. Reforms in the field of criminal law tend to establish new obligations on citizens in the form of the criminalization of an activity, and new constraints on officials in the form of procedures that should be followed when dealing with those accused of crime. In the United Kingdom there have been key constitutional events but no one defining moment has set the foundations of the modern system of criminal justice. In contrast to many modern republics the system has evolved over a very long period of time. One key modern participant in the criminal justice system, the Justices of the Peace, can be traced back to the Justices of the Peace Act 1361. Working alongside the Justices of the Peace, usually referred to in the modern era as magistrates, is the Crown Prosecution Service, an agency established as recently as 1985. Despite the gradual evolution of the key constitutional foundations to the criminal justice system—the rule of law, parliamentary democracy, and freedoms of the individual—since the 1980s there has been a new pace of change as matters of crime, justice, law and order have dominated the political headlines and the actions of both government and citizens.

The history of legislative reform in the field helps to illustrate the growing interest in criminal justice in England and Wales. In the first eighty years of the twentieth century there were only four statutes entitled Criminal Justice Acts, enacted in 1925, 1948, 1967, and 1972. The rate of change increased with Criminal Justice Acts in 1982, 1988, 1991, 1993, and 1994 and a major piece of criminal legislation in each year since 1994: Criminal Appeal Act 1995, Criminal Procedure Act and Investigations Act 1996, Crime (Sentences) Act 1997, Crime and Disorder Act 1998, and the Youth Justice and Criminal Evidence Act 1999.

In the busy parliamentary session 1999/2000 the following laws were enacted: Powers of the Criminal Courts (Sentencing) Act, Crown Prosecution Service Inspectorate Act, Regulation of Investigatory Powers Act, and the Criminal Justice and Court Services Act.

Such reforms are in part a response to internal pressures for more effective crime control, a desire to protect citizens from bias and unfair procedures, the pursuit of greater administrative efficiency, and technological change. Pressure for reform also results from Britain's membership in the European Union, which has brought greater cross-jurisdictional cooperation and coordination in an attempt to control cross-European organized crime and to incorporate reforms such as the European Convention on Human Rights (adopted by the United Kingdom in the Human Rights Act 1998). In October 2000 the Convention comes into effect in the United Kingdom and some of the legislation in the 1999/2000 parliamentary session was to ensure compliance with the European Convention especially with regard to the surveillance powers of the police (Regulation of Investigatory Powers Act 2000). Heralded as the most significant constitutional changes in recent British history, it is likely to have a widespread impact, especially on aspects of policing, bail, and prison procedures.

The criminal justice system in England and Wales has evolved over a considerable period of time and is a unique mix of traditional and modern institutions, agencies, and procedures. The main features of this system will be outlined briefly, followed by more detailed descriptions of policing and prosecution, criminal courts, sentencing and the penal system, and the governmental and administrative context of criminal justice.

The system of government in the United Kingdom, despite some devolution in recent years, is based primarily in London. The importance of central government funding for the criminal justice agencies and courts means that there is considerable cooperation and uniformity of approach found in the three criminal justice systems in the United Kingdom. The process of harmonization is further enhanced by the increasingly important effect the European Union is having on matters such as cooperation between police forces across Europe to combat transnational crimes (particularly organized crime, money laundering, and drugs).

In the United Kingdom there is no penal code. The sources and interpretation of the criminal laws are to be found in individual Acts of Parliament (statutory sources) and decisions by judicial bodies, in particular the Court of Appeal (case law). Increasingly, decisions of the European Court of Justice have an influence on the operation of the criminal law in all member states of the European Union, including the United Kingdom.

The definition of many criminal offenses can be found in statutes. New laws introduced as bills need to pass through both the House of Commons and the House of Lords before they become Acts of Parliament. Thus the definition of burglary and the maximum punishment for it is defined in the Theft Act 1968. The other principal source of criminal law is common law, which derives not from legislation but from what originally were the customs of the people; these were subsequently used as the basis of decisions made by judges in individual cases. There are some criminal offenses that exist only in the rulings of judges. Murder and manslaughter, for instance, are common law offenses. However, the punishments and partial defenses for these two offenses are set out in statutes—Homicide Act 1957, Murder (Abolition of the Death Penalty) Act 1965, and the Criminal Justice Act 1991.

In any criminal justice system it is important to understand the origins of the definitions of criminal conduct, be it through statutory or common law sources. However, it is equally important to appreciate that laws do not enforce themselves; it is therefore necessary to understand the influences on those agencies and participants in the system who interpret and implement the law.

The "law in practice" depends on the activities and decisions of the police, prosecutors, probation and prison officers, professionals (lawyers), and lay participants (magistrates). They do not work from a single document but an array of regulations, requirements, and guidelines as to how they should undertake the task of implementing the criminal law. Thus they will have to refer to specific statutes that relate to their activity and a number of policy documents from central and local government. Furthermore, an agency's approach to making the law work in practice will be determined by the available resources, as well as the organizational culture that has developed over time regarding the appropriate way of doing business.

Although there are many factors that affect the way the criminal law is enforced in England and Wales it is particularly important to understand the influence of "adversarial justice" and the "rule of law" and how these principles shape the way that criminal justice is defined and implemented.

The defining logic determining the nature of the criminal law and its operation in England and Wales is provided by the adversarial principle. This means that a person is not considered to be guilty of a crime simply on the word of a government official. Conviction in a court requires presentation of admissible evidence that convinces the fact finder—a jury, in the case of serious crimes; for less serious crime, a stipendiary (professional and salaried) magistrate (renamed District Judges in 2000), or a panel of lay magistrates—that the evidence demonstrates the guilt of the defendant "beyond reasonable doubt." This test of the evidence is in contrast to the much lower standard of proof used in the civil courts, where facts are determined by a judge on the balance of probability ("more likely than not").

The nonconviction of a defendant following a trial or an appeal does not mean that the defendant is innocent in the common-sense meaning of the word, that is, he or she had nothing to do with the crime. The adversarial system in England and Wales does not ask whether a defendant is innocent or guilty but only whether they are "guilty" or "not guilty."

The adversarial nature of criminal justice in England and Wales means that in many respects the process of conviction for crime is the same as in the United States. The burden is on the prosecutor to establish that a crime has been committed and that they have sufficient evidence to be able to persuade a jury, beyond reasonable doubt, that the person accused both carried out the act alleged in the crime and was responsible in the sense of being considered blameworthy for the crime. This distinction between committing an illegal act and being blameworthy or culpable, reflects the distinction in English law, as in the United States, between the principles of *actus reus* and *mens rea*. Actus reus refers to the events that took place; for example, a named person, on a specified time, date, and place inflicted a knife wound on a named victim. The mens rea refers to the culpability, responsibility, or blameworthiness of the act. If the wound was inflicted by accident and without fault the defendant is not regarded as criminally responsible for the injury.

The principle of adversarial justice has been developed over many centuries, and is designed to protect the liberty and freedom of citizens. Although in any system there is a difference between the principles of a system and the way it operates in practice, government officials are answerable to the law; under this system, known as the "rule of law," police, prosecutors, courts, and prisons may only make decisions and exercise powers that are permitted through the law.

Although most criminals are convicted through their own admission of guilt and therefore a contested trial about the guilt of a defendant is not necessary, the possibility of a trial is the main safeguard of a citizen who has been wrongly accused of a crime. A citizen who becomes a suspect will normally cooperate to help establish his innocence but should he choose not to the onus is on the police to collect sufficient evidence about the crime and to pass this on to the prosecuting body to make a decision on whether or not to prosecute. The citizen accused of a crime has a number of safeguards that start at the point of questioning and arrest for a crime.

Finally as part of this introduction to the criminal justice system in England and Wales it is important to understand the different classifications of crime. The significance of the classification system is, firstly, symbolic—to indicate society's distinction between minor and more serious crimes; secondly, to determine the powers of arrest and detention of suspects; and thirdly, for procedural purposes such as deciding whether the offender is dealt with in the magistrates' court or the Crown Court. The latter deals with more serious crimes.

The Criminal Law Act 1967 abolished the distinction between felony crimes and misdemeanors and introduced the concept of arrestable and non-arrestable offenses. An arrestable offense is defined as any offense for which the sentence is fixed by law (for example, murder, which carries a mandatory sentence of life imprisonment); or for which an offender may be sentenced to imprisonment for a term of five years or more, as well as certain other specified offenses, such as going equipped for stealing. Anyone who is suspected of committing an arrestable offense may be arrested by the police or a member of the public without a warrant. Otherwise, an arrest warrant, signed by a magistrate, is required. Most serious offenses have statutory maxima that exceed five years; for instance, burglary of a dwelling house has a maximum sentence of fourteen years, and the maximum sentence for rape is life imprisonment.

For procedural purposes all criminal offenses are classified into one of three categories:

indictable only, triable-either-way, or summary. An indictable-only offense may only be tried in a Crown Court before a jury, and requires an indictment which is a formal document setting out the charges against the person. Offenses in this category include murder, manslaughter, kidnapping, robbery, and rape.

Summary offenses may only be dealt with by summary justice, that is, proceedings in the magistrates' courts that deal with less serious crimes. Summary offenses are generally those that are punishable by no more than six months imprisonment or a fine of £5,000. These are the maximum sentencing powers in the magistrates' courts. Examples of summary offenses include motoring offenses such as driving after consuming alcohol or taking drugs, careless driving, and driving without a license. Non-motoring offenses that are summary include less serious forms of assault, drunkenness, and prostitution offenses.

Triable-either-way refers to the third category of offenses, examples of which include burglary, theft, and handling stolen goods, many offenses involving the possession, use, and supply of illegal drugs, and many types of assault. With this category of offense an individual case may be dealt with either in the magistrates' court or the Crown Court, and hence a pretrial decision becomes necessary, known as the mode of trial decision, which is discussed below in the section on the criminal courts.

But before a case reaches the trial stage there must first be a crime and a suspect. As the case proceeds the suspect becomes the accused and in court the defendant. These pretrial processes are outlined in the following section.

Table 1 gives statistical data for the year 1999, showing case volume at each stage of the criminal process, beginning with estimates of victimization.

Law enforcement: the police and prosecution

The first English police were medieval constables and the unpaid parish constables who were responsible for maintaining the King's Peace. The urban Watchman had a similar duty. It was not until 1829 that a paid, full-time organized and disciplined police force became established in London: the Metropolitan Police.

Today, the investigation of crime and the arrest, questioning, and charging of those suspected of committing criminal offenses in England and Wales is primarily in the hands of

Table 1

Criminal justice data—England and Wales 1999	
Amount of crime	
Crimes estimates by British Crime Survey	14,716,000
Offenses recorded by the police	5,301,185
Police	
Offenses cleared up by the police (25 percent of all recorded)	1,497,000
Number of arrests for notifiable* offenses	1,300,000
Diversion	
Police-issued formal cautions in lieu of prosecution	266,100
Cases discontinued by Crown Prosecution Service	164,700
Cases written off (defendants cannot be traced)	86,100
Proceedings in the courts	
Total proceeded against	1,881,700
indictable offenses	512,700
summary non-motoring	560,000
summary motoring	809,000
Committed for trial at the Crown Court	72,000
Total convicted in all criminal courts	1,408,500
Numbers sentenced all courts	
Sentence distribution:	
absolute and conditional discharges	129,900
fines	992,400
probation orders	58,400
community service orders	40,600
combination orders	20,700
attendance center orders	8,700
curfew orders	1,600
custody - young offender institution	24,800
custody - prison	79,700
suspended prison sentence	3,200
other	39,000

*Notifiable offenses are crimes recorded by the police and include all indictable and triable-either-way offenses plus a few of the more serious summary offenses.

SOURCE: Home Office. *Criminal Statistics: England and Wales 1999*. London: Stationery Office, 2000. Home Office. *Home Office Statistical Bulletin, The 2000 British Crime Survey*. London: Stationery Office, 2000.

forty-three regional police forces. As of 2000 there were 124,418 police officers and 53,227 civilian staff; the Metropolitan Police is the largest force with 25,485 officers covering the whole of the London area. They are not armed with guns unless working in a special unit such as those assigned to protect diplomats and public officials, or are in armed response units ready to respond to incidents where weapons are used.

The organization of the police in England and Wales is very different from that found either in the United States or in the rest of Europe.

Unlike the United States, there are far fewer police forces and there is no equivalent to the distinctions made between federal, state, county, and city police forces. Unlike many European police forces, there is no national police force answerable to a central government department. However, regional and national police work has been developing in recent decades and there is now a National Crime Squad, set up in 1998, with a cross-jurisdictional role. Furthermore, the Home Secretary, the political head of the Home Office, has considerable influence (although not direct operational control), through the system of central government grants that, along with local council taxes, funds police work. The control of the police is shared between central government, local government, and the police as semi-autonomous professionals.

Special laws and codes govern the operation of police work. Decisions to stop, search, arrest, or question suspects are governed by rules set out in administrative codes pursuant to the Police and Criminal Evidence Act 1984. The act requires the publication of a series of Codes of Practice to regulate police work when dealing with criminal suspects. Code A deals with the powers to stop and search a suspect in the street; Code B is concerned with the search of premises and seizure of property; Code C relates to the detention, treatment, and questioning of suspects; Code D regulates identification procedures; and, Code E specifies the procedures to be followed for tape recorded interviews with suspects.

The function of the police is to be the main agency responsible for responding to crime, but they also have several other important responsibilities: crime prevention; the maintenance of public order at large events such as royal ceremonies, sporting occasions and public meetings; traffic control, and road safety; custody of lost property; and the provision of emergency service to a variety of persons in need (e.g., those who have lost their door keys, or who have been involved in motoring accidents).

There are other agencies responsible for responding to lawbreaking such as Her Majesty's Customs and Excise, in the case of smuggling, and the British Transport Police, who deal with crime on the railways and at ports and docks. In contrast to other European countries, the responsibility for most crime is given to the local police force, who have the duty of responding to both major and minor crimes. In England and Wales the prosecutor plays no part at the crime investigation stage, and there is no investigating

magistrate as there is in France. Within the police there is a functional division between the detective branch and the regular uniformed police officer. The detective branch is called the Criminal Investigation Department (CID). They respond to major crimes such as murders and have units responsible for investigating more routine crimes such as burglary.

Since 1950 the crime trend has been steadily upward, but it leveled off in the 1990s. Recorded crime figures collected by the police and published annually by the Home Office show that in the year between April 1999 and March 2000 there were 5.3 million crimes recorded by the police. However, a more reliable guide to the extent of crime is provided by the British Crime Survey. Organized by the Research, Development and Statistics Directorate of the Home Office, the survey is now regularly conducted every two years and gives an estimate of the total amount of crime based on a sample of 19,500 respondents. In 2000 it was estimated that there were over 16.5 million crimes reported by victims in this survey. The survey only relates to crimes against the individual and therefore does not include public order offenses (e.g., involving drugs), property crimes committed at the workplace, or crimes involving public bodies such as the railways or tax fraud.

The crime pattern is very different from the United States, with the latest British Crime Survey showing that 22 percent of crimes are violent (homicide, robbery, rape, wounding, sexual offenses) and 80 percent are property crimes. In the twelve months from April 1999 to March 2000 across the whole of England and Wales, there were 765 offenses recorded as homicide (murder, manslaughter and infanticide) and 749 attempted murder offenses recorded (Povey et al.).

The police have a duty to respond to criminal incidents but they are not required to prosecute in every case. Investigations often result in no prosecution because there is not sufficient evidence to charge the suspect, or there may not even be a suspect. Where there is sufficient evidence and a person is charged, the police have the option of not sending the case papers on to the Crown Prosecuting Service, but rather diverting the case from the normal system by issuing an official caution in lieu of prosecution. For this to happen the police should have sufficient evidence against a suspect to be able to have the CPS prosecute the case, and the suspect must admit his or her guilt for the offense. He may then be given a formal caution that is placed on the offender's record. This system of diversion is used primarily with young offenders; indeed the majority of youngsters aged ten to seventeen are given a caution. For young offenders the use of cautioning was reformed in the Crime and Disorder Act 1998 to a system of reprimands and final warnings.

In most cases where the police have sufficient evidence against a suspect, the case papers are forwarded to the prosecuting agency. There are a number of prosecuting bodies for criminal offenses in England and Wales such as the Post Office and the Inland Revenue (responsible for collecting taxation). Since the Prosecution of Offences Act 1985 there has been one agency responsible for the great bulk of routine criminal cases dealt with: the Crown Prosecution Service, known as the CPS.

Prosecutors: Crown Prosecution Service

The CPS was established by the Prosecution of Offences Act 1985, and for the first time provided for a systematic and standardized approach toward prosecution decisions across England and Wales. Before its introduction the police were responsible for most criminal prosecutions, and so procedures and practices varied across the forty-three regional policing areas.

The reform of prosecution was designed to encourage a more cost-effective approach and to promote fairness. The latter was to be achieved by providing for the review of each case by independent and legally qualified prosecutors. Greater consistency and accountability was to be sought through the use of a nationwide code, the details of which are published by the CPS. Each decision to prosecute should only be taken if it satisfies the "evidential" and the "public interest" tests described below. The annual report of the Crown Prosecution Service sets out the Code for Crown Prosecutors and the details of these tests.

The evidential sufficiency test is that the prosecutors must be convinced that the evidence in a case will provide "a realistic prospect of conviction." To make this judgement they must review the evidence to ensure that it is usable in court and not excluded because of the rules of evidence or because of the way it has been collected. After this they must decide whether the evidence is reliable in the sense of coming from an honest and competent witness who is available to attend court.

The public interest test asks whether it would be in the public's interest to continue with the prosecution. For example, a case of a very minor offense committed by a defendant close to death due to a terminal illness is unlikely to be prosecuted. The Code for Prosecutors sets out factors that are in favor of prosecution and those that are against prosecuting a case.

A prosecution might be dropped—discontinued in the language of the CPS—for the following public interest reasons: the likely penalty would be very small or nominal (e.g., an absolute or conditional discharge); the crime was committed as a result of a mistake; the loss or harm involved could be described as minor; there has been a long delay between the trial and the date of the offense (except when a case is serious or the delay has been caused by the defendant, or the complexity of the offense has required a lengthy investigation); the victim's health is likely to be adversely affected by the trial; the defendant is elderly, or mentally or physically ill; the defendant has made reparation to the victim; or there are security reasons for not revealing information that might be revealed during a trial.

The CPS has no investigative function. However, in addition to their main task of reviewing all cases sent to them by the police, they discuss and negotiate with the police on matters of charging standards, for example the offense characteristics that should be taken into consideration when deciding whether a sexual offense should be charged as a rape or as an indecent assault. Finally, a high-profile aspect of their role is they act as advocates to present cases in the magistrates' courts as prosecutors. In 2000 there were 2,100 lawyers and 3,700 other staff working for the CPS.

Some cases do not go through the standard procedure because of the status of the offender. Special rules of procedure apply to those offenders who are young or are diagnosed as mentally ill. Criminal liability starts at the age of ten in England and Wales. There are different stages relating to the age of the offender that determine both the criminal procedure and the range of dispositions for younger offenders. Under ten years of age the person has no criminal liability; from ten to fourteen they are regarded as children; from fifteen to seventeen as young offenders.

Criminal courts: pre-trial and trial

Criminal courts include the magistrates' court, the youth court, the Crown Court, and the

Court of Appeal. All routine cases will start in the magistrates' court with a pretrial decision about granting or refusing bail. Another important pretrial decision concerns the mode of trial for cases where a person has pleaded not guilty and the offense is triable-either-way. As noted previously, some indictable offenses, such as murder and rape, are "indictable only"; these must be sent on to the Crown Court. Other indictable offenses are triable-either-way, and these can either be heard by the magistrates' court or in the Crown Court. The mode of trial decision determines in which court the case will be heard.

In the magistrates' court, decisions are made about guilt and sentence by lay magistrates or District Judges. Lay magistrates are members of the local community appointed by the Lord Chancellor's Department. They are part-time and usually sit one day every two weeks. They do not need legal qualifications and typically sit in panels of three, known as the "bench." Stipendiary magistrates are paid, full-time lawyers with experience of criminal practice. In 2000 there were 30,308 lay magistrates (48 percent of them women), 93 District Judges, and 45 Deputy District Judges. District Judges and lay magistrates have the same powers and jurisdiction. They make pretrial decisions about bail conditions or pre-trial detention (remands in custody), legal representation, and committal for trial or sentence to the Crown Court.

Magistrates in summary trials determine issues of guilt and sentence convicted offenders. They are responsible for the overwhelming majority of criminal convictions and sentencing decisions. They are assisted on matters of law by a legally trained Clerk to the Justices.

The more serious criminal cases are heard in the Crown Court where a judge presides over the trial and a lay jury determines guilt. However, most cases are resolved without a trial because in the overwhelming majority of cases the defendant pleads guilty, induced by the advantage of a reduction in sentence length if a plea of guilt is entered early in the proceedings. When guilt is contested the trial proceeds with the presentation of prosecution and defense evidence and witnesses are subject to cross-examination by opposing counsel.

Criminal liability is often contested not by denial that the events took place but by a claim that the defendant was not responsible for the actions that occurred, or that the actions of the defendant were justified. Such defenses include self-defense, mistake, duress, provocation, automa-tism (involuntary act), or diminished responsibility. These defenses can sometimes persuade the jury or District Judges that the person is not guilty; even if the defendant is convicted, such defenses may suggest mitigating circumstances resulting in a less severe sentence. Where a suspect is below the age of criminal responsibility or is certified as mentally ill, he or she will not be regarded as responsible under the criminal law for their actions. The decision on guilt is made by a twelve-person jury, who are able to make a majority verdict (10–2 or 11–1) if, after a length of time, a unanimous verdict is unlikely.

The judge's role is threefold: to ensure a fair trial, for example, by excluding unreliable evidence; to sum up the evidence at the end of the trial and summarize the legal issues for the jury before they make a decision; and, if the defendant is convicted, to decide on the sentence. The judge should act as the umpire and ensure a fair trial. If the evidence is insufficient, unreliable, or unfair the judge can order a directed acquittal.

In criminal cases, appeals can be made against conviction, against the sentence, or both. Appeals against decisions made in the magistrates' court are heard by the Crown Court; routine appeals against conviction or sentence in the Crown Court are heard in the Court of Appeal.

Where a serious miscarriage of justice is alleged, a review body has the role of deciding whether to refer the case back to the Court of Appeal. The Criminal Cases Review Commission was established by the Criminal Appeal Act 1995, and its function is to review suspected miscarriages of justice. It can refer a conviction, verdict, or sentence to the Court of Appeal if it feels there are grounds for re-examining the case. It came into operation in 1997 and by March 2000 had made eighty referrals to the Court of Appeal. The leading reasons for referrals are breach of identification or interview procedures; use of questionable witnesses; problems of scientific evidence such as DNA or fingerprints; nondisclosure by the prosecution of evidence that could have helped the defense case; and problems with other types of evidence such as alibis, eyewitnesses, and confessions.

Cases involving defendants above the age of legal responsibility—ten years of age—who have not yet reached the age of eighteen will normally be heard by the youth court, which is attached to the magistrates' court; the public is not allowed to observe events in the youth court. For certain grave crimes such as murder, a child or youth will have their case heard in a Crown Court adapted in some measure to the needs of children.

Sentencing and the penal system

The aims of sentencing were set out in a 1990 Home Office report that preceded the Criminal Justice Act 1991. The law sought to provide a sentencing framework for those making sentencing decisions in the courts and those responsible for operating the penal system (the Probation Service, Prison Service, and Parole Board). The report stated:

The first objective for all sentences is the denunciation of and retribution for the crime. Depending on the offence and the offender, the sentence may also aim to achieve public protection, reparation and reform of the offender, preferably in the community. This approach points to sentencing policies which are more firmly based on the seriousness of the offence, and just deserts for the offender. (Home Office, 1990, p. 6)

Sentencing decisions for those convicted of a crime are made by the magistrates in magistrates' courts and the judge in the Crown Court. Decisions about individual cases are made with the help of voluntary guidelines in the case of magistrates and presentence reports provided by the Probation Service. The general sentencing framework is determined by the maximum sentences set out in statutes, a few mandatory sentences (such as life imprisonment for murder), and statutory criteria such as those related to the use of custody. A major influence on judges in the Crown Court are the decisions made by the Court of Appeal and particularly the Court of Appeal Sentencing Guideline Cases.

In England and Wales in recent decades the sentencing process has been reformed with the aim of reducing disparities, promoting consistency, and reassuring the public about the purpose of sentencing. But the reforms have not introduced the degree of constraint found in those parts of the United States where the courts are subject to sentencing guidelines (as in Minnesota) or determinate sentencing laws (as in California). The constraints on judges and magistrates in England and Wales are provided by statutory factors, the appeal process, judicial training, and the use of voluntary guidelines by magistrates.

Appeals against sentences are allowed, with appeals from the magistrates' court being heard in the Crown Court and the appeals against sentence in the Crown Court being heard by the Court of Appeal. Only the defendant has the general right of appeal, although in 1988 the Attorney General was given the right to appeal unduly lenient sentences for grave offenses that are triable only in the Crown Court.

The twentieth century has witnessed an increase in the range of available penalties; the abolition of corporal and capital punishment; and the introduction of a variety of community sentences. The death penalty was abolished for homicide in 1965. For adults convicted of murder the mandatory sentence is life, although this rarely means a person spends the rest of their life in prison. The average length served in prison on a life sentence before first release under license (parole) is fourteen years, but release is not automatic. A life sentence is indeterminate, not fixed; release from a mandatory life sentence is authorized by the Home Secretary following recommendations of the Parole Board and consultation with the Lord Chief Justice and the trial judge. A life sentence is also possible (but not mandatory) in a number of other grave offenses such as rape and robbery.

All prisoners given a fixed prison sentence are eligible for remission. Remission is automatic for those sentenced to less than four years at the halfway point of the sentence so that a person sentenced to six months will be released after three months and a person sentenced to three years will be released after eighteen months. If the defendant had time spent on remand in custody this time will be taken into account as time served.

Some inmates will be supervised in the community following their release. A distinction is made between those who are sentenced to over twelve months but less than four years. These will be supervised in the community after release from custody for a period equal to a quarter of their sentence length. Those sentenced to less than twelve months will not be subject to supervision in the community after release. Where supervision in the community is required it is undertaken by the Probation Service; there is not a separate parole service as there is in the United States.

Those sentenced to periods of four years and greater have their sentence remission counted differently. They are allowed one-third off their sentence length but may apply for parole after serving 50 percent of their time. Thus a person sentenced to twelve years becomes eligible to apply for parole after serving six years, and must be released after eight years. The decision on whether to release the inmate between the six- to eight-year period is made by the Parole Board. Compulsory community supervision applies to these released inmates.

Home Detention Curfew was introduced in 1999 to allow inmates early release up to sixty days before their automatic release date. During the period they are subject to a curfew and electronic monitoring.

The prison system held on average 64,631 prisoners a day in the year 1999/2000. This is five hundred more than the prison system was designed for, and thus overcrowding occurred in some, mainly male, local prisons (Prison Service).

The same range of community penalties are available for adults in the magistrates' courts and the Crown Court. In 1907 probation was introduced; in 1972 community service orders became available; and in 1991 the combination order and curfew order were established as sentencing options. However, the typical sentence is a fine, accounting for 992,400 out of 1.47 million sentenced offenders in 1999 (see Table 1). To promote the use of community sentences the Criminal Justice and Court Services Act 2000 introduced Drug Abstinence Orders and Exclusion Orders and renamed Probation Orders as Community Rehabilitation Orders; Community Service Orders became Community Punishment Orders; and Combination Orders were redesignated as Community Punishment and Rehabilitation Orders.

Governmental and administrative context of criminal justice

The Parliament at Westminster is the source of all legislation that covers criminal procedure and criminal law. The system of case law means that the courts are the source of common law. Increasingly European Community regulations and decisions by the European Court of Human Rights are coming to affect criminal procedure in England and Wales.

Although there are similarities between the principles of the criminal justice system in England and Wales and the United States, especially with respect to the adversarial system of justice, there are important differences in the system of government. There is far less separation of power in the British constitution than in the United States. The executive and legislative branches of government are brought closely together through the parliamentary system of government whereby the executive branch of government is formed by the political party with a majority of seats in the House of Commons. The General Election simultaneously determines the political party that will form the government and gives the governing party control of the legislature. Thus the constitution allows for a considerable degree of overlap between the executive and legislative branches. Secondly, the administration of government in England and Wales is more centralized than in the United States. There are no separate states with their own laws, jurisdictional authority, and criminal procedures.

The major government offices are based in London. The key government departments are the Home Office and the Lord Chancellor's Department. The Home Office has overall responsibility for policing, prisons, and the probation service. The head of the Home Office is called the Home Secretary who has political responsibility for crime policy in England and Wales. For example, the Home Secretary sets the key objectives and priorities for the police. The Lord Chancellor's Department has responsibilities relating to the judiciary, and the head of this department, the Lord Chancellor, is both a political appointee and the head of the judiciary in England and Wales.

Most of the public sector employees of the criminal justice system work for the central government; this includes 177,645 employees (officers and civilians) of the police forces, 43,088 employees of the Prison Service, and 7,200 probation officers.

The pressure to adopt a more centralized and systematic approach to crime has been apparent since the 1980s. Government policies have encouraged a greater degree of interagency cooperation within regions. The Criminal Justice Consultative Council was established in 1991 to promote greater awareness of the problems facing the different agencies in the system. Increased cross-regional coordination of law enforcement was the purpose behind the establishment of the National Crime Squad, set up by the Police Act 1997. The National Criminal Intelligence Service (NCIS) was established in 1992 to coordinate law enforcement efforts with regard to organized crime, illegal immigration, drugs, and counterfeiting.

A comparison of the criminal justice systems in the United Kingdom and the United States would lead to the correct conclusion that the system in England and Wales is more centralized and dependent on central government. However, there are some important counterinfluences that make the role of central government less powerful than first appears to be the case.

First, there are strong regional divisions and responsibilities based primarily on the big metropolitan cities and the old shire counties. For instance, the organization of the police is based on forty-three police forces with jurisdictions that are geographically determined primarily by the old county boundaries of England and Wales such as Hampshire and Essex. An important role is played by local government (cities, boroughs, and counties), especially with regard to crime prevention work in the community, and these governments play a vital role coordinating interagency strategies in response to youth crime.

Second, the independence of the judiciary is a real and effective constraint on the activities of the executive branch of government. The legal professions, represented by the Law Society (representing solicitors) and the Bar Council (representing barristers, or trial lawyers) are powerful protectors of the liberties of the citizen.

Third, the involvement of nonprofessional lay participants such as magistrates, lay visitors to police stations, the Board of Visitors responsible for the oversight of prisons, and Victim Support volunteers ensures that the system is not solely accountable to central government. These nonprofessional groups include well over fifty thousand citizens who each week play a vital role within the system, and bring with them a degree of independence in their approach to issues of crime and justice.

Fourth, there is vociferous and well-organized system of pressure and lobby groups based on the voluntary sector, such as the Magistrates' Association, who help to shape policy developments. These voluntary associations also play a role in cooperative projects and schemes to help offenders and victims (Victim Support). Two key volunteer organizations in the penal system are the Howard League for Penal Reform and NACRO (National Association for the Care and Resettlement of Offenders).

Fifth, interest groups play a part in the process of shaping criminal justice policies. The existence of powerful trade unions such as the Prison Officers Association and the Police Federation ensure that the views of these officers are heard in public debate. In recent years the advance of the private sector has become apparent with privately run prisons operated by commercial companies such as Group 4. An extensive private security industry includes companies such as Securicor and Wells Fargo. It is estimated that 400,000 people are employed in the private sector associated with the criminal justice system in England and Wales.

Finally, the European Court of Human Rights has become increasingly important as the final court of appeal for those citizens who feel that the system has infringed their rights. The international dimension of criminal justice is bound to increase under the influence of greater European harmonization of laws and cooperation between law enforcement agencies; organizations such as Europol (policing agencies) and Eurojust (prosecutors) have already linked officials in different European countries.

Is a European criminal justice system likely to come into being in the near future? Given the great diversity of legal systems, the range of criminal justice agencies in the countries that form the European Union, and the variations in crime problems and public attitudes to law and order, it will be some time before it would be realistic to talk of a single European criminal justice system with harmonized laws and procedures that are the same regardless of where a suspect is arrested in Europe. On matters of crime and justice, parochial attitudes are very difficult to overcome, although the experience of the United States has shown that greater harmonization is not an impossibility. Whether it is desirable or not is a very different question.

MALCOLM DAVIES

See also ADVERSARY SYSTEM; CRIMINAL JUSTICE SYSTEM; CRIMINAL LAW REFORM: ENGLAND; CRIMINAL PROCEDURE: COMPARATIVE ASPECTS; PROSECUTION: COMPARATIVE ASPECTS.

BIBLIOGRAPHY

ASHWORTH, ANDREW. "The Decline of English Sentencing and Other Stories." In *Sentencing and Sanctions in Western Countries.* New York: Oxford University Press, 2001.

BARCLAY, G., ed. *Criminal Justice Digest 4: Information on the Criminal Justice System in England and Wales.* London: Home Office, 1999.

DAVIES, MALCOLM; CROALL, HAZEL; and TYRER, JANE. *Criminal Justice: An Introduction to the Criminal Justice System in England and Wales,* 2d ed., London and New York: Longman, 1998.

Home Office. *Crime, Justice and Protecting the Public.* London: Home Office, 1990.

————. *Criminal Statistics: England and Wales 1999*. London: Stationery Office, 2000.

————. *Criminal Statistics: England and Wales*. London: Stationery Office. Published annually.

————. *A Guide to the Criminal Justice System in England and Wales*. London: Home Office, 2000.

KERSHAW, C.; BUDD, T.; KINSHOTT, G.; MATTINSON, J.; MAYHEW, P; and MYHILL, A. *The 2000 British Crime Survey England and Wales*. Home Office Statistical Bulletin, issue 21/98. London: Home Office, 1998.

POVEY, D.; COTTON, J.; and SISSON, S. *Recorded Crime Statistics*. Home Office Statistical Bulletin 12/00. London: Home Office, 2000.

Prison Service. *H M Prison Service Annual Report and Accounts April 1999 to March 2000*. London: Stationery Office, 2000.

SISSON, S.; SMITHERS, M.; and NGUYEN, K. T. *Policing Service Personnel*. Home Office Statistical Bulletin Issue 15/00. London: Home Office, 2000.

INTERNET RESOURCES

Court of Appeal, Decisions and Docket, http://www.courtservice.gov.uk/homemap.htm.

Criminal Cases Review Commission, http://www.ccrc.gov.uk.

Criminal Justice System, http://www.criminal-justice-system.gov.uk/.

Crown Prosecution Service, http://www.cps.gov.uk.

Her Majesty's Prison Service, http://www.hmprisonservice.gov.uk/statistics.

Home Office, The Criminal Justice Digest, http://www.homeoffice.gov.uk/rds/digest4/.

Home Office, Legislation, http://www.hmso.gov.uk/legis.htm.

Home Office, Public Acts, http://www.hmso.gov.uk/acts.htm.

Home Office, Research Development and Statistics Directorate, http://www.homeoffice.gov.uk/rds/.

Interpol, http://www.interpol.int.

Law Commission for England and Wales, Criminal Laws, http://www.open.gov.uk/lawcomm/misc/criminal.htm.

Lord Chancellor's Department, http://www.open.gov.uk/lcd/.

Metropolitan Police, http://www.met.police.uk/.

National Criminal Intelligence Service, http://www.ncis.gov.uk/.

Parliament, Public Act Bills, http://www.parliament.the-stationery-office.co.uk/pa/pabills.htm.

Police Forces in England and Wales, http://www.police.uk/.

Serious Fraud Office, http://www.sfo.gov.uk/.

Youth Justice Board, http://www.youth-justice-board.gov.uk/.

COMPARATIVE CRIMINAL LAW AND ENFORCEMENT: ISLAM

Islamic law is traditionally equated with the *shari'a*, the compendium of rules and applications devised over the centuries by the jurists of the Islamic empire. The main form and content of the *shari'a* arose during the first three and a half centuries after the death of Muhammad in A.D. 632, through the development of "schools of law," which were groupings of legal specialists. There are today four major surviving schools of law in orthodox, or Sunni, Islam. They are the Maliki, the Hanafi, the Shafi, and Hanbali. But Islamic law is far broader than the *shari'a*, particularly in regard to the law on crimes.

The portion of the *shari'a* dealing with criminal matters is one of its least developed parts. Early on, the Islamic state removed criminal (and other) jurisdiction from the *qadi*, the religious judge, and vested it in state-appointed judges serving under the direction of the political authorities. A number of political devices of the empire outflanked the requirements of the *shari'a* and continued in some form or other in later centuries. To begin with, the police or *shurta* began to investigate, apprehend, try, and punish offenders independently of the *shari'a* courts.

One of the most important jurisdictions belonged to the *muhtasib*, or inspector of the market, who not only established regulations for the conduct of merchants and traders, but enforced them as well. With so much of the commercial activity of the Islamic empire centered on trading, the jurisdictional power of the *muhtasib* was enormous. In fact, it fell to him to enforce Islamic morals as well.

In addition to his powers of appointing *qadis* and constricting their jurisdiction at will, the Islamic sovereign has always possessed an independent right of legislation. Called the *siyasa shar'iyya*, it signifies the ability of the caliph to pass "administrative regulations" to help effectuate the *shari'a*. Strictly speaking, "sovereign" and "legislation" are misnomers when applied to the Islamic state. Only God is sovereign, and only He "legislates," that is, only He can literally "make law." Nonetheless, through the mechanism of *siyasa*, the Islamic state (including conservative modern states like Saudi Arabia) has been able to contend with problems in ways that are outside of, and in some ways even contradictory to, the approach of the *shari'a*.

Without the constant contact with real cases, the jurists' thinking on criminal matters became dormant. In contrast to the portions of the *shari'a* dealing with civil law, such as contracts and property, the criminal law sections seem intellectually undeveloped. After about A.D. 1000, the development of the *shari'a* as a whole slowed almost to a halt. The jurists themselves disparaged jurisprudential thinking and innovation. Both practically and intellectually, then, the criminal parts of *shari'a* had little chance of further growth.

Today, when some radical Islamic regimes seek to "restore" the ancient *shari'a*, they often turn to the formulas of the criminal law as a first step. In doing so, they impose a criminal structure that was often ignored by the Islamic empire itself. Its relation to applied criminal law was frequently tangential.

Much research still needs to be done on the actual application of criminal laws in different eras and different parts of the Islamic empire. However, because the jurists of Islam redacted the rules of the *shari'a* over the centuries, we have a source of the Islamic law of crimes that represents the juridical tradition, if not the entire political and legal practice. What follows then, is a summary of the Islamic law of crimes as found in the books of the *shari'a*.

The *shari'a* categorizes its offenses by the types of punishments they engender:

- offenses to which are affixed a specified punishment (*hadd*);
- those for which the punishment is at the judge's discretion (*ta'zir*);
- those offenses in which a form of retaliatory action or blood money is inflicted against the perpetrator or his kinsmen by the victim's kinsmen (*jinayat*);
- offenses against the public policy of the state, involving administrative penalties (*siyasa*); and
- offenses that are corrected by acts of personal penance (*kaffara*).

The *shari'a*, however, deals primarily with *hadd*, *ta'zir*, and *jinayat* offenses. Those offenses are to be adjudicated before the *qadi* unless the state has removed jurisdiction to one of its own courts. At the very least, secular tribunals handle administrative offenses under the state's *siyasa* jurisdiction. Acts of personal penance, or *kaffara*, are usually undertaken voluntarily by the individual outside of any tribunal or court.

Hadd offenses

Islamic law denotes five "Qur'anic offenses," which are regarded as offenses directly against Allah and which compel a specific punishment. Theoretically, these offenses find their source in the Qur'an, although many aspects are post-Qur'anic developments.

Unlawful intercourse (*zina*). Unlawful intercourse consists in having sexual relations with any person not one's lawful spouse or concubine. Thus, if a man marries and has intercourse with a woman not legally capable of becoming his wife, such as a near relative, a fifth wife while four are still living, or a girl below the age of puberty, he violates the prohibition against unlawful intercourse. Necrophilia is included in the prohibition. There is, however, no prohibition against concubinage. *Zina* should not be confused with the Western notion of adultery as a violation of the marital contract between two persons. In Islam, adultery is not a legal basis for divorce.

The punishment for *zina* is either death by stoning or lashes. Some Hanbali jurists require flogging and stoning for the offender. The penalty of death by stoning is not in the Qur'an but was inflicted as punishment by the first caliphs who succeeded Muhammad. According to some scholars, stoning was adopted from Mosaic law and was incorporated into Islamic law by a later tradition in which Muhammad was said to have approved the practice. Stoning can only be inflicted on one who has been convicted of unlawful intercourse, is not a minor, is mentally competent, is free, and has already had lawful sexual intercourse in marriage. For all others, the punishment is one hundred lashes, or fifty lashes if the convicted person is a slave. In some cases, banishment is added as a penalty.

As with most *hadd* offenses, an action for *zina* must normally be brought against an accused within one month of the offense. The proof must affirmatively show not only that unlawful intercourse took place but also that the act was voluntary. Islamic law requires either the testimony of four eyewitnesses, instead of the normal two, or the confession of the accused. Some jurists require that the confession must be repeated four times. The pregnancy of an unmarried woman can be sufficient proof against her.

The witnesses must be competent adult male Muslims. Non-Muslims may testify in cases in which a non-Muslim is charged with *zina*. The witnesses must testify that they all saw the same act of unlawful intercourse at the same time. The magistrate who receives their testimony is charged with examining the witnesses assiduously, for they must not only testify to the fact of intercourse, but also to its unlawfulness—that is, they must testify that the parties were not married to each other and that the act was voluntary.

Many jurists hold that it is meritorious for witnesses to refrain from coming forward so that the accused can settle the offenses privately with God. An additional incentive for silence lies in the fact that if the accusation is dismissed, those who testified are subject to the *hadd* punishment for false accusation of adultery (*kadhf*). Even if the case is dismissed for a technical reason, such as the minority of one of the witnesses, all the other witnesses can be charged with false accusation of adultery. If one is convicted by testimony, the four witnesses must be present at the execution and must throw the first stones. Otherwise, the death penalty is not carried out.

Alternatively, one can be convicted of *zina* by a personal confession. Again, however, the offender is encouraged to be silent and to turn to God privately for forgiveness. If he does confess, a retraction at any time will void the confession and the sentence. The magistrate should give the self-accused every opportunity for retraction. Some opinions hold that if the convicted person attempts to escape from his place of execution, it will be presumed that it is a retraction of his confession and the sentence may no longer be carried out. If one is convicted of multiple counts of adultery, the *hadd*—whether by stoning or lashes—is satisfied by a single punishment. Any person who is not liable for the *hadd* punishment for *zina* because of any of the limitations listed above may still be prosecuted under the criminal law of discretionary punishment, or *ta'zir*.

False accusation of unlawful intercourse (*kadhf*)

Anyone who is competent and adult, whether male or female, Muslim or not, slave or free, is liable if he falsely charges another person with unlawful intercourse if the slandered party is free, adult, competent, Muslim, and not previously convicted of unlawful intercourse. False accusation (*kadhf*) occurs also when one is charged with being illegitimate. Only those who are the objects of the slander (the alleged fornicator or the alleged bastard) or their heirs may bring a

charge of *kadhf*. The prohibition arose in the Qur'an after a man insinuated that an escort of the Prophet's wife A'isha may have engaged in intimate conduct with her.

The *hadd* punishment for *kadhf* is eighty lashes for free persons or forty lashes for a slave. Proof is obtained by normal Islamic penal procedure, either by confession (in this case retraction will not be suggested by the judge) or by the testimony of two adult male free Muslims. The person accused of slander may defend himself by proving that unlawful intercourse actually took place, but he would have to produce the four male witnesses as required by the law on *zina*. Those slanders not falling under the strict rules regarding *kadhf* are punished under *ta'zir*.

Islamic law treats as a special case the accusation by a husband of his wife's adultery, either directly or by denying paternity of her child. The procedure is known as *li'an*. A husband may charge his wife with infidelity without risk to himself if he swears four times by Allah that he is speaking the truth and, at a fifth oath, calls down a curse upon himself if he is lying. The wife may answer the charge similarly by swearing four times by Allah that she has not sinned and, at a fifth oath, by calling down a curse upon herself if she is not speaking the truth.

If the husband makes an accusation of adultery without using the *li'an* formula, he is liable to the *hadd* punishment for *kadhf*. The Hanafi school would imprison the husband until he pronounces the *li'an*. If he still refuses, he is declared a liar and given the lashes. If, after an accusation by *li'an*, the wife does not deny the charge by the *li'an* formula, this is taken as a tacit confession, and she is subject to the *hadd* punishment for *zina*. The *li'an* is the only legal means by which a man may contest the paternity of his child.

Drinking of wine (*shurb*)

The animus against drinking wine grew by historic stages in the Qur'an. It was not, in the beginning, completely forbidden. Ultimately, drinking was prohibited altogether as Muhammad became scandalized at the drunkenness present in much of Arabic society at the time.

The punishment for drinking intoxicants or for drunkenness is eighty lashes for a freeman and forty for a slave. The punishment is not prescribed in the Qur'an but was established later and analogized from the punishment for the *kadhf*. In many cases, the schools extend the prohibition to other intoxicating substances, such as drugs.

Besides proof by a retractable confession, evidence can be given by two male adult Muslims who saw the accused drinking an intoxicant, smelled the odor of alcohol on his breath, or saw the accused in a state of drunkenness. The Hanafi school punishes drinking wine but not the imbibing of other alcoholic beverages unless drunkenness ensues.

Theft (*sariqa*)

The *hadd* punishment for theft is the amputation of a hand. To be guilty of theft, one must be a competent adult and have the mental intention to steal. The act must consist of the removal by stealth of a certain kind of item of a minimum value that is owned by another person.

Stealth.   The item taken must be in a place of safekeeping (*hirz*), such as a private residence, or a storehouse where goods are kept under guard. Invited guests cannot be charged with theft, nor can pickpockets, nor even one who enters a *hirz* stealthily but has not yet departed when apprehended or has left the place openly. An accessory who receives the stolen good is not normally subject to the *hadd*.

Minimum value (*nihab*).   Unless the value of stolen goods meets or exceeds a certain value, the *hadd* penalty may not be applied. The jurists of the different schools set varying minimum values, but for all, the minimum was not negligible, and roughly corresponds with the common law offense of grand as opposed to petty theft.

Type of good (*mal*).   The crime of theft applies only to chattels that are capable of being owned by a Muslim. Thus, the stealing of wine or pork does not incur the *hadd*. Nor do items of idle amusement, such as games or pets. Holy items are also exempt, as is real and intellectual property.

Property of another.   Taking a piece of property in which one, knowingly or not, has a part interest, does not constitute theft. Thus, embezzlement or stealing from the public treasury is not theft, because every Muslim has a part interest in the fisc. The taking of the property of a near relative will not make one subject to the penalty nor things in a wild state, such as game.

If one is convicted of theft, the right hand is amputated and the wound cauterized. Demonstrating that much of the law on crimes in the *shari'a* came from jurists' speculations rather than actual practice, the rule requires that if there are subsequent thefts, amputation of the left foot, left hand, and right foot will proceed respectively.

Highway robbery (*qat'al-tariq*)

The crime of highway robbery is an extremely serious offense, since it threatens the calm and stability of society itself. Two kinds of offenses are covered by the prohibition: robbery of travelers who are far from aid and armed entrance into a private home with the intent to rob it. Both Muslims and non-Muslims are protected from robbers by this law.

If one is convicted of *qat'al-tariq*, the punishment is amputation of the right hand and left foot for the first offense and amputation of the left hand and right foot for the second offense. If murder took place during an attempted robbery, the punishment is death by the sword. If there was murder accompanied by an actual theft, the penalty is crucifixion. The body is to be hung for three days. Unlike the normal case of murder, where the relatives of the victim have a choice of retaliation, blood money, or pardon of the offender, the death penalty here is mandatory. All accomplices must be treated in the same way. If one (a minor, for example) cannot be given the *hadd* punishment, neither can any of the others.

Discretionary punishment (*ta'zir*)

Ta'zir developed in the early Islamic empire of the Umayyads (A.D. 661–750) and grew out of the discretionary punishments the *qadi* imposed when he was part of the imperial bureaucratic apparatus.

The objectives of the punishment were prevention of the recurrence of the crime, deterrence to others, and reform of the guilty party. The judge attempted to accomplish those objectives by varying the punishment according to the circumstances of the case, of the convicted party, and of society. Consequently, acts of reparation and repentance by the offender are relevant to a judge's sentence. So also are interventions made before the court on behalf of the offender; though such interventions are forbidden in cases dealing with *hadd* offenses.

The punishments cover a range of severity:

- private admonition to the guilty party, sometimes by letter;
- public reprimand in court;
- public proclamation of the offender's guilt;
- suspended sentence;
- banishment;
- fine;
- flogging;

- imprisonment; and
- death.

The general rule in all of the schools, except the Maliki, is that no punishment in *ta'zir* can exceed a *hadd* penalty. Although the death penalty is to be used only in extreme cases, all the schools allow it.

The standard of proof is less strict than in cases of *hadd*: either a confession or the testimony of two witnesses is sufficient for conviction. In *ta'zir*, a confession is not retractable.

Offenses under *ta'zir* include perjury, usury, and slander. Many thefts, acts of unlawful intercourse, and false accusations of adultery that escape the rigorous rules under the *hadd* punishments can be dealt with under *ta'zir*. Selling wine may be punishable under this rule of discretionary jurisdiction.

For example, only under *ta'zir* can a non-Muslim be protected from the *kadhf*. Analogizing from adultery, jurists declare sodomy punishable by death, sometimes by stoning, but often with a public ignominy attached to the execution, such as being thrown from a high building or buried alive. As with adultery, four witnesses are required. Similarly, one who accuses another of homosexual acts or child molestation can be liable under *kadhf*. Bestiality, however, is not analogized with adultery because another person is not involved. The perpetrator, though not executed, is severely punished, and, in the Hanbali school, the animal is killed.

Because the central aspect of *ta'zir* is discretionary punishment by the judge, and because Islamic law categorizes offenses according to their penalties, there has never developed a rigorous code of penal offenses under *ta'zir* within the classical schools of law.

Homicide and bodily harm (*jinayat*)

Pre-Islamic Arabia treated attacks against one's tribesman as an attack on the tribe itself. Such an attack could result in a blood feud between the two tribes where any member of the other tribe was an object of vengeance. Through arbitration, justice could sometimes be secured by retaliation against the specific offender or by the payment of blood money to the victim's tribesmen.

Islamic law accepted the basic structure of the traditional Arabic law of homicide and bodily harm, but modified it in three ways:

- the blood feud was abolished;

- vengeance could be exacted only after a trial before a judicial authority, which determined the guilt of the accused; and
- punishment was scaled according to the offender's degree of culpability and the harm inflicted on the victim.

There is a wide variety in the interpretation of the rules by the various schools of law.

Three kinds of punishments can be permitted in cases of proven homicide or bodily harm:

- retaliation (*qisas*),
- blood money (*diya*),
- penitence (*kaffara*).

Where retaliation (*qisas*) is applied, the guilty party is liable to the same degree of harm as he inflicted on his victim. In the case of homicide, the nearest kinsman of the victim performs the retaliation. Where there is bodily harm, the victim himself is entitled to perform the act of vengeance.

In most schools, the general rule is that retaliation is allowed only in cases in which the victim was equal or superior to the attacker in terms of freedom and religion. So, for example, with a few exceptions among the opinions of the jurists, a father may not be killed in retaliation for murdering his child, but the child can be subject to the penalty for patricide. The same formula applies to homicidal actions between masters and slaves. The Hanafi school is alone in holding that a freeman may be subject to retaliation if he kills the slave of another.

Retaliation can come about if, after proper conviction, the nearest relative of the victim (or the master, in the case of a slave) demands it. The schools differ on the question of which relatives have standing to demand retaliation and which have the right to inflict a capital retaliation. If the victim has no living relatives, the right of retaliation falls to the state, which can execute the offender.

In the case of wounding, only the victim can demand retaliation. Before he dies from his injuries, a wounded man can, on his own, remit retaliation for the offender. If the guilty party dies before retaliation can be inflicted, the cause lapses entirely in the Maliki and Hanafi schools, but the shafi'i and the Hanbali schools allow blood money (*diya*) to be paid. If many persons participated in the murder, all can suffer retaliation if the action of any one of them would have resulted in death.

A murderer is to be killed in the same way as he killed, according to the Maliki and shafi'i schools. The Hanafi require execution by the sword and punish any other form of execution by ta'zir. The Hanbali jurists are divided on the issue. If a person is entitled to inflict retaliation but inflicts it before proper judicial procedure has been completed, he is subject to ta'zir. If a man avenges a killing without any possible legal entitlement, he himself is subject to the law of retaliation.

In cases of bodily harm, an exact equivalence of harm is inflicted on the perpetrator: a hand for a hand, a tooth for a tooth. Loss of sight can be avenged, but not the loss of an eyeball, for the injury cannot be exactly duplicated. Neither can retaliation be inflicted for the loss of the nose or penis. Only blood money is permitted as punishment in those cases.

If there was an attack by many, all the perpetrators suffer the same loss as the wounded victim, but this is not permitted in the Hanafi school. Nor do the Hanafi permit retaliation for wounding between men and women or between slaves. When retaliation is allowed, all schools except the Maliki allow the victim to return the wound. The Maliki assign an expert to inflict the punishment. Any excess harm is punishable by ta'zir.

The second form of punishment is blood money. The diya is sometimes an alternative to retaliation, at the option of the nearest relative of the slain person or of the wounded victim. At other times, depending on the circumstances of the crime, diya and forgiveness are the only options available.

The traditional diya, as taken over from Arabic custom, is set at two levels. In serious cases the heavier diya is imposed, set at one hundred female camels equally divided between one, two, three, and four year olds. In less serious cases the lighter diya is imposed, amounting to eighty female camels, similarly divided by age, in addition to twenty one-year-old male camels.

The near relatives of the offender pay the diya to the heirs of the deceased, or to the wounded victim. If the near relatives cannot be found, the state assumes the obligation to pay the diya. In all but the Hanafi school, the full amount of the diya is due only when the victim is a free male Muslim. If the victim is a dhimmi (a non-Muslim protected by treaty) or a musta'min (a non-Muslim under safe-conduct pass), the diya ranges from one-third to one-half of that for a Muslim except in the Hanafi school, which requires full pay-

ment. The diya for a murdered slave is his market value.

The diya for bodily injury is a proportion of the payment for loss of life. If there is only one of a bodily part, such as the nose, the diya is the same as for loss of life. If there are more than one, the diya is proportionately smaller—for example, one-half for an arm, a leg, or an eye; one-tenth for a finger; a third of one-tenth for each joint of a finger; and one-twentieth for a tooth. The jurists have established an elaborate scale of payments. If an injury falls outside of the defined examples, compensation is paid on the basis of the "actual harm suffered" (but does not include any pain and suffering endured). The diya for a woman is half that of a man, but in no case, such as for partial injuries, is it to fall below a third of what a man would receive.

The third form of punishment is penitence (kaffara), but penitence is never the sole required punishment. When imposed, it is attached in certain kinds of cases to the payment of diya. An act of penitence consists in freeing a Muslim slave or, if one has no slaves, in fasting during daylight hours for two consecutive months. Generally speaking, Islamic law holds that those entitled to retaliation or diya may remit the punishment on their own accord or may agree to any level of settlement, although not normally higher than the legal diya.

Procedurally, the charge of homicide must be brought by the nearest relative of the deceased, or by the wounded victim prior to his death. Proof is by retractable confession or by testimony of two male witnesses. In addition, there is the unusual procedure known as kasama, whereby the oaths of fifty reliable persons who are not witnesses are accepted as proof where incomplete evidence has created a presumption of guilt. The Maliki school utilizes kasama to complete proof. The Hanafi use it to prevent a conviction.

In a number of instances, killing or inflicting bodily injury is excused. Of course, retaliation properly applied after an adjudication of guilt is permitted. There is no culpability if a man kills his wife, daughter, or sister as well as her lover if he discovers them in an act of unlawful intercourse, and none, except in the Maliki school, for harm or death inflicted with the consent of the victim.

Self-defense is permitted if it is an act of resistance to an unlawful assault and if it is proportionate to the danger. Preemptive action is allowed to forestall an imminent attack. However, in the Hanafi school, one must pay the heavier *diya* if he uses a deadly weapon to kill a minor or insane person in self-defense. Killing combatants in lawful war is, of course, permitted and, in many cases, may take on an obligatory nature. One is permitted to kill male non-Muslims who refuse to pay the obligatory poll tax and who also refuse to convert to Islam.

Most schools divide homicide into three categories (the Hanafi have developed five):

- Willful homicide is an action resulting in death that was undertaken with no legal excuse, with the intention to wound or kill, and by means of an instrument that normally causes death. The punishment is retaliation or, if remitted, the heavier *diya*, plus loss to the offender of any rights of inheritance from the deceased. All schools except the Hanafi categorize as willful homicide death resulting from intentional false testimony at trial, as well as death caused by intentionally withholding food and water. The *shafi'i* and the Hanbali also term as willful homicide any fatal action resulting from repeated blows, no one of which would normally cause death.
- Quasi-willful homicide is intent to kill or wound with an instrument not normally known to be fatal. If death results, the punishment consists of the heavier *diya*, acts of penitence, and loss of inheritance rights. If only bodily harm results, the offense is then one of willful wounding, the punishment for which is retaliation or, if remitted, the appropriate proportion of the *diya*.
- Accidental homicide occurs when the offender either did not intend to kill a person or he did intend to kill a person but believed that he was acting legally. For example, if one shoots at an animal but misses and kills a person instead, or if one believes he is shooting at a deer but in reality is shooting at a human being, or if during wartime one kills a Muslim under the impression that he is a non-Muslim, the case will be treated as accidental homicide. The punishment is payment of the lighter *diya*, the obligation to perform acts of penitence, and in some schools the loss of inheritance rights.

Apostasy (*ridda*)

There is also the special case of the apostate from Islam. Many jurists classify apostasy as a *hadd* offense. He who kills an apostate is, in some schools, free from the law of retaliation. In the Hanafi school, a male apostate is given three days to repent before execution; a female is imprisoned and beaten until she repents. Some modern Muslim jurists assert that the penalty for apostasy was a later accretion from the offense of treason and has no authority from the Qur'an or elsewhere. In addition to apostasy, some jurists classify rebellion (*baghi*) as a *hadd* offense, but not in the Hanafi school.

Discretionary administrative penalties (*siyasa*)

Under Islamic law, the secular authorities do not possess a power to legislate independently of the *shari'a*, but the state may develop public policies by enacting and enforcing administrative regulations. The regulations are designed to help effectuate the *shari'a* and to regulate those areas in which the *shari'a* has left gaps. *Siyasa* regulations are not supposed to conflict with the provisions of the *shari'a*. Nonetheless, it has been through the mechanism of *siyasa* that the Islamic states have supplanted many of the penal requirements of the *shari'a*. The combination of *siyasa* and the power over jurisdiction effectively shifted the definition and enforcement of criminal regulations to the state, although the *shari'a* significantly influenced the content of the secular criminal law.

Acts of penitence (*kaffara*)

Kaffara consists in the performance of certain acts of penitence to cover or expiate sinful acts. The acts of penitence are the freeing of a Muslim slave, fasting during daylight hours (while also abstaining from sexual intercourse), or, in some cases, giving alms to the poor. In rare cases, *kaffara* is accomplished by the sacrifice of a goat, sheep, camel, or cow.

Although the law books prescribe *kaffara* for certain sins, the imposition of the penance is almost always voluntary. Only in exceptional cases can a *qadi* require *kaffara*. Offenses for which *kaffara* is prescribed include breaking an oath, perjury, breaking fast during the holy month of Ramadan, or hunting or breaking other rules while in a consecrated state for the holy pilgrimage to Mecca.

At the dawn of the twenty-first century, the criminal portions of the *shari'a* remain an artifact. In an unhappy irony, some modern Islamists believe they are reinstituting a purer Islam when they use the formulaic notions of crime of the ancient *shari'a*. By an unreflective copying of that part of a legal code that was at once undeveloped and often impractical of application, they obscure the grander sweep of classical Islamic civilization, and, in some cases, erect an unnecessary barrier to the full realization of fundamental human rights.

DAVID F. FORTE

See also CORPORATE PUNISHMENT; CRIMINAL PROCEDURE: COMPARATIVE ASPECTS.

BIBLIOGRAPHY

ANDERSON, JAMES N. D. "Homicide in Islamic Law." *Bulletin of the School of Oriental & African Studies, University of London* 13 (1951): 811–828.

———. *The Maliki Law of Homicide.* Zaria, Nigeria: 1959.

BASSIOUNI, M. CHERIF. *The Islamic Criminal Justice System.* London and New York: Oceana, 1982.

DONALDSON, DWIGHT M. *Studies in Muslim Ethics.* London: SPCK, 1953.

FAIRCHILD, ERIKA S. *Comparative Criminal Justice Systems.* Delmont, Calif.: Wadsworth, 1993.

FORTE, DAVID F. *Islamic Law: Classical and Contemporary Applications.* Lanham, Md.: Austin and Winfield, 1999.

IBN DUYAN, IBRAHIM IBN MUHAMMAD IBN SALIM MANAR AL-SABIL. *Crime and Punishment under Hanbali Law.* Translated by George M. Baroody. Cairo: 1962.

KHALIL IBN ISHAK, AL JUNDI. *Maliki Law* (The Mukhtasar of Sidi Khalil). Translated by F. H. Ruxton. London: Luzac & Co., 1916.

AL-KHIRAQI. "The 'Mukhtasar' of al-Khiraqi: A Tenth-Century Work on Islamic Jurisprudence." Translated by Anas Khalid. Ph.D. diss., New York University, 1992.

LIEBESNY, HERBERT J. *The Law of the Near and Middle East: Readings, Cases, and Materials.* Albany: State University of New York Press, 1975.

LIPPMAN, MATTHEW; MCCONVILLE, SEAN; and YERUSHALMI, MORDECAI. *Islamic Criminal Law & Procedure: An Introduction.* New York: Praeger, 1988.

AL-MARGHINANI. *The Hedaya.* Translated by C. Hamilton. London: W. H. Allen, 1870.

MAYER, ANN ELIZABETH. "Libyan Legislation in Defense of Arabo-Islamic Sexual Mores." *American Journal of Comparative Law* 28 (1980): 287–313.

NAWAWI (MAHIUDIN ABU ZAKARIA YAHYA IBN SHARIF ENNAWAWI). *Minhaj al–talibin: A Manual of Muhammadan Law According to the School of Shafi'i.* Translated by E. C. Howard from the French translation of L. W. C. Van Den Berg. London: W. Thacker & Co., 1914.

QUERRY, A. *Droit Musulman: Receuil de Lois Concernant les Musulmans Schyites.* Paris: Imprimerie nationale, 1871. Page 470.

RAHIM, ABDUR. *The Principles of Muhammadan Jurisprudence According to the Hanafi, Maliki, Shafi'i, and Hanbali Schools.* (1911). Reprint. Westport, Conn.: Hyperion Press, 1981.

SCHACHT, JOSEPH. *An Introduction to Islamic Law.* Oxford: Clarendon Press, 1964.

SIDDIQI, MUHAMMAD IQBAL. *The Penal Law of Islam.* Tahore: Kazi Publications, 1979.

SOLAIM, SOLIMAN A. "Saudi Arabia's Judicial System." *Middle East Journal* 25 (1971): 403–407.

VICKER, RAY. "Moslem Justice." *Wall Street Journal* 11 May 1979, pp. 1, 30.

VINCENT, M. B. *Études sur la Loi Musulmane: Législation Criminelle.* Paris: Joubert, Librarie de la Coar de Cassition, 1842.

COMPARATIVE CRIMINAL LAW AND ENFORCEMENT: PRELITERATE SOCIETIES

Emerging problems

Preliterate societies do not constitute a single type of society but a whole assortment of societies. Just as most people speak about English, Russian, or Chinese Law, an anthropologist might speak about Tongan, Tiv, or Zapotec law. Any study of criminal law in preliterate societies must take this diversity into account. The comparative perspective, however, need not stress only the differences among preliterate societies, or between preliterate societies and our own, but may uncover similarities as well. The inhabitants of Mexican mountain villages are generally peaceful, whereas New Guinea highland communities tend to be warlike. Melanesians settle most of their disputes through negotiation, and so do Americans. Both the Lenje of Zambia and the Japanese stress restitution.

However, Western concepts present difficulties. The concept of crime, for example, an idea related to the development of the state, becomes problematic when applied cross-culturally in societies with little or no government. The world of preliterate and literate societies presents rich contexts in which to examine the problem of universal categories.

Early studies. Nineteenth-century anthropologists interested in preliterate law were armchair speculators who first investigated the differences between Western and non-Western law. Some theorists, such as Emile Durkheim, described primitive law as penal and repressive in contrast with that of more advanced and specialized societies, which generally used restitutive sanctions. Others, like Leonard Hobhouse, challenged that distinction, arguing instead that as human societies become more advanced, their legal systems progress from a reliance on self-redress to formal sanctions of punishment or restitution.

Later generations of anthropologists studied societies through firsthand fieldwork, which revealed that the models developed by armchair anthropologists were either oversimplified or wrong. These "newer" anthropologists were struck by the wide diversity in social organization and attempted to understand and then explain the ways in which different societies manage the serious wrongs that might endanger peace and security in what appeared to be bounded societies.

The most powerful break with the past was made by Bronislaw Malinowski, a field observer of the first rank who used his detailed observations to destroy widespread law-and-order myths about preliterate peoples. In *Crime and Custom in Savage Society* (1926) he argued persuasively that people do not automatically conform to rules of conduct in what were then called the "simpler societies": positive inducements were as important as sanctions in inducing social conformity. Malinowski also called attention to the important connection between social control and social relations, an idea that foreshadowed a generation of anthropological research on how peace could be achieved in societies lacking in central authority, codes, courts, and constables. His definition of *crime* was "the law broken." Precision in definition defied Malinowski, who wrote that crime in Trobriand societies could be only vaguely defined as an "outburst of passion, sometimes the breach of a definite taboo, sometimes an attempt on person or property (murder, theft, assault), sometimes an indulgence in too high ambitions or wealth, not sanctioned by tradition, in conflict with the prerogatives of the chief or some notable" (p. 99).

A. R. Radcliffe-Brown, a contemporary of Malinowski, was more jurisprudential. In 1933 he made use of Roscoe Pound's definition of *law* as "social control through the systematic application of the force of politically organized society" (p. 202). Radcliffe-Brown had studied the Andaman Islanders of the Bay of Bengal, a people he described as without any law at all. By defining *law* in terms of organized legal sanctions, Radcliffe-Brown concluded that in some simpler societies there is no law. He did not find terms such as *civil law* and *criminal law* useful in analyzing data from other societies; instead, he observed a distinction between public law (which made use of penal or repressive sanctions) and private law (which emphasized restitutive sanctions). Like Malinowksi, Radcliffe-Brown viewed crimes as acts that engender a collective feeling of moral indignation.

Modern approaches. Today most anthropologists of law do not define *crime*, nor do they attempt to impose such distinctions as those between crime, tort, delict, sin, and immorality on their data. Boundaries are porous. Hardly any anthropologist would accept as valid the distinction between public and private law. Distinctions are discussed, but anthropologists increasingly report data without attempting to categorize them in terms of Western legal thought (unless Western implants are at issue); instead they adopt, for purposes of analysis, the categories used by the people studied or of the social scientist, and eschew attempts to define *crime* in a universal manner.

Diverse concepts of crime. Antisocial conduct is a universal aspect of group life, but the forms it takes and the reactions it provokes vary. In some societies today infanticide, cannibalism, theft, or the selling of products known to be harmful fall in the area of conduct approved by authorities, but standards of good and bad behavior are not constant over time. Records covering the Tswana peoples of Africa over a hundred-year period indicate not only that "crimes" are in a state of flux but also that crime is not necessarily disapproved of by all members of society. In one example, Isaac Schapera observed that a "civil" wrong was treated as such by one chief, made a "penal" offense by another, and denied legal recognition by a third. Notions of specific wrongs may be internalized by and reflect the behavioral norms of a group, or they may be ordered from above. Schapera's study indicates that native law is not static and that it was founded on deliberate enactment as well as custom.

Since there are no wrongs that are universal to preliterate societies and no behavior that is bad in itself, the nature of an act alone cannot be used to determine its social or legal meaning. For the Ontong Javanese, as for many societies, killing kin is murder and killing non-kin is not. Among the Tiv of Nigeria, killing thieves or witches may be permissible.

The relationship of the parties concerned may determine whether an act is regarded as a crime. For the Kapauku of New Guinea, intra-confederacy killing is murder, whereas killing outside the confederacy is warfare if approved by the elders; otherwise, starting a war is a crime punishable by death. In New Guinea an offense is defined more by social context than by the nature of the act; there are no broad distinctions between types of offenses, and opinions about what constitutes the "same" crime vary widely from group to group or among individuals in a group. Among the Kipsigi of Kenya the same offense will meet with different consequences according to political differences between the opposing parties.

The task of discovering factors that determine the seriousness of an act has encouraged a relativistic approach, since categories in some societies may bear no resemblance to standard Western ones. There is, for example, no special Lozi term for *crime*, although Max Gluckman (1965, p. 4) reports a distinction between *wrong* and *great wrong*. The Tiv rank acts by their social consequences, the most serious being incest, homicide, and sometimes adultery. The Yakan of the Philippines distinguish between wrongs that can lead to disputes, and wrongs against God (or moral wrongs), which do not bring legal consequences to the offender. Among the Jalé, now of Irian Jaya, intention is less important than consequence in defining an act as an offense. Attempted murder is not a crime since it inflicts no harm, but if a woman dies in childbirth the husband is as responsible for the death (since he impregnated her) as is a man who kills another in a fight. Among the Zinacantecan of southern Mexico, circumstances surrounding an offense are crucial; if an offense is committed when the offender is not under the influence of alcohol, or is a repeated offense, the act is considered serious enough to require punishment as well as the compensation sufficient for lesser offenses.

Radcliffe-Brown's distinction between public and private law has not been useful for modern anthropologists because of the difficulty in determining whether an offense is against the individual or the society, as Karl Llewellyn and E. Adamson Hoebel have shown with regard to Cheyenne society. Often it is both.

Diverse concepts of punishment. Early notions about sanctions in preliterate societies are not supported by data. Durkheim's theory that repressive and penal law characterizes the "inferior societies" is incorrect. Indeed, restitution plays a predominant role in face-to-face societies. Restitution is the process whereby money or services are paid by the offender or the offender's family to the victim or the victim's family: it may be paid in kind (a life for a life) or in equivalence (a wife for a life). There are various forms of liability: absolute and contingent, collective and individual. Klaus-Friedrich Koch has proposed that the distinction between absolute and contingent (relative) liability depends upon the availability of third parties to facilitate a case. Without formal governmental control in indigenous third-party mechanisms, liability will be absolute. Similarly, collective responsibility is likely to prevail where decent groups are the primary units in social organization.

Among the Berbers of the Atlas Mountains of Morocco, restitution follows a pattern of collective and contingent liability. After an act of physical aggression, the culprit and his close kinsmen escape to a sanctuary provided by religious leaders for a cooling-off period, which is then followed by a period of mediated negotiation between the victim's group and that of the offender. Compromises usually recognize degrees of seriousness of the act and the status of the victim; the higher the victim's status, the greater the restitution. The Egyptian bedouin of the western desert regard the consequence of the act and the status of both parties as the primary determinants of the amount of restitution. The Ifugao of northern Luzon recognize a scale of payment that varies according to the social position of the injured party and the offender; higher payments accompany higher positions.

The reparation process may function as a deterrent, since the process implicates kin groups on both sides. Once a reparation has been agreed on, the victim is often urged to avoid further conflict with the offender so as not to forfeit the kin's right to compensation, and the members of the offender's group usually have a vested interest in keeping him in line because they are paying for his actions. The threat of a mutually destructive feud gives added incentive to abide by the agreement. However, a society that uses restitution as a strategy may also use retaliation, raids, property seizures, and fines. Retaliative sanctions are systematized through rules governing how the injured party may strike back and how much the injured parties should demand for righting a wrong or punishing an individual.

Restitution can be found in societies both with and without formalized political systems. Even societies without centralized systems—the Yurok of California, the Ifugao of Luzon, or the bedouin of Egypt—can have very sophisticated, even if unwritten, indemnity codes. Such substantive law can develop independently of legal procedures, courts and complex political organization. On the other hand, people can have a formal court system and not use it. In Japan restitution is settled almost entirely extrajudicially, by agreements between victim and offender.

Finally, restitution is used sparingly in preliterate societies, most often in cases of murder, theft, debt, adultery, and property damage. The restitutive sanction, whether collective or individual, restores social equilibrium by addressing the needs of the victim or the victim's kin, by restating social values, and by providing a means for reintegrating the offender into the mainstream without too much stigma. Among the Valley Zapotec of Mexico, who follow both village and state law, the process of reintegration into the village begins after offender's release from jail. This process entails a gradual resumption of relationships between offender and community by means of material and interpersonal exchanges. By Zapotec definition, ex-offenders build up social relationships by exchange as a means of removing stigma. The Zapotec do not keep the deviant permanently on the margin of society but reintegrate him through the resumption of social interchange and through a "collective amnesia," which serves to deny that the crime ever occurred in the first place.

Habitual misbehavior is considered more threatening than single offenses in preliterate as in complex societies. The custom of group lynching among the Kamba of East Africa was reserved for habitual thieves or sorcerers. These community killings involved no blood guilt but did require consent of an offender's nearest relatives. The Tiv are critical of Nigerian state law, which punishes single murders harshly while denying the community the right to execute habitual offenders for behavior that the Tiv see as more dangerous. The Tiv judge a person's general behavior, rather than a specific wrong.

Social control and the state. The evolution of the state and the growth of governmental machinery for regulating social relations provided the political context for the development of penal criminal law. In large and complex societies, in which social differentiation is great and conflicting values are juxtaposed, a small number of people representing powerful interests often define what the law will call criminal. The criminal act becomes an act against the state. As the initiator of third-party hearings, the offended merely becomes the victim, and loses the important status of plaintiff.

With the emergence of the state, there is an increasing reliance on penal sanctions to deter antisocial behavior. In preliterate or prestate societies the legal sanction, whether penal or restitutive, represents only one means of enforcing conformity to norms. Control mechanisms such as sorcery and suicide, which had often been labeled as criminal behavior by Western observers, were seen by Malinowski as legal and socially rehabilitative mechanisms—behaviors that supported the preliterate social order. Beatrice Whiting's work on Paiute Indians reported that sorcery was found in societies with decentralized political systems, and she argued that sorcery is an important mechanism of social control in decentralized systems. A study of purely criminal law among preliterate peoples misses just such important phenomena of their legal life.

Radcliffe-Brown argued that in preliterate societies there is a close connection between religious behavior and the sanctions of criminal law. In fact, supernatural sanctions may be more threatening to an offender than physical retaliation against him or material compensation to his victim, because they are so vague and unpredictable. Public shame and ridicule or the sanction of supernaturally imposed sickness both constitute a means for societal regulation. When formalized legal sanctions coexist with less formal controls, the latter have often been more effective in restraining disruptive social conduct and strengthening the cohesion of social relations. It is important to realize that courts, police, and the like are not necessary to achieve order in societies where there is a wide range of checks on human conduct that are functionally equivalent to enforcement agencies in state societies. Among the eighteenth-century Iroquois, for example, theft and vandalism were almost unknown. Public opinion in the form of gossip and ridicule was sufficient to deter most members of the tribe from such property crimes.

Crime and social structure

Order and disorder. Theories have been proposed to explain the relation between modes of production and the organization of social controls. For example, a number of anthropologists observed that hunters and gatherers do not develop means for adjudicating disputes, but rather for avoidance of disputes. Order and disorder are present in both small and large societies. For this reason, the presence or absence of order (however one measures order) is not easily explained by theories of size, means of livelihood, or ecology. Although understanding diversity in relation to law is crucial to understanding prestate societies as a group, law as it relates to order can never be comprehended by universal rules of evidence outside the context of the particular society that houses this law.

A productive approach to an examination of order and disorder is to analyze the influence of social organization. Most ethnographic studies of a specific society describe how relationships or institutions function to coordinate social activities or to organize social relations, or they describe how the society is disordered by just such factors. In the social organization of the Mexican Zapotec town of Talea, the binding force of reciprocity and the principles of social organization provide systematic ordering (Nader). The ties that link citizens are those of kinship, locale, common work interests, friendships, and shared obligations and values. Three dimensions of Talean social organization best indicate the manner in which principles of social and cultural control operate outside of governmental organization.

First, in Talea all groups, whether kinship, governmental, or religious, are organized hierarchically according to sex, age, wealth, or experience. Second, a value is placed on symmetry (a term that translates as *equality* only in some contexts), which serves to level relationships. Such leveling mechanisms as those that redistribute wealth from the rich to the poor mediate the harsher aspects of hierarchy but do not sabotage the virtues of superordinate-subordinate relationships. The third dimension of Talean social organization brings people together as groups or as individuals, and at the same time divides them by linking some of them with different groups. These three dimensions stratify, level, and integrate the town: they reinforce hierarchy and symmetry by buttressing traditional and changing values, and they strengthen the linkages by ensuring the presence of third parties in case of dispute. Asymmetry is both unappealing and dangerous; it is often the underlying cause of envy, witchcraft accusations, and court disputes. The integrative links between individuals and groups provide a safety valve and with the aid of harmony ideology cool most disputes before excessive pressure builds up.

The Taleans are therefore a relatively peaceful people, unlike their neighbors in the mountains, the people of Yalalag, who have a high annual rate of violent killings. Yalalag, divided into two traditionally opposed parts, each with its own leaders, illustrates that without social and cultural principles that link groups together, discourse in the peaceful settlement of disputes does not develop. Although Talea and Yalalag are similar in cultural history, size, ecology, and economy, differences in social organization have produced different means for managing problems and disputes. The Taleans tend to use third-party mechanisms and coercive harmony, whereas the people of Yalalag use self-help tactics such as assault, battery, and killing.

The social correlates of relatively violent or peaceful societies have been the subject of extensive research. For example, studies on preliterate societies have correlated place of residence after marriage with the management of conflict. H. U. E. Thoden van Velzen and W. Van Wetering have examined the question of residence and violence cross-culturally and have found a consistent relationship between the predominant use of passive means of managing conflict, and the use of matrilocal residency rules, which locate married couples with maternal relatives. They also recognized the relationships between residence with the paternal relatives of the group, the development of mutually exclusive fraternal interest groups, and the frequent use of physical violence among males within such societies.

Koch found a relationship between patrilocality and the use of physical violence in the Jalé society of western New Guinea (Irian Jaya). In the New Guinea highlands most disputes are of the intermunicipal sort, like contemporary international conflicts in which a sovereign power does not exist. The Jalé are a farming people who live in villages divided into two or more wards. The wards form the principal war-making units in intravillage and intervillage conflicts. There are no political and judicial offices, and thus self-help—often in the form of violent retaliation—is an institutionalized method of resolving conflicts when negotiation fails.

A number of problems are evident in Jalé conflict management. The first is the snowball effect of inadequate procedures to deal with grievances: if there are no authorities capable of settling conflicts, even minor disagreements may escalate into war between whole villages. A second is the potential of every retaliation to generate new troubles. Brakes are provided by kinship and residence, but these are not strong enough to prevent escalation in any particular conflict. Such observations support the proposition that both the style of conflict resolution and the occurrence of conflict derive from a society's principles of human association.

The factor of early environment. A cross-cultural study of the correlates of crime by the psychologists Margaret Bacon, Irvin Child, and Herbert Barry examined the frequency of theft and personal crimes (defined to include assault, rape, suicide, sorcery, murder, and making false accusation) in forty-eight preliterate societies. They found that both types of offense are more frequent in societies having polygymous mother-child households than in those societies with monogamous, nuclear households.

Whiting expanded on this work and examined the idea associating household organization and conflict frequencies in six cultures. Her study combined social, structural, and psychological variables to test this hypothesis: If, during the first two or three years of life, a boy is frequently with the mother and only infrequently with the father, he will identify strongly with his mother; if, later in life, he is living in a world dominated by men, he will face internal conflict, which may lead to attempts to prove his masculinity. The "masculine protest hypothesis" was concerned with the sex identity conflict theory: where the father has less importance in infancy and where men have higher prestige and salience from childhood on, violence becomes an expression of "protest masculinity," as among the Gusii of Kenya or the Khalapur Rajput of India.

Witchcraft in preliterate societies. Like killing, the act of sorcery or witchcraft is not necessarily a wrong; rather, it depends for its cultural meaning on the context and locus of the action and on who is involved. Furthermore, in many societies there is no division between the natural and the supernatural. For the Mexican Zinacantecans, earthly conflicts are only manifestations of conflicts between supernatural beings and people, often expressed by means of witchcraft. The Kapauku of New Guinea consider kill-ing by arrow, by sorcery, or by forced violation of food taboos to be identical crimes, since all are attacks on people. The Gwembe Tonga of Zambia treat poisoning and sorcery in the same manner; the Tonga reason that they are functionally identical, since both are covert attacks that make people fall sick. The Barotse and Gisu of Zambia and Kenya and the Sepik of Melanesia believe that no death or illness is entirely natural. Each death brings the question, "Who has caused this?"

In witchcraft societies people usually fear sorcery, although not everyone condemns it. At times sorcery is condemned, but sorcerers are not punished. The Sepik rarely accuse anyone of sorcery, because they fear reprisals from evil spirits. Among the Gisu, a sorcerer will be killed if the whole community agrees to the killing. In many societies sorcery was formerly sanctioned by death, but today this penalty is considered illegal under state law, and, indeed, such traditional punishment is now defined as murder by some national legal systems.

The identity of the initiator of witchcraft is important, especially since witchcraft itself is frequently inferred from death or sickness rather than directly observed. Among the Azande of the Sudan, people accused of witchcraft are usually those whom people in the community already had cause to hate. Women can be vulnerable to charges of witchcraft in partrilineal societies, where they are seen both as outsiders and as a divisive force. Men may or may not accuse lineage members, depending on whether rivalry or solidarity is paramount.

Some have examined witchcraft as an index to social disorder. Agricultural, rather than pastoral, communities tend to have witchcraft outbreaks as a response to overpopulation, scarcities, or inequalities. Witchcraft in such settings allows people an excuse to leave the community either because they have been accused or because they are afraid of being witched (Colson). Gluckman connected the witchcraft outbreak of 1957–1958 among the Barotse with societal strain caused by the young going off to work and bringing back money, which resulted in loss of prestige by powerful tribal elders. The accusations of witchcraft in this instance were by the young against the old. Waves of witchcraft accusations may be connected with changing times, as among the Barotse; with stress and periods of unrest, as among the Tonga; and with the absence of centralized political machinery, as among the Paiutes of the United States. During

Great Britain's colonial period, the use of witchcraft by indigenous peoples led to heated debates among British administrators, who were called upon to maintain the native customary law according to their policy of indirect rule, which incorporated indigenous law.

Generalizing about small-scale societies

Most stereotypes of preliterate societies have not withstood the empirical test. Preliterate societies, like modern ones, support various, and sometimes contradictory, systems of rules. Adjectives that apply to the law of some African societies—communal, restitutive, cloaked with magic-religious beliefs—do not apply to the Australian aborigines, the Plains Indians of North America, or other societies that may be more individualistic and dominated by consensual, rather than litigious, thinking in relation to law.

One can no longer argue that small, face-to-face societies are more peaceful or that large and complex societies, where relations between strangers predominate, are more naturally crime-prone. It is not true that preliterate societies use negotiation to the exclusion of arbitration or mediation, or that industrial societies use adjudication to the exclusion of negotiation. Collective liability is as much a part of the thinking of contemporary insurance companies as it is of traditional Berbers. Preliterate law may be flexible and highly effective or highly unpredictable and destructive because of the absence of formalized controls. There are wide differences in the degree to which societal wrongs are recognized and punished. Research on exogamy rules (patterns of marrying outside the group) has revealed that official sanctions vary from one society to another in response to violation of these rules and include death, fines, beating, banishment, and invoking the disapproval of supernatural forces.

The rare attempts by anthropologists to define the nature of "primitive" crime have frequently placed undue emphasis on categories drawn from Western cultures. Although few efforts have been made to produce a definition of crime that can be applied cross-culturally, it seems clear that the results of norm violations across cultures are loss of status and change in social position. The development of a cross-cultural understanding of "crime" may lie in the study of those normative violations that consistently result in downward change in the social rank for the violator. Such patterns will vary in meaning with authority structures that may be consensual or authoritarian. In preliterate societies the numerous combinations of structures provide means for preventing the escalation of conflicts, and yet they also generate interconnecting systems of behavior in the domains of kinship, economics, politics, and law that give the air of suitability to acts which, to the Western mind, may appear deviant.

Essentially, similarities in social structure and culture will produce similarities in criminal offenses and in the management of such offenses. In small-scale settings, where people know one another and share a broad range of personal ties, there is a special kind of indirect social control that is absent from, or almost inoperative in, settings where anonymity functions as an escape from the controls of kin and neighbor. In this second setting, criminal offenses are increasingly a result of the interaction between people who do not know one another. In the West, such offenses are met directly with sanctions that are likely to be repressive and penal rather than restitutive. Gluckman has noted that the range of relevance is narrow in cases involving strangers and broad in those involving kinsmen. A dispute between two parties who are strangers need not end in reconciliation, but rather can be adjudicated and end in a clear decision. Changes in relationships between disputants and population movements accompany modernization processes. With development new states use transplant law to monopolize the legitimate use of violence and social control in general. Other systems of control either cease to be important, in which case there is increased dependence on police enforcement, or they compete with imported law. In other words, political encapsulation brings into contact different systems of right and wrong and different ideas about who is a wrong doer and how to treat them.

Preliterate societies in the modern world

Surviving preliterate societies are increasingly being encapsulated by the modern bureaucratic state, a process that began under colonial governments and has developed further under conditions of independence. Creating central administrations has had a pervasive influence on local communities by acting as a brake on intervillage hostilities. Elizabeth Colson reports that before becoming subjects of the British colonial administration, the Valley and Plateau Tonga of Zambia lived in fear of intervillage raids. Of course, the fear of violence in such societies led to avoiding and preventing violence, but where insecurity was common, colonial governments may have been welcomed as allies.

On the other hand, political encapsulation forces collision and collusion. The Indonesian state and Papua New Guinea entered into economic development by invading indigenous territory, whereby local people became trespassers on their own land. Resisters are considered criminals. In addition, encapsulation may establish "insider-outsider" distinctions that were absent prior to the introduction of modern politics, and may open opportunities for those who see an advantage in using violence. Power is now an issue. Among the Maya Indians of Guatemala, an encroaching Guatemalan state system has been associated with the disintegration of village leadership and with increased resort to homicide for the management of problems and disputes in the community. Alternatives to, and controls over, the use of physical violence resulted from the nature of contact between the two types of systems—state and village. The contact between local and state organizations produced a similar result among the Sidamo of southwest Ethiopia. The Sidamo have increasingly neglected procedural rules of community law, developed a preference for revenge, and refused to accept traditional sanctions. The increased use of national courts underlies these changes in the manner of labeling and processing.

However, not all contacts between indigenous and state systems of control produce similar results. The mountain Zapotec use harmony legal models to control the amount and impact of state judicial involvement in village affairs. It is considered a serious offense against the autonomous Zapotec village to aid the state in gaining control over the processing of a dispute settlement. Most villages are able to maintain control over their customary boundaries of authority by maintaining effective mechanisms for local dispute settlement. Indigenous communities may not define state law as "legal" when the state actively participates in disputes that villagers wish to settle among themselves.

Although crimes, from the Western perspective, are violations of the law, violations of the law from the cross-cultural perspective are not necessarily crimes. Radcliffe-Brown's definition of *crime* in primitive societies as a violation of public order is cross-culturally inapplicable if the exercise of a penal, rather than a civil, sanction is at issue. Research on preliterate societies has not yet established that the cost to the victim is the criterion commonly applied in classifying behavior as criminal or in establishing the severity of the offense. What has been established is that societies without criminal populations are those that prevent individuals from obtaining criminal status through their behavior, not those that prevent violations of the "law." The record on world societies has well illustrated that crime is a cultural construct.

LAURA NADER

See also ADVERSARY SYSTEM; CIVIL AND CRIMINAL DIVIDE; CRIMINAL LAW REFORM: CONTINENTAL EUROPE; CRIMINAL LAW REFORM: ENGLAND; CRIMINAL PROCEDURE: COMPARATIVE ASPECTS; RESTORATIVE JUSTICE; SHAMING PUNISHMENTS.

BIBLIOGRAPHY

BACON, MARGARET K.; CHILD, IRWIN L.; and BARRY, HERBERT, III. "A Cross-cultural Study of Correlates of Crime." *Journal of Abnormal and Social Psychology* (1963): 291–300.

BOHANNAN, PAUL. *Justice and Judgement among the Tiv.* London: Oxford University Press for the International African Institute, 1957.

COLSON, ELIZABETH. *Tradition and Contract: The Problem of Order.* Chicago: Aldine, 1974.

DURKHEIM, ÉMILE. *The Division of Labor in Society* (1893). Translated by George Simpson. New York: Free Press, 1964.

GLUCKMAN, MAX. *The Judicial Process among the Barotse of Northern Rhodesia.* 2d ed. With corrections and two additional chapters. Manchester, U.K.: Manchester University Press for the Institute for Social Research, University of Zambia, 1967.

———. *Politics, Law, and Ritual in Tribal Society.* Chicago: Aldine, 1965.

HOBHOUSE, LEONARD T. *Morals in Evolution: A Study in Comparative Ethics* (1906). 7th ed. With a new introduction by Morris Ginsburg. London: Chapman & Hall, 1951.

KOCH, KLAUS-FRIEDRICH. *War and Peace in Jalemo: The Management of Conflict in Highland New Guinea.* Cambridge, Mass.: Harvard University Press, 1974.

LLEWELLYN, KARL N., and HOEBEL, E. ADAMSON *The Cheyenne Way: Conflict and Case Law in Primitive Jurisprudence.* Norman: University of Oklahoma Press, 1941.

MALINOWSKI, BRONISLAW. *Crime and Custom in Savage Society.* New York: Harcourt, Brace, 1926. Reprint. New York: Humanities Press, 1951.

NADER, LAURA. *Harmony Ideology. Justice and Control in a Zapotec Mountain Village.* Stanford, Calif.: Stanford University Press, 1990.

RADCLIFFE-BROWN, A. R. "Primitive Law." *Encyclopedia of the Social Sciences*, vol. 9. Edited by Edwin R. A. Seligman, Alvin Johnson, et al. New York: Macmillan, 1933. Pages 202–206.

SCHAPERA, ISAAC. "Some Anthropological Concepts of 'Crime'" The Hobhouse Memorial Lecture." *British Journal of Sociology* 23 (1972): 381–394.

STARR, JUNE, and COLLIER, JANE F. eds. *History and Power in the Study of Law.* Ithaca, N.Y.: Cornell University Press, 1989.

THODEN VAN VELZEN, H. U. E., and VAN WETERING, W. "Residence, Power Groups, and Intrasocial Aggression: An Inquiry into the Conditions Leading to Peacefulness within Nonstratified Societies." *International Archives of Ethnography* 49 (1960): 169–200.

WHITING, BEATRICE V. "Sex Identity Conflict and Physical Violence: A Comparative Study." *American Anthropologist* 67, no. 6, part 2 (Special Publication: The Ethnography of Law. Edited by Laura Nader) (1965): 123–140.

COMPARATIVE CRIMINAL LAW AND ENFORCEMENT: RUSSIA

Russia belongs to the continental European civil law tradition although its long history of autocracy and Soviet totalitarianism has left a distinct imprint on its system of criminal justice. Three great historical watersheds have left their imprint on Russian law: (1) the legal reforms of Tsar Alexander II in 1864; (2) the Bolshevik Revolution in 1917; and (3) the collapse of the Soviet Union in 1991 and the ensuing period of legal reform aimed at moving to a capitalist market economy, pluralist democracy, and a state under the rule of law and eliminating the worst abuses of the Soviet criminal justice system.

The modern reform movement commenced during *perestroika*, the attempt to transform the Soviet Union under the leadership of Mikhail Gorbachev (1985–1991). Its goals received their clearest expression in a document entitled the "Concept for Judicial Reform," which was approved by the Supreme Soviet of the Russian Federation on 21 October 1991 and which looked to the 1864 reforms for inspiration. The most important of these goals were: (1) creating an independent judiciary by reducing its dependence on local officials and making it self-governing; (2) introducing adversary procedure and trial by jury; (3) stripping the office of the public prosecutor or procuracy (*prokuratura*) of its oversight over the courts and its quasi-judicial powers to order invasions of constitutionally protected rights of the citizens; and (4) strengthening the right to counsel and the rights of defendants to protect against abusive practices by law enforcement organs.

Significant reform legislation was passed by the Supreme Soviet of the Russian Federation in 1992 and 1993 during the presidency of Boris Yeltsin. This consisted of amendments to the 1978 Constitution of the Russian Soviet Federated Socialist Republic (RSFSR) and, most notably, the Law on the Status of Judges, passed on 26 June 1992, and a law introducing trial by jury, passed on 16 July 1993 (Jury Law). After Yeltsin's violent dissolution of the Supreme Soviet in October of 1993 and the passage by referendum of the Constitution of the Russian Federation on 12 December 1993, strengthening presidential powers at the expense of a weakened bicameral legislature, the pace of reform slowed but the new lower house, the State Duma, continued to pass significant legislation, most notably, the Law on Operational Investigative Activities, passed on 12 August 1995, the Criminal Code of the Russian Federation, signed into law on 13 June 1996, and the Federal Constitutional Law on the Judicial System of the Russian Federation, signed on 31 December 1996. The long-awaited new draft Code of Criminal Procedure, which was presented to the Duma on 3 July 1995 (1995 Draft CCP), and passed first reading, has, as of early 2000, still not made it out of the lower house, leaving the heavily amended 1960 Code of Criminal Procedure of the RSFSR (CCP) in force.

Another important impulse for criminal justice reform in Russia, as in other post-socialist states of Europe, has been its petition for, and subsequent admission into, the Council of Europe, a condition of which was the signing of the European Convention on Human Rights, which took place on 28 February 1996. Article 15(4) of the Constitution gives this treaty, and the other most important human rights treaty, the United Nations International Covenant on Civil and Political Rights, which the Soviet Union signed in 1976, priority over domestic law and makes them directly applicable by the courts.

Criminal procedure

The principle of adversary procedure has been constitutionally rooted since 1992 and was codified in the 1993 Jury Law. Although the new jury system has been preliminarily limited to just nine of Russia's eighty-nine political subdivisions, the new provisions have begun to be applied in nonjury cases. Three of the prime aspects of the turn to adversary procedure that were at the heart of the reform movement were: (1) reducing the role of the procuracy to that of prosecutor of criminal cases with powers equal to that of the defense; (2) transforming the judge from an inquisitor, duty-bound to determine the truth and empowered to perform quasi-prosecutorial functions, into an impartial arbiter, who guarantees the equal rights of the parties during the trial; and (3) strengthening defense rights, including the right to counsel.

The criminal investigation

The criminal investigation in serious cases is divided into two stages: an informal inquest (*doznanie*), performed by the police (*militsiia*), and a formal preliminary investigation (*predvaritel'noe sledstviia*), usually conducted by a legally trained investigator (*sledovatel'*) who works for the Ministry of Internal Affairs but is subordinate to the procuracy. Less serious cases are investigated by the police and their reports are submitted in writing directly to the courts, bypassing the formal preliminary investigation. The investigator's role is similar to that of investigating magistrates in France or Spain, who are, however, part of the judiciary. The modern European trend, however, is to entrust the public prosecutor with the formal criminal investigation, this change having been made in Germany in 1974 and Italy in 1988.

The activity of the police during the inquest is supposed to be limited to arresting suspects, securing the crime scene, and taking initial statements from available suspects and witnesses. The police should inform the procuracy within twenty-four hours of the arrest of a suspect and the case should then be turned over to the investigator who decides whether to initiate a formal criminal investigation. The investigator's actions are limited by strict rules of evidence-gathering laid down in the CCP. All investigative acts are meticulously documented in writing and collected in an investigative dossier that follows the case into the courts and serves as a repository for vital evidence during trial and appeal. The procurator has forty-eight hours after notification to either issue an order of preventive detention or release the suspect.

Most suspects against whom a preliminary investigation is initiated remain in custody in preventive detention facilities until trial. Although the maximum time for pretrial detention is fixed at two months, many extensions are available up to a maximum of eighteen months. Detention is authorized if there is fear the defendant will not appear for trial, will destroy evidence, commit more crimes, or just because of the seriousness of the offense. A Special Rapporteur for the United Nations has found that Russia's eighteen-month limit on pretrial detention violates Article 9(3) of the International Covenant on Civil and Political Rights and that the rate of detention is excessive (from 30 to 50 percent of persons facing at least one-year imprisonment). The figure in France, for comparison, is around 10 percent. The population in Russia's preventive detention centers rose from 238,000 in 1994 to about 300,000 in 1999.

Article 22(2) of the Constitution states that deprivation of liberty, including preventive detention, is only possible with a "judicial decision" and that such decision must be taken within forty-eight hours of arrest. Unfortunately, the Russian legislature has never enacted legislation implementing this constitutional protection. A halfway measure was enacted on 23 May 1992, which provided for the first time in modern Russian history a mechanism to appeal the procurator's decision on preventive detention to the courts. A detained person's petition for release must be conveyed to the court and procurator within twenty-four hours. Documents relevant for the decision of the case must be transferred to the court within an additional twenty-four hours (Art. 220.1 CCP). The judge must then decide the issue within three days of receiving the aforesaid documents (Art. 220.2 CCP). Although judges began granting such motions for release, officials of the procuracy and the Ministry of the Interior, which controls the police and prisoner transport, flouted the law and often refused to produce the prisoner or the papers required to decide the issue within the statutory time limit. They would also often re-arrest persons released by judges before they could leave the courtroom. On 14 June 1994, President Yeltsin himself violated the Constitution by issuing an edict on "immediate measures to defend the population from banditry and other manifestations of organized crime" that allowed detention of suspects for up to thirty days without charges.

To protect suspects against being coerced to confess to crimes, a recurrent problem in Soviet times, a constitutional right to counsel from the moment of arrest or detention was introduced (Art. 48(2) Const. RF). In addition, Article 51 of the Constitution guarantees the right not to testify against oneself, and the Supreme Court has interpreted this to mean that the police, procurator, or investigator must advise a suspect of the right to remain silent and of the right to counsel before commencing an interrogation. Counsel will be appointed for the indigent. Unfortunately the police routinely coerce suspects into "waiving" their right to counsel. Even where investigators try to supply a suspect with appointed counsel, lawyers sometimes refuse to represent indigent defendants because of the low pay for court-appointed lawyers. If suspects refuse to give a statement they are often tortured. There have been estimates that around 40 percent or higher of all suspects are tortured, usually through beating, but also by asphyxiation or electric shock. Police give other inmates in the pretrial detention facilities special privileges to beat, rape, or otherwise force suspects into confessing. Just the veiled threat of torture induces suspects to confess, even sometimes to crimes they did not commit.

Article 23(2) of the Constitution requires a judicial decision for any invasions of the right to privacy in one's writings, telephone conversations, and postal or telegraphic communications, and Article 24 requires a judicial decision for invasions of the home. Despite this and comparable provisions in the European Convention of Human Rights, such searches and seizures may still be authorized by the procurator alone. To prevent crimes the 1995 Law on Operational Investigative Activities has also given the police broader powers than those enumerated in the CCP to engage in both open and secret investigative activities. The law includes provisions dealing with wiretapping, electronic interception of conversations, controlled deliveries and the use of undercover informants but lacks adequate guidelines for issuance of warrants, or notifying targets of the measures after they have been undertaken. Russia's failure to eliminate the procurator's power to authorize invasions of constitutionally protected citizens' rights, a power recognized as belonging exclusively to a judge in modern human rights documents, can be attributed to the procuracy's staunch opposition to all reforms aimed at undermining its power.

Created by Peter the Great in 1722, the procuracy came to be known as the "eye of the emperor" due to its exercise of oversight over all judicial and administrative bodies. Although the procuracy was stripped of these "supervisory" functions pursuant to the reforms of 1864, and restricted for the most part to the prosecution of criminal cases, the Bolsheviks resurrected the pre-1864 model of the procuracy in 1922, vesting it again with general powers to supervise the legality of acts of administrative officials and the courts. The Soviet procuracy was undoubtedly the most powerful institution in the administration of justice. When citizens complained of a violation of their rights, their remedy, ironically, was to appeal to the procurator, not a court, at a time when the procuracy itself was working closely with the Committee of State Security (KGB) in investigating, arresting, and prosecuting dissidents. The only success reformers have had in limiting the institutional power of the procuracy was the elimination of its oversight of the courts, which was accomplished by the Law on the Procuracy passed by the Supreme Soviet on 17 January 1992.

When the investigator determines that there is sufficient evidence to hold the accused to answer for trial he prepares an accusatory pleading and forwards it to the procurator for review. The accused and his counsel have, at this point, the right to full discovery of the entire contents of the investigative dossier. The procurator may dismiss the case, amend the pleading, or forward the case to the court for trial.

Fair trial and independent judiciary

Article 120 of the Constitution proclaims that "judges are independent and are subordinate only to the Constitution of the Russian Federation and federal law." Article 6 of the European Convention of Human Rights also guarantees the right of every criminal defendant to an independent judge. Prior to 1864 the courts were subservient to notoriously corrupt provincial governors. The 1864 reforms set up the framework for a genuinely independent judiciary with life tenure and introduced trial by jury to further liberate judges from the influence of local officialdom. The Bolshevik Decree on the Courts of 7 December 1917, however, put an end to an independent judiciary and the jury court was eventually replaced by a mixed court composed of one career judge, elected for a term of five years by local party officials, and two "people's assessors" also selected by party-controlled collectives. Although the Soviet mixed court looked superficially similar to the German *Schöffengericht*, the court became dependent on local officials (of the government and party), much as had the pre-1864 courts. The people's assessors were nicknamed the "nodders" because they virtually never outvoted the professional judge. The professional judge, on the other hand, relied on local officials for being nominated, retained in office, and for obtaining housing and technical and material support for the court's functioning. In controversial cases "telephone law" prevailed, that is, local officials would telephone the judge and indicate the way the case should be resolved.

The 1992 Law on the Status of Judges increased the social and legal protection of judges and, as amended, guaranteed their tenure in office until the retirement age of sixty-five, after a probationary period of three years. As in 1864, trial by jury was introduced in 1993 as a means of providing citizen participation in the administration of justice but also to insulate judges from outside influences. The reforms have not yet had their desired effects. In 1999 Russia had only 14,352 judges, about half the number of judges as in the Netherlands and far less than the projected number of 35,742. The Russian government has also refused to allocate sufficient budgetary resources to the court system to allow it to function properly. The situation was especially critical in 1998; when many courts were unable to pay their bills and electricity, telephone and other services were cut off. Many courts stopped hearing criminal and civil cases and the ancient Russian menace of judicial subservience to local officialdom resurfaced. As many as half of all district trial courts receive money and other support from regional or local governments or even private businesses, which usually is coupled with demands of the sponsoring parties. Bribery of judges is widespread. To ease the overburdening of the courts, which affects the quality of justice rendered, the 1996 Law on the Judicial System provided for a reinstitution of local justices of the peace (*mirovye sud'i*), a system introduced by the 1864 reforms, as the lowest level in the judicial hierarchy. Justices of the Peace would be competent to handle trials of minor civil and criminal cases and administrative law violations. The Draft Law on Justices of the Peace, however, was vetoed by President Yeltsin in March of 1998 for financial reasons.

Most criminal cases are tried in the district (*rayonnyy*) courts. Cases punishable by no more than five years imprisonment are tried by a single professional judge. Most cases punishable by from five to fifteen years imprisonment, and all juvenile cases, are tried by the Soviet-era mixed court of one professional judge and two "people's assessors." The "people's assessors" are no longer appointed by Communist-controlled collectives, of course, and it has become increasingly difficult to get them to attend court because of the meager pay they receive. The second-level trial courts (one in each of the eighty-nine political subdivisions of the country) hear cases of aggravated (capital) murder and selected other grave felonies. The cases are usually tried by the mixed court. In the areas in which trial by jury functions (as of 2000 only in Moscow, Ivanovo, Riazan, Saratov, Rostov-on-the-Don, and Ul'ianovsk regions and Altay, Krasnodar, and Stavropol territories), the defendant has a choice of being tried by a jury of twelve, presided over by one professional judge, by a panel of three professional judges, or by the mixed court with people's assessors. These courts handle appeals from the district courts as well. A special system of military courts exercises jurisdiction over crimes committed by military personnel.

Under the Jury Law, jurors are randomly selected from Russian citizens at least twenty-five years of age who are registered voters in the region in which the crime was committed. Jurors are required to serve only once a year for not more than ten days or for one case. They are paid one-half of the pro-rata salary of a judge, substantially higher than lay assessors, and this has helped guarantee their attendance at trial. Russia and Spain (1995) have been the only countries on the European continent to return to trial by jury after the institution was virtually eliminated by the totalitarian regimes of the first half of the twentieth century. Although the new constitutions of Belarus (Art. 114) and Kazakhstan (Art. 75(2)) provide for trial by jury, no implementing legislation has been passed.

Judgments and decisions of the second-level courts (whether acting as trial or appellate courts) may be appealed to the Supreme Court of the Russian Federation, the highest normal appellate court in civil and criminal matters. Appeals at all levels are heard by three professional judges without lay participation. The Supreme Court also hears a select number of cases as a trial court composed of one judge and two people's assessors. The Supreme Court consists of 115 judges, divided into criminal, civil, military and cassational panels. It has a governing body called the Presidium, consisting of the president and twelve other judges, which has a power of review over the decisions of the panels.

The Constitutional Court of the Russian Federation, modeled on that of the Federal Republic of Germany, was created in 1991, suspended following Yeltsin's attack on parliament in October of 1993, and reconstituted following the passage of the 1993 Constitution. It now consists of nineteen judges elected by the Federation Council, the upper house of the new parliament, upon nomination by the president. The Constitutional Court can decide the constitutionality of the application of the criminal law in particular cases upon a petition of a citizen or of a lower court in which the particular case is pending. On 31 October 1995, the Supreme Court articulated a policy that the regular courts had authority to determine whether laws, or their application in a particular case, were consistent with the Constitution and international human rights conventions. This power was codified in the 1996 Law on the Judicial System. A criminal defendant who has exhausted all remedies in the Russian courts may file a petition with the European Court of Human Rights in Strasbourg, France, if there is a claim that the authorities violated a right protected by the European Convention on Human Rights. In 1999 the European Court of Human Rights received more complaints from Russian citizens than from any other country, 972 of the 8,396 cases lodged.

The admissibility of evidence

Upon receipt of the case the trial judge reviews the accusatory pleading and, depending on the sufficiency of the evidence, may set the case for trial, return the case to the investigator for further investigation, or dismiss all or some of the charges. This pretrial hearing is often the setting for motions to suppress evidence due to violations of the law committed by investigative officials. The prohibition against the use of illegally seized evidence has been constitutionally based since 1992 (Art. 50(2) Const. RF) and was codified as part of the 1993 Jury Law (Art. 69(para. 3) CCP). In jury cases there is a special preliminary hearing before trial at which motions to suppress illegally seized evidence may be made based on the documents in the investigative dossier (Art. 433 (para. 3) CCP). Motions to suppress evidence have been common in jury tri-

als and are beginning to be made in nonjury trials. The Supreme Court has ruled, for instance, that a statement made by a suspect without having been advised of the right to remain silent or without waiving the right to counsel must be excluded from the trial, a ruling quite similar to the famous decision of the U.S. Supreme Court in *Miranda v. Arizona*. Courts have also routinely excluded evidence seized following unlawful searches or other procedural violations. The Russian exclusionary rule applies to evidence gathered in violation of a statute, even if the violation was not of constitutional magnitude.

The exclusionary rule has not been effectively applied, especially in relation to alleged use of torture or other coercion to compel confessions by suspects. Allegations of the use of improper methods are commonly rejected by the trial judge after at most a perfunctory investigation by the procuracy. The Supreme Court has also ruled that a finding by the trial judge that a confession was voluntary will preclude the defendant or other witnesses from testifying before the jury that the confession was the product of torture, threats, violence, promises, or other inducements and should not therefore be believed.

The criminal trial and the presumption of innocence

In Russian criminal trials, the victim (*poterpevshiy*) has rights equal to the defendant and prosecutor to attend the trial, make a statement, summon witnesses, examine witnesses, argue at the time of sentencing, and even prosecute the case (in jury trials) if he or she disagrees with the procurator's motion to dismiss. As in other European countries, the victim, or anyone else suffering a loss as a result of the allegedly criminal acts of the defendant, has the right to file a civil suit for monetary damages or restitution that will be heard along with the criminal case. The civil party may then join civil defendants other than the accused to answer the claim, such as an insurance company or guardian of the accused.

In jury cases, the trial judge summons twenty prospective jurors selected at random from the jury lists to appear in court on the trial date. The judge questions the jurors to make sure they are qualified and the parties (including the victim) may submit questions in writing to be posed by the judge to determine whether the jurors are biased and thus subject to challenge. The prosecution and defense each have two peremptory challenges that may be used to exclude jurors without cause. The jury is composed, in the end, of twelve jurors with two alternates.

After the reading of the accusatory pleading the defendant is then asked to enter a plea. If the defendant pleads guilty, this does not end the case as it does in the United States. A guilty plea is just considered to be a piece of evidence and the procurator must present other evidence to corroborate the guilty plea. In jury trials, however, upon an admission of guilt by the defendant, the court may then proceed to closing arguments if there is no dispute about the evidence and the defense and prosecution agree. Legislation was proposed in 1998 to extend this procedure to normal trials but it was defeated in the State Duma. In the late 1990s much interest was shown in introducing some kind of plea-bargaining to reduce court caseloads.

After entry of a plea the defendant is given an opportunity to make a statement. Before doing so, the judge advises the defendant of the constitutional right to remain silent. While defendants usually give their testimony at the beginning of the trial (this is common practice in continental European countries), some judges in jury cases have allowed the defendant to testify later in the proceedings. After the defendant makes a statement (they rarely remain silent), the witnesses and experts testify. In standard inquisitorial fashion it is normally the judge who calls the witnesses and asks them to narrate what they know about the facts that are the subject of the criminal charge. This is quite different from the question-and-answer format followed in direct examination in common law trials. Only after the judge finishes asking follow-up questions to the witnesses, do the other parties have a chance to formulate questions. In Russian mixed courts the lay assessors may also ask questions of the defendant and witnesses, but rarely do. In jury courts, the jurors may submit written questions to be formulated by the presiding judge. The new principle of adversary procedure has led, especially in jury trials, to the judge taking a more passive role and allowing the parties to summon witnesses and do the bulk of the questioning. The 1995 Draft CCP also provides for party control of the summoning and questioning of witnesses.

During Soviet times the presumption of innocence was considered to be "bourgeois nonsense" inconsistent with the inquisitorial nature of Soviet criminal procedure. Although Article 49 of the Constitution now guarantees the presumption of innocence in criminal cases certain old practices persist that seem to contradict such

a presumption. One is having the defendant speak first. Another is the provision requiring the trial judge to review the entire investigative dossier before trial to determine whether there is sufficient evidence to convict the defendant. In nonjury cases this ensures that the judge, whether deciding the case alone or as the dominant force in the mixed court, will be practically unable to give the defendant the benefit of a presumption of innocence when the trial begins. For this reason Italian judges are not permitted to read the investigative dossier. The most problematic procedural rule, however, is the power of the trial judge to return the case to the investigator to perform supplementary investigative acts after the trial has begun, in a jury case requiring dissolution of the jury. In Soviet times this rule enabled judges, in cases where there was insufficient evidence to convict, to avoid having to acquit the defendant and thereby impugn the integrity of the investigative organs. On 20 April 1999, the Constitutional Court ruled that this practice violates the constitutional presumption of innocence and the right to adversary procedure. The Constitutional Court indicated that courts should acquit the defendant in such situations.

When all the evidence has been presented, the parties give their closing summations. The last word in the trial is always personally that of the defendant. In jury trials the judge also instructs the jury on the law that is to be applied in the case and must summarize all the evidence that supports both the prosecution and defense theories of the case. It is reversible error for the judge to in any way indicate his or her opinion as to the guilt or innocence of the defendant in doing so.

In cases before the mixed court, the professional judge and the two lay assessors retire to deliberate together, where they must collegially decide all questions of law and fact relating to guilt and sentence. A majority vote is sufficient, whereupon the professional judge formulates a written judgment including the reasons for the findings on guilt and sentence. Prior to deliberation in jury cases the judge formulates a list of questions that the jury must answer. The list must minimally contain questions dealing with whether the acts constituting the crime were committed, whether the defendant was the person who committed them, and whether the defendant is guilty of their commission. Questions are asked separately as to each defendant and some judges formulate separate questions relating to all relevant conduct charged against the defendant as well as to all excuses or justifications raised by the defense and all aggravating or mitigating factors. In one case over one thousand questions were asked of the jury. Such "question lists" were typical in continental European jury systems during the nineteenth and early twentieth centuries and were meant to give the professional judge the possibility of formulating a reasoned judgment after a jury verdict. Guilty verdicts or answers unfavorable to the defendant require seven votes; not guilty verdicts or answers favorable to the defendant require six votes to be valid. After the jury reaches a verdict, the presiding judge evaluates the legal sufficiency of the jury's answers to the questions and enters a judgment of guilty or not guilty as to each charge. The Supreme Court has ruled that the jury must only decide questions of fact and has reversed many cases because the trial judge has formulated questions that call for legal conclusions.

The shakiness of the presumption of innocence in Russian criminal trials is reflected by the fact that acquittals are almost nonexistent. They occurred in only 0.36 percent of all cases in 1998. During the *perestroika* years the Soviet public was shocked by many stories of innocent people having been convicted due to coerced or tortured confessions and this was one reason why reforms were pushed, among them, that of returning to trial by jury. Indeed, juries have acquitted substantially more than nonjury courts, anywhere from 18–22 percent of the time. A disturbing development has been the refusal of law enforcement organs to accept acquittals. For instance, in November 1999 in Moscow, officers of the Federal Security Service, the successor of the KGB, entered a courtroom in camouflage uniforms and black masks and re-arrested two defendants who had been acquitted at trial by a military court. Such occurrences are not rare.

Review of judgments

The defendant, the procurator, and the victim may appeal judgments at each level of the court structure. The appellate courts are empowered to review questions of fact as well as law. If the accused appeals, the appellate court may not find the defendant guilty of a more serious offense or impose a more severe punishment. The procurator or the victim may appeal, however, and seek to have the judgment overturned, and a more severe punishment may be imposed upon

retrial. Unlike in the United States the procurator or the victim may appeal an acquittal. (This is also allowed in many continental European countries.)

The procuracy is quick to appeal nearly every acquittal and the Supreme Court is just as quick to reverse them. In 1997, for instance, the Supreme Court reversed 33.1 percent of all acquittals and only 2.5 percent of guilty verdicts. The Cassational Panel of the Supreme Court, responsible for hearing appeals of jury cases, overturned 66 percent of all jury acquittals in 1998. In a few jury cases persons have been acquitted two or three times, only to have their acquittals reversed and new trials ordered by the Supreme Court. Grounds for reversals of jury acquittals have been faulty preparation of the question list, defense testimony relating to unlawful methods used by the police to obtain confessions, and erroneous exclusion of incriminating evidence (i.e., a confession), thus depriving the state of the right to a fair trial. Although many of the acquittals were for atrocious murders, the Supreme Court seems to be reversing acquittals as an obedient warrior in the battle against crime, not as an impartial institution of the rule of law as it was supposed to become as a result of the democratic reforms.

The appellate courts may also reverse a lower court judgment on grounds not pleaded by the parties. Finally, final judgments may still be subject to "review" (*nadzor*). Pursuant to this procedure, higher courts may, on their own initiative or upon petition of the procurator (but not the defense), review final judgments of lower courts, and court presidiums may review decisions of their own panels and overturn them if they are not to their liking. This inquisitorial mode of review has been criticized as being in violation of the constitutional right to adversary procedure and equality of the parties in the trial. It is also a tool used by the higher courts to enforce conformity in decision-making in the lower courts and to discipline judges who seek to be independent in their resolution of cases. At least one of the successor states of the Soviet Union, Georgia, has abolished this type of "review" in its new Code of Criminal Procedure.

Substantive criminal law

The de-sovietization of criminal law began during the latter years of *perestroika* when the Penal Code of 1960 was heavily amended to eliminate offenses such as anti-Soviet agitation, defaming the Soviet State, and parasitism, alleged violations of which had sent hundreds of thousands of Soviet citizens to the Gulag. But the code was also obsolete, especially due to the profound economic changes triggered by the massive privatization of state property and the move to a capitalist market economy. The 1996 Criminal Code is divided into a General Part, containing general principles relating to criminal responsibility and assessment of punishment, and a Special Part, listing the various offenses and the punishments threatened for the commission thereof. Although Russians continue to define crime, as in Soviet times, as a "socially dangerous act," the "goals" of the code and the interests it protects are no longer related to "the socialist legal order" as was the case under the old code. In most Western countries neither a substantive general definition of crime, nor a list of protected interests is provided. A purely formal notion prevails, whereby any act punishable in the criminal code is a crime. The new Russian code incorporates universally recognized principles of criminal law such as that of no punishment without a written law, no retroactive laws, and so on.

The general part.   Persons are subject to the criminal law when they reach the age of sixteen years for normal crimes, and fourteen years for murder and other grave crimes. Persons who are insane at the time of commission of a crime may not be convicted thereof. A person is insane under the Russian Criminal Code if he or she "could not understand the factual character and social dangerousness of his acts (omissions) or control them as a result of chronic psychic disturbance, temporary psychic disturbance, imbecility or any other sick state of the psyche" (Art. 21 CC). Though Soviet criminal law did not recognize any form of diminished criminal responsibility for those who suffered from mental illness but were not legally insane, this has been included in the new code, but only as a mitigating factor in sentencing. Due to the staggering rate of alcohol-induced violent criminality throughout Russian history, being intoxicated has never been admissible to diminish criminal responsibility or mitigate punishment. While this remains true under the new code, being drunk is no longer an aggravating circumstances in sentencing as it was under the old code.

The new Criminal Code introduces some new factors that exclude guilt to go along with traditional justifications such as self-defense or necessity, or excuses such as duress. These include "innocent infliction of harm," by persons who, due to objective or subjective (mental) circumstances, could not have appreciated the dangerousness of their acts or have prevented the harm (Art. 28 CC), or who inflict harm while taking a socially useful justified risk (Art. 41 CC). Other innovations are that first-time offenders who commit less serious crimes can be freed of criminal responsibility if they engage in "active remorse" in the form of turning themselves in, aiding in the solving of the crime, or making restitution (Art. 75 CC). Reconciliation with the victim (Art. 76 CC) or a change in conditions that has caused either the offender or the crime to no longer be socially dangerous (Art. 77 CC) will also lead to release from criminal responsibility. Prosecutors have used these provisions to fashion bargains with offenders to work with the authorities in exchange for a dismissal, practices that compensate for the lack of statutorily recognized plea bargaining and a relative lack of prosecutorial discretion.

The goal of punishment under the new code is the re-establishment of social justice, the rehabilitation of the convicted person, and the prevention of the commission of new crimes (Art. 43 CC). The widely used Soviet punishment of banishment was abolished toward the end of the *perestroika* period, but the 1996 Criminal Code still includes the death penalty and other common forms of punishment: fine, prohibition to engage in a profession, confiscation of property, and deprivation of liberty among others. The death penalty can only be imposed for especially grave crimes against life and may not be imposed against women, men under eighteen years of age at the time of the commission of the offense, or men over sixty years of age at the time of judgment (Art. 59 UK). Whereas fifteen years was the maximum period of imprisonment under the old code, the 1996 code introduces life imprisonment as an alternative to the death penalty, and a maximum imprisonment of twenty years for noncapital crimes and thirty years if a person is sentenced for multiple crimes.

The death penalty.   Although Empress Elizabeth was one of the first monarchs to abolish the death penalty in 1753, the ban remained in force only for a short time. Besides the extrajudicial murders of millions by Soviet authorities during its rule, death sentences were handed down by Soviet courts often and not only as punishment for murder. Because the Soviet Union did not publish criminal justice statistics it is difficult to know how many people were judicially executed until the *glasnost* reforms instituted under Mikhail Gorbachev. Executions decreased during the *perestroika* years from 770 in 1985 to 195 in 1990. It was only in 1991 that the death penalty was eliminated for economic crimes, such as theft of socialist property, bribery, and illegal currency transactions, and not until 1994 that it was eliminated as a punishment for counterfeiting. The number of executions during Yeltsin's presidency fluctuated depending on presidential politics. In 1992 the president established a Clemency Commission that commuted 337 of the 378 death sentences submitted to it. Suddenly, however, Yeltsin proclaimed a tougher policy in the fight against crime and only five of 129 death sentences were commuted, and fifty-six persons were executed in 1996 after Russia had declared a moratorium on executions as a condition of its entry into the Council of Europe. Russia was strongly criticized by the Council of Europe and no executions have apparently taken place since August of 1996. The Sixth Protocol of the European Convention of Human Rights declares the death penalty to be a violation of the right to life.

Between 1989 and 1992 most of the former socialist countries of non-Soviet Europe abolished the death penalty. With respect to the successor states to the Soviet Union, Latvia declared a moratorium on executions in 1996 and finally eliminated the death penalty in 1999. The Lithuanian Constitutional Court struck down the death penalty in 1998 and eliminated it from its Criminal Code in 1999. Both countries, as well as Estonia, which has declared a moratorium on the death penalty, are full members of the Council of Europe. Like Russia, Ukraine agreed to a moratorium on executions as a condition of entering the Council of Europe, but outraged that body by secretly executing thirteen people in 1997. The Ukrainian parliament finally eliminated the death penalty in February of 2000. Membership in the Council of Europe has also pushed Moldavia (1995), Georgia (1997), and Azerbaijan (1998) to abolish the death penalty and Armenia to abide by an unofficial moratorium. Belarus, which has still not been accepted into the Council of Europe, executed thirty persons in 1997 and still enforces the death penalty. In Soviet Asia, Kyrgystan declared a moratorium (December 1998), though courts continued to impose death sentences as of January 2000. Turkmenistan executed around four hundred persons in 1996 and sentenced seven hundred to death in 1997, mostly for drug-related crimes. In 1999, however, it also declared an official moratorium. In 1996 Ka-

zakhstan executed forty-two persons and made a reduced number of offenses punishable by death in its new Criminal Code, which went into effect 1 January 1998. Death sentences continue to be imposed and executed in Tadjikistan and Uzbekistan as well, six having been executed in the latter republic in January 2000. All Soviet Asian states with the exception of Kyrgystan still impose the death penalty for drug trafficking.

Even after Russian executions stopped in August 1996, trial courts continued to sentence people to death in aggravated murder cases and these sentences were often affirmed by the Supreme Court. On 2 February 1999, however, the Constitutional Court declared that the death penalty could no longer be imposed on equal protection grounds. Inasmuch as Article 20 of the Constitution guarantees the right to trial by jury for anyone facing the death penalty and the jury system only functions in nine Russian regions and territories, the Court held that no death sentences could be imposed anywhere until trial by jury was available throughout Russia.

The special part of the criminal code. The Criminal Code contains a typical list of crimes against the person (homicide, sexual offenses, assaultive conduct), but also includes an offense punishing the transmission of venereal diseases or the HIV virus (Arts. 121–122 UK). Chapter 19 of the Criminal Code punishes violations against "the constitutional rights and freedoms of the person and citizen," among them acts infringing on the inviolability of one's private life, correspondence, and dwelling or on the liberty of confession or assembly, rights that went unprotected in Soviet times.

Among the most radical changes in the 1996 Criminal Code are those contained in Section VIII relating to "Crimes in the Economic Sphere." Under Soviet Law all types of private enterprise were illegal and, at times, severely punished. Theft of state property was considered a more serious crime than theft of private property. Entrepreneurial activity is now protected by the Constitution and regulated in the criminal law, with offenses punishing the hindering of legal entrepreneurial activity, but also engaging in illegal business dealings such as money laundering, restricting competition, false advertising, securities or credit fraud, fraudulent bankruptcy, tax evasion, and consumer fraud. Drafters of these provisions used the American Model Penal Code as a model. New provisions punish "ecological crimes" and "crimes in the sphere of computer information," including hacking and creating viruses (Arts. 272, 273 CC). Russia has suffered disastrous ecological consequences from the near complete absence of laws regulating defense and heavy industry during Soviet times. The new code punishes seventeen separate environmental crimes, some relating to general violation of rules, others to improper handling of dangerous substances such as biological agents or toxins, still others protecting distinct resources such as water, the atmosphere, the sea, the continental shelf, the soil, the subsoil, and flora and fauna (Arts. 248, 250–262 CC).

The new code punishes incitement to national, racial, or religious hatred (Art. 282 CC), an important provision in a racially, ethnically, and religiously diverse country with a history of conflict among the various groups. Chapter 30 punishes abuse of public office, bribery, and so on (Arts. 285–293 UK). Despite the rampant corruption at all levels of Russian government there have been no prosecutions during the Yeltsin years of the ruling political elite connected with the corrupt privatization of Soviet industry and the granting of sweetheart export and customs privileges. Nor have the provisions of Chapter 31 relating to "crimes against the administration of justice" (Arts. 294–316 CC) been enforced, despite the open refusal of executive organs of the administration of justice to abide by judicial decisions and the increase of violent attacks on judges.

Finally, the 1996 Code has aimed to strengthen the provisions designed to fight organized crime. The general part of the code provides for aggravation of sentences if a crime is committed by a group of persons pursuant to a conspiracy, by an organized group or criminal organization (Art. 35 CC). Chapter 24 punishes individual "crimes against social security" such as terrorism, taking hostages, organizing an illegal armed group, and formation of a criminal organization. In 1998, 28,633 crimes were committed by organized groups or criminal organizations (including 152 contract killings).

Sentencing and the prison system

On 1 July 1997, the "Criminal-Execution Code of the Russian Federation" was passed. In light of the notoriously brutal conditions in prison camps during Soviet times, the new Code explicitly lays out the rights and duties of prisoners. With some exception, persons sentenced to imprisonment are required to serve their sentences in correctional institutions within the territory of the Russian Federation in which they lived or were sentenced. Most sentenced prisoners do their time performing hard labor in "correctional colonies" with various levels of regimes depending on the severity of the crime committed.

In 1998 Russia imprisoned 700 persons per 100,000 population, the second highest rate in the world after Rwanda, slightly higher than the United States (668 per 100,000) and around fifteen times higher than in most European countries. As of 1 July 1997, the total prison population in Russia was 1,017,848, of which 275,567 were in pretrial detention centers intended for a maximum of 182,358 detainees. To alleviate the overcrowding of Russia's prisons the State Duma adopted an amnesty law on 18 June 1999 to compel the release of around 100,000 detainees and prisoners. Tuberculosis caused the death of 178 prisoners out of every 100,000 in 1995. In 1998 nearly 100,000 prisoners were diagnosed as being infected with the disease, 10 percent of the total number of inmates, and thirty thousand have an untreatable and deadly form thereof. Overall, 720 of every 100,000 prisoners died in confinement in 1995, a great number thereof from tuberculosis, asphyxiation, and suicide.

Crime in post-Soviet Russia

According to Soviet ideology, crime was a "bourgeois" phenomenon, an excrescence of capitalist society that would disappear in a mature communist system. Crime statistics were not published until Gorbachev's *glasnost* reforms so one does not have a clear idea of the level of crime in Soviet society. But there is little doubt that crime has risen dramatically since the dismantling of the Soviet administrative-command economy. Not only is corruption rampant at every level of local and national government, but the new capitalist economy is widely controlled either by organized crime or by so-called oligarchs who obtained large chunks of the former state economy for a fraction of their value in exchange for sweetheart relationships with government officials at all levels. Russia's immense wealth is being pillaged through the selling off of former state assets and natural resources as well as transfer-pricing and stock manipulations, and the proceeds are being invested overseas instead of in Russia. Organized criminal gangs, estimated in the mid-1990s to number around three thousand (in about fifty overarching syndicates), are active throughout Russia. The catastrophic fall in gross national product, the inability to collect taxes, and two devastating and costly wars in the breakaway Republic of Chechnya have left the Russian government in a continuing fiscal crisis. The number of registered crimes was 16.3 percent higher in 1999 than in 1998 and has risen every year since the early 1990s. Violent crimes, and especially murders, have reached shocking proportions. The number of intentional murders reported in 1999 was 31,140 (in a population of around 147 million), compared with "only" 16,910 in the United States in 1998 (in a population of around 270 million). The government of Vladimir Putin, elected to succeed Boris Yeltsin as president of the Russian Federation on 26 March 2000, must redirect the executive branch of government to fighting crime, instead of participating in it, to strengthening the judicial branch of government, instead of sabotaging its enforcement of the presumption of innocence and the right to a fair trial, and to pushing to perfect the reforms, instead of obstructing them at every step of the way.

STEPHEN C. THAMAN

See also ADVERSARY SYSTEM; COMPARATIVE CRIMINAL LAW AND ENFORCEMENT: CHINA; CRIMINAL LAW REFORM: CONTINENTAL EUROPE; CRIMINAL PROCEDURE: COMPARATIVE ASPECTS; PROSECUTION: COMPARATIVE ASPECTS.

BIBLIOGRAPHY

BARRY, DONALD D., ed. *Toward the "Rule of Law" in Russia? Political and Legal Reform in the Transition Period.* Armonk, N.Y.: M. E. Sharpe, 1992.

BERMAN, HAROLD J. *Justice in the U.S.S.R. An Interpretation of Soviet Law.* Cambridge, Mass.: Harvard University Press, 1963.

BUTLER, WILLIAM E., AND HENDERSON, JANE E. *Russian Legal Texts. The Foundations of a Rule-of-Law State and a Market Economy.* The Hague: Kluwer Law International, 1998.

FELDBRUGGE, F. J. M. *Russian Law: The End of the Soviet System and the Role of Law.* Boston: Martinus Nijhoff Publishers, 1993.

FEOFANOV, IURII, AND BARRY, DONALD D. *Politics and Justice in Russia: Major Trials of the Post-Stalin Era.* Armonk, N.Y.: M. E. Sharpe, 1996.

FOGLESONG, TODD. "Habeas Corpus or Who Has the Body? Judicial Review of Arrest and Pre-trial Detention in Russia." *Wisconsin International Law Journal* 14 (1996): 541–578.

Human Rights Watch. *Confessions at Any Cost. Police Torture in Russia.* New York: Human Rights Watch, 1999.

HUSKEY, EUGENE. *Russian Lawyers and the Soviet State: The Origins and Development of the Soviet Bar.* Princeton, N.J.: Princeton University Press, 1986.

KAISER, FRIEDHELM B. *Die russische Justizreform von 1864.* Leiden, Netherlands: E. J. Brill, 1972.

KRUG, PETER. "Departure from the Centralized Model. The Russian Supreme Court and Constitutional Control of Legislation." *Virginia Journal of International Law* 37 (1997): 725–787.

KUCHEROV, SAMUEL. *Courts, Lawyers and Trials Under the Last Three Tsars.* New York: Frederick A. Praeger, 1953.

———. *The Organs of Soviet Administration of Justice: Their History and Operation.* Leiden, Netherlands: E. J. Brill, 1970.

LUPINSKAIA, P. A. *Ugolovno-prostessual'noe pravo Rossiyskoy Federatsii.* Moscow: Yurist, 1997.

MARSHUNOV, M. N. *Komentariy k zakonodatel'stvu o sudoustroystve Rossiyskoy Federatsii.* Moscow: Torgovyy Dom (Gerda), 1998.

NAUMOV, ANATOLYI V. "The New Russian Criminal Code as a Reflection of Ongoing Reforms." *Criminal Law Forum* 8 (1997): 191–230.

PETRUKHIN, I. L. *Lichnye tayny (chelovek i vlast').*

Sbornik kodeksov Rossiyskoy Federatsii. II. Kniga. 1999. Moscow: Institut Gosudarstvo i prava, 1998.

SCHITTENHELM, ULRIKE. *Strafe und Sanktionensystem im sowjetischen Recht.* Freiburg im Breisgau, Germany: Max Planck Institute for Foreign and International Criminal Law, 1994.

SCHROEDER, F-C., ed. *Die neuen Kodifikationen in Rußland",* 2d ed. Berlin: Berlin Verlag A. Spitz, 1999.

SKURATOV, YU I., AND LEBEDEV, V. M. *Kommentariy k Ugolovnomu kodeksu Rossiyskoy Federatsii,* 2d ed. Moscow: Norma-Infra, 1998.

SMITH, GORDON B. *Reforming the Russian Legal System.* New York: Cambridge University Press, 1996.

SOLOMON, PETER H., JR. *Soviet Criminal Justice under Stalin.* New York: Cambridge University Press, 1996.

———, ed. *Reforming Justice in Russia, 1864–1996.* Armonk, N.Y.: M.E. Sharpe, 1997.

Sudebnaia i pravookhranitel'naia sistemy, 2d ed. Moscow: Bek, 1998.

THAMAN, STEPHEN C. "The Resurrection of Trial by Jury in Russia." *Stanford Journal of International Law* 31 (1995): 61–274.

———. "Reform of the Procuracy and Bar in Russia." *Parker School Journal of East European Law* 3 (1996): 1–29.

———. "Europe's New Jury Systems: The Cases of Spain and Russia." *Law and Contemporary Problems* 62 (1999): 233–259.

TOPORNIN, B. N.; BATURIN, YU. M.; AND OREKHOV, R. G., eds. *Konstitutsiia Rossiyskoy Federatsii. Komentariy.* Moscow: Yuridicheskaia Literatyra, 1994.

COMPETENCY TO STAND TRIAL

If at any time in the criminal proceedings the defendant appears to be suffering from a mental illness, the issue of competence to proceed may be raised. This may occur when the defendant seeks to plead guilty or to stand trial. It may occur when the defendant seeks to waive certain constitutional rights, such as the Fifth Amendment or *Miranda v. Arizona*, 384 U.S. 436 (1966), or the Sixth Amendment right to counsel or to a jury trial. Even after conviction, the issue may be raised at a sentencing hearing, or when the government seeks to administer punishment, including capital punishment. The issue usually is raised by defense counsel by oral or written motion, but also may be raised by the prosecution or by the court itself, even over the objection of the defendant, who may prefer to proceed despite the existence of mental illness.

Several studies conclude that the vast majority of defendants are referred inappropriately for competency evaluation and have suggested that the competency process often is invoked for strategic purposes. The issue may be raised by both sides to obtain delay, by prosecutors to avoid bail or an expected insanity acquittal, or to bring about hospitalization that might not otherwise be available under the state's civil commitment statute, or by defense attorneys to obtain mental health recommendations for use in making an insanity defense, in plea bargaining, or in sentencing.

Under *Drope v. Missouri*, 420 U.S. 162 (1975), and *Pate v. Robinson*, 383 U.S. 375 (1966), the court must conduct an inquiry into competence whenever a bona fide doubt is raised concerning the issue. Even after the criminal trial has commenced, the court must order a competency evaluation when reasonable grounds emerge to question the defendant's competence. If this does not occur even though a bona fide question of competence exists, any resulting conviction will violate due process.

When is such a bona fide doubt raised? According to *Drope v. Missouri*, "[e]vidence of a defendant's irrational behavior, his demeanor at trial, and any prior medical opinion on competence to stand trial are all relevant in determining whether further inquiry is required, but . . . even one of these factors standing alone may, in some circumstances, be sufficient." The Court noted that there are "no fixed or immutable signs which invariably indicate the need for further inquiry;" instead, "the question is often a difficult one in which a wide range of manifestations and subtle nuances are implicated" (p. 180). As a result of *Drope* and the rule of *Pate* that due process is violated if an incompetent defendant is subjected to trial, courts typically order a formal competency evaluation in virtually every case in which doubt about the issue is raised.

What happens when the court fails to order a competency determination when the evidence raises a bona fide question concerning the issue? When the defendant is subjected to trial in the absence of such a determination, any ensuing conviction would violate due process and must be reversed under *Pate v. Robinson*. Can a court retrospectively conduct the needed inquiry into competence after the trial has occurred? Although *Pate* seemed to indicate that an automatic reversal of such a conviction would be required, lower courts have sometimes permitted such a retrospective competency assessment when such a determination is thought to be feasible in the circumstances.

The competency standard and its application

Mental illness alone, even a diagnosis of schizophrenia, will not automatically result in a finding of incompetence. The question is the degree of functional impairment produced by such illness. To be found incompetent, such mental illness must prevent the defendant from understanding the nature of the proceedings or from assisting counsel in the making of the defense. This standard focuses upon the defendant's mental state at the time of trial. By contrast, the legal insanity defense focuses upon the defendant's mental state at the time when the criminal act occurred, and seeks to ascertain whether he or she should be relieved of criminal responsibility as a result. The Supreme Court's classic formulation of the standard for incompetency in the criminal process was adopted in the case of *Dusky v. United States*, 362 U.S. 402 (1960). The Court held that a court was required to determine whether a defendant "has sufficient present ability to consult with his lawyer with a reasonable degree of rational understanding and whether he has a rational as well as factual understanding of the proceedings against him" (p. 402). Although some courts had applied a more demanding standard of competency when the defendant attempted to plead guilty or waive counsel, requiring the ability to make a reasoned choice, in *Godinez v. Maran*, 509 U.S. 389 (1993), the Supreme Court rejected such a higher standard. Instead, the Court found that the *Dusky* formulation was the appropriate test of competency throughout the criminal process, at least as a constitutional minimum. The *Dusky* standard emphasized the cognitive ability to understand and the behavioral ability to consult with counsel, not necessarily the ability to engage in rational decision-making. In *Godinez*, the Court distinguished between competency and the knowledge and voluntariness requirement for the waiver of certain fundamental rights. The competency inquiry, the Court noted, focuses on the defendant's mental capacity. The question is whether he or she has the ability to understand the proceedings. In contrast, the Court noted, the inquiry into "knowing" and "voluntary" is to determine whether the defendant actually does understand the significance and consequences of a particular decision and whether the decision is uncoerced.

Although the Court thus clarified that its competency standard was not as broad as some courts had thought, the standard is still broad, open-textured, and vague, permitting clinical evaluators substantial latitude in interpreting and applying the test. The clinical instruments available for competency assessment compound the problem. These instruments typically list the many potentially relevant capacities that a defendant may need without prescribing scoring criteria for how these capacities should be rated. Moreover, because clinical evaluators rarely consult with counsel to ascertain the particular skills the defendant will need to have to function effectively in the case, the assessment instruments encourage clinical evaluators to apply a generalized, abstract standard of competency, rather than following a more appropriate contextualized approach to competency assessment.

By simply relying upon clinical judgment based on all the circumstances, these instruments make competency assessment a highly discretionary exercise in clinical judgment. Many clinical evaluators are paternalistically oriented, and without more concrete guidance, tend to classify marginally mentally ill patients as incompetent. The literature documents the tendency of clinical evaluators in the criminal courts to misunderstand the legal issues involved in incompetency, frequently confusing it with legal insanity or with the clinical definition of psychosis.

This discretion is both increased and made more troubling by the fact that appellate courts rarely review and almost never reverse trial court competency determinations, and that trial judges almost always defer to clinical evaluators. Vesting broad and unreviewable decision-making discretion in clinical evaluators tends to obscure the distinction between the clinical and legal components of incompetency in the criminal process, and allows clinicians to regard a competency assessment as largely an exercise in clinical description. The question of who is competent to stand trial, however, is more legal than clinical. Courts and legislatures thus should define the concept of competency with greater precision. Bonnie's efforts to delineate in detail the various components of competency to stand trial are helpful in this connection. Bonnie (1992) suggests that competency is best viewed as containing two related but separable constructs—a foundational concept of competence to assist counsel, and a contextualized concept of decisional competence. Bonnie persuasively argues that while the first should be required, the second should not always be necessary for a defendant to be considered competent. Also useful in this connection are the efforts of Bonnie's coresearchers in the MacArthur Network on Mental Health and the Law to develop detailed assessment instruments and to conduct empirical research on the decision-making abilities of mentally ill defendants (Hoge et at., 1997). The MacArthur group developed the MacSAC-CD (MacArthur Structured Assessment of the Competencies of Criminal Defendants), a structured, standardized psychometric instrument that can be used by clinicians in their assessment of competence and which has been validated for inter-rater reliability and validity.

The competency assessment process

When the competency issue is raised, the court typically will appoint several clinical evaluators to conduct a formal assessment of the defendant's competence. These evaluators, usually psychiatrists or psychologists, will examine the defendant and then submit written reports to the court. The evaluation may be performed on an inpatient basis, but increasingly is done outpatient, in a court clinic or the jail. The court then decides the issue, sometimes following a hearing at which the examiners testify and are subject to cross-examination. When both parties stipulate to the findings made in the reports, a hearing will be unnecessary. When the issue is contested, state law will allocate the burden of persuasion, and under *Medina v. California*, 505 U.S. 437 (1992), it will not violate due process to place the burden on the party asserting incompetence, even if that party is the defendant. Under *Medina*, such a burden may be required by statute to be carried by a preponderance of the evidence, but the Supreme Court held in *Cooper v. Oklahoma*, 517 U.S. 348 (1996) that due process would be violated if the burden is required to be carried by clear and convincing evidence.

Disposition following competency determination

If the court finds the defendant competent, the trial proceedings will resume; if not, they will be suspended and the defendant will be ordered into treatment, typically on an inpatient basis. Treatment is designed not to cure the defendant, but to restore competence. If such restoration is thought to have been achieved, a new round of evaluations and hearings will occur, and if the court is satisfied concerning the defendant's competence, the criminal proceedings will be resumed.

In excess of thirty-six thousand defendants are evaluated for competency each year and the number appears to be increasing. The vast majority (as high as 96 percent in some jurisdictions and probably 75 percent in most) are found competent. Nearly all of those found incompetent are hospitalized for treatment, where they are treated with psychotropic drugs and typically returned to court within several months as restored to competence. Some are hospitalized for longer periods, and some are never restored to competence.

Although designed largely based on considerations of paternalism and fairness to the defendant, the competency doctrine frequently imposes heavy burdens on the defendant and considerable costs upon the criminal justice system. Prior to the Supreme Court's decision in *Jackson v. Indiana* (406 U.S. 715 (1972)), defen-

dants hospitalized for incompetency to stand trial received what amounted to an indeterminate sentence of confinement in a mental hospital, typically exceeding many years and often the maximum period authorized as a sentence for the crime charged, and sometimes lasting a lifetime. In *Jackson*, the Court recognized a constitutional limit on the duration of incompetency commitment, holding that a defendant committed solely based upon trial incompetence could not be held more than a reasonable period of time necessary to determine whether there is a substantial probability that he will obtain capacity in the foreseeable future. Any continued confinement, the Court held, must be based upon the probability that the defendant will be restored to competence within a reasonable time. If the treatment provided does not succeed in advancing the defendant toward that goal, then the state must either commence customary civil commitment proceedings or release the defendant. Although *Jackson* marked an end to the most egregious cases of incompetency commitment, many states have responded insufficiently to the Court's decision and abuses persist. The delay often imposed by the incompetency process, much of it unnecessary, frequently produces unneeded and unnecessarily restrictive hospitalization and undermines the defendant's Sixth Amendment right to a speedy trial.

Psychotropic medication in the incompetency process

Psychotropic medication is the principal treatment technique used in the restoration to trial competence. Although some courts and hospitals had once followed an approach that precluded a defendant from being considered competent when competency was maintained by ongoing medication, this practice has now been rejected.

The reverse problem is raised when a defendant seeks to refuse psychotropic medication. This occurred in *Riggins v. Nevada* (504 U.S. 127 (1992)), in which the defendant had been receiving antipsychotic medication in the jail, but sought to refuse the continuation of such medication during his trial. The trial judge refused, and he was convicted. The Supreme Court reversed, finding that the defendant's trial while on a heavy dose of unwanted antipsychotic medication violated due process because the trial court had failed to make findings sufficient to justify such forced medication. The Court's holding was a narrow one, but in important dicta it suggested the kinds of findings that would have justified involuntary medication during trial. Such medication would have been justified if the trial court had found it to be a medically appropriate and least intrusive alternative method of protecting the defendant's own safety or the safety of others in the jail. In addition, the Court noted that the state might have been able to justify such medication if medically appropriate and the least intrusive means of restoring him to competence and maintaining his competency.

Although *Riggins* does not resolve the question of whether the state's interest in competency restoration would outweigh a defendant's assertion of a right to refuse psychotropic medication, this dicta suggests that the Court would find such a state interest sufficient, and most lower courts have so held. *Riggins* leaves open many issues concerning when psychotropic medication can be authorized in the criminal trial process and the disposition of those for whom it may not that the lower courts must face. *Riggins* also alerts the courts to the need to insure that the side effects of psychotropic medication do not impair the defendant's demeanor and trial performance in ways that would be prejudicial, and should lead to increased judicial attention to drug administration practices in the competency to stand trial process.

BRUCE J. WINICK

See also BURDEN OF PROOF; CIVIL AND CRIMINAL DIVIDE; CRIMINAL PROCEDURE: CONSTITUTIONAL ASPECTS; DIMINISHED CAPACITY; EXCUSE: INSANITY; MENTALLY DISORDERED OFFENDERS.

BIBLIOGRAPHY

American Bar Association. *Criminal Justice Mental Health Standards.* Washington, D.C.: American Bar Association, 1989.
BONNIE, RICHARD J. "The Competence of Criminal Defendants: A Theoretical Reformulation." *Behavioral Sciences and the Law* 10 (1992): 291–316.
———. "The Competence of Criminal Defendants: Beyond Dusky and Drope." *University of Miami Law Review* 47 (1993): 539–601.
BONNIE, RICHARD J.; POYTHRESS, NORMAN; HOGE, STEVEN K.; and MONAHAN, JOHN. "Decision-making in Criminal Defense: An Empirical Study of Insanity Pleas and the Impact of Doubted Client Competence." *Journal of Criminal Law and Criminology* 87 (1996): 48–62.
GRISSO, THOMAS. *Evaluating Competencies: Forensic Assessment and Instruments.* New York: Plenum Press, 1986.
HOGE, STEVEN K.; POYTHRESS, NORMAN G.; BONNIE, RICHARD J.; MONAHAN, JOHN T.; EISENBERG, MARLENE; and FEUCHT-HAVIAR, THOMAS. "The MacArthur Adjudicative Competence Study: Development and Validation of a Research Instrument." *Law and Human Behavior* 21 (1997): 141–179.
OTTO, RANDY; POYTHRESS, NORMAN G.; NICHOLSON, ROBERT; EDENS, JOHN F.; MONAHAN, JOHN T.; BONNIE, RICHARD J.; HOGE, STEVEN K.; and EISENBERG, MARLENE. "Psychometric Properties of the MacArthur Competence Assessment Tool—Criminal Adjudication (MacCat-CA)." *Psychological Assessment* 10 (1998): 435–443.
PERLIN, MICHAEL L. *Law and Mental Disability.* Charlottesville, Va.: Michie & Co, 1994.
WINICK, BRUCE J. "Restructuring Competency to Stand Trial." *UCLA Law Review* 32 (1985): 921–985.
———. "Psychotropic Medication in the Criminal Trial Process: The Constitutional and Therapeutic Implications of *Riggins v. Nevada.*" *New York Law School Journal of Human Rights* 10 (1993): 637–709.
———. "Reforming Incompetency to Stand Trial and Plead Guilty: A Restated Proposal and a Response to Professor Bonnie." *Journal of Criminal Law & Criminology* 85 (1995): 571–624.
———. *The Right to Refuse Mental Health Treatment.* Washington, D.C.: American Psychological Association Books, 1995.

CASES

Cooper v. Oklahoma, 517 U.S. 348 (1996).
Drope v. Missouri, 420 U.S. 162 (1975).
Dusky v. United States, 362 U.S. 402 (1960).
Godinez v. Moran, 509 U.S. 389 (1993).
Jackson v. Indiana, 406 U.S. 715 (1972).
Medina v. California, 505 U.S. 437 (1992).
Miranda v. Arizona, 384 U.S. 436 (1966).
Pate v. Robinson, 383 U.S. 375 (1966).
Riggins v. Nevada, 504 U.S. 127 (1992).

COMPUTER CRIME

Computerization significantly eases the performance of many tasks. For example, the speed and ability to communicate with people is fostered by the Internet, a worldwide network that is used to send communiqués and provide access to the world-wide web. But this same speed and ability to communicate also opens the door to criminal conduct. Computer crime plays a significant role in the criminal law of the information age. Accompanying the influx of computers is an increase in criminal acts and, as a result, an increase in the number of statutes to punish those who abuse and misuse this technology.

Computer crime, sometimes known as cybercrime, is a serious concern. The crime can be perpetrated instantaneously and its effects can spread with incredible quickness. Furthermore, the ever-increasing use of computers, especially in serving critical infrastructure, makes computer criminality increasingly important.

There is an endless list of possible crimes that can occur through use of the Internet. For example, the Internet can be a medium used for committing hate crimes, pornography, consumer fraud, stalking, terrorism, theft of security or trade secrets, software piracy, economic espionage, and financial institution fraud. The threat of computer crime is underlined by the fact that a security organization such as the Federal Bureau of Investigation was forced to temporarily take down its Internet site in 1991 after an attack by hackers. Companies have been equally vulnerable and have incurred millions of dollars in damage due to the effect of certain viruses.

Misuse of the computer threatens individual and business privacy, public safety, and national security. There have been considerable efforts made by state, federal, and international governments to curb computer crime.

Categorizing computer-related crime

A precise definition of computer crime is problematic. This is because of the array of different forms and forums in which the crime may appear. A single category cannot accommodate the wide divergence of conduct, perpetrators, victims, and motives found in examining computer crimes. Adding to this confusion is the fact that computer crimes also can vary depending upon the jurisdiction criminalizing the conduct. The criminal conduct can be the subject of punishment under a state statute. There is also an odd mixture of federal offenses that can be used to prosecute computer crimes. But computer crimes are not just domestic. Because computers operate internationally, the definition of computer crime can be influenced by the law of other countries as well. Despite debate among leading experts, there is no internationally recognized definition of computer crime.

At the core of the definition of computer crime is activity specifically related to computer technologies. Thus, stealing a computer or throwing a computer at another person would not fall within the scope of the definition of computer crime in that these activities do not use the technology as the means or object of the criminal act.

Computers serve in several different roles related to criminal activity. The three generally accepted categories speak in terms of computers as communication tools, as targets, and as storage devices.

The computer as a communication tool presents the computer as the object used to commit the crime. This category includes traditional offenses such as fraud committed through the use of a computer. For example, the purchase of counterfeit artwork at an auction held on the Internet uses the computer as the tool for committing the crime. While the activity could easily occur offline at an auction house, the fact that a computer is used for the purchase of this artwork may cause a delay in the detection of it being a fraud. The use of the Internet may also make it difficult to find the perpetrator of the crime.

A computer can also be the target of criminal activity, as seen when hackers obtain unauthorized access to Department of Defense sites. Theft of information stored on a computer also falls within this category. The unauthorized procuring of trade secrets for economic gain from a computer system places the computer in the role of being a target of the criminal activity.

A computer can also be tangential to crime when, for example, it is used as a storage place for criminal records. For example, a business engaged in illegal activity may be using a computer to store its records. The seizure of computer hard drives by law enforcement demonstrates the importance of this function to the evidence-gathering process.

In some instances, computers serve in a dual capacity, as both the tool and target of criminal conduct. For example, a computer is the object or tool of the criminal conduct when an individual uses it to insert a computer virus into the Internet. In this same scenario, computers also serve in the role of targets in that the computer virus may be intended to cripple the computers of businesses throughout the world.

The role of the computer in the crime can also vary depending upon the motive of the individual using the computer. For example, a juvenile hacker may be attempting to obtain access to a secured facility for the purpose of demonstrating computer skills. On the other hand, a terrorist may seek access to this same site for the purpose of compromising material at this location. Other individuals may be infiltrating the site for the economic purpose of stealing a trade secret. Finally, unauthorized computer access may be a display of revenge by a terminated or disgruntled employee.

In addition to computer crimes having several roles, the individuals who commit the crimes do not fit one description. The only common characteristic of the individuals committing these crimes is their association with a computer. The perpetrator of a computer crime could easily be a juvenile hacker, sophisticated business person, or terrorist. Likewise, the victims of computer crimes do not fit a specific category in that the spectrum of possible victims includes individuals, financial institutions, government agencies, corporations, and foreign governments.

Computer crimes often fit within traditional criminal law categories in that computers can be used to commit crimes such as theft, fraud, copyright infringement, espionage, pornography, or terrorism. In some instances, existing criminal categories adapt new terminology to reflect the computer nature of the crime. For example, cyberterrorism is used when the terrorist activity involves computers, and cyberlaundering relates to money laundering via computer. Trespass crimes take on a new dimension when the unauthorized access occurs in cyberspace. For example, in 2000, the website for the American Israel Public Affairs Committee was defaced by intruders who downloaded e-mail addresses and credit card numbers from the site.

Criminal conduct that may appear to have no connection with computers can, in fact, be affected by technology. For example, stalking presents itself as a serious concern growing from increased use of the Internet. Cyberstalking generally involves the stalking of a person via the Internet or other electronic communication. Access to personal information on the Internet makes cyberstalking particularly problematic. Recognizing the need to consider the effect of technology on crimes such as stalking, the Attorney General issued the "1999 Report on Cyberstalking: A New Challenge for Law Enforcement and Industry" that describes the efforts that law enforcement can take to deter this criminal activity. First Amendment concerns factor into whether these and other legal initiatives regarding computer crimes will withstand constitutional challenges.

Computer crimes do not always correlate with traditional descriptions of illegality. Some activities present unique forms of criminal conduct that bear no resemblance to common law or existing crimes. For example, computerization allows for new types of crimes, such as trafficking in passwords.

Other computer crimes may have a resemblance to traditional crimes but the conduct may not fit neatly into an existing category. For example, a "page-jacker" who misappropriates material from another individual's website may face criminal liability for a copyright violation. If the "page-jacker," however, manipulates a website to redirect individuals to his or her own website, it remains uncertain whether this fraudulent conduct fits within classic theft or fraud offenses. Specific computer crime statutes are tailored to meet these new forms of criminal conduct. The ability the Internet provides in accessing information with a degree of anonymity makes some crimes, such as identity theft, important priorities for the criminal justice system.

The technical and changing nature of computer technology can make it difficult for those who are drafting criminal statutes. The array of new terms and new meanings given to existing terms requires a certain level of expertise in order to understand the computer activity. Examples of simple words used in the context of computer activity are the terms "virus" and "worm." A federal court explained, "A 'worm' is a program that travels from one computer to another but does not attach itself to the operating system of the computer it 'infects.'" This differs from a computer "virus," which does attach to the computer operating system that it enters (*United States v. Morris*, 928 F.2d 504, 505n.1 (2d Cir. 1991)).

Computer crime statutes

Legislation at both the federal and state level provide for the prosecution of computer crime. Although computer crimes can be prosecuted using federal statutes that are exclusively focused on computer crime, many prosecutors do not use these specific computer-related statutes. Instead, prosecutors often continue to use traditional criminal law statutes in computer crime prosecutions. Although computer crime laws develop to accommodate new forms of criminal activity, the law has moved relatively slowly in comparison to the rapid development of computer technology.

Federal statutes. At the forefront of federal computer-related offenses is the computer fraud statute, 18 U.S.C. § 1030. Initially passed in 1984 (Counterfeit Access Device and Computer Fraud and Abuse Act of 1984), the statute has been amended on several occasions, including a significant expansion of the statute in the Computer Fraud and Abuse Act of 1986.

This computer fraud statute prohibits seven different types of computer-related activity. These can basically be described as: (1) electronic espionage; (2) unauthorized access to financial institution information, information from a United States department or agency, or information from any protected computer involved in interstate or foreign commerce; (3) intentionally browsing in a government computer or affecting a government computer; (4) using the computer for schemes of fraud or theft; (5) transmitting programs that cause damage or accessing a protecting computer and causing damage; (6) interstate trafficking of passwords; and (7) extortion threats to a protected computer. The statute includes both felony and misdemeanor provisions with different penalties depending on the specific conduct. Additionally, 18 U.S.C. § 1030(g) includes a civil remedy for those damaged through violations of the statute.

The Electronic Communications Privacy Act (ECPA) (18 U.S.C. §§ 2510 et. seq., 2701–2710) was initially enacted to criminalize eavesdropping. In 1986 Congress updated this privacy legislation so that it was not limited to conduct involving traditional wires and electronic communications. The EPCA now covers all forms of digital communications.

By providing privacy rights to Internet communications, the EPCA equips federal prosecutors with a tool for curbing criminal activity involving the Internet. This act allows prosecutors to proceed with criminal charges when a defendant compromises a victim's privacy rights by improperly accessing the victim's computer system. The ECPA details the statutory exceptions that are provided to system operators and to law enforcement. For example, where service providers can monitor traffic data on the system, they are precluded from reading material that is being transmitted over the Internet.

Another federal statute that permits prosecution of computer-related activity is the Economic Espionage Act (EEA). Passed by Congress in 1996, this act focuses on the protection of trade secrets. Trade secrets, a term defined in the statute, include an array of different types of information that have an actual or potential value and that an owner has "taken reasonable measures" to keep secret. The EEA offers trade secret protection to both businesses and the government. The significance of information to society, and the problems that are attached to protecting this information, make the EEA an important step in how the law can provide protection from computer crime.

The EEA includes statutes pertaining to both domestic and foreign trade secrets. The statute 18 U.S.C. § 1831 prohibits the misappropriation of trade secrets that benefit any foreign government. In contrast, 18 U.S.C. § 1832 prohibits the theft of domestic trade secrets. The EEA provides for extraterritorial application, allowing U.S. prosecutors to pursue cases that meet criteria set forth in the statute, despite the fact that the criminal activity may have occurred outside the United States. The EEA also permits forfeiture, such as forfeiture of computer equipment, as a possible penalty. In an effort to encourage businesses that are victims of a theft of trade secrets to cooperate in pursuing prosecution, the EEA attempts to preserve the confidentiality of the trade secret during the criminal prosecution.

The availability and dissemination of pornography is exacerbated by technology. The accessibility of pornography via the Internet is a concern of the Communications Decency Act of 1996 and the Child Pornography Prevention Act of 1996. The child pornography and luring statutes specifically include activities related to use of a computer (18 U.S.C. § 2251 et. seq., 18 U.S.C. § 2422(b)). These statutes and others have been added to the criminal code to provide additional protections to children. When reviewing these statutes, courts have the difficult task of determining the appropriate line between individual liberties, such as privacy and free speech, and criminal conduct.

Many federal statutes prohibit conduct in "technology-neutral" ways. These statutes permit prosecutors to proceed with the prosecution of criminal activity involving a computer without having to wait for lawmakers to create a specific computer-related crime. For example, the sale of drugs without a prescription can be prosecuted using a traditional drug statute, even though the activity occurs on the Internet (21 U.S.C. § 353(b)). Similarly, statutes prohibiting the sale, manufacture, or distribution of controlled substances present conduct in a "technology-neutral" way, permitting the use of existing statutes for the prosecution of these crimes (21

U.S.C. §§ 822, 829, 841). Improper gun sales on the Internet, likewise, may be prosecuted using existing gun commerce statutes (18 U.S.C. § 922).

Statutes that include the term "wires" as a means of committing the conduct may allow prosecutors to apply the statute to Internet-related crimes. For example, a statute that includes the language "wire communication facility" to describe the means by which the criminal conduct occurs, is broad enough to encompass Internet-related crimes. This language is found, for example, in a sports gambling statute (18 U.S.C. § 1081). Thus, businesses conducting sports gambling over the Internet can be prosecuted using the traditional federal gambling laws (18 U.S.C. § 1084).

In the federal arena, one commonly finds computer-related conduct charged using existing statutes that are not uniquely worded to provide for prosecutions involving activity related to computers. Despite the absence of specific reference to computers, individuals engaged in computer-related activity are charged with crimes such as securities fraud (15 U.S.C. § 77q), money laundering (18 U.S.C. § 1956), fraud and related activity in connection with access devices (18 U.S.C. § 1029), and conspiracy (18 U.S.C. § 371).

Three statutes that do explicitly refer to computers that prosecutors continue to use in charging computer-related activity are wire fraud (18 U.S.C. § 1343), copyright infringement (17 U.S.C. § 506 (a)), and illegal transportation of stolen property (18 U.S.C. § 2314).

Wire fraud presents a generic statute that is easily adaptable to a wide array of criminal conduct. Schemes to defraud of "money or property" or the "intangible right to honest services" that use the wires in their furtherance are prohibited by the wire fraud statute (18 U.S.C. § 1343). For example, individuals selling fraudulent products over the Internet can be subject to prosecution under the wire fraud statute.

Software piracy and intellectual property theft are important issues of the information age. Because the Internet offers an easily accessible means for transmitting copyrighted material, these crimes have the effect of costing U.S. businesses substantial sums of money each year. Often prosecutors use the copyright infringement statute (17 U.S.C. § 506 (a)) in proceeding against individuals committing these crimes. The No Electronic Theft Act (P.L. 105–147), passed by Congress in 1997, extends the reach of criminal copyright law to specifically include electronic means as one method for committing the crime (17 U.S.C. § 501 (a) (1)). The act also expands the scope of the criminal conduct covered under this crime, allowing for prosecutions without a showing that the distributor of the copyrighted material profited from the activity.

Computer crimes also have been prosecuted under the National Stolen Property Act. This was particularly true prior to the passage of the specific computer-related statute, the Computer Fraud and Abuse Act (18 U.S.C. § 1030). The National Stolen Property Act prohibits certain described activities involving the illegal transportation of stolen property (18 U.S.C. § 2314). There are, however, specific statutory limitations that preclude this offense from being used widely to prosecute computer crimes.

State statutes. All states have enacted computer crime laws. These laws offer different coverage of possible computer criminality. In some instances the state law resembles provisions found in the federal Computer Fraud and Abuse Act. Some states incorporate computer activity into theft and criminal mischief statutes, while others provide laws addressing sophisticated offenses against intellectual property. Computer fraud, unauthorized access offenses, trade secret protection and trespass statutes also exist in some state codes. In some state statutes, there is explicit legislative recognition that the criminal activity is a problem in both the government and private sector.

A state may use different degrees of an offense to reflect the severity of the computer violation. For example, a state may penalize what it terms an aggravated criminal invasion of privacy, which carries a higher penalty than a privacy invasion that is not aggravated. Several states have included forfeiture provisions, which permit the forfeiture of computers and computer systems as a consequence of the illegal conduct. State statutes include civil relief, allowing individuals harmed by violations of the computer statute to sue civilly for damages. Realizing the skills necessary for investigating computer crime, a state may include provisions for the education of law enforcement officers as part of its efforts to combat criminal activity related to computers.

International initiatives

Computers can operate globally. Thus, the perpetrator of a computer crime can affect the computers of another country without leaving home. As stated by Attorney General Janet Reno, "[a] hacker needs no passport and passes no checkpoints." The global nature of the Internet raises a host of international questions, such as what should be considered computer crime and who will have the jurisdiction to prosecute such crime. There are also issues regarding how evidence necessary for a criminal prosecution may be obtained. Mutual assistance treaties between countries often assist in procuring necessary evidence from other countries that may be needed for a criminal prosecution within the United States.

Although the Internet operates internationally, there is no uniformly accepted set of international laws that criminalize computer misuse and abuse. Several international conferences and initiatives, however, have focused on computer crime.

The Council of Europe (COE), an international organization with more than forty member countries, has been at the forefront in promoting international cooperation regarding computer crime. Mutual assistance in the investigation of cybercrime is also a discussion topic of the Group of Eight (G-8) countries (United States, United Kingdom, France, Germany, Italy, Canada, Japan, and Russia). In May 1998, the G-8 countries adopted a set of principles and an action plan to combat computer crimes.

Other international initiatives also have considered computer-related issues. For example, consumer protection policies have been formulated through the Organization for Economic Co-operation and Development ("OECD"). Computer crime issues have also been discussed in international forums such as the Vienna International Child Pornography Conference. Additionally, the United Nations produced a manual on the prevention and control of computer-related crime. The manual stresses the need for international cooperation and global action.

Agencies focused on computer crimes

The Federal Bureau of Investigation (FBI) and Department of Justice (DOJ) are the agencies at the forefront of investigation and prosecution of computer crimes. Each of these entities has established separate bodies within the agency that concentrates on computer crimes. There are also interagency groups that focus on computer crimes. In some cases, private businesses are included as a part of the cybergroup. Since most of the victims of computer crimes are businesses, the FBI has stressed the importance of having close business cooperation in the investigation and prosecution of these crimes.

The National Infrastructure Protection Center (NIPC), established in 1998, focuses on protecting "critical infrastructures." The NIPC is an interagency body located within the FBI. The NIPC is divided into three sections: (1) the Computer Investigations and Operations Section (CIOS), which coordinates computer crime investigations; (2) the Analysis and Warning Section (AWS), which analyzes information and warns the government and private industry of possible system threats; and (3) the Training, Outreach and Strategy Section (TOSS), which provides training to law enforcement and outreach to private businesses. In addition to the NIPC, the FBI has cybercrime programs in individual FBI offices.

The Computer Crime and Intellectual Property Section (CCIPS) of the DOJ is the prosecutorial body coordinating federal computer crime cases throughout the United States. Founded in 1991, CCIPS became a formal section of the DOJ in 1996. CCIPS assists federal prosecutors and law enforcement agents throughout the country. CCIPS works particularly closely with the assistant U.S. attorneys in the individual offices that are handling computer crime cases. Each U.S. attorney's office designates an assistant U.S. attorney, known as Computer and Telecommunications Coordinators (CTCs), to receive special training for the prosecution of computer crime cases.

The CCIPS also serves a key role in the national and international coordination of efforts to curb computer crimes. It is associated with the National Cybercrime Training Partnership (NCTP), a body that is focused on making certain that law enforcement receives adequate technical training to handle computer crimes. CCIPS also participates in discussions with international bodies such as the G-8 Subgroup on High-Tech Crime and the Council of Europe Experts Committee on Cybercrime.

Numerous other government agencies can play a role in the investigation of computer crimes. For example, if the computer activity involves bomb threats, the Bureau of Alcohol, Tobacco, and Firearms (ATF) may be involved in the investigation. The investigation of Internet fraud involving the mails may include the U.S. Postal Inspection Service. The U.S. Customs service may play a role in an investigation involving imported software, and the U.S. Secret Service is likely to be involved if the alleged crime is counterfeiting of currency. Likewise, Internet securities fraud may include individuals from the Securities and Exchange Commission (SEC) as part of the investigation team.

In some instances the government agency may have developed a particular group focused on computer activity. For example, in July 1998 the Securities and Exchange Commission created the Office of Internet Enforcement (OIE). A key focus of this body is Internet securities fraud. In addition to providing training, the OIE oversees the investigation of improper securities activity involving the Internet. The office also refers matters to other government agencies.

There are also study groups to consider approaches to eradicating computer crimes. On 5 August 1999, President Clinton issued Executive Order 13,133 establishing a working group to consider and make recommendations regarding the existence of unlawful conduct on the Internet. The report of the group, issued in March 2000, recommends a three-part approach for addressing unlawful conduct on the Internet. It calls for analysis through a "policy framework" of Internet regulation of unlawful conduct to assure consistency in the treatment of online and offline conduct and ensure the protection of privacy and civil liberties. It stresses the need for law enforcement funding, training, and international cooperation. It also calls for continued support from the private sector. A key focus of the report is the need to develop educational methods to combat computer crime.

The private sector has been included in many of the agency efforts to curtail computer crime. An example of a joint effort between the government and business is seen in the Cybercitizen Partnership, an alliance between high-tech industry and the government. As an aspect of this partnership, the government and private industry will share computer knowledge to achieve a more secure system. An aim of this partnership is to promote computer ethics and educate users.

In an effort to become more aware of computer crimes, the FBI and the National White Collar Crime Center established the Internet Fraud Complaint Center (IFCC). Established as a result of this partnership is a website that offers victims of Internet fraud a way to report Internet fraud online.

Government agencies have also been involved in educating consumers about computer abuses. For example, the Federal Trade Commission (FTC) uses the computer to alert and educate consumers and businesses on privacy and fraud issues that pertain to the Internet.

Privacy issues

Computers present new considerations for both substantive criminal law and criminal procedure. At the heart of many of the questions is the appropriate balance between privacy rights and necessary criminal investigation. It is particularly problematic with respect to computer crimes, since serious national security issues can arise when computers are misused.

The tension between the government's need to secure information to investigate criminal conduct and privacy concerns of individuals and businesses appears prominently in the debate concerning encryption. Encryption offers individuals and businesses the ability to protect the privacy of data being transferred on the Internet. Encryption is particularly useful in protecting trade secrets in the commercial market. Encryption, however, also can be used to avoid detection by individuals who are committing unlawful activities. By encrypting data, individuals can store data, transmit data, and harmfully use data for criminal purposes. The Department of Justice has expressed concern that securely encrypted material can undermine law enforcement efforts. Unlike law enforcement's ability to obtain court authorized wiretaps for information transmitted over the telephone, securely encrypted matter may preclude the government from using the material.

Conclusion

Computers add a new dimension to criminal law, presenting many issues for law enforcement. At the forefront of law enforcement concerns is the necessity to secure adequate training to combat these crimes. This requires additional resources. The technical sophistication needed to follow the "electronic trail" far surpasses traditional methods of investigation. In some cases data are encrypted, making it difficult for police authorities to discern the contents of the information. The detection of criminal conduct may also be hampered by the reluctance of entities to report an unauthorized computer access. Corporations may fear the negative publicity that might result as a consequence of their systems being compromised. In many cases, unauthorized computer access may go undetected by the individual or entity whose computer system had been invaded.

Equally challenging are the policy and legal issues. It is necessary to enact legislation that will sufficiently prohibit the abuses of new and developing technology. The speed with which technology develops makes this a continual concern. In some cases, the line between what will be considered criminal conduct and what will be civil remains uncertain. A common debate in discussions of business crimes is whether the activity is an aggressive business practice, or alternatively a crime. Further, issues of jurisdiction and enforcement power present special problems given that the Internet operates internationally. This can become particularly problematic when countries adopt different standards of what constitutes crime and different penalties for computer-related criminal activity.

The Internet also presents national security concerns since computers serve instrumental roles in the delivery of emergency services, government operations, banking, transportation, energy, and telecommunications. As technology develops, the law needs to respond to these new developments to deter those who would abuse and misuse the new technology.

ELLEN S. PODGOR

See also EMPLOYEE THEFT: BEHAVIORAL ASPECTS; EMPLOYEE THEFT: LEGAL ASPECTS; FEAR OF CRIME; FEDERAL CRIMINAL JURISDICTION; POLICE: PRIVATE POLICE AND INDUSTRIAL SECURITY; SEX OFFENSES: CONSENSUAL; STALKING; THEFT; WHITE-COLLAR CRIME: HISTORY OF AN IDEA.

BIBLIOGRAPHY

ALEXANDER, KENT B., and WOOD, KRISTIN L. "The Economic Espionage Act: Setting the Stage for a New Commercial Code of Conduct." *Georgia State University Law Review* 15 (1999): 907–939.

BAKER, GLENN D. "Trespassers Will Be Prosecuted: Computer Crime in the 1990s." *Computer Law Journal* 12 (1993): 61–100.

BRANSCOMB, ANNE W. "Rogue Computer Programs and Computer Rogues: Tailoring the Punishment to Fit the Crime." *Rutgers Computer and Technology Law Journal* 16 (1990): 1–61.

CHARNEY, SCOTT, and ALEXANDER, KENT. "Computer Crime." *Emory Law Journal* 45 (1996): 931–957.

GOODMAN, MARC D. "Why the Police Don't Care About Computer Crime." *Harvard Journal of Law & Technology* 10 (1997): 465–495.

HATCHER, MICHAEL; MCDANNELL, JAY; and OSTFELD, STACY. "Computer Crimes." *American Criminal Law Review* 36 (1999): 397–444.

LEDERMAN, ELI. "Criminal Liability for Breach of Confidential Commercial Information." *Emory Law Journal* 38 (1989): 921–1004.

NIMMER, RAYMOND T. *The Law of Computer Technology,* 2d ed. Boston: Warren Gorham Lamont, 1992. Pages 12-1–12-50.

PARKER, DONN B. *Fighting Computer Crime.* New York: Wiley Computer Publishing, 1998.

PERRITT, HENRY H., JR.; CHARNEY, SCOTT; and MILLER, GREGORY P. "Computer Crimes Now on the Books: What Do We Do from Here?" *Temple Law Review* 70 (1997): 1199–1226.

PODGOR, ELLEN S., and ISRAEL, JEROLD H. "Computer Crimes." In *White Collar Crime in a Nutshell.* St. Paul, Minn.: West Publishing Co., 1997. Pages 236–242.

RENO, JANET. "Keynote Address by U.S. Attorney General Janet Reno on High Tech and Computer Crime." (Presented before the meeting of the P–8 Senior Experts' Group on Transnational Organized Crime, January 21, 1997, Chantilly, Virginia).

WHITLEY, JOE D., and JORDAN, WILLIAM H. "Computer Crime." In *White Collar Crime: Business and Regulatory Offenses.* Vol. 2. Edited by Otto G. Obermaier and Robert G. Morvillo. New York: Law Journal Press, 1999. Pages 21-1–21-43.

WISE, EDWARD M. "Computer Crime and Other Crimes Against Information Technology in the United States." In *International Review of Criminal Law* 64. Toulouse, France: Association Internationale De Droit Penal, 1992. Pages 647–669.

INTERNET RESOURCES

For information on the protection of critical infrastructure, see the website of the National Infrastructure Protection Center (http://www.nipc.gov).

For information on international issues regarding computer crimes, see the U.N. Crime and Justice Information Network (http://www.uncjin.org).

For information on U.S. enforcement of computer crimes, see the Computer Crime and Intellectual Property section of the Criminology Division of the U.S. Department of Justice (http://www.usdoj.gov/criminal/cybercrime).

For information on cyberstalking, see the website of the U.S. Department of Justice (http://www.usdoj.gov/criminal/cybercrime/cyberstalking.htm).

CONFESSIONS

Confessions have played an ambiguous and paradoxical role in Anglo-American cultural and legal history. In many religious traditions, a confession begins the process of expiation and forgiveness. Yet in the secular, legal sphere, it often lays the foundation for blame and punishment.

Moreover, there is a contradiction embedded within this contradiction. Because confessions appear to create unmediated access to the defendant's knowledge, thought processes, and beliefs, they seem to provide uniquely powerful evidence of both culpability and contrition. Yet because the access is in fact always mediated, confessions can also be uniquely dangerous and misleading. The upshot has been heavy reliance on confessions coupled with extensive regulation of their use.

In the United States, three separate constitutional provisions limit the legal use of confessions.

1. The Fifth and Fourteenth Amendments guarantee due process of law. This protection has been interpreted to prohibit the extraction of "involuntary" confessions.
2. The Sixth Amendment (made applicable to the states by the Fourteenth Amendment) guarantees the assistance of counsel in all criminal prosecutions. The Supreme Court has interpreted this provision to prohibit introduction of post-charge statements made by a defendant in the absence of a lawyer.
3. Finally, the Fifth Amendment's self-incrimination clause (also made applicable to the states by the Fourteenth Amendment) provides that "No person . . . shall be compelled in any criminal case to be a witness against himself." This language has been interpreted to bar from criminal prosecutions all compelled statements made by a criminal defendant and any evidence derived from such statements.

The role of confessions

A defendant can confess to guilt in a variety of different settings, and different legal rules govern admissibility in each setting. First, some defendants make inculpatory statements to friends or associates. In general, if the prosecution learns of these statements because of the cooperation of a person who hears them, the statements are admissible against the defendant.

The primary exception to this general rule arises when a government agent deliberately elicits statements made by an individual who has been formally charged with a crime. As we shall see, admission of statements secured in these special circumstances violates the defendant's Sixth Amendment right to counsel. In the more typical situation, there is no constitutional bar to admission of the statements. Although various evidentiary privileges may bar introduction of inculpatory statements made to a spouse, a lawyer, a member of the clergy, or a physician, the admissions exception defeats a general hearsay objection to the evidence. Moreover, the Supreme Court has repeatedly held that there is no "reasonable expectation of privacy" implicating Fourth Amendment rights when an individual voluntarily shares information with others. Nor is there usually the "compulsion" or "involuntariness" required to invoke self-incrimination or due process objections.

Second, defendants regularly admit culpability when they plead guilty to an offense. Indeed, confessions associated with guilty pleas are the most commonly used inculpatory statements in the criminal justice system. Approximately 90 percent of all criminal prosecutions end in guilty pleas. To be sure, the defendant need not always concede his factual guilt when he pleads guilty, but prosecutors frequently insist on such a concession, and most guilty pleas are accompanied by an admission of guilt. One might suppose that guilty pleas would implicate the Fifth Amendment's self-incrimination clause when they are extracted through a threat of harsher punishment if a guilty plea is not forthcoming. However, the Supreme Court has held that the mere risk of conviction does not constitute the kind of compulsion that implicates self-incrimination rights and that plea bargaining is therefore permissible, at least so long as the defendant's plea satisfies the looser "voluntariness" standard.

Third, whether or not they plead guilty, defendants frequently make inculpatory statements during the sentencing process in order to demonstrate contrition. The Federal Sentencing Guidelines grant defendants a reduction in their offense level if they "clearly demonstrate . . . acceptance of responsibility for [the] offense," and judges regularly take into account remorse or contrition even in the absence of formal guidelines requiring them to do so. Although the Supreme Court has held that self-incrimination rights attach at the sentencing phase, the Court has yet to decide whether harsher punishment for defendants who refuse to admit their guilt at sentencing violates Fifth Amendment rights.

Finally, many defendants confess as a result of police interrogation conducted after their arrest. Confessions in this setting have generated the most controversy, and a complex body of law, discussed below, regulates their use. Despite this regulation, it appears that a surprisingly large number of defendants make inculpatory statements to the police. Although there are no nationwide statistics, a smattering of local studies is suggestive. In a study published in 1996, Richard Leo reported on observations of 182 police interrogations, most of them in a major urban police departments. He found that 64.29 percent of the suspects gave incriminating information of some type and that 41.76 percent either confessed or made partial admissions. In 1994, Paul Cassell studied data on confessions and incriminating statements in cases submitted for prosecution to the Salt Lake County Attorney's Office. He found that in 33.3 percent of the cases, the suspect confessed, gave incriminating statements, or was locked into a false alibi (1996).

There has been considerable controversy over just how important these confessions are to successful law enforcement. In *Escobedo v. Illinois* (378 U.S. 478, 488 (1964)), a majority of the Justices implied that reliance on "extrinsic evidence independently secured through skillful investigation" could achieve the same results as a system that relied heavily on confessions. In contrast, Justice Byron White, dissenting in *Miranda v. Arizona* (384 U.S. 436, 541 (1966)), warned that limitations on confessions would "measurably weaken the ability of the criminal law to perform [its] tasks," and Justice Tom Clark, dissenting in the same case, argued that a limitation on confessions "inserted at the nerve center of crime detection may well kill the patient" (384 U.S. at 500).

Decades after Justice Clark's gloomy prediction, the patient seems to be alive and kicking, but there are no recent, systematic empirical studies that throw light on these rival claims. A group of studies conducted in the 1960s tended to show that confessions were necessary for convictions in about a quarter of all cases prosecuted, but the numbers varied widely in different studies, and there appears to be no solid, nationwide data from more recent years.

The voluntariness approach

As already noted, three separate constitutional provisions bear on the admission of confessions achieved through police interrogation. Before 1964, the principal means of control were the clauses in the Fifth and Fourteenth Amendments, guaranteeing due process of law. Beginning in 1936, a series of Supreme Court cases held that police tactics having the effect of "overbearing the suspect's will" or resulting in "involuntary" statements violate this guarantee.

Almost from the beginning, the scope and purposes of this protection were encrusted in ambiguity. To be sure, the earliest cases, suppressing confessions gained through overt police brutality and outright torture, seem uncontroversial, yet even here the Court never made entirely clear which of two rival theories led to exclusion of the evidence. On one theory, the coercive measures themselves entailed a deprivation of liberty, and due process was therefore denied when these measures were utilized without first providing the suspect with adequate process. On this view, the constitutional violation was complete at the point when coercion was applied, and the resulting confession was inadmissible only because this evidentiary rule served to deter future misconduct or prevented the tainting of the criminal justice system by misconduct that had already occurred. Alternatively, the Court sometimes suggested that the deprivation of liberty came when the defendant was convicted. On this theory, a trial at which unreliable statements were introduced did not amount to the process that was due to criminal defendants.

So long as the Court confined itself to the regulation of outright brutality, this ambiguity made little difference. Violence and torture are reprehensible both because this treatment of suspects "shocks the conscience" and because a trial dominated by statements secured by these means is a mockery. Over time, however, the Court began to focus on more subtle means of coercion. For example, the Court held that denial of food or sleep, incommunicado interrogation, and subtle psychological pressure might make a confession involuntary. It also began to focus on individual characteristics of the suspect. Statements made by suspects who lacked education or sophistication, who were illiterate, or who suffered from mental abnormalities were suspect even when there was no physical coercion.

This expansion of due process protection raised urgent questions as to the purpose the protection was meant to serve. In the early cases, the Court emphasized the unreliability of confessions secured by violence or torture. In later cases, however, the Court began to suggest a vaguer rationale based upon the appropriate limits of state power over the individual, even when the application of such power produced reliable evidence. For example, in *Rogers v. Richmond* (365 U.S. 534 (1961)), the trial judge found that the police tactics used in the case had no impact on the reliability of the defendant's statements and told the jury that the confession's admissibility turned on its trustworthiness. The Supreme Court reversed, holding that the involuntariness question should be resolved "with complete disregard of whether or not [the suspect] in fact spoke the truth" (365 U.S. at 543).

If one's concern is unreliability, then confessions secured through both brutality and more subtle coercion are suspect. Both techniques have at least the potential to lead innocent defendants to confess. It might follow that both types of confessions should be excluded as evidence because of the possibility that they will taint the verdict. But this rationale runs up against the fact that in many other contexts (most notably eye witness identification or testimony by accomplices), courts regularly depend upon juries to filter out unreliable testimony. Moreover, the rationale fails to explain why the Court has insisted on excluding reliable confessions. For example, a confession might contain extrinsic evidence that could be known only to the perpetrator. When such a confession is secured through brutal methods, its exclusion might be justified on the ground that the law should not encourage or sanction the use of these methods. But this rationale fails to explain the exclusion of reliable confessions, and reliable evidence gained as a result of these confessions, when police utilize trickery or manipulation rather than brutality.

The short of it, then, is that there is no rationale that adequately explains all of the Court's due process doctrine. Moreover, the voluntariness approach runs into serious philosophical and practical difficulties. On the philosophical level, the Court's approach requires it to distinguish between cases where the defendant confessed because of an act of "will" and cases where the confession was the product of external forces that "overbore" the will. This distinction poses philosophical problems encountered by any abstract effort to differentiate between freedom and coercion. On the one hand, there is a sense in which all confessions are the product of choice. Even a defendant who is brutally beaten or tortured in the end "chooses" to confess. Indeed, it is the very fact that the statement cannot be secured without the victim's cooperation that

makes torture so dehumanizing. Yet on the other hand, even the most "free" confession is in some sense a product of external forces. After all, a defendant who volunteers a statement to police would not have done so had there been no police to volunteer the statement to.

To be sure, this philosophical conundrum does not prevent us from sharing strong intuitions about polar cases. So long as we are in the world of the whips and electrodes on the one hand and of authentic contrition on the other, most people know where they come out. More serious problems arose, however, as the Court moved from the clear cases to the marginal ones. These difficulties, in turn, created practical problems. Because the Court never succeeded in formulating a coherent and administrable "test" for what police could legitimately do, it left the lower courts with scant guidance for resolving the many cases that the Supreme Court did not have room for on its docket. Perhaps more seriously, the police themselves lacked clear directions that they could rely upon before the fact when they decided what tactics to use against suspects.

Problems such as these ultimately led the Court to shift focus to alternative means of legal control—means that are discussed below. To be sure, as a formal matter, the Court has never abandoned the voluntariness requirement. But although due process protections remain as a theoretical limit on police tactics, the Court has shown much less interest in the voluntariness inquiry in recent years.

In the quarter century following the *Miranda* decision the Supreme Court reversed only two convictions on voluntariness grounds, whereas there had been twenty-three reversals during the comparable period prior to *Miranda*. This change might be attributable, at least in part, to improvements in police behavior, but judicial oversight of that behavior has also changed. For example, in *Colorado v. Connelly* (479 U.S. 157 (1986)), the Court held that personal characteristics of a defendant, including severe mental illness, did not make his statement involuntary in the absence of coercive police activity.

Moreover, even in cases where the police have resorted to various forms of coercive pressure, lower courts often admit the resulting statement after finding that under the "totality of the circumstances," the defendant's will was not overborne. These courts have routinely admitted confessions secured through threats of severe punishment, deceptive statements, and promises. They have also upheld the product of interrogations conducted with suspects who were mentally disabled or who were undergoing drug withdrawal or suffering from lack of food or sleep. As Chief Judge Richard Posner of the Seventh Circuit United States Court of Appeals has summarized the current state of the law, "The [voluntariness] formula is not taken seriously. . . . [V]ery few incriminating statements, custodial or otherwise, are held to be involuntary, though few are the product of a choice that interrogators left completely free" (*United States v. Rutledge*, 900 F.2d 1127, 1129 (7 B Civ. 1990)).

The right to counsel approach

By the mid-1960s, unhappiness with its own voluntariness jurisprudence led the Supreme Court to consider other, more clear-cut and rule-like approaches to the control of putatively improper interrogation techniques. A breakthrough came in 1964, when the Court decided *Massiah v. United States* (377 U.S. 201 (1964)). Massiah was arrested and, along with one Colson, indicted for possession of narcotics. Unbeknownst to Massiah, Colson thereupon agreed to cooperate with the government and permitted an agent to install a radio transmitter under the front seat of his car. The agent used the transmitter to overhear a lengthy and incriminating conversation between Colson and Massiah. The Supreme Court held that Massiah "was denied the basic protections of [the Sixth Amendment right to counsel] when there was used against him at his trial evidence of his own incriminating words, which federal agents had deliberately elicited from him after he had been indicted and in the absence of his counsel" (377 U.S. at 206).

In some respects, *Massiah* is a puzzling holding. After all, Massiah had a lawyer at the time of his incriminating conversation. The prosecution had done nothing to prevent Massiah from bringing his lawyer with him when he went to talk with Colson. It was Massiah's bad judgment, rather than government coercion, that led to his misguided discussion in the absence of counsel. Moreover, it is hard to see how the presence of his lawyer would have made that discussion less problematic. Indeed, eavesdropping on discussions between lawyer and client seems more invasive of Sixth Amendment rights than what actually transpired in *Massiah*. If the government's *Massiah* tactics were indeed offensive, the difficulty seems to lie not in the absence of a lawyer, but in the deceptive use of a confederate to extract incriminating information. Yet the Court has repeatedly held in the Fourth Amendment context that a defendant who talks to a confederate "assumes the risk" that this information will be conveyed to the police.

But although *Massiah* rested on debatable doctrinal premises, it nonetheless held out the promise of "solving" the confessions problem. If the Sixth Amendment required the presence of counsel even for a conversation between a defendant and his confederate, then surely it required counsel's presence during a formal police interrogation. And as a practical matter, there was little chance that a suspect would confess with a lawyer sitting at his elbow.

The Supreme Court seemed to be moving in just this direction in *Escobedo v. Illinois* (378 U.S. 478 (1964)), a case decided a few weeks after *Massiah*. Unlike Massiah, Escobedo had not yet been formally charged with an offense. He was arrested on suspicion of murder and interrogated in the absence of counsel despite his repeated requests to see his lawyer. Although the facts surrounding his confession could easily have led the Court to find it involuntary under the due process test, the Justices chose instead to focus on the absence of counsel. Even though there had been no formal charge, the Court found that Escobedo had been "accused" because the investigation had focused on him. It followed that he had a right to the presence of a lawyer and that his confession could not be used against him.

When the Supreme Court announced its decision in *Miranda v. Arizona* (384 U.S. 436 (1966)), some two years after *Escobedo*, many observers thought that the Court's newly minted self-incrimination approach would subsume its *Massiah-Escobedo* right to counsel jurisprudence, much as the Court lost interest in enforcing a due process, voluntariness standard in the post-*Miranda* period. In one important respect, the modern Court has indeed backed away from its earlier Sixth Amendment jurisprudence: subsequent cases have made clear that the Sixth Amendment right to counsel attaches only after adversary criminal proceedings have been formally initiated against the suspect. Despite the *Escobedo* Court's clear language to the contrary, the *Escobedo* opinion has been reinterpreted as resting on self-incrimination rather than Sixth Amendment grounds. This limitation on the Sixth Amendment right is important, because most police interrogations are conducted during the time period between the defendant's arrest and the filing of formal charges.

In other important respects, however, the Court has actually expanded upon Sixth Amendment protections against statements made in the absence of counsel. For example, in *Brewer v. Williams* (430 U.S. 387 (1977)), the Supreme Court reversed the conviction of a defendant convicted of murdering a ten-year-old girl on the ground that the defendant's confession was secured without the presence of counsel. (Williams was subsequently retried without the confession, and the Supreme Court affirmed his resulting conviction.) The murder in question occurred in Des Moines, Iowa, but Williams was arrested and formally charged in Davenport, some 160 miles away. Despite a promise not to interrogate Williams on the trip back to Des Moines, an officer delivered a long monologue designed to appeal to Williams's guilt and religious sensibility. Although Williams had been warned repeatedly of his right to remain silent, he responded to the speech by leading the officer to the body of the murdered child.

The Supreme Court's reversal of Williams's conviction is notable not only for its reaffirmation of *Massiah* rights in a highly emotional setting, but also for its clarification of the standards for interrogation and waiver in the Sixth Amendment context. Even though the police officer had not directly questioned Williams, the Court nonetheless found that he had been "interrogated" for *Massiah* purposes because the officer had "deliberately and designedly set out to elicit information" from him (430 U.S. at 399). Since Williams plainly knew that he had a right to remain silent, one might have supposed that he knowingly waived this right when he led the officer to the body. But the Court focused on the fact that the defendant had "effectively asserted his right to counsel" prior to making the statement (430 U.S. at 405). Having claimed this right, Williams was entitled to "every reasonable presumption against waiver" (430 U.S. at 404). In a later case, the Court made this presumption more concrete: once a defendant had been formally charged and had requested counsel, a defendant could waive the right only if the defendant himself initiated a subsequent conversation about the offense.

Chief Justice Warren Burger wrote a bitter dissenting opinion in *Williams*, but he arguably extended the *Massiah* doctrine still further in *United States v. Henry* (447 U.S. 264 (1980)). After Henry had been charged with armed robbery, the government placed an informant in his cell. The informant was told not to initiate conversa-

tion with Henry, but to pay attention to anything he might say about the offense. Writing for the majority, Chief Justice Burger held that the government had "deliberately elicited" Henry's statements in violation of the *Massiah* doctrine. True, the government had told the informant not to initiate conversations with Henry, but the informant testified that he had had "some conversations with Mr. Henry" and that the incriminatory statements were "the product of this conversation." Moreover, because Henry did not know that his cellmate was a government agent, he could not have knowingly and voluntarily waived his right to assistance of counsel.

In subsequent cases, the Court has made clear that *Henry* does not apply in circumstances where a government informant does no more than listen to the suspect and refrains from "deliberately eliciting" the statements. The Court has also held that the police may legally elicit and introduce statements from a charged defendant concerning a different crime for which the defendant has not yet been charged, and that even when a defendant invokes the right to counsel, the invocation does not bar interrogations about other offenses. Moreover, the Court has held, a defendant who receives *Miranda* warnings and waives his *Miranda* rights, discussed below, also waives his Sixth Amendment rights.

The self-incrimination approach— historical background

In 1966, the Supreme Court decided *Miranda v. Arizona* (384 U.S. 436 (1966)), one of the most famous decisions in its history. *Miranda* is best known for the warnings that take its name. As a doctrinal matter, however, the case is most important for shifting the Court's focus from due process and Sixth Amendment concerns to an analysis resting on compelled self-incrimination. In order to understand how this shift was accomplished, it is necessary briefly to review the history and structure of the self-incrimination guarantee.

Although the concern about self-incrimination can be traced back to Talmudic law and early Christian thinking, the modern privilege developed out of the events preceding the English Civil War in the mid-seventeenth century. Ecclesiastical courts—most notoriously the High Commission and the Star Chamber—utilized an "oath ex officio" in an effort to squelch religious dissent, mostly by Catholics and Puritans. The oath required the suspect to answer all questions truthfully, although the suspect did not know in advance what questions would be asked, and the authorities were not required to have a basis to believe that the suspect was guilty of any particular crime.

According to the standard view, associated with the scholarship of Leonard Levy, these courts were challenged by common law judges, in particular Edward Coke, who relied on the Latin maxim *nemo tenetur prodere seipsum* (no man is bound to accuse himself). More recent scholarship by Richard Helmholtz and John Langbein has thrown some doubt on this account. Helmholtz argues that objections to the oath officio were grounded in Roman canon law and European *ius commune*, rather than the English common law. Langbein has argued that the *nemo tenetur maxim* was in force only in political trials and had no effect on ordinary criminal trials until defense counsel was introduced on a regular basis over a century later.

However this may be, the colonists were surely aware of the English struggle over self-incrimination. It did not follow that they embodied this principle in their own criminal prosecutions, however. On the contrary, Eben Moglen has shown that early American criminal procedure was dominated by an "accused speaks" model. An investigating magistrate interrogated the accused who, without benefit of counsel, often confessed to criminal acts.

To be sure, state bills of rights, adopted in the 1770s and 1780s, often contained a privilege against self-incrimination. For example, section 8 of the Virginia Declaration of Rights, written by George Mason, provided "that in all capital and criminal prosecutions a man [cannot be] compelled to give evidence against himself." But Moglen argues that these provisions were meant merely to protect existing arrangements against British retrenchment, not to reform them. Accordingly, compelled incrimination before justices of the peace remained the norm.

When the 1787 Constitution was placed before the states for ratification, over half the ratifying states recommended amendments, and four conventions—Virginia, New York, North Carolina, and Rhode Island—recommended inclusion of versions of section 8 of the Virginia Declaration of Rights. After ratification, James Madison, initially an opponent of a bill of rights, introduced such a bill in the House of Representatives. Included in his proposal was a provision stating in part that "No person . . . shall be compelled to be a witness against himself." John Lau-

rence, a congressman from New York, moved that Madison's language be changed so as to limit the protection to criminal cases because it was "a general declaration in some degree contrary to laws passed." There was no opposition to this change, and the self-incrimination provision, as so amended, passed the House of Representatives unanimously. The Senate thereupon passed the provision without making any substantive change. With little debate, the states ratified the provision along with the rest of the Bill of Rights.

There is little evidence, however, that the Amendment had much immediate effect on criminal practice. At the time of its adoption, defendants were not permitted to give sworn testimony in their own defense, so there was little controversy about compulsion to testify. Defendants continued to be brought before magistrates, who placed considerable pressure upon them to cooperate with the prosecution. It was not until the 1820s, with the widespread introduction of defense counsel, that this practice began to die out.

The self-incrimination approach— *Miranda*

Although much of the history of the self-incrimination clause is contested, one fact is certain: When the provision was adopted, no one supposed that it applied to pretrial police interrogations in a custodial setting. The reason is simple: in late-eighteenth-century America, there were no organized police forces and there were therefore no police interrogations to which the self-incrimination clause could be applied.

Moreover, even when modern policing took hold, there were significant textual obstacles to application of the self-incrimination guarantee in the station house. By its terms, the self-incrimination clause requires two elements to trigger its protection: a defendant in a criminal prosecution must be *compelled*; and the defendant must be compelled to be *a witness against himself*. If one reads this language literally, a defendant who confesses in the station house has not been a "witness against himself" because the station house interrogation does not constitute a formal trial with witnesses. The Supreme Court has surmounted this hurdle by reading the clause to apply in circumstances where the defendant's compelled statements are subsequently introduced against him at a formal trial. Still, even this reading does not get over the compulsion hurdle. Police officers conducting station house interrogation are not ordinarily armed with subpoena power or, indeed, with any means of formal compulsion.

The *Miranda* Court's key analytic move was to equate compulsion with custodial interrogation. The Court said in effect that if a defendant was in custody, and if he was interrogated, then he was automatically compelled. And of course, if the defendant had been compelled, then he could not constitutionally be made a witness against himself. It followed that statements that were the product of custodial interrogation had to be excluded at trial.

If the Court had stopped at this point, the result would have been the effective outlawing of custodial interrogation. In the immediate wake of *Escobedo*, some members of the law enforcement community feared that this was precisely what the Court planned. In fact, however, this fear turned out to be baseless. Indeed, there is a sense in which *Miranda* facilitated confessions. Instead of the vague and amorphous voluntariness test, which left police guessing as to how they were to proceed, or the effective exclusion of virtually all confessions implied by *Escobedo*, *Miranda* provided the police with practical guidelines for making confessions admissible.

The first step was to dissipate the inherent compulsion created by custodial interrogation by administering the famous warnings. The Court insisted that before interrogation began, the suspect must be informed that he had a right to remain silent, that anything said by the suspect could be used against him in court, that he had the right to the presence of counsel during interrogation, and that if the suspect was indigent, a lawyer would be appointed to represent him. These last two warnings were not derived from the Sixth Amendment right to counsel, as the *Massiah* counsel right had been. Because station house interrogation most frequently occurs before a defendant has been formally charged, Sixth Amendment rights have not yet attached. Instead, in the Court's view, a person subject to custodial interrogation was entitled to counsel because "the right to have counsel present at the interrogation is indispensable to the protection of the Fifth Amendment privilege" (384 U.S. at 436).

Because it is the product of Fifth Amendment "compulsion" that has not yet been dissipated, any statement made by an unwarned suspect subject to custodial interrogation is automatically inadmissible. Moreover, the Court made clear that even after the defendant has been warned, police are obligated to refrain from interrogation if, at any time, he invokes his rights. On the other hand, once warned, a defendant can also waive his rights. Although a valid waiver cannot be presumed "simply from the silence of the accused after warnings are given or simply from the fact that a confession was in fact eventually obtained" (381 U.S. at 475), the Court held that an express statement that the defendant was willing to talk without the presence of counsel might constitute a valid waiver.

At first, *Miranda* generated tremendous controversy. Critics of the decision raised questions about its constitutional legitimacy. They argued that nothing in the text or history of the self-incrimination clause gave the Court the authority to promulgate a set of warnings, and that there was no warrant for the irrebuttable presumption that all custodial interrogation in the absence of these warnings was compelled. The Court's defenders responded that constitutional law was full of judge-made glosses on the text designed to give it practical force and that *Miranda* had to be understood against the backdrop of other, failed attempts to protect self-incrimination rights in the station house.

Whatever the merits of this theoretical argument, the practical effect of the Court's decision were certainly less devastating than its most vocal critics predicted. Suspects did not suddenly stop confessing. Instead, the decision provided police with a road map that they could and did follow in order to shield confessions from challenge. Officers throughout the country reduced the warnings to a card, which was read to defendants, and reduced the waiver procedure to a checklist, which defendants executed and signed. In theory, these waivers were subject to challenge on the ground that they were not knowing and intelligent; in practice, absent extraordinary circumstances, they were usually sufficient to meet the prosecution's burden.

Ironically, there is even a sense in which *Miranda*'s very success has undermined the argument for it. Over time, the warnings have become a fixture in popular culture, repeated endlessly in crime novels and on television police shows. Arguably, the warnings have become so well known as to reduce both the need for them and their effectiveness. Many criminal suspects already know of the warnings, and to many of them, their recitation is bound to seem like legal gobbledygook that must be ritually intoned before the real business of interrogation begins.

The self-incrimination approach—
Miranda doctrine

When the liberal Justices on the Warren Court were replaced by more conservative jurists, many predicted that *Miranda* would be quickly overruled. The Burger and Rehnquist Courts did cut back on some aspects of the decision but it has not yet been overruled, and in some important respects, its protections have actually been expanded.

Discussion of *Miranda* doctrine can usefully be organized around two questions: What factors trigger *Miranda* protection? And what rules govern the use of confessions after *Miranda* has been triggered?

Unlike Sixth Amendment rights, which are triggered by a formal charge, *Miranda* protection comes into play whether or not the suspect has been charged, so long as she is interrogated while in custody. With regard to the interrogation requirement, at least one subsequent case has actually expanded on the protection that *Miranda* first provided. In *Rhode Island v. Innis* (446 U.S. 291 (1980)), the Court held that *Miranda* applied not just to express questioning, but also to the "functional equivalent" of express questioning, which the Court defined as "any words or actions on the part of the police (other than those normally attendant to arrest and custody) that the police should know are reasonably likely to elicit an incriminating response from the suspect (446 U.S. at 301). This test is subtly different from the test for Sixth Amendment purposes, which focuses on whether the police "deliberately elicited" an incriminating response. Although it extends *Miranda* beyond express questioning, the test has the odd property of permitting the police to use techniques designed to get the defendant to confess so long as they are unlikely to succeed. For example, in *Innis*, the police appealed to Innis's fear that a still unrecovered gun might be found and used by an innocent child. Reasoning that the police had asked no direct questions and that there was no reason to suppose that this appeal would be effective, the Court held that Innis's statements were admissible.

In *Illinois v. Perkins* (496 U.S. 292 (1990)), the Supreme Court held that even if the interaction is likely to elicit incriminating statements, conversations with undercover agents are not within the purview of *Miranda*. A comparison with Sixth Amendment doctrine is again instructive. *Massiah* and *Henry* make clear that once a defendant has been formally charged with an offense, interaction with an undercover government agent may well violate the right to counsel. In contrast, the *Perkins* Court reasoned that *Miranda* was concerned with the risk that the pressure of station house interrogation would "compel" the suspect to speak and that this risk was absent when the suspect was unaware that he was conversing with a government agent.

The second element that triggers *Miranda* protection is custody. The *Miranda* Court defined "custody" as interference with a suspect's "freedom of action in any significant way." In the years since *Miranda*, the Court has made plain that a defendant can be in custody even if he is not at the station house. For example, the Court has applied *Miranda* to individuals under arrest at their home and to prisoners in jail for unrelated offenses. On the other hand, in an important qualification of the *Miranda* right, the Court held that an individual stopped briefly on the street for investigative purposes is not in custody in the *Miranda* sense. Moreover, even if the questioning occurs at the station house, the defendant is not necessarily in custody. According to the Court, the relevant question is neither what the police intend, nor what the suspect thinks. Instead, the question is whether a reasonable person would believe that he has the freedom to leave.

Once *Miranda* has been triggered, the next question is under what circumstances confessions can be utilized. For purposes of analysis, we can distinguish between three situations: cases where the warnings are not administered; cases where the warnings are administered, but the suspect does not expressly assert his rights; and cases where the warnings are administered, but the defendant does assert his rights.

In the first class of cases, the *Miranda* Court was unequivocal: in the absence of warnings, the suspect's statements were per se inadmissible. It is with regard to this situation that subsequent cases have cut back most severely on *Miranda*. Later Courts have fashioned a wide variety of exceptions to *Miranda*'s per se rule. For example, in cases decided in 1971 and 1975, the Court held that even if a defendant has not been warned of his rights, or has been warned and has asserted his rights, his statements can be used against him in cross-examination to throw doubt on the truth of his testimony if he chooses to take the stand.

Similarly, in *New York v. Quarles* (467 U.S. 649 (1984)), a case decided in 1984, the Court recognized a "public safety" exception to *Miranda*. The case arose when a woman told the police that she had just been raped by a man who had entered a supermarket. An officer chased after Quarles in the supermarket and stopped him. A frisk revealed that he was wearing a shoulder holster that was empty. The officer asked Quarles where the gun was, and Quarles responded by nodding in the direction of some empty cartons and saying "the gun is over there." The Court held that "the need for answers to questions in a situation posing a threat to the public safety outweighs the need for the prophylactic rule protecting the privilege against self-incrimination" (467 U.S. at 653) and allowed this statement and the gun to be used against the defendant.

The Court has also been generous in permitting the admission of other evidence gained as a result of statements secured in violation of *Miranda* so long as the *Miranda*-defective statement itself is excluded. For example, in *Michigan v. Tucker* (417 U.S. 433 (1974)), the Court held that the testimony of another witness, discovered through a *Miranda*-defective statement, could be admitted at trial. Similarly, in *Oregon v. Elstad* (470 U.S. 289 (1985)), the Court held that a suspect's second confession could be used as evidence, even though it was the product of a first confession that had been secured in violation of *Miranda*.

Most of these cases have a common structure. The Court has tended to characterize Miranda warnings as "procedural safeguards" that are "not themselves rights protected by the Constitution but . . . instead measures to insure that the right against compulsory self-incrimination [is] protected." Having removed the mantle of constitutional necessity from *Miranda*, the Court then typically balances the benefits and costs of exclusion and concludes that the costs outweigh the benefits.

This technique has provided the Court with a means of restricting *Miranda*'s reach without disowning the decision itself, but it has achieved this objective at the cost of considerable irony. It was, after all, *Miranda*'s opponents who initially complained that the Court lacked constitutional authority to impose the warnings requirement on the states without a constitutional mandate. In contrast, *Miranda*'s defenders insisted that the Court could legitimately place a gloss on the Constitution in order to secure self-incrimination rights. Now, critics and defenders seem to have switched places. The Justices who have participated in *Miranda* retrenchment have argued that the Court can appropriately require the police to obey procedural requirements not directly man-

dated by the Constitution, while the Justices criticizing retrenchment have insisted that *Miranda* can only be justified if the warnings are directly required by the Constitution.

In cases where warnings are given and the defendant does not assert his rights, the modern Court has hewed more closely to *Miranda*'s requirements. *Miranda* itself provided that the defendant could waive his rights in these circumstances, so long as the waiver was knowing, intelligent, and voluntary. It is fair to say that more recent decisions have not interpreted this requirement generously, but neither have they disowned it. The Court has not required the police to go out of their way to provide more information than contained in the warnings, but neither has it completely forsaken inquiry into the legitimacy of the waiver.

Perhaps surprisingly, in the third class of cases, where the defendant has claimed his rights, the Court has actually gone beyond the *Miranda* requirements. At first, it appeared that here, too, the Court might cut back. In *Michigan v. Mosely* (423 U.S. 96 (1975)), the defendant received *Miranda* warnings and invoked his right to remain silent. Two hours later, a different detective administered the warnings again and asked Mosely about a separate crime. Mosely executed a waiver and made incriminating statements. The Court upheld his resulting conviction, noting that the defendant's right to cut off questioning about the first offense had been "scrupulously honored."

However, six years later, in *Edwards v. Arizona* (451 U.S. 477 (1981)), the Court took a very different approach to invocation of the right to counsel. Edwards invoked his right to counsel, and the officers ceased questioning him. The next morning, two different detectives came to see Edwards, informed him of his *Miranda* rights again, and engaged in a colloquy with him, resulting in Edwards's confession. The Court reversed Edwards's conviction. In doing so, it created a new per se rule on top of the *Miranda* rule: In cases where a suspect invokes his *Miranda* right to counsel, "a valid waiver of the right cannot be established by showing only that he responded to further police-initiated custodial interrogation even if he has been advised of his rights. [Such a suspect] is not subject to further interrogation by the authorities until counsel has been made available to him, unless the accused himself initiates further communication, exchanges, or conversations with the police" (451 U.S. at 483). Moreover, in *Arizona v. Roberson*

(486 U.S. 675 (1988)), the Court went beyond even the *Edwards* requirements by applying the rule to a suspect questioned about a unrelated crime by an officer who was unaware of the first invocation of the counsel right. And in *Minnick v. Mississippi* (498 U.S. 146 (1990)), the Court held that the *Edwards* rule applied even in a case where the defendant had been allowed to talk to his lawyer prior to police questioning.

The continuing controversy

Although *Miranda* no longer excites the strong emotions that it did in the 1960s, the controversy over its holding has not entirely dissipated. Scholars continue to debate the effect of the decision. For example, Paul Cassell, a strong *Miranda* opponent comprehensively reviewed empirical data about the decision's impact. He concluded that approximately 3.8 percent of all criminal cases are lost due to the *Miranda* rule. Stephen Schulhofer, a strong *Miranda* defender, reviewed the same data and concluded that the attrition rate was only .78 percent. Even if this empirical disagreement could be settled, it is doubtful that empirics alone can resolve the underlying dispute. Any judgment about whether "too many" convictions are lost because of *Miranda* will depend upon normative judgments about the investigatory techniques that would have secured those convictions, and no empirical study can settle this disagreement.

There is also a lingering controversy over the legal question. Shortly after *Miranda* was decided, Congress enacted 18 U.S.C. section 3501, which provides that a confession "shall be admissible in evidence if it is voluntarily given." For thirty years, this statute remained dormant, with successive Justice Departments declining to invoke it, presumably because of a belief that it was unconstitutional. However, in 1999, the Fourth Circuit Court of Appeals ordered briefing on the effect of the statute. Relying upon language in *Miranda* itself suggesting that other techniques might displace the warning requirement and on post-*Miranda* decisions holding that the warnings were not, themselves, constitutionally required, the Court upheld the statute and concluded that it had the effect of "overruling" *Miranda*. In a 7-2 decision written by Chief Justice Rehnquist, the Supreme Court reversed this judgment and strongly reaffirmed Miranda in *Dickerson v. United States*, U.S. (2000). Emphasizing that "Miranda is a constitutional decision," the Court noted that it has become embedded in routine police practice to the point where the warnings have become part of our national culture."

LOUIS MICHAEL SEIDMAN

See also ADVERSARY SYSTEM; COUNSEL: RIGHT TO COUNSEL; CRIMINAL PROCEDURE: CONSTITUTIONAL ASPECTS; EXCLUSIONARY RULE; PERJURY; POLICE: CRIMINAL INVESTIGATIONS; POLICE: POLICE OFFICER BEHAVIOR; PUBLICITY IN CRIMINAL CASES.

BIBLIOGRAPHY

ALSCHULER, ALBERT W. "A Peculiar Privilege in Historical Perspective: The Right to Remain Silent." *Michigan Law Review* 94 (Aug. 1996): 2625–2672.

———. "Constraint and Confession." *Denver University Law Review* 74, no. 4 (1997): 957–978.

AMAR, AKHIL REED. *The Constitution and Criminal Procedure: First Principles.* New Haven, Conn.: Yale University Press, 1997.

BAKER, LIVA. *Miranda: Crime, Law, and Politics.* New York: Atheneum, 1983.

BROOKS, PETER. "Storytelling without Fear? Confession in Law and Literature." *Yale Journal of Law and the Humanities* 8 (winter 1996): 1–29.

———. *Troubling Confessions: Speaking Guilt in Law and Literature.* Chicago: University of Chicago Press, 2000.

CAPLAN, GERALD M. "Questioning Miranda." *Vanderbilt Law Review* 38 (Nov. 1985): 1417–1476.

CASSELL, PAUL G. "Miranda's Social Costs: An Empirical Reassessment." *Northwestern Law Review* 90 (winter 1996): 387–499.

———. "The Guilty and the 'Innocent': An Examination of Alleged Cases of Wrongful Conviction from False Confessions." *Harvard Journal of Law and Public Policy* 22 (spring 1999): 523–603.

CASSELL, PAUL G., and FOWLES, RICHARD. "Handcuffing the Cops? A Thirty-Year Perspective on Miranda's Harmful Effects on Law Enforcement." *Stanford Law Review* 50 (April 1998): 1055–1145.

CASSELL, PAUL G., and HAYMAN, BRET S. "Police Interrogation in the 1990s: An Empirical Study of the Effects of Miranda." *UCLA Law Review* 43 (Feb. 1996): 839–931.

DOLINKO, DAVID. "Is There a Rationale for the Privilege against Self-incrimination?" *UCLA Law Review* 33 (April 1986): 1063–1148.

DONOHUE, JOHN J. III. "Did Miranda Diminish Police Effectiveness?" *Stanford Law Review* 50 (April 1998): 1147–1180.

GRANO, JOSEPH D. "Prophylactic Rules in Criminal Procedure: A Question of Article III Legitimacy." *Northwestern University Law Review* 80 (March 1985): 100–164.

———. *Confessions, Truth, and the Law.* Ann Arbor: University of Michigan Press, 1993.

HELMHOLTZ, R. H. "Origins of the Privilege against Self-Incrimination: The Role of the European Ius Commune." *New York University Law Review* 65 (1990): 962–990.

INBAU, FRED E. "Police Interrogation: A Practical Necessity." *Journal of Criminal Law, Criminology, and Police Science* 52 (1961): 16–20.

———. *Criminal Interrogation and Confessions.* 3d ed. Baltimore, Md.: Williams & Wilkins, 1986.

KAMISAR, YALE. *Criminal Justice in Our Time.* Charlottesville: University Press of Virginia, 1965.

———. *Police Interrogation and Confessions: Essays in Law and Policy.* Ann Arbor: University of Michigan Press, 1980.

———. "Confessions, Search and Seizure and the Rehnquist Court." *Tulsa Law Journal* 34 (1999): 465–500.

LANGBEIN, JOHN H. "The Historical Origins of the Privilege against Self-Incrimination at Common Law." *Michigan Law Review* 92 (1994): 1047–1085.

LEO, RICHARD A. "Inside the Interrogation Room." *Journal of Criminal Law and Criminology* 86 (winter 1996): 266–303.

LEO, RICHARD A., and OFSHE, RICHARD J. "The Consequences of False Confessions: Deprivations of Liberty and Miscarriages of Justice in the Age of Psychological Interrogation." *Journal of Criminal Law and Criminology* 88 (winter 1998): 429–496.

LEVY, LEONARD WILLIAMS. *Origins of the Fifth Amendment: The Right against Self-Incrimination.* New York: Macmillan, 1986.

———. "Origins of the Fifth Amendment and Its Critics." *Cardozo Law Review* 19 (Dec. 1997): 821–859.

MOGLEN, EBEN. "Taking the Fifth: Reconsidering the Origins of the Constitutional Privilege against Self-Incrimination." *Michigan Law Review* 92 (March 1994): 1086–1130.

OGLETREE, CHARLES J. "Are Confessions Really Good for the Soul?: A Proposal to Mirandize Miranda." *Harvard Law Review* 100 (May 1987): 1826–1845.

SCHULHOFER, STEPHEN J. "Reconsidering Miranda." *University of Chicago Law Review* 54 (spring 1987): 435–461.

———. "Miranda's Practical Effect: Substantial Benefits and Vanishingly Small Social Costs." *Northwestern University Law Review* 90 (winter 1996): 500–563.

SEIDMAN, LOUIS MICHAEL. "Brown and Miranda." *California Law Review* 80 (May 1993): 673–753.

———. "Rubashov's Question: Self-incrimination and the Problem of Coerced Preferences." *Yale Journal of Law and the Humanities* 2 (winter 1990): 149–180.

STRAUSS, DAVID A. "The Ubiquity of Prophylactic Rules." *University of Chicago Law Review* 55 (winter 1988): 190–209.

STUNTZ, WILLIAM J. "The Substantive Origins of Criminal Procedure." *Yale Law Journal* 105 (Nov. 1995): 393–447.

THOMAS, GEORGE C. III "Aristotle's Paradox and the Self-Incrimination Puzzle." *Journal of Criminal Law and Criminology* 82 (summer 1991): 243–282.

———. "Is Miranda a Real-World Failure? A Plea for More (and Better) Empirical Evidence." *UCLA Law Review* 43 (Feb. 1996): 821–837.

WHITE, WELSH S. "Confessions Induced by Broken Government Promises." *Duke Law Journal* 43 (March 1994): 947–988.

———. "False Confessions and the Constitution: Safeguards against Untrustworthy Confessions." *Harvard Civil Rights–Civil Liberties Law Review* 32 (winter 1997): 105–157.

WITT, JOHN FABIAN. "Making the Fifth: The Constitutionalization of American Self-Incrimination Doctrine 1791–1903." *Texas Law Review* 77 (March 1999): 825–922.

CASES

Arizona v. Robertson, 486 U.S. 675 (1988).
Brewer v. Williams, 430 U.S. 387 (1977).
Dickerson v. United States, U.S. (2000).
Edwards v. Arizona, 451 U.S. 477 (1981).
Escobedo v. Illinois, 378 U.S. 478 (1964).
Illinois v. Perkins, 496 U.S. 292 (1990).
Massiah v. United States, 377 U.S. 201 (1964).
Michigan v. Mosely, 423 U.S. 96 (1975).
Michigan v. Tucker, 417 U.S. 433 (1974).
Minnick v. Mississippi, 495 U.S. 146 (1990).
Miranda v. Arizona, 384 U.S. 436 (1966).
New York v. Quarles, 467 U.S. 649 (1984).
Oregon v. Elstad, 470 U.S. 289 (1985).
Rhode Island v. Innis, 446 U.S. 291 (1980).
Rogers v. Richmond, 365 U.S. 534 (1961).
United States v. Henry, 447 U.S. 264 (1980).
United States v. Rutledge, 900 F.2d. 1127 (7RCiv. 1990).

CONSPIRACY

Introduction

The crime of conspiracy is traditionally defined as an agreement between two or more persons, entered into for the purpose of committing an unlawful act. At first carefully delimited in scope, conspiracy evolved through a long and tortuous history into a tool employed against dangerous group activity of any sort. The twentieth century in particular has witnessed an expansion of conspiracy law in the face of modern organized crime, complex business arrangements in restraint of trade, and subversive political activity. At the same time, indiscriminate conspiracy prosecutions have sparked great controversy, not only because the vagueness of the concept of agreement and the difficulty in proving it frequently result in convictions with only a tenuous basis for criminal liability, but also because conspiracy law involves a number of extensions of traditional criminal law doctrines. The principal extensions are the following:

1. Conspiracy criminalizes an agreement to commit a crime, even though an attempt conviction would not be permitted because of the highly preparatory nature of the act.
2. Although conspiracy is now generally limited in most jurisdictions to agreements to commit statutorily defined crimes, traditionally persons agreeing to commit tortious acts, or indeed any acts resulting in "prejudice to the general welfare," could be held liable for conspiracy.
3. All conspirators are liable for crimes committed in furtherance of the conspiracy by any member of the group, regardless of whether liability would be established by the law of complicity.
4. Contrary to the usual rule that an attempt to commit a crime merges with the completed offense, conspirators may be tried and punished for both the conspiracy and the completed crime.
5. Special procedural rules designed to facilitate conspiracy prosecutions can prejudice the rights of defendants. For example, all conspirators may be joined for trial, with resultant danger of confusion of issues and of guilt by association; and rules of evidence are loosened to alleviate the difficulties of proving the existence of a clandestine agreement.

In order better to understand and evaluate these doctrines, it is necessary to examine the elements of the crime of conspiracy. Like most crimes, conspiracy requires an act (actus reus) and an accompanying mental state (mens rea). The agreement constitutes the act, and the intention to achieve the unlawful objective of that agreement constitutes the required mental state.

The agreement

One of the fundamental purposes of the criminal law is to prevent conduct that is harmful to society. Accordingly, the law punishes conduct that threatens to produce the harm, as well as conduct that has actually produced it. However, the law does not punish all persons shown to harbor a criminal intent. Everyone occasionally thinks of committing a crime, but few actually carry the thought into action. Therefore, the law proceeds only against persons who engage in acts that sufficiently demonstrate their firm intention to commit a crime.

The act of conspiracy. The rationale of conspiracy is that the required objective manifestation of disposition to criminality is provided by the act of agreement. Agreement represents an advancement of the intentions that a person conceives in his mind. Intervention of the law at this point is said to be justified because the act of agreement indicates a firm intention to promote the crime, and because the agreement enhances the likelihood that unlawful action will ensue. The greater probability of action is believed to stem from the dynamics of group activity: the group exerts psychological pressure against withdrawal of its members, a single individual cannot deflect the will of the group as easily as he can change his own mind, and the group can bring greater resources to bear on its objective than could an individual acting alone. Conspiracy law, then, seeks to counter the special dangers incident to group activity reaching back to incipient stages of criminal behavior.

Ironically, conspiracy was initially directed neither at preparatory activity nor at group crime in general. Rather, it was a narrowly circumscribed statutory remedy designed to combat abuses against the administration of justice. According to Edward Coke, it consisted of "a consultation and agreement between two or more to appeal or indict an innocent man falsely and maliciously of felony, whom accordingly they cause to be indicted and appealed; and afterward the party is lawfully acquitted" (p. 142).

A writ of conspiracy would lie only for this particular offense, and only when the offense (including acquittal of the falsely indicted party) had actually taken place. However in 1611 the Court of Star Chamber extended the law by upholding a conspiracy conviction even though the rarely accused party was not indicted (*Poulterers' Case*, 77 Eng. Rep. 813 (K.B. 1611) (Coke)). The court reasoned that the confederating together, and not the false indictment, was the gist of the offense. The ramifications of this decision were twofold. First, if it was not necessary that the intended injury occur, then conspiracy punished the attempted crime. Second, if the agreement and not the false indictment was the target of conspiracy law, then conspiracy was loosed from its mooring: subsequent decisions logically could and in fact did hold that agreement to commit any unlawful act was criminal conspiracy.

There is a serious question as to whether the act of agreement is not too slender a reed to support such a vast extension of conspiracy law. First, agreement—a "conscious union of wills upon a common undertaking" (Developments in the Law, p. 926)—is an act primarily mental in nature. This is emphasized by the fact that parties to an agreement need not communicate directly; a tacit understanding may constitute an agreement. Conspiracy thus comes perilously close to criminalizing an evil state of mind without any accompanying act. Most jurisdictions have therefore bolstered the act element by requiring an overt act in pursuance of the conspiracy. The function of the overt act is "to manifest that the conspiracy is at work . . . and is neither a project still resting solely in the minds of the conspirators nor a fully completed operation no longer in existence" (*Yates v. United States*, 354 U.S. 298, 334 (1957)). However, this requirement rarely hinders a conspiracy prosecution because almost any act, however trivial, will suffice. For example, if two persons plan to rob a bank, the purchase of disguises would be a sufficient overt act. An act of this nature is highly equivocal; it would not support an attempt conviction because it is not a substantial act that sufficiently demonstrates the defendants firm intention to rob the bank. There is reason, then, to support the position of a few states that set a stricter standard by requiring a substantial step in pursuance of the object of the conspiracy, and thereby render conspiracy more comparable to the law of attempt (Note, pp. 1153–1154).

Second, conspiracy is a clandestine activity. Persons generally do not form illegal covenants openly. In the interests of security, a person may carry out his part of a conspiracy without even being informed of the identity of his co-conspirators. Since an agreement of this kind can rarely be shown by direct proof, it must be inferred from circumstantial evidence of cooperation between the defendants. What people do is, of course, evidence of what lies in their minds. Since a person's acts might, by extension of this principle, create an inference concerning what he has agreed to do, it is fair to infer an agreement to join a conspiracy from the performance of acts that further its purpose. However, this evidentiary rule can obscure the basic principle that conspiracy is not established without proof of an agreement. Conspiracy is not merely a concurrence of wills, but a concurrence resulting from agreement. Even if a conspiracy between two parties is established, not every act of a third party that assists in accomplishment of the objective of the conspiracy is a sufficient basis to demonstrate his concurrence in that agreement.

Unfortunately, many courts have not adhered strictly to the requirement of an agreement. The decision of the United States Supreme Court in *Interstate Circuit Inc. v. United States*, 306 U.S. 208 (1939) is more representative of the courts' loose treatment of the requirement of an actual agreement. In this case, the manager of Interstate, a motion picture exhibitor that dominated the motion picture business in certain cities in Texas, sent a letter to eight motion picture distributors demanding certain concessions as conditions for continued exhibition of those distributors' films. He requested that, in selling their products to "subsequent run" theaters, the distributors impose the restrictions that the films never be exhibited below a certain admission price or in conjunction with another film as a double feature. Both of these restrictions constituted significant departures from prior practice.

The Court found that the distributors conspired with one another and with Interstate to impose the demanded restrictions in violation of the Sherman Antitrust Act. Agreement among the distributors was inferred from several strands of evidence. First, the letter named all eight distributors as addressees; hence each distributor was aware that the proposals were being considered by the others. Second, the distributors were in active competition; hence without unanimous action with respect to the restrictions, each risked substantial loss of business, and, conversely, unanimity yielded a prospect of increased profits. Finally, the distributors did in fact act with substantial unanimity. However, since the actions of each distributor might just as easily have resulted from the exercise of self-interest in the absence of any illegal agreement, the Court had to take one step further. It declared, "We think that in the circumstances of this case such agreement for the imposition of the restrictions upon subsequent run exhibitors was not a prerequisite to an unlawful conspiracy. It was enough that, knowing that concerted action was contemplated and invited, the distributors gave their adherence to the scheme and participated in it" (*Interstate Circuit Inc.*, 226). Such a dilution of the requirement of agreement may be necessary in view of the special problems of enforcing the nation's antitrust policy. However, difficulties of proof lead courts to extend the principle to conspiracy prosecutions generally.

The scope of a conspiracy. Another large problem that arises in connection with the requirement of an agreement is that of determining the scope of a conspiracy—who are the parties and what are their objectives. The determination is critical, since it defines the potential liability of each defendant. Ascertaining the boundaries or scope of a conspiratorial relationship is crucial for resolving several major questions. Among these are (1) the propriety of joint prosecution; (2) the admissibility against a defendant of hearsay declarations of other conspirators; (3) the satisfaction of the overt-act requirement; (4) the liability of a defendant for substantive crimes committed by other conspirators pursuant to a conspiracy; and (5) the possibility of multiple convictions for conspiracy and substantive crimes.

The problems generated by the question of the scope of conspiracy are among the most troublesome in conspiracy law. They derive from the necessity of applying the theoretical idea of agreement to the reality of ongoing, fluctuating partnerships engaged in diverse criminal activity. Can a single agreement embrace persons unknown to one another in a sprawling, far-flung illegal operation? Can separate decisions made over a course of time to commit various crimes be said to stem from a single agreement? Generally, does the multiplicity of relationships making up a criminal organization constitute one large conspiracy or several smaller ones?

The law has developed several different models with which to approach the question of scope. One such model is that of a chain, where each party performs a role that aids succeeding parties in accomplishing the criminal objectives of the conspiracy. An illustration of such a single conspiracy, its parts bound together as links in a chain, is the process of distributing an illegal foreign drug. In one such case, smugglers, middlemen, and retailers were convicted of a single conspiracy to smuggle and distribute narcotics (*United States v. Bruno*, 105 F.2d 921 (2d Cir.), *rev'd on other grounds*, 308 U.S. 287 (1939)). On appeal, the defendants argued that there were separate conspiracies—one between the smugglers and the middlemen, and the other between the middlemen and the retailers. The court rejected this view and found a single overall conspiracy despite the absence of cooperation or communication between the smugglers and retailers, stating:

The smugglers knew that the middlemen must sell to retailers; and the retailers knew that the middlemen must buy of importers of one sort or another. Thus the conspirators at one end of the chain knew that the unlawful business would not, and could not, stop with their buyers; and those at the other end knew that it had not begun with their sellers. . . . The accused were embarked upon a venture, in all parts of which each was a participant, and an abettor in the sense that the success of the part with which he was immediately concerned, was dependent upon the success of the whole [922].

Another prototype, denominated the wheel conspiracy, exists where one central figure, the hub, conspires with several others, the spokes. The question is whether there is a rim to bind all the spokes together in a single conspiracy. A rim is found only when there is proof that the spokes were aware of one another's existence and that all promoted the furtherance of some single illegal objective. In the celebrated case of *Kotteakos v. United States*, 328 U.S. 750 (1946), one man, Brown, agreed with a number of different persons to obtain loans for each of them from the Federal Housing Authority through fraudulent means. Since each of these transactions was entirely distinct and independent of the others, there could not be a finding of a single conspiracy. Instead, there were a number of separate conspiracies consisting of Brown and each of his customers.

On the other hand, a single conspiracy may be found where each person's success depends on continued operation of the hub, which in turn depends on success of all the spokes. In this situation each spoke can be said to contribute to the separate objectives of all the other spokes. In the case of *Anderson v. Superior Court*, 78 Cal. App. 2d

22, 177 P.2d 315 (1947), a woman who referred pregnant women to a physician for abortions was indicted for a conspiracy to commit abortion with him and with other persons who referred pregnant women to him. She was also indicted for the illegal abortions committed upon the women she referred, as well as for the abortions committed upon women referred by the other persons who had made such referrals. The court held that the evidence permitted the inference of a conspiracy among all the referring persons and the physician, because the defendant knew that the others were referring business to him, and because his continued functioning and hence the woman's commission depended upon continuance of all these sources of referral. For these reasons it might be said that she contributed to each separate instance of abortion.

These models deal with situations in which various parties conspire to promote a single unlawful objective. The traditional concept of agreement can also accommodate the situation where a well-defined group conspires to commit multiple crimes; so long as all these crimes are the objects of "the same agreement or continuous conspiratorial relationship," a finding of one large conspiracy is appropriate (Model Penal Code, 1962, § 5.03(c)).

However, traditional conspiracy law is inadequate when applied to criminal organizations in which highly diverse objectives are pursued by apparently unrelated individuals. Hence, Congress enacted the Racketeer Influenced and Corrupt Organizations Act of 1970 [RICO] to cope with the growing problem of organized crime (18 U.S.C. §§ 1961–1968 (1999)). This act facilitates conspiracy prosecutions by modifying the traditional idea of a conspiratorial objective. Instead of proving that each defendant conspired to commit a particular crime or crimes—a task that is exceedingly difficult in the context of a large, sprawling criminal organization—the prosecution need only show that each defendant conspired to promote the enterprise through his individual pattern of criminal activity. No matter how diverse the goals of a large criminal organization, there is but one objective: to promote the furtherance of the enterprise.

The problem with this tendency to view conspiracy as an ongoing criminal enterprise is that it beclouds the idea of an act of agreement. Many persons may thereby be snared in the coils of a single conspiracy whose nature and membership were unknown to them. The effect may be to convict people in circumstances where the tradi-

tional requirement of personal guilt is not present. The Model Penal Code has attempted to reformulate the definition of conspiracy to avoid this consequence. For each defendant, it would ask whether and with whom he agreed to commit which parts of the entire illegal scheme, thus reaffirming the centrality of the agreement in a conspiracy prosecution (MPC, 1960, commentary on § 5.03). A number of state criminal codes have now adopted this approach.

Mental state

The two elements of mental state required by conspiracy are the intent to agree and the intent to promote the unlawful objective of the conspiracy. The first of these elements is almost indistinguishable from the act of agreement. Agreement is in any case morally neutral; its moral character depends upon the nature of the objective of agreement. It is the intention to promote a *crime* that lends conspiracy its criminal cast.

Some crimes do not require an intention to cause the prohibited result. Manslaughter, for example, may be committed by a person who kills another by his act of driving carelessly. These crimes may not be the basis of a conspiracy, however, since two people could not be said to agree together to kill another carelessly. The nature of the requirement of agreement, therefore, limits the objectives of conspiracy to those crimes that are committed by intentional actions.

Problems arise, however, in determining the sense of intention that is required. Does it include acting with knowledge of the probable results of one's action, or is it confined to acting with a purpose to attain such results? The question has most frequently arisen in the case of suppliers who furnish goods to members of a conspiracy with knowledge of their intended illegal use. Examples include the supplying of yeast and sugar to a group known to be using them to engage in illegal production of whiskey (*United States v. Falcone*, 311 U.S. 205 (1940)), or the furnishing of medical drugs by a manufacturer that knows they will be used for nonmedical and illegal purposes (*Direct Sales Co. v. United States*, 319 U.S. 703 (1943)).

Some courts have found it enough to convict the supplier for an illegal conspiracy with the user when the supplier knew of the illegal use. The justification for this position is that the supplier has knowingly furthered a crime and has no interest in doing so that is worthy of protection (MPC, 1960, commentary on § 5.03). However, the majority view is to the contrary: the supplier must be shown to have had a purpose to further the illegal objectives of the user (MPC, 1962, § 5.03(1)). In the language of Judge Learned Hand, "he must in some sense promote their venture himself, make it his own, have a stake in its outcome" (*United States v. Falcone*, 109 F.2d 579, 581 (1949)). This might be demonstrated by evidence of the sale of unusually large quantities of goods, particularly where such goods are legally restricted; by evidence of inflated charges or of the sale of goods with no legitimate use; or by evidence that sales to an illegal operation have become a dominant proportion of the seller's business.

The reasons for requiring a stake in the venture are twofold. First, the act of agreement necessarily imports a purpose; indifference to illegal use by another of what one supplies him for otherwise legitimate reasons does not constitute an agreement. Second, making the supplier liable in these situations whenever a jury decides that he knew of the illegal use imposes an undue burden on legitimate business since to avoid liability suppliers would be obliged to police the intended uses of their purchasers. By taking into account the social usefulness of the commercial activity and the magnitude of the seller's contribution to the crime, the majority rule strikes a balance between the needs of business enterprises to operate without oppressive restriction and of society to protect itself against crime.

Sometimes the issue arises whether a mistake of fact that would not defeat liability for the object offense nevertheless defeats liability for conspiracy. The argument that it does is sometimes couched in logical or conceptual terms: "While one may, for instance, be guilty of running past a traffic light of whose existence one is ignorant," Judge Learned Hand wrote in another famous decision, "one cannot be guilty of conspiring to run past such a light unless one supposes that there is a light to run past" (*United States v. Cummins*, 123 F.2d 271, 273 (1941)). But other courts, including the U.S. Supreme Court in *United States v. Feola*, 420 U.S. 672, 693 (1975), have taken a more pragmatic stance, reasoning that the mental state element of the conspiracy charge should mirror that of the substantive offense "unless one of the policies behind the imposition of conspiratorial liability [would] not [be] served by such a result." The Model Penal Code makes this an issue to be resolved on a case-by-case basis (MPC 1985, commentary on § 5.03, at 4.13).

The object of a conspiracy

Common law conspiracy encompassed agreements to commit an unlawful act. The key word is *unlawful:* it refers not only to criminal, but also to tortious acts, or even to acts that, in the opinion of a court, result in "prejudice to the general welfare or oppression of an individual of sufficient gravity to be injurious to the public interest" (*Commonwealth v. Dyer*, 243 Mass. 472, 138 N.E. 206 (1922)). This rule owed its origin to seventeenth-century expansion of the scope of conspiracy, which was stimulated by impatience with the narrow technicalities of medieval law, coupled with a tendency to identify criminality with immorality. It was thought that courts had authority to correct

errors and misdemeanors extra-judicial, tending to the breach of peace, or oppression of the subjects, or to the raising of faction, controversy, debate, or to any manner of misgovernment; so that no wrong or injury, either public or private, can be done, but that it shall be here reformed or punished by due course of law. (*Bagg's Case*, 77 Eng. Rep. 1271 (K.B. 1616) (Coke))

The doctrine's most significant use in the United States occurred in the early nineteenth century, when many courts sustained criminal-conspiracy prosecutions against unions of workers seeking to organize in order to pressure employers to meet their employment demands by collectively withholding their labor (Wellington, pp. 7–46).

In affording discretion to judges to punish as a crime the group pursuit of any objectives they determined to be against morality and the public interest, the law of conspiracy contravened the classic principle of *nulla poena sine lege* (no punishment without law). It also went contrary to the principle forbidding ex post facto punishment (criminalizing conduct not previously declared to be criminal). Today, such discretionary criminal liability is vulnerable to constitutional attack as violative of due process of law (*Musser v. Utah*, 333 U.S. 95 (1948)). Although the common law rule still prevails in some jurisdictions—notably in the federal provision directed against conspiracy to commit "any offense" against or to defraud the United States (18 U.S.C. § 371 (1999))—the modern approach limits the scope of conspiracy to statutorily defined criminal objectives, except where the legislature has identified and prohibited specific kinds of concerted activity.

Conspiracy and complicity

Conspiracy is not only a substantive crime. It also serves as a basis for holding one person liable for the crimes of others in cases where application of the usual doctrines of complicity would not render that person liable. Thus, one who enters into a conspiratorial relationship is liable for even reasonably foreseeable crime committed by every other member of the conspiracy in furtherance of its objectives, whether or not he knew of the crimes or aided in their commission. The rationale is that

criminal acts done in furtherance of a conspiracy may be sufficiently dependent upon the encouragement and support of the group as a whole to warrant treating each member as a causal agent to each act. Under this view, which of the conspirators committed the substantive offence would be less significant in determining the defendant's liability than the fact that the crime was performed as part of a larger division of labor to which the defendant had also contributed his efforts [Developments in the Law, p. 998].

This rationale, however, becomes attenuated in many situations in which the doctrine is applied. For example, in the leading case of *Pinkerton v. United States*, 328 U.S. 640 (1946), a defendant who had earlier conspired with his brother to operate an illegal still was held liable for his brother's later acts of operating the still, despite the fact that by the time those acts were committed, the defendant was in prison for another offense.

Although dilution of the strict concepts of causality and intention may be required to cope with the dangers of organized crime, serious objections have been raised to this aspect of the law of conspiracy. Liability for substantive crimes is predicated on the loose evidentiary standards of conspiracy law; liability attaches for crimes not actually intended or even necessarily foreseen; and holding each member of a conspiracy liable for all crimes committed by the group without regard to the character of that person's role within the group yields overly broad liability without penal justification. This is particularly true in those jurisdictions that allow the finding of a single conspiracy, rather than several smaller ones, in cases of large, sprawling, and loosely confederated criminal enterprises. As a consequence, some states, following the lead of the Model Penal Code, have eliminated this feature of traditional conspiracy by declaring that one is liable for the criminal actions of another only if he is made liable by the doctrines of the law of complicity.

Procedural rules

Perhaps the most significant advantage of a prosecutor's decision to charge several defendants with conspiracy is that he may invoke special procedural rules that apply only to conspiracy cases. The major prosecutorial advantages of conspiracy are that it enables the prosecution to join all the conspirators for trial and to use out-of-court statements of each conspirator against all the others.

Joinder of conspirators for trial, coupled with relaxation of the rules of venue to allow the trial to take place wherever acts in pursuance of the conspiracy have occurred, is a measure designed to promote efficiency and convenience for courts, prosecutors, and witnesses. Where evidence pertaining to all defendants substantially overlaps, joinder avoids multiple trials involving the same issues and evidence. Even where the cases against various defendants are more distinct, the rule is helpful to the prosecution, since such constraining factors as prosecutorial resources and availability of witnesses often dictate a choice between joint trial and dismissal of charges against some of the conspirators.

In some situations, however, joinder may well yield not increased efficiency but rather a profusion of evidence, a multiplication of issues, and consequently much ambiguity and confusion. Moreover, joinder may substantially impair the rights of defendants. Where the jury is asked to hear a large amount of complex evidence, to remember which evidence applies to which defendant, and to make fine discriminations of individual guilt or innocence, there are several problems. First, there is serious danger of guilt by association. Second, conspirators may be hampered in their defense if optimal group strategy conflicts with the best course for an individual. Frequently, defendants attempt to cast the blame on someone else, and end up by convicting one another.

Loosened standards of admissibility of evidence prevail in a conspiracy trial. Contrary to the usual rule, in conspiracy prosecutions any declaration by one conspirator, made in furtherance of a conspiracy and during its pendency (hearsay), is admissible against each coconspirator. For example, in a conspiracy prosecution of a sheriff and a magistrate for extorting money from a coal company, an executive of the company testified that the sheriff told him that the magistrate was his (the sheriff's) agent in the extortion scheme and would pick up the extortion payments (*United States v. Vinson*, 606 F.2d 149 (6th Cir. 1979)). This testimony would normally be inadmissible because it is hearsay as against the magistrate—that is, it is testimony by the declarant (the witness) of what someone else said (the sheriff), offered to prove the truth of the matter asserted by that other person (that the magistrate was his agent in the scheme). However, since there was enough evidence of a conspiracy, the hearsay testimony was admitted as further evidence of the conspiracy and of the magistrate's participation in it.

The conventional reason for the exclusion of hearsay evidence is that such evidence is thought to be untrustworthy. The witness may report it poorly, either from faulty memory or from motive to misstate, and more importantly, the jury has no means of evaluating the credibility of the declaration unless the original declarant is available for cross-examination. Despite the unreliability of hearsay evidence, it is admissible in conspiracy prosecutions. Explaining this rule, Judge Hand said, "Such declarations are admitted upon no doctrine of the law of evidence, but of the substantive law of crime. When men enter into an agreement for an unlawful end, they become ad hoc agents for one another, and have made 'a partnership in crime.' What one does pursuant to their common purpose, all do, and as declarations may be such acts, they are competent against all" (*Van Riper v. United States*, 13 F.2d 961, 967 (2d Cir. 1926)).

Thus conspirators are liable on an agency theory for statements of co-conspirators, just as they are for the overt acts and crimes committed by their confreres. Although this theory may explain why co-conspirators are liable for each other's declarations, it does not really dispel the concerns of the hearsay rule regarding the trustworthiness of evidence. By requiring that the declarations be made within the scope of the agency relationship and with intent to advance the objectives of that relationship, the rule excludes declarations made before the agreement or after the termination of the conspiracy as peripheral and hence too unreliable. It thereby creates a nexus between the declarations and the criminal goals of the conspiracy, with whatever assurance of truth that might import.

However, the justification for circumventing the hearsay rule in conspiracy prosecutions is the practical need for such evidence—since conspiracy is a type of crime of which direct evidence is usually unavailable, the choice may be between admitting inferior evidence and admitting no evidence at all. Nevertheless the practice of admitting this evidence conflicts with the policy of the hearsay rule.

The problems encountered in applying the exception to the hearsay rule for co-conspirators were aptly described by justice Robert Jackson in his concurring opinion in *Krulewitch v. United States*, 336 U.S. 440, 453 (1949):

Strictly, the prosecution should first establish prima facie the conspiracy and identify the conspirators, after which evidence of acts and declarations of each in the course of its execution are admissible against all. But the order of proof of so sprawling a charge is difficult for a judge to control. As a practical matter, the accused often is confronted with a hodgepodge of acts and statements by others which he may never have authorized or intended or even known about, but which help to persuade the jury of existence of the conspiracy itself. In other words, a conspiracy often is proved by evidence that is admissible only upon assumption that conspiracy existed. The naive assumption that prejudicial effects can be overcome by instructions to the jury . . . all practicing lawyers know to be unmitigated fiction.

Conclusion

Conspiracy, a crime special to common law jurisdictions and largely unknown, except in modest forms, in continental European countries, is one of the most controversial of all substantive crimes. It affords great advantages to law enforcement, since it avoids multiple trials, permits prosecution of preparatory activity at an early stage, facilitates prosecution against organized criminality, and extends a number of evidentiary and procedural advantages to the prosecution. At the same time, it constitutes what Justice Jackson in *Krulewitch* termed an "elastic, sprawling and pervasive offense" (445) that departs from traditional requirements of liability: (1) the crime of conspiracy is vaguely defined and its contours are often unpredictable; (2) it permits conviction on acts largely mental in character; (3) its essential feature, an agreement, is often diluted to something approaching suspicion of agreement; and (4) it affords a highly tenuous basis for holding the defendant for substantive crimes committed by others. Moreover, the procedural advantages to the prosecution impose corresponding disadvantages on the defendant, disadvantages thought inappropriate and unfair when other crimes are charged.

The balance has been struck on the side of retaining the offense with modest revisions, despite long-standing criticism (Johnson). The crime of conspiracy will in all likelihood remain an integral part of the prosecutor's arsenal. Whether it will be kept within tolerable bounds depends on how sensitively and critically prosecutors employ it, courts administer and interpret it, and legislators act to preclude its excesses.

JAMES ALEXANDER BURKE
SANFORD H. KADISH
DAN M. KAHAN

See also ACCOMPLICES; ATTEMPT; SOLICITATION.

BIBLIOGRAPHY

American Law Institute. *Model Penal Code: Proposed Official Draft.* Philadelphia: ALI, 1962.
———. *Model Penal Code: Tentative Draft No. 10.* Philadelphia: ALI, 1960.
COKE, EDWARD. *The Third Part of the Institutes of the Laws of England: Concerning High Treason, and Other Pleas of the Crown, and Criminal Causes* (1641). London: E. & R. Brooke, 1797.
Developments in the Law. "Criminal Conspiracy." *Harvard Law Review* 72 (1959): 920–1008.
FILVAROFF, DAVID B. "Conspiracy and the First Amendment." *University of Pennsylvania Law Review* 121 (1972): 189–253.
HARNO, ALBERT J. "Intent in Criminal Conspiracy." *University of Pennsylvania Law Review* 89 (1941): 624–647.
JOHNSON, PHILLIP E. "The Unnecessary Crime of Conspiracy." *California Law Review* 61 (1973): 1137–1188.
LEVIE, JOSEPH H. "Hearsay and Conspiracy: A Reexamination of the Co-conspirators' Exception to the Hearsay Rule." *Michigan Law Review* 52 (1954): 1159–1178.
MARCUS, PAUL. *The Prosecution and Defense of Criminal Conspiracy Cases.* New York: M. Bender, 1978–1990.
MITFORD, JESSICA. *The Trial of Dr. Spock, the Rev. William Sloane Coffin, Jr., Michael Ferber, Mitchell Goodman, and Marcus Raskin.* New York: Knopf, 1969.
Note. "Conspiracy: Statutory Reform since the Model Penal Code." *Columbia Law Review* 75 (1975): 1122–1188.
SAYRE, FRANCIS. "Criminal Conspiracy." *Harvard Law Review* 35 (1922): 393–427.
TURNER, MARJORIE B. S. *The Early American Labor ConspiracyCases—Their Place in Labor Law: A Reinterpretation.* San Diego. Calif.: San Diego State College Press, 1967.
U.S. National Commission on Reform of Federal Criminal Laws. *Final Report: A Proposed New Federal Criminal Code (Title 18, United States Code).* Washington, D.C.: The Commission, 1971.
———. *Working Papers,* vol. 1. Washington, D.C.: The Commission, 1970.
WELLINGTON, HARRY H. *Labor and the Legal Process.* New Haven, Conn.: Yale University Press, 1968.
WRIGHT, ROBERT S. *The Law of Criminal Conspiracies and Agreements.* Philadelphia: Blackstone, 1887.

CONTRIBUTING TO THE DELINQUENCY OF MINORS

The offense of contributing to the delinquency of minors (CDM) originated in the United States in the 1900s. Colorado enacted the first statute defining CDM in 1903. Since that time, virtually all states have enacted some form of CDM legislation.

CDM is a statutory crime with no precedent in the common law. As a result, its application and elements vary considerably across jurisdictions. In general, CDM statutes make it a crime to "aid, encourage, cause, or allow" a child to become delinquent or neglected by "words, acts, threats, commands, or persuasions." Though usually a misdemeanor, some states grade the crime as a felony. Many statutes define the people who may be prosecuted for the crime as "parents, legal guardians, and any other person having care or custody of the child" (Geis, p. 64). Notably, in the jurisdictions where this language has been interpreted, it has not been construed to exclude strangers. In addition, courts have interpreted this language to include minors, making it possible for a minor to contribute to the delinquency of another minor. Each jurisdiction also has the power to define the age at which majority is reached. Hence, states vary in their definition of a minor though most states establish minors as individuals under the age of eighteen or seventeen.

Delinquent behavior, as defined by the statutes and the case law, falls into one or more of the following categories: (1) violation of laws by a child; (2) conduct by a child that tends to injure his own health or morals or those of another; (3) behavior by the child that displays a risk that the child might become involved in criminal activity. Delinquent behavior covers a broad spectrum, including acts such as truancy, loitering, gambling, purchasing and consuming alcohol, inappropriate sexual conduct, violating curfew ordinances, and associating with known criminals. Similarly, the term "contributing" is broadly defined. A few states, such as Montana, have attempted to enumerate specific acts constituting "contribution," but most states have left the decision to the jury or judge. The de facto practice of relying on judges and juries to constrain and interpret ostensibly vague words such as "tendency," "contributing," and "delinquency" began with the inception of CDM statutes and still continues today, despite serious scholarly criticism of the practice.

Currently, the substantive disagreements among jurisdictions have to do with two major issues: (1) whether the alleged offender's behavior must lead to prohibited conduct by the child; and (2) what level of mens rea (the requisite mental state) is required for a conviction. Since most statutes have been construed as preventive as well as punitive in their purpose, the prevailing view is that a delinquent act is not required. Often buttressed by statutory language covering acts "causing delinquency or tending to cause delinquency," most CDM laws do not make delinquency an element of the crime.

On the question of mens rea, some states only require the intent to do the act charged. In these jurisdictions, ignorance as to the age of the minor or to the existence of the law is no defense. Other states either make some level of mens rea an element of the offense or allow lack of mens rea as an affirmative defense to the crime.

Almost without exception, CDM statutes have been upheld against all legal challenges. Due to the imprecision of the words used in the various laws, opponents of CDM legislation have repeatedly attempted to have such laws declared void for vagueness, arguing that the laws provide inadequate notice and produce inconsistent enforcement. Courts have rejected vagueness challenges, however, based on the view that judges and juries understand the purpose of the law and that the statutory words have been developed sufficiently in the case law to have reasonably accessible meanings (e.g., *Williams v. Garcetti*). In addition to vagueness challenges, CDM laws have been challenged unsuccessfully on three other grounds: (1) as substantive due process violations of the rights of parents to raise their children; (2) as violations of the Eighth Amendment prohibition against cruel and unusual punishment; and (3) as violations of the Eighth Amendment prohibition against crimi-

nalizing the status of being a bad parent or guardian.

Significantly, discussion of CDM is conspicuously missing in most major criminal law texts. This may be in part because a defendant who can be charged with CDM is also generally subject to prosecution for other offenses covered by sex offense, drug, or accomplice liability laws, which tend to carry much stiffer penalties than CDM.

The American Law Institute takes the view that the offense of CDM should not be continued in the criminal law canon. In lieu of a CDM statute, the Model Penal Code defines the offense of "Endangering Welfare of Children," which covers only a limited range of misconduct solely by people legally responsible for a child's supervision (MPC, § 230.4). In addition, section 230.4 necessitates that the defendant "knowingly endanger" the child, which has been interpreted to require that the actor be aware of her conduct and know of the facts giving rise to her duty of supervision, though it does not require that the actor be aware that her conduct constitutes a criminal offense. Though no American jurisdiction has adopted the Model Penal Code conception without modification, some states have followed the Code's approach by defining the offense as a violation of a legal duty of care, and some jurisdictions that formerly graded CDM as a felony have revised the grade to a misdemeanor.

PRATHEEPAN GULASEKARAM
EMILY BUSS

See also FAMILY ABUSE AND CRIME; FAMILY RELATIONSHIPS AND CRIME; JUVENILE STATUS OFFENDERS; JUVENILE VIOLENT OFFENDERS.

BIBLIOGRAPHY

DAVIDSON, HOWARD. "No Consequences—Reexamining Parental Responsibility Laws." *Stanford Law and Policy Review* 7 (1996): 1.
GREENWOOD, CHRISTINE T. "Holding Parents Criminally Responsible for the Delinquent Acts of Their Children: Reasoned Response or 'Knee-Jerk Reaction.'" *Journal of Contemporary Law* 23 (1997): 401.
GEIS, GILBERT. "Contributing to Delinquency." *St. Louis University Law Journal* 59 (1963): 59–81.
GEIS, GILBERT, and BINDER, ARNOLD. "Sins of Their Children: Parental Responsibility for Juvenile Delinquency." *Notre Dame Journal of Legal Ethics and Public Policy* 5 (1991): 303.

LUDWIG, FREDERICK. *Youth and the Law.* Brooklyn, N.Y.: The Foundation Press, 1955.

WEINSTEIN, TONI. "Visiting the Sins of the Child on the Parent: The Legality of Criminal Parental Liability Statutes." *Southern California Law Review* 64 (1991): 859.

CASES

Powell v. Texas, 392 U.S. 514 (1968).

Vachon v. New Hampshire, 414 U.S. 478 (1974).

Territory v. Delos Santos, 42 Hawaii 102 (Haw. 1957).

State v. Flinn, 208 S.E.2d 538 (W.Va. 1974).

Jung v. State, Wis. 2d 714, 201 N.W.2d 58 (Wis. 1972).

State v. Simants, 182 Neb. 491, 155 N.W.2d 788 (Neb. 1968).

Dabney v. State, 239 S.E.2d 698 (Ga. Ct. App. 1977).

State v. Norflett, 67 NJ 268, 337 A.2d 609 (N.J. 1975).

Williams v. Garcetti, 20 Cal Rptr. 2d 341, 5 Cal. 4t 561, 853 P.2d 507 (Cal. 1993).

CONVICTION: CIVIL DISABILITIES

When a person leaves prison, or is released from probation or parole, the most long-lasting aspect of his criminal conviction may only be beginning. Every state, to a greater or lesser degree, prohibits an ex-felon from exercising some of the most basic rights of free citizens, ranging from the right to vote to the right to employment by the state. Although some states impose civil disabilities only if the convicted felon has been imprisoned, where this limitation does not exist, "collateral" consequences for the 50 percent of felons who are not imprisoned are anything but collateral; they may well be the most persistent consequences inflicted for crime.

Historical background

The view that criminals forfeit their rights as citizens is not new. Both the Greeks and Romans imposed on a convicted person the punishment of "infamy," which forbade him to exercise the rights of a free citizen. Early English law followed the same principle: a person convicted of a felony was declared "attainted," losing all his civil rights and forfeiting his property; collectively, these sanctions were called "civil death." More dramatic was the doctrine, based on the fiction that the criminal's act evidenced his entire family's corruption, of "corruption of the blood," which prohibited the felon's heirs from inheriting his estate. Since in most instances the felon in England was executed, this consequence of his act fell upon his family and heirs, who lost whatever property he had owned. When the death penalty was abolished for many crimes in nineteenth-century England this sanction might have died as well. Indeed, the U.S. Constitution specifically prohibited corruption of blood except in the case of a person convicted of treason. Nonetheless, the notion of civil death persisted, and many of the rights that would have died with the executed felon in medieval England continued to be denied to the felon who, in nineteenth-century America and England, was merely imprisoned and later released. The vast majority of states have now rejected the idea of a blanket death as an adjunct of conviction for a crime, but every state, to some degree, still imposes civil disabilities on ex-offenders.

The predicates for imposing civil disabilities

Considerable variation exists among the states as to which civil disabilities are imposed and when they apply. By far the most common basis for imposing civil disabilities is a conviction for a felony. Although the term *felony* is not always consistently defined, it typically means a crime for which a year or more of imprisonment may be imposed. Thus, the same civil disability is often visited both on a person convicted of first-degree murder and on one convicted of a relatively minor crime. Some states, however, impose such disabilities only after conviction for certain enumerated felonies. As a third alternative, in some states conviction of a "crime of moral turpitude" or of an "infamous crime" is the basis for civil disabilities. Thus, the distinction between a felony and misdemeanor, which often plays a role in many aspects of criminal law, is ignored, thereby subjecting to civil disabilities a person convicted of misdemeanors that are thought to reflect some weakness of morals or moral behavior. This attempt to be more discerning actually widens the net. One court, for example, has ruled that the term *moral turpitude* includes any offense that is "contrary to justice, honesty, principle, and good morals" (*In re Hatch,* 10 Cal. 2d 147, 73 P.2d 885 (1937)). The ambiguity of this standard was revealed in a later decision by the same court, which held that failure to report for the Selective Service draft during World War II was not a crime of "moral turpitude" (*Otsuka v. Hite*, 64 Cal. 2d 596, 414 P.2d 412 (1966)).

Civil disabilities are usually imposed without any necessary connection between a specific disability and the crime that has been committed. Thus, a person convicted for a drug violation may find himself forbidden to vote or even to make contracts, even though his crime has no obvious bearing on his ability capably to engage in these activities. Although the issue is not clear, such provisions are probably constitutional (*Hawker v. New York*, 170 U.S. 189 (1898)). Yet it surely seems sensible, at least if the notion of civil death is abjured, to require that there be some "rational connection" between the crime and the specific disability imposed. Under such a scheme, a person convicted of bribery might be disqualified from public employment or from serving on a jury, and an embezzler might be prohibited from working as a bank teller or in another capacity involving funds or records. But neither could be barred from exercising private rights, or suffer other disabilities unrelated to the crime for which he was convicted.

Specific rights lost

Public rights. Apparently on the premise that violation of the criminal law indicates a general lack of respect for law and for the obligations of citizenship, most states, as well as the federal government, have barred former offenders from participating in a number of public activities normally open to citizens—some of which indeed are considered obligations of citizenship.

The right to citizenship. No right is more basic or all-encompassing than citizenship itself. In a number of decisions, the U.S. Supreme Court has either directly invalidated or cast substantial doubt upon attempts by Congress to revoke naturalized citizenship for such crimes as desertion in time of war or residing for three years in a foreign country of birth (*Trop v. Dulles*, 356 U.S. 86 (1958); *Schneider v. Rusk*, 377 U.S. 163 (1964)).

The right to vote. Next to citizenship itself, the right to vote is probably the single most important political right held by a citizen. Yet fourteen states now provide for the permanent disenfranchisement of convicted felons, while most others allow restoration of the right. (On the other hand, some states provide prisoners with absentee ballots, thus encouraging them to remain politically aware.) Many of these provisions are found in state constitutions rather than in statutes, reflecting a deeply and widely held belief that the right to participate in democracy's most basic exercise is forfeited by criminal action. In 1974 the Supreme Court upheld such a provision in the California constitution, relying on a provision of the Fourteenth Amendment to the U.S. Constitution that was interpreted to allow such disenfranchisement (*Richardson v. Ramirez*, 418 U.S. 24 (1974)).

The right to hold public office. Twenty-five states have constitutional or statutory provisions disqualifying persons convicted of certain crimes from holding or retaining public office. These disabilities sometimes extend beyond the term of sentence of the crime, and generally apply to local as well as state public offices, and to appointive as well as elective positions. Court decisions have held, for example, that the term *public office* includes the positions of city manager, postmaster, school board member, county treasurer, and justice of the peace. Congress has similarly enacted legislation providing that persons convicted of certain offenses cannot hold federal office (for example, 18 U.S.C. §§ 593, 1901, 2071). Yet nothing in the U.S. Constitution prohibits such persons from being elected to Congress itself or, for that matter, from being elected president. Whether or not one agrees with the disqualification of former offenders from holding appointive office, barring them from elective public office seems particularly hard to defend. Theoretically, the electorate should be able to assess for itself the offense's bearing on the candidate's ability to perform the job.

Judicial rights. Various provisions affect what might be called judicial rights. Some state laws provide that a person convicted of or imprisoned for certain offenses cannot litigate in the state's courts for the period of disability, often the term of imprisonment. In most instances these statutes allow the prisoner to bring his suit after the disability is lifted. However, this is far from a perfect remedy, since the passage of time may affect the memories or availability of witnesses, or result in other difficulties that the litigant would encounter on release. Moreover, it still leaves the offender, while encumbered with the disability, without the right to appear in court and to represent his own interests. Some state statutes make provision for the appointment of a substitute or counsel for the prisoner, but impediments to receiving the full protection of the courts and the legal system still remain substantial.

A second judicial right clouded by a criminal conviction is the right to testify in court. Most states do not automatically disqualify offenders from appearing as witnesses, unless the conviction was for perjury; these statutes are all that remains of the common law doctrine that persons convicted of serious crimes were incompetent to testify. However, in virtually every state, a previously convicted witness may be questioned about his past record. This rule has the valid purpose of informing the jury about facts that may be relevant to the witness' credibility, but discourages witnesses—and particularly persons charged with new crimes—from testifying in court. Some states, as well as the federal courts, have restricted the use of such "impeachment" evidence to recent convictions, on the ground that older convictions are no longer sufficiently relevant.

A third judicial right sometimes rescinded is the right to perform fiduciary duties. A criminal conviction may prevent the offender from holding a court-appointed position of trust, from serving as the executor of a will or administrator of an estate, or from being a guardian of a person or estate. For example, a testamentary guardian named in a will by the parents of a minor or of an incompetent person must be approved by the court. A few jurisdictions disqualify any nominee who has been convicted of a felony or infamous crime.

By far the most symbolic disqualification from judicial rights is the barrier to serving on a jury. Although only a handful of states automatically prohibit such service for all convicted felons, approximately thirty states expressly exclude permanently from jury service persons who have been convicted of certain crimes. Such an automatic disqualification might be rational when applied to perjury, but less persuasive when applied to assault. Furthermore, where a state statute provides that a juror must have "good character," evidence of a conviction may be sufficient to result in disqualification. A requirement that a juror be a qualified elector will, of course, result in incapacity to be a juror in those states that disfranchise felons. As with the issue of holding public office, the concern that motivates this disqualification is clear, but as with that concern, there is a less drastic approach—disclosure of the potential juror's criminal record should be sufficient to protect the interests of the parties.

Registration. Pursuant to what amounts to a federal mandate, virtually all states now require persons convicted of sexual offenses (variously defined) to register their addresses with police after they have been released from prison. Many of these states also provide for dissemination of this information to the community, in an apparent attempt to prevent future sexual offenses, primarily, but not solely, against children. Moreover, a majority of states now require such registration (but not community notification) of all convicted felons.

Private rights

Family and personal rights. Conviction of a crime may jeopardize the offender's relationship to her family in several ways. Incarceration, of course, severely hampers this relationship. But beyond this, in many states conviction alone, or conviction and imprisonment, may provide the impetus to legal dissolution of family ties. A convict subject to civil death may be forbidden to marry; many others, either while incarcerated or on conditional liberty, may find their right to marry subject to the scrutiny and approval of a warden, or a probation or parole officer. More commonly (twenty-nine states), a conviction may be declared grounds for divorce; in some states, a divorce will be automatically granted if the convicted spouse is actually incarcerated, or when civil death is incurred.

Nineteen states provide statutorily that conviction or imprisonment may result in the forfeiture of parental rights. Even in those states not so providing, imprisonment may serve as a basis for a finding of abandonment; in dependency and neglect proceedings a parent's criminality may be grounds for terminating parental rights. In virtually every state, a conviction is evidence of unfitness in a custody proceeding. Further, some states rule that a person's imprisonment renders unnecessary his consent to the adoption of his children by others, although most provide such a draconian penalty only in the event of lengthy incarceration.

At common law, the convicted felon generally possessed the right to inherit. The aversion of the colonists to bills of attainder generally ensured that this right would continue. But in the twentieth century many jurisdictions have legislated an exception, providing that a felonious slayer cannot inherit from his victim. This new doctrine has been universally upheld as constitutional.

Government benefits. A criminal conviction may also prevent the offender from participating in insurance, pension, workers' compensation, or other public benefit programs. The federal government, for example, disqualifies some felons from public housing. Similarly, a number of states have enacted statutes that directly prohibit convicted criminals from benefiting from pension funds in some instances. Finally, a criminal conviction adversely affects the offender's right to receive worker's compensation benefits; in most states, convicts are not entitled to such benefits for injuries sustained while they are incarcerated, even during the course of work at prison jobs.

Employment.   Certainly the most pervasive private right disqualification is the exclusion, by statute or by administrative decision, of the convicted felon from specific types of employment. Because it significantly reduces the convicted offender's ability to reenter society as a working citizen, this exclusion is thought by many either to restrict offenders to menial jobs, or to impel them to return to crime.

Certain crimes disqualify offenders from holding a job with the federal government. More importantly, government and private employers alike may generally refuse to hire any applicant who has been convicted. For example, the civil service provides that "criminal, infamous, dishonest, immoral or notoriously disgraceful" conduct may be grounds for dismissal or for refusal to hire an applicant (see 5 C.F.R. 302. 303(a)(2)).

State and municipal governments as well may bar convicted persons from official positions. Nearly half the states bar some convicted persons from certain official jobs, but only six deny public employment permanently; the typical pattern is one of discretionary judgment rather than statutory exclusion. At the other extreme lie municipalities and states that hire ex-offenders as police or, more typically, as correctional or parole officers. The latter help rehabilitate other ex-offenders and at the same time demonstrate to sentenced offenders that the state is concerned about their future employment.

Other provisions deal with the licensing of convicted persons for work at certain jobs. Thus, convicted lawyers, doctors, or others automatically lose their licenses in some states, and are subject to loss of license in all. The courts have seen such statutes as nonpunitive, and upheld them without much dissent. In the nineteenth and early twentieth centuries, when only "professions" were licensed by the state, the barring of convicted persons from such employment, although onerous, was not catastrophic. Today, however, the situation has changed dramatically.

In one state, for example, brokers, dry cleaners, cosmetologists, embalmers, and trainers of guide dogs for the blind must be licensed. Another state licenses (among others) minnow dealers. In all, nearly six thousand occupations are licensed in one or more states; the convicted offender may find the presumption of ineligibility against him either difficult or impossible to overcome, even though there is no apparent link between his offense and the skills needed for the job, or any character trait supposedly required by the occupation.

Access to licensed employment is usually determined by licensing boards, which are generally composed of persons engaged in the given occupation. Concerned with upholding the public image of their trade, many such board members tend to react adversely to any convicted applicant, even if the crime committed bears no relation to the trade in question. Furthermore, some of the most frequently licensed occupations are those taught in prison vocational rehabilitation programs. Thus, the released prisoner may find himself blocked from plying the very skills he was taught during incarceration, thereby frustrating both the prisoner and the correctional authorities.

Some courts have restricted the discretion of boards to deny licenses automatically on the basis of a criminal record, requiring that the board consider the circumstances of the criminal conviction and the extent of rehabilitation, the relation (if any) of the crime to the duties of the job, and the person's character at the time he applies. On the whole, however, courts have been extremely reluctant to interfere with the discretion of licensing boards, even when that discretion has thwarted rehabilitative goals both in and out of prison. In most states, therefore, ex-offenders remain barred from many licensed occupations.

Private employers, like their government counterparts, frequently simply refuse to hire ex-convicts. They usually fear that the ex-criminal will recidivate; neither clear indications that he has been rehabilitated nor the fact that the crime was unrelated to the job sought can erase that fear or the taint he allegedly retains. Although federal (and some state) statutes may prohibit discrimination in hiring on the basis of such factors as sex and race, a past criminal record is not among these factors.

Punishment and procedure

A significant legal question that permeates all of these disabilities is whether they are punishment, or civil sanctions. If they are considered punishment, then a number of protections, both procedural and substantive, would surround their imposition. For example, under the Eighth Amendment no punishment may be cruel and unusual; there is no explicit parallel provision for civil sanctions. Similarly, punishments cannot be imposed unless the state proves the predicate beyond a reasonable doubt, but civil sanctions may be imposed on the basis of far lesser standards of proof.

Almost uniformly, however, the courts have held that whether a specific loss or disability is punishment depends on the intent of the legislature, and courts have been eager to find nonpunitive motives for such statutes. Thus, for example, forfeiture of one's goods may be imposed civilly because there courts have found a remedial purpose in the sanction. Similarly, preventive detention, which could be characterized as pre-conviction civil disability, has been upheld on the basis that it serves the regulatory purpose of crime prevention. Most recently, courts have wrestled with whether requiring convicted sex offenders to register with police upon their release from prison is punitive, thus activating the rights mentioned above. Universally, the courts have found that the legislature's purpose was not punitive, but preventive, even though many states require such registration for the offender's entire life. Indeed, public notification of the offender's history, current address, and employment has been upheld as nonpunitive on the same basic theory.

That some states impose civil disabilities in a wide-ranging manner, while others forego or limit such disabilities, suggests that the nonpunitive purposes espoused by proponents are at least suspect. But even if that conclusion is debatable, these examples suggest either the need for reevaluation of the notion of punishment, or a more nuanced exploration of the disability being imposed. Thus, one might suggest a sliding scale in which the standard of proof, or procedural rigor, might be increased as the intensity and duration of these civil disabilities increased. The Supreme Court has adopted such an approach in analogous areas, for example in civil commitment where the Court held that the standard of proof should be by clear and convincing evidence, rather than by a mere preponderance. Similarly, one might impose rules of evidence, or appointed counsel, in some instances where the disabilities are both intrusive and long-lasting.

Restoration of rights

Once a person has lost civil rights as a result of a conviction, he may never be able to regain them. Disfranchisement in many states is lifelong; there is no mechanism for restoring the right to vote. A prospective employer, public or private, may use a decades-old conviction for a minor offense as grounds for denying employment to an applicant. The stigma of conviction lasts long after a sentence has been served, and may constitute a permanent barrier to reintegration into the community. Some states limit the duration of at least some civil disabilities, usually providing for automatic restoration of certain rights at the end of imprisonment, probation, or parole. Many states take a middle ground, providing some discretionary mechanism, either judicial or administrative, for the restoration of at least some civil rights.

A substantial and growing number of states have enacted legislation providing for the "expungement" of a criminal conviction, under specific circumstances and for specific crimes. The statutes are usually vague about the scope of expungement and even less clear about its effect on those civil rights that would otherwise be lost or suspended. For example, it is uncertain whether a person whose conviction has been "expunged" may validly deny, on employment application forms or in other settings, that she has been convicted of a crime.

Similar difficulties arise with regard to specific rights that are generally lost upon conviction. In California, for example, the expungement statute provides that the defendant convicted of a misdemeanor "shall be released from all penalties and disabilities resulting from the offense or crime" (Cal. Penal Code § I 203.4a (1981 Supp.)). The California courts have interpreted this language in varying ways. Thus, expungement restores the voting franchise and releases the offender from the obligation to register with local police, but does not automatically restore either his right to possess a firearm or his right to regain professional licenses. Nor does expungement prohibit the civil service from relying on evidence of a conviction in dismissing a public employee. Similar confusion has attended efforts to provide for the restoration of other civil rights that are lost as a result of conviction.

Analysis and future of civil disabilities

Imposition of collateral civil disabilities on those convicted of crime raises perplexing problems of both policy and law. The major problem encountered in analyzing civil disabilities is the existence of competing views concerning their purpose. If the primary purpose of the criminal justice system is to rehabilitate the offender, no civil disabilities should be imposed on him, at least after incarceration, since this will only jeopardize his reintegration into the community. Critics of civil disability laws and practices point out with particular anguish that it is often government itself, although allegedly seeking the rehabilitation of offenders, that refuses to hire ex-offenders, erects legal barriers to their acceptance by the community, and allows private employers and others to indulge their fears about them. These critics urge complete restoration of rights immediately upon release, as well as strict prohibition against any search for information about a person's past criminal record.

At the other extreme is the view that civil disabilities are merely additional components of the offender's sentence and punishment, and are implicit in the verdict, which is surrounded by procedural and substantive protections. Even if this view were accepted, however (and note the number of instances, cited above, in which the courts have held that these disabilities are not punitive), imposing the same disabilities—in some cases lifetime ones—on all offenders regardless of the seriousness of their crimes seems to violate the cardinal principle of proportionality.

On the other hand, non-offenders surely have the right to inquire about an offender's past record in order to avoid becoming victims of his possible future crimes. Employers have a particular concern since some courts, either on an absolute basis or on the basis that the employer did not sufficiently investigate the ex-felon's character, have held liable employers who have hired ex-felons who have then committed crimes against customers. Arguably, then, potential future victims should have the right to exclude the offender from situations in which they would be particularly vulnerable, or at least the right to know about the past conviction so that they can decide whether to take a risk such as that of employing him. Thus, even if only one out of every thousand former embezzlers might embezzle again, it seems at first blush questionable to prohibit a prospective employer from learning of an applicant's past background, including his past convictions, and from acting on that information. Prohibiting such an inquiry, however, could be supported on the utilitarian grounds that the fear of recidivism is greatly exaggerated and can-

not outweigh the benefits that employment would bring to ex-offenders; and that on retributivist grounds, the offender has "paid the price" of his crime and should be allowed to re-enter society without continuing impediments and burdens.

Balancing the rights of the ex-offender against the rights of others is no easy task. Where the conflict concerns such potential victims as the state, and the issue is the right to vote or to serve as a juror, perhaps the balance should be weighted differently than where the potential conflict is between the right of one individual—the ex-offender—and that of another individual—the potential employer or crime victim.

As indicated earlier, civil disabilities have been imposed on offenders for over two millennia. This well-established practice is unlikely to cease anytime in the foreseeable future. The good news, however, is that while, in the past fifteen years, there has been an explosion in the number of states requiring registration by ex-offenders, there was a only a minimal escalation in the imposition of other consequences. Since there was otherwise a marked increase in the length and intensity of criminal punishment generally, it may be that we have reached the apogee of the movement.

Numerous reforms have been suggested for dealing with these problems. The Model Penal Code (§ 306.6) provides for automatic restoration of all civil rights to any successful probationer or parolee, as well as to all persons who have completed their incarceration and have not committed a crime for two years; yet it does allow licensing boards to deny licenses when there is a prior criminal record. The National Advisory Commission on Criminal Justice Standards and Goals recommends automatic restoration of civil rights upon completion of sentence, and would require a licensing board to show a "direct relationship between the offense committed or the characteristics of the offenders and the license or privilege being sought" before denying a license. Similar standards adopted by the American Bar Association and the National Conference of Commissioners on Uniform State Laws extend the requirement to private employers as well. The National Council on Crime and Delinquency goes further, calling for automatic restoration of rights by a court on completion of parole, probation, or incarceration, and allowing licensing boards (and possibly private employers) to inquire only whether the applicant has ever been arrested for or convicted of a crime "which has not been annulled by a court."

Civil disability statutes are vague and uncertain of application, and would seemingly provide fertile grounds for legal challenges in terms of both due process and equal protection. If change is to occur, however, it seems unlikely to come from the courts. A few sporadic judicial decisions have invalidated state actions, but the imposition of civil disabilities is within the province of the legislature, and except in extreme cases it does not violate the offender's constitutional rights. Moreover, as noted above, most courts find these provisions nonpunitive in purpose, thereby granting states wide discretion as to how to deal with such disabilities.

In effecting change, legislatures will have to confront the philosophic and policy dilemmas posed by civil disabilities laws, as well as the practices of private employers and others who seek information about a person's criminal background. The predicament of former offenders is unquestionably real, but public concern about their future behavior is equally real. This is the problem that will confront the legislatures in the future.

RICHARD G. SINGER

See also CIVIL AND CRIMINAL DIVIDE; PRISONERS, LEGAL RIGHTS OF; PROBATION AND PAROLE: HISTORY, GOALS, AND DECISION-MAKING; PROBATION AND PAROLE: PROCEDURAL PROTECTION; PROBATION AND PAROLE: SUPERVISION; SENTENCING: ALTERNATIVES; SEXUAL PREDATORS.

BIBLIOGRAPHY

American Bar Association. "Legal Status of Prisoner Standards." *Standards for Criminal Justice.* Washington, D.C.: ABA, 1981.

FELLNER, JAMIE, and MAUER, MARK. *Losing the Vote: The Impact of Felony Disenfranchisement Laws in the United States.* Washington, D.C.: The Sentencing Project, 1998.

FLETCHER, GEORGE P. "Disenfranchisement as Punishment: Reflections on the Racial Uses of Infamia." *UCLA Law Review* 46, no. 6 (1999): 1895–1907.

HUNT, JAMES W.; BOWERS, JAMES; and MILLER, NEAL. *Laws, Licenses, and the Offender's Right to Work: A Study of State Laws Restricting the Occupational Licensing of Former Offenders.* Washington, D.C.: National Clearinghouse on Offender Employment Restrictions for the ABA Commission on Correctional Facilities and Services and Criminal Law Section, 1974.

MILLER, HERBERT. "The Closed Door: The Effect of a Criminal Record on Employment with State and Local Public Agencies. Prepared for the Manpower Administration, U.S. Department of Labor." Springfield, Va.: National Technical Information Service, 1972.

National Conference of Commissioners on Uniform State Laws. *Uniform Law Commissioners' Model Sentencing and Correction Act.* Washington, D.C.: U.S. Department of Justice, Law Enforcement Assistance Administration. National Institute of Law Enforcement and Criminal Justice, 1979.

Note. "The Loss of Parental Rights as a Consequence of Conviction and Imprisonment: Unintended Punishment." *New England Journal on Prison Law* 6 (1979): 61–112.

OLIVERAS, KATHLEEN; BURTON, VELMER; and CULLEN, FRANCIS. "The Collateral Consequences of a Felony Conviction: A National Study of State Legal Codes 10 Years Later." *Federal Probation* 60 (September 1996): 10.

RUDENSTINE, DAVID. *The Rights of Ex-offenders.* New York: Avon, 1979.

Special Project. "The Collateral Consequences of a Criminal Conviction." *Vanderbilt Law Review* 23, no. 5 (1970): 929–1241.

U.S. Department of Justice, Law Enforcement Assistance Administration, National Advisory Commission on Criminal Justice Standards and Goals. *Corrections.* Washington, D.C.: The Commission, 1973.

VON HIRSCH, ANDREW, and WASIK, MARTIN. "Civil Disqualifications Attending Conviction: A Suggested Conceptual Framework." *Cambridge Law Journal* 56 (1997): 599.

CASES

Hawker v. New York, 170 U.S. 189 (1898).
In re Hatch, 10 Cal. 2d 147, 73 P.2d 885 (1937).
Otsuka v. Hite, 64 Cal. 2d 596, 414 P.2d 412 (1966).
Richardson v. Ramirez, 418 U.S. 24 (1974).
Schneider v. Rusk, 377 U.S. 163 (1964).
Trop v. Dulles, 356 U.S. 86 (1958).

CORPORAL PUNISHMENT

Corporal punishment is the infliction of physical pain as a penalty for an infraction. Past forms of corporal punishment included branding, blinding, mutilation, amputation, and the use of the pillory and the stocks. It was also an element in such violent modes of execution as drowning, stoning, burning, hanging, and drawing and quartering (in which offenders were partly strangled and, while still alive, disemboweled and dismembered). In most parts of Europe and in the United States such savage penalties were replaced by imprisonment during the late eighteenth and early nineteenth centuries, although capital punishment (usually by hanging) remained. Physical chastisement became less frequent until, in the twentieth century, corporal punishment was either eliminated as a legal penalty or restricted to beating with a birch rod, cane, whip, or other scourge. In ordinary usage the term now refers to such penal flagellation.

Prevalence

Although corporal punishment has been widely banned, the extent to which it continues to be used is difficult to determine. Countries that strictly observe Islamic law inflict both amputation and whipping as penalties. In South Africa, until the mid-1990s, males under twenty-one years of age could be whipped for any offense in lieu of other punishment, and adult males between the ages of twenty-one and thirty could be whipped either in addition to or instead of other punishment for many offenses, including robbery, rape, aggravated or indecent assault, burglary, and auto theft. In the 1970s an annual average of 335 adults were sentenced to "corporal punishment only." Whipping was used more extensively to chastise juveniles, but official statistics were not kept.

In Great Britain the Cadogan Committee, appointed in 1937 to review the application of corporal punishment, reported that this penalty had been abolished for criminal offenses by adults in every "civilized country" in the world except those whose criminal code was influenced by English criminal law—that is, in some of the British dominions and American states, where it could still be legally imposed for offenses by juveniles and for violations of prison discipline (Cadogan Committee). The committee's recommendation that corporal punishment be abandoned as a judicial penalty in England was adopted in the Criminal Justice Act, 1948, 11 & 12 Geo. 6, c. 58 (Great Britain), which abolished the penalty for all offenses except serious violations of prison discipline; in 1967 it was also eliminated for these. The Advisory Council on the Treatment of Offenders (ACTO) reported in 1961 that corporal punishment had not been reintroduced in any country which had abolished it and that in those few countries which contin-

ued to prescribe such penalties various limitations had been introduced, so that infliction had become uncommon (Advisory Council on the Treatment of Offenders). The last two American states to use corporal punishment as a judicial penalty were Maryland, where it was seldom inflicted before being abolished in 1952, and Delaware, where the last flogging took place in 1952 although formal abolition did not occur until 1972. Corporal punishment remains available, however, as a penalty for serious breaches of prison discipline in a number of states. Milder forms of corporal punishment for students remain a possible penalty in many states.

In 1994, the caning of a young American in Singapore for a property offense drew wide political condemnation from American political leaders, although it also had the effect of temporarily raising public debate over the merits of judicial corporal punishment. As a result of a growing public concern over crime rates, as well as prison overcrowding, public support of corporal punishment for petty criminals and juvenile offenders increased, and bills were introduced in several state legislatures to reintroduce judicial corporal punishment as an alternative to imprisonment. Most efforts failed, however, because of potential constitutional infirmities.

More serious forms of corporal punishment, including flogging and amputation, have undergone a revival in certain Islamic countries that have experienced a resurgence in fundamentalism. The United Nations Human Rights Committee and other organizations have suggested that the prohibition of cruel, inhuman, or degrading punishment under Article 7 of the International Covenant on Civil and Political Rights could be extended by customary law to include corporal punishment. Nevertheless, while some of the practices of some Islamic countries have drawn rebuke and condemnation by the United Nations Commission on Human Rights, that body has as recently as 1997 suggested only that certain forms of corporal punishment may be violative of international law, leaving open the question of the extent to which evolving standards or general principles of law will tolerate other forms.

Normative arguments

Corporal punishment satisfies demands for reprisal and is seen as a just penalty for certain kinds of offenses. Both sentiments are resurgent among the public in countries in which such punishment has been abolished. Apparent or real increases in crime, particularly violent offenses, spark public demands for the restoration of corporal punishment. A 1960 poll in England revealed that 74 percent of the population thought it an appropriate penalty for some crimes. The idea that corporal punishment is particularly fitting for certain offenses—for example, those involving personal violence—is ultimately a moral or political judgment that reflects the retributive theory of punishment. Various modern expressions of human rights policy, however, condemn corporal punishment. Article 3 of the European Convention on Human Rights declares that "no one shall be subjected to torture or to inhuman or degrading treatment or punishment" (Council of Europe, p. 25), and in 1978 the European Court of Human Rights found corporal punishment to be "degrading" under the terms of this article (*Tyrer v. United Kingdom*, 2 Eur. Human Rights R. 1, 58 I.L.R. 339 (Eur. Ct. Human Rights 1978)). Moreover, the United Nations' "Standard Minimum Rules for the Treatment of Prisoners" specifically states that "corporal punishment . . . shall be completely prohibited as punishment for disciplinary offenses" (United Nations Secretariat, Rule 31, p. 69).

In the mid-1990s, several proponents of corporal punishment asserted an "economic" approach: that technology could enable the use of more effective forms of corporal punishment designed to provide temporary and specific physical incapacitation rather than imprisonment, which "over-incapacitates." Others have argued in favor of reintroduction of corporal punishment as a solution to overcrowding and the negative effects of long-term imprisonment.

Effectiveness

Advocates of corporal punishment argue that it is more likely than any alternative to prevent offenders from committing further criminal acts, and that it is also an exceptionally strong deterrent to potential offenders. These claims have been subjected to some empirical investigation, especially by the Cadogan Committee, whose research was continued in 1960 by the Home Office Research Unit for ACTO.

Individual deterrence.   Part of the research carried out by the Cadogan Committee and ACTO covered 3,023 cases of robbery with violence (virtually the only offense for which corporal punishment was imposed) between 1921 and 1947. Offenders were divided into two groups: those previously convicted of serious crimes and those not previously convicted. In both categories, offenders who were not flogged showed slightly better subsequent records. Those who were flogged seemed slightly more likely to be convicted again of robbery with violence, although the numbers were small and the differences not statistically significant (Cadogan Committee; Advisory Council on the Treatment of Offenders). These findings suggested that flogging was not especially effective as an individual deterrent, but they were not conclusive: the groups of those flogged and not flogged were not properly matched, nor were the sentences randomly assigned, for some judges habitually made more use of the penalty than others.

General deterrence.   The Cadogan Committee devoted special attention to five cases of corporal punishment used as an exemplary sentence in response to major outbreaks of crimes for which, according to public opinion, the penalty was particularly suitable. The committee found that in some cases the facts plainly contradicted such beliefs and that reductions in crime could just as plausibly be attributed to causes other than the penalties imposed on offenders. It also noted that the incidence of robbery with violence in England and Wales had declined steadily in the years before World War I notwithstanding infrequent and decreasing use of corporal punishment, whereas in the postwar years it had tended to increase despite a much greater and increasing resort to floggings. It was also shown that between 1890 and 1934 the incidence of robbery in England and Wales (where corporal punishment might have served as a deterrent) declined more slowly than in Scotland, where corporal punishment was not inflicted for those offenses (Cadogan Committee).

ACTO also compared the incidence of robbery with violence in England and Wales before and after corporal punishment was abolished as a judicial penalty in 1948. The number of robberies reported to the police increased steadily during and after World War II, although corporal punishment was employed more frequently than before the war. After 1948, however, there was a marked downward trend, and until 1957 instances of robbery remained well below the 1948 level. The causes of this reduction were unknown, but ACTO inferred that corporal punishment had not been a strong deterrent immediately before its abolition and noted that abolition was not followed by an increase in the offenses for which it had previously been imposed (Advisory Council on the Treatment of Offenders). In short, no evidence proved that corporal punishment provided more deterrence than imprisonment, to which it commonly served as an alternative penalty before abolition. Canadian and New Zealand studies confirmed these findings (Canada, Parliament; New Zealand Department of Justice).

Conclusion

Repudiation of the infliction of pain as a penal method and the substitution of corrective incarceration for physical punishment have been conspicuous features of penal history since the late eighteenth century. Corporal punishment has come to be seen as incompatible with "modern" penal methods and as likely to militate against the success of reformative or rehabilitative treatment. The decline of corporal punishment was once hailed as a sign of the progress of humanitarianism, enlightenment, and civilization. In the latter part of the twentieth century, however, such optimism has been questioned by certain writers, notably Michel Foucault, who have argued that the rehabilitation theory and the creation of "noncorporal" penal systems generally meant only the insidious expansion and refinement of penal repression. However, Foucault and most other critics of the rehabilitative ideal have not expressed approval of earlier penal practices, nor have they recommended that corporal punishment be revived as a penal method.

GORDON HAWKINS
RICHARD S. FRASE

See also CAPITAL PUNISHMENT: LEGAL ASPECTS; CAPITAL PUNISHMENT: MORALITY, POLITICS, AND POLICY; COMPARATIVE CRIMINAL LAW AND ENFORCEMENT: ISLAM; CRUEL AND UNUSUAL PUNISHMENT; PUNISHMENT; SHAMING PUNISHMENTS.

BIBLIOGRAPHY

Advisory Council on the Treatment of Offenders. *Report: Corporal Punishment.* Cmnd. 1213. London: Her Majesty's Stationery Office, 1961.

BAHRAMPOUR, FIROUZEH. "The Caning of Michael Fay: Can Singapore's Punishment Withstand Scrutiny of International Law?" *American University Journal of International Law & Policy* 10 (1995): 1075–1108.

Cadogan Committee. *Report of the Departmental Committee on Corporal Punishment.* Cmnd. 5684. London: Her Majesty's Stationery Office, 1938. Reprint, 1963.

CALDWELL, ROBERT G. "The Deterrent Influence of Corporal Punishment on Prisoners Who Have Been Whipped." *American Sociological Review* 9 (1944): 171–177.

Canada, Parliament. *Reports of the Joint Committee of the Senate and House of Commons on Capital Punishment, Corporal Punishment, Lotteries.* Ottawa: Queen's Printer and Controller of Stationery, 1956.

Council of Europe. *The European Convention on Human Rights.* Strasbourg, France: Directorate of Information, 1968.

FOUCAULT, MICHEL. *Discipline and Punish: The Birth of the Prison.* New York: Pantheon, 1977.

KAN, STEVEN S. "Corporal Punishments and Optimal Incapacitation." *Journal of Legal Studies* 25 (1996): 121–130.

MATTHEWS, MICHAEL P. "Caning and the Constitution: Why The Backlash against Crime Won't Result in the Backlashing of Criminals." *New York Law School Journal of Human Rights* 14 (1998): 571–614.

MIDGLEY, JAMES O. "Corporal Punishment and Penal Policy: Notes on the Continued Use of Corporal Punishment with Reference to South Africa." *Journal of Criminal Law & Criminology* 73 (1982): 388–404.

NEWMAN, GRAEME. *Just and Painful: A Case for the Corporal Punishment of Criminals.* Harrow & Heston/Macmillan Book, 1983.

New Zealand Department of Justice. *Crime in New Zealand.* Wellington, New Zealand: Government Printer, 1968.

PHILLIPS, BARRY. "The Case for Corporal Punishment in the United Kingdom: Beaten into Submission in Europe?" *International & Comparative Law Quarterly* 43 (1994): 153–163.

RODLEY, NIGEL S. *The Treatment of Prisoners under International Law.* 2d ed. New York: Oxford University Press, 1999.

SCOTT, GEORGE RYLEY. *The History of Corporal Punishment: A Survey of Flagellation in Its Historical, Anthropological, and Sociological Aspects.* Reprint. London: T. Werner Laurie, 1942.

United Nations Secretariat. "Standard Minimum Rules for the Treatment of Prisoners." *First United Nations Congress on the Prevention of Crime and the Treatment of Offenders, Geneva, 22 August–3 September 1955.* New York: United Nations. Department of Economic and Social Affairs, 1956. Pages 67–73.

WEIDMAN, WHITNEY S. "Don't Spare the Rod: A Proposed Return to Public, Corporal Punishment of Convicts." *American Journal of Criminal Law* 23 (1996): 651–673.

CORPORATE CRIMINAL RESPONSIBILITY

Criminal prosecutions of corporations and other fictional entities have occurred routinely in the United Kingdom since the nineteenth century and in the United States since the beginning of the twentieth century. During the later portion of the twentieth century the Netherlands, Canada, and France enacted standards for holding fictional entities criminally liable. Elsewhere in the world, legislative bodies and courts are being urged to recognize corporate criminal liability by advocates who point to the major role played by organizations in modern day life and argue that active prosecution of organizations is essential to effective crime control efforts. Even so, because of theoretical and practical problems in prosecuting fictional entities, corporate criminal liability is controversial. The debate centers on the issues of how to measure a fictional entity's liability, how to sanction a fictional entity, and whether criminal prosecution of organizations is effective.

History

By the fourteenth century, fictional entities were well recognized in English law. These early corporations were created by grants from the Crown or Parliament and consisted almost entirely of ecclesiastical bodies. By the sixteenth and seventeenth centuries the importance of corporations grew as industrialization spread. Municipalities, craft guilds, hospitals, and universities incorporated. Soon thereafter, massive business frauds and failures to perform duties (i.e., repair public bridges and roads) led to criminal prosecution of corporations for *nonfeasance*. By the mid-nineteenth century, English courts were willing to hold corporations criminally liable for wrongful acts as well as wrongful omissions. However, the courts drew a distinction at crimes of "immorality," since these required some proof of criminal intent. By the twentieth century, however, English courts had developed an "identification" doctrine by which corporations were prosecuted for crimes of intent. This doctrine merges the personalities of the corporation and its controlling individuals, and holds a corporation criminally liable for crimes committed by persons who "represent the directing mind and will of the corporate entity" (de Doelder and Tiedemann, p. 372).

In the North American colonies, the English Crown or Parliament granted the first corporate charters. After the colonies obtained freedom from England, state legislatures issued such grants. As in England, corporations initially were held criminally liable only for failure to comply with legal duties, then for wrongful acts under regulatory statutes that carried no mens rea requirement, and finally, for crimes of intent through use of anthropomorphic doctrines that identified an organization with individuals within the organization. Beyond these similarities, however, the American development of corporate criminal liability doctrines has been more complex, in part because of the dual state/federal judicial systems in the United States. Throughout the latter part of the twentieth century, two competing doctrines prevailed in the United States for holding organizations criminally liable: the Model Penal Code, section 2.01, which, like the English approach, holds an organization liable for the acts of certain leaders of the organization, and *respondeat superior*, which holds an organization criminally liable for the acts of any of its agents. The Model Penal Code approach has been adopted by a number of states; the respondeat superior approach is followed by the federal courts and some states.

American standards of corporate criminal liability

Both of the American standards for holding organizations criminally liable employ the "identification" approach pioneered in England. This approach imposes *vicarious liability* on an organization for the acts committed by agents of the organization. Respondeat superior is the broader of the two standards. It is a common law rule developed primarily in the American federal courts and adopted by some American state courts. Derived from agency principles in tort law, it provides that a corporation "may be held criminally liable for the acts of any of its agents [who] (1) commit a crime (2) within the scope of employment (3) with the intent to benefit the corporation." (Note, p. 1247). This standard is quite broad, permitting organizational liability for the act of any agent, even the lowest level employee.

The U.S. Supreme Court first recognized the respondeat superior standard as appropriate for imposing corporate criminal liability for intentional crimes in *New York Central & Hudson River Railroad v. United States* (1909). New York Central Railroad had been convicted of bribery because an assistant traffic manager gave "rebates" on railroad rates to certain railroad users. As a result of the rebates, the effective shipping rate for some users was less than mandated rates; this violated the Elkins Act, which imposed criminal sanctions. In affirming the conviction of New York Central the Supreme Court applied the respondeat superior standard, holding that since an agent of New York Central committed a crime while carrying out his duties, New York Central was liable. The Court applied this broad standard to New York Central with almost no analysis of whether respondeat superior was an appropriate standard for assessing criminal intent. The Court noted that the principle of respondeat superior was well established in civil tort law, then simply stated that "every reason in public policy" justified "go[ing] only a step farther" and applying respondeat superior to criminal law (p. 495). Other American courts have followed the lead of *New York Central*, stating: "There is no longer any distinction in essence between the civil and criminal liability of corporation, based upon the element of intent or wrongful purpose" (*Egan v. United States*, 137 F.2d 369, 379 (8th Cir.), *cert. denied*, 320 U.S. 788 (1943)).

New York Central and its progeny have been criticized as failing to appreciate the inherently different nature of civil and criminal liability, failing to consider civil alternatives to imposing corporate criminal liability, and failing to examine alternative standards for imposing criminal liability upon corporations.

Critics point to the fact that tort lawsuits are designed primarily to compensate one party for the damage caused by another party. The assumption underlying tort liability is that it is more equitable for the employer of the *tort-feasor* to absorb the financial loss caused by its agent's conduct than for the individual victim to do so. Except in rare tort cases, intent is not an issue in holding a corporation liable. There is no effort to assess corporate intent since even the most honorable corporation becomes liable simply because its agent engaged in certain conduct. Moreover, even though the threat of tort liability may deter conduct, collection of damages, not deterrence of future conduct, is the paramount concern of a tort action. Lastly, in all but unusual cases, tort liability carries no moral or punitive stigma; it is simply a cost of doing business.

In all criminal cases, however, intent, deterrence, and stigma are key ingredients. Intent to violate the law is an essential element of almost every crime. Criminal prosecutions are pursued precisely because of their deterrent impact. The stigma and shame of a criminal conviction, coupled with the disabilities a conviction carries, helps conveys this impact. In short, while the notion of respondeat superior is well suited to torts, it is anathema to the criminal law.

The second flaw regularly identified in *New York Central* is its failure to consider civil options to imposing criminal liability on corporations. The Court stated in *New York Central* that failure to impose criminal liability on corporations would "virtually take away the only means of effectually controlling the subject matter and correcting the abuses aimed at" (p. 496). This statement is inaccurate. There are two major options to imposing criminal liability on corporations: criminal liability of responsible individuals within the corporation, and civil remedies against the corporation. Granted, when the Court decided *New York Central* in 1909, prosecution of responsible corporate officials was unusual. Since then, however, such prosecutions have become more routine and much easier through the development of the "responsible corporate official" and strict liability doctrines. In addition, in 1909, administrative regulation and supervision was in its infancy. During the twentieth century, however, agencies grew dramatically in size, expertise, and power to regulate. Unfortunately, courts and legislatures have failed to reexamine the propriety of using respondeat superior to hold corporations criminally liable. As one court noted in affirming the conviction of a corporation, failure to impose criminal liability against the corporation "[was] to immunize the offender who really benefits and open wide the door for evasion" (*United States v. George F. Fish, Inc.*, 154 F.2d 798 (2d Cir.), *cert. denied*, 328 U.S. 869 (1946), p. 801).

The third flaw highlighted in *New York Central* is the Court's failure to consider the conceptual alternatives to respondeat superior for imposing corporate criminal liability. In *New York Central*, the Court assumed that the only standard available for imposing corporate criminal liability was respondeat superior. Such a rigid view of its options is understandable given the posture of the case before the Court and the historical place of the opinion. However, in light of the considerable scholarship throughout the twentieth century identifying the problems with the respondeat superior approach and proposing alternative conceptual models, there is little reason to adhere to the overly simplistic choice facing the Court in 1909.

The Model Penal Code, section 2.01, remedies some of the problems of the respondeat superior standard because it more narrowly imposes corporate criminal liability. The Code approach more closely tracks the approach taken worldwide for imposing corporate criminal liability. The Code imposes corporate criminal liability only for the acts of some corporate agents. It provides that a corporation is criminally liable for criminal conduct that was "authorized, requested, commanded, performed or recklessly tolerated by the board of directors or by a high managerial agent acting in behalf of the corporation within the scope of his office or employment." A high managerial agent is anyone "having duties of such responsibility that [their] conduct may fairly be assumed to represent the policy of the corporation or association."

While praised as an improvement over respondeat superior's breadth, the Code standard has been criticized on several grounds. The first such criticism is that it is unrealistic, given the size of many modern corporations. Because illegal activities rarely are conducted openly, it would be difficult if not impossible to obtain the required proof that a high managerial agent conducted, or even recklessly tolerated, illegal activity. Second, the Code standard has been criticized because it encourages high managerial agents to avoid learning of wrongdoing within a corporation. Since the Code imposes corporate liability only if higher-level corporate officials are involved in or tolerate wrongdoing, a lack of knowledge of wrongdoing avoids liability under the Code. Lastly, the Code standard has been criticized as inappropriately narrow, since even if a clear corporate policy encouraged a lower echelon employee to commit an offense, the corporation is not liable unless there is evidence of participation or knowledge by a specific corporate director or high managerial agent.

Both the respondeat superior and the Code standards contain two requirements that could substantially limit their applicability and cure some of the problems they pose, but the courts have interpreted these requirements so broadly that they mean almost nothing. Both standards require that the illegal act be "within the scope of the agent's employment" and undertaken "for the benefit of the corporation" (p. 1247). Courts have interpreted "within the scope of employment" as applying to acts within an agent's apparent scope of employment. Under this broad interpretation even acts undertaken by a corporate employee contrary to specific corporate instructions have been held to warrant imposition of corporate criminal liability. The rationale for this view is that the agent's actions, taken while the agent is serving in the corporation's employ, would appear to outsiders to be within the agent's authority. *United States v. Hilton Hotels Corporation*, 467 F.2d 1000 (9th Cir. 1972), provides an example of this broad interpretation. The purchasing agent at Hilton Hotel in Portland, Oregon, threatened a supplier of goods with the loss of the hotel's business if the supplier did not contribute to an association formed to attract conventions to Portland. The corporate president testified that such action was contrary to corporate policy. Both the manager and assistant manager of the hotel testified that they specifically told the purchasing agent not to threaten suppliers. Nevertheless, the court convicted Hilton Hotel Corporation of antitrust violations under the respondeat superior standard because to outsiders, the assistant manager appeared to be acting on behalf of the corporation.

Although the respondeat superior test was applied in *Hilton Hotels*, the problem of the maverick employee arises even under the narrower Model Penal Code standard since the Code also relies on vicarious liability. Thus, for example, if the Hilton Hotel purchasing agent had "duties of such responsibility that his conduct may fairly be assumed to represent the policy of the corporation or association," the agent would be a "high managerial agent" (MPC § 2.01) and Hilton Hotels Corporation would be criminally liable.

Courts also have interpreted the second requirement, "with intent to benefit the corporation," almost out of existence. As one court noted, "[t]here have been many cases . . . in which the corporation is criminally liable even though no benefit [to the corporation] has been received in fact" (*Standard Oil Co. v. United States*, 307 F.2d 120 (5th Cir. 1962), p. 128). Courts have found this element of corporate criminal liability met, even when the corporation is a victim of its agent's act. *United States v. Sun-Diamond Growers of California*, 138 F.3d 961 (D.C. 1998), provides an example. Sun Diamond, a large agricultural cooperative owned by member cooperatives, was convicted of making illegal gifts to a public official, wire fraud, and making illegal campaign contributions. A vice president of Sun-Diamond made the improper payments and engaged in all of the illegal conduct. Sun-Diamond argued that its vice president did not act with intent to benefit Sun-Diamond, but with intent to defraud Sun-Diamond. Acknowledging that

Sun-Diamond "look[ed] more like a victim than a perpetrator," the court nevertheless rejected Sun-Diamond's argument, finding that the jury could have concluded that the vice president acted with an intent, "however befuddled," to further his employer's interest (p. 970). The court explained its holding by noting the policy justification for holding corporations criminally liable for acts of their agents: "to increase incentives for corporations to monitor and prevent illegal employee conduct" (p. 971). This analysis is typical of judicial creation and application of corporate criminal liability. The court relied upon a utilitarian rationale with no discussion of whether corporate liability for crimes is consistent with principles of criminal law. Yet even if courts wanted to require stringent proof of "intent to benefit the corporation," it is unclear how they could. It seems impossible to apply literally. For example, if an employee takes bribes for favors to corporate customers, has the corporation benefited? If so, how do courts measure the benefit? Do the disadvantages, such as poor relationships with other customers, a criminal conviction, detrimental publicity, internal dissension, and poor morale, outweigh the benefit?

In addition to watered-down interpretations of "within the scope of employment" and "for the benefit of the corporation," adoption of the notion of "collective intent" has rendered the respondeat superior and Model Penal Code standards extremely broad. The doctrine of "collective intent" allows courts to find intent on the part of a corporation even when it is not possible to identify a corporate agent with criminal intent. *United States v. Bank of New England*, 821 F.2d 844 (1st Cir. 1987), demonstrates this. The Bank of New England was convicted of failing to file U.S. Treasury reports of cash transactions over $10,000. On thirty-one occasions, a bank customer withdrew more than $10,000 in cash from a single account by simultaneously presenting multiple checks in sums less than $10,000 to a single bank teller. Acknowledging that under applicable law a corporation's criminal intent is imputed from an agent's intent, the bank argued that it was not liable because there was no bank employee with sufficient criminal intent to violate the reporting requirements. According to the bank, the teller who conducted the transactions did not know that the law required the filing of the reports in the circumstance presented by the customer. And, the bank employee who knew of the reporting requirements did not know of the customer's transactions. Thus argued the bank, there was no single bank employee with sufficient *mens rea* to impute to the corporation. The trial court rejected the bank's argument because of the "collective intent" of bank employees. The court explained that "the bank's knowledge is the totality of what all of the employees know within the scope of their employment" (p. 855).

Critique of corporate criminal liability

Several arguments are made against recognizing corporate criminal liability. The most consistent argument is that corporate criminal liability is inconsistent with basic tenets of criminal law. A corollary argument is that using the criminal justice system inappropriately, by imposing corporate criminal liability, distorts, cheapens, and ultimately weakens the criminal justice system. Proponents of this view argue that corporate criminal liability is inconsistent with the criminal law in two respects. First, the current standards of corporate criminal liability, which are based upon principles of vicarious liability, are incompatible with the criminal law's requirement that an actor be held responsible only for its own action and intent. Since fictional entities have no intent, they are not suitable for criminal prosecution, and the subterfuge of imputing another actor's act and intent to the corporation (even that of a corporate agent) cannot substitute for this deficiency in proof. This argument also points to imprisonment as a defining characteristic of the criminal law and argues that since fictional entities cannot be imprisoned, corporate criminal liability is inappropriate.

A variety of arguments against corporate criminal liability concern the harm such liability poses to businesses. One argument is that the vague and broad standards of corporate criminal liability confer too much discretion in prosecutors, too little guidance to courts as to how to apply the standards, and too little notice to businesses as to how to avoid criminal liability. Another argument is that the broad standards for corporate criminal liability, along with aggressive use of expansive statutes such as money laundering and RICO (Racketeer Influenced and Corrupt Organizations Act), have led to "overcriminalization." Actions once handled administratively through dialogue between regulator and regulated are now prosecuted criminally. Overcriminalization has caused American businesses to expend resources on expensive internal policing efforts that, in turn, leaves American companies less competitive in a global business environment.

Another argument advanced against corporate criminal liability is that it is unclear whether imposing such liability does any good. In fact, argue some critics, criminal prosecution with its heavy penalties and dire consequences for the corporation and its employees may encourage cover-ups of illegal activity. These critics suggest that regulatory oversight with continuing dialogue between regulator and those regulated is more effective in detecting and deterring corporate misbehavior.

The last argument advanced against corporate criminal liability is that imposing it hurts innocent actors: the shareholders, who especially in the context of a large publicly held corporation are powerless to effect the conduct of corporate executives; bondholders and other creditors; employees; the community in which the corporation is located and that may be adversely affected by serious consequences imposed on the corporation; and consumers, who likely will pay higher prices because of the criminal penalties imposed. This argument is, of course, just as applicable to imposition of civil penalties as to criminal penalties.

The major argument offered for corporate criminal liability is utilitarian: corporations are major actors in today's world and crime cannot be fought effectively without tools to pursue all major actors. A corollary argument is that allowing corporations to engage in criminal activity gives illegal corporations a competitive edge over law-abiding corporations. This, in turn, distorts and undermines market forces in a capitalist economy. This view is based upon the belief that criminal prosecution of corporations can change corporate behavior. Advocates of corporate criminal liability suggest that corporate behavior can be altered in two ways by criminal prosecutions. First, general deterrence of similar behavior by many corporations is achieved through publicity about corporate prosecutions. Second, options for sentencing convicted corporations, such as probation, which requires implementation of an effective corporate compliance plan, forces changes within a corporation.

The obvious alternative to corporate criminal liability is prosecution of culpable individuals within an organization. Proponents of corporate criminal liability argue that this alternative is inadequate because it is not always possible to identify the responsible individuals within a large organization; individuals are fungible and can be replaced by others who are willing to break the law; individuals are more likely than organizations to be judgment-proof and thus immune to financial penalties that accompany criminal liability and deter future unlawful conduct.

Most proponents of corporate criminal liability acknowledge many of the problems identified with the manner in which corporate criminal liability is imposed and urge adoption of a more appropriate standard for assessing such liability. These commentators agree that the problem with all current standards of corporate criminal liability is their reliance on vicarious liability, which is inconsistent with criminal law's focus on personal guilt through one's own conduct and intent. They argue that corporate criminal liability should hinge on an organization's own conduct and intent. Many commentators have suggested models for assessing corporate criminal liability. One view is that corporate criminal liability should not be imposed until an organization's "intent" is proven. Such proof would focus on corporate policies and procedures such as the effectiveness of corporate hierarchy in monitoring activities of employees; corporate goals; education and monitoring programs for employees; an organization's reaction to past violations and violators; and an organization's compensation incentives for legally appropriate behavior. This suggested approach is similar to that taken in the U.S. Sentencing Guidelines for assessing the culpability of a convicted organization about to be sentenced.

Another proposal focuses on a corporation's response to a violation of the law by corporate agents. Termed *reactive corporate fault*, this approach examines the corporate reaction after the crime is brought to the attention of the policy-making officials within the corporation. Although this approach provides a conceptual paradigm for measuring corporate intent, it measures it only after the criminal conduct has occurred. This is a problem since the relevant time to measure intent for any crime is at the time the offense was committed.

Another conceptual approach toward corporate criminal liability that respected scholars have advocated for years is a *due diligence defense*. The Netherlands and some American courts currently permit such a defense. A due diligence defense allows a corporation, otherwise criminally liable, to show that it exercised due diligence to prevent the crime. Presumably corporate policies and procedures existing at the time of the offense, such as the presence of a corporate compliance plan, would be relevant in assessing due diligence. The weakness in this approach is that it becomes available only after a corporation has been found liable under the inappropriately broad vicarious liability standard.

Procedural rights of corporate defendants

Corporate defendants in the United States, like individual defendants, enjoy certain protections available only in the criminal context: the right to have all elements of the offense proven beyond a reasonable doubt instead of by a preponderance of the evidence; the right to indictment by a grand jury; the right to trial by jury; the right to confront adverse witnesses; freedom from double jeopardy; and the right to effective counsel. Of these, the burden of proof and the right to jury trial may be the most significant. Proof of most complex crimes, which will be the bulk of crimes charged against a corporation, are difficult to prove. Requiring proof beyond a reasonable doubt will be difficult and likely will dissuade prosecutors from proceeding in many cases. Trial by jury presumably means that a jury must understand the charges before they convict. Clarifying a corporation's role in a complex crime may not be feasible and should lead to acquittal. In addition, juries may not approve of the broad standards of corporate criminal liability; jury nullification is a possibility.

Corporations do not enjoy what is perhaps the most significant right belonging to defendants in the American criminal justice system. They do not have the right not to incriminate themselves. Considering that most statements against corporate interest will be made by corporate agents over whom a corporation may have little control, the inability to assert this right is a serious disability for the corporate defendant.

Sentencing

A practical problem in prosecuting corporations for crimes is what to do with them after conviction. Options include cash fines and forfeiture of proceeds of the criminal activity or property used to commit the offense; compensation to victims; public acknowledgment of wrongdoing; community service; appointment of a trustee to supervise some or all of the convicted corporation's affairs; required implementation of a corporate compliance plan; revocation of business licenses; debarment from conducting future business with the government or other entities;

revocation of the corporate charter (the corporate equivalent of a "death penalty"); and probation, through which some of the above options may be implemented.

In 1991, the U.S. Sentencing Commission implemented sentencing guidelines for organizations. The guidelines are based upon the following four principles: a convicted organization should remedy any harm caused by the offense; if the organization "operated primarily for a criminal purpose or primarily by criminal means, the fine should be set sufficiently high to divest the organization of all of its assets"; the fine for any other organization should be based upon its conduct and culpability; and, probation is appropriate "when needed to ensure that another sanction will be fully implemented, or to ensure that steps will be taken within the organization to reduce the likelihood of future criminal conduct" (*U.S. Sentencing Guidelines Manual*, chap. 8, Introductory Commentary).

One of the more innovative aspects of the Sentencing Guidelines is the effort to describe an organization's "culpability." For most organizations (those not operated primarily for a criminal purpose or primarily by criminal means), the fine assessed upon conviction will depend, in part, upon the organization's culpability. A court is to examine the following factors to assess such culpability: involvement in or tolerance of criminal activity; prior regulatory and criminal history; violation of a judicial order; obstruction of justice during the investigation; installation of an effective program to prevent and detect violations of the law; self-reporting, cooperation; and acceptance of responsibility. In essence, the Sentencing Commission has provided a model for judging corporate intent.

Experts identify at least two potential side-effects of the Sentencing Guidelines. First, the guidelines may be partially responsible for the increase in prosecutions of organizations. From 1995, when the impact of the Sentencing Guidelines was just being felt, to 1998, there was a 197 percent increase in U.S. federal courts in convictions of organizations. Although the guidelines are intended to apply after conviction, they provide a model for assessing organizational culpability. This clarifies the law of corporate criminal liability for prosecutors and courts. The guidelines also make meaningful sentences more likely, which, in turn, gives prosecutors an incentive to pursue corporate offenders. Second, the guidelines have made it imperative that corporations have meaningful corporate compliance plans. The existence of such a plan affects an organization's culpability score under the guidelines, thereby reducing any criminal fine by as much as 400 percent.

Conclusion

There is global discord on whether corporations should be held criminally liable. The jurisprudential and practical problems in imposing criminal liability on fictional entities ferment this disagreement. The arguments against imposing such liability focus on its incompatibility with the criminal justice system; the hardship such liability, especially under the broad vicarious liability standards employed, causes for businesses; and the unfairness of punishing innocent actors, such as shareholders and creditors, when corporate criminal liability is imposed. The arguments in favor of corporate criminal liability focus on the major role corporations play in today's world; the corrupting influence of corporate crime; and the ineffectiveness of alternatives such as prosecuting individuals involved or pursuing civil remedies. The existing standards for assessing corporate criminal liability are universally criticized as simplistic, unrealistic, and inconsistent with fundamental tenets of criminal law. These standards rely upon vicarious liability and hold a corporation liable by imputing the actions and intent of a corporate agent to the corporation.

Change is likely in the years ahead for there is growing support, worldwide, for imposing corporate criminal liability. It is likely, however, that the anthropomorphic standards currently employed to assess corporate criminal liability will evolve into more sophisticated standards that assess corporate culpability.

PAMELA H. BUCY

See also CIVIL AND CRIMINAL DIVIDE; ECONOMIC CRIME: ANTITRUST OFFENSES; ECONOMIC CRIME: TAX OFFENSES; ECONOMIC CRIME: THEORY; STRICT LIABILITY; VICARIOUS LIABILITY; WHITE-COLLAR CRIME: HISTORY OF AN IDEA.

BIBLIOGRAPHY

American Law Institute. *Model Penal Code: Proposed Official Draft.* Philadelphia, Pa..: ALI, 1962.

ARLEN, JENNIFER. "The Potentially Perverse Effects of Corporate Criminal Liability." *Journal of Legal Studies* 23 (1994): 833–867.

AYERS, IAN, and BRAITHWAITE, JOHN. *Responsive Regulation.* Oxford, U.K.: Oxford University Press, 1992.

BALL, HARRY V., and FRIEDMAN, LAWRENCE M. "The Use of Criminal Sanctions in the Enforcement of Economic Legislation: A Sociological View." *Stanford Law Review* 17, no. 1 (1965): 197–218.

BRAITHWAITE, JOHN. *To Punish or Persuade, Enforcement of Coal Mine Safety.* Albany, N.Y.: State University of New York Press, 1985.

BRICKEY, KATHLEEN. *Corporate Criminal Liability,* 2d ed. New York, N.Y.: Clark Boardman Callaghan, 1991.

———. "Corporate Criminal Accountability: A Brief History and an Observation." *Washington University Law Quarterly* 60, no. 2 (1982): 393–423.

BUCY, PAMELA H. "Corporate Ethos: A Standard for Imposing Corporate Criminal Liability." *Minnesota Law Review* 75, no. 4 (1991): 1095–1184.

———. "Organizational Sentencing Guidelines: The Cart Before the Horse." *Washington University Law Quarterly* 71, no. 2 (1993): 329–355.

COFFEE, JOHN C., JR. "Does 'Unlawful' Mean 'Criminal'?: Reflections on the Disappearing Tort/Crime Distinction in American Law." *Boston University Law Review* 71, no. 2 (1991): 193–246.

———. "No Soul to Damn; No Body to Kick: An Unscandalized Inquiry into the Problem of Corporate Punishment." *Michigan Law Review* 79, no. 3 (1981): 386–459.

COHEN, MARK A. "Corporate Crime and Punishment: An Update on Sentencing Practice in the Federal Courts, 1988—1990." *Boston University Law Review* 71, no. 2 (1991): 247–280.

DE DOELDER, HANS, and TIEDEMANN, KLAUS, eds. *Criminal Liability of Corporations.* The Hague, The Netherlands: Kluwer Law International, 1996.

"Developments in the Law—Corporate Crime: Regulating Corporate Behavior through Criminal Sanctions." *Harvard Law Review* 72, no. 6 (1979): 1229–1375.

FISSE, BRENT. "Reconstructing Corporate Criminal Law." *Southern California Law Review* 56 (1983): 1141–1148.

FRENCH, PETER. *Collective and Corporate Responsibility.* New York: Columbia University Press, 1984.

GRUNER, RICHARD S. "Towards an Organizational Jurisprudence: Transforming Corporate Criminal Law through Federal Sentencing Reform." *Arizona Law Review* 36 (1994): 407–472.

HUGHES, GRAHAM. "Administrative Subpoenas and the Grand Jury: Converging Streams of Criminal and Civil Compulsory Process." *Vanderbilt Law Review* 47, no. 3 (1994): 573–672.

KADISH, SANFORD H. "Some Observations on the Use of Criminal Sanctions in Enforcing Economic Regulations." *University of Chicago Law Review* 30, no. 3 (1963): 423–441.

KHANNA, V. S. "Corporate Criminal Liability: What Purpose Does It Serve?" *Harvard Law Review* 109, no. 7 (1996): 1477–1534.

LAUFER, WILLIAM S. "Corporate Bodies and Guilty Minds." *Emory Law Journal* 43, no. 2 (1994): 647–730.

LEIGH, L. H. *The Criminal Liability of Corporations in English Law.* London: London School of Economics and Political Science, 1969.

———. "The Criminal Liability of Corporations and Other Groups: A Comparative View." *Michigan Law Review* 80, no. 7 (1982): 1508–1528.

MUELLER, GERHARD O. W. "Mens Rea and the Corporation: A Study of the Model Penal Code Position on Corporate Liability." *University of Pittsburgh Law Review* 19, no. 1 (1957): 21–46.

ORLAND, LEONARD. "Reflections on Corporate Crime: Law in Search of Theory and Scholarship." *American Criminal Law Review* 17, no. 4 (1980): 501–520.

SYKES, ALAN O. "The Economics of Vicarious Liability." *Yale Law Journal* 93 (1984): 1231–1280.

United States Sentencing Commission. *Sourcebook of Federal Sentencing Statistics.* Washington, D.C.: U.S. Government Printing Office, 1995.

———. *United States Sentencing Guidelines Manual,* chapter 8. Washington, D.C.: U.S. Government Printing Office, 1995.

———. *Sourcebook of Federal Sentencing Statistics.* Washington, D.C.: U.S. Government Printing Office, 1998.

WALSH, CHARLES J., and PYRICH, ALISSA. "Corporate Compliance Programs as a Defense to Criminal Liability: Can a Corporation Save Its Soul?" *Rutgers Law Review* 47, no. 2 (1995): 605–691.

WELLS, CELIA. *Corporations and Criminal Responsibility.* Oxford: Clarendon Press, 1993.

WILLIAMS, CYNTHIA. "Corporate Compliance With the Law in the Era of Efficiency." *North Carolina Law Review* 76, no. 4 (1998): 1265–1385.

CASES

New York Central & Hudson River Railroad v. United States, 212 U.S. 481 (1909).

Egan v. United States, 137 F.2d 369 (8th Cir.), *cert. denied,* 320 U.S. 788 (1943).

In re Caremark International Inc. Derivative Litigation, 698 A.2d 959 (De. Ch. 1996).

Standard Oil Co. v. United States, 307 F.2d 120 (5th Cir. 1962).

United States v. Bank of New England, 821 F.2d 844 (1st Cir. 1987).

United States v. George F. Fish, Inc., 154 F.2d 798, 801 (2d Cir.), *cert. denied,* 328 U.S. 869 (1946).

United States v. Hilton Hotels Corp., 467 F.2d 1000 (9th Cir. 1972).

United States v. Sun-Diamond Growers of California, 138 F.3d 961 (D.C. 1998).

CORPUS DELICTI

Corpus delicti literally means the body or substance of the crime. In law the term refers to proof establishing that a crime has occurred.

Although misunderstanding about corpus delicti has been common, the term does not refer to a dead body. There is a corpus delicti of robbery, tax evasion, and, indeed, of every criminal offense. Moreover, even in a homicide case, a "dead body" is neither necessary nor sufficient to establish the corpus delicti. Testimony that a ship's passenger pushed the deceased overboard can establish the corpus delicti of murder even if the body is never recovered. Conversely, the body of a child killed in a fire would *not* establish the corpus delicti of murder, absent proof that the fire was caused by some criminal act (Perkins).

When a failure to prove some fact essential to the charge implies that the offense was not committed by anyone, the courts sometimes say that reversal of the conviction is required by the absence of a corpus delicti. It would be equally accurate, and less mysterious, to say simply that the reversal results from the prosecutor's failure to prove an essential element of the case.

The principal significance of corpus delicti is its effect on the admissibility of evidence. Under the traditional rule, still followed in most states, a confession is inadmissible unless there is independent evidence of a corpus delicti. But some American jurisdictions now reject this traditional rule. In federal courts and in several states, a confession is admissible if its trustworthiness is established, even without independent proof of a corpus delicti. Some commentators argue that this approach offers a better way to meet concerns about the truthfulness of a confession (Mullen).

Many murder convictions have been obtained even though the body of the alleged victim was never found. In several early cases, dating from the seventeenth century and before, the "deceased" turned up alive and well shortly after the defendant had been executed (Perkins). Such miscarriages of justice contributed to the development of the rule requiring independent corroboration of any confession. In the modern era, numerous murder convictions continue to be found by juries and upheld by the courts even in the absence of a dead body. In nearly all of these cases the defendant confessed, and the proof of corpus delicti, together with the defendant's direct admissions, afforded strong evidence of guilt (e.g., *Jones v. State*, 701 N.E.2d 863 (Ind. App. 1998)).

More troublesome, and less common, are murder prosecutions in which there is no dead body, no confession, and no eyewitness to the alleged crime. In these cases the proof of guilt is necessarily "circumstantial"—that is, based entirely on inferences drawn from suspicious facts. Although the potential for a miscarriage of justice in such cases is evident, the legal system must have some means for dealing with the offender who is able to obliterate all trace of the victim (Morris). In many cases, circumstantial evidence of guilt has been held sufficient to warrant a conviction of murder, even though neither a dead body, a confession, nor an eyewitness was available (e.g., *State v. Nicely*, 529 N.E.2d 1236 (Ohio 1988)).

STEPHEN J. SCHULHOFER

See also CONFESSIONS; DISCOVERY.

BIBLIOGRAPHY

MORRIS, NORVAL. "Corpus Delicti and Circumstantial Evidence." *Law Quarterly Review* 68 (1952): 391–396.

MULLEN, THOMAS A. "Rule without Reason: Requiring Independent Proof of the Corpus Delicti as a Condition of Admitting an Extrajudicial Confession." *University of San Francisco Law Review* 27 (1993): 385–418.

PERKINS, ROLLIN M. "The Corpus Delicti of Murder." *Virginia Law Review* 48 (1962): 173–195.

CORRECTIONAL REFORM ASSOCIATIONS

Throughout U.S. history nongovernmental organizations (NGOs) have played a decisive role in correctional reform and the evolution of the penal system. As governmental control of the justice system has grown, NGOs have continued to exert a large influence on public policy decisions that involve the corrections system; indeed, their role has increased in the last quarter century.

Historical role of nongovernmental organizations

The Pennsylvania Prison Society was founded in 1787 in Philadelphia with the goals of improving the conditions of prisons and humanizing the treatment of prison inmates. Leaders of the society were Quaker clergy who sought to reduce the use of corporal punishment in prisons and jails. They tried to reframe corrections as a religious experience in which convicts could seek expiation for their sins through Bible reading and contemplation of their misdeeds. The society was successful in promoting the use of "separate and solitary" confinement as a novel penal method to achieve their philosophic objectives (Barnes). Most prisons at the end of the eighteenth century had congregate living situations in which inmates worked in jail-based workshops. Pennsylvania Prison Society members felt that congregate living contributed to prisons becoming "schools for crime" where more criminally sophisticated convicts recruited younger ones for their criminal exploits. The Philadelphia Quakers also believed that solitary contemplation of God could lead to genuine individual reformation.

During the early part of the nineteenth century the so-called Philadelphia System of separate and solitary confinement competed with the older congregate system as the dominant penal approach. French philosopher Alexis de Tocqueville traveled to America to study the two approaches and make recommendations on correctional practices to European governments (Beaumont and Tocqueville).

Over time the system of congregate imprisonment became more popular, and was more amenable to efforts to create industrial enterprises behind the walls (Rusche and Kirchheimer). Ironically, separate and solitary confinement, initially advocated as a humanitarian reform, became one of the principal methods of disciplining recalcitrant convicts in lieu of corporal punishment.

Today the Pennsylvania Prison Society remains a leading proponent of enlightened responses in corrections. The society continues to advocate for programs that assist prisoners and their families during the period of incarceration, and pushes for programs that help offenders reintegrate into the community. The Pennsylvania Prison Society operates a range of educational programs for the general public and attempts to depoliticize the debate on criminal justice policy.

As America entered the nineteenth century, concern was growing over the common practice of holding children in jails and adult workhouses. Another NGO, the Society for the Prevention of Pauperism, stepped forward to transform the justice system. Founded in New York City this NGO, later renamed the Society for the Prevention of Juvenile Delinquency (SPJD), lobbied for the establishment of the first specialized penal institution for youngsters in the United States. The SPJD argued that pauperism led to delinquent behavior, and that the cure was to remove children from inadequate parents or the streets and place them in institutions known as houses of refuge. The first such institution was opened in New York City in 1825 (Pickett).

The house of refuge was to be the combination of a school and a prison that was operated by a private, charitable agency. Wayward youths were educated, but within an unwavering daily regimen that emphasized worship, work, and discipline. Upon release these young inmates were generally placed as indentured servants. Youths were often "rescued" forcibly and placed in the houses of refuge by members of the SPJD. When parents of the "rescued" youths complained to the legal system that they had been deprived of their property rights to control their children, the courts often supported the SPJD to save children from dire living circumstances (Mennel).

The leadership of the SPJD consisted of prominent religious leaders who were frightened over the growth of a large, urban, immigrant underclass that they believed would threaten democracy. They asserted that the practice of placing children in adult facilities increased the chances that these children would be recruited into criminal lives. Moreover, the SPJD claimed that juries were acquitting guilty youths rather then sending them to prisons and jails. The SPJD lobbied for the establishment of more houses of refuge in most American cities.

Despite the very effective propaganda campaign of the SPJD, the houses of refuge encountered many problems. These facilities were plagued with violence, riots, and large numbers of absconders. Robert Mennel, a historian of the houses estimated that 40 percent of the inmates ran away. The Catholic Church criticized that youngsters were not allowed to practice their religion. Others charged that the private contractors who ran the work programs in the houses of refuge were brutally exploiting the young wards.

As scandals surrounding the houses of refuge mounted, government agencies were forced to inspect these private facilities, and in some cases converted them to state-run institutions. Another influential NGO, the Children's Aid Society, engaged in the public policy debate and offered a very different solution to the growing problem of youth criminality. Founded by Charles Loring Brace, the Children's Aid Society set out to rescue impoverished children from urban streets, providing food, clothing, and temporary shelter to wayward youth. But, Brace and his followers also criticized the houses of refuge, which they believed were criminogenic. The Children's Aid Society pioneered the practice of "placing out" urban children with farm families in the Midwest and the West. Brace believed that the American farm family embodied all of the best virtues of the nation, and held out great hope for rehabilitating urban youngsters (Mennel). Critics of the "placing out" strategy claimed that children were sometimes exploited by the farm families, and there were concerns that brothers and sisters who had been separated might never see one another again. Proponents of the houses of refuge and of "placing out" battled for public acceptance for the next several decades.

The growing concern about scandals and abuses in correctional facilities led to the establishment, in 1870, of the National Prison Association (later renamed the American Correctional Association, or ACA). The first head of the ACA was former U.S. President Rutherford B. Hayes. At its inaugural meeting the ACA put forth a progressive agenda for reforming the nation's prisons, jails, and juvenile facilities. Seeking to develop ethical and professional standards for the field, the ACA became the major source of training materials, professional recognition, and resources for practitioners. The organization later sought to provide accreditation for correctional programs. Today the ACA is the largest professional group in the corrections field. Its annual meetings are attended by over four thousand members, although some have expressed concern that the association has become overly dependent on the financial largesse of businesses that sell products to the corrections system.

Toward the close of the nineteenth century, influential NGOs such as the Chicago Women's Club and the Chicago Bar Association lobbied to create a special legal system for children, and in 1899 helped enact the Illinois Juvenile Court Act, the first comprehensive child welfare law in U.S. history. Famous leaders of these groups, especially Julia Lathrop, Lucy Flowers, and Jane Addams, practically invented the modern profession of social work in the United States. These child welfare pioneers raised funds to sponsor some of the earliest research on juvenile delinquency.

The Illinois law spawned a juvenile court movement that spread quickly across the nation. One key component of these laws was the establishment of probation officers to supervise wayward youths in the community. The actual invention of probation in the last quarter of the nineteenth century is generally credited to a Boston shoemaker, John Augustus, who would post bail for adults and juveniles, promising to personally supervise them and assure their appearance in court. Interestingly, the first juvenile court laws specified that probation officers should not be paid, but were instead directed to volunteer their services.

In 1901 Chicago became the founding city for the U.S. version of the John Howard Association. Named for the eighteenth-century British penal reformer, the John Howard Association (JHA) organized citizens who were concerned about the abhorrent conditions in Illinois prisons and jails. The JHA initiated the practice of citizen visits to penal facilities to monitor the conditions of confinement and to investigate grievances made by inmates. The JHA expanded its mission to push for rational sentencing policies and to provide educational programs for the public.

In 1907, a group of fourteen probation officers met at Plymouth Church in Minneapolis, Minnesota, to create the National Probation Association, which later became the National Council on Crime and Delinquency (NCCD). This new NGO attempted to establish professional standards for the education and training of probation officers, advocating that probation officers be paid court staff. The NCCD then lobbied to enact state laws permitting the use of community supervision, both probation and parole, in lieu of

sentences of imprisonment (Krisberg). The NCCD assumed the mantle as the major organization trying to reform the juvenile justice system, focusing on removing children from jails and creating standards for the juvenile court. Later the NCCD helped organize the nation's business leaders in behalf of progressive reforms of the justice system. Today the NCCD specializes in research, training, and advocacy on sensible responses to juvenile crime and safe alternatives to incarceration for adult offenders.

Two other notable NGOs that were founded in the early part of the twentieth century are the American Civil Liberties Union (ACLU) and the American Friends Service Committee (AFSC). The ACLU was founded by noted lawyer Roger Baldwin in 1920. Its mission is to protect and promote the Bill of Rights. This overarching goal has led the ACLU to be a forceful advocate against "cruel and unusual" punishments, and to fight for the protection of the rights of the accused, as well as guarding the due process rights of institutionalized persons. The AFSC was established in 1917 as a vehicle for conscientious objectors to aid civilian victims during World War I. AFSC members have participated in a broad range of international and domestic human rights issues. They have worked to protect the rights of incarcerated persons, and they have exposed what they believe to be inhumane correctional practices. In 1972, the AFSC published *Struggle for Justice*, which provided a compelling case for the replacement of indeterminant sentencing with a system of fixed (and determinant) sentencing.

More recent sentencing reforms and NGOs

The pace of new NGOs that have taken up the cause of sentencing corrections reform has not slowed over the last several decades. These groups have aggressively pursued litigation on behalf of prisoners' rights, raised awareness about the human rights violations committed by the U.S. justice system, and campaigned against mandatory prison sentences.

In 1961 Lois Schweitzer established the Vera Institute of Justice in New York City. The Vera Institute took on the issue of crowding in jails, and through its Manhattan Bail Project tested new methods by which indigent defendants could be released from jail without having to make large payments to bail bondsmen. The research promulgated by Vera led to a nationwide movement to create pretrial service agencies to allow poor people with community ties to effect release on their own recognizance. The Vera Institute has also launched a number of demonstration projects proving the public safety of a variety of alternatives to incarceration. The institute works closely with New York City government to initiate innovative service programs for drug addicts, the homeless, and mentally ill offenders.

An outgrowth of the ACLU, the National Prison Project (NPP) launched a successful effort to advance the constitutional rights of prisoners. NPP lawsuits led to numerous legal orders and agreements to improve the conditions of confinement and to protect the rights of prisoners. The work of the NPP caused many states to end the practice of double- and triple-celling inmates, thus creating the need either to consider alternatives to incarceration or to construct costly new prisons. In the juvenile arena, the Youth Law Center and the National Center for Youth Law filed lawsuits challenging conditions of confinement in youth corrections facilities. In particular, these juvenile litigation groups focused on the horrendous practice of holding children in adult jails. Besides litigation, all three of these NGOs have produced resource materials and conducted training for correctional practitioners to teach them how to avoid further legal actions.

Human Rights Watch was formed in 1978 in Helsinki in response to complaints about human rights violations taking place in Soviet bloc nations. The group set out to monitor and support the provisions of the historic Helsinki Accords. In 1987, President Ronald Reagan argued that human rights violations in democratic nations were more "tolerable" than violations occurring in totalitarian counties. Human Rights Watch/America was founded to counteract this thinking. Human Rights Watch has produced a series of investigative reports pointing to human rights violations in areas such as capital punishment, the use of super maximum security prisons, and the growing practice of sentencing children to adult prisons. Human Rights Watch has assisted community organizing efforts in the United States, and has raised international consciousness about grave problems of the American criminal law system.

An interesting recent NGO is Families Against Mandatory Minimums (FAMM). Founded in 1991, FAMM was created by family members of persons who were sentenced to extremely long mandatory prisons terms, often for relatively minor drug offenses. FAMM conducts public education efforts, and actively opposes tougher penalties at the state and federal level. FAMM has worked to gain clemency for those serving unduly harsh sentences. A related group is Citizens United for the Rehabilitation of Errants (CURE), which is a nationwide advocacy group that opposes the death penalty, looks for creative alternatives to incarceration, and fights for the humane treatment of inmates. CURE includes a diverse membership, including ex-offenders and the families of current prison inmates. In 2000 CURE organized a voter registration drive for inmates of the Baltimore City Jail to dramatize the disenfranchisement of offenders. Another goal for CURE is to make telephones more accessible to inmates and to lower the cost of the phone calls, so that incarcerated persons can stay in touch with their families.

Conclusion

NGOs have played a major and significant role in the evolution of the American justice system. Indeed, some have argued that most of the truly significant reforms have been energized and pushed by groups outside the formal governmental channels (Sutton). The last several decades have witnessed the continued creation and growth of NGOs devoted to the causes of sentencing and corrections reform. These groups operate with modest funding derived from private philanthropy and public memberships. Some NGOs have been successful at attracting limited governmental funding in jurisdictions in which progressive criminal justice professionals have sought their assistance.

While he was studying American prisons in the early nineteenth century, Tocqueville commented on the vibrancy of civic life, and on the fact that Americans were always forming new voluntary associations to improve their communities. He believed that these voluntary groups or NGOs were essential to preserving American democracy. The NGOs that have focused on justice issues have certainly contributed to a lively debate and struggle for those core American principles that are celebrated the U.S. Declaration of Independence and the Constitution. Without the efforts of NGOs the justice system might easily embrace pragmatic and expedient policies, regardless of the threats to human and civil rights. Not all of the reforms introduced by the NGOs stood the test of time, but these organizations continue to press for innovations, and for greater humanity in our treatment of wayward youth and adult lawbreakers.

BARRY A. KRISBERG

See also CAPITAL PUNISHMENT: LEGAL ASPECTS; CAPITAL PUNISHMENT: MORALITY, POLITICS, AND POLICY; CONVICTION: CIVIL DISABILITIES; CORPORAL PUNISHMENT; CRUEL AND UNUSUAL PUNISHMENT; INTERNATIONAL CRIMINAL JUSTICE STANDARDS; JAILS; PRISONERS, LEGAL RIGHTS OF; PRISONS: CORRECTIONAL OFFICERS; PRISONS: HISTORY; PRISONS: PRISONERS; PRISONS: PRISONS FOR WOMEN; PRISONS: PROBLEMS AND PROSPECTS; REHABILITATION; SENTENCING: ALLOCATION OF AUTHORITY; SENTENCING: ALTERNATIVES; SENTENCING: DISPARITY; SENTENCING: GUIDELINES; SENTENCING: MANDATORY AND MANDATORY MINIMUM SENTENCES; SENTENCING: PRESENTENCE REPORT; SENTENCING: PROCEDURAL PROTECTION.

BIBLIOGRAPHY

American Friends Service Committee. *Struggle for Justice.* New York: Hill and Wang, 1981.
BARNES, HARRY ELMER. *The Repression of Crime.* New York: George H. Doran Co., 1926.
BEAUMONT, GUSTAVE, and TOCQUEVILLE, ALEXIS DE. *On the Penitentiary System in the United States and its Application in France* (1833). Translated by Francis Leiber. Carbondale: Southern Illinois University Press, 1979.
KRISBERG, BARRY. "The Evolution of an American Institution." *Crime and Delinquency* 44, no. 1 (1988): 5–8.
MENNEL, ROBERT M. *Thorns and Thistles: Juvenile Delinquents in the United States, 1825–1940.* Hanover, N.H.: University Press of New England, 1973.
PICKET, ROBERT S. *Houses of Refuge: Origins of Juvenile Reform in New York State, 1815–1857.* Syracuse, N.Y.: Syracuse University, 1969.
RUSCHE, GEORG, and KIRCHHEIMER, OTTO. *Punishment and Social Structure.* New York: Columbia University Press, 1939.
SUTTON, JOHN R. *Stubborn Children: Controlling Delinquency in the United States, 1640–1981.* Berkeley: University of California Press, 1981.
TOCQUEVILLE, ALEXIS DE. *Democracy in America* (1835, 1840). Translated by Henry Reeve. Cambridge, U.K.: Sever and Francis, 1862. Revised by Francis Bowen and Philips Bradley. New York: Vintage Books, 1945, 1961.

COUNSEL: RIGHT TO COUNSEL

The Sixth Amendment to the United States Constitution provides that "[i]n all criminal prosecutions, the accused shall enjoy the right . . . to have the Assistance of Counsel for his defense." Over the past seventy-five years, the contours of this constitutional right have expanded dramatically. Originally, the Sixth Amendment simply ensured that the defendant in a federal criminal case who could afford to hire counsel would be entitled to appear through a lawyer, rather than being forced to defend himself. But beginning in the early 1930s, and expanding over the next three decades, the U.S. Supreme Court and state supreme courts came to require the government to provide lawyers to the vast majority of criminal defendants who could not afford to hire a lawyer. As other aspects of criminal law and procedure have become increasingly complex, the need for counsel has grown correspondingly. Moreover, the greater complexity of constitutional criminal procedure—for example, the intricate rules governing the admission of evidence and appropriate jury instructions—means that defendants need not only a lawyer's physical presence; they need effective assistance. Much of the doctrinal development of the past twenty years, then, has focused not on when a lawyer must be provided—a question largely answered by the 1980s—but on how a lawyer must perform in order to realize the Sixth Amendment's guarantee.

The sources of the constitutional right to counsel

The constitutional right to counsel has its roots in four separate constitutional provisions. The most explicit of these is the Sixth Amendment, quoted above. Like the rest of the Bill of Rights, the Sixth Amendment applied originally only to criminal prosecutions brought by the federal government.

As with most of the other provisions dealing with the criminal justice process, however, the Sixth Amendment came to be "incorporated" against the states through a second constitutional provision—the due process clause of the Fourteenth Amendment. In a series of cases beginning in the 1930s (*Palko v. Connecticut*, 302 U.S. 319 (1937)), the Supreme Court held that provisions of the Bill of Rights that were "implicit in the concept of ordered liberty" and thus necessary for a trial to be fundamentally fair were to be applied in state-court proceedings as well. In *Gideon v. Wainwright*, 372 U.S. 335 (1963), the Supreme Court held that the Sixth Amendment's guarantee of counsel to indigent defendants was so fundamental and essential to a fair trial that the due process clause required states to provide counsel to all indigent defendants in felony cases.

In addition to the Sixth Amendment–based right, the Supreme Court has found a right to counsel within the Fifth Amendment's privilege against self-incrimination (also made applicable to the states through incorporation). In *Miranda v. Arizona*, 384 U.S. 436 (1966), the Court held that an individual who is taken into police custody "must be clearly informed that he has the right to consult with a lawyer and to have that lawyer with him during interrogation" since otherwise he may be unable to protect his right not to be a witness against himself.

Finally, the equal protection clause of the Fourteenth Amendment has been held to require the appointment of counsel for indigent defendants in first appeals as of right following their convictions (*Douglas v. California*, 372 U.S. 353 (1963)). The precise analytic contours of the equal protection right to counsel are somewhat fuzzy, perhaps because the cases applying the equal protection clause to the criminal justice process arose largely during a period when the Warren Court seemed to be moving toward treating wealth as a quasi-suspect classification. The Burger and Rehnquist Courts have repudiated that position, but they have left *Douglas* and *Griffin v. Illinois*, 351 U.S. 12 (1956), in place. In the end, the equal protection rationale seems mostly to reflect the Court's discomfort in using the due process clause to require the appointment of counsel on appeal when the Court had declined to hold that the due process clause requires providing appeals in the first place (see, e.g., *Martinez v. California*, 526 U.S. 152, 161 (2000), reiterating that "the Sixth Amendment does not apply to appellate proceedings").

A framework for thinking about when the constitutional right to counsel attaches

While both the Fifth Amendment and the Sixth Amendment contain guarantees of the right to counsel, their applications differ significantly along two important dimensions. First, the Fifth Amendment right is *spatially* limited, while the Sixth Amendment right is *temporally* limited. Second, the Supreme Court treats waiver of the Fifth Amendment right to counsel far less skeptically than it treats waiver of the Sixth Amendment right to counsel.

Almost always, Fifth Amendment right-to-counsel issues arise in the context of a defendant's attempt to suppress evidence: the defendant claims that an incriminating statement was taken either without her being informed of her right to a lawyer or in disrespect of her invocation of that right. The Fifth Amendment right applies only to government-civilian interactions in particular places: it applies to "custodial interrogation." Thus, the question whether the Fifth Amendment right to counsel has attached depends, first, on whether an individual is in custody and, second, on whether she has been subjected to interrogation.

With respect to the former question, a suspect is not in custody—and, therefore, is not entitled to her Fifth Amendment right to counsel—if she is merely briefly detained against her will by the police. Instead, a person is only in custody if she is under arrest or if a reasonable person in the suspect's situation would understand herself to be subject to restraint comparable to that associated with a formal arrest (*Berkemer v. McCarty*, 468 U.S. 420 (1984)). With respect to the matter of interrogation, this requirement is met if the suspect is formally questioned or is subjected to words or actions that the police should know are likely to elicit an incriminating response (*Rhode Island v. Innis*, 446 U.S. 291 (1980)).

Assuming that the appropriate *Miranda* warning is given and the suspect understands her rights, as a practical matter the government is free to question a suspect in the absence of counsel unless and until the suspect affirmatively and unambiguously invokes her right to counsel (*Davis v. United States*, 512 U.S. 452 (1994)). If the suspect later claims that her statements should be suppressed, the government need prove waiver only by a preponderance of the evidence (*Colorado v. Connelly*, 479 U.S. 157 (1986)), and such waiver need not be explicit; it may be inferred from the suspect's actions or words (*North Carolina v. Butler*, 441 U.S. 369 (1979)).

By contrast, once the Sixth Amendment attaches—a subject addressed in the remainder of this section—there is a heavy presumption against waiver. Indeed, although the Supreme Court has recognized a constitutional right to self-representation (*Faretta v. California*, 422 U.S. 806 (1975)), an entitlement that involves waiving the right to counsel, it has erected barriers in the way of exercising that right of self-representation that depend on the assumption that few defendants would choose to waive the assistance of a lawyer; and the Court has expressed the view that courts should aim at preserving the sanctity of the attorney-client relationship, rather than freely permit its waiver (*Patterson v. Illinois*, 487 U.S. 285 (1988)).

Instead of being spatially limited, as the Fifth Amendment is, the Sixth Amendment right is *temporally* limited: a literal reading of the amendment's text means that it comes into play only once a "criminal prosecution" has begun. Thus, for example, arrest alone is insufficient to trigger the Sixth Amendment right to counsel. In *Brewer v. Williams*, 430 U.S. 387 (1977), the Supreme Court explained, that "[w]hatever else it may mean, the right to counsel granted by the Sixth and Fourteenth Amendments means . . . that a person is entitled to the help of a lawyer at or after the time that judicial proceedings have been initiated against him—'whether by way or formal charge, preliminary hearing, indictment, information, or arraignment'" (quoting *Kirby v. Illinois*, 406 U.S. 682 (1972)).

Although the Sixth Amendment right to appear through a lawyer applies to all criminal cases—as the Supreme Court long ago observed in *Powell v. Alabama*, 287 U.S. 45 (1932), if in "any case" a court were "arbitrarily to refuse to hear a party by counsel, employed by and appearing for him, it reasonably may not be doubted that such a refusal would be a denial of . . . due process in the constitutional sense"—the Sixth Amendment entitlement to appointed counsel for indigent defendants is more limited. *Gideon* requires the appointment of counsel in all cases where the defendant is charged with a felony, but *Argersinger v. Hamlin*, 407 U.S. 25 (1972), and *Scott v. Illinois*, 440 U.S. 367 (1979), require the appointment of counsel in misdemeanor cases only if the defendant is actually sentenced to imprisonment. As a practical matter, this means that a trial judge who anticipates any possibility that she will wish to sentence a misdemeanor defendant to prison in the event of his conviction will appoint counsel at the outset of the case, so defendants in cases involving serious misdemeanors will receive appointed counsel.

Once the Sixth Amendment right to counsel has been triggered, and the defendant has either retained or been appointed counsel, the question becomes whether counsel must be present on a given occasion. In *United States v. Wade*, 388 U.S. 218 (1967), for example, the Court held that because a post-indictment lineup was a "critical stage" of the proceedings, "the presence of counsel is necessary to preserve the defendant's basic right to a fair trial." But a substantial number of other government-defendant interactions do not require counsel's presence. For example, in *Gilbert v. California*, 388 U.S. 263 (1967), the Court held that defense counsel's presence was not required during the taking of handwriting exemplars. And in *United States v. Ash*, 413 U.S. 300 (1973), the Court held that a lawyer is not required when identifications are made through a photo array. Most significantly, although the Supreme Court had held in *Coleman v. Alabama*, 399 U.S. 1 (1970), that counsel is required at a hearing to determine whether there is probable cause sufficient to justify charging the defendant with a crime, it held in *Gerstein v. Pugh*, 420 U.S. 103 (1975), that a preliminary hearing to determine whether there is probable cause to detain a defendant pending trial does not require the provision of counsel because it is not a "critical stage." Thus, while federal and state statutes may require the provision of counsel at bail hearings or preventative detention hearings, the Constitution has not been extended that far. And in a somewhat odd hybrid holding, the Court has required that defense counsel be given notice of state-requested psychiatric evaluations of a defendant, but has refused to hold that counsel have a right to be present during the evaluation (*Estelle v. Smith*, 451 U.S. 454 (1981)).

Finally, in a different vein, the line of cases stemming from *Massiah v. United States*, 377 U.S. 201 (1964), and its progeny have held that it is a violation of the Sixth Amendment right to counsel for the government deliberately to elicit incriminating statements from an already charged defendant in the absence of his counsel unless the defendant has knowingly and intelligently waived the right to have counsel present. *Massiah* has its greatest bite in cases involving undercover officers or informants; clearly in such cases there is no possibility of waiver, so the key question becomes whether the government's agent actively extracted the incriminating statement or was merely a passive recipient of an unsolicited statement.

Once a trial has begun, a defendant is entitled to the continued presence of counsel throughout the trial, including at sentencing (*Mempa v. Rhay*, 389 U.S. 128 (1967)). There are some lower court cases, however, that have declined to find a Sixth Amendment violation in a defense lawyer's absence from the courtroom for some portion of the trial period—finding, for example, that a defendant has not been denied the right to counsel if his attorney is absent only during a part of the case involving evidence against a codefendant or the introduction of stipulated evidence.

Finally, the Sixth Amendment and equal protection clause rights to counsel end after the conclusion of the first appeal as of right. There is no constitutional right to counsel for discretionary appeals, either to state supreme courts or to the U.S. Supreme Court (*Ross v. Moffitt*, 417 U.S. 600 (1974)). Nor is there any constitutional right to counsel in postconviction processes such as coram nobis (a procedure in which a defendant can present newly discovered evidence) or habeas corpus proceedings (*Pennsylvania v. Finley*, 481 U.S. 551 (1987); *Murray v. Giarratano*, 492 U.S. 1 (1992)). This limitation is important for three distinct, but related, reasons. First, defendants often are not given appointed counsel, and thus must proceed *pro se*, which substantially reduces their likelihood of successfully obtaining discretionary review (if an appellate court does decide to hear a defendant's case on the merits, it usually appoints an attorney at that point) or post-conviction relief. Second, if a defendant in one of these noncovered procedures is represented by a lawyer, either because he has retained counsel, volunteer counsel, or counsel appointed gratuitously or pursuant to statutory authorization, he does not have a constitutional right to effective assistance. Thus, if his lawyer makes an error—even an error that falls below the acceptable level of attorney performance and that adversely affected the outcome of his case—that error provides no grounds for later reversal. Absent the constitutional right to counsel, a defendant has no right to effective counsel (*Coleman v. Thompson*, 501 U.S. 722 (1991)). Finally, the first opportunity many defendants will have to establish that they have been denied effective assistance of counsel at trial or in their appeal as of right will often be in postconviction proceedings, either because they were represented throughout the direct appeal process by the lawyer who allegedly was ineffective (and who presumably did not claim his own ineffectiveness as a ground for reversal) or because establishing constitutional ineffectiveness requires an evidentiary hearing. Thus, the fact that defendants are not entitled to counsel to prove that they were deprived of their constitutional entitlement to counsel may effectively foreclose many such claims.

The right to "effective" assistance of counsel

While "[i]t has long been recognized that the right to counsel is the right to the effective assistance of counsel" (*McMann v. Richardson*, 397 U.S. 759, 771, n. 14 (1970)), it was not until the mid-1980s that the Supreme Court began to articulate a test for deciding when a defendant has been denied the right to effective assistance. The seminal cases were *Strickland v. Washington*, 466 U.S. 668 (1984), and *United States v. Cronic*, 466 U.S. 648 Ct. 2039 (1984).

Strickland identified a performance-and-prejudice test. Under the performance prong, a defendant must show that his lawyer "made errors so serious [he] was not functioning as the 'counsel' guaranteed the defendant by the Sixth Amendment" (*Strickland*, 466 U.S. at 687). The Court announced "a strong presumption" (*Kimmelman v. Morrison*, 477 U.S. 365, 381 (1986)), that counsel's performance falls within the "wide range of [acceptable] professional assistance" (*Strickland*, 466 U.S. at 689). Moreover, the reasonableness of a lawyer's performance is to be evaluated from counsel's perspective at the time of the alleged error and in light of all the circumstances, and the standard of review is highly deferential. Courts often find that a defense lawyer's decision to forego a particular line of inquiry or action was strategic or tactical; even if the decision was ultimately unsuccessful, that failure does not establish inadequate performance. The performance prong of the *Strickland* inquiry is descriptive. It measures defense counsel's behavior with reference to the professional norm. As the Court insisted in *Strickland*, "the purpose of the effective assistance guarantee of the Sixth Amendment is not to improve the quality of legal representation," but rather to ask whether the defendant received the level of performance generally observed.

With respect to the prejudice prong, a defendant must show that "counsel's errors were so serious as to deprive the defendant of a fair trial, a trial whose result is reliable." That is, a defendant must show that there was "a reasonable probability that, but for counsel's unprofessional errors, the result of the proceeding would have been different." The Court elaborated that a reasonable probability is "a probability sufficient to undermine confidence in the outcome." Thus, the prejudice prong is ex post: it looks at the outcome of the defendant's trial and asks whether the result might have been different in the absence of counsel's deficient performance. Moreover, while the prejudice prong is generally treated as a descriptive matter—in *Kimmelman v. Morrison,* for example, the Court found prejudice from counsel's failure to make a timely suppression motion when, had the evidence been suppressed, there was a reasonable probability the defendant would not have been convicted—the Court has on occasion taken a more normative view. In *Nix v. Whiteside,* 475 U.S. 157 (1986), the Court refused to find that a defendant had been prejudiced by his lawyer's threats to reveal his client's perjury because a defendant has no entitlement to "the luck of a lawless decisionmaker," and thus the defendant had not suffered cognizable prejudice. And in *Lockhart v. Fretwell,* 506 U.S. 364 (1992), the Court extended this rationale to hold that a defendant suffered no cognizable prejudice when the lawyer failed to make an objection that, at the time of the defendant's sentencing, would have resulted in his death sentence being overturned because a subsequent appellate decision overruled the case from which the defendant would have benefited. Thus, even though Fretwell as a descriptive matter was prejudiced by his attorney's failure to make the objection, this failure did not render the sentence less "reliable" in a more normative sense.

Two other facets of the prejudice prong deserve mention. The first is how prejudice is defined in the vast majority of cases in which defendants plead guilty, rather than going to trial. In *Hill v. Lockhart,* 474 U.S. 52 (1986), the Court held that in order to satisfy the prejudice prong, the defendant must show that there is a reasonable probability that, but for counsel's errors, he would not have pleaded guilty and would have insisted on going to trial. This articulation of the prejudice prong makes it extremely difficult for defendants to prove ineffectiveness in the plea bargaining process. In reality, the likely effect of most defense attorney shortcomings is not that a defendant pleads guilty instead of going to trial, but that he gets a less advantageous plea bargain than would otherwise be the case. But showing simply that, but for defense counsel's unprofessional errors, one would have pleaded to a less serious offense or received a lighter sentence does not establish prejudice. The upshot of *Hill* is that it is exceptionally difficult for a defendant to prevail in attacking a conviction pursuant to a plea on grounds that counsel was ineffective.

Second, in *Strickland* and *Cronic,* the Court identified three categories of cases in which prejudice is presumed because an adverse effect on the defendant "is so likely that case-by-case inquiry into prejudice is not worth the cost." First, courts will presume prejudice in a case of denial of counsel altogether. Second, "various kinds of state interference with counsel's assistance" can warrant a presumption of prejudice (*Cronic,* 466 U.S. at 659, and n. 25). Third, "prejudice is presumed when counsel is burdened by an actual conflict of interest" (*Strickland,* 466 U.S. at 692) and the defendant can show that the conflict actually affected counsel's performance. *Gideon v. Wainwright* would be an example of the first category: faced with an outright denial of counsel, a reviewing court will not ask whether counsel might have changed the outcome of a defendant's trial. Rather, it will simply reverse the conviction and order retrial with counsel. *Geders v. United States,* 425 U.S. 80 (1976), is an example of the second category: there, a judge unconstitutionally barred defense counsel from consulting with his client during an overnight recess; again, the reviewing court did not ask whether there was a reasonable likelihood that the prohibited consultation would have changed the outcome. An example of the third category is *United States v. Malpiedi,* 62 F.3d 465 (2d Cir. 1995). There, the court of appeals reversed a defendant's conviction because his lawyer had represented a key government witness in her first appearance before the grand jury and therefore curtailed his cross-examination of her at trial.

But the Court has made clear that cases of presumed prejudice are relatively rare. Thus, for example, in *Burger v. Kemp,* 483 U.S. 776 (1987), the Court declined to find an actual conflict of interest even though the defendant was represented by the law partner of the attorney who represented his co-indictee in a capital murder case and, at each defendant's trial, the defense strategy was to emphasize the co-indictee's culpability in order to avoid the death penalty. And in several "sleeping lawyer" cases, lower courts have refused to hold that a defense lawyer who has fallen asleep gives rise to a presumption of prejudice without regard to what was occurring when the lawyer nodded off.

Strickland also clearly held that defendants challenging their convictions must establish both inadequate performance and prejudice, and that courts faced with ineffectiveness claims can address the two prongs of the test in either order. Thus, a reviewing court need not determine whether a lawyer's actions fell outside the bounds of reasonable attorney behavior if it concludes that there is no reasonable probability that the outcome would have been different had the lawyer acted differently.

The right to self-representation

In *Faretta v. California*, the Supreme Court held that the Sixth Amendment also guarantees the defendant in a criminal trial "a constitutional right to proceed without counsel when he voluntarily and intelligently elects to do so." *Faretta* was based on three interrelated arguments. First, historical evidence showed that a right of self-representation had existed since the founding. Second, the Court interpreted the structure of the Sixth Amendment, in the light of its English and colonial background, to embody a right of self-representation. The Sixth Amendment protected a defendant's personal right to make his defense and spoke of the "assistance" of counsel, and to require a defendant to accept counsel he did not want would undermine the amendment's structure. Finally, *Faretta* concluded that even though as an objective matter most defendants would receive a better defense if they accepted a lawyer's representation, a knowing and intelligent waiver "must be honored out of that respect for the individual which is the lifeblood of the law."

The reasons why a defendant might choose to represent himself vary. With respect to the roughly one-in-five defendants who do not qualify for appointed counsel, self-representation might reflect an inability to find a lawyer to take the case for an amount the client is willing to spend. Other times, a defendant may insist on representing himself because he is dissatisfied with the quality of appointed counsel and is unable to persuade the court to appoint a different lawyer. In these cases, the choice to represent oneself might realistically be viewed as not really a choice at all—in the Court's trenchant phrase in *Martinez v. Court of Appeal*, 528 U.S. 152 (2000), "comparable to bestowing upon the homeless beggar a 'right' to take shelter in the sewers of Paris." But in other cases, the defendant may have political or personal reasons for insisting on representing himself that are affirmatively served by presenting his own case rather than proceeding through a lawyer.

The right to self-representation is not absolute. First, a defendant must "'voluntarily and intelligently'" elect to conduct his own defense, and must assert his right in a timely manner. Unlike most rights, where waiver requires a knowing

and intelligent relinquishment, a defendant need not be informed of his right to self-representation, and a court must warn him against asserting it. Second, a trial judge may terminate self-representation or appoint "standby counsel"—even over a defendant's objection. (On the other hand, a defendant has no constitutional right to the appointment of standby counsel; see *McKaskle v. Wiggins*, 465 U.S. 168 (1984)). Finally, in *Martinez v. Court of Appeal*, the Court held that a defendant has no right to represent himself on appeal.

The right to counsel of one's choice

From the very outset of its modern Sixth Amendment jurisprudence, the Supreme Court has recognized that "it is hardly necessary to say that, the right to counsel being conceded, a defendant should be afforded a fair opportunity to secure counsel of his own choice" (*Powell v. Alabama*, at 53). Thus, lower courts have reversed defendants' convictions when they are unreasonably deprived of the ability to be represented by counsel of their choice through such practices as a court's failure to grant a continuance—see, for example, *United States v. Rankin*, 779 F.2d 956 (3d Cir. 1986); *Gandy v. Alabama*, 569 F.2d 1318 (CA5 1978); or failure to admit otherwise qualified lawyers *pro hac vice*, *Fuller v. Diesslin*, 868 F.2d 604 (3d Cir.), *cert. denied*, 493 U.S. 873 (1989)—without asking whether the lawyers who actually represented them were ineffective.

On the other hand, the right to choose one's lawyer, like most other aspects of the Sixth Amendment, is not unqualified. In particular, a defendant cannot insist on representation by an attorney he cannot afford or who for other reasons refuses to represent him. Nor can a defendant insist on being represented by a lawyer who has a previous or ongoing relationship with an opposing party. In *Wheat v. United States*, 486 U.S. 153 (1988), the Supreme Court held that although "the right to select and be represented by one's preferred attorney is comprehended by the Sixth Amendment," that right can be outweighed by the judicial system's "independent interest in ensuring that criminal trials are conducted within the ethical standards of the profession and that legal proceedings appear fair to all who observe them." In particular, the Court held that multiple representation not only poses a risk to a defendant's interest in having a lawyer who acted on his behalf but also can jeopardize "the institutional interest in the rendition of just ver-

COUNSEL: RIGHT TO COUNSEL 277

dicts in criminal cases." It thus refused to allow Wheat to waive his right to conflict-free representation in order to retain a lawyer who would otherwise be disqualified.

The right of indigent defendants to counsel of their choice is far more constrained. First, of course, it is constrained by their economic circumstances: they cannot afford to retain a lawyer in the first place, and thus are subject to state-run systems for providing counsel. The two most prevalent are public-defender systems, in which an organization contracts with a jurisdiction to provide representation for indigent defendants, and appointed-counsel systems, in which judges appoint particular lawyers who are otherwise in private practice to represent a given defendant for a specified fee or hourly rate. Within either system, the indigent defendant may have little control over the lawyer assigned to his case. In *Morris v. Slappy*, 461 U.S. 1 (1983), the Supreme Court rejected the claim that "the Sixth Amendment guarantees a meaningful relationship between an accused and his counsel." Slappy's Sixth Amendment claim revolved around the substitution of one staff attorney at the public defender's office for another. Slappy's request for a continuance was denied. The Court found that, as long as Slappy was adequately represented by the lawyer who actually defended him at trial, his Sixth Amendment rights had been fully respected. In short, as the Court later explained in *United States v. Cronic*, "the appropriate inquiry focuses on the adversarial process, not on the accused's relationship with his lawyer as such" (466 U.S. at 657, n. 21). Thus, the question for indigent defendants devolves back to an ineffective assistance claim, rather than operating as a discrete constitutional protection.

The Supreme Court's perception of the role and value of criminal defense attorneys has been powerfully shaped by the kinds of cases in which it observes them operating. It was easy, in cases like *Powell v. Alabama* and *Gideon v. Wainwright*, to see defense lawyers as the first line of protection for weak and possibly innocent individuals. Today, the Court sees far fewer cases involving arguably innocent defendants, precisely because the provision of lawyers has worked: defendants are acquitted, obtain reversals of their convictions, or agree with the prosecutor on a plea bargain in the vast bulk of criminal cases. Still, the Court's unwillingness to recognize that many defense attorneys fail to provide their clients with truly competent representation has hindered the full realization of the constitutional promise proclaimed in cases like *Powell* and *Gideon*.

PAMELA S. KARLAN

See also ADVERSARY SYSTEM; APPEAL; ARRAIGNMENT; BAIL; CAPITAL PUNISHMENT: LEGAL ASPECTS; COUNSEL: ROLE OF COUNSEL; CRIMINAL PROCEDURE: CONSTITUTIONAL ASPECTS; EXCLUSIONARY RULE; EYEWITNESS IDENTIFICATION: CONSTITUTIONAL ASPECTS; FORFEITURE; HABEAS CORPUS; PRELIMINARY HEARING; PROBATION AND PAROLE: PROCEDURAL PROTECTION; SENTENCING: PROCEDURAL PROTECTION.

BIBLIOGRAPHY

American Bar Association. *ABA Standards for Criminal Justice: Providing Defense Services*, 3d ed. Washington, D.C.: American Bar Association, 1992.
BRIGHT, STEPHEN B. "Counsel for the Poor: The Death Sentence Not for the Worst Crime, But for the Worst Lawyer." *Yale Law Journal* 103 (May 1994): 1835.
COLBERT, DOUGLAS L. "Thirty-Five Years after Gideon: The Illusory Right to Counsel at Bail Proceedings." *University of Illinois Law Review* 1 (1998): 1.
DRIPPS, DONALD A. "Ineffective Assistance of Counsel: The Case for an Ex Ante Parity Standard." *Journal of Law and Criminology* 88 (Fall 1997): 242.
GEIMER, WILLIAM S. "A Decade of Strickland's Tin Horn: Doctrinal and Practical Undermining of the Right to Counsel." *William and Mary Bill of Rights Journal* 4 (1995): 91.
GREEN, BRUCE A. "Lethal Fiction: The Meaning of 'Counsel' in the Sixth Amendment." *Iowa Law Review* 76 (March 1993): 433.
KARLAN, PAMELA S. "Discrete and Relational Criminal Representation: The Changing Vision of the Right to Counsel." *Harvard Law Review* 105 (January 1992): 670.
KLEIN, RICHARD. "The Constitutionalization of Ineffective Assistance of Counsel." *Maryland Law Review* 58, no. 4 (1999): 1433.
LaFAVE, WAYNE R., and ISRAEL, JEROLD H. *Criminal Procedure*, 2d ed. St. Paul, Minn.: West Publishing Co., 1992.
LEFSTEIN, NORMAN. *Criminal Defense Services for the Poor: Methods and Programs for Providing Legal Representation and the Need for Adequate Financing*. Chicago: American Bar Association, 1982.
SCHULHOFER, STEPHEN J., and FRIEDMAN, DAVID D. "Rethinking Indigent Defense: Promoting Effective Representation Through Consumer

Sovereignty and Freedom of Choice for All Criminal Defendants." *American Criminal Law Review* 31 (1993): 73.

SPANGENBERG, ROBERT L., and BEEMAN, MAREA L. "Indigent Defense Systems in the United States." *Law and Contemporary Problems* 58, no. 1 (1995): 31.

STUNTZ, WILLIAM J. "The Uneasy Relationship between Criminal Procedure and Criminal Justice." *Yale Law Journal* 107 (October 1997): 1.

WHITEBREAD, CHARLES H., and SLOBOGIN, CHRISTOPHER. *Criminal Procedure: An Analysis of Cases and Concepts,* 4th ed. New York: Foundation Press, 2000.

ZEIDMAN, STEVEN. "To Plead or Not to Plead: Effective Assistance and Client-Centered Counseling." *Boston College Law Review* 39 (July 1998): 641.

CASES

Argersinger v. Hamlin, 407 U.S. 25 (1972).
Berkemer v. McCarty, 468 U.S. 420 (1984).
Brewer v. Williams, 430 U.S. 387 (1977).
Burger v. Kemp, 483 U.S. 776 (1987).
Coleman v. Alabama, 399 U.S. 1 (1970).
Coleman v. Thompson, 501 U.S. 722 (1991).
Colorado v. Connelly, 479 U.S. 157 (1986).
Davis v. United States, 512 U.S. 452 (1994).
Douglas v. California, 372 U.S. 353 (1963).
Estelle v. Smith, 451 U.S. 454 (1981).
Farreta v. California, 422 U.S. 806 (1975).
Fuller v. Diesslin, 868 F.2d 604 (3d Cir.), *cert. denied,* 493 U.S. 873 (1989).
Gandy v. Alabama, 569 F.2d 1318 (CA5 1978).
Geders v. United States, 425 U.S. 80 (1976).
Gerstein v. Pugh, 420 U.S. 103 (1975).
Gideon v. Wainwright, 372 U.S. 335 (1963).
Gilbert v. California, 388 U.S. 263 (1967).
Griffin v. Illinois, 351 U.S. 12 (1956).
Hill v. Lockhart, 474 U.S. 52 (1986).
Kimmelman v. Morrison, 477 U.S. 365 (1986).
Kirby v. Illinois, 406 U.S. 682 (1972).
Lockhart v. Fretwell, 506 U.S. 364 (1992).
Martinez v. California, 526 U.S. 152 (2000).
Martinez v. Court of Appeal, 528 U.S. 152 (2000).
Massiah v. United States, 377 U.S. 201 (1964).
McKaskle v. Wiggins, 465 U.S. 168 (1984).
McMann v. Richardson, 397 U.S. 759 (1970).
Mempa v. Rhay, 389 U.S. 128 (1967).
Miranda v. Arizona, 384 U.S. 436 (1966).
Morris v. Slappy, 461 U.S. 1 (1983).
Murray v. Giarratano, 492 U.S. 1 (1992).
Nix v. Whiteside, 475 U.S. 157 (1986).
North Carolina v. Butler, 441 U.S. 369 (1979).
Palko v. United States, 302 U.S. 319 (1937).
Pennsylvania v. Finley, 481 U.S. 551 (1987).
Powell v. Alabama, 287 U.S. 45 (1932).
Rhode Island v. Innis, 466 U.S. 291 (1980).
Ross v. Moffitt, 417 U.S. 600 (1974).
Scott v. Illinois, 440 U.S. 367 (1979).
Strickland v. Washington, 466 U.S. 668 (1984).
United States v. Ash, 413 U.S. 300 (1973).
United States v. Cronic, 466 U.S. 648 (1984).
United States v. Malpiedi, 62 F.3d 465 (2d Cir. 1995).
United States v. Rankin, 779 F.2d 956 (3d Cir. 1986).
United States v. Wade, 388 U.S. 218 (1967).
Wheat v. United States, 486 U.S. 153 (1988).

COUNSEL: ROLE OF COUNSEL

In the eyes of many people, the criminal defense lawyer (*defense counsel*, or *defender*, for short) represents all that is best about the legal profession; in the eyes of others, all that is worst. Defense counsel is the innocent defendant's last refuge against the horror of wrongful conviction—or, as lawyers sometimes say in their hyperbolic fashion, the defender is the only friend that an accused person has left in the world. Defense counsel is also the guilty defendant's chief instrument for defeating justice and getting away with crime. Paradoxically, the defender is at once the indispensable condition for justice and the enemy of justice. The trait on which defenders most pride themselves—a fierce, undivided loyalty to the client—seems to many people a virtue, while to others it is a vice. Heightening the paradox is the fact that the better a legal system is—the fewer wrongful arrests and prosecutions it engages in—the more often the defender will be working to exonerate the guilty. Although a vigorous, independent defense bar is often thought to be a sign of a first-rate legal system, improving the legal system inevitably makes the defender's role more morally problematic.

The classic statement of the defender's ethical outlook was offered in 1820 by a British barrister, Lord Henry Brougham: "An advocate, in the discharge of his duty, knows but one person in all the world, and that person is his client. To save that client by all means and expedients, and at all hazards and costs to other persons, and, amongst them, to himself, is his first and only duty; and in performing this duty he must not regard the alarm, the torments, the destruction which he may bring upon others. Separating the duty of a patriot from that of an advocate, he must go on reckless of consequences, though it should be his unhappy fate to involve his country in confusion" (Nightingale, p. 8). Brougham's credo displays both sides of the dilemma. On the one hand, it eloquently extols the loyalty and personal courage that a defender must possess to represent someone accused of wrongdoing and perhaps despised by the entire community. On the other hand, it states plainly that defenders will discount to zero the alarm, torments, and destruction that they may bring on the community, a position that seems hard to justify on any plausible theory of morality.

The moral basis of defense counsel

Why should the role of defense counsel exist in the first place? If this question seems peculiar, it is only because the moral assumptions built into the defender's role are taken for granted in modern societies. Chief among these assumptions is a particular horror at the prospect of condemning the innocent—a horror that goes back as far as the Hebrew Bible (Genesis 18:29–32). A society that placed higher importance on convicting the guilty than on acquitting the innocent would eliminate defense counsel from its criminal justice system. Modern societies instead profess belief in the old slogan that it is better that ten guilty criminals escape than that one innocent person be wrongfully convicted.

The reasons for this repugnance at convicting the innocent are straightforward. First, criminal law is usually enforced through corporal punishment—imprisonment, and in some legal systems flogging, mutilation, or even death. Second, criminal conviction carries with it the stigma of moral condemnation. Third, criminal litigation pits the defendant against the state: cases bear names like *People v. X, the Crown v. Y,* and *State v. Z.* Within liberal polities, at any rate, the danger that state power will be abused by those who wield it is thought to warrant special precautions—not just the protection of individual rights against the state, but in some cases the overprotection of those rights. Thus, liberal polities always grant the presumption of innocence, so that the state always bears the burden of proof in criminal cases. The special horror at convicting the innocent explains why in many societies criminal conviction requires proof beyond a reasonable doubt rather than some lesser standard. And prominent among the safeguards against wrongful conviction is the right to defense counsel.

A more subtle moral assumption behind the defender's role is this: any decent legal system must presume that the accused person has a good-faith story to tell, a defense to offer. A society which respects the human dignity of its inhabitants withholds its verdict in abeyance until the defendant's side of the story has been heard—even in an open-and-shut case such as the knife-point rapist caught in the very act (Donagan, pp. 128–33). Once society presumes that defendants have good-faith stories to tell, fairness requires that the ability of defendants to tell their stories should not be undercut merely because they may be uneducated, ignorant of the law, poor public speakers, or unintelligent. They must be provided an advocate—a "mouthpiece" in a nonpejorative sense of the word—who can help them tell their stories, just as non-native speakers must be provided with translators at their trials.

Of course, nothing in these arguments implies that the defender must be a partisan advocate. Perhaps the prosecutor could be required to present the accused's side of the story along with the state's version; or perhaps the judge could assume the burden of defense. Experience, however, teaches that systems designed along these lines fail. For centuries, English felony defendants were prohibited from employing defense counsel, on the theory that the court would look out for the defendant's interests and that partisan defense counsel would merely muddy the waters. Instead of safeguarding defendants, however, judges often joined with prosecutors in reviling defendants to their faces, and this was one reason for the Prisoners' Counsel Bill of 1836, which established the right to defense counsel (Mellinkoff). Likewise, American prosecutors are required by their ethics codes to seek justice, not victory—but before the right to counsel was granted in 1963, defenderless trials often led to convictions based on evidence so flimsy that any competent defender would have demolished it; and prosecutors routinely sought victory without worrying overmuch about justice. It seems, then, that to be effective the defender's loyalty must be undivided, just as Lord Brougham suggested; and, if it is undivided, the moral ambiguities of the role emerge fully.

Defending the guilty

The dilemma is at its most intense when the client is guilty, for then the lawyer seems not much different from the driver of a getaway car:

both aim to help the criminal escape just punishment for his crime. Morally if not legally, the defender becomes an accomplice in the criminal's escape.

Lawyers respond with several arguments about the importance of representing the guilty and, moreover, representing the guilty as vigorously as the innocent. Each of these arguments has force, but each is open to criticism.

The adversary system.   The system of criminal justice, which pits prosecution against defense, requires undivided partisanship. Because the prosecutor will present the state's case, the defender must concentrate entirely on the accused's, and present it as forcefully as possible. A corollary to this *principle of partisanship* is that the lawyer should not be held morally accountable for zealously defending the client; otherwise, moral compunctions might compel defenders to restrain their zeal, in violation of the principle of partisanship. Taken together, the principles of partisanship and nonaccountability are thought by many to define the advocate's role (Luban, 1988; Schwartz; Simon, 1978).

This argument grounds the defender's ethic of partisan zeal in the nature of the adversary system (see Freedman's 1975 work for a classic statement of this argument). However, the adversary system has often been criticized on the ground that it turns the system of legal justice into a contest of skill and resources and encourages amoral ruthlessness on the part of prosecutors and defenders alike. That is, the very system that is supposed to justify partisan zeal can be criticized precisely on the ground that it encourages too much partisan zeal. In this way, the argument based on the adversary system begs the question of how partisan a defender should be. In addition, the argument based on the adversary system may apply with less force to legal cultures with different procedural systems.

Another version of the argument focuses on liberal fear of the state. It seems too unfair to pit the might of the state against a solitary defendant, even a guilty one, without providing the defendant with a champion (Luban, 1993). Critics, however, point out that criminals seldom if ever face "the bogey of the state"; in reality, they are pitted against "a small number of harassed, overworked bureaucrats" (Simon, 1998, p. 174), and there is little reason to suppose that "the state" poses a greater threat to the public than do the criminals it prosecutes.

Usurping the court's role.   A defender who refuses to defend the guilty, or offers a less vigorous defense, has substituted his or her own judgment that the client is guilty for the verdict of the judge or jury. Not only does this violate the trial's division of labor, it denies the defendant the due process that trials are meant to provide by, in effect, convicting the defendant before the trial. Sometimes this argument is phrased as a point about the nature of truth in law: when Boswell asked Dr. Johnson how he could represent a cause known to be bad, Johnson replied, "Sir, you do not know it to be good or bad till the Judge determines it."

Skeptics may reply that the defender is not literally substituting his or her judgment for that of the judge and jury, because the defender is not rendering a legal verdict on the defendant. The defender is merely deciding how vigorously to defend based on what he or she knows of the client's guilt or innocence. As for Johnson's argument that the lawyer cannot "know" the client is guilty, it rests on a play on words. If Johnson meant that only the judge is authorized to establish forensic facts, he was wrong to couch the point in terms of knowledge rather than authority; if he meant that lawyers can never know more than judges about a case, he was simply mistaken.

The political activist's reason.   Many defenders view their job as fighting for society's outcasts and underdogs. Violent criminals have themselves often grown up as victims of violence and oppression; the criminal justice system operates in a racist manner; criminal sentences are often savagely harsh; and conditions of imprisonment in many jurisdictions are inhuman. For these reasons, as one writer puts it, "A lawyer performs good work when he helps to prevent the imprisonment of the poor, the outcast, and minorities in shameful conditions" (Babcock, p. 177).

Here too, the argument, strong as it is, is open to doubt. It does not apply to prosperous white-collar criminals, racial-majority defendants, or those whose punishments are not excessively harsh. More importantly, the argument glosses over the fact of guilt, including the legitimate interests of past and potential crime victims in having dangerous criminals isolated from society. Victims too have rights, and often the victims of crimes are themselves the poor, the outcast, and minorities in shameful conditions (Simon, 1998).

Making the screens work.   Only when the defense bar makes a practice of vigorously challenging prosecutors, even in cases where the defendant is guilty, will prosecutors and judges take precautions to ensure that only valid cases, backed by solid evidence, are brought. The aggressive defender disciplines the prosecutors, making them do their jobs, and thus, "by defending the guilty, the defense attorney protects the freedom of the innocent" (Mitchell, p. 320; see Kaplan, pp. 231–232). To this argument, one critic responds by asking whether vigorously challenging prosecutors includes misleading them and the court, as vigorous partisan advocacy may require when the defendant is guilty. If so, then it seems less plausible that vigorous defense "makes the screens work" than that vigorous defense makes the system fail (Simon, 1998, pp. 178–179).

One other version of this argument seems valid and uncontroversial, however. Prosecutors often charge defendants with multiple crimes, or choose the most serious among several possibilities in the statute book. One crucial role the defender plays is to keep the prosecution honest by resisting overcharging, or by arguing vigorously that the facts support only a less serious crime (manslaughter rather than murder, for example). Likewise, when prosecutors press for the harshest sentence, the defender highlights facts that point toward leniency. Without the defender, prosecutors have little incentive to be careful in their charging decisions and sentencing recommendations.

Confidentiality and zeal.   Recall that in liberal polities, respect for human dignity requires a defender to present the defendant's good-faith story as the defendant would if he or she was knowledgeable about the law and skilled at public speaking. The defender cannot present the client's story, however, unless the defendant can tell the defender the facts of the case, and defendants will not do this unless they believe they can do it safely. That is the root justification of confidentiality: lawyers must keep client confidences to encourage clients to tell them everything they need to present the case. Some argue that this policy behind confidentiality is so strong that clients must be assured that what they tell their lawyers will never work to their disadvantage. For that reason, counsel cannot curtail vigorous defense merely because the client has admitted guilt.

The implications of this argument are far-reaching, and, it may prove, too much so. It means, to take a characteristic ethical problem facing defenders, that a defender must treat the client's perjurious testimony as if it was true, because otherwise the client's confidences about the actual facts will be used to the client's disadvantage (Freedman, 1966, 1975). This conclusion, however, is not commonly accepted by legal professions anywhere in the world. American ethics rules, like those in many countries, typically require defenders to inform courts about client perjury, and never permit defenders to argue perjurious testimony as if it were true. True, this rule forces clients to choose between concealing facts from their defenders—thereby running the risk of inadequate defense—or confiding in the defenders but giving up the opportunity to commit perjury. In that case, the defender is not presenting the client's fabricated story as the defendant would; but respecting the client's human dignity requires only that the client be allowed to present a good-faith defense through the lips of the defender, not a fabricated one. It follows that the argument that confiding in the defender must never be permitted to harm the client is too strong: client confidences must never be used to harm the client's good-faith defense, but if the client's defense is not in good faith, defenders should not offer it, even if the result harms the client.

Defense counsel's battle against truth

It seems likely that popular revulsion to the defense counsel arises partly from a kind of irrational transference—a projection of revulsion for the client onto the client's lawyer. It has another, more rational, source as well, however. That is the concern, dating back to Plato, that lawyers win cases by perverting the truth. When clients are guilty, how can it be otherwise? If the client is guilty, the defender labors mightily to keep damning evidence away from the judge or jury. The defender tries to discredit opposing witnesses, often by making them seem like liars or fools, even when the defender knows that they are telling the truth. In addition, the defender will try to sell the judge or jury on some alternative story that—supposing the client is guilty—is false: that the robber was elsewhere at the time, or that the rape victim consented to sex, or that the police planted the incriminating evidence, or that the killer was acting in self-defense. In the extreme case, the defender will try to pin the blame on someone else, combining the injustice of freeing the guilty with the far greater injustice of framing the innocent.

Defenders justify these practices by reminding us that the prosecution bears the burden of proving each and every element of a crime beyond a reasonable doubt. When defenders brutally cross-examine truthful prosecution witnesses, their purpose is to expose reasonable doubts a judge or jury might entertain about the witnesses' testimony, including truthful testimony. After all, if the witness lacks credibility, a conscientious jury should find reasonable doubt even if the witness happens to be telling the truth. Similarly, when the defender vigorously argues that the evidence supports an alternative story, even one that the defender knows is false, the argument is a valid tactic because it raises reasonable doubts about the prosecution's case. Jurors will never find reasonable doubt if the defender merely argues the abstract possibility of doubt; that is why defenders argue concrete alternative stories—not because they are true, but because they are consistent with the evidence and reasonably plausible, which should suffice for acquittal. Of course, the defender will not explicitly say, "My client's alibi may not be true, but on this evidence it could very well be true": such an admission would cause jurors to discount the alibi and convict even in the face of reasonable doubt. The defender will behave as though the alibi is true, because that is the only way to ensure that jurors vividly perceive that there are reasonable doubts about the prosecution's case. The defender's battle against truth is part of a larger war for justice.

There is much to be said for this argument. However, it fails to justify some of the defender's favorite tactics.

Misleading investigators and prosecutors. Particularly in the defense of white-collar crime, where arrest and indictment are typically preceded by lengthy investigation, defenders devote most of their efforts to forestalling the indictment. Defenders will caution potential witnesses that cooperating with prosecutors may be bad for their business careers. They will try to coordinate the stories of all the targets of investigation, and persuade them to stonewall investigators. Avoiding overt lies, defenders will shower prosecutors with half-truths to throw them off the track. And, in order to avoid being put in the position of lying to prosecutors, they will intentionally refrain from asking their clients questions when hearing the "wrong" answers would prevent them from arguing a plausible falsehood (Mann, 1985). None of these tactics can plausibly be described as merely testing the prosecution's case by raising reasonable doubts. They are attempts to prevent the prosecution from assembling a case in the first place.

Undermining the fairness of the forum. Where it is possible, defenders will "forum shop" for a venue with favorable jury demographics. They will try to disqualify any juror whom they suspect will be skeptical of their defense. And they will energetically seek to delay trials so that witnesses have time to forget details, leave town, or die. (It should not be forgotten, however, that prosecutors also have a formidable repertoire of dirty tricks, and defenders argue that they are merely fighting fire with fire.)

Playing to bias and emotion. The defender will make sure that the accused arrives for trial neatly coiffed, cleanly shaven, and dressed in a suit and tie (which actually may belong to the defender); the defendant's sweet, sorrowful wife and adorable children will be arrayed behind him, even if in reality he deserted them months before. The exploitation of appearance and manipulation of emotion have always been the defender's stock in trade. When Phryne, the most famous and beautiful courtesan in classical Athens, was tried for impiety, her defense counsel Hyperides delivered the greatest oration of his life. But, observing that the jury remained unmoved, Hyperides dramatically bared Phryne's breasts and secured her acquittal by telling the Athenians that it would be sacrilegious to condemn Aphrodite's own representative among mortals (Davidson, p. 134). Today, mafia lawyers borrow stirring paragraphs from the speeches of Martin Luther King to defend charismatic but murderous dons, and demagogic defenders play the "race card" to secure acquittals in racially charged cases (Dannen). Two thousand years ago, Plato's *Apology* and *Gorgias* criticized trials and lawyers for substituting emotionalism and sentiment for truth, and today as in Plato's time this criticism remains fundamental.

Who calls the shots?

Recall that the standard conception of the advocate's role combines a principle of partisanship with a principle of moral nonaccountability, according to which the advocate bears no moral responsibility for lawful actions taken on the client's behalf. This principle flows from the legal understanding that the lawyer is the client's agent or servant, that is, that the client is the primary decision-maker and the lawyer merely executes the client's decisions. In fact, however, everyone recognizes that the description of a client-principal directing a lawyer-agent represents little more than a legal fiction.

In the United States, even the formal rules of legal ethics allocate virtually all tactical decision-making to the lawyer, not the client. The client certainly chooses the ends of representation. The client also has a constitutional right to testify even if his defender objects. Finally, the client chooses how to plead, and thus whether to accept a negotiated plea. Apart from these limitations, however, the defender makes the remaining choices. Yet, although the lawyer must consult with the client about the means, lawyers need not abide by clients' tactical preferences. The lawyer decides which witnesses to call, what theory of the case to offer, and what strategy to pursue. In reality, then, the client probably possesses even less autonomy than the rules envisage: defenders can and do present options to their clients in a way so skewed that the client will choose what the defender wants him to choose. Defenders justify such overbearing behavior by insisting that clients are often foolish and that lawyers know better than clients what is in the client's best interests. Often, perhaps, the defenders are right.

However, it is important to realize that the more defenders become the real decision-makers in their clients' cases, the more accountable they are for the choices they make. In addition, overriding their clients' preference raises the important issue of how much paternalism can be justified in the lawyer-client relationship.

The unsung problem: indifferent defense

The preceding discussion has centered on the moral problems of zealous defense that spares nothing and no one in pursuit of victory. While these are central to understanding the defender's role, it would be irresponsible to conclude without noting that they form only a small part of the landscape of criminal defense. In reality, very few criminal defendants are fortunate enough to have a defender who fits the excessive-zeal picture. In the United States, three-fourths of all criminal defendants are indigent, represented either by overworked public defenders or by private counsel paid bargain-basement fees by the state. The result is perfunctory defense, little or no fact investigation, and quick negotiated pleas—"meet 'em, greet 'em, plead 'em," as observers describe the typical lawyer-client interaction. One study in New York City found that private counsel for indigent defendants interviewed prosecution witnesses in fewer than 5 percent of their felony cases, and other studies

reveal equally shocking lapses (Luban, 1993). In practical terms, the greatest moral problem of criminal defense is not excessive zeal, but incompetence and indifference. For these lead to the kind of bureaucratic mass-processing of faceless, interchangeable defendants that the defense counsel's role as champion of individual dignity was supposed to counteract.

DAVID LUBAN

See also ADVERSARY SYSTEM; CAREERS IN CRIMINAL JUSTICE: LAW; CONFESSIONS; COUNSEL: RIGHT TO COUNSEL; CRIMINAL JUSTICE PROCESS; GUILTY PLEA: ACCEPTING THE PLEA; GUILTY PLEA: PLEA BARGAINING; SENTENCING: PROCEDURAL PROTECTION; TRIAL, CRIMINAL.

BIBLIOGRAPHY

BABCOCK, BARBARA. "Defending the Guilty." *Cleveland State Law Review* 32, no. 2 (1983): 175–187.

DANNEN, FREDERIC. "Annals of the Law: Defending the Mafia." *The New Yorker,* 21 February 1994, pp. 64–89.

DAVIDSON, JAMES N. *Courtesans and Fishcakes: The Consuming Passions of Classical Athens.* New York: St. Martin, 1997.

DONAGAN, ALAN. "Justifying Legal Practice in the Adversary System." *The Good Lawyer: Lawyers' Roles and Lawyers' Ethics.* Edited by David Luban. Totowa, N.J.: Rowman & Allanheld, 1983. Pages 123–149.

FREEDMAN, MONROE H. "Professional Responsibility of the Criminal Defense Lawyer: The Three Hardest Questions." *Michigan Law Review* 64 June (1966): 1469–1484.

———. *Lawyers' Ethics in an Adversary System.* Indianapolis: Bobbs-Merrill, 1975.

KAPLAN, JOHN. "Defending Guilty People." *University of Bridgeport Law Review* 7 (1986): 223–255.

LUBAN, DAVID. *Lawyers and Justice: An Ethical Study.* Princeton, N.J.: Princeton University Press, 1988.

———. "Are Criminal Defenders Different?" *Michigan Law Review* 91 (1993): 1729–1766.

MANN, KENNETH. *Defending White Collar Crime: A Portrait of Attorneys at Work.* New Haven, Conn.: Yale University Press, 1985.

MELLINKOFF, DAVID. *The Conscience of a Lawyer.* St. Paul, Minn.: West Publishing, 1973.

MITCHELL, JOHN B. "The Ethics of the Criminal Defense Attorney—New Answers to Old Questions." *Stanford Law Review* 32, no. 2 (1980): 293–337.

NIGHTINGALE, J. *The Trial of Queen Caroline*, vol. 2. London: J. Robins & Co., Albion Press, 1820–1821.

SCHWARTZ, MURRAY L. "The Professionalism and Accountability of Lawyers." *California Law Review* 66, no. 4 (1978): 669–697.

SIMON, WILLIAM. "The Ideology of Advocacy: Procedural Justice and Professional Ethics." *Wisconsin Law Review* no. 1 (1978): 29–144.

———. *The Practice of Justice: A Theory of Lawyers' Ethics*. Cambridge, Mass.: Harvard University Press, 1998.

COUNTERFEITING

Counterfeiting is one of the few crimes mentioned in the text of the Constitution, perhaps because "[t]he general power over currency . . . has always been an acknowledged attribute of sovereignty" (*Legal Tender Cases*, 79 U.S. 457, 545 (1870)). Congress quickly made use of its authority to prohibit counterfeiting; the Act of 30 April 1790 authorized the death penalty for counterfeiting U.S. securities (contemporary punishments include fines, forfeiture, and prison). Comprehensive federal regulation of counterfeiting, however, emerged only with the adoption of a national currency amid the economic turmoil of the Civil War. The act of 30 June 1864, as modified and extended, forms the backbone of the statutory scheme codified at 18 U.S.C. §§ 470–514.

An obligation or security is counterfeit if it "bears such a likeness or resemblance to any of the genuine obligations or securities issued under the authority of the United States as is calculated to deceive an honest, sensible and unsuspecting person of ordinary observation and care when dealing with a person supposed to be upright and honest" (*United States v. Wethington*, 141 F.3d 284, 287 (6th Cir. 1998)). The definition of *counterfeit* also includes objects such as slugs that can be used to procure goods and services from vending machines and other coin or currency activated devices (18 U.S.C. § 491).

Counterfeiting is similar to forgery, and both are covered in the same chapter of the United States Code. Courts sometimes use the terms interchangeably, but *counterfeiting* generally refers to "a crime based upon a preexisting genuine instrument," while *forgery* does not always "carry such presumption but indicates that there is a genuine or real obligor in existence whose obligation has been simulated" (*Stinson v. United States*, 316 F.2d 554, 555 (5th Cir. 1963); see also 18 U.S.C. § 513(c)). To the extent the distinction between these offenses could create confusion or suggest a gap in coverage, federal statutes prohibit the counterfeiting, forging, or false making of securities and obligations, as well as the creation of fictitious obligations (18 U.S.C. § 514).

Federal law prohibits counterfeiting or forging a wide variety of specific obligations, securities, and public records, ranging from currency and coins to postage stamps and meter stamps; state and private securities; lending agency notes and obligations; federal contractor bonds, contracts, and related records; visas and other entry documents; customs documents and letters patent; military passes and permits; money orders; court, department, and agency seals; and ship's papers and federal transportation requests. Related offenses include the counterfeiting or pirating of copyrights and trademarks (18 U.S.C. §§ 2318, 2320). The counterfeiting within the United States of foreign obligations, securities, bank notes, and postage stamps is a crime as well. In response to the widespread use of U.S. currency in other countries and the increasingly international scope of counterfeiting efforts, federal law also has a broad extraterritorial component that bars counterfeiting of U.S. obligations or securities even when such activities occur entirely outside the United States (18 U.S.C. § 470).

In addition to the crime of making counterfeits, federal law prohibits the distinct offenses of possessing, passing, uttering, and dealing in domestic or foreign counterfeit items with intent to defraud. *Uttering* is the crime of representing a counterfeit item as genuine (*United States v. Heller*, 625 F.2d 594, 598 (5th Cir. 1980)). Making, possessing, and dealing in the things used to make domestic or foreign counterfeits, with intent that they be so used, is also a crime.

Intent to defraud need not be directed at a specific person or entity; "a general intent that some innocent third party in the chain of distribution be defrauded" is sufficient (*United States v. Mucciante*, 21 F.3d 1228, 1235 (2d Cir. 1994)). Proof of intent against a claim of innocent possession usually comes from circumstantial evidence, such as a rapid series of passings, passing false bills at different establishments, the use of large counterfeit bills for small purchases rather than using the change from prior purchases, and the segregation of counterfeit bills from genuine bills (*United States v. Armstrong*, 16 F.3d 289, 292 (8th Cir. 1994)).

Not every counterfeiting offense requires intent to defraud. The mere possession of a counterfeit with intent to sell or otherwise use it is a crime (*United States v. Parr*, 716 F.2d 796, 808 (11th Cir. 1983)). Copying or reproducing all or part of an obligation or security of the United States is a crime regardless of intent (*Boggs v. Bowron*, 842 F. Supp. 542, 559–560 (D.D.C. 1993), *aff'd* 67 F.3d 972 (D.C. Cir. 1995)). Because there are sometimes good reasons to reproduce currency—for example, to illustrate news articles on monetary policy—Congress created limited exceptions to the blanket prohibition for certain purposes. Congress liberalized these exceptions after the Supreme Court found the "purpose" clause too narrow for the First Amendment (*Regan v. Time, Inc.*, 468 U.S. 641 (1984); 18 U.S.C. § 504). Although these exceptions allow some versions of expressive counterfeiting, the U.S. Secret Service—which enforces the counterfeiting statutes—has applied the copying prohibition strictly against artists and satirists whose works call into question the integrity, value, or meaning of currency (*Boggs v. Rubin*, 161 F.3d 37 (D.C. Cir. 1998); *Wagner v. Simon*, 412 F. Supp. 426 (W.D.Mo. 1974), *aff'd* 534 F.2d 833 (8th Cir. 1976)).

Counterfeiting of federal obligations is generally a crime under state law as well as under federal law. State and federal governments have concurrent jurisdiction, states to protect their citizens against fraud, and the federal government to protect the integrity of the currency (*United States v. Crawford*, 657 F.2d 1041, 1046 n.6 (9th Cir. 1981); *State v. McMurry*, 907 P.2d 1084, 1086–1087 (Az. App. 1995)).

JOHN T. PARRY

See also FEDERAL CRIMINAL JURISDICTION; FEDERAL CRIMINAL LAW ENFORCEMENT; FORGERY.

BIBLIOGRAPHY

CUMMINGS, NATHAN K. "The Counterfeit Buck Stops Here: National Security Issues in the Redesign of U.S. Currency." *Southern California Interdisciplinary Law Journal* 8, no. 2 (spring 1999): 539–576.

GOLDSTONE, DAVID J., and TOREN, PETER J. "The Criminalization of Trademark Counterfeiting." *Connecticut Law Review* 31, no. 1 (fall 1998): 1–76.

STAPEL, JULIE K. "Money Talks: The First Amendment Implications of Counterfeiting Law." *Indiana Law Journal* 71, no. 1 (winter 1995): 153–182.

TORCIA, CHARLES E. *Wharton's Criminal Law.* 15th ed. Deerfield, Ill.: Clark Boardman Callaghan, 1993. Vol. 4, pp. 106–112.

United States Secret Service. Counterfeit Division—History of Counterfeiting. http://www.ustreas.gov/usss/counterfeit.htm (visited 28 August 1999).

United States Secret Service. Know Your Money—Illustrations of Currency, Checks, or Other Obligations. http://www.ustreas.gov/usss/money-illustrations.htm (visited 28 August 1999).

WESCHLER, LAWRENCE. *Boggs: A Comedy of Values.* Chicago: University of Chicago Press, 1999.

COURTS, ORGANIZATION OF

See CRIMINAL JUSTICE SYSTEM.

CRIME: DEFINITION

A crime is an act proscribed by law and subject to punishment. It can also be an omission instead of an act, namely a failure to act where the law imposes a duty to act. Traditionally, crimes have been restricted to acts and omissions that harm the interests of others. Sometimes, however, a legislature will criminalize an act or omission because it is harmful to the perpetrator himself, or because the conduct is morally reprehensible. Such criminal provisions are known as "victimless" crimes. The possibility of a victimless crime underscores the central difference between criminal and civil law: a crime is an offense against public welfare, whereas a civil wrong is an offense against private interests. While civil damages are awarded to compensate a victim for harm he has suffered at the injurer's hands, criminal punishment is inflicted to allow the state to vindicate its interest in the common good.

In our history, the concept of the public wrong emerged after the Norman Conquest, replacing what was essentially a system of private plea-bargaining under the Anglo-Saxons. Prior to the conquest, an injurer would pay his victim a sum of money in order to buy off the latter's right to revenge. These payments, known as *wer*, *wíte*, and *bót*, were not determined by law, but instead depended on what injurer and victim could negotiate. We can already discern the concept of a public harm at this time, however, in the fact that some injuries were *bóteás*, or beyond monetary redemption, and for these a man might be put to death. A later possible source of the offense against the state may be the jurisdictional concept of the "king's peace." Under this concept, the Crown reserved the right to control for violent acts that might occur along any route on which the king traveled. Finally, while an even later development, the advent of a public police force made the concept of a public wrong institutionally feasible.

Civil and criminal divide

In recent years, the distinction between civil and criminal wrongs has become somewhat blurred. On the civil side, for example, there is the institution of "punitive damages," by which an individual is punished for the intentional infliction of an injury or a malicious breach of contract. Punitive damages are intended as punishment for the injurer, unlike the ordinary civil remedy of compensatory damages that cannot exceed the amount required to make the victim whole. On the criminal side, there is the increasingly common use of monetary penalties in lieu of incarceration. Such penalties are often paid as compensation to the victim in the form of restitution. There is also increasing use of the criminal sanction against corporations. Since a corporation can only be punished with monetary sanctions, and since punitive damages are increasingly awarded in civil suits, the distinction between civil and criminal in such cases is a nominal one. It would appear to consist mostly of procedural differences, such as the different standards of proof and different rules of evidence. Finally, there is a recent movement to enhance the role of the victim in criminal proceedings, stemming from the belief that crime victims have a right to representation in the prosecution of their attackers. The idea of victim's rights most strongly suggests a shift away from the conception of crime as a public offense. It suggests that the punishment of the offender serves, at least in part, to satisfy the victim's need for vengeance. This trend toward the "privatization" of crime finds expression in various proposed institutional reforms as well, such as the proposal to convert prisons to private ownership.

The acceptability of these various modifications of the traditional notion of crime depends partly on what we take a crime to be. Is a crime simply a prohibition that appears in one of the state or federal penal codes under the heading "criminal"? Or is the criminal category a deeper one, one that does not derive its meaning from any particular use to which the notion of crime is put? The first would be what we might call a "positivistic" stance toward the notion of an offense. It treats crime entirely as a legislative concept. The second would be a normative stance toward the notion of an offense identifying the criminal category by a theory of justified prohibition. On a positive approach, there can be no objection to punishing corporations or enhancing the role of the victim, since there is no obligatory content to the notion of an offense. On a normative approach, by contrast, there may be grounds for objecting to these modifications to the traditional treatment of crime. For it may turn out that punishing an offender at the behest of the victim, especially if associated with the payment of restitution, is not legitimate according to our best theory of justified punishment.

The positivistic approach

The prevailing approach of the American legal system toward crime is positivistic. As Henry Hart once wrote facetiously: "a crime is anything which is *called* a crime, and a criminal penalty is simply the penalty provided for doing anything which has been given that name" (p. 404). By refusing to recognize constitutional boundaries on the notion of an offense, this is precisely the position the U.S. Supreme Court has articulated over the course of the last fifty or so years. The Court has held, for example, that a legislature may criminalize conduct without including a mental state element (*mens rea*) in the definition of the offense (*U.S. v. Dotterweich*; *U.S. v. Balint*). It has also found it a matter of legislative discretion whether to treat exonerating conditions like insanity as part of the definition of the offense to which they apply or as so-called affirmative defenses. The former approach would place the burden on the prosecution to prove, for example, that the defendant was not insane at the time he performed the criminal act, whereas the latter would place the burden on the defendant to prove he was. The Court famously articulated its commitment to the positivistic approach to crime in a case involving the defense of extreme emotional disturbance where it upheld a New York provision that shifted the burden to the defendant to prove the defense, instead of requiring the prosecution to prove the absence of the defense beyond a reasonable doubt (*Patterson v. New York*). Given its premise, the Court's reasoning was flawless: It argued that because a state has the power to eliminate the defense altogether, it must also have the power to shift the burden to the defendant to prove it, since "the greater power implies the lesser power" (p. 211). The same argument has been found applicable to other defenses as well, even one as fundamental as self-defense. Recently, however, the Supreme Court has indicated a renewed willingness to place limits on state burden-shifting. The case concerned a New Jersey hate-crime statute that authorized substantially increased penalties for any defendant whose crime was committed from the motive of racial animus. The Court found the statute unconstitutional on the grounds that it obviated the state's duty to prove mental state by treating racial bias as a sentencing factor instead of as an element of the offense. The implication of such a decision is that legislatures do not have unfettered discretion to decide how and whether to criminalize, even outside the area of fundamental rights. For if it is constitutionally impermissible for a state to shift the burden on a mental state element, it would seem to follow that it does not have unfettered discretion to decide whether to include such mental state elements in its offense definitions in the first instance. The question, then, is whether the Court's recent holding in the area of burden of proof signals a fundamental shift away from the positivist approach to crime, or whether its influence will be confined to the area of burden of proof. Is the Court embarking on a new constitutional jurisprudence of substantive criminal law or will it continue to shy away from any real attempt to place limits on the substantive criminal provisions legislatures can pass?

While the positivistic approach to crime has prevailed, there are some isolated areas in which the Supreme Court has traditionally attempted to place limitations on offense definition. For the most part, these limitations have consisted of a set of formal restrictions on how legislatures may draft offenses, stemming from the due process clauses of the Fifth and Fourteenth Amendments. While these restrictions purport to speak only to how conduct is criminalized, rather than what is criminalized, they often turn out to impose substantive conditions on offense definition as well. Consider, for example, the following four important limitations on the notion of an offense.

First, the doctrine of *vagueness* requires that criminal statutes define the prohibited conduct with sufficient specificity to place potential defendants on notice of their vulnerability to criminal prosecution. This doctrine has most notably been applied to loitering ordinances, many of which are thought to leave too much discretion to police officers to arrest individuals on grounds of physical appearance or demeanor. In many cases, the objection to such statutes would not be eliminated by more precise drafting. As the Court made clear in a recent case involving a Chicago loitering ordinance, sometimes a statute cuts too deeply into the ordinary activities of everyday life, with too little justification, to be constitutionally acceptable (*City of Chicago v. Morales*). A second, related doctrine is that of *overbreadth*, which forbids a legislature from drafting criminal statutes in a way that risks prosecution and conviction for ordinary, noncriminal behavior. The Court will strike down criminal statutes on overbreadth grounds mostly where the prohibition risks infringing freedom of speech and expression (*R.A.V. v. City of St. Paul*). A third doctrine is also articulated under the heading of "due process," namely the doctrine of *legality*. Criminal statutes must provide clear notice of a citizen's potential subjection to criminal punishment in order to afford ordinary citizens a fair opportunity to conform their behavior to the law. For example, punishment must not be retroactive, and it must be certain and definite. Finally, the Eighth Amendment ban on "cruel and unusual punishment" has been interpreted as containing a doctrine of *proportionality* that serves to restrict the punishment selected for a given offense (*Solem v. Helm*; see *Harmelin v. Michigan*). While this doctrine retains its force mostly in the death penalty area, it has served in the past to ensure that the sanction authorized for a given offense is roughly on a part with the sanction for the same offense in other jurisdictions, and that it is appropriate given the sanction authorized for other offenses in the same jurisdiction.

Nonpositivist approaches

The foregoing limitations on the notion of an offense suggest that while the positivistic approach to offense definition may be the prevailing one in our constitutional jurisprudence, there is reason to question the depth of our commitment to it. We do not in fact accept that any conduct a legislature wishes to make criminal is rightly punished, and the restrictions we impose on the use of the criminal sanction cannot be entirely accounted for as restrictions imposed by the first eight amendments to the Constitution. Some conduct seems so unsuitable as an object of criminal prohibition that we feel it stretches the concept of crime to apply it to those cases. In extreme cases the point would be clear: Statutes that made criminal punishment retroactive rather than prospective, that punished for thoughts without any accompanying deeds, that enacted a separate set of prohibitions for each separate member of the community, that established a separate count of theft for each thirty-second period that a thief withheld the stolen item from its owner, or that adopted an arbitrary class of subjects to whom the prohibition would apply, would be so out of keeping with the way we think of crime that we might be inclined to reject the suggestion that the statutes made the conduct (or thoughts) crimes. In what sense would they be crimes? Simply arresting a person and subjecting him to incarceration or other harsh treatment does not by itself make the conduct for which he was arrested criminal. It does not even do so when the legislature has authorized the behavior in the form of a law. While one might hope to limit the use of the criminal sanction in such cases by the sorts of ancillary constitutional restrictions on legislative discretion discussed above, these will prove insufficient to capture our current understanding of crime. It may be, therefore, that it is the concept of crime itself that limits what a legislature may prohibit and how it may ensure adherence to those limits.

At least to some extent, then, our understanding of crime is normative as well as descriptive. In particular, there may be conditions of justification that are themselves part of the notion of crime. If this is correct, then part of what we mean when we speak of a criminal offense is that the infringement of liberty the statute authorizes is justified by the importance of inducing conformity with the criminal prohibition. This approach would suggest not only that punishing an individual for something he had no reason to know was forbidden is not, properly speaking, punishment, but that the conduct thus penalized could not be correctly called "criminal," even if the legislature has called it a crime and has attached the kinds of penalties to it that typically accompany so-called criminal conduct. The normative approach to crime would thus provide a way of evaluating legislative uses of the power to criminalize by establishing criteria that are internal to the notion of crime itself. Such criteria would make it possible to say quite directly that the legislature erred in prohibiting a certain kind of conduct and providing stringent penalties for its occurrence, on the grounds that the prohibited conduct is not an appropriate object of criminal prohibition. And while legislatures might have significant latitude in determining the acceptable objects of criminal prohibition, under a normative approach to crime, their decision-making would operate within certain broadly defined limits.

Legal moralism.   Unlike their judicial counterparts, criminal law scholars tend to favor some sort of normative approach to the notion of an offense. There is, however, no nonpositivistic definition of crime that would command uniform assent among them. One school of thought about crime is called "legal moralism." The legal moralist maintains that a crime is an immoral act, and accordingly that all and only immoral acts ought to be punished. Thus the legal moralist not only believes that every crime is in some way an immoral act, or that it tends to produce an immoral act, but also that there are no immoral acts that should go unpunished. One class of crime appears to pose a problem for the legal moralist, namely the crimes often referred to as *mala prohibita*. *Mala prohibita* crimes identify acts that are bad only because the legislature has forbidden them. By contrast, *mala in se* crimes prohibit acts that are bad in and of themselves. The legal moralist has difficulty with this distinction, because he seems to regard all crimes as *mala in se*, to the extent that he thinks it is the underlying immorality of an act that justifies prohibiting it under the criminal law. Legal moralists sometimes seek to solve the problem of *mala prohibita* crimes by saying that the acts they prohibit are instrumentally related to an act or state of affairs that is *mala in se*. While it is not immoral to drive on the left rather than on the right, it is immoral to impose grave risk of injury on one's fellows. In this way, the legal moralist explains the law mandating driving on the left, in the United States, or on the right, in Britain, as a necessary prohibition in order to avoid the truly immoral act of plowing into cars coming in the opposite direction.

Social practice view.   A second nonpositivistic view of the notion of an offense sees crimes as prohibited acts, where the explanation for these prohibitions is that they are forbidden by certain social practices, or by those possessing authority to make criminalization decisions in light of a social practice allocating the power to do so. H. L. A. Hart, for example, thought of criminal law as a set of "primary rules" designed to regulate conduct. But the primary rules, he argued, are law only because they are made by officials whose authority rests on a social practice that identifies when a rule counts as law. The rule that men must remove their hats in church, he wrote, identifies a social practice. But not all social practices have the force of law. Unlike customs and ordinary, quotidian conventions, the social rules that are law are ones that are identified in a special way within the practice as having the force of law. Only those rules possessing a certain "pedigree," namely those created by individuals authorized by "secondary rules" to create, interpret, and apply primary rules, will be so recognized. The social practice view of crime may seem similar to the positivistic approach, given that both approaches treat crime as a set of prohibitions created by those authorized to do so. It might thus be thought simply a different brand of positivism. But unlike the Supreme Court's brand of positivism about crime, Hart's account would allow for evaluative judgments about a legislature's criminalization decisions, based on their fidelity to an underlying notion of crime. A legislature that created draconian criminal prohibitions under a social practice view could be found to be exceeding its authority as established by the relevant secondary rules. As such, its dictates would not have the force of law.

Economic account.   A third prominent nonpositivistic alternative is the economic account of crime. According to some theorists, a crime is an inefficient act—inefficient because it bypasses a voluntary market. Criminal sanctions are necessary to give individuals sufficient incentive to obtain what they want through the market, rather than to take what they want by force. In this, criminal sanctions are slightly different from civil penalties. While the legal economist sees rules of civil and criminal liability as serving the same purpose, namely to provide incentives for efficient behavior, the incentive structures needed to promote efficiency for the two kinds of acts diverge. According to the economic account of crime, the criminal sanction ought to apply to acts that are always inefficient. The criminal law must threaten potential defendants with sufficiently stringent punishment to ensure that criminal acts are never worthwhile. Sometimes, by contrast, the acts that violate civil law are in fact efficient, despite the fact that they are prohibited. It is thus sometimes efficient to allow individuals to break a contract or to run a risk of injuring another person. Unlike criminal sanctions, which must always induce conformity, the penalty for civil wrongs need only be equal to the damage caused in order to provide the incentives for efficient behavior. By forcing injurers or those wishing to breach a contract to "internalize" the cost of the damage they cause, they will injure or breach only when it is efficient to do so. Criminal penalties are just like civil penalties, with the exception that civil sanctions must contain a "kicker" added to the damage caused, in order to ensure that it is never sufficiently advantageous to violate the prohibitory norm. Indeed, the decreasing distance between tort law and criminal law in recent years may itself be testimony to the influence of law and economics on judicial and legislative methodology.

While the positivistic view of crime enjoys a rhetorical advantage in our system, the actual understanding of crime our legal system presupposes seems rather to display an admixture of descriptive and normative facts. We look to legislative pronouncement to learn the content of those prohibitions we call "crimes," but we also make normative judgments about criminal statutes based on an implicit sense of what constitutes a correct application of the notion of crime. It is perhaps, moreover, because the conceptual limits of "crime" are reasonably well ensconced in our public use of the term that states do not attempt to eliminate the defense of self-defense or, for the most part, make chatting on a street corner a crime.

Harm-based theory.   Jeremy Bentham is often thought of as the father of legal positivism. But even Bentham recognized that the notion of crime must incorporate normative elements. Bentham took the standard positivist line that laws, and criminal laws in particular, are commands of the sovereign. Whatever is commanded has the force of law. But Bentham also argued interestingly that a command does not count as law if it is not "complete." In order for a law to be complete, it has to identify a discrete harm or evil at which the legal prohibition aims. Thus even for Bentham, the notion of crime rests on a pre-legislative concept, namely the notion of harm. Building an account of crime on the idea of harm represents a fourth nonpositivistic approach. The beginnings of such an account were suggested by John Stuart Mill, who articulated what has come to be knows as the "harm principle." In *On Liberty* Mill wrote: "The only purpose for which power can rightfully be exercised over any member of a civilized community against his will is to prevent harm to others" (pp. 10–11). More recently, Joel Feinberg has developed Mill's basic approach in greater detail. He has argued, however, that harm may not provide the only legitimate grounds for making criminal sanction. Even if Feinberg is right that we do not adhere to the harm principle without exception, the harm principle may nevertheless lie at the heart of American criminal law's approach to the notion of an offense.

CLAIRE FINKELSTEIN

See also ACTUS REUS; BURDEN OF PROOF; CAUSATION; CIVIL AND CRIMINAL DIVIDE; GUILT; MENS REA; PUNISHMENT; STRICT LIABILITY; VICTIMLESS CRIME.

BIBLIOGRAPHY

BENTHAM, JEREMY. *Of Laws in General.* New York: Oxford University Press, 1970.

COLEMAN, JULES L. "Crimes, Kickers and Transaction Structures." Repr. in *Markets, Morals and the Law.* New York: Cambridge University Press, 1988. Pages 153–166.

FEINBERG, JOEL. *The Moral Limits of the Criminal Law.* Vols. 1–4. New York: Oxford University Press, 1984–1998.

FINKELSTEIN, CLAIRE. "Positivism and the Notion of an Offense." *California Law Review* 88: (2000): 335–394.

FLETCHER, GEORGE P. *With Justice For Some: Protecting Victims' Rights in Criminal Trials.* Reading, Mass.: Addison-Wesley Publishing Co., 1996.

GOEBEL, JULIUS, JR. *Felony and Misdemeanor: A Study in the History of English Criminal Procedure.* University of Pennsylvania Press, 1937. Reprint, 1976.

HART, H. L. A. *Punishment and Responsibility.* Oxford, U.K.: Clarendon Press, 1967.

HART, HENRY M. "The Aims of the Criminal Law." *Law and Contemporary Problems* 23 (1958): 401.

MILL, JOHN STUART. *On Liberty* (1859). Reprint. New York: W. W. Norton, 1975.

MOORE, MICHAEL. *Placing Blame.* New York: Oxford University Press, 1997.

POLLOCK, SIR FREDERICK, AND MAITLAND, FREDERIC WILLIAM. *The History of English Law before the Time of Edward I.* Lawyer's Literary Club Edition, 1959.

POSNER, RICHARD. "An Economic Theory of the Criminal Law." *Columbia Law Review* 85 (1985): 1193.

CASES

Apprendi v. New Jersey, 120 S. Ct. 2348 (2000).
City of Chicago v. Morales, 119 S. Ct. 1849 (1999).
R.A.V. v. City of St. Paul, 505 U.S. 377 (1992).
Harmelin v. Michigan, 501 U.S. 957 (1991).
Martin v. Ohio, 480 U.S. 228 (1987).
Solem v. Helm, 463 U.S. 277 (1983).
Patterson v. New York, 432 U.S. 197 (1977).
United States v. Dotterweich, 320 U.S. 277 (1943).
Lambert v. California, 355 U.S. 225 (1957).
Leland v. Oregon, 343 U.S. 790 (1952).
United States v. Balint, 258 U.S. 250 (1922).

CRIME CAUSATION: THE FIELD

Crime causation is a daunting and complex field. For centuries, philosophers have pondered the meaning of the concept of *cause* as it pertains to human behavior. Increasingly, research suggests that individuals are unaware of the causes of other people's behaviors as well as the causes of much of their own conduct. It is no longer sufficient to ask people, "Why did you do that?" (Davison and Neale, p. 167), because they may only think they know. Instead, modern research offers a bevy of approaches in an attempt to answer that question.

The "why did you do that?" inquiry is particularly perplexing when it applies to crime. Criminal behavior is, by definition, outside of normative conduct. Many criminals engage in behaviors that most people could not conceive of doing themselves. There is also a wide range of criminal misconduct that may not always share the same source. For example, the causes of violent crime can differ from the causes of property crime; the causes of chronic and repeat criminality can differ from the causes of one-time or infrequent criminality. This type of variation makes the field of crime causation all the more challenging.

There are two basic questions concerning cause-and-effect relationships: (1) What evidence is needed to support a legitimate inference that "A" caused "B"? (2) Assuming that the evidence in question (1) is acceptable, what inferences can be drawn from such evidence, and how? These questions are difficult in part because there are no clear semantics for describing causal chains nor the proper empirical tools for raising causal questions and deriving causal answers. Yet the questions are critical for determining the causes of crime. The concept of cause structures the way we perceive and think about the "why did you do that?" inquiry, as well as the legal action courts may take in response to it.

Some causal questions are particularly troublesome to researchers because of the strong ties between criminology, philosophy, and law. For example, the concepts of *cause and effect* are intertwined with the concepts of *free will* and *determinism*, which are in turn associated with the legal concepts of *responsibility* and *reasonable person*. More philosophically detached fields of study (such as engineering or mathematics) appear to encounter fewer problems with causal investigations because they can more easily sidestep moral and value-laden issues. While increasingly quantitative approaches in criminology may succeed in restructuring the way researchers investigate the causes of crime, the field of criminology cannot avoid tackling philosophical questions altogether; the semantic roots of law and morality run too deep and they frame the disciplinary lense that criminologists use for study.

Modern crime causation models favor an interdisciplinary lense that recognizes how different fields complement, rather than contrast with, one another. This approach acknowledges that no single theory can explain all the many types of criminality nor the legal and moral issues that accompany them.

The entries that follow highlight this disciplinary interaction among theories within five different fields: biology, sociology, psychology, economics, and politics. *Biological theories* of crime locus on the physiological, biochemical, neurological, and genetic factors that influence criminal behavior. However, such theories also stress the complex link between a person's biology and the broad span of social or environmental factors that *sociological theories* examine. For example, the three major sociological theories of crime and delinquency—strain, social learning, and control—all explain crime in terms of social environmental factors, such as the family, school, peer group, workplace, community, and society. However, sociologists also recognize the significance of biological, psychological, and related theories of crime as well as the importance of individual traits such as intelligence, impulsivity, and irritability. These theories and traits help explain how individuals respond to their social environment. Similarly, *psychological theories* study in particular two types of crime factors that look at individuals in the context of their social environment: (1) family influences, such as broken homes, poor child-rearing methods, and criminal parents; and (2) individual influences, such as intelligence, personality (e.g., impulsivity), and cognitive processes (e.g., thinking, reasoning, and decision-making). A more comprehensive psychological theory of crime highlights the importance of motivational, inhibiting, decision-

making, and learning processes, as well as the need to incorporate biological, individual, family, peer, school, and neighborhood factors.

On the surface, *economic theories* of crime appear to be relatively unusual. Predicated on a model of rational behavior, they attempt to explain a behavior (crime) that is largely considered irrational. The standard economic model of crime proposes that individuals choose between criminal behavior and legal behavior on the basis of a number of factors, including the expected gains from crime relative to earnings from legal work and the risk of being caught and convicted. While an economic model of crime may not explicitly profess a mutidisciplinary approach, such an approach can be implied in the broad selection of variables that economists study (e.g., sex, age, intelligence, income, education, peer-group effects).

Lastly, *political theories* recognize that any crime theory may be linked with some political ideology (conservative, liberal, or radical), and therefore may be used for political purposes. For example, criminologists seem to associate biological and psychological theories more closely with a conservative ideology and align some sociological and economic theories more closely with a liberal or radical ideology. Consequently, any theory of crime can be viewed as a political theory.

In general, then, the following entries show that modern approaches to crime causation are integrative. They emphasize a wide range of possible influential variables, methodologies, and ideologies. If criminal behavior is as diverse and multifaceted as criminologists believe, then the causal theories and philosophies that explain that behavior should be also.

DEBORAH W. DENNO

See also CAUSATION; CRIME CAUSATION: BIOLOGICAL THEORIES; CRIME CAUSATION: ECONOMIC THEORIES; CRIME CAUSATION: POLITICAL THEORIES; CRIME CAUSATION: PSYCHOLOGICAL THEORIES; CRIME CAUSATION: SOCIOLOGICAL THEORIES; CRIMINOLOGY: INTELLECTUAL HISTORY; CRIMINOLOGY: MODERN CONTROVERSIES.

BIBLIOGRAPHY

DAVISON, GERALD C., and NEALE, JOHN M. *Abnormal Psychology*, 8th ed. New York: Wiley, 2001.
DENNO, DEBORAH W. "Human Biology and Criminal Responsibility: Free Will or Free Ride?" *University of Pennsylvania Law Review* 137, no. 2 (1988): 615–671.

———. *Biology and Violence: From Birth to Adulthood.* New York: Cambridge University Press, 1990.

HIRSCHI, TRAVIS, and SELVIN, HANAN C. "False Criteria of Causality in Delinquency." *Social Problems* 13 (1966): 254–268.

MCCORD, JOAN. "Developmental Trajectories and Intentional Actions." *Journal of Quantitative Criminology* 16 (2000): 237–253.

MESSNER, STEVEN F.; KROHN, MARVIN D.; and LISKA, ALLEN E., eds. *Theoretical Integration in the Study of Deviance and Crime: Problems and Prospects.* Albany: State University of New York Press, 1989.

PEARL, JUDEA. *Causality: Models, Reasoning, and Inference.* New York: Cambridge University Press, 2000.

REISS, JR., ALBERT J., and ROTH, JEFFREY A. *Understanding and Preventing Violence.* 4 vols. Washington, D.C.: National Academy Press, 1993–1994.

WELLFORD, CHARLES F. "Controlling Crime and Achieving Justice: The American Society of Criminology 1996 Presidential Address." *Criminology* 35 (1996): 1–11.

WILKINS, LESLIE T. "The Concept of Cause in Criminology." *Issues in Criminology* 3 (1968): 147–165.

CRIME CAUSATION: BIOLOGICAL THEORIES

Criminal behavior results from a complex interplay of social and biological factors. Social factors are a reflection of environmental sources of influence, such as socioeconomic status. The terms "biological" and "genetic" are often confused, in part due to the fact that they represent overlapping sources of influence. Biological factors are more inclusive, consisting of physiological, biochemical, neurological, and genetic factors. Genetic factors refer to biological factors that are inherited. Social factors, on the other hand, cannot be inherited. Until recently, the majority of criminological research focused solely on social contributors, either minimizing or negating the importance of genetic and biological influences on criminal behavior. In the past fifteen years, however, a large body of evidence has accumulated that suggests that the etiology of criminal behavior may be better understood when genetic and biological factors are also taken into account. Evidence for the role of genetic factors in the etiology of criminal behavior carries the assumption that biological factors mediate this relationship. Therefore, in this entry, we will first discuss the role of genetics in the etiology of criminal behavior, followed by evidence outlining the importance of biological factors.

Genetic epidemiological studies

Epidemiological evidence that genetic factors contribute to criminal behavior come from three sources: family, twin, and adoption studies. The limitation of family studies is the inability to separate the genetic and environmental sources of variation. Therefore, given the limited utility of family studies to separate issues of nature versus nurture, this section will focus on two other epidemiological research designs that are better equipped to test for genetic effects.

Twin studies. Twin studies support the contention that a heritable trait may increase risk for criminal behavior. Twin studies compare the rate of criminal behavior of twins who are genetically identical or monozygotic twins (MZ) with twins who are not, or dizygotic twins (DZ) in order to assess the role of genetic and environmental influences. To the extent that the similarity observed in MZ twins is greater than that in DZ twins, genetic influences may be implicated.

The twin design, however, does present some problems to this interpretation. The use of twin studies to test questions of heritablilty are limited in that it is a rare occurrence for the twins to be reared in separate environments. Moreover, Dalgaard and Kringlen suggest that the greater similarity of MZ twins may be attributed to their shared environmental experiences. In line with this hypothesis, Carey (1992) suggests that MZ twins may imitate one another more than DZ twins, and that this phenomenon could lead to an overestimation of heritability. Consequently, any review of twin studies must keep these limitations in mind.

Earlier twin studies reported considerable variations in the pairwise concordance rates (among monozygotic twins from 100 percent to 25 percent and in dizygotic twins from 81 percent to 0 percent). Several methodological flaws in earlier twin studies made it difficult to draw conclusions regarding genetic liability to criminal behavior. First, the operational definition of "criminal behavior" varied from mild incidental offenses to long-term incarceration. A potentially more serious methodological concern is that, with the exception of Dalgaard and Kringlen's study and the twin study that follows, all other twin samples suffered from biased samples.

Using an unselected sample of 3,586 twin pairs in Denmark, Christiansen reported 52 percent of the monozygotic twins were (probandwise) concordant for criminal behavior whereas only 22 percent of the dizygotic twins were (probandwise) concordant for criminal behavior. A marked increase of probandwise concordance for criminal behavior among monozygotic twins suggests that the MZ twins inherit some biological charactcristic(s) that increases their joint risk for criminal involvement.

Results from more recent twin studies are largely in agreement with results obtained from earlier twin studies. Variability in criteria for criminal behavior and sample composition does not appear to change the genetic effect, an outcome which suggests that criminal behavior and correlates of antisocial behavior (i.e., antisocial symptom counts, conduct disorder) may be genetically mediated. The twin design, as discussed earlier, is limited in that the assumption of equal environments is often violated. Studies comparing the concordancc ratcs in MZ twins reared apart can avoid this problem, but it is difficult to obtain such subjects. Christiansen has noted that several of the earlier twin studies had cases in which a set of monozygotic twins were raised in separate environments; these preliminary data suggest that studying MZ twins reared apart may be an important behavioral genetics tool to investigate the etiology of criminal behavior. To the present authors' knowledge, only one modern twin study has employed this type of research design to test whether criminal behavior may be genetically mediated.

Twins reared apart.   Grove and others investigated the concordance of antisocial problems, as measured by the Diagnostic Interview Schedule (DIS), among a sample of thirty-two sets of monozygotic twins reared apart (MZA) who were adopted by nonrelatives shortly after birth. Because this was a nonclinical sample, very few subjects met Diagnostic and Statistical Manual-III criteria for antisocial personality. To remedy this limitation, symptoms that contribute to the overall DSM-III diagnoses were counted to assess for subclinical manifestations of antisocial problems. Grove found substantial overlap between the genetic influences for both childhood conduct disorders (correlation of .41) and adult antisocial behaviors (correlation of .28). Although these findings are based on a small number of subjects, the Grove findings are congruent with the findings from other twin studies and extend the twin literature by evaluating MZ twins raised in separate environments.

Adoption studies.   Another epidemiological design that may more cleanly parcel out most environmental effects is the adoption design. Adoption studies provide a natural experiment to test the existence and strength of inherited predispositions. Adoptees are separated at birth from their biological parents. Thus, similarities between the adoptee and biological parents can be regarded as estimates of genetic influences, while similarities between the adoptee and the adoptive parents may be thought of as estimates of environmental influences. Moreover, the adoption design allows for the assessment of interaction effects between environmental and genetic influences. Adoption studies have been carried out in three different countries: the United States, Sweden, and Denmark.

Iowa.   The first adoption study to explore the genetic transmission of criminal behavior was carried out in Iowa by Crowe. The sample consisted of fifty-two adoptees (including twenty-seven males) born between 1925 and 1956 to a group of forty-one incarcerated female offenders. A group of control adoptees were matched for age, sex, race, and approximate age at the time of adoption. Seven of the fifty-two adoptees sustained a criminal conviction as adults whereas only one of the control adoptees had a conviction. Since these adoptees were separated from their incarcerated mothers at birth, this tends to implicate a heritable component to antisocial behavior.

A separate series of adoption studies carried out in Iowa by Cadoret and colleagues (1980, 1983, 1985, 1987, 1995) have supported Crowe's original findings. These independent replications lend support to the notion that criminal behavior may have important genetic influences.

Several characteristics of the Iowa adoption studies carried out by Cadoret and colleagues should be noted. First, the genetic factors of interest, namely the antisocial status of the biological parents, were ascertained from "poorly maintained adoption agency records" or incomplete prison and hospital records. Second, a high refusal rate of adoptee interviews introduces the possibility that adoptees who consented to be interviewed may be qualitatively different from those who declined. Third, in two of the Cadoret studies, antisocial status of the adoptees was determined from telephone interviews (1987, 1995). In short, what is needed is the use of criminal national registries that would provide a better opportunity to assess lifetime, cumulative records for all subjects (both biological and adoptive parents and adoptees). This condition is difficult if not impossible to meet in the United States. Such requirements, however, have been met by adoption studies from two Scandinavian countries, Denmark and Sweden.

Sweden. Bohman examined the criminality and alcoholism rates among 2,324 Swedish adoptees and their biological parents, as determined by a check with national criminal and alcohol registries. Preliminary findings led Bohman to conclude prematurely that biological fathers who were criminal only (without alcohol abuse) were not more likely to have criminal, adopted-away children than biological fathers with no criminal record (12.5 percent vs. 12 percent). He did not differentiate between criminality alone in the biological fathers and criminality accompanied by alcohol abuse in the biological fathers. Further statistical analysis reveals that when these two groups are separated, there are significantly more criminal-only sons (without alcohol abuse) of criminal-only biological fathers than there are criminal-only sons of other fathers (8.9 percent vs. 4.9 percent, p (significance level) < 0.05).

One of the chief findings to emerge from the Swedish Adoption Study is evidence for a distinct, highly heritable form of alcoholism and criminality that may be transmitted from father to son (Cloninger et al., 1981). Cross-fostering analyses revealed the emergence of two distinct subtypes of alcoholism that could be differentiated based upon genetic and environmental influences. The first subtype proposed by Cloninger, Type I alcoholism, appears to be affected by environmental factors, such as the socioeconomic status of the adoptive parents. Type I alcoholics were found to have a late onset of alcohol abuse (i.e., after age twenty-five) and did not engage in criminal behavior.

Type II alcoholism, in contrast, appears to have a strong genetic component. Type II alcoholics are typically males with alcohol and criminal registrations. The biological fathers of these Type II alcoholics had an early onset (i.e., before age twenty-five) of recurrent alcoholism and criminality (sample size, n = 36). Environmental factors, such as low socioeconomic status and alcoholism in the adoptive parents, were not found to influence the frequency of Type II alcoholism. Moreover, the male adoptees' risk of Type II alcoholism was not increased by an interaction between genetic and environmental factors. These findings were later replicated in independent adoption studies carried out in Sweden by Sigvardsson and others (1996) and in a reanalysis of the Danish Adoption Project (Tehrani and Mednick, forthcoming). Although the utility of the Type I, Type II paradigm in clinical samples has received mixed support, these data suggest the existence of a highly heritable form of criminality and alcoholism that is genetically transmitted from father to son.

Denmark. Mednick, Gabrielli, and Hutchins carried out a study of the genetic influence on criminal behavior using an extensive data set consisting of 14,427 Danish adoptees (ranging in age from twenty-nine to fifty-two years) and both sets of biological and adoptive parents. They found that adopted-away sons had an elevated risk of having a court conviction if their biological parent, rather than their adoptive parent, had one or more court convictions. If neither the biological nor adoptive parents were convicted, 13.5 percent of the sons were convicted. If the adoptive parents were convicted and the biological parents were not, this figure only increased to 14.7 percent. When examining sons whose biological parents were convicted and adoptive parents remained law-abiding, however, 20 percent of the adoptees had one or more criminal convictions. Moreover, as the number of biological parental convictions increased, the rate of adoptees with court convictions increased.

There were cases where a biological father, mother, or both contributed more than one child to this population. Some of these children, either full or half-siblings, were placed in different adoptive homes. There were 126 male-male half-sibling pairs placed in separate adoptive homes. Of the 126 male-male half-sibling pairs in the study 31 pairs had at least one member of the sibship convicted. Of these 31 pairs, 4 pairs were concordant for convictions (concordance rate = 12.9 percent for half-siblings). The study yielded 40 male-male full-sibling pairs who were adopted into separate homes. Fifteen pairs had at least one member of the sibship sustain a criminal conviction; of these 15 pairs, 3 pairs were concordant for convictions (concordance rate = 20 percent for full siblings). Although the numbers are small, these findings suggest that as the level of genetic relationship increases, the level of concordance increases.

These data, obtained from three different countries and in different laboratories, lend support to the notion that criminal behavior appears to have a strong genetic component. In addition, the combination of genetic *and* environmental factors, or gene-environment interactions, has also been the subject of investigation. Accordingly, several adoption studies have noted significant interactive effects when environmental variables are also taken into account.

Gene-environment interactions

The importance of gene-environment interactions are illustrated in several adoption studies. For example, the effects of socioeconomic status (SES) on inhibiting or promoting the expression of the genetic vulnerability to criminality have been examined in two large-scale adoption studies, the Danish and Swedish adoption studies. Cloninger and others (1982) and Van Dusen and others (1983) have reported that adoptive parent SES appears to interact with genetic vulnerability for criminality. Specifically, the risk of criminality among adoptees of criminal biological parents was significantly reduced if they were adopted into middle to high SES adoptive homes. Conversely, low adoptive parent socioeconomic status interacted with criminality in the biological parents to increase the adoptee's risk of criminality.

Other adverse environmental influences, such as adoptive parental registrations for alcohol and crime, and later age of placement, were found to interact with the genetic risk for criminal behavior. Crowe (1975) found that adoptees who had a criminal biological mother and spent longer time in an orphanage or foster placement had the highest rates of criminal conviction. In a separate series of adoption studies carried out by Cadoret and colleagues, evidence for the importance of gene-environment interactions in the development of antisocial problems in adoptees has been presented. Cadoret and others (1983) reported in a Missouri adoption sample (n = 108) that adoptees with an alcoholic or antisocial biological parent who were placed in an adoptive home at a later age had the highest rate of adolescent antisocial problems. In an Iowan adoption study (n = 246 male and female adoptees), Cadoret and Cain found that the presence of alcohol or antisocial symptoms in the biological parents interacted with adverse environmental conditions, such as the presence of alcohol and antisocial problems in the adoptive parents, time spent in foster care, and divorced status of the adoptive parents, to produce a marked increase in the incidence of adolescent antisocial behavior. Cadoret and others (1995) reported that a biological background of antisocial prob-

lems interacted with adverse environmental conditions, such as the presence of a psychiatric condition in the adoptive family, separation or divorce of the adoptive parents, adoptive parent alcohol or drug abuse, to increase the risk of childhood conduct disorder and adolescent aggressivity. Taken together, these studies demonstrate the utility of the gene-environmental model to our understanding of the etiological correlates of criminal behavior.

Sex differences in genetic liability to criminality

There is some evidence to suggest that genetic and environmental factors may differentially contribute to the risk of criminality for males and females. It has been hypothesized that females who engage in criminal activity may have a stronger genetic propensity for this type of behavior than males (Sellin). Evidence for this contention is provided by two independent adoption studies in which female property offenders had a much higher percentage of biological parents who were property offenders than did male adoptees (Sigvardsson et al.; Baker et al.). This finding is supportive of the contention that females are faced with more social pressures to remain law-abiding than males and therefore females who violate these social norms may have an added genetic push toward these behaviors.

Taken together, twin and adoption studies provide convincing evidence that criminal behavior, in both males and females, may have genetic influences. Establishing a heritable component to criminal behavior begs the question as to whether serious forms of criminal behavior, such as violent criminal offending in particular, may also be a heritable trait. Perhaps impulsive violent acts may reflect a genetic predisposition toward this type of behavior while property offending may be driven more by economic or social factors.

Is there a genetic liability to violence?

Twin and adoption studies have been employed to address this question, yielding mixed results. Relying on criminal arrest data, Cloninger and Gottesman reanalyzed the twin data collected by Christiansen and grouped subjects as either violent offenders or property offenders. Heritability for property offenses was found to be .78 while heritability for violent offenses was .50. Although the genetic effect for property offenses was greater than for violent offenses, the data suggest that violent offenses, as assessed by official crime statistics, may also have a heritable underlying component.

Two independent adoption studies, however, have failed to provide support for the hypothesis that violence is a heritable trait (Bohman et al.; Mednick et al.). The largest adoption study to date was carried out in Denmark by the present authors' research group (n = 14,427). Mednick, Gabrielli, and Hutchins had previously reported a significant relationship between the number of criminal convictions in the biological parent and the number of convictions in the adoptees. Subsequent statistical analyses revealed that this relationship held significantly for property offenses, but not significantly for violent offenses.

Perhaps a genetic predisposition toward violence may exist in the presence of some other unidentified mediator. A study in Oregon provided an important clue in that mental illness, particularly severe mental illness, may be genetically related to violence. In a classic study, Heston followed up a sample of forty-seven offspring born to schizophrenic mothers and compared them to a group of matched controls from the same orphanage. These offspring were separated from their mothers shortly after birth and placed in foster care or orphanages. Heston was primarily interested in determining if adopted-away offspring were at increased risk of becoming schizophrenic themselves. The findings supported the original hypothesis, as five of the forty-seven offspring became schizophrenic. An interesting finding is that an even greater number of the adopted-away offspring of schizophrenic biological mothers actually had been incarcerated for violent offenses. Eleven (23.4 percent) of the adoptees had been incarcerated for violent offenses. Since these offspring were not raised by their schizophrenic mothers, this suggested the possibility that mental illness and criminal violence may share a common genetic basis.

With the Heston study in mind, Moffit investigated the role of parental mental illness in the emergence of violent offending among the Danish adopted-away sons. When only the criminal behavior of the biological parents is considered, she found no increase in violent offending in the adoptees. A significant increase in the rate of violent offending is noted only among offspring whose biological parents were severely criminal (typically the biological father) and had been hospitalized one or more times for a psychiatric condition (typically the biological mother).

These findings suggest that a biological background positive for mental disorders appears to be associated with an increased risk of violent offending in the children. Other disorders in the biological parents may also increase the risk of violent offending in the adopted-away offspring. One such disorder that may elevate the risk of violent offending in children is the presence of alcoholism in the biological parents.

The genetic link between violence and alcoholism

Recent molecular genetics studies report that a gene related to the serotonin system may be associated with increased risk for the co-occurrence of violence and alcoholism. These efforts have been fueled by the robust finding that alcoholism and violence, in humans and nonhuman primates, may be related to serotonergic dysregulation (Virkkunen et al., 1989; Higley et al., 1992). In a reanalysis of data from the Swedish Adoption Study, Carey (1993) noted that paternal violence is linked to alcoholism in adopted-away males.

The present authors are currently investigating the possible genetic link between violence and alcoholism (Tehrani and Mednick, forthcoming). Within the context of the Danish Adoption Cohort, we found that alcoholic biological parents were twice as likely to have a violent adopted-away son than nonalcoholic parents. In contrast, the risk for property offenses in adopted-away sons of biological parents with alcohol problems was not significantly elevated. The significant genetic effect was specific to violent offenders. Moreover, violent offending, but not property offending, among the biological parents was associated with severe alcohol-related problems in the adopted-away males. These findings from our adoption cohort are in agreement with data from the Swedish adoption study, and support the overall interpretations from recent molecular genetic studies.

Genetic factors, as determined by a biological background positive for criminality or mental illness, may represent one pathway through which the risk for a certain negative outcome is conferred. Our research group has also explored the role of prenatal factors in the development of criminal behavior.

Prenatal factors

Another pathway that has been investigated as a potential determinant in the etiology of violence is prenatal factors. The prenatal period presents a nine-month window in which the developing fetus may be exposed to a variety of stressors and agents. There are reasons to suspect that these stressors or agents may operate differently depending on when they are introduced. Recently, an increasing amount of attention has been paid to pinpointing the gestational periods of highest risk for negative outcomes. One such teratogen that has been extensively investigated is the timing of maternal influenza exposure in relation to negative outcomes in the exposed fetuses.

Maternal prenatal influenza. In Helsinki, our research group reported that second-trimester maternal influenza significantly increased the risk of adult schizophrenia (Mednick et al., 1988) and major affective disorder (Machon and Mednick) in the exposed fetuses. The data have been replicated in numerous studies in various countries.

The "second-trimester schizophrenics" were interviewed and found to differ from non-influenza exposed schizophrenics in that their symptom picture was dominated by suspiciousness and delusions (Machon and Mednick). As both Volavka and Hodgins suggest, delusional paranoid individuals are characterized by elevated levels of violent behavior. Mednick, Machon, and Huttenen hypothesized that a common etiological link between schizophrenia and violence may be a disturbance in fetal neural development in the second trimester.

Accordingly, Mednick, Machon, and Huttenen (1996) hypothesized that maternal influenza during the second trimester was associated with an increased risk for violent offending, but not property offending among exposed fetuses. To test this hypothesis, the Finnish criminal register was searched for all of the Helsinki residents born in the nine months after the 1957 influenza epidemic. The results indicated that property crime was not significantly associated with period of exposure to the influenza virus. Individuals who had been exposed to the influenza virus during the second trimester of gestation, however, were significantly more likely to have a criminal conviction for violence than individuals who were exposed to the influenza virus during the first or third trimesters of gestation or not exposed to the virus at all.

The impact that the influenza virus has on fetal neural development, either negative or neutral, appears contingent upon the timing of the virus, relative to the stage of gestation. It may also be difficult if not impossible to identify a specific month or trimester associated with the highest risk of negative outcome in cases where the teratogen is present throughout development, or when the long-term effects of the teratogen may linger and have residual effects throughout the period of gestation. Introduction of some types of teratogens, such as illegal drugs, alcohol, and nicotine, may represent substances that, regardless of when they are introduced, could potentially be harmful to the exposed fetus. Much attention has recently been paid to the association between maternal smoking during pregnancy and negative behavioral outcomes among exposed fetuses. These negative outcomes include impulsivity and attention problems. Prenatal nicotine exposure has also been associated with criminal offending.

Maternal prenatal smoking. An investigation conducted in Finland by Rantakallio and colleagues, examined the criminal records of 5,966 members of a birth cohort and found that prenatal maternal smoking predicted to criminal offending at age twenty two. These findings persisted after controlling for the effects of social variables such as socioeconomic status. With these recent studies in mind, Brennan, Grekin, and Mednick investigated the association between maternal smoking and criminal violence using a Danish birth cohort of 4,129 males. It was hypothesized that maternal smoking would be related to an increased risk of violent offending among males. One of the major strengths of the study was that maternal prenatal smoking was assessed through interviews during the pregnancy as opposed to retrospectively. Moreover, the study relied on the Danish criminal register to identify cases where the individuals were arrested for property or violent offenses.

The findings indicate a linear dose-response relationship between the number of cigarettes the mother smoked on a daily basis in her third trimester of pregnancy and the percent of offspring who became violent offenders. This relationship persists despite controlling for various potential confounds such as socioeconomic status, parental psychiatric hospitalization, and father's criminal history.

The recent finding that maternal smoking during pregnancy is linked to criminal violence in exposed offspring, along with Rantakallio's study, suggests the possibility that chemicals contained in cigarette smoke may alter fetal brain neurochemistry. Moreover, exposure to cigarette smoke prenatally may increase risk for asphyxia.

Biological factors

Biological influences, including psychophysiological and biochemical measures are thought to mediate the relationship between genetics and criminal behavior. Psychophysiological measures, including electroencephalogram (EEG) activity, heart rate (HR), event-related potentials (ERP), and skin conductance (SC), have been identified as potential biological markers that may help to distinguish criminals from noncriminals. This literature has been thoroughly reviewed by Raine.

Other, more direct measures of biological functioning, may provide additional information regarding the role of biological factors in the etiology of criminal behavior. One such factor that has been widely investigated since the last edition of this volume is the role of serotonergic dysregulation in criminal behavior.

Serotonin

Serotonin (5-HT; 5-hydroxytryptamine), a neurotransmitter produced by the raphe nuclei, is thought to be involved in the modulation of impulsivity. Consequently, serotonergic dysregulation may result in a decreased ability to inhibit certain externalizing behavioral patterns and may reflect a deficit in behavioral inhibition. It seems reasonable to hypothesize that violent criminal behavior, an outcome often marked by behavioral disinhibition, may be linked to some type of dysregulation of the serotonin system. A review of biochemical studies that have investigated the role of low serotonin concentrations in the emergence of criminal behavior follows. These studies have primarily examined levels of the cerebrospinal fluid (CSF) 5-HT metabolite, 5-hydroxyindolacetic acid, CSF 5-HIAA.

Recently, an impressive body of evidence, primarily obtained from biochemical studies, has accumulated regarding the role of the serotonin system in criminal behavior. Linnoila and colleagues have reported that within the context of a Finnish forensic population, violent offenders and impulsive fire-setters evidenced lower mean CSF 5-HIAA than normal controls (Virkkunen et al., 1989). This seems to suggest that serotonin

dysfunction may play an etiologic role in more severe forms of antisocial behavior, such as violent offending. These studies have been extended to investigate whether serotonin levels can differentiate offender populations based upon type of the index offense and the presence or absence of alcohol abuse and violence in first-degree family members.

Virkkunen and others (1996) report that a combination of paternal violence and alcoholism, as measured by questionnaires to the first-degree relatives, was associated with low CSF 5-HIAA concentration levels in the male subjects, irrespective of subgroup classification (i.e., impulsive vs. nonimpulsive). The authors suggest that a familial trait may be associated with early-onset alcohol abuse, violent and impulsive offending, and low CSF 5-HIAA concentrations.

Subjects who had committed violent crimes during the 4.5-year follow-up period had lower CSF levels compared to nonrecidivists. Moreover, violent recidivists were more likely to have experienced paternal absence than nonrecidivists, suggesting the importance of both biological and environmental factors in the prediction of recidivistic violent offending. Due to the highly selective nature of the sample, results must be interpreted cautiously. A significant relationship between aggressiveness, parental absence, and low levels of serotonin was also noted in a study of nonhuman primates (Higley et al., 1993).

Virkkunen and others (1994) reported that impulsive violent offenses and impulsive fire-setters were found to evidence lower CSF 5-HIAA concentration levels; violent alcohol offenders whose index crime was not found to be impulsive had normal CSF 5-HIAA concentrations. The emphasis on the index offense as opposed to the qualitative nature of the cumulative criminal history, however, may be interpreted as a weakness of this study. On the basis of these findings, Virkkunen and colleagues propose that low serotonin may be a biological marker specific to impulsive violent offending accompanied by alcoholism. These conclusions, however, are drawn from a subject pool of forensic patients, representing a sample of heavily violent individuals. Within the context of a community sample, Hibbeln and others found that relative to the nonviolent control group, the violent group evidenced significantly lower concentration levels of CSF 5-HIAA.

One of the limitations of the biochemical studies is that CSF metabolites reflect presynaptic neurotransmitter activity; therefore, it is not known what is occurring at the postsynaptic level. Apart from the lack of specificity in information, efforts to investigate the role of serotonin in behavioral outcomes in humans have been challenging due to the fact that CSF levels of serotonin are collected via a lumbar puncture. More importantly, examination of the CSF does not provide information about the role of specific brain regions. Results from neuropsychological measures, for example, have consistently found neurological deficits to be present among antisocial persons than in nonantisocial persons. The limitation of neuropsychological indices, however, is that they present an indirect measure of brain functioning. Other, more recent techniques, have been applied to uncover the structural and functional properties of the brain in relation to criminal behavior. Brain imagining techniques, for example, have received an increasingly prominent role in the study of criminal behavior. These recent advances may in fact represent an important sector of the future of biological research in the field of criminal behavior.

Future directions: brain imaging and criminal behavior

The field of neuroscience, through the use of brain imaging techniques, has provided illuminating data on the etiology of severe mental disorders, including depression and schizophrenia. These recent technological innovations are computerized tomography (CT) and magnetic resonance imaging (MRI), which provide information on brain structure, and positron emission tomography (PET) and regional cerebral blood flow (RCBF), which provide information on brain functioning. The advances and disadvantages of each method are thoroughly discussed in Raine (1993). These methods have recently been applied to the study of criminal behavior, lending support to the theory that criminal behavior may be associated with brain dysfunction.

To date, over 20 studies using these techniques have been published (see Raine, 1996). Taken together, these studies suggest that frontal and temporal dysfunction may be associated with violent behavior. The link between frontal dysfunction and impulsive, violent criminality is consistent with the notion that frontal lobe damage may be associated with a variety of correlates of violent behavior, including impulsivity, behavioral disinhibition, and poor concentration (Raine, 1993). It should be noted that these brain abnormalities may be caused by genetic, biological, or environmental agents. Criminals may be more likely to be involved in physical fights than noncriminals, and sustain head injuries as a result. Frontal lobe damage may also be attributed to birth or delivery complications, for example. Another concern relates to the issue of timing. Are structural and functional deficits present prior to the onset of criminal behavior, or are these changes in the brain triggered after the individual has begun their criminal career? To our knowledge, no study has been conducted examining pre-morbid measures of brain structure and function among criminals. Despite these issues, it is likely that our understanding of the biological and genetic underpinnings of criminal behavior will be greatly advanced through continued developments in brain imaging research.

Conclusions

1. Twin and adoption studies lend support to the notion that criminal behavior has important genetic influences. The role of genetics in violent offending, however, is less clear. Our research, along with other epidemiological studies and molecular genetic investigations, have shown that violence may be genetically related to mental illness and to alcoholism.

2. Violent offending, but not property offending, may be associated with a disturbance in fetal development. We have demonstrated that prenatal disturbances, such as exposure to the influenza virus during the second trimester of gestation and maternal smoking during pregnancy, is linked to offspring violent offending. These data suggest the possibility that the introduction of some type of teratogen during gestation may alter normal fetal development.

3. Lower levels of serotonin have been found to distinguish criminals from noncriminals in both forensic and community samples. Serotonergic dysregulation appears to be specific to violent offenders who have committed impulsive crimes.

4. Technological advances, such as the use of brain imaging, will undoubtedly provide exciting new data on the biological underpinnings of criminal behavior. The data thus far suggest that frontal lobe deficits may be

marked among violent offenders. Continued efforts to pinpoint specific brain regions associated with an increased risk in violent offending will advance our understanding of the etiology of violent criminal behavior.

JASMINE A. TEHRANI
SARNOFF A. MEDNICK

See also DIMINSHED CAPACITY; EXCUSE: INSANITY; INTELLIGENCE AND CRIME; MENTALLY DISORDERED OFFENDERS; PREDICTION OF CRIME AND RECIDIVISM; PSYCHOPATHY; SCIENTIFIC EVIDENCE; VIOLENCE.

BIBLIOGRAPHY

BAKER, LAURA A.; MACK, WENDY; MOFFITT, TEMI E.; and MEDNICK, SARNOFF A. "Sex Differences in Property Crime in a Danish Adoption Cohort." *Behavior Genetics* 19 (1987): 355–370.

BOHMAN, MICHAEL. "Some Genetic Aspects of Alcoholism and Criminality." *Archives of General Psychiatry* 35 (1978): 269–276.

BOHMAN, MICHAEL; CLONINGER, C. ROBERT; SIGVARDSSON, SOREN; and VON KNORRING, ANNE LIS. "Predisposition to Petty Criminality in Swedish Adoptees." *Archives of General Psychiatry* 39 (1982): 1233–1241.

BRENNAN, PATRICIA A.: GREKIN, EMILY R.; and MEDNICK, SARNOFF A. "Maternal Smoking during Pregnancy and Adult Male Criminal Outcomes." *Archives of General Psychiatry* 56 (1999): 215–219.

CADORET, REMI J., and CAIN, COLLEEN. "Sex Differences in Predictors of Antisocial Behavior in Adoptees." *Archives of General Psychiatry* 37 (1980): 1171–1775.

CADORET, REMI J.; CAIN, COLLEEN; and CROWE, R. R. "Evidence for Gene-Environment Interaction in the Development of Adolescent Antisocial Behavior." *Behavior Genetics* 13 (1983): 301–310.

CADORET, REMI J.; O'GORMAN, THOMAS W.; TROUGHTON, ED; and HEYWOOD, ELLEN. "Alcoholism and Antisocial Personality: Interrelationships, Genetic and Environmental Factors." *Archives of General Psychiatry* 42 (1985): 161–167.

CADORET, REMI J.; TROUGHTON, ED; and O'GORMAN, THOMAS. "Genetic and Environmental Factors in Alcohol Abuse and Antisocial Personality." *Journal of Studies on Alcohol* 48 (1987): 1–8.

CADORET, REMI J.; YATES, WILLIAM R.; TROUGHTON, ED; WOODWORTH, GEORGE; and STEWART, MARK A. "Genetic-Environmental Interaction in the Genesis of Aggressivity and Conduct Disorders." *Archives of General Psychiatry* 52 (1995): 916–924.

CAREY, GREGORY. "Twin Imitation for Antisocial Behavior: Implications for Genetic and Family Environment Research." *Journal of Abnormal Psychology* 101 (1992): 18–25.

———. "Multivariate Genetic Relationships among Drug Abuse, Alcohol Abuse and Antisocial Personality." *Psychiatric Genetics* 3 (1993): 141.

CAREY, GREGORY, and GOLDMAN, DAVID. "The Genetic of Antisocial Behavior." In *The Handbook of Antisocial Behavior.* Edited by Stoff, D. M., Breiling, J., and Maser J. D. New York: John Wiley, 1996.

CHRISTIANSEN, KARL O. "A Preliminary Study of Criminality among Twins." In *Biological Bases of Criminal Behavior.* Edited by S. A. Mednick and K. O. Christiansen. New York: Gardener Press, 1997. Pages 89–108.

CLONINGER, C. ROBERT, and GOTTESMAN, IRVING. "Genetic and Environmental Factors in Antisocial Behavior Disorders." In *The Causes of Crime: New Biological Approaches.* Edited by S. A. Mednick, T. E. Moffit, and S. A. Stack. New York: Cambridge University Press, 1987.

CLONINGER, C. ROBERT; BOHMAN, MICHAEL; and SIGVARDSSON, SOREN. "Inheritance of Alcohol Abuse." *Archives of General Psychiatry* 38 (1981): 861–868.

CLONINGER, C. ROBERT; CHRISTIANSEN, KARL O.; REICH, THOMAS; and GOTTESMAN, IRVING I. "Implications of Sex Differences in the Prevalences of Antisocial Personality, Alcoholism, and Criminality for Familial Transmission." *Archives of General Psychiatry* 35 (1978): 941–951.

CLONINGER, C. ROBERT; SIGVARDSSON, SOREN; BOHMAN, MICHAEL; and VON KNORRING, ANNE LIS. "Predisposition to Petty Criminality in Swedish Adoptees. II. Cross-fostering Analysis of Gene-Environment Interaction." *Archives of General Psychiatry* 39 (1982): 1242–1247.

CROWE, RAYMOND R. "An Adoption Study of Antisocial Behavior." *Archives of General Psychiatry* 31 (1974): 785–791.

DALGAARD, OLE S., and KRINGLEN, EINAR A. "A Norwegian Twin Study of Criminality." *British Journal of Criminology* 16 (1976): 213–232.

GROVE, WILLIAM M.; ECKERT, E. D.; HESTON, L.; BOUCHARD, T. J.; SEGAL, NYAND; and LYKKEN, D. Y. "Heritability of Substance Abuse and Antisocial Behavior: A Study of Monozygotic Twins Reared Apart." *Biological Psychiatry* 27 (1990): 1293–1304.

HALLIKAINEN, TERO; SAITO, TAKUTA; LACHMAN, HERBERT M.; and VOLAVKA, JAN. "Association between Low Activity Serotonin Transporter Promoter Genotype with Habitual Impulsive Violent Behavior among Antisocial Early Alcoholics." *Molecular Psychiatry* 32 (1999): 432–438.

HEINZ, ANDRES; HIGLEY, J. DEE; GOREY, JULIA G.; SAUNDERS, RICHARD C.; JONES, DOUGLAS; HOMMER, DANIEL; ZAJICEK, KRISTIN; SOUMI, STEPHEN; LESCH, KLAUS-PETER; WEINBERGER, DANIEL; and LINNOILA, MARKKU. "In Vivo Association between Alcohol Intoxication, Aggression and Serotonin Transporter Availability in Nonohuman Primates." *American Journal of Psychiatry* 155 (1998): 1023–1028.

HESTON, LEE L. "Psychiatric Disorders in Foster-Home Reared Children of Schizophrenics." *British Journal of Psychiatry* 112 (1996): 819–825.

HIBBELN, J. R.; LINNOILA, M.; UMHAU, J. C.; RAWLINGS, R.; GEORGE, D. T.; and SALEM, N. "Essential Fatty Acids Predict Metabolites of Serotonin and Dopamine in Cerebrospinal Fluid among Healthy Control Subjects, and Early and Late-Onset Alcoholics." *Biological Psychiatry* 44 (1998): 235–242.

HIGLEY, J. DEE; THOMPSON, W.; CHAMPOUX, M.; GOLDMAN, D.; HAERT, M. F.; KRAEMER, G. W.; SCANLAN, J. M.; SUOMU, S. J.; and LINNOILA, M. "Paternal and Maternal Genetic and Environmental Contributions to Cerebrospinal Fluid Monoamine Metabolites in Rhesus Monkeys." *Archives of General Psychiatry* 50 (1993): 615–662.

LAPPALAINEN, JAAKKO; LONG, JEFFREY C.; EGGERT, MONICA; OZAKI, NORIO; ROBIN, ROBERT W.; BROWN, GERALD L.; NAUKKARINEN, HANNU; VIRKKUNEN, MATTI; LINNOILA, MARKKU; and GOLDMAN, DAVID. "Linkage of Antisocial Alcoholism to the Serotonin 5-HT1B Receptor Gene in 2 Populations." *Archives of General Psychiatry* 55 (1998): 989–994.

LYONS, MICHAEL J. "A Twin Study of Self-Reported Criminal Behavior." In *Genetics of Criminal and Antisocial Behavior*. Edited by C. Foundation. Chichester, U.K.: Wiley, 1996. Pages 61–69.

MACHON, RICARDO A., and MEDNICK, SARNOFF A. "Adult Schizophrenia and Early Neurodevelopmental Disturbances." In *Confrontations Psychiatriques: Epidemiologie et Psychiatrie*, no. 35. Specia Rhone-Poulenc Rorer, 1994. Pages 189–215.

MACHON, RICARDO A.; MEDNICK, SARNOFF A.; and HUTTENEN, MATTI O. "Adult Major Affective Disorder following Prenatal Exposure to an Influenza Epidemic." *Archives of General Psychiatry* 54 (1997): 322–328.

MEDNICK, SARNOFF A.; GABRIELLI, WILLIAM F.; and HUTCHINGS, BARRY. "Genetic Influences in Criminal Convictions: Evidence From an Adoption Cohort." *Science* 224 (1984): 891–894.

MEDNICK, SARNOFF A.; MACHON, RICARDO A.; HUTTUNEN, MATTI O.; and BARR, CHRISTOPHER E. "Influenza and Schizophrenia: Helsinki vs. Edinburgh." *Archives of General Psychiatry* 47 (1990): 875–876.

MEDNICK, SARNOFF A.; MACHON, RICARDO A.; HUTTUNEN, MATTI O.; and BONNET, D. "Adult Schizophrenia following Prenatal Exposure to an Influenza Epidemic." *Archives of General Psychiatry* 45 (1988): 189–192.

MEDNICK, SARNOFF A.; MACHON, RICARDO A.; and HUTTENEN, MATTI. "Second Trimester Influenza Virus Predicts to Violent but not Property Offending." In TEHRANI, JASMINE A.; BRENNAN, PATRICIA A.; HODGINS, SHELEIGH; and MEDNICK, SARNOFF A. "Mental Illness and Criminal Violence." *Social Psychiatry and Psychiatric Epidemiology* 33 (1998): 81–85.

MOFFIT, TEMI E. "Parental Mental Disorder and Offspring Criminal Behavior: An Adoption Study." *Psychiatry: Interpersonal and Biological Processes* 50 (1987): 346–360.

RAINE, ADRIAN. *The Psychopathology of Crime: Criminal Behavior as a Clinical Disorder*. San Diego, Calif.: Academic Press, 1993.

———. "Antisocial Behavior and Psychophysiology: A Biosocial Perspective and a Prefrontal Dysfunctional Hypothesis." Edited by D. M. Stoff, J. Breiling, and J. D. Maser. New York: Wiley, 1996.

RANTAKALLIO, P.; LAARA, E.; ISOHANNI, M.; and MOILANEN, I. "Maternal Smoking during Pregnancy and Delinquency of the Offspring: An Association Without Causation?" *International Journal of Epidemiology* 1992. 21, 1106–1113.

SIGVARDSSON, SOREN; BOHMAN, MICHAEL; and CLONINGER, C. ROBERT. "Replication of the Stockholm Adoption Study of Alcoholism." *Archives of General Psychiatry* 53 (1996): 681–687.

SIGVARDSSON, SOREN; CLONINGER, C. ROBERT; BOHMAN, MICHAEL; and VON KNORRING, ANNE LIS. "Predisposition to Petty Criminality in Swedish Adoptees. III. Sex Differences and Validation of the Male Typology." *Archives of General Psychiatry* 39 (1982): 1248–1253.

SLUTSKE, WENDY S.; HEATH, ANDREW C.; DINWIDDIE, S. H.; and MADDEN, PAMELA. "Modeling

Genetic and Environmental Influences in the Etiology of Conduct Disorder: A Study of 2,682 Adult Twin Pairs." *Journal of Abnormal Psychology* 106 (1996): 266–279.

TEHRANI, JASMINE A.; and MEDNICK, SARNOFF A. "Genetic Cross-relationships between Criminal Behavior and Severe Alcohol-related Problems." (Manuscript submitted.)

VAN DUSEN, KAREN T.; MEDNICK, SARNOFF A.; GABRIELLI, WILLIAM F.; and HUTCHINGS, BARRY. "Social Class and Crime in an Adoption Cohort." *The Journal of Criminal Law and Criminology* 74 (1983): 249–261.

VIRKKUNEN, MATTI; DE JONG, JUDITH; BARTKO, F.; GOODWIN, FREDRICK; and LINNOILA, MARKKU. "Relationship of Psychobiological Variables to Recidivism in Violent Offenders and Impulsive Fire Setters." *Archives of General Psychiatry* (1989): 600–604.

VIRKKUNEN, MATTI; EGGERT, MONIKA; RAWLINGS, ROBERT; and LINNOILA, MARKKU. "A Prospective Follow-up Study of Alcoholic Violent Offenders and Fire Setters." *Archives of General Psychiatry* 53 (1996): 523–529.

VIRKKUNEN, MATTI; RAWLINGS, ROBERT; TOKOLA, RIITA; POLAND, RUSSELL; GUIDOTTI, ALESSANDRO; NEMEROFF, CHARLES; BISSETTE, GARTH; KALOGERAS, KONSTANTINE; KARONEN, SIRKKA-LIISA; and LINNOILA, MARKKU. "CSF Biochemistries, Glucose Metabolism, and Diurnal Activity Rhythms in Alcoholic, Violent Offenders, Fire Setters and Healthy Volunteers." *Archives of General Psychiatry* 51 (1994): 20–27.

VOLAVKA, JAN. *Neurobiology of Violence.* Washington D.C.: American Psychiatric Press, 1995.

WOLFGANG, MARVIN; FIGLIO, R. M.; and SELLIN, T. *Delinquency in a Birth Cohort.* Chicago: University of Chicago Press, 1972.

CRIME CAUSATION: ECONOMIC THEORIES

The roots of crime are diverse and a discipline like economics, predicated on rational behavior, may be at something of a disadvantage in explaining a phenomenon largely viewed as irrational. The foray by economists into this area is relatively recent, dating back to Gary Becker's pathbreaking contribution in 1968. As part of a larger model designed to explore optimal criminal justice policy, he developed the "supply of offense" function, which indicates the factors affecting the number of crimes a rational individual commits. Since then there has been much progress in both expanding on this important relationship and utilizing it for more theoretically grounded analyses of criminal behavior.

A recent survey suggests that three general issues are of central concern in the economics of crime literature: the effects of incentives on criminal behavior, how decisions interact in a market-setting, and the use of cost-benefit analysis to assess alternative policies to reduce crime (see Freeman, 1999a). In this entry we will focus on the role of incentives on criminal behavior.

Crime is a major activity for young males. Crime is like basketball; it's a young man's game. As one researcher has observed: "Actual rates of illegal behavior soar so high during adolescence that participation in delinquency appears to be a normal part of teen life" (Moffit, p. 675). By the age of eighteen possibly 90 percent of young males have participated in delinquent acts and approximately half have been arrested for non-traffic offenses by the time they are thirty. Only 50 to 60 percent of young females have been involved in delinquent acts by the time they are eighteen and less than 10 percent have been arrested by the age of thirty (Witte, 1997).

Explaining the secular trend in criminal participation rates in most industrialized economies is a difficult task. Many social scientists argue that crime is closely related to work, education, and poverty and that truancy, youth unemployment, and crime are by-products or even measures of social exclusion. "Blue-collar" criminals often have limited education and possess limited labor market skills. These characteristics partly explain the poor employment records and low legitimate earnings of most criminals. These sort of issues originally led economists to examine the relationship between wages and unemployment rates on crime. More recently economists have also considered the benefits and costs of educational programs to reduce crime.

A related question concerns the impact of sanctions. For example, does increased imprisonment lower the crime rate? How does the deterrent effect of formal sanctions arise? Although criminologists have been tackling such issues for many years, it is only recently that economists have entered the arena of controversy. This is not surprising given the high levels of crime and the associated allocation of public and private resources toward crime prevention. The expenditure on the criminal justice system (police, prisons, prosecution/defense, and courts) is a significant proportion of government budgets. In addition, firms and households are spending increasingly more on private security.

The incentive-based economic model of crime is a model of decision-making in risky situations. Economists analyze the way in which individual attitudes toward risk affect the extent of illegal behavior. In most of the early literature, the economic models of crime are single-period individual choice models. These models generally see the individual as deciding to allocate time with criminal activity as one possible use of time. A key feature is the notion of utility; judgments are made of the likely gain to be realized (the "expected utility") from a particular choice of action. Individuals are assumed to be rational decision-makers who engage in either legal or illegal activities according to the expected utility from each activity. An individual's participation in illegal activity is, therefore, explained by the opportunity cost of illegal activity (for example, earnings from legitimate work), factors that influence the returns to illegal activity (for example, detection and the severity of punishment), and by tastes and preferences for illegal activity.

Economists see criminal activity as being similar to paid employment in that it requires time and produces an income. Clearly, the dichotomy between either criminal activity or legal activity is an oversimplification. For example, individuals could engage in criminal activities while employed since they have greater opportunities to commit crime; similarly, some criminals may jointly supplement work income with crime income in order to satisfy their needs. A secondary problem with the economist's choice model, which was highlighted in our opening comments, is that young people are more likely to participate in crime long before they participate in the labor market. This observation raises questions about the appropriateness of the economic model of crime in explaining juvenile crime.

Economic models of criminal behavior have focused on sanction effects (e.g., deterrence issue) and the relationship between work and crime. In the main, these models have not directly addressed the role of education in offending. It could be argued that unemployment is the conduit through which other factors influence the crime rate. For example, poor educational attainment may be highly correlated with the incidence of crime. However, this may also be a key determinant of unemployment. Although educational variables have been included as covariates with crime rates, they have not received a great deal of attention in correlational studies.

The remainder of the entry is organized as follows. In the next section, we outline the economic model of crime; the section following considers two extensions to the basic theory; then a section provides a brief overview of the empirical evidence; the final section examines recent work on juvenile crime and education.

Economic model of criminal behavior: basic theory

As mentioned in the overview, the economic model of crime is a standard model of decision-making where individuals choose between criminal activity and legal activity on the basis of the expected utility from those acts. It is assumed that participation in criminal activity is the result of an optimizing individual responding to incentives. Among the factors that influence an individual's decision to engage in criminal activities are (1) the expected gains from crime relative to earnings from legal work; (2) the chance (risk) of being caught and convicted; (3) the extent of punishment; and (4) the opportunities in legal activities. Specifying an equation to capture the incentives in the criminal decision is a natural first step in most analyses of the crime as work models. The most important of these gives the relative rewards of legal and illegal activity. For example, the economic model sees the criminal as committing a crime if the expected gain from criminal activity exceeds the gain from legal activity, generally work.

Just as in benefit-cost analysis, when comparing alternative strategies, interest centers on the returns from one decision vis-à-vis returns from another decision. For example, a preference for crime over work implies the earnings gap between legal and illegal activities must rise when the probability of being caught and the severity of punishment increases. Attitudes toward risk are central to economic models of criminal choice. For example, if the individual is said to dislike risk (i.e., to be risk averse) then he will respond more to changes in the chances of being apprehended than to changes in the extent of punishment, other things being equal. Becker developed a comparative-static model that considered primarily the deterrent effect of the criminal justice system. As we will see, how individuals respond to deterrent and incapacitation effects of sanctions has generated considerable theoretical and empirical interest from economists.

Any reasonable economic model has crime dependent on (1) legal and illegal opportunities; (2) the chance of being caught; and (3) the extent of sentencing; in the terminology of Freeman (1999a), they are *intrinsically related*. Thus, severe sentencing and improvements in legal work opportunities of criminals must be expected jointly to reduce crime. Of course, this assumes that crime and work are determined by the same factors and that higher legitimate earnings increase the probability of working. Early literature applied static one-period time allocation models to analyze criminal behavior. In other words, crime and work are assumed to be substitute activities; if an individual allocates more time to work, he will commit less crime because he will have less time to do so. The basic economic model of crime is static or comparative static in economic jargon because it does not see the potential criminal as considering more than a single time period when making his decision.

Extensions of the basic model

The incentive-based model of crime has experienced significant theoretical and empirical developments. The model by Becker has been developed subsequently by Ehrlich (1973). Since at least Ehrlich there has been an awareness of a correspondence between any crime-work decision and time allocation. In the 1970s and 1980s, the influential contributions of Ehrlich (1975) and Witte (1980), among others, made this connection much more precise and the awareness more widespread. For example, Ehrlich allowed for three different criminal justice outcomes, whereas Witte utilized a model in which the time allocations between legal and illegal activities entered the utility function directly. See Schmidt and Witte for a survey of these first-generation economic models of crime.

Early studies of criminal behavior by economists can be criticized for being set in a static framework. Economic models of crime are typically estimated as static models, though there are many reasons to suspect dynamic effects matter, both theoretically through habit formation, interdependence of preferences, capital accumulation, addiction, peer group effects, and so on, and empirically through improvements in fit when lagged dependent variables or autocorrelated residuals are included in the model. Labor economists have long been interested in state dependence, the fact that activities chosen in the current period may be strongly affected by the individual's activities in the previous period (e.g., Heckman). Examples of state dependence in economic models of criminal behavior in-

clude: the effect of education today on future criminal activities; and the effect of crime in one period on future legitimate and criminal earnings. Becker and Murphy, Flinn, Grogger (1995), Nagin and Waldfogel, Tauchen and Witte, and Williams and Sickles exemplify attempts at describing a causal dynamic economic model of crime.

Flinn incorporates human capital formation in a time-allocation model. In his model, human capital is accumulated at work, not at school. Consequently, crime takes time away from work and hence diminishes the amount of human capital accumulated. The diminished human capital leads to lower future wages and hence less time spent working. Since crime and work are substitutes in his model, the decline in time allocated to work leads to increased participation in criminal activities.

Becker and Murphy build on consumer demand theory and develop a model of rational addiction. Their model relies on "adjacent complementarities" in consumption to produce habit formation. Under their model, the marginal utility of consuming a good that is an adjacent complement is higher if the good has been consumed in the previous period. They also incorporate myopia to explain why people become addicted to harmful goods.

Grogger estimates a distributed lag model to allow arrests and prosecution to affect both current and future labor market outcomes. Using data from the California Adult Criminal Justice Statistical System, he found that arrest effects on employment and earnings are moderate in magnitude and fairly short-lived. Nagin and Waldfogel consider the effects of criminality and conviction on the income and job stability of young male British offenders. Their analysis uses a panel data set assembled by David Farrington and Donald West as part of the Cambridge Study in Delinquent Development (CSDD). The authors present results which at first sight appear somewhat paradoxical. They find that conviction increases both the job instability and legal income of young offenders. To rationalize these results Nagin and Waldfogel outline a characterization of the labor market in which young men participate. The basic idea underlying the model is that young men have two types of jobs available to them—skilled and unskilled—where wage profiles are rising in the former (due to accumulation of human capital, training and experience) and flat in the latter (no training). If discounted wages are equalized across jobs, the unskilled wage would start above and end below skilled wage. Also, human capital theory suggests that job stability will be greater in skilled sector than in the unskilled sector. Given these predictions, and assuming that a criminal conviction adversely affects prospects of getting a skilled job, it is likely that conviction is associated with higher pay and higher job instability. Note that Nagin and Waldfogel found criminal activity without conviction had no significant effect on labor market performance. They conclude that this result implies stigma, rather than withdrawal from legal work, explains the effects of conviction.

Dynamics arising from the impact of private and social programs (e.g., police treatments in cases of domestic violence) have been dealt with by including the lag of the dependent variable (actual violence) and the latent variable (Tauchen and Witte). Tauchen and Witte use data from the Minneapolis Domestic Violence Experiment to determine how police treatments in cases of domestic violence (advising the couple, separating the individuals temporarily, or arresting the suspect) affect the couple's subsequent violence. Estimating a dynamic probit model for the probability of observing violence in the follow-up periods, the authors find that arrest is more effective than advising or short-term separation but that the differential effect is transitory.

In an interesting paper, Williams and Sickles provide an extension of Ehrlich (1973) by including an individual's social capital stock into his utility and earnings functions. Social capital, including things like reputation and social networks, is used as a proxy to account for the effect of social norms on an individual's decision to participate in crime. This assumes that the stigma associated with arrest depreciates an individual's social capital stock. Williams and Sickles clarify this point further by arguing that employment and marriage create a form of state dependence, which reduces the likelihood of criminal involvement. In other words, an individual with a family, job, or good reputation has more to lose if caught committing crimes than those without such attachments. Dynamics arise from current decisions affecting future outcomes through the social capital stock accumulation process. The main result is that criminals behave rationally in the sense that they account for future consequences of current period decisions.

A brief sketch of the empirical evidence on the supply of crime

The motivation behind most early applications of Becker's model was to examine the impact of legitimate labor market experiences (e.g., unemployment) and sanctions on criminal behavior. Broadly speaking, the empirical findings are that (1) poor legitimate labor market opportunities of potential criminals, such as low wages and high rates of unemployment, increases the supply of criminal activities; and (2) sanctions deter crime.

The empirical evidence on the relationship between unemployment and criminal activity has been the subject of much investigation (see literature review by Freeman, 1999a). Unemployment could be taken to influence the opportunity cost of illegal activity. High rates of unemployment growth could be taken to imply a restriction on the availability of legal activities, and thus serve to ultimately reduce the opportunity cost of engaging in illegal activities. Although theoretically well-defined, most empirical studies of the unemployment-crime relationship have provided mixed evidence.

Not all early studies used aggregate time-series data to test the relationship between unemployment and crime. Thornberry and Christenson use individual level data from the 1945 Philadelphia cohort to find that unemployment had significant effects on crime. Farrington et al., using data from the CSDD, showed that property crime rates were higher when offenders were unemployed.

Witte and Tauchen (1994) exploit the panel data dimensions of the Philadelphia cohort used by Thornberry and Christenson. Instead of primarily focusing on crime as a function of unemployment, they use a richer set of controls, like deterrence, employment status, age, education, race, and neighbourhood characteristics. The results reported by Tauchen and Witte on the relationship between employment and crime were consistent with the previous findings of Thornberry and Christenson and Farrington. Recent work, of which Levitt and Witt et al. (1999) are representative, proceeded to use pooled time-series cross-section data and find, inter alia, positive associations between unemployment and property crime.

One problem with most work and crime models is that they assume both activities are mutually exclusive. This may be a problematic assumption when considering disadvantaged youths (see Freeman, 1999b). The fact that a youth can shift from crime to an unskilled job and back again or can commit crime while holding a legal job means that the supply of youths to crime will be quite elastic with respect to relative rewards from crime vis-à-vis legal work or to the number of criminal opportunities.

From the 1970s through the 1990s the labor market prospects for unskilled workers in most OECD countries has deteriorated considerably. In particular, the real earnings of young unskilled men fell, while income inequality rose. This suggests that as the earnings gap widens, relative deprivation increases, which in turn leads to increases in crime. Empirical research into the relationship between earnings inequality and crime generally find that more inequality is associated with more crime. For example, in a study based on a sample of the forty-two police force areas in England and Wales, Witt et al. (1999) report a positive association between earnings inequality and crime rates for vehicle crime, theft, and burglary. For the United States, see the evidence reviewed in Freeman (1999a).

Much of the empirical work on testing the Becker model has focused on the role of deterrence in determining criminal activity. Deterrence refers to the effect of possible punishment on individuals contemplating criminal acts. Deterrence may flow from both criminal justice system actions and from social actions (i.e., the negative response of friends and associates to criminal behavior). To date, attempts to measure deterrent effects have concentrated on the effects of the criminal justice system. See Nagin (1998) for a survey of this literature.

This section discusses a variety of practical problems that arise in testing for deterrent effects. In particular, we consider three estimation issues: measurement error, endogeneity, and nonstationarity.

Models of criminal behavior are usually estimated using official reported crime statistics. Such recorded offenses are influenced both by victims' willingness to report crime and by police recording practices and procedures. At the level of the individual police department, both administrative and political changes can lead to abnormalities in reported data or to failures to report any data. For example, the measurement error in crime rates may arise because hiring more police leads to more crimes reported. Consequently, estimates derived from regressing crime rates on the number of police (or on arrest rates) may be severely distorted by the impact of measurement error.

The potentially serious problem of simultaneity between sanctions and crime has been the subject of much debate. Here, the main point is that increases in sanctions may cause decreases in crime, but increases in sanctions may be in response to higher crime rates. Since the 1970s there has been a considerable effort to find instruments (i.e., exogenous factors) to identify the effects of sanctions on the supply of crime. For example, Levitt (1996) uses instrumental variables to estimate the effect of prison population on crime rates. Prison-overcrowding litigation in a state is used as an instrument for changes in the prison population.

In order to identify the effect of police on crime, Marvell and Moody and Levitt (1997) proposed different procedures. Marvell and Moody are concerned with the timing sequence between hiring police and crime. Using lags between police levels and crime rates to avoid simultaneity, they test for causality in the spirit of Granger. Although they find Granger causation in both directions, the impact of police on crime is much stronger than the impact of crime on police. In a recent paper Levitt (1997) uses the timing of elections (when cities hire more police) as an instrumental variable to identify a causal effect of police on crime. He finds that increases in police instrumented by elections reduces violent crime, but have a smaller impact on property crime.

A substantial problem that has been ignored in the vast majority of empirical studies is nonstationarity of crime rates. A time-series is said to be nonstationary if (1) the mean and/or variance does not remain constant over time; and (2) covariance between observations depends on the time at which they occur. In the United States, index crime rate appears strongly nonstationary, for the most part being integrated of order one with both deterministic and stochastic trends (a random variable whose mean value and variance are time-dependent is said to follow a stochastic trend). See, for example, Witt and Witte (2000). Here, the authors have attempted to estimate and test a model using linear nonstationary regressor techniques like cointegration and error correction models. The empirical results suggest a long-run equilibrium relationship between crime, prison population, female labor supply, and durable consumption.

Recent developments: juvenile crime and education

Recently some researchers have focused their attention on juvenile crime and education. Levitt (1998) and Mocan and Rees provide evidence to show that the economic model of crime applies to juveniles as well as adults. Levitt uses state-level data over the period 1978–1993 for making comparisons between the adult criminal justice system and delinquents. The dependent variable is juvenile crime (either violent or property crime) per number of juveniles. The explanatory variables include the number of juveniles or adults in custody per crime; the number of juveniles or adults in custody per juvenile or adult; economic variables, including the state unemployment rate; and demographic variables, including race and legal drinking age, and dummy variables for year and state. Levitt finds that juvenile crime is negatively related to the severity of penalties, and that juvenile offenders are at least as responsive to sanctions as adults. Interestingly, he finds that the difference between the punishments given to youths and adults helps explain sharp changes in crimes committed by youths as they reach the age of majority.

Mocan and Rees estimate the economic model of crime for juveniles using individual-level data from a nationally representative sample of 16,478 students in grades 7 through 12. The data set contains rich information on offenses and deterrence measures, as well as on personal, family, and neighborhood characteristics. They find that probit estimates for young males selling drugs and assault are strongly affected by violent crime arrests (i.e., increases in arrests per violent crime reduce the probability of selling drugs and committing an assault). Violent crime arrests for females reduces the probability of selling drugs and stealing. Mocan and Rees also find higher levels of local unemployment and higher levels of local poverty associated with higher levels of crime. Family welfare status, a proxy for family poverty, has a positive impact on juvenile offending. Finally, family structure and the education of the juveniles' parents also have an impact on delinquent behavior.

Up to now, we have primarily concerned ourselves with research on crime reduction that focuses on labor market experiences and deterrent effects. The issue of education and training has generally been neglected. It is only recently that economists have begun to explicitly model work, education, and crime. Witte (1997) reviews the literature on education and crime and discusses models that suggest possible crime-reducing effects of education. She carefully traces the various attempts made over the past two decades at a full integration of education and crime but finds that the empirical evidence regarding the effects of education on crime is limited. In recent work, using data from the National Longitudinal Survey of Youth and Uniform Crime Reports, Lochner (1999) developed and estimated a dynamic model in which all three activities—work, investment in human capital, and crime—are endogenized. He finds that education, training, and work subsidies can reduce criminal activity.

Summary and conclusions

Most economic work on crime has focused on the deterrent effect of the criminal justice system and on the interrelationship between work and crime. Empirical work provides some, but not unambiguous support for the deterrence hypothesis. Recent work by economists suggest that the relationship between work and crime may be far more complicated than implied by economic models.

The rise in juvenile crime rates has focused increasing attention on youth crime. This has forced economists to expand their thinking to incorporate such things as education, peer group effects, and the influence of family and community.

Increasingly both theoretical and empirical work on the economics of crime has come to use dynamic models. Theoretical work is developing multi-period models of crime. Empirically economists are using both panel data techniques and modern time series techniques to examine the dynamics of criminal behavior.

ROBERT WITT
ANN DRYDEN WITTE

See also CLASS AND CRIME; CRIME CAUSATION: BIOLOGICAL THEORIES; CRIME CAUSATION: POLITICAL THEORIES; CRIME CAUSATION: PSYCHOLOGICAL THEORIES; CRIME CAUSATION: SOCIOLOGICAL THEORIES; RACE AND CRIME; UNEMPLOYMENT AND CRIME.

BIBLIOGRAPHY

BECKER, GARY. "Crime and Punishment: An Economic Approach." *Journal of Political Economy* 76 (1968): 169–217.

BECKER, GARY, and MURPHY, KEVIN. "A Theory of Rational Addiction." *Journal of Political Economy* 96 (1988): 675–700.

EHRLICH, ISAAC. "Participation in Illegitimate Activities: A Theoretical and Empirical Investigation." *Journal of Political Economy* 81 (1973): 521–565.

———. "The Deterrent Effect of Capital Punishment: A Question of Life and Death." *Journal of Political Economy* 65 (1975): 397–417.

FARRINGTON, DAVID; GALLAGHER, BERNARD; MORLEY, LYNDA; ST. LEDGER, RAYMOND; and WEST, DONALD. "Unemployment, School Leaving and Crime." *British Journal of Criminology* 26 (1986): 335–356.

FLINN, C. "Dynamic Models of Criminal Careers." In *Criminal Careers and "Career Criminals."* Edited by A. Blumstein. Washington, D.C.: National Academy Press, 1986.

FREEMAN, RICHARD. "The Economics of Crime." In *Handbook of Labor Economics.* Vol. 3c, chap. 52. Edited by Orley Ashenfelter and David Card. Amsterdam, Netherlands: North Holland Publishers, 1999a.

———. "Disadvantaged Young Men and Crime." In *Youth Employment and Joblessness in Advanced Countries.* Edited by David Blanchflower and Richard Freeman. Chicago, 1999b.

GRANGER, CLIVE. "Investigating Causal Relations by Econometric Models and Cross-Spectral Methods." *Econometrica* 37 (1969): 424–438.

GROGGER, JEFFREY. "The Effect of Arrests on the Employment and Earnings of Young Men." *Quarterly Journal of Economics* 110 (1995): 51–71.

HECKMAN, JAMES. "Statistical Models for Discrete Panel Data." In *Structural Analysis of Discrete Data with Econometric Applications.* Edited by C. F. Manski and D. F. McFadden. Cambridge, Mass.: MIT Press, 1981.

LEVITT, STEVEN. "The Effect of Prison Population Size on Crime Rates: Evidence from Prison Overcrowding Litigation." *Quarterly Journal of Economics* 111 (1996): 319–351.

———. "Using Electoral Cycles in Police Hiring to Estimate the Effect of Police on Crime." *American Economic Review* 87 (1997): 270–290.

———. "Juvenile Crime and Punishment." *Journal of Political Economy* 106 (1998): 1156–1185.

LOCHNER, LANCE. "Education, Work, and Crime: Theory and Evidence." *University of Rochester, Working Paper No. 465* (1999).

MARVELL, THOMAS, and MOODY, CARLISLE. "Specification Problems, Police Levels, and Crime Rates." *Criminology* 34 (1996): 609–646.

MOCAN, NACI, and REES, DANIEL. "Economic Conditions, Deterrence and Juvenile Crime: Evidence from Micro Data." *NBER Working Paper 7405* Cambridge, Mass., 1999.

MOFFIT, TERRIE. "Adolescence-Limited and Life-Course-Persistent Antisocial Behavior: A Developmental Taxonomy." *Psychological Review* 100 (1993): 674–701.

NAGIN, DANIEL. "Criminal Deterrence: A Review of the Evidence on a Research Agenda for the Outset of the 21st Century." In *Crime and Justice: An Annual Review of Research.* Edited by Michael Tonry. University of Chicago Press. Vol. 23, pp. 1–42.

NAGIN, DANIEL, and WALDFOGEL, JOEL. "The Effects of Criminality and Conviction on the Labor Market Status of Young British Offenders." *International Review of Law and Economics* 15 (1995): 109–126.

SCHMIDT, PETER, and WITTE, ANN DRYDEN. *An Economic Analysis of Crime and Justice.* New York: Academic Press, 1984.

TAUCHEN, HELEN, and WITTE, ANN DRYDEN. "The Dynamics of Domestic Violence." *American Economic Review* 85 (1995): 414–418.

THORNBERRY, TERRENCE, and CHRISTENSON, R. L. "Unemployment and Criminal Involvement: An Investigation of Reciprocal Causal Structures." *American Sociological Review* 56 (1984): 609–627.

WILLIAMS, JENNY, and SICKLES, ROBIN. "Turning from Crime: A Dynamic Perspective." Paper presented in the Econometric Session on Structural Models at the ASSA Meetings in Boston, January, 2000.

WITT, ROBERT; CLARKE, ALAN; and FIELDING, NIGEL. "Crime and Economic Activity: A Panel Data Approach." *British Journal of Criminology* 39 (1999): 391–400.

WITT, ROBERT, and WITTE, ANN DRYDEN. "Crime, Prison, and Female Labor Supply." *Journal of Quantitative Criminology* 16, no. 1 (March 2000): 69–85.

WITTE, ANN DRYDEN. "Estimating the Economic Model of Crime with Individual Data." *Quarterly Journal of Economics* 94 (1980): 59–87.

———. "Crime." In *The Social Benefits of Education.* Edited by Jere Behrman and Nevzer Stacey. Ann Arbor: University of Michigan Press, 1997.

WITTE, ANN DRYDEN, and TAUCHEN, HELEN. "Work and Crime: An Exploration Using Panel Data." *Public Finance* 49 (1994): 1–14.

CRIME CAUSATION: POLITICAL THEORIES

From its inception criminology has been embedded in politics (Radzinowicz). Despite frequent claims to scientific objectivity, criminological inquiry has been defined and sustained by political concerns. Affinities between political orientations and explanations of crime have often been noted, and debates over theoretical differences have typically included references to such affinities. Indeed, pointing out the ideological assumptions and implications of theories has been a standard element in assessments of their worth with or without regard for research findings.

In the eighteenth and early nineteenth centuries the idea of studying crime and criminals was closely associated with that of making governance more effective. European intellectuals saw the arbitrariness and cruelties of despotic rule as threats to social order. Their views were crystallized in 1764 by Cesare Beccaria, one of the Italian *illuministi*, who forcefully and concisely argued that punishment of offenders should be "public, necessary, the minimum possible under the circumstances, [and] proportionate to the crime" (quoted in Beirne, p. 38). By the 1830s the movement to rationalize governmental social control through law promoted statistical studies of the "dangerous classes" (ultimately leading to Cesare Lombroso's search for "born criminals") and the mapping of associations between crime and various indicators of moral deficiency (for the detailed history see Beirne).

Until the 1960s, disagreements among criminologists centered almost entirely on how best to measure and explain the characteristics of people who ran afoul of the law, or who were statistically likely to do so. It was generally assumed that the goal of criminology is to learn what pathologies, individual and/or environmental, cause criminal behavior. That assumption was challenged by a growing number of "conflict" criminologists who argued (1) that criminality is defined by a lawmaking process influenced mainly by the more powerful classes in society, and (2) that the prime directive of law enforcement is to protect the interests of the higher classes, so that (3) the lower classes are more likely both to commit the kinds of acts legally defined as crimes (while the often much more harmful behaviors of the higher classes are not so defined) and to be labeled as criminals regardless of their behavior.

Where criminologists stand on the issues raised by traditional and conflict criminological studies largely determine the research questions they ask, and the theories they find most promising in looking for answers. Although the com-

plexity of theories may sometimes leave them open to differing political interpretations and uses, there are affinities between conservative, liberal, and radical political orientations and major statements about crime causation.

Political orientations and theoretical affinities

Each orientation is characterized by distinctive assumptions regarding (1) the nature of social order, both as current reality and as an ideal; (2) human nature; and (3) criminality and crime causation. Affinities between political orientations and specific criminological theories will be noted in considering those assumptions.

Conservatism and restraining defective people. Conservative ideologies assume that the ideal society is one in which authority is unquestioned. The hierarchy of wisdom and virtue is accepted by all as based on recognizing natural inequalities. Because human nature is basically egoistic, people need discipline—instruction for those with the requisite capacity, restraint for those lacking the capacity to understand. An approximation of the ideal is found in contemporary society, characterized by limited democracy and free market capitalism, which is basically sound. Unfortunately, society is threatened by defective people—individuals and population groups—who cannot or will not accept the authority and direction of their superiors, and resort to crime to profit from the labors of others. Criminals are predators, and their crimes are the results of pathologies of mind and body.

The influence of conservatism is evident in the politics of "law and order" (Scheingold). Fear of crime is promoted by focusing attention on heinous crimes and emphasizing the "failures" of rehabilitation, probation, and parole. The public is encouraged to believe they are threatened by a surrounding army of murderous psychopaths, epitomized in racial and class stereotypes ("folk devils"). Demonization of offenders is compatible with calls for "taking the handcuffs off the police" (i.e., reducing legal restraints and accountability, as in expanding their powers of discretionary search and seizure). At the same time, rights of the accused (and of the convicted) are constricted; and the "victims' rights" movement is fostered—which goes beyond ensuring concern and support for victims and survivors, instead to promoting the demand for more severe penalties. Punishment in the name of deterrence is stressed, rejected are liberal calls for institutional reforms and greater investment in preventive and custodial treatment, support for the families of offenders, job training, diversion to community service, and other alternatives to punitive crime control policies.

Theories positing that criminal behavior must have some pathological sources are obviously most congenial with conservative thinking about crime and criminals. The search for criminogenic genes, glands, body types, minds, and personality traits has become increasingly more sophisticated in research designs and techniques, but the underlying assumption remains: there must be "something wrong" with lawbreakers, at least those whose offenses are heinous or repeated.

Biological theories suggest that the fundamental sources of psychological abnormalities, and thus of criminal behavior, are to be found in genetic or other organic defects and anomalies. The history of research along such lines is at best spotty and inconclusive, but studies such as those of Sarnoff Mednick and his colleagues encourage the view that genetic factors are involved in causing crime. Efforts to link crime causation to inferior intelligence, brain disorders, nutritional deficiencies, and glandular disorders have been similarly inconclusive. Still, the imagery of the inferior and inherently dangerous criminal is given wide currency, and fits readily the ideological assumptions of conservatism—and at the extreme, of racism.

Psychological theories of unconscious problems and failures in moral development have been compatible with conservatism insofar as they support the view that criminals are unable to resist their impulses. Similarly, theories emphasizing childhood emotional and material deprivations imply that it is probably too late for many offenders, whose limited capacities for healthy social interaction make it very unlikely that they can become normal law-abiding citizens. And though an enormous body of research comparing criminal and noncriminal personalities has failed to confirm significant and consistent differences, attempts to find such differences have continued. Such studies as those of Halleck, Yochelson and Samenow, and Gough and Bradley support the notion that criminals (at least serious persistent and violent ones) are sociopaths, or psychopaths, who have only contempt for others, unbounded egoism, no sense of responsibility, and no self-control.

Assuming that people are inherently egoistic, and thus criminally inclined, Travis Hirschi has offered a theory of internal social control to explain why everyone does not commit crimes. In its original formulation (considerably expanded in Gottfredson and Hirschi, pp. 85–120) his theory posited four social bonds that keep people from committing criminal acts: attachment, commitment, involvement, and belief. Strong attachments to parents and schoolteachers outweigh peer attachments, which are nonetheless significant in promoting respect for others. Commitments to such conventional norms as working hard to get ahead educationally and occupationally help to keep young people out of trouble, as does involvement in the kinds of activities required to achieve success. More abstractly, conformity is also the product of belief in the values of society, which means respecting its institutions and laws. To the extent that people fail to establish such bonds early in life, there is nothing in them to inhibit criminal behavior—that clearly implies the need for external restraint. External controls include both the detention and elimination of individual offenders and the manipulation of the social environment so as to reduce opportunities for crime and make its detection more probable.

If criminal types are presumed, the theories and research offering to identify them encourage the conclusion that little or nothing can be done to change criminals. For those who have not been "habilitated" in the first place, rehabilitation is a meaningless notion. Accordingly, the criminal threat must be dealt with by external controls. As noted above, conservatism favors "get tough" measures aimed at making the apprehension and incapacitation of offenders easier, and at making it as difficult as possible for crimes to be committed without risking detection, apprehension, and punishment.

Situational ("opportunity") theories assume the existence of criminally motivated people, and promote efforts to learn what kinds of social environmental factors increase or reduce the opportunities available to them. Environmental theory (Brantingham and Brantingham) focuses on crime patterns, using mapping techniques to relate the location of criminal incidents to features of the social setting (e.g., the location of schools, businesses, recreational facilities; the flow of vehicular and pedestrian traffic; the availability of security personnel and devices; the racial, class, age, and other characteristics of local populations). Rational choice theory (Clarke) emphasizes the "choice-structuring properties" of specific types of crime, assuming that offenders choose to commit a particular kind of crime (e.g., theft) in regard to such factors as the number and accessibility of targets, skills, and resources needed to optimize the chances of success, the likely payoff, and the risks of injury and apprehension. Routine activities theory (Felson) predicts an incident whenever the everyday activities of people (such as going to school or work, shopping, attending recreational events) lead to the conjunction of a likely offender (someone intending to commit a crime), a suitable target (something or someone), an absent guardian (no one to see or prevent the act), and no personal handler (no associate to dissuade the offender).

Liberalism and reforming defective environments. Liberalism assumes that the ideal society is one in which there is equality of opportunity and a general consensus to accept differences in rewards as the outcomes of fair competition. Social stratification is functional if based on merit, that is, differences in achievement; it is dysfunctional insofar as it is based on ascription (e.g., inherited status or other attributes independent of performance) or mere power differences. Contemporary society is basically sound, grounded in the principles of representative democracy and enlightened capitalism.

However, there are structural and administrative problems in applying those principles. And illiberal racial and other prejudices remain to be eliminated. Though naturally inclined to peaceful and mutually supportive relations with others, people whose opportunities for enlightenment and achievement are blocked—by the organizational and operational shortcomings and cultural biases of social institutions—are at risk of falling into crime as they try to cope with the stresses imposed on them. The institutional shortcomings that cause stress, and therefore crime, are to be remedied by legal and social reforms.

Liberalism has had minimal success in challenging the dominance of conservatism in crime control policymaking. The efforts of its advocates have included: refocusing debate on the historical failure to give rehabilitation a fair chance; searching for the sources of crime in social environments instead of individual pathologies; redirecting budgeting decisions so as to reward lawful behavior rather than punish criminal behavior; examining the greater punitiveness of the American criminal justice system as compared to the systems of other advanced Western industrial societies; and providing the public with more accurate information about crime and criminals. All of these efforts have failed to overcome the conservative ascendancy (Currie; see also Stenson and Cowell, pp. 33–61).

Theories of crime emphasizing institutional sources of stress are obviously congenial with liberal ideology. Social disorganization or strain theories explain criminal behavior in terms of associations between crime rates and various indices of institutional malfunctioning or breakdown. An extension of social disorganization theory is ecological theory, which focuses on the negative effects of political and economic decisions (e.g., zoning, investment) on land use patterns, resulting in the deterioration of neighborhoods (Bursik and Grasmick).

The core notion of stress resulting from institutional defects is derived from the classic concept of anomie—referring to either the breakdown of social norms or, later, the discrepancy (notably in American society) between the cultural norms defining material success and how it is to be achieved, and the institutional barriers denying minorities and poor people opportunities to compete and succeed. The primary criticism of strain theory is that the stressful impact of institutional shortcomings has been assumed rather than demonstrated, and that the causal role of stress in causing criminal behavior has not been adequately specified.

Accepting the postulate that institutional deficiencies have stressful consequences, Robert Agnew offers a refinement of strain theory that identifies three types of stress that may lead to crime. First, stress may be caused by failure to achieve positively valued goals, such as material success. Second, it may result from the removal of positively valued stimuli (e.g., the actual or feared loss of someone or something valued). Third, stress may be caused by the presentation of negative stimuli—for example, experiencing child abuse, being a victim of a crime, being taunted or threatened. Each type produces anger, fear, or depression. The type of stress most likely to result in crime is anger, which increases the urge for revenge, helps to justify aggression, and stimulates action. Because people vary in their capacity to cope with frustration and anger, not everyone under stress will resort to crime. Whether criminal behavior is the ultimate outcome depends on the nature and degree of strain experienced in relation to the person's capacity to handle it by noncriminal means.

Given that people are not naturally inclined to crime, it is assumed that they must learn both the attitudes and the behaviors necessary to commit crimes. Thus, there is an affinity between liberalism and social learning theories of crime causation. Differential reinforcement, operant conditioning, imitation, and the many theories of socialization and acculturation all begin with the assumption that criminals are made, not born (Akers). Therefore, understanding how people learn to be criminals is closely tied to explanations of how they individually and collectively are influenced by stressful environments.

Theories of criminal subcultures may explain how institutional barriers generate stresses on individuals who then band together to support one another in trying to cope—prototypically by forming gangs (explained in Albert Cohen's famous statement as a process of "mutual conversion"). More often, subculture theories begin with the assumption that criminal subcultures exist as a part of the malfunctioning social environment, adding to the consequent stress while at the same time offering at least some resources for coping with it (Sanchez Jankowski). At the extreme, a "subculture of violence" may in time emerge as populations react to the strains imposed by repression, exploitation, and discrimination (Wolfgang and Ferracuti).

Radicalism and replacing defective societies. Whether left or right, radical ideology envisions the ideal society as one in which people—naturally creative and freedom-loving—are able to do as they please in going about their peaceful business, without interference by anyone—especially those claiming or representing some presumed higher authority. Contemporary society is viewed not merely as falling well short of the ideal, but as a massive obstacle, blocking progress toward it. Liberal democratic society is a sham, camouflaging social realities that are obvious in openly despotic societies—namely, political oppression and economic exploitation. Capitalism is institutionalized exploitation.

Stratification is intrinsically dysfunctional. The rich manipulate the poor so as to divide and conquer, by pitting workforces and races against one another. A common theme in rightist ideology is that racial and ethnic minorities are favored to keep more capable groups from becoming strong enough to challenge "the system." To leftists, particularly those inspired by Marxism, class, racial, and other forms of discrimination are promoted by the "ruling classes" to keep the work force divided, thus more easily controlled.

The current social order is doomed, and will be replaced by a truly free society. Rightists em-

phasize moral deterioration, reflected in crime rates, as the harbinger of society's political and economic collapse into war among racial and other groups fighting to survive. Leftists posit fundamental and ultimately fatal contradictions in the structuring of capitalist liberal democracy—for example, the inherent clash between capitalists' interest in maximizing profits and workers' interest in maximizing wages, as well as the contradiction between capitalists' interest in minimizing labor costs and their interest in maximizing consumer purchases. The conflict between capitalists and workers encourages selfishness ("possessive individualism") leading to acts of force and fraud in an insatiable quest for material gains.

Radical rightist ideology is most congenial with the same theories of crime causation found to have affinities with conservative ideology, especially those emphasizing biological and psychological abnormalities. Crime is distinguished from "acts of war." Biologically, psychologically, and morally inferior human beings (most notably racial minorities) commit crimes. Governmental and corporate "goons" commit crimes in a war against survivalists and other rightists resisting tyranny. Resisters, on the other hand, are forced to commit acts of war, ranging from bank robbery and fraud to assassination and terrorism, in order to carry on the struggle.

Radicalism, particularly of the left, has had even less impact on crime control policymaking than has liberalism, which has led radical leftists to divergent strategies for accomplishing the replacement of contemporary society (Lanier and Henry, pp. 235–297; Turk). The major difference is between confrontational and incremental strategies. Classic instrumental Marxism and militant anarchism encourage an uncompromising confrontation with the political, economic, and intellectual defenders of liberal democratic capitalism. Whether reactive or provocative, militant defiance of authorities is assumed to be an effective strategy for bringing attention to the rottenness of the social order and to mobilizing public outrage and support.

Recognizing the limited success of confrontation (indeed its likelihood of reinforcing the conservative bias of public debate and policy on crime control), "left realists" and allied proponents of constitutive, critical, humanist, and peacemaking criminologies have adopted an incremental strategy of promoting short-term "progressive" measures to alleviate the immediate situational problems of the socially disadvantaged. In practice, this has meant overlapping and even cooperating with liberals. However, the ultimate objective remains the transformation of the current social order into the radical ideal of a society combining the best features of participatory democracy, socialist economics, and cultural emphasis on the free expression of human creativity.

Leftist radicalism not only has affinities with theories emphasizing the significance of social conflicts in crime causation, but also has directly inspired some of them. "Labeling theory" and "conflict" theories grounded in Marxism or anarchism have been developed not simply out of intellectual interest to understand the world, but with the aim of changing the world.

Labeling theory is based on the premise that definitions of crime, and of criminal responsibility, are socially constructed in interactions between more and less powerful people. Emphasizing the problematic outcomes of creating and interpreting laws, and of applying them to individuals, labeling theorists such as Howard Becker and Edwin Lemert have concluded that individuals should, as far as possible, be shielded from the criminal process. It is argued that the experience of being treated and labeled as a criminal negatively affects the offender's self-image, with repeated experiences likely to result in an alienated and brutalized person whose identity is that of a criminal.

Marxist criminologists have generally moved from instrumentalism (positing a conspiracy model of political and economic capitalist domination) to structuralism (locating the mechanisms of domination and the sources of crime in the structuring and functioning of institutions). The theoretical contributions of William Chambliss (Chambliss and Zatz; Turk) exemplify the shift, and have contributed significantly to it. In brief, Chambliss argues that liberal democratic capitalist society has basic structural contradictions that are evident in the discrimination built into criminal and civil laws. The alienating impact of such institutionalized discrimination on the disadvantaged precipitates conventional street crime, while the relative immunity afforded the advantaged encourages white collar (including governmental) crime.

Beginning with a Marxist approach, Richard Quinney (see also Pepinsky and Quinney; Turk) has refined his views to set out a Judeo-Christian socialist theory, which posits the criminogenic impact of the conflicts of values fomented by the impersonal oppressiveness of the liberal demo-cratic capitalist order. Nonviolent peacemaking measures are necessary to prevent or resolve the conflicts underlying criminal events. Violence and oppressive social institutions must be ended; people and institutions must become more compassionate.

Constitutive criminologists (Henry and Milovanovic) offer the most philosophically radical theory, linking the definition of criminality to the biases intrinsic to prevailing legal, criminological, and other languages of social control. Various types of critical "discourse analysis" reveal the discriminatory and repressive meanings of criminality contained and perpetuated in such languages. Crime causation is a highly problematic notion, neither determinate nor predictable in terms of measurable variables, and can only be inferred from the totality of all aspects of social reality.

Theories of crime and explaining political crime

Given that any theory of crime may be shown to have an affinity with some political ideology, it follows that any theory may be used for political purposes. In this general sense, therefore, any theory of crime is a political theory. And any form of crime may be given political significance. Indeed, radical criminologists have sometimes argued that all crimes are political, as are all theories of crime. And some theorists have offered explanations of crime (and criticisms of one another's views) that obviously support conservative or liberal political perspectives and agendas. Their theories may thus be considered political theories (e.g., Wilson and Herrnstein; Currie).

An alternative conception of political theories of crime causation is that they are characterized by their emphasis on social conflict and power relationships. Although such theories, as we have seen, may be applied to any form of crime, they have not historically focused on explaining individual criminal behavior, but rather have focused on explaining variations in crime rates, and especially on the differing risks (among class, racial, and other population sectors) of being labeled as criminal. Insofar as the criminal justice system is seen as an instrument of political control or repression, the politicization of all crime is implied. More narrowly, it is occasionally argued that political crimes, as such, are especially amenable to explanation by labeling and conflict theories; but the counterargument is that any theory with an affinity to a political ideology can be invoked to account for political criminality.

Given affinities between political ideologies and crime causation theories, it may be conjectured that the more explicitly political the theory, the more likely it is to assign political significance to criminality. Theories having affinities with conservatism and radicalism appear to be more likely than theories with affinities to liberalism to explain crime and criminals in political terms, whether as threats to political stability or as resistance to political oppression. As previously noted, theories having affinities with conservative images of crime and criminals tend to encourage the view that crime threatens the political order, while radical Marxist theories assert or imply that crimes may either be acts of accommodation or resistance, to oppression or oppressive acts by agents of governmental and corporate domination (Quinney). In any event, how theorists define and explain political criminality, and what policy options are favored, vary with whether their theories have greater affinities with conservatism, liberalism, or radicalism. Accordingly, conservatives will assume the pathology of political offenders (especially violent ones), liberals will assume that political offenders are mostly normal but misguided people who are reacting to the stresses imposed on them by faulty social institutions, and radicals will assume that political offenders are reasoning people who perceive and resist the oppressive and exploitative nature of liberal democratic capitalist society.

Conclusion

This entry provided an overview of the various political theories of crime, which may be summarized as follows:

1. Criminology has always been a politically oriented discipline.
2. Differences among theories of crime causation are associated with their affinities with conservative, liberal, or radical political ideologies.
3. Any crime may have political significance, whether as a source or a consequence of political instability.
4. Explanations of political crimes are not necessarily the province of labeling and conflict theories but may be derived from any theory.

5. Every theory of crime causation is at bottom a political theory.

AUSTIN T. TURK

See also ASSASSINATION; CLASS AND CRIME; CRIME CAUSATION: BIOLOGICAL THEORIES; CRIME CAUSATION: ECONOMIC THEORIES; CRIME CAUSATION: PSYCHOLOGICAL THEORIES; CRIME CAUSATION: SOCIOLOGICAL THEORIES; POLITICAL PROCESS AND CRIME; TERRORISM; WAR AND VIOLENT CRIME.

BIBLIOGRAPHY

AGNEW, ROBERT. "Foundations for a General Strain Theory of Crime and Delinquency." *Criminology* 30, no. 1 (1992): 47–87.
AKERS, RONALD L. *Social Learning and Social Structure: A General Theory of Crime and Deviance.* Boston: Northeastern University Press, 1998.
BECKER, HOWARD S. *Outsiders: Studies in the Sociology of Deviance.* New York: The Free Press, 1963.
BEIRNE, PIERS. *Inventing Criminology: Essays on the Rise of 'Homo Criminalis.'* Albany: State University of New York Press, 1993.
BRANTINGHAM, PAUL J., and BRANTINGHAM, PATRICIA L., eds. *Environmental Criminology.* Prospect Heights, Ill: Waveland, 1991.
BURSIK, ROBERT J., and GRASMICK, HAROLD G. *Neighborhoods and Crime: The Dimensions of Effective Community Control.* New York: Lexington Books, 1993.
CHAMBLISS, WILLIAM J., and KATZ, MARJORIE S., eds. *Making Law: The State, the Law, and Structural Contradictions.* Bloomington: Indiana University Press, 1993.
CLARKE, RONALD V. "Situational Crime Prevention." *Building a Safer Society: Strategic Approaches to Crime Prevention.* Edited by Michael Tonry and David P. Farrington. Chicago: University of Chicago Press, 1995. Pages 91–150.
COHEN, ALBERT K. *Delinquent Boys: The Culture of the Gang.* New York: Free Press, 1955.
CURRIE, ELLIOTT. *Confronting Crime: An American Challenge.* New York: Pantheon, 1985.
FELSON, MARCUS. *Crime and Everyday Life: Insights and Implications for Society.* Thousand Oaks, Calif.: Pine Forge Press, 1994.
GOTTFREDSON, MICHAEL R., and HIRSCHI, TRAVIS. *A General Theory of Crime.* Stanford, Calif.: Stanford University Press, 1990.
GOUGH, HARRISON G., and BRADLEY, PAMELA. "Delinquent and Criminal Behavior as Assessed by the Revised California Psychological

Inventory." *Journal of Clinical Psychology* 48, no. 3 (1992): 298–308.

HALLECK, SEYMOUR L. *Psychiatry and the Dilemmas of Crime.* New York: Harper & Row, 1967.

HENRY, STUART, and MILOVANOVIC, DRAGAN. *Constitutive Criminology: Beyond Postmodernism.* London: Sage Publications, 1996.

HIRSCHI, TRAVIS. *Causes of Delinquency.* Berkeley, Calif.: University of California Press, 1967.

LANIER, MARK M., and HENRY, STUART. *Essential Criminology.* Boulder, Colo.: Westview Press, 1998.

LEMERT, EDWIN M. *Human Deviance, Social Problems, and Social Control.* Englewood Cliffs, N.J.: Prentice-Hall, 1972.

MEDNICK, SARNOFF; MOFFITT, TERRIE; and STACK, SUSAN eds. *The Causes of Crime: Biological Approaches.* London: Cambridge University Press, 1987.

PEPINSKY, HAROLD E., and QUINNEY, RICHARD. *Criminology as Peacemaking.* Bloomington: Indiana University Press, 1991.

RADZINOWICZ, LEON. *Ideology and Crime.* New York: Columbia University Press, 1966.

SANCHEZ JANKOWSKI, MARTIN. *Islands in the Street: Gangs and American Urban Society.* Berkeley: University of California Press, 1991.

SCHEINGOLD, STUART A. *The Politics of Law and Order: Street Crime and Public Policy.* New York: Longman, 1984.

STENSON, KEVIN, and COWELL, DAVID, eds. *The Politics of Crime Control.* London: Sage Publications, 1991.

TURK, AUSTIN T. "Conflict Theory." *Encyclopedia of Criminology and Deviant Behavior.* Edited by Clifton D. Bryant. Vol. 1. New York: Taylor & Francis, 2000. Pages 46–51.

WILSON, JAMES Q., and HERRNSTEIN, RICHARD. *Crime and Human Nature.* New York: Simon and Schuster, 1985.

WOLFGANG, MARVIN E., and FERRACUTI, FRANCO. *The Subculture of Violence.* London: Tavistock, 1967.

YOCHELSON, SAMUEL, and SAMENOW, STANTON. *The Criminal Personality.* New York: Jason Aronson, 1976.

CRIME CAUSATION: PSYCHOLOGICAL THEORIES

It is hard to specify distinctively psychological theories of crime. The guiding principle in this entry is that psychological theories focus especially on the influence of individual and family factors on offending. Psychological theories are usually developmental, attempting to explain the development of offending from childhood to adulthood, and hence based on longitudinal studies that follow up individuals over time. The emphasis of such theories is on continuity rather than discontinuity from childhood to adulthood. A common assumption is that the ordering of individuals on an underlying construct such as criminal potential is relatively constant over time.

Psychologists view offending as a type of behavior that is similar in many respects to other types of antisocial behavior. Hence, the theories, methods, and knowledge of other types of antisocial behavior can be applied to the study of crime. Lee Robins popularized the theory that offending is one element of a larger syndrome of antisocial behavior, including heavy drinking, drug-taking, reckless driving, educational problems, employment problems, difficulties in relationships, and so on. This is the basis of the psychiatric classification of antisocial personality disorder. Robins also argued that antisocial personality is obvious early in life and that it tends to persist from childhood to adulthood, with different behavioral manifestations.

Typically, psychological theories may include motivational, inhibiting, decision-making, and learning processes (Farrington, 1993). The most common motivational idea is that people (and especially children) are naturally hedonistic and selfish, seeking pleasure and avoiding pain, and hence that children are naturally antisocial. Another classic idea is that people are motivated to maintain an optimal level of arousal; if their level falls below the optimum, they will try to increase it, whereas if it is above the optimum they will try to decrease it. Thus, someone who is bored might seek excitement.

Since offending is viewed as essentially natural, most psychological theories attempt to explain the development of mechanisms that inhibit offending such as the conscience. The conscience is often assumed to arise in a conditioning process (depending on the association between antisocial behavior and the anxiety created by parental punishment) or in a learning process (where the probability of behavior increases or decreases according to parental rewards or punishments). Psychological theories often include cognitive (thinking or decision-making) processes that explain why people choose to offend in a particular situation. A common assumption is that offending is essentially rational, and that people will offend if they think that the expected benefits will outweigh the expected costs.

Generally, psychologists are committed to the scientific study of human behavior, with its emphasis on theories that can be tested and falsified using empirical, quantitative data, controlled experiments, systematic observation, valid and reliable measures, replications of empirical results, and so on. Much research in recent years has been carried out within the risk factor paradigm (Farrington, 2000), focusing on the extent to which risk factors such as impulsiveness or poor parental supervision predict offending. This research also investigates possible causal mechanisms or processes that intervene between and explain the link between risk factors and crime.

The following sections discuss the most important categories of risk factors that influence crime: (1) family influences, such as broken homes (associated with attachment theories), poor child-rearing methods (associated with social learning theories), and criminal parents (associated with intergenerational transmission theories); and (2) individual influences such as personality. The most important personality factor in relation to crime is impulsiveness, while the most influential theory of the link between personality and crime is that put forward by Hans Eysenck. A significant theory focusing on impulsiveness was propounded by James Q. Wilson and Richard Herrnstein. The section also examines cognitive theories, which emphasize thinking, reasoning, and decision-making processes. Lastly, this entry describes a more comprehensive theory than those discussed under family and individual influences. The more comprehensive theory includes motivational, inhibiting, decision-making, and learning processes.

Family influences

Broken homes and attachment theories. Psychologists have approached broken homes and attachment theories from a broad range of perspectives. Psychoanalytic theories emphasized the importance of loving relationships and attachment between children and their parents. These theories suggested that there were three major personality mechanisms: the id, ego, and superego. The id contained the instinctual, unconscious desires (especially sexual and aggressive) with which a child was born. It was governed by the pleasure principle, seeking to achieve pleasure and avoid pain. The ego, which was the seat of consciousness, developed out of the id by about age three. The ego tried to achieve the desires of the id while taking account of the reality of social conventions, and hence could delay immediate gratification in favor of long-term goals. Children would only develop a strong ego if they had a loving relationship with their parents.

The superego developed out of the ego by about age five, and contained two functions, the conscience and the ego-ideal. The conscience acted to inhibit instinctual desires that violated social rules, and its formation depended on parental punishment arousing anger that children then turned against themselves. The ego-ideal contained internalized representations of parental standards, and its formation depended on children having loving relationships with their parents. According to psychoanalytic theories, offending resulted from a weak ego or a weak superego, both of which followed largely from low attachment between children and parents. These ideas inspired counseling and social work approaches, trying to rehabilitate offenders by building up warm relationships with them.

Most studies of broken homes have focused on the loss of the father rather than the mother, because the loss of a father is much more common. In agreement with attachment theories, children who are separated from a biological parent are more likely to offend than children from intact families. For example, in a birth cohort study of over eight hundred children born in Newcastle-upon-Tyne, England, Israel Kolvin and his colleagues discovered that boys who experienced divorce or separation in their first five years of life had a doubled risk of conviction up to age thirty-two (53 percent as opposed to 28 percent).

However, the relationship between broken homes and delinquency is not as simple as that suggested by attachment theories. Joan McCord (1982) conducted an interesting study in Boston of the relationship between homes broken by loss of the biological father and later serious offending by boys. She found that the prevalence of offending was high for boys from broken homes without affectionate mothers (62 percent) and for those from unbroken homes characterized by parental conflict (52 percent), irrespective of whether they had affectionate mothers. The prevalence of offending was low for those from unbroken homes without conflict (26 percent) and—importantly—equally low for boys from broken homes with affectionate mothers (22 percent). These results suggest that it might not be the broken home that is criminogenic but the parental conflict that often causes it. They also suggest that a loving mother might in some sense be able to compensate for the loss of a father.

Modern theories of the relationship between disrupted families and delinquency fall into three major classes. *Trauma theories* suggest that the loss of a parent has a damaging effect on a child, most commonly because of the effect on attachment to the parent. *Life course theories* focus on separation as a sequence of stressful experiences, and on the effects of multiple stressors such as parental conflict, parental loss, reduced economic circumstances, changes in parent figures, and poor child-rearing methods. *Selection theories* argue that disrupted families produce delinquent children because of preexisting differences from other families in risk factors, such as parental conflict, criminal or antisocial parents, low family income, or poor child-rearing methods.

Hypotheses derived from the three theories were tested in the Cambridge Study in Delinquent Development (Juby and Farrington), which is a prospective longitudinal survey of over four hundred London males from age eight to age forty. While boys from broken homes (permanently disrupted families) were more delinquent than boys from intact homes, they were not more delinquent than boys from intact high-conflict families. Overall, the most important factor was the post-disruption trajectory. Boys who remained with their mother after the separation had the same delinquency rate as boys from intact low-conflict families. Boys who remained with their father, with relatives, or with others (e.g., foster parents) had high delinquency rates. It was concluded that the results favored life-course theories rather than trauma or selection theories.

Child-rearing methods and learning theories. Many different types of child-rearing methods predict a child's delinquency. The most important dimensions of child-rearing are supervision or monitoring of children, discipline or parental reinforcement, and warmth or coldness of emotional relationships. Of all these child-rearing methods, poor parental supervision is usually the strongest and most replicable predictor of offending, typically predicting a doubled risk of delinquency. This refers to the degree of monitoring by parents of the child's activities, and their degree of watchfulness or vigilance. Many studies show that parents who do not know where their children are when they are out of the house, and parents who let their children roam the streets unsupervised from an early age, tend to have delinquent children. For example, in the classic Cambridge-Somerville study in Boston, poor parental supervision in childhood was the best predictor of both violent and property offending up to age forty-five (McCord, 1979).

Parental discipline refers to how parents react to a child's behavior. It is clear that harsh or punitive discipline involving physical punishment—sometimes approaching physical abuse—predicts a child's delinquency. In a follow-up study of nearly seven hundred Nottingham children, John and Elizabeth Newson found that physical punishment at ages seven and eleven, predicted later convictions; 40 percent of offenders had been smacked or beaten at age eleven, compared with 14 percent of nonoffenders. Erratic or inconsistent discipline also predicts delinquency. This can involve either erratic discipline by one parent, sometimes turning a blind eye to bad behavior and sometimes punishing it severely, or inconsistency between two parents, with one parent being tolerant or indulgent and the other being harshly punitive.

Cold, rejecting parents also tend to have delinquent children, as Joan McCord (1979) found more than twenty years ago in the Cambridge-Somerville study. In a 1997 study, McCord concluded that parental warmth could act as a protective factor against the effects of physical punishment. Whereas 51 percent of boys with cold, physically punishing mothers were convicted in her study, only 21 percent of boys with warm, physically punishing mothers were convicted, similar to the 23 percent of boys with warm, nonpunitive mothers who were convicted. Similar results were also obtained for fathers.

Apart from attachment theories, most theories that examine the link between child-rearing methods and delinquency are learning theories. One of the most influential early learning theories was propounded by Gordon Trasler. Trasler's theory suggested that when a child behaved in a socially disapproved way, the parent would punish the child. This punishment caused an anxiety reaction, or an unpleasant state of physiological arousal. After a number of pairings of the disapproved act and the punishment, the anxiety became conditioned to the act, and conditioned also to the sequence of events preceding the act. Consequently, when the child contemplated the disapproved act, the conditioned anxiety automatically arose and tended to block the tendency to commit the act, so the child became less likely to do it. Hence, Trasler viewed the conscience as essentially a conditioned anxiety response. This response might be experienced subjectively as guilt.

Trasler emphasized differences in parental child-rearing behavior as the major source of disparity in criminal tendencies or in the strength of the conscience. According to Trasler, children were unlikely to build up the link between disapproved behavior and anxiety unless their parents supervised them closely, used punishment consistently, and made punishment contingent on disapproved acts. Hence, poor supervision, erratic discipline, and inconsistency between parents were all conducive to delinquency in children. It was also important for parents to explain to children why they were being punished, so that they could discriminate precisely the behavior that was disapproved.

Trasler argued that middle-class parents were more likely to explain to children why they were being punished and more likely to be concerned with long-term character-building and the inculcation of general moral principles. This approach was linked to the greater facility of middle-class parents with language and abstract concepts. In contrast, lower-class parents supervised their children less closely and were more inconsistent in their use of discipline. Therefore, lower-class children committed more crimes because lower-class parents used less effective methods of socialization.

More recent social learning theories (e.g., Patterson) suggested that children's behavior depended on parental rewards and punishments and on the models of behavior that parents represent. Children will tend to become delinquent if parents do not respond consistently and contingently to their antisocial behavior and if parents themselves behave in an antisocial manner. These theories have inspired the use of parent training methods to prevent delinquency.

Intergenerational transmission theories. Criminal and antisocial parents tend to have delinquent and antisocial children, as shown in the classic longitudinal surveys by Joan McCord in Boston and Lee Robins in St. Louis. The most extensive research on the concentration of offending in families was carried out in the Cambridge Study in Delinquent Development. Having a convicted father, mother, brother, or sister predicted a boy's own convictions, and all four relatives were independently important as predictors (Farrington et al., 1996). For example, 63 percent of boys with convicted fathers were themselves convicted, compared with 30 percent of the remainder. Same-sex relationships were stronger than opposite-sex relationships, and older siblings were stronger predictors than younger siblings. Only 6 percent of the families accounted for half of all the convictions of all family members.

There are several possible theories (which are not mutually exclusive) for why offending tends to be concentrated in certain families and transmitted from one generation to the next. First, the effect of a criminal parent on a child's offending may be mediated by genetic mechanisms. In agreement with this, twin studies show that identical twins are more concordant in their offending than are fraternal twins (Raine). However, the greater behavioral similarity of the identical twins could reflect their greater environmental similarity. Also in agreement with genetic mechanisms, adoption studies show that the offending of adopted children is significantly related to the offending of their biological parents. However, some children may have had contact with their biological parents, so again it is difficult to dismiss an environmental explanation of this finding.

In a more convincing design comparing the concordance of identical twins reared together and identical twins reared apart, William Grove and his colleagues found that heritability was 41 percent for childhood conduct disorder and 28 percent for adult antisocial personality disorder. Hence, the intergenerational transmission of offending may be partly attributable to genetic factors. Crime cannot be genetically transmitted because it is a legal construct, but some more fundamental construct such as aggressiveness could be genetically transmitted. An important question is how the genetic potential (genotype) interacts with the environment to produce the offending behavior (phenotype). David Rowe (1994) argued that genetic influences should always be estimated in studying the links between family factors and delinquency.

An alternative theory focuses on assortative mating; female offenders tend to cohabit with or get married to male offenders. In the Dunedin study in New Zealand, which is a longitudinal survey of over one thousand children from age three, Robert Krueger and his colleagues found that sexual partners tended to be similar in their self-reported antisocial behavior. Children with two criminal parents are likely to be disproportionally antisocial. There are two main classes of explanations concerning why similar people tend to get married, cohabit, or become sexual partners. The first is called *social homogamy*. Convicted people tend to choose each other as mates because of physical and social proximity; they meet each other in the same schools, neighborhoods, clubs, pubs, and so on. The second process is called *phenotypic assortment*; people examine each other's personality and behavior and choose partners who are similar to themselves.

Other intergenerational transmission theories focus on the intergenerational continuity in exposure to multiple risk factors, on direct and mutual influences of family members on each other, and on risk factors that might intervene between criminal parents and delinquent children (such as poor supervision or disrupted families). It seems likely that both genetic and environmental factors are involved.

Individual influences

The Eysenck personality theory. Studies show that antisocial behavior is remarkably consistent over time; or, to be more precise, the relative ordering of individuals is remarkably consistent over time (Roberts and Del Vecchio). Psychologists assume that behavioral consistency depends primarily on the persistence of individuals' underlying tendencies to behave in particular ways in particular situations. These tendencies are termed personality traits, such as impulsiveness, excitement seeking, assertiveness, modesty, and dutifulness. Larger personality dimensions such as Extraversion refer to clusters of personality traits.

Historically, the best-known research on personality and crime was that inspired by Hans Eysenck's theory and personality questionnaires. Eysenck viewed offending as natural and even rational, on the assumption that human beings were hedonistic, sought pleasure, and avoided pain. He assumed that delinquent acts such as theft, violence, and vandalism were essentially pleasurable or beneficial to the offender. In order to explain why everyone was not a criminal, Eysenck suggested that the hedonistic tendency to commit crimes was opposed by the conscience, which he (like Gordon Trasler) viewed as a conditioned fear response.

Under the Eysenck theory, the people who commit offenses have not built up strong consciences, mainly because they have inherently poor conditionability. Poor conditionability is linked to Eysenck's three dimensions of personality, Extraversion (E), Neuroticism (N), and Psychoticism (P). People who are high on E build up conditioned responses less well, because they have low levels of cortical arousal. People who are high on N also condition less well, because their high resting level of anxiety interferes with their conditioning. Also, since N acts as a drive, reinforcing existing behavioral tendencies, neurotic extraverts should be particularly criminal. Eysenck also predicted that people who are high on P would tend to be offenders, because the traits included in his definition of psychoticism (emotional coldness, low empathy, high hostility, and inhumanity) were typical of criminals. However, the meaning of the P scale is unclear, and it might perhaps be more accurately labeled as psychopathy.

A review of studies relating Eysenck's personality dimensions to official and self-reported offending concluded that high N (but not E) was related to official offending, while high E (but not N) was related to self-reported offending (Farrington et al., 1982). High P was related to both, but this could have been a tautological result, since many of the items on the P scale were connected with antisocial behavior or were selected in light of their ability to discriminate between prisoners and nonprisoners. In the prospective longitudinal study of over four hundred London boys, those high on both E and N tended to be juvenile self-reported offenders, adult official offenders, and adult self-reported offenders, but not juvenile official offenders. These relationships held independently of other criminogenic risk factors such as low family income, low intelligence, and poor parental child-rearing behavior. However, when individual items of the personality questionnaire were studied, it was clear that the significant relationships were caused by the items measuring impulsiveness (e.g., doing things quickly without stopping to think). Hence, it seems likely that research inspired by the Eysenck theory mainly identifies the link between impulsiveness and offending.

Since 1990 the most widely accepted personality system has been the "Big Five" or five-factor model. This suggests that there are five key dimensions of personality: Neuroticism (N), Extraversion (E), Openness (O), Agreeableness (A), and Conscientiousness (C). Openness means originality and openness to new ideas, Agreeableness includes nurturance and altruism, and Conscientiousness includes planning and the will to achieve. Because of its newness, the "Big Five" personality theory has rarely been studied in relation to offending. However, in an Australian study, Patrick Heaven (1996) showed that Agreeableness and Conscientiousness were most strongly (negatively) correlated with self-reported delinquency.

Impulsiveness theories. Impulsiveness is the most crucial personality dimension that predicts offending. Unfortunately, there are a bewildering number of constructs referring to a poor ability to control behavior. These include impulsiveness, hyperactivity, restlessness, clumsiness, not considering consequences before acting, a poor ability to plan ahead, short time horizons, low self-control, sensation-seeking, risk-taking, and a poor ability to delay gratification. In the longitudinal study of over four hundred London males, three groups of boys all tended to become offenders later in life: (1) boys nominated by teachers as lacking in concentration or exhibiting restlessness; (2) boys nominated by parents, peers, or teachers as the most daring or risk-taking; and (3) boys who were the most impulsive on psychomotor tests at ages eight to ten. Later self-report measures of impulsiveness were also related to offending. Daring, poor concentration, and restlessness all predicted both official convictions and self-reported delinquency, and daring was consistently one of the best independent predictors (Farrington, 1992).

The most extensive research on different measures of impulsiveness was carried out in another longitudinal study of males (the Pittsburgh Youth Study) by Jennifer White and her colleagues. The measures that were most strongly related to self-reported delinquency at ages ten and thirteen were teacher-rated impulsiveness (e.g., "acts without thinking"), self-reported impulsivity, self-reported under-control (e.g., "unable to delay gratification"), motor restlessness (from videotaped observations), and psychomotor impulsivity. Generally, the verbal behavior rating tests produced stronger relationships with offending than the psychomotor performance tests, suggesting that cognitive impulsiveness (based on thinking processes) was more relevant than behavioral impulsiveness (based on test performance). Future time perception and delay of gratification tests were less strongly related to self-reported delinquency.

There have been many theories put forward to explain the link between impulsiveness and offending. One of the most popular theories suggests that impulsiveness reflects deficits in the executive functions of the brain, located in the frontal lobes (Moffitt). Persons with these neuropsychological deficits will tend to commit offenses because they have poor control over their behavior, a poor ability to consider the possible consequences of their acts, and a tendency to focus on immediate gratification. There may also be an indirect link between neuropsychological deficits and offending that is mediated by hyperactivity and inattention in school and the resulting school failure. A related theory suggests that low cortical arousal produces impulsive and sensation-seeking behavior.

James Q. Wilson and Richard Herrnstein (1985) also proposed an important criminological theory focusing on impulsiveness and offending, which incorporated propositions from several other psychological theories. Their theory suggested that people differ in their underlying criminal tendencies, and that whether a person chooses to commit a crime in any situation depends on whether the expected benefits of offending are considered to outweigh the expected costs. Hence, there is a focus on cognitive (thinking and decision-making) processes.

The benefits of offending, including material gain, peer approval, and sexual gratification, tend to be contemporaneous with the crime. In contrast, many of the costs of offending, such as the risk of being caught and punished, and the possible loss of reputation or employment, are uncertain and long-delayed. Other costs, such as pangs of conscience (or guilt), disapproval by onlookers, and retaliation by the victim, are more immediate. As with many other psychological theories, Wilson and Herrnstein (1985) emphasized the importance of the conscience as an internal inhibitor of offending, suggesting that it was built up in a social learning process according to whether parents reinforced or punished childhood transgressions.

The key individual difference factor in the Wilson-Herrnstein theory is the extent to which people's behavior is influenced by immediate as opposed to delayed consequences. They suggested that individuals varied in their ability to think about or plan for the future, and that this factor was linked to intelligence. The major determinant of offending was a person's impulsiveness. More impulsive people were less influenced by the likelihood of future consequences and hence were more likely to commit crimes.

In many respects, Gottfredson and Hirschi's (1990) theory is similar to the Wilson-Herrnstein theory and typical of psychological explanations of crime because it emphasizes individual and family factors as well as continuity and stability of underlying criminal tendencies. Despite their sociological training, Gottfredson and Hirschi castigated criminological theorists for ignoring the fact that people differed in underlying criminal propensities and that these differences appeared early in life and remained stable over much of the life course. They called the key individual difference factor in their theory "low self-control," which referred to the extent to which individuals were vulnerable to the temptations of the moment. People with low self-control were impulsive, took risks, had low cognitive and academic skills, were self-centered, had low empathy, and lived for the present rather than the future. Hence, such people found it hard to defer gratification and their decisions to offend were insufficiently influenced by the possible future painful consequences of offending. Gottfredson and Hirschi also argued that between-individual differences in self-control were present early in life (by ages six to eight), were remarkably stable over time, and were essentially caused by differences in parental child-rearing practices.

Cognitive theories. While most psychologists have aimed to explain the development of offenders, some have focused on the occurrence of offending events. The most popular theory of offending events suggests that they occur in response to specific opportunities, when their expected benefits (e.g., stolen property, peer approval) outweigh their expected costs (e.g., legal punishment, parental disapproval). For example, Ronald Clarke and Derek Cornish outlined a theory of residential burglary that included the following influencing factors: whether the house was occupied, looked affluent, had bushes to hide behind, had a burglar alarm, contained a dog, and was surrounded by nosy neighbors. This rational choice theory has inspired situational methods of crime prevention.

The importance of reasoning and thinking processes is also emphasized in other psychological theories of offending, for example in the moral development theory of Lawrence Kohlberg. According to this theory, people progress through different stages of moral development as they get older: from the preconventional stage (where they are hedonistic and only obey the law because of fear of punishment) to the conventional stage (where they obey the law because it is the law) to the postconventional stage (where they obey the law if it coincides with higher moral principles such as justice, fairness, and respect for individual rights). The preconventional stage corresponds to rather concrete thinking, where-

as abstract thinking is required to progress to the postconventional stage. Clearly, the developing moral reasoning ability is related to the developing intelligence.

The key idea of moral reasoning theory is that moral actions depend on moral reasoning. Specifically, the theory posits that offenders have poor powers of moral reasoning and are mainly stuck in the preconventional stage. There is a good deal of evidence that offenders indeed show lower levels of moral reasoning than nonoffenders, and some institutional treatment programs have been designed to improve moral reasoning ability.

Some theories of aggression focus on cognitive processes. Rowell Huesmann and Leonard Eron put forward a cognitive script model in which aggressive behavior depends on stored behavioral repertoires (cognitive scripts) that have been learned during early development. In response to environmental cues, possible cognitive scripts are retrieved and evaluated. The choice of aggressive scripts, which prescribe aggressive behavior, depends on the past history of rewards and punishments, and on the extent to which children are influenced by immediate gratification as opposed to long-term consequences. According to Huesmann and Eron, the persisting trait of aggressiveness is a collection of well-learned aggressive scripts that are resistant to change.

There are other cognitive social learning theories that emphasize the role of modeling instructions, thought processes, and interpersonal problem-solving strategies (e.g., Bandura). The individual is viewed as an information-processor whose behavior depends on cognitive processes as well as on the history of rewards and punishments received in the past. Robert and Rosslyn Ross explicitly linked offending to cognitive deficits, arguing that offenders tended to be impulsive, self-centered, concrete rather than abstract in their thinking, and poor at interpersonal problem solving because they failed to understand how other people were thinking and feeling. Cognitive-behavioral skills training programs for offenders are based on these ideas.

More comprehensive theories

Farrington's (1996) theory of offending and antisocial behavior attempts to integrate propositions from several other theories, and it distinguishes explicitly between the development of antisocial tendencies and the occurrence of antisocial acts. This theory suggests that offending is the end result of energizing, directing, inhibiting, and decision-making processes.

According to this theory, the main long-term energizing factors that ultimately lead to variations in antisocial tendencies are desires for material goods, status among intimates, and excitement. The main short-term energizing factors that lead to variations in antisocial tendencies are boredom, frustration, anger, and alcohol consumption. The desire for excitement may be greater among children from poorer families, for several reasons: excitement is more highly valued by lower-class people than by middle-class ones, poorer children think they lead more boring lives, or poorer children are less able to postpone immediate gratification in favor of long-term goals (which could be linked to the emphasis in lower-class culture on the concrete and present as opposed to the abstract and future).

In the directing stage, these motivations produce antisocial tendencies if socially disapproved methods of satisfying them are habitually chosen. The methods chosen depend on maturation and behavioral skills; for example, a five-year-old child would have difficulty stealing a car. Some people (e.g., children from poorer families) are less able to satisfy their desires for material goods, excitement, and social status by legal or socially approved methods, and so tend to choose illegal or socially disapproved methods. The relative inability of poorer children to achieve goals by legitimate methods could be because they tend to fail in school and tend to have erratic, low status employment histories. School failure in turn may often be a consequence of the unstimulating intellectual environment that lower-class parents tend to provide for their children, and their lack of emphasis on abstract concepts.

In the inhibiting stage, antisocial tendencies can be inhibited by internalized beliefs and attitudes that have been built up in a social learning process as a result of a history of rewards and punishments. The belief that offending is wrong, or a strong conscience, tends to be built up if parents are in favor of legal norms, if they exercise close supervision over their children, and if they punish socially disapproved behavior using firm but kindly discipline. Antisocial tendencies can also be inhibited by empathy, which may develop as a result of parental warmth and loving relationships. The belief that offending is legitimate (and anti-establishment attitudes generally) tend

to be built up if children have been exposed to attitudes and behavior favoring offending (e.g., in a modeling process) especially by members of their family, by their friends, and in their communities.

In the decision-making stage, which specifies the interaction between the individual and the environment, whether a person with a certain degree of antisocial tendency commits an antisocial act in a given situation depends on opportunities, costs and benefits, and on the subjective probabilities of the different outcomes. The costs and benefits include immediate situational factors such as the material goods that can be stolen and the likelihood and consequences of being caught by the police, as perceived by the individual. They also include social factors such as likely disapproval by the parents or spouses, and encouragement or reinforcement from peers. In general, people tend to make rational decisions. However, more impulsive people are less likely to consider the possible consequences of their actions, especially consequences that are likely to be long delayed. There is also a learning process that feeds back into the other processes, since people learn from the consequences of their actions.

Conclusions

There are many common features in existing psychological theories of offending (Farrington, 1994). Most theories assume the following: (1) there are consistent individual differences in an underlying construct such as criminal potential or antisocial personality; (2) hedonism or the pursuit of pleasure is the main energizing factor; (3) there is internal inhibition of offending through the conscience or some similar mechanism; (4) methods of child-rearing used by parents are crucial in developing this conscience in a social learning process; (5) where parents provide antisocial models, there can also be learning of antisocial behavior; (6) the commission of offenses in any situation essentially involves a rational decision in which the likely costs are weighed against the likely benefits; and (7) impulsiveness, or a poor ability to take account of and be influenced by the possible future consequences of offending, is an important factor, often linked to a poor ability to manipulate abstract concepts.

Future psychological theories of offending need to be more wide-ranging, including biological, individual, family, peer, school and neighborhood factors, as well as motivational, inhibiting, decision-making, and learning processes. It is plausible to propose sequential models in which, for example, neighborhood factors such as social disorganization influence family factors such as child-rearing, which in turn influence individual factors such as impulsiveness. Existing theories aim to explain all types of offenders, but different theories may be needed to explain occasional or situational offenders as opposed to persistent or chronic offenders with an antisocial lifestyle. However, it is important that theories do not become so complex that they can explain everything but predict nothing.

Theories need to be carefully specified, so that they lead to testable empirical predictions. The emphasis in the past has been on explaining well-known relationships between risk factors and offending rather than on predicting new findings. Future theorists should plan a program of theoretical development where theories and evidence advance together in a cumulative fashion, with the theories guiding the research and the findings leading to a better specification of the theories.

DAVID P. FARRINGTON

See also DIMINISHED CAPACITY; EXCUSE: INSANITY; INTELLIGENCE AND CRIME; MENTALLY DISORDERED OFFENDERS; PREDICTION OF CRIME AND RECIDIVISM; PSYCHOPATHY; REHABILITATION; SCIENTIFIC EVIDENCE.

BIBLIOGRAPHY

BANDURA, ALBERT. *Social Learning Theory.* Englewood Cliffs, N.J.: Prentice-Hall, 1977.

CLARKE, RONALD V., and CORNISH, DEREK B. "Modelling Offenders' Decisions: A Framework for Research and Policy." In *Crime and Justice,* vol. 6. Edited by Michael Tonry and Norval Morris. Chicago: University of Chicago Press, 1985. Pages 147–183.

EYSENCK, HANS J. "Personality and Crime: Where do we Stand?" *Psychology, Crime and Law* 2 (1996): 143–152.

FARRINGTON, DAVID P. "Juvenile Delinquency." In *The School Years,* 2d ed. Edited by John C. Coleman. London: Routledge, 1992. Pages 123–163.

———. "Motivations for Conduct Disorder and Delinquency." *Development and Psychopathology* 5 (1993): 225–241.

———, ed. *Psychological Explanations of Crime.* Aldershot, U.K.: Dartmouth, 1994.

———. "The Explanation and Prevention of Youthful Offending." In *Delinquency and Crime: Current Theories.* Edited by J. David Hawkins. Cambridge, U.K.: Cambridge University Press, 1996. Pages 68–148.

———. "Explaining and Preventing Crime: The Globalization of Knowledge—The American Society of Criminology 1999 Presidential Address." *Criminology* 38 (2000): 1–24.

FARRINGTON, DAVID P.; BARNES, GEOFFREY; and LAMBERT, SANDRA. "The Concentration of Offending in Families." *Legal and Criminological Psychology* 1 (1996): 47–63.

FARRINGTON, DAVID P.; BIRON, LOUISE; and LEBLANC, MARC. "Personality and Delinquency in London and Montreal." In *Abnormal Offenders, Delinquency, and the Criminal Justice System.* Edited by John Gunn and David P. Farrington. Chichester, U.K.: Wiley, 1982. Pages 153–201.

GOTTFREDSON, MICHAEL, and HIRSCHI, TRAVIS. *A General Theory of Crime.* Stanford, Calif.: Stanford University Press, 1990.

GROVE, WILLIAM M.; ECKERT, ELKE D.; HESTON, LEONARD; BOUCHARD, THOMAS J.; SEGAL, NANCY; and LYKKEN, DAVID T. "Heritability of Substance Abuse and Antisocial Behavior: A Study of Monozygotic Twins Reared Apart." *Biological Psychiatry* 27 (1990): 1293–1304.

HEAVEN, PATRICK C. L. "Personality and Self-Reported Delinquency. Analysis of the 'Big Five' Personality Dimensions." *Personality and Individual Differences* 20 (1996): 47–54.

HUESMANN, L. ROWELL, and ERON, LEONARD D. "Individual Differences and the Trait of Aggression." *European Journal of Personality* 3 (1984): 95–106.

JUBY, HEATHER, and FARRINGTON, DAVID P. "Disentangling the Link between Disrupted Families and Delinquency." *British Journal of Criminology* 41 (2001): 22–40.

KLINE, PAUL. "Psychoanalysis and Crime." In *Applying Psychology to Imprisonment.* Edited by Barry J. McGurk, David M. Thornton, and Mark Williams. London: Her Majesty's Stationery Office, 1987. Pages 59–75.

KOHLBERG, LAWRENCE. "Moral Stages and Moralization: The Cognitive-Developmental Approach." In *Moral Development and Behavior.* Edited by Thomas Lickona. New York: Holt, Rinehart and Winston, 1976. Pages 31–53.

KOLVIN, ISRAEL; MILLER, F. J. W.; FLEETING, M.; and KOLVIN, P. A. "Social and Parenting Factors Affecting Criminal Offense Rates: Findings from the Newcastle Thousand Family Study (1947–1980)." *British Journal of Psychiatry* 152 (1988): 80–90.

KRUEGER, ROBERT F.; MOFFITT, TERRIE E.; CASPI, AVSHALOM; BLESKE, APRIL; and SILVA, PHIL A.

"Assortative Mating for Antisocial Behavior: Developmental and Methodological Implications." *Behavior Genetics* 28 (1998): 173–186.

MCCORD, JOAN. "Some Child-Rearing Antecedents of Criminal Behavior in Adult Men." *Journal of Personality and Social Psychology* 37 (1979): 1477–1486.

———. "A Longitudinal View of the Relationship between Paternal Absence and Crime." In *Abnormal Offenders, Delinquency and the Criminal Justice System*. Edited by John Gunn and David P. Farrington. Chichester, U.K.: Wiley, 1982. Pages 113–128.

———. "On Discipline." *Psychological Inquiry* 8 (1997): 215–217.

MOFFITT, TERRIE E. "The Neuropsychology of Juvenile Delinquency: A Critical Review." In *Crime and Justice*, vol. 12. Edited by Michael Tonry and Norval Morris. Chicago: University of Chicago Press, 1990. Pages 99–169.

NEWSON, JOHN, and NEWSON, ELIZABETH. *The Extent of Parental Physical Punishment in the UK*. London: Approach, 1989.

PATTERSON, GERALD R. *Coercive Family Process*. Eugene, Oregon: Castalia, 1982.

RAINE, ADRIAN. *The Psychopathology of Crime: Criminal Behavior as a Clinical Disorder*. San Diego, Calif.: Academic Press, 1993.

ROBERTS, BRENT W., and DEL VECCHIO, WENDY F. "The Rank-Order Consistency of Personality Traits from Childhood to Old Age: A Quantitative Review of Longitudinal Studies." *Psychological Bulletin* 126 (2000): 3–25.

ROBINS, LEE N. "Sturdy Childhood Predictors of Adult Outcomes: Replications from Longitudinal Studies." *Psychological Medicine* 8 (1979): 611–622.

ROSS, ROBERT R., and ROSS, ROSSLYN D., eds. *Thinking Straight: The Reasoning and Rehabilitation Program for Delinquency Prevention and Offender Rehabilitation*. Ottawa: Air Training and Publications, 1995.

ROWE, DAVID. *The Limits of Family Influence*. New York: Guilford, 1994.

TRASLER, GORDON B. *The Explanation of Criminality*. London: Routledge and Kegan Paul, 1962.

WHITE, JENNIFER L.; MOFFITT, TERRIE E.; CASPI, AVSHALOM; BARTUSCH DAWN J.; NEEDLES, DOUGLAS J.; and STOUTHAMER-LOEBER, MAGDA. "Measuring Impulsivity and Examining its Relationship to Delinquency." *Journal of Abnormal Psychology* 103 (1994): 192–205.

WILSON, JAMES Q., and HERRNSTEIN, RICHARD J. *Crime and Human Nature*. New York: Simon and Schuster, 1985.

CRIME CAUSATION: SOCIOLOGICAL THEORIES

This entry focuses on the three major sociological theories of crime and delinquency: strain, social learning, and control theories. It then briefly describes several other important theories of crime, most of which represent elaborations of these three theories. Finally, efforts to develop integrated theories of crime are briefly discussed.

All of the theories that are described explain crime in terms of the social environment, including the family, school, peer group, workplace, community, and society. These theories, however, differ from one another in several ways: they focus on somewhat different features of the social environment, they offer different accounts of why the social environment causes crime, and some focus on explaining individual differences in crime while others attempt to explain group differences in crime (e.g., why some communities have higher crime rates than other communities).

Strain theory

Why do people engage in crime according to strain theory? They experience strain or stress, they become upset, and they sometimes engage in crime as a result. They may engage in crime to reduce or escape from the strain they are experiencing. For example, they may engage in violence to end harassment from others, they may steal to reduce financial problems, or they may run away from home to escape abusive parents. They may also engage in crime to seek revenge against those who have wronged them. And they may engage in the crime of illicit drug use to make themselves feel better.

A recent version of strain theory is Robert Agnew's 1992 general strain theory. Agnew's theory draws heavily on previous versions of strain theory, particularly those of Robert Merton, Albert Cohen, Richard Cloward and Lloyd Ohlin, David Greenberg, and Delbert Elliott and associates. Agnew, however, points to certain types of strain not considered in these previous versions and provides a fuller discussion of the conditions under which strain is most likely to lead to crime.

The major types of strain. Agnew describes two general categories of strain that contribute to crime: (1) others prevent you from achieving your goals, and (2) others take things you value or present you with negative or noxious stimuli.

While strain may result from the failure to achieve a variety of goals, Agnew and others focus on the failure to achieve three related goals: money, status/respect, and—for adolescents—autonomy from adults.

Money is perhaps the central goal in the United States. All people, poor as well as rich, are encouraged to work hard so that they might make a lot of money. Further, money is necessary to buy many of the things we want, including the necessities of life and luxury items. Many people, however, are prevented from getting the money they need through legal channels, such as work. This is especially true for poor people, but it is true for many middle-class people with lofty goals as well. As a consequence, such people experience strain and they may attempt to get money through illegal channels—such as theft, selling drugs, and prostitution. Studies provide some support for this argument. Criminals and delinquents often report that they engage in income-generating crime because they want money but cannot easily get it any other way. And some data suggest that crime is more common among people who are dissatisfied with their monetary situation—with such dissatisfaction being higher among lower-class people and people who state that they want "a lot of money."

Closely related to the desire for money is the desire for status and respect. People want to be positively regarded by others and they want to be treated respectfully by others, which at a minimum involves being treated in a just or fair manner. While people have a general desire for status and respect, theorists such as James Messerschmidt argue that the desire for "masculine status" is especially relevant to crime. There are class and race differences in views about what it means to be a "man," although most such views emphasize traits like independence, dominance, toughness, competitiveness, and heterosexuality. Many males, especially those who are young, lower-class, and members of minority groups, experience difficulties in satisfying their desire to be viewed and treated as men. These people may attempt to "accomplish masculinity" through crime. They may attempt to coerce others into giving them the respect they believe they deserve as "real men." In this connection, they may adopt a tough demeanor, respond to even minor shows of disrespect with violence, and occasionally assault and rob others in an effort to establish a tough reputation. There have been no large scale tests of this idea, although several studies such as that of Elijah Anderson provide support for it.

Finally, a major goal of most adolescents is autonomy from adults. Autonomy may be defined as power over oneself: the ability to resist the demands of others and engage in action without the permission of others. Adolescents are often encouraged to be autonomous, but they are frequently denied autonomy by adults. The denial of autonomy may lead to delinquency for several reasons: delinquency may be a means of asserting autonomy (e.g., sexual intercourse or disorderly behavior), achieving autonomy (e.g., stealing money to gain financial independence from parents), or venting frustration against those who deny autonomy.

In addition to the failure to achieve one's goals, strain may result when people take something one values or present one with noxious or negative stimuli. Such negative treatment may upset or anger people and crime may be the result. Studies have found that a range of negative events and conditions increase the likelihood of crime. In particular, crime has been linked to child abuse and neglect, criminal victimization, physical punishment by parents, negative relations with parents, negative relations with teachers, negative school experiences, negative relations with peers, neighborhood problems, and a wide range of stressful life events—like the divorce/separation of a parent, parental unemployment, and changing schools.

Factors influencing the effect of strain on delinquency. Strainful events and conditions make people feel bad. These bad feelings, in turn, create pressure for corrective action. This is especially true of anger and frustration, which energize the individual for action, create a desire for revenge, and lower inhibitions. There are several possible ways to cope with strain and these negative emotions, only some of which involve delinquency. Strain theorists attempt to describe those factors that increase the likelihood of a criminal response.

Among other things, strain is more likely to lead to crime among individuals with poor coping skills and resources. Some individuals are better able to cope with strain legally than others. For example, they have the verbal skills to negotiate with others or the financial resources to hire a lawyer. Related to this, strain is more likely to lead to delinquency among individuals with few conventional social supports. Family, friends, and others often help individuals cope with their problems, providing advice, direct assistance, and emotional support. In doing so, they reduce the likelihood of a criminal response.

Strain is more likely to lead to delinquency when the costs of delinquency are low and the benefits are high; that is, the probability of being caught and punished is low and the rewards of delinquency are high. Finally, strain is more likely to lead to delinquency among individuals who are disposed to delinquency. The individual's disposition to engage in delinquency is influenced by a number of factors. Certain individual traits—like irritability and impulsivity—increase the disposition for delinquency. Another key factor is whether individuals blame their strain on the deliberate behavior of someone else. Finally, individuals are more disposed to delinquency if they hold beliefs that justify delinquency, if they have been exposed to delinquent models, and if they have been reinforced for delinquency in the past (see below).

A variety of factors, then, influence whether individuals respond to strain with delinquency. Unfortunately, there has not been much research on the extent to which these factors condition the impact of strain—and the research that has been done has produced mixed results.

Social learning theory

Why do people engage in crime according to social learning theory? They learn to engage in crime, primarily through their association with others. They are reinforced for crime, they learn beliefs that are favorable to crime, and they are exposed to criminal models. As a consequence, they come to view crime as something that is desirable or at least justifiable in certain situations. The primary version of social learning theory in criminology is that of Ronald Akers and the description that follows draws heavily on his work. Akers's theory, in turn, represents an elaboration of Edwin Sutherland's differential association theory (also see the related work of Albert Bandura in psychology).

According to social learning theory, juveniles learn to engage in crime in the same way they learn to engage in conforming behavior: through association with or exposure to others. Primary or intimate groups like the family and peer group have an especially large impact on what we learn. In fact, association with delinquent friends is the best predictor of delinquency other than prior delinquency. However, one does not have to be in direct contact with others to learn from them; for example, one may learn to engage in violence from observation of others in the media.

Most of social learning theory involves a description of the three mechanisms by which individuals learn to engage in crime from these others: differential reinforcement, beliefs, and modeling.

Differential reinforcement of crime. Individuals may teach others to engage in crime through the reinforcements and punishments they provide for behavior. Crime is more likely to occur when it (a) is frequently reinforced and infrequently punished; (b) results in large amounts of reinforcement (e.g., a lot of money, social approval, or pleasure) and little punishment; and (c) is more likely to be reinforced than alternative behaviors.

Reinforcements may be positive or negative. In positive reinforcement, the behavior results in something good—some positive consequence. This consequence may involve such things as money, the pleasurable feelings associated with drug use, attention from parents, approval from friends, or an increase in social status. In negative reinforcement, the behavior results in the removal of something bad—a punisher is removed or avoided. For example, suppose one's friends have been calling her a coward because she refuses to use drugs with them. The individual eventually takes drugs with them, after which time they stop calling her a coward. The individual's drug use has been negatively reinforced.

According to social learning theory, some individuals are in environments where crime is more likely to be reinforced (and less likely to be punished). Sometimes this reinforcement is deliberate. For example, the parents of aggressive children often deliberately encourage and reinforce aggressive behavior outside the home. Or the adolescent's friends may reinforce drug use. At other times, the reinforcement for crime is less deliberate. For example, an embarrassed parent may give her screaming child a candy bar in the checkout line of a supermarket. Without intending to do so, the parent has just reinforced the child's aggressive behavior.

Data indicate that individuals who are reinforced for crime are more likely to engage in subsequent crime, especially when they are in situations similar to those where they were previously reinforced.

Beliefs favorable to crime. Other individuals may not only reinforce our crime, they may also teach us beliefs favorable to crime. Most individuals, of course, are taught that crime is bad or wrong. They eventually accept or "internalize" this belief, and they are less likely to engage in crime as a result. Some individuals, however, learn beliefs that are favorable to crime and they are more likely to engage in crime as a result.

Few people—including criminals—generally approve of serious crimes like burglary and robbery. Surveys and interviews with criminals suggest that beliefs favoring crime fall into three categories. And data suggest that each type of belief increases the likelihood of crime.

First, some people generally approve of certain minor forms of crime, like certain forms of consensual sexual behavior, gambling, "soft" drug use, and—for adolescents—alcohol use, truancy, and curfew violation.

Second, some people conditionally approve of or justify certain forms of crime, including some serious crimes. These people believe that crime is generally wrong, but that some criminal acts are justifiable or even desirable in certain conditions. Many people, for example, will state that fighting is generally wrong, but that it is justified if you have been insulted or provoked in some way. Gresham Sykes and David Matza have listed some of the more common justifications used for crime. Several theorists have argued that certain groups in our society—especially lower-class, young, minority males—are more likely to define violence as an acceptable response to a wide range of provocations and insults. And they claim that this "subculture of violence" is at least partly responsible for the higher rate of violence in these groups. Data in this area are somewhat mixed, but recent studies suggest that males, young people, and possibly lower-class people are more likely to hold beliefs favorable to violence. There is less evidence for a relationship between race and beliefs favorable to violence.

Third, some people hold certain general values that are conducive to crime. These values do not explicitly approve of or justify crime, but they make crime appear a more attractive alternative than would otherwise be the case. Theorists such as Matza and Sykes have listed three general sets of values in this area: an emphasis on "excitement," "thrills," or "kicks"; a disdain for hard work and a desire for quick, easy success; and an emphasis on toughness or being "macho." Such values can be realized through legitimate as well as illegitimate channels, but individuals with such values will likely view crime in a more favorable light than others.

The imitation of criminal models. Behavior is not only a function of beliefs and the reinforcements and punishments individuals receive, but also of the behavior of those around them. In particular, individuals often imitate or model the behavior of others—especially when they like or respect these others and have reason to believe that imitating their behavior will result in reinforcement. For example, individuals are more likely to imitate others' behavior if they observe them receive reinforcement for their acts.

Social learning theory has much support and is perhaps the dominant theory of crime today. Data indicate that the people one associates with have a large impact on whether or not one engages in crime, and that this impact is partly explained by the effect these people have on one's beliefs regarding crime, the reinforcements and punishments one receives, and the models one is exposed to.

Control theory

Strain and social learning theorists ask, Why do people engage in crime? They then focus on the factors that push or entice people into committing criminal acts. Control theorists, however, begin with a rather different question. They ask, Why do people conform? Unlike strain and social learning theorists, control theorists take crime for granted. They argue that all people have needs and desires that are more easily satisfied through crime than through legal channels. For example, it is much easier to steal money than to work for it. So in the eyes of control theorists, crime requires no special explanation: it is often the most expedient way to get what one wants. Rather than explaining why people engage in crime, we need to explain why they do not.

According to control theorists, people do not engage in crime because of the controls or restraints placed on them. These controls may be viewed as barriers to crime—they refer to those factors that prevent them from engaging in crime. So while strain and social learning theory focus on those factors that push or lead the individual into crime, control theory focuses on the factors that restrain the individual from engaging in crime. Control theory goes on to argue that people differ in their level of control or in the restraints they face to crime. These differences explain differences in crime: some people are freer to engage in crime than others.

Control theories describe the major types of social control or the major restraints to crime. The control theory of Travis Hirschi dominates the literature, but Gerald Patterson and associates, Michael Gottfredson and Travis Hirschi, and Robert Sampson and John Laub have extended Hirschi's theory in important ways. Rather than describing the different versions of control theory, an integrated control theory that draws on all of their insights is presented.

This integrated theory lists three major types of control: direct control, stake in conformity, and internal control. Each type has two or more components.

Direct control. When most people think of control they think of direct control: someone watching over people and sanctioning them for crime. Such control may be exercised by family members, school officials, coworkers, neighborhood residents, police, and others. Family members, however, are the major source of direct control given their intimate relationship with the person. Direct control has three components: setting rules, monitoring behavior, and sanctioning crime.

Direct control is enhanced to the extent that family members and others provide the person with clearly defined rules that prohibit criminal behavior and that limit the opportunities and temptations for crime. These rules may specify such things as who the person may associate with and the activities in which they can and cannot engage.

Direct control also involves monitoring the person's behavior to ensure that they comply with these rules and do not engage in crime. Monitoring may be direct or indirect. In direct monitoring, the person is under the direct surveillance of a parent or other conventional "authority figure." In indirect monitoring, the parent or authority figure does not directly observe the person but makes an effort to keep tabs on what they are doing. The parent, for example, may ask the juvenile where he or she is going, may periodically call the juvenile, and may ask others about the juvenile's behavior. People obviously differ in the extent to which their behavior is monitored.

Finally, direct control involves effectively sanctioning crime when it occurs. Effective sanctions are consistent, fair, and not overly harsh.

Level of direct control usually emerges as an important cause of crime in most studies.

Stake in conformity. The efforts to directly control behavior are a major restraint to crime. These efforts, however, are more effective with some people than with others. For example, all juveniles are subject to more or less the same direct controls at school: the same rules, the same

monitoring, and the same sanctions if they deviate. Yet some juveniles are very responsive to these controls while others commit deviant acts on a regular basis. One reason for this is that some juveniles have more to lose by engaging in deviance. These juveniles have what has been called a high "stake in conformity," and they do not want to jeopardize that stake by engaging in deviance.

So one's stake in conformity—that which one has to lose by engaging in crime—functions as another major restraint to crime. Those with a lot to lose will be more fearful of being caught and sanctioned and so will be less likely to engage in crime. People's stake in conformity has two components: their emotional attachment to conventional others and their actual or anticipated investment in conventional society.

If people have a strong emotional attachment to conventional others, like family members and teachers, they have more to lose by engaging in crime. Their crime may upset people they care about, cause them to think badly of them, and possibly disrupt their relationship with them. Studies generally confirm the importance of this bond. Individuals who report that they love and respect their parents and other conventional figures usually commit fewer crimes. Individuals who do not care about their parents or others, however, have less to lose by engaging in crime.

A second major component of people's stake in conformity is their investment in conventional society. Most people have put a lot of time and energy into conventional activities, like "getting an education, building up a business, [and] acquiring a reputation for virtue" (Hirschi, p. 20). And they have been rewarded for their efforts, in the form of such things as good grades, material possessions, and a good reputation. Individuals may also expect their efforts to reap certain rewards in the future; for example, one might anticipate getting into college or professional school, obtaining a good job, and living in a nice house. In short, people have a large investment—both actual and anticipated—in conventional society. People do not want to jeopardize that investment by engaging in delinquency.

Internal control. People sometimes find themselves in situations where they are tempted to engage in crime and the probability of external sanction (and the loss of those things they value) is low. Yet many people still refrain from crime. The reason is that they are high in internal control. They are able to restrain themselves from engaging in crime. Internal control is a function of their beliefs regarding crime and their level of self-control.

Most people believe that crime is wrong and this belief acts as a major restraint to crime. The extent to which people believe that crime is wrong is at least partly a function of their level of direct control and their stake in conformity: were they closely attached to their parents and did their parents attempt to teach them that crime is wrong? If not, such individuals may form an *amoral orientation* to crime: they believe that crime is neither good nor bad. As a consequence, their beliefs do not restrain them from engaging in crime. Their beliefs do not propel or push them into crime; they do not believe that crime is good. Their amoral beliefs simply free them to pursue their needs and desires in the most expedient way. Rather then being taught that crime is good, control theorists argue that some people are simply not taught that crime is bad.

Finally, some people have personality traits that make them less responsive to the above controls and less able to restrain themselves from acting on their immediate desires. For example, if someone provokes them, they are more likely to get into a fight. Or if someone offers them drugs at a party, they are more likely to accept They do not stop to consider the long-term consequences of their behavior. Rather, they simply focus on the immediate, short-term benefits or pleasures of criminal acts. Such individuals are said to be low in "self-control."

Self-control is indexed by several personality traits. According to Gottfredson and Hirschi, "people who lack self control will tend to be impulsive, insensitive, physical (as opposed to mental), risk-taking, short-sighted, and nonverbal" (p. 90). It is claimed that the major cause of low self-control is "ineffective child-rearing." In particular, low self-control is more likely to result when parents do not establish a strong emotional bond with their children and do not properly monitor and sanction their children for delinquency. Certain theorists also claim that some of the traits characterizing low self-control have biological as well as social causes.

Gottfredson and Hirschi claim that one's level of self-control is determined early in life and is then quite resistant to change. Further, they claim that low self-control is the central cause of crime; other types of control and other causes of crime are said to be unimportant once level of self-control is established. Data do indicate that low self-control is an important cause of crime.

Data, however, suggest that the self-control does vary over the life course and that other causes of crime are also important. For example, Sampson and Laub demonstrate that delinquent adolescents who enter satisfying marriages and obtain stable jobs (i.e., develop a strong stake in conformity) are less likely to engage in crime as adults.

In sum, crime is less likely when others try to directly control the person's behavior, when the person has a lot to lose by engaging in crime, and when the person tries to control his or her own behavior.

Labeling theory

The above theories examine how the social environment causes individuals to engage in crime, but they typically devote little attention to the official reaction to crime, that is, to the reaction of the police and other official agencies. Labeling theory focuses on the official reaction to crime and makes a rather counterintuitive argument regarding the causes of crime.

According to labeling theory, official efforts to control crime often have the effect of increasing crime. Individuals who are arrested, prosecuted, and punished are labeled as criminals. Others then view and treat these people as criminals, and this increases the likelihood of subsequent crime for several reasons. Labeled individuals may have trouble obtaining legitimate employment, which increases their level of strain and reduces their stake in conformity. Labeled individuals may find that conventional people are reluctant to associate with them, and they may associate with other criminals as a result. This reduces their bond with conventional others and fosters the social learning of crime. Finally, labeled individuals may eventually come to view themselves as criminals and act in accord with this self-concept.

Labeling theory was quite popular in the 1960s and early 1970s, but then fell into decline—partly as a result of the mixed results of empirical research. Some studies found that being officially labeled a criminal (e.g., arrested or convicted) increased subsequent crime, while other studies did not. Recent theoretical work, however, has revised the theory to take account of past problems. More attention is now being devoted to informal labeling, such as labeling by parents, peers, and teachers. Informal labeling is said to have a greater effect on subsequent crime than official labeling. Ross Matsueda discusses the reasons why individuals may be informally labeled as delinquents, noting that such labeling is not simply a function of official labeling (e.g., arrest). Informal labeling is also influenced by the individual's delinquent behavior and by their position in society—with powerless individuals being more likely to be labeled (e.g., urban, minority, lower-class, adolescents). Matsueda also argues that informal labels affect individuals' subsequent level of crime by affecting their perceptions of how others see them. If they believe that others see them as delinquents and troublemakers, they are more likely to act in accord with this perception and engage in delinquency. Data provide some support for these arguments.

John Braithwaite extends labeling theory by arguing that labeling increases crime in some circumstances and reduces it in others. Labeling increases subsequent crime when no effort is made to reintegrate the offender back into conventional society; that is, when offenders are rejected or informally labeled on a long-term basis. But labeling reduces subsequent crime when efforts are made to reintegrate punished offenders back into conventional society. In particular, labeling reduces crime when offenders are made to feel a sense of shame or guilt for what they have done, but are eventually forgiven and reintegrated into conventional groups—like family and conventional peer groups. Such reintegration may occur "through words or gestures of forgiveness or ceremonies to decertify the offender as deviant" (pp. 100–101). Braithwaite calls this process "reintegrative shaming." Reintegrative shaming is said to be more likely in certain types of social settings, for example, where individuals are closely attached to their parents, neighbors, and others. Such shaming is also more likely in "communitarian" societies, which place great stress on trust and the mutual obligation to help one another (e.g., Japan versus the United States). Braithwaite's theory has not yet been well tested, but it helps make sense of the mixed results of past research on labeling theory.

Social disorganization theory

The leading sociological theories focus on the immediate social environment, like the family, peer group, and school. And they are most concerned with explaining why some individuals are more likely to engage in crime than others. Much recent theoretical work, however, has also focused on the larger social environment, especially the community and the total society. This work usually attempts to explain why some

groups—like communities and societies—have higher crime rates than other groups. In doing so, however, this work draws heavily on the central ideas of control, social learning, and strain theories.

Social disorganization theory seeks to explain community differences in crime rates (see Robert Sampson and W. Bryon Groves; Robert Bursik and Harold Grasmick). The theory identifies the characteristics of communities with high crime rates and draws on social control theory to explain why these characteristics contribute to crime.

Crime is said to be more likely in communities that are economically deprived, large in size, high in multiunit housing like apartments, high in residential mobility (people frequently move into and out of the community), and high in family disruption (high rates of divorce, single-parent families). These factors are said to reduce the ability or willingness of community residents to exercise effective social control, that is, to exercise direct control, provide young people with a stake in conformity, and socialize young people so that they condemn delinquency and develop self-control.

The residents of high crime communities often lack the skills and resources to effectively assist others. They are poor and many are single parents struggling with family responsibilities. As such, they often face problems in socializing their children against crime and providing them with a stake in conformity, like the skills to do well in school or the connections to secure a good job. These residents are also less likely to have close ties to their neighbors and to care about their community. They typically do not own their own homes, which lowers their investment in the community. They may hope to move to a more desirable community as soon as they are able, which also lowers their investment in the community. And they often do not know their neighbors well, since people frequently move into and out of the community. As a consequence, they are less likely to intervene in neighborhood affairs—like monitoring the behavior of neighborhood residents and sanctioning crime. Finally, these residents are less likely to form or support community organizations, including educational, religious, and recreational organizations. This is partly a consequence of their limited resources and lower attachment to the community. This further reduces control, since these organizations help exercise direct control, provide people with a stake in conformity, and socialize people.

Also, these organizations help secure resources from the larger society, like better schools and police protection. Recent data provide some support for these arguments.

Social disorganization theorists and other criminologists, such as John Hagan, point out that the number of communities with characteristics conducive to crime—particularly high concentrations of poor people—has increased since the 1960s. These communities exist primarily in inner city areas and they are populated largely by members of minority groups (due to the effects of discrimination). Such communities have increased for several reasons. First, there has been a dramatic decline in manufacturing jobs in central city areas, partly due to the relocation of factories to suburban areas and overseas. Also, the wages in manufacturing jobs have become less competitive, due to factors like foreign competition, the increase in the size of the work force, and the decline in unions. Second, the increase in very poor communities is due to the migration of many working- and middle-class African Americans to more affluent communities, leaving the poor behind. This migration was stimulated by a reduction in discriminatory housing and employment practices. Third, certain government policies—like the placement of public housing projects in inner-city communities and the reduction of certain social services— have contributed to the increased concentration of poverty.

Critical theories

Critical theories also try to explain group differences in crime rates in terms of the larger social environment; some focus on class differences, some on gender differences, and some on societal differences in crime. Several versions of critical theory exist, but all explain crime in terms of group differences in power.

Marxist theories. Marxist theories argue that those who own the means of production (e.g., factories, businesses) have the greatest power. This group—the capitalist class—uses its power for its own advantage. Capitalists work for the passage of laws that criminalize and severely sanction the "street" crimes of lower-class persons, but ignore or mildly sanction the harmful actions of business and industry (e.g., pollution, unsafe working conditions). And capitalists act to increase their profits; for example, they resist improvements in working conditions and they attempt to hold down the wages of workers. This

is not to say that the capitalist class is perfectly unified or that the government always acts on its behalf. Most Marxists acknowledge that disputes sometimes arise within the capitalist class and that the government sometimes makes concessions to workers in an effort to protect the long-term interests of capitalists.

Marxists explain crime in several ways. Some draw on strain theory, arguing that workers and unemployed people engage in crime because they are not able to achieve their economic goals through legitimate channels. Also, Marxists argue that crime is a response to the poor living conditions experienced by workers and the unemployed. Some draw on control theory, arguing that crime results from the fact that many workers and the unemployed have little stake in society and are alienated from governmental and business institutions. And some draw on social learning theory, arguing that capitalist societies encourage the unrestrained pursuit of money. Marxist theories, then, attempt to explain both class and societal differences in crime.

Institutional anomie theory. Steven Messner and Richard Rosenfeld's institutional anomie theory draws on control and social learning theories to explain the high crime rate in the United States. According to the theory, the high crime rate partly stems from the emphasis placed on the "American Dream." Everyone is encouraged to strive for monetary success, but little emphasis is placed on the legitimate means to achieve such success: "it's not how you play the game; it's whether you win or lose." As a consequence, many attempt to obtain money through illegitimate channels or crime. Further, the emphasis on monetary success is paralleled by the dominance of economic institutions in the United States. Other major institutions—the family, school, and the political system—are subservient to economic institutions. Noneconomic functions and roles (e.g., parent, teacher) are devalued and receive little support. Noneconomic institutions must accommodate themselves to the demands of the economy (e.g., parents neglect their children because of the demands of work). And economic norms have come to penetrate these other institutions (e.g., the school system, like the economic system, is based on the individualized competition for rewards). As a result, institutions like the family, school, and political system are less able to effectively socialize individuals against crime and sanction deviant behavior.

Feminist theories. Feminist theories focus on gender differences in power as a source of crime. These theories address two issues: why are males more involved in most forms of crime than females, and why do females engage in crime. Most theories of crime were developed with males in mind; feminists argue that the causes of female crime differ somewhat from the causes of male crime.

Gender differences in crime are said to be due largely to gender differences in social learning and control. Females are socialized to be passive, subservient, and focused on the needs of others. Further, females are more closely supervised than males, partly because fathers and husbands desire to protect their "property" from other males. Related to this, females are more closely tied to the household and to child-rearing tasks, which limits their opportunities to engage in many crimes.

Some females, of course, do engage in crime. Feminist theories argue that the causes of their crime differ somewhat from those of male crime, although female crime is largely explained in terms of strain theory. Meda Chesney-Lind and others argue that much female crime stems from the fact that juvenile females are often sexually abused by family members. This high rate of sexual abuse is fostered by the power of males over females, the sexualization of females—especially young females—and a system that often fails to sanction sexual abuse. Abused females frequently run away, but they have difficulty surviving on the street. They are labeled as delinquents, making it difficult for them to obtain legitimate work. Juvenile justice officials, in fact, often arrest such females and return them to the families where they were abused. Further, these females are frequently abused and exploited by men on the street. As a consequence, they often turn to crimes like prostitution and theft to survive. Theorists have pointed to still other types of strain to explain female crime, like the financial and other difficulties experienced by women trying to raise families without financial support from fathers. The rapid increase in female-headed families in recent decades, in fact, has been used to explain the increase in rates of female property crime. It is also argued that some female crime stems from frustration over the constricted roles available to females in our society.

There are other versions of critical theory, including "postmodernist" theories of crime. A good overview can be found in the text by George Vold, Thomas J. Bernard, and Jeffrey B. Snipes.

Situations conducive to crime

The above theories focus on the factors that create a general willingness or predisposition to engage in crime, locating such factors in the immediate and larger social environment. People who are disposed to crime generally commit more crime than those who are not. But even the most predisposed people do not commit crime all of the time. In fact, they obey the law in most situations. Several theories argue that predisposed individuals are more likely to engage in crime in some types of situations than others. These theories specify the types of situations most conducive to crime. Such theories usually argue that crime is most likely in those types of situations where the benefits of crime are seen as high and the costs as low, an argument very compatible with social learning theory.

The most prominent theory in this area is the routine activities perspective, advanced by Lawrence Cohen and Marcus Felson and elaborated by Felson. It is argued that crime is most likely when motivated offenders come together with attractive targets in the absence of capable guardians. Attractive targets are visible, accessible, valuable, and easy to move. The police may function as capable guardians, but it is more common for ordinary people to play this role—like family members, neighbors, and teachers. According to this theory, the supply of suitable targets and the presence of capable guardians are a function of our everyday or "routine" activities—like attending school, going to work, and socializing with friends. For example, Cohen and Felson point to a major change in routine activities since World War II: people are more likely to spend time away from home. This change partly reflects the fact that women have become much more likely to work outside the home and people have become more likely to seek entertainment outside the home. As a result, motivated offenders are more likely to encounter suitable targets in the absence of capable guardians. Homes are left unprotected during the day and often in the evening, and people spend more time in public settings where they may fall prey to motivated offenders. Other theories, like the rational-choice perspective of Derek B. Cornish and Ronald V. Clarke, also discuss the characteristics of situations conducive to crime.

Integrated theories

Several theorists have attempted to combine certain of the above theories in an effort to create integrated theories of crime. The most prominent of these integrations are those of Terence P. Thornberry and Delbert S. Elliott and associates. Elliott's theory states that strain and labeling reduce social control. For example, school failure and negative labeling may threaten one's emotional bond to conventional others and investment in conventional society. Low social control, in turn, increases the likelihood of association with delinquent peers, which promotes the social learning of crime. Thornberry attempts to integrate control and social learning theories. Like Elliott, he argues that low control at home and at school promotes association with delinquent peers and the adoption of beliefs favorable to delinquency. Thornberry, however, also argues that most of the causes of crime have reciprocal effects on one another. For example, low attachment to parents increases the likelihood of association with delinquent peers, and association with delinquent peers reduces attachment to parents. Likewise, delinquency affects many of its causes: for example, it reduces attachment to parents and increases association with delinquent peers (an argument compatible with labeling theory). Further, Thornberry argues that the causes of crime vary over the life course. For example, parents have a much stronger effect on delinquency among younger than older adolescents. Factors like work, marriage, college, and the military, however, are more important among older adolescents.

The future of crime theories

Sociologists continue to refine existing theories and develop new theories of crime, including integrated theories of crime (e.g., Charles Tittle's control balance theory). Sociologists, however, are coming to recognize that it is not possible to explain crime solely in terms of the immediate social environment. As a consequence, they are devoting more attention to the larger social environment, which affects the immediate social environment. And they are devoting more attention to the situations in which people find themselves, which affect whether predisposed individuals will engage in crime. Further, sociologists are coming to recognize that they need to take account of the factors considered in biological, psychological, and other theories of crime. Most notably, they must take account of individual traits like intelligence, impulsivity, and irritability. These traits influence how individuals respond to their social environment. An irritable individual, for example, is more likely to respond to strain with crime. These traits also shape the individual's social environment. Irritable individuals, for example, are more likely to elicit hostile reactions from others and select themselves into social environments that are conducive to crime, like bad jobs and marriages. (At the same time, the social environment influences the development of individual traits and the ways in which individuals with particular traits behave.)

Further, sociologists are increasingly recognizing that their theories may require modification if they are to explain crime in different groups and among different types of offenders. As indicated above, theories may have to be modified to explain female versus male crime. And theories may have to be modified to explain crime across the life course. For example, the factors that explain why young adolescents start committing crime likely differ somewhat from those that explain why some older adolescents continue to commit crimes and others stop. Much recent attention, in fact, has been devoted to the explanation of crime across the life course, as described in the text by Vold, Bernard, and Snipes. Also, theories will have to be modified to explain crime among different types of offenders. Some offenders, for example, limit their offending to the adolescent years. Others offend at high rates across the life course.

Sociological theories, then, will become more complex, taking account of individual traits, the immediate social environment, the larger social environment, and situational factors. And modified versions of such theories will be developed to explain crime in different groups and among different types of offenders.

ROBERT AGNEW

See also CLASS AND CRIME; CRIME CAUSATION: BIOLOGICAL THEORIES; CRIME CAUSATION: ECONOMIC THEORIES; CRIME CAUSATION: POLITICAL THEORIES; CRIME CAUSATION: PSYCHOLOGICAL THEORIES; DELINQUENT AND CRIMINAL SUBCULTURES; DEVIANCE; FAMILY RELATIONSHIPS AND CRIME; GENDER AND CRIME; JUVENILE AND YOUTH GANGS; MASS MEDIA AND CRIME; RACE AND CRIME; RIOTS: BEHAVIORAL ASPECTS; UNEMPLOYMENT AND CRIME; WHITE-COLLAR CRIME; HISTORY OF AN IDEA.

BIBLIOGRAPHY

AGNEW, ROBERT. "Foundation for a General Strain Theory of Crime and Delinquency." *Criminology* 30 (1992): 47–88.

AKERS, RONALD L. *Social Learning and Social Structure*. Boston: Northeastern University Press, 1998.

ANDERSON, ELIJAH. *Code of the Street*. New York: Norton, 1999.

BANDURA, ALBERT. *Social Foundations of Thought and Action*. Englewood Cliffs, N.J.: Prentice Hall, 1986.

BRAITHWAITE, JOHN. *Crime, Shame, and Reintegration*. Cambridge: Cambridge University Press, 1989.

BURSIK, ROBERT J., JR.; and GRASMICK, HAROLD G. *Neighborhoods and Crime*. New York: Lexington, 1993.

CHESNEY-LIND, MEDA; and SHELDON, RANDALL G. *Girls, Delinquency, and Juvenile Justice*. Belmont, Calif.: West/Wadsworth, 1998.

CLOWARD, RICHARD; and OHLIN, LLOYD. *Delinquency and Opportunity*. Glencoe, Ill.: Free Press, 1960.

COHEN, ALBERT K. *Delinquent Boys*. Glencoe, Ill.: Free Press, 1955.

COHEN, LAWRENCE E.; and FELSON, MARCUS. "Social Change and Crime Rate Trends: A Routine Activities Approach." *American Sociological Review* 44 (1979): 588–608.

CORNISH, DEREK B.; and CLARKE, RONALD V. *The Reasoning Criminal*. New York: Springer-Verlag, 1986.

ELLIOTT, DELBERT S.; HUIZINGA, DAVID; and AGETON, SUZANNE S. *Explaining Delinquency and Drug Use*. Beverly Hills, Calif.: Sage, 1985.

FELSON, MARCUS. *Crime and Everyday Life*. Thousand Oaks, Calif.: Pine Forge Press, 1998.

GOTTFREDSON, MICHAEL; and HIRSCHI, TRAVIS. *A General Theory of Crime*. Palo Alto, Calif.: Stanford University Press, 1990.

GREENBERG, DAVID F. "Delinquency and the Age Structure of Society." *Contemporary Crises* 1 (1977): 189–223.

HAGAN, JOHN. *Crime and Disrepute*. Thousand Oaks, Calif.: Pine Forge Press, 1994.

HIRSCHI, TRAVIS. *Causes of Delinquency*. Berkeley, Calif.: University of California Press, 1969.

MATSUEDA, ROSS L. "Reflected Appraisals, Parental Labeling, and Delinquency: Specifying a Symbolic Interactionist Theory." *American Journal of Sociology* 97 (1992): 1577–1611.

MATZA, DAVID; and SYKES, GRESHAM M. "Juvenile Delinquency and Subterranean Values." *American Sociological Review* 26 (1961): 712–719.

MERTON, ROBERT K. "Social Structure and Anomie." *American Sociological Review* 3 (1938): 672–682.

MESSERSCHMIDT, JAMES W. *Masculinities and Crime*. Lantham, Md.: Rowman and Littlefield, 1993.

MESSNER, STEVEN F.; and ROSENFELD, RICHARD. *Crime and the American Dream*. Belmont, Calif.: Wadsworth, 1997.

PATTERSON, GERALD R.; REID, JOHN B.; and DISHION, THOMAS J. *Antisocial Boys*. Eugene, Oreg.: Castalia Publishing Co., 1992.

SAMPSON, ROBERT J.; and GROVES, W. BYRON. "Community Structure and Crime: Testing Social-Disorganization Theory." *American Journal of Sociology* 94 (1989): 774–802.

SAMPSON, ROBERT J.; and LAUB, JOHN H. *Crime in the Making*. Cambridge, Mass.: Harvard University Press, 1993.

SUTHERLAND, EDWIN H.; CRESSEY, DONALD R.; and LUCKENBILL, DAVID F. *Principles of Criminology*. Dix Hills, N.Y.: General Hall, 1992.

SYKES, GRESHAM; and MATZA, DAVID. "Techniques of Neutralization: A Theory of Delinquency." *American Journal of Sociology* 22 (1957): 664–670.

THORNBERRY, TERENCE P. "Towards an Interactional Theory of Delinquency." *Criminology* 25 (1987): 863–891.

TITTLE, CHARLES R. *Control Balance: Toward a General Theory of Deviance*. Boulder, Colo.: Westview, 1995.

VOLD, GEORGE B.; BERNARD, THOMAS J.; and SNIPES, JEFFREY B. *Theoretical Criminology*. New York: Oxford University Press, 1998.

CRIME COMMISSIONS

The emergence of crime as a national issue in America dates back to the early 1920s. The Volstead Act, providing for federal enforcement of the Eighteenth Amendment (which prohibited the manufacture, sale, or transportation of intoxicating liquors), went into effect in January 1920. This was followed by the rapid growth of organized crime in the form of large-scale smuggling, manufacture, and sale of alcoholic beverages. The open and well-publicized violence and lawlessness involved inspired a widely held belief that the nation was undergoing a crime wave.

This perception led President Calvin Coolidge in November 1925 to appoint the first national crime commission to investigate what steps could be taken to reduce crime. Members of the executive committee of the commission included Franklin D. Roosevelt (then assistant secretary of the navy), Charles Evans Hughes (a U.S. Supreme Court Justice and later the Court's Chief Justice), Richard Washburn Child (ambassador to Italy), Hubert Hedley (chancellor of Washington University), and Hugh Frayne (representing the American Federation of Labor).

The establishment of the commission was criticized on the grounds that its members lacked "expert knowledge" or "special experience" of the crime problem; that it had "no power"; and that consequently there was "little hope of any practical results from such a commission" (Wigmore, pp. 313–314). That prediction appears to have been fulfilled. The commission "met with little success and much opposition and jealousy from state counterparts" (Cronin, Cronin, and Milakovich, p. 28).

The commission did, however, make one significant discovery. As Roosevelt put it in 1929: "On the word of the National Crime Commission which has been studying the matter for three years . . . no one can today state with any authoritative statistics to back him, whether there is or is not a crime wave in the United States . . . . [A]s to whether or not there is a total increase in the number of crimes committed we have no knowledge whatever." No one could tell, "even in the most inaccurate way" how many murders took place per year (p. 369).

The second national crime commission was also the product of presidential concern that a crime wave had swept the country. President Herbert Hoover, who had campaigned in part on a law-and-order platform, declared in his inaugural address on 4 March 1929, that "the most malign of all these dangers today is disregard and disobedience of law. Crime is increasing. Confidence in rigid and speedy justice is decreasing" (1974, p. 2).

Hoover added that he would "appoint a national commission for a searching investigation of the whole structure of our Federal system of jurisprudence, to include the method of enforcement of the 18th amendment and the causes of abuse under it" (p. 4). Accordingly, in May 1929 he established the United States National Commission on Law Observance and Enforcement, with former attorney general George W. Wickersham as chairman, and requested it to "investigate and recommend action upon the whole crime and prohibition question" (1951–1952, p. 277).

Within the next two years the commission, which included among its members Roscoe Pound of the Harvard University Law School and Ada Comstock, president of Radcliffe College, issued fourteen separate reports totaling almost three and a half million words. The reports

were the product of an exhaustive investigation of all aspects of national law enforcement, and they made numerous recommendations for reform.

Unfortunately, what attracted most attention were the commission's contradictory and inconclusive findings in its *Report on the Enforcement of the Prohibition Laws of the United States*. By a large majority, the commission opposed the repeal of the Eighteenth Amendment, but at the same time it presented substantial evidence that effective enforcement was unattainable (U.S. National Commission on Law Observance and Enforcement, vol. 2).

As a result, the commission was attacked by both supporters and opponents of Prohibition. It was ridiculed by the press and even criticized by Hoover himself. In the national debate on Prohibition that culminated in the 1932 election, the commission's other recommendations were forgotten. Nevertheless, it is generally credited with exerting substantial influence in bringing Prohibition to an end.

Otherwise, the Wickersham Commission's reports and recommendations had little impact on the administration of criminal justice. But it was a first-rate effort that, for the first time in American history, attempted to present to a national audience a body of research into the problems of crime and its control. The reports have proved to be of enduring value to the community of criminal justice and criminological scholars.

More recent commissions

Since 1920 there have been ten major national crime commissions under presidential authority or that of the attorney general. But the Wickersham Commission was the last national crime commission appointed until the mid-1960s. After a lapse of more than three decades, the next six commissions were created, between 1965 and 1971. These were the President's Commission on Law Enforcement and Administration of Justice established in 1965; the United States National Advisory Commission on Civil Disorders (the Kerner Commission) (1967); the United States National Commission on the Causes and Prevention of Violence (1968); the U.S. Commission on Obscenity and Pornography (1968); the U.S. Commission on Marihuana and Drug Abuse (1970); and the Justice Department's National Advisory Commission on Criminal Justice Standards and Goals (1971). The most recent entries into this forest of blue-ribbon advice have been the Justice Department's National Advisory Committee for Juvenile Justice and Delinquency Prevention (1980); the Attorney General's Task Force on Violent Crime (1981); the President's Commission on Organized Crime (1983); and the Attorney General's Commission on Pornography (1986), which arose out of promises made during Ronald Reagan's presidential campaign.

The six national efforts that were reported between the mid-1960s and the early 1970s deserve briefer individual attention, at least in this context, because they overlap substantially in time and topic coverage. The first and most serious was a product of the 1964 presidential election, when Senator Barry Goldwater and the Republicans campaigned on a "law and order" "crime in the streets" platform. After his election victory, President Lyndon Johnson responded in 1965 to citizen concern about crime by creating the President's Commission on Law Enforcement and Administration of Justice, calling upon it to "give us the blueprints that we need to banish crime" (Johnson, p. 983).

Although it cannot be said to have fulfilled that demand, the President's Commission, with Attorney General Nicholas Katzenbach as chairman and James Vorenberg of the Harvard University Law School as executive director, produced a report, *The Challenge of Crime in a Free Society*, which is perhaps the best official expression of modern America's crime dilemmas ever produced. That report, together with the nine task force volumes that supplement it, has been described as constituting "the most comprehensive description and analysis of the crime problem ever undertaken" (Caplan, pp. 596–597). Thirty years later, the report was described as a "landmark document" that was still "in many ways as instructive and insightful" as when it was written (U.S. Department of Justice, 1997, p. iv).

The next two "crime commissions" were responses to emergencies. The Kerner Commission report reacted to the race riots of the mid-1960s with a highly ideological document that probably reflected the correct ultimate conclusion: the United States was unsuited for apartheid. Living as two societies (one black, one white) would be totally destructive of the American national mission. The U.S. National Commission on the Causes and Prevention of Violence appeared in June 1968, in the aftermath of the assassination of Robert Kennedy. This commission delegated to a body of scholars, task forces, and assistants the independent responsibility of producing volumes on the causes and prevention of violence in American life. The commission's report itself was not a tower of strength. The substantial body of scholarly knowledge in the task force reports was a tribute, as was the Wickersham Commission's report, to serious work and good intentions. The emphasis on task force efforts represented a deliberate departure from the procedure of the President's Commission on Law Enforcement and Administration of Justice, where the main report was the focus of the commission's senior staff effort.

At the close of the 1960s, two commissions were directed to study specific crime problems: pornography and marijuana. Each commission issued a report recommending reduced criminal enforcement, and both reports were almost immediately rejected by political leaders. The U.S. Commission on Obscenity and Pornography, after two years of scientific research but with few public hearings, issued a report that challenged many common assumptions with respect to the definition of pornography, and the causes and consequences of pornographic materials' production and distribution. The report recommended the dismantling of state and federal obscenity laws after having found no significant connection between sexually explicit materials and criminal sexual behavior. The Nixon Administration dismissed the report's findings as morally bankrupt.

The congressionally mandated U.S. Commission on Marihuana and Drug Abuse issued a multivolume report on the pharmacological and social effects of drug use and abuse, and concluded with a controversial proposal that the major thrust of policy should be to minimize the incidence and consequences of intensified and compulsive use of psychoactive drugs. The commission urged decriminalization of some recreational marihuana use to reflect social change, stating that the drug's potential for harm to the vast majority of individual users and its actual impact on society did not justify a policy designed to seek out and punish users. This proposal angered the Nixon Administration, which decidedly repudiated the report. Eventually, a federal "drug czar" was appointed, to coordinate a "war on drugs," and federal drug penalties were increased substantially. Nevertheless, federal and some state penalties for possession and use of marijuana were temporarily relaxed during and following the publication of the commission's report, and a few states subsequently approved limited marijuana use in connection with certain medical conditions.

The Justice Department's National Advisory Commission on Criminal Justice Standards and Goals issued its major report, *A National Strategy to Reduce Crime*, in 1973. It was a Nixon commission and a Nixon document. The commission's standards for immediate reform were too high. For example, most forms of predatory crime were to be cut in half by 1983. "Standards" and "goals" abounded in the report, the former including many platitudes and the latter awash in numerical fantasies.

By contrast to earlier efforts, the next two federal commissions to report on crime were low-budget affairs. The Justice Department's National Advisory Committee for Juvenile Justice and Delinquency Prevention reported in 1980. Its major contribution was a set of standards for the administration of juvenile justice. No scholarly tomes were at the foundation of this volume, and no great ambitions informed it. It was an intense and sincere effort, but as Oscar Wilde remarked about sincerity, a little of it "is a dangerous thing and a great deal of it is absolutely fatal."

Attorney General William French Smith's 1981 Task Force on Violent Crime was a modest, "no-nonsense" undertaking. Its report stood in sharp contrast to the basic strategy of crime commissions since their inception: seek expert advice and report on basic knowledge. Wickersham and the 1960s-era national crime commissions had taken years and produced large volumes; Attorney General Smith's task force was given 120 days, and during this period the task force members interrupted their deliberations to travel to seven cities for public hearings. Nevertheless, the task force produced a volume of ninety-six pages, documenting sixty-four individual recommendations. Many of the sixty-four recommendations were off-the-shelf conservative bromides; others were hastily conceived in an atmosphere of high enthusiasm and substantial misinformation.

The President's Commission on Organized Crime undertook an enormous effort to expand upon President Lyndon Johnson's effort twenty years earlier to identify and analyze organized crime. The commission produced twelve volumes of hearings and reports over a four-year period. Some of the most significant departures from previous efforts were the broadening of the definition of organized crime to reflect the multiethnic international expansion of organized

criminal activity, and the recommendation for expanded civil remedies to address private commercial corruption. Unlike President Johnson's effort, the Commission failed to evaluate federal prosecutorial roles in dealing with organized crime, which lead to dissension among the commission's members and little in the way of results.

In 1986 President Reagan's Attorney General, Edwin Meese, led the Attorney General's Commission on Pornography, which sought to eviscerate the U.S. Obscenity and Pornography Commission's conclusions and recommendations regarding the nature, extent, and impact on society of pornography in the United States. The new commission's report admitted, however, that its conclusions lacked independent research and were dependent almost exclusively on politically charged public hearings. Nevertheless, the Meese Commission justified its departure from the earlier commission report by noting that technological advances have enabled far more extensive private access to pornographic materials. As a result of the commission's work, the attorney general created a federal prosecutorial unit that specialized in prosecutions of obscenity-related crimes.

The political context of the crime commissions

Nationally chartered blue-ribbon commissions on the causes and prevention of crime have generated reports prolifically since 1925, and particularly since the mid-1960s. The question is, Why? The answers are manifold.

The federal government is only a limited partner with the states in direct crime control. When direct intervention is unavailable as a federal option, the appeal to national expertise and the capacity to recommend are immensely attractive. As a general matter, when the government does not know what to do, the tendency to turn to blue-ribbon commissions is irresistible.

Crime commissions and their causes cannot be understood without substantial awareness of the politics of crime control at the national level in the United States. In national politics, violent crime is a candidate's dream but an incumbent's nightmare. Running for office, the candidate confronts a national consensus against crime in the streets. Once he is president, the issue before him is no longer whether the American public would rather not be mugged, but what the federal government can do about street crime. The answer that has emerged over sixty years—

encompassing both free-spending and frugal administrations—is that the federal government cannot do much.

Why is American national government stymied when it comes to the control of street crime? The central problems are two. The first, while important, is elementary. At any level of government there are limits to the capacity of Western democracies to control crime without sacrificing the freedom of the general citizenry. Combining urban interdependence with Western liberty is a risky task in Europe as well as in the United States.

The American federal government operates under a second handicap unknown to other nations. The division of power between different levels of government in the United States hinders direct federal initiatives to counter street crime. The limited criminal justice role of the American national government has few parallels in the developed world. Aside from drug trafficking and bank robbery, street crime in the United States is largely the province of local police, county courts, and state prison systems.

A few comparative statistics make the point. As of 1999, the United States had more than 1.8 million accused or convicted criminals behind bars but only about one in fourteen were in the federal system. Several states had larger prison systems than the federal government. Prisons, moreover, are only the beginning. Decisions to arrest, prosecute, and send to prison are even more decentralized than decisions about prison administration. Here, cities and counties make the decisions, while state governments pay the prison bills. In criminal law enforcement there is nothing new about what has been called the "New Federalism," but much that frustrates the electorate.

The essential frustration is that—notwithstanding occasional programs providing federal money for state prison construction, more police officers, and (very occasionally) improved courts—street crime is a national problem without a federal solution. The remarkable fact about national crime commissions is not that there have been so many but so few. These documents, relying on recommendation where no power exists, range from deplorable to extraordinarily good. Almost invariably, a national crime commission is a response to a specific problem, a high crime period, a change in presidential leadership, or all three. The timing of these documents, their contents, and their legacies vary widely. But serious study of the relationship between the federal government and crime cannot ignore the blue-ribbon commission as a device for coping with the national dimensions of what the public perceives as the crime problem.

Whatever fault may be found with the national crime commissions, they have not been hesitant in making recommendations. Most prodigal was the National Advisory Commission on Criminal Justice Standards and Goals, which contributed 494 recommendations to a grand total of more than 1,200 for all the commissions. The National Advisory Commission's summary report referred to "the sweeping range of its proposals." Yet many of those proposals (such as those to "establish mandatory retirement for all judges at age 65" or to "open church facilities for community programs") seem unlikely to contribute greatly to crime reduction (pp. 153–158, 164). So great a profusion of proposals has a tendency to be counterproductive, weakening the impact that four or five targeted priorities might have. At the same time, proclaiming such unrealistic objectives as the reduction of robbery by "at least 50 percent" within ten years (p. 7) tends to undermine whatever credibility these documents might otherwise possess.

It is not at all clear to whom all the admonitions and injunctions in the various commission reports were addressed. Who, for example, was supposed to respond to the 1967 President's Commission's exhortations to "expand efforts to improve housing and recreation" or to "create new job opportunities" (pp. 293–294)? Sometimes unspecified "civic and business groups and all kinds of governmental agencies" are apostrophized (p. xi). Or, even less specifically, "all Americans" or "the citizens of this country" are called on to "work to bring about the necessary changes" (U.S. Department of Justice, National Advisory Commission on Criminal Justice Standards and Goals, p. 4). Most often the recommendations seem, like Longfellow's arrow, to be shot into the air to fall to earth "I know not where."

How is it that intelligent and responsible people produce these grandiose manifestos? The trouble is that national commissions are invariably problem specific. Yet the intractability of the American crime problem lies in its intimate connection with a multitude of other problems, such as race, poverty, unemployment, and drug abuse. It requires a leap of faith to believe that the criminal justice system can somehow surgically remove all the criminogenic elements from this complex of interrelated problems.

There is another aspect to the matter. Crime commissions are assigned to study a single problem in a world where problems are multiple. In the course of their studies they learn how serious their problem is, but they acquire little knowledge of the other ills that beset society. Thus the competition for scarce resources between national afflictions is almost invariably overlooked. This creates a disjunction between the blue-ribbon commission and the national political process, a process that must consider the multiplicity of problems in a multi-problem United States.

To summarize: some crime commissions take years to complete their work, others take months. Some issue huge numbers of volumes, and others produce slim reports. Their common problem is that the federal government can only serve as a limited partner in the administration of criminal justice. No matter how urgent a national issue mugging becomes, for example, the federal response must be limited: when this is the case, it is time to call for the experts and hope they will help. Sometimes they have done so and some times they have not. It would be an occasion for amazement rather than surprise if the United States has seen its last national commission on crime and justice.

FRANKLIN E. ZIMRING
GORDON HAWKINS
RICHARD S. FRASE

See also CRIMINAL JUSTICE SYSTEM; CRIMINAL LAW REFORM: ENGLAND; CRIMINAL LAW REFORM: HISTORICAL DEVELOPMENT IN THE UNITED STATES; CRIMINAL LAW REFORM: CURRENT ISSUES IN THE UNITED STATES; POLITICAL PROCESS AND CRIME; PUBLIC OPINION AND CRIME.

BIBLIOGRAPHY

ALBANESE, JAY S. "Government Perceptions of Organized Crime: The Presidential Commissions, 1967 and 1987." Federal Probation 52 (1988): 58–63.

CAPLAN, GERALD. "Reflections on the Nationalization of Crime, 1964–1968." Law and the Social Order 3 (1973): 583–635.

CRONIN, THOMAS E.; CRONIN, TANIA; and MILAKOVICH, MICHAEL E. U.S. v. Crime in the Streets. Bloomington: Indiana University Press, 1981.

HOOVER, HERBERT C. Memoirs. 3 vols. New York: Macmillan, 1951–1952.

———. Public Papers of the Presidents of the United States: Herbert Hoover, (1929). Washington, D.C.: Office of the Federal Register, National Archives and Records Service, General Services Administration, 1974.

JOHNSON, LYNDON B. Public Papers of the Presidents of the United States: Lyndon B. Johnson (1965), vol. 2. Washington, D.C.: Office of the Federal Register, National Archives and Records Service, General Services Administration, 1966.

MOWRY, GEORGE E. "Wickersham, George Woodward." Dictionary of American Biography, vol. 11, supp. 2. Edited by Robert Livingston Schuyler and Edward T. James. New York: Scribner, 1958. Pages 713–715.

NOBILE, PHILIP, and NADLER, ERIC. United States of America v. Sex: How the Meese Commission Lied About Pornography. New York: Minotaur Press, Ltd., 1986.

President's Commission on Law Enforcement and Administration of Justice. The Challenge of Crime in a Free Society. Washington, D.C.: The Commission, 1967.

President's Commission on Organized Crime. The Impact: Organized Crime Today. Washington, D.C.: U.S. Government Printing Office, 1986.

ROOSEVELT, FRANKLIN D. The Public Papers and Addresses of Franklin D. Roosevelt (1938) vol. 1. Special introduction and explanatory notes by President Roosevelt. Compiled by Samuel I. Rosenman. Reprint. New York: Russell & Russell, 1969.

ROSENTHAL, MICHAEL P. "The Legislative Response To Marihuana: When the Shoe Pinches Enough." Journal of Drug Issues 7, no. 1 (winter 1977): 61–77.

U.S. Commission on Marihuana and Drug Abuse. Drug Use in America: Problem in Perspective. Washington, D.C.: The Commission, 1973.

U.S. Commission on Obscenity and Pornography. The Report of the Commission on Obscenity and Pornography. New York: Random House, 1970.

U.S. Department of Justice. Attorney General's Commission on Pornography. Final Report. Washington, D.C.: The Commission, 1986.

U.S. Department of Justice. Attorney General's Task Force on Violent Crime. Final Report. Washington, D.C.: The Department, 1981.

U.S. Department of Justice. Beyond the Pornography Commission: The Federal Response. Washington, D.C.: The Department, 1988.

U.S. Department of Justice, Law Enforcement Assistance Administration, National Advisory Commission on Criminal Justice Standards and Goals. A National Strategy to Reduce Crime. Washington, D.C.: The Commission, 1973.

U.S. Department of Justice, Office of Justice Programs. *The Challenge of Crime in a Free Society: Looking Back, Looking Forward.* Washington, D.C: U.S. Department of Justice, 1997.

U.S. Department of Justice, Office of Juvenile Justice and Delinquency Prevention, National Advisory Committee for Juvenile Justice and Delinquency Prevention. *Standards for the Administration of Juvenile Justice: Report.* Washington, D.C.: The Committee, 1980.

U.S. National Advisory Commission on Civil Disorders [Kerner Commission]. *Report.* Washington, D.C.: The Commission, 1968.

U.S. National Commission on Law Observance and Enforcement [Wickersham Commission]. *Reports* (1930–1931). 15 vols. Reprint. Montclair, N.J.: Patterson Smith, 1968.

U.S. National Commission on the Causes and Prevention of Violence. *To Establish Justice, to Insure Domestic Tranquility.* Washington, D.C.: The Commission, 1969.

WICKERSHAM, GEORGE W. "The Work of the National Crime Commission." *Report of the Forty-ninth Annual Meeting of the American Bar Association Held at Denver, Colorado, July 14–16, 1926.* Reports of the American Bar Association, vol. 51. Baltimore: Lord Baltimore Press, 1926. Pages 233–237.

WIGMORE, JOHN H. "The National Crime Commission: What Will It Achieve?" *Journal of the American Institute of Criminal Law and Criminology* 16 (1925): 312–315.

CRIMINAL CAREERS

Since the early works of Sheldon and Eleanor Glueck, the concept of the criminal career has been well established within the field of criminology. Most generically, the criminal career is conceived of as the longitudinal sequence of delinquent and criminal acts committed by an individual as the individual ages across the lifespan from childhood through adolescence and adulthood. Four key structural elements are defined and applied to the study of criminal careers: *participation/prevalence, frequency/incidence, seriousness,* and *career length* (Blumstein, Cohen, Roth, and Visher). Participation is a macro-level measure of the proportion of the population that is involved in offending behavior, while frequency is the rate of offending for those individuals who are active offenders (often denoted as lambda, or λ). Seriousness refers to the level of seriousness of the offenses being committed by a given individual, while career length refers to the length of time that an individual is actively offending. When aggregated across individuals, criminal careers typically exhibit a unimodal *age-crime curve* for the population.

Frequency, seriousness, and career length can vary greatly among individuals, who may range from having zero offenses across the lifespan to having one offense of a nonserious nature to being *chronic* or *career criminals* with multiple, serious offenses across a broad span of their lives. In the United States, Blumstein and others (1986) suggested that population-level participation rates vary between 25 and 45 percent, depending on how "participation" is measured. Visher and Roth, in a meta-analysis of studies on both United States and British participation rates, found that the level of participation is about 30 percent for non-traffic related offenses. Averages are higher or lower depending on the measure of participation, which can range from the mild "contact with the police" (e.g., Shannon, 1988, 1991) to the more stringent measure of "convicted of a crime" (e.g., West and Farrington, 1973, 1977).

However, despite this consensus on the definition of the criminal career (and the career criminal) and the aggregate level age-crime curve typically found, controversy has emerged across many other areas within criminal careers research. For example, do juvenile delinquents/criminals comprise a unique segment of the population (e.g., Blumstein et al., 1986) or is delinquency a behavior that is a "typical" part of the growing-up process, from which most adults desist? Are criminal propensities relatively constant across the lifespan (e.g., Gottfredson and Hirschi, 1990) or do they vary with age (e.g., Sampson and Laub)?

Studying criminal careers implies the use of longitudinal panel data. In criminology, this has been difficult due to a lack of available resources, hampering the development of testable theories. As Sampson and Laub point out, "criminology has been dominated by narrow sociological and psychological perspectives, coupled with a strong tradition of research using cross-sectional data on adolescents" (p. 23). This combination of a lack of data and limited theoretical perspectives and methodological techniques has particularly hampered the ability to understand the criminal career, which is both longitudinal and dynamic in nature.

Historical background

Research has demonstrated that most offenders commit only a single offense and terminate their offending after first arrest. A smaller percentage go on to offend repeatedly, while a subset of these repeat offenders go on to chronic "career" patterns of offending. The focus on the concept of crime patterns as "careers" began with the early studies of Sheldon and Eleanor Glueck that followed the pathways of both criminals and noncriminals. In the work for which they are best known, *Unraveling Juvenile Delinquency* (1950), the Gluecks followed five hundred white males, ages ten to seventeen, who were adjudicated delinquent by the state of Massachusetts. This sample was matched case-by-case on such variables as neighborhood of residence, birthplace of the parents, and measured intelligence to a sample of five hundred white males of the same age drawn from the Boston public school system. Delinquent/criminal behavior was followed from 1939 to 1948 through self-reports, parental reports, and teacher reports. With these data, the Gluecks were instrumental in beginning to disentangle the relationship between age and crime (Sampson and Laub). In identifying age of onset and declining rates of offending with age as key components in the age-crime relationship, they contributed greatly to current criminal careers research. In addition to changing behavior over time (e.g., declining rates of offending with age), the Gluecks also found high levels of stability in offending behavior over time. The concept of stability versus change, or dynamic versus static models of offending, is a central argument in modern criminal careers research (Gottfredson and Hirschi, 1990; Sampson and Laub).

Building on work done by the Gluecks, several major cohort studies advanced the development of the criminal careers paradigm (Shannon, 1988, 1991; Tracy, Wolfgang, and Figlio; West and Farrington, 1973, 1977; Wolfgang, Figlio, and Sellin). Wolfgang, Figlio, and Sellin assembled data on the males of the 1945 birth cohort in the city of Philadelphia and followed their criminal activity through the young adult years, leading to a more complete conceptualization of the chronic or career offender. A particularly enduring finding of Wolfgang and his colleagues has been the existence of a small percentage of the general population (estimated at 5 to 10 percent), called "chronic recidivists" that is responsible for over 50 percent of the total offenses committed by cohort members. The 1945 Philadelphia Birth Cohort Study was followed up with a larger birth cohort study in 1958 that included both males and females, following

them into adulthood (Tracy, Wolfgang, and Figlio). While the researchers found increased rates of offending in the 1958 Philadelphia Birth Cohort, there remained a stable class of chronic offenders responsible for a large percentage of the cohort's offenses. In addition, it was found that females offended at significantly lower rates than their male counterparts, with approximately 1 percent being classified as chronic offenders. Later follow-ups of the 1958 cohort have found stability in offending among the most chronic of offenders, coupled with higher levels of desistance among other nonchronic offenders (Tracy and Kempf-Leonard).

West and Farrington (1973, 1977) continued the tradition of longitudinal studies of offending using panel data collected in Cambridge, England, beginning in 1961–1962 (West and Farrington, 1973, 1977). The Cambridge Study in Delinquent Development followed the development of 411 boys from the age of eight through the age of thirty-two and documented the existence of chronic offenders similar to the conclusions reached in studies conducted in the United States. In particular, Farrington and his colleagues found that indicators of future chronic or persistent offending are detectable as early as age eight, indicating a continuity or stability in criminal behavior over time; that delinquent and criminal offending tends to be diverse in nature as opposed to specialized; and that social factors such as family structure, economic conditions, and marital status influence the continuity of offending over time.

Lyle Shannon's work (1988, 1991) with the Racine, Wisconsin, birth cohorts of 1942, 1949, and 1955 has added to the body of knowledge on the development of the criminal career. Coupling police contact information for all members of the birth cohorts who remained within the city of Racine through at least their eighteenth birthday with more in-depth interview data, Shannon found evidence supporting the existence of the career or chronic criminal. In the Racine cohorts, about 5 percent of each of the total cohorts was responsible for approximately 80 percent of the felonies. In addition, substantial continuity existed among the most serious offenders in their offending patterns, while less serious offenders were prone to desist from their offending.

Contemporary issues and controversies

Taking the lead from earlier cohort studies, more current research on criminal careers and chronic offenders has centered on the continuing exchange between Blumstein and his associates (Barnett, Blumstein, and Farrington; Blumstein, Cohen, and Farrington, 1988a, 1988b) and Gottfredson and Hirschi (1988, 1990) on the stability of criminal careers over time. To test the validity of the criminal career concept, Barnett, Blumstein, and Farrington proposed a probabilistic model (with the conviction process following a Poisson distribution of rare events) to predict actual offense rates from arrest/conviction rates (Barnett and Lofaso; Blumstein, Farrington, and Moitra). Using the Cambridge Cohort, the researchers generated a model reflecting both individual rates of offending and termination, as well as heterogeneity in the population through the use of multiple parameters of offending. In support of the criminal career paradigm and its implications of both continuity and change in offending, it was found that the Cambridge cohort is comprised of nonoffenders as well as those who were both "occasional" (57 percent of offenders) and "frequent" (43 percent) offenders. In addition, there existed an intermittency in offending, in which periods of criminal activity were interspersed with periods of inactivity (possibly related to such factors as incarceration). A more dynamic view of offending, including both stability and change within criminal careers, was supported.

Sampson and Laub's *age-graded theory of informal social control* allows for both stability and change in behavioral trajectories such as offending over time. Sampson and Laub hypothesize that shifting social bonds to individuals and institutions (e.g., family, education, work) over the life-course cause an individual to either persist or desist in his/her offending. While life events such as marriage may increase ties to conventional society (Laub, Nagin, and Sampson) or decrease an individual's association with delinquent peers (Warr), therefore decreasing offending, failure to make such transitions may cause an individual to persist in offending.

Sampson and Laub make three major theoretical assertions: (1) the *structural context* of family and school social controls explains delinquency in childhood and adolescence; (2) this leads to a *continuity in antisocial behavior* from childhood through adulthood across many social domains; and (3) *social bonds* in adulthood to institutions such as family and employment explain changes in criminal behavior over the life-course, despite early criminal propensity. Sampson and Laub's developmental model acknowledges the

potential for both stability and change in criminal behavior over time. While other psychologically oriented models of individual criminal behavior provide a more static view of criminality within the individual over time (e.g., Gottfredson and Hirschi, 1990), the age-graded theory of social control allows for the possibility of changes in behavior fluctuating with changing levels of attachment or social bonding over time. At the population level, decreasing levels of offending at later ages are attributed to the termination in offending behavior of some, coupled with the persistence in offending behavior of others. While Sampson and Laub note that "there is considerable evidence that antisocial behavior is relatively stable across stages of the life-course," there also are many opportunities for the links in the "chain of adversity" to be broken over time (pp. 11, 15).

The most prominent of the "static" or "continuity" theories of crime is Gottfredson and Hirschi's (1990) *self-control theory of crime*. Gottfredson and Hirschi (1988, 1990) assert that both crime and *criminality* are stable across the life-course and that a singular underlying individual characteristic, self-control, is predictive of offending behavior. Self-control is established early in life (before the age of eight) and is related to parental child-rearing techniques. Those parents who are able to consistently and fairly discipline children and teach them to resist impulsive behavior will instill in their children a high level of self-control. Across the lifespan, an individual's level of self-control will remain stable but can manifest itself in many different ways. Childhood antisocial behavior, adolescent and adult criminality, problem drinking, excessive speeding, or any other impulsive or deviant activity could be traced back to low levels of self-control. Gottfredson and Hirschi (1990) attribute decreasing levels of offending at later ages in the age-crime curve to a gradual "aging-out" of all offenders, reflective of relative stability over time, as opposed to the termination of offending by some. Support for the existence of an underlying latent trait predictive of continuity in offending has been found by those such as Greenberg and Rowe, Osgood, and Nicewander.

Debates between those advocating a more dynamic versus a static view of offending behavior have spawned a related question on the relationship of past to future offending: Does prior offending have a subsequent causal impact on future offending or do time-stable individual differences cause persistence in offending over time? This question, framed in terms of the existence of either *state dependence* or *persistent heterogeneity*, has been advanced by Nagin and his colleagues (Nagin and Farrington, 1992a, 1992b; Nagin and Paternoster, 1991). State dependence implies that the commission of a crime may raise the probability that an individual will commit a subsequent crime. According to state dependence, prior participation in offending has an "actual behavioral effect" (Nagin and Paternoster, p. 163) on subsequent offending (a dynamic approach). On the other hand, *population heterogeneity* implies that past and future offending are related only inasmuch as they are both related to an unmeasured criminal propensity that is stable over time within the individual (a static approach). Mixed conclusions have been drawn from this vein of research—support has been found for both the hypotheses of state-dependence (Nagin and Farrington, 1992a; Nagin and Paternoster) and population heterogeneity (Loeber and Snyder; Nagin and Farrington, 1992a, 1992b).

The life course and offending categories

The criminal careers research of the 1980s and early 1990s, begun with several seminal longitudinal cohort studies, has been expanded with the addition of life-course or developmental criminology, as well as evidence supporting multiple age-crime curves or classes/categories of criminal careers. According to Loeber and Stouthamer-Loeber, studying criminal careers from a life-course or developmental perspective implies three major goals: (1) encouraging the description of within-individual changes in offending across time; (2) identifying the causal factors of the longitudinal course of offending; and (3) studying the impact of life transitions and relationships on offending behavior.

Support for a developmental perspective on criminal careers is abundant. Bartusch and others find that an individual's age is indeed important in the development of offending, which it would not be in a more static model. They suggest that "identical antisocial behaviors [e.g., delinquency] represent somewhat different underlying constructs when the behaviors are measured during childhood versus during adolescence" (p. 39). Paternoster and Brame find more limited support for the developmental perspective. While association with delinquent peers and prior offending behavior—both of which change over time—are important predictors of

serious delinquent activity, there also remains an element of time-invariance of between-individual differences in offending. Paternoster and Brame suggest that crime is best studied taking into account both static and dynamic models by assuming a "theoretical middle ground" (p. 49). Simons and others find a dynamic and reciprocal causal chain of events that support a developmental perspective of offending, as opposed to a direct relationship between childhood and adolescent misconduct, which would be suggestive of a latent trait or static approach.

The most recent criminal careers research has examined the possibility of heterogeneity in the unimodal age-crime curve. What this unimodal curve may mask is the possibility of heterogeneity between different kinds of offender groups that is lost at the aggregate level. Research by Nagin and Land and by D'Unger and others has suggested that the aggregated age-crime curve for the population may mask the existence of qualitatively different classes of criminal careers with distinct trajectories and differing ages of offending onset, peak ages and rates of offending. In addition, the assumption of a singular age-crime curve may hamper empirical research, particularly if different variables predict membership into different classes of offenders.

Theoretical developments in criminology have suggested that there are many different types of offenders, and empirical evidence for this assertion has been found. In particular, the development of *latent class analysis* (in the form of *semiparametric mixed Poisson regression models*) has allowed researchers to disaggregate offenders groups with multiple pathways of offending over time (Nagin and Land; Land, McCall, and Nagin; Land and Nagin; D'Unger et al.). The first major study that conjoined the criminal careers paradigm and latent class analysis of delinquent/criminal careers cohort data was Nagin and Land. Nagin and Land determined that four distinct categories of delinquent/criminal careers could be identified in the Cambridge cohort (West and Farrington, 1973, 1977): nonoffenders (i.e., those who did not have any recorded convictions), individuals whose offending was limited predominantly to the teen years, and two categories of chronic offenders—one with a low-rate and the other with a high-rate of offending.

The research was some of the first to provide empirical evidence of multiple types of offending trajectories with distinct patterns of offending over time. However, because it contained only a limited number of covariates, it was not able to establish the predictors of group membership. Subsequent latent class analysis of criminal careers offered further support for the notion of multiple types of delinquent/criminal offenders across many different types of data. D'Unger and others provide evidence that multiple categories of offenders are present across several data sets with a high level of consistency. Using all-male data from the Cambridge cohort, the 1958 Second Philadelphia Birth Cohort, and the Racine 1942, 1949, and 1955 Birth Cohorts, D'Unger and colleagues concluded:

Rather than merely representing a discrete approximation to an underlying continuous distribution of unobserved delinquent/criminal propensity, the small number of latent offending categories estimated in [the] models may *represent distinct classifications of cohort offenders with respect to age trajectories of offending that are meaningful in and of themselves* (emphasis added) (p. 1622).

Across all samples from various cohorts and with differing measures of offending (e.g., arrests, convictions) as the dependent variable, several basic patterns emerged: the *adolescent-peaked offender*, the *chronic offender*, and the *nonoffender*. These categories sometimes bifurcated into "higher-" and "lower-" rate groups, but the shape of the offending trajectories across samples was remarkably consistent. However, this research still did not answer the question: What predicts membership in various offender/nonoffender classes?

In another attempt to answer the above question, Nagin, Farrington, and Moffitt looked at the impact of several types of factors on the four offending categories initially delineated by Nagin and Land in the Cambridge cohort. Using both self-report and conviction data on the Cambridge cohort, several significant differences were found between the predictors of the four criminal career categories. In particular, evidence was found in support of the distinctiveness of the high-rate chronic offenders. At their peak, these offenders were more likely to be engaged in violent behavior, smoking cigarettes, using drugs, and having sexual intercourse. By age thirty-two, all three of the offending groups (high-rate chronic, low-rate chronic, and adolescence-limited) were more likely to be fighting, using drugs, and abusing alcohol than the nonoffenders, based upon their self-reported offending. All three offender groups also suffered in the

job market. Using data on males from the National Youth Survey, McDermott and Nagin also attempted to delineate the predictors of offending-class membership. It was determined that three classes of offenders exist in this sample, analogous to findings from other latent class research: nonoffenders, an adolescent-peaked group that rises to a peak early but then slows down and reaches zero by the age of twenty four, and a higher-rate group that exhibits an increasing rate of offending until the age of eighteen—characteristic of chronic offenders—but then acts erratically between the ages of eighteen and twenty-four. McDermott and Nagin determined that variables such as involvement with delinquent peers and deviant labels imposed by parents were most significant for predicting changes in the offending index, while measures of social control offered conflicting evidence.

Criminal career patterns

As discussed above, much research has detailed the existence of several different types of criminal career patterns. This notion is very important for the testing and further development of criminological theories, as most previous work in criminology has posited the existence of a simple dichotomy of classes: offenders and nonoffenders. Research challenging this dichotomy points to the existence of several stable types of categories beyond offenders and nonoffenders.

In particular, Moffitt's (1993, 1997a) work on *adolescence-limited* and *life-course persistent* offenders offers theoretical support for the existence of and distinctions between these two types of career patterns. It also suggests why there may be a continuity in offending behavior over time among some individuals, coupled with a dramatic increase in levels of offending in the teen years—one piece of evidence for what Cohen and Vila (1996) call the "paradox of persistence." The paradox is this: while most juvenile delinquents do not grow up to be adult offenders (e.g., deviant behavior is a "normal" part of the teen years), almost all adult offenders were juvenile delinquents.

Moffitt (1993) points to neuropsychological problems, often occurring in the fetal brain and inhibiting temperamental, behavioral, and cognitive development, interacting with a poor or "criminogenic" social environment, as the cause for chronic offending. Unlike the adolescence-limited offenders, the cause of the antisocial behavior exhibited by chronic offenders is often located in the earliest years of socialization. The early deficit identified by Moffitt, combined with the lack of a supportive childhood environment and problematic child-parent interactions, causes persistence in deviant behavior over time. Moffitt points out that, "children with cognitive and temperamental disadvantages are not generally born into supportive environments, nor do they even get a fair chance of being randomly assigned to good or bad environments" (1993, p 6681). Cumulative consequences of their behavior continue to narrow their options in the world of "legitimate" or normative behavior. Moffitt (1997b) goes one step further to assert that neuropsychological problems can interact specifically with neighborhood social context to either enhance antisocial or delinquent behavior. Looking at African American males from the Pittsburgh Youth Study (Loeber, Stouthamer-Loeber, Van Kammen, and Farrington), Moffitt (1997b) finds that living in a good neighborhood seemed to protect boys from involvement with delinquency, but only if they were neuropsychologically healthy. Boys suffering from neuropsychological problems were always more likely to be delinquent than those not suffering from such problems, regardless of neighborhood status.

Unlike their chronic counterparts, Moffitt hypothesizes that adolescence-limited offenders do not come from the same environmentally deficit backgrounds or have the same neurological problems, nor do they suffer from the effects of cumulative disadvantage. Rather, Moffitt asserts that such behavior confined in the teen years is, "motivated by the gap between biological maturity and social maturity" (1993, p. 685). Antisocial behavior, including involvement with juvenile delinquency, is "social mimicry" that is used by young individuals to achieve a higher level of status in the teenage world, with its subsequent power and privileges. Adolescence-limited offenders mimic the behavior that they see exhibited by chronic offenders during the teen years but, because they have not severed major bonds with society, may come from more stable families, and are not suffering from the same neurological damage, they are able to easily desist from offending as they reach the early years of adulthood.

The hypothesized existence of these two groups of offenders suggests two important points. First, it would explain the huge increase in individual rates of offending that happen in the adolescent years, followed by the precipitous decline exhibited in the unimodal population-level age-crime curve. It would seem to suggest that this change happens because fewer people are offending in the later years: the adolescence-limiteds have stopped, while the smaller group of chronic offenders keeps going—an argument for state dependence as opposed to population heterogeneity. Secondly, it also points to the necessity of conducting longitudinal research on criminal careers. If, at their peaks in offending, adolescence-limited and life-course persistent offenders are similar in their behavior, there is little way to distinguish between the two groups.

Conclusions and future research

Osgood and Rowe have suggested that the best ways to answer the current questions in criminal careers research is through building "bridges between theoretical criminology, the study of criminal careers, and policy relevant research" (p. 517). Offering suggestions for moving beyond the current debates, Land has suggested that only through empirical analysis of criminal behavior over time via competing statistical models will the questions of criminal careers research be answered. Loeber and LeBlanc have suggested that only by paying attention to how a criminal career unfolds (e.g., what causes some to begin offending, what predicts desistance, what leads to specialization in offending, what causes an escalation in severity of offending) will the tension between dynamic and static theories of crime be resolved. Future years undoubtedly will see many important contributions to this exciting area of research in criminology.

KENNETH C. LAND
AMY V. D'UNGER

See also DELINQUENT AND CRIMINAL SUBCULTURES; ORGANIZED CRIME; PREDICTION OF CRIME AND RECIDIVISM; TYPOLOGIES OF CRIMINAL BEHAVIOR; WHITE-COLLAR CRIME: HISTORY OF AN IDEA.

BIBLIOGRAPHY

BARNETT, ARNOLD; BLUMSTEIN, ALFRED; and FARRINGTON, DAVID P. "Probabilistic Models of Youthful Criminal Careers." *Criminology* 25 (1987): 83–108.

BARNETT, ARNOLD, and LOFASO, ANTHONY J. "Selective Incapacitation and the Philadelphia Cohort Data." *Journal of Quantitative Criminology* 1 (1985): 3–36.

BARTUSCH, DAWN R. JEGLUM; LYNAM, DONALD R.; MOFFITT, TERRIE E.; and SILVA, PHIL A. "Is Age Important? Testing a General versus a Developmental Theory of Antisocial Behavior." *Criminology* 35 (1997): 13–48.

BLUMSTEIN, ALFRED; FARRINGTON, DAVID P.; and MOITRA, SOUMYO D. "Delinquency Careers: Innocents, Desisters, and Persisters." In *Crime and Justice, Volume 6*. Edited by Michael Tonry and Norval Morris. Chicago: University of Chicago Press, 1985.

BLUMSTEIN, ALFRED; COHEN, JACQUELINE; ROTH, JEFFREY A.; and VISHER, CHRISTY A., eds. *Criminal Careers and "Career Criminals," Volume 1*. Washington, D.C.: National Academy Press, 1986.

BLUMSTEIN, ALFRED; COHEN, JACQUELINE; and FARRINGTON, DAVID P. "Criminal Career Research: Its Value for Criminology." *Criminology* 26 (1988a): 1–35.

———. "Longitudinal and Criminal Career Research: Further Clarifications." *Criminology* 26 (1988b): 57–74.

COHEN, LAWRENCE E., and VILA, BRYAN J. "Self-Control and Social-Control: An Exposition of the Gottfredson-Hirschi/Sampson-Laub Debate." *Studies on Crime and Crime Prevention* 5 (1996): 125–150.

D'UNGER, AMY V.; LAND, KENNETH C.; MCCALL, PATRICIA L.; and NAGIN, DANIEL S. "How Many Latent Classes of Delinquent/Criminal Careers? Results from Mixed Poisson Regression Analyses." *American Journal of Sociology* 103 (1998): 1593–1630.

GLUECK, SHELDON, and GLUECK, ELEANOR. *500 Criminal Careers*. New York: Knopf, 1930.

———. *One Thousand Juvenile Delinquents*. Cambridge, Mass.: Harvard University Press, 1934.

———. *Later Criminal Careers*. New York: The Commonwealth Fund, 1937.

———. *Unraveling Juvenile Delinquency*. New York: The Commonwealth Fund, 1950.

GOTTFREDSON, MICHAEL, and HIRSCHI, TRAVIS. "Science, Public Policy, and the Career Paradigm." *Criminology* 36 (1988): 37–55.

———. *A General Theory of Crime*. Palo Alto, Calif.: Stanford University Press, 1990.

GREENBERG, DAVID F. "Modeling Criminal Careers." *Criminology* 30 (1991): 149–155.

LAND, KENNETH C. "Models of Criminal Careers: Some Suggestions for Moving Beyond the Current Debate." *Criminology* 30 (1992): 149–155.

LAND, KENNETH C.; MCCALL, PATRICIA L.; and NAGIN, DANIEL S. "A Comparison of Poisson, Negative Binomial, and Semiparametric Mixed Poisson Regression Models with Empirical Applications to Criminal Careers Research." *Sociological Methods and Research* 24 (1996): 387–442.

LAND, KENNETH C., and NAGIN, DANIEL S. "Micromodels of Criminal Careers: A Synthesis of the Criminal Careers and Life Course Approaches via Semiparametric Mixed Poisson Regression Models, with Empirical Models." *Journal of Quantitative Criminology* 12 (1996): 163–191.

LAUB, JOHN H.; NAGIN, DANIEL S.; and SAMPSON, ROBERT J. "Trajectories of Change in Criminal Offending: Good Marriages and the Desistance Process." *American Sociological Review* 63 (1998): 225–238.

LOEBER, ROLF, and LEBLANC, MARC. "Toward a Developmental Criminology." In *Crime and Justice, Volume 12*. Edited by Michael Tonry and Norval Morris. Chicago: University of Chicago Press, 1990.

LOEBER, ROLF, and SNYDER, HOWARD N. "Rate of Offending in Juvenile Careers: Findings of Constancy and Change in Lambda." *Criminology* 28 (1990): 97–109.

LOEBER, ROLF, and STOUTHAMER-LOEBER, MAGDA. "The Development of Offending." *Criminal Justice and Behavior* 23 (1996): 12–24.

LOEBER, ROLF; STOUTHAMER-LOEBER, MAGDA; VAN KAMMEN, W.; and FARRINGTON, DAVID P. "Development of a New Measure for Self-Reported Antisocial Behavior for Young Children." In *Cross-National Research in Self-Reported Crime and Delinquency*. Edited by Malcolm Klein. Boston, Mass.: Kluwer-Nijhoff, 1989.

MCDERMOTT, SHAUN, and NAGIN, DANIEL. "Same or Different? Comparing Offender Groups and Covariates Over Time." In *Handbook of Law and Social Science: Youth and Justice*. Edited by S. O. White. New York: Plenum Press, 1998.

MOFFITT, TERRIE E. "'Life-Course-Persistent' and 'Adolescent-Limited' Antisocial Behavior: A Developmental Taxonomy." *Psychological Review* 100 (1993): 674–701.

———. "Adolescence-Limited and Life-Course Persistent Offending: A Complementary Pair of Developmental Theories." In *Developmental Theories of Crime and Delinquency: Advances in Criminological Theory, Volume 7*. Edited by Terence P. Thornberry. New Brunswick, N.J.: Transaction Publishers, 1997a.

———. "Neuropsychology, Antisocial Behavior, and Neighborhood Context." In *Violence and Childhood in the Inner City*. Edited by Joan

McCord. Cambridge, U.K.: Cambridge University Press, 1997b.

NAGIN, DANIEL S., and FARRINGTON, DAVID P. "The Onset and Persistence of Offending." *Criminology* 30 (1992a): 501–523.

———. "The Stability of Criminal Potential From Childhood to Adulthood." *Criminology* 30 (1992b): 235–260.

NAGIN, DANIEL S.; FARRINGTON, DAVID P.; and MOFFITT, TERRIE E. "Life-Course Trajectories of Different Types of Offenders." *Criminology* 33 (1995): 111–140.

NAGIN, DANIEL S., and LAND, KENNETH C. "Age, Criminal Careers, and Population Heterogeneity: Specification and Estimation of a Nonparametric, Mixed Poisson Model." *Criminology* 31 (1993): 327–362.

NAGIN, DANIEL S., and PATERNOSTER, RAYMOND. "On the Relationship of Past to Future Delinquency." *Criminology* 29 (1991): 163–189.

OSGOOD, D. WAYNE, and ROWE, DAVID C. "Bridging Criminal Careers, Theory, and Policy Through Latent Variable Models of Individual Offending." *Criminology* 32 (1994): 517–554.

PATERNOSTER, RAYMOND, and BRAME, ROBERT. "Multiple Routes to Delinquency? A Test of Developmental and General Theories of Crime." *Criminology* 35 (1997): 49–84.

ROWE, DAVID C., OSGOOD, D. WAYNE, and NICEWANDER, W. ALAN. "A Latent Trait Approach to Unifying Criminal Careers." *Criminology* 28 (1990): 237–270.

SAMPSON, ROBERT J., and LAUB, JOHN H. *Crime in the Making: Pathways and Turning Points Through Life.* Cambridge, Mass.: Harvard University Press, 1993.

SHANNON, LYLE W. *Criminal Career Continuity: Its Social Context.* New York: Human Sciences Press, 1988.

———. *Changing Patterns of Delinquency and Crime: A Longitudinal Study in Racine.* Boulder, Colo.: Westview Press, 1991.

SIMONS, RONALD L.; JOHNSON, CHRISTINE; CONGER, RAND D.; and ELDER, GLEN, JR. "A Test of Latent Trait versus Life-Course Perspectives on the Stability of Adolescent Antisocial Behavior." *Criminology* 36 (1998): 217–244.

TRACY, PAUL E., and KEMPF-LEONARD, KIMBERLY. *Continuity and Discontinuity in Criminal Careers.* New York: Plenum, 1996.

TRACY, PAUL E.; WOLFGANG, MARVIN E.; and FIGLIO, ROBERT M. *Delinquency in Two Birth Cohorts.* New York: Plenum, 1990.

VISHER, CHRISTY A., and ROTH, JEFFREY A. "Participation in Criminal Careers." In *Criminal Careers and "Career Criminals." Volume 1.* Edited by Alfred Blumstein, Jacqueline Cohen, Jeffrey A. Roth, and Christy A. Visher. Washington, D.C.: National Academy Press, 1986.

WARR, MARK. "Life-Course Transitions and Desistance From Crime." *Criminology* 36 (1998): 183–216.

WEST, DONALD J., and FARRINGTON, DAVID P. *Who Becomes Delinquent?* London: Heinemann, 1973.

———. *The Delinquent Way of Life.* London: Heinemann, 1977.

WOLFGANG, MARVIN E.; FIGLIO, ROBERT M.; and SELLIN, THORSTEN. *Delinquency in a Birth Cohort.* Chicago: University of Chicago Press, 1972.

CRIMINALIZATION AND DECRIMINALIZATION

The question of the proper scope of the criminal law—what to punish, and why—is a continuing and difficult one. What new criminal prohibitions should be enacted, and which existing prohibitions should be expanded, narrowed, or eliminated? Since all criminal laws in the United States are created or subject to modification by statute, this question is primarily addressed to the legislature. However, when courts are called upon to interpret the scope of criminal statutes, they sometimes address similar questions, either as a matter of presumed legislative intent, or as a matter of public policy or (very rarely) constitutional interpretation. Police, prosecutors, and other law enforcement officials also sometimes face these issues, when deciding how to interpret and enforce existing criminal laws.

How the criminal law has been used and abused

When most people think about "crime," they imagine serious, "common law" offenses such as murder, rape, assault, robbery, burglary, and traditional forms of theft, that is, the stealing of tangible property. There have been relatively few changes in the scope of the criminal law in these areas, although major issues of criminalization occasionally arise, for example: whether to permit any form of euthanasia or assisted suicide; how broadly to define rape and other criminal sexual conduct offenses, or crimes against children and fetuses; and whether to recognize broader duties to prevent harm, or new forms of vicarious liability. But the focus of debate on the criminalization question tends to be elsewhere, involving a host of miscellaneous offenses designed to protect public morality, discourage risk creation, support government regulation of the economy, preserve the environment, or otherwise promote the public welfare.

Despite efforts in many states to reform and recodify criminal codes, numerous "morals" and "public welfare" offenses remain on the books, and new offenses of these types are continually being added. Indeed, there appears to be a unidirectional tendency to adopt new criminal laws, without repealing or substantially restricting old ones that are not even enforced. New statutes are enacted in reaction to the scandals or crises of the day, by legislators who are eager to do something about these problems or who wish to demonstrate their strong support for public morality and good order. Rarely does any effective lobbying group or other impetus compel legislators to repeal or restrict existing laws. Moreover, the scope of government regulation and welfare programs has expanded enormously since the late nineteenth century, and each new program has brought with it new penal laws. Criminal penalties have been applied to widely varied activities in the effort to end the killing of endangered species; to regulate automobile traffic; to discipline school officials who fail to use required textbooks; to regulate commerce in foods, drugs, and liquor; to uphold housing codes; and to regulate the economy through price control and rationing laws, antitrust laws, export controls, lending laws, and securities regulations (Allen, 1964; Kadish, 1963; 1967; Packer).

In response to the ever-increasing number of criminal statutes, numerous proposals have been made to define more narrowly the scope of the criminal law and to decriminalize a large number of morals and public welfare offenses. The laws most often proposed for repeal relate to public drunkenness, vagrancy, disorderly conduct, homosexuality, sodomy, fornication, adultery, bigamy, incest, prostitution, obscenity, pornography, abortion, suicide, euthanasia, the use or sale of drugs and liquor, gambling, violations of child-support orders, passing of worthless checks, economic regulatory violations, minor traffic offenses, and juvenile offenses that would not be criminal if the actor were an adult (Allen, 1964; Kadish, 1963, 1967; Packer; Morris and Hawkins, 1970, 1977; Richards, 1982; Schur; U.S. Department of Justice). Some of these offenses have, in fact, been repealed or narrowed in a number of American jurisdictions, and decriminalization efforts have gone much farther in several Western European nations (Frase, 1990; Frase and Weigend).

The authors of decriminalization proposals do not always reject the same offenses, nor do they all agree on a common rationale or criterion for making these decisions. However, there is considerable consensus that many of the laws proposed for repeal are either inappropriately invasive of individual freedom of action, hypocritical, unenforceable, or too costly to enforce. These authors also appear to agree that the scope of the criminal law can and should be defined by a single set of objective, "neutral" principles capable of efficient application to all types of offenses, and should reflect general consensus among reasonable persons of widely differing moral and philosophical views. Such an approach has the advantage of avoiding narrow, subjective disputes about the wisdom of specific laws, although it also has the disadvantage inherent in any abstract, a priori schema. This article will describe the various criminalization criteria that have been proposed and will attempt to reconcile them and present a consensus of the consensus-seekers.

Definition of a "criminal" sanction

Before examining the wide variety of issues involved in the choice of the criminal sanction, it is useful to consider what it means to call something a crime and, in particular, how criminal prohibitions differ from various civil laws and regulations. Although criminal penalties tend to be more severe than civil and regulatory remedies, perhaps only the death penalty is unique to the criminal law. Property is taken by taxation, civil fines, civil forfeitures, and compensatory or punitive damages; individual liberty may be denied by such civil procedures as quarantine, involuntary civil commitment, and the military draft. Thus, what principally distinguishes the criminal sanction is its peculiar stigmatizing quality, even when sentence is suspended and no specific punishment follows conviction. Criminal sanctions have traditionally been viewed as expressing society's strong moral condemnation of the defendant's behavior and its "hatred, fear, or contempt for the convict" (Henry M. Hart, Jr., p. 405). This is probably still true, despite the dilution of "moral" blame that has resulted from the continuing expansion of the criminal law.

A second distinguishing feature of the criminal law, which follows naturally from the special stigma and severe sanctions that may be imposed, is the strict procedure of adjudication required. As a matter of constitutional law, criminal defendants are entitled to proof beyond a reasonable doubt, the privilege against compelled self-incrimination, and numerous other procedural guarantees. Criminal statutes may also violate due process if they are unduly vague (*City of Chicago v. Morales*, 527 U.S. 41 (1999)), and they are traditionally construed narrowly, both as a matter of public policy and as a means to avoid unconstitutional vagueness problems.

A third distinguishing feature of the criminal law, which follows in part from the first two, is that it employs specialized agencies of enforcement: police, prosecutors, criminal courts, and correctional agencies focus their efforts largely or entirely on the criminal law.

Criminal procedures and enforcement agencies are, however, sometimes also used to enforce "civil" sanctions. In Minnesota, for example, most moving-traffic violations, violations of certain ordinances, and numerous other minor offenses are classified as petty misdemeanors (punishable by a fine of up to $200); these are not deemed to be "crimes" (Minn. Stat. Ann. § 609.02, subd. 4a (2000)), but they are enforced by the police and criminal courts, and are governed by the code of criminal procedure (Minn. Rule of Crim. Procedure 1.01 (2000)). A similar hybrid offense category, classified as a "violation," is recognized under the Model Penal Code, section 1.04 (5), and under the laws of many European countries (Weigend). The latter, known as "administrative penal law," often includes violations that would be deemed "crimes," subject to jail or prison terms, in most American jurisdictions (Frase, 1990); such downgrading of offense classification, and resulting lower penalties, stigma, and procedural requirements, constitutes a form of partial "decriminalization."

The moral condemnation and stigmatizing effect of criminal penalties is related to one of the traditional purposes of criminal sanctions: to exact retribution by imposing "deserved" punishment in proportion to the offender's blameworthiness. Retribution is a nonutilitarian ethic that views punishment as being proper for its own sake, whether or not it has any effect on future wrongdoing by the offender or others. Various utilitarian theories, on the other hand, justify punishment because it discourages the offender from future wrongdoing (special deterrence), intimidates other would-be offenders (general deterrence), and strengthens behavioral standards in more indirect ways (the educative or moraliz-

ing function of punishment). Punishment sometimes also prevents further crime by the defendant through physical restraints on his liberty or privileges (incapacitation), or through education or other treatment aimed at changing underlying psychological or physical causes of his criminal behavior (rehabilitation) (Packer; Zimring and Hawkins). Clearly, the extent to which the enactment or enforcement of criminal penalties actually achieves any of these purposes of punishment must be an important factor in deciding whether to apply criminal sanctions to a given type of behavior.

How does the criminal law achieve these purposes, that is, what types of criminal sanctions are available? In addition to the punishments listed or implied above (death, imprisonment, fines), defendants may be given a conditional sentence (of imprisonment or a fine, or an unspecified (deferred) sentence). A conditional sentence is not carried out if the defendant complies with certain restrictions or requirements, such as periodic reports to a probation officer or other supervisor; limitations on travel, place of residence, or associates; home detention or electronic monitoring; abstinence from liquor or drugs; periodic random tests for drug or alcohol use; restitution to the victim, community-service work; participation in educational, counseling, or medical treatment programs; and refraining from further criminal behavior.

Persons convicted of crimes may also lose certain privileges or suffer other disabilities, either automatically or at the discretion of various officials (Schonsheck). These include revocation or denial of a driver's license or other permit; ineligibility for government or private employment, public office-holding, and government programs or contracts; loss of voting and other civil rights; forfeiture of property gained from or used to commit the crime; liability to greater penalties upon subsequent convictions; and loss of credibility as a witness, through rules permitting impeachment by prior convictions.

As suggested earlier, many of these sanctions can also be imposed by means of civil or regulatory procedures. The U.S. Supreme Court has had some difficulty in determining which of these various civil-criminal hybrids (in particular, involuntary civil commitment of dangerous persons, civil fines, civil forfeitures, and occupational disqualifications) are subject to constitutional criminal procedures. After some vacillation, the Court, in a series of cases decided in the late 1990s, seemingly held that constitutional criminal procedures are either fully applicable or do not apply at all; such procedures will be deemed applicable only to offenses that are labeled as criminal or which are overwhelmingly punitive in purpose or effect (Klein). However, at least some forfeitures are subject to the excessive fines clause of the Eighth Amendment (*United States v. Bajakajian*, 524 U.S. 321 (1998)), and principles of due process prohibit "grossly excessive" awards of punitive damages (*BMW of North Am., Inc. v. Gore*, 517 U.S. 559 (1996)).

How should one treat such quasi-criminal penalties when approaching the criminalization problem? Although they all could be viewed as criminal laws, this entry initially adopts a narrower approach and defines criminal laws as those that are generally labeled or regarded as criminal in a formal sense, enforced by the police and other traditional criminal justice agencies, and subject to constitutional and nonconstitutional rules of criminal procedure. However, it will be necessary at some point to consider the various hybrids as well. In its broadest sense, the criminalization question thus becomes several questions: Should the behavior in question be prohibited or regulated by law? If so, to what extent? What role should be given to purely civil or administrative laws, quasi-criminal sanctions, and formal criminal penalties? Which agencies should enforce these prohibitions and sanctions?

A review and typology of criminalization arguments

It is useful at the outset to distinguish between three fundamentally different types of arguments for and against the use of the criminal law. Arguments of principle assert that as a matter of political or moral philosophy, it is proper (or improper) to prohibit certain conduct. The second category, that of arguments of practicality, is logically relevant only if it has been determined that society may legitimately prohibit the conduct in question; practical arguments assert that, although legitimate, certain prohibitions are unwise because in practice they cause more harm than good. A third approach rejects the feasibility of devising a workable standard based on the substance of criminal prohibitions, and argues instead for additional procedural limitations on criminalization decisions and criminal law enforcement.

Arguments of principle. The broad question of whether, and to what extent, the law may enforce morality represents one of the classic debates in philosophical and criminal law literature. This debate has tended to focus on the use of formal criminal sanctions, and most of the arguments appear to make no distinction between criminal and noncriminal measures. Of course, if the law may not legitimately interfere at all with certain behavior, then neither criminal nor civil sanctions may be used. On the other hand, if the law may legitimately interfere, there is the further question of whether it is legitimate, necessary, or desirable to use criminal sanctions.

Arguments in favor of prohibition. Some writers have argued that society is permitted, and perhaps even obligated, to enforce morality by means of criminal or other legal sanctions. There are at least two distinct variations of this argument. What H. L. A. Hart calls the "conservative thesis" asserts that the majority in society have the right not only to follow their own moral convictions but also to preserve their "moral environment" as a thing of value and to insist that all members of society abide by their moral convictions (p. 2; see also Stephen). What H. L. A. Hart calls the "disintegration thesis" asserts that public morality is the "cement of society," which must be maintained to prevent social disintegration (p. 1). A major proponent of this thesis was Patrick Devlin, who argued that the law should protect society's political and moral institutions and the "community of ideas" necessary for people to live together. Devlin wrote, "Society cannot ignore the morality of the individual any more than it can his loyalty; it flourishes on both and without either it dies" (p. 22).

Even if it is conceded that the legal enforcement of morality is legitimate, however, several practical difficulties arise: whose "morality" is to be enforced, and how much of it? Although the United States has a highly "moralistic" criminal law (Morris and Hawkins, 1970), many types of behavior that would generally be considered "immoral" have never been considered criminal—for example, most breaches of contract (Packer). The nineteenth-century jurist James Fitzjames Stephen suggested that the criminal law should be limited to "extreme cases . . . [of] gross acts of vice," that public opinion and common practice must "strenuously and unequivocally condemn" the conduct, and that "a moral majority must be overwhelming" (1967 ed., pp. 159, 162). Although he saw no possibility of setting theoretical or a priori limits on the power of the law to enforce morality, Patrick Devlin conceded the need for "toleration of the maximum individual freedom that is consistent with the integrity of society"; only if the majority has "a real feeling of reprobation, intolerance, indignation and disgust" for the conduct may it be prohibited (pp. 16–17). But how are such judgments to be made, and by whom? Devlin answered that the standard should be that of the "reasonable" person, or the typical juror, because the "moral judgment of society must be something about which any twelve men or women drawn at random might after discussion be expected to be unanimous" (p. 15).

Although these formulations do suggest some limiting principles, they provide little concrete guidance to legislators. Moreover, in an increasingly secular, pluralist society there is less and less consensus about fundamental moral principles, and some doubt whether twelve persons "drawn at random" would be unanimous about anything. (However, as discussed more fully below, Stephen's and Devlin's overwhelming-moral-consensus standards do suggest potential procedural limits on criminalization decisions.) Finally, in deciding how much of morality to enforce with the law, there is no inconsistency in also considering the practical advantages and disadvantages of attempting to prohibit certain conduct. Indeed, Devlin accepted this, citing such practical considerations as the extent to which enforcement would be ineffective or would inevitably violate rights of privacy (pp. 18–22).

Principled arguments against criminalization. In sharp contrast to Devlin, other writers have argued that the law may not legitimately prohibit certain behavior. The classic statement of this position was made by the nineteenth-century English philosopher John Stuart Mill, who argued that society may interfere with the individual's freedom of action only "to prevent harm to others. His own good, either physical or moral, is not a sufficient warrant" (1946 ed., p. 15). Mill believed that the individual must be accorded the maximum degree of liberty and autonomy that is consistent with the rights of others. Although writers such as Devlin concede the importance of protecting individual liberty, Mill and his followers appear to give this factor much greater weight. They view the individual's freedom and self-determination as preeminent rights, which outweigh mere utilitarian considerations of the greatest good for the greatest number (Richards, 1979a, pp. 1222–1223).

To some extent, the Supreme Court and some state courts have adopted this approach, holding that individual rights of privacy and free expression, implicit in the First, Fourth, and Ninth Amendments, prevent the state from prohibiting certain acts that cause no direct injury to any other person (*Griswold v. Connecticut*, 381 U.S. 479 (1965) (use of contraceptives); *Stanley v. Georgia*, 394 U. S. 557 (1969) (possession of obscene material in the home); *Roe v. Wade*, 410 U.S. 113 (1973) (abortion during the first three months of pregnancy); *Ravin v. State*, 537 P.2d 494 (Alaska 1975) (possession of marijuana in the home); *Commonwealth v. Bonadio*, 490 Pa. 91, 415 A.2d 47 (1980) (sodomy between consenting adults in private)). The Supreme Court has also held that, under certain limited circumstances, the ban on cruel and unusual punishments, and principles of due process or equal protection, preclude criminal liability for morals or regulatory offenses (*Robinson v. California*, 370 U.S. 660 (1962) ("status" crime of being an addict); *Lambert v. California*, 355 U.S. 225 (1957) (crime of failing to register as a convicted person, with no showing of reasonable opportunity to become aware of the duty to act); *Loving v. Virginia*, 388 U.S. 1 (1967) (interracial marriage)). On the other hand, the Court has also stated that broad deference should be given to legislative judgments about the wisdom of prohibiting certain conduct, even if those judgments are based on moral assessments. Thus, for example, the Court has upheld punishment of obscenity in a private theater to which access was limited to consenting adults (*Paris Adult Theater I v. Slaton*, 413 U.S. 49 (1973)), and has also upheld criminalization of private acts of sodomy between consenting adults (*Bowers v. Hardwick*, 478 U.S. 186 (1986)).

Analysis of the earlier quotation from Mill reveals several distinguishable justifications for punishment: individuals might be punished for their own "moral" benefit, for their own "physical good," or to prevent "harm to others." Modern writers have tended to agree with Mill that the first purpose is clearly improper: as far as the law is concerned, the individual has "an inalienable right to go to hell in his own fashion, provided he does not directly injure the person or property of another on the way" (Morris and Hawkins, 1970, p. 2).

However, most modern writers do not share Mill's total opposition to prohibitions aimed at protecting the defendant's physical well-being. Mill apparently felt that paternalism was a rationale too easily abused (Richards, 1979b, p. 1424), but modern authors seem more willing to recognize some limited version of this rationale. Mill did approve of laws to protect children from their own lack of judgment, and some modern writers have broadened this justification to include protection against exploitation and corruption of other especially vulnerable groups, including those "weak in body or mind, inexperienced, or in a state of special physical, official or economic dependence" (*The Wolfenden Report,* para. 13; Morris and Hawkins, 1970; H. L. A. Hart; Feinberg, vol. 3). Other writers maintain that individuals must be given the maximum freedom to make choices that they may later regret; these writers would narrowly limit paternalism to cases of extreme irrationality or non-rationality "likely to harm irreparably serious human interests," such as rationality, freedom, or life itself (Richards, 1979b, p. 1424).

As for Mill's third category, "harm to others," it is unclear to what extent he would have distinguished between tangible and intangible harms. If intangible harms include the weakening of "public morality," there is obviously little point to Mill's other limitations. A related problem involves the use of the criminal law for "verbal vindication of our morals" (Kadish, 1967, p. 162), with no serious effort actually to enforce the law. Since such symbolic legislation provides intangible benefits to "others," and does not directly inhibit the individual's freedom of action or punish him for his own moral benefit, how does it violate either the letter or the spirit of Mill's philosophy? Modern followers of Mill usually respond with practical arguments about the collateral disadvantages of unenforced law (for example, diminished respect for law), rather than with arguments of principle (Kadish, 1972).

Also problematic is Mill's support for laws punishing offenses against public "decency" (Mill; H. L. A. Hart; Morris and Hawkins, 1970; Richards, 1979a). The offense caused to the "victims" of public indecency seems different in degree, but not in principle, from the revulsion that such victims feel toward similar acts performed in private. However, one distinction is that prohibition of public solicitation, nudity, and other "indecencies" does not totally eliminate the freedom of the individual to engage in such behavior (in private), or in the presence of those who are not offended. Nevertheless, the result is to limit individual freedom for the sake of preventing an intangible harm to others.

Another intangible harm to others, recognized by at least one modern follower of Mill as a proper justification for punishment, is the breach of promises of marital fidelity (Richards, 1979a). Traditional laws prohibiting adultery, bigamy, and prostitution would seem to be justified on this basis, yet the same author opposes such laws, apparently on the ground that they are over- or under-inclusive. That is, these laws purportedly cover some conduct that poses no threat to fidelity, yet they fail to punish other conduct that clearly does pose such a threat.

A third category of harm that might be viewed as intangible, at least from the point of view of human beings, is that of cruelty to animals. Several modern followers of Mill's philosophy appear to support prohibitions against such cruelty (H. L. A. Hart; Morris and Hawkins, 1970), without considering whether these laws are consistent with the harm-to-others criterion.

As for more tangible harm to others, such as physical injury or property loss, there is widespread agreement with Mill's position that this is a proper basis for punishment. However, as Herbert Packer has pointed out, it is almost always possible to argue that a given form of conduct involves some risk of harm to the interests of others; the harm-to-others criterion is thus a matter of degree—"a prudential criterion rather than a hard and fast distinction of principle" (p. 266). Packer goes on to argue that the risk of harm to others must be "substantial" and unjustified by reasons of social utility. He also asserts that the harm should not be trivial in two senses: it should not be so minor that the imposition of any criminal punishment would be disproportionate to the social harm caused, nor should it be so minor that law enforcement and sentencing authorities are unwilling to enforce the law or to make regular use of "real criminal sanctions," such as imprisonment (pp. 271–273).

Other modern followers of Mill appear to recognize a much broader authority to "protect the citizen's person and property" (Morris and Hawkins, 1970, p. 4). Difficult problems of remoteness of harms are also posed by conduct that, if widely practiced, might cause serious social disorganization—for example, drug addiction. Thus, one court, while upholding the right to use marijuana in the home, implied that such use could be punished if it ever became so widespread that it might "significantly debilitate the fabric of our society" (*Ravin, supra,* p. 509).

A strict application of the Mill philosophy thus poses a number of difficulties. As noted above, it is difficult to find a "pure case" of behavior that harms no one but the actor (Dripps). Clearly, however, the extent of harm to others, both in seriousness and probability, is an important factor to be considered in the criminalization decision. Second, depending on how broadly "harm to others" is defined and on how willing we are to recognize paternalistic legislation, the Mill principle may not be all that limiting, particularly if it is recognized that the legislature has at least some discretion to be both over- and under-inclusive in pursuit of its goals. Third, to the extent that a strict interpretation of Mill's philosophy is based on an elaborate theory of the moral or human rights of the person (Richards, 1979b), this approach to criminalization may prove too vague or too subjective to command broad consensus and application. Fourth, Mill and his followers offer little guidance in the choice of various noncriminal sanctions; indeed, a strict reading of the Mill philosophy would invalidate not only civil and criminal penalties but any interference with individual "liberty of action," including, for example, steep excise taxes on tobacco or alcoholic beverages (Greenawalt, p. 719). Finally, there is no reason why "moral" arguments against criminalization should preclude consideration of practical disadvantages as well, particularly since most of the moral arguments do not lend themselves to definitive, "bright line" distinctions.

Arguments of practicality. Although modern advocates of decriminalization have often cited Mill's philosophy in support of their arguments, they usually go on to argue that even if prohibition might be legitimate, it is unwise. One group of writers argues that all "victimless" crimes should be repealed. A less simplistic approach seeks to catalog the specific advantages and disadvantages of trying to prohibit certain behavior, and argues that, on balance, the total "costs" of criminalization often outweigh the benefits.

Victimless crime. The concept of victimless crime is frequently suggested as a basis for decriminalization (Schur). The term itself is somewhat misleading, since it has been applied to offenses such as public drunkenness and adultery, which often have direct, readily identifiable "victims." Furthermore, it is arguable that most other so-called victimless crimes, such as drug offenses and prostitution, do have at least potential victims: the participants themselves, relatives, taxpayers, or society at large. The users of this term tend to stress the practical disadvantages of trying to enforce victimless crimes—for example, that the lack of complaining witnesses leads to the use of intrusive police practices, bribery, and discriminatory enforcement. However, many of these problems arise in the enforcement of criminal laws that have not been labeled as victimless or proposed for repeal (for example, carrying an unregistered weapon). The victimless crime concept may draw some of its rhetorical appeal from largely unarticulated philosophical premises: if a crime is truly victimless, efforts to enforce it may not only be difficult but illegitimate (Morris and Hawkins, 1970). But whether the victimless crime criterion is best viewed as an argument of principle or one of practicality, the concept is of very limited utility in deciding the more difficult issues of criminalization. The criterion lacks a clear definition, fails to cover some of the offenses to which it has been applied, and applies equally well to other offenses that have not been proposed for repeal. The relative victimlessness of an offense is closely related to several important practical issues in the criminalization decision (discussed below). However, labeling a crime as victimless only begins what is, in most cases, a very difficult process of assessing complex empirical facts and fundamental value choices.

The cost-benefit approach. A more sophisticated (but less rhetorically effective) practical approach to the criminalization question seeks to identify the specific advantages and disadvantages of invoking the criminal law, in an effort to determine whether the total public and private "costs" of criminalization outweigh the benefits (Kadish, 1967). Strictly speaking, cost-benefit analysis involves the weighing of variables that are measurable in dollars or other quantitative units. The proponents of a cost-benefit approach to criminalization generally concede that there is little quantitative data in this area, but they argue that the approach is still a useful way of thinking about criminalization problems (Kadish, 1972).

The costs of criminalization include public and private burdens, both tangible and intangible. Beginning with tangible public costs, it is necessary (but often difficult) to separate out the police, court, attorney, and correctional expenditures properly attributable only to the enforcement of a specific criminal law. (Occasionally this "marginal" cost is fairly clear—the salaries and expenses of the police narcotics division, for example.) In some cases, apparent costs may not entirely disappear with decriminalization: many of the previous enforcement efforts (such as collecting and jailing public drunks) may have simply taken up the slack in police and jail resources that must still be maintained to handle peak loads. Moreover, decriminalization may require the police and other public officials to respond to the underlying behavioral problem in alternate ways that have their own costs: in the example above, removal of penalties for public drunkenness may lead to more arrests for disorderly conduct, or may increase the use of costly public and private medical facilities.

Private costs of criminalization include not only concrete items such as attorneys' fees and other litigation expenses, but also several factors that are harder to measure. These include the individual's loss of the freedom, pleasure, or other value derived from engaging in the forbidden conduct (for example, having sex with a prostitute; owning firearms); the anxiety and social ostracism imposed upon offenders, whether or not they are detected and prosecuted; the reduction or elimination of the offender's economic earning power during the period of pretrial and trial proceedings, while sentence is being served, and perhaps for the rest of his life; detention and other losses of physical freedom, before and after conviction; and the uncompensated costs and inconveniences imposed on witnesses and jurors.

Another set of costs, which may affect both public and private interests, is the tendency of criminalization to produce more, rather than less, socially undesirable behavior. Examples of illegal behavior that may result from criminalization are bribery of the police or other enforcement officials; extortion by officials of money or other favors in return for nonenforcement; private blackmail by threats to expose the offender; discriminatory enforcement of the law against unpopular groups or individuals, or in favor of defendants with more political or social influence; and the use of illegal methods of obtaining evidence, such as unauthorized searches and electronic surveillance, coercive interrogations, and entrapment. Indeed, some categories of crimes (for example, vagrancy and disorderly conduct) seem to have been specifically designed to undercut constitutional limitations on arrest, search, and interrogation (Kadish, 1967).

Even where the methods of law enforcement are not clearly illegal, they may be so contrary to widely held feelings of privacy or fairness that they cause a lowering of public respect for the law, particularly among social groups already alienated from society, including ethnic minorities and the poor. Examples of such questionable tactics include selective enforcement in order to conserve resources; the use of undercover agents, decoy officers, and informers from the criminal milieu who are paid in money or leniency; arrests for purposes of harassment or to "clean the streets," with no effort to prosecute; and "legal" searches, electronic surveillance, and intrusive physical surveillance (for example, peering through holes in the ceilings of public washrooms in order to observe possible homosexual or narcotic offenses). As may be noted, the problems listed above arise primarily when the behavior involves consenting parties and few, if any, witnesses. It is partly this relative invisibility of victimless crimes that makes their enforcement so costly.

Criminal laws may violate principles of equal justice even if not intentionally enforced in a discriminatory or selective manner. For example, poor or uneducated women are less likely to obtain a safe, although illegal, abortion and thus must either bear unwanted children or suffer the risk of death or severe medical complications. Efforts to enforce prostitution laws against "call girl" operations are costly and difficult, and therefore most arrests of prostitutes involve street solicitations by lower-class or minority-group women (Morris and Hawkins, 1970). Drug-law enforcement is likewise heavily biased against poor, nonwhite street dealers and users (Tonry). Unequal justice is inherently wrong, but it also has important practical consequences. Perceptions of unfairness, either in the law's procedures or its impact, undercut the legitimacy of legal prohibitions, making citizens less willing to obey the law (Tyler).

Other costs of criminalization arise when the prohibited conduct involves goods, activities, or services that are in great demand, such as gambling, drugs, liquor, illegal weapons, abortion, commercial sex, and pornography. When there is high demand, prohibition tends to limit supply more than demand, thus driving up the black-market price and creating monopoly profits for those criminals who remain in business. Organized criminals tend to have advantages over less organized ones in exploiting illegal markets and coping with law enforcement pressures, and consequently, criminalization tends to foster the growth of sophisticated, well-organized, and powerful criminal groups. Once in existence, organized crime tends to diversify into other areas of crime. Its high profits provide ample funds for bribery of public officials, as well as capital for diversification. Finally, whether or not the participants in black markets are highly organized, they tend to use violence to resolve their disputes; thus, the enactment and increased enforcement of alcohol and drug prohibitions in the twentieth century led to increased rates of lethal violence (Miron).

Although higher prices tend to discourage some would-be participants in prohibited activities, the underlying high demand, combined with restricted supply, maintains both high prices and high participation rates. In extreme cases of high and inflexible demand (for example, heroin or cocaine addiction), exorbitant prices force many participants to commit other crimes to pay for the illegal goods or services they want. These are generally nonviolent property crimes, such as shoplifting, or other forms of vice such as prostitution or sale of drugs, but violent property crimes may also be encouraged. Finally, because the illegal goods or services are in great demand, a large number of otherwise law-abiding citizens are driven into association with the criminal elements who supply these goods and services. There is a danger that these citizens will come to view themselves as criminals, since society labels them as such. As members of the criminal subculture, they may lose respect for the law and are more likely to be drawn into other forms of crime.

Another concrete cost of criminalization is the barrier that the law erects between the criminal and important social services and protections. For example, when the law forbids abortion or drug use, consumers are forced to make use of unsanitary instruments or medically unsound procedures, increasing the risk of death, injury, or infection (to themselves and, in the case of HIV, to all of their sexual or syringe-sharing partners). If harm occurs they are unwilling to seek the medical attention they need, for fear of exposing their criminal behavior; pregnant drug users may avoid all prenatal care. Laws against prostitution and homosexuality may have a similarly adverse effect: participants who contract a venereal disease are less likely to seek timely medical treatment. Moreover, although prostitution laws seek to prevent the exploitation and physical abuse of female prostitutes by their pimps, the existence of criminal penalties and enforcement efforts probably makes women more likely to seek the support and protection of the pimp, while discouraging them from seeking legal protection from exploitation and abuse.

Further costs of criminalization include overloading the criminal justice system with a mass of petty cases; creating a law enforcement bureaucracy with a "vested interest in the status quo" (Packer, p. 333), thus thwarting efforts at reform or even research; and fostering the illusion that a social problem has been taken care of, thereby discouraging the development of more effective alternative measures (Kadish, 1967).

Finally, it can be argued that extending the criminal law to behavior that is widely believed to be morally neutral or that is engaged in by the vast majority of citizens dilutes the stigmatizing quality of criminal sanctions generally, thus robbing them of their peculiar effectiveness in dealing with more serious conduct (Packer; Kadish, 1967). Of course, lack of widespread moral condemnation may also make the law difficult or impossible to enforce, thus limiting the benefit of prohibition.

Benefits of criminalization.   On the other side of the ledger, the benefits achieved by criminalization fall into several categories. To the extent that the criminal law is enforced with a view toward preventing specific social or individual harms, the likelihood of achieving such preventive benefits depends on the following factors:

1. The probability that the behavior defined as criminal will be observed or detected by anyone other than the immediate participants;
2. The probability that various parties will invoke formal criminal processes—that witnesses or participants will report the crime to the police and support prosecution efforts, that the police will be able and willing to make an arrest, that the prosecutor will approve the filing of formal charges, and that judges and juries will be able and willing to find the defendant guilty and impose significant sanctions;
3. The likelihood that conviction and sentence will reduce the future incidence of the behavior defined as criminal, either through general deterrence of other potential offenders, the "educative" effect of punishment, special deterrence or rehabilitation of the punished offender, or incapacitation of the offender; and
4. The likelihood that reducing the incidence of the behavior defined as criminal will reduce any more remote harms sought to be prevented (for example: the likelihood that reducing acts of drunken driving at low alcohol-concentration levels will reduce accident frequency or severity).

Of course, to the extent that punishment of criminal behavior is considered proper for its own sake (to impose "deserved" punishment, for example), the last two factors are irrelevant.

Even if criminal prosecution is not successful or is not even attempted, the mere existence of criminal prohibitions might have some indirect effect on the incidence of the behavior defined as criminal and thus, even more indirectly, on any more remote harm to be prevented. The labeling of behavior as criminal represents a social judgment that such behavior is morally wrong or at least undesirable, and this judgment may serve to reinforce similar feelings among members of the public. As with actual enforcement efforts, the extent of this symbolic effect depends on the strength of the perceived relationship between the prohibited behavior and the more remote social harm, if any, sought to be prevented (for example, the relationship between euthanasia and the devaluation of human life). Another important set of considerations here involves attitudes about unenforced law; to the extent that most people believe that the law should either be enforced or repealed, unenforced law promotes cynicism and disrespect for the law, particularly the criminal law (Kadish, 1967). Thus, legislative attempts to denounce certain behavior symbolically, with no intention or ability to enforce the law, may do more harm than good.

Perhaps the most critical determinant of the total "benefit" of criminalization, whether by means of actual enforcement efforts or symbolic denunciation, is the importance of the social harm involved. In the case of heroin possession or sales, for example, it must be decided how seriously society views the use of heroin itself—as well as undesirable behaviors (e.g., driving) of persons under the influence of heroin, and the risk of heroin addiction—in order to decide whether the costs of criminalizing heroin use and sale are worth bearing. A host of tangible and intangible factors must then be considered: the values of human rationality and full consciousness; the losses of life and health that are not attributable to prohibition itself; the potential loss of the economic productivity of users; and perhaps even the anguish that heavy use or addiction may impose on relatives and close friends of the user.

Costs and benefits of noncriminal measures.

Even if the benefits of criminalization exceed the costs, proponents of the cost-benefit approach point out that various civil, administrative, or regulatory measures may be more effective than criminal sanctions, less costly, or both. Examples of such noncriminal alternatives include the zoning or licensing of pornography and prostitution (Richards, 1979a); civil detoxification or civil commitment of public drunks (Kadish, 1967); medically supervised distribution of maintenance doses to heroin addicts (Morris and Hawkins, 1970); the use of civil fines for certain drug, traffic, and other minor violations; heavy taxation of unhealthy products; and general preventive measures such as product labeling and television advertising, seeking to discourage certain activities. Each such alternative must be subjected to a weighing of costs and benefits; whichever approach (criminalization or some alternative) produces the greatest excess of benefits over costs is the approach that should be followed, and if no approach produces a net benefit, then the ultimate alternative is to do nothing at all (Packer).

There are several reasons why noncriminal measures may be more effective or less costly than criminal sanctions. As discussed earlier, the former may not be subject to the strict procedural requirements applied to criminal statutes, and the personnel who administer noncriminal sanctions may be less highly trained and paid. An alternative solution to the problems of proving guilt in criminal cases would be to redefine crimes by reducing or eliminating the traditional criminal law requirement of culpable mental state (mens rea) or the requirement of personal guilt, thus imposing strict liability or vicarious liability for the acts or omissions of others. However, the latter alternatives create new problems of enforcement. To the extent that the redefined prohibited behavior is not generally viewed by witnesses, police, prosecutors, judges, and juries as morally blameworthy, criminal penalties will not be fully enforced (Kadish, 1963), whereas civil penalties for the same behaviors might be viewed as an appropriate compromise between condemning and condoning the behavior in question. Finally, noncriminal procedures may be better adapted to controlling and regulating violations of a continuing nature. An injunction proceeding, for example, uses past misconduct to formulate a rule of behavior specifically tailored to the situation, and then makes use of rather summary contempt proceedings each time that rule is violated in the future. Similarly, licensing and inspection regimes are better suited to detecting and enforcing limits on particularly problematic aspects of ongoing behaviors (for example, venereal disease among prostitutes). One of the key lessons of alcohol prohibition and its repeal is that it is not possible to effectively regulate behavior that is criminally prohibited (Morris and Hawkins, 1977).

On the other hand, noncriminal procedures are not always less costly or more effective than criminal penalties. Courts have occasionally applied criminal law procedural requirements to violations labeled as civil, because of the penalties authorized, the punitive intent of the legislature, or other indexes of punishment. In *Brown v. Multnomah County Dist. Ct.,* 280 Or. 95, 570 P. 2d 52 (1977), for example, the court invalidated an attempt to decriminalize first-offense drunk driving and dispense with right-to-counsel and proof-beyond-reasonable-doubt   guarantees. Even the requirements of civil due process may make enforcement difficult and costly. For example, *Heap v. Roulet,* 23 Cal. 3d 219, 590 P. 2d 1 (1979), held that state constitutional due process required proof beyond a reasonable doubt, as well as a unanimous jury in civil conservatorship and commitment proceedings. Moreover, the abuses of discretion and other nonfinancial costs of criminal law enforcement are not necessarily avoided by the use of civil enforcement procedures: civil inspectors and regulators would seem just as likely to discriminate invidiously, take bribes, use intrusive means of detection, and the like. Indeed, to the extent that noncriminal alternatives are governed by lower standards of proof and procedure, and enforced by less highly trained personnel, we might expect the results to be less reliable and more subject to abuse, and we should also expect these less formal procedures to be invoked much more often. Past experience with informal measures such as the juvenile court and pretrial diversion suggests caution in abandoning the procedural protections of the criminal law (Allen; Morris).

In terms of the effectiveness of sanctions, there are undoubtedly certain types of behavior that cannot be adequately controlled without the use of the criminal law. Given its greater stigmatizing effect and more severe penalties, the criminal law is more likely, all things being equal, to prevent future offenses through deterrence (general and special), norm-reinforcement, or incapacitation. Criminal penalties also have greater retributive impact. Moreover, even where the behavior in question (for example, nonpayment of support) can generally be prevented and controlled without the use of the most severe penalties, there is often a need to retain the criminal law to deal with aggravated cases and to encourage cooperation with lesser forms of regulation or treatment (Morris and Hawkins, 1970), as well as for the occasional case where the criminal law's coercive detention and investigatory powers are needed. Although efforts can and should be made to define the scope of the criminal law as narrowly as possible in these areas, the traditional reliance on administrative discretion to tailor the penalties to the offense reflects, in part, the difficulty of specifying in advance precisely when criminal penalties and procedures are appropriate.

Priorities.   The last and perhaps the most important step in the cost-benefit analysis is to consider whether, in a world of limited resources, the time and money spent attempting to control the behavior in question would be better spent elsewhere. A major criticism of attempts to prohibit such offenses as drunkenness, prostitution, and drug use is that these cases overload the police, courts, and correctional systems; thus these offenses distract those systems from their more important task of preventing serious crimes against persons and property and reduce the quality of justice in serious and nonserious cases alike. Implicit in this criticism is the assumption that other offenses are more socially harmful, easier to detect and prosecute, or subject to fewer collateral costs (police corruption and the like). The assessment of priorities thus involves yet another level of cost-benefit analysis, focusing on the marginal benefit that would be achieved by shifting resources from one type of offense to others. This analysis applies to resources spent on noncriminal as well as criminal sanctions. Finally, one must also consider whether it would be better to shift the resources completely away from law enforcement into other social uses, such as education or health care.

To summarize, the cost-benefit approach first examines the various costs and benefits of using the criminal law to control the behavior or social harm in question. If the costs outweigh the benefits, criminal prohibition is rejected. Even if the benefits of criminalization outweigh the costs, however, it is necessary to consider whether some noncriminal form of prohibition or regulation would produce not only a net benefit but a greater net benefit than criminalization. If neither criminalization nor a noncriminal alternative produces a net benefit, then the solution is to do nothing or leave the matter up to existing remedies and procedures—such as private civil damages actions—that exist for nonpunitive, nonregulatory reasons. If there is a net benefit, whichever form of prohibition yields the greatest net benefit must then be compared with the alternative uses of the resources involved, to see whether these resources would produce a still greater benefit if applied elsewhere (to control different behaviors, or for other public purposes).

Critique of the cost-benefit approach. In theory, the approach described above covers all relevant considerations and has the further advantage of relying, as much as possible, on matters that are subject to empirical verification. However, it seems unlikely that we will ever obtain reliable data on most of the relevant cost and benefit variables, and what data we have on each variable may not be commensurate with data on other variables. How does one compare, for example, the public safety benefits of extending drunk-driving prohibitions to lower alcohol concentrations, with the increased costs of enforcement—not only financial costs, but also lost freedom of action by drivers who would not have caused any public harm if left unregulated? Moreover, the cost-benefit calculus is too complex to provide much practical assistance in making specific criminalization decisions, nor does application of the calculus effectively limit such decisions—results are highly dependent upon the weight given to key variables, and the estimates used where (as is often the case) hard data is lacking. Finally, although practical problems of law enforcement are certainly very relevant considerations, they must not be allowed to overshadow the fundamental value choices that must be made: What purposes of prohibition are legitimate in a free, secular society? How much discretion should lawmakers have in defining prohibitions aimed at achieving concededly legitimate goals? How important are various harms (such as drug addiction) and values (such as the ideal of marital fidelity)? How important are the various unquantifiable costs of criminalization (such as loss of privacy or the right to use drugs or possess weapons for self-defense)?

In light of these complexities, it is tempting to fall back on more simplistic criteria: the law may (or must) enforce morality with few, if any, a priori limitations (Devlin); the law may only seek to prevent "harm to others" (Mill); the law may not violate the "human rights of the person" (Richards, 1979b); "victimless" crimes should be repealed (Schur); and so on. As this entry has attempted to demonstrate, however, the search for a single, simple criterion is illusory: both in matters of principle and of practicality, criminalization is almost always a question of degree, and seldom a matter of clear-cut alternatives.

The procedural (content-independent) approach. Given the inherent problems of criminalization arguments based on either principle or practicality, some writers have suggested that a more effective way to limit overbroad criminal laws would be to impose additional procedural limitations on criminalization decisions and criminal law enforcement. Donald Dripps proposes three such limits. First, the enactment of criminal prohibitions should require a two-thirds vote of the legislature, similar to the super-majority vote required to convict on impeachment, propose a constitutional amendment, or approve a treaty. Second, all criminal laws should have a built-in "sunset" provision, requiring reenactment (by two-thirds vote) every ten years. Third, courts should be given greater powers to require even-handed enforcement of criminal laws, thus increasing political pressures to limit their scope. Although Dripps admits that current equal protection doctrine is much narrower, he suggests that it might only be necessary to extend existing rules which, upon a showing of disparate impact on identifiable racial minorities, require the government to prove the absence of discriminatory intent.

Dripps's super-majority and sunset requirements are designed to prevent the enactment or continued enforcement of laws that are, or later become, strongly opposed by a substantial minority of citizens. These two requirements are thus consistent not only with the views of writers who argue for penal restraint based on political pluralism (Allen), but also with statements, summarized earlier, made by some of the most prominent advocates of "legislating morality." Thus, James Fitzjames Stephen conceded that criminal laws must be based on an "overwhelming" moral consensus; Patrick Devlin agreed that criminal laws must be based on moral judgments as to which a typical jury of twelve would be unanimous. And although Dripps does not go that far, something close to a unanimity requirement seems quite appropriate when the issue is whether to enact or continue the most severe penalties, such as the death penalty or life without parole (just as we require the most stringent procedures in order to impose the death penalty in any given case). Presumably, such super-majority and sunset requirements would have to be embodied in a constitutional amendment. Although there is reason to doubt that very many legislatures would propose such an amendment, some states permit this to be done by popular referendum.

Other writers have proposed additional, less ambitious procedural incentives for narrow criminal lawmaking. One idea, somewhat parallel to Dripps's super-majority requirement, is to force legislatures to consider—or even include in current budgets—the full costs of proposed criminal legislation, including costs to be incurred beyond the current budget cycle (Wright). This mechanism is already being used in a number of states with sentencing guidelines commissions, and has helped those states control the growth of their prison populations (Frase, 1995). Another proposal, paralleling Dripps's sunset rule, is to create a permanent law revision committee or commission, "charged with the task of constant consideration of the fitness and adequacy" of criminal laws and sanctions (Morris and Hawkins, 1970, p. 27).

Synthesis of criminalization theories

In the absence of any simple criminalization criterion or effective procedural limits on criminalization decisions, how should legislators proceed? How can the mass of interrelated, often conflicting substantive criteria discussed above provide any concrete guidance in the choice of the criminal sanction? The list below attempts to synthesize the views of classical and modern writers on this subject, and poses a series of questions that hypothetical legislators (or their constituents) should ask themselves.

1. What is the specific social or individual harm that the law seeks to prevent or minimize, how important is it, and how likely is it to follow from the behavior sought to be prohibited? Although the law may on occasion seek to go beyond concrete "harm to others" to achieve paternalistic goals (such as the safeguarding of children) or to protect intangible interests (such as "decency" in public places), the dangers of abuse of individual rights increase the closer one comes to basing the law on public morality, intangible harms, or protection of the criminal "for his/her own sake." In particular, protection of an adult person's private morality, solely for that person's own good, would seldom if ever be justified in a secular society.

2. What are the major pros and cons of criminalization? Like the cost-benefit approach described earlier, this question addresses the practical difficulties of enforcing the law (because, for example, there are few civilian witnesses, or the prohibited behavior is highly desired by the participants), and also takes into account the likely success of criminal penalties in preventing both the prohibited acts and any more remote social harms sought to be prevented. Even if the practical pros and cons cannot be quantified and rigorously compared with each other, their mere enumeration and description helps to ensure that no relevant considerations are overlooked, and may signal the need for legislative caution (even in the absence of super-majority, sunset, or other procedural limitations). One factor that deserves particularly close scrutiny is the long-term financial cost of proposed criminal laws and penalties, particularly when most of the proposal's benefits are likely to be achieved in the short term.

3. Are any noncriminal methods of control more effective or less costly? Here again, the legislator must consider the major advantages and disadvantages of civil, administrative, or quasi-criminal forms of prohibition or regulation. Given the procedural complexities of the criminal law, its more severe stigma and sanctions, and the need to permit the agencies of the criminal law to concentrate their energies on the most serious social harms, noncriminal procedures are often preferable. In such cases, residual, "last resort" criminal penalties will sometimes be necessary, but they should be kept to a minimum, both to avoid problems of discretionary enforcement and to prevent interference with noncriminal procedures (for example, by discouraging prostitutes or drug users from obtaining medical assistance). There are some cases, of course, for which the criminal law and its procedures are peculiarly appropriate, as in dealing with violent or imminently harmful behavior. In other cases, only certain aspects of the criminal law may be needed (such as the arrest powers of the police), but not its severe stigma or sanctions. It may also be administratively convenient to give the police, prosecutors, or other criminal justice agencies responsibility for enforcing certain noncriminal prohibitions, for example, minor traffic offenses. Even where criminal sanctions are retained, it may be possible to reduce enforcement costs and procedural complexity by lowering authorized penalties (since, in general, less serious offenses merit less elaborate procedural safe-

guards). Ultimately, the assessment of these practical advantages and disadvantages may not be possible without a willingness to experiment and evaluate carefully the actual results of switching to noncriminal modes of control.

4. Would the resources devoted to criminal or noncriminal prohibition produce greater benefit if applied to other undesirable behavior, or to public and private purposes unrelated to law enforcement?

5. What would happen if all prohibitions or regulatory efforts were discontinued? The alternative of doing nothing is almost always the least expensive, although it is politically the most difficult. Legislators and their constituents like to believe they are "doing something" about social problems, even if this is an illusion; moreover, the removal of all legal prohibitions may encourage the behavior in question, at least in the short run. As with the use of noncriminal alternatives, however, legislators must show a greater willingness to experiment with new approaches; this, after all, is one definition of leadership. Much guidance can be received from those jurisdictions (including those in other nations) that have pioneered deregulation. And of course, prohibition can be reinstated if the results of deregulation are unsatisfactory. The important point is simply that the existence of a criminal prohibition (or even a noncriminal one) must not create any presumption of its own validity. With or without formal "sunset" (required reenactment) provisions, the criminalization question is a continuing one that must be reexamined periodically, without preconditions, by the public and its elected officials. Similarly, new prohibitions should not be casually added without careful consideration of the lessons of past criminalization efforts

RICHARD S. FRASE

See also ABORTION; ALCOHOL AND CRIME: THE PROHIBITION EXPERIMENT; CIVIL AND CRIMINAL DIVIDE; CRIMINAL LAW REFORM: CURRENT ISSUES IN THE UNITED STATES; DRUGS AND CRIME: LEGAL ASPECTS; ENTRAPMENT; GAMBLING; HOMOSEXUALITY AND CRIME; JUVENILE STATUS OFFENDERS; OBSCENITY AND PORNOGRAPHY: BEHAVIORAL ASPECTS; POLICE: POLICING COMPLAINANTLESS CRIMES; PROSTITUTION; SEX OFFENSES: CONSENSUAL; VAGRANCY AND DISORDERLY CONDUCT; VICTIMLESS CRIME.

BIBLIOGRAPHY

ALLEN, FRANCIS A. The Borderland of Criminal Justice: Essays in Law and Criminology. Chicago: University of Chicago Press, 1964.

———. "Majorities, Minorities, and Morals: Penal Policy and Consensual Behavior." Northern Kentucky Law Review 9 (1982): 1–22.

American Law Institute. Model Penal Code: Proposed Official Draft. Philadelphia: ALI, 1962.

Canada, Special Committee on Pornography and Prostitution. Pornography and Prostitution in Canada: Report. Summary and 2 vols. Ottawa, Ontario: Justice Canada, 1985.

COOK, PHILLIP J. "An Introduction to Vice." Law and Contemporary Problems 51 (1988): 1–7.

CRANOR, CARL F. "Bibliographic Essay—The Hart-Devlin Debate." Criminal Justice Ethics 2 (winter/spring 1983): 59–66.

DEVLIN, PATRICK. The Enforcement of Morals. New York: Oxford University Press, 1965.

DRIPPS, DONALD A. "The Liberal Critique of the Harm Principle." Criminal Justice Ethics 17 (summer/fall 1998): 3–18.

FAGAN, JEFFREY. The Criminalization of Domestic Violence: Promises and Limits. Washington, D.C.: U.S. Dept. of Justice, National Institute of Justice, 1996.

FEINBERG, JOEL. The Moral Limits of the Criminal Law. 4 vols. Vol. 1, Harm to Others; Vol. 2, Offense to Others; Vol. 3, Harm to Self; Vol. 4, Harmless Wrongdoing. New York: Oxford University Press, 1984–1988.

FRASE, RICHARD S. "Comparative Criminal Justice as a Guide to American Law Reform: How Do the French Do It, How Can We Find Out, and Why Should We Care?" California Law Review 78 (1990): 539–683.

———. "State Sentencing Guidelines: Still Going Strong." Judicature 78 (1995): 173–179.

FRASE, RICHARD S., and WEIGEND, THOMAS. "German Criminal Justice As a Guide to American Law Reform: Similar Problems, Better Solutions?" Boston College International & Comparative Law Review 18 (1995): 317–360.

GREENAWALT, KENT. "Legal Enforcement of Morality" Journal of Criminal Law & Criminology 85 (1995): 710–725.

HARCOURT, BERNARD E. "The Collapse of the Harm Principle." Journal of Criminal Law and Criminology 70 (1990): 109–194.

HART, H. L. A. Law, Liberty, and Morality. Stanford, Calif.: Stanford University Press, 1963.

———. "Social Solidarity and the Enforcement of Morality." University of Chicago Law Review 35 (1967): 1–13.

HART, HENRY M., JR. "The Aims of the Criminal Law." *Law and Contemporary Problems* 23 (1958): 401–441.

KADISH, SANFORD M. "Some Observations on the Use of Criminal Sanctions in Enforcing Economic Regulations." *University of Chicago Law Review* 30 (1963): 423–449.

———. "The Crisis Of Overcriminalization." *Annals of the American Academy of Political and Social Science* 374 (1967): 157–170.

———. "More on Overcriminalization: A Reply to Professor Junker." *UCLA Law Review* 19 (1972): 719–722.

KAISER, GÜNTER. "Recent Developments in Criminalization and Decriminalization in West German Penal Policy." *EuroCriminology* 3 (1990): 27–45.

KLEIN, SUSAN R. "Redrawing the Criminal-Civil Boundary." *Buffalo Criminal Law Review* 2 (1999): 679–721.

MILL, JOHN STUART. "On Liberty" (1859). *On Liberty; Representative Government; The Subjection of Women: Three Essays*, by John Stuart Mill. Introduction by Millicent Garrett Fawcett. London: Oxford University Press, 1946. Pages 5–141.

MIRON, JEFFREY A. "Violence and the U.S. Prohibitions of Drugs and Alcohol." *American Law and Economics Review* 1 (fall 1999): 78–114.

MORRIS, NORVAL. *The Future of Imprisonment.* Chicago: University of Chicago Press, 1974.

MORRIS, NORVAL, and HAWKINS, GORDON J. *The Honest Politician's Guide to Crime Control.* Chicago: University of Chicago Press, 1970.

MORRIS, NORVAL, and HAWKINS, GORDON J. *Letter to the President on Crime Control.* Chicago: University of Chicago Press, 1977.

PACKER, HERBERT L. *The Limits of the Criminal Sanction.* Stanford, Calif.: Stanford University Press, 1968.

RICHARDS, DAVID A. J. "Commercial Sex and the Rights of the Person: A Moral Argument for the Decriminalization of Prostitution." *University of Pennsylvania Law Review* 127 (1979a): 1195–1287.

———. "Human Rights and the Moral Foundations of the Substantive Criminal Law." *Georgia Law Review* 13 (1979b): 1395–1446.

———. *Sex, Drugs, Death, and the Law: An Essay on Human Rights and Overcriminalization.* Totowa, N.J.: Rowman & Littlefield, 1982.

ROACH, KENT. "Four Models of the Criminal Process." *Journal of Criminal Law and Criminology* 89 (1999): 671–716.

SCHONSHECK, JONATHAN. *On Criminalization: An Essay in the Philosophy of the Criminal Law.* Dordrecht, The Netherlands: Kluwer Academic Publishers, 1994.

SCHUR, EDWIN M. *Crimes without Victims: Deviant Behavior and Public Policy-Abortion, Homosexuality, Drug Addition.* Englewood Cliffs, N.J.: Prentice-Hall, 1965.

STEPHEN, JAMES FITZJAMES. *Liberty, Equality, Fraternity* (1874). Edited with an introduction and notes by R. J. White. London: Cambridge University Press, 1967.

TONRY, MICHAEL. *Malign Neglect: Race, Crime, and Punishment in America.* New York: Oxford University Press, 1995.

TYLER, TOM R. *Why People Obey the Law.* New Haven, Conn.: Yale University Press, 1990.

U.S. Department of Justice, Law Enforcement Assistance Administration, National Advisory Commission on Criminal Justice Standards and Goals. *A National Strategy to Reduce Crime.* Washington, D.C.: U.S. Dept. of Justice, 1973.

WEIGEND, THOMAS. "The Legal and Practical Problems Posed by the Difference between Criminal Law and Administrative Penal Law." *Revue Internationale de Droit Pénal* 59 (1988): 57–93.

The Wolfenden Report: Report of the Committee on Homosexual Offenses and Prostitution. Authorized American edition. Introduction by Karl Menninger, M.D. New York: Stein & Day, 1963.

WRIGHT, RONALD F. "Three Strikes Legislation and a Sinking Fund Proposal." *Federal Sentencing Reporter* 8 (1995): 80–83.

ZIMRING, FRANKLIN E., and HAWKINS, GORDON J. *Deterrence: The Legal Threat in Crime Control.* Chicago: University of Chicago Press, 1973.

CASES

BMW of North Am., Inc. v. Gore, 517 U.S. 559 (1996).

Bowers v. Hardwick, 478 U.S. 186 (1986).

Brown v. Multnomah County Dist. Ct., 280 Or. 95, 570 P.2d 52 (1977).

City of Chicago v. Morales, 527 U.S. 41 (1999).

Commonwealth v. Bonadio, 490 Pa. 91, 415 A.2d 47 (1980).

Griswold v. Connecticut, 381 U.S. 479 (1965).

Heap v. Roulet, 23 Ca. 3d 219, 590 P.2d 1 (1979).

Lambert v. California, 355 U.S. 225 (1957).

Loving v. Virginia, 388 U.S. 1 (1967).

Paris Adult Theater I v. Slaton, 413 U.S. 49 (1973).

Ravin v. State, 537 P.2d 494 (Alaska 1975).

Robinson v. California, 370 U.S. 660 (1962).

Roe v. Wade, 410 U.S. 113 (1973).

Stanley v. Georgia, 394 U.S. 557 (1969).

United States v. Bajakajian, 524 U.S. 321 (1998).

CRIMINAL JUSTICE PROCESS

The criminal justice process consists of the procedures public officials follow in the course of imposing criminal punishment. Criminal justice specialists commonly distinguish the investigatory and adjudicatory stages of the process. Cases must come to the attention of officials before an investigation can begin, the boundaries separating the two stages are occasionally blurred, and the same officials may be involved in both investigation and adjudication. Despite these important qualifications, the investigatory/adjudicatory classification remains quite useful.

Overview of the process

Generally speaking, the investigative stage is an inquisitorial process run by the police and the adjudicatory stage is an adversary process run by judges and lawyers. Sometimes prosecutors play a leading role in the investigation, and sometimes the police investigation continues even after the adversary process of adjudication has begun. Despite the occasions when this broad-brush description is not entirely accurate, in general the distinction between police investigations conducted before any defendant is formally accused of an offense in court, and the adjudication in court of those charges that are filed, provides a sound overview of the criminal justice process.

Although the term *inquisitorial* carries some negative connotations in Anglo-American legal culture, all the term refers to here is the absence of named defendants. Obviously, without a defendant there can be no adversary proceedings. Equally obviously no criminal justice process can assume an adversarial form during the initial stages of an investigation, when the authorities may not know for sure whether an offense has taken place or the identity of the offender. It may not be so obvious but it is equally true that many long-standing criminal justice controversies, including those about police interrogation and eyewitness identification proceedings, involve disagreements about when the investigation should cease and the adjudicatory process should commence.

One vital point about the investigatory/adjudicatory distinction should be made at the outset. It is, of course, possible to authorize the police themselves to adjudicate by simply conflating the investigation and the trial. In such a system the police, whether officially or secretly, have the power not just to use violence such as arrest or search for the purpose of bringing about a trial according to due process. They have also the power to punish supposed offenders without judicial authorization. Such systems, to which the epithet "police state" properly applies, have operated in many places and many times. Even in societies with a deep political commitment to due process, the police occasionally disregard the judicial process and punish suspects without trial. Thus the distinction between investigation, which must for practical reasons be assigned to an executive agency with paramilitary qualities, and adjudication, which is made more rather than less necessary by the existence of a paramilitary police force, is not an accident. It is instead the best institutional arrangement people have yet discovered for protecting themselves from private crime without subjecting themselves to arbitrary official power.

The criminal justice process is not the only form of official coercive social control. Individuals who are mentally ill and a danger to themselves or others may be committed to institutions indefinitely after a civil, as distinct from a criminal, hearing. Contraband and the fruits or instrumentalities of crime, such as an airplane used to smuggle drugs, may be seized by the state in civil as well as criminal forfeiture proceedings. The government like private individuals may bring a civil action for punitive damages when authorized by statute or court decision. The criminal justice process is the most extensive and most prominent, but by no means the exclusive, system of coercive social control.

The criminal justice process in the United States varies widely. Federal practice differs from that in the states and the practice in one state varies from that in another. Different police departments pursue different investigative strategies, and different court systems follow different procedures. What follows will be liberally sprinkled with words such as "typically," "commonly," and "generally." It would be difficult to put forward a descriptive assertion about the American criminal justice process to which no exception could be found. Nonetheless, the following description may prove useful, given the recognition that real people go to jail only in particular cases governed by the laws of a single jurisdiction that may depart from the norm in any number of important ways.

The investigatory process

Investigation of crime usually involves three elements. First, public officials, usually the police, must learn that an offense may have been, or is to be, committed. Second, law enforcement agents must identify the likely offender or offenders. Finally, they must collect and preserve evidence that the courts will accept as proving the suspect's guilt beyond reasonable doubt.

Police may learn of crimes in two basic ways. Police officers may themselves observe the offense or evidence of it, or they may receive a report or complaint from someone else. It might seem that relatively few crimes would be directly observed by the police, but a surprisingly large number of offenses are in fact discovered in just this way. Police on patrol may observe suspicious behavior, as when a vehicle circling slowly in a commercial area after hours has a license plate registered to a vehicle recently reported stolen. Moreover, a great many crimes, prominently including prostitution, illegal weapons, and drug offenses, do not involve anyone inclined to complain to the police. Although voluntary informants often come forward in these cases, effective investigation largely depends on undercover police agents.

Citizen reports provide the other major source of information about crimes. Not all crimes that occur are reported to the police, and not all crimes that are reported in fact took place or took place as the initial informant described. False reports, motivated by revenge or insurance fraud, are relatively rare. The failure to report crime is far more frequent.

Victims or other witnesses of crime may not come forward for a variety of reasons. They may perceive the chance of apprehending the offender as too remote to justify the time of reporting and testifying. They may be afraid of vengeance by the offender or by those acting on his behalf. They may be related to, or on friendly or intimate terms with, the offender. When researchers estimate the crime rate by surveying sample populations and asking how often the respondents have been victimized (*victimization surveys*) the rate of actual crime appears to exceed the rate of reported crime by a very wide margin. It is generally agreed that homicide and auto theft are most frequently reported. It is also generally agreed that sexual assault and domestic violence are disproportionately underreported.

Once the police have determined that an offense has taken place, they must determine the likely perpetrator (or perpetrators). They must also gather evidence of guilt that will stand up in court. Although these two processes are closely related they are not identical, because some of the evidence police routinely use to identify the likely offender is not admissible in court. For example, police investigations often rely heavily on representations by informants that are based on what the informants have heard rather than what they have witnessed personally. Even if such an informant were willing to testify (and they typically are not), the *hearsay rule* usually would prevent the informant from testifying in court about what the informant has heard others say about the crime. Another important example is the criminal record of individuals previously arrested or convicted for crimes similar to the one under investigation. The police routinely consider the records of potential suspects, while the courts typically exclude such evidence under the *character-evidence rules*.

Even when the information before the police is admissible in court, the police must weigh its probative force in selecting potential suspects. Eyewitnesses are notoriously inaccurate and may give police completely incorrect descriptions of the offender. In rare cases individuals may confess to crimes they did not commit. Far more commonly they may attribute crimes in which they were involved to other persons who were not involved or involved to a lesser degree. Witnesses may shield the guilty with false alibis and the like. Physical evidence is not subject to the risk of deception but may mislead in other ways, as when illegal drugs are discovered in an automobile containing several passengers who accuse each other of sole possession.

The police must select potential suspects in the face of these challenges under severe time and resource constraints. As police departments often evaluate the work of their officers based on the clearance rate (the percentage of reported crimes that result in an arrest), the police may have an incentive to focus on the most likely suspect however unlikely his guilt is relative to that of persons unknown. On the other side of the equation the police may often have very strong suspicions about the identity of the suspect but be unable to prove his guilt beyond reasonable doubt by evidence admissible in court.

The U.S. Supreme Court has construed the Constitution to regulate many phases of police investigation. With many important qualifications, the police may not detain people on the street for investigation without some objective evidence of criminal activity; they may not search homes without a judicial warrant based on facts showing probable cause; they may search automobiles based on a determination of probable cause, without first obtaining a judicial warrant; and they may not arrest individual without probable cause to believe the individual has committed an offense. A suspected who is arrested may not be questioned without first receiving *Miranda* warnings and waiving his rights to silence and counsel, but the police may interview persons not yet arrested without following the *Miranda* rules (*Miranda v. Arizona*, 384 U.S. 436 (1966)).

These regulations are enforced almost exclusively by the judicial exclusion of evidence obtained in violation of the applicable constitutional rules. Police more interested in seizing a cargo of drugs than in prosecuting the courier may have little incentive to obtain a warrant before searching for the drugs. Police who are willing to lie about how they obtained their evidence likewise may feel little incentive to comply with the rules, so long as their testimony is likely to be accepted in court.

The police investigation thus follows a dialectical or give-and-take process, in which the investigators formulate a hypothesis about the identity of the offender and collect evidence tending to confirm that hypothesis until some new item of information surfaces to exonerate the suspect. It is hard to imagine the process operating any other way, because without some sense of the potential perpetrators' identities there would be no way to distinguish evidence from completely irrelevant facts. The police do not have the resources to conduct every investigation by a process of elimination in which they begin by establishing the alibi of every person in town. Yet the choice of suspects influences the evidence collected; if the police focus on Smith as the perpetrator, Jones will not be made to stand in a lineup.

"Realistic" fiction of the police-procedural variety, whether in print or on film, is not far wide of the mark in capturing the basic tenor of this process. But police fiction grossly overstates the epistemic power of the investigatory process. The fictional police always get their man. In real life, only about 20 percent of all reported crimes are cleared by an arrest.

Observers have always known that not all arrested persons are in fact guilty, but experience with DNA testing indicates that the investigatory process is more prone to false positives than many believed. Nationwide about a quarter of the conclusive DNA tests run at the request of the police exonerate the suspect. That is good news for the innocent (and bad news for the guilty) in cases where physical evidence permits a test. But it is not an encouraging sign about the frequency with which the police investigation identifies the wrong individual as the offender in the large majority of cases in which physical evidence does not permit scientific tests of identity.

In a world in which most crimes are not reported and only about one-fifth of the reported crimes result in an arrest, it is obvious that law enforcement officials must make difficult decisions about how to allocate their scarce resources. Patrol officers must be assigned to neighborhoods. Detectives and undercover operatives must be assigned to certain types of offenses. Should undercover officers be devoted to enforcing the drug laws or the prostitution laws? How heavily should the police concentrate patrol efforts in a high-crime neighborhood? Given too few officers, the residents (generally poor and often disproportionately racial minorities) may be unfairly denied police protection. Given too many police, there may be either the perception or the reality of discriminatory overenforcement.

The model of a police-dominated investigation followed by adjudication in court must be modified to include those situations in which the investigation is run primarily by prosecutors. Prosecutorial investigations usually involve either "white collar" crime of an economic or political nature, or organized crime of the narcotics, gambling, and loan-sharking variety. In the white-collar context prosecutors will not need much assistance from the armed police and will ordinarily interview witnesses and then take sworn testimony before an investigatory grand jury prior to filing charges. In the organized-crime case, prosecutors need to work closely with the police or federal agents. The prosecutors support the officers' applications for warrants for electronic surveillance and negotiate immunity for informants, while the officers recruit or plant informants and execute the searches and arrests.

The adjudicatory stage

In the United States the adjudicatory process varies considerably from one jurisdiction to another, although the process throughout the country is highly similar. Most cases originate with an arrest by the police. The Supreme Court has held that the Constitution requires a prompt judicial determination of probable cause to believe that the arrestee has committed an offense. If that judicial probable cause determination was not made prior to arrest by the issuance of a warrant or the return of an indictment by a grand jury, the arrestee must be brought before a judicial officer for a determination of probable cause. Although the time frame prior to this first appearance is not rigidly defined, the Court has recognized a presumption that detention without judicial authorization that lasts longer than forty-eight hours is unconstitutional.

The probable cause hearing need not be more elaborate than the process of issuing an arrest warrant. There does not need to be any formal charge filed at this point, and the Supreme Court has held that the right to counsel does not arise until a charge is filed, whether by indictment, information, or complaint. Nonetheless common practice is to perform several functions at the first appearance in court if the court finds that probable cause indeed exists. Bail or other conditions of pretrial release may be set, counsel for the indigent may be appointed, and a date for further proceedings may be set.

The period between arrest and presentment in court offers the police the opportunity to interrogate the suspect under the *Miranda* rules. Once the suspect is represented by counsel, it is highly unlikely that the suspect will volunteer information, and any questioning by the police after the right to counsel has attached is unconstitutional. The *Miranda* right to counsel is not the Sixth Amendment right to counsel at trial, but a right derived from the Fifth Amendment privilege against self-incrimination. If the adjudicatory process were understood to begin with arrest, there would be no period of time in which the suspect was in custody but unprotected by the Sixth Amendment right to counsel at trial. The Supreme Court in *Miranda* accepted the proposition that counsel may be waived without an appearance in Court or consultation with counsel for purposes of interrogation, but has never intimated that such a waiver of the right to counsel at trial would be valid.

After the arrest and a judicial determination of probable cause, the next step in the process is the selection of a charge by the prosecutor. Prosecutors enjoy extremely wide discretion in selecting charges. Consider, for example, a suspect who fired a gun at another man. This might be dismissed as no crime because the suspect was acting in self-defense (or because the prosecutor concludes that although the defendant was not acting in self-defense a jury might conclude otherwise). At the other end of the continuum the case might be charged out as attempted murder or aggravated assault. In between it might be charged out as illegal possession or discharge of a firearm, or a simple assault. If the suspect has prior convictions the prosecutor may but need not add a charge under a recidivism statute such as the *three strikes* laws. Thus prosecutors typically have discretion to expose the suspect to a range of liability extending from zero to a substantial term of years.

Prosecutors decline to proceed in a substantial percentage of cases. In some cases the police themselves never expected a prosecution and made the arrest solely for immediate social control purposes. For example, the police might arrest one or both of the drunks involved in a brawl simply to separate them and prevent further violence, or to prevent one of the inebriates from passing out outdoors on a cold night. In other cases the police might hope for an eventual conviction but the prosecutor may decide the evidence is unlikely to persuade a jury.

Often the prosecutor will agree to drop the criminal charges if the defendant will undertake some alternative program to prevent a recurrence of the offense. The prosecutor may agree with a defendant charged with an offense involving or induced by narcotics to abandon the criminal charge provided the suspect enters a drug treatment program. These so-called *diversion arrangements* are quite common, and there is great variety in the types of programs to which persons might be diverted from the criminal justice system.

Juveniles make up a substantial percentage of the population arrested. All U.S. jurisdictions have by statute created specialized juvenile courts, which deal not only with juvenile behavior that would constitute a criminal offense if committed by an adult (delinquency cases), but also with behavior that is legal for adults but not for juveniles, such as drinking alcohol (status offenses). The juvenile court often also has jurisdiction over child welfare cases. The applicable statutes typically permit juveniles suspected of serious felonies to be transferred to the general criminal justice system and tried as adults.

Although the courts have not applied all the procedural protections of the adult system to the juvenile system, the juvenile court system includes most of the same phases (investigation, accusation, presentment, bail, accusation, discovery, plea bargaining, motions, trial, etc.) as the adult system. The Supreme Court has not yet required trial by jury in juvenile cases, but the issue may fairly be regarded as open for consideration at some future time.

In jurisdictions that do not require grand jury indictment the prosecutor may unilaterally file an information accusing the defendant of the crime or crimes the prosecutor has chosen to pursue. About half the states and the federal government require grand jury indictment in felony cases. Whether the charging instrument takes the form of an indictment or an information, the basic purpose of the accusation is to enable the accused to prepare a defense to present at a subsequent trial.

The grand jury usually consists of twenty-three citizens who review cases presented by the prosecutor. Although the grand jurors have the power to refuse to indict, in practice the grand jury very rarely rejects a prosecutor's request for an indictment.

If the case originates with an indictment filed before arrest, the process will differ somewhat. The accused will be either arrested or will surrender to face the charge. At that point the process will continue just as in cases that begin with arrest, with the important qualification that the accused's Sixth Amendment right to counsel has attached even before the arrest. Absent a valid waiver of that right to counsel, so-called critical stages of the process require the presence of defense counsel. Critical stages include interrogation, lineups, and court appearances. They do not include photo identification sessions, the interviewing of witnesses other than the defendant, or the gathering or testing of physical evidence.

Once the charge selected by the prosecutor is filed in court, whether by indictment, information, or complaint, the next step in the process is an arraignment at which the defendant appears in court to hear the charges and enter a plea. If the defendant has not yet retained or been appointed counsel, counsel must be appointed, retained, or waived in open court before entering a plea. Likewise if bail has not been previously set or denied, a pretrial release decision will be made at this point.

If the defendant and the prosecution do not reach a plea agreement and the case goes to trial, there typically will be a *discovery* period, an opportunity for pretrial motions, a preliminary hearing, and a trial. The discovery process has become more extensive but still falls far short of the discovery permitted on the civil side. The principal reasons for the difference are fears that

criminal defendants are more likely than civil litigants to harass or intimidate witnesses and the belief that the defendant's right not to testify unfairly turns criminal discovery into a one-way street.

The Supreme Court's *Brady* doctrine requires the prosecution to turn over to the defense all material *exculpatory evidence* upon a timely request (*Brady v. Maryland*, 373 U.S. 83 (1963)). Court rules typically require both sides to disclose the names and addresses of the witnesses they intend to call, thus permitting the opposing side to interview the witnesses before trial. In many jurisdictions the defense must give advance notice of the intention to rely on certain defenses, such as insanity, alibi, entrapment, or consent.

The theory of the adversary system is that justice is most likely to emerge from a contest in which the two sides prepare their own cases. In practice the theory is compromised by limited resources. A majority of criminal defendants are represented by publicly provided counsel. There is widespread agreement that the funds provided for indigent defense do not permit anything like an independent investigation by defense counsel in every case. Caseload pressures, often in the range of hundreds of felony files per lawyer per year, require defense counsel to select a few cases for trial while arranging the most favorable plea agreement possible for the rest.

Pretrial motions can be made for a wide variety of purposes, including but not limited to: (1) suppression of otherwise admissible evidence because the evidence was improperly obtained; (2) change of venue; (3) admission or exclusion of evidence; (4) compelling discovery withheld by the other side; (5) determining competence to stand trial; and (6) court appointment of expert witnesses for an indigent defendant. Motions are decided by the court without a jury. If a ruling on a motion turns on disputed facts, the court will hold an evidentiary hearing to determine the facts. Pretrial rulings are ordinarily not appealable by the defense until after a conviction, but are commonly allowed for the prosecution, as otherwise the double-jeopardy principle might prevent a retrial even though the government lost the trial because the trial court erroneously ruled on a motion.

Like rulings on motions, the preliminary hearing is conducted by the court without a jury. In theory the preliminary hearing is designed both as a final test of probable cause for a trial and as a discovery tool. Actual practice varies a great deal. In some cases prosecutors introduce their full case, both to encourage a plea from the defense and to preserve the testimony of wavering witnesses. In other cases the prosecutor may put on the minimum needed to go forward to trial out of fear of giving the defense an opportunity for discovery.

The criminal trial

If the defendant demands trial by jury, the trial process begins with the selection of the jury. Potential jurors will be summoned to court in a venire. They will be questioned either by the court, by counsel, or both. Potential jurors will be excused for cause if they have an association with one side or the other or if they in some way manifest an inability to act impartially. Both sides will be given a limited number of peremptory challenges that may be exercised without giving a reason. The defense is usually allowed more peremptory challenges than the government. If either side uses peremptory challenges to excuse potential jurors in a way that might be perceived as racially motivated, the Supreme Court's *Batson* decision requires the trial court to demand a race-neutral explanation of the peremptory challenges (*Batson v. Kentucky,* 476 U.S. 79 (1986), *Georgia v. McCollum,* 502 U.S. 1056 (1992)).

Once the jury is empaneled the prosecuting attorney and defense counsel have the opportunity to make an opening statement. Then the prosecution begins its case by calling witnesses. Their testimony is subject to cross-examination by the defense. At the close of the government's case the defense may move for a directed verdict of acquittal if the government's evidence failed to enable reasonable jurors to find the elements of the charged offense beyond a reasonable doubt.

If the government has succeeded in making out a prima facie case, the defense has the opportunity to put on its case. The defendant may not be called to the stand by the prosecution, and may refuse to testify in his own defense. Jurors are likely to conclude that the defendant who refuses to testify is hiding something, but if the defendant testifies his prior convictions are admissible to impeach the credibility of his testimony. If the defense puts on a case, the prosecution will have an opportunity to call witnesses in a rebuttal case.

Once both sides have rested their cases, the court will instruct the jurors on the legal issues in the case and the two sides will have the opportunity for closing arguments. There is no fixed pattern as to whether the instructions follow the arguments of counsel or vice versa. During the argument stage the prosecution usually has the first argument, the defense the second, and prosecution is given a rebuttal argument to close the case.

The Supreme Court has upheld juries composed of six rather than twelve jurors. Most jurisdictions, however, continue to employs juries of twelve. The Court has also upheld nonunanimous jury verdicts of eleven to one, ten to two, or nine to three to convict, but many jurisdictions continue to require unanimity for a conviction. Although the Supreme Court has never recognized a constitutional right to an appeal, all jurisdictions allow at least one appeal as a right of a felony conviction. The double jeopardy clause prevents the government from appealing acquittals.

The double jeopardy clause does not prohibit a second prosecution following acquittal for an offense under the laws of a different sovereign. Thus an acquittal on federal charges does not bar a subsequent prosecution under state law, and an acquittal on state charges does not bar a subsequent prosecution under federal law.

Sentencing

Upon conviction, whether by plea or after a trial, the trial court imposes the sentence upon the offender. Many states still follow the traditional practice that allows the trial judge discretion to impose any sentence authorized by the statute, from the minimum to the maximum. The court's decision is usually informed by a presentence report prepared by agents of the correctional system. Both the government and the defense may recommend a sentence. Although legally the court is not required to accept a prosecutor's recommendation for a reduced sentence, judges know that disregarding such recommendations could impair the incentives for defendants to plead guilty. Purely discretionary sentencing systems have been widely criticized for treating defendants convicted of similar offenses more or less seriously based on arbitrary factors such as the ideology of the judge.

In 1984 Congress adopted legislation creating the Federal Sentencing Commission and authorizing the commission to promulgate sentencing guidelines for federal courts. The guidelines promulgated by the commission specify a recommended sentence based on the seriousness of the offense and the defendant's prior record. Factors such as post-crime cooperation with the prosecution may reduce the recommended sentence, and other factors such as the use of a weapon during the offense may increase the recommended sentence. The sentencing judge is authorized to depart from the recommended sentence, but must give reasons for doing so, and departures may be challenged on appeal by both the government and the defense. The federal guidelines have been criticized, especially by federal district judges, as unduly rigid.

Many states have taken a middle position between the traditional discretionary system and the more rigid federal guidelines by adopting nonbinding sentencing guidelines. These system vary widely, but their common aim is to reduce sentencing disparities without forcing sentencing judges into a result that may not fit the facts of the particular case.

Many but not all American jurisdictions authorize the death penalty for murder. The Supreme Court has held that capital punishment systems that give juries unguided discretion to impose the death sentence violate the Eighth Amendment's prohibition of cruel and unusual punishments. The Court also has struck down mandatory death penalty statutes for such crimes as the murder of a police officer or a murder committed by a prisoner serving a life sentence. The Court has held that the death penalty is inherently unconstitutional for the crime of raping an adult.

With respect to murder, the Court has upheld statutory schemes that require the sentencing jury to find the presence of statutorily defined aggravating factors, and to balance the aggravating factors against any mitigating factors that may be present in each case before imposing the death sentence. Typical death penalty statutes provide for a bifurcated trial. The sentencing issue will not be considered until the issue of guilt and innocence is tried. If the jury convicts at the guilt phase, the trial will enter a second, penalty phase, during which both sides may offer evidence that was not introduced during the guilt phase.

Whether the Supreme Court really has succeeded in reducing arbitrary decisions about capital punishment is open to question. Juries cannot impose the death penalty unless prosecutors ask for it, and the Court has not imposed any limitations on prosecutorial discretion to seek the death penalty. Moreover, by allowing defendants to introduce evidence of any relevant mitigating circumstance, whether authorized by statute or not, the Court effectively has tolerated very wide jury discretion in death penalty cases. Although some Justices of the Supreme Court have taken the view that the death penalty is inherently cruel and unusual, no Justice on the Court in early 2001 professes that opinion.

A convicted defendant who has exhausted the appeals process may still challenge the conviction by filing a petition for habeas corpus. Habeas corpus is an original civil action challenging the legality of detention. The criminal defendant becomes the civil plaintiff, and the warden or jailer becomes the civil defendant. The Supreme Court has taken an increasingly narrow view of when state prisoners may obtain habeas corpus review in federal court, and in 1996 Congress adopted legislation codifying and in some respects tightening the limitations recognized by the Court.

Plea bargaining

Relatively few criminal cases go to trial, fewer still are appealed, and fewer yet become the subject of collateral review. Prosecutors refuse to file charges or dismiss charges in a large number of cases. In the cases prosecutors choose to pursue, the majority end not in trial by jury but by a plea of guilty or a successful motion to dismiss. Statistics vary across jurisdictions, but it would not be uncommon for half of all arrests to result either in no charges or in charges that are later dismissed, for 80 percent of the cases that are not dismissed to end in guilty pleas, and for the remaining cases to be tried. The government typically wins a significant but not overwhelming majority of criminal trials; a 70 percent conviction rate at trial would not be unusual.

These statistics reflect the ubiquity of plea bargaining. Plea bargaining involves the prosecutor trading a reduction in the seriousness of the charges or the length of the recommended sentence for a waiver of the right to trial and a plea of guilty to the reduced charges. Both sides usually have good reasons for settlement. In a case in which the evidence of guilt is overwhelming, the prosecution can avoid the expense and delay of a trial by offering modest concessions to the defendant. When the evidence is less clearcut the government can avoid the risk of an acquittal by agreeing to a plea to a reduced charge. Because the substantive criminal law authorizes a wide range of charges and sentences for typical criminal conduct, and because the procedural law allows prosecutors wide discretion in selecting charges, the prosecution can almost always give the defense a substantial incentive to plead guilty.

A defendant who is sure to be convicted at trial is likely to take any concessions he can get. The weaker the government's case the more concessions the government will be willing to offer. For the most part the trial process comes into play when the two sides disagree about the likely outcome of a trial. Thus it is not surprising to see that in cases that are not dismissed a very large percentage end in guilty pleas but that the results of trials are far less one-sided. If trials resulted in convictions in 90 percent of cases more defendants would accept even minor concessions in exchange for a plea. If 90 percent of trials resulted in acquittals prosecutors would offer better deals or dismiss more cases unilaterally.

Plea bargaining is problematic for at least three reasons. First, because the substantive criminal law typically authorizes draconian penalties (the three strikes laws, for instance) the prosecution has the power to present defendants with unconscionable pressures. Imagine a defendant with two prior convictions charged with petty theft. The prosecutor offers to drop a three-strikes charge if the defendant pleads guilty. The defendant must now choose between the risk of life in prison if convicted at a trial or a very short term or a suspended sentence following a guilty plea. Although the Supreme Court has accepted such pleas as voluntary, they have every appearance of being practically coerced.

Second, the prosecution has the incentive to maximize the benefit of pleading guilty in the weakest cases. The more likely an acquittal at trial the more attractive a guilty plea is to the prosecution. Given caseload pressures prosecutors may simply dismiss the weakest cases. But in a borderline case that does go forward the prosecution may very well threaten the most serious consequences to those defendants who may very well be innocent.

Third, the indigent defense lawyers who represent most felony defendants do not have the resources to independently investigate every case. Prosecutors face acute resource limitations as well, but generally speaking the government can afford to go to trial in more cases than the defense. Moreover, the defense frequently must decide which cases to contest based on the evidence collected by the police rather than on the basis of an independent investigation. Despite these troubling dimensions, plea bargaining is the central feature of the adjudicatory process.

Racial aspects of the criminal justice process

The justice system undeniably arrests, prosecutes, and punishes African Americans in numbers out of proportion to their representation in the population. Some of the statistics are shocking. For example, it is not uncommon for there to be fewer young black men in a state's institutions of higher learning than are in prison, on probation or parole, or awaiting trial on a criminal charge. The percentage of the prison population that is African American is roughly four times the percentage of African Americans in the overall population.

To the extent this disparity reflects higher rates of criminal behavior among blacks the disparity is rational. Males are arrested, prosecuted, and punished out of proportion to their representation in the population, but no one regards this disparity as unjust. Since most crime is intraracial, the failure to prosecute black offenders will typically fail to protect black victims.

For some crimes (homicide, for example), the African American offense rate is dramatically higher than the rate among Caucasians. Yet even when social science evidence indicates that black and white offense rates are very similar, as with usage rates for marijuana and cocaine, blacks are far more likely to be arrested and prosecuted than whites. The cause of such racial disparities is debatable. What seems clear is that the reverse situation—one in which whites were disproportionately selected for arrest and prosecution despite similar offense rates—would not be tolerated politically.

The relationship between substance and procedure

Plea bargaining also offers an interesting perspective on the criminal justice process as a whole. The Constitution as construed by the Supreme Court places significant limits on police investigations and secures every defendant the right to a rigorous trial. But the limits on the police and the right to trial may be waived by defendants, and police and prosecutors have virtually limitless discretion in selecting targets for investigation and prosecution. The key features of the system are not due process and equal protection, but waiver and discretion.

If defendants could not waive their rights, the system would be required by the Constitution to devote much greater resources to the trial process. If prosecutors did not have discretion to drop and add charges, the state would be disabled from giving defendants an incentive to waive their rights. Because the courts have imposed extensive constitutional requirements on criminal procedure, but have left the substantive criminal law virtually unregulated, discretion and waiver have invited legislatures to authorize extremely harsh sentences. Legislature who adopt harsh penalties know that very few defendants will receive the maximums authorized by statute, because prosecutors have discretion not to bring every charge supported by the evidence. Long potential maximum sentences in turn give the prosecutor powerful leverage in plea negotiations.

Waiver and discretion are both perfectly defensible in theory. In practice they have given us not one criminal justice process, but two. In one system the accused really receives the protections promised by the Constitution. This system is reserved for those who know their legal rights and can afford to assert them. As discretion is generally not exercised to target such individuals anyway, this system only rarely comes into play. The other system tolerates pressures that in fact induce most suspects to waive their rights. In this, the everyday system, defense counsel enters the process only after the police have completed the investigation. Once counsel does enter the picture, defense lawyers cooperate with prosecutors in negotiating an acceptable plea in an environment in which the prosecution largely determines the terms of trade. The right to trial operates primarily as a bargaining chip the defense can play to counter the prosecution's ability to unilaterally determine the severity of the charges.

An honest view of the process does not necessarily entail cynicism. If defendants could not waive their rights it would not be long before those rights were substantially curtailed. If prosecutors were compelled to bring every charge supported by the evidence legislatures would be forced to modify the substantive criminal law or to ante up billions of dollars for prisons. The present arrangement permits society to retain a strong set of procedural safeguards that might protect sophisticated defendants against politically motivated prosecutions. Waiver keeps the cost of these safeguards, in terms of crime control, to a practical minimum.

The role played by wealth in determining the type of justice accorded to different defendants is certainly troubling, but so long as individuals have the right to use their own money to defend themselves against criminal charges it is hard to see how that role could be eliminated. Society could do much more to improve the process and reduce the disparity between rich and poor by raising the floor beneath which justice for the poor is not allowed to fall. This would require the commitment of additional resources, especially but by no means exclusively for indigent defense. Thus far the political will for such reforms has not developed.

DONALD DRIPPS

See also ADVERSARY SYSTEM; APPEAL; ARRAIGNMENT; BURDEN OF PROOF; CRIMINAL PROCEDURE: CONSTITUTIONAL ASPECTS; DISCOVERY; FEDERAL CRIMINAL JURISDICTION; GRAND JURY; GUILTY PLEA: ACCEPTING THE PLEA; GUILTY PLEA: PLEA BARGAINING; HABEAS CORPUS; INFORMAL DISPOSITION; JURY: LEGAL ASPECTS; PRELIMINARY HEARING; SENTENCING: ALLOCATION OF AUTHORITY; SENTENCING: ALTERNATIVES; SENTENCING: DISPARITY; SENTENCING: GUIDELINES; SENTENCING: MANDATORY AND MANDATORY MINIMUM SENTENCES; SENTENCING: PRESENTENCE REPORT; SENTENCING: PROCEDURAL PROTECTION; TRIAL, CRIMINAL.

BIBLIOGRAPHY

BEDAU, HUGO ADAM. *The Death Penalty in America*, 3d ed. New York: Oxford University Press, 1982.

COLE, DAVID. *No Equal Justice: Race and Class in the American Criminal Justice System*. New York: The New Press, 1999.

CONNORS, EDWARD, et al. *Convicted by Juries, Exonerated by Science: Case Studies in the Use of DNA Evidence to Establish Innocence after Trial*. Washington, D.C.: United States Department of Justice, Office of Justice Programs, National Institute of Justice, 1996.

DAMAŠKA, MIRJAN R. *Evidence Law Adrift*. New Haven, Conn.: Yale University Press, 1997.

EASTERBROOK, FRANK H. "Criminal Procedure as a Market System." *Journal of Legal Studies* 12 (1983): 289.

FORST, BRIAN, et al. *Arrest Convictability as a Measure of Police Performance*. Washington, D.C.: United States Department of Justice, National Institute of Justice, 1982.

FELD, BARRY C. *Bad Kids: Race and the Transformation of the Juvenile Court*. New York: Oxford University Press, 1999.

FEELEY, MALCOLM. *The Process is the Punishment: Handling Cases in a Lower Criminal Court.* New York: Russell Sage Foundation, 1979.

FRANKEL, MARVIN E. *Criminal Sentence: Law Without Order.* New York: Hill and Wang, 1973.

FRIEDMAN, LAWRENCE M. *Crime and Punishment in American History.* New York: Basic Books, 1993.

GOLDSTEIN, ABRAHAM S. *The Passive Judiciary: Prosecutorial Discretion and the Guilty Plea.* Baton Rouge: Louisiana State University Press, 1981.

KALVEN, HARRY. *The American Jury,* 2d ed. Chicago: University of Chicago Press, 1971.

KAMISAR, YALE. *Police Interrogation and Confessions: Essays in Law and Policy.* Ann Arbor: University of Michigan Press, 1980.

KENNEDY, RANDALL. *Race, Crime, and the Law.* New York: Pantheon Books, 1997.

LAFAVE, WAYNE R.; ISRAEL, JEROLD H.; and KING, NANCY J. *Criminal Procedure,* 3d ed. St. Paul: West Group, 2000.

LEWIS, ANTHONY. *Gideon's Trumpet.* New York: Random House, 1964.

LOFTUS, ELIZABETH F. *Eyewitness Testimony: Civil and Criminal,* 3d ed. Charlottesville, Va.: Lexis Law, 1997.

NARDULLI, PETER F.; FLEMMING, ROY B.; and EISENSTEIN, JAMES. *The Tenor of Justice. Criminal Courts and the Guilty Plea Process.* Urbana: University of Illinois Press, 1988.

PACKER, HERBERT L. *The Limits of the Criminal Sanction.* Stanford, Calif.: Stanford University Press, 1968.

SIMON, DAVID. *Homicide: A Year on the Killing Streets.* Boston: Houghton Mifflin, 1991.

SKOLNICK, JEROME H. *Justice Without Trial: Law Enforcement in Democratic Society,* 3d ed. New York: Macmillan, 1994.

STUNTZ, WILLIAM J. "Race, Class, and Drugs." *Columbia Law Review* 98 (1998): 1795.

TONRY, MICHAEL H. *Malign Neglect: Race, Crime, and Punishment in America.* New York: Oxford University Press, 1995.

United States Department of Justice, Bureau of Justice Statistics. *Sourcebook of Criminal Justice Statistics.* Washington, D.C.: United States Department of Justice, Bureau of Justice Statistics. Published annually since 1973.

WILSON, JAMES Q. *The Investigators: Managing FBI and Narcotics Agents.* New York: Basic Books, 1978.

WEINREB, LLOYD L. *Denial of Justice: Criminal Process in the United States.* New York: Free Press, 1977.

WHITEBREAD, CHARLES H., and SLOBOGIN, CHRISTOPHER. *Criminal Procedure: An Analysis of Cases and Concepts,* 4th ed. New York: Foundation Press, 2000.

CRIMINAL JUSTICE SYSTEM

A criminal justice system is a set of legal and social institutions for enforcing the criminal law in accordance with a defined set of procedural rules and limitations. In the United States, there are separate federal, state, and military criminal justice systems, and each state has separate systems for adults and juveniles.

Criminal justice systems include several major subsystems, composed of one or more public institutions and their staffs: police and other law enforcement agencies; trial and appellate courts; prosecution and public defender offices; probation and parole agencies; custodial institutions (jails, prisons, reformatories, halfway houses, etc.); and departments of corrections (responsible for some or all probation, parole, and custodial functions). Some jurisdictions also have a sentencing guidelines commission. Other important public and private actors in this system include: defendants; private defense attorneys; bail bondsmen; other private agencies providing assistance, supervision, or treatment of offenders; and victims and groups or officials representing or assisting them (e.g., crime victim compensation boards). In addition, there are numerous administrative agencies whose work includes criminal law enforcement (e.g., driver and vehicle licensing bureaus; agencies dealing with natural resources and taxation). Legislators and other elected officials, although generally lacking any direct role in individual cases, have a major impact on the formulation of criminal laws and criminal justice policy. Such policy is also strongly influenced by the news media and by businesses and public-employee labor organizations, which have a major stake in criminal justice issues.

The notion of a "system" suggests something highly rational—carefully planned, coordinated, and regulated. Although a certain amount of rationality does exist, much of the functioning of criminal justice agencies is unplanned, poorly coordinated, and unregulated. No jurisdiction has ever reexamined and reformed all (or even any substantial part) of its system of criminal justice. Existing systems include some components that are very ancient (e.g., jury trials) alongside others that are of quite recent origin (e.g., specialized drug courts). Moreover, each of the institutions and actors listed above has its own set of goals and priorities that sometimes conflict with those of other institutions and actors, or with the supposed goals and priorities of the system as a whole. Furthermore, each of these actors has substantial unregulated discretion in making particular decisions (e.g., the victim's decision to report a crime; police and prosecutorial discretion whether and how to apply the criminal law; judicial discretion in the setting of bail and the imposition of sentence; and correctional discretion as to parole release, parole or probation revocation, prison discipline, etc.).

Nevertheless, all of the institutions and actors in the criminal justice system are highly interdependent. What each one does depends on what the others do, and a reform or other change in one part of the system can have major repercussions on other parts. It is therefore very useful to think about criminal justice as a system, not only to stress the need for more overall planning, coordination, and structured discretion, but also to appreciate the complex ways in which different parts of the system interact with each other.

This entry describes the major components of contemporary American criminal justice systems, presents some of the available data on how these components typically operate in practice, and examines the various uses of the system concept. The entry will focus on aspects of criminal justice involving adult offenders and designed to enforce civilian criminal laws. There is, however, considerable overlap between the adult and juvenile systems. The police spend a substantial proportion of their time on juvenile suspects; serious juvenile offenders may be tried as adults; and juvenile court convictions (adjudications) may be taken into account in the sentencing of young adults.

Readers should also be aware that several legal regimes outside of the adult, juvenile, and military criminal justice systems can be used to impose serious deprivations of liberty and property (usually with far fewer legal safeguards than apply to criminal prosecutions). Of these, three deserve special mention. First, persons can be seized and detained, sometimes for lengthy periods, under the civil and administrative procedures used to enforce immigration laws. Second, state and federal law enforcement authorities often employ civil forfeiture procedures, permitting the confiscation of property alleged to be the fruit of criminal activity (for example, money earned from selling drugs) or to have served as an instrumentality of crime (for example, a car

used to carry the drugs). Third, persons found to be mentally ill and dangerous to themselves or others are subject to involuntary civil commitment. Such a commitment can lead to indefinite confinement in a secure mental health facility that, from the inmate's perspective, is not much different than a prison. A number of states have expanded these procedures to make it easier to commit sex offenders who have completed their criminal sentences but who are believed to be too dangerous to release into the community.

Structural and theoretical components of criminal justice systems

The principal components of American criminal justice systems are jurisdictional (resulting in separate federal and state systems), normative (the goals, values, and limitations provided by criminal and procedural laws), functional (the activities that typically occur at different stages of the process), and institutional (the officials, agencies, and other actors that handle these various stages).

Separate federal, state, and local criminal justice systems. Each of the fifty states has its own criminal justice system. Some components of the system are organized at the state level (e.g., courts of appeal, state prisons, parole boards, police crime labs); other components are organized at the city and county level (e.g., trial courts, local jails, and most police departments). Some components are found at both state and local levels (e.g., legislative bodies, prosecution and defense offices, probation officers). For minor crimes, a state's criminal justice system actually consists of many independent local systems. Minor crimes are often defined by local ordinances or by state statutes that authorize only local jail and other community sentences, and such crimes are usually processed entirely by local officials. For more serious offenses, it is meaningful to speak of a statewide "system," but one with very substantial local variations. Although such offenses are usually defined by state statutes authorizing state prison sentences, they are processed by local police, prosecutors, attorneys, pretrial and trial judges, and probation officers, who may be strongly attached to local values and traditions. Local variation also results from factors such as differing rates and types of crime, and problems of justice administration such as court congestion and jail overcrowding.

There is also a nationwide federal criminal justice system, consisting of Congress; general and specialized police agencies such as the FBI and the Secret Service; prosecutors in the Department of Justice and in over ninety local United States attorneys' offices; federal public defenders and private defense attorneys; trial (district) courts; intermediate (circuit) courts of appeal; the U.S. Supreme Court; the Federal Sentencing Commission; and the U.S. Bureau of Prisons. Under the American federal constitutional system, the general police power belongs to the states, and the federal government is, in principle, a limited government exercising the powers specified in the U.S. Constitution. Thus, most federal crimes and enforcement activities are limited to conduct jeopardizing a particular federal program (e.g., the federal income tax), or involving some aspect of international or interstate commerce or movement (e.g., mail fraud; interstate transport of stolen property).

State crimes and enforcement activities include a much broader range of behavior, indeed almost any conduct that could be considered criminal, with the exception of certain matters, such as immigration, which lie within the exclusive control of Congress. There is considerable overlap between state and federal criminal jurisdiction, particularly with respect to illegal drugs and prohibited weapons. Cases are sometimes investigated at one level, and prosecuted at the other. In general, federal police and prosecutors use their discretion to select and prosecute only the most serious crimes, or those which the states are unwilling or unable to handle effectively, for example: crimes involving activities in several states, organized crime, complex economic crimes, corruption of local law enforcement or political officials, or denial of civil rights guaranteed by the U.S. Constitution.

The District of Columbia has its own criminal justice system, operating under laws passed by Congress, but with a broad criminal caseload more similar to that of state systems.

State and federal criminal justice systems are generally very similar in their major features, but quite diverse in their details. No particular state is widely regarded as typical, and the specialized criminal jurisdiction of the federal courts precludes using that system to illustrate the entire country. The remainder of this entry will focus primarily on state and local systems. Although federal criminal jurisdiction and federal criminal caseloads have grown steadily over the years, and have increased dramatically since a "war on drugs" was declared in the 1980s, about 95 percent of criminal defendants continue to be prose-

cuted in state courts, under state criminal laws (Harlow, p. 4).

Normative dimensions: laws defining crimes and criminal procedure. Criminal justice systems exist to enforce criminal laws, and such enforcement is both structured and limited by rules of procedure. Although many aspects of criminal justice operate without—or even in violation of—legal rules, the goals, values, and specific provisions of the applicable criminal and procedural law have a major bearing both on how a given system functions and on any assessment of such functioning.

Criminal laws. In the United States, virtually all crimes are defined at least partially by statutes enacted by a legislative body. Within state systems, local legislative bodies usually only have power to enact ordinances creating minor offenses, and only if such local laws do not conflict with state criminal laws governing the same conduct. The power that early U.S. courts exercised to create or expand "common law" crimes is now seen as inconsistent with the fundamental requirement of "fair notice" to the citizen in advance of the acts that are criminally punished. However, many criminal statutes are written in general language, so that courts retain considerable power to interpret statutory terms defining the required elements of liability (actus reus and mens rea). Moreover, affirmative defenses (e.g., self defense, defense of property, necessity, duress, insanity) are often only loosely specified by statute, and some defenses have been recognized by courts without any statutory basis.

The legal categories of crimes in each system determine not only the type and severity of authorized penalties, but also the jurisdiction of trial courts and the applicable procedural rules (more serious offenses are governed by more elaborate procedural safeguards). U.S. criminal law traditionally recognizes three major classes of crime: felonies, misdemeanors, and a third category variously called violations, petty offenses, or petty misdemeanors. In most states, felonies are defined as offenses punishable with more than one year of imprisonment. Such lengthy terms are normally served in large, state-run prisons, but felons may also receive shorter custodial terms to be served in a local jail. Common examples of felonies include murder, manslaughter, rape, robbery, kidnaping, aggravated assault, arson, burglary, forgery, and non-petty cases of theft, possession of stolen property, criminal damage to property, fraud, drug possession or trafficking, illegal weapons, gambling, and prostitution.

Misdemeanors include less serious versions of most of the above offenses, various public order crimes (drunk in public or other disorderly conduct; violation of building or health codes), and serious moving traffic violations (drunk driving; driving without a license). Many states recognize more than one category of misdemeanor offense. In Minnesota, gross misdemeanors are punishable with up to one year in jail, and in most respects are treated procedurally the same as felonies. Ordinary misdemeanors are punishable with up to ninety days in jail, and are handled under simpler, less demanding procedures. The least serious category of offenses (labeled petty misdemeanors in Minnesota) is usually punishable with a fine or other noncustodial penalty. This category includes lesser traffic violations and various minor regulatory offenses. Such violations are not deemed to be "crimes" in many states, but they are generally enforced by the police, and some criminal procedures apply. Most of these cases are handled by payment of scheduled fines, without any court appearance.

Felony cases are generally prosecuted by government attorneys at the county or multi-county level, in a court of general jurisdiction organized at the same level. In many states, misdemeanor cases are handled by city attorneys, and are tried in a municipal or other court of limited jurisdiction, or in the municipal division of county or district court.

Sentencing laws and purposes. Criminal statutes specify the types and amounts of punishment authorized for a given offense, and sometimes even impose a specific penalty (e.g., life in prison without parole, for certain murders) or a minimum penalty (e.g., a mandatory minimum prison sentence of at least five years, for persons selling a certain type and quantity of drugs). Criminal codes sometimes further specify the general purposes that criminal sentences are supposed to serve; however, since these purposes are rarely specified in an exhaustive or detailed manner, courts retain substantial authority to interpret and apply sentencing goals.

Five major purposes of punishment have traditionally been recognized: rehabilitation, incapacitation, deterrence, denunciation, and retribution. The first four are designed to prevent crime. Rehabilitation does this through treatment, education, or training of offenders. Incapacitation prevents crime by imprisoning dangerous offenders, thus physically restraining

them from committing crimes against the public. Deterrence discourages future crimes by the defendant ("special" deterrence) and by other would-be offenders ("general" deterrence), through fear of punishment.

The theory of denunciation (sometimes referred to as the expressive function of punishment, indirect general prevention, or affirmative general prevention) views criminal penalties as a means of defining and reinforcing important social norms of behavior. Given the many difficulties of preventing crime by deterrent threats, incapacitation, or treatment (in particular, the fact that so few offenders are caught and punished—see statistics, presented below), this norm-reinforcement process may be one of the most important crime-preventive effects of punishment.

The fifth traditional sentencing goal, retribution, aims not to prevent crime but rather to give defendants their "just deserts" by imposing penalties directly proportional to the seriousness of the offense and the offender's blameworthiness. What some have called "defining" retributivism seeks to scale punishment precisely to each defendant's desert, while also ensuring that equally deserving offenders receive similarly severe sanctions (sentencing uniformity). A more modest version of desert theory, "limiting" retributivism, merely sets upper and lower bounds—sentences must not be excessively severe or unduly lenient; within these outer limits, punishment is scaled according to what is needed to achieve the crime-preventive goals listed above, and should be the least severe sanction necessary to achieve all of these goals (sentencing "parsimony") (Morris; Frase, 1997).

In addition to the principal goals outlined above, numerous other sentencing purposes, limitations, and theories have been recognized. Constitutional and international human rights norms forbid physically cruel or inhumane punishments. In recent years, more and more courts and other sentencing officials have applied the theory of restorative justice, which seeks to obtain restitution or other satisfaction for the victim or the community, promote victim-offender reconciliation and healing, and provide more opportunities for victims and community representatives to participate in the sentencing and punishment processes. Another new punishment goal in recent years is "truth in sentencing"—offenders should serve almost all of the sentence imposed by the trial court, and should not be released early on parole. However, reforms based on this goal usually allow sentence reductions for good behavior in prison, and this exception illustrates another important sentencing factor: the need to reward the offender's cooperation. Indeed, the entire criminal justice process, from investigation through punishment, relies heavily on such cooperation (for instance, in providing testimony against other offenders; pleading guilty or waiving jury trial and other legal rights; and cooperating with treatment and with conditions of release). Cooperation is induced by giving defendants leniency in the form of lower charges or less severe penalties. Such leniency may bear little relation to an offender's "deserts," and thus requires adoption of the more flexible, "limiting" theory of retribution, described above.

Sentencing judges and corrections agents are not the only officials who must interpret and apply purposes and limitations of punishment. Since police and prosecutors have discretion to set priorities in the use of limited law enforcement resources, they must decide, for example, whether to pursue enforcement policies that emphasize deterrence and incapacitation of drug sellers (the "supply" side) or close supervision and treatment of drug users ("demand"); within the goal of deterrence, they must decide whether to attempt to maximize the number of convictions (i.e., the certainty of punishment) or the severity of penalties.

Legislators also make "sentencing" decisions, based on at least an implicit theory or theories of punishment: mandatory-minimum penalties are believed to have a greater deterrent or incapacitation effect than discretionary penalties; laws punishing drugs possessed for personal use are premised in part on the retributive assumption that drug use is immoral and deserves to be punished, and on the belief that the threat or imposition of criminal penalties will reduce the incidence of drug use (via deterrence or one of the other crime-control theories summarized above).

Whether at the legislative, law enforcement, sentencing, or corrections stage, the definition and application of punishment purposes is highly problematic. Since these purposes are rarely specified in detail, criminal justice agents may apply differing purposes, thus producing disparate results for similarly situated offenders; indeed, the same agent may act inconsistently in different cases.

Beyond mere human error and differences of philosophy, another important reason for disparity is that the traditional goals of punishment often conflict with each other, posing difficult tradeoffs. For example, increased rates of imprisonment may increase the general deterrent effect on other would-be offenders, yet some of the incarcerated offenders may be made substantially worse (more dangerous, less able to cope with freedom) than they were before entering prison (an effect know as prisonization). An offender's mental illness or addiction to drugs reduces his or her capacity to obey the law, thus making the offender less deterable and less blameworthy, but more dangerous and in need of incapacitation. All of the sentencing goals premised on assessments of the individual offender's dangerousness or amenability to treatment inevitably produce disparate sentences for equally culpable offenders, thus violating retributive goals. Given all of these inherently conflicting values and goals, it is no wonder that many persons both inside and outside of the criminal justice system are strongly critical of law enforcement and punishment decisions.

Procedural laws and values. The day-to-day functioning of criminal justice systems is strongly influenced by rules of criminal procedure, which specify what should or should not be done at each stage of the investigation and prosecution of a suspected offense. In comparison with other nations (particularly continental European and other civil law countries), relatively few procedural matters are governed by statutes or codes in American systems; instead, many aspects of U.S. criminal procedure are regulated primarily by state and federal constitutional provisions (particularly the Bill of Rights), for example: limitations on searches and seizures, pretrial interrogations, and admissibility of evidence at trial. But most U.S. jurisdictions do have codes of criminal procedure or statutes that specify such things as arraignment procedures, charging documents, grand jury procedures, pretrial release, pretrial motion procedures, speedy trial rights, trial procedures, and appeal rights and procedures. Separate codes or statutes also regulate such things as electronic surveillance, general evidence rules, and professional responsibility, incorporating both constitutionally imposed and nonconstitutional rules. Some of these codes are promulgated by judicial authorities, others are legislative enactments. In addition, the courts in many states occasionally invoke "inherent" or "supervisory" powers, permitting them to create new procedural requirements.

Criminal procedure laws are based on certain fundamental goals and values that, like the goals and values of punishment mentioned above, sometimes conflict with each other. The central procedural goal is to promote the accurate, speedy, and efficient assessment of criminal liability and punishment—what is often loosely referred to as the "truth-seeking" goal. However, the values of promptness and efficiency often conflict with the need to allow sufficient time for accurate investigation and resolution of complex factual and legal issues. Furthermore, many procedural rules are designed to protect competing values that often limit the achievement of truth-seeking goals, at least in particular cases. These competing values include individual privacy, autonomy, freedom of movement, and dignity; the protection of certain family and confidential relationships (by means of evidence rules excluding "privileged" information); equal treatment of offenders (particularly those of different social classes or races); lay participation in the pretrial and trial processes (on grand juries and trial juries); victim participation at various stages; political accountability of key officials (in particular, judges and prosecutors); and sensitivity to local values and customs (as interpreted by local judges, prosecutors, police, and juries). Such collateral values also sometimes conflict with each other. For example, it may be difficult to increase the participation rights of crime victims without simultaneously reducing defense rights (and also making the process slower and more expensive).

Another procedural value underlying many aspects of American criminal justice is the preference for "adversary" procedures. The most common meaning of this term is that evidence should be gathered and presented by the principal parties (prosecution and defense) and their lawyers, rather than, as in some foreign systems, by a supposedly neutral investigator or presiding trial judge. However, it is easy to overstate the practical significance of this concept in American systems. Although trials and certain pretrial proceedings (e.g., hearings on motions to suppress evidence) are highly adversary, many other procedures are largely or entirely dominated by officials (e.g., police investigations, grand jury proceedings, and most of the decisions affecting the execution of sentence).

These conflicting procedural goals and values thus require constant balancing and compromise, and inevitably produce some disparity in the handling of similar cases, all of which leads to frequent dissatisfaction with the process and its results. These problems are made all the worse by the chronic shortage of resources, and the need to handle large numbers of cases in a more-or-less "assembly line" fashion.

Viewed from a broader perspective, however, the conflicts between procedural values may be less serious than they seem when viewed in the context of individual cases; the pursuit of procedural fairness does not necessarily compete strongly with the achievement of crime-control goals in the long term. Research suggests that people are more likely to obey the law if they feel they have been fairly treated (Tyler), and are more likely to accept the fairness of adjudication procedures in which they can directly participate (Freedman, pp. 87–88). These findings underscore the importance of maintaining respect for the criminal justice system on the part of the general public as well as suspects and defendants. Such respect seems particularly important if, as was suggested earlier, the long term, norm-reinforcing effect is one of the most important functions of punishment. Criminal sentences cannot achieve their vital "teaching" effect if the procedures leading to such sentences are seen as unfair and not worthy of respect.

Typical stages of criminal case processing. The following is a brief summary of the stages through which most criminal cases pass, and the various agencies involved at each stage. These agencies and their personnel are examined further in the following section. Additional detail on the stages of criminal procedure, procedural rules, and criminal justice agencies is provided in other entries in this encyclopedia.

Although any given criminal case usually begins with the commission of the offense, the criminal justice system actually begins to operate even earlier. First, the behavior must be defined as criminal, with specified penalties and resultant procedural requirements (see discussion above). Moreover, in some cases the police begin to act even before the offense is committed; given the difficulties of detecting and proving so-called victimless or consensual crimes (that is, crimes like drug selling, illegal gambling, prostitution, and other "vice" crimes, which have few if any witnesses other than the direct participants), the police often need to use undercover police agents and informants to infiltrate criminal groups and observe, or even propose, the particular criminal acts that are to be prosecuted.

Many minor crimes (traffic offenses, disorderly conduct, fish and game violations) are directly observed by law enforcement officers, but most offenses become known to the police because a victim or a witness has reported the crime. However, many crimes go undetected by anyone other than the offenders (e.g., attempted thefts; illegal drug use), and public surveys reveal that a large number of detected crimes are not reported to the police by victims (Bureau of Justice Statistics web page; see further statistics below). The most common reasons for not reporting to the police are either that the matter was seen as too minor or too personal, or that the victim felt that the crime could not be solved anyway (due to lack of evidence, delay, etc.). As will be seen, these reasons are quite similar to the reasons that police and prosecutors often give for not pursuing criminal charges.

Even if the police observe a crime or receive a report, they may be unwilling or unable to take further action, for a variety of reasons. First, they may decide that no crime was committed, for instance, because the reported behavior is not legally a crime, or because the police doubt the complainant's account (a process known as "unfounding" the complaint). Even if the police believe that a crime was committed, they may decline to take further action because they deem the offense to be too difficult to solve and not worth pursuing, given its relatively low seriousness (e.g., a stolen bicycle, taken from a front yard). Or, they may feel that the offense is so minor (e.g., driving only a few miles above the posted speed limit) that a warning or other informal measure will suffice.

If the police do take further action, it will depend very much on the nature of the crime, the suspected offender, and the particular circumstances. If the police directly observe the offense, or find the offender on the scene when they respond to a crime report, they may immediately arrest the offender or, in traffic and certain other minor crimes, issue a "ticket," or citation, which requires the offender to come to court at a later time. They may also detain and talk to the offender, which may lead to arrest or citation, a warning but no charges, a noncriminal disposition (e.g., taking a drunken person to a detoxification center), or a decision that no crime has occurred and no further action is required. In more complex cases the police may interview victims and witnesses, search places where they believe evidence, contraband, or crime fruits may be found, and compare the information obtained with police records of known offenders or other unsolved cases. One or more suspects may be approached, detained, and questioned. In many cases, especially those with no eye-witnesses, the police will be unable to solve ("clear") the offense by making an arrest or otherwise charging someone. In "white collar" and other highly complex cases, police and prosecutorial investigations may last for months or even years; if and when sufficient evidence is found to support charges, suspects in these cases may be issued a summons to appear in court, rather than being arrested and taken into custody.

Once a suspect is arrested, he or she is usually searched and then transported to the police station or other central facility for further processing (fingerprinting, interrogation, lineups, and other identification procedures). If the evidence is not strong, or the offense is relatively minor, the suspect may then be released without further charges. If the police decide to press charges, the suspect may be released on a promise to appear later in court (recognizance), if he or she is considered reliable enough to appear when required. The suspect may also obtain release by posting bail according to a preset bail schedule established by the court for that offense. If the suspect is not released, he or she will be transferred to jail. While in jail, the suspect may be subject to further searches, questioning, or identification procedures.

Within a few days, the detained suspect will make his or her first appearance in court. (Since priority is given to expediting cases of detained offenders, those who are released on citation or who receive a summons may not be scheduled to appear in court for several weeks.) By the time the suspect appears in court, the police will have given at least a preliminary report of the crime to the prosecutor, who will assess the strength of the evidence, the seriousness of the crime, and other factors bearing on whether the case merits prosecution, and if so, on what charges. Many cases are dismissed or charged down at this stage.

Prosecutors screen out cases for a variety of reasons (alone or in combination): evidence problems that would make it difficult to obtain a conviction (in particular, a lack of credible witnesses, or the reluctance of key witnesses to testify); attractive alternatives to prosecution such as victim-offender mediation or restitution; the defendant's agreement to enter a treatment program; and policy reasons that make prosecution inappropriate (such as the defendant's willingness to testify for or cooperate with the prosecution, or the minor nature of an offense or the defendant's role in it). American prosecutors exercise almost complete discretion in deciding what charges to file and to dismiss. Courts cannot order a charge to be filed, and have limited authority to dismiss charges; crime victims, the police, and other government agencies have no legal power to file or demand the filing of charges.

If charges are filed, the defendant will be advised of the charges at the first court appearance. Indigents will have counsel appointed to represent them. Minor crimes may be immediately adjudicated by trial or entry of a guilty plea. If the case is not disposed of at this hearing, issues of pretrial release and detention will be addressed. Offenders may be released on recognizance, or be given an opportunity to post bail (or request a reduction in bail). If the court decides that the defendant's pretrial release would jeopardize community safety, or that no release conditions will adequately assure later appearance in court, the defendant may be held without bail (preventive detention). Bail and release decisions may be facilitated by background reports prepared by probation or other court officials, or by private agencies; these officials and agencies may also provide supervision of defendants released and awaiting trial.

Although decisions about pretrial detention are collateral to the central goals of the criminal process—adjudication of guilt and imposition of sentence—detention decisions are closely related to, and sometimes interfere with, the pursuit of these goals. A decision to detain a suspect is often based in part on a prediction that a custodial sentence will be imposed later. But once pretrial detention has been ordered, it exercises a powerful influence on subsequent decisions, and may even render moot the formal processes of adjudication and sentencing. Detained offenders are more likely to plead guilty (in return for a sentence of "time already served"), and are less able to present an effective defense at trial; they are also disadvantaged at sentencing, having been deprived of the opportunity to demonstrate their ability to comply with release conditions. These effects illustrate not only the critical impact of pretrial detention decisions, but also the importance of system-wide analysis of criminal justice functioning.

Later formal stages of pretrial and trial procedure depend on the law of the particular jurisdiction, and also on the seriousness of the charges. In general, more serious charges receive more elaborate procedures—for instance, review by the grand jury; required disclosure of proposed trial evidence ("discovery") by the prosecution to the defense, and vice versa; and jury trial rights (none, for petty offenses; small juries for low-level offenses, and larger juries for the most serious crimes). All these procedures are described more fully in other entries in this encyclopedia.

Of course, not all prosecutions lead to conviction; many criminal cases are dismissed by the court or prosecutor (usually because of evidentiary weaknesses, or because the defendant has agreed to plead guilty to other charges), and some defendants who go to trial are acquitted of all charges.

Perhaps the most important pretrial and trial-court procedure—plea bargaining—occurs largely outside of court, and with very little legal structure or regulation. In most jurisdictions, 90 percent or more of convicted offenders have pled guilty rather than being convicted at trial, and most of these pleas are the result of negotiations between the prosecution and the defense. Such bargaining takes a variety of forms, including "vertical" charge bargaining (a plea of guilty in exchange for a lowering of the severity of the charges, or an agreement not to raise them); "horizontal" charge bargaining (a plea of guilty to some charges in exchange for a dismissal of other pending charges, or an agreement not to add additional ones); and sentence bargaining (a plea of guilty in exchange for leniency in sentencing, or at least a lenient sentence recommendation or position by the prosecutor).

Many view plea bargaining as a necessity that enables courts to dispose of large caseloads; in terms of money and time, criminal trials are costly for the state and the defendant, as well as for witnesses and victims. Some have also argued that offenders who plead guilty deserve less punishment and demonstrate that they are less likely to repeat their crimes, or are more amenable to treatment.

Criticisms of the practice of plea bargaining are leveled from many ideological perspectives. Some civil libertarians view plea bargaining as unfairly coercive, and as penalizing defendants who assert their constitutional rights by demanding a trial. It is also argued that, by avoiding the procedural safeguards of a full trial, plea bargaining risks convicting innocent persons who are unwilling to risk going to trial and possibly receiving a much more severe sentence. Moreover, plea bargaining, in effect, allows sentencing decisions to be made not by judges but by prosecutors, whose discretion is subject to few legal limits. Conservative critics, on the other hand, often object to plea bargaining because they believe it results in lenient sentences, and gives the impression that the courts, and by extension the criminal justice system, can be manipulated.

If the defendant is found guilty at trial (and sometimes, if conviction results from a guilty plea), the court may receive a presentence investigation report prepared by a probation or court services officer, providing additional background about the offender (e.g., prior record; employment history; family situation) and the conviction offense. More serious cases are more likely to benefit from a presentence report, and to have a separate sentencing hearing. Some jurisdictions allow the trial jury to recommend a sentence (and imposition of the death penalty often requires a jury recommendation), but the vast majority of sentences are imposed solely by the trial judge. The sentencing discretion afforded to trial judges varies considerably across jurisdictions. The federal system and about twenty states have some form of recommended sentencing guidelines, and several other states have determinate sentencing laws that limit the range of authorized penalties (Frase, 2000). In addition, most jurisdictions have enacted mandatory prison terms for some repeat offenders, as well as for those convicted of certain offenses (especially those involving drugs or weapons). As of the end of 1999, capital punishment was authorized in thirty-eight states (Snell, p. 2).

Although American courts make heavy use of custodial (jail or prison) sentences (see statistics, below), a wide variety of noncustodial sentences are also available. Such options include: treatment (residential or outpatient); home detention (with or without electronic monitoring); probation (with "intensive," regular, or minimal supervision); periodic drug or alcohol-use testing; the imposition of fines and court costs; compensation (restitution) to the victim or his/her family; victim-offender mediation; and community service. Most of these options are combined with some degree of probationary supervision and a suspended prison or jail term (or the option to hold a delayed sentencing hearing and impose such a term, if probation conditions are violated).

Once a sentence is imposed, the offender has a certain period of time in which to file an appeal. Only some jurisdictions, particularly those with sentencing guidelines, permit defendants to appeal the sentence; these jurisdictions also usually permit prosecution sentence appeals. Except for

a few jurisdictions that permit a second full trial (trial de novo) in a higher court (usually only for minor crimes initially tried without a jury), appeals on questions of guilt may only raise issues of law (e.g., jury instructions; rulings admitting or excluding evidence), not factual issues; thus, no witnesses or other forms of evidence are heard by an appeals court, and facts may not be reevaluated except as necessary to apply rules of law (including whether the evidence, viewed in the light most favorable to the prosecution, was legally sufficient to support a finding of guilt beyond a reasonable doubt). Many states now allow two stages of appeal: the first appeal, open to all offenders (except those who waive this right, as part of their guilty plea), is heard by a regional court of appeals; the second appeal, usually to the state supreme court, is often permitted only with the approval of that court. Offenders who were sentenced to prison are often required to begin serving their sentences even if they have filed an appeal. Once the time for direct appeals has passed, offenders may still be able to raise certain legal issues by seeking a writ of habeas corpus or other form of postconviction (or "collateral") relief.

The processes involved in the execution of the trial court's sentence are diverse, and depend both on the nature of the sentence and the defendant's postsentence behavior. Defendants who violate conditions of their release on probation may have those conditions tightened; if the violations are serious (for instance, committing further crime, repeatedly failing drug tests, failing to cooperate with treatment or home detention restrictions, or failing to perform required community service) probation may be revoked and the offender will then be sent to jail or prison (from which they may later be paroled, as explained below).

For felony crimes, custody sentences of over one year are usually served in a state prison, whereas shorter terms (as well as almost all misdemeanor custody sentences) are served in a local jail or workhouse. Offenders sentenced to prison are generally eligible to be released by the state parole board or similar agency after a certain portion of the sentence has been served. Both the date of earliest eligibility for parole release, and the maximum duration the inmate can be held if parole is never granted, are usually reduced as a reward for good behavior in prison (good time credits), based on evaluations made by prison officials. Parole is not available for extremely serious crimes; moreover, in a substantial number of jurisdictions parole release has been abolished for all prison inmates (although limited good time credits are still available). Jail sentences may also be eligible for parole (by decision of the sentencing judge or a separate agency), as well as good time credits. As with probation, parole release from prison or jail is conditioned on law-abiding behavior, cooperation with supervising parole agents, and other requirements; violation of these requirements will often lead the parole board or judge to revoke release, sending the offender back to jail or prison.

Major system actors: organization and function. The actual work of the criminal justice system is performed by a large number of public and private actors and agencies, many of which have already been mentioned. Some of them (for example, trial courts and private defense attorneys) operate only at the level of individual cases, while others (legislatures; sentencing commissions) have only general policymaking authority (Reitz, pp. 392–396). Still others (appeals courts; parole boards) operate at both levels, setting general policy as well as handling individual cases. This section provides a brief description of the principal public agencies and their personnel.

Legislatures. Legislative decisions determining the number and types of crimes, authorized or mandatory penalties, and levels of funding for various agencies have a significant impact on the functioning of criminal justice systems. These impacts are sometimes felt beyond a legislature's immediate jurisdiction (for example, when federal or state laws provide funding on condition that certain rules or procedures are adopted by the receiving state or local government).

Police and other law enforcement agencies. Law enforcement agencies are among the most diverse and decentralized components of criminal justice systems. There are some agencies with statewide jurisdiction (e.g., highway patrol, fish and game, tax agents, environmental inspectors), but most law enforcement agents work for counties or cities. Almost all counties have an elected sheriff, whose appointed deputies enforce the law outside of cities, operate the county jail, and perform certain court services such as service of legal process and transport of prisoners. City police departments are generally headed by a chief who is appointed by the city council or the mayor. Additional local police agencies, with limited subject matter and geographic jurisdiction, are operated by city or county depart-

ments responsible for public parks, transit, and other specialized functions. Colleges and universities often have their own police forces. Some of the law enforcement agencies described above have overlapping jurisdiction, for example, state and local police may both have enforcement power on state highways.

As of 1996, there were 663,535 full-time sworn law enforcement officers in the United States, broken down as follows: 54,587 state police officers, in forty-nine agencies; 410,956 local police officers, in 13,578 agencies (including five consolidated police-sheriff departments); 152,922 sheriff's department officers, in 3,088 agencies; and 45,070 special police officers, in 1,317 state or local agencies (including the Texas Constable) (Bureau of Justice Statistics web page).

Police functions are also frequently carried out by nongovernmental employees. As of 1999, it was estimated that there were about 2.5 million private security personnel in the United States (Forst and Manning, p. 34).

Courts and court services. Many states, as well as the federal system, have two levels of trial court. The lower court (city or municipal court, magistrate's court) is a court of limited jurisdiction; it may try misdemeanor crimes, but in felony cases it may only conduct pretrial hearings. Felony trials are held in the criminal division of the court of general jurisdiction (county court, district court, circuit court, superior court). Some states have a unified court system, in which all felony and misdemeanor hearings and trials are held in various divisions of the court of general jurisdiction. The area covered by such courts may be limited to a single, large county, or may, in less populated areas, include a group of several smaller counties. In addition to conducting pretrial hearings and trials, local courts supervise grand juries and operate various court services including probation departments and pretrial services agencies (which are used for bail screening and supervision, pretrial diversion, mediation programs, and the like).

In 1998 thirty-nine states had both an intermediate appellate court and a state supreme court (or other, higher appeals court); eleven states and the District of Columbia had only one level of appellate court (Rottman et al., p. ix). In addition to hearing appeals, state supreme courts exercise control over bar membership and judicial discipline. They also enact and revise rules of trial and appellate procedure, evidence, admission to the bar, professional responsibility, and so forth.

In 1998 there were about 9,100 full-time authorized judgeships in state trial courts of general jurisdiction, and about 1,300 appellate judges (Rottman et al., pp. ix, 13). Gubernatorial or legislative appointment was used to select general jurisdiction trial judges in eighteen states; for appellate judges, this method was used in twenty-four states. Nonpartizan or retention elections ("shall judge X be retained?") were used for trial judges in eighteen states, and for appellate judges in eighteen states; partizan elections were used for trial judges in ten states, and for appellate judges in eight states (other methods were used for trial judges, in four states) (Rottman et al., p. ix).

Prosecutors. In state systems, prosecutors are found at the state, county, and city levels. State attorneys general sometimes have concurrent authority to prosecute some or all crimes, though this power is seldom used except in the few states that have no separate county government. County or multicounty prosecutors (county attorney, district attorney, state's attorney) mainly handle felony-level crimes, while city prosecutors handle misdemeanors and ordinance violations.

In 1996 an estimated 2,343 state prosecutors' offices were authorized to file felony cases (DeFrances and Steadman, pp. 1, 2). These offices employed approximately 24,000 assistant prosecutors. Ninety-one percent of the offices also had jurisdiction to handle misdemeanor cases, 82 percent handled traffic violations, and 53 percent handled child support enforcement. Fifty-three percent represented the government in civil lawsuits.

Defense attorneys. Defendants may be represented by privately retained attorneys (some of whom specialize in criminal law), or by publicly paid, court-appointed counsel. In 1998 appointed counsel represented 82 percent of state felony defendants in the seventy-five largest counties (Harlow, p. 1). One or more of the following three systems of appointed counsel are used in state courts: (1) a *staff public defender system*, in which salaried defense attorneys work for a public or private nonprofit organization, or as direct government employees; (2) an *assigned counsel system*, in which judges appoint attorneys from a list of private bar members who accept cases on a judge-by-judge, court-by-court, or case-by-case basis; and (3) a *contract attorney system*, in which private attorneys, bar associations, law firms, groups of attorneys, or nonprofit corporations provide services based on contracts with state, county, or other local governmental units. In the general jursdiction courts as of 1994, these three public defense systems were in use in 68, 63, and 29 percent of the courts, respectively (Harlow, p. 4).

Detention and correctional facilities. In 1995 long-term sentenced inmates were being held in 1,084 state prisons and 291 community-based facilities (Bureau of Justice Statistics, 1997, p. 53). Short-term sentenced inmates, as well as persons awaiting trial or transfer to other authorities, were held in about 3,400 county or city jails (Beck 2000a, p. 7). As of 1999, there were 161 private adult correctional facilities, in thirty-two states and the District of Columbia, with a rated capacity of 132,933 inmates (Maguire and Pastore, p. 82, Table 1.65).

Sentencing and correctional agencies and agents. Most states have a statewide department of corrections or similar agency, responsible for operating prisons and some or all probation and parole functions. Some cities and counties also have a department of corrections, to operate their jails or probation services. Most states retain discretionary parole release, under a statewide parole board; most states also have some sort of board that reviews requests for pardons, commutations, and other extraordinary relief for convicts. As of the fall of 1999, about twenty states had a sentencing commission, responsible for implementing and monitoring sentencing guidelines (Frase, 2000, p. 70).

The systems in operation

Previous sections of this entry have described the structure and purposes of criminal justice systems, but it is equally important to examine how systems function in practice—which may be quite different from how they are commonly assumed to function. Perhaps the most striking finding derived from the available data on system operations is the very substantial case attrition between the start of the process (crimes committed) and the final stages of execution of sentence. This is not a new phenomenon, nor one limited to the United States; studies of American criminal justice in the early part of the twentieth century (Cleveland Foundation), and in several other Western countries (Frase, 2001, Table 3; Zeisel, p. 24), have reported similarly high rates of case attrition.

Citizens and their political leaders must keep these findings in mind when making criminal justice policy decisions. For most crimes, nothing even remotely approaching "full enforcement" has ever been achieved, nor is it likely to be achieved; it may even be undesirable. The high level of case attrition in all modern systems suggests that the criminal law has very substantial limitations as an instrument of direct crime control (by means of deterrence, incapacitation, and rehabilitation). Such limitations suggest that, in most cases, the primary value of criminal prosecution is symbolic. Criminal convictions and penalties impose deserved punishment (retribution), and reinforce important societal norms (denunciation)—but only if these penal consequences are imposed according to procedures that are widely perceived as fair and just (Tyler).

Case attrition results from the exercise of discretion by all system actors, both public and private, and from the nature of the criminal process itself. Several factors justify and require the exercise of discretion by public officials: (1) the practical inability of legislatures to specify in advance all of the conditions that properly bear on issues of criminal liability and the scope of criminal statutes, punishment, and criminal procedure (particularly when, as was noted earlier, basic goals and values often conflict with each other); (2) the need for case-specific assessments of the available evidence to convict an offender, as well as the available resources for investigation, conviction, and punishment of this and other offenders; (3) the desirability of taking into account local crime problems, community values, and the desires and needs of crime victims.

Citizens involved in the criminal justice process also exercise substantial amounts of discretion. Crime victims and witnesses may choose not to report a crime, or not to cooperate with prosecution. Suspects and defendants also have choices: to exercise their legal rights, rather than waiving them; to supply information helpful in convicting other offenders; and to comply with conditions of release or prison rules of conduct.

Apart from the exercise of discretion, another major reason why case volumes decline substantially as cases move through the system is that different standards apply at these stages: probable cause may be sufficient to justify an arrest or a search, with the hope of uncovering more evidence. But if such evidence does not become available within a reasonable time, cases must be dismissed or charged down; imposition of the severe social stigma and sanctions of the criminal law requires morally convincing evidence (proof beyond a reasonable doubt).

Statistics on case attrition at various stages. Many of the decisions made at crucial points in the criminal process are not easily observable, so it can be very difficult to determine what decisions are made, let alone the rationale for these decisions. For example, there is very little information regarding police and prosecutorial decisions to investigate. Likewise, there are few available statistics on decisions made in the correctional realm, such as parole and probation revocations, and sentence-reductions based on an inmate's good behavior in prison. However, data is available on decisions at several of the most important stages of the process.

Victim reporting of crime. Victim surveys reveal that substantially less than half of crimes committed are reported or otherwise made known to the police. The reporting rate is especially low for attempts and minor completed crimes, and is also probably very low for so-called victimless crimes (i.e., those with no immediate victim or witnesses other than the offender[s] and the police, such as drug offenses). On the other hand, the proportion of homicides that become known to the police (either by contemporaneous reporting or by discovery of the body) is probably close to 100 percent. For obvious reasons, neither victimless crimes nor homicide are included in victim surveys. These surveys also do not measure crimes against the environment, frauds, or crimes against businesses and government agencies.

In 1999 only 44 percent of violent crimes and 34 percent of property crimes were reported to the police (Rennison, p. 11). Table 1 illustrates the percent of crimes that victims claimed to have reported to the police, by crime type (including attempts).

Table 1 shows that the likelihood of a victim reporting an offense to the police varies significantly by crime type. Victim reporting is highest for auto theft (84 percent), probably because most auto insurance policies require police notification of a stolen vehicle. By contrast, personal thefts outside the home (e.g., a stolen bicycle) are reported to the police only about one-fourth of the time.

Police recording of crime. If the police doubt that any crime was actually committed they will "unfound" the report, take no further investigative action, and decline to include the report in their statistics of crimes known to the police. There are no official statistics on the rates

Table 1

Percent of crimes claimed to have been reported to police, by crime type, 1999

Crime type	Percent claimed reported
Rape/sexual assault	28%
Aggravated assault	55%
Simple assault	39%
Robbery	61%
Household burglary	49%
Motor vehicle theft	84%
Other household thefts	27%
Personal theft (away from the home)	26%

SOURCE: Rennison, p. 11.

Table 2

Percent of index crimes reported to police that are "cleared," 1999

Crime type	Percent cleared
Murder and non-negligent manslaughter	69%
Forcible rape	49%
Aggravated assault	59%
Robbery	28%
Burglary (including commercial property)	14%
Motor vehicle theft (including commercial)	15%
Other thefts (including commercial)	19%
Arson	17%

SOURCE: F.B.I. (2000), p. 203, Table 25.

of police unfounding, overall or for particular offenses.

Proportions of crimes solved (clearance rates). The only official statistics on police crime-solution (clearance) rates are for the eight "index crimes" (listed in Table 2) that the Federal Bureau of Investigation (FBI) uses as an overall measure of crime levels. For 1999, the FBI reported that 21 percent of index crimes were cleared—including 50 percent of violent crimes and 17 percent of property crimes (FBI, 2000, p. 203). Regarding specific crime types, Table 2 presents the percentages of index crimes known to police departments in the United States that were cleared by arrest, another charging procedure (e.g., a summons or citation) or, occasionally, by attribution to a dead or otherwise unavailable suspect.

As is the case with victim reporting, there is great variation in clearance rates across types of index crime. More than two-thirds of murder and non-negligent manslaughter cases and almost three-fifths of aggravated assaults were cleared by arrest, whereas less than one in six burglary and motor vehicle theft offenses was cleared. These differences are attributable both to the higher priority that the police give to more serious crimes, and to typical offense patterns: violent crimes often involve offenders who are already known to the victim.

It is likely that clearance rates are lower for other (non-index) crimes, since the latter are generally less serious, and receive less victim, witness, and police attention. On the other hand, the proportion of "victimless" crimes cleared is probably very high, since such crimes are rarely known to the police unless they are committed in the presence of a police officer or undercover informant.

It should be noted that clearance rate statistics are only roughly comparable to the victim-survey data reported previously. In particular, the surveys exclude offenses against victims under the age of twelve, exclude most property offenses committed against businesses, and include sexual assaults other than forcible rape.

Pretrial detention. Statistics on this critical issue are only available for defendants charged with felonies in a sample of the nation's seventy-five largest counties. In 1996 these counties accounted for 37 percent of the nation's population, 50 percent of serious violent crimes known to the police, and 40 percent of serious property crimes known to the police (Hart and Reaves, p. 1). Sixty-three percent of these defendants were released before case disposition and 37 percent were detained; one-sixth of those detained were denied bail, whereas five out of six failed to post bail. Those charged with a violent offense were less likely to be released (55 percent) than those charged with a property offense (65 percent) or a drug offense (66 percent). Table 3 shows the percent of those released and detained, and the type of release or detention, by the most serious arrest charge.

As Table 3 illustrates, the decisions whether to release suspects before trial, and whether to guarantee their appearance in court by setting bail, varied greatly across felony charges. Only 16 percent of those charged with murder were released before disposition, and 84 percent were detained; 61 percent were denied bail. In comparison, those charged with theft were released two-thirds of the time, and more than half of these releases were nonfinancial (not requiring

Table 3

Felony defendants released before or detained until case disposition:
type of release or detention by most serious charge, 75 largest counties, 1996

Arrest charge	Percent released before case disposition			Percent detained until case disposition		
	Total	Financial release	Nonfinancial release	Total	Held on bail	Denied bail
Murder	16%	16%	0%	84%	23%	61%
Rape	53%	31%	22%	48%	37%	12%
Robbery	42%	18%	25%	60%	48%	13%
Assault	66%	37%	28%	34%	29%	5%
Burglary	47%	22%	24%	53%	47%	6%
Theft (including motor vehicle theft)	66%	31%	36%	34%	29%	5%
Drug trafficking	62%	30%	31%	38%	32%	6%
Drug possession	69%	28%	42%	30%	25%	4%
Weapons	71%	31%	40%	30%	26%	5%

SOURCE: Hart and Reaves, pp. 16, 17, Tables 13 and 14.

deposit of bail or other security). For all charges except murder, the majority of those who were released before trial were released within a week of being arrested.

In regard to the relationship between pretrial detention and subsequent case processing, separate analysis of this data by the present authors confirms the results of previous studies: detained defendants were more likely to be found guilty, and were also more likely to receive a custody sentence. At the same time, a significant portion of the detained did not receive a formal conviction and custodial sentence. For example, 34 percent of those charged with burglary who were detained for more than two days before trial either were not convicted or received a noncustodial sentence. For defendants charged with theft or with drug violations, the proportions were 38 and 36 percent, respectively. Thus, even where the system has officially decided that an individual should not receive custodial punishment, a de facto custody "sentence" is often imposed.

Prosecutorial screening and diversion. Despite the critical importance of prosecutorial discretion, there is almost no current national data on charging decisions (for the most recent data, covering eleven states as of 1990, see Perez). Table 4 presents rough estimates of prosecution rates, for selected offenses in 1996, derived by comparing the total number of felony cases filed in a sample of the nation's seventy-five largest counties with the total number of adult arrests for each offense in those counties that year.

Table 4 indicates that offense-specific prosecution rates vary a great deal—one out of five theft cases, three out of four cases of murder and non-negligent manslaughter, and over nine out of ten forcible rape cases. It is important to recognize that these numbers are aggregates, and thus do not represent the disposition of individual cases as they flow through the system. These figures also exclude offenders who were prosecuted for a different crime (usually a less serious one) than their arrest offense. Yet these admittedly inexact numbers are the only available estimates, given the paucity of national data tracking individual cases beginning at the arrest stage (compare Perez, cited above). (It should also be noted that the offense-specific prosecution-rate data above (as well as the conviction-rate data below) is only roughly comparable to the victim-survey and FBI data presented previously.)

Final dispositions: conviction rates. Nationwide data on these issues are, again, only available for certain jurisdictions, offenses, and years. Table 5 shows, by arrest offense, the percentages of those charged with selected felonies who were convicted (including conviction on lesser charges) in the nation's seventy-five largest counties.

Guilty pleas and plea bargaining. There are no national data on the practice of plea bargaining per se; information is limited to the prevalence of guilty pleas, and, once again, is further limited to certain jurisdictions, offenses, and years. Implicit in a defendant's decision to plead guilty is the assumption that the sentence will be more lenient than it would have been had the de-

Table 4

Estimated percent of felony arrests for adults that are prosecuted, by most serious charge, 75 largest counties, 1996

Arrest charge	Percent of arrests prosecuted
Murder and non-negligent manslaughter	75%
Forcible rape	95%
Aggravated assault	41%
Robbery	81%
Burglary	64%
Theft (including motor vehicle theft)	20%

SOURCE: Hart and Reaves, p. 2, Table 1; Uniform Crime Reports data available from the Inter-University Consortium for Political and Social Research (ICPSR) web site (http://www.icpsr.umich.edu/).

Table 5

Percent of prosecuted felony cases resulting in a conviction, by arrest charge, 75 largest counties, 1996

Arrest charge	Percent of filed cases resulting in a conviction		
	Total	Felony conviction	Misdemeanor conviction
Murder	64%	62%	2%
Rape	62%	57%	5%
Assault	53%	33%	20%
Robbery	70%	57%	13%
Burglary	75%	62%	13%
Theft (including motor vehicle theft)	71%	55%	15%
Drug trafficking	78%	68%	11%
Drug possession	68%	59%	10%
Weapons charges	73%	59%	13%

SOURCE: Hart and Reaves, p. 24, Table 23.

fendant been convicted at trial, but the percent of plea agreements that are explicitly negotiated is unknown. The available data on felony dispositions in the nation's seventy-five largest counties show that, in 1996, 93 percent of felony charges resulting in a conviction (either felony or misdemeanor) were the result of a guilty plea, while only 7 percent were the result of a trial. Table 6 shows that guilty pleas are less likely when the stakes are highest. Murder convictions are almost as likely to result from a trial (47 percent of convictions) as from a guilty plea. By contrast, drug possession convictions were the product of a guilty plea in 97 percent of the cases.

Impact of method of disposition on case processing time. Table 7 shows the median time in days between arrest and sentencing, controlling for the manner of case disposition—trial (jury or bench) versus guilty plea.

It is evident from Table 7 that, across conviction types, guilty pleas and bench trials are associated with much shorter case processing times than are jury trials. For example, regarding cases in which the most serious conviction offense was murder, those disposed with bench trials (191 days) took only half as long as those with jury trials (377 days), and two-thirds as long as cases disposed with a guilty plea. For other offenses, median days to disposition by plea were roughly the same as for disposition by bench trial, with time to disposition for jury trials markedly longer.

The slower case processing associated with jury trials is partly due to court backlogs, but another contributing factor is that many jury trials occur only after the parties have failed to reach a plea agreement—often after lengthy negotiations and attempts to "wear down" the other side. It is therefore quite possible that, if plea bargaining were curtailed and cases were either pled as charged or set for trial, average disposition times might actually decrease. Indeed, this is what happened in the only state (Alaska) that has ever attempted to sharply limit plea bargaining (Zimring and Frase, pp. 678–679).

Sentencing outcomes. Once again, national data on sentencing in the United States is limited to certain jurisdictions, offenses, and years. Table 8 shows the distribution of prison, jail, and probation sentences for selected felonies, by most serious conviction offense, in the seventy-five largest counties; it also reports the median sentence length for prison and jail sentences.

Table 8 shows that the total percent incarcerated varies greatly across conviction offense charges. For example, all of those convicted for murder received a prison sentence, whereas roughly one-third of those convicted on theft, drug possession, and weapons charges received probation. Among those who are incarcerated, the likelihood of getting a prison sentence as opposed to a jail sentence varied too. Those convicted of robbery were over three times more likely to receive a prison sentence than a jail sentence (71 percent versus 19 percent), whereas those convicted of drug possession were almost twice as likely to receive a jail sentence as they were to get a prison sentence.

Table 6

Percent of convictions from guilty pleas versus trials, by arrest charge, 75 largest counties, 1996

Arrest charge	Percent of convictions from pleas	Percent of convictions from trials
Murder	53%	47%
Rape	87%	13%
Assault	89%	11%
Robbery	89%	11%
Burglary	93%	7%
Theft (including motor vehicle theft)	94%	6%
Drug trafficking	95%	5%
Drug possession	97%	3%
Weapons charges	92%	8%

SOURCE: Hart and Reaves, p. 24, Table 23.

In light of the high proportions of custodial sentences reported in Table 8, it should be noted that many other Western countries appear to make much less use of custodial sentences, particularly for nonviolent crimes (Tonry and Frase, 2001; Frase, 2001).

Table 8 also shows that maximum sentence lengths are by far the longest for murder (median of 360 months), followed by rape (96 months). By comparison, those arrested for theft or drug possession had a median maximum sentence of only 24 months. Sentence lengths for those receiving a sentence of jail are markedly shorter since, in most states, jail sentences can be no longer than one year.

Actual time served in prison is almost always less than the maximum sentence imposed (usually much less). In 1996 it was expected that those convicted of violent felonies would serve 51 percent of their sentence (e.g., murder, 50 percent). In comparison, it was expected that those who were convicted of felony property offenses, as well as drug trafficking, would serve 42 percent of their sentences (Brown et al., p. 4, Table 4).

At the end of 1999, 3,507 prisoners were being held under sentence of death; 98 prisoners, in twenty states, were executed during that year (Snell, pp. 1, 7).

Case volumes at various stages (by offense, over time, and across jurisdictions). Table 9 shows the number of cases nationwide at several different stages in the criminal court process for six felony offenses that have the greatest comparability across reporting series. These numbers are aggregates, and do not represent individual cases as they flow through the system. Yet, they are the best available national data showing case volume (and therefore, case attrition) at several different points in the criminal court process. For example, in 1996 the police arrested more than 322,000 adults for drug trafficking (which is almost always a felony). In that year more than 212,000 adults were convicted of drug trafficking, and about 84,000 received a prison sentence. The last three columns in Table 9 show that in 1996, for every 100 adult arrests for drug trafficking, there were 66 felony convictions, and 48 custodial sentences (26 sentences to prison, and 22 to jail).

The screening decisions carried out at each successive stage of the criminal process result in dramatic reductions in case volume, as cases move through the system. For example, among the four felony offenses in Table 9 for which there is information on the number of offenses committed (robbery, aggravated assault, burglary, and motor vehicle theft), for every 1,000 felonies committed 444 were reported by the police, 71 adults were arrested, 18 adults were convicted, 13 adults were incarcerated, and 9 adults were imprisoned. Although data are not available, it seems likely that case attrition is at least as great for less serious crimes. In 1996, for example, there were about 12.3 million adult arrests in the United States (FBI, 1997, pp. 214, 224), but there were only about one million felony convictions in state criminal courts in that year (Brown et al., p. 2, Table 1). On the other hand, the attrition data above reflect cases, rather than offenders; since many offenders commit more than one offense, and thus are likely to be eventually caught for one of their crimes, it is likely that the proportion of offenders arrested, prosecuted, convicted, and imprisoned is somewhat higher than the numbers above would suggest.

Number of individuals in prisons and jails (overall and by state). As of midyear 1999, 1,254,600 persons were held in federal and state prisons, and 606,000 federal and state prisoners were held in local jails (Beck, 2000a, p.1). These inmate counts represented a national average of 460 adults per 100,000 residents incarcerated in state and federal prisons, and 222 per 100,000 incarcerated in local jails. However, as Table 10 shows, these national averages belie great variation across states. Southern states such as Texas (726 state prisoners per 100,000) and Oklahoma (625 per 100,000) imprison at much higher rates than some Midwestern and Northeastern states

Table 7

Median number of days between arrest and sentencing by method of case disposition, felony cases disposed by state courts nationwide, 1996

Most serious conviction offense	Total	Trial			Guilty plea
		Total	Jury	Bench	
Murder	327 days	363 days	377 days	191 days	282 days
Sexual Assault (including rape)	220	279	307	192	209
Aggravated assault	165	247	295	181	178
Robbery	176	239	284	188	174
Burglary	139	202	267	165	153
Theft (including motor vehicle theft)	135	193	287	164	153
Drug trafficking	139	227	264	168	157
Drug possession	129	170	262	142	163
Weapons charges	148	232	300	163	161

SOURCE: Brown et al., p. 8, Table 11.

(Minnesota, 121 per 100,000; Maine, 131 per 100,000).

Jail rates also vary greatly across jurisdictions. In 1999 Louisiana jailed at a rate (585 jail prisoners per 100,000) that was six and a half times higher than Maine's rate (89 per 100,000). Moreover, the relative use of prison and jail varied greatly. For example, whereas Missouri's prison rate was 3.6 times its jail rate, the ratio of prison use to jail use was much lower in most other states; indeed, two states (Louisiana and Tennessee) had substantially higher jail rates than prison rates. These dramatic variations in the rate and type of incarceration are only partially explained by variations in crime rates and criminal caseloads.

Number of individuals on probation and parole. At the end of 1999 there were approximately 3,773,600 adults on probation and 712,700 on parole (Bureau of Justice Statistics, 2000 (press release), p. 1). These caseloads represented an aggregate rate of 1,848 probationers per 100,000 residents, and 317 persons on parole per 100,000.

Trends in the number of individuals under criminal justice control. The last quarter of the twentieth century witnessed a sharp increase in all forms of correctional supervision—both custodial (prison and jail) and noncustodial (probation and parole). Figure 1 provides a graphic illustration of these increases (some figures have been scaled up or down, to facilitate trend comparisons). Figure 1 shows that, from 1977 through 1999, the number of adults on state or federal probation increased from 816,525 to 3,773,624—an increase of 362 percent. Over the same period, the number of adults on parole increased at a slightly lower rate (from 173,632 to 712,713, or 310 percent). State and federal year-end prison populations increased from 291,667 to 1,263,226 (up 333 percent), while average daily jail populations increased from an estimated 155,200 in 1977, to 607,978 in 1999 (up 292 percent). As with the state-to-state variations shown in Table 10, only some of these dramatic increases can be attributed to rising crime rates—as shown in Figure 1, adult arrests increased by only 50 percent during the same time period.

Appeals. It is estimated that about 122,000 criminal appeals were filed in 1996. More than two-thirds of these were mandatory appeals—cases that the appellate courts must hear as a matter of a defendant's right. The balance were discretionary petitions that appellate courts agreed to hear (National Center for State Courts, 1997, pp. 71, 74).

Criminal justice budgets. In 1997 total direct criminal justice expenditures (in billions) at federal, state, county, and city levels of government were, respectively: $20.5, $42.4, $31.6, and $35.3 (Bureau of Justice Statistics web site). Federal government expenditures had grown the most since 1982 (4.8 times higher in 1997), reflecting the dramatic increase in federal prison populations (which rose even faster than state prison populations during this period). State and county expenditures were about four times higher in 1997 while city expenditures (mostly for police) were about three times higher. When examined by component, the direct expenditures in 1997 for policing, the courts, and corrections, respectively, were: $57.8, $28.5, and $43.5

Table 8

Most severe type of sentence received by convicted defendants, by conviction offense, 75 largest counties, 1996

Most serious conviction offense	Total percent incarcerated	Incarcerated in prison		Incarcerated in jail		Not incarcerated
		Percent receiving prison	Median length of sentence	Percent receiving jail	Median length of sentence	Percent receiving probation
Murder	100%	100%	360 months	0%	—	0%
Rape	77%	56%	96	21%	—	23%
Assault	73%	40%	48	33%	6 months	26%
Robbery	90%	71%	60	19%	12	10%
Burglary	74%	43%	41	31%	6	25%
Theft (including motor vehicle theft)	66%	32%	24	34%	6	34%
Drug trafficking	78%	44%	42	34%	6	22%
Drug possession	65%	23%	24	42%	3	34%
Weapons charges	64%	37%	32	27%	4	34%

Notes: Sentence medians are the medians of maximum sentences. One percent of defendants in both burglary and drug possession cases, and two percent of defendants in weapons cases, were fined only.

NOTE: Sentence medians are the medians of maximum sentences. One percent of defendants in both burglary and drug possession cases, and 2 percent of defendants in weapons cases, were fined only.
SOURCE: Hart and Reaves, pp. 30–33, Tables 30–32.

billion. Correctional expenditures (mostly to operate prisons and jails) grew the most (4.8 times higher than they were in 1982); police and court expenditures were 3.0 and 3.7 times higher, respectively.

The importance of viewing criminal justice as a system

Although criminal justice, in practice, is often highly un-"systematic," it is still very useful to take a system-wide approach when seeking to better understand and more effectively respond to problems of modern criminal justice.

Understanding criminal justice practices. A systemwide approach facilitates better understanding of the many ways in which decisions at earlier and later stages of the process affect each other (President's Commission, p. 7). Earlier decisions, such as those involving prosecutorial screening or pretrial detention, often anticipate later ones (conviction and sentencing), and provide the essential "inputs" for subsequent case processing. Later decisions react to or overrule earlier ones, and in some cases provide new system inputs (for instance, when unreformed offenders are released back into the community, or appellate courts adopt rulings limiting or expanding police powers).

Systemic analysis also helps to avoid the serious distortions that can occur when selected aspects of system functioning are compared across jurisdictions (or in the same jurisdiction over time). For example, a simple comparison of the proportion of convicted assault offenders who receive a custodial sentence in two jurisdictions will yield very misleading results if these two systems have different rates of case screening in earlier stages; convicted assault cases in the jurisdiction with higher screening rates will usually have stronger evidence and more aggravated offense and offender details, which would help to explain higher custody sentencing rates observed in that jurisdiction (Frase, 2001).

System-wide analysis also reveals common policies and principles that apply at very different levels or stages of the process. For example, although issues of criminal law, sentencing, and criminal procedure are usually analyzed separately, it is useful to recognize the common values that underlie legal rules in several of these areas, such as the need to limit state power (especially physical brutality); concern for crime victims; the value of equal justice (but also of flexibility and local control); and the critical importance of defendant cooperation. Similarly, an examination of the reasons for case attrition at different stages (victim nonreporting; police and prosecutorial dismissal; sentencing leniency) shows that cases are usually dropped (or charged down, or punished less harshly) for three basic reasons: because greater severity appears to be

Table 9

Number of cases at different stages of the criminal court process, United States, 1996

Offense	Estimated number committed*	Number reported to police	Number of adults arrested	Number of felony convictions	Number of felony sentences		For 100 adult arrests	Felony sentences	
					Incarceration	Prison	Felony convictions	Incarceration	Prison
Murder	—	19,650	16,161	11,430	10,833	10,505	71	67	65
Robbery	1,451,520	537,050	106,178	42,831	37,382	31,195	40	35	29
Aggravated assault	1,910,000	1,029,810	445,005	69,522	49,852	29,042	16	11	7
Burglary	7,267,500	2,501,500	229,745	93,197	66,101	42,252	41	29	18
Motor vehicle theft	1,664,400	1,395,200	102,578	17,794	13,242	5,919	17	13	6
Drug trafficking	—	—	322,393	212,504	154,977	83,913	66	48	26

* The National Crime Victimization Survey (NCVS) counts only victimizations of individuals and households, so the NCVS data were augmented by estimates of business victimizations, for each offense shown in the table. These estimates are based on the proportion of individual and business victims, among crimes reported to the police (F.B.I. data). The conviction and sentencing data in this table are from a sample of 344 counties, chosen to represent the entire country. Conviction data previously reported (Tables 6 and 8) are from a sample of the 75 largest counties.

SOURCE: Ringel, p. 3, Table 1; Brown et al., p. 5.

legally or factually unsupportable; because a less severe alternative seems more appropriate; or because the offense seems too minor to justify stricter measures. This similarity suggests a surprisingly broad policy consensus, but also raises questions as to which actor(s) should implement these agreed policies. Finally, the pervasiveness of case attrition (and of the various discretionary powers that produce it) becomes clear when all stages of the system are examined. The magnitude of this attrition, across the entire system, has important implications for our understanding of the limits of the criminal law, and the purposes it can feasibly achieve.

There is, unfortunately, also considerable system-wide disagreement on major issues and, in general, a lack of agreed goals, priorities, and performance measures for the whole system. The police measure their success primarily by arrest and clearance rates (even if no conviction results), and secondarily by reported crime rates (even if many crimes are unreported); prosecutors "keep score" according to their conviction rates (even if large numbers of cases are dismissed or charged down); judges saddled with heavy caseloads sometimes keep score in terms of how quickly they can dispose of cases (by any means); elected prosecutors and judges are tempted to emphasize how "tough on crime" they are (whether or not "tough" means "effective"). Systemic analysis promotes recognition of these conflicting standards, and the impact such conflicts have on the performance of the system and its separate parts.

Evaluating criminal justice reforms and operations. Systemic analysis also helps in evaluating the merits of proposed reforms, and the consequences of reforms that have been adopted. One consistent problem of criminal justice reform, which results from the pervasiveness of unregulated discretion, is the tendency for changes in one part of the system to be nullified or greatly weakened by compensating changes in other parts. This phenomenon is sometimes referred to as the system "hydraulic"; like a full tube of toothpaste, "squeezing" one part of the system causes it to "bulge" somewhere else. For example, mandatory minimum sentence reforms are often undercut by charging or plea bargaining decisions that prevent many eligible offenders from being convicted of the targeted offense.

Reforms that create new, intermediate options (pretrial diversion; strict supervision before or after conviction; prison "boot camps") provide another good example of the need for careful, systemic evaluation. Although many such reforms are designed to reduce the use of more severe options, in practice they are more likely (for reasons of public and political safety) to be applied to cases that would otherwise have received less severe treatment—thus increasing, not decreasing, the budgetary and other disadvantages

Table 10

**State jail and prison rates
per 100,000 residents, as of 30 June 1999**

	State	Jail rate	Prison rate
Northeast	Maine	89	131
	Massachusetts	174	179
	New Hampshire	133	187
	New Jersey	206	330
	New York	184	390
	Pennsylvania	225	304
South	Alabama	261	496
	Arkansas	189	399
	Florida	337	453
	Georgia	421	535
	Kentucky	262	284
	Louisiana	585	440
	Maryland	211	439
	Mississippi	320	344
	North Carolina	173	391
	Oklahoma	200	625
	South Carolina	226	546
	Tennessee	358	297
	Texas	288	726
	Virginia	266	447
	West Virginia	138	166
Midwest	Illinois	139	367
	Indiana	215	291
	Iowa	104	252
	Kansas	165	319
	Michigan	159	469
	Minnesota	105	121
	Missouri	127	464
	Nebraska	131	213
	North Dakota	92	147
	Ohio	148	417
	South Dakota	144	341
	Wisconsin	239	280
West	Arizona	216	545
	California	233	488
	Colorado	222	298
	Idaho	225	306
	Montana	172	281
	Nevada	270	504
	New Mexico	298	292
	Oregon	189	275
	Utah	188	245
	Washington	183	248
	Wyoming	209	276
U.S. Totals		**222**	**460**

Prison rates are based on the number of persons actually held in prison (regardless of sentence length). These rates thus exclude persons under the supervision of state prison authorities but held in local jails, or out of state.

NOTE: Excludes six states that lack locally operated jails.
SOURCE: Beck 2000a, pp. 8–9, Tables 10 and 11.

of severity, and greatly complicating the selection of matched comparison groups to evaluate offender impact (Zimring and Frase, pp. 349–387). A third example of the value of systemic analysis is its ability to identify strong linkages between existing practices that may preclude a particular reform, or show that it is unnecessary. Thus, an

American state may not wish to adopt the narrower, more flexible exclusionary rules found in many civil law systems if such rules depend on other practices—stricter police discipline or closer prosecutorial oversight of the police—which that state would be unable or unwilling to emulate (Frase, 1990, pp. 550, 553–564). Conversely, to the extent that civil law systems employ these compensating police and prosecution safeguards, they may have less need to adopt broader American exclusionary rules.

Beyond the assessment of specific reforms, the system concept underscores the need for system-wide planning and coordination, particularly of information systems. American criminal justice is highly balkanized; although planning agencies exist in many states and some local jurisdictions, it is rare that any agency has a mandate (and budget) to engage in detailed planning for all, or even many, components of the system. One notable exception is found in states with sentencing guidelines monitored by a permanent sentencing commission (Frase, 2000, pp. 70–71). Such commissions usually have members representing all major public and private agencies and interests involved in sentencing, and have the legal authority and resources to take a long-term, multiagency view of sentencing issues. Similar multiagency, criminal justice coordinating councils have existed in some metropolitan areas (National Advisory Commission, pp. 32, 35).

System analysis also encourages legislators and other criminal justice policymakers to keep the various components of the system in proper balance. This is particularly important in three areas:

Balancing the powers of the various sentencing agencies. The legislature, sentencing commission and parole board, prosecutors, defenders, courts, and corrections officials all share power over sentencing decisions, and thus serve as a check on each other (Frase, 2000). Reforms such as mandatory minimum sentencing tend to unduly concentrate power in the legislature and the prosecution (Reitz, pp. 396–398).

Balancing the funding provided to different agencies and levels of government. Funding for some agencies, especially courts and defense services, is less popular and tends to lag behind funding for the police and prosecution. States often pass criminal laws imposing unfunded mandates on local systems. Conversely, local judges have no direct stake in allocating scarce state resources, and thus are tempted to send too

Figure 1

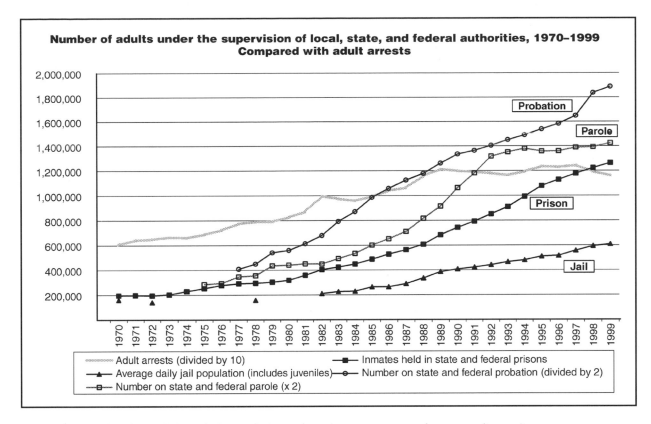

Number of adults under the supervision of local, state, and federal authorities, 1970–1999 Compared with adult arrests

SOURCE: Bureau of Justice Statistics web site (probation and parole); F.B.I. 2000 [and corresponding earlier reports] (arrests); Beck 2000a [and corresponding earlier reports] (jail inmates); Beck 2000b [and corresponding earlier reports] (prison inmates).

many offenders to state prison (the "correctional free lunch"; Zimring and Hawkins, p. 140).

Balancing short-term and long-term perspectives. As much as we may hate criminals, it is in our long-term interest to help them, since almost all of them return to the community (usually after only a few months or years). Moreover, extremely long custodial sentences, although politically popular and satisfying today, impose substantial added costs far in the future, when the benefits (e.g., of confining "geriatric" inmates) may be slight or even negative. As for shorter custodial sentences, these may be cheaper than noncustodial alternatives in the near term, but more expensive in the long run (the marginal cost of confining one more inmate is usually small, while noncustodial alternatives take time and money to set up).

Application of the system concept to criminal justice research and evaluation has many advantages. But the complexities and contradictions of modern criminal justice systems will always pose

a challenge to those seeking to improve the design and operation of these systems. Perhaps the greatest problem is that few researchers, and almost no officials or private citizens, have a stake in studying, improving, and explaining the whole system. This lack of systemwide experts and defenders helps explain (along with conflicting goals and values, poor coordination, and chronic funding shortages and misallocations) why these systems are so often maligned and misunderstood. Officials and other actors in each system, as well as researchers, must try to do a better job of understanding—and explaining to the public—the system's purposes, values, and operations.

RICHARD S. FRASE
ROBERT R. WEIDNER

See also BAIL; CAREERS IN CRIMINAL JUSTICE: CORRECTIONS; CAREERS IN CRIMINAL JUSTICE: LAW; CAREERS IN

CRIMINAL JUSTICE: POLICE; COMPARATIVE CRIMINAL LAW AND ENFORCEMENT: ENGLAND AND WALES; COUNSEL: RIGHT TO COUNSEL; COUNSEL: ROLE OF COUNSEL; CRIME COMMISSIONS; CRIMINALIZATION AND DECRIMINALIZATION; CRIMINAL JUSTICE PROCESS; CRIMINAL PROCEDURE: COMPARATIVE ASPECTS; CRIMINAL PROCEDURE: CONSTITUTIONAL ASPECTS; FEDERAL CRIMINAL LAW ENFORCEMENT; GUILTY PLEA: ACCEPTING THE PLEA; GUILTY PLEA: PLEA BARGAINING; INFORMAL DISPOSITION; INTERNATIONAL CRIMINAL JUSTICE STANDARDS; JAILS; JUVENILE JUSTICE: HISTORY AND PHILOSOPHY; JUVENILE JUSTICE: INSTITUTIONS; JUVENILE JUSTICE: JUVENILE COURT; JUVENILES IN THE ADULT SYSTEM; POLICE: HISTORY; POLICE: COMMUNITY POLICING; POLICE: CRIMINAL INVESTIGATIONS; POLICE: HANDLING OF JUVENILES; POLICE: ORGANIZATION AND MANAGEMENT; PRETRIAL DIVERSION; PROBATION AND PAROLE: PROCEDURAL PROTECTION; PROBATION AND PAROLE: SUPERVISION; PROSECUTION: HISTORY OF THE PUBLIC PROSECUTOR; PROSECUTION: PROSECUTORIAL DISCRETION; PROSECUTION: UNITED STATES ATTORNEY; PROBATION AND PAROLE: HISTORY, GOALS, AND DECISION-MAKING; PUNISHMENT; SENTENCING: ALLOCATION OF AUTHORITY; SENTENCING: ALTERNATIVES; SENTENCING: DISPARITY; SENTENCING: GUIDELINES; SENTENCING: MANDATORY AND MANDATORY MINIMUM SENTENCES; SENTENCING: PRESENTENCE REPORT; SENTENCING: PROCEDURAL PROTECTION; STATISTICS: REPORTING SYSTEMS AND METHODS; VICTIMLESS CRIME; VICTIMS' RIGHTS.

BIBLIOGRAPHY

AMERICAN BAR ASSOCIATION, Section of Criminal Justice. *The State of Criminal Justice*. Chicago: American Bar Association, 1998.

BECK, ALLEN J. *Prison and Jail Inmates at Midyear 1999*. Washington, D.C.: Bureau of Justice Statistics, 2000. Cited as Beck 2000a in this entry.

———. *Prisoners in 1999*. Washington, D.C.: Bureau of Justice Statistics, 2000. Cited as Beck 2000b in this entry.

BONCZAR, THOMAS P., and GLAZE, LAUREN E. *Probation and Parole in the United States, 1998*. Washington, D.C.: Bureau of Justice Statistics, 1999.

BROWN, JODI M.; LANGAN, PATRICK A.; and LEVIN, DAVID J. *Felony Sentences in State Courts, 1996*. Washington, D.C.: Bureau of Justice Statistics, 1999.

BUREAU OF JUSTICE STATISTICS. *Correctional Populations in the United States, 1995*. Washington, D.C.: Bureau of Justice Statistics, 1997.

———. *Compendium of Federal Justice Statistics, 1998*. Washington, D.C.: Bureau of Justice Statistics, 2000.

———. "U.S. Correctional Population Reaches 6.3 Million Men and Women—Represents 3.1 Percent of the Adult U.S. Population." Press release, 23 July 2000.

CLEVELAND FOUNDATION. *Criminal Justice in Cleveland: Reports of the Cleveland Foundation Survey of the Administration of Criminal Justice in Cleveland, Ohio*. Cleveland, Ohio: Patterson Smith, 1922.

COLE, GEORGE F., and SMITH, CHRISTOPHER E. *Criminal Justice in America*. Belmont, Calif.: Wadsworth Publishing Co., 1996.

DEFRANCES, CAROL J., and LITRAS, MARIKA. *Indigent Defense Services in Large Counties, 1999*. Washington, D.C.: Bureau of Justice Statistics, 2000.

DEFRANCES, CAROL J., and STEADMAN, GREG W. *Prosecutors in State Courts, 1996*. Washington, D.C.: Bureau of Justice Statistics, 1998.

EISENSTEIN, JAMES; FLEMMING, ROY B.; and NARDULLI, PETER F. *The Contours of Justice: Communities and Their Courts*. Boston: Little, Brown & Co., 1988.

FEDERAL BUREAU OF INVESTIGATION. *Crime in the United States 1996*. Washington, D.C.: Federal Bureau of Investigation, 1997.

———. *Crime in the United States 1999: Uniform Crime Reports*. Washington, D.C.: Federal Bureau of Investigation, 2000.

FEELEY, MALCOLM M. *The Process is the Punishment—Handling Cases in the Lower Court*. New York: Russell Sage Foundation, 1979.

FORST, BRIAN, and MANNING, PETER K. *The Privatization of Policing: Two Views*. Washington, D.C.: Georgetown University Press, 1999.

FRASE, RICHARD S. "Comparative Criminal Justice as a Guide to American Law Reform: How Do the French Do It, How Can We Find Out, and Why Should We Care?" *California Law Review* 78 (1990): 539–683.

———. "Sentencing Principles in Theory and Practice." *Crime & Justice: A Review of Research* 22 (1997): 363–433.

———. "Sentencing Guidelines in Minnesota, Other States, and the Federal Courts: A Twenty-Year Retrospective." *Federal Sentencing Reporter* 12 (2000): 69–82.

———. *Sentencing in Germany and the United States: Comparing Apfels with Apples*. Freiburg, Germany: Max Planck Institute for Foreign and International Criminal Law, 2001.

FREEDMAN, MONROE H. "Our Constitutionalized Adversary System." *Chapman Law Review* 1 (1998): 57–90.

GIFFORD, LEA S. *Justice Expenditure and Employment in the United States, 1995*. Washington, D.C.: Bureau of Justice Statistics, 1999.

HARLOW, CAROLINE WOLF. *Defense Counsel in Criminal Cases*. Washington, D.C.: Bureau of Justice Statistics, 2000.

HART, TIMOTHY C., and REAVES, BRIAN A. *Felony Defendants in Large Urban Counties, 1996*. Washington, D.C.: Bureau of Justice Statistics, 1999.

LAFAVE, WAYNE R. *Arrest: The Decision to Take a Suspect into Custody*. Edited by Frank J. Remington. Boston: Little, Brown, 1965.

MAQUIRE, KATHLEEN, and PASTORE, ANN L. *Sourcebook of Criminal Justice Statistics 1998*. Washington, D.C.: Bureau of Justice Statistics, 1999.

MILLER, FRANK W. *Prosecution: The Decision to Charge a Suspect with a Crime*. Edited by Frank J. Remington. Boston: Little, Brown, 1970.

MORRIS, NORVAL. *The Future of Imprisonment*. Chicago: University of Chicago Press, 1974.

National Advisory Commission on Criminal Justice Standards and Goals. *Criminal Justice System*. Washington, D.C.: The Commission, 1973.

National Center for State Courts. *State Court Caseload Statistics 1996*. Williamsburg, VA: National Center for State Courts, 1997.

———. *Examining the Work of State Courts*. Williamsburg, VA: National Center for State Courts, 1998.

OHLIN, LLOYD, and REMINGTON, FRANK, eds. *Discretion in Criminal Justice: The Tension between Individualization and Uniformity*. Albany: State Univ. of N.Y. Press, 1993.

PACKER, HERBERT L. *The Limits of the Criminal Sanction*. Stanford, Calif.: Stanford University Press, 1968.

PEREZ, JACOB. *Offender-Based Transaction Statistics: Tracking Offenders, 1990*. Washington, D.C.: Bureau of Justice Statistics, 1994.

President's Commission on Law Enforcement and Administration of Justice. *The Challenge of Crime in a Free Society*. Washington, D.C.: The Commission, 1967.

REAVES, BRIAN A., and GOLDBERG, ANDREW L. *Campus Law Enforcement Agencies, 1995*. Washington, D.C.: Bureau of Justice Statistics, 1996.

REAVES, BRIAN A., and GOLDBERG, ANDREW L. *Local Police Departments 1997*. Washington, D.C.: Bureau of Justice Statistics, 2000.

REAVES, BRIAN A., and HART, TIMOTHY C. *Federal Law Enforcement Officers, 1998*. Washington, D.C.: Bureau of Justice Statistics, 2000.

REITZ, KEVIN R. "Modeling Discretion in American Sentencing Systems." *Law & Policy* 20 (1998): 389–428.

RENNISON, CALLIE MARIE. *Criminal Victimization 1999*. Washington, D.C.: Bureau of Justice Statistics, 2000.

RINGEL, CHERYL. *Criminal Victimization 1996*. Washington, D.C.: Bureau of Justice Statistics, 1997.

ROACH, KENT. "Four Models of the Criminal Process." *Journal of Criminal Law & Criminology* 89 (1999): 671–716.

ROTTMAN, DAVID B., et al. *State Court Organization 1998*. Washington, D.C.: Bureau of Justice Statistics, 2000.

SNELL, TRACY L. *Capital Punishment 1999*. Washington, D.C.: Bureau of Justice Statistics, 2000.

STEPHAN, JAMES J. *State Prison Expenditures, 1996*. Washington, D.C.: Bureau of Justice Statistics, 1999.

TONRY, MICHAEL, ed. *Handbook of Crime and Punishment*. New York: Oxford University Press, 1998.

TONRY, MICHAEL, and FRASE, RICHARD S., eds. *Sentencing and Sanctions in Western Countries*. New York: Oxford University Press, 2001.

TYLER, TOM R. *Why People Obey the Law*. New Haven, Conn.: Yale University Press, 1990.

Vera Institute of Justice. *Felony Arrests. Their Prosecution and Disposition in New York City's Courts*. New York: Vera Institute of Justice, 1977.

WALKER, SAMUEL. *Taming the System: The Control of Discretion in Criminal Justice, 1950–1990*. New York: Oxford University Press, 1993.

ZEISEL, HANS. *The Limits of Law Enforcement*. Chicago: University of Chicago Press, 1982.

ZIMRING, FRANKLIN E., and FRASE, RICHARD S. *The Criminal Justice System: Materials on the Administration and Reform of the Criminal Law*. Boston: Little, Brown & Co., 1980.

ZIMRING, FRANKLIN E., and HAWKINS, GORDON. *The Scale of Imprisonment*. Chicago: University of Chicago Press, 1991.

INTERNET RESOURCES

Bureau of Justice Statistics. http://www.ojp.usdoj.gov/bjs/.

Federal Bureau of Investigation. http://www.fbi.gov/ucr.htm.

Federal Bureau of Prisons. http://www.bop.gov/.

Federal Justice Statistics Resource Center. http://fjsrc.urban.org/index.html.

U.S. Sentencing Commission. http://www.ussc.gov/.

CRIMINAL LAW REFORM: CONTINENTAL EUROPE

Creating a rational criminal law system has since the eighteenth century been an important issue of public policy on the European continent. In the course of time, the focus of reformers shifted from rationalization of existing legislation to more efficient crime control and prevention.

From Enlightenment to the rehabilitative ideal: early reform efforts

The radical intellectual renewal in eighteenth-century Europe known as the Enlightenment provided the cause of legal reform with its essential political and philosophical principles: the rule of law, reason, liberty, and humanitarianism. In France, Montesquieu advocated the separation of powers in order to preserve judicial independence from the executive; punishment was to correspond to the gravity of the offense. At the same time, Voltaire vigorously opposed capital punishment and demanded that criminal justice concentrate on the prevention rather than on the punishment of crime. The foundations of modern criminal policy were laid by Italian writer Cesare Beccaria (1738–1794) in his famous book *Dei delitti e delle pene* (1764). Like the French authors, Beccaria favored the abolition of the death penalty as well as corporal punishment, supported the principle of proportionality between crime and punishment, and insisted that prevention be the primary objective of criminal policy. Enlightened monarchs of the late eighteenth century—for example, Frederick II ("the Great") of Prussia, Joseph II and Leopold II of Austria, and Gustavus III of Sweden—introduced reform laws reflecting these ideas.

Early codification. At the beginning of the nineteenth century, a wave of codification of criminal law swept through Europe, led by the Criminal Code of Austria of 1803 and the French *Code pénal* of 1810. These codes, for the first time since the sixteenth century, aimed at providing comprehensive legislation on crimes and punishment based on the rationalistic ideas of the Enlightenment era. In the following decades, Bavaria (1813), Spain (1822), Greece (1834), Norway (1842), Prussia (1851), Portugal (1852), Sweden (1864), Belgium (1867), and the Netherlands (1881) adopted criminal codes, and after efforts at national unification were successful, the great codifications of Germany (1871) and Italy (1889) concluded the consolidation of criminal

laws in continental Europe. The criminal codes of Poland (1932), Romania (1936), and Switzerland (1937) were late fruits of the codification movement. Some of these codes, since frequently amended, still constitute the basis of criminal law in their countries.

Penitentiary reform. Under the ancien regime, criminal sentences were often for corporal punishment, and the prisons that existed were infamous for the maltreatment of prisoners. The move toward a modern penitentiary system with the aim of reforming offenders began as early as in 1595 with the foundation of the Amsterdam penitentiary. In 1775 a prison providing individualized treatment for prisoners was opened in Ghent. In the nineteenth century, penitentiary reform was strongly influenced not only by the movement of the Enlightenment but also by Anglo-American practices. Penology was a field of true internationalism. The first of a series of international prison conferences was held in 1846 in Frankfurt under the chairmanship of the liberal German jurist Carl J. A. Mittermaier, and in 1878 the International Penal and Penitentiary Commission was founded. In 1877 Charles Lucas and Bonneville de Marsagny established the Ecole Pénitentiaire in France, and at about the same time Eduard Ducpétiaux and Adolphe Prins reformed the penitentiary system in Belgium.

Reforms of the criminal law in the nineteenth century. The main goal of early reformers was the establishment of a rational system of criminal justice built mainly on the ideas of retribution and general deterrence. In the second half of the nineteenth century, the advances of natural sciences, the rise of psychology, anthropology, and sociology as new sciences, and the advent of philosophical positivism led to a change of paradigms in criminal justice. Punishment was no longer meant simply to visit an evil upon the offender in retribution for the crime he had committed, but criminality was viewed as a "moral disease." Criminal justice, in analogy to medicine, now aimed at curing the offender of his evil tendencies, which were alternatively regarded as genetically or environmentally caused (see Dubber; Frommel). Leading European theorists of that era were Italians Cesare Lombroso, Enrico Ferri, and Raffaele Garofalo. In Germany, Franz von Liszt, departing from the traditional idealist notion of justice, was the founding father of an influential "sociological" approach to criminal justice, regarding the reform or, with respect to "incurable" criminals, the incapacitation of offenders as the goal of the sanctioning system. Together with Belgian Adolphe Prins and Dutchman Gerard van Hamel, von Liszt founded, in 1889, the International Union of Penal Law. The reform demands of this organization included the introduction of probation, the abolition of short-term imprisonment, the long-term incarceration of professional criminals, the creation of a special criminal law for juveniles, and the substitution of other sanctions for deprivation of liberty. Many of these proposals have since been introduced by legislation.

The crisis of the rehabilitative ideal. Beginning in the early 1960s, the idea that criminal sanctions can reform and rehabilitate offenders was challenged from two sides: criminological studies found that rehabilitative efforts produced no measurable effect (Lipton, Martinson, and Wilks), and human rights advocates argued that harsh and sometimes undeserved punishment was concealed by the rhetoric of reform (American Friends Service Committee; von Hirsch). These insights led in many countries to a reorientation toward retribution ("just desert") and incapacitation as the foundations of the system of criminal law. Sanctions of indeterminate duration, in particular, came to be regarded as misplaced in the criminal justice system. Although European legal systems did not go as far as some United States jurisdictions in establishing by statute fixed sentences or narrow sentence ranges for individual offenses, the 1970s and 1980s saw a clear movement away from the earlier medical paradigm of crime control and toward greater strictness. At the same time, some writers criticized imprisonment, which had since the nineteenth century become the backbone of the sanctioning system. Imprisonment was denounced as a fundamentally desocializing sanction, and reformers called for its replacement by noncustodial sanctions (restitution, fines, community service, probation) or at least for more open forms of corrections including furloughs and work release (Morris, pp. 12–27; Jescheck, pp. 1975–1989; Albrecht, pp. 291–305). Many legislatures followed up on these demands and enacted laws promoting the use of alternatives to traditional prison sentences.

Criminal law reform in continental Europe

Several European countries have reformed their criminal laws since the 1970s. Many of the recently enacted codes, most notably those of Austria, France, Germany, Poland, Portugal, and Spain, share certain tendencies: in the general part, they tend to introduce differentiated rules on criminal responsibility (e.g., distinction among various forms of perpetratorship and accessorial liability, recognition of an inevitable mistake of law as an excuse); in the area of criminal policy, these modern codes strive to restrict imprisonment by implementing noncustodial penalties affecting the offender's financial means (fines, restitution) or his ability to dispose of his leisure time (community service, weekend arrest). Although modern criminal laws on the European continent have these and many other features in common, each country has its own style and methods in dealing with crime. These different styles reflect variances in policy, history, and national culture. For example, some legal systems (e.g., Switzerland and the Netherlands) have traditionally relied on short-term imprisonment as the primary sanction for offenses of medium seriousness, and continue to do so, whereas others (e.g., Germany and Austria) have long tried to restrict the use of this sanction because they regard it as dissocializing the offender (Th. Weigend). It is thus necessary to look at each country separately in order to fully comprehend European legal reform. For this article, France, Germany and its German-speaking neighbors, Italy, the Netherlands, Poland, Spain, and Sweden have been selected as examples of recent developments on the Continent.

France. In France, several reform efforts were undertaken since 1810 to replace the antiquated *Code Napoléon* with more modern legislation. After many partial revisions of the code, finally in 1994 a completely new penal code entered into force (see Lazerges; Pradel). Contrary to the ancient legislation, the new code places the protection of individual (rather than state) interests at the top of the list of offenses, which begins with the prohibition of genocide (Art. 211-1 Code pénal). Since the abolition of the death penalty in 1981, the most severe sentence is life imprisonment, which is reserved for the most serious offenses. For other offenses, the code provides for fines (imposed according to the day-fine system, allowing the court to adapt the amount of the fine to the offender's income); revocation of rights and privileges (e.g., prohibition to drive a motor vehicle or to use credit cards, closure of the defendant's business); and community service. The 1994 code also eliminates all minimum penalties (Tomlinson, p. 9). Other notable features of the new code include the criminal liability of legal entities (Art. 131-37 Code pénal), the introduction of a proportionality requirement in the defense of self-defense (Art. 122-5 Code pénal), and the recognition of an excuse of inevitable mistake of law (Art. 122-3 Code pénal). These and other changes have brought French criminal law to the forefront of European criminal policy and theory.

Germany. Reform efforts in Germany began at the start of the twentieth century. Piecemeal changes, especially a larger field of application for fines, were achieved in the 1920s, but the Nazi regime and World War II prevented the further adoption of liberal reform ideas. After the war, an official reform commission produced a rather conservative draft law in 1962. This provoked a response from a group of younger and more liberal law professors, who presented an "Alternative Draft" (*Alternativ-Entwurf*) of the general and sanctions part in 1966 (see Darby). In parliament, a compromise was achieved between these two drafts, with liberal ideas prevailing in the sanctions part and more conservative solutions adopted with respect to general theories of the criminal code. In the course of the reform, outdated offenses, especially in the area of sex crime, were abolished. Based on the parliamentary compromise, a largely revised version of the 1871 Penal Code came into force in 1975.

The revised code retained the traditional orientation toward individual responsibility based on subjective blameworthiness. This orientation has deep roots in German philosophy dating back to the idealist philosophers Kant and Hegel. Individual blameworthiness not only determines criminal liability but also the punishment an offender receives. Because this strictly guilt-oriented system cannot take account of an offender's future dangerousness, German criminal law has since 1933 provided for "measures of reform and security." Such measures, which include detention in a psychiatric hospital or a clinic for addicts as well as revocation of an offender's driving license, can be imposed even when subjective blameworthiness is absent, for example, because the offender is insane. The 1975 reform legislation has retained and even extended this dualistic system of sanctions.

As regards penal policy, the most important aspect of the 1975 reform law was its emphasis on restricting the use of imprisonment. The new law decreed that prison sentences of less than six months were to be imposed only under exceptional circumstances, and the court should always consider suspension of the sentence as a preferred option. At the same time, fines were made more attractive as sanctions even for serious crime by the introduction of the day-fine system. As a result of these reforms, the rate of prison sentences has declined markedly, from more than one-third of all convictions before the reform to 19.6 percent in 1999 (Statistisches Bundesamt, pp. 44–45). More than two-thirds of sentences of imprisonment (68 percent in 1999) are suspended, which means that only 6 percent of convicted offenders are sentenced to serve time in prison. This rate has remained almost stable over the years since 1975. However, the rate of lengthy prison sentences (of more than two years) has increased since then. Terms and conditions of imprisonment, including prisoners' rights with regard to furloughs and access to open institutions, have been regulated by statute since 1976.

Austria and Switzerland. Germany's smaller neighbors Austria and Switzerland have taken different approaches toward criminal law reform. Austria, in close cooperation with Germany, revised its ancient criminal code in 1975, adopting many provisions that parallel the new German legislation, including the day-fine system, a preference for fines over imprisonment, extensive decriminalization of sexual offenses and abortion, and such preventive measures as separate institutions for mentally disturbed criminals and dangerous recidivists. Switzerland, on the other hand, has retained its criminal code of 1937. Typical features of this code are its strong reliance on various forms of imprisonment, including short-term imprisonment, as the main sanction, and the distinction—as in Germany—between penalties and security measures as reactions to crime (see Bauhofer). In 1993, a reform draft was presented, which would replace short-term imprisonment by noncustodial sanctions (see Schweizer Kriminalistische Gesellschaft). This draft has not yet been passed into law at the beginning of the twenty-first century.

Italy. The Italian Penal Code stems from the Fascist area; it was adopted in 1930 and reflected the dominant authoritarian ideology of its time. After the end of World War II, numerous efforts were made to replace the *Codice Rocco* of 1930 by more modern and liberal legislation, but only with very limited success. The death penalty was abolished as early as in 1944, and the Constitution of 1948 incorporated the principles of personal criminal responsibility and rehabilitation as the goal of imprisonment. Based on these principles, the Constitutional Court released several landmark decisions affecting criminal law. For example, the court declared that imprisonment for nonpayment of fines constituted unconstitutional discrimination against the poor, and in another decision required criminal courts to recognize an inevitable mistake of law as a valid excuse. In the field of corrections, parole was introduced in 1962, and later legislation provided for probation, community service as a substitute penalty, and work release of prisoners.

The most comprehensive attempt to introduce a new criminal code was undertaken in 1992, when a draft code was presented by a commission consisting mainly of academics. This draft aimed at reducing the number of petty offenses and at consolidating the criminal law by integrating offenses proscribed in other legislation into the penal code (Pisani). The draft was discussed by the government but not acted upon by the Italian parliament.

The Netherlands. In the Netherlands, German and French influences on penal legislation are noticeable, but criminal policy is quite autonomous and independent. In 1811, the French penal code was imposed on the Dutch. It was superseded by the Dutch Criminal Code (*Wetboek van Strafrecht*), still in force today, in 1886. After World War II, Dutch criminal policy was well-known for its leniency and for the sparing use courts made of imprisonment. Many minor offenses do not even reach the courts but are disposed of by prosecutorial "transaction," that is, a fine to be paid by the culprit without trial and conviction. Since the 1980s, however, rates as well as duration of imprisonment have risen sharply, mostly due to more severe treatment of an increasing number of violent and drug offenses (Junger-Tas). Another noteworthy development is the frequent use made of community service sanctions.

Poland. Like all other Eastern European countries, Poland's criminal legislation in the wake of World War II was heavily influenced by the Soviet Union and its specific "socialist" criminal justice (see Schittenhelm). In 1969, Poland replaced its liberal criminal code of 1932 by new legislation reflecting, both in the general part and in the description of offenses, the guiding ideas of socialism, especially the priority of the protection of social interests and the "substantive" notion of criminal offenses linked to the offender's "social dangerousness" (arts. 1 and 26 § 1 Penal Code 1969). Penalties included capital punishment. The courts relied heavily on long-term imprisonment, especially in the 1980s when the government attempted to repress popular demands for greater freedom and democratic reforms. In the brief period between the onset of the Solidarity movement in 1980 and the imposition of military rule in late 1981, two independent commissions began work on a reform of the criminal law, yet their efforts seemed to lead nowhere when the political climate changed toward repressiveness and stagnation. It took until 1989 for the representatives of the reform movement to be able to participate again in the work of a commission installed two years earlier by the socialist government with the mandate of developing guiding principles for a new criminal code. In 1997 the efforts of this commission, which included conservatives and liberals but was dominated by the latter, eventually led to adoption, by the Polish parliament, of a new criminal code (for an overview see E. Weigend). The code of 1997 retained some features of its predecessor but in many ways went back to the traditions of the 1932 code and tried to integrate those with modern developments and criminal policy. By its orientation toward a rational, systematic, and humanitarian criminal law, Poland's new code differs to some extent from the criminal code of the Russian federation (1996), which relies much more heavily on the heritage of the Soviet past (see Schroeder).

The Polish code's general rules concerning criminal liability represent a mixture of traditional, indigenous solutions (e.g., the treatment of perpetratorship and accessories in art. 18), and formulations reflecting the latest advances of European criminal law theory (e.g., the definitions of intent and negligence in art. 9 and the treatment of necessity in art. 26). With respect to sanctions, Poland distinguishes between penalties, probationary measures, and security measures. The latter include commitment to an institution for the insane or for addicts (arts. 94–96 Penal Code). If the offender was criminally responsible at the time of the offense and therefore receives a criminal penalty, his sentence is reduced for time spent in an institution. Penalties include fines (to be imposed according to the day-fine system), imprisonment, and, as a holdover from the 1969 code, restriction of freedom (arts. 35, 36 Penal Code). Restriction of freedom consists alternatively in a duty to perform community service or a reduction of the offender's regular wages, coupled with a prohibition of changing one's place of residence without the court's permission. In an important general directive for sentencing, art. 58 sec. 1 of the Penal Code provides that imprisonment can only be imposed if other, less restrictive sanctions are unable to fulfill the purposes of punishment. Such alternative sanctions include not only fines and restriction of freedom but also probation and the conditional dismissal of prosecution (arts. 66–68 Penal Code), which spares the defendant a criminal conviction if the offense is of lesser seriousness, the offender makes restitution to the victim, and fulfills other conditions the court may impose.

Spain. Reform efforts began in Spain immediately after the restoration of democracy in 1975. Capital punishment was abolished by the constitution of 1978, which also declared rehabilitation to be the goal of custodial punishment. It took until 1996, however, to replace the authoritarian and outdated criminal code of 1944 by modern legislation.

The new Penal Code of 1996 modernized the general part of the criminal law (for an overview see Cerezo Mir). Art. 1 explicitly states the principle of legality and extends it to penalties as well as measures of security and rehabilitation, and art. 5 does away with objective criminal responsibility. An inevitable error of law excludes culpability (art. 14 Penal Code), and attempts are punishable only when there is some measure of objective dangerousness (art. 16 Penal Code). The offenses are listed in a sequence that expresses the idea that individual interests have priority over those of the state. Some remnants of ancient legal traditions, such as special rules for the enhanced punishment of patricide and lesser punishment of killing a child born out of wedlock, were abolished.

In its provisions on penalties and sentencing, the code of 1996 establishes principles of modern criminal policy. The multitude of different forms of imprisonment, a characteristic of earlier Spanish law, has been replaced by a unitary type of imprisonment, supplemented by weekend arrest (with a maximum of twenty-four weekends) as a milder form of custodial punishment (arts. 35, 37 Penal Code). Fines, to be imposed according to the day-fine system, as well as community service are to be imposed for less serious offenses.

Sweden. Sweden has been at the forefront of European criminal policy since the first half of the twentieth century. As early as 1921, Sweden abolished the death penalty in peace times (total abolition followed in 1974). In 1927 indeterminate sentences were introduced for recidivists, following the then modern trend toward preventive individualization of punishment. The day-

fine system of imposing fines was adopted in 1931, and in 1937 imprisonment for nonpayment of fines was restricted to offenders who willfully refused to pay, which led to a drastic reduction in the number of prisoners (Cornils and Jareborg, p. 6). In 1965 a new criminal code (*brottsbalken*) went into force. This code was built on the idea of rehabilitation as the main purpose of criminal law, again reflecting the prevalent ideology of the time. Shortly after introduction of the code, the winds changed again: skepticism set in with respect to the possibility of rehabilitation, especially in custody, and Sweden was again quick to implement new insights. Indeterminate imprisonment was abolished for juveniles in 1979 and for recidivists in 1981. Although rehabilitation is still seen as the goal of corrections, a 1988 amendment to the criminal code has defined the "penal value" (that is, the objective and subjective gravity of the offense) as the main criterion for the selection and gradation of punishment (see Jareborg). According to the new version of the code (ch. 29 § 1 sec. 2), the primary consideration in sentencing is the harm or risk brought about by the offense and the offender's subjective attitude (motive, intention, knowledge, or negligence) as to his deed.

Through all these changes, Sweden has remained wary of overusing imprisonment: in 1998, only 13 percent of all convicted offenders received prison sentences, and only 15 percent of those were for one year or more (Cornils and Jareborg, p. 38). For the great majority of offenders, noncustodial penalties are regarded as sufficient. Most frequently, they receive fines (which can be adjusted to the offender's income through use of the day-fine system) or probation or a combination of both. New alternatives include community service and (since 1998) house arrest with electronic surveillance, which is regarded as a special form of executing a sentence of imprisonment.

Efforts at assimilation and unification of European law

The process of European unification, which started after World War II and reached new dimensions after the end of the political partition of the continent in the 1990s, has extended to criminal law, though not as extensively as to private law.

The Council of Europe, of which almost all European states are members, has played an important role in setting common standards for criminal justice and in simplifying cooperation in transnational prosecutions. The most important European instrument in this area is the 1950 European Convention for the Protection of Human Rights and Fundamental Freedoms (ECHR), which has been signed and ratified by all member states of the Council of Europe. The Convention guarantees citizens a number of important basic rights, several pertaining specifically to the criminal process and—like the prohibition of torture and cruel punishment in art. 3 ECHR—to criminal sanctioning. The European Court of Human Rights in Strasbourg is the guardian of human rights under the Convention, and any citizen can, after exhausting the legal remedies of domestic law, bring a complaint against the state that has allegedly violated one of the rights guaranteed by the Convention. The decisions of the court have had considerable influence on the laws of the member states (Bengoetxea and Jung). The Council of Europe has also been the source of many recommendations on criminal policy and of several conventions on cooperation in the prosecution of offenders and the execution of sentences.

The European Union has until the end of the twentieth century not been given a clear competence for criminal legislation. The 1997 version of the European Community Treaty does provide for the Council to prescribe sanctions for violations of the Union's economic interests (EC treaty art. 280 sec. 4), but the application of penal law is left to the member states (see Deutscher). It is nevertheless obvious that the European Union is moving toward an assimilation and perhaps even unification of some parts of the criminal law, especially those relevant to economic and environmental issues central to the European unification movement. There exists a draft code for European economic criminal law (Delmas-Marty and Vervaele), and some authors have even suggested that a European Model Penal Code should be drafted to speed up the unification process (Sieber). Although it seems unlikely that a unitary European law might in the near future supersede national criminal codes, criminal law reform in Europe will probably be more and more a matter for continental rather than national policymaking.

THOMAS WIEGAND

See also ADVERSARY SYSTEM; CRIMINAL PROCEDURE: COMPARATIVE ASPECTS; PROSECUTION: COMPARATIVE ASPECTS.

BIBLIOGRAPHY

ALBRECHT, PETER-ALEXIS. *Kriminologie.* Munich: Beck, 1999.

American Friends Service Committee. *Struggle for Justice: A Report on Crime and Punishment in America.* New York: Hill and Wang, 1971.

Association of American Law Schools. "Symposium: The New German Penal Code." Foreword by J. Hall and W. J. Wagner. *American Journal of Comparative Law* 24 (1976): 589–778.

BAUHOFER, STEFAN. "Reform strafrechtlicher Sanktionen in der Schweiz." In *Reform der strafrechtlichen Sanktionen. Réforme des sanctions pénales.* Edited by Stefan Bauhofer and Pierre-H. Bolle. Zurich: Rüegger, 1994. Pages 225–265.

BENGOETXEA, JOXERRAMON, and JUNG, HEIKE. "Towards a European Criminal Jurisprudence? The Justification of Criminal Law by the Strasbourg Court." *Legal Studies* 11 (1991): 239–280.

CEREZO MIR, JOSÉ. "Das neue spanische Strafgesetzbuch von 1995." *Zeitschrift für die gesamte Strafrechtswissenschaft* 108 (1996): 857–872.

CORNILS, KARIN, and JAREBORG, NILS. "Einführung." *Das schwedische Kriminalgesetzbuch. Brottsbalken.* Translated from Swedish by Karin Cornils and Nils Jareborg. Freiburg im Breisgau, Germany: edition iuscrim, 2000. Pages 1–46.

DARBY, JOSEPH J., trans. *Alternative Draft of a Penal Code for the Federal Republic of Germany.* South Hackensack, N.J.: Rothman, 1977.

DELAMS-MARTY, MIREILLE, and VERVAELE, J. A. E., eds. *The Implementation of the Corpus Juris in the Member States.* Vol. 1. Antwerp: Intersentia, 2000.

DEUTSCHER, JÖRG. *Die Kompetenzen der Europäischen Gemeinschaften zur originären Strafgesetzgebung.* Frankfurt: Peter Lang, 2000.

DUBBER, MARKUS DIRK. "The Right to Be Punished: Autonomy and Its Demise in Modern Penal Thought." *Law and History Review* 16 (1998): 113–146.

FLETCHER, GEORGE P. *Rethinking Criminal Law.* Boston: Little, Brown, 1978.

FROMMEL, MONIKA. *Präventionsmodelle in der deutschen Strafzweck-Diskussion.* Berlin: Duncker & Humblot, 1987.

JAREBORG, NILS. "Zur Reform des schwedischen Strafzumessungsrechts." *Zeitschrift für die gesamte Strafrechtswissenschaft* 106 (1994): 140–162.

JESCHECK, HANS-HEINRICH. "Die Freiheitsstrafe und ihre Surrogate in rechtsvergleichender Darstellung." *Die Freiheitsstrafe und ihre Surrogate im deutschen und ausländischen Recht.* Edited by Hans-Heinrich Jescheck. Baden-Baden, Germany: Nomos, 1984. Pages 1939–2172.

JUNGER-TAS, JOSINE. "Dutch Penal Policies Changing Direction." *Overcrowded Times* 9, no. 5 (1998): 1, 14–20.

LAZERGES, CHRISTINE, ed. *Réflexions sur le Nouveau Code Pénal.* Paris: Editions A. Pedone, 1995.

LIPTON, DOUGLAS; MARTINSON, ROBERT; and WILKS, JUDITH. *The Effectiveness of Correctional Treatment: A Survey of Treatment Evaluation Studies.* New York: Praeger, 1975.

MORRIS, NORVAL. *The Future of Imprisonment.* Chicago: University of Chicago Press, 1974.

PISANI, MARIO, ed. *Per un nuovo codice penale.* Padua, Italy: Cedam, 1993.

PRADEL, JEAN. *Le Nouveau Code Pénal (Partie générale).* Paris: Dalloz, 1994.

SCHITTENHELM, ULRIKE. *Strafe und Sanktionensystem im sowjetischen Recht.* Freiburg im Breisgau, Germany: Eigenverlag Max-Planck-Institut, 1994.

SCHROEDER, FRIEDRICH-CHRISTIAN. "Einführung." *Strafgesetzbuch der Russischen Föderation.* Translated by Friedrich-Christian Schroeder and Thomas Bednarz. Freiburg im Breisgau, Germany: edition iuscrim 1998. Pages 1–37.

Schweizer Kriminalistische Gesellschaft. "Vernehmlassung zur Totalrevision des Allgemeinen Teils des Schweizerischen Strafgesetzbuches." *Schweizer Zeitschrift für Strafrecht* 112 (1994): 354–375.

SIEBER, ULRICH. "Memorandum für ein Europäisches Modellstrafgesetzbuch." *Juristenzeitung* 52 (1997): 369–381.

Statistisches Bundesamt. *Rechtspflege. Reihe 3: Strafverfolgung 1999.* Wiesbaden, Germany: Metzler-Poeschel, 2001.

TOMLINSON, EDWARD A. *The French Penal Code of 1994.* Littleton, Colo.: Rothman and Co., 1999.

VOGEL, JOACHIM. "Wege zu europäisch-einheitlichen Regelungen im Allgemeinen Teil des Strafrechts." *Juristenzeitung* 50 (1995): 331–341.

VON HIRSCH, ANDREW. *Doing Justice: The Choice of Punishments.* New York: Hill and Wang, 1976.

WEIGEND, EWA. "Einführung." *Das polnische Strafgesetzbuch. Kodeks karny.* Translated by Ewa Weigend. Freiburg im Breisgau, Germany: edition iuscrim, 1998. Pages 1–34.

WEIGEND, THOMAS. "Die kurze Freiheitsstrafe— eine Sanktion mit Zukunft?" *Juristenzeitung* 41 (1986): 260–269.

CRIMINAL LAW REFORM: ENGLAND

English criminal law, like almost every other English legal, political, religious, educational, and social institution, has undergone substantial reform since the second quarter of the nineteenth century; but reform has taken place piecemeal and very slowly. There has been no decisive break with the past as has occurred in many European countries with the promulgation of a penal code and code of criminal procedure. Not only is England still without either, but dozens of reforms cogently urged by publicists, parliamentary committees, and royal commissions in the first half of the nineteenth century had to wait until the second half of the twentieth to be implemented. Some, like the complete abolition of common law offenses, as well as codification itself, are still awaited.

Two factors have combined to make the pace of reform of the criminal law particularly slow. The first has been the influential presence in both houses of Parliament of considerable numbers of lawyers: many of the most senior judges, as well as other lawyers, sit in the House of Lords, and many magistrates and practicing lawyers have been members of the House of Commons. The second is the British parliamentary practice that permits the scrutiny and debate of the detail, and not just the principle, of proposed legislation. Until the 1900s, every substantial reform was opposed by either the judiciary or the practicing profession.

In 1786 the lord chancellor, Lord Loughborough, said that any proposal for changing the criminal law should either originate from the judges or be approved by them before being submitted to parliament, and this convention was generally followed (at least by governments). Many of the reforms would have curtailed the powers and discretion of the judiciary, the wide extent of which has always been one of the most striking characteristics of English criminal law. Judicial and professional opposition to reform remained the rule. Moreover, the breadth of this judicial discretion, coupled with both the absence of any rule or machinery compelling the prosecution of known offenders, and the uncontrollable liberty of juries to acquit in the teeth of the evidence, often made it possible for the worst of the law's defects to be palliated in response to public opinion. It could therefore be argued that in practice the law was nowhere near as objectionable as it was in theory, and that reforming legislation was, accordingly, unnecessary and might well result in unforeseen harm. At least two generations commonly elapse between the proposal and the enactment of a reform. Furthermore, the amount of parliamentary time likely to be consumed in considering any comprehensive legislation has constantly deterred the promotion of those reforms of the substantive law that even the legal profession has come to recognize as—in principle—desirable.

The unreformed law

In 1818 the youthful Thomas Macaulay described English criminal law as "a penal code at once too sanguinary and too lenient, half written in blood like Draco's, and half undefined and loose as the common law of a tribe of savages . . . the curse and disgrace of the country" (Cross, p. 520). He did not exaggerate. The law had been growing haphazardly for more than five centuries. Much had been added, often under the influence of temporary alarms. Very little had been taken away. As a result the criminal law was seriously defective both in substance and in form, and many aspects of the procedure under which it was applied were equally unsatisfactory.

For over a century and a half, Parliament had sought to compensate for the absence of any adequate nationwide machinery for enforcing law and order (such as police forces would later provide) by threatening the severest penalty for those few offenders unlucky enough to be caught. In 1818 there were more than two hundred statutes in force imposing the death penalty for a wide variety of offenses, both serious and trivial. These offenses ranged from treason and murder to forgery and even to criminal damage and petty theft when committed in a host of specified circumstances, as well as to several sex offenses, including sodomy. There was, however, no question of implementing all the death sentences that the judges were required by this undiscriminating legislation to pass whenever a prosecutor with the necessary nerve (or malice) found a jury willing to convict. Capital sentences were carried out, in 1810, in less than once case in twenty, although as might be expected the proportion varied greatly from crime to crime. Fewer than one convicted person in twenty was executed for theft unaccompanied by personal violence, but about one in six was put to death for the more serious offenses of murder, rape, arson, counterfeiting, forgery, and attempted murder.

Whether or not the convicted defendant was reprieved largely depended on the trial judge, although in cases tried in London his recommendations were reviewed by the Privy Council. His discretion was affected, but not controlled, by public opinion, professional expectations, and the influence of persons in high places. The judge did not have to give any reasons for his decision, which was as likely to be determined by matters irrelevant to the defendant's guilt and to the jury's verdict as by anything that the defendant himself had actually done: the defendant's past record, the reputed prevalence of his offense in the locality, the extent of the perjury committed by witnesses called on his behalf, and the number of other defendants sentenced to death at the same assizes. But although the trial judge had a wide (or, as many critics said, an arbitrary) discretion to decide whether a defendant convicted of a capital offense should die, he had no discretion as to what should happen to the defendant if he was allowed to live.

The alternatives to the death penalty were whipping, a short term of imprisonment, or transportation—after 1787, generally to an Australian colony (the American ones being no longer available for this purpose) for a fixed period, which was usually seven years, but for some offenses fourteen years, and for a few, life. However, by no means all the defendants who had been sentenced to death and then reprieved on condition of being transported left English shores. Whether a convict was in fact transported or merely served a short (two- or three-year) period in an English prison hulk before being released depended not on the nature of the offense, but on purely administrative and practical considerations with which the judges were not concerned—the Australian demand for convict labor, and the availability of the requisite shipping.

The law governing these capital offenses was thus inefficient, as well as cruel and capricious. The chances of an offender actually suffering the extreme penalty with which the law threatened him were small, and its deterrent effect was therefore slight. Yet the chance that he might suffer the death penalty deterred many victims from prosecuting, many witnesses from giving evidence, and many juries from convicting.

The form of the law was chaotic and extremely obscure. In 1821 it was estimated that there were 750 acts of Parliament concerning the criminal law in force, together with another 400 relating to proceedings before magistrates.

These statutes were the product of three centuries of parliamentary activity. Not only had almost all of them been enacted without regard to any of the others, but they also presupposed the "unwritten" common law of crime, without a knowledge of which the statutes themselves were more often than not quite unintelligible. Such matters as the definitions of the basic offenses (murder, rape, robbery, burglary, theft, forgery, and assault), the rules governing the liability of accomplices, and general defenses were a matter of judicial tradition sustained by three seventeenth- and eighteenth-century authorities—Edward Coke's *Third Institute* (1644); Matthew Hale's *History of the Pleas of the Crown* (first published in 1736); and William Hawkins's *Pleas of the Crown* (1716–1721). These were supplemented by a very small amount of reported case law. Although the judges recognized that either immemorial custom or an act of Parliament was required to make conduct a felony and a capital offense, they exercised a wide power to declare an act criminal as a misdemeanor, and to punish with the pillory, whipping, imprisonment, or a fine, any conduct which they happened to consider immoral or antisocial.

Trial procedure (and also powers of arrest and ancillary liability) was determined by whether the offense with which a defendant was charged was a treason, a felony, or a misdemeanor, although with the shifts and changes in the law that had occurred over the years these distinctions had become more than a little arbitrary. Theft, for example, was a felony, however small the amount stolen, but obtaining by false pretenses was a misdemeanor, however valuable the property obtained. A defendant could not be tried simultaneously for a felony and a misdemeanor, however closely related in point of fact the two charges might be (as, for example, the inchoate offense to the completed offense). Indeed, only one felony could be tried at a time. Most importantly, at a felony trial the defendant's counsel could only examine witnesses and argue points of law: he was not allowed to address the jury, although he might at treason or misdemeanor trials. A defendant was not entitled to any prior notice of the case against him beyond the information provided by the indictment itself; and since it was a general rule that neither party to the proceedings nor anyone who had any pecuniary interest in the result of a trial could give evidence at it, not only the defendant but frequently also the victim was excluded from the witness stand. (Defendants were, however, usually allowed to make a statement at the very end of the trial, when it was difficult for anyone to test its correctness.)

There were no special procedures for youthful offenders. Everyone over the age of seven was subject to the same law, modes of trial, and penalties; and though children were very rarely hanged, they were sentenced to death and imprisoned. This reflected the fact that the common law knew only one form of criminal trial, trial by jury. Statutes had in specific instances given to magistrates, sitting singly or in small groups, the power to try persons charged with certain statutory offenses (for example, under the game laws and the revenue legislation), but there was no general provision for the summary trial of offenses of a minor character. There was, finally, no system of criminal appeals, either on the facts, on account of the judge's misdirection of the jury, or from a sentence in those cases in which the judge had discretion. Only a very limited and rarely invoked remedy existed for the review of procedural and similar technical errors.

Movements for reform

The literary movement for the reform of English criminal law began in 1771 with the publication of William Eden's *Principles of Penal Law*. The parliamentary movement was initiated in 1810 by Samuel Romilly's (unsuccessful) attempt to make three forms of petty theft noncapital crimes, and by the establishment in 1819, on the motion of James Mackintosh, of a select committee of the House of Commons, "to consider so much of the criminal laws as relates to capital punishment in felonies, and to report their observations and opinions upon the same." Both Romilly and Mackintosh were the friends as well as the disciples of the philosopher Jeremy Bentham (1748–1832), whose ideas and writings (published and unpublished) pervaded every proposal for the reform not only of the criminal law but of most other legal and political institutions for more than half a century.

William Blackstone (1723–1780) had not been uncritical of several aspects of the criminal law in the fourth volume of his *Commentaries on the Laws of England*; but Eden's book, published when the author was only twenty-six, and strongly inspired by Montesquieu and Beccaria, was the first attempt at a critical examination of the law's structure and principles. It was also the first effort to evolve a comprehensive plan for its reform. Although he favored retaining the death penalty for a substantial number of crimes (including maiming, rape, sodomy, arson, and burglary), Eden argued that the severity of penal laws should be controlled first by "natural justice" and second by "public utility," and that punishments should bear some relation to the gravity of offenses. He accordingly identified scores of crimes that should no longer be capital—a bold suggestion at a time when Parliament was still readily adding to their number. Eden disapproved of transportation, on the ground that if it did not kill the convict, it often conferred a benefit on him. He also disapproved of imprisonment, which he considered a dead loss to everyone. On the other hand, he favored flogging, fines, and compulsory labor in public works. Finally, he proposed the outright repeal of all obsolete statutes, and the consolidation of those that were to remain. Nearly all of Eden's reforms (with the exception, of course, of the disuse of imprisonment) were ultimately implemented by Parliament, but the process took more than seventy years.

In 1808, Romilly sought the repeal of a statute imposing the death penalty—one dating from 1565, for stealing "privately" from the person (that is, pickpocketing)—but it was his speech in the House of Commons on 9 February 1810 (printed, with additions, as *Observations on the Criminal Law of England as It Relates to Capital Punishments, and on the Mode in Which It Is Administered*) that reopened public debate on the state of the criminal law. Romilly's argument was a masterly exposure (still well worth reading) of the fallacies of the orthodox justifications for the law's indiscriminate threats, but relatively infrequent and largely arbitrary imposition, of the death penalty. Since the three statutes whose repeal he unsuccessfully sought covered a considerable proportion of all nonviolent offenses against property, Romilly's proposed reform was a substantial one going to the heart of the existing law.

Mackintosh's committee of 1819 made the first official large-scale investigation into the criminal law and its effects, and its report, with detailed statistical returns of convictions and executions, as well as a chronological review of the statute law, served as a model for official reports on the criminal law for the rest of the nineteenth century. The committee recommended: (1) that twelve obsolete statutes be repealed and fifteen others amended; (2) that Romilly's proposed reform of 1810 (for the repeal of three capital theft offenses) be carried out; (3) that the statute law

of forgery be consolidated; and (4) that all forgery offenses other than the actual forging of Bank of England notes, as well as a second conviction for uttering forged notes, should cease to be capital. The fourth of these reforms was strongly supported by bankers and businessmen, who found it virtually impossible to obtain convictions while the offenses remained capital. Although the committee's recommendations met with determined opposition and were at first rejected by Parliament almost all of them were implemented during the 1820s after Home Secretary Robert Peel, keen that the government should control the pace and extent of reform, had in 1823 committed it to an extensive review of the criminal law.

Legislation, 1823–1849

The review promised by Peel resulted in very substantial improvements in the form of the law, but only in relatively minor reductions in its severity and arbitrariness. Peel was accordingly able to secure the support of the judiciary in carrying a considerable body of legislation through Parliament. Three hundred and sixteen acts of Parliament were consolidated in four statutes, which covered nearly four-fifths of all offenses (the Larceny Act, 1827, 7 & 8 Geo. 4, c, 29, consolidating ninety-two statutes; the malicious Injuries to Property Act, 1827, 7 & 8 Geo. 4, c, 30, consolidating forty-eight statutes; the Offences against the Person Act, 1828, 9 Geo. 4, c. 32, consolidating fifty-six statutes; and the Forgery Act, 1830, 11 Geo. 4 & 1 Will. 4, c. 66, consolidating 120 statutes). Peel's acts also totally repealed obsolete statutes, filled small gaps in the law, and made other minor amendments; but being merely consolidating statutes, they did not incorporate the common law rules. Thus, the Larceny Act contained no definition of larceny (which was not provided until 1916); the Forgery Act, no definition of forgery (not provided until 1913); and the Offences against the Person Act, no definitions of murder, manslaughter, assault, or rape (only rape has since been defined, and then not until 1976). This legislation did not therefore amount to codification, as Bentham and his followers would have wished, and as Edward Livingston was contemporaneously projecting for Louisiana. Nor did it do much to mitigate the severity and arbitrariness of the law relating to capital punishment. Even in 1830 Peel, against the wishes of the banking and commercial community, favored retention of the death sentence for forgery, although no one was in fact executed for this offense after that date.

Only four reforms were effected in the substance, as opposed to the form, of the law under Peel's leadership. First, in 1823, two of the three capital offenses of theft that Romilly had singled out in 1810 were repealed, as well as another eight whose abolition had been proposed by Mackintosh's committee. Four more were repealed in 1825, and two others (larceny in booths and larceny in churches), in 1827. Second, another statute of 1823 provided that death sentences should not be pronounced if the judge intended to recommend a reprieve. This meant that the judge had to decide openly for, rather than privately against, the carrying out of the death sentence. This statute thus increased the number of cases in which the death penalty was commuted. Third, in 1827 Parliament abolished the technicalities of benefit of clergy (a medical jurisdictional rule that had been manipulated so as to give, unless a statute otherwise provided, what was in effect a conditional discharge to every felon on his first conviction) and the distinction between grand and petty larceny, with the result that a second conviction for the theft of more than twelvepence was no longer capital. The practical consequence was not any reduction in the number of death sentences carried out but rather that such thefts became triable at quarter sessions, which was much more convenient for prosecutors than trial at assizes. Fourth, many changes were introduced in the scale of punishments for lesser offenses, which had the same effect.

The formation of Earl Grey's Whig reform ministry in November 1830 made possible more radical changes. In 1832 William Eden's son, George Eden, president of the board of trade and master of the mint, successfully sponsored the Coinage Offences Act, 1832, 2 & 3 Will. 4, c. 34 (repealed), which not only consolidated the existing law but also carried through the drastic reform of abolishing the death penalty for all counterfeiting offenses. During the next two years, and in the face of opposition from Peel and the judges, the death sentence was abolished for several forms of four offenses (larceny, housebreaking, forgery, and robbery), being replaced by mandatory sentences of transportation, either for life or for not less than seven years.

In 1835 the appointment as home secretary of Lord John Russell, a disciple of Romilly and a member of Mackintosh's committee, stimulated another reform. Between April and July 1837, Russell carried ten reforming bills through parliament, seven of them directly concerned with the death penalty. The total number of capital offenses was thereby reduced from thirty-seven to sixteen, nearly all of those that remained involving some element of violence against the person. The principle that no offense against property alone should be punishable by death, for which the reformers had long contended, was at last implemented. In the same year a motion in the House of Commons seeking the abolition of the death penalty for all crimes "save those of actual murder" failed by a single vote. By 1839 the only offenses still subject to the death penalty were treason, riot, arson of naval ships and of naval and military stores, murder and other offenses involving attempts on or risks to life, rape, buggery, sexual intercourse with girls under ten years of age, and robbery and burglary when accompanied by personal violence—much the same list as that proposed by Eden in 1771. Rape ceased to be a capital crime in 1840.

The opposition of twelve of the fifteen judges notwithstanding, Russell also carried in 1836 a bill that allowed counsel or solicitor (attorney) representing a defendant charged with a felony to address the jury on his behalf. (Previously he might only examine and cross-examine witnesses.) The law and practice governing proceedings before magistrates (both committal proceedings and summary trial), however, remained in its unreformed state until John Jervis, as attorney general, took the matter in hand, piloting through Parliament in 1848 and 1849 three statutes that laid down basic procedures and procedural standards for those jurisdictions. This reform made it politically possible to increase the number of minor offenses that might be tried summarily (a process inaugurated by the Criminal Justice Act, 1855, 18 & 19 Vict., c. 126) and, as a consequence, the number of offenders who were in fact prosecuted. And in 1847 the first step was taken toward creating a separate jurisdiction for young offenders, when it was provided that children under fourteen (after 1850, under sixteen) charged with simple larceny could be tried summarily with their parents' consent. This procedure was extended to all offenses, other than homicide, in 1879, but it was not until 1908 that juvenile courts, held at different times from those for adults, were established.

The criminal law commissioners, 1833–1849

The different shifts and compromises made when the death penalty was removed from various offenses had left the law governing maximum penalties for serious crimes in a chaotic state. This led Lord Brougham, lord chancellor in Earl Grey's ministry, and another of Bentham's friends and disciples, in 1833 to initiate what proved to be the first of three projects for the codification of English criminal law. (The second, initiated by James Fitzjames Stephen, was to come before Parliament between 1877 and 1881; the third, initiated by the Law Commission in 1967, is still notionally continuing.) A royal commission, composed of five practicing lawyers, was appointed to "digest into one statute all the enactments concerning crimes, their trial and punishment, and to digest into another statute all the provisions of the Common Law touching the same; and to enquire and report how far it might be expedient to combine both these statutes into one body of the Criminal Law, repealing all other statutory provisions; or how far it might be expedient to pass into law the first mentioned of these statutes." This was a mammoth assignment, but it was completed in a little over ten years, despite the commissioners' work on their principal task being interrupted by requests from Lord John Russell to consider and report on the special question of the right of counsel for a prisoner to address the jury in felony cases. He also asked the commissioners to consider which offenses should continue to incur capital punishment (*Second Report* (1836), which formed the basis for Russell's legislation on these matters), and procedures for the trial of juvenile offenders (*Third Report* (1837), which was applied, as noted above, to charges of simple larceny in 1847, but not to all other offenses until 1879).

The commission's *First Report* (1834) considered the need for codification and the best way of achieving it. It contained a draft digest, with a commentary, of the law of theft—as complicated and difficult a subject as any in the criminal law. As a result of this report, the commissioners' terms of reference were widened to include recommendations as to "what partial alterations may be necessary or expedient for more simply and completely defining crimes and punishments and for the more effective administration of criminal justice." That is, the commissioners were authorized to make recommendations for the reform, as well as the restatement, of the criminal law. In the ensuing years they accordingly reported (with draft legislation) on homicide, offenses against the person, theft, fraud, and criminal damage (*Fourth Report* (1839)); on burglary, offenses against the executive power and the administration of justice, forgery, and offenses against the public peace (*Fifth Report* (1840)); and on treason and other offenses against the state and religion, libel, coinage offenses, and offenses against the revenue (*Sixth Report* (1843)). The *Seventh Report* also contained a complete draft code of the substantive criminal law, revising the digests contained in previous reports, and was complemented in the *Eighth Report* (1845) by a draft code of criminal procedure.

The royal commission's eight reports contain the most thorough and principled examination of English criminal law ever made by an official body. The commissioners recommended many reforms that were ultimately to reach the statute book, though it was more than one hundred years before the felony-murder rule (under which a death accidentally caused while committing a felony amounted to murder) and of the distinction between a felony and a misdemeanor, and theft based on an appropriation rather than a taking and carrying away. They succeeded in producing codes that combined in legislative form the rules of both the common and the statutory law of crime. These codes would, therefore, have ended the judges' freedom to extend the criminal law to include any conduct of which they disapproved. Equally importantly, the commissioners, utilitarians to a man, followed Livingston's example and offered a classification of offenses that sought to reflect their relative gravity in an elaborate scheme of graduated penalties. To be justified punishments, they believed, must deter, and the graver the crime the greater the deterrent needed to be. They would, moreover, not deter unless they were imposed uniformly, not erratically. Had it been accepted, this classification would have considerably reduced judicial discretion in sentencing, which had by now replaced the mixture of rigidity and arbitrariness that had characterized the eighteenth century law. In an appendix to the *Fourth Report* (1839), the commissioners demonstrated that, leaving aside death and various obsolete penalties, forty different penalties were provided for felonies and ninety-six for misdemeanors. In the commission's *Seventh Report* (1843), only forty-five classes of punishment were specified. The number was reduced to thirteen by the revising commissioners (see below) in their *Second Report* (1846); it rose to thirty-one in their *Third Report* (1847), but finally dropped to eighteen in their *Fourth Report* (1849).

The draft code of substantive criminal law was introduced as a bill in the House of Lords by Lord Brougham in 1844 but it was withdrawn when the lord chancellor, Lord Lyndhurst, announced the appointment of a new royal commission to reconsider and revise it. This commission, which included three of the five 1833 commissioners, published five reports between 1845 and 1849 that recommended further reforms and revisions—but no radical alterations—in their predecessors' draft. The revised code of substantive law, which was published in the *Fourth Report* (1848), was introduced into the House of Lords in the same year by Lord Brougham, and referred to a select committee. Its report led to division of the draft code that was submitted to Parliament piecemeal. The Criminal Law Amendment (No. 1) Bill, dealing with the general principles of liability, defenses, homicide, and offenses against the person, was accordingly prepared and given a second reading by the House of Lords in 1853. A second bill, dealing with larceny and other offenses of dishonesty, was also tabled. Lord Cranworth, who had recently become lord chancellor, circulated these bills to the judges, seeking their comments. He asked in particular whether the policy of bringing the whole of the criminal law—statutory and common law—into one statute (that is, codification, not merely consolidation) was likely to be beneficial to the administration of criminal justice. The judges' replies showed them ready to concede the advantages of further consolidation, but unanimously opposed to reducing the common law to statutory form. As one judge put it, "to reduce unwritten law to statute is to discard one of the great blessings we have for ages enjoyed in rules capable of flexible application"; according to another, it was "inadvisable to lose the advantage of the power of applying the principles of the common law to new offenses, and combinations of circumstances, arising from time to time."

In the face of this adverse judicial reaction, the bills were not reintroduced. It was decided that the draftsman (C.S. Greaves, Q.C.) should confine himself to producing consolidating statutes that would replace Peel's acts, which were now obsolescent as a result, first, of the removal of the death penalty for many offenses in the 1830s and, second, of the abolition—by the Penal Servitude Act, 1857, 20 & 21 Vict., c. 3—of the

sentences of transportation that had taken the place of capital punishment. The latter reform, which had been urged by Eden in 1771, as well as by many subsequent publicists, had been strongly recommended by Molesworth's Select Committee in 1838. Six of these consolidating statutes were enacted in 1861. Since the 1840s only murderers had been executed (and by no means all of them), so this legislation brought the law into line with practice. The death penalty was retained only for murder, treason, and arson of naval vessels. Seven years later, public executions came to an end, when the Capital Punishment Amendment Act (1868) provided that executions should take place within the prison in which the prisoner was confined.

Substantial parts of two of the 1861 acts (the Accessories and Abettors Act and the Offences against the Person Act) still remain in force. The other four lasted well into the twentieth century: the Larceny Act until 1916, the Malicious Damage Act until 1971, the Forgery Act until 1913, and the Coinage Offences Act until 1936. Sexual offenses, many of which had been included in the Offences against the Person Act, were not consolidated again until 1956. In some of these twentieth-century statutes the draftsman was at last allowed to incorporate statutory formulations of some of the common law rules without provoking a howl of protest from the judiciary. Most notably, definitions of the offenses were incorporated in the Larceny Act (1916), the Forgery Act (1913), and the Perjury Act (1911). However, other statutes, such as the Sexual Offences Act of 1956, were merely consolidating statutes that presupposed, but did not state, the common law rules. This legislation, although a small step forward, was still, therefore, a long way from the codification recommended by the criminal law commissioners in 1834.

The Indian Penal Code, 1835–1860

While the criminal law commissioners were at work on a code for England, Macaulay, who had gone to India in 1834 to be the law member of the governor-general's council, was drafting a penal code that was intended to apply to the entire population—native and expatriate—of British India. Instructions were issued to four commissioners in June 1835, but because of the illnesses and absences of the others, Macaulay was virtually the sole author of the draft that he submitted in October 1837 to the governor-general, Lord Auckland. The governor-general maintained the Eden family's interests in the criminal law that he had demonstrated when promoting the Coinage Offences Bill in England in 1832. Macaulay's code was a most able piece of drafting, "the first specimen," as Stephen said, "of an entirely new and original method of legislative expression" (1883, p. 299). The work of a master of English prose, the code was concise, lucid, and free of legal jargon. It paid careful attention to the degree of fault required for each offense, and was accompanied by a well-argued introduction and set of notes. Influenced by the thinking of Bentham and John Austin (1790–1859), as well as by the *First Report* (1834) of the English commissioners (in which they had outlined their program for codification), the substance, but not the language, of Macaulay's code was to a large extent an improved version of the English law of the 1830s. He also, however, drew on Edward Livingston's code for Louisiana and on the French Code Pénal, for he was not under the restraints that forced the English commissioners to restate as closely as possible the existing law, and to justify any departure from it.

Despite, or because of, its virtues, Macaulay's draft had a very hostile reception from the contemporary Indian judiciary (composed of English lawyers doing a tour of duty abroad). It was not enacted until 1860, in the aftermath of the Indian Mutiny of 1857, with amendments that were by no means all improvements, and came into force in 1862. The code worked well, and is still law in India, Pakistan, Sri Lanka, and northern Nigeria (and, until recently, the Sudan) having been adopted while these latter territories were under the jurisdiction or influence of the British Colonial office. It also strongly influenced the second attempt—Stephen's—to provide England with a code of criminal law.

Stephen's codes, 1877–1883

James Fitzjames Stephen served in India as law member of the governor-general's council from 1869 to 1872, and was involved in the revision of the Criminal Procedure Code and the passing of the Indian Evidence Act of 1872 and the Indian Contract Act of the same year. He was much impressed by the Penal Code. "To compare [it] to English criminal law," he wrote on his return, "is like comparing cosmos with chaos." Shortly after his return to England, Stephen joined in the drafting of the Homicide Law Amendment Bill, which offered a statutory definition of murder, abolished the felony-murder rule, and made infanticide a lesser offense than murder. This bill was introduced in Parliament in August 1872. It was reintroduced in May 1874 and referred to a select committee, where it was to founder. Although the committee agreed that a redefinition of murder was "urgently needed," it found the judiciary very critical of the bill.

In particular, the Lord Chief Justice, Alexander Cockburn, although professing himself a strong supporter of codification (and, if so, the first chief justice of whom this could be said), argued that the "partial and imperfect codification" of the bill, which included clauses dealing with the insanity defense, necessity, and the presumption of intention, applying only to homicide cases, would be fatal to the prospects of a complete code (Stephen, 1877, p. v). Stephen responded to this challenge by publishing in 1877 *A Digest of the Criminal Law (Crimes and Punishments)*, in which he showed the form that a complete code might take, and outlined a program for the reform of the criminal law which has still scarcely been traveled beyond. Modeled on the Indian Code, and in marked contrast to the Criminal Law Commissioners' bills, the *Digest* was a masterly condensation of a mass of law into manageable form. As a result, Lord Cairns, the lord chancellor, later that year instructed Stephen to draft two bills: one a penal code, the other a code of criminal procedure. The first was introduced into Parliament as the Criminal Code (Indictable Offences) Bill in May 1878, and was sufficiently well received to be referred to a royal commission composed of three judges (two English and one Irish) and Stephen himself. The commission was to consider and report on the bill and also to suggest any other alterations in the existing law or procedure that seemed desirable, it being recognized that Parliament itself could not give the bill the detailed technical legal scrutiny required.

The commission sat daily from November 1878 to May 1879, discussing, according to Stephen, "every line of and nearly every word of each section" of the two bills. Although it added 127 sections to Stephen's draft (in particular, detailed provisions concerning the use of force in self-defense, defense of property, and the prevention of crime), the royal commission agreed to recommend to Parliament both the principle of codification and a revised bill. This was a considerable achievement, especially since the commission's chairman, Lord Blackburn, the most eminent judge of the day, had previously been opposed to codification.

The Criminal Code Bill had its first two readings in the House of Commons in April and May 1879, but no third reading that session. It was reintroduced in February 1880, but there was a change of government in April of that year, and although the part of the code dealing with criminal procedure was announced as a government measure in the Queen's Speech in both 1882 and 1883, Parliament's time and attention were dominated by the struggle for Irish home rule. Consequently, nothing further was done to secure the code's enactment. Since it not only consolidated and codified the existing law but also included a considerable number of reforms, its passage through Parliament would almost certainly have been controverted and, therefore, time-consuming.

The fact that Lord Chief Justice Cockburn was again highly critical (on the ground that even this code was incomplete, because it omitted some obsolescent statutory offenses, as well as all summary ones) inevitably cast a shadow. However, Cockburn's objections were easily answered by Stephen, and they need not have proved fatal to the code if parliamentary time had been made available for its consideration. More significantly, perhaps, the Statute Law Committee, which had been established in 1868 to promote statutory consolidation and revision, favored a more gradual program of reform and consolidation. In addition, doubts came to be felt about the quality of Stephen's drafting, and comparisons (not to Stephen's advantage) were drawn with the code that R.S. Wright had drafted between 1874 and 1877 for the colony of Jamaica to be a model, or so the Colonial Office hoped, for the rest of the empire.

Among the changes envisaged by Stephen's code that had to wait many years before they were finally effected were (1) abolition of the felony/misdemeanor distinction (first recommended in 1839 but implemented only in 1967); (2) abolition of the felony-murder rule (recommended in 1839 and implemented in 1957); (3) allowing words as well as acts to constitute provocation, reducing an intentional killing from murder to manslaughter (implemented in 1957); (4) the coalescence of larceny and the other offenses of dishonest appropriation in a single offense of theft (achieved in 1968); (5) abolition of the defense of marital coercion (still surviving); (6) allowing the defendant always to be competent witness at his own trial (implemented in 1898); and (7) establishment of a court of criminal appeal (a bill for which was first introduced in 1844 and which was finally implemented in 1907, after a protracted public campaign).

The public debate over Stephen's code showed that the judges were no longer opposed to codification in principle, as they had been in the 1850s. But the fact that the project was allowed to lapse reveals how little concerned they or the profession were that the law should, as Cockburn had put it, "be suffered to remain in its present state of confusion, arising from its being partly unwritten and partly in statutes so imperfectly drawn as to be almost worse than unwritten law" (Stephen, 1877, p. v). In 1901 Courtney Ilbert, the principal government draftsman, lamented that "it was impossible to view . . . without a certain degree of humiliation, the entire cessation during recent years of any effort to improve the form of English Law, and the apathy with which that cessation has been regarded" (p. 162). He observed that the lack of a criminal code and a code of criminal procedure "produced practical and substantial inconveniences." Revised versions of Stephen's codes were, however, adopted in Canada, New Zealand, Queensland, Western Australia, many of the British territories in East and West Africa, Cyprus, and Palestine, and proved quite satisfactory.

Royal commissions and departmental and select committees, 1900–1960

The first half of the twentieth century saw very few reforms in the criminal law. Such attention as was given to problems of criminal justice centered on the conditions and effects of—and alternatives to—imprisonment, and especially on ways of dealing with young and first offenders. As far as the criminal law itself was concerned, apart from the already-mentioned revisions of the 1861 acts and the consolidation of statutory offenses of perjury (which, being misdemeanors, had not previously been undertaken), the most important pieces of legislation were the act that established the Court of Criminal Appeal in 1907 (Criminal Appeal Act, 1907, 7 Edw. 7, c. 23 and the Indictments Act, 1915, 5 & 6 Geo. 5, c. 90), which effected a very substantial simplification in the form of indictments. All these statutes were sponsored by the reforming Liberal government that took office in 1906. Its principal reforms were, however, directed at other aspects of English life, politics, and law. For the rest, royal commissions and departmental and select committees were from time to time established to consider particular matters. Their recommendations were rarely implemented, and then only after considerable delay.

Among the chief of these bodies was the Departmental Committee on Insanity and Crime (1922), whose report, recommending widening the insanity defense to include cases of "irresistible impulse" (a meaningless phrase), was put aside after ten of the twelve King's Bench judges said they were opposed to its proposals. (A new offense of infanticide, punishable as manslaughter rather than murder, committed by the mentally disordered mother who killed her newly born child—a reform recommended by the 1866 Royal Commission on Capital Punishment—was, however, created.) Others were the Select Committee on Insanity and Crime (1930), the Departmental Committee on Sexual Offences against Young Persons (1925), and the Interdepartmental Committee on Abortion (1939). The Royal Commission on Betting, Lotteries and Gaming (1951) resulted in the Betting, Gaming and Lotteries Act, 1963, c. 2; the Royal Commission on Capital Punishment (1953), in the Homicide Act, 1957, 5 & 6 Eliz. 2, c. 11; the Select Committee on Obscenity (1958), in the Obscene Publications Act, 1959, 7 & 8 Eliz. 2, c. 66; and the Departmental Committee on Homosexual Offences and Prostitution (1957), in the Sexual Offences Act, 1967, c. 60, and the Street Offences Act, 1959, 7 & 8 Eliz. 2, c. 57.

This list shows that in the 1950s, after the interruptions and dislocations caused by two world wars and a major economic recession, there was a long-overdue revival of public interest in the need to reform the criminal law so that it would be less out of accord with contemporary standards and expectations. (Another sign was the foundation in 1957 of JUSTICE, the British section of the International Commission of Jurists, which has produced a valuable series of reports drawing attention to defects in criminal law and procedure, and proposed many reforms.) But all this interest was confined to very specific matters. The concern shown by the nineteenth-century reformers for the principles that should govern the criminal law, and for its overall structure, was absent.

Thus, when the Royal Commission on Capital Punishment returned to problems that had occupied the criminal law commissioners in the 1830s and the royal commission of 1866, its terms of reference were limited to considering ways in which the incidence of capital punishment might be restricted: it was not asked to say

whether capital punishment should be retained. The commission accordingly recommended (and the Homicide Act of 1957 implemented) the abolition of the felony-murder rule, the widening of the defense of provocation to include provocative words, and the creation of two new forms of manslaughter in cases where the intentional killer was mentally disordered (but not insane) or had acted in pursuance of a suicide pact. The commission recommended that degrees of murder (of which only the first would carry the death penalty) should not be introduced, but this recommendation was rejected by the Conservative government, which, in an attempt to stymie the campaign for the total abolition of capital punishment, distinguished in the 1957 act between capital and noncapital murders. This distinction quickly proved to be so unacceptable that it was discarded in 1965, when the death penalty for murder was suspended for an experimental period of five years, a suspension made permanent in 1970. The Homicide Act of 1957, did not, however, include a statutory definition of murder (or any other homicidal offense). There was, consequently, the astonishing spectacle of the definition of murder, still a matter of common law, being the subject of no less than six appeals to the House of Lords within the next forty years (*Director of Public Prosecutions v. Smith* [1961] A.C. 290; *Hyam v. Director of Public Prosecutions* [1975] A.C. 55; *Regina v. Cunningham* [1982] A.C. 566; *Regina v. Moloney* [1985] A.C. 905; *Regina v. Hancock* [1986] A.C. 455; *Regina v. Woollin* [1998] 4 All E.R. 103 (H.L.)).

The Criminal Law Revision Committee 1959–1986

The most important manifestation of the revival of interest in criminal law reform during the 1950s was the establishment in 1959 (by Home Secretary R. A. Butler, largely at the instigation of Glanville Williams, the leading academic writer on English criminal law) of a standing Criminal Law Revision Committee. It was "to examine such aspects of the criminal law of England and Wales as the Home Secretary may from time to time refer to the Committee, to consider whether the law requires revision and to make recommendations" (*First Report*, Cmd. 835, 1959, p. 3). (The standing Law Revision Committee, first appointed by the lord chancellor in 1934 and reconstituted as the Law Reform Committee in 1952, had never considered any aspect of criminal law.)

The Criminal Law Revision Committee always included three of four senior judges, one or two circuit judges, the chief London stipendiary magistrate, and the director of public prosecutions, as well as several practicing and one or two academic lawyers. It thus maintained the convention, recognized since the eighteenth century, that the government should sponsor only those reforms in the criminal law that had the support of the judiciary. The committee produced eighteen reports on specific matters, of which the most important were the seventh (Cmnd. 2659, 1965) recommending the abolition of the felony/misdemeanor distinction (implemented in 1967); the eighth (Cmnd. 2977, 1966), on theft and related offenses (implemented in 1968); the eleventh (Cmnd. 4991, 72), proposing many important changes in the law of evidence; the fourteenth (Cmnd. 7844, 1980), on offenses against the person, including homicide; and the fifteenth (Cmnd. 9213, 1984), on sexual offenses.

As might be expected from its composition and sponsoring department, the committee adopted a very pragmatic approach to its work (Glanville Williams inspired almost all of it, but he was far from being always successful in getting his ideas accepted). It eschewed all interest not only in codification but also in restating the common law in statutory form, and its reports showed a readiness to retain common law rules whose vagueness and uncertainty ("flexibility") was their chief attraction. Until the advent in 1979 of Mrs. Thatcher's conservative government the Home Office was, accordingly, usually ready to promote legislation giving effect to the committee's recommendations, though on the only occasion when radical proposals for rationalization and reform were made (in the eleventh report, on the law of evidence) it took fright after just one of many recommendations attracted a great deal of (ill-informed) criticism. This recommendation (to invite the drawing of inferences about the veracity of a defense which the defendant had failed to mention when first questioned by the police) had, therefore, to wait for more than twenty years before being implemented (by sections 34–38 of the Criminal Justice and Public Order Act 1994) though others were taken up when occasion offered, notably in the Police and Criminal Evidence Act 1984.

The Thatcher government was hostile to royal commissions and departmental committees, which had continued to flourish as a means of finding solutions to controversial issues from which governments wished to distance themselves. Its immediate predecessors had remitted the law relating to official secrets (1972), contempt of court (1974), abortion (1974), obscenity (1979), and pretrial criminal procedure (1981) to them. These bodies were now portrayed as slow and cumbersome: their real vice was that their members could not be required, as civil servants could be, to do ministers' bidding, who in turn were embarrassed by having to explain their failure to act on the advice they had been given. The Criminal Law Revision Committee was not, however, formally abolished: it was simply starved to death by not having further subjects referred to it. The Public Order Act 1986, a tawdry piece of lawmaking, which replaced the common law offences of riot, affray, and unlawful assembly with statutory substitutes, was produced without the committee's help.

The Law Commission, 1966 to present

The Law Commission, having been created by statute, could not be so easily disregarded: no government could be heard to say that the law was not in need of reform. It is a permanent governmental agency, composed of five lawyer commissioners (one of whom, in practice the chairman, must be a judge). It was established at the instigation of Lord Gardiner, lord chancellor in the labor government that came to office in 1964, who was convinced that too much of the law was in need of reform for the task to be left to commissions and committees appointed ad hoc. The Law Commissions Act, 1965, c. 22 (there is another commission for Scotland) places the commissioners under a duty "to take and keep under review all the law . . . with a view to its systematic development and reform, including in particular the codification of such law." In 1967, after Home Secretary Roy Jenkins had stated that in the government's view there was a pressing need for codification of the criminal law to begin, the commission included in its second program of law reform "a comprehensive examination of the Criminal Law with a view to its codification."

Since the commission has a responsibility to keep "all the law" (not just the criminal law) under review, it has devoted only a small proportion of its attention and staff to this work. Between 1967 and 1973 a working party (subcommittee) investigated the general principles governing criminal liability. (Here, too, Glanville Williams was the leading spirit.) It published several working papers (discussion documents) on particular matters, including the mental element in crime, inchoate offenses, the liability of accomplices, and defenses. These working papers, which were to a considerable extent modeled on, and influenced by, the tentative drafts prepared for the American Law Institute's Model Penal Code between 1952 and 1962, set out not so much to restate the existing law in statutory form, as to consider what the best rule on each point would be. This proved, however, to be too ambitious a project, and was discontinued.

The commission has nonetheless gone on to publish a series of reports recommending legislation on both the general principles of liability and the definitions of particular offenses. These include reports on the mental element in crime (1978), the inchoate offenses of conspiracy (1976) and attempt (1980), defenses of general application (1977), and the law's territorial extent (1978), as well as on the offenses of criminal damage (1970), forgery and counterfeiting (1973), and interfering with the course of justice (1979). These proposals although made piecemeal, and poorly coordinated (both with one another and with the contemporaneous work of the Criminal Law Revision Committee), were intended to ease the work of codification, for which the elimination of the remaining common law offenses and the statutory statement of the general part of the criminal law are essential prerequisites. The Home Office showed little interest in them. Only four reports were implemented by legislation (some of it badly drafted): those relating to criminal damage (in 1971), conspiracy (in 1977), attempt (in 1981), and forgery (also in 1981); while the common law offenses continued to expand under cover of the rubrics of "public nuisance," "conspiracy to defraud," and "outraging public decency."

In 1981, in order to give fresh impetus to its codification program, the Law Commission appointed a team of four academic lawyers "(1) to consider and make proposals in relation to—(a) the aims and objects of a criminal code; (b) its nature and scope; (c) its content, structure and the interrelation of its parts; (d) the method and style of its drafting; and (2) to formulate, in a manner appropriate to such a code—(a) the general principles that should govern liability under it; (b) a standard terminology to be used in it; (c) the rules which should govern its interpretation." Their report, with a draft bill governing the general principles of liability and (as an exemplar) offenses against the person was published in 1985 (Law Com. No. 143) and subsequently scru-

tinized by regional groups of judges and practicing lawyers before the commission itself published a revised, and more pusillanimous, version in 1989 (Law Com. No. 177).

All this work had proceeded on the (academically orthodox) basis that criminal liability ought to fall only on those who were aware that they were doing, or risking doing, what was forbidden, and that no one should be punished for causing harms that they had not actually foreseen. The intellectual climate was, however, changing and these assumptions were beginning to be challenged: retribution, as well as deterrence and rehabilitation, was once again being considered a proper function of criminal sanctions, and punishing people for causing more harm than they had contemplated, or for being careless, was no longer regarded as self-evidently unjust or unmerited. The 1989 draft code was also criticized for the selective and inconsistent way in which it incorporated certain reforms: changes in the law were, it was suggested, being smuggled in as part of a codification package without adequate public and parliamentary discussion. Doubts were also expressed as to whether all the time and effort required for the pursuit of the codifiers' ultimately unattainable goals of accessibility, comprehensibility, consistency, and certainty might not be better devoted to the many particular rules that needed reforming.

The commission appears to have felt the force of these criticisms. While not formally abandoning its objective of producing a code, it announced in 1992 that it would seek to (redraft and) "legislate the code" in installments: which is self-contradictory. Even very small installments have been slow in coming (Offenses against the Person and General Principles (1993; revised and curtailed by the Home Office 1998); Conspiracy to Defraud (1994); Intoxication and Criminal Liability (1995); Involuntary Manslaughter (1996); Misuse of Trade Secrets (1997); Corruption (1999)), and as of 2000, none had resulted in legislation. In 1992 the House of Lords' Appeal Committee endorsed a judicial foray into the field of law reform: the abolition of the centuries-old rule that a husband could not be convicted of raping his wife. And in 1998 the Lord Chief Justice, Lord Bingham, was to be heard asking whether England must wait for ever for a criminal code. These were remarkable instances of role reversal.

P. R. GLAZEBROOK

See also COMPARATIVE CRIMINAL LAW AND ENFORCE-MENT: ENGLAND AND WALES.

BIBLIOGRAPHY

BINGHAM, LORD. "A Criminal Code: Must We Wait for Ever?" *Criminal Law Review* (1998): 694–696.

BLACKSTONE, WILLIAM. *Commentaries on the Laws of England* (1765–1769). Vol. 4. Reprint. Chicago: University of Chicago Press, 1979.

COKE, EDWARD. *The Third Part of the Institutes of the Laws of England: Concerning High Treason, and Other Pleas of the Crown, and Criminal Causes* (1641). London: E. & R. Brooke, 1797.

CORNISH, WILLIAM R., et al. *Crime and Law in Nineteenth Century Britain*. Introduction by P. Ford and G. Ford. Dublin: Irish University Press, 1978. Contains full bibliographic information concerning parliamentary and governmental reports and papers referred to in this article.

Criminal Law Revision Committee. *Reports*. London: Her Majesty's Stationery Office, 1959–1986. Eighteen reports were issued by the committee; the most important of them are described in this article.

CROSS, RUPERT. "The Making of English Law: Macaulay." *Criminal Law Review* (1978): 519–528.

———. "The Making of English Law: Sir James Fitzjames Stephen." *Criminal Law Review* (1978): 652–661.

DE BURCA, G., and GARDNER, S. "The Codification of the Criminal Law." *Oxford Journal of Legal Studies* 10 (1990): 559–571.

EDEN, WILLIAM. *Principles of Penal Law*. London: White, 1771.

FRIEDLAND, M. L. "R. S. Wright's Model Criminal Code." *Oxford Journal of Legal Studies* 1 (1981): 307–346.

GARDNER, GERALD and CURTIS-RALEIGH, NIGEL. "The Judicial Attitude to Penal Reform." *Law Quarterly Review* 65 (1949): 196–219.

GLAZEBROOK, P. R., ed. *Reshaping the Criminal Law: Essays in Honour of Glanville Williams*. London: Stevens, 1978. The essays by Cross, Hodgson, and Spencer are especially relevant.

GLAZEBROOK, P. R. "Still No Code! English Criminal Law 1894–1994." In *City University Centenary Lectures in Law*. Edited by M. Dockray. London: Blackstone Press, 1996.

HALE, MATTHEW. *The History of the Pleas of the Crown* (1685; first publication, 1736). 2 vols. Edited by W. A. Stokes and E. Ingersoll. Philadelphia: Small, 1847.

HAWKINS, WILLIAMS. *Pleas of the Crown* (1716–1721). 8th ed. Edited by J. Curwood. London: Butterworth, 1824.

HOSTETTLER, J. *The Politics of Criminal Law Reform in the Nineteenth Century*. Chichester, U.K.: B. Rose, 1992.

ILBERT, C. P. *Legislative Methods and Forms*. Oxford, U.K.: Clarendon Press, 1901.

Justice (Society). *Annual Report*. London: The Society, annually.

KADISH, SANFORD H. "Codifiers of the Criminal Law: Wechsler's Predecessors." *Columbia Law Review* 78 (1978): 1098–1144.

Law Commission. *Annual Report*. London: Her Majesty's Stationery Office, annually.

PHILLIPSON, COLEMAN. *Three Criminal Law Reformers: Beccaria, Bentham, Romilly*. New York: Dutton, 1923.

RADZINOWICZ, LEON. *A History of English Criminal Law and Its Administration from 1750*. Vols. 1, 4, and 5. London: Stevens, 1948, 1968, 1986.

ROMILLY, SAMUEL. *Observations on the Criminal Law of England as It Relates to Capital Punishments, and on the Mode in Which it is Administered*. 3d ed. London: Cadell & Davies, 1813.

SMITH, J. C. *Codification of the Criminal Law*. London: Child Co. Lecture, 1986.

STEPHEN, JAMES FITZJAMES. *A History of the Criminal Law of England*. Vol. 3. London: Macmillan. 1883.

———. "Introduction." *A Digest of the Criminal Law (Crimes and Punishments)*. London: Macmillan, 1877. This introduction is absent from later editions.

WILLIAMS, GLANVILLE. "The Reform of the Criminal Law and of Its Administration." *Journal of the Society of Public Teachers of Law* 4 (1958): 217–230.

———. "The Work of Criminal Law Reform." *Journal of the Society of Public Teachers of Law* 13 (1975): 183–198.

———, ed. *The Reform of the Law*. London: Gollancz, 1951.

CRIMINAL LAW REFORM: HISTORICAL DEVELOPMENT IN THE UNITED STATES

Introduction

It is an incontrovertible fact that the law of crimes has historically suffered from a kind of malign neglect in America. In other branches of the law, from the beginning there has been a tradition of willingness, if not eagerness, on the part of judges, legislators, and legal commentators to examine basic premises and to promote doctrinal change if they thought society required it. But the dominant attitude of the American legal profession toward the penal law seems in general to have been that if it needed improvement, it would somehow improve itself. It is not surprising, therefore, that the criminal law long remained one of the least developed, most confused, and, in a sense, most primitive bodies of American law.

There are, to be sure, several significant exceptions to this general rule of neglect. From time to time in American history there have been bursts of interest in criminal jurisprudence, and reformers have arisen who have sought in one way or another to humanize the criminal law, to modernize it, or perhaps only to introduce a measure of clarity into it. These efforts have varied enormously in inspiration, in scope, and in caliber, and they have had varying impacts on the course of legal developments. But they have all represented a recognition of the crucial importance of the law of crimes and a readiness to come to grips with at least some of its inherent problems. As such, they stand out as bright landmarks in what is otherwise a rather gray landscape.

This article surveys the checkered history of criminal law reform in America. The principal emphasis is on the substantive penal law, by which is meant also the law governing the treatment of criminal offenders. However, there are some observations as well on attempts that have been made to reform criminal procedure and the administration of justice.

The colonial period

The New England colonies. It is appropriate to begin a discussion of the history of criminal law reform with the colonial period since that era witnessed the first efforts at improvement. All of the American colonies drew principally on the jurisprudence and laws of the mother country in fashioning their criminal law. Obviously, small bands of colonial settlers, few of them with any legal training, do not fabricate criminal codes out of nothing, but from the beginning, the colonists displayed a willingness to experiment with alterations in the English inheritance if their own values seemed to call for them. In the very first body of laws promulgated in British North America, the Plymouth Code of 1636, a notable divergence from the English model in the punishment of serious crimes was already apparent. Although the list of capital offenses in England was long and comprehended almost all serious misdeeds, the death penalty in Plymouth was limited to treason, murder, arson, and several morals offenses. One should not attach too much importance to this document, since it was a rudimentary code of laws in many respects and Plymouth was a tiny settlement that was destined soon to fade into insignificance. Still, its modifications in the criminal law signaled a trend that was later to be followed by other colonies.

A much more sophisticated document than the Plymouth Code, *The Laws and Liberties of Massachusetts* (1648), embodied in addition major changes in the common and statutory criminal law of the mother country. It, too, reduced the number of capital offenses, and in general prescribed more lenient penalties for noncapital offenses than did English law. Its general prohibition against "cruel and barbarous" punishments was itself an innovation. The inspiration for the whole code came as much from the Old Testament as from the English common law. Deuteronomy and other parts of the Pentateuch were repeatedly cited in justification of penal provisions, and this reliance on the Bible had the net effect of making the code less sanguinary than it might have been. Only those offenses for which Scripture clearly prescribed death were made capital offenses. The code included several significant improvements in criminal procedure as well. Conviction of a capital crime required the testimony of two witnesses (this requirement, too, was rooted in Scripture), and appeal was a matter of right in all capital cases.

Besides the inspiration of Scripture, *The Laws and Liberties of Massachusetts* was pervaded by a spirit of rationality and a healthy distaste for the many accidental features of English criminal jurisprudence. The device of benefit of clergy, for example, was perceived—accurately—as a result of historical accident, having no foundation in Scripture or reason, and as such was excluded from the code.

The significance of these New England criminal codes, especially that of Massachusetts Bay, lies as much in the fact that they were codes as it does in the modifications which they made in individual provisions of English penal law. Underlying the codes was the strong belief that the criminal law of a community was too important to be allowed to grow up piecemeal, as, in the opinion of many of these Puritan settlers, had been the case with the English common law.

Rather, it was something that ought to be crafted systematically and with deliberation to reflect the deepest moral sense of the community and to further the social purposes for which the community existed This insight was unfortunately lost sight of in later years.

The Pennsylvania experiment. Although the criminal law of the American colonies was in general less sanguinary than that of the mother country, it was certainly no less retributive, and was very harsh by any modern standards. Crime and sin were virtually identical in the colonial mind. The criminal was seen as a free moral agent, and punishment was justified as a kind of social revenge or a species of divinely ordained, if humanly implemented, retribution. Schedules of punishments were little more than crude attempts to proportion the penalty to the sinfulness of the offense, and virtually no attention was paid to the individual circumstances of the offender. Exhibiting a very different spirit, however, were the penal laws enacted by Pennsylvania colony in the closing decades of the seventeenth century. There, between 1682 and 1718, a most remarkable experiment in criminal law reform was undertaken under the aegis of William Penn and other Quaker notables. Although it came to an unhappy end, it planted seeds that were later to bear fruit.

One year after it was established by William Penn under a royal charter, Pennsylvania enacted a complete code of criminal laws—part of a larger codification known as the Great Law of 1682—that was quite unlike anything that had gone before it. The Quaker founders of the colony were opposed in principle to cruelty, to gratuitous bloodshed, and, barring the most unusual conditions, to the taking of human life. They were repelled by the existing English system of penal sanctions and felt compelled to look for alternatives. The alternative they found was the prison. In their code, imprisonment at hard labor or imprisonment coupled with a fine was the prescribed penalty for all crimes save willful and premeditated murder, the length of imprisonment varying according to the offense and the circumstances surrounding its commission. The terms of confinement were in general not severe. Thus, burglary was punishable by three months' imprisonment and quadruple restitution to the victim. Arson merited a year at hard labor and corporal punishment (usually whipping) according to the discretion of the court. Assault on a magistrate was punishable by a month's confinement. Common assault and battery, as well as manslaughter, were to be punished according to the nature and circumstances of the acts in question. In contrast to the rather mild sanctions accruing to these crimes, sex offenses were sternly dealt with in the Quaker code. Bigamy, for example, was punishable by life imprisonment upon first commission, and rape, upon second conviction.

Another remarkable feature of the Pennsylvania code was its approach to religious offenses—a popular category of offense in the criminal law of most jurisdictions. These kinds of crimes were completely abolished, and full freedom of conscience was assured to all inhabitants.

The Pennsylvania code of 1682 represented Quaker criminal jurisprudence at its purest. In the next three decades the colony's criminal law was modified by a series of legislative enactments and became somewhat severer. More offenses were made punishable by imprisonment, prison terms became longer, and harsh corporal punishments such as branding were introduced for certain crimes. Yet even after these alterations, Pennsylvania's criminal law remained a model of enlightenment and humanity in comparison with that of its neighbors. In 1718, however, the Quaker experiment came to an abrupt end. The colony had for some time been pressing the Crown to allow Quakers to testify on affirmation rather than on oath, and the Crown had been seeking to bring the colony's criminal law into closer conformity with that of the mother country. A bargain was struck under which Quakers received recognition for affirmation in exchange for the colony's agreement to substitute the English criminal law for its own.

The Revolution and its aftermath

The American Revolution stimulated several forays in the direction of criminal law reform, all of them interesting for the new attitudes toward punishment that they revealed, although only one produced any long-term results. In the aftermath of the break with Great Britain, the newly independent colonies all faced the question of how much of the mother country's law they wished to retain. Some patriots urged that American criminal law was in particular need of change. Its harsh provisions, they argued, reflected a British rather than an American ethos. These arguments struck a responsive chord in certain state capitals. In New Hampshire, the first state constitution (promulgated in 1784) exhorted the legislature to do something about the sanguinary penal laws with which the state was saddled. It opined that it was not wise to affix the same punishment to crimes as diverse as forgery and murder, "the true design of all punishments being to reform, not to exterminate, mankind" (art. 1, § 18). Regrettably, the legislature refused to respond to the invitation and the state's penal law changed in no significant respect. There were parallel developments in Virginia.

Jefferson's proposed reform of the penal law of Virginia.   A few weeks after the signing of the Declaration of Independence, the General Assembly of Virginia passed an act for the revision of the Laws (ch. 9 (1776), Hening's Virginia Statutes at Large 175 (Richmond, Va., 1821)), with a view to bringing the state's laws into greater harmony with the spirit of republicanism. The committee that was entrusted with the task of revision included George Mason and Thomas Jefferson. As part of the revision effort, Jefferson prepared a draft of a bill for a new system of criminal sanctions. This draft was the product of an exhaustive survey of theoretical writings on punishment and on the history of the treatment of criminal offenders from ancient to modern times. The footnoted version of the bill that appears in Jefferson's papers includes citations, in the original language, from the laws of the Anglo-Saxons. It is widely regarded as a model of literary draftsmanship (Boyd, p. 594).

Among the theorists Jefferson read, none had so great an impact on him as the great Italian criminologist Cesare Beccaria, whose essay *On Crimes and Punishments* (1764) was stimulating lively discussion in educated colonial circles. Beccaria urged a thoroughly utilitarian approach to the criminal law, and the influence of his ideals permeated the whole of Jefferson's penology. Jefferson's guiding principles were: (1) that the only goal of the penal law was the deterrence of crime; (2) that sanguinary laws were self-defeating because men recoiled at the idea of enforcing them to the full and thus left many crimes unpunished; (3) that if punishments were proportioned to the crime, men would be more likely to see that the laws were observed; and (4) that the reform of criminals was an object worthy of the law's promotion. Finally, Jefferson's criminal jurisprudence reflected a fascination for the theory of analogical punishments, which stated that punishments ought to be symbolic reflections of the offenses to which they were affixed, so that crimes and their consequences would be inextricably linked in the minds of citizens. This curious theory had first been suggested by Beccaria and

had an enormous impact on the course of penological thought in the late eighteenth and early nineteenth centuries.

These principles combined to produce a proposed system of punishments that in general was mild and enlightened but that was marred by some rather bizarre features. Jefferson cut drastically the long catalogue of offenses punishable by death under the prevailing law, limiting them to treason and murder, and prescribed much milder sanctions for most of these traditionally capital crimes. But the penalties designated for some offenses had, because of what might almost be called an obsession with analogy and proportionality, a somewhat ghoulish hue. Thus, the punishment for treason was burial alive. Murder by poison was punished by poisoning, rape by castration, and mayhem by maiming the offender. Jefferson's proposals were seriously debated in the Virginia legislature but eventually were defeated.

Pennsylvania and the degrees of murder.   The first state in which the new advocates of penal law reform were able to translate theory into reality was Pennsylvania, which had earlier experimented with large-scale changes in its penal regime. The ground may have been rendered even more fertile by the fact that during the Revolution many Pennsylvania political offices fell into the hands of a coalition of populist farmers and Philadelphia radicals. In any event, in 1776 the state approved a constitution that included provisions concerning the reform of the criminal law very similar to those later included in the New Hampshire Constitution of 1784. (New Hampshire may well have taken some of its language from the Pennsylvania document.) The difference was that Pennsylvania commanded, rather than exhorted, its legislature to reform the penal laws of the state and to make punishments more proportional to crimes. Echoing a favorite theme of the new generation of reformers, the constitution also articulated the view that crime was more effectively deterred by visible punishments of long duration—that is, by imprisonment—than by intense, bloody, but brief sanctions (Pa. Const. of 1776, §§ 38–39).

The first step toward the reform of the penal law was taken by the Pennsylvania legislature ten years later, when it eliminated the death penalty for robbery, burglary, and sodomy (Act of Sept. 15, 1786). In 1791 a statute was passed abolishing capital punishment for witchcraft and ending the barbarous practice of branding for adultery and fornication (Act of Sept. 23, 1791, §§ 5, 8).

Notwithstanding these developments, there were signs in the early 1790s that the momentum that had been generated during the Revolution in favor of fundamental and wide-scale reform of the criminal law was beginning to slow down. For example, a new Pennsylvania constitution, promulgated in 1790, failed even to mention the subject. Perhaps with this in mind, a number of very eminent Pennsylvanians began now to speak out publicly and vigorously on behalf of the reformist cause.

In 1790, James Wilson, the first professor of law at the University of Pennsylvania, a signer of the Declaration of Independence, and a co-drafter of the United States Constitution, delivered a series of lectures in Philadelphia on crime and punishment. Citing with approval the views of Beccaria and that other great eighteenth-century legal theorist, Montesquieu, Wilson argued forcefully that prevention was the sole end of punishment and that anything more severe than the minimum punishment necessary to deter crime ill became a civilized nation. In 1792, Benjamin Rush, professor of medicine at the same university, published a widely disseminated essay entitled "Considerations on the Injustice and Impolicy of Punishing Murder by Death," in which he argued that capital punishment was "contrary to reason and to the order and happiness of society." That same year, William Bradford, justice of the Pennsylvania Supreme Court, entered the fray. In a report on the death penalty as a deterrent to crime, prepared at the instance of Governor Thomas Mufflin, Bradford argued that the supreme penalty was totally unnecessary and adduced statistics to show that the penalty of imprisonment, provided by the act of 1786, had proved just as effective in deterring burglary, robbery, and sodomy as had the earlier punishment of death.

Governor Mufflin, taking his cue from Bradford's memorandum, proposed to the Pennsylvania legislature that further mitigations in the penal regime seemed warranted and urged it to consider implementing additional reforms. The legislature's response was ambivalent. It was quite unwilling to go the full distance down the path that Bradford, Wilson, and others were urging it to go, but it did agree that the punishment of death ought to be inflicted only when it was absolutely necessary to ensure the public safety. In light of this philosophy, it prepared a bill that for the first time in Anglo-American legal history divided the crime of murder into two degrees. The first degree, punishable by death, referred to homicides perpetrated by lying in wait or by poison, or to any other kind of willful, deliberate, and premeditated killing. (There were echoes here of the act of 1682.) All other kinds of murder were classified as murder in the second degree, punishable by imprisonment at hard labor or in solitary confinement or both for a term not to exceed twenty-one years. This bill was duly passed by the legislature in 1794 with the addition of felony murder to the category of the first degree (Act of April 22, 1794, § 2).

The division of murder into two degrees proved to be Pennsylvania's most lasting contribution to the general criminal jurisprudence of the United States. In 1796, Virginia enacted a similar law, to be followed in 1824 by Ohio, in 1835 by Missouri, in 1846 by Michigan, and eventually by the vast majority of American jurisdictions.

The antebellum period

The passage of the statute on the degrees of murder took much of the wind out of the sails of the Pennsylvania movement for the complete abolition of capital punishment. The movement remained quiescent for several decades but was to revive again in the 1820s as part of a larger anti-capital-punishment crusade that flourished on the national scene roughly between 1820 and 1850. This discussion will be resumed below, but attention must now be shifted to the state of Louisiana and to the work of the most fertile and imaginative of all nineteenth-century penal law reformers, Edward Livingston.

Livingston. Edward Livingston (1764–1836), born in New York State, had a distinguished political career before turning to the work of criminal law reform. He served as a member of the House of Representatives, as United States attorney, and finally as mayor of New York City. Livingston left New York in 1804 and moved to New Orleans, where he opened a law practice and quickly became involved in Louisiana politics. At the same time he continued to cultivate a long-standing interest in jurisprudence and the reform of the law.

In 1820, Livingston was elected to the Louisiana legislature and in the same year was instrumental in the passing of an act that authorized the preparation of a code of criminal law "founded on one principle, viz., the prevention of crime" (Livingston, vol. 1, pp. 1–2). The following year, he was appointed to direct the effort.

Livingston read all the available materials on criminal jurisprudence and conducted a wide correspondence with jurists and legal practitioners in other states and abroad in order to draw on their ideas and experience. In 1826, he finally laid before the General Assembly of the state of Louisiana a finished product.

The Livingston Code consisted of four separate parts: a code of crimes and punishments, a code of procedure, a code of evidence, and a code of reform and prison discipline. Each code was accompanied by an introductory report that described its background and explained its underlying philosophy. There were in addition two lengthy reports in which Livingston set forth his general views on criminal jurisprudence. In one of them he made it clear that he thought his code to be the first real attempt, at least in the Anglo-American world, to place the criminal law on a sound, scientific basis. He compared the previous criminal law to pieces of fretwork, the product of caprice, fear, and carelessness, which by reason of cruel or disproportionate punishment and inconsistent provisions endangered the lives and liberties of the people (Livingston, vol. 1, p. 11).

The theorist to whom Livingston owed his greatest intellectual debt—one he freely acknowledged—was the English utilitarian philosopher Jeremy Bentham, and the whole structure of the code rests solidly on Benthamite principles. There is first a commitment to the principle that the content of the laws should be fully accessible to all educated citizens. "Penal laws should be written in plain language, clearly and unequivocally expressed, that they may neither be misunderstood nor perverted," Livingston wrote (vol. 1, p. 5). It is remarkable how little of that technical jargon of which lawyers are so fond appears in the code. It is one of the few pieces of legislation of which it can truly be said that it is a delight to read.

Consistent with Benthamite philosophy, the code is also permeated with a deep distrust of judges and a thorough aversion to any species of judicial lawmaking. The code of crimes and punishments forbade the punishment of any acts not expressly made criminal by statute, and judges were forbidden to punish anything not made criminal by the letter of the law under the pretense that the act in question came within the law's spirit (vol. 2, p. 15). Livingston wished to leave no room for judges to infuse their own moral beliefs into the penal law.

Finally, again in the interest of the involvement of the ordinary citizen in the law's process, the code sought to make transparent the rationale for its specific provisions. Thus, individual prohibitions on types of conduct were often accompanied by illustrations and by explanations why they had been included. It was Livingston's view that if people saw that the laws were rational and were framed on the great principle of utility, they would be more disposed to obey them.

Livingston's code in general represented a major consolidation and clarification of the existing penal laws and the pruning away of much of its weedlike overgrowth; he believed firmly that there were too many crimes and that the criminal sanction was most unwisely used when the civil sanction would suffice. In addition, however, many particular substantive provisions of the code were quite innovative. This was especially true in the areas of civil liberties and of privacy. To open a letter addressed to another was made criminal (vol. 2, p. 166), and it was a misdemeanor to interfere with the exercise of anyone's right of free speech or free assembly (vol. 2, p. 69). Homosexuality was removed from the list of criminal offenses on the grounds that to describe such offenses in a code was potentially corrupting to youthful readers and, further, that making sexual deviance criminal was an invitation to blackmail (vol. 1, p. 27).

Of all the innovations in Livingston's code, the most striking was the abolition of the death penalty (vol. 1, pp. 185–224). Livingston devoted a large part of his "Introductory Report to the Code of Crimes and Punishments" to a defense of this proposal. His chief argument was that the state was justified in taking life only if it could demonstrate that this was absolutely necessary. But, he averred, it could be shown by logic and by experience that lesser penalties would suffice for the prevention of great crimes. He also pointed to the corrupting effect that public executions had on social morals, to the not infrequent instances of courts incorrectly convicting defendants, and to the impossibility of remedying these errors under a system that allowed capital punishment. In a part of his discussion that has been relatively unnoticed by commentators, Livingston also argued that capital punishment was insufficient for the deterrence of serious offenses. The fear of death was simply not enough to offset in the minds of potential offenders the powerful passions that drove them to commit their crimes. The rapacious spendthrift, he suggested, might risk the momentary, if intense, pain of death to promote his interest in a life of idleness and debauchery, whereas the prospect of a life spent under a hard prison regime might be sufficient to cool his thievish instincts (vol. 1, pp. 37–40).

The system that Livingston wished to introduce for the treatment of social deviance had never been proposed before. He recognized that conditions of poverty and idleness led to crime, and so his code of reform and prison discipline provided for a house of refuge, which would give employment to those who could not find work, and a house of industry for those who refused to work in the house of refuge. The latter institution would also offer employment to recently discharged convicts. For the treatment of genuinely criminal offenses he offered an exquisitely gradated schedule of penalties, ranging from fines to imprisonment. The conditions of imprisonment were themselves graded according to the nature of the offense. The purpose of imprisonment was both to rehabilitate the offender and to deter crime by means of example.

Livingston's code of reform and prison discipline was in most respects far in advance of its time. It forbade any mistreatment of inmates and prescribed that they be adequately clothed and fed. It also prescribed strict standards of training and behavior for prison personnel. But it had its less pleasing side as well, incorporating as it did rather crude techniques of psychological manipulation, both of the offender and of the members of the public who were to be deterred by his example. Murderers, for example, were for the remainder of their lives to have no contact with persons from the outside world other than official visitors, and little contact with their fellow prisoners. Their cell walls were to be painted black, and on the outside of the cells an inscription was to be hung affirming that the inhabitants were dead in all but body; their bodily existence was being prolonged solely in order that they might remember their crimes and repent of them, and in order that their tribulations might serve as an example to others (vol. 2, p. 573).

Livingston argued passionately in the legislature for the adoption of his penal law, but it was not to the liking of that body and was never enacted. It was, in retrospect, an odd growth in the regressive, slave-holding society that was antebellum Louisiana.

The movement to abolish the death penalty. As noted earlier, a movement to abolish capital punishment came to life and flourished on the national scene in the second half of the antebellum period. Beginning in New England and in Pennsylvania, it spread quickly to other states and soon comprised a national constituency. By the 1840s there were well-organized anti-capital-punishment societies in eleven states, and in 1845 a national society was launched with George Dallas, the vice-president of the United States, as its first president. Quakers and others who opposed the death penalty on grounds of Christian humanitarianism were in the forefront of the movement, but also prominent were those who took their inspiration from the tradition of enlightened rationalism and utilitarianism. These opponents, many of them lawyers, often drew on the penological theories of Edward Livingston in making their arguments.

The advocates were called abolitionists—a well-chosen word, for there was significant overlap between the antislavery crusade and the death-penalty movement. Wendell Phillips, for example, was one of the founders of the Massachusetts society. The abolitionists were especially active on the floors of state legislatures. Their strategy was usually to engineer inquiries by legislative or outside consultative committees into the efficacy and necessity of capital punishment. These inquiries led to varying results.

In 1836, Governor Edward Everett of Massachusetts appointed a committee headed by Robert Rantoul, the great Jacksonian lawyer and advocate of codification, to look into the question of whether capital punishment might be eliminated for all crimes save murder. The committee issued a report that quickly became a classic in the movement, intermixing utilitarian arguments with appeals to Scripture in calling for abolition. Rantoul did not persuade the legislature to adopt his views, but in 1839 the body did abolish the death penalty for burglary and highway robbery (Act of April 8, 1839). In New York, too, there was legislative agitation for reform.

Abolition of the death penalty repeatedly came up for debate on the floor of the New York Assembly during the 1830s and was the subject of several committee inquiries during that decade. Occasionally the results of these deliberations proved disappointing to the antagonists of capital punishment. Thus, in 1838 an assembly committee rejected the Livingstonian argument that prison was a more effective deterrent than death, contending instead that since most criminals were paupers, the prospect of free lodging and board in prison would be positively attractive to them.

The most signal success of the anti-capital-punishment movement occurred in 1846, when the Michigan legislature voted to abandon the death penalty for all crimes except treason (Mich. Rev. Stat. tit. 30, chs. 152–153, 658 (1846)). Rhode Island followed suit in 1852, and Wisconsin, in 1853. The movement crested with these events, however, and then began to lose vigor. By the eve of the Civil War it had ceased to have much impact on the national consciousness.

Much later, during the Progressive Era, the anti-capital-punishment movement enjoyed a brief renascence, and a half-dozen states were persuaded to abolish the death penalty. Some of these triumphs were short-lived, however, as popular pressure forced most of these states to reintroduce the death penalty within a few years of abolition.

The postbellum period

The second half of the nineteenth century was not marked by any great ferment in the field of substantive penal law reform. American lawyers and legislators were by and large preoccupied with other matters during this era of industrialization and commercial expansion. One notable exception to the rule, however, was the effort mounted in New York and presided over by David Dudley Field to completely reshape the state's criminal law.

Field's reforms in New York State. David Dudley Field (1805–1894) was one of the towering figures of the nineteenth-century American bar, and by the Civil War he had become the leading advocate of codification in the United States. His efforts on behalf of penal-law reform were part of his larger codification project. In 1846 a New York constitutional convention, convoked in large measure because of successful lobbying by Field and other Jacksonian Democrats, passed a resolution directing the New York legislature to reduce into a written and systematic code the whole body of the state's laws. A path-breaking code of civil procedure was prepared by Field and other members of a specially appointed commission and enacted by the New York legislature before the Civil War (1849 N.Y. Laws, ch. 438), but work on the other codes was not to be completed until after the war.

In 1857 a new commission, with Field again a member, was established and given the responsibility of preparing a civil code, a political code, and a penal code. Field played a predominant role in drafting the first two documents, but he had no professional or scholarly expertise in the criminal law, and the bulk of the work on the last code, which was presented to the New York legislature in 1865, was done by Field's two co-commissioners, Curtis Noyes and B. V. Abbot. Nonetheless, Field participated in the drafting to a limited extent, and, inasmuch as he was the guiding spirit behind the whole New York codification effort, it is fitting that the penal code, like all the other New York codes, has always borne his name.

The stated objectives of the drafters of the Field Penal Code were, first, to bring within the compass of a single volume the whole body of the state's criminal law. The drafters noted that the state's penal provisions were scattered helter-skelter through the collected statutes and that many acts were criminal by virtue of judicial decision only; if made criminal by statute, they could be defined solely by recourse to common law decisions. All this, they said, caused uncertainty to pervade New York's criminal jurisprudence. Second, the drafters intended to rectify deficiencies and correct errors in existing definitions of crimes. Third, they aimed to eliminate inequalities and disparities in punishments, and finally, they wished to criminalize acts that should be criminal but were not (New York State Commissioners of the Code, pp. iii–vi).

It was a comprehensive and bold agenda, and there seemed instinct in it at least the possibility of a searching, critical reexamination of the fundamental principles of American criminal jurisprudence, a task that had not been undertaken by anyone save Livingston. But the finished product that the commissioners delivered was in this respect a profoundly disappointing document. Field and his colleagues seem to have felt that their reform agenda was completed when the scattered parts of the state's penal law had been pulled together and a semblance of order introduced into this collection of provisions. Nowhere in the document is there any evidence of a desire to clarify or reformulate any of the confused or archaic common law concepts that lay at the base of Anglo-American criminal law, or to simplify or consolidate the enormous corpus of statutory crimes and regulatory offenses that had been added to the state's criminal law since the Revolution. This "reformist" code thus left the status quo quite unaltered.

What the Field Code did achieve in full was its objective of bringing all of the criminal law within the compass of a single volume. Every instance in which criminal penalties were imposed for any action was included in the code's provisions. Nothing was left outside, nor was there any attempt to consolidate. Thus there are separate, specific provisions on "the refilling of mineral bottles" (§ 417), on "omitting to mark packages of hay" (§ 449), and on "throwing gas tar into public waters" (§ 434). Four kinds of arson are described, ranging from maliciously burning an inhabited building at night to burning an uninhabited building in the daytime—each covered by a separate provision (§§ 531–539). In perhaps the most ludicrous example of overspecificity, separate provisions cover, respectively, malicious mischief to railroads, to public highways or bridges, to toll houses or turnpikes, to mile markers and guideposts, and to telegraph lines (§§ 690–695).

Notwithstanding these limitations, the Field Code proved extremely popular. It was eventually enacted by the New York legislature in 1881 (1881 N.Y. Laws, ch. 676), it was adopted almost in its entirety by California and the Dakotas, and it had significant influence on the penal law of several other western states, including Arizona, Idaho, Montana, Oregon, Utah, and Wyoming.

Progressivism and its fruits

In the last decade of the nineteenth century and the first decades of the twentieth, a dynamic, complex social reform movement known as Progressivism swept through the middle and upper sectors of American society. The Progressives were a varied lot, and they had a varied political and social agenda. But among their chief aims were the elimination of corruption from politics, the introduction of efficiency and scientific technique into the governmental process, the uplifting of the underprivileged, and the assimilation into society's mainstream of the immigrant masses who were then pouring into the United States in record numbers. The whole Progressive program rested solidly on two fundamental principles: faith in the perfectibility of man, and implicit trust in the state's ability to promote individual well-being. The major reforms in the treatment of criminal offenders—probation, parole, and the juvenile court—that were either introduced or came into vogue during this era may be seen as manifestations of the Progressive spirit.

Probation. Probation, whose philosophy is that at least some criminal offenders are more likely to be rehabilitated by being placed in the community under the supervision of a trained official than by being incarcerated, is an American invention and has its origins in the work done in Boston in the 1840s and 1850s by the shoemaker John Augustus. With the permission of the courts, Augustus had for almost two decades taken into his care persons convicted of (usually minor) criminal offenses, with a view to rehabilitating them. Augustus accumulated a rather impressive record, but his arrangement with the Boston courts remained entirely informal, and his example inspired no imitators elsewhere. The modern system of probation dates in actuality from 1878, when Massachusetts enacted a statute authorizing the mayor of Boston to appoint a paid probation officer, and in 1880 this authority was extended to all cities and towns in the state (Mass. Probation Act of 1880, 1880 Mass. Acts, ch. 129). Other states toyed with the idea of introducing similar reforms but hesitated because of doubts about the constitutional propriety of the scheme. For many, this cloud was removed in 1894 when the highest court of New York ruled that a state law authorizing judges to suspend sentence, a necessary prerequisite to any system of probation, was not an unconstitutional infringement on the executive power of pardon (*People ex rel. Forsyth v. Court of Sessions*, 141 N.Y. 288, 36 N.E. 386 (1894)). Between 1900 and 1905, twelve states adopted probation for juvenile offenders; the number grew to twenty-three by 1911. By 1925, all forty-eight states permitted the probation of juveniles. Adult probation proceeded at a somewhat slower pace, but it too made steady strides during the Progressive Era.

Parole. Probation emphasized the individualized treatment of the malefactor by professionals: criminals were now seen as ill and in need of therapy, rather than as evil and deserving of retribution. As such, it was in harmony with the deep-seated Progressive belief in the educability of all through the use of scientific method. The same was true of parole. Parole and the other reform with which it usually went hand in hand—the indeterminate sentence—were first implemented in New York's Elmira Reformatory, which began admitting youthful offenders in 1877. The reformatory was to detain its inmates so long as was necessary to rehabilitate them, and then was to turn them over to trained professionals for further noncustodial supervision or treatment in the outside world. New York passed a general indeterminate sentencing law in 1889 (1889 N.Y. Laws, ch. 382, § 74), and by 1891 eight other states had enacted some form of indeterminate-sentence or parole legislation.

The juvenile court. Of all the criminal justice reforms promoted by progressives, the most emblematic was the juvenile court. Progressivism was a child-centered movement, and child welfare was a major focus of Progressive activity. Before the advent of juvenile court, jurisdictions had often devised ways of sparing youthful offenders the full rigors of the legal process, but, as has been pointed out, what was missing was the conception that a young person who ran afoul of the law was to be dealt with *from the outset* "not as a criminal, but as a person needing care, education and protection" (Warner and Cabot, p. 600). During the 1890s a wide spectrum of enlightened professionals, including members of the bar and representatives of the emerging behavioral sciences, pressed for the removal of juvenile offenders from the adult criminal process and the introduction of a separate system for their treatment. Illinois was the first state to respond favorably to these appeals, in 1899 enacting a law that created a juvenile court for Chicago (1899 Ill. Laws, ch. 131). The statute had been drafted by a committee of the Chicago Bar Association, and it established the court essentially as a court of equity with corresponding administrative powers. The plan was that the court should, when circumstances so warranted, assume guardianship over wayward or neglected youths with a view to giving them the care, custody, and discipline that a good parent would give his own children. The court, in sum, was to be thrust into the role of *parens patriae*, a role not unknown to equity courts. The juvenile court was to operate under relatively relaxed, nonadversarial procedures, with the role of counsel reduced, and its role was to be seen as remedial rather than punitive. The question before the court would not be whether the accused juvenile was guilty of a crime, but whether he was "delinquent" and thus in need of the state's care and education.

After the passage of the Illinois statute, the juvenile court movement acquired some of the features of a crusade. Proponents of the reform pushed vigorously in other states for its adoption. In addition to theoretical arguments, they now had a practical example to offer in support of their proposals, and in the personnel of the Chicago juvenile court they found eager and willing allies. For example, Timothy Hurley, the court's chief administrator, published the monthly *Juvenile Court Record*, which detailed the success of his institution and recorded the progress of the movement. The proponents encountered little or no opposition and state after state rushed to imitate the Chicago model. To be sure, a few did raise the question of whether the loose, informal procedure that characterized juvenile court, and the immense discretion of the juvenile magistrate, adequately protected youths from arbitrary deprivation of liberty. But these voices were drowned out by the rising chorus of approbation. By 1920, all but three states had created juvenile courts.

Twentieth-century developments

By the 1920s, attention had shifted from improving the techniques of rehabilitating the individual offender to the control of criminal behavior in the aggregate. This was the period of the great national experiment of Prohibition, with its attendant rise in illegalities of all sorts. Citizens across the land, but especially in large cities, became increasingly agitated at what they perceived to be an alarming increase in crime and the seeming inability of the criminal justice system to deal with it. Some charged that the corruption of government officials by the criminal element was the root cause of the problem—and indeed, there were many instances of political corruption during the period. Others insisted that the system of criminal justice was itself at fault and was desperately in need of overhaul. There was a widespread demand for some kind of action.

The Cleveland survey. The city of Cleveland was the first to attempt to address the problem in systematic fashion. It had for several years been suffering from a rising crime rate, and a pall of distrust hung over the municipal criminal justice apparatus. Matters came to a head in the spring of 1920, when the chief judge of the city's municipal court was forced to resign because of complicity in an atrocious crime. A number of civic organizations, headed by the Cleveland bar, persuaded the Cleveland Foundation, a private philanthropic organization, to sponsor a survey of criminal justice in the city. A staff of investigators headed by Roscoe Pound, then dean of the Harvard Law School, and by Felix Frankfurter of the Harvard law faculty, was assembled. After two years of empirical observation and the accumulation of masses of statistics, they delivered a lengthy report on the criminal justice process in Cleveland. It was the most comprehensive, detailed, and accurate portrait of the problems of urban law enforcement that had ever been produced. Every nook and cranny of the machinery of criminal justice was explored, from police administration to the criminal courts and the city's correctional facilities. There was even a section on legal education in Cleveland and its impact on the criminal justice process.

The report highlighted many flaws in the existing machinery of criminal justice and made recommendations for change. However, these recommendations were ameliorative rather than revolutionary. The report proposed no radical redesign of the existing system, but rather the streamlining and modernization of its operation. The emphasis was on the introduction of greater efficiency into all phases of the criminal justice process. Much space was devoted, for example, to explaining how prosecutorial staffs and courts could process more smoothly and expeditiously the large criminal case loads with which they were confronted. The report also emphasized the need for the full professionalization of criminal justice staffs and for the elevation of the status of the criminal law practitioner.

The example of the Cleveland crime survey stimulated the establishment in other jurisdictions of crime commissions charged with similar responsibilities. Georgia in 1924, Minnesota and Missouri in 1926, Memphis in 1928, and Illinois and New York State in 1929 all launched investigations of their own into the conditions of local law enforcement. However, they were in general pale imitations of the original.

The Wickersham Commission.   At this time, the national government itself decided to enter the picture. In 1929, President Herbert Hoover appointed the National Commission of Law Observance and Enforcement, under the chairmanship of United States Attorney General George Wickersham. The Wickersham Commission, as it came to be known, was originally charged only with the responsibility of looking into problems of law enforcement under the Eighteenth Amendment, but it soon expanded its scope to include the entire field of criminal justice. Over the next two years it undertook a sweeping investigation into crime and law enforcement in America and published fourteen volumes of reports on all phases of the process. Its findings and recommendations in many ways paralleled those of the Cleveland survey, but it broke important new ground as well. Its report on police practices, for example, exposed patterns of police abuse of suspects and stressed the need for the elimination of these practices. An entire volume, *The Causes of Crime*, took a broad sociological view of criminal behavior and suggested methods for attacking the conditions that, according to the commission, bred crime.

The focus of the great crime surveys of the 1920s was almost entirely procedural, but Pound, the guiding spirit of the Cleveland survey, had on several occasions pointed to the enormous inconsistencies and anachronisms embedded in the American substantive law of crimes and had emphasized how these stood in the way of erecting a truly modern and efficient system of criminal justice. The Wickersham Commission as well called attention to the deplorable, chaotic state of the federal substantive criminal law. Furthermore, ever since the turn of the century and continuing into the 1920s, scholars in criminal law, in the behavioral sciences, and in the nascent field of criminology had been leveling broadsides at the theoretical foundations of the criminal law. They challenged the scientific soundness of such fundamental notions as "criminal intent," "deliberation," and "premeditation," and questioned the purpose served by the subtle and often bizarre definitional distinctions that had grown up over the centuries in the common law of crimes.

To be sure, some of these critiques were seriously marred by a naive determinism—a few went so far as to say that science had totally vitiated the concept of free will or was on the verge of identifying the biological and psychological types that inevitably led to criminal behavior. But the majority were far more subtle and tentative, and there can be no caviling with the point, made by all, that there was much that was amiss in the existing criminal law.

The Model Penal Code.   The American Law Institute, an organization of lawyers, judges, and legal scholars, was founded in 1923 for the purpose of clarifying and improving the law. One of the major causes that had led to its establishment was dissatisfaction with the state of the criminal law, and thus it is no surprise that criminal law reform occupied a high place on its agenda from the outset. However, it proved difficult to translate this concern into action. The institute was quick to decide that the method of restatement which seemed the appropriate way to proceed in other fields of law was inappropriate for the law of crime. As Herbert Wechsler, a leading theorist of penal jurisprudence, later explained, "The need . . . was less for a description and reaffirmation of existing law than for a guide to long delayed reform" (1974, p. 421). A proposal for a model penal code was advanced in 1931, but the project was large in scope, and the funding to carry it out was not forthcoming during the Depression years.

In 1950 the infusion of a large grant from the Rockefeller Foundation stirred the model penal code project to life again. An advisory committee, made up of distinguished scholars in the field of criminal law, was assembled by the American Law Institute. Wechsler was appointed chief reporter of the enterprise, and Louis Schwartz, another eminent authority in the field, was named coreporter.

Early in the project's life, Wechsler made it clear that he and his colleagues were confronting a task of immense magnitude. In Wechsler's view, American society had entered the twentieth century without having ever rationally articulated "the law on which men placed their ultimate reliance for protection against all the deepest injuries that human conduct can inflict on individuals and institutions" (1974, p. 420). Instead, the penal law of the various states was a hopelessly disorganized and internally inconsistent mass of common and statute law—with the statutes often more important in their gloss than in their text—less the product of informed, deliberate choice than of accident, chance, and unreflecting imitation. As Wechsler put it, American penal law was "a combination of the old and the new that only history explains" (1955, p. 526).

From beginning to end, Wechsler was the code project's guiding spirit, and he deserves most of the credit for leading the enterprise to successful completion. But the drafting of the Model Penal Code was no solo performance by Wechsler. It was very much a collaborative effort, drawing on the talents of virtually the whole of the academic criminal law establishment of a goodly number of judges, and of a handful of practitioners. It was also an effort that proceeded carefully and deliberately. The writing of the Code took ten years, from 1952 to 1962, during which time thirteen tentative drafts were circulated for general discussion and comment after debate in the project's advisory committee and on the floor of the American Law Institute.

In 1962 the institute's Proposed Official Draft of the Model Penal Code was promulgated, the greatest attempt since Livingston's time to put the house of penal jurisprudence into some kind of rational order. In truth, the Proposed Official Draft was in many respects a very Livingstonian document. This was seen particularly in its commitment to the principle that the sole purpose of the criminal law was the control of harmful conduct, and in its adherence to the notion

that clarity of concept and expression were essential to that purpose's fulfillment. The draft was wholly lacking, however, in that ideological smugness and imperiousness which at times had tarnished the work of Livingston and of his mentor, Bentham. As befitted a product of the mid-twentieth-century American mind, the draft was suffused with a spirit of pragmatism, albeit a pragmatism tempered by principle.

The Code was divided into four parts: general provisions definitions of specific crimes, treatment and correction, and organization of correction. Each contained significant innovations with respect to existing law. In keeping with the principle that the criminal law's only purpose was to deter blameworthy, harmful conduct, and the converse principle that faultless conduct should be shielded from punishment, new standards of criminal liability were established in the Code's general provisions. In the area of inchoate crimes, for example, the law of attempt was rewritten to sweep away all questions as to factual impossibility and to focus attention on the actor's perception of the circumstances surrounding the commission of his act (§ 5.01). In conspiracy, on the other hand, the traditional common law rule that made every member of the conspiracy liable for any reasonably foreseeable crime committed by any other member of the conspiracy was rejected. Instead, an accomplice's liability was limited to those crimes of the principal that the accomplice intended to assist or encourage (§ 5.03). Thus too, in the interest of protecting faultless conduct, the use of defensive force was declared justifiable in cases of apparent, as opposed to actual, necessity (§ 3.04). Reasonable mistake of fact was affirmed as a defense in crimes such as bigamy (§ 230.1). In addition, a limited defense of *ignorantia legis* was made available to defendants who harbored good faith beliefs regarding the innocence of their conduct as a result of reliance on official opinion or as a result of the unavailability to them of the enactment they were accused of violating (§§ 2.02, 2.04).

The most striking provisions in the Code's general part were those that sought to articulate a new definition of the mental element in crime. The common law used a bewildering variety of terms to designate the mental blameworthiness (mens rea) that had to be present if a person were to be convicted of a criminal offense. For this profusion of terms the Code drafters substituted four modes of acting with respect to the material elements of offenses—purposely, knowingly, recklessly, and negligently—one of which would have to be present for criminal liability to attach (§ 2.02). The Code achieved a creative compromise in the area of strict liability, allowing for the possibility of such offenses by classifying them as violations punishable only by fines.

In addition to attempting to order and rationalize the general, underlying principles of criminal liability, the Model Penal Code wrought numerous innovations in the definitions of specific offenses. Perhaps the most signal achievement in this regard was its substitution of a unified law of theft for the potpourri of common law offenses that went under the names of larceny, larceny by trick, false pretenses, and embezzlement. It sought, too, to bring greater rationality and fairness to the sentencing of those convicted of crimes. It proposed a scheme of determinate sentencing, under which all felonies were classified into three punishment categories and all misdemeanors into two. Upper and lower limits of sentences were set out for each category, with the determination of the exact length left to the discretion of the judge (§§ 6.06, 6.08). Extended terms were authorized for persistent offenders and professional criminals (§§ 7.03, 7.04).

The American Law Institute neither expected nor intended that its Model Penal Code would be adopted in toto anywhere, or that it would lead to the establishment of a uniform national penal law. Diversity of political history and of population makeup in the various states made that kind of expectation quite unrealistic. Rather, the institute hoped that the Code would spark a fresh and systematic reevaluation of the penal law in many jurisdictions and that its provisions would be liberally drawn on. The institute was not to be disappointed in this hope. By 1980, in large part owing to the Model Penal Code's example, some thirty states had adopted revised criminal codes, and another nine had code revisions either under way or completed and awaiting enactment. It is no exaggeration to say, as did Sanford Kadish, that within three decades of the time when Code drafts began to be circulated, the Model Penal Code had "permeated and transformed" American substantive law (p. 1144).

A final salutary impact of the Model Penal Code must be mentioned, namely, the impetus that it gave to the effort to codify—for the first time in the true sense of the word—the federal penal law. In 1962, when the Code's Proposed Official Draft was promulgated, the federal criminal law was in a sorrier condition than that of most of the states. It had grown up in an unsystematic, piecemeal fashion since the beginnings of the republic, and the several efforts that had been previously undertaken to place it on a more rational basis had not come to very much. In 1866 Congress, alarmed at the uncontrolled manner in which the corpus of federal criminal law seemed to have been growing since 1800, had impaneled a commission to introduce some order into the confusion. The work of this commission led to the passage of a body of revised statutes, which at least had the virtue of arranging federal penal provisions into some sort of coherent order (U.S. Congress). In 1897 and later in 1909, revisions and rearrangements of federal penal statutes were again undertaken (Appropriations Act of June 4, 1897, ch. 2, 30 Stat. 11; Act of March 4, 1909, ch. 321, 35 Stat. 1088 (codified in scattered sections of 18 U.S.C.)). Finally, in 1948, after eight years of work by another commission, Congress enacted Title 18 of the United States Code, which purported to be the first codification of the federal criminal law. If it was a codification, it was one in the Fieldian rather than the Benthamite-Livingstonian sense—and even that may be a charitable overstatement.

In 1966 Congress established the National Commission on Reform of Federal Criminal Laws to examine the state of the federal penal law and to propose a reformulation. The action was in part taken to appease an anxious public which was insisting that Congress do something about dramatically escalating crime rates, but it was motivated as well by an authentic desire to reform and improve the law. Congress left no doubt that it wished to see a thorough rethinking of the federal law of crimes, and its mandate was heeded. In due course the commission produced a thorough revision of the federal substantive law of crimes, and several bills were promptly introduced for the enactment of some version of it into law.

The middle decades of the twentieth century, thanks in part to the work of Wechsler and his colleagues, witnessed a widespread quickening of interest in the field of criminal justice, as well as considerable activity aimed at the reformation of the criminal law. Whether this signaled the reversal of past patterns of inattention and the beginning of a new, long-term trend or whether it was merely another episode of flirtation with the subject, only the future can determine.

CHARLES MCCLAIN
DAN M. KAHAN

See also CAPITAL PUNISHMENT: LEGAL ASPECTS; CAPITAL PUNISHMENT: MORALITY, POLITICS, AND POLICY; CRIME COMMISSIONS; JUVENILE JUSTICE: HISTORY AND PHILOSOPHY; PRISONS: HISTORY.

BIBLIOGRAPHY

American Law Institute. *Model Penal Code: Proposed Official Draft.* Philadelphia: ALI, 1962.

BARNES, HARRY ELMER. *The Evolution of Penology in Pennsylvania: A Study in American Social History* (1927). Reprint. Montclair, N.J.: Patterson Smith, 1968.

BECCARIA, CESARE. *On Crimes and Punishments* (1764). Translated with an introduction by Henry Paolucci. Indianapolis: Bobbs-Merrill, 1963.

BOYD, JULIAN P., ed. *The Papers of Thomas Jefferson,* vol. 2. Princeton, N.J.: Princeton University Press, 1950.

"Colony of New Plymouth: Laws of 1636." *The Compact with the Charter and Laws of the Colony of New Plymouth.* Edited by William Brigham. Boston: Dutton & Wentworth, 1836, pp. 35–57.

"Constitution of Pennsylvania, 1790." *The Federal and State Constitutions, Colonial Charters, and Other Organic Laws of the States, Territories, and Colonies Now or Heretofore Forming the United States of America,* vol. 5. Edited by Francis Newton Thorpe. Washington, D.C.: Government Printing Office, 1909, pp. 3092–3103.

DAVIS, DAVID BRION. "The Movement to Abolish Capital Punishment in America, 1798–1861." *American Historical Review* 63 (1957): 23–46.

DRESSLER, DAVID. *Practice and Theory of Probation and Parole.* New York: Columbia University Press, 1959.

FRIEDMAN, LAWRENCE M. *Crime and Punishment in American History.* New York: Basic Books, 1993.

GOEBEL, JULIUS, JR., and NAUGHTON, T. RAYMOND. *Law Enforcement in Colonial New York: A Study in Criminal Procedure (1664–1776)* (1944). Reprint. Montclair, N.J.: Patterson Smith, 1970.

GREEN, THOMAS A. "Freedom and Criminal Responsibility in the Age of Pound: An Essay on Criminal Justice." *Michigan Law Review* 93 (1995): 1915–2053.

HALL, JEROME. "Edward Livingston and His Louisiana Penal Code." *American Bar Association Journal* 22 (1936): 191–196.

HALL, LIVINGSTON. "The Substantive Law of Crimes: 1887–1936." *Harvard Law Review* 50 (1937): 616–653.

HARNO, ALBERT J. "Some Significant Developments in Criminal Law and Procedure in the Last Century." *Journal of Criminal Law, Criminology, and Police Science* 42 (1951): 427–467.

HIRSCH, ADAM J. *The Rise of the Penitentiary: Prisons and Punishments in Early America.* New Haven: Yale University Press, 1992.

KADISH, SANFORD H. "Codifiers of the Criminal Law: Wechsler's Predecessors." *Columbia Law Review* 78 (1978): 1098–1144.

KEEDY, EDWIN R. "History of the Pennsylvania Statute Creating Degrees of Murder." *University of Pennsylvania Law Review* 97 (1949): 759–777.

The Laws and Liberties of Massachusetts. Reprinted from the copy of the 1648 edition in the Henry B. Huntington Library. Introduction by Max Farrand. Cambridge, Mass.: Harvard University Press, 1929.

LIVINGSTON, EDWARD. *The Complete Works of Edward Livingston on Criminal Jurisprudence. Consisting of Systems of Penal Law for the State of Louisiana and for the United States of America* (1873). 2 vols. Introduction by Salmon P. Chase. Reprint. Montclair, N.J.: Patterson Smith, 1968.

NELSON, WILLIAM E. *The Americanization of the Common Law: The Impact of Legal Change on Massachusetts Society, 1760–1830.* Cambridge, Mass.: Harvard University Press, 1975.

New York State Commissioners of the Code. *Draft of a Penal Code for the State of New York.* Albany: Weed, Parsons, 1864.

POUND, ROSCOE. *Criminal Justice in America* (1930). Reprint. New York: Da Capo Press, 1972.

———, and FRANKFURTER, FELIX, eds. *Criminal Justice in Cleveland: Reports of the Cleveland Foundation Survey of the Administration of Criminal Justice in Cleveland, Ohio.* Cleveland Foundation, 1922.

ROTHMAN, DAVID J. *Conscience and Convenience: The Asylum and Its Alternatives in Progressive America.* Boston: Little, Brown, 1980.

———. *The Discovery of the Asylum: Social Order and Disorder in the New Republic.* Boston: Little, Brown, rev. ed. 1990.

SAYRE, FRANCIS. "Public Welfare Offenses." *Columbia Law Review* 33 (1933): 55–88.

U.S. Congress. "Title LXX." *Revised Statutes of the United States.* 2d ed. 43d Cong., 2d sess., 1873–

1874. Washington, D.C.: Government Printing Office, 1878, pp. 1035–1075.

WALKER, SAMUEL E. *Popular Justice: A History of American Criminal Justice.* New York: Oxford University Press, 1980.

WARNER, SAM B., and CABOT, HENRY B. "Changes in the Administration of Criminal Justice during the Past Fifty Years." *Harvard Law Review* 50 (1937): 583–615.

WECHSLER, HERBERT. "American Law Institute: II. A Thoughtful Code of Substantive Law." *Journal of Criminal Law, Criminology, and Police Science* 45 (1955): 524–530.

———. "The Model Penal Code and the Codification of American Criminal Law." *Crime, Criminology, and Public Policy: Essays in Honor of Sir Leon Radzinowicz.* Edited by Roger G. Hood. New York: Free Press, 1974, pp.419–468.

———, and MICHAEL, JEROME. "A Rationale of the Law of Homicide." *Columbia Law Review* 37 (1937): 701–761, 1261–1325.

CRIMINAL LAW REFORM: CURRENT ISSUES IN THE UNITED STATES

Since World War II, American penal law has undergone a fundamental transformation that has reached each of its three aspects: the definition of offenses and the consequences of their violation (substantive criminal law, or criminal law), the imposition of these norms (procedural criminal law, or criminal procedure) and their infliction (prison or correction law). The first phase of that transformation—peaking in the 1960s and 1970s—brought the legislative codification and the judicial constitutionalization of criminal law, procedural law, and prison law. The second phase, which is still ongoing, has seen the abandonment of the codificatory ideal by legislatures and the deconstitutionalization of penal law by the courts. The end result has been a dramatic expansion in the reach and severity of penal law.

This article focuses on the second phase and speculates on what may come after it. In general, an indefinite continuation of the current unprincipled punitiveness is as unlikely as a return to the days of comprehensive postwar reform. The challenge for penal law reform in the years ahead will be the development of an approach to penal law that steers a middle path between the abstract rationality of the early reforms and the ad hoc reflexiveness of the backlash to them.

Overview of recent developments in criminal law reform

The stimulus for and paradigm of the first phase of postwar American criminal law reform was the American Law Institute's Model Penal Code. The second phase coincides with the waning of the Code's influence. As the following overview makes plain, most of the recent developments in American penal law were pioneered or at least influenced by the two major jurisdictions that escaped wholesale recodification based on the Model Penal Code: the United States (federal) and California. The current issues in American penal law reform therefore are framed not by the Model Penal Code, but by jurisdictions that have remained untouched by the Code's influence.

Modern federal criminal law deserves our attention not merely as a catalyst for similar developments throughout the country, but also in its own right. The last decades of the twentieth century were marked by Congress' use of the commerce clause to reach behavior that traditionally had been the exclusive province of state criminal law. In general, courts have done little to stem the tide of federal criminalization based on the commerce clause, at least until 1995 when the U.S. Supreme Court surprisingly struck down a federal statute criminalizing the possession of firearms in a designated school zone (*United States v. Lopez*, 514 U.S. 549 (1995)). Five years later, the Court invoked Lopez to invalidate a section of the Federal Violence against Women Act that provided a civil remedy for victims of gender-motivated crimes of violence (*United States v. Morrison*, 529 U.S. (2000)). Whether these cases signal the end of federal crime law as we have come to know it remains to be seen. So far, constitutional scrutiny has not interfered with the creation of federal laws criminalizing carjacking, drive-by shootings, the possession of firearms by those convicted of domestic violence or under a restraining order, theft of major artwork, murder of a state official assisting federal law enforcement agents, odometer tampering, the failure to pay child support, computer fraud, and the disruption of laboratories where research on animals is performed, to pick only a small sample.

The current phase of American penal law has been marked by the war on crime. This comprehensive effort to suppress crime has manifested itself in often radical reforms in each aspect of penal law, from substantive criminal law to criminal procedure to the law of corrections. Before we turn to these and other specific changes, however, it is worth highlighting three general developments that span all three aspects of penal law.

The concentration of penal power in the executive. Responsibility and, therefore, power has been passed from the legislature through the judiciary onto the executive to strengthen the enforcement, the execution, of penal law. In the wake of the global chaos of lawlessness in World War II, the first phase of modern American criminal law reform sought to put the legality principle of *nulla poena sine lege* (no punishment without law) into legislative action. The second phase turned the legality principle on its head, in the name of an all-out effort to exterminate crime: *nulla poena sine lege* became *nullum crimen sine poena* (no crime without punishment).

As we will see, power has been transferred onto the executive in each stage of the penal process, including the police officer (who first determines whether an offense has been committed), the prosecutor (who decides whether or not a sanction should be imposed), and eventually the prison administrator (who inflicts that sanction).

The rise of the victims' rights movement. The victim today plays a role in every aspect of American penal law, from the substantive criminal law to the imposition of penal norms in the criminal process and, eventually, to the actual enforcement of norms upon suspects and convicts. New offenses turn on the characteristics of victims, victims may participate in all stages of the criminal process, and victims have even been integrated into the infliction of punishment either as observers or as participants. In the words of one state appellate court, the traditional view that "criminal prosecutions should punish the guilty and protect society from any future criminal misdeeds of the defendant" has given way to the view that "the law should serve as a salve to help heal those whose rights and dignity have been violated" (*People v. Robinson*, 298 Ill. App. 3d 866, 877 (1998)).

The emergence of incapacitation as the primary function of penal law. The dominant penal ideology of the postwar reforms, rehabilitation, gave way in the 1970s to a revival of retributive punishment, that is, of punishment for its own sake. The retributive interlude, however, proved short-lived. It soon gave way to its crude utilitarian analogue, vengeance, and the simplest of all penal ideologies, incapacitation, which can be reduced to the truism that someone who can-

not commit crimes will not commit crimes. In practice the growing influence of incapacitation has meant an expansion of the reach of penal law, an increase in the severity of punishments, an acceleration and simplification of the criminal process, the reemergence of capital punishment, and the abandonment of efforts to rehabilitate prison inmates.

Definition of sanctions, including crimes and punishments (substantive criminal law)

The substantive criminal law has two components, the definition of crimes and the consequences of their commission (punishments). Both components are undergoing significant changes. These changes include a reassignment of legislative emphasis among the two components. In many jurisdictions, the locus of substantive criminal law has moved from the penal code to a set of sentencing guidelines, and therefore from the law of crimes to the law of punishment. This shift has been particularly pronounced in federal law, which established a comprehensive and mandatory system of punishment law while failing to undertake a similarly ambitious reform of its law of crimes. As a result, the federal sentencing guidelines today address and resolve more questions of substantive federal criminal law than does the federal criminal code.

In the federal model, this shift from a code of crimes to guidelines of punishment also has resulted in shifts of power from the legislature to a sui generis commission and then from the judiciary to the executive. Based on a general—and generally unchecked—delegation of authority from the legislature, the federal sentencing guidelines were drawn up and are continuously amended by the federal sentencing commission. Despite occasional shows of force, the legislature effectively has ceded the power to make the law of punishment to this unelected commission. The mandatory guidelines drafted by the commission then transfer judicial discretion at the sentencing phase to prosecutorial discretion at the charging phase. In the end, federal criminal law is made by an unelected commission and applied by the executive.

Crimes

The transfer of power from the legislature to the judiciary and, most important, to the executive has not been confined to the law of punishment. The law of crimes, too, has been transformed to place flexible crime-fighting tools at the disposal of enforcement officials. The paradigmatic crime here is RICO (Racketeer Influenced and Corrupt Organization), added to the federal criminal code in 1970. Widely hailed as an innovation in American criminal lawmaking (and the envy of many countries eager to fight corruption), RICO, as its name suggests, does not define any kind of criminal conduct at all. Instead, RICO liability turns on one's association with an organization. On its face, RICO violates at least two of the most sacred principles of substantive criminal law: the prohibition of criminal liability based on mere association rather than on conduct and the prohibition of vague criminal statutes. RICO and the many statutes it has spawned in federal criminal law and throughout the states has survived scrutiny in the legislatures and, perhaps more remarkably, in the courts on the basis of a widely shared belief that law enforcement officials were incapable of rooting out elusive criminal networks within the traditional constraints of the legality principle. To combat organized crime, American criminal law had to be radically refocused from criminal acts to criminal actors and ultimately to the organizations to which they belonged.

Attempts to extend this technique of enforcement-driven penal lawmaking to street gangs have met with mixed success. The U.S. Supreme Court struck down on vagueness grounds a Chicago gang loitering statute that criminalized the failure promptly to obey a dispersal order by a police officer directed at anyone "reasonably believe[d] to be a criminal street gang member loitering in any public place with one or more other persons" (*Chicago v. Morales*, 119 S. Ct. 1849 (1999)). It remains to be seen whether the Court will continue to reaffirm its commitment to specificity when confronted with a more carefully drafted gang loitering law.

The war against street gangs instead has been fought with a far more potent weapon in the arsenal of modern American law enforcement: the drug crime. The war on crime first and foremost has been a war on drugs. In a sense, drug criminal law therefore combats the very gangs it brought into existence by criminalizing drug possession and distribution in the first place. However internally inconsistent the notion of a drug criminal law may be, its explosion in scope and severity has been the single most important development in American penal law since the 1970s.

As late as 1962, the Model Penal Code could treat drug offenses in a casual note relating to "additional Articles dealing with special topics such as narcotics, alcoholic beverages, gambling and offenses against tax and trade laws." Today, drug offenses ranging from simple violations to the most serious felonies occupy a central place in the criminal law of all American jurisdictions. Legislators have shown considerable imagination in creating new and ever more serious drug offenses, with innumerable variations according to the nature and weight of the drug and the circumstances of its distribution.

As in the case of offenses designed to aid the destruction of criminal networks, the criminal law of drugs was driven by federal law. In fact, the nationwide impact of federal drug law far exceeds even that of RICO and its offspring. The tripling of the federal prison population since the 1970s is largely attributable to the expansion and harshening of federal drug criminal law, with the number of federal drug offenders increasing eighteen-fold from three thousand to over fifty thousand, or 60 percent of federal prisoners. In 1993, the number of drug offenders in American prisons reached 350,000, almost twice the total number of prison inmates at the time of the original Model Code.

The federal law also has been at the forefront of the creation of so-called regulatory offenses. Today, the criminal law has become a necessary ingredient of any regulatory enterprise. Following the federal model, no comprehensive piece of environmental legislation, for instance, would be complete without a list of environmental offenses (ranging from violations to misdemeanors and felonies) or a catch-all provision criminalizing the contravention of some or all of its provisions, or both.

Take, for example, the New York State Environmental Preservation Law. It contains a general provision declaring a violation of any of its hundreds of provisions a criminal violation, which according to New York law carries a maximum jail sentence of fifteen days. In addition, the environmental code defines dozens of criminal offenses ranging in severity from violations to misdemeanors and felonies and in content from hunting while intoxicated to the illegal commercialization of fish, shellfish, crustaceans, and endangering public health, safety, or the environment. Other than in the state penal code, criminal offenses appear in the following New York state codes: Agriculture and Markets; Alcoholic Beverage Control; Arts and Cultural Affairs; Banking; Business Corporation; Civil Rights; Civil Service; Cooperative Corporations; Correction; County; Defense Emergency Act; Domestic Relations; Education; Election; Energy; Environmental Preservation; Estates, Powers, and Trusts; Executive; Family Court; General Business; General City; General Municipal; General Obligations; Highway; Indian; Insurance; Judiciary; Labor; Legislative; Local Finance; Lost and Strayed Animals; Mental Hygiene; Military; Multiple Dwelling; Multiple Residence; Municipal Home Rule; Navigation; New York City Civil Court; New York City Criminal Court; Not-For-Profit Corporation; Parks, Recreation and Historical Preservation; Personal Property; Public Authorities; Public Health; Public Lands; Public Officers; Public Service; Racing, Pari-Mutuel Wagering and Breeding Law; Railroad; Real Property; Real Property Actions and Proceedings; Real Property Tax; Retirement and Social Security; Second Class Cities; Social Services; State Finance; Tax; Town; Transportation; Transportation Corporations; Uniform Justice Court; Vehicle and Traffic; Village; Volunteer Ambulance Workers' Benefit; Volunteer Firefighters' Benefit; and Workers' Compensation.

This modern mode of regulatory penal lawmaking has certain characteristics. First, as the above list indicates, many of the new regulatory offenses do not appear in penal codes. Instead, they are dispersed among the multitude of laws dealing with the multitude of objects of modern regulation.

Second, many of these *malum prohibitum* offenses are strict liability offenses, that is, they do not require mens rea of any kind, not even negligence. The mere commission of an act suffices for criminal liability.

Third, the new offenses often disregard not only the traditional common law requirement of mens rea. They similarly loosen the actus reus requirement. Unlike the common law, the modern law of criminal regulation has not hesitated to criminalize the mere failure to act. In fact, the paradigm of modern corporate criminal law is an omission, the failure of executives to supervise their subordinates. The job responsibilities of executives are supervisory by their very nature. As criminal liability creeps up the corporate ladder, the distinction between commission and omission dissipates.

The spread of possession offenses also has contributed to the erosion of actus reus. Today, the criminal law heavily regulates possession not only of narcotics but also of firearms. Penalties for possession offenses can run as high as life imprisonment without the possibility of parole. Modern criminal codes that attempt to bring possession, a status, into line with actus reus, can do no better than redefine possession as a failure to end possession, which of course is not an act, but an omission.

Fourth, this spread of strict liability has also been accompanied, particularly in federal law, by a spread of vicarious liability, that is, criminal liability based exclusively on one's relationship to another person who has committed an unlawful act or unlawfully has failed to engage in an act.

Fifth, the expansion of vicarious liability has gone hand in hand with an expansion of corporate criminal liability. As a result, not only are corporate executives more likely to incur criminal liability for the acts of their subordinates, but criminal liability also is more likely to attach to the corporate entity itself.

Sixth, the expansion of regulatory criminality has not been confined to consolidated laws, or codes. The New York legislature, to return to our example, has not only found it impossible to find room for its regulatory offenses in the state's penal code. It also has found it necessary to include criminal offenses in that state's diverse collection of unconsolidated laws, which by definition are unavailable in official statutory compilations. Criminal offenses, again ranging from violations to felonies, appear in these New York state unconsolidated laws: Boxing, Sparring and Wrestling; General City Model; Local Emergency Housing Rent Control Act; New York City Health and Hospitals Corporation Act; New York State Financial Emergency Act for the City of New York; Police in Certain Municipalities; Regulation of Lobbying Act; and the Yonkers Financial Emergency Act.

Seventh, many of the new regulatory offenses are not promulgated by the legislature at all, but by the executive. In New York, the following executive agencies are entitled to issue rules and regulations the first violation of which amounts to a criminal violation punishable by up to fifteen days imprisonment, with repeat violations subject to higher punishment: Department of Motor Vehicles; Banking Board; Civil Service Commission; Department of Corrections; Department of Economic Development; Department of Education; Board of Elections; Department of Environmental Conservation; Department of Transportation; Office of Parks, Recreation and Historic Development; Department of Health; New York State Racing and Wagering Board; State Board of Real Property Services; Department of Taxation and Finance; and Workman's Compensation Board, as well as local utilities. This delegation of penal lawmaking to regulatory agencies quietly transfers the very penal power onto the executive that the legislature had assumed from the judiciary during the postwar phase of codification in the wake of the Model Penal Code.

Finally, not only the states and the federal government, but also lower level governmental entities throughout the country are busy generating new regulatory offenses. County codes, city codes, town codes, and village codes today contain criminal offenses covering everything from disorderly conduct and bingo games to hazardous waste and tax fraud.

The proliferation of regulatory offenses in all corners of American law is symptomatic of a general mode of penal lawmaking that also extends to offenses that no one would characterize as regulatory or malum prohibitum. With the federal legislature once again taking the lead, American penal law in recent years has become cluttered with topical offenses, many of which either duplicate existing offenses or do not fit into existing categories of criminal wrongdoing, or both. The paradigmatic example of a duplicative offense is carjacking, an offense that reaches conduct that long had been criminalized under standard robbery statutes. Legislatures also felt the need to respond to the spread of computers by inserting chapters on computer crimes into their penal codes, which tend merely to collect already criminal conduct under a new heading. Hate crimes likewise have struggled to find a home in American penal codes, largely because they duplicate or aggravate existing criminal offenses, including homicide, assault, and the destruction of property. To the extent that the federal RICO and its dozens of state law versions can be read as criminalizing conduct rather than mere association, they merely duplicate offenses already defined elsewhere.

Legislatures occasionally have found it difficult to integrate these offenses into existing codes. So one finds the New York version of RICO in title X of Part N (Administrative Provisions) of the New York Penal Law, sandwiched between titles W and Z, dedicated to "Firearms, Fireworks, Pornography Equipment and Vehicles Used in the Transportation of Gambling Records" and "Laws Repealed; Time of Taking Effect," respectively. The preamble to this title of the New York Penal Law attempts to explain why

a New York RICO is necessary to combat "such criminal endeavors as the theft and fencing of property, the importation and distribution of narcotics and other dangerous drugs, arson for profit, hijacking, labor racketeering, loansharking, extortion and bribery, the illegal disposal of hazardous wastes, syndicated gambling, trafficking in stolen securities, insurance and investment frauds, and other forms of economic and social exploitation," each of which is criminalized under the threat of often severe punishment elsewhere in the New York Penal Law, which also contains broad provisions on complicity as well as on conspiracy, facilitation, solicitation, and attempt, generic inchoate offenses applicable to any offense defined in the penal code.

The federal legislature has not faced similar problems of classification. The special part of the federal criminal code is arranged alphabetically, from Aircraft and Motor Vehicles to Wire and Electronic Communications Interception and Interception of Oral Communications. By contrast, the special part of the Model Penal Code and of codes based on it, including the New York Penal Law, is organized by interests, including Offenses Against Existence or Stability of the State, Offenses Involving Danger to the Person, Offenses Against Property, Offenses Against the Family, Offenses Against Public Administration, and Offenses Against Public Order and Decency.

The Model Penal Code's conceptual structure makes it difficult to insert new offenses that protect no particular interest, more than one interest, or an interest that already is protected by one or more existing offenses. As a result, penal codes whose special part follows the Code's general structure force legislatures to consider which recognized interest a new offense might protect before simply adding it to the list of existing offenses.

The growing influence of federal penal lawmaking, which is unconstrained by such conceptual constraints, therefore reflects a general abandonment of the ideal of systematic codification. According to this ideal, the state bore the responsibility of carefully weighing all available policy options before resorting to the coercive power of the penal law. The ideal found its most complete manifestation in the penal code, which transferred the power to make penal law from a judiciary bound by the limitations of particular cases or controversies into the hands of a legislature whose elected representatives were free to explore the short- and long-term implications of adopting a particular penal provision within the context of the penal law as a whole.

Instead, legislatures have increasingly abandoned their newfound responsibilities for considered penal lawmaking. In the era of the new punitiveness, careful distinctions have been abandoned as technical luxuries that recall the quainter times of postwar America when crime rates were lower and Americans felt safer, but are entirely inappropriate for a war on crime. The casualties of this war of crime extermination through the incapacitation of criminal elements included not only nice distinctions among offenses by the interests they set out to protect, but also the willingness to place certain infringers of these interests beyond the pale of punishment. Since the 1980s, the two defenses to criminal liability based on the actor's incapacity to engage in truly criminal conduct in the first place, insanity and infancy, have been eroded steadily. As the minimum age for criminal liability, as opposed to juvenile delinquency, has dropped throughout the United States, so the insanity defense, largely in response to John Hinckley's insanity acquittal for the attempted assassination of Ronald Reagan, has either been abandoned altogether or radically restricted in federal criminal law and the criminal law of many states. Today, someone who would have been acquitted as criminally insane in the 1970s may well be found "guilty but mentally ill."

The campaign of incapacitation even has led to the relaxation of the one remaining bedrock principle of American penal law, that no one may be punished absent the conviction of a criminal offense, no matter how dangerous he or she might be. So the Supreme Court has upheld preventive detention of suspects pending trial based merely on a finding of dangerousness, as well as the continued and indefinite incarceration of persons classified as "sexual predators" beyond their punishment for a criminal offense.

Punishments

The law of punishment has become more significant, mere complex, and more draconian. Once the province of judicial discretion, punishment today increasingly is governed by comprehensive guidelines. Particularly in jurisdictions with incomplete criminal codes, these guidelines have become the major source of innovation in substantive criminal law. Much of the general and special part of federal criminal law, for example, today can be found not in the federal criminal code, but in the federal sentencing guidelines.

To begin with the general part of federal criminal law, the federal criminal code (title 18 of the U.S. Code) contains no general provision on jurisdiction, voluntariness, actus reus, mens rea, causation, mistake, entrapment, duress, infancy, justification, self-defense, or inchoate offenses. The federal sentencing guidelines, by contrast, cover mens rea, complicity, duress, intoxication, mistake, consent, necessity, and inchoate crimes.

The special part of the federal criminal code, as we saw earlier, arranges its underinclusive collection of thousands of federal crimes in alphabetical order. In drafting the sentencing guidelines, the federal U.S. Sentencing Commission assigned most, but not all, of these title 18 offenses, along with thousands of other federal crimes dispersed through the fifty titles of the U.S. Code, to a classificatory scheme of eighteen offense categories. It then drafted guidelines on the basis of this novel scheme, not the legislative definitions of offenses in the U.S. Code. Instead of merely linking punishments to legislatively defined crimes, an impossible task given the disorganized state of federal crime definitions, the commission thus created an entirely novel system of federal crimes, clustered around the commission's definition of certain groups of basic offense conduct. The legislative definitions of offenses appear in the federal guidelines only as an appendix—literally—to facilitate the process of linking up guidelines categories to actual federal offenses.

The federal criminal code provided the sentencing commission with no more guidance on the law of punishment than it has on the law of crimes. The code generally assumes virtually unlimited discretion on the part of the sentencing judge. Its sentencing provisions are accordingly sporadic and vague. The code contains no general law of punishment applicable to all federal offenses. Punishment provisions instead are attached to particular offense definitions, thus suffering from the problems of inconsistency and inaccessibility that plague the offense definitions themselves.

As a result, federal criminal law today largely begins and ends with the sentencing guidelines. The guidelines' superior organization, comprehensiveness, and accessibility, combined with their determinate and mandatory nature, have turned them into a shadow code of federal penal law that shapes actual practice while federal legislators enjoy unfettered discretion in continuously adding offenses to the U.S. Code, secure in the knowledge that ultimate responsibility for the making of penal law rests with the sentencing commission.

This shift from codes of crime to guidelines of punishment as the paradigmatic sources of criminal law also has meant the transfer of penal lawmaking power from the legislature onto sentencing commissions. The significance of this transfer has been proportional to the quality of a jurisdiction's criminal code. The less comprehensive and coherent the code, the more complete the transfer of legislative power, with the most complete transfer occurring in federal law.

This transfer is troubling to the extent that the legislatively made criminal law enjoys a particular legitimacy because of the legislature's representativeness and freedom from the narrow constraints of particular cases or controversies. These considerations played an important role in transferring penal lawmaking power from the judiciary onto the legislature in the first phase of American criminal law reform. Their failure to prevent the transfer of that power from the legislature onto a quasi-agency illustrates the decline of the ideal of codification as a prerequisite for a legitimate law of crimes and punishments.

As the form and source of the law of punishment have changed, so has its substance. The reemergence of capital punishment since the 1970s stands for a general increase in the severity of punishments. In fact, the death penalty, which despite recent expansions applies only to a minuscule percentage of criminal offenders, should not obscure the enormous increase in noncapital penalties, ranging from short-term imprisonment for minor offenses to life imprisonment without the possibility of parole. As constitutional law has focused on capital punishment, harsh noncapital penalties have spread without constitutional constraints of any kind.

The qualitative difference between capital and noncapital punishment also has led to the bizarre situation that the consideration of the offender's personal circumstances and background, the mainstay of the rehabilitative ideology of penal law that dominated the first phase of American criminal law reform, now is often limited to capital defendants, that is, the very people who are facing the one punishment that could never rehabilitate. By contrast, defendants in noncapital cases often are punished according to sentencing guidelines that, like the federal ones, calculate penalties based primarily, if not exclusively, on the basis of the offender's current and past criminal conduct and preclude the consideration of rehabilitative factors.

Mandatory minimum penalties and recidivist statutes are characteristic of recent increases in the severity of criminal punishment. Mandatory minimums have been particularly popular in the war on drugs; recidivist statutes such as the three strikes laws, have been the weapon of choice in the overall war on crime. Federal criminal law spearheaded the implementation of mandatory minimum sentences for drug offenders. California criminal law was most influential in the spread of Draconian repeat offender statutes. By the end of the twentieth century, mandatory minimums for some drug offenses had escalated to life imprisonment without the possibility of parole, while some recidivist statutes mandated the same penalty for a third felony conviction and death penalty statutes throughout the country listed prior convictions as an aggravating factor upon which a sentence of death may be based.

The penalty enhancements for a previous conviction or convictions in particular are so harsh that they can best be explained by a desire to incapacitate certain persons identified as incurable "recidivists." As such, they fall into a growing category of punishments that attach to certain individuals rather than to their acts. For these punishments, criminal conduct is significant only insofar as it is symptomatic of the individual's characteristics, including his or her "dangerousness." Punishments of this sort include not only those reserved for "recidivists," "career offenders," and the like, but also those triggered by a classification as "sexual predator," "sex offender," or "gang member."

At some point, punishments based upon characteristics, rather than acts, become detached from the law of crimes. The less a punishment turns on a particular criminal act, that is, a crime, the more it resembles a regulatory measure. The distinction between criminal punishment and civil commitment erodes, so that ultimately punishment ceases to be punishment. Then offenders are no longer punished for their acts, but are disposed of according to society's incapacitative needs, much like they were once treated according to their rehabilitative needs. The second, incapacitative, phase of American criminal law reform thus reveals itself as the flip side of the first, rehabilitative, phase. Both proceeded from the classification of offenders as abnormal, with the only difference being that the rehabilitationists of the first phase held a firm belief in the possibility of correcting this abnormality, a belief that their incapacitationist successors abandoned. The paradigmatic measures of this new, incapacitative, mode of penal law are preventive detention and civil in rem forfeiture, not punishment. The cutting edge of the second phase of American criminal law reform, in other words, extends beyond the boundaries of criminal law itself into the realm of administration, with a concomitant shift of power from the legislative to the executive aspect of government.

The current ideology of incapacitation has been eager to differentiate those who deserve protection (us) from those against whom we need to be protected (them). It has shown little interest in differentiating among members of the latter group. The trend has been toward the development of a uniform law of punishment—or guidelines of incapacitation—for all dangerous persons, including the criminally insane and the young, who previously had remained outside the bounds of the law of crimes and the law of punishments.

The differentiation at the heart of modern incapacitative penalty has been subjected to frequent and vociferous criticism, so far without effect. Recently, attempts have been made instead to reduce current levels of incarceration through alternative sanctions without requiring a wholesale abandonment of the current mode of punishment. Insofar as these well-intentioned proposals presume the identification of offenders as criminologically abnormal (though "shaming" via the public assignment—and perhaps also the display—of labels like "thief" or "embezzler") and unworthy of the company of upstanding members of the community (perhaps through banishment), they affirm the differentiating impulse at the core of the incapacitative ideology that manifested itself in the costly explosion of imprisonment they hope to undo. Assuming that a system of criminal law can consistently be based on this impulse—and this assumption remains doubtful—time will tell whether an essentially irrational impulse can be divorced from its immediate manifestation, imprisonment and execution, through rational considerations of cost efficiency. So far, legislatures have been slow to put these proposals into action, although some judges have begun to experiment with unconventional punishments of this sort.

Imposition of sanctions (criminal procedure)

This article focuses on issues in substantive criminal law reform. Still, some reforms in procedural criminal law and the law of corrections will be mentioned, especially if they complement developments in substantive criminal law.

In general, recent decades have seen increased legislative activity in the area of criminal procedure, with a concomitant increase in the significance of statutory law. In the first phase of American penal law reform, the U.S. Supreme Court had taken over the field and reinvented it on constitutional grounds. The ultimate beneficiary of this development, however, once again has been the executive. The discretionary void left by the retraction of judicial—constitutional—constraints has not been filled with legislative—statutory—action. As in the field of substantive criminal law, legislative activity in the current phase of American penal law has been spotty and ad hoc, rather than comprehensive and long-term. While the codification efforts characteristic of the first phase of American penal law reform, which included not only the Model Penal Code but also a Model Code of Pre-Arraignment Procedure, were designed to constrain administrative discretion, recent legislative reforms have been eager to free that discretion in the name of maximum enforcement.

The transfer of substantive criminal law from codes to guidelines, and from the law of crimes to the law of punishments, also has resulted in a parallel paradigm shift in procedural criminal law, from the guilt phase of a criminal proceeding to its sentencing phase. Here, too, federal law has set the standard. The vast majority of criminal cases today are resolved not through a trial before a jury or a judge, but through plea bargaining. Although recent decades have seen an expansion of plea bargaining, this practice of course is nothing new in American criminal procedure. What may be new is that even in the few cases that still make it before a jury, the decisive findings of fact often do not occur until after the trial, at sentencing. Under the federal sentencing guidelines, for instance, the judge at sentencing now is free to consider all "relevant conduct," including, among other things, uncharged conduct and charged conduct of which the defendant was acquitted at the trial.

The significance of the sentencing hearing also has been bolstered by reforms implemented in response to the victims' rights movement as well as by the revival of capital punishment. Some victim-based reforms have affected the guilt phase of the criminal process, including rape shield laws and the right of victims to be consulted on proposed plea bargains. More important, however, victims now enjoy the right to submit victim impact statements at the sentencing hearing, either in writing or in person.

The inclusion of victim impact statements has been most controversial in the capital cases. Since the 1970s the U.S. Supreme Court has crafted an elaborate set of constitutional constraints on the sentencing of capital defendants. In the process, the Court created a separate sentencing trial in death penalty cases. It is in this trial, often but not necessarily before a jury, that the decision about life and death is made. And it is this separate and highly regulated proceeding that settles the constitutionality of the death penalty statute in general and of its application in a particular case. Since 1989, the sentencer may be presented with "victim" impact statements by surviving friends and relatives of the victims, at least one of whom will not have survived the crime, since the Supreme Court effectively has limited capital punishment to homicide.

Mirroring the curtailment of the infancy defense in the law of crimes and the incorporation of juvenile penalties into uniform sentencing guidelines in the law of punishments, the law of criminal procedure also has begun to collapse the distinction between adults and juveniles in the process of sanction imposition as more and more younger and younger persons are tried "as adults." Similarly, the criminally insane are increasingly adjudicated in regular criminal trials, rather than in civil commitment proceedings, as the newly created verdict of "guilty but mentally ill" has replaced the traditional one of "not guilty by reason of insanity."

Infliction of sanctions (prison or correction law)

Recent reforms in the law of the infliction of sanctions—prison or correction law—have generally developed along the lines of reform in the law of sanction imposition—criminal procedure. The ambitious codification projects of the immediate postwar era have met with little success. The subsequent massive effort by federal courts, led by the Supreme Court, to reform the infliction of punishment in American prisons through constitutional law also has ground to a halt. Recent legislation in this area has sought to restore executive discretion over prison management and to implement the incapacitative ideology characteristic of the second phase of American penal law reform. The abandonment of rehabilitation in favor of incapacitation has brought the cancellation of educational and rehabilitative programs, the removal of recreational facilities, and—in keeping with similar developments in the substantive and procedural criminal law—the restriction of probation, the abolition of parole, as well as the incarceration of young and mentally ill offenders in regular adult prisons. The paradigmatic modern prison is the Special Housing Unit, prisons surrounded with high voltage barbed wire and patrolled by heavily armed guards in flak jackets, where inmates are kept in bare concrete cells twenty-three hours a day, with one hour of solitary supervised exercise.

Legislatures recently have shown so little interest in the law of correction that they have delegated prison administration to private firms. In effect, the law of correction has all but disappeared, as one might expect at a time when the ideal of rehabilitation has been thoroughly discredited.

In stark contrast, the American Law Institute's Model Penal Code, the central document of the first phase of postwar reform, included a full-fledged correction code, a fact that has long since been forgotten. In fact, the "correctional" component of this self-styled "Penal and Correctional Code" covered two of the Code's four parts and was far more elaborate than the notoriously narrow special part of its "penal" half (part 2), which contained definitions of only a limited number of specific offenses, leaving the remainder to the individual legislatures. The penal component of the code (parts 1 and 2), in fact, should be read from the vantage point of its correctional component (parts 3 and 4). The Model Penal Code drafters saw the significance of the Code's first two parts as identifying offenders' correctional needs, with the Code's last two parts (entitled "treatment and correction" and "organization of correction," respectively) specifying how these needs were to be met by the correctional system. Nonetheless, despite the widespread adoption of the Model Penal Code, the Correctional Code has been widely ignored.

Conclusion

The second phase of American penal law reform has yet to run its course. Driven by an all-consuming desire to incapacitate, it placed into the hands of the executive formidable crime suppression tools. But run its course it will, as the pursuit of crime suppression at all costs will either reveal itself as futile or meet with sufficient apparent success to calm the punitive passions, which at any rate cannot be sustained indefinitely at their current fever pitch, no matter how hard the media and some politicians might try.

Still, the next phase of American penal law reform cannot simply recapture the sense of expert confidence that gave rise to the Model Penal Code. It remains to be seen in particular whether the American Law Institute today could produce a piece of model penal legislation that would deserve and gain widespread acceptance among American legislatures. Unless the status of the study and practice of American criminal law dramatically and quickly improves, this body of distinguished jurists, not many of whom can claim an expertise in penal law, may find it difficult to muster the considerable personal resources required for such an ambitious project, nor will the necessary financial support from private foundations materialize.

The original Model Penal Code was drafted with generous foundation support over the course of a decade under the exceptional leadership of Herbert Wechsler, who uniquely combined in him absolute command of the law and a sense for legal codification with a remarkable ability for leadership and similarly formidable powers of persuasion. As the fast waning of the original Code's significance has made clear, the long-term success of the new Model Penal Code project would require an even greater commitment of personal and financial resources, as well as technical expertise.

The original Code soon lost influence over penal law reform partly because it remained frozen in the ideology of its time. The penal policy of postwar America was rehabilitation and the entire Penal and Correctional Code was built around that policy, with the penal code guiding the diagnosis of abnormalities to be treated according to the prescriptions outlined in the correctional code. As rehabilitation faded, so did the Code's influence.

A new Model Penal Code could not resurrect rehabilitationism. It need not adopt wholesale incapacitationism, either. A retributive justice approach might suggest itself as an alternative. Rehabilitationism and incapacitationism after all share a morally suspect common core, the assumption of the offender's abnormality. Rehabil-

itation and incapacitation are two sides of the same treatment coin. Rehabilitation is treatment for the curable; incapacitation is how the incurable are treated.

The arguments for retributivism are familiar from the determinate sentencing debate of the 1970s and 1980s. At least in theory if not necessarily in policy, retributivism carried the day then, though its triumph proved short-lived. As the substantially incapacitative federal sentencing guidelines powerfully illustrate, the actual implementation of the idea of determinate sentencing need not have much to do with the idea's retributive foundation.

Regardless of which theory of punishment it takes as its starting point, a new Model Penal Code will not succeed unless it manages to shift the burden of penal justification back onto the state, thereby reestablishing the presumption against criminalization. Neither maximum punitiveness nor the acting out of communal vengeance is a principle of rational, and therefore minimally justifiable, penal lawmaking. A new Code would have succeeded if it managed to remind American legislatures that the penal law, as any other exercise of their power to coerce through law, must be justifiable to all members of the political community, including importantly those who stand to suffer its consequences.

Even the most thoughtful Model Penal Code, however, will find it difficult to retain its influence over time unless it is continuously reviewed by a standing commission of experts. With the onset of the war on drugs in the 1970s, the original Model Code was condemned to irrelevance. Anticipating a trend that would peak in the 1960s, the Code drafters had relegated drug offenses to a class of regulatory offenses unworthy of consideration in a major comprehensive codification of crimes. Today, drug offenses occupy a central place in the criminal law of every American jurisdiction. They carry very severe penalties, and occupy police departments, prosecutors offices, courts, and wardens throughout the country, and especially in the federal system. No modern Model Penal Code with any hope of serving as a model for actual codes today can afford to ignore drug offenses or any of the other new offense types that poured out of noncodified jurisdictions in the years after the promulgation of the original Code, including RICO and its offspring.

A standing criminal law commission would ensure that the Model Code speaks to the concerns of the day. By carefully considering if and how proposals for penal law reform might be integrated into the existing purposes and structure of the Code, as well as by drafting model provisions on particular subjects of concern, such a group of criminal law experts could provide principled legislators with the kind of general and specific guidance that they have lacked since the publication of the original Model Penal Code in 1962.

MARKUS DIRK DUBBER

See also CIVIL AND CRIMINAL DIVIDE; CRIMINAL LAW REFORM: HISTORICAL DEVELOPMENT IN THE UNITED STATES; HATE CRIMES; POLITICAL PROCESS AND CRIME; SENTENCING: GUIDELINES; SENTENCING: MANDATORY AND MANDATORY MINIMUM SENTENCES; SEXUAL PREDATORS; SHAMING PUNISHMENTS.

BIBLIOGRAPHY

ALLEN, FRANCIS A. *The Decline of the Rehabilitative Ideal: Penal Policy and Social Purpose.* New Haven, Conn.: Yale University Press, 1981.

American Law Institute. *Model Penal Code and Commentaries: Official Draft and Revised Comments.* Philadelphia: ALI, 1980.

BRAITHWAITE, JOHN. *Crime, Shame and Reintegration.* Cambridge and New York: Cambridge University Press, 1989.

DUBBER, MARKUS DIRK. "Recidivist Statutes as Arational Punishment." *Buffalo Law Review* 43 (1995): 689–724.

FELD, BARRY C. *Bad Kids: Race and the Transformation of the Juvenile Court.* Oxford University Press, 1999.

FLETCHER, GEORGE P. *With Justice for Some: Victims' Rights in Criminal Trials.* Reading, Mass.: Addison-Wesley, 1995.

FREED, DANIEL J. "Federal Sentencing in the Wake of Guidelines: Unacceptable Limits on the Discretion of Sentencers." *Yale Law Journal* 101 (1992): 1681–1754.

HENDERSON, LYNNE N. "The Wrongs of Victim's Rights." *Stanford Law Review* 37 (1985): 937–1021.

VON HIRSCH, ANDREW. *Doing Justice: The Choice of Punishments.* New York: Hill and Wang, 1976.

JACOBS, JAMES B., and POTTER, KIMBERLY. *Hate Crimes: Criminal Law & Identity Politics.* New York: Oxford University Press, 1998.

KADISH, SANFORD H. "Fifty Years of Criminal Law: An Opinionated Review." *California Law Review* 87 (1999): 943–982.

KAHAN, DAN M. "What Do Alternative Sanctions Mean?" *University of Chicago Law Review* 63 (1996): 591–653.

KAHAN, DAN M., and MEARES, TRACEY L. "The Coming Crisis of Criminal Procedure." *Georgetown Law Journal* 86 (1998): 1153–1184.

LYNCH, GERARD E. "RICO: The Crime of Being a Criminal, Parts I & II." *Columbia Law Review* 87 (1987): 661–764.

———. "RICO: The Crime of Being a Criminal, Parts III & IV." *Columbia Law Review* 87 (1987): 920–984.

"Symposium: The Model Penal Code Revisited." *Buffalo Criminal Law Review* 4 (forthcoming 2000): 1.

"Symposium: Rethinking Federal Criminal Law." *Buffalo Criminal Law Review* 1 (1997): 1–272.

"Symposium: Toward a New Federal Criminal Code." *Buffalo Criminal Law Review* 2 (1998): 1–365.

"Symposium: Victims and the Criminal Law." *Buffalo Criminal Law Review* 3 (1999): 1–315.

TONRY, MICHAEL H. *Malign Neglect: Race, Crime, and Punishment in America.* New York: Oxford University Press, 1995.

WECHSLER, HERBERT. "The Challenge of a Model Penal Code." *Harvard Law Review* 65 (1952): 1097–1133.

WILSON, JAMES Q. *Thinking about Crime.* 2d ed. New York: Basic Books, 1983.

WINDLESHAM, DAVID. *Politics, Punishment, and Populism.* New York: Oxford University Press, 1998.

ZIMRING, FRANKLIN E., and HAWKINS, GORDON J. *Incapacitation: Penal Confinement and the Restraint of Crime.* New York: Oxford University Press, 1995.

CRIMINAL PROCEDURE: CONSTITUTIONAL ASPECTS

Criminal procedure is literally at the center of the U.S. Bill of Rights, as a quick glance at the Fourth, Fifth, and Sixth Amendments makes evident. But as a subfield of constitutional law, constitutional criminal procedure stands as an anomaly, with shaky historical and conceptual foundations.

In many other areas of constitutional law, major opinions of the Marshall Court helped lay the groundwork upon which modem jurisprudence builds. In thinking about judicial review and executive power, lawyers and their fellow citizens still look to *Marbury v. Madison*, 5 U.S. (1 Cranch) 137 (1803); in considering the basic structure of federal jurisdiction, we ponder *Martin v. Hunter's Lessee*, 14 U.S. (1 Wheat.) 304

(1816); in reflecting on the scope of Congress' enumerated powers, and related issues of federalism, we refer back to *McCulloch v. Maryland* 17 U.S. (4 Wheat.) 316 (1819); in considering vested property rights, we return to *Fletcher v. Peck*, 10 U.S. (6 Cranch) 87 (l810), and *Dartmouth College v. Woodward* 17 U.S. (4 Wheat.) 518 (1819); and so on. But no comparable Marshall Court landmarks dot the plain of constitutional criminal procedure.

It is often thought that the explanation for this anomaly lies in another Marshall Court landmark, *Barron v. Baltimore*, 32 U.S. (7 Pet.) 243 (1833). Most criminal law, the argument goes, is state law: murder, rape, robbery, and the like are generally not federal crimes. Under *Barron*, the constitutional criminal procedure rules of the Bill of Rights did not apply against states, and so the Marshall Court predictably heard few cases raising issues of constitutional criminal procedure.

Barron is indeed part of the story, but only part. The federal government was very much in the crime-fighting business in the first century of the Bill of Rights. For constitutional scholars, perhaps the most vivid example of early federal criminal law comes from the infamous Sedition Act of 1790, but we must also not forget the territories. Perhaps the most central and sustained project of the federal government in its first century was the "Americanization" of this continent through territorial expansion, organization of territorial governments, and eventual admission to statehood of these territories. In the territories, the federal government did indeed enforce criminal laws against murder, rape, robbery, and so on. And the Bill of Rights applied to these criminal cases, even under *Barron*. Territorial law was, constitutionally speaking, federal law.

But for virtually the entire first century of the Bill of Rights, the U.S. Supreme Court lacked general appellate jurisdiction over federal criminal cases. This little-known fact helps explain why, for example, the Sedition Act prosecutions in the late 1790s—which raised the most important and far-reaching constitutional issues of their day—never reached the Supreme Court for ultimate judicial resolution.

By the time Congress decided to give the high court general appellate review over federal criminal cases in 1891, the sun was already setting on the territorial era. Thus, the criminal cases the Supreme Court heard under the new jurisdictional regime were a skewed lot, with disproportionately more federal customs violations,

tax evasions, and bootleggings than murders, rapes, and robberies. It was during this era that the intellectual and conceptual foundations of some of today's most controversial criminal procedure rules were laid.

In the 1886 case *Boyd v. United States*, 116 U.S. 616, the Court melded the Fourth Amendment rule against unreasonable searches and seizures with the Fifth Amendment ban on compelled self-incrimination to suppress various papers that the government had in effect subpoenaed and sought to use in court against the target of the subpoena. The *Boyd* Court thus laid the intellectual groundwork for what later become known as the Fourth Amendment exclusionary rule: inculpatory evidence discovered in violation of the ban on unreasonable searches and seizures cannot be introduced in criminal cases. (Today, of course, this "rule" has many exceptions.)

The history of the exclusionary rule is interesting to trace, and nicely illustrates some of the larger problems of modern American constitutional criminal procedure—in particular, the awkward relationship between current doctrines and founding principles. Prior to *Boyd*, no court in America—state or federal—had ever excluded evidence on the ground that it was unconstitutionally obtained. Virtually every state had a state constitutional counterpart to the Fourth Amendment, so the sheer number of cases admitting such evidence is staggering to contemplate. Indeed, in a famous 1822 circuit court case (*United States v. La Jeune Eugenie*, 26F. Cas. 832), the scholarly Justice Story rejected the exclusionary rule in a dismissive opinion proclaiming that he had never heard of such an outlandish idea in Anglo-American law. (England never had anything like the modem American exclusionary rule—in the words of one famous 1861 English case (*The Queen v. Leathram*, 121 Eng. Rep. 589 (Q.B.)), "It matters not how you get it [evidence, that is]; if you steal it even, it would be admissible.")

Post-*Boyd* cases, like *Weeks v. United States*, 232 U.S. 383 (1914), helped crystalize the emerging American exclusionary rule in situations where various papers and other testimonial materials were seized; the key theory of these cases was that to introduce the seized papers against their owner in a criminal case would be akin to forcing the defendant to testify against himself in violation of the Fifth Amendment ban against compelled self-incrimination. Thus the exclusionary rule was born not simply to undo or remedy a past (out-of court) violation of the Fourth Amendment, but also to prevent a later (in-court) violation of Fifth Amendment principles. Only this fusion of the Fourth and Fifth Amendments can explain basic features of the exclusionary rule—for example, the fact that unconstitutionally seized evidence may be used in civil cases, as in *United States v. Janis*, 428 U.S. 433 (1976), or against persons other than the searchee, as in *Agnello v. United States*, 269 U.S. 20, 35 (1925). These limits are hard to explain in purely Fourth Amendment terms—for example, the amendment nowhere distinguishes between civil and criminal cases. But these limits are more readily explicable under a Fifth Amendment theory: under the explicit words of this amendment a person cannot be compelled to be a witness against himself in his own criminal prosecution, but he can, for example, be obliged to testify against himself in a civil case—and so the use of his seized papers in a civil context likewise presents no Fifth Amendment problem.

Post-*Weeks* cases then began to exclude from criminal cases even nontestimonial evidence—physical things rather than private papers—that had been unconstitutionally seized from the searchee. The theory seems to have been that a person's lawful private property was an intimate part of himself, and, therefore, forcing a person's property to "testify" against him was akin to forcing him to testify against himself. This odd property fetishism harmonized with the strong protections of property characteristic of federal case law at the turn of the twentieth century—often referred to today as the *Lochner* era, in recognition of the famous case *Lochner v. New York*, 198 U.S. 45 (1905).

By mid-century, the Court was explicitly using the exclusionary rule even in situations where the seized evidence was plainly not the searchee's property but was instead contraband or stolen goods. The Court, however, did not squarely confront the logical implications of this extension, and most major Supreme Court exclusionary rule cases from 1920 through 1960 continued to rely upon an interplay of the Fourth and Fifth Amendments, explicitly invoking both. For example, in *Mapp v. Ohio*, 367 U.S. 643 (1961), which held that states, too, were bound by the federal exclusionary rule, Justice Black's critical fifth vote was explicitly premised on a *Boyd*-brained theory of Fourth-Fifth fusion; and Justice Clark's opinion for the Court contained no less than six express or implied invocations of the Fifth Amendment.

In several more recent landmark cases, however—such as *Schmerber v. California*, 384 U.S. 757 (1966), *Fisher v. United States*, 425 U.S. 391 (1976), and *United States v. Leon*, 468 U.S. 897 (1984)—the Justices have explicitly and emphatically rejected the Fourth-Fifth fusion theory. *Boyd* itself is no longer good law, in many respects. The result, critics have argued, is a modem exclusionary rule without a firm conceptual basis. Once Fourth-Fifth fusion is rejected (and properly so, say the critics), what is the constitutional principle requiring exclusion? If the idea is that government should never profit from its own wrong, then must it return stolen goods to the thief, and a kidnap victim to the kidnapper, if it finds them in an unconstitutional search? Must it likewise refrain from using the evidence in civil cases? If evidentiary use of unconstitutionally seized material violates judicial integrity, why is such use generally admissible in civil cases, or in criminal cases against someone other than the searchee? If the rule is really justified by deterrence, aren't other possible remedial schemes capable of providing more deterrence, with more careful remedial tailoring between right and remedy, and at less overall social cost? Critics in particular try to point to the obvious conceptual and practical advantages of alternative remedial systems: damage awards and administrative remedies that would provide more compensation and justice for innocent citizens for whom the exclusionary rule rings hollow. (If the police find no incriminating evidence there is nothing to exclude; if they know they will find no evidence, but simply seek to harass, there is no deterrence whatsoever.) And many forms of unreasonable police behavior—police violence for example—have little or no causal nexus to the finding of evidence. To the critics, the exclusionary rule cannot work to remedy these Fourth Amendment violations; and so they believe there is need to devise sound alternative mechanisms. But once these mechanisms are truly in place, exclusion would not be necessary or proper—at least as a constitutional mandate. Or so the critics argue. (Many also argue that the current system of alternatives to exclusion is inadequate and should be beefed up in a variety of ways.)

The Court, however, has never squarely confronted this set of basic remedial questions, because the Justices, as explained above, did not originally conceive of exclusion in modern deterrence-based remedial terms. Indeed, as late as 1961, when the Court imposed the rule on states, there was not in place anything remotely like a proper system of federal damage remedies for state constitutional torts: A federal law allowing damages for constitutional violations had lain dormant for almost a century, and was only revitalized by the Court in the early 1960s, beginning with the landmark case of *Monroe v. Pape*, 365 U.S. 167 (1961). Nor had the Court yet decided that the Fourth Amendment itself provided a cause of action for damages against offending federal officials (*Bivens v. Six Unknown Named Agents of the Federal Bureau of Narcotics*, 403 U.S. 388 (1971)). As a result, the exclusionary rule took root in a remedially impoverished milieu, and without clear analysis of the relative advantages and disadvantages of alternative remedial schema.

The conceptual confusion surrounding the current exclusionary rule is mirrored by considerable confusion about the basic meaning and purpose of the Fifth Amendment rule prohibiting compelled self-incrimination. Soon after *Boyd* was decided, the Court began to develop its Fifth Amendment self-incrimination jurisprudence. In *Counselman v. Hitchcock*, 142 U.S. 547 (1892), the Court faced the following question: what immunity must a person receive before he may be obliged to speak outside his own criminal case, for example, in a civil case brought against him, or a grand jury proceeding, or a legislative hearing? The *Counselman* Court insisted that a person be given total ("transactional") immunity from prosecution in such a situation. Not only could his compelled words never be used against him, but also no physical evidence discovered as a result of his testimony could be used against him; indeed, no prosecution could ever be brought against him, even if all the evidence adduced was proved to be wholly independent and nonderivative. Building on *Boyd*, the *Counselman* Court thus held that the self-incrimination clause should be read expansively to support broad principles of evidentiary exclusion. Later cases have restricted *Counselman*—allowing prosecution where all the evidence introduced is shown to be independent—but none of these cases has explained exactly where the new rule of "use plus use-fruits" immunity (or the old rule of "transactional immunity," for that matter), comes from. Nor have these cases explained exactly what the Fifth Amendment stands for, and why.

Some modern critics have argued for a narrower rule of "testimonial immunity" under which a person may be compelled to speak outside his criminal case, with the secure immunity

that his compelled words cannot ever be introduced against him in a criminal proceeding. But, say proponents of testimonial immunity, fruits of the immunized statement—any leads that the government tracks down as a result of the statement—should generally be admissible. The Constitution prohibits only the introduction of the words themselves; if those words are never introduced at trial, a person never will have been impermissibly compelled to be a testifying "witness" against himself in a criminal case (i.e., a trial). And the purpose of this narrow rule of immunity and of the Fifth Amendment itself, it is argued, it to protect an innocent person from erroneous conviction, rather than to protect a guilty person as such. Innocent folk, when questioned by clever prosecutors, can sometimes be made to look guilty, and so they should not be forced to speak before the jury, or in some deposition that can later be read to the jury. But if their words lead to reliable "fruit"—a murder weapon with fingerprints, for example—that fruit should itself be admissible under the letter and spirit of the Fifth Amendment, say the critics. This was indeed the dominant rule in America (and in England) prior to *Boyd* and *Counselman*. The critics' account also helps explain the intuition behind more modern cases like *Schmerber* (1966), which allow the government to force a criminal defendant to give a blood sample or a handwriting exemplar or voice sample, on the theory that these reliable bits of physical evidence are not the kind of unreliable "witnessing" that the Amendment seeks to protect against. Current Fifth Amendment self-incrimination doctrine, however, has not embraced the critics' revisionist account; but the Court has left the field in a state of intellectual disarray, in which it is far from clear what the main purpose of the Amendment truly is. Lacking even the most basic consensus on the big idea (or ideas) underlying the Amendment, the Court has had difficulty defending the many ways in which it has invoked or limited the clause.

Boyd and the Fourth and Fifth Amendment cases that followed it for the next two generations mostly dealt with corporate and regulatory offenses, because these amendments at the time applied only against the federal government, and the federal government had a rather limited criminal agenda at the turn of the twentieth century. These cases established controversial, pro-defendant rules, but almost none of them dealt with violent crime. It was not until the Warren Court (1953–1969) incorporated these and many other criminal procedure clauses against the states that they began to be applied regularly to violent crimes. Under an approach eventually labeled "selective incorporation"—the theory whereby the Fourteenth Amendment incorporates against the states those provisions of the Bill of Rights deemed "fundamental"—the mid-century Court began to apply the criminal procedure clauses to the states. Although most of this incorporation took place during the Warren Court, some of its roots lie in the 1930s and 1940s.

In the famous "Scottsboro Boys" case of *Powell v. Alabama*, 287 U.S. 45 (1932), involving poor black defendants tried in a highly racially charged and unfair proceeding, the Court held that the right to a fair trial and the right to appointed counsel in capital cases were necessary components of due process of law under the Fourteenth Amendment, and thus enforceable against the states. In the 1948 case *In re Oliver*, 333 U.S. 257 (1948), the Court in effect held that the right to a public trial—a right explicitly protected against the federal government by the Sixth Amendment—is also an inherent part of Fourteenth Amendment due process, and thus no state trial can ever take place in secret. And in the 1949 case *Wolf v. Colorado*, 338 U.S. 25, the Court made the Fourth Amendment's protection against unreasonable searches and seizures applicable to the states, but declined to saddle states with the exclusionary rule, choosing instead to allow states to fashion their own remedies for unreasonable searches and seizures.

In one of the most important criminal procedure decisions of the Warren Court, *Mapp v. Ohio* (1961), the Justices modified *Wolf* and incorporated the exclusionary rule against states. Two years later, the Court held that defense counsel is a necessary part of a fair criminal case. Thus, in *Gideon v. Wainwright*, 372 U.S. 335 (1963), the Court decided that the states must provide attorneys to indigent defendants in all felony cases, not just capital cases, as the *Powell* Court held.

The next year, in *Malloy v. Hogan*, 378 U.S. 1 (1964), the Court explicitly began to conceptualize its task as deciding which clauses of the Bill of Rights were so fundamental as to apply against states in every jot and tittle—the approach now known as "selective incorporation." Eventually, this process would lead to the application of almost all of the Bill of Rights against the states. This application derives strong support from the original intent of the Fourteenth Amendment, whose framers saw the provisions of the Bill of Rights as paradigmatic "privileges and immunities of citizens" that no state should be allowed to abridge. (The Justices have tended to emphasize the language of "due process" rather than "privileges and immunities," however, in part to avoid the need to confront an early emasculation of the Fourteenth Amendment's privileges or immunities clause in the *Slaughterhouse Cases*, 83 U.S. (16 Wall.) 36 (1873)).

Malloy held that the Fifth Amendment right against self-incrimination was made applicable to the states via the Fourteenth Amendment, and the year after that, in *Pointer v. Texas*, 380 U.S. 400 (1965), incorporated the defendant's Sixth Amendment right to confront witnesses against him. Soon thereafter, the Court incorporated the Sixth Amendment right to speedy trial (*Klopfer v. North Carolina*, 386 U.S. 213 (1967)); the Sixth Amendment right to compulsory process (*Washington v. Texas*, 388 U.S. 14 (1967)); the Sixth Amendment right to jury trial (*Duncan v. Louisiana*, 391 U.S. 145 (1968); the Fifth Amendment right against double jeopardy (*Benton v. Maryland*, 395 U.S. 284 (1969)); and the Eighth Amendment right to bail (*Schlib v. Kuebel*, 404 U.S. 357 (1971) (dictum)).

At the same time that the incorporation movement was gaining speed, the Warren Court also profoundly revised the law of police station interrogation. In *Escobedo v. Illinois*, 378 U.S. 478 (1964), the Court excluded a confession obtained during a prolonged interrogation of a suspect who had been advised of neither his right to an attorney nor his right to remain silent. Escobedo had asked for a lawyer several times at the police station, but his request was denied. In fact, Escobedo's mother had retained a lawyer for him, who came to the police station but was not allowed to confer with the client. Two years later, in *Miranda v. Arizona*, 384 U.S. 436 (1966), Chief Justice Warren went much further, holding that prosecutors could never use statements made by defendants while in custody unless the prosecutors could demonstrate the use of procedural safeguards to protect against Fifth Amendment violations. These safeguards, the Court suggested, should amount to informing the defendant of her right to remain silent, of the fact that any statement she did make could be used against her, and of her right to an attorney, either hired by her or appointed by the state. Under the *Miranda* regime, a defendant in custody was free to remain silent without any adverse inference of guilt. Perhaps even more exuberant than *Miranda* (though less politically salient) was the Court's ruling in *Massiah v. United States*, 377 U.S. 201

(1964), which held inadmissible statements obtained from a sting operation of an indicted defendant, who—while not in custody, and free from any compulsion whatsoever—bragged about his crimes to someone who, unbeknownst to him, was an undercover agent.

These and other Warren Court cases constituted nothing less than a revolution in criminal procedure. By the end, the Court's "selective incorporation" resulted in the application of all of federal constitutional criminal procedure against the states, except the Fifth Amendment right of grand jury indictment. In the process, the nature of the defendants invoking constitutional criminal procedure rights changed radically. Now the exclusionary rule, the right against self-incrimination, and the rest, were no longer limited to cases of corporate and regulatory offenses, but also applied to murder and robbery. To many ordinary persons and some scholars, it seemed outrageous to see murderers and thieves going free because, for instance, clearly relevant and inculpatory evidence was found in technical violation of the Fourth Amendment. Many other scholars, however, have lamented the passing of the Warren Court "revolution," which they believe provided a needed antidote to alleged governmental overreaching.

The mid-century Court's constitutional criminal procedure doctrine also seemed to some to suffer from some serious legal flaws. For instance, the Court repeatedly held that the Fourth Amendment generally requires warrants and probable cause for all searches and seizures. But the Amendment, when read carefully, does not say this. No early state constitution says this; and no leading Founder or early case or treatise says this, either. The Amendment says simply that all searches and seizures must be reasonable, without further saying that reasonableness always or even presumptively means a warrant or probable cause. Historically, a vast number of serious intrusions—arrests and border searches, to name just two—have not required warrants; and as a practical matter, there are many situations where it would not be sensible to require even probable cause. (Consider for example metal detectors at airports and in court houses.) The Warren Court itself admitted as much in the 1968 case *Terry v. Ohio*, 392 U.S. 1, authored by Earl Warren himself speaking for eight Justices. *Terry* upheld a police weapons "frisk" for self-protection even though no probable cause existed—and thus a warrant could never have been properly issued (since the Amendment does insist that all warrants be backed by probable cause). But *Terry* nowhere explained how this result could be squared with the Court's general insistence that the Amendment did ordinarily require warrants and probable cause. Critics have argued that the warrant requirement is textually incorrect, historically mistaken, and functionally suspect, and that the Court's efforts to adhere to this requirement while also recognizing various exceptions is intellectually bankrupt. By 1991, Justice Scalia counted about twenty exceptions to the warrant "requirement" (*California v. Acevedo*, 500 U.S. 565, 582-83 (1991) (Scalia, J., concurring in judgment)).

As noted above, the Court's self-incrimination case law is likewise a conceptual muddle. Moreover, the Court's interpretation of the Fifth Amendment's self-incrimination clause seems to conflict with the Sixth Amendment right to compel testimony in one's defense. Under the Court's 1972 ruling in *Kastigar v. United States*, 406 U.S. 441, a person compelled to testify against himself outside his own criminal case (say, in a legislative hearing, or someone else's criminal prosecution) must receive "use plus use-fruits immunity"—that is, neither the testimony nor any evidence it led to could later be used against him. As a result of *Kastigar*, an innocent defendant will often be denied the right to compel the testimony of a witness who, the defendant claims, is in fact the guilty culprit. To give every defendant the right to compel another suspect to take the stand, as the Constitution's Sixth Amendment seems to require, would, under *Kastigar*, enable a guilty defendant to give all of his partners in crime a general "immunity bath"—an obviously unacceptable result. But this conflict between Fifth and Sixth Amendment rights exists only because of the broad "use plus use-fruits" immunity rule. The more narrow and historically supportable principle of testimonial immunity would restore to every defendant the right to compel defense witnesses on equal terms with the prosecutor: immunity baths are not a problem because the government loses nothing when a defendant forces another suspect to take the stand. Thus, the unhappy result of current doctrine is that an overbroad, nontextual, ahistorical reading of the Fifth Amendment requires an underprotective, nontextual, and ahistorical reading of the Sixth Amendment. Even worse, the Court's regime ends up overprotecting the interests of guilty defendants at the expense of innocent ones. And this overprotection—say critics—is a more general feature of the current landscape of constitutional criminal procedure. The Fourth Amendment exclusionary rule, Fifth Amendment immunity doctrine, Fifth Amendment double jeopardy doctrine, Sixth Amendment speedy trial rules concerning dismissal with prejudice—all these, say critics, end up in various ways protecting the guilty at the expense of (or with indifference to) the innocent.

In defense of the Warren Court, it must be said that the Justices were reacting to a regime that often seemed to run roughshod over the legitimate interests of the poor and racial minorities. Police departments were not integrated; remedial systems like section 1983 were not in place; and the third degree prevailed in a great many places. In many cases, juries were all-white because many blacks were disenfranchised, others were not allowed to be part of the jury venire, and still others were excluded by race-based peremptory challenges. One of the most impressive accomplishments of late twentieth-century constitutional criminal procedure has been a gradual integration of the jury, created by a combination of voting rights case law, voting rights statutes, jury reform statutes, and federal jury case law.

But, critics say, in many other areas of constitutional criminal procedure, the Warren Court overreacted by overconstitutionalizing, and by moving too quickly with rules that far outstripped the problems to be solved. More direct focus on civil remedies, on issues of class and poverty, on the rights of the innocent, on the nature of police brutality and police discretion, on the racial composition of police departments, and on other racial dimensions of the crime problem, may have been better than some of the indirect and overbroad strategies devised by the Court in cases like *Mapp*, *Miranda*, and *Massiah*. The interests of victims of crime—themselves disproportionately poor and black or brown, not to mention female—also seemed to get inadequate attention.

In sum, many of the criminal procedure rulings to come out of the Warren Court lacked firm grounding in constitutional text and structure. Key rulings ran counter to early case law both in lower federal courts and in state courts construing analogous provisions of state constitutions. Precisely because so few Marshall Court cases existed, the many breaks with Founding-era understandings were not highly visible. On key issues, the Warren Court seemed to contradict itself, laying down sweeping rules in some cases that it could not quite live by in other cases. On a politi-

cal level, many of the Warren Court's constitutional criminal procedure pronouncements did not sit well with the American people. The guilty—who now included murderers, thieves, and rapists, and not merely the corporate and regulatory offenders of pre-incorporation days—too often seemed to go free because of Warren Court rules. Indeed, many of these rules seemed tailor-made to protect guilt per se.

The result was, predictably, something of a political backlash. Accusations that the Warren Court was too easy on the guilty have given way to accusations that the Burger (1969–1986) and Rehnquist (1986–) Courts are too hard on the innocent. Habeas corpus rules, expanded by the Warren Court in ways that may have overprotected the guilty, have been retracted by later Justices and by Congress in ways that may now underprotect the innocent.

As noted above, the post–Warren Courts have continued to carve out exceptions to the warrant requirement without replacing it with a clear concept of what reasonableness entails. Moreover, the Court has crafted an increasing number of exceptions to the Fourth Amendment exclusionary rule, most dramatically a habeas exception, *Stone v. Powell*, 428 U.S. 465 (1976); an impeachment exception, *United States v. Havens*, 446 U.S. 620 (1980); and a good faith exception, *United States v. Leon* (1984). The post–Warren Court has also chipped away at the self-incrimination clause doctrine of the Warren Court. For example, in *Harris v. New York*, 401 U.S. 222 (1971), a five-Justice majority held that incriminating statements made without a *Miranda* warning could be used to impeach the accused's testimony at trial. *Miranda*, the Court seemed to say, was merely a prophylactic rule, and not all *Miranda*-defective statements were truly "compelled" in a way that would trigger the underlying Fifth Amendment right. And in *Oregon v. Elstad*, 470 U.S. 298 (1985), the Court suggested that the physical evidence and other fruits generated by a "mere" *Miranda* violation need not be suppressed at trial.

In many other areas, however, the Burger and Rehnquist Courts have not reacted against Warren Court rulings, and, in some cases, they have furthered the Warren Court's trends. In dealing with the Sixth Amendment speedy trial clause, the Court has continued to insist that dismissal with prejudice—that is, dismissal with no possibility of refiling charges later—is the only possible remedy for violations (*Strunk v. United States*, 412 U.S. 434 (1973)). Perhaps most fa-

CRIMINAL PROCEDURE: CONSTITUTIONAL ASPECTS 443

mously, since its ruling in *In re Winship*, 397 U.S. 358 (1970), the Court has continued to hold that the Fifth Amendment guarantee of due process of law requires that the prosecution prove guilt beyond a reasonable doubt—though defining the precise difference between offense elements governed by *Winship* and sentencing factors and affirmative defenses beyond the scope of *Winship* has not proved easy.

In one accepts the critical analysis set out above, this leaves the current state of constitutional criminal procedure in something of a mess. The Court has often seemed to proceed by indirection, at times distinguishing away precedent, at times ignoring it, at times adhering to it. When this new confusion is added to the contradictions that existed within the Warren Court, the state of constitutional criminal procedure becomes truly perplexing. The time thus seems ripe for an overhauling of the law. This seems even more likely given the current state of Court personnel: no one on the Court today served with Chief Justice Warren, and two-thirds of the Court never served with Chief Justice Burger. The question is how today's Justices should go about reorganizing the law. Precedent alone certainly cannot guide the way: precedent in this field is too often contradictory or perverse.

Some have recently suggested that constitutional criminal procedure be reevaluated with the protection of innocence as its primary purpose. Under this reading, the Fourth Amendment exclusionary rule would be discarded, as it protects only the guilty, as such. The exclusionary rule does not provide a direct remedy to innocent victims of unreasonable searches and seizures; no evidence is found in such searches, and so there is nothing to exclude. Instead, the exclusionary rule provides the most help to the most guilty—the proverbial murderer found with a bloody knife. A scheme of innocence protection would provide civil remedies, including but going beyond what the Court has done in *Bivens* and section 1983 cases. Such remedies would be available as a remedy for guilty defendants, as well as innocent ones, but would not aid guilty defendants because of their guilt, as does the exclusionary rule. Similarly, current Fifth Amendment self-incrimination case law could be profitably rethought. It makes sense in terms of protecting innocence (and innocents) to exclude compelled testimony itself: a cunning prosecutor may be able to make an innocent but inarticulate or unattractive defendant look guilty on the stand, even though he is not. However, the use of physical evidence does not raise these concerns. Indeed, the Fifth Amendment exclusion of physical evidence, like the Fourth Amendment exclusionary rule, protects defendants in direct proportion to their guilt. Thus, the rule of exclusion of "use fruits" as demanded by *Kastigar*, is dubious indeed. A scheme of only testimonial immunity—excluding possibly unreliable words without excluding reliable fruits—would continue to protect innocents while avoiding windfalls to the guilty. And as noted earlier, a regime of testimonial immunity would allow the Sixth Amendment to be construed more broadly, in ways that would aid innocent defendants who seek to prove their innocence at trial by compelling other suspects to take the stand. More generally, the due process clause, the double jeopardy clause, and the Sixth Amendment rights of speedy trial, counsel, compulsory process, and confrontation, should all be seen as having a strong unifying thread: The Constitution, rightly read, seeks to protect innocent defendants from erroneous convictions—it seeks to find the truth, not suppress it, in the interest of both the innocent, and society as a whole. Thus, by viewing innocence-protection as the primary purpose of the constitutional criminal procedure clauses, we may achieve a more unified, and more normatively attractive, interpretation linking the Fourth, Fifth, and Sixth Amendments—the centerpiece of the Constitution's Bill of Rights.

AKHIL REED AMAR

See also BURDEN OF PROOF; CAPITAL PUNISHMENT: LEGAL ASPECTS; CONFESSIONS; COUNSEL: RIGHT TO COUNSEL; DISCOVERY; DOUBLE JEOPARDY; EXCLUSIONARY RULE; EYEWITNESS IDENTIFICATION: CONSTITUTIONAL ASPECTS; HABEAS CORPUS; JURY: LEGAL ASPECTS; PROBATION AND PAROLE: PROCEDURAL PROTECTION; PUBLICITY IN CRIMINAL CASES; SEARCH AND SEIZURE; SENTENCING: PROCEDURAL PROTECTION; SPEEDY TRIAL; TRIAL, CRIMINAL; WIRETAPPING AND EAVESDROPPING.

BIBLIOGRAPHY

AMAR, AKHIL REED. *The Constitution and Criminal Procedure: First Principles.* New Haven, Conn.: Yale University Press, 1996.

AMSTERDAM, ANTHONY G. "Perspectives on the Fourth Amendment." *Minnesota Law Review* 58 (1974): 349.

CORWIN, EDWARD S. "The Supreme Court's Construction of the Self-Incrimination Clause." *Michigan Law Review* 29 (1930): 1.

DAVIES, THOMAS Y. "Recovering the Original Fourth Amendment." *Michigan Law Review* 98 (1999): 547–750.

FRIENDLY, HENRY J. "The Fifth Amendment Tomorrow: The Case for Constitutional Change." *University of Cincinnati Law Review* 37 (1968): 671.

———. "A Postscript on Miranda." In *Benchmarks*. Chicago: Chicago University Press, 1967. Page 266.

———. "The Bill of Rights as a Code of Criminal Procedure." *California Law Review* 53 (1965): 929.

STUNTZ, WILLIAM J. "The Substantive Origins of Criminal Procedure." *Yale Law Journal* 105 (1995): 393.

———. "The Uneasy Relationship between Criminal Procedure and Criminal Justice." *Yale Law Journal* 107 (1997): 1.

TAYLOR, TELFORD. *Two Studies on Constitutional Interpretation*. Columbus: Ohio State University Press, 1969.

CASES

Agnello v. United States, 232 U.S. 383 (1914).
Barron v. Baltimore, 32 U.S. (7 Pet.) 243 (1833).
Benton v. Maryland, 395 U.S. 284 (1969).
Boyd v. United States, 116 U.S. 616 (1886).
California v. Acevedo, 500 U.S. 565, 582–83 (1991).
Counselman v. Hitchcock, 142 U.S. 547 (1892).
Duncan v. Louisiana, 391 U.S. 145 (1968).
Escobedo v. Illinois, 378 U.S. 478 (1964).
Fisher v. United States, 425 U.S. 391 (1976).
Gideon v. Wainwright, 372 U.S. 335 (1963).
Harris v. New York, 401 U.S. 222 (1971).
In re Oliver, 333 U.S. 257 (1948).
In re Winship, 397 U.S. 358 (1970).
Kastigar v. United States, 406 U.S. 441 (1971).
Klopfer v. North Carolina, 386 U.S. 213 (1967).
Lochner v. New York, 198 U.S. (1905).
Malloy v. Hogan, 378 U.S. 1 (1964).
Mapp v. Ohio, 367 U.S. 643 (1961).
Massiah v. United States, 377 U.S. 201 (1964).
Miranda v. Arizona, 384 U.S. 436 (1966).
Monroe v. Pape, 365 U.S. 167 (1961).
Pointer v. Texas, 380 U.S. 400 (1965).
Powell v. Alabama, 287 U.S. 45 (1932).
The Queen v. Leatham, 121 Eng. Rep. 589 (Q.B.).
Schlib v. Kuebel, 404 U.S. 357 (1971).
Schmerber v. California, 384 U.S. 757 (1966).
Slaugherhouse Cases, 83 U.S. (16 Wall.) 36 (1873).
Stone v. Powell, 428 U.S. 465 (1976).
Strunk v. United States, 412 U.S. 434 (1973).
Terry v. Ohio, 392 U.S. 1 (1968).
United States v. Janis, 428 U.S. 433 (1976).
United States v. Havens, 446 U.S. 620 (1980).
United States v. La Jeune Eugenie, 26 F. Cas. 832 (1822).
United States v. Leon, 468 U.S. 902 (1984).
Weeks v. United States, 232 U.S. 383 (1914).

CRIMINAL PROCEDURE: COMPARATIVE ASPECTS

In the light of growing dissatisfaction with the realities of American criminal procedure, the criminal process of foreign countries has since the 1970s attracted growing interest among American scholars. They have sought possible models for domestic reform not only in other jurisdictions of the common law family but also in continental Europe, where the criminal process has followed a format quite different from the Anglo-American tradition.

Purposes and problems

The purpose of comparative research into foreign ways of conducting the criminal process is not limited to the satisfaction of scholarly curiosity, its results can also be put to practical use in various ways. Observation of foreign laws and practices can demonstrate that it is feasible to depart from one's own traditional solutions and thus back up reform proposals against conservative criticism. Looking abroad can also generate a pool of new ideas for law reform—ideas whose attractiveness increases in proportion to the perceived dysfunctionality of a system's own procedural system (cf. Frase, 1999; Frase and Weigend). Solutions that have thrived in a foreign system should, however, not be embraced without a healthy dose of skepticism. Even achieving a proper understanding of foreign legal systems is not as simple as it may appear. Domestic procedural institutions rarely have exact equivalents abroad, but their functions may be fulfilled by procedural arrangements that appear under a different name and sometimes in a totally different legal context, or practitioners may have developed functionally similar solutions without any explicit support in statutory law. To cite just one example: in continental procedure law, pleas of guilty or not guilty are unknown. Yet the main effect of a guilty plea, namely the radical abbreviation of the criminal trial, can be achieved by other means, for example, by a brief confession made at the beginning of the trial immediately followed by imposition of a sentence, or by the defendant's submission to being adjudicated on the record of pretrial proceedings. This example shows that it is crucial for comparativists to look not only beyond nominal parallels but even beyond a country's law on the books and to take procedural practice into account.

The second step, adaptation of a solution proven to "work" abroad creates even greater problems. Because of the interdependence of all elements of the criminal process, a procedural device that functions excellently in its original environment may be ineffectual or even counterproductive as a transplant severed from its roots. For example, the authors of the German Code of Criminal Procedure of 1877, fascinated by what they had seen flourish in England, introduced the possibility of examination and cross-examination of witnesses by the parties (Strafprozessordnung (StPO) vom 7. April 1987, Bundesgesetzblatt 1987 I, p. 1074, § 239). This option, which does not fit into the judge-dominated mode of the German trial, has almost never been used and is hardly known among German lawyers. Another possible pitfall for reformers intent on "borrowing" foreign solutions is the attitude of judges and lawyers: if they reject the transplant, perhaps because it seems to disturb the well-ingrained ways of doing justice, they can easily ignore or "integrate" any new institution into the old mold and thus prevent substantive change.

Two models of the criminal process

This entry does not advocate any particular legal reform but limits itself to providing outlines of the criminal process in some European countries, especially France, Germany, Italy, and Spain (for more detailed information on these and other systems see, Bradley, 1999 and Van den Wyngaert; for in-depth comparisons of two or three legal systems, see Fennell et al. (England and the Netherlands) and Hatchard et al. (England, France, and Germany)). Of these systems, France and Germany still represent, with great variations, the "inquisitorial" model of the criminal process, whereas Italy and Spain have procedural systems that represent intermediate solutions between the inquisitorial style of proceeding and the adversarial model practiced in the systems of the common law tradition.

One basic difference between the inquisitorial and the adversarial modes of conducting the criminal process lies in the definition of the goals of the process. The inquisitorial model is geared toward determining the truth of what has happened, and the judgment is based on findings of fact that approximate the historical truth as closely as possible; the adversary model regards the criminal process as a tool for the resolution of a dispute between the accuser (usually, a public prosecutor) and the accused, and it emphasizes the search for the truth only to the extent that truth-finding is necessary for the resolution of this dispute (cf. Damaska, 1998). Moreover, the adversary system, determined to provide both sides with a fair opportunity to win the contest, closely circumscribes the means by which facts can be established in court, and it excludes from the fact finder's consideration evidence that might unfairly prejudice one party. This basic contrast in outlook explains, for example, one of the conspicuous differences in evidence law between continental and common law systems: whereas hearsay evidence is generally admissible in inquisitorial systems (because even hearsay, regardless of its lesser reliability, can help the finder of fact in his or her attempt to find out what actually happened), common law systems exclude hearsay (with several exceptions) because its introduction would prevent the opposing party from effectively testing the truthfulness and reliability of the source of information (Damaska, 1997, pp. 79–81).

Inquisitorially oriented systems typically rely on neutral agents of the state (a judicial magistrate or a state's attorney cast in an objective role) to initially collect the evidence and to prepare the case for trial. At the trial stage, the court, in particular the presiding judge, is responsible for introducing the relevant evidence, and the attorneys for the state and for the defense play only supplementary roles. In the adversary system, by contrast, each party (i.e., the prosecutor and the defense) collects and presents the evidence favoring its position. The judge plays the role of an umpire at the trial stage, whereas a jury of laypersons is typically responsible for finding the verdict. The Italian approach is similar to the adversary model in that trial proceedings are adversarial, but trial is preceded by a thorough pretrial investigation conducted by the public prosecutor, who at that stage is expected by the law to act in an "objective" fashion and to also investigate facts favoring the suspect (Codice di procedura penale, allegato al decreto del Presidente della Repubblica 22 sept. 1988, n. 447 (Italian CP), art. 358). Before a case can go to trial, the results of the pretrial investigation must be submitted to a magistrate; he or she determines whether there is sufficient evidence against the suspect and whether the case can be resolved—if the defendant consents—by convicting and sentencing him on the spot, without trial (Italian CCP, arts. 416–433). Spanish procedure similarly provides for a combination between an inquisitorial investigation and a party-dominated trial (for an overview, see Vogler, pp. 394–396).

The existence of such eclectic systems—of which there are more—demonstrates that the inquisitorial and adversarial models of the process are merely ideal-types (Damaska, 1975), convenient for reference in scientific debate but with limited relevance for the understanding of a particular country's procedural system. It is unclear to what extent either of these models has historically existed in pure form; today, in any event, every system of criminal procedure includes inquisitorial as well as adversarial features.

Investigation

Investigation of a reported offense is the first step in the criminal process. The law typically entrusts either an investigating magistrate, as in France (Code de Procédure Pénale, Loi n. 57-1426 du 31 déc. 1957 (French CPP), arts. 80, 81) and Spain (Ley de Enjuiciamiento Criminal, promulgada por real decreto de 14 de sept. de 1882 (LEC), art. 306), or the state's attorney, as in Germany (StPO, § 160) and Italy (Italian CPP, art. 327), with conducting the investigation, but in fact it is almost invariably the police who interrogate suspects and witnesses, seize physical evidence, and do everything else necessary to collect proof for a later trial (see StPO, § 163; Italian CPP, Art. 348).

Whenever it is necessary, in the course of an investigation, to seriously interfere with citizens' privacy or liberty interests, for example, by searching a home or placing a person under arrest, the police need prior judicial permission or, if exigent cirumstances have precluded the police from requesting a judicial warrant, at least a magistrate's subsequent authorization of the relevant measure. Pretrial custody, as the most serious invasion of personal liberty, invariably requires a judicial warrant (French CPP, art. 146; StPO, § 114; Italian CPP, art. 292; LEC, art. 502). Provisional arrest and short-term detention (up to two or three days) can, however, be imposed by nonjudicial officers when there is strong suspicion against a person, especially when he or she has been apprehended while committing an offense or shortly thereafter (French CPP, art.

63; StPO, § 127; Italian CPP, arts. 380–386; Spanish Constitution, art. 17 sec. 2).

When suspects are interrogated by the police, most of these systems require informing the suspect of the right to consult an attorney (French CCP, art. 63–4 (1); StPO, §§ 136 (1), 163a (4); Italian CCP, art. 350(2); LEC, art. 118). Germany and France (in custodial interrogations) also require a warning about the right to remain silent (French CCP, art. 63–1(1); StPO §§ 136(1), 163a (4)).

Searches and seizures must on principle be ordered by a magistrate, but they can be conducted without such authorization when it is necessary to act immediately, for example when illegal drugs or weapons have been seen on someone's premises and there is the risk that they will be concealed or destroyed while the police attempt to obtain a judicial warrant (French CPP, art. 56; StPO, §§ 105, 111e; Italian CPP, art 352). Searches can legally be conducted only if the police suspect that evidence of a crime or items subject to confiscation will be found. Required standards of suspicion tend to be lower in continental systems than under U.S. law (Bradley, 1983). Because the law accords the individual less extensive protection against invasions of privacy in the course of a criminal investigation, cases involving the issue of rule-breaking by the police occur less frequently than in the United States. Conflicts between the interests of vigorous law enforcement and individual rights nevertheless arise, and the protection of citizens from overzealous police is an important policy issue in all systems.

Control of police

One possible way of controlling police is the imposition of individual civil and criminal liability for unlawful invasions of citizens' rights. Such remedies are available in most legal systems, but they are notoriously ineffectual in cases of misconduct below the level of outright brutality. The same must be said of formal disciplinary proceedings. Internal discipline generally functions comparatively well within hierarchical statewide or nationwide police forces, yet disciplinary measures are often regarded as being out of proportion with respect to routine violations and therefore are initiated only for the most egregious offenses.

In many systems, the police are formally regarded as auxiliaries of the state's attorney and subject to his or her orders and supervision (see, e.g., French CPP, arts. 12, 13; German Gerichts-verfassungsgesetz (GVG) vom 9. Mai 1975, Bundesgesetzblatt 1975 I, p. 1077, § 152). But prosecutorial supervision does not provide an effective check on police activities because prosecutors typically remain aloof from routine investigations and police agencies do not look favorably upon "outside" interference.

Another approach toward guaranteeing the legality of pretrial proceedings is to entrust an impartial magistrate with conducting the investigation. The institution of the investigating magistrate has long been a hallmark of continental criminal procedure. At the beginning of the twenty-first century, this institution still exists in France, Spain, and the Netherlands but has been abolished in Germany and Italy, among other countries. In those systems that still retain the investigating magistrate procedure, its practical relevance is limited to the most serious cases, and even there many of the steps in collecting evidence are delegated to judicial police. It would indeed be unrealistic to expect that a magistrate could single-handedly conduct or even effectively control the investigation as long as the police monopolize the requisite manpower, information, equipment, and experience. The "myth of judicial supervision" (see Goldstein and Marcus, pp. 246–259) as well as the formal authority of state's attorneys over pretrial proceedings may in fact provide a convenient legal smokescreen behind which the police are shielded from effective control.

Lacking the legal and institutional mechanisms described above, American law has adopted an indirect approach designed to give maximum protection to the individual. According to U.S. law, evidence obtained in violation of a suspect's rights cannot be used in court to support a conviction (*Mapp v. Ohio*, 367 U.S. 643 (1961); *Dickerson v. U.S.*, 120 S.Ct. 2326 (2000)). Proponents of this rule expect its operation to deter police from illegal conduct, on the assumption that police have a professional interest in the conviction of offenders. To a surprisingly large extent, legal rules providing for the exclusion of illegally obtained evidence have spread from the United States to Europe. Such rules are, however, not always designed to control police conduct.

Even more sweeping exclusionary rules than in the United States apply in Italy and Spain. Italian law simply states that evidence obtained in violation of a legal prohibition cannot be used; this rule is to be applied at any stage of the proceedings, even on the court's own motion (Italian CPP, art. 191). In Spain, the relevant statute provides that evidence obtained in violation of fundamental rights shall not have any direct or indirect effect (Ley orgánica 6/1985 of July 1, 1985, del poder judicial, art. 11 sec. 2). Such fundamental rights include the right to defense and to counsel, the right to be informed about the accusation, the privilege against self-incrimination, and the presumption of innocence (cf. Spanish Constitution, art. 24 sec. 2). Spanish courts have interpreted this provision to require exclusion even of the "fruits of the poisonous tree" (see Picó i Junoy). There is little information available about how these far-reaching rules of exclusion actually operate in Italian and Spanish practice.

In Germany, statutory law mandates exclusion of statements obtained from suspects or witnesses by force, deception, hypnosis, or similar illicit methods of interrogation (StPO, § 69 sec. 3, § 136a). The courts have gone further and refused to use as evidence, for example, a suspect's diary (Judgment of the Federal Court of Appeals of Feb. 21, 1964, 4 StR 519/63, 19 Entscheidungen des Bundesgerichtshofes in Strafsachen (BGHSt) 325), the results of an illegal wiretap (Judgment of the Federal Court of Appeals of March 17, 1983, 4 StR 640/82, 31 BGHSt 304), a statement elicited from the suspect by a police informer illegally placed in the suspect's cell during pretrial custody (Judgment of the Federal Court of Appeals of April 28, 1987, 5 StR 666/86, 34 BGHSt 362), and a suspect's statement made to the police without the requisite prior warning of his right to remain silent (Judgment of the Federal Court of Appeals of Feb. 27, 1992, 5 StR 190/91, 38 BGHSt 214). Exclusion in these cases was mainly based on the argument that admission of the evidence would violate the principle of due process (*Rechtsstaatlichkeit*). Since this is a rather vague and pliable concept, it is not surprising that German courts have admitted evidence in other, factually quite similar cases, arguing that the violation of the suspect's rights was outweighed by the state's interest in determining the truth (see, e.g., Judgment of the Federal Court of Appeals of July 9, 1987, 4 StR 223/87, 34 BGHSt 397, admitting into evidence the suspect's diary in a murder case). Because deterrence of police misconduct is not the rationale for exclusion of evidence, German courts tend to admit evidence obtained through illegal searches (Judgment of the Federal Court of Appeals of Feb. 15, 1989, 2 StR 402/88, 1989 Neue Zeitschrift für Strafrecht 375 at 376) as well as evidence found through investigations based on illegally obtained evidence ("fruits of the poisonous tree"; Judgment of the Federal Court of Appeals of August 24, 1983, 3 StR 136/83, 32 BGHSt 68).

According to French law, results of investigatory acts can be stricken from the record of the investigation when the court in charge of controlling pretrial procedure (*chambre d'accusation*) determines that they were performed illegally. In a few instances, for example with respect to the rules governing the conduct of a domicile search, the Code of Criminal Procedure explicitly provides for annulment of the act and its consequences when the relevant rules are violated (French CCP, art. 59 sec. 3). Beyond that, annulment occurs whenever a substantial rule of procedure was misapplied and prejudice to the complaining party resulted (French CCP, arts. 171, 802).

Prosecution

Prosecutorial discretion. American prosecutors enjoy practically unlimited discretion in their decision whether to file charges against a suspect, and what charges to bring. This can frustrate victims of crime, who have no legal recourse against a district attorney's refusal to prosecute and who are in most states precluded from directly involving the courts by filing criminal charges.

Foreign legal systems offer alternatives to unfettered prosecutorial discretion. Three methods of limiting or controlling discretion can be distinguished: (1) the law can impose a duty to prosecute whenever, given the evidence available, conviction appears likely; (2) the prosecutor's refusal to bring charges can be subject to judicial review; (3) the complainant (or any citizen) can be given the right to file criminal charges directly with the court. Most European systems employ at least one of these checks upon prosecutorial discretion.

In Italy and Spain, the prosecutor cannot legally decline to prosecute a case if there is enough evidence to convict (Constituzione della Repubblica italiana, approvata dall'Assemblea Costituente il 22 dic. 1947, art. 112; Italian CCP, art. 50; LEC, art. 105). In Germany, the same principle applies, but only with respect to serious felonies (StPO, § 152 sec. 2, § 160). Observers of practice report, however, that prosecutors in these countries only pay lip service to the law; they claim insufficiency of the evidence even in convictable, but less serious cases that do not merit prosecution (Guarneri, pp. 143–152; Tak, pp. 38–41; Volkmann-Schluck, pp. 44–45). Prosecutorial discretion, it seems, cannot be abolished by legislative fiat. Rules of mandatory prosecution were introduced in many European countries in the nineteenth century, when prosecutorial offices were still suspected of being tied too closely to the political interests of the government; their rationale was to achieve equality through strict application of the criminal code without exception and political favoritism. Yet the rule of mandatory prosecution tries to exorcise the evil of inequality by the even greater evil of systematic overenforcement. This has proved to be not only unwise but also impracticable. Since prosecutors in all systems view as their function the elimination of cases in which conviction would do more harm than good, they will do so even in the face of law to the contrary.

External judicial review of prosecutorial dismissals is available in Germany and Italy. When a German prosecutor closes a case because he or she deems the evidence insufficient for conviction, the prosecutor must notify the private victim-complainant and state the reasons for dismissal. The victim can then file a complaint with the state attorney general and, if the original dismissal is upheld, can file a further appeal with the regional appellate court. The court mandates the prosecutor to file charges if the victim's claim is justified. The victim can then join the proceedings as a "supplementary prosecutor" to make sure that the prosecution case is presented forcefully (StPO, §§ 171–175, 395 sec. 1). Successful mandamus motions by victims are extremely rare in Germany, but the fact that the option is available serves as a check on prosecutorial arbitrariness. Paradoxically, victims are precluded from challenging a discretionary dismissal in court when the prosecutor's decision not to file charges is not based on lack of evidence but on policy grounds, as is possible with lesser felonies and misdemeanors (StPO, §§ 153, 153a). In Italy, dismissal of a case for lack of sufficient evidence (*archiviazione*) requires a judicial decree. The prosecutor must inform the victim of his or her intention to apply for *archiviazione*, and the victim can then file a brief in opposition with the magistrate in charge (Italian CCP, arts. 408, 410). If the magistrate deems the victim's argument in favor of prosecution well-founded, he or she orders the prosecutor to conduct additional acts of investigation or to file a formal accusation (Italian CCP, Art. 409 secs. 4, 5).

A third way of confining prosecutorial discretion is to permit criminal prosecution by private citizens. Many countries grant victims this right. They do not share the concern of U.S. courts that private victims may be so strongly involved in the case that they are unable to conduct the prosecution in a professional and detached manner. The most far-reaching provision can be found in Spain, where the constitution guarantees not only the victim of the offense but every citizen the right to bring criminal charges (Spanish Constitution, art. 125). Upon receipt of a citizen's complaint, the investigating magistrate is obliged to conduct a regular preliminary investigation. The court cannot dismiss charges preferred by a private complainant unless it finds that the act in question does not constitute a crime (LEC, arts. 637, 645). In Germany, the right to bring a private accusation is limited to certain minor offenses such as slander, simple assault, trespass, and destruction of private property (StPO, § 374). In these instances, the victim can go forward with the criminal case even without the state attorney's consent, but the public prosecutor can take over if the public interest so requires (StPO, §§ 376, 377).

Neither in Spain nor in Germany does private prosecution play a significant role in practice. This is hardly surprising because the task of collecting and presenting evidence in court places a heavy burden on a private individual. German law confronts private complainants with an additional impediment by requiring them to attempt reconciliation with the opposing party with the help of a mediator appointed by the community (StPO, § 380); only when mediation has failed can the case be brought before the court. Chances of actually obtaining a conviction are low even if the victim has cleared all formal hurdles. In cases of minor guilt, the court can simply dismiss the case even though all elements of the offense have been established (StPO, § 383 sec. 2), and it may well be that the complainant is then left with nothing but the bill for his own and his adversary's expenses (StPO, § 471 secs. 2, 3).

Most legal systems under consideration here permit victims who have suffered harm by an offense to join the prosecution with their claim for civil damages (French CCP, art. 2; German StPO, §§ 403–406c; Italian CCP, arts. 74, 76); in Spain, the public prosecutor demands civil damages for the victim unless the latter objects (LEC, art. 108). With the exception of France, however, the victim's ability to sue for civil damages in criminal court is dependent on the existence of a public action, so that the public prosecutor's unwillingness to file or maintain charges eliminates the victim's ability to recover in criminal court. In the French system, the victim can file a private criminal action (*action civile*) directly with the investigating magistrate or the criminal court. Since the victim's *action civile* is deemed to initiate a "regular" prosecution (French CCP, arts. 1 sec. 2, 418) the public prosecutor must fulfill his or her regular functions in the process even though the prosecutor may not have wished to file charges. The right to bring an *action civile* can be exercised not only by individuals directly affected by an offense but also by organizations representing certain interests or classes of victims, for example victims of war or of discrimination (French CCP, Arts. 2-1–2-15).

The French system evidently provides an effective check on the prosecutor's decision not to file charges. It may even go too far in subordinating the prosecutor's decision-making to the judgment of an individual victim. The German and Italian systems seem to offer a more balanced solution: if a conflict arises between the prosecutor and the victim, a neutral judge decides whether prosecution is warranted. It would be desirable to extend this system to policy-based decisions to refrain from prosecution. Prosecutors should undoubtedly have some leeway in making policy decisions on how to allocate limited resources, but the possibility of external review might at least persuade them to formulate and adhere to rational standards of decision-making in this area.

Diversion.   Whenever a prosecutor dismisses a "convictable" case he or she diverts a suspect from the criminal process. Diversion can be unconditional and thus amount to a prosecutorial grant of impunity, but it can also be tied to the imposition of obligations on the suspect. In France, the prosecutor can in some areas (e.g., criminal violations of environmental and fiscal laws) enter into a "transaction" with the suspect, promising to drop the case in exchange for a payment to be made to the fisc (French CCP, art. 6 sec. 3; Conte and Maistre du Chambon, pp. 106–108; see also French CCP, arts. 41-2 and 41-3, authorizing conditional dismissal of certain less serious charges). German law provides for a similar scheme. In cases of misdemeanors and less serious felonies, the prosecutor can offer to the suspect to dismiss the case if the suspect fulfills obligations imposed on him (StPO, § 153a). In practice, such obligations almost invariably involve payments to be made to the state, a charitable organization, or the victim. The suspect can refuse to enter into this quid pro quo, but if he does he risks prosecution and eventual conviction. On the other hand, if the suspect makes the required "penance payment," he or she avoids the publicity of a trial as well as having a criminal record.

Since the 1980s, diversion from the criminal process has also been promoted and practiced as a tool of reconciliation between offenders and victims. In various systems, the prosecutor can make nonprosecution dependent on the suspect's willingness to meet with the victim and to work out an agreement involving restitution (cf. French CCP, art. 41-1 sec. 7; StPO, § 155a). Such efforts, which have led to the creation of a host of local victim/offender mediation programs (for Germany, see Bundesministerium der Justiz), rest on the notion that there is no public interest in prosecution and conviction when the offender (of a less serious offense) has satisfied the victim.

Diversionary practices are popular because they save time and money, relieve the courts' workload, and allow marginal offenders to avoid the stigma of criminal conviction. Critics have, however, pointed out several real or potential drawbacks of diversion: sentencing authority is effectively shifted from the judiciary to prosecutors; standards are lacking for diversion eligibility and obligations; the availability of conditional diversion may enlarge rather than reduce the overall scope of state control over individuals' lives ("net widening effect"); and the presumption of innocence is neglected because mere suspects are coerced into accepting diversionary sanctions by threatening them with harsher treatment after trial and conviction (Kuhlen). Yet the practical advantages of diversionary practices for prosecutors, defense attorneys, courts, and most defendants have proved so overwhelming that theoretically valid criticism was unable to stop the rapid expansion of diversion. In Germany, conditional dismissal, originally designed for petty offenses, is frequently being used for resolving even very serious cases of white-collar crime, especially those which present problems of proof: the suspect makes a high payment (sometimes equivalent to more than U.S. $100,000) in exchange for nonprosecution (Meinberg, pp. 115–127). This resolution offers benefits to both sides: the defendant can still maintain his or her innocence whereas the prosecutor can claim that the state has obtained sufficient vindication without the trouble and risk of a trial.

In order to avoid abuses, it is important to develop proper safeguards for the fair and equitable application of diversionary measures. Prosecutors should develop guidelines for diversion eligibility, including limits on the amount of payments to be demanded of suspects; suspects and victims should be given the right to have decisions on granting or refusing diversion reviewed by a judge; and there should be guarantees against penalizing the defendant at trial and sentencing for refusing to accept diversion. Such limitations on prosecutorial discretion would be justified in light of the fact that the prosecutor in the diversionary process assumes a judge-like position.

Adjudication

The contrast between adversarial and inquisitorial styles of conducting the criminal process becomes most evident at the trial stage. In inquisitorial systems, the trial is typically dominated by the presiding judge, who selects and calls up the evidence to be presented at trial, makes procedural rulings as necessary, and interrogates defendants, witnesses, and experts. In adversarial systems, the judge's role is limited to presiding over the parties' presentation of the evidence. Advantages and disadvantages of either system have long been the subject of scholarly debate. To some extent, the difference between the modes of trial is technical rather than substantive: as long as the court as well as the parties have the right to question witnesses, the sequence of interrogation is of little relevance. Yet there is one basic difference between adversarial and inquisitorial systems that relates back to differing definitions of the purpose of the process: the inquisitorial judge has the responsibility of making certain that a complete account of the relevant facts is given in court so that the verdict can be based on "the truth"; in the adversary system, by contrast, the finder of fact decides on the factual basis as it is presented by the parties, and neither the court nor the jury have the right to probe into the factual background or (in most systems) to introduce evidence on their own initiative.

In inquisitorial systems, the court has complete freedom in evaluating the evidence. The French Code of Criminal Procedure leaves the judgment on guilt or innocence to the "internal conviction" (*intime conviction*) of the judges

(French CCP, art. 427; cf. StPO, § 261; Italian CCP, art. 192). This means that there are, in principle, no rules of law determining the weight to be given to particular items of evidence. As a further consequence of the court's independent duty to determine the truth, the court cannot be bound by parties' factual admissions or stipulations.

Inquisitorial and adversarial systems also typically differ with respect to the relationship between pretrial and trial proceedings. Systems that place great emphasis on the adversarial presentation of evidence tend to shield the trial process from being influenced by the results of the pretrial investigation—only what is presented and discussed at the trial can form the basis of the judgment. Inquisitorial systems, on the other hand, are much less adamant in keeping the various stages of the process separate, because they regard the trial as the culmination of a continuous effort at determining the "truth." Thus, a French or Dutch lawyer would not regard it as a violation of procedural principle that a witness's prior police testimony can be introduced at the trial by reading from the police transcript in the absence of the witness; and this is indeed common practice in both countries' lower criminal courts (Frase, 1999, p. 171; Swart, p. 298).

Beyond these characteristics, it would be misleading to say that continental systems universally adhere to a strict inquisitorial style of proceeding. On the contrary, a closer look reveals a great variety of trial styles, some of which are surprisingly similar to the common law trial. One can, in fact, determine an advance of the adversary trial mode on the continent, for which several explanations can be given. On the one hand, "trial by combat" is attractive to skilled and competitive lawyers everywhere; on the other hand, the European Convention on Human Rights, which has been adopted by virtually all European countries, guarantees certain trial rights typical of the common law style, most importantly the defendant's right to present evidence in his defense and to confront witnesses against him (European Convention on the Protection of Human Rights and Basic Freedoms of Nov. 4, 1950, art. 6 sec. 3 lit. d). The jurisprudence of the European Court of Human Rights in Strasbourg, which tends to give broad interpretations to the clauses of the Convention, has indeed cast doubt upon the continued permissibility of some traditional practices of inquisitorial systems in the light of the European Convention's trial rights (see, e.g., *Unterpertinger v. Austria*, Reports of Judgments and Decisions, Series A, Nr. 110 (1987); *Lüdi v. Switzerland*, Reports of Judgments and Decisions, Series A, Nr. 238 (1992)).

French criminal procedure is still closest to the prototype of the inquisitorial model. The Code of Criminal Procedure confers upon the presiding judge discretionary authority to take, "on his honor and conscience," all measures he or she deems useful to discover the truth (French CCP, art. 310). When the formal document of accusation has been filed by the prosecutor, the presiding judge reviews the evidence gathered before trial. In addition to witnesses suggested by both parties, he or she can have any other witnesses called, can appoint experts and have physical evidence produced. It is the presiding judge who interrogates the defendant and all witnesses. Members of the court may ask additional questions (French CPP, art. 311) whereas the parties are limited to suggesting additional questions but may not themselves examine witnesses (French CCP, art. 312).

In the most serious cases, tried before a mixed court of three professional and nine lay judges (the *cour d'assises*), the presiding judge formulates the specific questions for the court to answer (French CCP, art. 348). Since the professional and lay judges deliberate on the verdict together, the presiding judge also has ample opportunity to explain the law and advise the other judges on the evidence behind closed doors. The presiding judge's role is even greater in the lower courts, where he sits alone or together with two associate professional judges (French CCP, arts. 398, 398-1, and 523); these courts handle over 99 percent of criminal trials (Frase, 1999, p. 163).

In Germany, the great majority of cases are decided by a single professional judge, who can impose penalties of up to four years imprisonment (Gerichtsverfassungsgesetz in der Fassung der Bekanntmachung vom 9. Mai 1975 (Bundesgesetzblatt 1975 I, p. 1077), § 24 sec. 2). More serious cases are adjudicated by mixed courts of professional judges and lay persons sitting and deliberating together (cf. Dubber, pp. 556–567). As in France, the court is responsible for having all relevant evidence available at the trial (StPO, § 244 sec. 2). Parties can, however, bring their own witnesses and experts, and the court must hear them unless it can determine in advance that their testimony will be irrelevant or duplicative (StPO, §§ 244 sec. 3, 245). The presiding judge initially interrogates the defendant (if he or she wishes to testify), witnesses, and experts. In that interrogation, the dossier of the pretrial investigation, assembled by the public prosecutor and submitted to the court, often plays an important role: the presiding judge frequently confronts witnesses with prior statements contained in the dossier and asks them to explain contradictions between their trial testimony and what they had earlier told the police or the prosecutor. The other judges as well as counsel for the prosecution and the defense have the right to ask additional questions. The court can reject parties' questions only if they are inappropriate or irrelevant (StPO, § 241 sec. 2)—a standard that German courts have interpreted narrowly (Judgment of the Federal Court of Appeals of April 22, 1952, 1 StR 96/52, 2 BGHSt 284). In routine cases, parties tend to make sparing use of their right to ask additional questions; yet in contested cases, the defense may employ the right to interrogate prosecution witnesses to much the same effect as an Anglo-American cross-examination. At the end of the trial, the prosecution and the defense sum up their views of the evidence, and the defendant has the opportunity to speak last. As in France, professional and lay judges deliberate together. A two-thirds majority is required for conviction (StPO, § 263). Given the composition of German mixed courts (one, two, or three professional judges sitting with two lay judges), this means that lay judges can in any event block a conviction if they vote together.

In Spain, it is the parties who primarily determine what evidence will be presented at the trial (LEC, art. 728), but the court can add evidence to the extent it regards such evidence as necessary for proving one of the offenses listed in the formal accusation (LEC, art. 729 No. 2). The allocation of roles is similar with respect to the actual presentation of evidence: examination and cross-examination by the parties is the primary method of taking oral testimony. The presiding judge can, however, not only reject misleading and irrelevant questions (LEC, art. 709 sec. 1), but can also change the sequence in which witnesses are interrogated and ask additional questions (LEC, arts. 701 sec. 6, 708). The presiding judge thereby fulfills his or her role as the guardian of the proceedings and of their orientation toward determining the truth (LEC, art. 683). Even apart from these remnants of the inquisitorial process, party domination of the trial is of lesser relevance in Spain than in common law jurisdictions because the results of judicial

pretrial investigations can filter through to the trial stage and form the basis of the judgment, especially when a witness's trial testimony deviates from his or her earlier statements (LEC, art. 714).

A similar structure exists in Italy where, since 1989, the trial is supposed to be party-dominated and strictly separated from the pretrial process. It is the parties who present lists of evidence to be taken, and it is they who examine and cross-examine witnesses (Italian CCP, arts. 468, 498). But the presiding judge can strike manifestly superfluous witnesses from the list (Italian CCP, art. 468 sec. 2), reject irrelevant lines of questioning (Italian CCP, art. 499 sec. 6), ask additional questions of witnesses and experts (Italian CCP, art. 506 sec. 2), and can even, "if absolutely necessary," order additional evidence to be taken (Italian CCP, art. 507). The supposed strict separation between pretrial and trial proceedings has not survived the very first years after the reform of the Italian criminal process: the law and the jurisprudence of the courts have since permitted the introduction of pretrial statements under more and more liberal rules (see Italian CCP, arts. 510-513; Grande).

The examples of Spain and Italy demonstrate how resistant the inquisitorial heritage is to efforts to inoculate it with elements of a foreign system; they also show to what extent procedural practice is shaped by the traditions and attitudes of the lawyers involved rather than by the letter of the law. On the other hand, adherence to certain basic tenets of the inquisitorial process, in particular the quest for the truth as the overriding purpose of the process, is obviously compatible not only with a recognition of defendants' rights, such as the presumption of innocence and the privilege against self-incrimination, but also with procedural features commonly associated with the adversary trial, such as party examination of witnesses and the defendant's right to confront witnesses against him. It seems that the choice among procedural styles is of much lesser importance for the "quality" of the process than has long been assumed; what is important is an effort to respect parties' individual rights even in light of systemic and political pressures toward greater efficiency and speed.

Trial and sentencing. In common law countries, trial and sentencing are kept strictly separate. Sentencing hearings usually take place a few weeks after the defendant has been found guilty. In continental systems, by contrast, issues of both guilt and sentence are argued and decided upon in one single trial: the court's judgment at the end of the trial includes a finding on the issue of guilt and, if there is a conviction, the sentence. Consequently, no distinction is made between evidence relevant to guilt and evidence relevant to sentence; even sensitive information concerning the offender's personality and prior offenses is admissible at the trial because of its impact on sentencing. The unitary trial, though saving time, creates a number of problems. Material relevant to the sentence can be prejudicial to the defendant, and in contested trials the focus is often so much on the issue of guilt that the determination of the sentence may not be based on sufficient argument and information. The continental tradition of conducting a unitary trial has nevertheless survived academic criticism, and even those systems that have adopted American-style adversary trials have not seriously considered the introduction of separate sentencing hearings. This may be an area in which vested bureaucratic interests in efficiency are too strong to be overcome by considerations of fairness.

Juries and lay judges. Trial by a jury of one's peers was one of the great demands of liberal reformers of the European criminal process in the nineteenth century. Several countries at that time followed the example of England and introduced trial juries, but the jury system often did not survive. In France, the jury was introduced in 1791 but merged into a mixed court of professional and lay judges in 1941. Germany established juries for the most serious offenses in 1877, but likewise abolished the jury as an independent fact finder and replaced it by mixed panels in 1924. The jury had a particularly interesting history in Spain: it was introduced in 1888, abolished in 1924 and recreated, for the most serious offenses, in 1995 (Ley Orgánica 5/1995, de 22 de mayo 1995 del Tribunal del Jurado; see Thaman), on the basis of a constitutional provision guaranteeing every Spanish citizen the right to participate in the administration of criminal justice as a juror (Spanish Constitution, art. 125 sec. 1).

Americans tend to regard trial by jury as one of the hallmarks of a civilized system of criminal justice. And it is certainly true that the vagaries of decision-making by a group of lay persons introduces into the criminal process an element of chance that often benefits the accused. On a more rational basis, one can argue that a verdict of guilty is valid only if it can be based both on the law and on the moral persuasion of a group of citizens. Paradoxically, however, decision-

making by juries has in the United States led to an enormously complex system of rules on the presentation of evidence at trial (Damaska, 1997, pp. 28–46): the attempt to shield jurors from overly prejudicial evidence and to make difficult issues of fact and law palatable to lay persons goes a long way in explaining why American trials are so costly, protracted, and often far removed from the actual facts of the case.

The mixed record of juries on the European continent may be related to this and other defects. Juries were useful historically as long as trials dealt with simple issues of fact and the verdict depended largely on whether the testimony of one or the other witnesses was to be believed. With the growing complexity of factual and legal issues—white-collar offenses are paradigmatic in this regard—jurors have lost much of their capacity to reliably adjudicate cases without professional advice and guidance. If one wishes to retain a lay element in criminal justice it may thus be preferable to turn to mixed panels as can be found in many European jurisdictions (see Langbein). This system, which combines the freshness of judgment and worldly experience of non-lawyers with the sophistication of professional judges, may produce more rational and predictable verdicts than the traditional jury system.

Adjudication of uncontested cases. Anglo-American law makes a sharp distinction between contested and uncontested criminal cases. The latter are adjudicated without trial on the basis of the defendant's plea of guilty, which is often brought about through plea bargaining, that is, offering the defendant a reduced sentence in exchange for a waiver of his or her trial rights. Civil law countries traditionally did not provide for distinctive modes of processing cooperative and uncooperative defendants. The inquisitorial ideal requires a full investigation of the facts even if the defendant confesses guilt; credible admissions can do no more than reduce the amount of extrinsic evidence necessary for a finding of guilt.

At the beginning of the twenty-first century, law and practice in many continental legal systems differ from that ideal, however. The idea of disposing of uncontested cases without a full trial, which had been regarded as a typical American aberration as late as in the 1970s, has quickly spread to a large number of European jurisdictions. The main reason for this development is the jurists' common interest in efficiency: where there is no issue, the argument goes, there is no need for going through the motions of a trial.

The law has in various ways been adapted to fit this argument.

One instrument of avoiding trial in clear-cut cases is conviction and sentence by written decree. This instrument, called a penal order (*ordonnance pénale, Strafbefehl, decreto penale*), exists in France, Germany, and Italy (French CCP, arts. 524–528-2; StPO, §§ 407–412; Italian CCP, arts. 459–464). The basic idea is the same in all three systems: at the close of an investigation for a minor offense, the prosecutor drafts a judgment including a sentence. The draft is submitted to the magistrate, who issues it as a provisional judgment unless he detects obvious defects. Typically, only monetary penalties can be imposed by penal order; yet in Germany the defendant can also receive a suspended prison sentence of up to one year by written decree without a trial (StPO, § 407 sec. 2). The defendant can accept the penal order or file an appeal; in the latter case, the verdict and sentence imposed by the penal order lose effect, and the matter is set for trial. At the trial, the court is not bound in any way by the contents of the penal order; the defendant thus risks more serious punishment if he or she declines to accept the penal order (see Italian CCP, art. 464 sec. 4, explicitly stating that the judge can impose a more serious sentence after trial). Although the defendant's prior consent is not required for the issuance of a penal order, prosecutors are well-advised to ascertain in advance that the defendant will accept the sentence, because in the event of an appeal the prior attempt to avoid a trial only serves to draw out the process. In Italy, the statute explicitly invites bargaining by permitting a sentence reduction of one half of the "deserved" penalty in case of a *decreto penale* (Italian CCP, art. 459 sec. 2). German law does not provide for a similar discount, but it is well-known that the content of a penal order is a frequent subject of negotiations between the prosecutor and defense counsel, with defense counsel indicating what sentence his or her client would be willing to accept without demanding a trial (Dahs, pp. 644–646).

Another means to simplify the process is to hold an abbreviated trial instead of the ordinary full trial. In France, there exists a long-standing practice of *correctionnalisation*, that is, trying felony cases in the lower court designed to adjudicate misdemeanors (*tribunal correctionnel*). In lower court, oral testimony of witnesses can largely be replaced by the record of their interrogation by the police, parties' closing statements are often limited to perfunctory remarks, and sentences are generally lower than in the nine-judge felony court (*cour d'assises*). The practice of "reducing" what really appear to be serious felonies requires a silent understanding among all parties to omit from the facts presented to the court certain aggravating factors that would turn the offense into a felony (Stefani, Levasseur, and Bouloc, pp. 430–433). Parties' interests to do so tend to coincide in noncontested cases: the prosecutor saves the time and effort necessary to try the case in felony court, and the defendant has reason to hope for a more lenient sentence.

Italian law provides for several forms of abbreviated adjudication. The most interesting of these is *giudizio abbreviato* (Italian CCP, arts. 438–443), that is, adjudication of the case by a magistrate on the basis of the record of the pretrial investigation, possibly augmented by additional evidence offered by the defense (see Pizzi and Marafioti, pp. 27–35). As with the penal order, the Italian Code offers the defendant an incentive to agree to this form of conviction without trial by providing for a mandatory reduction of the "deserved" sentence by one-third (Italian CCP, art. 442 sec. 2). French and German statutes also provide for speedy, simplified trials in straightforward cases (French CCP, arts. 393–397-6; StPO, §§ 417–420). In France the defendant's advance consent for immediate adjudication is needed (French CCP, art. 397) whereas in Germany a short-cut trial with reduced opportunities of presenting defense evidence can be forced upon the defendant.

Even closer analogies to American plea bargaining have developed in Italy, Spain, and Germany. Spanish law has long provided for the possibility that the defendant submit to the penalty demanded by the prosecutor at the beginning of the trial (*conformidad*, LEC arts. 655, 694). In that case, the court takes no evidence but imposes the sentence demanded by the prosecutor. Originally, the prosecutor's sentence demands tended to be close to the statutory maximum, thus making it unattractive for the defendant to waive trial. Through a few small changes in the law, the Spanish legislature (Ley orgánica 7/1988 de 28 de dic. 1988) invited the parties to negotiate before trial with a view toward determining a sentence acceptable both to the prosecutor and the defendant. In its 1989 version, the Code of Criminal Procedure refers to the possibility of filing the formal accusation with a sentence demand signed both by the prosecutor and defense counsel (LEC, art. 791 sec. 3) and alludes to the possibility of reducing the original sentence demand (LEC, art. 793 sec. 3)—two subtle indications of the desirability of avoiding trial through prior bargaining on mutually acceptable conditions of *conformidad* (see, generally, Ortells Ramos).

Italian law is even more candid in facilitating and encouraging sentence negotiations between the prosecution and the defense. The Code provides that the parties can jointly propose, in the preliminary hearing or at the beginning of the trial, a sentence of up to two years imprisonment; this sentence is to include a discount of one-third from the penalty (hypothetically) applicable after trial (Italian CCP, art. 444). If the judge finds, based on the dossier and the representations of the parties, that the penal law has correctly been applied to the facts of the case, he or she imposes the penalty as requested by the parties (Bogner, pp. 135–208).

German law does not provide for an analogue to plea bargaining, but German lawyers have nevertheless developed informal practices that have the same effect as the Spanish and Italian laws. Especially in more complex criminal cases, it has become commonplace in Germany for defense counsel to approach the presiding judge (or for the presiding judge to approach defense counsel) with suggestions for an abbreviation of the process in exchange for a lenient sentence (Herrmann). A noncooperative defense can, under German evidence law, indefinitely protract the trial by compelling the court to take additional evidence; by making a full confession in open court, the defendant can, on the other hand, relieve the court of the necessity to hear many (or any) witnesses. In contrast to Spain and Italy, bargaining in Germany is done directly between the defense and the court; the public prosecutor has an informal veto power but usually is not one of the primary negotiators. The practice of "sentence bargaining," which has become known since the early 1980s, is of dubious legality because it not only lacks any foundation in written law but even runs counter to basic tenets of German law, especially the court's duty to independently establish the "truth" (Weigend, p. 57). The Federal Court of Appeals nevertheless gave in 1997 its general approval to bargaining, subject to certain conditions of "fair deal" to be respected by the negotiating parties (Judgment of the Federal Court of Appeals of August 28, 1997, 4 StR 240/97, 43 BGHSt 195). This development is an impressive sign of the times: it shows that the desire to be "functional" tends to override and neutralize the normative principles on which the inquisitorial criminal process was built. The advent and universal acceptance of bargained justice may indeed indicate that the traditional criminal trial is no longer adequate to deal with factually and legally complex matters that increasingly are the subject of criminal cases.

Agenda for comparative research

Comparative research has concentrated for too long on juxtaposing trial models, especially the inquisitorial and adversarial features of civil law and common law systems. The development of similar techniques for dealing with the large bulk of uncontested cases in various systems shows that the style of presenting evidence at trial is only one, comparatively insignificant aspect of the criminal process. There does remain a difference with respect to systems' overall orientation toward conflict resolution or "truth-finding." But even that theoretical contrast may be less important for the resolution of practical issues than appears at first blush. Research should thus refrain from spelling out again and again the supposed differences between adversarial and inquisitorial systems, but should focus on two other sets of issues.

One area of potentially fruitful research is the delineation of new paradigms by which to evaluate individual legal systems. The standard inquiry into the extent to which participants' human rights are respected in the criminal process could be augmented, for example, by research into the (comparative) relevance of bureaucratic interests and lawyers' professional interests in shaping the process, by studying the relationship and interactions between public security (police) law and criminal procedure law, and by looking into the influence of economic considerations on the criminal process. Another promising approach might be "micro" studies on particular aspects of the criminal process, where practical solutions developed in various systems could be compared and their potential for borrowing be explored. From an American perspective, areas of interest might include the law and practice of pretrial detention, protection of victims' interests, reduction of delay, and the organization of defense services. In studying foreign achievements in these and other problem areas, one should, however, keep aware of the pitfalls of transplanting foreign solutions—there is a rather large step from theoretical comparison to successful implementation in practice.

THOMAS WEIGEND

See also ADVERSARY SYSTEM; COMPARATIVE CRIMINAL LAW AND ENFORCEMENT: CHINA; COMPARATIVE CRIMINAL LAW AND ENFORCEMENT: ENGLAND AND WALES; COMPARATIVE CRIMINAL LAW AND ENFORCEMENT: ISLAM; COMPARATIVE CRIMINAL LAW AND ENFORCEMENT: RUSSIA; CRIMINAL JUSTICE PROCESS; CRIMINAL JUSTICE SYSTEM; CRIMINAL LAW REFORM: CONTINENTAL EUROPE; CRIMINAL LAW REFORM: ENGLAND; CRIMINAL PROCEDURE: CONSTITUTIONAL ASPECTS; INTERNATIONAL CRIMINAL COURTS; INTERNATIONAL CRIMINAL JUSTICE STANDARDS; PROSECUTION: COMPARATIVE ASPECTS.

BIBLIOGRAPHY

BOGNER, UDO. *Absprachen im deutschen und italienischen Strafprozessrecht.* Marburg, Germany: Elwert, 2000.

BRADLEY, CRAIG M. "The Exclusionary Rule in Germany." *Harvard Law Review* 96 (1986): 1032-1066.

BRADLEY, CRAIG M., ed. *Criminal Procedure: A Worldwide Study.* Durham, N.C.: Carolina Academic Press, 2000.

Bundesministerium der Justiz, ed. *Täter-Opfer-Ausgleich in Deutschland.* Bonn: Forum, 1998.

CONTE, PHILIPPE, and MAISTRE DU CHAMBON, PATRICK. *Procédure pénale.* Paris: Masson, 1995.

DAHS, HANS. *Handbuch des Strafverteidigers,* 6th ed. Köln, Germany: Otto Schmidt, 1999.

DAMASKA, MIRJAN. "Structures of Authority and Comparative Criminal Procedure." *Yale Law Journal* 84 (1975): 480–544.

———. *Evidence Law Adrift.* New Haven and London: Yale University Press, 1997.

———. "Truth in Adjudication." *Hastings Law Journal* 49 (1998): 289–308.

DUBBER, MARKUS DIRK. "American Plea Bargains, German Lay Judges, and the Crisis of Criminal Procedure." *Stanford Law Review* 49 (1997): 547–605.

FENNELL, PHIL; HARDING, CHISTOPHER; JÖRG, NICO; and SWART, BERT, eds. *Criminal Justice in Europe.* Oxford, U.K.: Clarendon Press, 1994.

FRASE, RICHARD S. "Comparative Criminal Justice as a Guide to American Law Reform: How Do the French Do It, How Can We Find Out, and Why Should We Care?" *California Law Review* 78 (1990): 539–583.

———. "France." *Criminal Procedure. A Worldwide Study.* Edited by Craig M. Bradley. Durham, N.C.: Carolina University Press, 1999. Pages 143–185.

FRASE, RICHARD S., and WEIGEND, THOMAS. "German Criminal Justice as a Guide to American Law Reform: Similar Problems, Better Solutions?" *Boston College International and Comparative Law Review* 18 (1995): 317–360.

GOLDSTEIN, ABRAHAM S., and MARCUS, MARTIN. "The Myth of Judicial Supervision in Three 'Inquisitorial' Systems: France, Italy, and Germany." *Yale Law Journal* 87 (1977): 240–283.

GRANDE, ELISABETTA. "Italian Criminal Justice: Borrowing and Resistance." *American Journal of Comparative Law* 48 (2000): 227–259.

GUARNERI, CARLO. *Pubblico Ministerio e Sistema Politico.* Padova, Italy: Cedam, 1984.

HATCHARD, JOHN; HUBER, BARBARA; and VOGLER, RICHARD. eds. *Comparative Criminal Procedure.* London: British Institute of International and Comparative Law, 1996.

HERRMANN, JOACHIM. "Bargaining Justice—A Bargain for German Criminal Justice?" *University of Pittsburgh Law Review* 53 (1992): 755–776.

KUHLEN, LOTHAR. *Diversion im Jugendstrafverfahren.* Heidelberg, Germany: C. F. Müller, 1988.

LANGBEIN, JOHN H. "Mixed Court and Jury Court: Could the Continental Alternative Fill the American Need?" *American Bar Foundation Research Journal* (1981): 195–219.

MEINBERG, VOLKER. *Geringfügigkeitseinstellungen von Wirtschaftsstrafsachen.* Freiburg, Germany: Eigenverlag Max-Planck-Institut für ausländisches und internationales Strafrecht, 1985.

ORTELLS RAMOS, MANUEL. *El proceso penal abreviado.* Granada, Spain: Comares, 1997.

PICÓ I JUNOY, JOAN. "Nuevas perspectivas sobre el alcance anulatorio de las pruebas ilícitas." *Justicia* (1997): 881–909.

PIZZI, WILLIAM T., and MARAFIOTI, LUCA. "The New Italian Code of Criminal Procedure: The Difficulties of Building an Adversarial Trial System on a Civil Law Foundation." *Yale Law Journal of International Law* 17 (1992): 1–40.

STEFANI, GASTON; LEVASSEUR, GEORGES; and BOULOC, BERNARD. *Procédure pénale.* 16th ed. Paris: Dalloz, 1996.

SWART, A. H. J. "The Netherlands." *Criminal Procedure Systems in the European Community.* Edited by Christine Van den Wyngaert. London: Butterworths, 1993. Pages 279–316.

TAK, PETER J. P. *The Legal Scope of Non-Prosecution in Europe.* Helsinki: Helsinki Institute for Crime Prevention and Control, 1986.

THAMAN, STEPHEN T. "Europe's New Jury Systems: The Cases of Spain and Russia." *Law and Contemporary Problems* 62 (1999): 233–259.

VAN DEN WYNGAERT, CHRISTINE, ed. *Criminal Procedure Systems in the European Community.* London: Butterworths, 1993.

VOGLER, RICHARD. "Spain." In *Criminal Procedure: A Worldwide Study.* Edited by Craig M. Bradley. Durham, N.C.: Carolina University Press, 1999. Pages 361–393.

VOLKMANN-SCHLUCK, THOMAS. *Der spanische Strafprozess zwischen Inquisitions-und Parteiverfahren.* Baden-Baden, Germany: Nomos, 1979.

WEIGEND, THOMAS. "Eine Prozessordnung für abgesprochene Urteile?" *Neue Zeitschrift für Strafrecht* 19 (1999): 57–63.

CRIMINOLOGY: INTELLECTUAL HISTORY

Criminology is the study of crime and the various responses to it. Over the long span of human history, going back even to ancient times, many of the world's greatest thinkers have addressed this subject in books and articles. It can be useful to look briefly back over this long history, in order to put modern views of crime into their historical context.

Early thinking about crime and punishment

The earliest form of punishment was private revenge, in which the victim or the victim's kin retaliated for injury and the community did not interfere. The problem was that private revenge often escalated into blood feuds that could continue for many years until one or the other family was completely wiped out. The loss of life and property became so great that the communities slowly started to impose trials and official penalties on offenders in order to restrict private vengeance.

For many centuries, this community trial and punishment largely was carried out in the context of religion. Criminal acts were said to be affronts to the gods, who might express their anger through plagues, earthquakes, or other desolation. Punishment proportionate to the wrongdoing was said to lessen the gods' anger. For example, the *lex talionis* ("an eye for an eye and a tooth for a tooth"), as found in the Bible, prescribed this correspondence between crime and punishment. Properly read as "no more than an eye for an eye" it also significantly limited the excesses of private revenge in an attempt to reduce the consequences of the blood feuds.

While these religious and spiritual approaches to crime and punishment dominated early thinking, naturalistic approaches also go back to antiquity. For example, Plato (429?–347 B.C.) argued that the basis of law was the prevailing social morality rather than the laws of the gods. Thus, every action against that morality constituted a crime. In his *Republic* and *Laws* he delineated four types of offenses: (1) against religion (theft within a temple, impiety, or disrespect); (2) against the state (treason); (3) against persons (poisoning, use of drugs, witchcraft, sorcery, infliction of injury); and (4) against private property (killing a thief caught stealing at night was not punishable). Plato also made various other arguments: that crime was the product of a faulty education, that the severity of punishment should be determined by the degree of culpability, that criminals are sick individuals who must be cured, and that if they cannot be cured they must be eliminated.

In Aristotle's (384–322 B.C.) view, humans were a synthesis of a body and a soul, endowed with intelligence, emotion, and desire. In his *Nicomachean Ethics*, Aristotle defined crime as the act of free will, stimulated by desire. Thus he argued that children, idiots, the mentally ill, and individuals in a state of ecstasy should not be held responsible for criminal actions.

According to Aristotle, societal responses to crime could be preventive or repressive. Preventive responses could be: (1) eugenic (some children should be nurtured and educated while others should be abandoned and left to die because of some deformity); (2) demographic (the number of births should be limited, and unnecessary pregnancies should be terminated); and (3) deterrent (punishment should be designed to intimidate the offender and deter the onlookers). Repressive responses originally were limited to allowing private revenge, but later were extended to include such measures as banishment and turning the offender over to the victim's family.

Rome was the source of the world's most powerful legal influences. The Twelve Tables are considered the basis of all Roman law, public and private, and it is thought that they were promulgated about 450 B.C. The tables were secular laws, clearly different from religious or moral rules, and included some forty clauses.

The Eighth Table was similar to a body of criminal law and detailed crimes and their punishments. Intentional homicide, setting fire to a dwelling or harvested crop, treason, and parricide were all were punished by death. The intentional infliction of injury was punished by a fine or by the infliction of a comparable injury if the fine was not paid. Punishment for theft generally was compensation equal to double the value of the stolen goods, although a thief caught in the act could be killed. If the thief was a free man, he could be given to his victim as a slave. Death sentences were also imposed on judges or arbitrators caught taking bribes and on witnesses giving false testimony. However, the sentences could only be carried out with the consent of the whole assembly of citizens, and citizens of Rome were rarely put to death. After the second century A.D., exile and banishment became common punishments. The institution of slavery decisively influenced the evolution of the penal system in Rome because the very severe sanctions devised for slaves were later extended to the entire population, with the exception of a limited number of privileged and wealthy citizens. When the population of Rome reached one million, during the second century A.D., permanent tribunals were established, composed of thirty or more jurors presided over by a praetor. At first the jurors had to be of the senatorial class, but gentlemen, wealthy citizens, and soldiers later became eligible. These tribunals were empowered to deal with cases of treason, homicide, adultery, corruption, and kidnapping, and there was no appeal from their decisions.

The Middle Ages

The acceptance of Christianity in Europe turned the thinking about crime and punishment in a spiritual direction, away from the naturalistic thinking found in Roman law. The influence of the devil was the most common explanation for crime, and punishments were primitive and cruel. Crime was identified with sin, and the state claimed that it was acting in the place of God when it inflicted these horrible punishments.

In the Middle Ages, this spiritual and religious basis for punishment was joined to the political and social organization of feudalism to produce the beginnings of the criminal justice system. In an attempt to further limit the blood feuds, the feudal lords instituted official methods by which God could indicate who was innocent and who was guilty. One such method was "trial by ordeal," in which the accused was subjected to difficult and painful tests. The belief was that an innocent person (protected by God) would emerge unharmed while a guilty person would die a painful death. For example, a common method of determining whether a woman was a witch was to tie her up and throw her into the water. If she floated she was considered innocent, but if she sank she was guilty. Other forms of ordeal included running the gauntlet and walking on fire. Trial by ordeal was condemned by the pope in 1215 and was replaced by compurgation, in which the accused gathered together a group of twelve reputable people who would swear that he or she was innocent. The idea was that no one would lie under oath for fear of being punished by God. Compurgation ultimately evolved into testimony under oath and trial by jury.

Shortly after the pope condemned trial by ordeal, St. Thomas Aquinas (1225–1274) began writing his theology, which included an important spiritual explanation of crime and punishment. Aquinas argued that there was a God-given "natural law" that was revealed by observing, through the eyes of faith, people's natural tendency to do good. People's tendency to commit evil, in contrast, was a manifestation of original sin and the Fall from grace, when Adam and Eve were expelled from the Garden of Eden. The criminal law was based on and reflected the "natural law," so that people who commit crime (i.e., violate the criminal law) also commit sin (i.e., violate the natural law). Aquinas argued that crime not only harmed victims, but it also harmed criminals because it harmed their essential "humanness"—their natural tendency to do good. He also regarded human misery as a cause of crime and he offered an impassioned defense of those who steal because of extreme misery.

The Renaissance

The end of the Middle Ages in Europe brought the beginning of the modem search for natural explanations of the phenomenon called crime. This was the time of the Renaissance, an age of great humanists who were interested in human character and personality, society and politics. Especially prominent were the utopian writers, whose name derives from the *Utopia* of Thomas More (1478–1535), and the "social contract" writers, whose name derives from *The Social Contract* of Jean-Jacques Rousseau (1712–1778).

Beginning with Thomas Hobbes (1588–1678), "social contact" writers substituted naturalistic arguments for the spiritual and religious arguments of people like Aquinas. Where Aquinas argued that people naturally do good rather than evil, Hobbes argued that people naturally pursue their own interests without caring whether they hurt anyone else. This leads to a "war of each against all." But people are rational enough to realize that this "war" is not in anyone's interests, so they agree to give up their own selfish behavior as long as everyone else does the same thing. This is the "social contract"—something like a peace treaty when everyone is exhausted from the war of each against all. But the social contract needs an enforcement mechanism to prevent people from cheating. According to Hobbes, that is the role of the state: Everyone who agrees to the social contract also agrees to grant the state the right to use force to maintain the contract.

Later social contract writers protested the criminal laws and punishments of the day and suggested ways to reform them. In *The Spirit of the Laws*, Montesquieu (1689–1755) insisted that prevention of crime was better than punishment of the criminal, and that punishment merely for its own sake was evil. Voltaire (1694–1778) became the leader of a movement against the arbitrariness of the French criminal justice system and the prevailing barbaric treatment of prisoners. He advocated rehabilitation and suggested employing prison inmates in dangerous public works as an alternative to enforced idleness. Rousseau was convinced that the institution of property, with the resulting poverty among some groups, caused most criminality. He strongly opposed the existing criminal justice system, which assumed that crime reflected the influence of the devil, declaring instead that humans are basically good and that only untenable social conditions transform them into criminals.

Utopian writers took a position similar to Rousseau's—that humans are basically good and that this basic goodness would emerge under the proper social conditions. Thus, their books criticized existing social institutions and described imaginary societies in which this basic human goodness was revealed. The most important such book was Thomas More's *Utopia*. More used sarcasm and satire to criticize social institutions in England. In particular he criticized the current economic conditions in England, discussed their relationship with criminality, and decried the extreme harshness of English justice under Henry VIII. More's book then went on to describe an imaginary land (Utopia) where humans were uncorrupted; where reason, love, and law worked in harmony to make a perfect society, pervaded by a sense of brotherhood among all educated people; where everyone worked and no one was idle; and where justice was designed to eliminate vice rather than to destroy the criminal.

Classical criminology

By the middle of the 1700s, the ideas of the utopian and social contact writers were well known and widely accepted by the intellectuals of the day, but they did not represent the thinking of politically powerful groups. Those ruling groups still held to the spiritual explanations of crime, so that crime was seen as resulting from the fall from an original state of grace and as manifesting the work of the devil. For example, this spiritual and religious thinking about crime and punishment appeared in the Puritan colony on Massachusetts Bay. During the first sixty years of its existence, this colony experienced three serious "crime waves" thought to be caused by the devil. The most serious of these "crime waves" occurred in 1792, when the community was said to have been invaded by a large number of witches. These supposed "witches" were subjected to extreme and horrific punishments.

In direct confrontation with these religious and spiritual views stood the utopian and social contract writers, who advocated rationalism and criticized the prevailing social conditions. Their protests against the abuses of judges, prosecutors, and jailers in the treatment of offenders evolved into the classical school of criminology, whose most outstanding representative was Cesare Beccaria (1738–1794).

Beccaria was an Italian writer who sought to change these excessive and cruel punishments by applying the rationalist, social contract ideas to crime and criminal justice. His small book, *Dei deliti e delle pene (On Crimes and Punishments)*, was published in 1764 and was well-received by intellectuals and some reform-minded rulers who had already accepted the general framework of social contract thinking. Even more important for the book's acceptance, however, was the fact that the American Revolution of 1776 and the French Revolution of 1789 occurred soon after this book's publication. These two great revolutions were both guided by naturalistic ideas of the social contract philosophers. To these revolutionaries, Beccaria's book represented the latest and best thinking on the subject of crime and criminal justice. They therefore used his ideas as the basis for their new criminal justice systems. From America and France, Beccaria's ideas spread to the rest of the industrialized world where they have formed the basis for most modern systems of criminal justice.

Beccaria argued that the legislatures should establish a fixed legal scale of crimes, ranging from the least serious to the most serious, and a corresponding fixed scale of punishments, proportional to the offenses, ranging from the least severe to the most severe. Judges should determine guilt or innocence at trials, which should be public and speedy, and then should apply the punishment that has been fixed in law by the legislature. Any other actions by a judge would be considered tyrannical. Beccaria also argued that the prevention of crime is more important than punishment, and the certainty and quickness with which a punishment is imposed has a greater preventive effect than the severity of the punishment. He thought capital punishment should be abolished, and that prisons should be improved, with inmates segregated on the basis of age, sex, and type of crime.

Beccaria did not deal with the causes of crime but rather established a clear and easily administered system for responding to it. On the whole, it worked quite well and eliminated many of the injustices and abuses that had been the focus of protest writers for several hundred years. The major problem was that the fixed scale of crimes and punishments focused solely on the criminal act and not on the intent of the offender or the circumstances of the crime. As a practical matter, this meant that there were no distinctions between first offenders and recidivists, the sane and insane, or juveniles and adults. Eventually, this exclusive focus on the act was modified in the so-called neoclassical school, which retained the essential principles of the classical school but modified the concept of "the same punishment for the same crime." It allowed judges some discretion and individualization, so that the particular circumstances of each case were taken into account. The neoclassicists recognized that an individual's free will could be affected by pathology as well as by other factors. They introduced the concept of premeditation, admitted the validity of physical, environmental, and psychological mitigating circumstances as bases for attributing only partial responsibility, and accepted expert testimony as to whether an accused was capable of distinguishing and choosing between right and wrong. All of these issues later gave raise to what became known as the "positivist" school of criminology.

Positivist criminology

The first annual national crime statistics were published in France in 1827, about sixty years after Beccaria wrote his book. It soon became clear that the rates of crime in general and of particular crimes such as murder and rape remained relatively constant from year to year. In addition, some places in the nation had higher crime rates while others had lower, and these differences remained relatively constant from year to year. All of this suggested that there might be some broader social causes to crime, instead of it being merely a matter of individual free will.

One of the first people to analyze these statistics was Adolphe Quetelet (1796–1874). He found that some people were more likely to commit crime than others, especially those who were young, male, poor, unemployed, and undereducated. Young males were more likely to commit crime under any circumstances, so that places with more young males tended to have more crime. But places with more poverty and more unemployment actually had less crime. As it turned out, the poor and unemployed tended to commit crimes in places where there were many wealthy and employed people. Quetelet suggested that opportunities might have something to do with explaining this pattern. He also pointed to an additional factor: the great inequality between wealth and poverty in the same place excites passions and provokes temptations of all kinds. This problem is especially severe in those places where rapidly changing economic conditions can result in a person suddenly passing from wealth to poverty while all around him still enjoy wealth. In contrast, provinces that were generally poor had less crime as long as people were able to satisfy their basic needs. Quetelet found that people with more education tended to commit less crime on the whole but they also tended to commit more violent crime. He therefore argued that increased education itself would not reduce crime.

Quetelet concluded that the propensity to engage in crime was actually a reflection of moral character. Relying on Aristotle's views, he identified virtue with moderation: "rational and temperate habits, more regulated passions . . . [and] foresight, as manifested by investment in savings banks, assurance societies, and the different institutions which encourage foresight." Young males often did not have these virtues, and so they committed high levels of crime. Similarly, these virtues tended to break down among poor and unemployed people who were surrounded by wealth. Thus, his main policy recommendations were to enhance "moral" education and to ameliorate social conditions to improve people's lives.

Quetelet retained the view throughout his life that crime essentially was caused by moral defectiveness, but increasingly took the view that moral defectiveness was revealed in biological characteristics, particularly the appearance of the face and the head. This also made him a direct predecessor of Lombroso, whose major book was published two years after Quetelet's death.

Cesare Lombroso (1835–1909) was a physician who became a specialist in psychiatry, and his principal career was as a professor of legal medicine at the University of Turin. His name came into prominence with the publication of his book *L'uomo delinquente (The Criminal Man)* in 1876. In that book Lombroso proposed that criminals were biological throwbacks to an earlier evolutionary stage, people more primitive and less highly evolved than their noncriminal counterparts. He used the term *atavistic* to describe these less-evolved people.

The idea of evolution was quite recent at the time. Darwin had proposed the evolution of animals in 1859 in his book *On The Origin of Species.* In 1871, in his book *Descent of Man*, Darwin argued that humans were the same general kind of creatures as the rest of the animals, except that they were more highly evolved or developed. He also suggested that some individuals might be reversions to an earlier evolutionary stage. In that same year, Lombroso conducted a postmortem examination on a certain Vilella, a highwayman who died in prison, during which he found certain unusual characteristics of the skull. Those anomalies that led him to conclude that Vilella was not as highly evolved as other people. Lombroso then discovered a second subject, Vincenzo Verzeni, who had raped, strangled, and dismembered women, who was physiologically similar. As a result, he concluded that criminals in general are atavistic, less evolved than noncriminals.

Lombroso is known principally for his theory of the atavistic criminal, but the real basis of the positive school is the search for the causes of criminal behavior. That search is based on the conception of multiple factor causation, where some of the factors may be biological, others psychological, and still others social. Lombroso did much by way of documenting the effects of many of these factors. As his thinking changed over the years, he looked more and more to environmental rather than biological factors. By the end of his life, Lombroso included as causes of crime such things as climate, rainfall, the price of grain, sex and marriage customs, criminal laws, banking practices, national tariff policies, the structure of government, church organization, and the state of religious belief. It had also become clear that his theory of the atavistic criminal was much too simple and naive, and it has since been largely abandoned.

Modern criminology as the search for the causes of crime

Criminology today is positivistic in the sense that it studies the causes of crime. But there are really two different methods of studying the causes of crime and therefore two different types of theories in positivist criminology. These can be illustrated with the work of Quetelet and Lombroso. Quetelet initially looked at different areas of France and tried to determine which social characteristics were associated with higher or lower crime rates in those areas. In contrast, Lombroso initially looked at individual criminals and tried to determine which individual characteristics were associated with more or less criminal behavior.

These are two very different approaches to the study of the causes of crime. On the other hand, by the end of their careers, both of these theorists had incorporated elements of the other's approach in their explanations of crime. This suggests that these approaches are not incompatible, but that they represent separate questions: Why are some people more likely to commit crime than others? and Why do some social units have higher crime rates than others? Answering these two questions has been the focus of and enormous amount of theory and research in criminology over the last one hundred years. In general, biological and psychological theories in criminology attempt to answer the first of these two questions, while social theories attempt to answer the second.

Biological theories in criminology

Studies of twins and adoptees lend general support for the notion that there is a connection between biology and crime. For example, some studies have found that identical twins (who develop from a single fertilized egg and thus have identical genetic heritage) are more likely to have similar criminal records than fraternal twins (who develop from two different fertilized eggs and thus have the same genetic relationship as ordinary siblings). In addition, some studies of adopted children have found that the criminal records of adopted children are similar to the criminal records of their biological parents, regardless of the criminal records of their adopted parents. These studies suggest at least some connection between biological heritage and the tendency to commit crime. On the other hand, it is possible that the increased criminality may instead be due to social conditions. For example, identical twins are physically more similar than fraternal twins, and so they may have more similar social experiences while growing up. These more similar social experiences then may explain the tendency for identical twins to have more similar criminal records than fraternal twins.

Other biological research attempts to identify specific biological factors associated with an increased risk of criminality. For example, recent studies have found that certain neurotransmitter imbalances in the brain such as low seratonin, and certain hormone imbalances such as extra testosterone, are associated with some greater likelihood of committing crime. Other studies have found that criminals tend to have slower reactions in their autonomic nervous systems. While some criminologists infer that these biological conditions increase the tendency to commit crime, other criminologists point out that all of these biological factors can be influenced by the environmental conditions. Thus, it may be that low seratonin and high testosterone increases a person's tendency to commit crime, but it may also be that committing crime tends to lower seratonin levels and increase testosterone levels.

At least some biological conditions result from a person's interaction with the environment. There has been considerable research, for example, on the influence of diet on crime, with some people arguing that excessive sugar intake results in increased aggression in juveniles. Consuming alcohol has a strong relationship with increased aggression in the short run, as does the consumption of certain illegal drugs. Ingesting various toxic substances such as lead tends to result in long-term increases in the tendency to commit crime. In addition, complications during pregnancy or birth and certain types of head injuries increase the risk of crime in the long run. There is, however, a similar problem with inferring that these environmentally based biological conditions cause crime. For example, some other factor such as poverty could cause both crime and the increased tendency to experience complications during pregnancy and birth, to ingest lead and other toxins, and to drink alcohol. If this were the case, then these biological factors would not themselves have any causal impact on crime.

Even if these biological factors are eventually shown to have a direct causal impact on crime, they would not determine absolutely that people with these factors would turn out to be criminal. Rather, the relationship between biological factors and crime is similar to the relationship between being tall and being a basketball player. Most basketball players are tall, but most tall people are not basketball players. Similarly, it may turn out that a fairly large number of criminals have low seratonin or high testosterone, but most people with these biological factors would not be criminals at all.

Psychological theories

The earliest psychological approaches to crime were based on Sigmund Freud's (1870–1937) psychoanalytic theory, which divided the human personality into id, ego, and superego. The id (the Latin word for "it") described all the instinctual drives that come from our biological heritage. The "ego" (Latin for "I") is the rational and conscious self that mediates between the drives of the id and the restraints of the superego. The "superego" consists in the restraints on behavior ("conscience") that children internalize as a result of their great love for and attachment to their parents. Criminality largely was explained as a failure of the superego, a consequence of a failure to form healthy and loving attachments to parents. Later theories of crime were based on behavioral psychology, as originating in the work of B. F. Skinner (1904–1990). In Skinner's view, all human behavior is the product of its consequences—its rewards and punishments. In this approach, criminal behavior is acquired and retained if people experience rewards from it, and it is abandoned if they experience punishments. Somewhat later, social learning theory expanded Skinner's behavior theory to include social rewards and punishments, such as the approval or disapproval of family and friends. It also expanded the ways in which behavior can be acquired to include learning through observation of what other people do, including observations in the media, particularly television.

Mental illness does not cause very many crimes, but mentally ill people occasionally commit crimes that are extreme or bizarre, and thus highly publicized. Thus, the public might get the impression that mental illness is a major cause of crime. In addition, following the closing of most mental institutions in the United States in the 1960s and 1970s, many mentally ill people began to be sent to prisons and jails because they were troublesome and appeared threatening and because there was no other way to remove them from the community. One particular personality disorder—antisocial personality disorder—has been found in many studies to be associated with criminality. However, the official criteria for diagnosing this disorder include the commission of crimes and crime-like behavior. Thus, it is not entirely clear whether this personality disorder is a cause of crime or whether the term "antisocial personality disorder" is just a fancy label that psychiatrists use to describe people who are criminals. Current psychological research focuses on impulsivity (a tendency to engage in high levels of activity, to be easily distracted, to act without thinking, and to seek immediate gratification) rather than antisocial personality as a personality characteristic associated with criminality.

Sociological theories

Sociological theories generally assert that crime is the normal response of a biologically and psychologically normal individual to social conditions that are abnormal and criminogenic. A large number of these theories have been proposed. For example, Edwin Sutherland (1883–1950) proposed differential association theory, which argues that criminal behavior is normal learned behavior, that the learning takes place in a process of interpersonal communication with other people, that it consists primarily in the learning of ideas about whether laws are to be obeyed, and that the learning of criminal behaviors is determined primarily by the extent of the person's contact with other people who themselves engage in criminal behaviors. Robert K. Merton proposed a theory of social structural strain. He argued that American culture emphasizes the goal of monetary success at the expense of adhering to the legitimate means to achieve that success. This results in high rates of profit-oriented crimes. He also argued that American

society has an unequal distribution of the legitimate opportunities to achieve monetary success. That is, people in the upper classes have very many legitimate opportunities to make money, while people in the lower classes had very few. Merton argued that this resulted in the reverse distribution of profit-oriented crimes, with the lowest classes having the highest rates of such crime and the highest classes having the lowest rates. Clifford Shaw presented an ecological theory that looks at crime at the neighborhood level. He generally found that neighborhoods with high poverty, frequent residential mobility, and family disruption (e.g., many divorced or single parents) have higher crime rates. Travis Hirschi proposed a social control theory that focused on the ability to resist the natural temptations of criminal behavior. Individuals who are more strongly attached to parents, more involved in conventional activities, have more to lose from criminal behavior, and have stronger beliefs in conventional moral values, will tend to commit less crime. Michael Gottfredson and Travis Hirschi later proposed a general theory of crime as being the result of low self-control. Where Hirschi's earlier social control theory concerned the restraints on an individual's behavior that are found in the person's immediate environment, self-control theory focuses on certain stable characteristics that people have after age eight or so. People with low self-control, and therefore a higher tendency to commit crime, tend to be impulsive, insensitive to others, oriented toward physical rather than mental activities, prone to take risks, shortsighted, and nonverbal. Labeling theories, by contrast, argue that people who become involved in the criminal justice system tend to be labeled as criminals by that system, rejected by law-abiding people, and accepted as criminals by other criminals. All of this results in their taking on a criminal self-concept, in which they come to think of themselves as criminals. The criminal self-concept then becomes the major cause of crime. Radical criminologists focus on the structure of society, in particular its political and legal systems. In one way or another, often with a considerable degree of subtlety, the criminal law is seen as a tool by which rich and powerful people maintain and preserve their own privileges and status.

THOMAS J. BERNARD

See also CRIMINOLOGY: MODERN CONTROVERSIES; PRISONS: HISTORY; PUNISHMENT; STATISTICS: HISTORICAL TRENDS IN WESTERN SOCIETY.

BIBLIOGRAPHY

BARNES, HARRY ELMER. *The Story of Punishment.* 2d ed., revised. Montclair, N.J.: Patterson Smith, 1972.

BECCARIA, CESARE. *On Crimes and Punishments* (1764). Translated and with an introduction by Henry Paolucci. Indianapolis: Bobbs-Merrill, 1963.

BEIRNE, PIERS. *Inventing Criminology.* Albany: State University of New York Press, 1993.

DOWNES, DAVID, and ROCK, PAUL. *Understanding Deviance.* 2d ed. Oxford, U.K.: Oxford University Press, 1988.

JONES, DAVID A. *History of Criminology: A Philosophical Perspective.* Westport, Conn.: Greenwood Press, 1986.

LOMBROSO, CESARE. *Crime: Its Causes and Remedies* (1876). Translated by Henry P. Horton. Introduction by Maurice Parmelee. Boston: Little, Brown, 1911.

MANNHEIM, HERMANN, ed. *Pioneers in Criminology.* London: Stevens, 1960.

MARTIN, RANDY; MUTCHNICK, ROBERT J.; and AUSTIN W. TIMOTHY. *Criminological Thought: Pioneers Past and Present.* New York: Macmillan, 1990.

NEWMAN, GRAEME. *The Punishment Response.* Philadelphia: Lippincott, 1978.

RENNIE, YSABEL. *The Search for Criminal Man.* Lexington, Mass.: Heath, 1973.

SCHAFER, STEPHEN. *Theories in Criminology: Past and Present Philosophies of the Crime Problem.* New York: Random House, 1969.

VOLD, GEORGE B; BERNARD, THOMAS J.; and SNIPES, JEFFREY B. *Theoretical Criminology.* 4th ed. New York: Oxford University Press, 1998.

CRIMINOLOGY: MODERN CONTROVERSIES

Controversy among criminologists and between criminologists and others is endemic. It could hardly be otherwise. Problems of definition, once merely legally technical regarding behavior defined as crime, are joined by both ideological and postmodern concerns with what crime, criminality, and criminology are about. Because crime is by definition behavior that is so specified in the criminal law, criminology involves study of, and controversy concerning, how and why behaviors become "criminalized." Be-cause the purpose of criminal laws is to control behavior so defined, the efficacy—and necessarily the fairness and moral status—of prescribed penalties is subject to challenge and debate in many circles.

These concerns intersect with controversy concerning the stance of criminology vis-à-vis social policy. They intersect, also, with theoretical and empirical issues of mainstream criminology, regarding, for example, the scope of the criminal law and of criminological inquiry, empirically and theoretically, and the extent to which the focus of inquiry should be on particular crimes, patterns of crime (e.g., careers), the broader field of deviance or, indeed, on all human behavior. General theories that attempt to explain deviance, such as Robert K. Merton's classic "Social Structure and Anomie" (1938) and, more recently, Charles Tittle's *Control Balance* theory (1995), imply theoretical explanations for all human behavior. Control theories tend to regard behavior that is not deviant as residual, to be explained by processes and forces that are left undefined.

Because human behavior is ever-changing in response to social change, the search for general etiological principles is both extraordinarily complex and changing. New technologies, evolving social structures, and cultural adaptations constantly pose new questions, and modify social distributions of crime and etiological processes.

This entry focuses primarily on issues—some persisting, some emergent—related to elements of Edwin Sutherland's classic definition of criminology. Criminology, wrote Sutherland, is "the body of knowledge regarding . . . crime as a social phenomenon," including "the processes of making laws, of breaking laws, and of reacting toward the breaking of laws" (p. 3). The inclusiveness of Sutherland's vision notwithstanding, controversy continues concerning the scope and purposes of criminology.

Models of criminology and ideology

Although Sutherland's definition of the field was broad enough to accommodate all scientific approaches to the study of crime and criminals, controversy continues concerning a variety of issues: (1) whether—or the extent to which—criminology is an independent or an integrative discipline; (2) challenges to the adequacy of science as the basis of knowledge in criminology; and (3) the role of criminology and criminologists in the application of knowledge. Although they intersect in quite different ways, ideological considerations as well as intellectual concerns are especially important to the latter two issues.

Marvin Wolfgang and Franco Ferracuti argued that criminology is sufficiently integrated, as discipline and profession, to be intellectually independent of other disciplines. In contrast, Donald Cressey argued that although criminology has of necessity been integrative, it can never be independent of other disciplines inasmuch as it must depend on basic knowledge generated by more basic social and behavioral science disciplines. Both positions have attracted followers, and there is a good deal of academic and professional activity independent of other disciplines. It seems fair to say, however, that the vast majority of criminologists regard criminology as necessarily integrative and to a large extent dependent on other disciplines.

Regarding issues 2 and 3, more than a century after his most seminal writings, a variety of "new criminologies" emerged, based in large measure on the works of Karl Marx. These perspectives challenged conventional views of lawmaking, lawbreaking, and crime control. The more radical views challenged science as well (Taylor, Walton, and Young), under several rubrics: "critical theory," "post-modern theory," "peacemaking criminology," and "consitutive theory." In varying ways, each of these perspectives enlarged upon the conflict theory critique of consensus as the basis for law. In its most extreme form the critique charges mainstream criminology with "investing in constructing the existing structures of power and oppression," and urges active participation by criminologists in "replacement discourse" aimed at development of "new, less harmful structures" (Henry and Einstadter, 1997, p. 418).

In the absence of convincing data to support such arguments, and because upholding human rights values does not distinguish between "new" and traditional criminologists, this "human rights" position has attracted few supporters. Indeed, many criminologists point to the likelihood that such a broad extension of the definition of crime would exacerbate problems already associated with the political use of the criminal law process. Beyond this, most criminologists do not agree with the basic premise that social science research contributes to a status quo of power and oppression. Quite to the contrary, most criminologists—indeed, most social scientists—choose their disciplines, in part, based firmly on the belief that knowledge will contribute to solutions to crime and to the alleviation of human misery.

Because this belief has proven to be delusive, the second type of controversy (the role of criminologists in the application of criminological, and more broadly, social and behavioral science knowledge) is more salient for most criminologists. Here controversy tends to be based on conflicting models of the relationship between social science knowledge, social policy, and other types of ameliorative action. Morris Janowitz characterized opposing positions on this issue as the "engineering" versus "enlightenment" models of social science. In the former, social scientists enter directly into the design and implementation of programs designed to ameliorate some social condition, for example, a delinquency prevention program or a program to rehabilitate delinquents or criminals. Classic programs of this type were the Chicago Area Project developed by Clifford Shaw and his followers, based on Shaw's research (see Kobrin), and Saul Alinsky's more confrontational community organization tactics, as described in his book, *Reveille for Radicals* (1946). More recently, the engineering model has proven to be attractive to governmental agencies in many countries seeking advice and participation in programs designed to control crime and delinquency.

The enlightenment model eschews direct intervention in action programs, holding instead to a more traditional "arm's length" posture regarding the involvement of researchers with social policies and programs. Here the production of basic knowledge concerning human behavior is the primary and sufficient goal. The distinction between social engineering and enlightenment sometimes becomes blurred, however, as researchers move beyond conducting and disseminating their findings to dispensing advice and consultation on policy options, even though they may not actively participate in the implementation of policies.

Research that evaluates the performance and outcomes of programs and policies also falls within the enlightenment model. Here, too, controversy exists, however; for example, concerning the validity of standard evaluation research measures of "before and after" recidivism or crime rates. The basis for controversy lies in the fact that criminal and juvenile justice systems play many roles in the social and political life of communities, as do programs of social agencies that are designed to aid in the socialization of the young or the rehabilitation of delinquents, or that seek to address in other ways problems related to crime and delinquency. In addition, many factors beyond the control of law enforcement and social programs influence crime rates and individual offending. The "weak stimulus" of any particular program, therefore, is likely to be only one of many, sometimes conflicting, influences on individual offending or crime rates. Moreover, the experience of researchers and theorists who have actively participated in program design and implementation suggests that even the most carefully designed, planned, and monitored programs rarely function as designed (see Klein and Teilmann, eds.). A variety of proposals for more nuanced approaches to measuring the results of juvenile criminal justice policy and practice, and of the effects of efforts to prevent offending and change offenders, have been suggested (see Bureau of Justice Statistics).

This type of controversy also occurs in debates over the proper role of scholarly organizations in relation to social policy. Here, also, engineering and enlightenment models conflict, adherents of the former urging that scholarly organizations such as the American Society of Criminology (ASC) ought to go on record in support of, or in opposition to, particular social policies. Failure to engage in social policy debate, adherents of the engineering model maintain, denies the purpose of knowledge building and is socially irresponsible. A "middle ground" position that individual scientists have the right, as citizens, to advise and consult on social policy, is rejected. A major argument of those favoring the enlightenment model, however, is that scientific evidence rarely, if ever, is sufficient to warrant endorsement of particular social policies. In addition, disagreements among organization members concerning which policies to favor or oppose is inevitable. More importantly, because policy decisions are inherently political in nature, the credibility of science and scientific associations is likely to be compromised by policy advocacy.

These arguments are as unending as they are inevitable among scholars and others in democratic societies with representative governments. For scholarly organizations the controversies they spark are often unsettling and they may be destabilizing. Although they seem unlikely ever to be resolved to everyone's satisfaction, scientific scholarly organizations have upon occasion come together in support of a few fundamental principles, such as freedom of research and teaching, and scientific standards. An example of the latter occurred in 1997 when the American Society of Criminology governing board was asked to support a "friend of the court" brief in behalf of an experimental effort to evaluate the efficacy of a treatment program for domestic violence offenders. For ASC, the case posed the issue of whether it was ethical to withhold treatment (counseling) from a control group of offenders who were to be compared with a similar group, randomly chosen, for whom counseling would be provided. The ASC board voted unanimously to support the research on the grounds that random assignment was the best method of determining the efficacy of the proposed treatment (see Short et al.; Feder).

At the most fundamental level these controversies reflect deep divisions among scholars regarding their responsibilities, their integrity, and the integrity of science. For such issues of values science can provide no answers, only relevant information. Although the implications of scholarly research for social policy are rarely clear and unambiguous, the two often seem clearly at odds with one another, leading to the frustration of criminologists and the urge to influence social policy. Regrettably, when scholars do so they often generalize beyond available, time- and place-bound data and theory. Examples from each of criminology's major divisions are not hard to find.

Sociology of law and crime control

Crimes are social constructions. Controversy concerning the behaviors so labeled—which to include or exclude, and how to define the former—and the circumstances under which invocation of the criminal law is warranted, change in response to legal and social changes. Historically, such controversies have taken many turns, from the status of witches to substance use and abuse (and efforts to enforce statutes related to them); from criteria of citizenship to the legal standing of corporations and other organizations; from "victimless" crimes and common "street crimes" to international commerce and terrorism. Here, only a brief sampling from the vast literature of research and debate addressing such issues is possible.

Hate crimes. Although the behaviors so labeled are as old as human history, crimes motivated by "hate" or "bias" became a part of the legal and social lexicon of the United States only in the 1980s. By bringing hate or bias motivation under the criminal law, the United States, in effect, embarked on a social and legal experiment to sanction and control behavior that has long been a part of the history of the country (Jacobs and Potter; American Sociological Association). Although every state passed some form of hate crime legislation in a very short time, there is great variation in the categories singled out for recognition as victims and in penalties for offending. Researchers note that social movements have been important in identifying some but not other categories for protection under hate crime legislation: for example, race, ethnicity, and religion most frequently; sexual orientation, physical and mental disability in several states; age, gender, interference with civil rights, marital status, physical appearance, political affiliation, and service in the armed forces in only a few states (Jenness and Grattet). Critics point to inconsistency and vagueness in such criteria as major faults of the laws.

Hate crime laws are not the first to reference motivation. Distinctions are made between "simple" and "aggravated" assault, and between "degrees" of homicide, rape, and burglary, for example. Most such distinctions, however, are based on some observable quality of behavior, rather than or in addition to motivation. Hate crimes frequently must rely on inferences drawn from speech or an offender's associates and reading material, still another basis of ambiguity requiring often questionable inference, and subject to abuse. The constitutionality of such laws has been challenged, as well, based on the First Amendment to the U.S. Constitution.

Sentencing enhancement—frequently employed as a device for distinguishing the relative seriousness of crimes—is the most common form of hate crime sanction. Here again, there is great variation among states, most providing for (varying) terms of incarceration in addition to those previously specified for an offense. Other statutes specify as hate crimes behaviors long considered too vague and subject to unreliable reporting and recording for inclusion in statistical systems, for example, harassment, intimidation, simple assault, and vandalism. For all these reasons, critics argue that statistics on hate crimes (required by federal law) are incomplete and lacking either reliability or validity. Such vagaries notwithstanding, some social scientists, journalists, politicians, and civil rights and social movement organization spokespersons argue that the United States has experienced a "rising tide of bigotry and bloodshed" based on hate (Levin and McDevitt). Yet, bias and hate toward selected groups, and behavior related to bias and hate,

have a long history in the United States and throughout the world (Graham and Gurr). Against this background, the rate of victimization of others by virtue of their categorical identity (race, ethnicity, sexual orientation, etc.) in the United States at the close of the twentieth century almost certainly was lower than in the past. Much has changed, however, including the cast of characters.

Labor disputes, for example—once the focus of violent confrontations between union organizers and members and plant owners and officials (often with government connivance and support of owners)—are now subject to regulation, and most are settled by agreed upon legal processes. Although religious prejudice continues to exist, and to be monitored by a variety of organizations, it is no longer as blatant or as volatile as it once was. Survey data suggest that racial and ethnic prejudice has decreased, and legal protections against many forms of discrimination are in place, prompted by civil rights movements— changes that have made it possible for many to escape poverty and enter mainstream society.

Pressure for hate crime laws is related also to the increasing concentration of poverty, especially among minorities living in inner-city areas. The gap between the most and the least affluent has increased in many nations. Scholars also note that declines in the perceived legitimacy of traditional institutions were associated with rising rates of violent crimes during the 1980s and early 1990s (see Harris and Curtis 1998; LaFree). Although violent crimes are overwhelmingly intraracial and intra-ethnic (that is, both victims and perpetrators occur within racial and ethnic categories), biases and fears are fueled by the overrepresentation of these minorities in crime statistics.

Although high crime rates are not associated with most other categories (religion, sexual orientation, age, gender) singled out for protection against hate crimes, all such laws may be counterproductive. Hate crime laws, Jacobs and Potter write, "are both a cause and a consequence of identity politics" that base political and other relationships among individuals and groups on membership in particular categories, thus accentuating existing divisions and resentments (p. 132).

Controversy over hate crimes is not likely to abate in the near future. Especially heinous killings that are clearly associated with racial or sexual orientation fan public outrage and encourage strengthening of such laws. Extreme behavior motivated by bias and hate has a long history—not only in the U.S. but in other countries, often in the form of "ethnic cleansing," which has become of increasing interest to the international community. It will be important in the future to monitor the effects of "natural experiments" such as hate crime legislation and enforcement, and international attempts to control such behavior. Similarly, we have much to learn from controversies regarding a host of other emerging problems and responses to them: "assisted suicide," computer crimes and message content, efforts to prevent, halt, or compensate for "ethnic cleansing," impacts of the globalization of commerce (some of which almost certainly will involve violations of criminal laws and other regulatory statutes within and between nations), and other behaviors that heretofore have been restricted to national boundaries. Increasingly, controversy concerning the legal status of behaviors that were the province solely of nation states is likely to transcend national boundaries, as global processes accelerate throughout the world.

Explanations of crime—social distribution and causation

Scholars from several disciplines and professions focus on different *levels of explanation* as they study and theorize about crime and criminals, and participate in control efforts. These differing perspectives give rise to often bitterly contested disagreements concerning the causes and correlates of crime. The *macrosocial* level of explanation seeks to determine what it is about the structural conditions and cultural variations of societies, communities, and organizations that explains variations in *crime rates* among them. The *individual* level seeks explanation of the criminal (and other) behavior of individuals, focusing primarily on biological and personal variations among individuals, only occasionally seeking to understand how macro-level phenomena influence the behavior of individuals. Until late in the twentieth century macro-level perspectives were fairly clearly associated with social sciences such as sociology, anthropology, and political science, as were individual-level perspectives with psychological and psychiatric disciplines. Distinctions between disciplines became blurred when scholars began to realize that their disagreements often were the result of the sorts of questions they were asking; that they

were often "talking past each other" as they contested explanatory principles and processes.

Several developments offer the hope, if not the promise, that disciplinary hegemony with respect to crime causation will further erode. *Integrative* theories necessarily must take into account both macro- and individual-level variables and processes. Emphasis on behavioral *contexts* brings into focus a third level of explanation that has heretofore been neglected: the *microsocial*, comprising both characteristics of situations and ongoing interactional processes (Short, 1997). Bridging theoretical levels remains, nevertheless, difficult and contentious.

Theoretical and empirical controversies exist at each level of explanation. Two long-standing controversies seem especially important because they cut across levels of explanation: (1) the role of poverty in crime; (2) the nature and role of youth groups and other collectivities in delinquency, violence, and other criminal activity.

Clearly, poverty does not cause crime. The vast majority of poor people are law-abiding. Yet poverty is associated with crime, and social class and other stratification variables often associated with poverty figure prominently in theories of crime.

Controversy centers on measurement, methodological, empirical, and theoretical issues. Examination of the reliability and validity of measures of crime has generated a large body of research and interpretation. Challenges to the adequacy of official records have led to innovations in such records, such as the U.S. Federal Bureau of Investigation's Uniform Crime Reports, as well as to self and victim reports, the latter having been institutionalized in the form of the National Crime Victimization Surveys in the U.S. and in similar systems in other countries. Researchers often triangulate such measures, and supplement them with observational studies in order to achieve better representations of the nature of criminal activity. Measures of the correlates of crime—including poverty and social class—and of processes associated with criminal activity, are equally controversial (Hagan). Much depends on the assumptions and theoretical linkages that are made by those who study these relationships. We first examine Douglas Massey's interpretation of possible consequences of "concentrated affluence and poverty in the twenty-first century" (p. 395).

Massey's broad historical review notes that the industrial revolution radically changed both the amount and the distribution of wealth, leading to increased density of both affluence and poverty and behaviors and problems associated with each. Citing population trends and research on the ecological distribution of crime in U.S. cities, Massey argues that, in the future, the affluent and the poor will be increasingly segregated spatially, and separated socially. Because social separation typically results in cultural differentiation, crime and violence will increase among the poor, leading to further withdrawal of the affluent and greater isolation of the poor, in an accelerating cycle of alienation between social classes.

Massey's bleak scenario (which he deplores, but advances in hopes of galvanizing preventive research and action) depends on several assumptions: (1) the continuation of world trends toward urbanization; (2) increased urbanization will lead to increased segregation of the affluent from the poor; (3) crime and violence in poor communities will lead to further protective measures by the affluent, such as gated communities; and (4) that poor communities will be left to cope with disorder with only their own diminished resources. The first of these assumptions seems quite likely, and the second may well be. As Massey acknowledges, however, the last two are by no means inevitable. The association of urbanization with crime is also controversial (Gillis). Moreover, the Chicago research by Sampson and others suggests that proximity of poor communities to those that are more affluent is advantageous to poor communities' "collective efficacy" with respect to children. Collective efficacy (social cohesion among neighbors and willingness to intervene on behalf of the common good) is, in turn, linked to reduced violence in those communities (Sampson et al., 1997).

These arguments are not necessarily incompatible. Sampson and his colleagues suggest "that residents take a more active role in child supervision and intergenerational exchange when others around them are doing likewise" (p. 647). To the extent that the more affluent seal themselves off from the poor, with gated communities and other security measures, this spillover effect may not obtain.

Time and place limitations of these studies make resolution of controversy impossible. Thus, Sampson and colleagues find that residential stability, as well as concentrated affluence, are important to collective efficacy, and that the advantage of these relationships characterize white neighborhoods to a greater extent than black neighborhoods. Future interethnic, interracial, and social class relationships, as well as res-

idential stability, remain quite uncertain. In addition, global urbanization and its impacts vary greatly along many dimensions, and will continue to do so as a result, for example, of different levels of technological development among nations and cities, access to global markets, political regimes, institutional, and structural and cultural traditions—each of which will influence crime and its control.

The nature and role of youth groups. Despite decades of research demonstrating that most delinquent behaviors are committed by young people in the company of others, the nature of youth groups and their role in such behaviors remain controversial. In large part this is due to the lack of a theoretically viable typology of youth collectivities—most notably, gangs. So confusing are the varying criteria used by law enforcement officials, academics, and the media even to define gangs that many who study phenomena so loosely grouped under that rubric do not use the term, referring instead to "co-offending" (Reiss; Reiss and Farrington), "bands of teenagers congregating on street corners" (Skogan), "unsupervised peer groups" (Sampson and Groves), "networks" of juveniles who violate the law (Sarnecki), or simply "delinquent groups" (Warr, 1996). Clifford Shaw and his colleagues, whose early work inspired much of the subsequent research and theory concerning gangs, had little to say about gangs (Shaw; Shaw and McKay; Shaw and Moore). Instead they emphasized patterns of friendship, association of younger with older offenders, and the coexistence in "delinquency areas" of organized crime and other forms of adult criminality. Even Frederic Thrasher's classic 1927 study presents a bewildering variety of descriptions of groups among the 1313 gangs he studied.

The goals of gang researchers vary, often determining the research methods they employ. The most common method used to count gangs in communities, for example, is to seek reports from police departments (Maxson and Klein, 1996; Curry et al., 1996; Moore and Terrett, 1999). Although this is reasonable, given the universality of law enforcement presence in communities, police resources and gang intelligence vary a great deal. It is significant that some participants in the Second Eurogang Workshop (an ongoing project involving researchers from many countries) asked specifically that planned surveys of gangs in their countries not be limited to inquiries of the police.

The consistency of police reports of gang activity suggests that street gangs have spread to many cities and rural areas throughout the United States; yet, many questions remain. For example, although violence accompanies the spread of gangs in nearly all reporting areas, the reported prevalence of other forms of criminal behavior varies greatly. Little is known about such variation. Nor is there agreement concerning criteria for classifying gangs and other youth groups. How, for example, do gangs relate to drug crews, "wilding" groups, milling crowds, networks involved in delinquency, "tagger crews," punks, socker hooligans, skinheads, bikers, and so on (Cummings and Monti; Klein)? *Diversity* of gangs—their behavior, organization, inter- and intra-gang relationships and relationships with their communities—hinders generalizations about them. Moreover, gangs change, as researchers who have studied them over time attest.

Police knowledge about change and diversity is variable and uncertain. Importantly, ethnographic studies document variations and changes that are not found in police reports. The *age range* of many gangs, especially among gangs in inner-city areas of the United States, has changed. Street gangs in some cities in the United States and Europe no longer consist entirely of adolescents, as many older members—unable to find attractive legitimate employment, or finding illicit sources of income attractive—remain active, often in leadership roles. Patterns of *gang ethnicity* vary among nations and change in response to patterns of immigration and settlement.

Ordinances targeting gang members also raise constitutional issues. Courts have in some cases upheld such laws, but some have been ruled unconstitutionally vague and restrictive (*City of Chicago v. Morles*). Sociologically, researchers note that gang membership may become a "master status" for police and others, and that it may serve to justify prejudicial attitudes and discriminatory behavior toward minorities (Miethe and McCorkle 1997; Roleff).

Although it is clear that violence among adolescents is not always attributable to gangs, however they are defined, both surveys and field observations in a variety of settings suggest that similar forces often are associated with the emergence and maintenance of gangs and other violent collectivities. They also share group and collective behavior processes that help to account for diversity and change, and for continuity in the forms taken by such collectivities.

Several characteristics are common to virtually all serious studies of gangs. Gangs are groups whose members meet together with some regularity, over time, on the basis of group-defined criteria of membership and group-defined organizational characteristics; that is, they are non-adult-sponsored, self-determining groups that demonstrate continuity over time. These elements do not include the characteristic of primary interest to law enforcement, that is, criminal behavior. Police are unlikely to be knowledgeable about all of these elements; nor should they be expected to be. Note, also, that defining gangs in this way avoids the logical inconsistency of including in the definition the behaviors that require explanation. Arguments that study of variations in criminal orientation and involvement among gangs avoids the tautology beg important questions regarding the conditions under which a criminal identity is acquired by gangs. Resolution of controversy concerning youth groups is unlikely, absent greater conceptual clarity and theoretical rigor.

Crime control controversies

Controversy concerning crime control led, during the last decades of the twentieth century, to the proliferation of new laws and interventions aimed at preventing crime and delinquency, punishing or treating criminals and delinquents. Many of these interventions either were explicitly experimental or accompanied by requirements that they be evaluated. Many such interventions, however, bear little relationship to criminological research or theory.

Political and ideological perspectives frequently enter into both theoretical controversies and crime control policy. Marxist, conflict, and critical criminologists argue that control interventions that fail to address macro-level political, economic, and social conditions are politically motivated by those who are committed to the political, economic, and social status quo. Regardless of their ideological, theoretical, or empirical preferences, however, all criminologists agree that macro-level conditions are important and should be addressed by control efforts.

Sweeping changes have generated controversy at every level of juvenile and criminal justice. Some followed the decline of the rehabilitative ideal that had served as the basis for penal policy from the beginning in the

United States—and in some countries dating back to the eighteenth century. Dissatisfaction with the performance of the juvenile court, once conceived primarily as a social service agency, and negative evaluations of treatment programs aimed at rehabilitation, led many to the conclusion that "nothing works" (Lipton et al.). The vacuum left by rehabilitation's fall has been filled by "spasmodic and overlapping interest in policies of incapacitation, retribution, and deterrence" (Reitz, p. 545).

Yet, rehabilitation and prevention efforts never completely lost their appeal, in part perhaps because of excesses following their abandonment. Prison populations exploded in the United States, out of all proportion to fluctuating serious crime rates and continuing after official rates declined dramatically during the 1990s. Rates of incarceration of blacks increased several times those of whites (Tonry). Widespread disillusionment over these developments, among corrections leaders, affected communities, and others were fueled by concerns over the effects of high rates of incarceration on families and local communities, as well as civil rights concerns, and the high costs of prison construction and imprisonment. Systematic studies demonstrated only marginal and very expensive reductions in crime attributable to high rates of incarceration. Innovation in corrections and crime prevention strategies escalated rapidly. Here we comment briefly on a few of the more controversial of these.

The well-established finding that a relatively small proportion of offenders accounts for a much larger proportion of crimes committed encouraged the hope that identification and incarceration of those relatively few would pay large dividends in crime control. Policies aimed at such *selective incarceration* have sparked a great deal of controversy and research, of which the most rigorous suggests that scales based on past behavior and experience in criminal justice systems perform poorly in terms of both reliability and validity (Auerhahn). Prediction of high-rate offenders yields unacceptably high proportions of "false positives" of future offending. Ethical issues thus are raised as well.

Restorative justice is an amalgam of ideas and policies aimed at securing justice for victims, offenders, and communities. For victims, it emphasizes restoration of property, physical injury, security and dignity, and satisfaction that justice has been done. For offenders and communities the goal is reintegrative shaming. Offenders should experience shame for their actions through a democratically deliberative process that may involve their family members or surrogates, victims and their family members, and other community members, and through this process be brought into mutual harmony with the community. Hundreds of such programs have been established in many countries. A leading proponent and theorist, John Braithwaite, describes restorative justice as "the emerging social movement for criminal justice reform of the 1990s" (p. 324). Programs exist in many countries, some closer than others to traditional juvenile and criminal justice components. Some begin and end with the police (Sherman), while others involve special court procedures and collaboration with prosecutors. In theory and in practice, however, restorative justice challenges traditional criminal justice systems at every level. Although their effects are as yet inadequately evaluated, they are likely to foment a great deal of controversy and further change.

Conclusion

The appalling monetary and social costs of incarceration—the former more obvious, but the latter even more devastating to families and communities—have led increasingly to the examination of alternatives and to experimental attempts to lessen or compensate for those costs. Community policing, strategies of reintegrative shaming and restorative justice, special courts, focus on "accountability"—all, in varying degrees, testify to the continued strength of the motivation to rehabilitate offenders, compensate victims, and restore communities, rather than merely punish those who offend criminally.

The politicization of crime and its control, especially in the United States, constitutes a major stumbling block to innovations such as those discussed. Social complexity and the rapidity of social change, resentment over bureaucratic procedures and intransigency, challenge all social institutions but especially those with coercive power. Some of that power would be transferred to individuals and communities if the goals of restorative justice were realized. The hope, if not yet the promise, is that individual self-reliance might also thereby be enhanced and communities strengthened.

JAMES F. SHORT, JR.

See also CRIME: DEFINITION; CRIMINOLOGY: INTELLEC-TUAL HISTORY; HATE CRIMES; JUVENILE AND YOUTH GANGS; RESTORATIVE JUSTICE.

BIBLIOGRAPHY

ALINSKY, SAUL. *Reveille for Radicals*. Chicago: University of Chicago Press, 1946.

American Sociological Association. *Hate in America: What Do We Know?* Washington, D.C.: American Sociological Association, 2000.

AUERHAHN, KATHLEEN. "Selective Incapacitation and the Problem of Prediction." *Criminology* 37 (1999):703–734.

BRAITHWAITE, JOHN. "Restorative Justice." In *The Handbook of Crime & Punishment*. Edited by Michael Tonry. New York: Oxford, 1998. Pages 323–344.

Bureau of Justice Statistics. *Performance Measures for the Criminal Justice System: Discussion from the BJS-Princeton Project*. Washington, D.C.: U.S. Department of Justice, 1993.

CRESSEY, DONALD R. "Crime: I. Causes of Crime." *International Encyclopedia of the Social Sciences*, vol. 3. New York: Macmillan and Free Press, 1968. Pages 471–476.

CUMMINGS, SCOTT, and MONTI, DANIEL J., eds. *Gangs: The Origins and Impact of Contemporary Youth Gangs in the United States*. Albany: State University of New York Press, 1993.

CURRY, G. DAVID; BALL, RICHARD A.; and DECKER, SCOTT H. "Estimating the National Scope of Gang Crime from Law Enforcement Data." In *Gangs in America*. 2d ed. Edited by C. Ronald Huff. Thousand Oaks, Calif.: Sage, 1996.

FEDER, LYNETTE. "Using Random Assignment in Social Science Settings." American Association for the Advancement of Science, Scientific Freedom, Responsibility and Law Program. *Professional Ethics Report* 9, no. 1 (Winter 1998): 1, 7.

GILLIS A. R. "Urbanization, Sociohistorical Context, and Crime." *Criminological Controversies: A Methodological Primer*. Edited by John Hagan, A. R. Gillis, and David Brownfield. Boulder, Colo.: Westview, 1996. Pages 47–74.

GRAHAM, HUGH DAVIS, and GURR, TED ROBERTS, eds. *Violence in America: Historical and Comparative Perspectives*. Rev. ed. Beverly Hills, Calif.: Sage, 1986.

HAGAN, JOHN. "The Class and Crime Controversy." In *Criminological Controversies: A Methodological Primer*. Edited by John Hagan, A. R. Gillis, and David Brownfield. Boulder, Colo.: Westview, 1996. Pages 1–16.

HENRY, STUART, and MILOVANOVIC, DRAGAN. "Constitutive Criminology: The Maturation of Critical Theory." *Criminology* 29 (1991): 293–315.

JACOBS, JAMES B., and POTTER, KIMBERLY. *Hate Crimes: Criminal Law & Identity Politics*. New York: Oxford, 1998.

JANOWITZ, MORRIS. "Professionalization of Sociology." *American Journal of Sociology* 78 (1972): 105–125.

JENNESS, VALERIE, and RYKEN GRATTET. *Building the Hate Crime Policy Domain: From Social Movement Concept to Law Enforcement Practice*. A volume in the Rose series, sponsored by the American Sociological Association. New York: Russell Sage Foundation, 2000.

KLEIN, MALCOLM W. *The American Street Gang*. New York: Oxford, 1995.

KLEIN, MALCOM W.; KERNER, MANS-JURGEN; MAXSON, CHERYL L.; and WEITEKAMP, ELMAR G. M. *The Eurogang Paradox: Street Gangs and Youth Groups in the U.S. and Europe*. New York: Kluwer/Plenum, 2000.

KLEIN, MALCOLM W., and TEILMANN, KATHERINE S., eds. *Handbook of Criminal Justice Evaluation*. Beverly Hills, Calif.: Sage, 1980.

KOBRIN, SOLOMON. "The Chicago Area Project: A Twenty-Five-Year Assessment." *The Annals of the American Academy of Political and Social Science* (March 1959): 657–658.

LAFREE, GARY. *Losing Legitimacy: Street Crime and the Decline of Social Institutions in America*. Boulder, Colo.: Westview, 1998.

LEVIN, JACK, and McDEVITT, JACK. *Hate Crimes: The Rising Tide of Bigotry and Bloodshed*. New York: Plenum, 1993.

LIPTON, DOUGLAS; MARTINSON, ROBERT; and WILKS, JUDITH. *Effectiveness of Correctional Treatment*. Springfield, Mass.: Praeger, 1975.

MASSEY, DOUGLAS. "The Age of Extremes: Concentrated Affluence and Poverty in the Twenty-first Century." *Demography* (November 1996): 395–412.

MAXSON, CHERYL, and KLEIN, MALCOLM W. "Defining Gang Homicide: An Updated Look at Member and Motive Approaches." In *Gangs in America*. 2d ed. Edited by C. Ronald Huff. Thousand Oaks, Calif.: Sage, 1996.

MIETHE, TERRENCE D., and McCORKLE, RICHARD C. "Gang Membership and Criminal Processing: A Test of the 'Master Status' Concept." *Justice Quarterly* 14, no. 3 (1997): 407–428.

MERTON, ROBERT K. "Social Structure and Anomie." *American Sociological Review* 3 (1938): 672–682.

MOORE, J. P., and TERRETT, C. "Highlights of the 1997 National Youth Gang Survey." *Fact Sheet #97*. Washington, D.C.: U.S. Department of

Justice, Office of Juvenile Justice and Delinquency Prevention, 1999.

REISS, ALBERT J., JR. "Co-offender Influences on Criminal Careers." In *Criminal Careers and Career Criminals*. Vol. 2. Edited by Alfred Blumstein, Jacqueline Cohen, Jeffrey A. Roth, and Christy A. Visher. Washington, D.C.: National Academy Press, 1986.

REISS, ALBERT J., JR., and FARRINGTON, DAVID P. "Advancing Knowledge about Co-offending: Results from a Prospective Longitudinal Survey of London Males." *Journal of Criminal Law & Criminology* 82, no. 2 (1991): 360–395.

REITZ, KEVIN R. "Sentencing." In *The Handbook of Crime & Punishment*. Edited by Michael Tonry. New York: Oxford, 1998. Pages 542–562.

ROLEF, TAMARA L., ed. *Crime and Criminals: Opposing Viewpoints*. San Diego: Greenhaven Press, 2000.

SAMPSON, ROBERT J.; MORENOFF, JEFFREY D.; and EARLS, FELTON. "Spatial Dynamics of Collective Efficacy for Children." *American Sociological Review* 64 (1999): 633–660.

SAMPSON, ROBERT J.; RAUDENBUSH, STEPHEN; and EARLS, FELTON. "Neighborhoods and Violent Crime: A Multilevel Study of Collective Efficacy." *Science* 277 (1997): 918–924.

SAMPSON, ROBERT J., and GROVES, WALTER B. "Community Structure and Crime: Testing Social-Disorganization Theory." *American Journal of Sociology* 94, no. 4 (1989): 774–802.

SARNECKI, JERZY. *Co-offending Youth Networks in Stockholm*. Cambridge, U.K.: Cambridge University Press, 2000.

SHAW, CLIFFORD R. *The Jack-Roller*. Chicago: University of Chicago Press, 1930.

SHAW, CLIFFORD R., and MCKAY, HENRY D. *Social Factors in Juvenile Delinquency*. Washington, D.C.: U.S.G.P.O., 1931.

SHAW, CLIFFORD R., and MOORE, MAURICE E. *The Natural History of Delinquent Career*. Chicago: University of Chicago Press, 1931.

SHERMAN, LAWRENCE W. "American Policing." In *The Handbook of Crime & Punishment*. Edited by Michael Tonry. New York: Oxford, 1998. Pages 429–456.

SHORT, JAMES F., JR. "The Natural History of an Applied Theory: Differential Opportunity and 'Mobilization for Youth.'" In *Social Policy and Sociology*. Edited by N. J. Demerath, III, Otto Larsen, and Karl F. Schuessler. New York: Academic Press, 1975.

SHORT, JAMES F., JR. "The Level of Explanation Problem Revisited." *Criminology* 36 (1997): 3–36.

SHORT, JAMES F., JR.; ZAHN, MARGARET; and FARRINGTON, DAVID. "Experimental Research in Criminal Justice Settings: A Role for Scholarly Associations." *Crime and Delinquency*. Forthcoming (2000).

SKOGAN, WESLEY G. *Disorder and Decline: Crime and the Spiral of Decay in American Neighborhoods*. New York: Free Press, 1990.

SUTHERLAND, EDWIN H. *Criminology*. Philadelphia: Lippincott, 1924.

TAYLOR, IAN; WALTON, PAUL; and YOUNG, JOCK. *The New Criminology: For a Social Theory of Deviance*. London: Routledge & Kegan Paul, 1973.

THRASHER, FREDERIC M. *The Gang: A Study of 1313 Gangs in Chicago*. Chicago: University of Chicago Press, 1927.

TITTLE, CHARLES R. *Control Balance: Toward a General Theory of Deviance*. Boulder, Colo.: Westview, 1995.

TONRY, MICHAEL. "Crime and Punishment in America." In *The Handbook of Crime & Punishment*. Edited by Michael Tonry. New York: Oxford, 1998. Pages 3–27.

WOLFGANG, MARVIN E., and FERRACUTI, FRANCO. *The Subculture of Violence: Towards an Integrated Theory in Criminology*. Translated from the Italian. London: Tavistock, 1967.

CRIMINOLOGY AND CRIMINAL JUSTICE RESEARCH: METHODS

Those interested in the study of criminology and criminal justice have at their disposal a wide range of research methods. Which of the particular research methods to use is entirely contingent upon the question being studied. Research questions typically fall into four categories of research: (1) descriptive, (2) exploratory, (3) explanatory, and (4) evaluative (Schutt). Descriptive research attempts to define and describe the social phenomena under investigation. Exploratory research seeks to identify the underlying meaning behind actions and individual behavior. Explanatory research seeks to identify the cause(s) and effect(s) of social phenomena. Evaluation research seeks to determine the effects of an intervention on individual behavior. These four areas of research are not mutually exclusive; rather, they are designed to be used interactively in order to gain a deeper understanding of the question under investigation.

With this background, the purpose of this entry will be to introduce the reader to the two major research paradigms and issues that organize the field of criminology and criminal justice: quantitative and qualitative research strategies. After describing the different research methodologies several issues related to internal and external validity are identified that are important to bear in mind when assessing the adequacies of distinct research methodologies. The entry closes by highlighting what appears to be the most promising research strategy for criminology and criminal justice.

Quantitative research methods

Quantitative research methods are typically concerned with measuring criminological or criminal justice reality. To understand this process several terms must first be identified. Concepts are abstract tags placed on reality that are assigned numerical values, thus making them variables. Variables are then studied to examine patterns of relation, covariation, and cause and effect. At the most basic level, there exists at least one dependent variable and one independent variable. The dependent variable is commonly referred to as the outcome variable. This is what the researcher is attempting to predict. The independent variable is commonly referred to as the predictor variable, and it is the variable that causes, determines, or precedes in time the dependent variable (Hagan). Consider the following examples.

Criminological theorists may be interested in studying the relationship between impulsivity (independent variable) and criminal behavior (dependent variable). In studying such a relationship, scholars create a summated scale of items that is designed to indirectly measure the concept of impulsivity. Then, this impulsivity scale is used to predict involvement in criminal behavior. Criminal justice scholars may be interested in studying the effects of a mandatory arrest policy (independent variable) on future patterns of domestic violence (dependent variable). In studying such a question, scholars typically evaluate the effect of an arrest, compared to some other sanction, on the future criminal behavior of the arrestee. Thus, quantitative research methods involve a pattern of studying the relationship(s) between sets of variables to determine cause and effect.

Three criteria are needed to establish causality. The first is association. That is, the independent and dependent variables must be related to one another. The second is time order; the independent variable must precede the dependent variable in time. Finally, there is the issue of nonspuriousness. This occurs if the relationship between the independent and dependent variables is not due to variation in some unobserved third variable.

There are a number of different quantitative research methods available to researchers, most of which fall under the rubric of a research design, which loosely can be defined as the plan or blueprint for a study that includes the who, what, where, when, why and how of an investigation (Hagan). These research methods include: survey research, experimental and quasi-experimental research, cross-sectional research, longitudinal research, time series research, and meta-analysis.

Survey research. Serving as the most frequently used mode of observation within the social sciences, including criminology (Maxfield and Babbie), survey research involves the collection of information from a sample of individuals through their responses to questions (Schutt). Survey research is generally carried out via mail, telephone, computer, or in person.

Typically, surveys contain a combination of open- and closed-ended questions. Open-ended questions ask the respondent to provide an answer to a particular question. For example, the respondent may be asked: "What do you think is the most important problem facing residents in your neighborhood today?" Then in their own words, the respondent would provide his or her answer. On the other hand, closed-ended questions ask the respondents to select an answer from a list of choices provided. For example, the question asked above would read exactly the same only now respondents are provided with a list of options to choose from: "What do you think is the most important problem facing residents in your neighborhood today? (a) crime, (b) drugs, (c) education, (d) employment, (e) family structure, (f) poverty, (g) health care, (h) child care, (i) extracurricular activities, (j) other."

Surveys offer a number of attractive features that make them a popular method of doing research. They are versatile, efficient, inexpensive, and generalizable. At the same time, survey methods may be limited due to problems in sampling, measurement, and overall survey design. When creating a survey, researchers should take care in making sure that the items in the survey are clear and to the point.

Experimental and quasi-experimental research. Some scholars believe that experimental research is the best type of research to assess cause and effect (Sherman; Weisburd). True experiments must have at least three features: (1) two comparison groups (i.e., an experimental group and a control group); (2) variation in the independent variable before assessment of change in the dependent variable; and (3) random assignment to the two (or more) comparison groups (Schutt).

Many experiments contain both a pre-test and a post-test. The former test measures the dependent variable prior to the experimental intervention while the latter test measures the outcome variable after the experimental group has received the treatment. Randomization is what makes the comparison group in a true experiment a powerful approach for identifying the effects of the treatment (Schutt). Assigning groups randomly to the experimental and comparison groups ensures that systematic bias does not affect the assignment of subjects to groups. This is important if researchers wish to generalize their findings regarding cause and effect among key variables within and across groups.

The classic experimental design is one in which there is a pre-test for both groups, an intervention for one group (i.e., the experimental group), and then a post-test for both groups. Consider the following criminal justice example. Two police precincts alike in all possible respects are chosen to participate in a study that examines fear of crime in neighborhoods. Both precincts would be pre-tested to obtain information on crime rates and citizen perceptions of crime. The experimental precinct would receive a treatment (i.e., increase in police patrols), while the comparison precinct would not receive a treatment. Then, twelve months later, both precincts would be post-tested to determine changes in crime rates and citizen perceptions.

There have been several experimental designs in criminology and criminal justice including the Domestic Violence Experiment (Sherman), where offenders were randomly assigned to one of three interventions (arrest, mediation, separation). The Jersey City Police Department's Program to Control Violent Places also utilized an experimental design (Braga et al.). For this study, twenty-four high-activity, violent crime places were matched into twelve pairs and one member of each pair was allocated to treatment conditions in a randomized block field experiment.

On the other hand, quasi-experimental research lacks the random assignment to experimental and control groups, but can be approximated by close and careful matching of subjects across the two groups on several key variables. The two major types of quasi-experimental designs are: (1) nonequivalent control group designs, which have experimental and comparison groups that are designated before the treatment occurs and are not created by random assignment; and (2) before-and-after designs, which have both a pre- and post-test but no comparison group (Schutt).

An example of a nonequivalent control group design is a study of the effect of police actions on seat-belt law violations. For example, Watson selected two communities of comparable size where police enforcement of the law was low. In the experimental community, Watson instituted a media campaign to increase seat-belt usage, followed by increased police enforcement of the seat-belt law. Watson found that the percentage of drivers using seat belts increased in the experimental community but remained stable or declined slightly in the comparison community.

An example of the before-and-after design is the Pierce and Bowers analysis of the impact of the Massachusetts Bartley-Fox gun law. This law carried a one-year minimum prison sentence for the unlicensed carrying of firearms. Their early evaluation showed a decrease in gun related assaults, robberies, and homicides, but was offset by increases in nongun assaults and robberies using other weapons.

Cross-sectional research. Cross-sectional designs involve studies of one group at one point in time. Therefore, they offer a quick glimpse or snapshot of the phenomena being studied. Typically, they refer to a representative sample of the group and thus allow researchers to generalize their findings (Hagan). Cross-sectional research designs permeate criminology and criminal justice research. Hirschi's famous study of causes of delinquency utilized a cross-sectional design in which he asked male respondents a series of questions related to involvement in delinquent activities and emotional ties to social bonds.

Longitudinal research. There are two commonly used longitudinal research designs, panel and cohort studies. Both study the same group over a period of time and are generally concerned with assessing within- and between-group change. Panel studies follow the same group or sample over time, while cohort studies examine more specific populations (i.e., cohorts) as they change over time. Panel studies typically interview the same set of people at two or more periods of time. For example, the National

Crime Victimization Survey (NCVS) randomly selects a certain number of households from across the United States and interviews a member from each a series of seven times at six-month intervals. Cohort studies follow individuals or specific cohorts as they change over time. One classic example of a cohort study was conducted by Marvin Wolfgang and his colleagues in Philadelphia. The authors traced the criminal records of all boys born in Philadelphia in 1945 through the age of eighteen. Similarly, Tracy, Wolfgang and Figlio tracked the criminal history of males and females born in Philadelphia in 1958.

Time-series designs. Time-series designs typically involve variations of multiple observations of the same group (i.e., person, city, area, etc.) over time or at successive points in time. Typically, they analyze a single variable (such as the crime rate) at successive time periods, and are especially useful for studies of the impact of new laws or social programs (Schutt). An example of a time-series design would be to examine the murder rate in the United States over the last twenty years or to compare the murder rate of the United States and Canada over the same period of time.

An interrupted time-series design analyzes a single variable at successive time periods with measures taken prior to some form of interruption (i.e., intervention) and other observations taken after the intervention. An example of an interrupted time-series design may be found in Spelman and Eck (1987). These authors studied the number of larcenies from automobiles in Newport News, Virginia. The intervention in this study was a problem-oriented policing program that consisted of special tracking and investigation of crime incidents. The results showed that the number of larcenies dropped significantly immediately after the intervention took place and remained significantly small for over one year after the intervention. In another interrupted time series study, D'Alessio and Stolzenberg investigated the impact of Minnesota sentencing guidelines on jail incarceration. They found that the onset of the sentencing guidelines increased judicial use of the jail sanction beyond the effect of preexisting trends.

Although time-series designs are especially useful in studying trends over time and how such trends are influenced by some sort of intervention, researchers should be aware of one key feature of time-series designs: the inability to control for all potential spurious effects. Consider the following example. Suppose that a re-searcher is studying the effect on robberies of a mandatory convenience store law that requires stores to have at least two clerks working during hours of operation. After examining the number of robberies before and after the law took effect, the researcher observed that the number of robberies significantly decreased after the law was instituted. Therefore, the researcher claimed that the law led to the decrease in the number of robberies committed and concluded that the law should be generalized to other locales. However, what the researcher may have failed to consider was the recent capture of two offenders who were committing 75 percent of all convenience store robberies, and who just happened to be captured about the time the law took effect. In sum, researchers need to be careful in making sure that their interpretations of interrupted time-series analyses take into consideration as much information, both empirical and nonempirical, as possible.

Meta-analysis. A recent advent in research methodology is the use of meta-analysis. This research approach is the quantitative analysis of findings from multiple studies. At its core, meta-analysis involves researchers pulling together the results of several studies and making summary, empirical statements about some cause and effect relationship. A classic example of meta-analysis in criminology was performed by Wells and Rankin and concerned the relationship between broken homes and delinquency.

After observing a series of findings showing that the broken-homes-causes-delinquency hypothesis was inconclusive, Wells and Rankin identified fifty studies that tested this hypothesis. After coding the key characteristics of the studies, such as the population sampled, age range, measures (both independent and dependent) used, the authors found that the average effect of broken homes across the studies was to increase the probability of delinquency by about 10 to 15 percent. Perhaps more importantly, they found that the different methods used across the studies accounted for much of the variation in estimating the effect of broken homes. For example, the effect of broken homes on delinquency tended to be greater in studies using official records rather than self-report surveys.

Although the research community has not spoken with one voice regarding the usefulness of meta-analysis, one thing is clear: meta-analysis makes the research community aware that it is inappropriate to base conclusions on the findings of one study. It is because of this important lesson that meta-analysis has become a popular technique in criminological and criminal justice research (Lipsey and Wilson).

Threats to validity

Validity refers to the accuracy of measurement or whether the instrument is in fact measuring what it is suppose to measure (Hagan). While quantitative research methods have permeated criminological and criminal justice research, they are not without problems. Threats to validity are perhaps the most profound and should be acknowledged. Some of these threats are internal and are concerned with whether the observational process itself produced the findings, while external threats are concerned with whether the results were unique and applicable only to the group or target studied (Hagan).

Internal threats. According to Campbell and Stanley, a number of internal threats need to be considered, including: (1) history, (2) maturation, (3) testing, (4) instrumentation, (5) statistical regression, (6) selection bias, (7) experimental mortality, and (8) selection-maturation interaction. In determining whether a particular design rules out threats to internal validity, Cook and Campbell suggest that "estimating the internal validity of a relationship is a deductive process in which the investigator has to systematically think through how each of the internal validity threats can be ruled out" (p. 55).

External threats. Campbell and Stanley also identify several threats to external validity, including: (1) testing effects, (2) selection bias, (3) reactivity or awareness of being studied, and (4) multiple-treatment interference. These threats are greater for experiments conducted under more carefully controlled conditions (Maxfield and Babbie). Perhaps one of the best methods for assessing threats to external validity is replication, or the repetition of experiments or studies utilizing the same methodology. By replication of key findings, researchers can gain confidence that the results observed in one study may not be due to external validity threats. One of the key examples of replication occurred in the late 1980s when the Minneapolis Domestic Violence Experiment was replicated in six cities throughout the United States (Sherman). Importantly, these replications yielded both similar and contradictory conclusions to those observed in the initial experiment.

Qualitative research methods

Unlike quantitative research methods, qualitative approaches are designed to capture life as participants experience it, rather than in categories predetermined by the researcher. These methods typically involve exploratory research questions, inductive reasoning, an orientation to social context and human subjectivity, and the meanings attached by participants to events and to their lives (Schutt). There are a number of distinctive research designs under this paradigm: (1) participant observation, (2) intensive interviewing, (3) focus groups, and (4) case studies and life histories. Each of these will be discussed in turn.

Participant observation. At its most basic level, participant observation involves a variety of strategies in data gathering in which the researcher observes a group by participating, to varying degrees, in the activities of the group (Hagan). Gold discusses four different positions on a continuum of roles that field researchers may play in this regard: (1) complete participant, (2) participant-as-observer, (3) observer-as-participant, and (4) complete observer. Complete participation takes place when the researcher joins in and actually begins to manipulate the direction of group activity. In the participant-as-observer strategy, the researcher usually makes himself known and tries to objectively observe the activities of the group. The observer-as-participant strategy is very much like a one-visit interview, where the interviewees are also short-term participant observers. Typically, these interviews are conducted with individuals who are known to participate in a designated activity. For example, Jacobs interviewed known active drug dealers in order to gain a better understanding of how the crack business actually operates on the streets. Finally, the complete observer strategy relies on sole observation absent participation from the researcher.

Although several issues must be confronted when engaging in this sort of research, two are of vital importance: (1) objectivity, and (2) "going native." The former deals with the researcher's ability to avoid not only overidentification with the study group, but also aversion to it (Hagan). The latter deals with a situation in which the researcher identifies with and becomes a member of the study group, and in the process abandons his or her role as an objective researcher (Hagan). Even with these cautions, a number of important participant observation studies have been undertaken in criminology and criminal justice including Polsky's study of pool hustlers and con artists, as well as Marquart's study of prison life.

Intensive interviewing. Intensive interviewing consists of open-ended, relatively unstructured questioning in which the interviewer seeks in-depth information on the interviewee's feelings, experiences, or perceptions (Schutt, 1999). Unlike the participant observation strategy, intensive interviewing does not require systematic observation of respondents in their natural setting. Typically, interviewing sample members, and identification and interviewing of more sample members, continues until the saturation point is reached, the point when new interviews seems to yield little additional information (Schutt).

A prominent example of the intensive interviewing technique can be found in a series of studies with active residential burglars (Wright and Decker, 1994) and robbers (Wright and Decker, 1997) in St. Louis. These authors have conducted in-depth interviews with active criminals in their natural environment. Some of these interviews have yielded important theoretical insights that perhaps may not have been garnered via traditional survey methods. Other prominent examples may be found in Fagan and Wilkinson's study of gun-related violence in New York and Jacobs's study of crack addicts in St. Louis.

Focus groups. Focus groups are groups of unrelated individuals that are formed by a researcher and then led in group discussions of a topic (Schutt). Typically, the researcher asks specific questions and guides the discussion to ensure that group members address these questions, but the resulting information is qualitative and relatively unstructured (Schutt).

Although generalizations from focus groups to target populations cannot be precise (Maxfield and Babbie), research suggests that focus group information, combined with survey information, can be quite consistent under certain conditions (Ward et al.). One such criminal justice example is provided by Schneider and her colleagues. These authors examined the implementation process and the role of risk/need assessment instruments for decisions about the proper level of supervision among parolees and probationers. Their use of focus group was able to provide a context for a more complete understanding of the survey results from the probation officers interviewed.

Case studies and life histories. In general, case studies and life histories are in-depth, qualitative studies of one or a few illustrative cases (Hagan). Several criminological examples using this approach exist, and a few in particular have produced some of the most important, baseline information in the discipline today. The classic example is Sutherland's *The Professional Thief* (1937). In this case study, Sutherland's informant, Chic Conwell, described the world of the professional thief. Other examples include Shaw's *The Jack-Roller* (1930), which tells the autobiographical story of a delinquent's own experiences, influences, attitudes, and values. Finally, Horatio Alger's tale of street life in New York tells the story of Young Dick, a street boy who is involved in a delinquent life but who is also honest and hardworking. Life-history methods generally involve the analysis of diaries, letters, biographies, and autobiographies to obtain a detailed view of either a unique or representative individual (Hagan). A classic example of the life-history method is Teresa and Renner's *My Life in the Mafia* (1973).

Future of research methods in criminology and criminal justice

Although the preceding discussion has portrayed the two main research paradigms, quantitative and qualitative research methods, as two ends of the research continuum, it was not meant to imply that the two are mutually exclusive. On the contrary, the future of research methods in criminology and criminal justice lies in the combination of quantitative and qualitative research approaches. Illustrated below are two successful integrations.

The first, by Eric Hirsch, used a combination of methods, including participant observation, intensive interviewing, and a standardized survey, to study the 1985 student movement that attempted to make Columbia University divest its stock in companies dealing with South Africa. Hirsch believed that the combination of research methodologies provided a more comprehensive picture of student's motivations.

The second example is from John Laub and Robert Sampson. For quite some time, these two scholars have been working on the reanalysis of one of the classic data sets in criminology, the Unraveling Juvenile Delinquency (UJD) study that was initiated by Sheldon and Eleanor Glueck in 1940. The data contain the original case records of all one thousand sample members as well as detailed archival life records that included information from the "home investigation," which consisted of an interview with family members and offered an opportunity for the investigators to observe the home and family life of sample members. Furthermore, the UJD study included interviews with key informants such as social workers, settlement house workers, clergymen, schoolteachers, neighbors, employers, and criminal justice and social welfare officials. When this detailed information is combined with the statistical information on criminal behavior and other life events, one can begin to appreciate the richness with which Laub and Sampson have been able to document these one thousand lives and contribute much needed information regarding crime over the life course.

The future of criminological and criminal justice research will likely come full circle. Early studies of crime and criminality began with qualitative observations almost to the exclusion of quantitative research. New research topics were observed and highlighted by scholars who wished to forge ahead in the understanding of crime and criminality. Once these topics were brought to the forefront of the field, quantitative research became the choice method of analysis. The future of criminological research must focus on the blending of the two. As John Clausen notes, both case history and statistical data are required "if we are to understand the influences on the lives of persons who have lived through a particular slice of American history" (p. 43).

ALEX R. PIQUERO
NICOLE LEEPER PIQUERO

See also CRIMINOLOGY AND CRIMINAL JUSTICE RESEARCH: ORGANIZATION.

BIBLIOGRAPHY

ALGER, JR., HORATIO. *Ragged Dick or, Street Life in New York with the Boot-blacks* (1867). New York: Signet Classic, 1990.

BRAGA, ANTHONY. A.; WEISBURD, DAVID L.; WARING, ELIN J.; MAZEROLLE, LORRAINE G.; SPELMAN, WILLIAM; and GAJEWSKI, FRANCIS. "Problem-Oriented Policing in Violent Crime Places: A Randomized Controlled Experiment." *Criminology* 37 (1999): 541–580.

CAMPBELL, DONALD T., and STANLEY, JULIAN C. *Experimental and Quasi-Experimental Designs for Research.* Chicago: Rand McNally, 1963.

CLAUSEN, JOHN. *American Lives: Looking Back at the Children of the Great Depression.* New York: Free Press, 1993.

COOK, THOMAS D., and CAMPBELL, DONALD T. *Quasi-Experimentation: Design and Analysis Issues for Field Settings.* Chicago: Rand McNally, 1979.

D'ALESSIO, STEWART J., and STOLZENBERG, LISA. "The Impact of Sentencing Guidelines on Jail Incarceration in Minnesota." *Criminology* 33 (1995): 283–302.

FAGAN, JEFFREY, and WILKINSON, DEANNA L. "Guns, Youth Violence, and Social Identity in Inner Cities." In *Youth Violence, Crime and Justice: An Annual Review of Research, Volume 24.* Edited by Michael Tonry and Mark H. Moore. Chicago: University of Chicago Press, 1998. Pages 105–188.

GOLD, RAYMOND L. "Roles in Sociological Field Observations." *Social Forces* 36 (1958): 217–223.

HAGAN, FRANK E. *Research Methods in Criminal Justice and Criminology.* 3d ed. New York: Macmillan, 1994.

HIRSCHI, TRAVIS. *Causes of Delinquency.* Berkeley: University of California Press.

HIRSCH, ERIC L. "Sacrifice for the Cause: Group Processes, Recruitment, and Commitment in a Student Social Movement." *American Sociological Review* 55 (1990): 243–254.

JACOBS, BRUCE A. *Dealing Crack: The Social World of Streetcorner Selling.* Boston: Northeastern University Press, 1999.

LAUB, JOHN H., and SAMPSON, ROBERT J. "Integrating Quantitative and Qualitative Data." In *Methods of Life Course Research: Qualitative and Quantitative Approaches.* Edited by Janet Z. Giele and Glenn H. Elder, Jr. Newbury Park, Calif.: Sage, 1998. Pages 213–230.

LIPSEY, MARK W., and WILSON, DAVID B. "Effective Intervention for Serious Juvenile Offenders: A Synthesis of Research." In *Serious and Violent Juvenile Offenders: Risk Factors and Successful Interventions.* Edited by Rolf Loeber and David P. Farrington. Newbury Park, Calif.: Sage, 1998. Pages 313–345.

MARQUART, JAMES W. "Doing Research in Prison: The Strengths and Weaknesses of Full Participation as a Guard." *Justice Quarterly* 3 (1986): 15–32.

MAXFIELD, MICHAEL G., and BABBIE EARL. *Research Methods for Criminal Justice and Criminology.* Belmont, Calif.: Wadsworth, 1995.

PIERCE, GLEN, and BOWERS, WILLIAM. "The Impact of the Bartley-Fox Gun Law on Crime in Massachusetts." Boston: Northeastern University Press, 1979.

POLSKY, NED. *Hustlers, Beats and Others.* Chicago: University of Chicago Press, 1967.

SCHNEIDER, ANNE L.; ERVIN, LAURIE; and SNYDER-JOY, ZOANN. "Further Exploration of the Flight from Discretion: The Role of Risk/Need Instruments in Probation Supervision Decisions." *Journal of Criminal Justice* 24 (1996): 109–121.

SCHUTT, RUSSELL K. *Investigating the Social World: The Process and Practice of Research,* 2d ed. Thousand Oaks, Calif.: Pine Forge Press, 1999.

SHAW, CLIFFORD R. *The Jack-Roller: A Delinquent Boy's Own Story.* Chicago: University of Chicago Press, 1930.

SHERMAN, LAWRENCE W. *Policing Domestic Violence.* New York: Free Press, 1992.

SPELMAN, WILLIAM, and ECK, JOHN E. "Problem-Solving: Problem-Oriented Policing in Newport News." *Research in Brief.* National Institute of Justice. Washington, D.C., 1987.

SUTHERLAND, EDWIN H. *The Professional Thief.* Chicago: University of Chicago Press, 1937.

TERESA, VINCENT, and RENNER, THOMAS C. *My Life in the Mafia.* New York: Doubleday, 1973.

TRACY, PAUL E.; WOLFGANG, MARVIN E.; and FIGLIO, ROBERT M. *Delinquency Careers in Two Birth Cohorts.* New York: Plenum, 1990.

WARD, VICTORIA M.; BERTRAND, JANE T.; and BROWN, LISANNE F. "The Comparability of Focus Group and Survey Results: Three Case Studies." *Evaluation Review* 15 (1991): 266–283.

WATSON, ROY E. "The Effectiveness of Increased Police Enforcement as a General Deterrent." *Law and Society Review* 20 (1986): 293–299.

WEISBURD, DAVID. "Design Sensitivity in Criminal Justice Experiments." In *Crime and Justice: A Review of Research.* Vol. 17. Edited by Michael Tonry. Chicago: University of Chicago Press, 1993.

WELLS, L. EDWARD, and RANKIN, JOSEPH H. "Families and Delinquency: A Meta-Analysis of the Impact of Broken Homes." *Social Problems* 38 (1991): 71–93.

WOLFGANG, MARVIN E.; FIGLIO, ROBERT M.; and SELLIN, THORSTEN E. *Delinquency in a Birth Cohort.* Chicago: University of Chicago Press, 1972.

WRIGHT, RICHARD T., and DECKER, SCOTT H. *Burglars on the Job.* Boston: Northeastern University Press, 1994.

———. *Armed Robbers in Action.* Boston: Northeastern University Press, 1997.

CRIMINOLOGY AND CRIMINAL JUSTICE RESEARCH: ORGANIZATION

Prior to the 1960s in the United States, criminological research resulted from individual efforts. The reliance on individual investigators to conduct (and oftentimes fund) their own research agenda was primarily a function of a lack of funding sources devoted to issues surrounding criminology and criminal justice. Since the 1960s, however, research in criminal justice has dramatically increased. The period between 1960 and 1980 saw the emergence of a concerted effort in the federal government to initiate research projects that were designed to understand the extent of criminal behavior, including the etiology of criminal behavior as well as the reaction of the criminal justice system to criminal behavior. Although still noticeably undersupported financially, funded research efforts during this time period gathered much information that helped set the stage for the continuation and expansion of criminological research efforts. Since 1980 there has been a substantial increase in the financial resources afforded to criminological research, which has led to a proliferation of scholarly activity within criminology and criminal justice.

Government-sponsored research

The interest in understanding the causes and consequences of crime can be traced back to the U.S. presidential campaign of 1964 and the consequential passage of the 1968 Omnibus Crime Control and Safe Streets Act (Pub L. No. 90–351, 82 Stat. 197). Since that time, the focus on crime-related issues has emerged as an important matter for the federal government. As a result of the elevated importance of crime and its consequences, monetary allocations for researching and understanding this phenomenon have been elevated dramatically.

The organization of criminological and criminal justice research can best be described at four levels: international, federal, state, and local. International efforts have consisted of coordinated efforts by countries with an interest in understanding and preventing problems associated with crime both within and across country boundaries. For example, the United Nations has funded a number of criminological studies focusing on transnational and transatlantic crime, terrorism, espionage, and white collar offenses. In addition, the federal governments of many European countries, as well as Australia and New Zealand, have funded a number of longitudinal studies that have attempted to unravel the complexities associated with criminal behavior over an individual's life span.

In the United States, participation in criminological research has been most extensive at the federal level. The largest funding agencies within the federal government have been the National Institute of Justice, Bureau of Justice Assistance, Bureau of Justice Statistics, Office of Juvenile Justice and Delinquency Prevention, the National Institutes of Health and Mental Health, the National Science Foundation (and the National Consortium on Violence Research), the Federal Justice Research Program, and the Department of Housing and Urban Development.

Since 1980 funding at the state level has increased. For example, state planning agencies, state commissions on crime and delinquency, and state analysis centers (SACs) have proliferated across the United States. These agencies perform a number of functions, including statewide research activities, program development, and program evaluation. State-level police and correctional departments plan, support, conduct, and encourage the study of criminal justice issues, particularly as they relate to resources within the system. At the local level, planning agencies and police departments plan and carry out research activities. With the advent of geographic information systems (GIS), a mapping system designed to pinpoint the location of crimes, these agencies are now better equipped to understand the nature of the local crime problem(s), and develop strategies aimed at curbing the problem. An additional advancement in aiding state and local agencies inform the public on matters of crime is the Internet. The Internet allows researchers and citizens to access and review the collected information on criminal justice issues. In fact, some agencies like the Philadelphia Police Department allow users to explore the nature and distribution of homicides throughout the city. Many other big-city police departments such as Baltimore, Phoenix, New York City, Charlotte, and Edmonton, Canada, have followed suit. Although state and local agencies have developed research capabilities that far surpass what was available to them in the 1960s and 1970s, it is the federal government that possesses the resources to conduct and sponsor large-scale studies.

Development of research centers

In addition to the increase in funding from the federal government for crime-related issues, a number of private (both not-for-profit and for-profit) research centers have also increased the distribution of resources available to the study of criminal justice issues. Some of the most notable include the Institute for Law and Justice, the Vera Institute, the Urban Institute, Rand Corporation, Abt Associates, Police Foundation, and the Police Executive Research Forum. Various private foundations have also entered the criminal justice arena, including the John D. and Catherine T. MacArthur Foundation, the Ford Foundation, the Edna McConnell Clark Foundation, the William T. Grant Foundation, the Robert Wood Johnson Foundation, and the Harry Frank Guggenheim Foundation.

Located in northern Virginia, the Institute for Law and Justice (ILJ) is a private, nonprofit corporation dedicated to consulting, research, evaluation, and training in criminal justice issues related to policing, courts, and corrections. ILJ fields a comprehensive research staff who also works with cities, counties, states, federal agencies, and private industries in matters associated with criminal justice. In addition, ILJ organizes the Annual Research and Evaluation Conference held in Washington, D.C.

The Vera Institute designs and implements innovative programs that encourage "just practices" in public services toward improvement in the quality of life. Located in New York City, Vera operates the programs it designs only during the demonstration stage; if these programs succeed, the demonstrations often lead to the creation of new government programs, the reform of old ones, or the establishment of nonprofit organizations to carry them out. In addition to a focus on applied criminal justice and social reform issues, Vera also has projects that examine child welfare and juvenile justice, a neighborhood drug crisis center, the citizen jury project, support for people with disabilities, and a Bureau of Justice Assistance Project in South Africa.

Located in Washington, D.C., the Urban Institute is a nonprofit policy research organization established in 1968. The goals of the institute are to sharpen thinking about society's problems and develop efforts to solve them, improve government decisions and their implementation, and increase citizens' awareness about important public choices. The Urban Institute is comprised of a variety of centers that fall under various domains, including economics, social welfare, community building, and policy briefs. The crime/law and behavior program, which handles much of the institute's criminal justice research, is part of the State Policy Center located within the community-building domain. The law and behavior program conducts evaluations and analyses of federal, state, and local crime programs and policies. Research foci include the police, courts, and programs designed to prevent and respond to drug use, delinquency, and family and youth violence. Recent projects include evaluation of comprehensive community-based anticrime initiatives, evaluation of Washington, D.C., drug courts, a gun control policy evaluation, and an assessment of the gains from criminal activity.

With its main headquarters in Santa Monica, California, one of the largest research centers in the country is the RAND Corporation. Originally designed to study matters associated with national security, the 1960s witnessed RAND's entrance into domestic policy concerns. Areas of research within RAND include national defense, education and training, health care, and criminal justice. RAND's criminal justice program started in 1976 and has been analyzing issues and policy related to three domains: sentencing and corrections, drug policy, and violence prevention. RAND's work in the criminal justice area has included projects on criminal careers, the effects of determinant sentencing, violence prevention, efficiency, effectiveness, and equity within the criminal justice system, and drug use trends and drug use reduction strategies.

Founded in 1965, Abt Associates is a for-profit government and business consulting and research firm based in suburban Boston that uses research-based approaches to help solve social and business problems and guide government policy decisions. Abt maintains proficiency in four large areas: social and economic policy, international economic development, business research and consulting, and clinical trials. Within the social and economic policy domain, Abt fields the law and public policy area. Abt's work in this area focuses on issues related to crime and substance abuse. It includes policy-oriented research and evaluation and translation and synthesis of research for nonscientific professionals in criminal justice and substance abuse areas. One recent development is a Neighborhood Problem Solving System that was designed for community crime prevention organizations in Hartford. The software package developed by Abt enables community groups to produce computerized maps showing the location of crimes and arrests.

The Police Foundation was established in 1970 with a $30 million fund from the Ford Foundation to assist a limited number of police departments in experiments and demonstrations aimed at improving operations, and to support special education and training projects. Since then, the Police Foundation has been at the forefront of several major police studies, including: the Kansas City Preventive Patrol Experiment; the Newark Foot Patrol Experiment; the Minneapolis Domestic Violence Experiment; the Status of Women in Policing Project; the San Diego Patrol Staffing Project; the Houston-Newark Fear of Crime Project; the Washington, D.C., Metropolitan Police Department's Repeat Offending Project; the Police Use of Force Project; and the Big Six Project, which studied the six largest police departments in the country. In addition, the foundation produced Crime File, a twenty-two-part criminal justice videotape series that focused on topics such as deadly force, domestic violence, and gun control.

Another organization that focuses on police research, the Police Executive Research Forum (PERF), is a national membership organization of police executives from the largest city, county, and state law enforcement agencies. PERF originated in 1975 when ten police executives from some of the nation's largest cities met informally to discuss common policing concerns. After a successful initial meeting, the chiefs decided to meet on a regular basis to explore issues related to improving the quality of policing. The twofold mission statement of PERF includes the improvement of policing, and the advancement of professionalism through research and involvement in public policy debate. PERF is primarily concerned with research and experimentation that generates knowledge, discussion, and debate about policing. Some of the projects undertaken by PERF include the effect of fatigue on officer performance, police use of force, and the potential effect of the police on reducing homicide.

Created in 1978 by John D. MacArthur, the John D. and Catherine T. MacArthur Foundation is a private, independent grant-making institution dedicated to helping groups and individuals foster lasting improvement in the human condition. Based in Chicago, the MacArthur Foundation supports research, policy development, dissemination, education and training, and practice. Of all private foundations, MacArthur provides the most financial support for criminal justice research. It makes grants through two major integrated programs: Human and Community Development, and Global Security and Sustainability. The former program supports national research and policy work, while the latter program focuses on arms reduction and security policy, ecosystems conservation and policy, and population. The foundation also supports two other programs: the general program, which undertakes special initiatives and supports projects that promote excellence and diversity in the media, and the MacArthur Fellows Program, which awards fellowships to exceptionally creative individuals, regardless of field of endeavor. The Program on Human and Community Development focuses broadly on social conditions, including community and child development. One focus of the foundation is its infusion of teams of collaborators that are comprised not only of interdisciplinary scholars, but also policy analysts, policymakers, and the individuals who do their jobs, work with civic and neighborhood organizations, and support the growth and development of children, families, communities, and friends. The foundation approaches this mission with two strategies: projects and networks. Foundation projects are large-scale and are designed to document social conditions, evaluate the effectiveness of social policies, and track the progress of major policy reform initiatives. One of these projects is the multiagency funded Project on Human Development in Chicago Neighborhoods, a project that is tracking the developmental histories of several cohorts of individuals throughout Chicago. The second strategy pursued by the foundation is the formation of research networks. Referred to as "research institutions without walls," the foundation networks bring together individuals from a broad spectrum of disciplines, perspectives, and research methods to explore basic theoretical issues and empirical questions that deal with fundamental social issues. Several networks deal with issues related to criminology and criminal justice (Psychopathology and Development, Mental Health and the Law, Successful Pathways through Middle Childhood). Principle among these is the Network on Adolescent Development and Juvenile Justice. This network has brought together a team of researchers and practitioners to study issues associated with development and juvenile justice. Two main studies are being undertaken by this particular network. The first is

a two-site, longitudinal study of the process by which serious offenders navigate the criminal justice process, and the patterns by which they persist or desist from criminal offending. The second project consists of a multisite study on issues related to competence and culpability regarding young offenders in the criminal justice system. The MacArthur Foundation is able to provide all of these research services because it has assets of $4 billion and makes grants totaling more than $170 million annually.

Founded in 1936, the Ford Foundation operated as a local philanthropy in Michigan until 1950 when it expanded to become a national and international foundation. Since its inception, it has been an independent, nonprofit, nongovernmental organization that has provided more than $9.3 billion in grants and loans. The Ford Foundation has as its goals the strengthening of democratic values, the reduction of poverty and injustice, the promotion of international cooperation, and the advancement of human achievement. To accomplish these tasks, the foundation encourages initiatives by those living and working closest to where problems are located; promotes collaboration among the nonprofit, government, and business sectors; and assures participation by men and women from diverse communities and at all levels of society. Three domains of research mark the foundation's funding: human and community development, peace and social justice, and education, media, and arts.

The Edna McConnell Clark Foundation grew out of financial resources from the Avon Company. The main funding priorities for the McConnell-Clark Foundation cut across four areas: the poor, children, the elderly, and the developing world. These topical areas have turned into research programs studying children, tropical diseases, New York neighborhoods, student achievement, youth development, and justice. Within the area of criminal justice, several grants have been awarded to youth law centers in Philadelphia and San Francisco, and to the law institute at the University of Minnesota.

Started in 1936 by William T. Grant, the William T. Grant Foundation's mission is to "assist research, education, and training through the sciences which have their focus in the study of man and the fundamental principles of human relations." Support from the Grant Foundation is available within three broad areas: research on the development of children, adolescents, and youth, research to evaluate broadly based social interventions; a faculty scholars program; and a small grants program. One current project being supported by the foundation concerns the disrupted transition of high school dropout from adolescence to adulthood, and the implications high school dropout has for successful life development, including involvement in antisocial behavior.

The purpose of the Robert Wood Johnson Foundation is to test promising ideas, evaluate results, and give heightened visibility to particular issues. Although the Robert Wood Johnson Foundation concentrates their grants in the health care arena, recent funding has been awarded to researchers interested in promoting health and reducing the harm associated with substance abuse in the form of tobacco, alcohol, and drugs, as well as the criminal events that arise from substance use and abuse problems.

The Harry Frank Guggenheim Foundation sponsors scholarly research on problems of violence, aggression, and dominance. The Guggenheim Foundation also provides funding for grants that explore various aspects of violence related to youth, family relationships, media effects, crime, biological factors, intergroup conflict related to religion, ethnicity and nationalism, political violence deployed in war and substate terrorism, as well as processes of peace and the control of aggression.

Research centers have also sprung up in universities nationwide. Early centers were attached to law schools and social science departments; however, since the early 1980s, research centers have been made part of a variety of criminal justice and sociology departments around the country. Perhaps the most interesting advent since the late 1960s has been the proliferation of graduate programs in criminology and criminal justice. In the 1970s, there were only two programs granting the Ph.D. degree in criminology and criminal justice. As of 1999, there were over twenty such programs within criminal justice, and many more that distribute Masters-level degrees in criminal justice. Further, a large number of programs granting the Ph.D. degree in sociology and psychology exist in which students can specialize in issues surrounding crime, law, psychopathy, deviance, and antisocial behavior. Many of these graduate programs are leaders in the dissemination of criminological, criminal justice, and violence research, including the University of Maryland, Carnegie Mellon University, State University New York–Albany, University of Cincinnati, Florida State University, Pennsylva-

nia State University, University of Pennsylvania, Temple University, Northeastern University, Michigan State University, University of Missouri–St. Louis, Arizona State University, University of California–Irvine, University of Illinois–Chicago, American University, Rutgers University, University of Washington, Cambridge University, University of Montreal, University of Chicago, University of Wisconsin, Harvard University, and others.

The federal impact on research

The federal government's interest in appropriating funds for the research and understanding of crime has continued to grow since its early interest in the 1960s. Housed within the U.S. Department of Justice (DOJ), the Office of Justice Programs (OJP) is principally in charge of allocating research funds. OJP is topically divided into bureaus and programs that provide research support per topic area, including: Bureau of Justice Statistics, Bureau of Justice Assistance, National Institute of Justice, Office of Juvenile Justice and Delinquency Prevention, and Office of Victims of Crime.

The Bureau of Justice Statistics (BJS) was created in 1979 and is primarily in charge of criminal justice statistics, including the collection, analysis, publishing, and disseminating of all information related to crime and criminal victimizations at all levels of government. BJS also administers the National Criminal History Improvement Program (NCHIP), which provides funding and technical assistance to improve the quality and accessibility of criminal history and related records, to support the interface between state and national record systems, and for data collection on presale firearm background checks. Finally, BJS assists states in technical and financial support of Statistical Analysis Centers (SACs), state-level agencies that are responsible for statistical activities concerning criminal justice issues and policies in each state. The national organization of the SACs is the Justice Research and Statistics Association (JRSA). This association is comprised of state SAC directors, analysts, researchers, and practitioners throughout the justice system. JRSA performs three main functions: it provides a clearinghouse of information on state criminal justice research, programs, and publications; offers training in computer technology as it relates to criminal justice issues; and reports on the latest research being conducted within federal and state criminal justice agencies.

In addition, JRSA holds an annual conference in which grantees, researchers, and practitioners convene for information dissemination and sharing.

The Bureau of Justice Assistance (BJA) was established by the Omnibus Crime Control and Safe Streets Act of 1968 and administers the Edward Byrne Memorial State and Local Enforcement Assistance Program. BJA provides funding and technical support to assist state and local agencies to combat crime and drug abuse. BJA also identifies, develops, and shares programs, techniques, and information with the states to increase the efficiency of the criminal justice system, and provides training and technical assistance to enhance the expertise of criminal justice personnel. In addition, BJA provides funding for the National White Collar Crime Center (NWCCC), which offers national support for the prevention, investigation, and prosecution of economic crimes.

The National Institute of Justice (NIJ), also created by the Omnibus Crime Control and Safe Streets Act of 1968, is authorized to support research, evaluation, and demonstration programs, development of technology, and both national and international information dissemination. NIJ funds a number of programs covering a variety of issues within criminal justice. Among its many funded programs are: Arrestee Drug Abuse Monitoring Program (ADAM), Breaking the Cycle, Correctional and Law Enforcement Family Support Program (CLEFs), Crime Mapping Research Center, Data Resources Program, International Center, Sentencing and Adjudication Program, Violence Against Women, and Family Violence Research and Evaluation Program. In particular, ADAM tracks trends in the prevalence and types of drug use among booked arrestees in urban areas within the United States, and has also expanded to rural areas and a site in England. Breaking the Cycle is a systemwide intervention designed to identify and treat all defendants in need of substance abuse treatment throughout the entire justice system. CLEFS is designed to find ways to prevent and treat the negative effects of stress experienced by law enforcement and correctional officers and their families. The Crime Mapping Research Center was established in 1997 with the goal of promotion, research, evaluation, development, and dissemination of GIS (geographic information systems) technology and the spatial analysis of crime. The International Center takes as it mission the comparison and study of criminal behavior and criminal justice systems in an international context. Although NIJ holds an annual conference in which grantees present work-in-progress to other researchers and practitioners, many of the programs within NIJ, such as ADAM and the Crime Mapping Research Center, also hold annual conferences.

The Office of Juvenile Justice and Delinquency Prevention (OJJDP) was established in 1974 and provides funding to states, territories, localities, and private organizations on matters related to juvenile delinquency and juvenile justice. There are seven divisions within OJJDP: missing and exploited children, concentration of federal effort, information dissemination, state relations and assistance, research and program development, training and technology assistance, and a special emphasis unit. Since the mid-1980s, the office has been engaged in a number of important research projects including Blueprints for Violence Prevention, Safefutures, and a three-site longitudinal study known as the Causes and Correlates of Delinquency. This last program, with sites in Rochester, Pittsburgh, and Denver, employs a team of researchers who have been collecting data for cohorts of individuals since middle/late childhood through early adulthood in an effort to understand the development and desistance of criminal offending.

The Office of Victims of Crime (OVC) was formed by the U.S. Department of Justice in 1983 and formally established by Congress in 1988 through an amendment to the Victims of Crime Act of 1984 (VOCA). The office provides federal funds to support victim assistance and compensation programs around the country and advocates for the fair treatment of crime victims. OVC administers formula and discretionary grants for programs designed to benefit victims, to provide training for diverse professionals who work with victims, and to develop projects to enhance victims' rights and services. The mission of OVC is to enhance the nation's capacity to assist crime victims and to provide leadership in changing attitudes, policies, and practices to promote justice and healing for all victims of crime. The office accomplishes these tasks by administering the Crime Victim's Fund, supporting demonstration projects with national impact, and publishing and disseminating materials that highlight promising practices in the effective treatment of crime victims that can be replicated throughout the country. A major responsibility of OVC is the administration of the Crime Victims Fund, which is derived not from tax dollars but from fines and penalties paid by federal criminal offenders. In 1997, $363 million was collected and distributed to states to assist in funding their victim assistance and compensation programs. Since 1988, OVC has distributed over $2 billion to the states to support victim services and compensation.

In addition to providing monetary support to crime victims, OVC also sponsors training on a variety of victims' issues for many different professions, including victim service providers, law enforcement, prosecutors, the judiciary, the clergy, and medical and mental health personnel. OVC also provides discretionary grants for innovative projects and has funded important reports on civil legal remedies for victims, on model antistalking laws, and on protocols for handling offenses on native tribal lands. The office has also established the OVC Resource Center, an information clearinghouse that provides current research findings, statistics, and literature on emerging victim issues. Finally, OVC has established the OVC Training and Technical Assistance Center (TTAC). This center serves as a centralized access point for information about OVC's training and technical assistance resources.

In addition to OJP's bureaus, which provide monetary funds for research, OJP has also developed specialized programs to aid in furthering criminological research. The corrections program office was established in 1995 to implement the correctional grant programs created by the Violent Crime Control and Law Enforcement Act of 1994. The Drug Courts Program Office was established to administer the drug court grant program and provide financial and technical assistance, training, guidance, and leadership. Operation Weed and Seed is a program that seeks to "weed" out criminal behavior and "seed" the target area through social and economic revitalization. State and Local Domestic Preparedness Support is offered to aid local public safety personnel in acquiring the equipment and skills to safely respond to domestic terrorist activities. The Police Corps is a college scholarship program designed to pay for education expenses for students who agree to work in a state or local police force for at least four years after graduation.

In addition to the funding available from the Office of Justice Programs, the National Science Foundation (NSF), under the Law and Human Behavior Program, has provided researchers with funding opportunities to study criminological and criminal justice issues. In 1994, NSF called for proposals for an interdisciplinary, multi-university effort to be supported by a five-year, $12 million grant. The funding for the grant was primarily from NSF with an additional $2 million from Housing and Urban Development (HUD), and $400,000 from the National Institute of Justice. Of the thirteen proposals received, one from Carnegie Mellon University was selected and has been the distributor of funds under the name National Consortium on Violence Research (NCOVR). The purpose of NCOVR is to employ a "virtual" consortium whereby the top researchers in the social and behavioral sciences use communication technology (i.e., e-mail) that was largely unavailable twenty years ago to study issues related to violence. Each summer, the consortium members convene for a summer workshop that involves the reporting of research results and development of future plans. As of 1999, the consortium had seventy members at thirty-eight universities in twenty-two states and four nations, including England, New Zealand, Canada, and the United States.

NCOVR is comprised of three research program areas that are designed to cover the array of violence-causing factors: individual, situational, and community. The individual level is concerned with individual characteristics and developmental experiences that lead some individuals to become more violent than others. The area on Continuity and Change uses a variety of longitudinal data sets to examine developmental processes and how they affect differential individual responses to a variety of violence-inducing stimuli. The situational level is concerned with identifying those factors that contribute to escalation in violence in some conflict situations and to peaceful resolution in others. The area on Situational Dynamics uses data on individual experiences in conflict situations that range from unstructured ethnographic observation to structured interviews to identify when conflicts turn into violence and when they are resolved otherwise. Specific attention is directed at studying guns, relationships, and the presence of drugs, including alcohol. The community level is concerned with identifying the differences between communities with high and low rates of violence, even after controlling for demographic and socioeconomic compositions. The Time and Space area is concerned with identifying factors that contribute to both long-term trends in violence as well as short-term variation around those trends.

In the late 1990s NCOVR initiated a series of projects in two other research areas: Race and Ethnicity, and Women and Violence. Research in the Race and Ethnicity area focuses on the factors that contribute to the differences and similarities among racial and ethnic groups in their involvement in violence as both victims and perpetrators. An important emphasis within the Race and Ethnicity area is the explanation of ethnic differences within racial or broader ethnic categories. Research in the Women and Violence area explores violence involving women, both as offenders and victims.

NCOVR provides two main sources of funding and operates four educative programs. The two main funding opportunities are grants and research initiative funds. The former are the kinds of awards that are typically awarded to those interested in studying criminological issues, while the latter entail small amounts of monies (under $5,000) that are designed to field small-scale pilot studies that are hoped to result in larger-scale research projects. The four educative programs operated by NCOVR include: predoctoral fellowships, postdoctoral fellowships, professional career-development fellowships, and an undergraduate training program. Predoctoral fellowships are designed for students pursuing a doctoral degree with an NCOVR member and with a secondary advisor of a different discipline. The pre-doctoral stipend is $10,000 per year. Postdoctoral fellowships are new Ph.D.s who work on one of the ongoing NCOVR research projects. The stipend is $30,000 for full-time work. The Professional Career Development Fellowships are designed for faculty members at minority-serving institutions who work with one or more NCOVR members on research projects to improve their research and grant-writing skills. These fellowships are eligible for funding to support their research efforts. The Undergraduate Training Program is designed to reach out to minority-serving institutions in an effort to provide undergraduates an opportunity to learn about research and education opportunities related to the study of violence.

In addition to grant-making and education, NCOVR also fields the NCOVR Data Center. Accessed through the NCOVR web site, the Data Center maintains a number of important data sets that can be readily linked. As of 1999, NCOVR had the complete set of Uniform Crime Reports from 1980 through 1996 as well as the complete 1980 and 1990 census data. The Data Center also retains Supplemental Homicide Report Data on details of individual homicide incidents. These crime and census data are available to the broader research community and are not restricted to NCOVR members. Finally, the Data Center has a special version of the National Crime Victimization Survey. This data set is provided to NCOVR by BJS through the Census Bureau, which collects the data for BJS, and indicates the census tract of each respondent, and so permits examination of victimization risk based on community characteristics. Because of Census Bureau policies designed to limit disclosure risk, these data can only be used in the Regional Census Data Center located at Carnegie Mellon University. Importantly, NCOVR believes that this can be an important resource for violence research, and as a result, it is prepared to cover the out-of-pocket costs of anyone wanting to pursue research with these data.

Research tools

A variety of research tools are available to individuals interested in studying criminological and criminal justice issues. Located at the University of Michigan, the Inter-University Consortium for Political and Social Research (ICPSR) is a membership-based, not-for-profit organization serving member colleges and universities in the United States and abroad. ICPSR provides access to the world's largest archive of computerized social science data, training facilities for the study of quantitative social analysis techniques, and resources for social scientists using advanced computer technologies. Currently, ICPSR supports five topic data archives: health and medical care archive, international archive of education data, national archive of computerized data on aging, substance abuse and mental health data archive, and the national archive of criminal justice data (NACJD). For those interested in the study of crime, the NACJD contains over five hundred data collections on a variety of issues related to criminology and criminal justice. For many of the data sets supported at ICPSR, users can download data, codebooks, and oftentimes the SAS and SPSS syntax statements to create ready-to-analyze data sets.

Information on criminological and criminal justice issues can be obtained primarily through two sources: agency clearinghouses, and academic journals, book, and serials. Federal agencies involved in the study of crime, primarily OJP, deposit their research reports and research briefings with the National Criminal Justice Reference Service (NCJRS). This service, accessible via the Internet, phone, or fax-on-demand, provides individuals with information on an array of criminal justice topics including issues related to the police, courts, corrections, and crime statistics. Each year BJS distributes, via NCJRS, the *SourceBook* on criminal justice statistics that contains a wealth of information on the justice system, as well as topical reports in *Crime Victimization, Capital Punishment,* and *Recidivism.* The other avenue for research information and dissemination occurs through academic outlets. A variety of journals publish topics regularly on issues related to criminology and criminal justice, including: *Criminology, Justice Quarterly, Journal of Research in Crime and Delinquency, Journal of Criminal Justice, Journal of Quantitative Criminology, Justice Research and Policy, Journal of Criminal Justice Education, Journal of Crime and Justice, Violence and Victims, Prison Journal, Journal of Drug Issues, British Journal of Criminology, Canadian Journal of Criminology, Australian and New Zealand Journal of Criminology, Studies on Crime and Crime Prevention, Development and Psychopathology, Deviant Behavior, Journal of Criminal Law and Criminology, Crime and Delinquency, Journal of Adolescent Research, Journal of Research on Adolescence, Journal of Abnormal Psychology, Psychological Bulletin, Psychological Review, Theoretical Criminology, Youth and Society, Criminal Justice, Criminal Justice Policy Review, Criminal Justice and Behavior, Criminal Behaviour and Mental Health, American Sociological Review, Western Criminological Review, American Journal of Criminal Justice, Homicide Studies, Social Forces, Social Science Quarterly, American Journal of Sociology, Psychology, Crime and Law, Policing, Police Quarterly, Federal Probation, Law and Human Behavior,* and a number of law school journals. In addition to academic journals, a number of different serials contain information on criminological and criminal justice issues. Three of the most popular serials include: *Crime and Justice: An Annual Review of Research, Advances in Criminological Theory,* and *Sociology of Crime, Law, and Deviance.* The first of these serials, *Crime and Justice,* publishes lengthy, review articles on a variety of crime-related topics, with a slight emphasis on issues related to criminal justice. *Advances in Criminological Theory* publishes theoretical and empirical articles on criminological theory, while the *Sociology of Crime, Law, and Deviance* publishes articles of criminological interest from a sociological perspective. Finally, academic books continue to operate as important sources of research

information. Many of the large academic presses, such as University of Chicago Press, Northeastern University Press, Cambridge University Press, Sage Publications, and Plenum Press, publish books related to crime issues on a regular basis.

In addition to these publication outlets, the field of criminology and criminal justice has two professional organizations: American Society of Criminology (ASC) and the Academy of Criminal Justice Sciences (ACJS). ASC is an international organization concerned with criminology, embracing scholarly, scientific, and professional knowledge concerning the etiology, prevention, control, and treatment of crime and delinquency. This includes the measurement and detection of crime, legislation and practice of criminal law, as well as the law enforcement, judicial, and correctional systems. The society's objective is to bring together a multidisciplinary forum fostering criminology study, research, and education. Its members include practitioners, academicians, and students in the many fields of criminal justice. ASC also conducts annual meetings for its membership, each devoted to a discussion of a particular topic of general interest. In addition, members of ASC receive the journal *Criminology,* published four times a year, and the *Criminologist,* a newsletter published six times per year. There are four specialized divisions in ASC: critical criminology, women and crime, international criminology, and people of color and crime. Each distributes newsletters and announcements on a regular basis. The Academy of Criminal Justice Sciences is an international organization established in 1963 to foster professional and scholarly activities in the field of criminal justice. ACJS is comprised of a number of scholars and practitioners that are international in scope and multidisciplinary in orientation. In addition to its annual conference, ACJS oversees publication of two academic journals: *Justice Quarterly* and the *Journal of Criminal Justice Education.* Unlike ASC, ACJS also has regional organizations that come together once a year for meetings and information dissemination. These regional organizations include the Western, Southern, Mid-Western, and Northeastern Academy of Criminal Justice Sciences. These regional organizations also sponsor several academic journals, including: *Western Criminological Review* (Western), *Criminal Justice Policy Review* (Northeastern), *Journal of Crime and Justice* (Midwestern), and the *American Journal of Criminal Justice* (Southeastern). In addition to these main criminological associations, other disciplines have annual meetings and sponsor academic journals that have substantive import for criminologists. These include the American Sociological Association, the American Psychological Association, Society for Research on Adolescence, and the Southern Sociological Society.

Future trends

The history of criminological and criminal justice research suggests at least six important trends that will affect the research and practitioner communities. First, while private foundations did not show substantial interest in funding criminological research during the 1970s and 1980s, interest has picked up in the 1990s with private foundations distributing millions of dollars earmarked for research on crime and violence. Second, the federal government continues to be one of the main grant providers to researchers interested in crime issues. Interestingly, in his original essay, Charles Wellford hypothesized that federal research efforts would be further consolidated such that many of the branches of OJP would be brought into closer coordination. Although this has yet to occur formally, Wellford's premonition appears to be taking shape. For example, many of the agencies who were tangentially involved in criminological research and grantmaking have been either consolidated or eliminated. Toward this end, an OJP reorganization plan was proposed in the late 1990s to consolidate all research, including juvenile justice research currently being conducted by OJJDP, within NIJ. It would also consolidate all statistics within BJS. The plan would eliminate the presidentially appointed directorships of the five bureaus (NIJ, BJS, OJJDP, BJA, and OVC). Under the reorganization plan, the directors of the NIJ and BJS would become appointees of the Attorney General. As of late 1999, the plan and its recommendations had yet to be voted upon, but whatever the outcome, it is likely to influence future funding for criminological research. Third, crime research is likely to continue on an interdisciplinary trajectory, while remaining cognizant of both qualitative and quantitative research, and relevant across macro, meso, and micro levels of analysis. Much of the current work employs researchers from different fields of study, including psychology, sociology, political science, biology, neuropsychology, and criminology, to approach criminological and criminal justice issues via a number of different methodologies and disciplinary training. Funding agencies are becoming more likely to administer grant awards to researchers working from this multidisciplinary, multimethod perspective. Fourth, the Internet has become a powerful research tool. Researchers can download data from police, courts, and corrections databases, view crime maps for a number of different cities, and retrieve journal articles and publications via *ProQuest Direct* in many more ways than ever before. These advents will make doing research, sharing data, and publishing results much easier than ever before. Fifth, with continued work on emerging methodological tools, researchers will likely revisit many secondary data archives in an effort to apply these new tools to old data to determine the usefulness of the new tools. Sixth, research will continue to be associated with universities and research centers (both private and nonprivate). Toward this end, crime research will probably expand to involve undergraduate students in more significant ways than ever before as universities continue to encourage undergraduate research projects and honors theses.

Since the 1980s, through the Office of Justice Programs, the National Science Foundation, and the National Institutes of Health, the federal government has created a solid, long-term program of research in criminology and criminal justice. In addition, private foundations have entered the criminological research area with a fervor of interest. Across both the federal and private domains, important and timely research programs have been created and sustained. The future of criminological and criminal justice research will probably anticipate and embody a working partnership between federal and private agencies. One exemplar of this working relationship is the Project on Human Development in Chicago Neighborhoods. This project is a major interdisciplinary study aimed at deepening society's understanding of the causes and pathways of juvenile delinquency, adult crime, substance abuse, and violence. Directed by the Harvard School of Public Health, this project is a joint venture among a variety of public and private agencies including the MacArthur Foundation, the National Institute of Justice, the National Institute of Mental Health, the U.S. Department of Education, the Stein Foundation, the Turner Foundation, and the Administration for Children, Youth, and Families. It is believed that these partnerships will continue the multidisciplinary, multiagency, multi-methodological approach to studying criminal behavior and the criminal justice system response to such behavior. This approach should continue to contribute to the knowledge base regarding the understanding and control of crime.

ALEX R. PIQUERO
NICOLE LEEPER PIQUERO

See also CRIMINOLOGY AND CRIMINAL JUSTICE RESEARCH: METHODS; STATISTICS: COSTS OF CRIME; STATISTICS: REPORTING SYSTEMS AND METHODS.

BIBLIOGRAPHY

Bureau of Justice Statistics. *Sourcebook of Criminal Statistics.* Washington, D.C.: National Institute of Justice, 1998.

INTERNET RESOURCES

ICPSR web site: http://www.icpsr.umich.edu.
NCJRS web site: http://www.ncjrs.org.
NCOVR web site: http://www.ncovr.heinz.cmu.edu.
Office of Justice Programs web site: http://www.ojp.usdoj.gov.
Project on Human Development in Chicago Neighborhoods web site: http://www.phdcn.harvard.edu.
ProQuest Direct web site: http://www.proquestdirect.com.

CROSS-EXAMINATION

During a trial, virtually all evidence is presented to the fact finder (usually a jury in criminal cases, but sometimes a judge) through witnesses called by each party during that party's *case*. The party that has called a witness first has an opportunity to elicit testimony from that witness in *direct examination*. At the conclusion of direct examination, and usually with little delay, the opposing party will have a chance to *cross-examine* the witness (although he is not obliged to do so).

The art and style of cross-examination

During direct examination, the party who has called the witness to the stand will, if at all possible, appear to let the witness tell his story on his own. The style of direct examination—*non-leading* questions, which do not point the way to a particular answer—is generally required by the rules of evidence. It also makes tactical sense for the examiner, since the fact finder will probably not believe someone who sounds like he is just agreeing to words that a lawyer puts into his mouth. The picture presented may be quite artificial, since the examining lawyer may have done a lot during trial preparation to structure the witness's account. But much of the persuasiveness of a witness's account will come from the integrity of his narrative—i.e., the degree to which the witness conveys a plausible story in language appropriate to both the story and to the witness himself (or at least what the witness seems to be).

If the key to a successful direct examination is constructing a narrative, the key to cross-examination is deconstructing that narrative, and perhaps developing an alternative one. The goal of the cross-examining attorney (at least when she thinks her side has been disadvantaged by a witness's testimony) is to highlight the artificiality of the narrative presented on direct examination, showing it to be selective and willful. And the style of cross-examination is calculated to achieve this goal. Here, where is it less likely that the witness will cooperate with the examiner's project, the rules of evidence will permit counsel to proceed through leading questions, and she is apt to do so. Indeed, cross-examination will generally be done through a sequence of short questions that cannot plausibly be denied, and that are barely "questions" at all. A lawyer conducting a good direct examination will often seem to fade into the background. On cross-examination, the lawyer takes center stage, sometimes even overshadowing the witness. The effect is rarely, if ever, that depicted in the movies or on television, when the browbeaten witness collapses on the stand and admits having committed the crime himself. Nor must cross-examination be done in a loud voice, five inches from the witness's face. Judges tend to protect witnesses against such abuse, and it is rarely a productive tactic anyway. Nevertheless, a good cross-examination can still be quite dramatic.

Keeping a tight rein on the witness through leading questions to which the witness can answer only "yes" or "no," the good cross-examiner may use a variety of tactics to lessen or even reverse the impact of the witness's direct examination. She may make the witness go back over some of the terrain covered during direct examination, forcing the witness to concede "facts" inconsistent with the previous narrative. She may confront the witness with statements the witness made before trial that are inconsistent with the witness's direct testimony. She may challenge the witness's ability to have perceived the events in question, or to have remembered them. She will, if possible, *impeach* the witness's credibility by eliciting admissions concerning his bias toward or against a party in the case. She may question the witness about previous instances in which he lied or acted deceitfully, in an effort to suggest that the witness is the kind of person likely to lie or shade the truth. She may also try to show the "true" character of the witness, by baiting him into shedding the calm demeanor with which he responded to questions on direct examination. Sometimes, the cross-examiner will not even care what the witness says. The point is to let the jury see him squirm. The judge will generally instruct that questions are not "evidence," but that the jury can still consider the witness's responses in the context of the questions. The difference between taking assertive questions as fact and taking them as mere "context" may seem small or nonexistent, particularly to a lay juror.

The general rule used to be that a party could not impeach the credibility of people it had called to the stand, the rationale being that a party had "vouched" for the credibility of those witnesses. Recent years have seen the rejection of this rule, however. Rulemakers have generally come to recognize that parties may be forced to put on witnesses whose testimony is true only in certain parts, so far as the parties are concerned, and may need to impeach the witness on other parts.

Protection of the right to cross-examine: the hearsay rule

The value that the American legal system places on cross-examination as a fact-finding tool is reflected in the *hearsay rule*. This rule (legislatively imposed in many jurisdictions, including federal, but a matter of common law in others) bars the introduction of statements made out of court if those statements are being offered to prove the truth of what the out-of-court declarant intended to say. (If the statements are offered to prove something other than their "truth"—perhaps the mere fact that they were said is relevant—the hearsay rule poses no bar to their consideration.) The rationale for the rule is that a fact-finder ought not to rely on the truth of a statement that someone made when no one had a chance to cross-examine him. Rather than trust a jury to discount the reliability of these untested

statements, the hearsay rule categorically excludes them from trials, even in those trials in which the person who made the out-of-court statement actually testifies as a witness. The fear is not simply that the jury would not be able to tell the difference between a first-hand account and a second- or third-hand account, but that the jury would be more ready to credit evidence from an out-of-court declarant (who would not be subject to cross-examination) that is presented through documentary proof or a naive trial witness than to credit evidence from an in-court witness subject to cross-examination. In the absence of the hearsay rule, parties would thus have a disincentive to present their cases through witnesses with personal knowledge of the matters at issue.

There are, of course, many exceptions to the hearsay rule. Some, like those covering business records or statements made in response to a startling event, arose because legislators or courts decided that out-of-court statements under these special circumstances were sufficiently reliable to be considered at trial for their truth even in the absence of cross-examination. Other exceptions, like those permitting one party to introduce any out-of-court statements by the opposing party, developed out of considerations of fairness and accountability. Notwithstanding the proliferation of such exceptions in recent years, however, the hearsay rule cuts deeply, frequently preventing the introduction of highly relevant out of court statements, and encouraging the use of in-court witnesses who can be cross-examined at trial.

The confrontation clause

While the hearsay rule, which applies to both criminal and civil trials, recognizes the value of in-court cross-examination only by implication, criminal defendants can also assert an explicit constitutional right to cross-examination under the confrontation clause of the Sixth Amendment. That clause, which technically addresses only proceedings in federal court, has been interpreted to apply to state cases by virtue of the due process clause of the Fourteenth Amendment. It provides that, in all criminal prosecutions, the accused shall enjoy the right "to be confronted with witnesses against him."

When drafting the confrontation clause, the Framers were doubtless influenced by the English jurist William Blackstone, whose *Commentaries on the Laws of England*, first published in 1765–1769, had noted that "open examination of witnesses *viva voce*, in the presence of all mankind, is much more conducive to the clearing up of truth, than the private and secret examination taken down in writing before an officer, or his clerk." They also had a dramatic demonstration, in the well-known trial of Sir Walter Raleigh, of how a criminal defendant could be oppressed through the denial of confrontation. When Raleigh was tried in 1603 for treason against the Crown, the main piece of prosecution evidence was a sworn "confession" that Lord Cobham, an alleged co-conspirator, had made to officers of the Crown in proceedings at which Raleigh was neither present nor represented by counsel. Aware that Cobham had thereafter recanted his confession, Raleigh demanded that Cobham be produced, to give testimony in open court. The prosecution responded by producing not Cobham but a boat pilot, who told of having heard an unidentified Portuguese gentleman say that Raleigh and Cobham were plotting to kill the king. Raleigh was convicted and eventually executed, never having had a chance to test the reliability of the principal witnesses against him.

Over the years, the Supreme Court has interpreted the confrontation clause with an eye to Raleigh's plight. At its most basic, the clause has been read to give defendants the right to actually see and confront the witnesses the prosecution has called to give testimony under oath. The importance of this physical confrontation should not be underestimated. Seeing a witness testify will make a defendant better able to assist in his own defense, and seeing a defendant before her may help impress a witness with the importance of truthful testimony. There are to be no secret witnesses, and no trial witnesses identified but excused from giving live testimony.

The focus, in recent years, on prosecuting child abuse cases, and the recognition of the lasting harm that the criminal justice system can inflict on child witnesses, has put a special pressure on settled confrontation clause doctrine. In 1990, in *Maryland v. Craig* (497 U.S. 836 (1990)), a case involving a child witness testifying about alleged child abuse, the Supreme Court held that "the face-to-face confrontation requirement" is not absolute, and may be trumped by an important state interest, such as the need to protect young victims of child abuse from the trauma of testifying against the alleged perpetrator, so long as the reliability of the testimony is otherwise assured. The Court went on to suggest that a procedure wherein a child testified and was cross-examined by defense counsel, outside the

presence of the defendant, judge, and jury—who all watched the proceedings via close-circuit television—might well pass constitutional muster, so long as there were specific findings of need in a particular case. *Craig* is an important case doctrinally because it envisions trials in which the jury never sees the interaction between a criminal defendant and his primary accuser. At least so far, however, it should be seen more as a response to the plight of the most vulnerable witnesses than as a rejection of the virtues of face-to-face confrontation.

Because there are limits to the benefits of a silent confrontation, the Supreme Court has also read the confrontation clause to allow criminal defendants a reasonable opportunity to cross-examine the witnesses whom the prosecution calls to the stand. The defendant whose lawyer is cut off in the middle of a prolonged inquiry into a witness's prior bad acts and prior inconsistent statements will rarely have a serious objection, even when good ammunition was left unused. Yet appellate courts have recognized the constitutional dimension of this right to inquire, and have reversed convictions where the defendant was prevented from pursuing an especially significant line of impeachment, even when the trial court's ruling was in accordance with state evidentiary law. The key Supreme Court cases have demanded that trial courts take particular care not to foreclose cross-examination that probes a prosecution witness's bias—their deal with the government to testify in exchange for leniency, or other reasons a witness might have to fabricate evidence against the defendant. These cases give a constitutional bite to the demand of defense counsel that she be permitted to cross-examine on matters that a witness believes private, even embarrassing. Where the privacy or dignitary interests of a witness have been given special protection by law, cross-examination may still be foreclosed. Thus, confrontation clause claims against the prohibition of inquiry into an alleged rape victim's prior sexual history have failed in a number of cases. But confrontation clause concerns do lead some (but certainly not all) courts to give defense lawyers more leeway in cross-examination than they give prosecutors, who have no constitutional right to assert.

Constitutional values can clash in this area when a criminal defendant asserts his constitutional right to probe a witness's credibility but the witness invokes his constitutional right against self-incrimination and refuses to answer questions that might expose him to future prosecution. When this happens, the witness's invocation, if valid, will trump the defendant's constitutional right to inquire. The witness will be able to remain silent. If this silence prevents the defendant from pursuing an important line of impeachment, a trial court might, if possible, prevent the witness from testifying in the first place. Alternatively, the court might seek to cure the prejudice by striking all or part of the witness's direct testimony from the record.

Interaction between confrontation clause and hearsay rules

The Supreme Court has also recognized that the guarantee of reasonable cross-examination of witnesses who appear in court can be of limited value when those witnesses simply repeat what some out-of-court declarant said at some previous time. It did not do Sir Walter Raleigh much good to be able to cross-examine the boat pilot, when the pilot could shed no light on the reliability of the unidentified Portuguese gentleman and could only repeat what he heard the gentleman say. The Court therefore has read the confrontation clause's reference to "witnesses" to include out-of-court declarants on whose extrajudicial statements the prosecution seeks to rely. This reading, at least in theory, might have paved the way to an entire body of constitutional evidentiary doctrine that paralleled the hearsay rule in its concern with the reliability of out-of-court statements, but put more of an emphasis on in-court confrontation. That has not occurred, however. The important move the Court made was to reason that, under the confrontation clause, physical confrontation and cross-examination are largely means to the more general end of assuring the reliability of evidence. And because the Court has seen well-established hearsay doctrine as serving this same end, it has generally found that the confrontation clause requires no more in the way of reliability or physical confrontation than does standard hearsay doctrine. If, for example, the circumstances under which an out-of-court statement was made are found to satisfy the requirements of the "dying declaration" hearsay exception, or those of the rule allowing statements "made for the purposes of medical diagnosis or treatment," the Court would allow a jury to consider it, without any separate inquiry into the reliability of the particular statement, or into why the party offering the statement failed to produce the out-of-court declarant for cross-examination.

Even where cross-examination is required by the confrontation clause, it does not necessarily have to be particularly effective in order for the clause to be satisfied (at least under recent interpretations). An opportunity to confront a witness ready and willing to answer questions will generally suffice. Thus, where the victim of an assault could testify to having previously identified the defendant as his attacker while in the hospital, but could not recall having seen his assailant or whether any of his hospital visitors had suggested that the defendant had committed the crime, the Court found it sufficient that defense counsel could inquire into such matters as the witness's bias, his eyesight, and his memory. "The weapons available to impugn the witness's statement when memory loss is asserted," the Court noted in *United States v. Owens*, 484 U.S. 554, 560 (1988), "will of course not always achieve success, but successful cross-examination is not the constitutional guarantee" (p. 560).

A criminal defendant may be found to have forfeited his confrontation clause right to challenge the introduction of an unavailable witness's out-of-court statements if the defendant had a hand in preventing that witness from appearance in court by, say, bribing the witness to stay away, threatening the witness, or having the witness murdered.

DANIEL C. RICHMAN

See also ADVERSARY SYSTEM; BURDEN OF PROOF; CONFESSIONS; COUNSEL: ROLE OF COUNSEL; CRIMINAL JUSTICE PROCESS; CRIMINAL PROCEDURE: CONSTITUTIONAL ASPECTS; TRIAL, CRIMINAL; VICTIMS' RIGHTS.

BIBLIOGRAPHY

BERGER, MARGARET A. "The Deconstitutionalization of the Confrontation Clause: A Proposal for a Prosecutorial Restraint Model." *Minnesota Law Review* 76 (1992): 557–613.
BENNETT, W. LANCE, and FELDMAN, MARTHA S. *Reconstructing Reality in the Courtroom: Justice and Judgment in American Culture.* New Brunswick, N.J.: Rutgers University Press, 1981.
BLACKSTONE, WILLIAM. *Commentaries on the Law of England*, vol. 3. (1768). Chicago: University of Chicago Press, 1979.
BURNS, ROBERT P. *A Theory of the Trial.* Princeton, N.J.: Princeton University Press, 1999.
LEMPERT, RICHARD O.; GROSS, SAMUEL R.; and LIEBMAN, JAMES S. *A Modern Approach to Evidence: Text Problems, Transcripts and Cases*, 3d

ed. St. Paul, Minn.: West Publishing Co., 2000.

MAUET, THOMAS A. *Trial Techniques*, 5th ed. Gaithersburg, Md.: Aspen Publishing Inc., 1999.

CASES

Maryland v. Craig, 497 U.S. 836 (1990).
United States v. Owens, 484 U.S. 554 (1988).

CRUEL AND UNUSUAL PUNISHMENT

The prohibition of cruel and unusual punishments is one of the most important constitutional limitations upon the penal process. Like the general guarantees of due process and equal protection, it has been applied to every aspect of that process, ranging from the definition of criminal norms and the consequences of their violation (the subject of substantive criminal law), to the imposition of punishment (criminal procedure), and to its eventual infliction (prison or correction law). As such, it addresses participants at all stages of the penal process, including the legislature, the judiciary (whether professional or lay, permanent or temporary), and the executive at the end of the punishment line, including wardens, prison guards, and the literal "executioner."

The prohibition appears in federal and state constitutions alike, with occasional slight variations ("cruel or unusual" or "cruel and unusual"). This article focuses on the scope of the federal provision, as interpreted by the U.S. Supreme Court. It should be noted, however, that the scope of the federal prohibition does not necessarily match that of its state analogues. For example, in 1992 the Michigan Supreme Court overturned on state constitutional grounds the very penalty that the United States Supreme Court had upheld under the federal cruel and unusual punishments clause the previous year (*Harmelin v. Michigan*, 501 U.S. 957 (1991); *People v. Bullock*, 485 N.W.2d. 866 (Mich. 1992)).

The federal version of the principle appears in the Eighth Amendment, which provides in its entirety that "[e]xcessive bail shall not be required, nor excessive fines imposed, nor cruel and unusual punishments inflicted." The excessive bail and fines clauses have proved far less significant as limitations on the state's power to punish than has the general proscription of cruel and unusual punishments.

The history of the prohibition of cruel and unusual punishments is uncontroversial in one sense, hotly contested in another. Everyone agrees that its wording stems from an identical provision in the English Bill of Rights of 1689. There is no similar consensus on the nature, or the contemporary significance, of the Framers' intent behind its insertion in the Bill of Rights.

One of the most important disagreements about the Framers' intent concerns the extent to which they meant to constrain the legislative definition of crimes and their punishments. Some argue that the Framers intended the prohibition of "cruel and unusual punishments" to apply only to the definition of punishments. Others discern an intent to limit also the definition of crimes as well as the relation (or "proportionality") of crimes and their punishments.

Disagreements about the contemporary significance of the Framers' intent, whatever it might be, reflect the more general debate about the proper approach to constitutional interpretation and related conceptions of the Supreme Court's role. Those who favor a restrictive role for the Court prefer that it stick to fathoming the Framers' intent behind a given constitutional provision. Others advocate a more flexible interpretative approach, occasionally appropriating the restrictive approach by claiming that the Framers intended that a given provision be interpreted flexibly.

The Supreme Court in recent decades has favored a more expansive approach to the clause, one that takes into account the "evolving standards of decency that mark the progress of a maturing society." This test was first announced in a plurality opinion by Chief Justice Earl Warren in the 1958 case of *Trop v. Dulles*, 356 U.S. 86, which invoked the principle to strike down the punishment of denationalization for military desertion as "obnoxious" in an "enlightened democracy such as ours" (p. 100).

The malleable *Trop* test itself has been interpreted more or less expansively since its appearance. Its references to evolution, progress, and maturation have been used to disregard historical intent and practice alike. At the same time, its reference to societal standards has been invoked to limit the courts' power to invalidate existing legislation. As with similarly broad tests framed in terms of the sense of justice or the conscience of the community, which used to be far more common in constitutional law than they are today, society's standards of decency have been difficult to pin down.

This epistemic difficulty has been resolved in two ways. On the one hand, the Supreme Court has invoked general principles, such as "humanity" and "the dignity of man," from which it deduced more particular limitations on the power to punish, as in *Trop* itself. On the other hand, the Court more recently has turned to empirical evidence of society's attitude toward a particular punishment, including legislative activity, prosecutorial charging practices, and jury verdicts. For example, the constitutionality of capital punishment was upheld based on evidence that, following the Court's decision to strike down all existing death penalty statutes in *Furman v. Georgia*, 408 U.S. 238 (1972), legislators passed new death penalty statutes, prosecutors continued to seek the death penalty, and jurors persisted in imposing it. In its search for standards of decency in American society, the Court has not consulted abolitionist developments in the laws of other countries and in the international law of human rights.

In addition to speculating about the Framers' intent and plumbing societal standards, the Supreme Court has also parsed the precise formulation of the principle to define its scope. It has been argued, for instance, that the clause's prohibition of cruel *and* unusual punishments (rather than cruel *or* unusual, or simply cruel, punishments) insulates common punishments from constitutional scrutiny—at least under the Eighth Amendment—regardless of their cruelty, no matter how cruel they might be. The plural "punishments" may suggest a similarly restrictive interpretation of the clause, which would limit its application to particular penalties, rather than treating it as the source for a wide range of constraints on punishment generally speaking.

The reference to "punishments" in the principle limits its scope in other ways as well. Most generally, this reference has been interpreted as rendering the principle inapplicable outside the penal process, including the use of corporal "punishment" in schools (*Ingraham v. Wright*, 430 U.S. 651 (1977)). Within the realm of the penal process, it has been invoked to remove nonintentional acts of prison officials from the reach of the principle on the ground that the concept of "punishment" presumes intention (*Wilson v. Seiter*, 501 U.S. 294, 300 (1991)). Moreover, even intentional acts of prison officials fall outside the principle's scope if they are perpetrated against inmates prior to their conviction, the formal prerequisite for the imposition and eventual infliction of "punishment" (*Ingraham v. Wright*, 430 U.S. 651, 671–672, n. 40 (1977)). The constitutional constraints upon the treatment of students

and pretrial detainees instead derive from the general guarantees of due process and equal protection, both of which apply to all state actions, regardless of their classification as punitive or not. The due process clause, for example, in keeping with the presumption of innocence prohibits the infliction of any kind of punishment on pretrial detainees, even if it is neither cruel nor unusual (*Bell v. Wolfish*, 441 U.S. 520, 537 (1979)).

Definition (substantive criminal law)

The primary addressee of the prohibition against cruel and unusual punishments as a limitation on the power to define crimes and their punishments is the legislature. In this case, however, care should be taken not to confuse the question of the principle's scope with that of its addressee. This common error derives from the assumption that the legislature enjoys a monopoly over the definition of crimes and punishments. This assumption holds, at least formally, only in federal law, where courts are precluded from generating a common, that is, nonstatutory, criminal law. The same does not hold for the bulk of American criminal law, which is state law and until recently relied heavily on judge made common law. The principle, therefore, would apply to any definition of crimes and their punishments, regardless of its author. In this context, it should be noted that the *federal* prohibition of cruel and unusual punishments was not applied to state criminal law until 1962 (*Robinson v. California*, 370 U.S. 660 (1962)).

Crimes. The cruel and unusual punishments clause has the potential of serving as the constitutional backbone for the basic principles of substantive criminal law. To begin with, the clause presumably would prohibit the state today from providing for the punishment of nonpersons, such as animals and inanimate objects, familiar in premodern punishment. Within the class of persons, the state also would be barred from criminalizing the behavior of certain individuals who lack basic capacities, such as the insane and infants. The proscription of cruel and unusual punishment, however, would not apply to other state controls directed at these persons, provided that they do not qualify as punishment, such as civil commitment of one form or another.

These restrictions upon the object of punishment are distinguished from those upon the ground of punishment, that is, that which may trigger the threat, the imposition, or even the infliction of punishment. The material criminal law teaches us that even a person who would generally qualify for punishment may not be punished unless certain formal and substantive conditions are met, which generally mirror the distinction between the general part and the special part of criminal law.

Attempts to interpret the principle as a constitutional foundation for these conditions of criminalization and punishability have met with little success. The Supreme Court, for example, has yet to declare mens rea a constitutional prerequisite, even if mens rea is expansively defined to include negligence, a nonintentional mental state. Strict liability crimes, that is, crimes that require no mental states whatsoever, persist on the books and, in fact, continue to multiply with the expansion of modern regulatory offenses.

Even the constitutional status of actus reus, the best candidate for a bedrock prerequisite for punishability, remains in doubt. The Supreme Court invoked the principle in a 1962 opinion to strike down a California law making it a misdemeanor "to be addicted to the use of narcotics, excepting when administered by or under the direction of a person licensed by the State to prescribe and administer narcotics." The Court reasoned that drug addiction is a disease and, as such, could not be punished under the proscription of cruel and unusual punishments (*Robinson v. California*).

Robinson has been interpreted more generally to proscribe all status offenses, including those based upon a status other than that of a sick person. Six years later, in *Powell v. Texas*, 392 U.S. 514 (1968), the Supreme Court clarified that *Robinson* should not be read to constitutionalize another aspect of actus reus, the voluntariness requirement. Other components of actus reus find a constitutional basis, if any, elsewhere. So punishing mere thoughts may run afoul of the first amendment's free speech guarantee, while the boundaries of omission liability are drawn by the due process clause (*Lambert v. California*, 355 U.S. 225 (1957)).

Attempts to derive from the cruel and unusual punishments clause substantive limitations on criminalization, as opposed to punishability, have been even less successful. The *Robinson* opinion, for example, has not been interpreted broadly to condemn the criminalization of drug possession, rather that of drug addiction, but has in fact been interpreted narrowly, as the *Powell* case makes clear. More recent cases on the scope of the state's power to criminalize often ignore the Eighth Amendment altogether (e.g., *Bowers v Hardwick*, (478 U.S. 186 (1986)), upholding anti-sodomy statute against due process attack).

Punishments. In contrast to the question of whom the state may punish for what, that of how the state may do the punishing falls squarely within the scope of the cruel and unusual punishments clause. So the clause prohibits torturous and barbaric punishments. What constitutes torture and barbarity depends on the application of the *Trop* decency standard. As we have seen, the Eighth Amendment does not condemn capital punishment. A state today presumably would not be free to provide for other corporal punishments, such as mutilation, lobotomy, and castration, at least if they are to be inflicted without explicit consent. The Supreme Court, however, has not seen fit to impose Eighth Amendment limitations on the quantity of noncorporal punishment, including life imprisonment without the possibility of parole.

Similarly, certain punishments, though generally unobjectionable under the Eighth Amendment, are cruel and unusual when imposed on certain defendants. So the death penalty may be imposed on defendants who are mentally retarded without being criminally insane (*Penry v. Lynaugh*, 492 U.S. 302 (1989)), but not on those who were under sixteen years of age at the time of the offense, though such defendants may be sentenced to life imprisonment without the possibility of parole (*Harris v. Wright*, 93 F.3d 581 (9th Cir. 1996)).

Crimes and punishments (proportionality). Whether the Eighth Amendment reaches the relation between crimes and punishments, that is, the proportionality of punishment, may depend on the nature of the punishment in question. There is consensus that the punishment must be proportionate to the crime in death penalty cases. The Supreme Court has been less clear on the question of whether a proportionality requirements also attaches to noncapital punishments, and, assuming it does, what it looks like. In the capital context, the Supreme Court has invoked the proportionality principle to strike down a statute that provided the death penalty for the rape of an adult woman. The proportionality principle may also constrain a legislature's discretion to specify death as the punishment for certain types of felony murder.

In noncapital cases, the Supreme Court has struggled to find a workable proportionality test. In an irreconcilable series of opinions on recidivist statutes decided within a space of three years, the Supreme Court upheld a life sentence and a forty-year prison term, but struck down another life sentence (*Rummel v. Estelle*, 445 U.S. 263 (1980); *Hutto v. Davis*, 454 U.S. 370 (1982); *Solem v. Helm*, 463 U.S. 277 (1983)). The last case in the series attempted to steady the jurisprudence in this area with a three-prong test that looked to the gravity of the offense compared to the severity of the penalty, the sentences imposed for other crimes in the same jurisdiction, and the sentences imposed for the same crime in other jurisdictions. The *Solem* test, however, proved short lived. Only eight years later, in a case upholding a sentence of life imprisonment without the possibility of parole for simple drug possession, a majority of the Supreme Court rejected the test, with two justices in the majority going so far as to suggest that the Eighth Amendment places no proportionality requirement on noncapital punishments, while the remaining three opined that the Amendment forbids only grossly disproportionate noncapital punishments (*Harmelin*).

Imposition (procedural criminal law)

The Eighth Amendment has had its greatest impact on procedural criminal law in capital cases. There the Supreme Court has required a process that guarantees an individualized sentencing decision to avoid arbitrary and capricious death sentences. The Supreme Court has rejected attempts to extend this requirement to noncapital cases, even those involving a maximum sentence of life imprisonment without the possibility of parole (*Harmelin*). Presumably, the imposition of penal norms upon an incompetent defendant would also be considered cruel and unusual. The Eighth Amendment alone, however, would not prohibit the conviction—or even the execution—of an innocent person, assuming the impositional process satisfied due process requirements (*Herrera v. Collins*, 506 U.S. 390 (1993)).

Infliction (prison or correction law)

Even if neither the legislative threat of a particular punishment nor its imposition on a particular defendant violates the Eighth Amendment, its actual infliction may. After all, the amendment specifically prohibits the *infliction* of cruel and unusual punishments, in contrast to the *imposition* of excessive bail or fines. Legislatures enjoy considerable latitude in determining the mode of punishment. Although burning at the stake and quartering would presumably run afoul of the Eighth Amendment, the Supreme Court has been unwilling to constrain legislatures' choice among other modes of execution, including electrocution, hanging, gassing, and lethal injection.

Still, the cruel and unusual punishments clause reaches the actual infliction of punishment, even if it does not deviate from the general mode specified by the legislature (say, by electrocuting a condemned man rather than hanging him). Paradoxically, the infliction of noncapital punishment has received much greater Eighth Amendment scrutiny than has the infliction of capital punishment. So the Supreme Court has consistently rejected claims based on botched execution attempts, while at the same time developing a complex jurisprudence of prison conditions, which critics have characterized as a National Code of Prison Regulations (*Hudson v. McMillian*, 503 U.S. 1 (1992) (Justice Thomas dissenting)).

In the law of prisons, different tests govern the infliction of legislatively defined and judicially imposed punishments, on the one hand, and the disciplining of inmates for prison misconduct, on the other. The former amounts to cruel and unusual punishment if it reflects "deliberate indifference" on the part of prison officials. The latter violates the Eighth Amendment, for example, only if it reflects "malice and sadism" (*Hudson*).

Conclusion

The cruel and unusual punishments clause today speaks to all aspects of the penal process. It remains to be seen whether it will ever realize its potential as the single most important source of substantive constitutional constraints upon American penal law, alongside the due process clause, which has long been recognized as the root of significant procedural rights.

MARKUS DIRK DUBBER

See also CAPITAL PUNISHMENT: LEGAL ASPECTS; CORPORAL PUNISHMENT; PRISONERS, LEGAL RIGHTS OF; PUNISHMENT; SHAMING PUNISHMENTS.

BIBLIOGRAPHY

DRESSLER, JOSHUA. "Kent Greenawalt, Criminal Responsibility, and the Supreme Court: How a Moderate Scholar Can Appear Immoderate Thirty Years Later." *Notre Dame Law Review* 74 (1999): 1507–1532.

Granucci, Anthony F. "'Nor Cruel and Unusual Punishments Inflicted': The Original Meaning." *California Law Review* 57 (1969): 839–865.

Greenawalt, Kent. "'Uncontrollable' Actions and the Eighth Amendment: Implications of *Powell v. Texas.*" *Columbia Law Review* 69 (1969): 927–979.

Note. "The Cruel and Unusual Punishment Clause and the Substantive Criminal Law." *Harvard Law Review* 79 (1966): 635–655.